Praise for *Reagan's Ruling Class*

"This is a clear and comprehensive guide, the best I have seen, to the governing ethos of the Reagan Administration. Taken as a whole, these profiles of the people in charge provide a deep and objective portrait of the Reagan managers who are, with few exceptions, hostile to the laws they are administering."

— William Greider, National editor,
Rolling Stone, author "The Education of David Stockman"

"If you want to know what is really going on in Washington, you must have this book. A monumental work of investigative research, *Reagan's Ruling Class* lays bare how public policy is distorted by concealed private interests, old-boy networks, and a militaristic mentality. This is in the Naderesque tradition of *Unsafe At Any Speed.*"

— Jack Newfield, senior editor of the
Village Voice

"If we are lucky *Reagan's Ruling Class* will form the raw material for a satiric musical comedy by Gilbert and Sullivan of the year 2000. For this book casts together in potentially comic conjunction the new Napoleons of commerce, ideological purists and Machiavellian maneuverers whose tense relations would convulse a Pirandello.

Brownstein and Easton are empiricists. Their fact-infested book will invigorate that saving remnant among Mr. Jefferson's inheritors who insist on a real world basis for real world policies. The authors tell us who the officers are, where they come from, what others say about them, and where they get their money and their ideas. New interviews let the Reaganites speak in their own argot.

Citizens who care enough to reach beyond the fluff, swoop and tinkle of the daily news will find solid fare in these pages. Professors who presume to instruct the next generation about the Washington big time really ought not to claim preparation until they possess this up-to-date volume."

— James David Barber, professor of
political science at Duke University,
author, *The Pulse of Politics*

"In its careful documentation of who the leaders of this Administration are, *Reagan's Ruling Class* goes far towards illuminating the Administration's values and explaining why it has chosen its present course. All people with an interest in how the national government actually functions—be they journalists or professors, lobbyists or lawyers, or active voters—should have this book at close reach on their shelf."

— James Fallows, Washington editor,
The Atlantic Monthly and author
National Defense

Reagan's Ruling Class

Reagan's Ruling Class

Portraits of the President's Top 100 Officials

Ronald Brownstein
and
Nina Easton

Introduction by Ralph Nader

The Presidential Accountability Group
Washington, D.C.

Published by:

Presidential Accountability Group
Box 19312
Washington, D.C. 20036
First printing
Printed in the United States of America
ISBN 0-936486-03-1
Library of Congress Card Catalogue Number 82-60917

AUTHOR'S NOTE

This book describes the major appointed officials of President Reagan's Administration. Whether they finish their terms or leave later in the Administration, the detailed road map has been laid out in the first year and a half of the Reagan presidency and recorded in *Reagan's Ruling Class*. Notwithstanding any later personnel changes, the future direction of the Reagan Administration, by its own declarations, has already been established during the period chronicled by this book.

Spicy, crisp, and comprehensive, *Reagan's Ruling Class* tells us not only what the Reagan Administration is doing, but *why*. It is a detailed roadmap to the men and women who spend your tax dollars, design the national defense and determine the margins of safety and health for millions of Americans.

An incisive examination of the links between public policy and private interest, the book is the most penetrating close-up of the Reagan government to date. James MacGregor Burns, the distinguished Pulitzer Prize-winning historian, says of *Reagan's Ruling Class:* ''A massive research and editorial job executed with sophistication and style, this book gives Americans the surest guide to their ruling class that they possess.''

Ronald Brownstein and **Nina Easton** are both staff writers for Ralph Nader. **Mr. Brownstein** is an editor of two previous books: *Who's Poisoning America* and *Selecting a President*. **Ms. Easton** is the author of *Reagan's Squeeze on Small Business*. Their work has appeared in many national magazines and newspapers including the *Los Angeles Times*, the *Boston Globe*, the *Christian Science Monitor, Newsday*, the *Village Voice, Parade, Reader's Digest* and the *Nation*.

Cover design by Kandy Jean Littrell

The Presidential Accountability Group
Box 19312, Washington D.C. 20036

TABLE OF CONTENTS

AUTHOR'S PREFACE

This book was a year in the making. It required the review of tens of thousands of pages of testimony, speeches, articles and other books, hundreds of interviews, thousands of hours of transcribing, proofreading, checking and rechecking.

Obviously a work of this magnitude cannot be done alone. And it was not. Many people assisted with this project. Several wrote profiles, others helped to research, and many more donated their time to review portions of the manuscript.

Kathy Hughes in particular assisted throughout, writing several profiles (many in collaboration with Brad Zweck, who worked on the project in the summer of 1981),fact-checking many more, and putting in long hours at the proofreading and production stage. Even with other deadlines, she handled her responsibilities for this book with good humor and steady performance.

In addition to Brad Zweck, who wrote or assisted in the writing of about two dozen profiles, Larry Elveru, Mike Fortun, Robert Bragdon, Christal Kyriacou, Jane Stone and Anne Urban all contributed profiles, devoting hours of research and writing. The profile of James Buckley is based largely on an article by Carl Mayer and Bill Taylor of the Public Interest Research Group. The work of all these people was an integral part of the final project.

Many other people helped with the research. But two made particular contributions. Rodman Low spent several months digging through the Library of Congress for information on two dozen of the officials profiled; he found many telling facts that we would have otherwise missed. Tom Street also performed valuable research on a number of profiles, then donated weeks of his time to assist in proofreading. Research assistance was also provided by Clark Roberts, Brad Martin, Karen Burns, Andy Broderick, Rich Collins, Phillip Simon, and David Schwartz. Doug King managed the files that made this book possible. Marilyn Osterman and Phyllis Mc-Carthy typed drafts of the manuscript that most people would have considered illegible. We give our special thanks to Kandy Jean Littrell who put many hours into designing the cover and the book.

Throughout Washington, dozens of people gave time and assistance. But, again, some were particularly generous with their time, either reviewing portions of the manuscript, suggesting further ideas, and redirecting us when we strayed. These included: Stan Norris, Seymour Hersh, Alan Morrison, Fred Townsend, Joan Claybrook, Matthew Rothschild, Matt Finucane, Sam Simon, Joe Waz, John Alter, Richard Udell, Peter Kirby, Rolfe Larson, Eleanor Randolph, Clarence Ditlow, Gary Sellers, David Wise, John Brown, Dr. Sid Wolfe and the Health Research Group, Strobe Talbott, Arthur Fox, Paul Levy and Dave Bradley.

There will never be total agreement, of course, on which are really the "top 100" officials in the federal government, and there may well be some who would quarrel with some of those included. We have profiled only appointees in the executive branch; hence, judges were excluded. And if there is a bias in the selection procedure, it is towards officials with line responsibilities rather than general authority—i.e., the assistant secretary of labor for occupational safety and health rather than the undersecretary was profiled.

We began this book with the proposition that the federal government belongs to the governed, that officials who carry out laws in the name of the people should be known to the people. Of the 100 officials profiled in this book, 57 graciously gave time out of busy schedules to be interviewed, some for up to two hours. We requested interviews with all 100. Below we list the officials who granted our request, and those who declined.

OFFICIALS WHO GRANTED INTERVIEWS

Thorne Auchter (Occupational Safety and Health Administration)
Malcolm Baldrige (Commerce)
Ray Barnhart (Federal Highway Administration)
William Baxter (Justice)
Robert Blanchette (Federal Railroad Administration)
Lawrence Brady (Commerce)
Shelby Brewer (Energy)
Robert Burford (Interior)
Frank Carlucci (Defense)
Gerald Carmen (General Services Administration)
William Casey (Central Intelligence Agency)
John Crowell (Agriculture)
Richard DeLauer (Defense)
Chris DeMuth (Office of Management and Budget)
Carol Dinkins (Justice)
Roscoe Egger (Internal Revenue Service)
Mark Fowler (Federal Communications Commission)
Rudolph Giuliani (Justice)
Anne Gorsuch (Environmental Protection Agency)
Edwin Harper (White House)
James Harris (Interior)
Arthur Hayes (Food and Drug Administration)
A. Alan Hill (Council on Environmental Quality)
Robert Hormats (State)
Lowell Jensen (Justice)
Phillip Johnson (Commodity Futures Trading Commission)
Rex Lee (Justice)
John Lehman (Defense)
Drew Lewis (Transportation)*
Richard Lyng (Agriculture)
John Marsh (Defense)
C. W. McMillian (Agriculture)
James Miller III (Federal Trade Commission)
Ernst Minor (Council on Environmental Quality)
Robert Nimmo (Veterans Administration)
William Niskanen (Council of Economic Advisers)
Paul Nitze (Arms Control and Disarmament Agency)
Verne Orr (Defense)
Nunzio Palladino (Nuclear Regulatory Commission)
Raymond Peck (National Highway Traffic Safety Administration)
Richard Perle (Defense)
Samuel Pierce (Housing and Urban Development)
Richard Pratt (Federal Home Loan Bank Board)
Donald Regan (Treasury)
Thomas Roberts (Nuclear Regulatory Commission)

*Lewis met with Ralph Nader though not directly in connection with this book.

Eugene Rostow (Arms Control and Disarmament Agency)
Edward Rowny (Arms Control and Disarmament Agency)
Timothy Ryan (Labor)
James Sanders (Small Business Administration)
Danford Sawyer (Public printer)
Edward Schmults (Justice)
Nancy Steorts (Consumer Product Safety Commission)
John Svahn (Social Security Administration)
Arthur Teele (Urban Mass Transportation Administration)
Norman Ture (Treasury)
Caspar Weinberger (Defense)
Murray Weidenbaum (Council of Economic Advisers)

OFFICIALS WHO DECLINED TO BE INTERVIEWED

James Baker III (White House)
Terrel Bell (Education)
John Block (Agriculture)
William Brock (Trade Representative)
James Buckley (State)
Charles Butler (Federal Energy Regulatory Commission)
William Clark (White House)
W. Kenneth Davis (Energy)
Michael Deaver (White House)
Donald Devine (Office of Personnel Management)
Raymond Donovan (Labor)
William Draper (Export-Import Bank)
Lawrence Eagleburger (State)
James Edwards (Energy)
Ford B. Ford (Mine Safety and Health Administration)
Alexander Haig (State)
J. Lynn Helms (Federal Aviation Administration)
Donald Hodel (Interior)
Donald Hovde (Housing and Urban Development)
Fred Ikle (Defense)
Mary Jarratt (Agriculture)
Jerry Jordan (Council of Economic Advisers)
Richard Kennedy (State)
Jeane Kirkpatrick (United Nations)
C. Everett Koop (Health and Human Services)
James Malone (State)
Peter McPherson (Agency for International Development)
Edwin Meese III (White House)
Edward Noble (Synthetic Fuels Corp.)
Lionel Olmer (Commerce)
William Olson and William Harvey (Legal Services Board Members)
Thomas Pauken (Action)
William Bradford Reynolds (Justice)
Richard Schweiker (Health and Human Services)
John Shad (Securities and Exchange Commission)

William French Smith (Justice)
Beryl Sprinkel (Treasury)
David Stockman (Office of Management and Budget)
Walter Stoessel (State)
Reese Taylor (Interstate Commerce Commission)
Joseph Tribble (Energy)
John Van de Water (National Labor Relations Board)
James Watt (Interior)

As the above lists make clear, some departments were extremely cooperative. In the Defense Department, seven of the eight officials profiled—from Secretary Weinberger on down—granted interviews, which in most cases lasted more than an hour. In the State Department, despite repeated requests, only one official (assistant secretary Robert Hormats) agreed to be interviewed. The Energy Department similarly chose to stonewall us. We felt that the interviews added a vital dimension to the profiles, allowing the officials to explain in their own words what they believe, how their experiences have shaped those beliefs, and how they respond to critics of their policies.

The master of evasion, though, was the Justice Department's Thomas DeCair, spokesman for Attorney General William French Smith. Though we had arranged interviews with the assistant attorney generals, DeCair refused for literally several months to give a final answer on a meeting with the attorney general, even after a conversation between Ralph Nader and Attorney General Smith about the interview. DeCair never did give us an answer. Through Deputy Attorney General Edward Schmults (who did meet with us) we finally learned that Smith would not grant an interview. Schmults said, however, that Smith would respond to written questions. We sent the questions to Smith, with a copy to Schmults. Smith never answered the questions. (Both Raymond Donovan and Ford B. Ford in the Labor Department also asked for written questions, then refused to respond.)

In all, though, almost 60 percent of the officials profiled agreed to make themselves available for what they knew would be some tough questions. We applaud their accessibility for these interviews.

In addition to the 57 officials profiled in the book, we conducted more than 500 other interviews over a one-year period. We spoke with people who worked with or knew the officials, and experts in the field under their purview. Many of their predecessors in the Carter Administration granted interviews. Among them were: Secretary Bob Bergland (Agriculture) and Patricia Harris (HUD and HHS); Eula Bingham (OSHA); Doug Costle (EPA); Paul Warnke (ACDA); and many others. Since many of the Reagan officials (particularly in the national security area) were part of the Nixon and Ford Administrations, we spoke with dozens of officials from those administrations as well, including virtually all the major figures involved in arms control and many of Henry Kissinger's closest aides.

For the sections involving the officials' current activities, we relied on congressional analysts who track the agencies. In addition, useful information and varying perspectives were provided by industry and public interest lobbyists in areas from environmental protection to arms control to trade with the Soviet Union.

As any Washington reporter knows, most people are very reluctant to speak candidly on the record about current government officials. That is particularly true for people still active in their field, who subsequently might have to deal with these officials. Congressional aides, for their part, are generally under an injunction to keep their names out of the newspaper—hence they usually appear as an "aide at the Senate _____ Committee."

Since we relied extensively on those two sources, the book uses a sizable number of anonymous quotes. Wherever possible, we sought to hold interviews on the record—indeed many of the interviews represented in the profiles are clearly identified. But in other cases, where the granting of anonymity appeared to be the best way to obtain the most candid and complete portrayals, we chose to accept those ground rules.

In addition to interviews, we extensively reviewed documentary evidence. In most cases, we read all of the speeches and testimony given by the official since he or she took office. We also read most (if not all) of their previous congressional testimony, and any speeches that were available, as well as newspaper and magazine articles and books relating to their activities before assuming office. We also reviewed the confirmation hearings for all of those profiled in the book.

Most profiles contain five sections. We begin with the *Responsibility of Office*, which lays out the statutory responsibilities of each official. Unless otherwise noted, the quotes in these sections that explain each agency's legal responsibilities are taken from the official *United States Government Manual, 1980-81* (published by the Office of the Federal Register, National Archives and Records Services).

The next section covers the official's *Background*. In addition to basic biographical data, this section includes a sketch of the official's career, and a sampling of their stands and beliefs, gleaned from speeches and articles they may have written over the years, and interviews with them and others that have known them.

The third section, *Major Issues*, examines the official's activities in Washington. This section, of course, does not deal with *all* of the major issues facing each agency; it discusses those that we determined to be the most significant to the most people. Where appropriate, we have included in this section a short list summarizing the major points for quick reference.

The fourth section deals with the official's *Financial Background*. All information in this section, unless otherwise noted, is taken from the financial disclosure form filed with the Office of Government Ethics (of the Office of Personnel Management).

Because of the manner in which financial assets are reported to the Office of Government Ethics, the figures on wealth (assets) can be merely suggestive. Currently, the disclosure forms require government officials to list assets in one of six broad categories as follows: $1,000-$5,000; $5,000-$15,000; $15,000-$50,000; $50,000-$100,000; $100,000-$250,000; $250,000 and over. In all cases we have used the *lowest* figure in calculating the total holdings of any individual. (Hence, a holding reported between $100,000 and $250,000 on the form would be calculated as $100,000.) So the data on holdings in this section represent the minimum total; the actual figures may be many times greater, as is quickly demonstrated when other information is available.

The uncertainty created by the current form is too large to truly assess the financial interests of any given official in the performance of a particular industry. We suggest the form be amended to include three additional categories: $250,000-$500,000; $500,000 to $1 million; and $1 million and above. For most nominees, this would require no additional disclosure. In those few cases where it would be required, that information should be available to the public.

The salary figures listed in the *Financial Background* section should also be considered merely suggestive. For shorthand, we have labeled these figures as the officials' 1980 earnings. Under the 1981 financial disclosure form, though, the officials report their earnings during the 1980 calendar year, plus their earnings in 1981 for up until 30 days prior to filing. For some officials appointed late in the Administration this means some of the income reported was actually earned in 1981. When an individual broke down their earnings between 1980 and 1981 we have reported that information. Where they did not, we did not attempt to disaggregate the figure, having no way to apportion it between 1980 and 1981 earnings. So, again, these numbers generally give a range, not a precise total.

Finally, we must thank Ralph Nader, who prompted, prodded, reviewed, interviewed, edited, rewrote and helped carry the book through to completion. We hope this book exemplifies the value of citizen inquiry. Government, after all, holds its power only in trust for that citizenry and must always be reminded of that simple fact.

Ronald Brownstein & Nina Easton
Washington, D.C., June, 1982

INTRODUCTION

BY
RALPH NADER

Most Presidential inaugurals in this century would not have pleased Andrew Jackson. They have been opulent affairs, often with upper crust pomp, ceremony and guests quite at variance with the folksy imprints making up the cross-country campaigns completed only a few weeks earlier. But, the inauguration of Ronald Reagan overwhelmed even the limousine rental companies as they rolled out their huge steel carriages for the multimillionaire couples who attended the lavish receptions, dinners and dances.

It was a gala Hollywood East that neither high inflation nor high unemployment could temper. Donnie Radcliffe, the veteran social reporter for *The Washington Post*, observed that "The Republican aristocracy took over Washington this weekend, making it safe again to put on diamonds, designer gowns and—speaking generally—the dog . . . the women came prepared in their full-length minks and sables over their St. Laurents, Oscar de la Rentas, Halstons and Bill Blasses . . . ;" "a bacchanalia of the haves" was the pithy phrase of reporter Elisabeth Bumiller. Nancy Reagan was not to be outdistanced by her social peers. She came to Washington with a $25,000 inaugural wardrobe, including a Maximilian mink coat replacing her old black mink that designer Adolfo had thoughtfully recycled into her raincoat lining.

Fortune magazine painted a portrait of regal congestion: "an armada of 400 corporate jets snarled traffic at National Airport. The streets were bumper-to-bumper with limousines . . . cloakrooms all around the capital were chockablock with mink." As many Americans were to learn in the coming months, such ostentation spoke less of festival than of a ruling culture's way of life.

Inaugurals always attract their share of the super-rich, coming to see and be seen. However, in this case, some came to stay. They were part of the new government whose leaders were invested by an electoral college landslide produced, in turn, by securing half of the half of the voters who bothered to come to the polls on November 4, 1980. This is, unabashedly, a government of the wealthy. Its top six members—President Reagan, Vice-President George Bush, Attorney General William French Smith, Secretary of Defense Caspar Weinberger, Secretary of State Alexander Haig, and Secretary of the Treasury Donald Regan are all multimillionaires. Mr. Regan, fresh from heading the world's largest brokerage company, Merrill Lynch, suggested in a *New York Times* interview that his material worth is $35 million. The Midas touch does not stop with these gentlemen. Over a fourth of the top one hundred Reagan Administration officials have net worths of seven figures, or more. In 1981, public financial reports[*] indicated that Secretary of Commerce Malcolm Baldrige received income just that year between $1.5 and $2.5 million, on top of his government salary. Secretary of Transportation Drew Lewis received nearly one million dollars in the same period.

---

[*]On June 8, 1981 Assistant Attorney General Jonathan Rose declared the Reagan Administration is studying proposals to repeal the requirements that high federal officials file public reports on their financial holdings.

Little of this wealth was inherited. The nouveau riche status may help to explain the absence of noblesse oblige which has characterized the paternalism of the Old Rich who entered politics. "The preponderance of these people are self-made," noted foreign propaganda director Charles Z. Wick, head of the International Communications Agency and a close friend of the President. "They followed the American dream." As reported in *The New York Times*, "Mr. Wick said he thought that economically pinched Americans of today enjoyed viewing the luxurious Washington way of life of the Reagan Administration members, much as Americans who suffered in the Depression enjoyed watching Hollywood stars in the movies."

Ronald Reagan knew only a small fraction of the one hundred men and very few women whom he appointed to his government's top positions. But, his recruiters knew how to find his mirror images. Our studies and interviews of the officials in this book demonstrate a remarkable sameness among them—of attitudes, ideologies, and even styles of thinking and explaining. It was difficult to find a maverick, apart from a few to the extreme right of Mr. Reagan.

The recruitment drive was directed by the "Kitchen Cabinet," a group of close-knit, wealthy friends of Mr. Reagan who groomed him for the California governorship and the Presidency. The hard core of this Kitchen Cabinet included Attorney General William French Smith, Justin W. Dart, industrialist and drug store chain mogul, Holmes P. Tuttle, a Los Angeles automobile dealer, William A. Wilson, a California rancher and real estate developer, Henry Salvatori, an oil producer, and Earle M. Jorgenson, president of a steel company. Joseph Coors of Coors Brewing Company and Walter H. Annenberg, publisher, were active in the post-election, pre-inaugural period. Meeting regularly in California and Washington as an executive advisory committee to recommend prospective nominees for high level appointments in the new Administration, the group left little to chance. As described by Henry Salvatori, three criteria guided their selection procedure: "One, was he a Reagan man? Two, a Republican? and three, a conservative?" Salvatori told the *National Journal* that the committee members agreed with one another 99 percent of the time on the final decisions, and Reagan accepted almost all their recommendations.

White House Chief of Staff James A. Baker III was engaging in understatement when he said: "Anytime the President's friends—members of the kitchen cabinet—want to see him we put them on the schedule." Early on in the Administration, these evangelists of a corporatist political ideology set the tone for the ethical short-circuits which later began to plague high Reagan officials. They were given offices in the Old Executive Office building next to the White House, a private influence group using federal property. The offices were vacated only when the irregularity became too prominent. Parallel to this transgression was the drive by Dart and Wick to raise corporate funds for the purpose of promoting Reagan's economic program through a group called "The Coalition for a New Beginning." This dunning, implying that the new regime would be good to them, turned off some corporate executives, and adverse publicity ended that endeavor.

Around the same time, Holmes Tuttle was soliciting tax deductible contributions of $10,000 or more from oil executives and other wealthy businessmen which provided about $250,000 to finance Nancy Reagan's plans to redecorate the White House. This effort began a month after Reagan had decontrolled oil prices which allowed the oil industry to reap profits in the billions of dollars. Former Watergate special prosecutor and Harvard Law Professor Archibald Cox commented that this fund-raising "shows a surprising insensitivity" to the danger of mixing money and politics. For Senator William Proxmire (D-Wis.) these oil company donations were "as blatant a presidential conflict of interest as I can recall in the more than 20 years I've been in Congress." Since these contributions were deductible, Representative Patricia Schroeder, (D-Colo.) complained that "if the oil donors are in the 50 percent tax bracket, it could cost the government $130,000 in lost revenues." Perhaps the aristocratic attitude was best observed by Professor Cox who said: "The White House belongs to all the people and should be refurbished by all the people, not just representatives of a select special interest." As an ideal, Cox was right on the board. But the Reagan White House did not belong to all the people, just to what Mary McGrory has called "the deserving rich." Such a description of some Administrations might be considered a normative statement. For the Reagan Administration, it was simply a statement of fact, reaffirmed day in and day out by its actions, inactions and profound absence of either a public philosophy or public compassion. Boundaries or limits to their ideology are hard to ascertain. Programs for the poor and the mentally and physically disabled are undergoing callously sharp cuts that include a medical diagnosis and treatment program for two million poor children. And Rep. David Obey (D-Wis.), who does not usually use such strong words, called the 1983 Reagan budget passed by the House, "a venal, vicious attack on the working poor."

Reagan officials, along with their President, have difficulty projecting popular political symbols in their departmental operations, in contrast to candidate Reagan's adept use of electioneering symbols and slogans during the campaign. While the Reagan leadership was daily alerting the public to the need for belt-tightening, top officials were spending ample sums redecorating their offices and enjoying illicit perquisites. The number of White House limousines is distinctly higher than in the Carter years. The President did not oppose or even criticize the passage of a notoriously huge tax deduction privilege by members of Congress for themselves, late in 1981.

The top Reaganites are reluctant to mix with ordinary people—injured workers, consumers and afflicted elderly. They avoid direct contact with victims who suffer from the harmful conditions they are supposed to be regulating. Their forays out of Washington are almost invariably to appear before party contributors or business audiences. It is not easy to envision the Environmental Protection Agency's (EPA) Anne Gorsuch visiting ghetto children ill from lead poisoning or learning from communities contaminated by toxic waste dumps. One awaits in vain for Thorne Auchter of the Occupational Safety and Health Administration (OSHA) to expose his mind to the realities of workers maimed or sickened from workplace hazards. Belatedly aware of unfavorable imagery that they create, some agency heads have retained outside public relations consultants for assistance. Others simply do not care. They flaunt their identity with the affluent instead of emphasizing duties of public trusteeship. As a principal fundraiser for the Republican Party, James Watt leaves his daily watch as Interior Secretary to speak with exclusive audiences whose minds are on tax shelters and cheap leaseholds of public lands.

Reaganites lend their presence to gatherings of the Eagles, a rarified club established by the Republican National Committee (RNC). Membership is assured by a $10,000 contribution to RNC. An admiring President Reagan attended their annual dinner at the Washington Hilton Hotel on January 20, 1982. "This is a very impressive gathering," he said. "When I walked in I thought I was back in the studio on the set of 'High Society'." Donnie Radcliffe spotted a guest in flowing pink chiffon offering a discordant note: "Actually, I think this whole thing is rather ridiculous," she said. "I mean the country's in a recession and on the first anniversary we're all here throwing away thousands of dollars."

Corporate executives in the audience might have disagreed with this evaluation. Their thousands of dollars were an investment in Congress and the White House with a rate of return which, historically, has been well worth the effort. Politicians, indeed, have much to offer to these high bidders—shunting aside regulations, preserving subsidies and monopolistic licenses, going soft on corporate crime prosecutions, expanding profitable government contracts and keeping other excluded American publics from challenging the consolidation of the corporate state.

The persons who run the federal government with Mr. Reagan are largely from the business world. They view the role of government as largely a many-splendored accounts receivable for the business community. They speak repeatedly of the mandate of November 1980, involving reduced government deficits, larger military budgets, and fewer safety regulations. Contradictions between these objectives were to be resolved by lower taxes leading to an expanding economy which would produce the needed revenues. This was generally speaking "supply-side economics" writ large. University of Michigan Professor Arthur H. Miller, the director of the 1980 American national election survey at the Institute of Social Research in a June 1981 article titled "What Mandate? What Realignment?" criticized what he called "The Year of the Invented Mandate" with these words:

> Treasury Secretary Donald Regan, defending the administration's three-year tax cut plan proclaims that the president "was elected on this basis." Vice President George Bush declares that congressional opponents of the president's spending and tax cut proposals would "in effect thwart the mandate of the people."

> Budget chief David Stockman adds his assertions that cuts in social programs are dictated by the elections, and Nevada Senator Paul Laxalt defends anti-abortion, pro-capital punishment and other conservative social causes by contending: "That's what the election was all about. It is part of the Reagan mandate."

> All this may or may not be good politics but it certainly is nonsense, and awfully repetitious nonsense at that. If administration officials are going to keep it up, there is little choice but to repeat back, emphatically: That is not what the election was about. The accumulating evidence makes it quite clear that the November returns provided none of these claimed mandates, just as they did not represent the broader "historical political realignment" that more than a few observers have suggested.

Repeated references to The November Mandate were attempts by a new Administration to legitimize its policies, notwithstanding diverse and numerous national polls to the contrary in areas such as price controls, pollution reduction, consumer protection, tax reform, and business crime. The omnibus slogan for the language of mandate was "Getting government off your backs." Behind the semantic curtain something quite serious was going on in the Reagan Administration. Power was being reshuffled in the age old game of politics but this time swiftly away from consumers, small taxpayers, receivers of social programs and workers toward large corporations, especially the multinational corporate variety. Not that these popular constituencies ever had that much control under previous administrations. However, the shift to more concentrated power in the hands of the few certainly became more pronounced. The rich indeed are getting richer and more powerful and the middle class and poor are finding their meagre economic and political assets slipping, the former less able to buy homes and find jobs, and the latter less able to receive sustenance for the bare necessities of life.

Contrary to the claims of Reaganites that all can prosper if the President's economic policies are adopted is the almost categorical way that they have made choices in favor of corporate demands when these conflict with popular need. Across the board—from the allocation of taxpayer revenue to deeper inequities in the tax system to the disposition of public lands to the abandonment of health and safety programs to severe reductions of social services to antagonistic policies toward freedom of information, civil rights and civil liberties—the Reagan Administration has chosen to increase the control of corporations and to decrease the rights of citizens and their access to government while the national security state has become more unaccountable.

A supporter of President Reagan, columnist George Will, scoffed at suggestions that the 1980 election constitutes a mandate. In his words, "it was not a national conversion to conservative ideology. It was a desire to see Carter gone . . . Reagan won because he kept the election from being a referendum on conservative ideology."

At the onset of any Administration, the rhetoric of legitimacy assumes a cloud-like proportion. But, well into the second year of Reagan's tenure, his record is displacing his rhetorical veneer. The motifs of the Republican regime are now well-established.

The regime is foremost a homogenized government by elites. Even organized labor leaders are out; also gone are the minorities, the poor, the elderly, consumers and environmentalists. Their clientele agencies have either disappeared or become moribund. Most of the laws respecting their rights are, of course, still intact. But their interpretation, implementation and enforcement reflect heavily corporatist or elitist mentalities. Top officials, while they would not use such words, are quite forthright in expressing their meaning. Their logic runs this way. They truly believe that the rich are simply more talented and skilled people. If unleashed and assisted, corporations can bring economic progress. If the U.S. is equipped with more awesome weaponry, war can be deterred. Washington lawyer Fred Dutton's description of Attorney General William French Smith's view typifies this perspective: "Smith's philosophy is that a small central establishment of a few people who have proven successful should run the rest of our lives."

It is erroneous to describe the Reaganites as anti-government or against big government. They are systematically redefining those terms to accord with their ideology of power. Instead of the political government curbing the power of economic government (or the excesses of the monied interests, as Thomas Jefferson put it) the Reagan rulers are pointing the might of the state in other directions. Certainly, greatly expanding the military budget, increasing government secrecy, closing off avenues of citizen participation in government, releasing the FBI and CIA from post-Watergate restraints, weakening the national defense against endemic polluters, monopolists and corporate defrauders, and invading poor citizen privacies can scarcely be viewed as a drive for smaller government. Moreover, despite the talk about reducing government deficits and taxes, Reagan's deficits will reach historic highs while citizens with incomes under $30,000 (79% of all tax-payers) will pay more in federal taxes in 1984 than they did in 1980, according to data from the Joint Congressional Committee on Taxation.

Many Americans must be puzzled by what reducing child immunization and infant nutrition programs or weakening nursing home inspection enforcement standards have to do with getting "government off the backs of the people" or lessening "big government" for that matter. The low priority given to prosecutions of most corporate crimes, such as the multi-billion dollar oil company overcharges of consumers and underpayment of royalties to the government, is a strange application of campaign law and order rhetoric. "The new federalism" engine stalls when corporations want to overturn state laws they do not like. Federal pre-emption of state laws relating to the transportation and storage of radioactive wastes, and attempts to override state usury and due-on-sale provisions, and coastal zone management authority all illustrate that, as in the regulatory area, the ideology of the Reaganites is, in fact, principally one of consistent expediency.

What is really at work here is the dismantling of government's traditional public role in defending victims abused by established private powers. Reagan's government is getting off the backs of the powerful who coerce the powerless. This translates into a loss of freedom from corporate toxic waste dumps, price-fixers, joblessness, racialism, sexism, and dangerous products or services.

The bulwark and fabric of the Reagan Administration are the major industrial and commercial corporations. There are, to be sure, resident libertarians who would like government to dissolve as there are moral majoritarian adherents who would like government to regulate the most personal of human behavior. Although both are part of the Reagan leadership coalition, they appear not to be very important elements in Reagan's actual priorities. Apart from soothing assurances, White House aides, who say economic and defense policy must take precedence, politely put off both constituencies. Of course, given the public's expectation of government's responsibility for remedying the chronic problems of what is essentially a big business run private economy, economic policies will always take precedence along with defense questions. Thus, from the original perspective of the groups who believed they elected Ronald Reagan, the focus of the Administration is narrowing to four objectives: give more power and fewer tax obligations to the rich; expand the weapons arsenal; sharply reduce the regulatory rule of law from application to the business world; and transfer many social programs to the states under sharply reduced bloc grants.

Accomplishing these goals requires people who have prejudged the array of public policies with a studied insensitivity to facts and a calculated indifference to alternate means to solve undeniable problems. Such officials need a strong ideological fealty and an unwillingness to collect information about injustice and human suffering. In department after department, for example, in energy, environment, and human services, the data base required for informed policy making, is being restricted or abolished outright.

In interviews, the officials were asked about their sense of mission and place in history. Many said they want to make their agency or department more efficient ("streamline" is a favorite word) and less burdensome on business. Many revealed a restlessness in their position, a desire to "get it over with" and return to or start a lucrative private career. Others expressed an enthusiasm at finding themselves in positions where their adversaries were sitting a short time earlier. They believed that it was their day in the sun and they were going for broke. In both camps there was little idealism expressed for alleviating the agonies of human beings. Statements of compassion are viewed as a sign of softness or of becoming a dreaded "bleeding heart"; they are not in style. Their speeches and testimony leave little sense of legacy, of humane vision, of what James MacGregor Burns called a "transforming or moral leadership." The top Reaganites are generally power holders, not leaders. For many, their pride is in managing well a blueprint handed down by their superiors. Again and again in the social services and regulatory agencies, the blueprint calls for doing nothing or repealing or reducing operations. Even anticipated responsiveness to the needs of Vietnam veterans has been placed in reverse. Problems that their agencies are supposed to address are minimized, denied, or considered the business of the states.

The lack of diverse viewpoints and program experience in the Reagan Administration is profound. Even the Nixon Administration had people who cared such as Russell Train who headed the Environmental Protection Agency and John Volpe, who was the Secretary of Transportation. In their uniformity of outlook and class background, the top Reaganites appear as a product of a giant cloning process whose sameness further insulate the President and themselves from the pressing needs and the realities of American society. Lyndon Johnson's press secretary, George Reedy, now a professor of journalism, offered a contrasting view of the dynamics within the Executive branch: "government should be vulgar, sweaty, plebian, operating in an environment where a fool can be called a fool and the motivations of ideological pimpery duly observed and noted."

President Reagan's advisory style is to stay with people of long acquaintance—the tight circle of the Kitchen Cabinet and a few trusted aides. "The glue which holds us together," said Attorney General Smith, "is our friendship with [Reagan] and the traditions and associations we share." The *Washington Post* analyst, Haynes Johnson, commenting on Reagan's isolation, wrote:

> He remains singularly committed to the absolute rightness of his beliefs. He gives no hint of being willing to accept any responsibility for the problems his economic plan had produced. He shows every indication of being truly convinced of the ultimate correctness of his course. The President sounds his own bells, sticks to his guns. Either, he doesn't hear the dissonant sounds crashing around him, or he doesn't want to hear.

A predictable consequence of isolation is Mr. Reagan's recurrent factual mistakes and fictional renderings at public gatherings. Whether these pertain to the number of Interstate Commerce Commission decisions (42 trillion rate decisions in 85 years!) or to the sources of air pollution (mostly from trees!) or to descriptions of budget cuts (there was no reduction in student aid!) or to asserting that unemployment had declined since he took office (when it had clearly increased!), the process of spinning these unreal webs is unabated by anything except the infrequencies of news conferences. It is an extremist Republican world that prevails in the White House with a contagious permissiveness allowing top officials to engage in Newspeak and Dr. Strangelove pronouncements.

At the Environmental Protection Agency, Anne Gorsuch firmly says she will protect more of the environment at the same time that she massively cuts the budget and personnel and severely impedes the standards and the enforcement process. At a media-packed October 1981 press conference, reporters could scarcely contain their demeanor when they heard Raymond Peck, the National Highway Traffic Safety Administrator, announce that his revocation of a major crash-safety regulation, ten years in the making, was done to save lives.

Murray Weidenbaum, James Miller and Raymond Peck continually speak about the costs to industry of health and safety standards which they want repealed without bothering to indicate the benefits in lives and injuries and costs saved.

While the Reaganites justify their deeds by referring to the mandate of November 1980, specific national poll after national poll shows overwhelming public opinion contrary to their drive to weaken the air and water pollution laws, or to stop the auto, worker, and food safety improvement programs, or to abolish the Legal Services Corporation. (The latter move prompted a joint letter by the former chief executive officers of DuPont, General Motors and General Electric asking the Reagan Administration to save the successful program that provides lawyers for the poor.)

Other polls show that the American people want to maintain the social welfare and job training programs for the poor but want fraud and waste stopped. The Reaganites assail fraud and waste but do little in such areas as criminal fraud by physicians against medicare. They deny cutting back on "the truly needy" but the record shows that they are cutting back on "the truly needy," including vital health and educational assistance to disadvantaged school children—among the most vulnerable of Americans. A *New York Times* editorial in June, 1980 declared:

"Almost any way you slice the budget figures, spending for people in need is being cut. The poor are being penalized. The special pleaders, if that's how Mr. Reagan thinks of advocates for the voiceless poor, are right." The *Times* was reacting to a repeated Ronald Reagan claim: "There have been no budget cuts"—only slower spending growth. Gallup polls report that 65 percent of the public thinks he doesn't care about the poor while 75 percent thinks he does care about the rich, added the editorial.

The almost unanimous opposition to Reaganomics by Black, Hispanic, Indian and other minority groups appears to be discounted by the White House as politically expected and inconsequential. When the moderate National Urban League condemned the Administration for a "betrayal of basic civil rights protections," it was only civic pressure on Congress that induced the Executive Branch to back down on some of the more extreme civil rights erosions.

Such facts and such polls do not give the Reagan leadership much pause. In interviews, they always have an explanation to discount the message. The public is "under a misconception," or the public is just "the most vociferous," "not the silent majority or the responsible viewpoint," or that the opinion wave is a temporary fad which will pass.

Facing down the facts is a persistent trait. It was again illustrated in yet another setting by the following exchange at a Senate hearing between Senator Claiborne Pell (D.-R.I.) and Eugene Rostow, director of the Arms Control and Disarmament Agency:

Pell: In the event of a full nuclear exchange between the Soviet Union and the United States, do you envision either country surviving to any substantial degree?

Rostow: It depends on how extensive the nuclear exchange is . . . Japan, after all, not only survived but flourished after the nuclear attack . . .

Pell: My questions is, in a full nuclear exchange, would a country survive?

Rostow: The human race is very resilient, Senator Pell.

Pell: Oh, the race is; but I asked if either country would survive.

Rostow: Well, there are ghoulish statistical calculations that are made about how many people would die . . . some estimates predict that there would be 10 million casualities on one side and 100 million on the other. But that is not the whole population.

There are some in the higher echelons of power in the country who are becoming more worried over the disruptive consequences of rupturing the social compact between government and less fortunate citizens. Social programs have been viewed by many political analysts as a form of pacification as well as a mode of redistributive justice. Predictions of riots in the cities reflect these concerns. But Reaganite philosophy believes that the culture of poverty and discrimination has no relation or, at least, cannot be recognized as a cause of riots or ghetto crimes. Therefore, social service reductions become principally a matter of budgetary imperatives, despite studies showing higher social costs will be incurred from such mindless neglect.

Conditions that could be treated with a more sophisticated and varied human response are reduced to dollar numbers. This process gives a robotized character to the Reagan leadership. The formula is often called a cost-benefit one. But whose cost-benefit? The formula, as applied, considers only the costs and benefits affecting the short-term profits and politics of an industry based on industry's figures. This book abounds with illustrations of this point. Reaganomics here means maintaining official price-setting and cartel schemes that are repugnant to people like Treasury Secretary Donald Regan, Council of Economic Advisers Chairman Murray Weidenbaum, and Administrator of the Office of Management and Budget's Regulatory Affairs Office Christopher DeMuth. But, because corporate power is behind these anathemas, it prevails over their free market ideology—as Weidenbaum and DeMuth wistfully implied to our interviewers. On the other hand, regulations that clearly prevent human casualties and economic waste are revoked or imperiled (for example, the auto crash protection or the lead poisoning standard) are delayed until tragedy occurs (for example, nutrition standards for infant formula), again, because power rejects sound policy.

Draped by false analytic pretense, the cost-benefit formula has repealed or undermined standards which curb known dangers to health and safety; it has jettisoned well-documented rules which would save taxpayers' money and inform buyers of possible product hazards and deficiencies. When officials like James Miller, who in secret as an OMB staff member rode herd on regulatory agencies, lose the cost-benefit argument, they raise the cost-effective challenge (for example, the use of worker respirators instead of engineering prevention of cotton dust in textile mills) and when that challenge is effectively rebutted, the Millers sometimes retreat to inapposite, inter-modal arguments (for example, money for preventing cotton dust lung disease could save more lives if applied to reducing worker alcoholism). When interviewers asked Mr. Miller whether there were any specific safety/health regulations that should be issued or stengthened by the Reagan Administration, this long-time student of all regulatory agencies replied ''Most of the relevant and needed regulations are on the books in some form or another.'' Not from any agency dealing with pollution or product hazards would he give a single example of the need for stronger standards.

So, the monetization of basic human values into a corporate-shaped calculus continues with greater force than ever. Vice-President George Bush proudly boasts to business audiences about his role in eliminating health and safety regulations. He makes no mention of how many lives and limbs his advocacy is also eliminating or mutilating. For Bush, it is purely a matter of how many such regulations he can stop, a sterile numbers game.

Apparently, few of these contradictions cause the regulators any unease. They were, after all, chosen to administer these programs because they would follow orders to abolish or weaken them. Consider a sample of illustrations. Robert Burford is a rancher and state legislator who was fined more than once by the Bureau of Land Management, the agency he now heads. In office he is proposing changes to loosen federal grazing policy, despite studies showing much of federal land is already overgrazed. James Watt, as Secretary of the Interior, cannot wait to lease one billion acres of offshore lands to the oil companies and to accelerate corporate exploitation of the public lands at bargain basement prices. John Crowell, formerly an attorney for two paper company giants, can now continue his mission as head of the U.S. Forest Service. Thorne Auchter, whose Florida construction firm received 48 safety violations from OSHA from 1972 to 1980, now is running OSHA into the ground. John Van de Water, chairman of the National Labor Relations Board, is the former president of a leading West Coast anti-union consulting firm. James C. Miller, an anarchist when it comes to regulating business, heads the Federal Trade Commission whose mission is to police deceptive and anti-competitive practices. He even objects to consumer labeling requirements for food and household fabrics. Raymond Peck, administrator of the National Highway Traffic Safety Administration, had a long record of resisting governmental curbs on coal strip-mining. Chosen for his new task because of his background as a true-believer, he has proceeded to strip-mine the auto safety standards and programs.

In the national security area, individuals who have made careers out of opposing arms control efforts are now responsible for arms control policies and negotiations. Edward Rowny is one such official. A former Army General, he has been chosen to negotiate START, the Strategic Arms Reduction Talks. Rowny had left the SALT II delegation to join forces with Senator Henry Jackson and fight the ratification of the SALT II treaty. In a 1980 speech, Rowny said: "You will note to date that I have had little to say about arms control. I have done this because my six and one-half years with SALT have led me to the conclusion that we have put too much emphasis on the *control* of arms and too little on the *provision* of arms." Attention to international human rights suffers from similar attitudes.

The circulation of elites between business and government will continue in the Reagan Administration. Too many temptations are being dangled before high government officials to expect anything but a turnover of these officials in search of the affluent groves of commerce. Replacements are quite likely to be drawn from the same strata as the officials profiled herein. Already, cases involving personal financial dealings, conflicts of interests, or misuse of public funds have matured into public condemnations and some resignations. Old Washington hands sense a fertile breeding ground for larger scandals later in the Administration. *The New York Times* noted that "a large number of Reagan appointees come from the industries they regulate, including those with ties to mining, forestry, trucking, securities, commodities futures, nuclear, drug, banking, oil, cattle and broadcasting industries." Most of these officials intend to return to their industries at enhanced levels of status and remuneration. It may be difficult for some of them to avoid what historian L.H. Jenks once described as the "unblushing confusion of the business of government with the promotion of private fortune."

This volume is about the President's top one hundred officials. Its significance is clear, when one considers the immense authority and power, both direct and derived, that these people and their predecessors have over 225 million Americans and future generations. We wish this work to start, in civic and scholarly circles, a tradition of continual scrutiny of the people who run the government for the President. The diffusion of reliable, empirical data about them could encourage more citizen interest in holding them accountable and in encouraging them toward operational and moral heights. Perhaps there could come a time when more of these officials would become household names like athletes and actors, as a result of greater public dialogue on important civic matters. The materials in this book should help develop a practical expectation of leadership which embraces, in the words of James MacGregor Burns, the "qualities of integrity, authenticity, initiative, and moral resolve."

Professor Burns concludes his study, *Leadership*, with these thoughts:

In real life the most practical advice for leaders is not to treat pawns like pawns, nor princes like princes, but all persons like *persons*. Woodrow Wilson called for leaders who, by boldly interpreting the nation's conscience, could lift a people out of their everyday selves. That people can be lifted into their better selves is the secret of transforming leadership and the moral and practical theme of this work.

And, it may be added, citizens can assist in generating this transforming leadership to a much greater degree than many present leaders think possible, or desirable.

Washington, D.C.
June, 1982

CHAPTER 1

ECONOMIC AFFAIRS

TREASURY DEPARTMENT

DONALD REGAN
SECRETARY

RESPONSIBILITY OF OFFICE

As secretary of the Treasury, Regan faces considerably broader concerns as the government's chief financial officer than did Alexander Hamilton. Regan has a dual role as both administrator of the Treasury Department and as fundamental adviser to the President on developing and implementing domestic and international economic policies.

Regan manages the Treasury's 112, 258 employees and its $110.3 billion budget. The department pays the government's bills (involving close to 740 million checks a year), collects the taxes, controls imports and exports, issues bonds, prints currency and manufactures coins, supervises many banks, controls tobacco, alcohol, and firearms and protects the President.

Regan serves as chairman of the Cabinet Council on Economic Affairs, the U.S. governor at the International Monetary Fund and a number of international development banks, and the main conduit for the Administration's views to the Federal Reserve Board.

BACKGROUND

Asked at his confirmation hearing why he would make the considerable financial sacrifice of leaving private business to enter the government, Regan told Sen. Russell Long (D-La.) "Without trying to wrap myself in the American flag, the country is in a predicament at this moment. The President of the United States asked me to be in his cabinet. How could you refuse when you get a call of duty of that nature?"

Making refusal more difficult undoubtedly was that Regan had long been sitting by the phone. Like his near-namesake in the White House, Regan has been campaigning for his current job for more than a decade.

"That job is something Don has wanted for a long time," one old associate said. "He had a long-term plan to get it."

Regan began his campaign in earnest around the time that he took over in 1971 as chairman and chief executive officer for Merrill Lynch, Pierce, Fenner & Smith, the world's largest stock brokerage and the nation's most aggressive financial supermarket. With the help of a former *Fortune* editor hired as speechwriter, he increased his public visibility, authored a short, inoffensive, relentlessly epigrammatic book—"Change might be described as experience in the present tense," he wrote in one typically reflective moment—that praised Richard Nixon's economic policies. And he began to spend more days in Washington, including time with White

House aides and the President himself. But the call never came. Not for Treasury; not for Commerce. Not from Nixon; not from Ford.

Regan's ascension into the Reagan hierarchy, paradoxically, began through his friendship with Nixon Secretary of State William Rogers, a pillar of the Eastern Republican community often repudiated by the Reagan forces. As recounted in an outstanding article on Regan by Chris Welles, in *Institutional Investor*, the Merrill Lynch head invited Rogers onto the company's board in early 1974. And he cemented the relationship by switching most of the firm's legal work to Rogers's firm, a lucrative contract that netted Rogers & Wells over $2 million in 1979 alone.

Regan edged closer to a top Washington post in 1976 when William Casey, the former chairman of the Securities and Exchange Commission (SEC), who ran Reagan's 1980 campaign and now runs the CIA, joined Rogers's firm. Through Casey and Rogers, Regan dramatically expanded his Washington connections. During the 1980 race he hosted two successful fund-raisers for Reagan. Through these displays of hospitality he also gained an ally in Helene von Damm, Reagan's long-time personal secretary, who was handling campaign financing in the Northeast. When William Simon, the Administration's first choice for the job, presented a series of unacceptable demands, Regan got the job. And Rogers sat in the audience at his confirmation hearing.

That path was not unusual for Donald Regan. Joining Merrill Lynch after serving in the Marines during World War II, he quickly worked his way to the top—again with the help of an invaluable connection.

At the time Regan joined Merrill Lynch, the company was dominated by Winthrop Smith, who was assuming greater control each year as founder Charles Merrill's health faded. Regan was married to the niece of Smith's second wife, the former Ann Buchanan. Ann was very close to Smith, so close that she called him "Daddy." As Chris Welles observed, "Daddies counted for a lot in those days, even at Merrill Lynch."

And so a golden boy was born. Six years after joining the firm, Regan became manager of the over-the-counter department in New York. Two years after that, he became a general partner. The next year he became manager of the firm's Philadelphia office. In 1960, he returned to New York as administrative division director. And on upward: in 1964, Regan became executive vice president; in 1968, president; in 1971, chairman and chief executive officer; and then in 1973, chairman and chief executive officer of Merrill Lynch & Co., the parent of the brokerage firm.

Known since its inception as a Wall Street innovator in mass merchandising to the general public, Merrill Lynch continued to expand under Regan's reign. His most dramatic accomplishment was the intricately conceived diversification into insurance, real estate, and banking-type functions. Walter Wriston, Citicorp's chairman, once summed up his vision of the future's dream bank, by saying: "Don Regan runs it and it's called Merrill Lynch, Pierce, Fenner and Smith."

Making extensive use of staff and task forces to develop new proposals, Regan himself did not conceive most of the company's innovations. He was an organizer, a decisionmaker and a tough boss. "He was," one long-time Merrill Lynch worker said, "an absolute dictator." One current senior official added: "People are afraid of him. He gets things done not because people agree with him, but because they felt if they don't go along, it will be their ass."

Regan's book offers very little of that personality. Instead, it is a friendly, almost folksy homily about the virtues of Wall Street, Richard Nixon, and of course, Merrill Lynch. In the book, designed to explain and at the same time defend the workings of the stock market to the average investor, Regan even manages to suggest that Congress and the Securities and Exchange Commission are understaffed. Some of its other observations are almost poignant in light of the manner in which Reaganomics has unfolded during its first year. If Regan had reread his book recently he might not have been so quick to assure Congress the Administration would balance the budget by 1984 or to blame "Wall Street" for dropping its confidence in that claim. Consider these observations:

- "Interest rates are not amenable to oral persuasion."

- "[T]he events of 1970 raised the question whether an Administration can in the course of a couple of years get control over the government's expenditures."

- "[T]he stock market is a mood, and moods can never be fully explained."

Then there is one other comment that Regan has probably never sent to his President, who has blamed the stock market for failing to reflect what he sees as popular confidence in his program: "The market," wrote Regan, "is people, after all."

Born in Cambridge, Massachusetts on December 21, 1918, Regan was graduated from Harvard with a B.A. in English in 1940. With the former Ann Buchanan, he has four children.

FINANCIAL BACKGROUND

After a career on Wall Street, Donald Regan is a wealthy man. His financial disclosure form lists holdings of greater than $250,000—probably a lot greater—in Merrill Lynch common stock in both his name and his wife's. In addition, Regan lists two oil and gas partnerships and a housing partnership, each valued between $100,000 and $250,000, and 19 separate holdings—ranging from bonds to other land development partnerships—valued at between $15,000 and $50,000. He also holds a cash management account valued at between $50,000 and $100,000.

Dividends on his Merrill Lynch holdings totalled over $100,000 in 1980. According to the firm's filing with the SEC, during the 1980 fiscal year, Merrill Lynch paid Regan $954,986. On January 16, 1981, Merrill Lynch paid Regan $441,000 in incentive compensation and book value appreciation rights; another $200,000 payment was deferred until the end of 1983.

Regan's worth is a matter of speculation—but it is undoubtedly considerable. In an April, 1982 profile of the secretary, the *New York Times* reported that, "He was disappointed that many reporters missed his total worth when writing stories about his nomination. Asked if it was $10 million, the secretary waved his hands toward himself, as if saying 'more' in a game of charades. $20 million? He beckoned more again. $35 million? 'No comment.'"

NORMAN TURE
UNDERSECRETARY FOR TAX AND ECONOMIC AFFAIRS

RESPONSIBILITY OF OFFICE

As Treasury's top tax official, Ture has been at the center of the "Reagan Revolution" in taxes, forcefully pressing the position of the supply-side true believers at the highest levels of government. An economist rather than a lawyer, (who usually holds the job), Ture demonstrates far less interest in revising the tax code than in employing taxes as an instrument in broadgauged economic policy.

BACKGROUND

For Ture, the comfortable office and spacious surroundings of a Treasury undersecretary represent the conclusion of an odyssey across the political spectrum that began in the early 1950s in a tax office now under his supervision.

An aide to Sen. Paul Douglas (D-Ill.), a sharp critic of tax breaks favoring the wealthy during the 1950s, Ture had transformed by the mid-1970s into a well-paid consultant whose work was funded by the right-wing Olin and Scaife foundations. From a transition team tax adviser to John F. Kennedy, Ture became a member of the Heritage Foundation squadron that presented Reagan with its massive blueprint for reordering the federal government.

Along the way he became among the most ardent of all supply-siders. Proud of his own contribution to that embattled economic theory, he dismissed our question of whether he considered Arthur Laffer the father of supply-side economics with a snitty "oh no." Said Rudolph Penner, director of tax policy studies at the American Enterprise Institute (AEI), a conservative think-tank with close ties to Reagan: "Ture is the highest level supporter" of supply-side theory within the Administration.

Ture snagged his first Washington job in the Treasury Department Office of Tax Analysis in 1951. There he worked for Joseph Pechman, a prominent economist now with the Brookings Institution. "At that time, I would have labeled him a liberal," Pechman told us.

After four years with Treasury, Ture joined the staff of the Joint Economic Committee, chaired by Douglas, and worked on a massive series of hearings on federal tax policy with Rep. Wilbur Mills (D-Ark.), who chaired the subcommittee on tax policy. "I certainly didn't consider him a supply-sider at the time," Mills told us. "I thought he was down the middle of the road." Added Pechman: "You weren't a conservative if you worked for Paul Douglas."

During 1955, Ture orchestrated a series of hearings on tax policy for Mills's subcommittee that culminated in a January, 1956 report which he wrote on "Federal Tax Policy for Economic Growth and Stability." The report is within the classical mainstream of liberal tax reform efforts, decrying inequities that funnel disproportionate benefits to the wealthy and powerful. Among its observations:

- "The inequities in the present tax system are to be found primarily in those provisions which afford some taxpayers preferential treatment as compared with others in fact similarly situated and *which serve to reduce, very markedly, progression in tax burdens.''* (Emphasis added.) By the late 1970s, Ture was describing the progressive rate structure as ''a penalty tax on increasing one's productivity. . .[that] certainly strikes one as counterproductive socially.''

- Commenting on special tax breaks afforded the powerful, Ture wrote: ''Experience has shown that preferential tax provisions tend to produce chain reactions; each such provision leads to claims for similarly preferential treatment from taxpayers who do not quite qualify for the initially provided benefits.'' (Those words proved prophetic during the summer of 1981, when special breaks on the inheritance tax, the capital gains tax, and the windfall profits tax cascaded upon each other in the final Reagan tax bill.)

- Looking at the impact of tax laws on increasing economic concentration Ture wrote: ''Present law provisions with respect to loss carryovers, corporate reorganizations, and nontaxability under the income tax of gains on property transferred by gift or at death appear to be of major significance in this connection.'' And in a comment that would make the Reagan Justice Department cringe, Ture added: ''While this development [increasing economic concentration] does not uniquely involve small businesses, their position is weakened by any tendency toward concentration of enterprise in fewer and fewer hands.'' (Today, Ture calls it a ''myth'' that ''the private sector has this terrible inclination to become monopolized and to concentrate the ownership of wealth and to concentrate the distribution of income.'')

- Noting that small businesses ''have limited access to credit and equity capital. . .as compared with larger, better established firms,'' the report concludes that federal tax policy should ''protect the competitive position of small and new businesses.'' (That conclusion echoes particularly ironic with the passage of Reagan's accelerated depreciation business tax cut, which directs 80 percent of its benefits to the 1,700 largest corporations and has generated billions of dollars to fund acquisitions and expensive advertising campaigns that can erode the position of small business.)

After Kennedy's election, Ture left Washington for the National Bureau of Economic Research, where he directed tax studies through 1969. By 1968, his views had altered enough that he was invited to sit on President-elect Nixon's task force on taxation, and a subsequent Nixon task force on business taxes. In 1971, he formed an economic consulting firm, and six years after that began the Institute for Research on the Economics of Taxation (IRET), a conservative group funded by corporate grants that produces studies and testimony, sometimes in collaboration with the Heritage Foundation. (See Financial Background section for supporters.) In 1977, Ture joined the board of the American Council for Capital Formation, a business group headed by Charls Walker, a former Nixon deputy secretary of Treasury. (Walker, a close adviser to Reagan, is credited with developing the accelerated depreciation plan appended to the Administration's supply-side individual tax cut in 1981.)

By this time, after years of consulting for business groups, Ture's views had hardened. ''In the outside world he has drifted into this [business-oriented] viewpoint,'' said one tax expert who has followed Ture's work for over two decades. ''You know, once you get a religion, the bible follows.'' Through the late 1970s, Ture repeatedly argued—as he does today—that the tax system was biased against savings and investment and that efforts to redistribute income through tax policy were both economically and morally indefensible. ''If it [the Carter Administration] continues the futile chase of that tax policy will-o'-the-wisp—redistribution of income," he wrote in 1977, "the result will be even more severe tax burdens on those activities which provide the momentum for economic progress."

Earlier that year he had condemned on ethical grounds efforts to promote "economic equality": "Unless it can be demonstrated that public policies that succeed in equalizing us economically would not at the same time herd us into sameness in all other aspects of our culture, we should find such policies ethically and aesthetically distasteful."

Ture moved his views into the political arena through Rep. Jack Kemp (R-N.Y.). In 1975, Kemp hired Paul Craig Roberts, who in turn brought Ture to work as an adviser on tax policy. Ture produced studies that predicted cuts in business taxes and new investment credits proposed by Kemp would generate tremendous growth in the GNP, $80 billion in increased capital outlays and 10 million new jobs within three years of enactment.

The rest, of course, is history.

Ture takes a longer, more elegant view of supply-side economics than the proponents with which it is most closely associated, Arthur Laffer and Jude Wanniski.

"Its antecedents," he asserted in an October, 1981 speech, "are to be found in the work of the classical economists of the modern era, from Adam Smith, David Ricardo, John Stuart Mill and Alfred Marshall through Irving Fisher and Milton Friedman." Closer to the present, he told us, "in terms of who first set out to consistently [analyze] the consequence of tax change and tax instruments for economic averages, I think I would take credit for it." For the celebrated cocktail napkin on which his rival drew the Laffer curve more immediately identified in most minds with the doctrine, Ture has nothing but contempt. "The cocktail napkin," he told the *Wall Street Journal*, "has nothing to do with supply-side economics."

Indeed, Ture told us he found the "Laffer curve"—which postulates that cutting tax rates will so increase the GNP that government tax revenues will actually increase—to be "spurious." "You cannot across the board reduce marginal tax rates and expect to get more revenue than you would have had," he said. "I never believed that, never asserted that. Maybe Art did, but he shouldn't have." Another tax cut proponent who made that assertion was candidate Ronald Reagan, who said in a February, 1980 interview that "an across the board reduction in tax rates every time it has ever been tried, it has resulted in such an increase in prosperity. . . that even the government winds up with more revenue."

Over the years, Ture has served on a variety of professional and business groups, from the U.S. Chamber of Commerce's Taxation Committee, to the National Association of Business Economists to the National Tax Association, of which he was President through 1981.

Born on September 8, 1923 in Cleveland, Ohio, Ture received his M.A. and Ph.D. in economics from the University of Chicago in 1947 and 1968 respectively. He has taught at George Washington University, Wharton and Illinois College. Ture is married with six children.

FINANCIAL BACKGROUND

Ture reported income of just under $100,000 in 1980, split almost evenly between his consulting firm, Norman B. Ture, Inc., and his salary as president of IRET.

That salary constituted a substantial chunk of IRET's expenditures.

According to the group's 1979 tax return, Ture earned $52,500 for 25 weekly hours of work. That was exactly one-half of their salary budget, and almost one-third of their entire $175,000 budget. Funding for the group came from the following sources:

Olin Foundation $100,000

Scaife Foundation $57,000

Norman B. Ture, Inc. $6,000

Mobil $3,500

Heritage Foundation $3,000

Tax Council $3,000

American Council for Capital Formation $2,500

In 1978, Scaife gave the group $122,000

Throughout the past decade, Ture has generally sought to present himself as a disinterested academic, even as his livelihood depended on business contracts and grants. At times, he has appeared to cross even the subtle line which upholds that distinction. In May, 1974, Ture appeared before a Senate committee to deliver a study which concluded that the natural gas industry was competitive and told them, "I approached the assignment of doing this study. . .in quite a detached way, most assuredly. I have no vested interest in the industry." One month later, he argued in Senate testimony against natural gas price controls on behalf of the Gas Supply Committee, an association of natural gas producers.

When he entered office, Ture became involved in a similar situation. This controversy, in which Ture was eventually cleared by the department's inspector general, involved a noncompetitive $230,000 contract for an economic forecasting model that Ture had developed.

Ture initiated the procurement process on January 28, 1981 when he urged the head of Treasury's Procurement Office to call the accounting firm of Coopers & Lybrand and discuss a possible contract for the model. Ture had been negotiating with the firm since early in the month to sell his interest in the model.

According to the inspector general's report, Ture and the company "believed that the essential components of what was to be the final sales agreement had been worked out" by January 16. But the final agreement was not signed until February 2—five days after Ture began the procurement process.

In an original outline of the agreement prepared on January 19, Ture was to be paid $42,500 for the model, with a "contingency" fee of $20,000 payable at a later date. A revised draft delivered to Ture on January 26, however, set the fee at a flat $60,000. That was the final purchase price.

Though exonerating Ture of all but "at most, an extremely debatable and highly technical violation of the statute," the inspector general did conclude that "Dr. Ture's failure to disclose formally his corporation's ownership of the economic model is open to question and to legitimate criticism."

WHAT OTHERS ARE SAYING ABOUT HIM

- Mills retains great respect for Ture. "He was very devoted to me," Mills told us. "But it was a different world then."

- Others we spoke with, particularly tax reformers, were less complimentary. "Ture is what we call a corporatist," said one Washington tax attorney. Several economists and tax attorneys we spoke with suggested that Ture's reputation in the field was minimal until he hitched his star to Kemp's tax cut proposals. Asked if he had seen a critique of Ture's work, one liberal economist responded: "Other than the latest economic indicators?"

BERYL SPRINKEL
UNDERSECRETARY FOR MONETARY AFFAIRS

RESPONSIBILITY OF OFFICE

Sprinkel has two responsibilities: to be the principal Treasury representative to foreign treasuries, central banks abroad, and to international monetary organizations; and to implement policy aimed at financing the public debt. The former involves a combination of diplomatic savvy and an understanding of international monetary issues. Sprinkel must make Treasury policy coherent to other governments, not always an easy task.

Sprinkel presented a third duty at his confirmation hearings: to coordinate the Federal Reserve Board and the Administration on monetary policy. While the Fed is statutorily independent, it is rarely deaf to the pleas of the Administration, and Sprinkel's hardline monetarism is no secret to the Fed governors.

BACKGROUND

Serving as a Treasury undersecretary does have its rewards, one of which is the responsibility of explaining U.S. economic policy to our European allies—often over dinner. "The first requirement for a dinner speech," Sprinkel said at one such occasion in Paris, "is that it be brief. It occurred to me that that is why you asked a monetarist to speak tonight. Our views are reputedly straightforward and concise: *only money matters*. Control the money supply and everything else falls into place. Thank you, and good night."

Actually, there is a bit more to Sprinkel's economic view of the world. But not much. He has followed the monetary path for almost three decades, helping to propel it from a theory on the fringe of polite economic society, to a cornerstone of Reagan Administration policy. "The Age of Aquarius," he wrote a little over a decade ago, when that development seemed pendant, "may become more aptly known as the Age of Monetarism."

Historians may well pass over this era without attaching either label, but certainly not for want of effort by Sprinkel. A prolific writer and speaker, he repeatedly affirms in no uncertain terms the fundamental importance of the money supply to the nation's economic health. "Excessive monetary growth," he wrote in his most well-known book, *Money and Markets*, "has accounted for all known sizable inflations, domestic and foreign, modern and ancient." And that is that.

Sprinkel fit this writing and speaking into a busy schedule as a high official of the Harris Trust and Savings Bank, Chicago's third largest. In 1974, Sprinkel was named executive vice president and economist, running the bank's economic research office. From that post, he published "Harris Economics," a subscription service analyzing economic issues. Despite those demands, Sprinkel found time to make regular trips to Washington to appear before congressional committees, joined various economic associations and sat on a number of panels, including the economic advisory committee of the American Bankers Association, and the Shadow Open Market Committee, a group of economists that meet regularly to critique the Fed.

In 1969, Sprinkel joined *Time* magazine's first board of economists, where his hardline monetarism often placed him at odds with other participants. In October, 1979, for instance, Sprinkel vigorously backed the Fed's efforts to tighten the money supply. A "delighted" Sprinkel felt if the policy was continued it would bring "inflation under control in the long run." Among the board members with whom this left him in conflict: Murray Weidenbaum, now chair of the Council of Economic Advisers. While the tight money policy offered "no guarantee" of reduced inflation, Weidenbaum said, it did produce "more certainty" of a recession.

Regan has said Sprinkel was appointed because "I wanted the best monetarist I could get." Political connections, of course, did not hurt. Among them was Republican Senator Charles Percy of Illinois, who introduced Sprinkel at his confirmation hearing with a vignette that captures the interwoven nature of politics and business.

As Percy recounted it, 25 years ago when he was president of Bell & Howell and a board member of the Harris Bank, Sprinkel, then a "young fellow. . .from the economics department," came out to advise him on a pending business deal in London. "I didn't know what he was talking about," said Percy. "I am still not sure I know." But the advice proved lucrative, Percy continued, and so he told the top people at the bank, "Keep your eye on this young fellow." They did: Sprinkel steadily advanced, and, concluded Percy, "when the President nominated him to be Undersecretary of Treasury for Monetary Affairs I hope this is the last time I have to pay off his help to me, 25 years ago."

Born November 20, 1923, on a farm near Richmond, Missouri, Sprinkel first broke with farm life as a tail gunner in World War II. Returning to the state, he was graduated from the University of Missouri in 1947 with a degree in public administration. From there he went to the University of Chicago, where he fell under the influence of Henry Gunnison Brown, a student of Irving Fisher, the leading American advocate of the quantity theory. Sprinkel received his M.A. in 1948, and his Ph.D. in economics and finance four years later. He is married with four children.

FINANCIAL BACKGROUND

Sprinkel earned $269,865 from Harris, which he supplemented with almost $11,000 in consulting ($5,000 from *Time's* Board of Economists) and speaking fees. His financial disclosure form lists assets, together with his wife, of at least $790,000, including his shares in the Harris profit sharing and pension plans, each of which are valued at above $250,000. His portfolio lists stock holdings in a number of major companies, including Emerson Electric, Caterpillar, Amax, Hughes Tool, Standard Oil of Indiana, Pfizer, and Texas Oil & Gas.

WHAT OTHERS ARE SAYING ABOUT HIM

- For all his after-dinner humor, Sprinkel has not been winning the hearts and minds of Europe. Reported *Business Week*: "It is difficult to separate personal criticism of Sprinkel from criticism of the policies themselves. 'He is self-deprecating, blunt, and dogmatic,' says a top international monetary official."

- And Sprinkel has had the misfortune to cross Evans and Novak as well. As keepers of the supply-side scrolls, they pilloried Sprinkel for leading Ronald Reagan down the dreaded road of Thatcherism. "[T]he supply-side view inside and outside the administration is that Sprinkel is not only the messenger but creator of the swollen deficit," they wrote in a bitter October, 1981 column. "They [the supply-siders] believe that the burgeoning deficit is the product not of tax cuts but tight-money policy promoted by Sprinkel, the disciple of Prof. Milton Friedman's monetarist school."

MAJOR ISSUES

- Regarded suspiciously by supply-siders at the outset of the Administration, Regan emerged as the most consistent opponent of tax increases, even as the swelling deficit made his former colleagues on Wall Street leap from the Reagan ship.

- The failure of business to invest its tax savings, as the Administration hoped, in productive investments has turned Regan into something of a critic of business management, suggesting the current generation of managers is "timid".

- Regan has also criticized the Federal Reserve Board, first for turning the monetary screws too tightly and then for letting the money supply expand too quickly.

- After the economic package, the Treasury leaders have devoted most of their attention to increasing the opportunities available to banks and savings and loans under financial deregulation legislation.

- Sprinkel and Regan have led the Administration's effort to choke off aid offered to Third World countries through the multilateral lending institutions.

"All history," Donald Regan once wrote, "is the unfolding of miscalculations."

And so too with Reaganomics. In less than a year, the rosy forecasts of untrammeled economic growth, balanced budgets and plummeting inflation have withered beneath the gloomy reality of recession and huge deficits, the prospects of the highest unemployment levels since World War II, record high interest rates for much of the year and the unwillingness of corporate America to invest its unprecedented tax savings in the new factories and shops the Administration expected them to build.

The resulting economic morass has strained the always uneasy accord between the Administration's supply-siders, monetarists and more traditional budget-balancing conservatives. As each side scrambles for its alibi, the finger-pointing has degenerated into occasionally acrid struggles between Administration policymakers, with one unnamed supply-sider—sounding suspiciously like Paul Craig Roberts—charging in print that the "OMB is going to destroy the President and destroy his program," and Regan chastising the Federal Reserve Board for turning the monetary screws too tightly or too erratically.

The pressure has even turned Regan, late of the Business Roundtable and the upper echelons of Wall Street, into a born-again critic of American management. In a September, 1981 speech he asked: "Is this generation of business people too timid, too accustomed to direction and too comfortable with regulations from outside to seize the initiative and generate the kind of effect we simply must have to achieve a better future for all Americans?"

The spectacle of Donald Regan (and Commerce Secretary Malcolm Baldrige) dressing down America's boardrooms, proves that, as *Fortune* put it, "Business's dismal record of putting its parochial interest above the general good is the darkest cloud over Washington's new approach to taxes."

Or, perhaps it merely proves, as Regan told the Senate Budget Committee in October, 1981, "Things seldom turn out the way you think they're going to."

Surely, though, the Administration thought things would turn out better than they have.

As recently as May, 1981, Ture could confidently assure the House Small Business Committee that "implementation of the President's program . . .will lead to diminishing deficits in fiscal 1982 and 1983 and the achievement of a balanced budget in fiscal 1984, with growing surpluses in the ensuing years." By November, Ture was telling us that the budget would not be balanced by 1984, echoing an admission first made by Regan on October 30. "Well, the basic economic variables are going to turn out differently than what I anticipated at that time," Ture said. To say the least; the Administration has publicly forecast deficits of almost $250 billion over the next three years alone.

It was all enough to make even Budget Director David Stockman recant his devotion to supply-side dogma. But Regan, reflecting the influence of Ture and Roberts, has held firm, arguing successfully against increasing taxes to reduce the deficit, and looking outside of Washington to assess blame for the economy's failure to perform as the Administration had forecasted. "The nice thing about being an economist," said the AEI's Penner, "is that there are always enough things going on in the economy to make up excuses for why your forecasts didn't work out."

Reagan's economic plan rests on four legs: cutting taxes, particularly for the wealthy and business, to spur investment; cutting domestic government spending; sharply increasing military spending, and reducing government regulation. Making barely a nick on supply-side dogma, Congress gave Reagan his 5-10-10 tax cut for individuals, and greatly accelerated depreciation for businesses. That sharply reduced expected revenue. Congress also went along with Reagan's increases in military spending. Those two trends are forcing a series of unprecedented federal deficits through the decade.

Wall Street's problems with Reagan's economic program begin with the prospect of those continued, and even expanding, high deficits, which worry supply-siders far less than the money-managers or traditional conservatives. "There is no inherent virtue in balancing the budget," Ture told us. "Balancing the budget is a way of imposing discipline as such." Treasury's top policymakers now argue that deficits are not inflationary if they are financed through increased private savings, rather than an expansion of the money supply. But, as *Business Week* observed, "the markets remain to be convinced."

Sprinkel has expressed more concern about the deficit than Ture, arguing that even if it is financed out of increased savings "you absorb savings . . .[which]

means you cannot have capital formation . . .to the extent that you desire.''

In an interview, Secretary Regan agreed that concern over the budget was one factor keeping interest rates high. Business people ''don't believe us and our budgets,'' Regan told us. ''Whether it's David Stockman or Don Regan or whoever it is, they don't believe we're going to hit $91 billion [deficit in 1982] . . .they think we're going to hit $150, $140 [billion] items in through there. So therefore they think the demand for the Treasury on and off budget for financing are going to be much greater than we're saying. They think we've got a lot of blue smoke in our budget. So therefore they're demanding a premium because we may crowd out [private borrowing].''

That's what Sprinkel's old colleagues at the Shadow Open Market Committee said in mid-March, 1982. The group wrote that if the deficits persist, ''the economy may continue to limp along the path characterized by low productivity growth, rising real transfer payments and a rising size of government.''

Agnostics too were the significant faction within the Administration—headed by Stockman—who sought to raise taxes to moderate the deficit. But the supply-siders within Treasury won that battle, indicating that Regan's influence was on the rise even before Stockman was sunk in the *Atlantic*.

The strongest supply-siders are depending instead on rapid economic growth to swell the tax rolls and restrain the deficit. Here, though, they are facing the greatest irony of the Reagan presidency: the refusal of the tax cut's corporate recipients to invest in new facilities that the Administration had predicted would bolster productivity and invigorate the economy. According to Commerce Department figures, after inflation is accounted for, manufacturers are projecting no increase in capital spending for 1982. As the recession deepens even those modest spending plans will likely be rolled back; General Motors, for example, faced with a staggering drop in sales, has cancelled one proposed new plant and delayed another.

As the *Wall Street Journal* recently observed, ''Manufacturers see no reason to expand. U.S. factories have been running at less than 80 percent of capacity for months . . .Companies don't see plant capacity being strained next year either.'' Asked why companies would expand when existing capacity is idle, Ture chose instead to attack the messenger: ''Have you ever noticed that every time there is a tax break, somebody—it's always the *Wall Street Journal*, it's almost as if the *Journal* was purging itself of the contention of bias in favor of business—will come back with a story which says in effect the recently enacted tax changes are not going to have any effect on our capital formation.''

Critics point out that the tax cuts, not the *Journal's* questions, were simply directed at the wrong businesses. Eighty percent of the benefits of the accelerated depreciation package will go toward just the 1,700 largest corporations. A study recently completed by Treasury's Office of Tax Analysis concluded that only about 40 percent of corporate investment tax breaks were reinvested into new productive assets. It would be more cost effective, one of the authors later remarked, to ''have government buy the new plants and equipment and give them to business.''

Where then does the money go? Since the largest corporations include many multinational firms, much of it goes abroad, where American multinationals hold fully a quarter of all their assets. That is reflected, for example, in the world car strategies of Ford and General Motors. And billions of dollars are also going into mergers and acquisitions, over $60 billion during the first nine months of 1981 alone—$16 billion more than had been recorded for the entire year in 1980. U.S.

Steel's $6 billion plus offer for Marathon Oil stunned even many conservatives, who had been listening for years to steelmakers complain about their inability to generate enough capital to modernize their plants.

Said Republican Representative Clarence Brown of Ohio: "U.S. Steel might better have used its money investing in steel mills." Even Commerce Undersecretary Olmer said it "calls into question the seriousness of the steel industry's efforts to modernize its steel-making facilities."

To many economists these activities vitiate the expected benefits of the tax cuts. "Mergers compete directly with capital investments, research and development, and other investment type expenditures for cash flows and management decision-making capacities," economist Dennis Mueller has written. "While a manager is perhaps indifferent between whether a given rate of expansion is achieved through internal or external growth society is likely to be better off through the creation of additional assets."

Ture rejects that view out of hand. "We could care less [where companies spend their tax savings]," he told us. "The market works very effectively. And I would certainly not impose any governmental judgments."

Regan displayed a similar view toward mergers during our interview. But he did agree that the tax bill was weighted toward big industry. "Our Economic Recovery Tax Act of '81 benefits—the business portion of it now—benefits for the most part the so-called smokestack companies," he said. "Yet, a little better than 70 percent of all jobs in the United States are in the service industries. And you know the studies as well as I do, of 1966 to 1976—during that decade—something on the order of 80 percent of all new jobs came from companies that had less than 100 employees. I'm not sure we've designed taxes to help that portion of our economy. And I think it well that we should."

One factor holding down capital spending is continuing high interest rates, which ran at record levels through much of 1981, before moderating late in the fall. Sprinkel and Ture see no conflict between a tight money supply and expansive fiscal policy; indeed they see the combination as essential. But many others ranging from supply-siders such as Jude Wanniski to Keynesians like John Kenneth Galbraith, see the combination as an inherent contradiction. "The program now put in place by the Administration is the equivalent of stepping hard on the gas at the same time as you slam on the brakes," said Rep. Jim Jones (D-Okla.), chairman of the House Budget Committee. "The result will sound spectacular—until either the brakes fail or the engine blows. It is a gamble of titanic proportions." Wanniski put the matter even more colorfully: "The public flogging of Beryl Sprinkel would do wonders for the bond market."

Simply put, critics see the tight money policy as an unavoidable check on the expanding growth that Reaganomics is supposed to generate. If the Fed does not expand the money supply to cover the debt, they argue, the Treasury's vast borrowing needs, swelled by growing deficits, will force out private credit seekers and force up the prime interest rate at a time when burgeoning economic activity will increase demands on the credit markets. And as high interest rates and tight credit restrain growth and deepen unemployment, the deficit in turn deepens, twisting the spiral down again.

Though Treasury officials argue this proves only the need for further budget cuts, the opportunities there are clearly limited—particularly, as OMB officials have pointed out, since military spending and Social Security are relatively exempt. And the resistance to Reagan's 1983 budget indicates that it will be politically impossible to make further reductions of anything approaching the magnitude of the tax cuts. For that reason, Treasury's hardliners will probably be eventually overcome by other Administration forces seeking tax increases. "Tax increases as compared to the 1981 act are probably going to become inevitable just because the deficit outlook is so grim," said Penner, who has worked with Administration policymakers such as Weidenbaum. Even Republican senators are looking critically at the hundreds of billions of dollars in subsidies dispensed as tax expenditures—or loopholes. First to go might be the tax leasing provisions inserted into the tax bill, which was designed to help money-losing companies by allowing them to sell their tax credits to profitable companies. Treasury originally wrote the implementing regulations tightly, to minimize the plan's drain on the budget. But, under pressure from Chrysler and other firms, Treasury redrafted the rules in November, 1981 and business has been brisk. With estimates on the cost of this largess escalating, and evidence appearing that profitable firms, such as General Electric, Amoco, Occidental Petroleum and LTV Corp., are using the credits to substantially reduce their tax liability, Congress may soon reconsider the idea.

And indeed if the economic situation continues to weaken, the supply-siders may even lose Regan, who came to Washington without passionate attachment to the concept. In his book, he defends Arthur Burns's support for price controls with a simple, but reverent, phrase he no doubt would like to see applied to himself: "He is a pragmatic man." As he told us, "I'm a financier, not an economist."

After the tax and budget issues, Regan has labeled as his top priority "the deregulation of financial institutions." Following extensive negotiations with Richard Pratt, chairman of the Federal Home Loan Bank Board, Regan in October, 1981 proposed legislation that allows savings and loan institutions to expand into services now restricted to commercial banks, such as making consumer loans and leasing equipment. At the same time, the legislation would allow the commercial banks to expand through affiliates into the operation of money market funds and the underwriting of municipal revenue bonds. The result would be that banks would look more like their diversified financial competitors, like Merrill Lynch.

"The financial regulatory system—as it exists today—is like a baseball manager who won't let a fastball pitcher use a slider, or a change of pace, even though he's competing with a lot of heavy hitters who can swing from both sides of the plate," Regan said in a major September, 1981 speech. "With this principle in mind, the Administration believes that all depository institutions—commercial banks, savings and loan associations, mutual savings banks, credit unions—all—should be free to compete for the financial consumer's dollar."

To some, that concern for competition is disingenuous. Many in the financial industry maintain that Regan's proposals would ultimately diminish competition by increasing concentration. "Essentially they [Regan's proposals] propose a great leap backward into the laissez-faire days of Coolidge and Hoover," said Robert McCormick, first vice-president of the Independent Bankers Association of America, a nationwide organization of smaller banks. "The oft-stated prescriptions of the Treasury secretary and the parallel prescriptions of the Justice Department under [William] Baxter inevitably will lead to significantly increased financial concentration and a dramatic reduction in the number of financial decision-making centers in our nation."

To others, the scheme blurs the historic separation between banking and commerce. Federal Reserve Board Chairman Paul Volcker, who generally opposes the expansion of banking powers proposed by Regan said recently that, "the laws and traditions of this country embodying a separation of banking and commerce still seem to us valid . . . Underwriting and marketing of long-term corporate securities to the general public by banks raises questions of risk, self-dealing and conflict-of-interest.''

Entrusting these additional powers to a subsidiary, rather than the bank itself, offers only paper-thin protection, Volcker maintained. ''[O]ur experience very clearly suggests that you cannot insulate the fortunes of a banking institution from the fortunes of its nonbanking affiliates.''

Deregulation of interest rate ceilings is proceeding, fitfully, in the Depository Institution Deregulation Committee (DIDC) established by 1980 legislation. Under pressure from the savings and loans industry, Regan in fall, 1981 reversed an earlier vote on the DIDC which would have allowed interest rates on passbook savings accounts to rise one-half percentage point. Regan had originally urged a 1.5 percentage point hike. ''Demonstrably not in the interest of the consumer,'' he said in his September speech, only a few weeks before reversing his vote, ''are interest rate ceilings.''

Regan did press the DIDC to remove interest ceilings on deposits of four years or more. But the U.S. League of Savings Association went to court and overturned the decision leaving the committee scrambling for a new tactic. In September, 1981 the group raised a proposal for three-and-a-half year certificates that could skirt the legal objections.

The needs of the financial community, of course, are not monolithic, and the conflictive pressures on federal regulators anxious to please the differing constituencies were starkly apparent at a November 20, 1981 meeting of the committee. With only Pratt dissenting, the DIDC voted at that meeting, over the objections of the savings and loans, not to impose an interest rate ceiling on Individual Retirement Accounts (IRAs) begun after January 1, 1982. Bankers hailed that decision, which the S&Ls called ''irresponsible and arrogant.'' But at the same time, the committee voted 3-2, with Regan in the majority, to impose substantial penalties on savers who transfer their funds from existing IRAs to the more lucrative accounts.

Regan's relationship with the Federal Reserve Board has also been fitful. He has criticized the Fed for allowing the money supply to grow too quickly, and for contracting the supply too tightly. ''I criticized the Fed last August and got taken to the woodshed for it, to use a phrase that's in vogue now,'' he told us in March, 1982. ''Yet I think I was right and I wouldn't back off again if I had to do it all over again, because that was right in the days when they were admittedly now too tight . . . I again was critical of them in December and January of this year. Why? Just the opposite—15 percent rate of growth on the money supply in December, 20 percent in January. If the secretary of the Treasury didn't speak up under those conditions, I think somebody would have a right to say to him, what the hell are you doing?''

In response to a question, Regan implied that he would like to see the President's influence over the Fed increase. Saying he was ''wrestling'' with the question ''right now,'' Regan told us, ''All I'm suggesting is that if we're going to be held responsible for the effects of monetary policy should we not have a voice in it?''

The Fed's current independence, Regan suggested, is at odds both with policies in all the other major industrial nations and our own history. ''As you know, we are the only nation in the world where the central bank does not come under the finance minister,'' he said. ''If the regime that is elected to do a political job is thwarted by the monetary authority of that country, you allow the political leaders a cop out, to say that it wasn't my fault, it was the fault of somebody else. The elected officials of England or in Japan cannot say that. Here we can cop that plea. And I think that Jimmy Carter for one might have a right to say 'Look at what the Fed did to me in 1980' . . .and surprisingly enough I find in history—and we've got to research this more—I was reading the other night that the secretary of the Treasury, up until the mid-1930s, was actually a member of the Board of Governors of the Federal Reserve, ex officio.''

Regan has spearheaded the Administration's tough line on aid provided through the international financial institutions, the World Bank and the International Monetary Fund (IMF). U.S. posture toward the two institutions has generated widespread debate within the Administration and the business community, with many conservatives urging the curtailment of aid and the international banking community and the State Department generally supporting the institutions as a stabilizing force on the economies, and political situations, of the Third World.

Generally, the Administration has sided with the critics, telling Third World countries that instead of aid they should, in the President's phrase, ''believe in the magic of the marketplace'' and rely more on private investment. That has translated into policies urging tougher restrictions on countries receiving IMF loans and pressure on the World Bank to ''make more use of the private sector,'' as Regan put it shortly before the Bank/IMF annual meeting in October, 1981. The Administration is also planning to sharply reduce U.S. contributions to the multilateral institutions.

For Third World countries, that in turn translates into tighter credit, and leaders argue, greater hardship. ''As a general rule,'' Bangladesh Finance Minister Saifur Rahman told the IMF/World Bank meeting, ''the market smiles at the rich but frowns on the poor.'' Private investors, he noted, are unlikely to invest in the basic infrastructure—construction of harbors or small rural agricultural projects—that the World Bank supports. Others have called the Reagan policy ''supply-side imperialism'' and an ''international trickle-down.''

In September, 1981 Regan criticized the IMF—whose financial austerity requirements are often criticized as draconian by Third World leaders—for not demanding enough austerity of its loan recipients. ''We will be telling them that our representatives will be watching, and insisting upon more strict fiscal policies and more strict monetary policies within the countries themselves as conditions [for the loans],'' the Treasury secretary said. That pressure, noted the *Wall Street Journal*, is meeting with ''at least grudging acceptance.'' Over U.S. objections, however, the IMF approved in October, 1981 a $5.8 billion loan to India, the largest it has ever made. (The U.S. abstained on the vote.)

Regan has also taken a tough stand toward the World Bank, urging that some nations be ''graduated'' from the soft lending terms of the bank's International Development Association (IDA), or perhaps out of the bank entirely. At the same time, the Administration has cut its contribution to the IDA and convinced other major industrial nations to follow its lead, while Sprinkel has suggested it may cut off funding entirely. ''[H]ere in the U.S.,'' Regan said, ''we have stringent budget limitations on what we can do and can't do for the [Third World].'' Added Sprinkel: ''The Bank will be a vastly different institution over time.''

These policies are reflected in the Administration's position on the World Bank's proposed energy-lending affiliate. Reversing Carter policy, the Reagan Administration has also come out against the affiliate. Designed to help Third World countries struggling with mammoth oil bills to develop their own energy resources, the affiliate has been resisted by the major international oil companies, who fear that it will strengthen the development of state-owned competitors.

Reagan officials have argued that a new agency would create an unnecessary bureaucracy. But the Treasury Department has also been sharply critical of existing energy lending programs within the bank, aligning itself closely with the views of the oil firms. The major "U.S. objective," in the international energy field, the Treasury Department stated bluntly in an August, 1981 study, is "encouraging private investment in the oil and gas area" in Third World countries.

Instead of expanding aid, the report concludes, "The World Bank has an important role to play . . . by encouraging host countries to remove impediments and adopt policies which facilitates private investment in energy development." To pressure recalcitrant governments, the report argues, the World Bank should require recipients of energy loans to increase the involvement of private oil companies in joint ventures and to allow multinationals to share in exploration and development.

While satisfying the oil companies, this view does little for many members of the international banking community who fear the mounting oil debt—to say nothing of the Third World itself. Said Frank G. Zarb, a former Federal Energy Administration chief now with Lazard, Freres and Co., "I don't have answers for the desperate position of those underdeveloped countries that would have a better chance to develop if it were not for their oil payments . . ."

After a year in Washington, Regan has made great strides. In the early months, he was overshadowed by the media wizardry of David Stockman, and only cautiously accepted by the supply-siders who had searched in vain for evidence of his prior adherence to the faith.

Regan told us there are "natural tensions" between the Treasury secretary, who worries about the entire economy, and the budget director who is "very tense to accomplish his objectives, which is to get his budget through in the shape that he originally had for it." Said Regan: "I never felt that Dave and I were rivals for anything. As a matter of fact, I've offered him my job at several times and said 'If you want it, take it. And I'll go back to the private sector and make money.' In a joshing way, naturally. And he in turn has said he doesn't want the damn job, that he's satisfied with what he's got."

But, perhaps inevitably, the President increasingly came to rely on the counsel of a man who, like himself, was old enough to be the budget director's father. And when it was spectacularly revealed that it was Stockman who harbored in his heart doubts about the supply-side path, Regan's role as preeminent economic spokesman was cemented.

The concrete has a few faults in it, however. Reagan's refusal to dismiss Stockman was a tacit admission that none of his other top economic officials were equally capable of manipulating the intricacies of the federal budget. And Regan's style on Capitol Hill has been criticized as too "blunt." Those deficiencies have kept Regan from clearly outstripping his rivals as the lead figure identified with Reagan's economic plans. As the promises of Reagonomics continue to unravel, though, the Treasury secretary may ultimately find that failure a blessing.

A CONVERSATION WITH THE TREASURY SECRETARY

On March 3, 1982, Ralph Nader, Ronald Brownstein and John Brown sat down with Donald Regan in a quiet boardroom dominated by a huge portrait of Andrew

Mellon, one of the Secretary's predecessors. Portions of the 45-minute conversation appear in Secretary Regan's profile. Additional excerpts follow:

QUESTION—David Stockman said he was stunned by the greed that came to the forefront during the negotiations on the tax bill. Would you agree with that characterization?

REGAN—I wouldn't want to comment on what Dave had to say. I think what happened in the final analysis was it's just as though you were on the platform at, where, Stamford, Connecticut and the 8:05 is leaving for Grand Central Station, and with hundreds of commuters waiting there to get aboard, the announcer says 'there will be no other train after this one.' You could imagine what would happen, everybody trying to get aboard that train. . .once it became apparent that there's going to be a whole list of things [added to the tax bill], everybody wanted to get his on—I'm talking there about members of Congress, particularly members of the Ways and Means Committee. Then the outsiders began to hear what was going on and they wanted theirs. And then when we split apart and it became sort of a test of wills or political might, as to whose bill would be passed, and we came up with the Hance-Conable bill and Dan [Rostenkowski, chair of the House Ways and Means Committee] had his own bill, then he'd hang one bauble on; we'd hang a bauble on ours and that's what Dave was referring to. Now to my point of view that was to have been expected once you got away from the original two-track bill and it became apparent that the Administration was going to have only one bill.

QUESTION—Would you support abolition of the corporate income tax and just tax corporate dividends?

REGAN—That's an interesting idea. I have asked for studies on that; I don't know. I keep hearing. . .economists saying, 'Corporations don't pay taxes, people do.' Well that's a fine idea and it's a great theory, but being more of a pragmatist I'd want to know more about the effects of that, and how we'd collect it and how you'd apportion it among the various stockholders.

QUESTION—Are you worried about the amounts of investment money that are going into what can be described as non-productive outlets such as collectibles, forced condominium conversions, mergers and acquisitions—now they're futures trading in New York Stock Exchange indices. When you take it all together, we're seeing a massive diversion into what was once called speculation.

REGAN—Well, let's split it down for a moment. . .If you take the various commodity type of speculation, that was a creature of inflation, the virulent inflation that we've had over the last several years. You cannot blame people for trying to escape that. . .When you have year after year double digit inflation, Latin America—the whole of Latin America is a classic example of it now—you must as an individual citizen take steps to protect yourself against that. Paper money won't do it. It used to be thought that stocks were the best investment. Well it turned out that stocks were far from the best investment. That's when collectibles became the thing to do.

When you come to mergers: why does U.S. Steel want to buy an oil company? This has many ramifications, not the least of which are the corporate objectives. If you're going to be up-down, up-down, following or lagging the business cycle, the prudent management tries to get something else to hedge against that. So instead of up-down, up-down, hopefully, it will be narrower swings along an increasing path. It looked to U.S. Steel as if that was the way to do it, to go into the oil business.

QUESTION—Some are saying it makes good sense for company A or company B, but for the overall economy?

REGAN—Being a free market fellow, you make management make its own mistakes and its own victories.

QUESTION—If there's only a limited amount of money available to the company—if it's credit or whatever, they're going to have to pay it back at some point—would you rather see them invest in a greenfield steel plant or. . .

REGAN—You have to take a look at what industry you're talking about. If there is no demand for the product what's the sense of a greenfield plant. To the extent that we don't need steel, or there's no demand for steel, or steel is at a 56 percent capacity or whatever, why bother with a greenfield. The idea, hopefully, would be that they'd start into a new industry or something brand new, a new product that would either have been shown to them or come out of their own labs, that they would do. . .steel companies can't do that.

QUESTION—We interviewed Mr. [William] Baxter, the antitrust division chief [of the Justice Department]. We said, 'what do you think about the deductibility of interest, paid for borrowed funds to facilitate mergers and acquisitions?' And he said that's a tax question. He kept refusing to answer it. So. . .

REGAN—This has to assume there's such a thing as good interest and bad interest. And with all due respect to the people who work over at IRS, I don't think they're competent to distinguish between good interest and bad interest. So that would leave it up to the Congress to distinguish between good interest and bad interest. And again, I'm not sure they could. I hope it doesn't go any further. Now if somebody borrows money to buy up an ailing thrift should that be deductible? And if U.S. Steel buys Conoco should that be deductible? How do you determine which is good and which is bad? Is it a good thing to buy up a bad company, or a failing company?

QUESTION—So you'd let the market do it?

REGAN—I'd let the market do it, sure.

QUESTION—You've been critical of business behavior. Commerce Secretary Baldrige's famous comment that too many managers of large corporations are 'fat, dumb and happy'. We understand there is an undercurrent. . .

REGAN—I never said they were fat.

QUESTION—An undercurrent in the Administration. You said they were timid. There's a lot of talk privately in the Reagan Administration about when are these guys going to start moving?

REGAN—Business I think is copping a plea. It's a good plea. We've put all these things in place for business. We've given them the ACRS, we've made stock options easier, we've made the estate tax easier so that if they make it they can leave it, all these types of things and yet the business recovery has not started. I admit, having been for ten years a CEO [chief executive officer] myself, I understand what they're saying. You get a printout from your computer in which you factor in a new building—a warehouse or a factory—in my case it would be a new program or a new office building. And you would see that if you had to borrow money, construction money, at 17 or 18 percent, if you had to then look at permanent financing over a 20 or 30 year period—AAA bonds are right now around 16 percent—the figures don't come out on that printout the way that you want them, the rate of return and the assets that you're devoting to the project, so they're saying 'uh, uh, not with the current high rates of interest.'

Now therein lies a separate tale all by itself. Why the current high rates of interest? As one of my banking friends said, interest rates are performing an act of levitation that defies the eyes and the imagination as to how they're staying up there when literally they should be way down. The real premium on interest now, if you take anything of historic standards [is unprecedented]. . .That premium has never been in real interest rates since—well, anytime. Not even in the bad days of the Continental Army, let alone the Civil War or any other panicky period of this country. So they have to come down. And I think that's what businessmen are waiting for.

QUESTION—In that context do you have some fear that there are experiments being run, which we haven't in the past, that may change that relationshp between inflation and interest rates? The two I have in mind are continuing reliance on monetary policy, not just for a six-month period but for a three- or four-year period, to wring inflation out of the economy, and two, at the same time, deregulation of financial markets, which seems to be exerting some upward pressure on interest rates. Is it possible that the combination of those two factors could lead to continuing high interest rates, even though inflation subsides?

REGAN—Well Jerry Voorhis was a Congressman [from California] for quite a few years [1937-1947] and I just read a chapter out of his book in which he deals with the Federal Reserve and monetary policies. And one of the things he says, he was a student, age 17, at the time that this happened back in 1920, he says that the 1920 recession was entirely induced by the monetary—monetary!—policies of the Federal Reserve, that the then chairman of the Federal Reserve decided that we were living beyond our means in the post-World War One era and wanted to see credit restrained . . . So monetary policy and the Fed go that far back. So it shouldn't be anything new in monetary policy that's causing it.

I think what's caused it, these real rates of interest is belief on the part of three separate elements of society. One business people, and I include in there the Wall Street money market types, will not believe either the Federal Reserve or this Administration as to what they are doing with money at this time. They don't believe that the Fed can control money because of the extreme volatility.

That volatility wrecks markets and produces uncertainty. That's one reason for this premium being there, because they've been burned.

The second one is that they don't believe us and our budgets . . .

I think the third factor is they don't believe the Congress. They don't think the Congress has the will to cut a budget. . .so with that that's why the premium is in there.

QUESTION—How about the point on deregulation?

REGAN—Deregulation has nothing to do with the rates of interest in my honest judgment, because everybody says it will never happen or it's way out there. If anything, deregulation would tend to cut that premium and cut it sharply.

QUESTION—You mentioned that the Fed had problems hitting its monetary targets and I was thinking of the problem of even defining the monetary target that you want to hit, in terms of what is the best definition of the money supply. Do you think there may be some utility in focusing more on a credit target?

REGAN—The monetarists tell me—and as you know I'm a financier, not an economist—the monetarist economists in particular tell me if they'd look at the base and forget M1, M2, M3, because people will shift back and forth . . .Just follow the base, the Fed, if they did that, could adjust quickly enough to that base without worrying about the other.

QUESTION—Have any business leaders from large corporations urged upon you that they look at the question of focusing more on credit aggregates?

REGAN—No. Most of the businessmen do not think that credit controls will [work], credit controls by any other name.

QUESTION—We know that a lot of officials in the Reagan Administration are very antagonistic toward all these corporate subsidies, to the slow pace in trucking deregulation, to the reassertion of the international airline cartel and all of that. Why do you think they don't speak out more on it?

REGAN—I myself being pro-competitive do not believe that self-proclaimed capitalists can be closet cartelists. If you're going to be a capitalist you have to live by capitalist rules, which are the rules that allow you to fail or succeed on your own, without government intervention, except to protect. I think one of the reasons people haven't spoken up here more or faster is that people in the Reagan Administration [have needed time to] begin to learn the system. You can't get through the Congress fast enough. And if you keep bopping a Congressman on the nose, pretty soon you get hit back on some other program that you're trying to get through.

QUESTION—Will the time come before '84 for business subsidies and cartelization?

REGAN—Hopefully, we'll be able to do as much as possible in those areas.

QUESTION—The criticism that has come of the quality of some top management of large corporations—that they're rigid, they're not flexible enough, they're too bureaucratic—something like what was behind Baldrige's statement: Do you think that top management in the U.S. needs to be subjected to broader constructive criticism and do you think they are a bit too stick in the mud?

REGAN—It's very uneven. Now if you're talking about smokestack companies, I do think that many of those companies [that] stayed in their products and in their methods of producing their products [were] a lot too rigid in view of the competition that was international and the like and didn't change soon enough. And I think they have learned a bitter lesson in that; I think they're now starting to change. I do think that in high technology, in medicine and in other areas like that we're probably as innovative as any management, including Japan, and a lot less rigid than many of the Japanese companies are that are very structured, or the German companies that are very structured.

ROSCOE EGGER, JR.
COMMISSIONER, INTERNAL REVENUE SERVICE

RESPONSIBILITY OF OFFICE

As the nation's highest-ranking tax collector, Egger administers the IRS through an elaborate network of regional,
district and local offices. Established by Congress in 1862,
the IRS did not acquire its biggest responsibilities until 1913
when the Sixteenth Amendment was enacted giving Congress authority to tax the income of individuals
and corporations.

As commissioner, his mission "is to encourage and achieve the highest possible
degree of voluntary compliance with the tax laws and regulations and to conduct
[himself] so as to warrant the highest degree of public confidence in the integrity
and efficiency of the Service."

In 1982, the IRS operated with 77,831 employees and a budget of $5.8 billion.

BACKGROUND ·

Egger comes to the federal government after a 25-year career with Price,
Waterhouse & Co., a major Washington accounting firm.

He has headed the firm's Office of Government Services since 1973. Since 1956,
he had been partner-in-charge of the firm's tax department in Washington, D.C.

His only recent government experience was as one of seven private sector
members appointed to the Commission on Administrative Review of the House of
Representatives, which was charged with evaluating the House's administrative
operations. The Commission made 42 proposals dealing with such issues as accounting and management functions, committee reform, congressional travel and
member allowances and perquisites.

Egger has also been a member of the board of directors of the U.S. Chamber of
Commerce and was active in the Chamber's committees on federal taxation and
governmental and regulatory affairs. He is a member of the American Institute of
Certified Public Accountants (AICPA), federal taxation division, and former chairman of the AICPA's federal government executive committee.

Egger began his career as the tax specialist for a small accounting firm, which he
joined after a brief period with the U.S. General Accounting Office in 1947.

He received his bachelor's degree from Indiana University in 1942 and a law
degree from George Washington University Law School in 1950.

Born on September 19, 1920 in Jackson, Michigan, Egger is married with two
daughters.

MAJOR ISSUES

- Original Administration intentions to cut IRS enforcement personnel have
  been reversed, and staff will be added, though former officials explain this will
  only restore what Reagan had originally taken away.

- Services to aid individuals on their taxes, though, are being sharply reduced
  and in some cases eliminated.

- Egger unsuccessfully opposed the Administration's policy shift on granting tax exemptions to schools that racially discriminate.

- Though dismayed by the Administration's regressive tax policies, and the decision to severely curtail taxpayer services, tax reform advocates believe Egger has generally managed the IRS well, though his influence on policy has been slight.

The Washington consensus is that Egger will be more of an administrator and even less of a policy-maker than his predecessor, Jerome Kurtz. Consequently, when the tax experts talk about Egger's stance on major issues they first make the point that they are essentially talking about Administration policy. Egger has been careful to follow the company line, and his influence on the setting of that line is considered small.

"I think he sort of steps aside and lets things happen around him," said one of Egger's predecessors, who requested anonymity. Added an aide who watches the IRS for the House Ways and Means Committee: "I think that he's lost a lot of battles."

Egger's response to the Administration's hiring constraints makes the point clear. When entering office, the Reagan Administration decided to spend less than President Carter budgeted for 1981 for the IRS "examination" staff, the people who audit tax returns. Treasury Secretary Donald Regan told Congress that the cuts in personnel will not pose a problem because, with the new tax cuts, taxpayers will be less compelled to cheat on their returns.

Most people have a less sanguine view of human values. As Sen. Max Baucus (D-Mont.) said at Egger's nomination hearing, "I am concerned that the more the public gets the feeling the IRS is laying people off, the more some Americans are going to feel, 'Well, I guess I don't have to pay as much attention to the tax returns that I otherwise might. I can fudge a little here, fudge a little there and not report here, not report there, et cetera.'"

Baucus attempted to draw out Egger's personal opinion on the cuts. Egger conceded, "It goes without saying that if you reduce the amount of enforcement, you are going to reduce the amount of revenues that would normally be achieved." Moreover, he told senators, "if we add more people in certain enforcement areas of the [IRS] the amount of revenue collected, in general, tends to exceed the cost and sometimes by several multiples."

Yet when the senator pressed Egger for his personal opinion of the enforcement rollback, he repeatedly side-stepped the question. Finally, he said he "certainly wouldn't object to [the hiring freeze] the way it was done."

Tax experts are especially concerned about maintaining auditing personnel because of the growing underground economy and the surge of tax resistance movements. Egger's predecessor, Kurtz, had been especially sensitive to the problem, launching an unreported income program. And another of Egger's predecessors told us that he considers the underground economy the most important issue facing the IRS. "I think it is very frightening," said Mortimer Caplin, IRS Commissioner from 1961 through 1964. "The commissioner has to do everything he can to get better compliance. That problem is getting bigger and bigger; it's a creeping octopus." The GAO estimated in March, 1982 that tax fraud is costing the Treasury more than $70 billion a year. It found, however, that audits had dropped from 26 per 1,000 in 1976 to only 16 in 1982.

When we spoke with Egger in August, 1981 he stressed that auditing personnel will actually be increased in fiscal year 1982, though he admitted the 1981 budget provided funds for 600 less auditors than Carter's proposal. Egger was especially enthused about new proposals before Congress which will give the IRS greater authority to impose fines and penalties for such abusive tax shelters as mail-order ministries.

As for Secretary Regan's comment that taxpayers will be less likely to cheat, Egger said he was sure Regan had been quoted slightly out of context.

"There is probably some truth to that statement," Egger said. "However, I'm sure that was not the Secretary's only consideration in discussing those [personnel] cuts."

Anxious to reduce huge deficits without raising taxes, though, the Administration has found the logic of increasing the IRS enforcement staff inexorable. Where it cut IRS employment from 78,425 in 1981 to 77,830 in 1982, the Administration is proposing an overall increase of about 4,000 employees for 1983. Specifically, the enforcement staff will be increased by more than 5,000 under the 1983 budget. (The IRS budget for investigations and enforcement will rise from $603 million in 1982 to $772 million.) These new employees would implement proposed changes in the tax code that would impose withholding on interest and dividends, and accelerate the payment of whatever corporate income taxes are left after the 1981 tax bill. The Office of Management and Budget expects this increased enforcement to generate $5.5 billion annually in 1983 and 1984.

But the personnel gains are somewhat illusory, according to Kurtz. With an annual 2 percent staff increase needed to handle the increased number of tax returns, and another 1,000 employees needed for the windfall profits tax, Kurtz said, the proposed additional employees only returns IRS to approximately where it should have been in 1983 without the original cuts.

Other areas that help the public, however, are facing cuts. According to budget documents, the cuts will reduce the number of taxpayers assisted by IRS from 41.4 million this year to just 19.3 million in 1983. The IRS will no longer prepare at no cost tax return forms for individuals. It proposes to no longer answer telephone or walk-in questions on matters of tax law. The Administration is reportedly considering the complete elimination of the taxpayers services division.

"The idea of taxpayer assistance is very important because it encourages compliance," said Caplin. "To the extent that you're being helpful to taxpayers, you've made better taxpayers of them."

Tom Fields of Tax Analysts, a tax reform group, said the one decidedly "stern" action Egger has taken was in response to the much-publicized tax revolt threat by auto workers in Flint, Michigan in the spring of 1981. Egger issued a strongly-worded statement warning the auto workers that such an act would be met by a swift reprisal by the IRS, and he has since seen to it that the major leaders have been tried and convicted.

"I imagine those workers were rather surprised," said Fields. Noting the Reagan Administration's anti-taxation theme, he added, "They went for the poor man's loophole, but they found out in a hurry that the loopholes in our tax system are only meant for the rich."

Another hot issue facing the service is its role in general law enforcement. The Administration is backing legislation to facilitate disclosure of IRS information to federal investigators. Strongly supported by the Justice Department, such measures were also backed by Egger at December, 1981 hearings. The Administration's bill,

Egger told the House Ways and Means Oversight Subcommittee, "strikes the proper balance between protection of our self-assessment tax system and enhancing nontax related criminal law enforcement efforts." But three former commissioners, including Kurtz, opposed the measure. Said Donald Alexander, commissioner from 1973-77: "IRS now has the right to report criminal activities, and the better course is to improve administration, not to impose a duty which might well be interpreted to force IRS into a role as a general law enforcement agency." Kurtz maintained the legislation would "diminish the confidentiality of tax information which taxpayers have a right to expect, seriously interfere with efficient tax administration, distort the mission of the [IRS] and open the potential for great mischief."

Egger has consistently stated his intention to go after "abusive tax shelters."

Kurtz told us Egger seems to be achieving this objective. The already existing IRS program to combat abusive tax shelters "has a life of its own" and Egger is not likely to soften it because "once you see the abuse it is hard for anyone to ignore it," Kurtz said. Egger has announced plans to reduce tax shelter litigation, aiming to settle more cases out of court and concentrate the agency's resources on more egregious cases.

Egger has some politically "hot" issues confronting him, but for the time being he does not have to decide on them because Congress has tied his hands. One of these is the issue of which fringe benefits ought to be counted as income. IRS has been eager to draw guidelines, but Congress is still grappling with the issue.

Egger has said fringe benefits are a top priority issue for him because "clearly we have to come up with a rule of reason." However, he adds the matter requires careful study "to give consideration to the impact of any possible changes done in such fashion as to make it palatable to the tax paying public." Acting over IRS' head, Treasury offered not to write any regulations until July, 1982. But even that wasn't enough for the business-oriented 97th Congress. In the 1981 tax act, Congress decided to bar IRS from acting through December 31, 1983.

The IRS drew the most attention early this year for a policy decision it had nothing to do with. On January 8, 1982 Reagan revoked the IRS policy of denying tax exemptions to schools that racially discriminate. After White House aides initially sought to isolate Reagan from the decision, it was revealed that the President in December personally gave Treasury Secretary Regan instructions to make the policy change. Egger has testified that he disagreed with the decision (See profiles of Ed Meese, James Baker and Michael Deaver). In an internal memo to Treasury Secretary Regan, he wrote: "The courts have held that organizations that violate a clearly defined public policy are not charitable in the broad sense of the word. At least since the 1954 *Brown* decision there has been a clear federal policy against racial discrimination in education."

Beyond these headlines, the IRS faces more fundamental, long-term challenges. In a June, 1981 article, Kurtz laid out some of these issues. "The urgent problems cannot be ignored, nor should they be," Kurtz wrote. "The risk is that they will not leave time for consideration of important long-range issues, the impact of which may not be fully apparent." Key issues identified by Kurtz included:

* resources and compensation for IRS staff, necessary "to attract the talent necessary to administer the tax system adequately."

- tax shelter and reporting problems
- withholding on interest and dividends (which has been embraced by the Administration)
- tax code simplification
- taxpayer privacy

"These problems," Kurtz concluded, "were not for the most part solved in the last four years and will not be solved in the next four. But substantial effort must be devoted to these concerns if progress toward solutions is to be made."

FINANCIAL BACKGROUND

Egger received $251,000 for his services at Price, Waterhouse in 1980. He has placed his stock holdings into a trust. These include small holdings in a number of firms including R.J. Reynolds, Time, American Brands and Geico.

WHAT OTHERS ARE SAYING ABOUT HIM

- Though dismayed by Reagan's tax policies, tax groups consider Egger something of a pleasant surprise. When Egger was first nominated for the job, "everybody was saying 'Who is this guy,'" said Fields. "Egger comes into this job a relative unknown."

Several of the tax groups we talked to echoed Field's statement. Few of them knew anything about Egger's background.

But after a year, Fields said, "the more I see of Egger the more I'm impressed with the job he's doing." Fields cites two points of particularly good performance on Egger's part: his opposition to granting tax exempt status to racially-discriminatory schools, and his administrative handling of the division. "I thought his memo [to the Treasury Department opposing the policy shift] was impressive and well-reasoned," Fields said. And he thought that Egger artfully managed the difficult cuts imposed on the agency for 1982. "If he had to make cuts, it seems to me he made them in the right place." In all, Fields said, Egger appears a "very practical, down-to-earth, unaffected pragmatic man."

- "I have a lot of respect for Egger," Kurtz told us. "He is obviously going to be calling some of the shots differently than I did, but that is more due to the new Administration than anything else."

COMMERCE DEPARTMENT

MALCOLM BALDRIGE
SECRETARY

RESPONSIBILITY OF OFFICE

Responsible for encouraging the nation's "economic development and technological advancement," the Commerce Department has recently picked up increased trade responsibilities to augment its traditional role of collecting data, analyzing the economy, developing standards and representing the interests of big business.

Baldrige is responsible for all "functions and authorities assigned" to the department. Its major operating divisions include: the International Trade Administration, the National Bureau of Standards, the National Oceanic and Atmospheric Administration (NOAA), the Patent and Trademark Office, the Bureau of the Census, the Bureau of Economic Analysis and the National Telecommunications and Information Administration. The department lost two divisions when the Reagan Administration eliminated the Economic Development Administration and transferred the Maritime Administration to the Transportation Department, but picked up another when Baldrige established a Bureau of Competitive Assessment, which charts the ability of each industrial sector to meet worldwide competition. If Congress agrees with the Administration's plans to dismantle the Department of Energy (DOE), Commerce will pick up most of its functions, including the production of nuclear weapons. (See Major Issues.)

The Commerce Department had a 1982 budget of about $2.1 billion and 26,000 employees.

BACKGROUND

Baldrige is probably the kind of person kitchen cabinet member Alfred Bloomingdale had in mind when he told reporters last fall that: "What we are doing is just trying to find the best guy for the job—the ones we'd hire for our own business."

A successful businessman, a long-time Republican activist often considered a potential candidate for elected office, and a life-time cowboy, Baldrige, according to a breathy *New York Times* profile, "is known as a man's man."

He is also a study in contradiction. A Marlboro chainsmoker who likes to dress as if he lives in the Marlboro Country—and was graduated from Connecticut's exclusive Hotchkiss School (1940) and Yale University (1944). A top corporate executive who sits on half a dozen major boards—and rides in professional rodeos. An Eastern Republican who backed William Scranton against Barry Goldwater in 1964—and is now serving the heir to Goldwater's conservative mantle. On his coffee table in his office is a copy of *The 1982 Official Pro Rodeo Media Guide*; beneath it is *The Arts of Japan, Ancient and Medieval*. The office is elegant, with spacious ceilings and exquisite chandeliers; behind his desk is a saddle and rope, won, he said proudly "a couple of years ago in California. . .against the pros."

When Reagan called the Baldrige household to offer him the Commerce job, so the story goes, his wife told the President-elect that Malcolm couldn't come to the phone; he was out riding. "That," said the President, "is my kind of guy." And so he has been, occasionally joining the President for a recreational ride. But the demands of the new job have cut back his riding schedule. Before coming to Washington, Baldrige has said, he used to practice steer roping three times a week; now he gets away less often. "I think I'll get to two or three rodeos this year, that's all," he said in an interview. "I can get down on Sunday afternoons and practice; they have some roping in Virginia and Maryland. . .They're putting up $50 and they do it for the money. You can't think about anything else; it just wipes everything else off of your mind. It's good exercise, but it's kind of exciting and it's very pleasing to me bacause you have to be partners with a good horse and you're in competition with 30 other people all the time, 50 in some cases, I really like that."

Baldrige managed to fit those steer-roping sessions—and occasional rodeo competitions—into a schedule that included the chairmanship of the Connecticut-based conglomerate Scovill, Inc., and directorships with AMF, Asarco, Bendix, Connecticut Mutual Life Insurance, Eastern Company and Uniroyal. Baldrige is credited with transforming Scovill from a slumping brass manufacturer into a diversified, expanding conglomerate. He did so in a manner that has become common for American business: downplaying basic productive industries—in this case brass manufacturing—and entering new businesses primarily by buying existing companies. On the other hand, Baldrige stressed to an unusual degree individual accountability among managers and stamped the company with his imprint, a rare pattern in an era of faceless chief executives.

When he came to Scovill as an executive vice-president in 1962, brass mill earnings accounted for over half of the company's sales. But Baldrige had other ideas. Through a series of acquisitions in the late 1960s and early 1970s—including the 1972 purchase of Westinghouse's small appliance division— Baldrige steered the company into consumer products where it became the nation's largest vendor of door chimes, corn poppers, sewing notions and blenders.

By the mid-1970s, Baldrige concluded that Scovill had to abandon the brass business it had run since the early 19th century. He decided to sell the company's brass mills in Waterbury, where it was the oldest and largest employer. When negotiations with prospective buyers stalled, Baldrige received permission from his board to shut down the mills. Buyers were eventually found, but only after the state interceded and the union acquiesced to a no-raise contract.

During Baldrige's tenure, Scovill's business boomed. Sales totalled $169 million when he arrived and $941 million when he left. The son of a one-term Republican congressman from Nebraska, Baldrige has long been active in national business advocacy groups and Republican political organizations. A former member of the National Finance Republican Committee, and a vice-chairman of the Business for Reagan-Bush campaign, he also ran Bush's 1980 Connecticut campaign, in which Bush defeated Reagan. That last assignment reportedly caused ill-will between Baldrige and Connecticut Republican Senator Lowell Weicker, who was at the time organizing a presidential bid of his own. By his own account, Baldrige has given between $5,000 and $7,500 annually to various local and national political candidates over the past ten years.

Baldrige is also a member of the Business Council, the Council on Foreign Relations, the Conference Board and the International Chamber of Commerce, not to mention the Professional Rodeo Cowboys Association. Turning professional at the age of 42, Baldrige was once the nation's fifth-ranked steer roper.

And he likes to affect the cowboy's legendary taciturnity. "If people in Washington got paid by the words," he once sneered, "they would all be billionaires." When one reporter asked him what the main difference was between the Washington circuit and the rodeo circuit, Baldrige told us, he responded: "A cowboy doesn't say anything unless he's got something to say."

Baldrige has let his subordinates know that such bureaucratic staples as "finalize," "interface" and "impact" were no longer acceptable in memos. The prose style he was seeking, he announced, was "halfway between Ernest Hemingway and Zane Grey." We asked Baldrige which of his cabinet colleagues came close to matching that ideal. "Well, not Al Haig, you can rule him out right away," he said with a laugh. "I tell you: I could answer that—Drew Lewis. Drew Lewis is definitely among the more short-winded cabinet members and he gets to the point."

Rumored as a possible candidate for governor in 1966 and 1970, Baldrige may eventually test the electoral waters in Connecticut, though he denies electoral ambitions. "I fully intend to serve out the term," he said. "You know some people talk to me about Connecticut politics but I honestly like what I'm doing. I don't think I've got the patience to be a good senator or congressman. It's just difficult for me to imagine myself doing that."

Baldrige, of course, is in many ways the prototypical member of the Reagan Cabinet: a wealthy, white, male industrialist active in Republican politics. But his other life in the rodeo has given him a perspective far different than his colleagues on some matters. "It used to be when I was at Scovill," he said, "some great friend of yours was married, had two kids and was trying to make a living on the rodeo circuit. He'd start off the year, he'd take maybe $2,500, $3,000 with him. I've been in campers with those guys, they'd invited me to go from Amarillo to Denver to the rodeo, and so we went up. And it was my turn to fix supper—and this is a true story—there'd be half a loaf of bread and some peanut butter in there. Period. And the guy'd say, 'Well, I got to win something in Denver.' Then you'd go home and see a vice-president arguing because he didn't have a key to the washroom. . .or because his office wasn't in quite the right place or something, and it kind of puts the world in perspective. It really does. . .I recommend a dose of that for everybody." Baldrige told that story without a hint that he recognized the irony of working for a President whose economic policies have been labeled "Robin Hood in reverse."

Born in Omaha, Nebraska on October 4, 1922, Baldrige came to Scovill from the nearby Eastern Iron Company, where he started as a foreman after World War II and worked his way up to president in 13 years. As a teenager he worked as a ranchhand in Nebraska. He is married, with two daughters.

MAJOR ISSUES

- As the economic situation has worsened, and business has failed to produce the surge of growth the Administration predicted, Baldrige has turned into a born-again critic of American management, complaining that "management has been too fat, dumb and happy in the past ten years."

- Baldrige, though, has filled the secretary's usual function of carrying business's water on a number of other issues, from regulations governing leasing of off-shore oil, to the Justice Department's antitrust case against American Telephone and Telegraph (AT&T).

- In an ostensibly free-market Administration, Baldrige has pressed European nations to "voluntarily" restrict steel exports, in response to pressure from domestic manufacturers.

- If the Administration's plan to dismantle the Department of Energy goes through, Baldrige will assume broad new powers, including oversight of the nation's nuclear-weapons building facilities and responsibility for drawing up the national energy plan.

In the past, the secretary of Commerce's job has been to serve as business' chief cheerleader in the federal bureaucracy. But in an Administration where the chief executive is the chief cheerleader, and business has installed its own pep squad in key posts throughout the government, Commerce's historical function has become redundant.

Searching for a new mission, Baldrige hit upon an unusual deviation: castigating business for the Administration. As the summer glow faded from Reaganomics, and Wall Street refused to lay out its money as Reagan had hoped, Baldrige even suggested that business was breaking its "contract" with the Administration.

That is not to say Baldrige has abandoned the department's functions of excoriating government regulation—Commerce compiled and released a "Terrible 20" list of regulations business most detests—complaining about over-taxation and pressuring other agencies engaged in activities business finds objectionable.

But Baldrige, who prides himself on direct speech, has been blunt about the shortcomings of American business. Consider these remarks, made during his first year in office:

On American management: "It's overstaffed. It concentrates on one-year goals, which is costly. It's not close enough to labor to understand labor's problems. It's insulated from what goes on in the world, even from what goes on at home. It's not as innovative in working on new ideas and generating money for research as the Japanese, the Germans and I will even include the Mexicans, are. I know Mexican businessmen that are a lot more efficient than many Americans."

On stagnating productivity: "I don't think it's labor productivity that's a problem. It's management. And I speak as a former manager. Management has been too fat, dumb and happy in the past 10 years. Management hasn't been sharp enough or hungry enough or lean enough."

On business' responsibility in Reaganomics: "You in the private sector asked for these programs, and now you have a friend in the White House who agrees with you. He's gone out on a limb for you. . .What we need is for the private sector to pick up its responsibility. With the transfer of funds—from the federal government's treasury and into the private sector's—comes a partial transfer of responsibility for the social well-being of this country."

Through the fall of 1981, Baldrige picked up that theme repeatedly, suggesting that as the economy fails to perform up to Reagan's expectations, an Administration that came to Washington draping laurels over American business will soon be pinning blame on it instead. "When candidate Reagan last year talked about tax cuts to help the private sector it wasn't just talk. He has delivered on his end of the bargain—you might say his half of the contract has been fulfilled," Baldrige told the National Alliance of Business in October, 1981. "It wasn't a contract that anyone signed, but it was a contract just the same. Much of what the President has done he did because he expected the business community to hold up its end of the contract—to respond as it should. . ."

A few moments later, Baldrige delivered the contract's penalty clause: "If you don't pick up on this responsibility," he told the assembled business leaders, "that obligation [to support the community] will fall back in the hands of the government—and we've seen where that leads—higher taxes, bigger government, over-regulation, overtaxation and overgovernment. The tax package may not be forever—it will depend on the responses by business." Baldrige told us: "I think it needs some initiative from business, some going the extra mile. . .not just sitting back and saying 'if I raise my contributions from one percent of after-tax income to 1.2 percent I have fulfilled my role as a corporate citizen.'"

In our interview, Baldrige backed off his criticisms somewhat, and gave an indication of the sorts of pressures those remarks have generated. "In that Springfield speech [where he used the phrase 'fat, dumb and happy'] I was talking about exporting to medium and smaller sized manufacturers and I was making the point that because we had such a large domestic market that enough medium and small sized manufacturers hadn't taken the trouble to investigate export opportunities, unlike our trading competitors around the world. . .And I said U.S. manufacturers—and I was thinking of a phrase, you know, it wasn't in the speech, probably 'complacent' might have been a little better choice of words—but I said fat, dumb and happy and in some cases that's been exactly true. I wouldn't categorize every businessman that way. But in a lot of cases it's true, with the domestic market and they had to get hungry enough about exports so that the country as a whole could compete in this worldwide race. . ."

At best, the reaction to that now legendary remark has been mixed. "I had a good many businessmen tell me, get up and say 'I'm glad somebody said that.' I also had some comments from the U.S. Chamber of Commerce to the effect of 'Why would I say anything like that? It looks like we've got a secretary of Labor who's more sympathetic with businessmen than the secretary of Commerce is, the secretary of Commerce is more sympathetic to labor than the secretary of Labor is.' Well, I think that was said tongue in cheek. But evidently the press made more out of it [my statement] than I intended."

A few moments later, though, Baldrige essentially reiterated his criticism. "In the 1950s we were the acknowledged worldwide and industrial leader," he said.

"We just had come through World War II when American industry had done a phenomenal job of out-producing everybody else. That led, in my opinion, to almost a generation of complacent managers who had been raised on the theory that American productivity [and] industrial power was unparalleled in the industrial world and so forth. For the next oh, 20 years, Americans went into business with the feeling that we were ahead of everybody else, that everything we did was probably the best possible to do in the entire world. Well, in the meantime, a lot of other countries were rebuilding their industrial capacities, which were damaged by World War II, and they were what I would describe, by necessity, as lean and hungry managers. They had a lot of catching up to do, they were building new plants, they made them as modern as possible because they had to export to get along in international competitive markets, they kept overheads and staff lean and they picked up a lot of our techniques and added on to them—I've seen this personally in country after country. And in the meantime our people were still complacent for too long. . .We were not modernizing our plants, we were falling behind in the age of our plants compared to competitors abroad. I can remember hearing them discussed, but there wasn't enough realization and action at the time. . .

"So what we're seeing now and I think we've seen for about the last five years, and slowly building up to where it's a common realization now, [is that] we simply have to accept the fact that in some areas we've really fallen behind and we've got to do something about it if we're going to be competitive worldwide—and that realization comes hard to a lot of American managers."

Such difficult new circumstances come hard for labor leaders as well, Baldrige continued. "I think we're seing kind of a painful evolution. . . When you see [United Auto Workers President] Doug Fraser and [General Motors Chairman] Roger Smith having their picture taken together, both of them smiling—or trying to smile— that's a kind of a new departure. What it means is they both recognize there's a problem and they're trying to work it out together. . .They're trying to get away from that adversarial relationship. . .In the process you see unions going through some really traumatic times now. . .you got to have sympathy for them. You see union presidents and local presidents particularly who may have spent their lives in certain industries and seen president after president ahead of them negotiate higher contracts. And all of a sudden his term comes and he's in that seat and he's faced with giving up some things. . .and I'll guarantee that is hard on him."

In the meantime, Baldrige has carried the department's concern about over-regulation into two highly controversial areas involving other departments: offshore drilling for oil and gas and the antitrust case against American Telephone and Telegraph. In this, his efforts have been guided by a straightforward philosophy: "Reforming the bureaucrats is much too important to America's future to be left to the bureaucrats," as he told a business group in April, 1981.

Baldrige has waded into the controversy over Interior Secretary James Watt's plan to greatly accelerate oil and gas development on the Outer Continental Shelf (OCS). From the early days of the Administration, Watt, quite presciently, foresaw that the "consistency" provisions of the 1972 Coastal Zone Management Act—which is administered by NOAA and falls under Baldrige's jurisdiction—posed a serious threat to his plans. Those provisions allow the states to review federal actions that "directly affect" their coastlines for "consistency" with their state coastal development plans. California, Alaska and other states quickly suggested that Watt's plans were not consistent with their own.

No one disputes that OCS exploration or drilling activities are covered by the law. But Watt, like Cecil Andrus before him, argued that preleasing activities were not covered. In March, 1981, Watt sent a private letter to Baldrige, urging that NOAA omit leasing activities from pending regulations defining actions that directly affect the coast. On the side of the letter, Watt scrawled: "Mac, this letter is of critical importance to us. I want to personally discuss it with you. Jim."

When the regulations were issued in July, Watt's concerns were addressed and preleasing was left out. But California, which had earlier sued Watt over disputed tracts off its coast (See Watt profile), went back into court to challenge the rules. Many analysts felt the state's case would be successful. Eldon Greenberg, the former NOAA general counsel predicted the regulations would be struck down: "We always took the position that pre-lease was subject to [the] consistency [provisions]," he told us.

Baldrige's decision stirred up a sharp Congressional backlash as well. Since NOAA's regulations are subject to Congressional veto, resolutions moved forward in both houses to reject the rules. "If state governments are not accorded a fair voice in these decisions," said Rep. Gerry Studds (D-Mass.), who sponsored one of the resolutions, "they will have no substantive role at all in the events that have an undeniably major impact on their local economies, their coastal environments, and the quality of life in their beachfront communities." Faced with a major rebuff, Watt and Baldrige backed down in October, 1981 and withdrew the rules.

Watt also sought Baldrige's help in opening up to drilling the Channel Islands marine sanctuary off the California coast. Watt will only be able to lease the marine sanctuary tracts if NOAA, which supervises the sanctuaries, withdraws its regulations banning oil exploration there. The agency issued its prohibition in October, 1980, but they were caught by the Administration's freeze on pending regulations and have since been suspended, waiting the outcome of a new cost/benefit analysis.

And even as the Interior Department readies to offer one billion acres of the OCS—virtually every tract on the entire shelf—for lease over the next five years, the Commerce Department sought to drastically reduce the funds granted to states to manage their coastal programs. Commerce sought the complete elimination of 1981 and 1982 funding for grants to help states manage coastal energy development, and to eliminate in 1982 grants to support state administration of the program. Congress has tentatively decided to save the administrative grants by transferring funds from the energy program. For 1983, the Administration is seeking the complete elimination of coastal zone aid to the states.

As chairman of the Cabinet Council on Commerce and Trade, Baldrige also took the lead in the White House's efforts to convince Assistant Attorney General William Baxter to drop the Justice Department's antitrust case against American Telephone & Telegraph. At the White House's request, Baldrige established and chaired a task force on telecommunications policy that concluded the suit posed a threat to the U.S. ability to keep up with foreign competition.

Baldrige then worked with the Defense Department to swing Administration support behind a telecommunications deregulation bill that allowed AT&T to offer unregulated activities through separate subsidiaries, rather than forcing the giant company to divest those operations, as the Justice Department suit would do. Baxter, though, pressed on to an agreement with AT&T. (See profile of William Baxter.)

And Baldrige strenuously defends the bias toward large corporations built into the Administration's business tax cuts, advancing a sort of industrial trickle-down theory in the process. "I think it's true that the depreciation reform helped big businesses more than small businesses because to be a capital-intensive industry you have to be of a certain size," he said. "Well, you say philosophically do we want to do that? And I would come back and say I think there are so many small businesses that live off capital intensive industries—all kinds of local businesses, suppliers—all of the things that go into a large business have to be helped by that. . . the small business's growth comes—and I don't have any statistics on this, but just from personal experience—except for consumer small businesses, a lot of their growth comes from sales to larger businesses. They're not just a lot of small businesses selling to each other around the room or the consumer."

Despite the comments in his speeches, he even defends business for not investing as the Administration had predicted. "It's too much to ask business to expand capacity in the middle of a recession when we have 71 percent utilization of manufacturing capacity. So that's close to 30 percent unused. What businessmen do—you can't lecture them or say change your ways. I wouldn't want to. It wouldn't make sense. Before they're going to expand to increase capacity, they're going to want to see the country coming out of a recession. And they want to see interest rates coming down, so they can come out ahead on whatever they do," he said.

Baldrige has also stepped into the secretary's usual role of pushing for increased U.S. exports—he prepared an Administration policy to expand coal exports—and complaining that foreign competitors are unfairly subsidizing exports. (Though conflict was anticipated, Baldrige has reportedly worked fairly well with Trade Ambassador William Brock.) In November, 1981, Baldrige succumbed to steady pressure from the domestic steel industry and took the unusual step of instituting unfair trade practice proceedings against five nations he charged were subsidizing their sale of steel here. Baldrige announced the action one day after a private meeting with the president of the American Iron and Steel Institutes and the chairmen of U.S. Steel, Bethlehem Steel and Republic Steel companies.

Against Baldrige's wishes, U.S. Steel subsequently announced plans to file an anti-dumping case of its own, thereby ensuring—if Baldrige's action alone was not sufficient—an escalating trade war with the Europeans. The battle escalated in predictable steps through the winter. On December 2, 1981, 16 leading steel companies and the steelworkers union announced they would file unfair trade practice charges against Western European nations exporting specialty steel; two days later Baldrige announced he would ask the Europeans to "voluntarily" restrict steel shipments to the U.S.

But that wasn't enough for the steel companies. So in January, 1982, U.S. Steel and six other manufacturers filed their long-threatened formal trade complaints. In February, the Commerce Department agreed to investigate most of the complaints (including all of those filed by U.S. Steel), and thereby took an Administration that came into office committed to free trade another step down the road of protecting an ailing domestic industry.

Baldrige is considered less of a hardliner on controlling trade with the Soviets than his counterparts in the Pentagon and even his subordinate Larry Brady. That ambivalence came through during our conversation. "In general, on non-strategic areas we should be able to ship the Soviets what's not going to help them in the military sense because it provides jobs for American workers that someone else would get. . .We ought to ease up at the bottom and be tougher at the top," he said. But when a gray-area product is available from other countries, Baldrige hesitates. "I think there is a limit of practicality because what you're doing is balancing American jobs against something they could really get, you know, from five countries."

Baldrige believes restraint of credit to the Soviets may be a more effective measure. "If you compare our restraints on trade with what we could do with credit restraints, in unity with the Europeans, the latter is a far stronger action to take because the Soviets are having trouble with hard currency."

Baldrige's department is involved in many other activities, though he has taken little interest in them. One of the most important areas is patent policy, an area of federal activity that rarely makes the press.

The Administration's patent policy reflects its ideological consistency: it is biased against small business in favor of big business. The Commerce Department is demonstrating this bias in both administrative and legislative policy.

Gerald Mossinghoff, the commissioner of patents and trademarks, has endorsed legislation that would allow all businesses conducting government research to keep the patents developed at public expense.

Under legislation passed in 1980, small businesses, universities and non-profit corporations were granted rights to the patents they develop from federal contracts. Congress passed the bill to rectify an imbalance. Large businesses with their large legal staffs and economic clout often convinced federal agencies to cede them patent rights when negotiating research contracts. (Agencies have been permitted since a 1971 executive order by Richard Nixon to exercise "judgment and flexibility" in granting patent rights.) Small businesses were left at a disadvantage, since they often lacked the political leverage to obtain patent rights on their research contracts. And in any case they received less than 4 percent of the total federal research and development (R&D) budget.

Now, with the support of the Reagan Administration, large businesses are trying to junk the entire convention of public patent ownership. To Sen. Howard Metzenbaum (D-Ohio), the dangers in that approach are considerable:

> Since the vast majority of government R&D expenditures go to the largest corporations, the granting of exclusive licenses to such corporations for government-financed inventions runs the risk of furthering concentration of economic power in the hands of large companies.

In March, 1982 testimony before a House subcommittee Mossinghoff said "the Administration is strongly supporting" the bill. "By permitting government contractors to retain commercial rights to their inventions. . .the bill is intended to encourage the most qualified and competent contractors to participate in government programs, thereby stimulating the introduction of new products into commerce and promoting competition." Rep. Robert Kastenmeier (D-Wis.) would like to attach to this bill a provision that would return most inventions not directly related to a company's business to the employee who developed the invention. "We're just not going to give this all away without getting something in return," said Bruce Lehman, an aide to Kastenmeier. The Administration has not taken a stand on that proposal.

The Commerce Department is proposing other changes in the patent system that work against small entrepreneurs. As part of a plan to make the processing of patents self-sustaining, Mossinghoff has recommended substantial fee hikes for patents. The base filing fee would increase from its present $65 to $300, and the fee for the actual issuing of the patent would increase from $100 plus $10 per page to a flat rate of $500. These increases will hardly be noticed by major corporations; but small businesses and individuals will have a harder time securing the rights to their inventions.

If Congress agrees to dissolve the Department of Energy, Baldrige's influence will increase greatly. Commerce would pick up the lion's share of DOE programs, including the $6 billion a year nuclear weapons building program. That program, along with basic nuclear, solar, and conservation research, and the government's uranium enrichment facilities, would be housed in a new Energy Research and Technology Administration under the department's aegis. Military experts generally opposed the transfer to Commerce of the weapons responsibility, with Defense Secretary Weinberger reportedly urging the President to place the program under the Pentagon or in a new independent agency. Drawing up the national energy plan will also become a Commerce responsibility.

FINANCIAL BACKGROUND

As is not unusual for chief executives of Fortune 500 companies—or, for that matter, Reagan cabinet officials—Baldrige is a wealthy man. In 1980, Baldrige earned $369,004 from Scovill; he took in another $90,176 from his board and trustee seats, though he lost about that much from various mining and other partnerships in which he was involved. Baldrige reports assets of at least $1.4 million, primarily through his holdings in Scovill, and two large farming partnerships, Southwest Grazing and Macron Farms. He is also involved in a number of mining ventures including: Texas Yellowcake, Bluebell Uranium, Venture Mining Co. and SBM Oil. He also reports liabilities of at least $715,000 in loans and a mortgage. According to documents obtained under the Freedom of Information Act by the Better Government Association Baldrige spent over $118,000 to redecorate his office—including the installation of a new sink and vanity, the refurbishing of his private elevator, and the expenditure of $12,444 to spruce up his private dining area.

WHAT OTHERS ARE SAYING ABOUT HIM

- According to department sources, Baldrige has been preoccupied with international trade issues. "He is an invisible man around the department," said one high-ranking Commerce official. "He was quite content to see the agency have a sharply diminished focus on the [domestic-oriented] things the members [in Congress] most care about." Baldrige bitterly resisted OMB Director Stockman's effort in 1981 to wipe out several Commerce Department export subsidies, such as the Foreign Commercial Service, and succeeded in restoring virtually all of the proposed cuts. But on the domestic front he has apparently been disinterested, leaving the day-to-day operation for his deputy, Joseph Wright, who has since moved over to OMB.

During our interview, Baldridge discussed those charges at length. "I don't know if 'invisible' is too strong, but let's say tending towards that. . .It's because of the way I look at getting the job done. . .This is a very interesting subject because it gets into the whole technique of management. . .I began being a foreman, well I really began being a company commander in the 27th infantry where you lived and died with 180 men. You knew every one of them like your brother. I was a foundry foreman when I came out, after working pouring iron. I became a foreman, then a superintendent, then a division manager of a small division when I was about 27. At the most 400 people—you knew every one of them. And you went down, got them out of jail, you went to their weddings, you were really close to them and you could manage that way if you weren't phony. Then you start to go up and the last company I ran had over 20,000 people. You've got a choice there: You can either be a kind of political symbol and constantly be on a jet going around to see everybody—we had 80 plants around the world. Or, if you come down here, you can get sucked into constant visits trying to reach 30,000 people somehow, and it's impossible to do. You could do a half-assed job at it, you could get to see 5,000, then the other 25,000 are still going to say what you said [about me being invisible]. The thing you want to aim for is not your own personal shaking the hand with everybody—although you'd love to do it—it's how are you going to effectively make this a strong department. . .To do that, 'a' number one and it's far above everything else, you've got to take the time initially and get the right assistant secretaries, undersecretaries, deputy secretaries. . .I would pick 15 then you talk about the kind of people they're going to pick and all of a sudden that gets up to 150 or 200. If you've done that right you can sit down and set the goals with them. . .and then you have to multiply yourself by 150 to get the job done. The fact that somebody down in Boulder or something hasn't seen you is sad—I miss that—but I know my time is better used on this."

LIONEL OLMER
UNDERSECRETARY FOR INTERNATIONAL TRADE

RESPONSIBILITY OF OFFICE

Olmer heads the Commerce Department's International Trade Administration (ITA), which is responsible for non-agricultural U.S. trade operations. ITA programs are intended to develop U.S. export markets, coordinate international trade policies, and implement export and import regulations.

The Office of the U.S. Trade Representative is charged by Congress with setting international trade policies, but these policies are largely administered by Olmer and his three assistant secretaries for international trade policy, trade development and trade administration. An early move by Reagan to shift many of the trade representative's policy-setting prerogatives to the Commerce Department was rebuffed by Congress. Since then the trade representative, and Commerce and State Department officials have been jockeying for the lead trade policy role.

Besides encouraging U.S. exports, Undersecretary Olmer administers the Export Administration Act's restrictions on exports for foreign policy, national security or short-supply reasons. These are among the most controversial trade decisions, particularly the restrictions on sales to Soviet-bloc countries. ITA is also charged with enforcing anti-dumping and countervailing duty laws on certain categories of imports.

BACKGROUND

Olmer comes from a foreign intelligence background. From 1972 to 1977, he worked for the President's Foreign Intelligence Advisory Board (FIAB), eventually as staff director.

Established in 1956 by President Eisenhower to advise him on U.S. intelligence activities, FIAB was discounted by President Kennedy but then reactivated after the Bay of Pigs debacle in 1961.

Under President Nixon, FIAB was responsible for reviewing and assessing intelligence activities, but was not a watchdog group. In fact, its only source of information about CIA activities was the CIA itself, according to a Senate study.

As FIAB staff director, Olmer obviously acquired a thorough knowledge of U.S. foreign intelligence matters, including clandestine activities and economic intelligence.

While still consulting with FIAB's successor, the Intelligence Oversight Board from September 1977 to January 1981, Olmer worked for Motorola, Inc., as director of international programs in Washington, D.C. At his Senate confirmation hearing Olmer testified that he "analyzed and wrote for the corporate leadership [his] assessments of business opportunities vs. risks in many countries of the world. . ." Apparently further drawing on his knowledge of U.S. foreign intelligence, Olmer also developed successful trade strategies for the multinational corporation in Japan, Western Africa and Latin America.

The Commerce Department's biographical sketch of Olmer states that: "Partly as a result of his efforts, Motorola has become the first major U.S. high technology manufacturer to penetrate the highly competitive Japanese public telecommunications market. In Africa, Olmer assisted Motorola to succeed in markets long dominated by French telephone equipment manufacturers.''

Before going to work for FIAB, Olmer served as an officer in the U.S. Navy in assignments which included a stint on the staff of the Chief of Naval Operations in the late 1960s. In 1973, he was graduated from the National War College, a political/military academy run by the defense department.

Olmer also holds a bachelor's degree from the University of Connecticut (1956) and a law degree from the American University in Washington, D.C. (1963). He is a member of the Connecticut and District of Columbia bars. Born on November 11, 1934 in New Haven, Connecticut, Olmer is married with two children.

MAJOR ISSUES

- Olmer's top priority has been the weakening of the Foreign Corrupt Practices Act, passed in the wake of the corporate bribery scandals of the mid-1970s. Olmer's former employer, Motorola, was one of the companies that admitted making illegal payments.

- With a national security background, Olmer has backed the hardline policies of his subordinate, Lawrence Brady, on restricting trade to the Soviets, more enthusiastically than his boss, Malcolm Baldrige, who has been receptive to business entreaties to expand trade.

- At the same time, Olmer has been a strong proponent of increased trade with mainland China.

The Reagan Administration's trade agenda is geared to removing government restrictions businessmen decry as ''disincentives'' to increasing American exports. Already income taxes for Americans employed overseas who earn $75,000 or less have been eliminated, and in April, 1981 the Senate voted 93-0 to relax banking and antitrust laws to allow banks and exporters to band together to set up trading companies. Reagan eliminated a Carter policy that restricted the export of hazardous products. The Administration's other major trade initiative is weakening the Foreign Corrupt Practices Act (FCPA). (Also see profile of Edward Schmults.)

FCPA was enacted in 1977 in the wake of disclosures by 450 American companies that they had made questionable payments totalling $300 million to foreign officials. One of those companies was Motorola, Inc. Six months before Olmer went to work for Motorola, Inc., the company advised the Securities and Exchange Commission (SEC) that it had failed to report about $400,000 in questionable payments overseas between January 1, 1972 and March 15, 1977, including payments ''on behalf of independent sales representatives to foreign government officials'' and direct payments to foreign government officials ''who were in a position to influence foreign government decisions to make purchases,'' and ''small gifts'' that were made to foreign nationals on holidays or ''to obtain services to which the company in most cases was clearly entitled.''

''The international business community has long been troubled by the Foreign Corrupt Practices Act,'' Olmer told participants in the 36th Annual World Trade Conference just three months after leaving Motorola to become an undersecretary of Commerce. ''The problem is that there is a lack of precision and clarity in the law'' that scares off prospective exporters, Olmer told them. ''We are particularly concerned about the provision which makes it a crime to pay a commission to your agent in a foreign country if you had 'reason to know' that any part of the commission would be passed on as a bribe.''

When asked to testify before the Senate Committee on Governmental Affairs several weeks later on a proposal to create a Department of International Trade and Investment, Olmer took the opportunity to again suggest modifying the anti-bribery act as ''one way to improve our international competitiveness. . .''

Sen. William Proxmire (D-Wis.), the author of FCPA, says members of the Reagan Administration are making ''a determined effort to gut the FCPA.'' Before the FCPA was enacted in 1977, Proxmire says much competition abroad ''was conducted on the basis of bribery, not price and quality of product.'' Because of American corporate bribery abroad, Proxmire maintains, ''our image as a democracy was tarnished, we suffered severe foreign policy setbacks in Japan and in Europe, [and] third world emerging democracies were corrupted. . .''

Olmer and other Administration officials support a bill introduced by Sen. John Chafee (R-R.I.) and Rep. Matthew Rinaldo (R-N.J.) that would amend the anti-bribery statute to allow payments ''customary in the country where made'' intended to ''secure prompt performance'' of official duties. (See also profiles of Edward Schmults and John Shad.)

Olmer's extensive foreign intelligence background apparently will come directly into play in implementing the Reagan Administration's get-tough policy on U.S.-Soviet trade, a policy run by his subordinate, Lawrence Brady. The policy imposes strict limits on sales of goods with potential military applications. It also restricts exports of critical technology for chemical processes, metallurgy and energy development. Olmer has been more supportive of tight controls on exports to the Soviet bloc than Commerce Secretary Malcolm Baldrige, perhaps because of Olmer's past association with U.S. intelligence agencies.

At the same time, though, Olmer has pushed to remove remaining regulations ''which run counter to our strategic interests. . .in developing the full potential of our economic and trade relations with China.'' In a July, 1981 statement to the House Subcommittee on Asian and Pacific Affairs, Olmer argued that the regulations ''discriminate against China on the basis of its earlier association with the Soviet Union.''

Olmer has been equally aggressive in promoting U.S. exports to American industries' arch trade rivals, the Japanese. At a June, 1981 meeting of the Japan-United States Businessmen's Conference, Olmer warned participants the $10 billion U.S. trade deficit with Japan could swell to $48 billion by 1990 unless the Japanese lower barriers to imports. ''Our goal must be to eliminate substantially our deficit with Japan. . .not by restricting imports from Japan, but by obtaining a Japanese market as open to all nations as ours is and by becoming more competitive ourselves,'' Olmer told them.

During the Administration's internal debate on Japanese auto imports, though, the Commerce Department backed the restrictions that were eventually imposed over the objections of a ''free-trade'' faction within the Cabinet that included the Office of Management and Budget and the Council of Economic Advisers.

FINANCIAL BACKGROUND

Olmer, his wife and children, have assets exceeding $22,000 in mutual and investment trust funds, as well as interests in family-owned restaurant and real estate ventures valued at more than $115,000. His children also hold more than $5,000 worth of stock in Wilamette Industries, a wood products manufacturing company.

When he was appointed, Olmer also was a participant in several employee benefits programs through his employer, Motorola, Inc. Under the benefits program, Olmer reported he expected to receive about a $1,000 payment from a profit-sharing fund and an undetermined amount as a bonus on April 1, 1981, from Motorola for past services.

LAWRENCE BRADY
ASSISTANT SECRETARY FOR TRADE ADMINISTRATION

RESPONSIBILITY OF OFFICE

As the Commerce Department's foreign trade administrator, Brady handles the export controls mandated for strategic, foreign policy or short-supply reasons under the Export Administration Act.

Brady is also in charge of Commerce Department investigations of anti-dumping and countervailing duty complaints; he oversees the trigger price mechanism on steel imports; and he administers industrial mobilization, import, and foreign trade zone programs.

BACKGROUND

President Reagan named Brady head trade administrator little more than a year after Brady resigned under pressure from a civil service post in Commerce's Office of Export Administration (which he now supervises).

In May, 1979, while still in the government, Brady told Congress that U.S. export controls were "in a shambles." American foreign policy over the preceding 10 years aimed at reducing political tensions through increasing East-West trade and cultural exchanges had allowed the Soviet Union to acquire American equipment and technology that could be diverted to military use, Brady insisted.

In particular, Brady pointed to the export of "dual-use" equipment, including an IBM 370 computer, to the Soviet's Kama River truck plant between 1971 and 1975. Some of the civilian heavy-duty trucks manufactured there were later reported to have been used in support of the Russian invasion of Afghanistan.

Questioned by Sen. Jake Garn (R-Utah), following Brady's resignation, then Commerce Sec. Philip M. Klutznick denied that official or unofficial reprisals had been taken against Brady: "Had Mr. Brady investigated his allegations as was his responsibility [and] had he referred the Kama case and intelligence to the Compliance Division. . .he would [still] be a major participant in the export administration. . . ."

Klutznick explained that Brady's recommendation prior to the invasion of Afghanistan that the U.S. block shipments to the Kama River plant "were general in nature. His recommendations were never based on a careful investigation of the alleged facts and never incorporated a legal analysis of any kind to support his recommendation."

After resigning in January, 1980, Brady returned to his home state where he organized the New Hampshire Coalition for Peace Through Strength—an umbrella organization supported by hawkish groups like the American Security Council and the American Conservative Union. At the same time, he campaigned for Ronald Reagan and ran unsuccessfully for the Republican nomination for a U.S. Senate seat.

Brady briefed Reagan on trade issues before the New Hampshire presidential primary and found that Reagan shared his worries that the West's trade policies have benefitted the Soviet military. "I wouldn't be here [back in the Commerce Department] if that weren't the case," Brady noted. In fact, trade sources maintain that at one point Brady was considered for an even higher job at Commerce—undersecretary.

Between 1970 and 1980 Brady worked in various Commerce, State Department and White House international trade posts. Before that, he spent 12 years as a Congressional staffer, working for both Sen. Norris Cotton (R-N.H.) and Sen. Everett Dirksen (R-Ill.).

Brady attributes his own political views in part to the influence of Senators Dirksen and Cotton, as well as to Richard Allen, President Reagan's controversial, and now departed national security adviser. "I've known Dick Allen since the early 1970s, so I work fairly closely with that office," Brady told us.

Brady says another major influence on his thinking was Catholic University politics professor William Roberts, who advised him while he completed course work there for a Ph.D. (never finished) in international relations and economics.

Professor Roberts, now deceased, "was a very conservative fellow, but he was also a super geopolitician," Brady said. "He would impress upon us, over and over again, that the thing to remember was. . .that a government sharpens a country, but it doesn't necessarily alter it from the geopolitical standpoint." That lesson, Brady believes, is particularly valuable in dealing with the Soviet Union; since the days of the czars, Brady maintains, the Russians have "always wanted Western Europe but they don't want to march into Western Europe, at least not in the 1980s, what they want is its productive capacity."

Having once dipped into the electoral waters, Brady looks as though he has the bug, and is likely to try again, particularly since his stature has been enhanced by his key role in the Administration's economic response to the Polish crackdown. He is articulate, energetic, and aggressive, with solid conservative credentials. "I think that anyone who runs [for office] and likes it would have to answer in the affirmative," he responded when we asked if he might run again. "I enjoyed myself, I really enjoyed it. I'm not saying I will, what I am saying is that it's not a profession I'm dubious about at all. But it's become a very, very expensive proposition. . . ."

Born in Berlin, New Hampshire, on April 22, 1939. Brady received his undergraduate degree from Catholic University in politics and economics in 1962. He is married with three children.

MAJOR ISSUES

- Echoing President Reagan's harsh anti-Soviet rhetoric, since taking office Brady has pressed for stringent new controls on exports to Russia and Eastern Europe that American multinational corporations fear will merely shift business to their Japanese and West European competitors. These pressures were heightened after the imposition of martial law in Poland, to the consternation of Reagan's business supporters.

- At the same time, Administration pressure on the allies to restrict "foreign availability" of technology to Soviet bloc countries have been resisted.

- Brady's endorsement of expanded trade with China, including sales of military support equipment, may alienate hardline conservative backers of his tough export control policies.

The Reagan Administration's declaration of "economic warfare" on the Soviet Union has no more stalwart soldier than Larry Brady—a man intent on keeping the Russians from someday turning Western technology against the United States.

"I can't tell you the intelligence information we have, but we know what the Soviets are doing," Brady told us. "They're using the best of Western technology to help them build up their military-industrial complex.

"And my very strong view is that, at a time when you're going to spend billions to increase your own defenses, it doesn't make sense to undermine that by allowing some of the very technology you're infusing into your own military to go to your adversary," Brady added.

To beef-up enforcement of export controls Brady has proposed adding 33 new members to his staff, some of which he would assign to the "Silicon Valley" near San Francisco to ensure that advanced American computer technology doesn't end up in Russian hands. Brady also wants to work more closely with the FBI and the U.S. Customs Bureau to be certain "there is a well coordinated approach to this whole problem."

Detente is dead, so far as he and other Administration officials are concerned, Brady told us. "They [the Soviets] have not played the game, and I think the Secretary of State [Alexander Haig] agrees with that," he said.

"I think we've learned that we've not moderated [the Soviets'] behavior by exporting high technology to them. They control their dissidents more today than they did in the early '70s, for godsake, and we sure as hell have not moderated their external behavior," Brady insists. "They are undermining areas of the world that we are resource-dependent on and it's a problem."

Brady says the Administration is determined to keep "major defense priority industries" from the Russians, including: heavy vehicle manufacturing, chemicals, microelectronics, computers and metallurgy. "Our objective is not to deny the technology to the Soviet Union—they'll get it eventually—it's to maintain the lag time. . . ."

Ironically, some of this country's major corporations have suddenly found themselves dangling from a very slender political limb as the Reagan Administration reverts to Cold War polemics and tightens trade constraints. While they don't want to seem unpatriotic, lobbyists for many high-technology manufacturers don't want to lose sales either. They argue that export controls may simply divert business to foreign competitors unless the Japanese and West European reverse their cool stance towards President Reagan's call to economically isolate the Warsaw Pact countries. Dozens of American corporations worked to develop trade ties with Soviet bloc countries during the 1970s at the urging of U.S. government officials, including Presidents Nixon, Ford and Carter. Now, many feel they've been left in the lurch.

The multinationals' fears are largely focused on a list being compiled by Brady and Defense Department experts of "critical technologies" to control. "We are concerned that the definition of 'strategic critical technologies' may be too broad,'' said Robert L. McNeill, vice chairman of the Emergency Committee for American Trade, a lobby group financed by 63 large multinationals. McNeill points out that the Export Administration Act (EAA) requires that "foreign availability" be considered by the executive branch in deciding which specific products should not be exported. "We're scared to death 'foreign availability' may not be considered and they may decide to just restrict everything," McNeill told us.

Sperry UNIVAC, the nation's 14th largest defense contractor, finally pulled out of the Soviet market, according to Edward Goldman, the firm's former director of legislative issues, trade and planning, because "it accounted for only half a percent of our business, but 10 to 15 percent of our headaches." Goldman said that he is pessimistic about the future of East-West trade because "the politics are dominant. I think we're going to create a hell of a market for our competitors," he added.

Although American multinationals pin their hopes on "foreign availability," Brady and other committed economic warriors in the Administration have already moved to counter that argument by pressuring Japan and Western Europe to cut back high technology sales to the Soviet bloc as well. Reagan may have fatally undercut the credibility of that approach, however, by lifting the embargo on American grain shipments to Russia and then quickly moving to sign a new Soviet-U.S. grain deal.

Brady maintained dropping the grain embargo is not inconsistent with Reagan's hard line on Soviet trade, explaining that food has only an "indirect link" to Russian military capabilities. "I think they [the allies] understand that we've got two concerns—technology and trade dependency—and I don't think grain is technology trade. . .[or that] there is a danger of creating a dependency, a vulnerability, with regard to grain," he said.

"There is a place for non-strategic trade, so long as you don't create a dependency," Brady told us. "Then you have a problem. That's an economic security problem."

For the same reasons Brady also publicly defends an Administration decision in August, 1981 allowing Caterpillar Tractor Co. to sell 100 pipe-laying machines to the Soviets that could speed construction of a planned natural gas pipeline running 3,000 miles from Siberia to West Germany. "They're not high technology products. We have to and we do draw that distinction with our allies." he explained.

But at the same time the Reagan Administration has opposed construction of the Siberian pipeline, arguing that it would make Western Europe, particularly West Germany, dependent on the Soviets for an undue percentage of its energy supplies. At the July, 1981 economic summit in Ottawa, President Reagan asked West German Chancellor Helmut Schmidt to cancel the plan. Schmidt rejected Reagan's offers to replace the pipeline with U.S. coal and nuclear power, however, and the project is moving ahead.

"Most people think it [Reagan's proposal] can't be really an alternative" to the Siberian pipeline, an official at the West German embassy told us. When asked whether the allies could be expected to back tougher overall restrictions on trade with the Soviet Union, the embassy spokesman suggested that existing constraints on sales of technology administered by the allies' Coordinating Committee (CoCom) on east-west trade policy "have worked quite well." While conceding that CoCom can't prevent people from making "some good business deals," he noted that many Europeans still believe that "reasonable coexistence" could be fostered through increased trade with the Soviets.

"Brady is known to be a very tough customer on trade with the Soviet Union," he acknowledged. The West German spokesman pointed out, though, that there are still those in the Commerce and State Departments who say, "'Don't mix business and foreign policy.'"

"You get different perceptions on how successful we'll be with the allies, there's no question about that," Brady conceded. "There are some people in this government who say, 'Nothing will happen, nothing will happen.' They're hand-wringers in my view," he said.

Despite the Reagan Administration's pressure, the pipeline proceeded steadily through the fall, with western European utilities—including German firms largely owned by U.S.-based multinational oil companies—signing the necessary agreements.

With the imposition of martial law in Poland, the U.S. government redoubled its efforts to stop the pipeline, but with mixed success. Ignoring U.S. objections, France agreed to buy 280 billion cubic feet of Siberian natural gas annually, for the next 25 years. That would increase its dependence of Soviet natural gas from about 15 percent now to as much as 40 percent by the end of the decade.

But the Administration in late December, 1981 imposed economic sanctions against the Soviet Union that blocked General Electric (GE) from providing rotor shafts and blades that would be used for compressor stations on the pipeline. And the sanctions blocked Caterpillar from delivering another 200 pipelayers, though the Administration allowed the original order to go through. Of the two moves, the former is considered far more damaging to the Soviets. (Japan quickly stepped in to fill the pipelayer order.) Even finding European firms that can provide substitute suppliers will be difficult; and the Reagan Administration is arguing to its allies that sale to the Soviets of compressors already built with the GE parts would violate U.S. export laws. The key question, Commerce officials say, is how to enforce that view if the allies disagree.

Poland also prompted the Administration to ban the future sale of high-technology and oil and gas transmission and refining equipment. (In total these actions affected about $300 million of the annual $3.7 billion U.S. sales to the Soviets.) In January, 1982, the U.S. pressed its allies to impose similar restrictions. But a few days after the CoCom meeting in Paris at which the issue was raised, the French government announced its agreement for natural gas imports from the Soviets.

With the heavy media attention devoted to the sanctions, Brady suddenly became a high-profile official. Accordingly, he went on an early 1982 rhetorical offensive, charging that Moscow had created a "veritable Soviet lobby" among Western business and government leaders to promote trade that increased its military might. And he renewed his attacks on the pipeline. "We must never forget," he told one audience, "the words of Vladimir Lenin, who prophesized that the capitalists would gladly sell the rope with which they would be hung. The Siberian pipeline represents such a rope."

One of Brady's chief supporters in Congress, Sen. Jake Garn (R-Utah), has proposed a bill to consolidate U.S. export controls now shared by the Commerce, State, and Defense Departments. The proposed Office of Strategic Trade (OST) would centralize decisions as to what constitutes non-exportable "critical technologies" under a single administrator, who could well be Brady. Brady had, in 1980, testified in favor of the OST.

Sen. Garn's assistant, Joe Maher, told us "the senator has had some concerns" about trade moves made by the Reagan Administration, such as the Caterpillar decision. Garn was not concerned about Brady's role in the decision, however.

"Obviously, Brady would not have approved it [the Caterpillar export license]," said Maher. In fact, Brady was responsible for "end-use restrictions" added to the license aimed at preventing the Soviets from using the new equipment in building the proposed Siberian gas pipeline, Maher maintained. According to Senate Foreign Relations Committee Chairman Charles Percy, a Republican from Illinois—Caterpillar's home state—Reagan personally approved the license after discussing the application with Percy.

Brady himself concedes the Soviets may ignore the restrictions placed on their use of the pipe-laying machinery. But, he insists the Administration will take into account any violations in deciding on future Soviet sales.

Perhaps even more perplexing to conservative ideologues than Reagan's Caterpillar decision is the Administration's determination to expand trade—including the sale of military hardware—with the People's Republic of China (PRC). The PRC, until a few years ago "Red China," has replaced the Soviet Union as America's "largest nonmarket economy trading partner," according to an April, 1981 report by the U.S. Trade Representative's Office.

The report notes that after the PRC was granted most-favored nation tariff status and commercial trade credits in January, 1980, total trade doubled to about $4.9 billion. Since then, both the Commerce and State Departments have relaxed "licensing policies on exports of U.S. high technology. . .including. . .non-weapons, military support equipment" to the PRC.

Despite Reagan's continuing overtures towards the Nationalist Chinese on Taiwan, the Administration has asked Congress to remove the few roadblocks that remain to expanding trade with the PRC. During a February, 1982 trip to China, Brady announced the U.S. was willing to increase the level of U.S. technology—including items with potential military use—the Chinese could purchase. "[W]e're willing to license in a manner that is different from the past," he said. When explaining the apparent inconsistency of the Administration's push to foster trade with the PRC while engaging in economic warfare with the Soviets, Brady falls back on terminology generally associated with detente.

"I think we've made a decision that geopolitically, strategically, our interests coincide with China and that's something that's going to develop over the years," Brady told us. "My conservative colleagues get very upset with me when I say this, but we've got to look at countries not necessarily only from a Marxist-Leninist standpoint. . .Yeah, it can come back and haunt you, but the world changes, you know."

Foreign policy shifts can sometimes make such rationales seem weak in retrospect, as Brady should well know from his own criticism of the Commerce Department's approval of U.S. technology exports to the Soviets during the thaw of the early 1970s. As the director of the General Accounting Office's international division recently told Congress: "The. . .rapid increase in exports of products with dual-use potential to [the PRC] could be subject to strong criticism and concern sometime in the future if relations with the PRC were to deteriorate."

FINANCIAL BACKGROUND

During his year's absence from the Commerce Department Brady reported little income except for consultant's fees paid him by the American Security Council, about $1,050, and $8,000 paid him by a manufacturing firm called Geophysical Survey Systems. Other than his residence and three savings accounts, each valued between $1,000 and $5,000, he reported no financial assets when appointed.

WHAT OTHERS ARE SAYING ABOUT HIM

- "Mr. Brady never personally conducted an investigation of the allegations he made respecting so-called military diversion of U.S. technology," said former Commerce Secretary Philip Klutznick.

- "I look at that situation [Brady's denunciation of exports to the Soviets' Kama River truck plant] as one where Brady did what he did for political reasons," said Edward Goldman, former director of legislative issues, trade and planning for Sperry UNIVAC.

OFFICE OF MANAGEMENT AND BUDGET

DAVID STOCKMAN
DIRECTOR

RESPONSIBILITY OF OFFICE

Armed with a staff of 604 and a budget of $34.4 million, Stockman has set out to fulfill his duties "reviewing the organizational structure and management procedures of the executive branch," assisting in "developing efficient coordinating mechanisms to implement Government activities and to expand interagency cooperation," keeping the President informed of the "progress of activities by agencies," and of course, the responsibility which has riveted Stockman in his early tenure, the duty to "supervise and control the administration of the budget." In recent months, OMB's influence over regulatory decisions has also expanded dramatically, with the passage of the Paperwork Reduction Act which gives it authority to review agency paperwork requirements on industry, and the promulgation of Executive Order 12291 in February, 1981 which gives it review power over agency regulations. Originally established as the Bureau of the Budget in 1921, the "M" in OMB was added in 1970.

BACKGROUND

Stockman entered OMB after a decade on Capitol Hill, having spent the previous four years as a representative from Michigan. During his time as a representative, he had been a strident critic of federal spending and federal regulatory programs—the areas in which he now exerts the most influence.

Raised in St. Joseph, Michigan, a rural town in the southwest corner of the state, Stockman is the eldest of five children and the son of fruit farmers. Growing up in an historically conservative area, Stockman recalls thinking Goldwater was the "greatest thing since sliced bread." Intending to study agriculture, Stockman set out for Michigan State University in 1964. His move to Michigan State was the start of Stockman's ideological travels.

Switching his major from agriculture to U.S. History, Stockman also switched from Goldwater conservatism to radicalism under the tutelage of his first professor, an "atheist and socialist from Brooklyn." Active in the anti-war movement at Michigan State, Stockman's activities earned him his own "Red Squad" file compiled by the state's anti-communist police unit. Receiving a cum laude degree in 1968, Stockman enrolled in the Harvard Divinity School, where he spent two years without receiving a degree.

Although enrolled in the study of theology, Stockman expended most of his energy studying politics. At Harvard, he took courses from such disaffected liberals as Nathan Glazer and James Q. Wilson. In a 1979 interview Stockman said, "It was one of Wilson's courses in organizational theory that totally changed my outlook. I decided that political parties, business enterprises and fraternal organizations—the building blocks of a society—are motivated by the preservation instinct, by the need to survive and thrive." From this revelation, Stockman derived his belief that "self-interest is an inherent part of the human condition and what we need to do is harness it not abolish it."

Of equal importance for Stockman's future was his job as a live-in babysitter for Daniel Patrick Moynihan. With Moynihan's aid, Stockman went to Washington to work for the House Republican Conference in 1970, then chaired by John Anderson. Two years after joining the staff, Stockman was named executive director of the conference.

In 1975, while still running the conference, Stockman published a widely circulated article entitled "The Social Pork Barrel" in the neoconservative journal *The Public Interest*. In the piece, Stockman attacked the "dominant liberal forces in Congress" and declared "what may have been the bright promise of the Great Society has been transformed into a flabby hodge-podge" that "increasingly looks like a great social pork barrel."

His article shocked at least one person, Stockman's employer, John Anderson, who recently described the 1975 piece as "savaging practically every effort government had made to improve the lot of people." Upon hearing of Stockman's admissions in William Greider's famous *Atlantic Monthly* article on Stockman, Anderson commented, "I was struck with a sense of deja vu. . .Dave did something very similar to me." Anderson insists that Stockman had never previously confided his doubts about social welfare policy and had appeared to support the programs he attacked in the article.

In a 1979 interview, Stockman related that after a time as conference director he "came to the conclusion that I ought to run for Congress as soon as I had the opportunity." With this in mind, "I started to plot how to get myself in a position to do that." Edward Hutchison, Michigan's Fourth District representative since 1962 was standing in the way of David Stockman's plotting.

The Watergate hearings gave Stockman his opportunity. As senior ranking Republican on the House Judiciary Committee during the hearings, Hutchison failed to distinguish himself. Indeed, one of the few, if not the only, notable contribution which Hutchison made to the proceedings was his contention at the start of the inquiry that Nixon should not be removed "for every little impeachable offense."

The hearings came as something of a revelation to the fourth district. Chester Byrns, one of the area's constituents, said of Hutchison, "Nobody realized what a nonentity he was until the Watergate investigation...He didn't know what to do. That came as a dreadful shock to the people around here." Stockman's evaluation of Hutchison's role is more to the point: "Simply put he missed the brass ring."

Few public figures have proven as adept at grabbing the "brass ring" as David Stockman. Having gained a minor national following with his article, Stockman saw his chance to win a seat in Congress. His success in lining up key party supporters and in convincing his mother to make a successful bid for Republican chair of a key area in the district, Berrien County, made him a candidate to be reckoned with.

Stockman was easily elected to three terms from the staunchly Republican area in 1976, 1978, and 1980, largely for a reason pithily expressed by Bunny Hoover, a party activist, who told the *Detroit News* in 1979, "When Dave first came on the scene I was skeptical. . .I said, 'Prove you're really a conservative.' He has." Money helped too: a month before the November, 1978 election, Stockman had spent $28,783 while his opponent, a Benton Harbor Democrat, had spent $622. In his 1980 campaign, Stockman's two largest contributors were the Automobile and Truck Dealers Election Action Committee ($4,000) and the Realtors Political Action Committee ($3,000).

Once in Congress, Stockman assumed a post position on the right, leading the charge against social programs and government intervention in the economy. He took on all the familiar conservative shibboleths: welfare, legal services, federal spending, and government regulation.

At a September, 1977 hearing on welfare for example, he offered a proposal to "provide no entitlements whatsoever to employable adults" meaning everyone except "the aged, blind, disabled and mothers with infants." He also took regular shots at the efforts of the Envirnmental Protection Agency (EPA), Occupational Safety and Health Administration (OSHA), National Highway Traffic Safety Administration (NHTSA)—all of which were in regular conflict with the auto companies, the industrial mainstay of his state.

In 1979, Stockman led a fight to overrule a 1977 Transportation Department order requiring passive restraints (air bags and automatic safety belts) on all cars by 1984. Stockman claimed in a March, 1979 speech, "Transportation Secretary Adams is an economic illiterate," and fumed, "We don't need cheerleaders like Mr. Brock Adams or [NHTSA Administrator] Joan Claybrook who don't know a damn thing about the auto industry. . ." He insisted the establishment of an independent Consumer Protection Agency was totally unnecessary because "we already have 'free enterprise' or the 'free market economy.' People will simply not buy products if they are bad or uneconomical."

Despite his cries of outrage over federal spending, Stockman engaged in his own share of "pork barreling." In December, 1980, one of his aides worked to obtain a multi-million dollar federal grant for Agriculture Power, Inc., a corporation seeking to build a fuel alcohol distillery in Stockman's district. On another occasion Stockman urged the Economic Development Admin. (EDA) to approve a $266,000 grant for an industrial plant in his district—though he later voted to eliminate the EDA in 1979. A Stockman aide was quoted as saying, "He [Stockman] tried to do his share to get a piece of the pie for his district once the program was in place."

According to Stockman, quoted in the *Atlantic*, "I went around and cut all the ribbons and they [his fourth district] never knew I voted against the damn programs.''

Stockman garnered a 94 percent voting rating from the U.S. Chamber of Commerce in 1980 and an 84 percent rating in the same year from the Americans for Conservative Action. Public Citizen gave Stockman 30 percent in 1978, 13 percent in 1979 and 33 percent in 1980.

Although Stockman originally supported John Connally in the 1980 presidential race he quickly switched his allegiance to Reagan when Connally's campaign crashed. Stockman was first brought to Reagan's attention when he impersonated first Anderson and then Carter in mock debates staged to gear up Reagan for the actual contests.

Shortly after the election, Stockman was again brought before the President's eye when he and Rep. Jack Kemp (R-N.Y.) collaborated on their famous memo warning of a "GOP Economic Dunkirk" unless swift action was taken to "dominate, shape and control the Washington agenda."

Originally considered a likely Energy secretary, as he had written the bulk of the GOP energy plank, Stockman won the OMB post largely through the concerted lobbying efforts of Jack Kemp and his supply-side allies.

Born on November 10, 1946 in Cape Hood, Texas, Stockman is the eldest of five children and remains unmarried.

MAJOR ISSUES

- Stockman's early offensive on the budget—forcing unprecedented cuts onto social programs, while slashing taxes for the wealthy and business—made him the most visible member of the Administration in early 1981.

- But Stockman's claims that the budget treated the wealthy and business as harshly as it did the poor wilted under closer examination. And Stockman's efforts to cut military spending and raise taxes to ameliorate an expanding deficit were rejected by the President in late 1981, indicating that his influence was waning even before his deepest feelings appeared in *The Atlantic Monthly*.

- The *Atlantic* article was a miscalculation of catastrophic proportions. Gambling that the President would support his position—which increasingly estranged him from supply-siders—Stockman sought to cement his position through the interviews. When Reagan refused to go along, Stockman was left out on a limb.

Stockman exhibited such zeal and grabbed so many headlines in the first few months of the Reagan Administration that budget cutting often appeared to be not merely the major but the *only* issue in Washington. Stockman got off to a remarkably quick start on the budget during the transition, ferreting into the details of departmental programs before most Cabinet officials had figured out the quickest way to commute to the office. He had the advantage of a clear head start, having drawn up a "counter budget" in 1980 with Rep. Phil Gramm (D-Tex.), who became a key ally in the final stages of the 1981 budget battle in June. Stockman's quick action left most Cabinet appointees with little time to repudiate massive cuts in their programs; most of the assistant secretaries, who do much of the budget battling, weren't even appointed when the cuts were made.

Stockman revealed his justification for drastic budget cuts in a controversial statement made in a March, 1981 interview:

> I don't believe that there is any entitlement, any basic right to legal services or any other kind of services, and that the idea that's been established over the last ten years that almost every service that someone might need in life ought to be provided, financed by the government as a matter of basic right, is wrong. We challenge that. We reject that notion.

Stockman has been willing to go to great lengths in order to keep his vision of the budget moving forward—his handling of the budget reconciliation bill is a case in point. House Democrats reported budget cuts out of their committees in excess of the amounts asked by the Reagan Administration. But Stockman was quick to denounce these cuts as "phony." Instead, he conceptualized the idea of offering a substitute package of budget cuts on the House floor, bypassing the committee process entirely. The cuts were passed on June 26, 1981. Rep. Leon E. Panetta (D-Calif.) was one of many infuriated by this near usurpation of legislative power by the executive and fumed, "We are dealing with more than 250 programs with no hearings, no deliberation, no debate."

A few months after the cuts had been passed Panetta told us that while Stockman was on Capitol Hill as a congressman he had often exhibited a "basic antagonism towards the process." Stockman "wound up being a loner. . .saying to hell with the rest of you." In his current position as head of OMB, mused Panetta, "it's almost as if he is coming back to defy the process—coming back to get us good."

The *Washington Star* described the substitute as "1,000 pages of scrawled, unindexed legislation" resulting from a "chaotic 24-hour rush." Some House members did not receive copies of the bill at all; others were presented with it two hours before floor action was convened and everyone was faced with "unnumbered pages and long-hand insertions of last minute changes."

Indeed, the legislation was so hastily put together it was later discovered that a woman's name and telephone number "Ruth Seymour, 225-4844" had accidently been written into the bill.

The substitute bill allows House members to avoid going on record as voting against specific social programs and Stockman claimed it would prevent pork-barreling. But the Administration was not adverse to offering sweeteners of its own in the form of support for expensive sugar subsidies to wavering members of the House.

When questioned about these heavy lobbying efforts Stockman insisted there were no "deals made" but some simple "adjustments and considerations."

There is little dispute that Stockman spearheaded the reconciliation effort. Indeed, he conferred so frequently with House Republicans on his proposal that James B. Hedlund, minority staff director of the Budget Committee quipped, "We know every tie in his wardrobe."

When pushing the budget, Stockman said it hurt big business as much as the poor, but critics quickly pointed to the myriad of subsidies left untouched. A particularly ironic item present in the budget were funds for the Clinch River Breeder Reactor. As a congressman, Stockman insisted the reactor was a tremendous waste of taxpayer's money: "Today it is the nuclear power lobby looking for a large uneconomic subsidy. Tomorrow, it will be the solar power gang, then the windmill freaks, and so on in a never ending stream of outstretched palms." When asked how the programs had escaped his ax, Stockman modestly replied, "I would suggest to you here that I am not running this government single handedly." Most tax loopholes were also left untouched, amounting to tens of billions of dollars for such favored institutions as the oil and nuclear industries.

The speed with which the budget was revised stunned, and troubled, much of Congress. When Stockman was asked whether a 5 percent cut in aid would be difficult for a family at poverty level, he replied, "I don't know." And in a particularly fiery exchange with Stockman concerning the decision (later revoked) to eliminate the Federal Trade Commission's antitrust authority, Rep. Benjamin Rosenthal (D-N.Y.), quoted a *Legal Times* article that stated, "The decision was made on the basis of a 2-page memo after less than a minute's deliberation by the OMB director, David Stockman." In reply Stockman insisted this was untrue and in fact claimed he had been "deliberating on it for about ten years" and further maintained that this consideration of the subject had begun "at a very early age." Childhood ruminations on antitrust aside, Stockman later admitted, "We were doing that whole budget cutting exercise so frenetically. . .trying to cut housing programs here and rural electric there, and we were doing it so fast we didn't know where we were ending up for sure. . ."

Stockman has acquired a reputation for using strong-arm tactics to press his points. These tactics have emerged most notably in his confrontations with Energy Secretary James Edwards—a former dentist and South Carolina governor who knew little about energy issues or the ways of Washington during the early months of his tenure. Stockman has clashed with Edwards on at least two occasions, the first when Stockman pushed for immediate decontrol of oil prices despite Edwards's strong objections and again in the heat of the summer over the signing of major synfuels contracts. Remarked Secretary Edwards of the synfuels incident, "I'd like to believe that Dave Stockman was trying to help me. . .I'd like to believe that he was."

The OMB director has not been uniformly successful. Early on, he and Secretary of State Alexander Haig became embroiled in a dispute over cutting foreign aid, which sent Stockman scurrying to make amends with the State Department. Stockman's proposal in May, 1981 to slash Social Security benefits for the elderly created such a public outcry that by September Reagan found it wise to publicly disown Stockman's proposal, although he had originally favored the idea. Edwards faced him down over the synfuels contracts.

For Stockman, September, 1981 was a grueling month. Soon after his Social Security proposals were sent rattling into the trash, the budget director became embroiled in another losing battle over defense expenditures. Believing that the Defense Department harbored $10 to $30 billion in "blatant inefficiency, poor deployment of manpower, [and] contracting idiocy," Stockman set about his task, confident that Defense Secretary Caspar Weinberger could be persuaded to support him. But Weinberger, an OMB director under Nixon, vigorously defended his department from virtually any cuts. Without the backing of Weinberger, Stockman had to settle for a $13 billion cut over three years from a massive defense budget which would total over a trillion dollars in the next five years. (See profile of Caspar Weinberger.) Yet despite Stockman's two great falls in September, nothing can rival mid-November which marked the breaking of the now legendary *Atlantic* story by *Washington Post* editor William Greider.

If one were to take President Reagan or Stockman's press secretary, Edwin Dale, at their word, one would believe Stockman had been tricked into giving the *Atlantic* interviews by an irresponsible journalist. Following his "visit to the woodshed" with Reagan, Stockman told reporters that, "I understood it to be off the record" and spoke of the incident as a "gross misunderstanding." Such after-the-fact explanations strain credibility. Having spent ten years in Washington, the last four as a congressman, Stockman is certainly wise to the ways of the nation's capital and it is hard to imagine such a "gross misunderstanding" between two people who met regularly for almost eight months.

More likely, in consenting to the *Atlantic* interview with Greider, Stockman saw an opportunity to assure his name would be "writ large" in the history of Reagan's Administration. It was a chance that was almost too good to be true—not only would Stockman be part of history, he would be able to mold that history by giving his own interpretation of events.

Conducting the interview with a *Post* editor had still additional rewards. Stockman's relationship with Greider allowed the OMB director to use the newspaper as a mighty mouthpiece against his adversaries in the Administration. As the "anonymous source from OMB" Stockman used the press to mobilize support for his positions which placed him increasingly at odds with Treasury's ardent supply-siders.

Although Stockman had relied on the supply-siders to win him his OMB position, he quickly turned his back on their agenda and allied himself with more traditional economists such as Alan Greenspan and Herbert Stein. While generally supporting the supply-siders publicly, Stockman often undercut their aims in his private conversations with Greider. Those doubts seeped into the *Post's* influential news columns. For Stockman, the balancing act was to placate his former colleague and erstwhile rival, Rep. Jack Kemp (R-N.Y.). "As long as Jack is happy with what's happening it's hard for the [supplyside] network to mobilize itself with a shrill voice. Jack's satisfied, although we're sort of on the edge of thin ice with him," he told Greider.

Early on, the supply-siders had become disturbed by Stockman's mania for slashing budgets. Supply-siders like Kemp, economist Arthur Laffer and writer Jude Wanniski were primarily worried that Stockman was drawing too much attention away from their tax cut. In addition, they were opposed to the kinds of deep budget cuts Stockman was proposing. Wanniski recalls his first serious misgivings about the OMB director shortly after his appointment when Wanniski spied Stockman and Alan Greenspan sitting in a corner of the Harvard Club in New York City contemplating drastic budget cuts. According to Wanniski:

> A hundred million here, a hundred million there, in cuts that's how they were talking. So I walked over and picked up some peanuts from a bowl and began to drop them in, one by one. 'Peanuts,' I said. 'Here's $100 million worth of widows, here's $100 million worth of orphans you'll drive into the snow.

While assuring supply-siders that he was a rank and file believer, Stockman had his own doubts. "I've never believed that just cutting taxes alone will cause output and employment to expand," he told William Greider. Harboring a traditional Republican fear of the huge deficits a steep tax cut could produce, Stockman had initially counted on House Democrats to reduce the size of the tax cuts. When the House gave him more than he had bargained for—$750 billion over the next five years—Stockman launched a determined drive to increase taxes.

Part of that drive—which ultimately failed despite support of virtually all other key advisers—was to focus political attention on the deficit by directing the *Post*, through Greider, to that subject. In all likelihood, Stockman had assumed that by the time the *Atlantic* article was printed, the Administration would have decided to push for higher taxes to cover the deficit. If that were the case, his admissions would not have seemed so extraordinary—indeed he might be all the more acclaimed for his advanced thinking.

But Stockman had miscalculated. Although a good many officials had resigned themselves to raising taxes by the time the *Atlantic* article appeared on the scene, Stockman had failed to convince the only official who really mattered—President Reagan. Faced with the possible loss of his job, Stockman struggled to stay on: "I would not be here now, nor would I have worked 16 hours a day for nearly a year if I did not believe in the President and his policies."

Although Reagan kept Stockman, the budget director's true beliefs were not as much an issue as that Reagan simply had no ready replacement for him.

FINANCIAL BACKGROUND

Stockman is vice president of the Birchlawn Corporation, a family-owned business. He lists property holdings in the corporation as between $15,000 and $50,000. In 1980, Stockman received speaking fees from such groups as Eli Lilly ($1,000), General Motors ($1,000), the American Hospital Association ($1,000) and the American Medical Association ($1,000).

As a congressman, Stockman raised a few eyebrows when he accepted a $2,000 campaign contribution from the American Medical Association (AMA) in April of 1978 and then came out vehemently against the Hospital Cost Containment Act in June, an act which was also strenuously opposed by the AMA. Stockman denies any link between the two incidents.

WHAT OTHERS ARE SAYING ABOUT HIM

- "I'm very worried, frankly, about what I'm hearing. Compassion. That's what I'm looking for from David," said Rev. Truman Morrison who counseled Stockman in the late 1960s.

- Rep. Jack Brooks (D-Tex.) commented in a House operations hearing at which the OMB director appeared, "My guess, Mr. Stockman, is that the heart of the problem is the fact that you use economic projections that represent your political and your economic hopes as fiscal and management tools. . ."

- "I'll tell you one thing about Dave Stockman. I've never thrown a question at him that he didn't have an answer to. Only trouble is, I'm never sure if he's telling the truth," said Ort Middough, a former constituent in the fourth district.

- John Anderson's wife, Keke, attempted to explain the initial wedge which led to strained relations between her husband and his former legislative aide: "John began to sense that there was just too much drive and not enough human aspects there."

- Rep. Jack Kemp (R-N.Y.), former football pro and more recently a close associate of David Stockman's, commented half jokingly, "I'm tired of Dave Stockman pushing me off the front pages. The next thing, I'll be seeing him on the cover of a sports magazine with his arm cocked back ready to throw a pass."

- Sen. Howard Metzenbaum (D-Ohio) blasted Stockman at a recent budget hearing: "I think you have been brilliant, but I also think you have been cruel. . .I think you have been inhumane; I think you have been unfair, and I think you are causing a perversion of justice for the poor and middle-class Americans."

- Stockman's modus operandi has incurred the wrath of more than one Reagan official. Walter W. Wriston, chairman of Citicorp observed that Treasury Secretary Regan was among those disenchanted with the Administration's "wunderkind": "One of these days Don Regan is going to eat Dave Stockman for breakfast."

- It looked as if Energy Secretary James Edwards might join Regan for lunch after Stockman outraged Edwards and his staff by pushing too hard, too loudly, for an immediate decontrol of oil prices. "That little gray-haired ideologue punched our clock good," steamed one Edwards aide. "He made points with the political types in the White House and left us to clean up the mess under the hot lights."

- When asked by the Joint Economic Committee whether Stockman had done anything about his suggestions to cut waste in the Defense Department, Admiral Hyman Rickover replied, "No. I never heard from him. This is what I call the 'Say-Do.' When you take the job, you make a lot of fine speeches and everybody applauds what you're going to do and that's the end of it. You say it and then I call it 'Say Do.' You don't have to do anything after that."

CHRISTOPHER DEMUTH

ADMINISTRATOR, OFFICE OF INFORMATION AND REGULATORY AFFAIRS
EXECUTIVE DIRECTOR, PRESIDENTIAL TASK FORCE ON REGULATORY RELIEF

RESPONSIBILITY OF OFFICE

With these two positions, DeMuth is one of the most powerful domestic officials in the Administration, though certainly among the least well-known. When we asked him, he readily agreed he was one of the Administration's top 100 officials.

Created in the 1980 Paperwork Reduction Act, the office's powers were increased tremendously—and many attorneys believe illegally—by Reagan's February 17, 1981 Executive Order (12291) on regulation. That order gave OMB unprecedented authority to review agency regulatory proposals before they are published in the *Federal Register*, and directed it to establish standards for conducting cost-benefit analysis, which the order mandated for "major" regulations.

Existing regulations are to be dealt with through the task force. Composed of the secretaries of Treasury, Commerce, and Labor, the attorney general, the OMB director, the chairman of the Council of Economic Advisers, the President's Domestic Policy Adviser and chaired by Vice-President Bush, the Task Force is run by the staff and directed to "assess executive branch regulations already on the books, especially those that are burdensome to the national economy or to key industrial sectors."

BACKGROUND

Running the most centralized regulatory review process ever established by the White House is a man who just two years ago wrote that it is an "unpromising idea that regulatory decisions will be improved by centralizing decision-making within the government."

In that same article, DeMuth—who now must ensure that regulatory agencies not issue regulations "unless the potential benefits to society. . .outweigh the potential costs"—concluded that "no single organization. . .could ever apply a strict cost/benefit test to the decisions of another organization (a regulatory agency)."

Asked about that conclusion in an interview, DeMuth joked, "I take back everything I ever said."

Like his predecessor, James C. Miller III, now chair of the Federal Trade Commission (FTC), DeMuth is a long-time critic of federal regulatory agencies. But he is far more critical than Miller of the tools designed by conservative economists and other regulatory reformers to rein in those agencies. If, in his own words, "policies that seek to harness regulatory decisions to the conclusions of economic analyses. . .put their faith in the possibility of making regulation more rational and scientific," DeMuth, in his previous work at least, has been an agnostic.

Consider his writings on cost/benefit analysis, the high totem of regulatory critics like Miller, Murray Weidenbaum, chairman of the Council of Economic Advisers, the Business Roundtable and the U.S. Chamber of Commerce. In a speech early in 1981, DeMuth worried that "if. . .cost-benefit analysis is simply used as another weapon in the battle of competing private interests [it could]. . .delay the regulatory process even further and introduce additional uncertainty." In a 1980 series of articles for *Regulation* magazine, which Weidenbaum then edited, DeMuth laid out the basis of his doubts:

> The heart of the problem is that cost/benefit analysis is an internal decision procedure for a single organization—an exercise in which the organization attempts to set out with exactitude its purposes and what it must give up to achieve them. But the political process is not a single organization and it has no "purpose." It consists of a multitude of organizations with conflicting purposes—purposes that are persistently obscured because of the need to maintain political support while achieving practical compromise. . . The most that can be done is to require some unspecified "reasonable relationship" between benefits and costs.

DeMuth there acknowledged one of the inherently crippling drawbacks to the use of cost-benefit analysis, one generally ignored by its proponents: that the costs and benefits of regulatory actions are generally borne by different groups. (What an employer considers a "reasonable" effort to control exposure to a cancer-causing chemical, in other words, may be considered less so by the worker actually exposed to it.) And DeMuth acknowledged that decisions which spring from the political process are bound to be influenced by the degree to which conflicting groups can make their voices heard in the decision-making. "Nobody pretends that this is an exact science," DeMuth told us. "It's not perfect. It's not a matter of a computer telling us what the results are going to be." Despite these reservations, and the conclusions of his academic work, DeMuth is finding the religion, energetically administering the executive order—with its requirements for formal cost-benefit analysis and centralized review.

DeMuth has developed these ideas since 1977 as a lecturer at the Harvard School of Government and director of the Harvard Faculty Project on Regulation. "He's very much in the mold of old-fashioned Harvard," said one friend. "Along the lines of 'let's sit down over a cup of sherry and discuss this.' He has kind of an aristocratic air."

Though he has Washington experience, DeMuth is less of a political operator than his predecessor, who revels in the earthiness of political jousting. "He's less rough and tumble than Miller, much less of a hardball player than Miller," continued the friend. With a self-contained demeanor, and a proclivity for bow ties, "the 'George Will' image is sort of on the mark," said the friend.

In his office, DeMuth still possesses a scholarly carriage. When we asked what he considered the major differences between the Carter and Reagan regulatory review policies, he launched into a disquisition tracing the history of regulatory criticism back to the 1950s.

Like his boss David Stockman, DeMuth parlayed a connection with Daniel Patrick Moynihan into a Washington job fresh out of Harvard. After graduating in 1968, DeMuth landed on the Nixon domestic policy staff, handling first urban issues and then chairing a White House Task Force on the Environmental Message that Nixon delivered in February, 1970. The task force sent Nixon a 65-page report in November, 1969 that recommended, among other things, the creation of a massive new Department of Environment and Natural Resources that would have subsumed the Department of Interior, the Rural Electrification Administration, the Forest Service, the Soil Conservation Service, and all the functions that eventually became the National Oceanic and Atmospheric Administration (NOAA) and the Environmental Protection Agency (EPA). (Eventually Nixon backed creating an EPA instead, in part because he felt then-Interior Secretary Walter Hickel was incapable of running the new department.) It also suggested stiffer penalties for polluters, increased federal acquisition of park land, and federal procurement of unconventionally powered, low-pollution automobiles, recognizing that the auto companies would not develop such a car on their own.

"The Nixon Administration was the Middle Ages as far as environmental regulation was concerned," DeMuth told us. "The main difference was there was a lack of awareness of the economic magnitude of these programs." Nor was the Administration receptive to the replacement of regulation with the economic incentives that anti-regulatory economists still espouse today, DeMuth recalled. "I had been something of an internal advocate for using the price system and tax mechanisms rather than direct regulations," he said. "It really didn't get very far."

DeMuth also handled some odd jobs. In May, 1970, Nixon sent DeMuth and seven other young staff members on a tour to assess the mood on college campuses; they came back, according to contemporary reports, "stunned by the depth of student hostility toward the Administration and the rapid erosion of respect for the government."

A year later, DeMuth left the White House to enter the University of Chicago Law School. After graduating in 1973, he practiced law with the prominent Chicago firm of Sidley & Austin until 1976 and then joined Conrail as general counsel. From there, he went to Harvard in 1977 where he devoted increasing attention—in scholarly work and articles published from his vantage point as contributing editor of *The American Spectator*, a conservative magazine based in Indiana—to health and safety and environmental regulation.

Despairing of centralized regulatory review, DeMuth in the past two years has advanced several other proposals. In the 1980 series of articles for *Regulation*, he suggested instead the use of a regulatory budget—an oft-advanced proposal which would limit the costs that regulatory agencies could impose on the private sector to some sum specified by Congress and the President. And in a 1981 paper on regulation and competition, he supported the replacement of the adversarial, courtroom-modeled regulatory procedure with a "consensual alternative" that would bring together business, regulators and members of the public to informally hammer out agreements.

But DeMuth has despaired of these ideas as well. In his article on the regulatory budget he concluded that accounting procedures it requires "may simply be infeasible" to develop and then worried that the concept would legitimize and institutionalize the government's right to impose costs on outside parties, a right he did not wish to see solidified. The consensual idea, he concluded, may simply add "an additional layer to the regulatory process" which produces standards "that are harmful to consumer welfare."

So what alternative does DeMuth finally embrace? Reading his work it is difficult to tell; he burns his bridges even as he crosses them. But, the end of his 1981 paper on competition—in which he concludes there is no evidence that regulation has significantly harmed either domestic productivity or our international competitiveness—offers perhaps the clearest indication of his thinking: "In the end," he wrote, "our business community may simply learn to live with—and eventually acquire a stake in—the current regulatory style. . . . As business comes to master the techniques of policy-making under the new health, safety and environmental statutes, the 'uncertainty costs' of regulation may greatly diminish."

Having reached that conclusion—letting business influence the regulators—will surely make it easier for DeMuth to reconcile his academic work with the Reagan regulatory review process he now directs, a process that many critics argue is less interested in reforming regulation than in removing those rules major industries find most objectionable. And for all his academic agonizing over the proper way to reduce government regulation of business, he has surely not lost sight of that goal. Consider the eloquence he mustered to defend advertising aimed at children, the subject of a nowended FTC investigation. "The deeper issue," he wrote in 1979, "is the unplanned, imperfect, sweaty reality of the market itself, especially its open acquiescence in the self-interestedness of the individual; whether its range should be constricted one little bit further, here as in a thousand other proceedings in Washington, giving way to the government's higher claim to provide a more planned, disinterested, 'rational' order."

DeMuth was Stockman's first choice as EPA administrator. Last summer, surveying the chaos that Anne Gorsuch had wrought on Waterside Mall, DeMuth told friends he thought he could have handled the job better and would not have alienated the career staff. His style is far less confrontational than that of the slashing, hard-driving Gorsuch.

Born on August 5, 1946 in Kenilworth, Illinois, DeMuth is married with two children.

MAJOR ISSUES

- The OMB regulatory review process has been directly condemned as illegal by the Congressional Research Service in a scathing study.

- In its cotton dust decision, the Supreme Court suggested that the requirement that agencies perform cost-benefit analyses of their regulations may also be illegal, unless specifically called for by the statute.

- Critics have focused on the process's lack of public accountability, which encourages backdoor appeals by powerful lobbies and its avoidance of records. DeMuth has not agreed to keep a publicly available log of his outside meetings. Nor are all OMB's communications with agencies publicly available.

DeMuth sits at the center of an historic power shift from the regulatory agencies to the White House. Under the February 17, 1981 Executive Order on regulation, the OMB has become the nerve center of Reagan's efforts to roll back federal health and safety regulation. Its new authority is unquestionably vast. But it may well be illegal.

Within 24 hours in June, 1981 the plan received two severe legal jolts. These separate actions challenged both its requirements for cost-benefit analysis and the right of the President to grant OMB such an expanded regulatory role. First, on June 17, the Supreme Court let stand the Occupational Safety and Health Administration (OSHA) standard for workplace exposure to cotton dust, rejecting arguments by the textile industry that the agency had not properly balanced the cost to industry with the benefits to the public. Cost-benefit analysis is a tenet of the Reagan regulatory reform effort. The following morning, the Congressional Research Service (CRS) reported in a stinging legal study that the process centralizing authority for regulatory review within OMB may be illegal. That analysis concluded the policy faced "substantial risk" if challenged in court "on the ground that the President exceeded his authority."

In the cotton dust case, the court ruled, first, that Congress did not require formal cost-benefit analysis on OSHA health standards and, second, that Congress had already made a cost-benefit analysis itself "by placing the 'benefit' of worker health above all other considerations save those making attainment of this 'benefit' unachievable." Of equal importance for the regulatory plan, the court ruled that when Congress didn't mention cost-benefit analysis, it didn't intend to require the agencies to justify their decisions by that measure. "Congress uses specific language when intending that an agency engage in cost-benefit analysis," the court concluded.

Throughout, the Administration has been maintaining the opposite: that it could require cost-benefit analysis unless Congress had specifically prohibited it under individual laws. "I believe the Supreme Court has not made up its mind on that point," said DeMuth after the cotton dust ruling. "The question whether the agencies may do it, whether the Administration may within the play in the joints given them by regulatory standards and regulatory statutes, may exercise their discretion with an eye toward economic efficiency was not presented to the court." But many other regulatory attorneys disagree. "What Reagan in effect is trying to do," said a Washington lawyer who works on regulatory issues, "is amend the environmental law or the occupational health law to include cost-benefit analysis without going to Congress."

It is also unclear to what degree the OMB is complying with its own cost-benefit requirements. Under questioning at a congressional hearing, DeMuth's predecessor, Miller, admitted that some of the regulations revoked had benefits that exceeded their costs. Patrick McLain, counsel to the House Oversight and Investigations Subcommittee, pressed the point:

Is it not true that based upon the analysis of those regulations which you have cited, that your regulatory reform efforts in holding them up could have cost the American people money?

Miller: It is conceivable.

Congressional investigators have been unable to more firmly track OMB's use of cost-benefit analysis because the regulatory review process has been designed to minimize record-keeping. (Jim Tozzi, DeMuth's deputy, joked that he avoids memos because "I don't want to leave fingerprints." Tozzi told us he avoids documents "because I believe in paperwork reduction.") The House oversight subcommittee, which obtained supporting documents on regulations rejected by OMB after a long struggle with David Stockman, observed there is a "total lack of supporting documentation evidencing the reasons why a particular regulation was found to be inconsistent with the Executive Order. Obviously, such lack of documentation makes efforts to oversee the implementation of the Executive Order difficult."

The lack of records is a key element also in the CRS's legal concerns. From the start, critics have charged that business groups seeking to ease their way out of federal regulations could avoid meeting with agency administrators—where they might be identified in a public docket—and instead effect major changes in law just through private meetings with sympathetic OMB officials.

In its analysis, the CRS agreed, noting that the order lacked "safeguards against secret, undisclosed and unreviewable contacts by governmental and nongovernmental interests seeking to influence the substance of agency actions." Continued the CRS analysis:

The Order provides no safeguards whatsoever to protect the integrity of the policy-making process or the interest of the public from such influences. On its face, then, the order deprives interested persons, now and in the future, of their right to the most essential elements of fair treatment embodied in the notion of due process and is therefore unconstitutional.

Business groups that came into OMB for meetings through last summer under Miller's reign included the Chemical Manufacturers Association, the American Mining Congress, the National Association of Manufacturers, the U.S. Chamber of Commerce, General Motors, Ford, Atlantic Richfield, the Sun Oil Company, the Business Roundtable and International Paper.

These meetings were revealed only after persistent inquiry by the oversight subcommittee. Like Miller, DeMuth has refused to keep a log of his outside meetings, as other government officials, such as former Attorney General Griffin Bell have done. DeMuth told us that such a requirement would be "very, very burdensome" given his crowded schedule. "I have a resistance to it on policy grounds that goes beyond the inconvenience to me," he added. "It seems to me that when you're making broad policy you have to talk to all sorts of outside groups simply to get out the information you need to make the decision. And the appropriate place for public participation and scrutiny of what the government has done is in the writing of the proposed and the final rule."

In January, 1979, the Justice Department recommended that the White House reveal its contacts with private parties involving ongoing rulemaking proceedings and eschew such contacts after the close of comment periods on the rules. But, as

Charles E. Ludlam, the former chief legal adviser to the White House Task Force on Regulatory Reform, noted in a recent study, "OMB now refuses to comply with the January 17, 1979 Justice Department recommendations, applicable judicial precedent and acknowledged standards of conduct. It has, in effect, declared its right to meet at any stage of a proceeding to discuss any matter under consideration by the agency."

Questioned about the problem, DeMuth expressed exasperation with the whole issue. "I'd rather limit my role to looking at the regulations and analyses they [the agencies] do," he told us. Meeting with outside groups, "takes too much time," and so he may soon decide to completely bar meetings with outside organizations, he said.

Communications between OMB and other government agencies are also shrouded in secrecy by the procedure. While OMB has agreed to publicly file with the agencies factual information given to it by outside groups, it will not guarantee to make available "nonfactual" information—presumably such as political considerations—it transmits to agencies. Such selective disclosure practices led George Eads, a former member of the Council of Economic Advisers who has been critical of the agencies, to declare that "the Reagan process is intended to impose a virtual information blackout on intragovernmental decisions."

Particularly dangerous in that context is OMB's authority to review regulations before they are even proposed in the Federal Register. As Ludlam notes, "OMB pre-clearance of proposed rules means that agencies cannot even solicit public comments on an idea unless OMB wishes to permit such discussion. Thus, OMB can censor a proposal before the public debate begins."

And even if OMB allows the regulation to go through, it can order changes that reshape the issues considerably. "If the real decision is made before the public has had an opportunity to participate," wrote Ludlam, "then the public comment period is illusory." DeMuth contends that OMB does not have "veto power" over agency rules. "If we think that some proposal does not comply with the executive order. . .we thrash it out," he said. "We're part of the same Administration. If we just can't agree with the people from the agencies. . .they can take it up with others. It starts out on the staff level, it can come to me, it can go to Dave Stockman, it can go to the Task Force on Regulatory Relief, it can go to the President."

DeMuth hopes to resolve some of these issues by using a computer system OMB has installed to track the regulatory process. That system could include a periodic list of regulations that have come over to OMB, OMB's objections to those rules, and any regulations that were withdrawn. Both the regulation as it was sent to OMB, and the rule that emerged, could be placed in the record of the rulemaking procedure, DeMuth said.

An even more fundamental question is whether OMB has the legal authority to review agency regulations at all. To the CRS, that power is in "clear and direct opposition" to the requirements of the Administrative Procedure Act (APA), which sets standards for fair and impartial rulemaking. "The Order does no less than supplant the agency role in informal rulemaking contemplated by the APA," wrote the CRS. Particularly, it concluded, the Executive Order violated the APA by:

- prescribing "the types of procedures an agency must use in its rulemaking";
- imposing "the requirement that substantive principles of cost-benefit analysis . . . be applied by all agencies";

- superimposing "over all agency rulemaking a central coordinating authority. . .in direct and irrevocable conflict with [the act]."

Considering the severity of the legal challenges raised by the Supreme Court and the CRS, OMB has modified the process to a remarkably small degree. DeMuth has reportedly agreed to send letters to the agencies explaining why regulations were returned (which Miller did not agree to do in all cases). But he told representatives of three consumer groups that met with him in October, 1981 that he would "refuse, except under a subpoena or a Freedom of Information request, to provide notice of rules under review, designated as 'major' or rejected by OMB, with explanations as to why OMB returned them to the agencies," according to the representatives' account of the meeting. And, while OSHA has abandoned its cost-benefit efforts in light of the Supreme Court decision, OMB continues to impose that requirement on other agencies, though that same decision suggested it had no authority to do so.

Though different in style than his predecessor, DeMuth is likely to be as critical of agency regulatory initiatives. Generally, he told us, he is "skeptical" of "the ability of government to make any significant changes for the better" in areas "where there is a direct relationship between the parties"—such as the purchase of consumer goods—or where there are significant behavioral aspects to the question, such as whether people will wear seatbelts. "But in the area of environmental protection [and occupational health] where there is no direct relationship," he said, the government role should be greater. The same should be true for occupational health problems where "obviously the human behavior aspect is a smaller one," he said. Nonetheless, DeMuth opposes mandatory passive restraints (such as airbags), the engineering response that does not require behavioral changes (such as wearing seatbelts) to reduce death on the highway.

DeMuth has mixed feelings about the government's proper role in providing the information—such as the identities of the chemicals that workers must handle—that most economists would agree is necessary for proper functioning of the free market. "I'm not sure that information is so different than shoes that we should say that although the government probably does a bad job of deciding who needs what kind of shoes when, government can always do a good job of bettering the market in deciding what kind of information ought to be available," he said. "I'm not trying to inveigh against the approach; I think it's often the correct one. But I don't think it's quite that simple." DeMuth had his most serious run-in with OSHA over that agency's proposed chemical labeling standard. Already watered-down from an earlier Carter Administration proposal, the standard was held up at OMB through the winter of 1981. "We have substantial problems with it," DeMuth told us. It was issued in March of 1982, when a congressional committee threatened hearings on its delay.

As a rule of government life, DeMuth said, you have to pick your shots. And so while he probably won't get heavily involved in fighting Reagan Administration policy supporting the international aviation cartel or maritime price fixing—policies with which he is ideologically uncomfortable (as evidenced by his grimace when we asked about them)—he does expect to make "progress" in stripping away the marketing order system that inflate food prices "[Agriculture Secretary] Block is very sympathetic," he said.

Almost ironically, the job that the Office of Information and Regulatory Affairs was created to do—implementing the Paperwork Reduction Act—has been virtually submerged in the rivers of paper surging into the OMB from the regulatory agencies. Through 1981, the office had reviewed 2,715 regulatory submissions, approved 2,412 of them, required changes in 134 and sent 91 back to the agencies. But processing that much paper has taken its toll on the government's efforts to streamline the paperwork that it imposes on private groups. In October, 1981, the General Accounting Office (GAO) said that OMB had directed "little or no effort. . .to key requirements of the Act" and was misallocating its resources toward regulatory review, when Congress intended the "funds to be appropriated for carrying out the purposes of the Act but for no other purpose." And, true to form, the GAO told Congress, "The Office of Management and Budget has denied us access to documents and information essential to reaching a full understanding of its processes and an assessment of its efforts."

FINANCIAL BACKGROUND

DeMuth earned $63,950 as a lecturer at Harvard University in 1980, and another $12,210 as a consultant to Polaroid Corp. of Cambridge, Massachusetts.

Upon assuming office, DeMuth placed most of his stock holdings in a blind trust. These holdings included shares in the following companies: American Home Products, Arco, Central & Southwest Corporation, Continental Corporation, Inland Steel, IMC, Josyln Manufacturing and Supply, Kansa-Nebraska Natural Gas, Motorola, NL Industries, Northwest Industries, Nortrust, Pennzoil, Standard Oil of Indiana, United Energy, U.S. Steel, United Telecommunications, and Wisconsin Public Service Company.

DeMuth held onto his stock in the family business, the DeMuth Steel Company and its subsidiary, the DeMuth Properties Co., but resigned from the parent firm's board of directors and recused himself from any particular matter affecting it. DeMuth reports his holdings in the two companies at between $100,000 and $250,000 each.

WHAT OTHERS ARE SAYING ABOUT HIM

- Noting DeMuth's prior academic criticism of regulatory review, one highly-regarded academic studying the regulatory system told us, "What he is may not be what he was."

- One of DeMuth's associates, a prominent regulatory critic who asked not to be identified, praised his work, but questioned his ability to survive in Washington. "If there's any reason why the appointment may not be a good one," said the associate, "it is that he may not have enough political savvy."

- Those who have met with DeMuth describe him as low-key and self-assured. "He exudes a quiet confidence, of being very much in control of himself and his emotions," one friend told us. "A quiet competence kind of thing."

COUNCIL OF ECONOMIC ADVISERS

MURRAY WEIDENBAUM
CHAIRMAN

RESPONSIBILITY OF OFFICE

Created, perhaps ironically, by the Employment Act of 1946, the council has, in Weidenbaum's words, a "most modest statutory authorization." It "advises the President on economic developments" and writes the President's annual economic report.

Though Weidenbaum is part of the Administration's economic "troika," the council has been overshadowed in policy-making by its other components, the Office of Management and Budget (OMB) and Treasury. And the role that recent councils played of opposing government regulatory efforts—a role for which Chairman Weidenbaum was ideologically well-suited—has instead been institutionalized in OMB's Office of Information and Regulatory Affairs. These developments, perhaps combined with Weidenbaum's modest stature as a macroeconomist, have created a less visible, less influential council than in recent years. Weidenbaum has been a regular loser in Administration debates on economic policy.

Weidenbaum sees a further role for the council, to serve as "the custodian for the economic profession, of the role of economic analysis in government," he told us. "At a time when all sorts of experiments in supply-side economics and monetarism are being conducted, it's important to make sure that whatever departures are made in the government have a sound analytic basis of good economics."

In 1982, CEA will operate with a budget of $1.96 million and a staff of just 35.

BACKGROUND

A prolific, facile author with a wide range of interests, Weidenbaum might nevertheless have remained part of the faceless legion of conservative economists despairing of big government were it not for the 1976 study where he first produced *the number*.

That number—an estimate of the cost imposed on business by government regulation—has become embedded in Reaganite Republicanism. It is frequently cited by opponents of federal health and safety regulation—most notably the President—as proof of the excesses of regulatory bureaucrats. And it undoubtedly propelled Weidenbaum into the inner circle of Reagan economic advisers.

For all that, Weidenbaum's number is considered by many serious economists a sham. Concluded the House Oversight and Investigations Subcommittee: "That Dr. Weidenbaum's figure—which is the result of a flawed study that, by itself, is irrelevant to the debate—has played such a major role in the clamour for reduction in Federal regulations merely confirms the fact that the derivation and meaning of a figure is often lost in the public debate."

In his study, Weidenbaum gathered what he considered the best estimates of the costs to business of complying with federal regulation and compared them with the administrative budgets of the agencies promulgating the rules. From those figures, he calculated that the agencies imposed costs on the private sector 20 times greater than their budgets. To update the figure—which he now says is over $120 billion annually—Weidenbaum simply multiplies the agencies' most recent budgets by 20.

Critics have pointed out numerous flaws in that approach, which cumulatively make the number not only economically meaningless but misleading. First, as the subcommittee observed, "Dr. Weidenbaum's study misses the mark even in calculating the costs of regulation because it mixes apples and oranges" adding to the cost of health and safety regulation the costs of "old line cartel regulation agencies such as the Interstate Commerce Commission." The budget estimates for the agencies are so arbitrarily set that Weidenbaum even includes, for example, the money that the federal government gives states to develop highway safety programs. The multiplier—which was called "a questionable procedure" by the Congressional Research Service—is further bloated by the inclusion in the compliance cost total of a $25 billion estimate for filling out federal paperwork. That estimate, generated by a federal commission in 1977, included IRS and census forms, as well as forms for government contracts and subsidies. A subsequent analysis by the General Accounting Office put the total non-IRS paperwork burden at only $1 billion; health and safety regulation made up less than 10 percent of the total. "If the multiplier were revised to reflect the evidence presented above on paperwork expenditure," concluded the authors of *Business War on the Law*, "it would shrink almost in half." And, as the oversight subcommittee report pointed out, the number completely ignores the offsetting benefits the regulations produce.

These criticisms have left Weidenbaum undaunted. "The numbers are now far too low," he recently said. When we asked him if he could see himself putting out a press release revising the number downward to reflect the Reagan Administration's cuts in regulatory budgets, he replied with a laugh, "No, I can't. I can't imagine doing that." Popularizing that study with congressional testimony and frequent articles, Weidenbaum emerged in the 1970s as a leading critic of federal regulation. Fighting government regulation was a ticket into the big-time not only for Weidenbaum, but for the American Enterprise Institute (AEI), which he joined in 1971 and used as a platform to push many of his ideas. Regulatory criticism "began to have a lot of influence on the American Enterprise Institute, which before then had been kind of a small organization doing an occasional study on this and that," said Christopher DeMuth, now the OMB's chief regulatory reformer, in an interview.

Along with James C. Miller III, DeMuth's predecessor at OMB, and now Federal Trade Commission chairman, Weidenbaum relentlessly promoted the concept of cost-benefit analysis. As the studies opposing government regulation poured out of the AEI in the 1970s, the contributions poured in. Over the past decade, the AEI's budget—swelled by contributions from the Lilly Endowment, Exxon, Bethlehem Steel and the Chase Manhattan Bank—has increased by a factor of ten, from $1 million to $10 million. It began to publish a number of slick magazines, including one entitled *Regulation* that Weidenbaum edited until his appointment.

From 1975 until his appointment, Weidenbaum also ran the Center for Study of American Business at Washington University, where he had been a professor since 1964 (with the exception of a two-year stint in the Nixon Treasury Department).

The center also produced a steady stream of anti-regulatory studies. Major funding sources for the center in the years after Weidenbaum took over included James S. McDonnell, Jr., chairman of the McDonnell-Douglas Corp.; the Olin Foundation; General Electric and the Scaife Foundation.

At times, Weidenbaum acknowledged some of the obvious limitations of cost-benefit analysis, noting in 1979 testimony that, "Reliable measures of costs and benefits are not easily achieved. Reasonably precise quantification of benefits and costs is not always possible." Despite those drawbacks, the Reagan Administration is now requiring the regulatory agencies to promulgate rules only if it can demonstrate that the benefits of proposed regulations to the public exceed its costs to industry.

Weidenbaum has also written extensively about military spending, spinning out such articles as "Could the U.S. Afford Disarmament?" and "The Need for Reforming the Military-Industrial Relationship." As those titles indicate, Weidenbaum has had mixed feelings about military spending, and the symbiotic relationship between the Pentagon and its prime contractors. As a former economist for Boeing, he has been careful in his work to clear the contractors of any hint of profiteering. Ironically, in light of the Reagan antitrust view that the American economy is not particularly concentrated, Weidenbaum has defended the limited pool of military contractors by noting that, "Concentration of economic activity is a longstanding and pervasive attribute of the American economy."

But Weidenbaum also made more critical observations he might do well to reread today, as the Reagan Administration embarks on its military buildup. If not a leading gadfly of military procurement and weapons design procedures, he at least in the past acknowledged the inefficiency problems that the Reagan military bureaucracy ignores. "A good deal of the high cost of weapons systems has resulted from *excessive sophistication* of military requirements," he wrote in 1973. (Emphasis added.) And for all that cost, he noted, "The environment of rapid technological change dictates a relatively short product life cycle; frequently new products just emerging from the production lines may be made obsolete by even newer products on the design boards. . . ." (Witness the B-1 bomber.) As he testified in 1974, "To a considerable extent, simpler weapons may also turn out to be better as well as cheaper."

In that 1973 article, Weidenbaum criticized the military for cancelling several weapons systems after billions of dollars had already been invested. In so doing he raised an argument that many critics see as the inevitable flaw in the Reagan Administration's avowed aim to spend its way to military superiority over the Soviets. Wrote Weidenbaum:

> Although precise conclusions are difficult, the available statistics (both public and private) do show that in recent years the USSR has escalated its weapons production in an effort to catch up with the United States. It is hard to think of something that reduces our real national security more than a crash effort to build a new weapons system that does not work, but that evokes a strong response by a rival power. And the rival power may succeed in developing the weapon that we failed to develop.

Weidenbaum's most well-known writing on military subjects is his analysis of the economic impact of the Vietnam War. Weidenbaum's study of the defense build-up associated with Vietnam—which essentially concluded that the Johnson Administration fueled inflation by failing to raise taxes to cover the increasing military expenditures—became controversial last year when critics such as MIT economist Lester Thurow charged the Reagan build-up will have the same effect. (See Major Issues.)

For Weidenbaum, that kind of analysis has been mostly supplanted in recent years by more popular writing, not only on regulation but a potpourri of other economic subjects. His extensive publication list reveals little macroeconomic work, and Weidenbaum is considered far less of an authority in that field than previous CEA chairmen. Instead, he has become a leading apologist for American business, castigating government regulators, labor unions and consumer groups for harming "the American economy and ultimately. . .the consumer." His rallying cry, as he expressed it in a 1980 speech, was "Free The Fortune 500."

Free them, for example, from "the monopolization of labor markets by labor unions," as he wrote in a July 3, 1979 article in the *Los Angeles Times*, that suggested outlawing industry-wide strikes. "The time may have come to consider restoring some of the virtues of competition to the labor market by imposing certain limits on unions' monopoly powers," he began. Later in the article he observed, with an apparent tone of disappointment, that "it is not realistic to consider changes in our legal institutions which would eliminate this basic factor [unions]."

Free them from "representatives of public interest groups [who] confuse their personal prejudices with the national well-being," as he said in 1980. Free them from "an unprecedented expansion of government involvement in private enterprise. . . ." Along those lines, Weidenbaum recently called affirmative action "just morally wrong." Weidenbaum even found the time to pen a piece, "In Defense of Tax Loopholes," that concluded, "tax expenditures, in the main, are not special benefits to the highest-income classes or the product of ingenious accountants or attorneys." Weidenbaum is not one of the economists increasingly critical of the quality of top American business management. But, as he told us, "I've never been on the board of a railroad or steel company. I might have a different view."

This is Weidenbaum's third tour of duty with the federal government. From 1949 to 1957 he crunched numbers at the old Bureau of the Budget. Then from 1969 to 1971 he served as assistant Treasury secretary for economic policy.

Weidenbaum kept busy with a wide variety of interests there as well. He worked on and energetically pushed the Nixon Administration's revenue sharing plan. At a January, 1970 seminar, he spoke in favor of cutting the defense budget. In June, he proposed "pollution taxes"—an idea still popular with many conservative economists. That November, he reversed his earlier opposition to wage price guidelines and called for a "conscious effort to create a new climate in which more reasonable and sensible wage-cost-price decisions are made," especially in areas "where substantial concentrations of private power exist." One month later, Weidenbaum went even further, saying, "I think the time has come to give some serious consideration to some form of incomes policy." (At his confirmation hearing in April, 1981 Weidenbaum voluntarily scourged himself for those now heretical thoughts, telling the senators, "I have learned that government attempting to interfere with private wage and price decisionmaking, interfering directly, is counterproductive.")

After resigning from Treasury in June, 1971, Weidenbaum returned to Washington University, where he remained until tapped by Reagan. Weidenbaum also taught at the University of Washington, from 1959 through 1963. He has worked in the corporate world for Boeing, General Dynamics and the Stanford Research Institute.

In addition to his academic work, Weidenbaum served on *Time's* board of economists; the board of directors of the American Council on Capital Formation, a business group; and the Council on Foreign Relations. Weidenbaum headed the Reagan transition team on regulatory reform—he insisted it not be called the task force on deregulation—and was a member of the overall transition economic policy group.

Weidenbaum has always considered himself something of a toastmaster, with a fondness for the well-placed verbal barb. "It's nice to work for a boss who is a great one-line collector and user of one-liners," he told us. "In fact, I once made a tactical goof. [Former White House aide] Lyn Nofziger, the President and I were at lunch together and I started making wise-cracks. That was deadly. Because Nofziger started. And Reagan matched him. To avoid getting caught in the cross fire, I just shut up for the next 10, 15 minutes. Those guys are pros."

A sample of the Weidenbaum wit: Recently, Weidenbaum shared a Gridiron Club platform with New York Mayor Ed Koch and Harvard economist John Kenneth Galbraith. Hearing Galbraith criticize the Administration on deficit financing and inflation, Weidenbaum said, "reminds me of the cartoon showing one of Custer's scouts approaching when he was in the valley surrounded by all the Indians. And Custer turns to his aide and says 'what does this guy want?' And he says, 'Oh, that's the scout who led you into this. He's back to give you more advice.' History doesn't record Custer's answer but I had it on authority from a descendant of an Indian who was back there up on the hill, who could lip read, and his response was, 'Send the bastard back to Harvard.'"

Born on February 10, 1927 in the Bronx, Weidenbaum still carries a New York City demeanor. He received his undergraduate degree from City College of New York in 1948, an M.A. from Columbia a year later and a Ph.D. from Princeton in 1958. He is married with three children.

FINANCIAL BACKGROUND

Weidenbaum has supplemented his academic income with a steady stream of speeches to business groups, articles and a lucrative consulting operation. In 1980, he earned $53,357 from Washington University and $18,333 from the AEI. His financial disclosure form lists numerous additional "honorariums"—presumably for speaking engagements—including: the Chemical Manufacturers Association ($2,500), the American Farm Bureau Federation ($3,500), the Soap and Detergent Association ($2,450), the National Building Metals Association ($2,450), and PPG, Inc. ($3,500).

In addition, Weidenbaum served on the board of directors of May Department Stores, Co., ($6,650), and consulted for the First National Bank in St. Louis ($3,000) and the Business Roundtable ($500) among other clients. He also ran Murray L. Weidenbaum, Inc., a consulting firm whose clients included:

May Department Stores ($5,000-$15,000)
U.S. Chamber of Commerce ($5,000-$15,000)
Johnson & Johnson ($1,000-$2,500)
Eli Lilly and Co. ($2,500-$5,000)
Kansas Bankers Association ($2,500-$5,000)

Exxon ($2,500-$5,000)
American Die Casting Institute ($2,500-$5,000)
Shell Oil ($2,500-$5,000)

The firm's total revenue for 1980 was $45,000.

Weidenbaum also reported stock holdings of between $5,000 and $15,000 in Coca Cola, IBM and Exxon, and holdings of between $1,000 and $5,000 in United Technologies as well as assorted other bonds, savings, and money market funds. Weidenbaum has resigned his business positions, taken leaves from the University and the AEI, and placed his holdings in a blind trust.

JERRY JORDAN
MEMBER

BACKGROUND

Along the road to power and influence in the economic world, Jerry Jordan took an unusual mid-life detour. From the hard-driving world of the eastern banking establishment, he diverted in 1980 to the quiet corridors of academia, as dean of the School of Management at the University of New Mexico (UNM).

As far as economic influence goes, he might as well have moved to New Zealand. "People don't realize I prefer the obscurity I achieved in New Mexico," he said recently.

When Jordan arrived at UNM, he pledged, like his predecessor, not to serve more than ten years in the job. He fulfilled the pledge. Less than a year after arriving, he was tapped by Murray Weidenbaum to be the CEA's resident monetarist and run its forecasting operation.

The CEA job will also allow Jordan to fulfill his stated aim at the time he went to New Mexico—"to be involved as an economist" in public policy decisions. The new job allows him to do a bit more than that. Particularly, his key role as a forecaster will enable him to inject his monetarist beliefs into the fundamental assumptions that underlie the Reagan budget.

Jordan earned a reputation as a monetarist during his years at the Federal Reserve Bank of St. Louis, which was the first outpost of monetarism in the Federal system. Jordan worked at the bank from 1967 through 1975, rising ultimately to the position of senior vice president and director of research.

His early work on the importance of controlling the money supply to control inflation has been praised by, among others, Beryl Sprinkel, another monetarist who is now undersecretary at Treasury for monetary policy. Jordan sat with Sprinkel on the Shadow Open Market Committee, a private group of economists that have been meeting since 1973 to criticize the Fed's policies and urging it to limit growth of the money supply, instead of attempting to moderate interest rates.

"The Shadow Committee was formed in 1973 and its sole job was to persuade the world that the Fed was screwing up badly because they were looking at the wrong thing," Jordan told a local reporter in March, 1981. "People thought all the central bank was supposed to do was provide the amount of money and credit demanded by the economy, but mainly focus on the level of interest rates, the cost of credit, not the quality."

Jordan and the Shadow, needless to say, thought differently. More important than managing interest rates was restraining money growth, they argued: "Our argument is that as long as you continue to inflate, you can't get unemployment down and keep productivity up."

In congressional testimony, Jordan succinctly laid out what he considers the proper policy for the Fed, a policy the Reagan Administration has generally backed. "There are two objectives in setting money targets that the Federal Reserve should be held to," he said. "One is to gradually lower the trend growth of money so you lower the rate of inflation, and the other is to eliminate the fluctuations in money growth so that it does not contribute to fluctuations in unemployment that occur."

In that same testimony, Jordan stated the monetarist defense against calls—heard frequently in the fall of 1981—for reducing interest rates:

> It is tempting to try to push interest rates down to help the economy. My point is, it would be self-defeating because investors in the market would look at the rapid growth of money supply and would expect future inflation to be higher and they would try to protect themselves from the losses in capital markets and rising interest rates. They would invest in short-term assets. They would avoid long-term commitments. Long-term interest rates would rise. You would get rates rising, not declining.

The only way to reduce interest rates, he argued, was to "wait it out" until the tight money policies reduce inflation. Now that the tight money policies are in place, the wait has been difficult to take, though. Jordan, along with other Reagan economic advisers, such as his colleague William Niskanen, have admitted puzzlement at the current stickiness of interest rates in the face of moderating inflation.

"As we enter a new decade," he said in 1980, "the central issue concerning stabilization policies is not the role of the money supply versus interest rates, and it is not the relative importance of monetary versus fiscal policies as was the case in the past decade. Now. . . The importance of restoring our central bank's reputation and credibility as an inflation fighting institution cannot be overemphasized."

Before becoming dean at New Mexico, Jordan spent five years as senior vice president and economist for the Pittsburgh National Bank. For six months in 1971-72, he served as a consultant to the central bank of West Germany. From 1979-80, he served on the U.S. Chamber of Commerce's Council on Trends and Perspectives.

Born November 12, 1941 in Hawthorne, California, Jordan received his B.A. in economics from California State University at Northridge in 1963 and his Ph.D. from the University of California at Los Angeles in 1967. He is married with three children.

FINANCIAL BACKGROUND

Jordan's largest financial assets are two land holdings in northern California, each of which are valued at between $15,000 and $50,000. He earned $25,000 in his half year as dean, less than half of the $64,000 he earned in the first half of the year from the Pittsburgh National Bank.

WILLIAM NISKANEN, JR.
MEMBER

BACKGROUND

Niskanen has been hovering around the edge of the Reagan entourage since at least 1973 when Reagan, then governor of California, appointed him to an economic task force. A prominent economist with experience in government, universities and business, Niskanen also served as a Reagan economic adviser during the 1976 and 1980 presidential campaigns.

Niskanen became a public figure during the last days of his five-year career as director of economics for the Ford Motor Company. In 1980, the company dismissed him after he openly criticized its plans to stifle free competition in the American automobile market.

Worried about the slump in automobile sales, Ford wanted to pressure Washington to negotiate an "orderly marketing agreement" that would restrict Japanese auto exports to the U.S. (Such an agreement was arranged by the Reagan Administration early last year, though without the support of the CEA.) Niskanen objected, first of all, to the idea of pressuring the government for favors—a tactic which he compared to "stealing." He also pointed out to Ford that its sales problems were largely attributable not to the Japanese but to the U.S. recession, high gasoline prices, and "bad production decisions" by Ford managers. Niskanen's indictment of auto management has since been widely echoed in American business literature.

In a 1980 press interview, he denounced the Ford philosophy that executives should " 'wait until they hear their superiors express their view and then contribute something in support of that view.' That wasn't and isn't my style." Added Niskanen: "The philosophy instilled in many corporate managers is almost a bureaucratic rather than a business ethic. When even highly paid, high status managers have little discretion in implementing a program and little incentive to take risks to improve it, it's to be expected that they contribute little."

Today, Niskanen believes the increases in gas prices since 1973 are the "primary" reason for the declining fortunes of the U.S. auto manufacturers. "What has happened since 1973. . .is that the U.S. new car market came to look much more like that against which the Germans and the Japanese and so forth had been producing all along," he told us. "And the U.S. never was competitive in making small cars, never was, it isn't. It isn't that the U.S. makers have become less competitive in making cars over time; it's just that the market has shifted towards those cars that they were never competitive in." Making matters worse, Niskanen argued, was that, "During this period in which the U.S. companies as a whole had an effective monopoly over the supply of new cars in the United States they allowed their wages to get way out of line. . . . The UAW [United Auto Workers] was able to extract that difference during a period of time in which the UAW effectively monopolized the U.S. auto market. And now they [the auto companies] find themselves with $20 an hour labor costs in a world in which they don't have that monopoly any more. And that is the key fact of life for the U.S. auto industry."

Niskanen's published work pillories government officials who muffle dissenting views. Niskanen has stated that his "professional unease" about the responsiveness of bureaucracies to national problems dates back to his first governmental appointment—as a director of special studies in the Pentagon in 1962. "Something was seriously wrong with. . .the management of the public sector," he later wrote. Precisely what was wrong was presumably clarified by Niskanen's experience in OMB under the Nixon Administration from 1970-72. In a book and major article published in 1971 and 1975, he examined the reasons for bureaucratic unresponsiveness and proposed some remedies. One suggestion: "Maybe class-action suits against the government for demonstrably inefficient performance should be authorized."

Niskanen's stint at OMB may also have contributed to his critical analysis of fiscal management in *Structural Reform of the Federal Budget Process*. Completed while he was a professor at University of California, Berkeley's School of Public Policy 1972-75, the book concludes that:

- Budget deficits damage the economy; those that are financed by borrowing from the public limit private investment and slow down economic growth.

- Deficits that persist after excess government spending is slashed should be reduced by raising personal income taxes.

Such findings, of course, are almost heretical in the Reagan Administration. Although corroborated by recent economic trends and accepted by many other economists, Niskanen's expressed views on the budget appear to collide with the "supply-side" theories of the current Administration at every turn, though his views on the deficit have changed. (See Major Issues.)

Working in big government and big business is "much the same," Niskanen believes. "I worked for [Defense Secretary] Bob McNamara when I was in the Pentagon, who had just come from being the head of Ford and it's not unusual for big businessmen to pick up one or more cabinet posts. In general, people probably work harder when they're here, just in terms of the number of hours they put in. I know I do when I'm here. . .It's also much more frustrating here in that businesses have a more clear hierarchy than this place and the authority to hire and fire and shape the organization in the direction [you want] is much more clear."

Although described derisively by a Ford Company vice-president as a "newly fledged professor," Niskanen appears to be highly regarded in the economics profession as an expert on public finance and administration. Like many Reagan officials, he has worked at the U.S. Chamber of Commerce, serving on the Council on Trends and Perspectives. Niskanen also serves on the board of the libertarian Reason Foundation (he has advocated increasing "the competition to the bureaucracy by greater use of private sources of supply of public services"), founded the National Tax Limitation Committee, which promotes state amendments limiting government spending, and served on the Board of the International Institute of Economic Research.

Niskanen started his career at the Rand Corp. and then took the director of special studies post in the Defense secretary's office in 1962. After two years there, Niskanen joined the Institute for Defense Analyses, a private think-tank similar to Rand, where he continued to conduct weapons system analysis and military economics studies. In 1970, he joined the OMB as assistant director for evaluation. Two years later, he once again left government for a post in the University of California at Berkeley's public policy school. He then joined Ford in 1975.

"Basically, I started out as a technocrat," said Niskanen, who still carries the pipe-smoking, unhurried air of an academic. "It was an outgrowth of the Rand Corporation, McNamara period in the Pentagon and things like that, in which my view was that all the world really needed was some smart hardworking people in the right places, without very much thought about the nature of institutional structure and incentives and all of that. In some ways [I was] getting caught up in the New Frontier image of the world: If you only put some Harvard grads in high office and worked them pretty hard, you'd solve all the problems of the world. . .My experience in the Pentagon was in that sense very disillusioning."

Vietnam was not the spur for that disillusionment, though Niskanen said he now has "mixed" feelings about the war. While he considered the intervention "largely generous in spirit," he lost faith in the war "when it became clear our efforts weren't effective"—around the late 1960s.

"No, it [my disillusionment] was largely a personal growing up realization that defense decisions. . .were made on the basis of a lot of criteria that had nothing to do with effectiveness or efficiency," he said.

Politically, Niskanen isn't much different today than he always was—"I suppose for the most part I voted Republican"—but his ideology has shifted since the can-do days at the Pentagon. "I've changed. . .from the point of view of in general being an optimist about government to being a pessimist about government," he told us. He calls himself a libertarian and sums up his philosophy of government with a simple declaration: "The government's responsibility is not to ensure that everything is done right in this country, but to focus on actions in which it is fairly clear that what is happening is wrong. . ."

Those beliefs have occasionally collided with Administration policy that bends to the needs of powerful supporters. Niskanen chaired the Administration working group that considered the request from the consortium building the Alaskan Natural Gas Pipeline for waivers in law that would allow them to "prebill" consumers for the gas, even if the pipeline was never completed. (See Charles Butler profile.) When we asked Niskanen how that squared with his libertarian principles, he replied, "It doesn't square. I was. . .the leading spokesman for either granting no waivers or at most having a special provision relative to the Canadian segment of the pipeline. . .I almost won. But I didn't. . .I could not publicly defend that particular [decision]."

Niskanen first met Reagan when the governor formed a Tax Limitation Task Force in 1973. Niskanen served on the group, which produced the spending limit proposal that California voters eventually defeated as Proposition One. Reagan addressed the group's first meeting, Niskanen recalled. "He [Reagan] said that we could not count on the election of a Republican president to ensure fiscal responsibility. . .and he was quite correct," Niskanen said.

Born in Bend, Oregon on March 13, 1933, Niskanen received a B.A. from Harvard (1954), and an M.A. (1955) and Ph.D. (1962) from the University of Chicago. Niskanen, a member of the board of several economic and public policy associations and journals, served on Reagan transition groups on the budget and regulatory policy. He is married with three children.

FINANCIAL BACKGROUND

Niskanen earned $117,212 in his last year with Ford, and another $27,000 as a graduate professor from UCLA. His only substantial stock holding, besides an investment in a Merrill Lynch fund, was an investment valued at over $250,000 in Mt. Hood Stages, a bus company.

WHAT OTHERS ARE SAYING ABOUT HIM

Niskanen's December remarks about the deficit (see Major Issues) kept the Senate floor hopping the next morning.

- Sen. William Armstrong, a conservative Republican from Colorado, said Niskanen's ideas "would make it impossible for us to survive as a viable, governing party in this country." And Republican Slade Gorton of Washington asked, "If we can safely and without adversely affecting our economy or rate of inflation borrow $100 billion, then why can we not borrow $200 billion or $400 billion or perhaps $700 billion?"

- Said Sen. Howard Metzenbaum (D-Ohio): "The fact is, the Republicans have fallen flat on their faces. They have fallen flat on their faces because anybody who could add 2 and 2 could understand that you could not increase defense spending by billions of dollars, cut taxes by billions of dollars, far more than anybody ever possibly envisioned, and then balance the budget at the same time."

MAJOR ISSUES

For Murray Weidenbaum, the American Enterprise Institute's Public Policy Week during December, 1981 should have been a triumphant homecoming. It was, after all, only one year ago at the previous Public Policy Week that Weidenbaum headed a panel of economists offering regulatory advice to the incoming Administration. Now, surrounded by colleagues and eminent conservative economists in the elegant surroundings of the Mayflower Hotel in Washington, he had returned as the President's chief economic adviser, an alumnus made good.

Flanked by his colleagues Niskanen and Jordan, Weidenbaum glowed with pride as Herbert Stein, the clipped, witty former CEA chair introduced him as the most successful CEA chairman ever.

Of the many wise things that Arthur Okun said, Stein continued, was that "Treasury had the revenue, the Budget Bureau had the expenditures and the CEA had the deficit." Since "Murray has the largest deficit," Stein concluded, he must be the most successful.

It was, of course, a joke, and the room's collection of gray suits bubbled with laughter. But it was a joke with a hard edge—made harder by the revelations in the morning's newspaper: The government's latest calculations put the 1982 deficit at a record $109 billion and the 1983 and 1984 deficits at a staggering $152 and $162 billion respectively.

For the conservative economists gathered there, many of them alumni of the Nixon and Ford years, such figures were heretical, almost unthinkable, for a Republican—or indeed any—administration. For Weidenbaum, those headlines were not an auspicious banner beneath which to be returning home.

Before the morning was over, the group heard an even greater heresy that left most of them—including, perhaps, Weidenbaum—stunned and made the White House scramble to disassociate itself from the remarks of its Council of Economic Advisers. Niskanen, who earned a reputation for speaking his mind at Ford, told the group—who had heard Ronald Reagan preach the balanced budget for years—that federal deficits were not, after all, inflationary. Said Niskanen: "The simple relationship between deficits and inflation is as close to being empty as can be perceived." And, "there are no necessary relationships between the deficit and money growth." Not only that, said Niskanen, but the "evidence doesn't support" the assertion that deficits crowd out private borrowers, a view held by, among others, Budget Director David Stockman, Fed Chairman Paul Volcker, and Treasury Undersecretary Beryl Sprinkel, not to mention Weidenbaum. In sum, Niskanen presented a view close to that of the most dedicated supply-siders, who find the traditional Republican preoccupation with the deficit a musty anachronism.

"The economic community has reinforced an unfortunate perspective on the deficit which is not consistent with the historical evidence," he concluded. Niskanen passed out a series of charts to buttress his points, which his listeners greeted with the skepticism that the Vatican might muster for a newly discovered book of the Bible. Even Weidenbaum looked pointedly uncomfortable, particularly when Stein turned the screws, in his acerbic manner, quipping pleasantly, but firmly, that President Reagan "seems to be the only member of this Administration who believes that deficits are inflationary."

Actually, Weidenbaum himself had long advocated that view. In 1976, Weidenbaum criticized the Humphrey-Hawkins full-employment bill for not acknowledging "deficit spending as a basic cause of inflation." As he asserted in an article, "financing large budget deficits reduces the money available for capital formation (new factories, production equipment, etc.) which is fundamental to creating new jobs." Two years earlier, he said in Senate testimony, "an excess of Government outgo over income increases the purchasing power in the private sector and this is inflationary."

Only a few weeks before the AEI forum, Jordan had also commented on the importance of reducing the deficit to help bring down interest rates. "[T]he very fact that deficits are believed by so many in the financial markets to cause high rates makes this view important," he said. "In a sense, it has all the aspects of a self-fulfilling prophecy. High real rates dampen economic activity and reduce revenue at the same time they add to the cost of carrying the national debt and thus increase the deficit. Therefore, to reduce interest rates, it is important that the Administration and Congress convince the public that we will continue to make credible progress toward reducing the deficit." At the forum, though, Jordan predicted interest rates would decline despite the swelling deficits.

When the meeting broke up, we asked Weidenbaum whether he supported Niskanen's assertions. "Those are the conclusions to his research," he replied brusquely. "That's all." A week later he told reporters, "It wasn't intended to be a statement of Administration policy—and it wasn't." And he subsequently told us: "I'm the chairman and by statute all of the authority of the council is lodged in the chairman. . .I'm just saying don't attribute anyone else's views to me."

At the same time, though, Weidenbaum said that a balanced budget was not "one of the fundamentals of the [Reagan economic] program." Those two remarks captured the Administration's contradictory response to the entire episode, indeed to the overall budget problem that compelled Niskanen to defend deficit spending.

Immediately after Niskanen's remarks hit the press, Republican senators hit the ceiling, with such staunch Reagan supporters as William Armstrong (R-Colo.) proclaiming that those sentiments presaged "economic disaster" and the "death knell of the Republican Party.'' Treasury Secretary Regan assured reporters, "we have to get our deficits down.'' From the White House came the rebuff that the "statement did not reflect the President's opinion or Administration policy.''

On the other hand, it was only Administration policy that forced Niskanen to contemplate such huge deficits in the first place. As he told the conference, "It is now recognized that some of the expected economic effects of the Reagan economic program are inconsistent and something has to give.'' And, condemned though his remarks were, he was certainly reflecting the President's apparent beliefs when he said: "It is preferable to tolerate deficits of these magnitudes either to reinflating [the money supply] or to raise taxes. Other things being equal, I would like to see lower deficits too, but other things are not equal.''

Several weeks after the incident, we suggested to Niskanen that, despite the White House denials and the boilerplate condemnations of deficits added to the council's 1982 annual report, his remarks at the conference only made explicit what is implicit in the 1983 budget. "In the budget,'' he jumped in, "and in the President's message, that's right. . . . I found myself in the awkard position of being criticized by some parties for being an apologist for the Administration and being criticized internally in the Administration for not following the party line.''

Niskanen will probably recede back into the relative obscurity of the council, or he might retreat back into private life. But the fundamental economic riddle of the Reagan Administration, posed first in the Iowa primary by John Anderson, will not go away. That question—how do you cut taxes, increase defense spending, and balance the budget at once—has become increasingly difficult for Administration officials to answer. Niskanen's remarks may have been a trial balloon suggesting that they would stop trying.

The Administration's original economic forecasts muted the issue, by projecting growth, inflation and unemployment rates that would eliminate the deficit by 1984. Supply-siders, stressing the importance of putting the economy in the proper psychological frame of mind to grow, originally pressed for a forecast that projected real Gross National Product (GNP) growth in 1982 of 7 percent and inflation of only 6.5 percent. Weidenbaum, among others, successfully watered those numbers down in the budget presented in February, 1981.

"In the range of whatever you think is a reasonable forecast every Administration to my knowledge has come down toward the optimistic end of that range,'' Weidenbaum told us. "But if you exceed the range and you discredit yourself, and the media, the financial markets and the economists don't take the forecasts seriously you're not doing yourself or your boss any service.''

But the numbers were still optimistic. For 1982, the Administration projected a growth rate of 4.2 percent, an increase in the Consumer Price Index of 8.3 percent and unemployment of 7 percent, with inflation and unemployment dropping through 1986 and growth continuing at a robust 4 percent annually.

Steadily, over the resistance of supply-siders who have taken to guerrilla warfare in the pages of the *Wall Street Journal*, those figures have been pared back. Weidenbaum has been sent forth to deliver the bad news more than once, and by November, 1981, with the economy mired in recession, was predicting a 1982 growth rate of only 1 percent. And he said that unemployment would climb "well over'' the current rate of 8 percent, perhaps as high as 9 percent, the highest level recorded since World War II. (In April, 1982 it went even higher.) In its fiscal year 1983 budget, the Administration predicted 1982 growth of only .2 percent, inflation of 7.3 percent and unemployment of fully 8.9 percent.

Niskanen argues that the growth projections are not "unusual" based on past performance of the economy coming out of recession. "What is different and what is something we don't understand and we don't really have modern experience with is what kind of growth we can expect during a period of time in which we expect to continue to deflate the economy," he said. "That is what's different. And I must acknowledge that it's a risk. . .we believe it can be done, but there really isn't a post-war experience."

As the optimistic economic assumptions have unraveled, so have the rosy forecasts of balanced budgets. That development has generated the jarring deficit projections that steadily expanded through the fall of 1981. (Though moderated by economic projections still highly optimistic, deficits forecast for the next three years total $273 billion.) It also set those who wanted to recognize the deficits against those "who support a crazy forecast" as an unnamed member of the CEA told the *Journal*. That battle will continue throughout the upcoming years and is unlikely to ever be resolved to either side's full satisfaction: The entrenched powers are too strong on both fronts.

"They are among the more political numbers in the system and there is a lot of internal political bargaining on those numbers," acknowledged Niskanen.

One battle summarily concluded during the summer of 1981 was the attempt by budget officials to trim the defense buildup. Weidenbaum sided with OMB Director Stockman and White House Chief of Staff James Baker in that ill-fated effort. But, as has often been the case, Weidenbaum did not play a lead role in the struggle.

In any event, Weidenbaum's involvement was ironic, for he spent most of his first months in office defending the increase in military spending against critics who cited, among other works, Weidenbaum's own study of the Vietnam War. In that work, Weidenbaum blamed the late 1960s surge of inflation on the Johnson Administration's failure to raise taxes to pay for the rapid increase in defense spending. "Should another major escalation occur in the level of U.S. commitment in Southeast Asia," he wrote in 1967, "it would be important to promptly develop the restraining fiscal measures [tax increases] needed to offset the inflationary impacts."

In a detailed critique of the Administration's plans, economist Lester Thurow argued that the planned buildup was "three times as large as the one that took place during the Vietnam War" and would fuel inflation, divert civilian high technology industries and swell the deficit. When the Administration was still projecting a balanced budget by 1984, Weidenbaum argued that the buildup was not that large—a conclusion disputed later by the Congressional Budget Office—and was being imposed on an economy with a larger amount of underutilized capacity than was the case in the mid-1960s. But Thurow and other critics point out that aggregate utilization figures explain little about the specific requirements of military production and the likelihood of bottlenecks in key sectors. Wrote Thurow: "Given the time it takes to train new skilled blue collar workers and engineers, there is no way that the supply of skills can keep up with that growth rate."

The tight supply of skilled personnel will also inevitably drain talent away from domestic high technology industries—such as the semiconductor field—a point on which, Thurow noted, "the economic defenders of the Reagan Administration's defense budget have been completely silent." Not always so, though. In words that echo Thurow, Weidenbaum once wrote, "There still may be an important opportunity cost involved in some of the highly specialized resources required by DOD and NASA. . .Those who decry private affluence amid public poverty may reflect on the allocation of one of our most vital resources, science and technology."

Weidenbaum also defended the buildup by saying it would only increase the military budget's share of the GNP by 1 percentage point, as compared to 1.8 percentage points during Vietnam. But those figures, Thurow points out, assume the original rapid growth and productivity estimates that the Administration is already finding untenable. Given a more realistic rate of productivity growth, Thurow calculated the military's share of the GNP would rise by 2.4 percentage points, and for all its carping about Thurow's (and other critics') assertions, the Administration has implicitly recognized their validity in the projections of massive deficits in the upcoming years.

And the council's 1982 annual report displays far more concern about "potentially adverse economic effects of the defense buildup" than Weidenbaum had previously acknowledged. For starters, it calculates that "real purchases of defense durables"—weapons procurement and research and development—would rise faster between 1981 and 1987 than they did "during the 3 peak years of the Vietnam buildup." This "large increase" in military spending could have three negative impacts on the economy, the report predicts:

- It may "increase relative prices" in defense-related industries, hurting both the military and "private purchasers" that buy from those sectors;
- It may create production bottlenecks;
- It may result in a "temporary crowding out of private investment" and force firms that rely on production sources which will be monopolized by the military to "turn to foreign sources for materials."

The report also questions the Pentagon's assurances that it can meet Reagan's military goals without a draft. "Declining unemployment rates and a reduction in the available manpower pool because of the decline in the recruiting-age population will make these goals difficult to achieve and will increase pressure to shift the costs of achieving them from taxpayers onto the young—that is, by reinstituting the draft," the council wrote.

These remarks suggest the battle over defense spending is still flickering. "There is, I think, an almost uniform recognition within the Administration that substantially greater defense spending than was the case during the 1970s is appropriate. . .Now whether that should commit us to a 7 percent real growth path or a 5 percent real growth path and how long we should keep it going, has been settled for the moment but I don't expect it to be settled forever," Niskanen told us.

Niskanen, a veteran of eight years in the upper levels of the Pentagon, has his own ideas about how to "discipline" defense spending. "All of our major military missions—with the sole exception of anti-submarine warfare— are now provided by at least two different services and in some cases three services. And relative performance of one service against the other can be used—in terms of how effectively it buys its weapons, develops its concepts and strategies and so forth—can be used to discipline the department as a whole, if the secretary is prepared to use that. And in order to do that he has to be willing to say 'Look, if the Navy performs the tactical air mission better than the Air Force we're willing to commit some money to it.' But if you're not prepared to use the competition among services it's in many cases just redundant [to have parallel missions]. . .and the incentives to use competition,

I must acknowledge, are usually greatest when budgets are tight rather than when they're growing."

Weidenbaum has continued to speak against government regulation, though his formal role has been limited to the President's Task Force on Regulatory Relief. "Informally," he told one interviewer, "I take a very strong interest in specific issues. I view my role here as almost that of an elder statesman providing support and guidance for the people on the firing line—those in the Office of Management and Budget and the Vice-President's office. It has been a happy and productive two-way relationship. They don't hesitate coming to me for advice, and I don't hesitate volunteering it."

On a number of issues Weidenbaum has privately taken a stand ultimately rejected by the President. Weidenbaum opposed the liberal tax leasing provisions that allow money-losing corporations to sell their tax breaks to profitable firms and was a leader in the fight against the auto import agreement Reagan imposed on Japan. He doesn't think much of the trigger pricing mechanism erected to protect the domestic steel industry against foreign competitors. And, for that matter, he doesn't think much of the efforts by other Cabinet secretaries to convince business leaders that they have a patriotic duty to reinvest their tax savings in job-producing investments. "I was at a meeting with Baldrige and other members of the Administration and leading business people and several members of the Administration gave them patriotic pep talks. You should be patriotic. You should be supportive. You should now go out and invest all of this money. I got up and I said, 'You know, I don't want to contradict my distinguished colleagues, but I have a somewhat different view of this. I really believe in the private enterprise system. I don't think you should make any investment that you don't think is warranted as a sheer business investment. I appeal to your business judgment not to your guilt feelings.'"

NISKANEN AT LARGE

Over the years, William Niskanen has acquired a reputation as a straight talker. During a wide-ranging 90-minute interview with us, he reaffirmed that reputation. What follows are selections of Niskanen's views on a broad variety of subjects:

THE BUSINESS TAX CUTS APPROVED IN 1981: "I think as far as I can trace the history on that nobody except maybe [lobbyist] Charlie Walker really knew what was going on."

SYNTHETIC FUELS: "I don't see any reason why we [the government] should be in that business."

GOVERNMENT PLANNING: "The institutions of government, the political processes, the bureaucratic processes and the nature of the reward structure in this town are such that the government has a shorter time horizon than almost any institution other than that which expects to go broke in the morning. If you're a businessman and you've got to pay your bank $100,000 in the morning or else you're going to go broke, you're the one who's got to go to Las Vegas and even draw at long odds. But that's a rare phenomena. The problem is that the government acts as if it has to go to Las Vegas every other year."

THE PROSPECTS FOR THE ADMINISTRATION'S 1983 BUDGET: "We're almost asking Congress to act as if they don't have to run for reelection this fall and that's unrealistic. My expectation is that there will be a great deal of posturing by Congress between now and November but they won't have a budget. There will be no budget as of election day. . . . And that will permit some Congressmen to run on an austerity program, a discipline in government, and other Congressmen to run on a program doing this, that or the other for whatever group. And they can both be personally honest because there won't be any budget.''

CHRYSLER: ''I would not be surprised to see Chrysler merge. . .I think the most attractive merger target for Chrysler would be Mitsubishi.''

ROLE OF GOVERNMENT: ''The government shouldn't be in the position of telling the rest of the world what is right behavior, as being quite clear about what kind of behavior it is likely to intervene [against]. I think the burden of proof ought to be on the exercise of police powers and not on the defenders against that exercise.''

NATO: ''I think that between now and the end of the century it will be a real race as to whether the Soviet bloc or NATO breaks up faster. . . . There are enormous internal strains on NATO which I find it hard to believe can last the century.''

THE ENVIRONMENTAL PROTECTION AGENCY: ''I'm not happy about much of anything that's going on at EPA right now. . . . I'm not sure you would be happy about what I would do over there either.''

OMB OVERSIGHT OF REGULATORY AGENCIES: ''It cannot be both the advocate and the judge of regulatory change. . . . We really don't have our act in order on this yet.''

THE ROLE OF THE COUNCIL IN THE ADMINISTRATION: ''Nobody has to deal with us. The easiest thing to do with the council is to ignore us. We have to pick our targets.''

RONALD REAGAN: ''In a rather fundamental way, he's much more of a radical in that he wants to change the character of the American government more than any President since the New Deal.''

U.S. TRADE REPRESENTATIVE

WILLIAM BROCK III

RESPONSIBILITY OF OFFICE

As U.S. trade representative, Brock holds a Cabinet-level position with the rank of ambassador and answers directly to the President. He is responsible for directing all trade negotiations for the United States and for formulating overall foreign trade policy.

Created by executive order in 1963, the post was incorporated within the Executive Office of the President under the Trade Act of 1974 to administer all U.S. trade programs and expanded by executive order in 1979 to include policy-setting responsibilities. The trade representative is the chief U.S. spokesman when trade and commodity issues are the primary subjects of bilateral or multilateral negotiations, and represents the U.S. in many international organizations such as the United Nations Conference on Trade and Development, the Organization for Economic Cooperation and Development, and the General Agreement on Tariffs and Trade.

He also heads the Cabinet-level Trade Policy Committee, and coordinates three other interagency groups—the Trade Policy Staff Committee, the Trade Negotiations Committee, and the Trade Policy Review Group.

Brock operated in 1982 with a budget of $8.6 million and a staff of 113.

BACKGROUND

After some initial turf fights with Secretary of State Haig and Agriculture Secretary Block, Brock has emerged as President Reagan's chief trade spokesman by developing a consensus between opposing views within the Administration and on Capitol Hill. Brock, who developed a reputation as a skillful political operative by successfully rejuvenating the Republican Party while chairman from 1977 until January, 1981, appears to have won confidence with his softspoken diplomatic methods even among hardline Reaganites.

In 1962, Bill Brock became the first Republican in more than 40 years elected to Congress from Tennessee's third district. In the House from 1963-70, Brock served on the Banking and Currency Committee and its subcommittees on monetary policy, international finance, and international trade.

While serving on the House committee responsible for federal banking regulations, Brock had investments exceeding $5,000 each in two banks— the Hamilton National Bank of Chattanooga, and the Hamilton National Bank of Knoxville—according to his financial disclosure report for fiscal 1968. Brock reported capital gains in excess of $5,000 on those investments in 1969.

In 1970, Brock took a U.S. Senate seat away from Democrat Albert Gore, a veteran of 32 years in Washington. Outspending Gore nearly 3-to-1, Brock devoted large sums to television ads, direct mail and billboards. His major billboard message was "Bill Brock Believes." About $1.25 million was spent on his campaign that year, but the most controversial contribution came after he had already won the election.

The *New York Times* reported that Brock accepted $2,500 from BANKPAC, the political action committee of the American Banking Association, fully one week after his narrow victory over Gore. Brock took the money despite allegations that the bankers' check was aimed at influencing the fate of a regulatory bill pending during the lameduck session of Congress. At least 16 of Brock's colleagues on the House Banking and Currency Committee and two senators had refused similar checks from the banking group, the *Times* pointed out.

During his six years in the U.S. Senate, Brock again served on committees charged with overseeing regulation of the banking and securities industry, as well as those responsible for housing and urban affairs, finance, and government operations. His voting record throughout his 14-year Congressional career was consistently pro-military and conservative on social welfare, environmental, civil rights and consumer issues.

Brock was a staunch hawk on the war in Southeast Asia, repeatedly voting against attempts to curb the President's power to deploy troops and wage war without congressional approval. Brock also had a conservative record on civil rights. He opposed both the Civil Rights Act of 1964 and the Voting Rights Act of 1965. On labor legislation, Brock voted while in the House not to repeal so-called "right-to-work" laws, against a $1 minimum wage for farmworkers and in favor of compulsory arbitration of transit strikes, positions which helped earn him an anti-labor reputation.

But Brock was not so conservative when it came to extending government subsidies to business. He voted for reimbursements to American aircraft manufacturers after their ill-fated attempts to build a commercial supersonic transport (SST) plane. He also voted to have taxpayers guarantee a $250 million loan for the financially and scandal troubled Lockheed Aircraft Corporation.

In addition to his substantial banking investments, Brock's financial disclosure report for fiscal 1968 listed interests worth more than $5,000 in 17 companies, including seven doing business directly with the government, or subject to substantial federal regulation—Gulf Oil, Texaco, Texas Instruments, Eastman Kodak, IBM, McDonnell-Douglas, and United Aircraft. Four of those seven brought Brock more than $5,000 each in capital gains that year. At that time he served on the Joint Defense Production Committe and the Joint Economic Committee, in addition to his regular legislative committee assignments.

Despite campaign contributions totaling $1.3 million in 1976—including sizeable contributions from banking interests—Brock was defeated in his bid for reelection by Democrat James Sasser, who spent $470,000 less than Brock. He wasn't long unemployed, though. Outgoing President Gerald Ford named him to head the Republican National Committee, a position he held through the 1980 election year.

The Republican sweep in 1980 clearly indicates that Brock handled his role well as conciliator between the moderate and ultra-conservative wings of the GOP. Respected as a political "technician," Brock helped rebuild the Republican organization with the help of burgeoning campaign contributions. After the election, Brock let it be known he would be interested in becoming Commerce secretary or deputy secretary of State. But Reagan insiders weren't interested. Realizing the value of his political expertise, though, they picked Brock for the trade role.

William Emerson Brock III was born in Chattanooga on November 23, 1930, an heir to the Brock (not Brachs) Candy Co. He also inherited a diverse family political history, which suggests he was forced to employ his skills in the art of compromise at an early age.

The first W.E. Brock, his grandfather, served Tennessee as a Democrat in the U.S. Senate from 1929-32. But at the same time his maternal grandfather was a staunch Republican and was reputed to be in line for a Cabinet post had Wendell Wilkie won the presidency in 1940.

Brock's affiliation with the Republicans began in 1960 when he quit the Democratic Party to work on county-level GOP committees. Soon he had become a national committeeman for the Young Republican National Federation, and less than two years later was elected to Congress.

Before undertaking his political career, Brock had graduated in' 1953 from Washington and Lee University in Virginia, where he studied business administration and commerce. After three years in the U.S. Navy (1953-56), he joined the family candy business in Chattanooga as vice president in charge of marketing.

Bill Brock married Laura Handly in January, 1957. They have three sons and a daughter.

MAJOR ISSUES

- Despite proclaiming a survival-of-the-fittest, free-trade policy, Brock has helped shield the auto and steel industries from foreign competition.

- Brock has pressured developing countries to lower barriers to investments by American multinational corporations, while supporting cuts in U.S. foreign aid programs intended to foster native enterprise.

- Brock is a leader of efforts by the Reagan Administration to gut corporate anti-bribery laws.

Despite trade policy pronouncements by Ambassador Brock couched in laissez-faire rhetoric, he has moved to protect politically powerful industries from foreign competition.

In May, 1981, for example, Brock triumphantly announced in Tokyo that Japanese trade officials had agreed to reduce automobile exports to avoid the imposition of stringent import quotas by the U.S. Congress. That was a victory for Brock and Transportation Secretary Drew Lewis over a free-trade faction in the Administration led by OMB Director David Stockman and Murray Weidenbaum, the chairman of the President's Council of Economic Advisers.

The U.S. International Trade Commission (ITC) previously had ruled that imports were not a primary cause of American automakers' economic problems. Indeed, by December, 1981, General Motors Chairman Roger Smith had acknowledged reluctantly that the ITC's analysis had been correct.

Just two months after he had convinced Japanese trade officials to restrict their U.S. auto exports, Brock appeared before Congress to outline the Reagan Administration's avowed dedication to market-oriented, free-trade policies. "We should be prepared to accept the competitive challenge, and strongly oppose trade distorting interventions by government," Brock testified.

When asked how the Japanese auto export restrictions could be reconciled with this policy statement, Brock referred to "the fact that the economic vitality of certain sectors of our domestic economy is clearly essential to national security." This same logic has since encouraged domestic steel producers to seek additional protection from foreign competition.

U.S. Steel and others in the declining American steel industry have renewed their cries for protection from the "dumping" of foreign steel allegedly being sold below costs and aggravated by the rapid depreciation of foreign currencies in the face of steep U.S. interest rates. Free trader Brock has noisily warned Common Market countries that they have been too "aggressive" in marketing steel in the United States. (See profile of Malcolm Baldrige.)

Trade relations with Japan have steadily soured as well. Prompted by a record $18 billion trade deficit with Japan in 1981, U.S. lawmakers have been studying ways to restrict Japanese access to U.S. markets. One approach being considered is legislation to apply "reciprocity"—forcing Japanese exporters to meet the same conditions here that Japan imposes on U.S. exporters. Considered by many trade experts a poorly disguised form of protectionism, reciprocity is under study by the Administration. Though no formal position has been issued, Brock has said, "Reciprocity will not become a code word for protectionism, but it will be used to state clearly our insistence on equity." Meanwhile, the Administration is considering invoking rarely-used national security provisions of U.S. trade law to restrict imports of Japanese state-of-the-art 64K computer chips, a product in which the Japanese now hold 70 percent of the U.S. market.

Brock's acquiescence to increasing protections for textile manufacturers in industrialized countries under terms of the December, 1981 extension of the international Multifiber Arrangement (MFA), raises additional questions about his commitment to free trade. The U.S. sided with European Common Market countries in negotiating the 51-nation treaty that calls for slowing the growth of textile imports, in contradiction of the original 1973 treaty. It had guaranteed developing countries a minimum 6 percent annual increase in their textile exports to industrialized countries.

Prior to the start of negotiations on extending the MFA, Brock replaced Ryder Webb, an experienced textile negotiator, with Peter O. Murphy, Webb's 33-year-old assistant, reportedly at the urging of lobbyists for American textile and apparel manufacturers. As Brock's representative at the MFA talks, Murphy made it clear from the outset that he was not a free-trade purist and acknowledged that considerable political clout of textile and apparel workers and manufacturers would have a "meaningful impact" on his negotiating position. "We're trying to formulate a pragmatic approach. . .and give some stability to the marketplace," Murphy told the *National Journal*.

Yet even while he is helping shield American business from foreign competition, Brock has pressured developing countries to lower their barriers to investments by U.S. multinational corporations.

Rather than rely on outside business interests to develop their economies, most Third World countries want to nurture indigenous industries with the help of foreign aid and development loans. Non-military U.S. foreign aid programs, however, have been severely cut by the Reagan Administration. In place of development aid, Brock and his staff have promised to ease strictures on imports from developing countries in return for policies allowing rapid expansion of American business interests in those same countries.

This tradeoff constitutes the substance of the so-called "Caribbean Basin Initiative" announced by Reagan in February, 1982. That approach may prove politically unpalatable on Capitol Hill, however, one high ITC aide suggested, if it appears lowered U.S. trade barriers will cost congressmen the jobs of too many constituents.

Brock is helping multinationals expand their operations in another way, as one of the Administration's legion of lobbyists working to gut the Foreign Corrupt Practices Act (FCPA). The anti-bribery legislation was enacted in 1977 following disclosures by 450 major American corporations that they had made questionable payments to foreign government officials to secure business abroad.

In testimony before a House subcommittee in December, 1981, Brock insisted that "changes in this law are urgent and necessary" to remove "one very serious barrier to our exports." Claiming that the FCPA is "ambiguous, complicated and difficult to comply with," Brock complained that "it is almost impossible for American businessmen to make differentiation between so-called 'grease payments' and corruption of foreign officials." Gratuities to encourage timely performance of duties by low-level officials—commonly called "grease payments"—already are exempted from prosecution under the anti-bribery act.

In support of his contention that the FCPA has cost American businesses export trade, Brock's office submitted unverified anecdotal evidence to the Senate and House committees considering the law. When questioned about the sources for his information, Brock conceded that some of the situations could not be documented—since many had been supplied to his office by the U.S. Chamber of Commerce. The remainder of his case histories had been gathered by U.S. embassy officials in response to a cable soliciting information that could be used to bolster the Reagan Administration's efforts to substantially weaken the anti-bribery act, Brock acknowledged under questioning by subcommittee Chairman Timothy Wirth (D-Colo.). Commerce Department trade statistics do not support the Administration's contention that export trade had suffered after the enactment of the anti-bribery law in 1977; from 1977-1981 U.S. merchandise exports increased by 98 percent.

Beyond these immediate concerns, perhaps the idea Brock is pushing hardest is that there is a need for international negotiations to establish agreements on trade in services—one of the few exports in which the U.S. remains dominant. The insurance and banking industries are especially intent on gaining assured access to foreign economies, but American communications, advertising, construction, aviation, computer and engineering firms are also concerned they might be precluded from doing business in some countries.

"Services trade is the frontier for expansion of export sales," Brock told the Organization for Economic Cooperation and Development in April, 1981. "Aggressive cultivation of foreign markets by U.S. service industries is as critical to our economic recovery as is increased export of goods."

Brock now is trying to lay the ground work for future multilateral trade negotiations on services in time to head off what he sees as a "disturbing trend" towards restrictions. Before other countries are likely to take him seriously, though, the laws governing services in the U.S. itself will have to become more uniform and open to foreign business enterprises.

"The big trade issue of the '80s will be trade in services," an ITC staffer acknowledges, "but it's still some ways down the road."

FINANCIAL BACKGROUND

Brock's business and real estate holdings in Tennessee (combined with his wife's assets) are worth in excess of $1.9 million, according to his 1981 financial disclosure statement. Besides an interest in the Brock Candy Company valued at more than $350,000, Brock also has a small investment (between $5,000 and $15,000) in a Hilton hotel franchise, resort and convention center complex located in a converted railroad station in Chattanooga, called the Chattanooga Choo Choo Company. In addition, Brock owns more than $250,000 worth of stock in Green Acres of America, a private real estate holding company that operates mobile home parks and recreational vehicle campgrounds in the southeastern states.

Both Brock and his wife are beneficiaries of stock trust funds, valued at more than $250,000 each. As a result, they retain interests in many American multinational corporations involved in the oil, insurance, textile, banking, retail, food, communications and manufacturing industries. In their trust portfolios, Brock and his wife held investments of $50,000 or more in: Provident Life & Accident Insurance; Xerox Corp.; General Motors Corp.; AMP, Inc.; Dow Chemical Co.; IBM; General Electric Co.; Exxon Corp.; Eastman Kodak Co.; Mobil Corp.; Caterpillar Tractor Co.; Corning Glass Works; Texaco; Standard Oil of Ohio; and Gulf.

In 1980, Brock was paid $62,500 in his position as chairman of the Republican

Party. In addition, he earned $4,500 as a speaker before four business groups and Georgetown University during 1980.

WHAT OTHERS ARE SAYING ABOUT HIM

- "He's sort of the [U.S.] Chamber of Commerce spokesman for the Administration," said one House telecommunications subcommittee staffer.
- "Basically, Bill Brock's in control of trade. There's a great deal of respect for him up on the Hill," said an official at the ITC.
- "He'll go wherever [political] expediency will take him," said another House telecommunications staffer.
- "He's a very capable, and good representative of the Administration's positions," said Steve Hilton, an aide to Sen. John Danforth (R-Mo.)

SMALL BUSINESS ADMINISTRATION

JAMES SANDERS
ADMINISTRATOR

RESPONSIBILITY OF OFFICE

Sanders oversees all SBA programs designed to help the nation's 14 million small businesses—including management, educational programs, procurement assistance, direct and guaranteed loans and disaster relief.

Congress established the agency under the Small Business Act of 1953, in part to stem growing levels of concentration in the post-war economy. Under the act, SBA is responsible for assuring that small businesses get a "fair share" of government procurement contracts. Though the federal agencies themselves generally determine how many, if any, contracts to set aside for small businesses, the SBA does supply procurement assistance and an appeals process for small business owners who have been denied a federal contract. In addition, SBA manages the controversial "8a program," which grants federal contracts to firms owned by socially and economically disadvantaged individuals.

The agency is best known for its loan programs. Under the guaranteed loan program, SBA provides a 90 percent guarantee on bank loans to the owners of qualifying small firms. Less credit-worthy small businesses can apply for a loan directly from the SBA.

The agency also licenses and offers financial assistance to Small Business Investment Companies (SBICs), which make venture commitments in small firms by supplying equity capital and extending unsecured loans. SBA also licenses a special SBIC to help socially or economically disadvantaged entrepreneurs, commonly known as MESBIC or Minority Enterprise SBIC.

During 1982, SBA has a staff of more than 4,500, a $569 million budget, and 65 district offices.

BACKGROUND

Jim Sanders has never been a professional advocate for small business. He probably never dreamed he would be. Indeed, his initial appointment to the SBA, in 1981 as associate administrator for management assistance, was the product of the President's patronage network, not any inordinate desire to help the small business community.

"I just went through presidential personnel," Sanders told us. "They sifted from agency to agency looking for a spot for me, and they finally decided this was the place."

Neither is he experienced in the pugilism of Washington politics. His career has been as an insurance broker in San Jose, California.

But close observers say that because of Sanders's business experience, his administrative ability, and—perhaps just as importantly—one of his personal connections, Sanders will be able to put back the pieces left by his predecessor, Michael Cardenas, who was fired after less than a year on the job.

Sanders's promotion to administrator is viewed favorably by both Democrats and Republicans, and by small business groups. Observers say he has the potential to be the Administration's saving grace with the small business community, which was short-changed not only by many of Reagan's economic policies but also by the performance of his first choice for SBA administrator, Michael Cardenas. Cardenas, who came into office declaring that he would be the chief government advocate for small business, succeeded in alienating small business groups with public statements sympathetic to big business, and the SBA staff with his iron-grip management style. "No tears were shed when he left," said Tom Gray of the SBA's Office of Advocacy. "He was a man in over his head, the more he did to tighten control over the agency the less he was able to control."

Though Cardenas was the highest-ranking Hispanic in the Administration, Hispanic groups didn't think much of him either. "His image was of blatant insensitivity, arrogance, and total disregard for the concern of minority small businessmen," Arnoldo Torres of the League of United Latin Citizens told the *San Jose Mercury*.

However, the final straw was an internal investigation of Cardenas over charges of conflict-of-interest in SBA contracting.

Sanders may not have much experience as a small business advocate, but at least he has an easy act to follow.

After working as an insurance broker with Aetna Life and Casualty Company in San Francisco during the 1950s, Sanders co-founded an insurance partnership, Sanders and Sullivan, in San Jose, California. He and his partner built the company from the ground up —according to his resume it became one of the top 100 privately owned brokers in the country—and in 1979 merged with the sixth largest broker in the country—Corroon and Black. "It took me 13 years to do that," Sanders told us, "so I guess that qualifies me" as a man familiar with small business problems.

After the merger Sanders gained a lucrative position as chairman and chief executive officer of the resulting subsidiary. Because of his experience managing a large organization Sanders is expected to be a more successful day-to-day administrator than Cardenas, who, coming from a small accounting firm, attempted to maintain personal control over the entire operation. Sanders knows how to delegate, according to those who have worked with him.

Sanders's other asset is his close friendship with top White House aide Michael Deaver. Though that does not guarantee Sanders will have access to the White House, as Alan Chvotkin, minority chief counsel to the Senate Select Committee on Small Business, noted: "More important in this town is the perception of access." Cardenas had no such connections.

Sanders dabbled in politics during his business career in California. He ran unsuccessfully for the Republican nomination to a state assembly seat in 1962. He has served as finance chairman for the Santa Clara County Republican Party and as a member of the State Republican Central Committee.

He served as a Saratoga city councilman from 1968 to 1971, where he says he helped develop the town's parks, purchasing land out of current income rather than financing them through bonds.

Sanders appears to still be formulating his views on small business assistance and he is reluctant to talk about specifics. Even his confirmation hearing in March, 1982, focused only on generalities. But he is a conservative Republican who can be expected to, as he put it, "help the Reagan Administration translate its philosophy to the small business arena." That will probably mean more emphasis on management assistance, primarily through volunteer programs, and less on costly loan programs. "There is no question that right now, in February, 1982, the high cost of money is the biggest problem facing small businesses," Sanders told us. However, he added, the reason most businesses fail is not capital or the availability of it, "but the lack of management understanding—how much capital is required, how to do a marketing study—all those little techniques of marketing, personnel, etc. that are involved in the making of decisions in small businesses." Before his confirmation, Sanders told the U.S. Chamber of Commerce's Small Business Council: "We will be using the private sector more and more in management assistance to help small business owners run their businesses effectively."

Born November 7, 1926 in Kansas City, Missouri, Sanders studied economics at Stanford University's graduate school between 1948 and 1949 and received a B.S. in civil engineering from the University of Kansas in 1948. He is married with seven children.

MAJOR ISSUES

- Without dissent from SBA officials, the Administration succeeded in implementing an economic program that is geared toward large corporations and will seriously erode the economic position of the small business community.

- In a period when small businesses are finding it harder and more expensive to obtain private credit, the Administration is slashing the SBA's loan programs, considered a vital safety net to the small business community.

- The Administration has been reluctant to support expansion of the small business set-aside program, traditionally a tool used to give small firms a fighting chance in the federal contracting system.

Despite Administration promises to restore the health of the small business community, and Ronald Reagan's amazing ability to portray himself as champion of the independent entrepreneur, it is widely agreed that the nation's 12 million small businesses have been dropped from the White House agenda—if, indeed, they were ever there. "Small business suffers from a perceived lack of political clout, from Reagan Administration disinterest in distinguishing between small business and big business and from a lack of coordinated lobbying," concluded the conservative American Political Research Corporation in 1981.

During its first year the Administration implemented a tax plan that provided huge tax breaks to large corporations, encouraged a more concentrated economy through its weakened antitrust policies, supported a monetary policy that has led to bankruptcy for thousands of small companies, and drastically cut the SBA's loan programs—all without dissent from Cardenas, the SBA's first administrator, who was by his own assertion the small business community's chief government advocate.

While the Administration was pushing through its accelerated depreciation tax break, which conferred nearly 80 percent of its benefits to the largest 1,700 companies, Cardenas told the National Small Business Association: "Big business will be getting more under the Administration's tax plan, but they are risking bigger bucks."

During last minute bargaining on the $750 billion tax break, the Administration finally agreed to $5.8 billion in small business tax breaks through 1986—drafted by the Democratic-controlled House—to be divvied up between millions of enterprises. At the same time it accepted twice that, $11 billion, for a handful of oil companies already flush with cash and profits.

But most detrimental to small business has been the Reagan Administration's support of a tight money supply, which resulted in record high interest rates and a leap in the number of business bankruptcies during 1981. High and fluctuating interest rates are particularly detrimental to small firms that are more dependent on short-term debt and require more frequent financing than large corporations.

For small business, interest rates have choked off opportunity. Small companies in the last quarter of 1981 reported the largest decline in employment since 1974. A survey by the National Federation of Independent Businesses showed an employment decline of 0.76 employees per firm during that quarter. More than 80 percent of the new jobs created between 1969 and 1976 were generated by firms with less than 100 employees.

Having locked small businesses out of the private capital market through its tight monetary policies, the Reagan Administration then began closing the public credit window through its tight budgetary policies. SBA's credit assistance programs were cut 32 percent in fiscal year 1982. More drastic cuts are slated for 1983.

The Administration's intention to cut back on SBA lending was revealed as early as November, 1980 when a Reagan transition small business issues task force concluded that the Administration's small business policy "should *not* consist of more small business subsidies and loan programs. . .If anything your Administration should work to remove small business advantages of this kind." Said Cardenas: "Giving away money is not the answer" to small businesses' problems. Like Cardenas, Sanders maintains that the bulk of small businesses fail because of mismanagement.

SBA's budget reflects that view. Management assistance programs received a boost in funding, from $20 million in 1981 to $28 million in 1982, while loan programs continue to be slashed. Direct loans, for example, were cut from $609 million in 1981 to $326 million in 1982, and the Administration wants to cut the program to $143.7 million in 1983. Similarly, the agency's guaranteed loans were cut from $3 billion in 1981 to $2.7 billion in 1982, and to $2.4 billion in 1983 if the Administration budget is passed. It is interesting to note that while the Administration slashed the small business loan program, which serves thousands of small companies, it *increased* the Export-Import Bank guaranteed loan program from $7.4 billion to $8 billion. The Ex-Im loan program primarily serves a handful of large corporations, including Lockheed, Westinghouse, Boeing, McDonnell-Douglas, and Fluor Corp.

The SBA's loans—particularly guaranteed loans—have been a lifeline for thousands of small business owners and individuals wanting to start a small business who have been squeezed out of the private capital market by tight money policies and an increasingly concentrated economy. "A lot of people I know would not have gotten started without SBA guaranteed loans," said Randy Martin of the Mid-Continent Independent Small Business Association. "The SBA should be expanding that program, not cutting it."

In another attempt to cut SBA's outlays, the OMB authorized only $40 million in guaranteed loans to help small firms buy pollution control equipment, while Congress had authorized $250 million.

"I don't know whether there is any point in having an SBA if they are not concerned about small business over there," Rep. Berkley Bedell (D-Iowa), member of the House Small Business Committee, told an SBA official after OMB's decision. "Administration policy is to let big business sell [transfer] their loss to other big business, with a $27 billion loss to the Treasury," he said referring to a provision in the Reagan tax package that has enabled profitable companies to escape, or drastically reduce, their federal income taxes. "But [the Administration] is unwilling to do something to help small business—even though you admit the [pollution control] program doesn't cost the government anything."

According to a number of congressional investigations, both the direct and guaranteed loan programs have a relatively high default rate, so the Administration is operating in a sympathetic atmosphere. The General Accounting Office blames the problem on mismanagement. Other SBA programs are similarly wrought with problems, including fraud. But many congressional experts say the answer is improved management, not across-the-board cuts.

Cardenas entered his office proclaiming his major goal as reducing waste and fraud in SBA programs. Ironically, he and several of his appointees came under investigation for possible conflict of interest in the awarding of SBA contracts. Officially Cardenas was cleared by the internal investigation. But his later firing raised many eyebrows.

SBA's 8a program, which sets aside government contracts for socially and economically disadvantaged small business owners, was the principal target of Cardenas's cleanup campaign. Critics charge, with justification, that most of the 2,130 businesses in the program have become addicted to government contracts and rarely "graduate" into the private sector, thereby preventing new firms from entering. The SBA is reviewing the largest 40 firms in the program to see if they should be ejected.

In the area of procurement, SBA officials have said they oppose small business set-asides, traditionally a tool used to give small firms a fighting chance in the government contract system. Small firms account for only 23 percent of the federal government's goods and services contracts, and 3.5 percent of research and development contracts. Frank Swain, head of the agency's Office of Advocacy, told Congress in September, 1981: "I am philosophically very opposed to set-asides."

And while Reagan has boasted of his support of a bill in Congress that would require all major federal science and research agencies to devote at least 1 percent of their research and development money to small businesses, testimony by SBA officials tells a different story. During a July, 1981 hearing before a House subcommittee, SBA's deputy administrator, Donald Templeman, said of the Small Business Innovation Research Act: "While strongly supporting an expanded Small Business Innovation Research Program, the Administration objects to the' mandatory 1 percent set-aside. We feel that the rigid application of a fixed set-aside does not provide sufficient flexibility."

After taking office, Cardenas sent a chill through SBA's Office of Advocacy, traditionally an aggressive, autonomous office set up to report to Congress rather than the President. In April, 1981 Cardenas issued a memorandum to all employees forbidding them to "speak with members of Congress or their staff, give congressional testimony, speak to organizations or groups, or write articles for publication concerning the official business of the SBA without first clearing it with this office."

The memo ran directly counter to Congress's intentions in establishing the office of advocacy as an independent office within the SBA. Cardenas's policy also runs counter to recommendations made by the White House Conference on Small Business in 1980 (to which Cardenas was a delegate). The conference report recommended that the Office of Advocacy, which has been frequently at odds with Administration line, be expanded and encouraged. In the words of one staff member, Cardenas's action undermined "the independent, aggressive role of the office."

With these kinds of changes in the Small Business Administration and the direction of the Reagan Administration's economic policies, there are growing signs of dissatisfaction within the small business community, which once made up the heart of Ronald Reagan's support. A survey by the Chicago-based Heller Institute for Small Business indicated that small business owners gave Reagan little more than a "C" on his economic policies: While 59 percent of small business owners surveyed during the summer of 1981 felt that Reagan's policies were supportive of small business, only 47 percent felt that way by the beginning of 1982.

Said a legislative aide of the House Small Business Committee: "The cuts proposed by the SBA, and the muzzling of the Office of Advocacy will cause a dramatic restriction for the voice and capital available to small business. This will inevitably reduce any opportunity for economic diversity."

FINANCIAL BACKGROUND

James Sanders is not a typical small businessman. In fact his holdings indicate that he is well into the millionaire category. His net worth is at least $2 million, according to his financial disclosure statement.

Sanders has investments worth more than $250,000 in his former firm, Corroon and Black; over $250,000 in an E.F. Hutton Muni Bond Fund; over $250,000 in Bank of America; and over $250,000 U.S. Treasury Bills. Other investments in a trust include AT&T, M.L. Corp., Standard Oil of California, F.S. James, Goodyear Tire Co., Allegheny Power, FMC Corp., Safeway Stores, Western Airlines, and Cities Service.

Between January and August, 1981, at which time he was appointed to the SBA as associate administrator for management assistance, Sanders received a bonus and salary from Corroon and Black of $63,500.

WHAT OTHERS ARE SAYING ABOUT HIM

- Sanders has received favorable reviews from a wide range of small business experts. Said one former high SBA official, and a regular critic of Reagan's policies: "I haven't heard a bad word about him."

- Said Tom Gray, of SBA's Office of Advocacy: "Sanders seems to be one of those people who understands the use of power without being power hungry, which is rare around here."

- Sanders is likely to escape criticism of his leadership style that so pervaded Cardenas's tenure. "He has already managed an organization similar in size to the SBA," noted Alan Chvotkin of the Senate Select Committee on Small Business. But in an Administration that vigorously tailors its economic policies to the interests of large corporations, observers also note that Sanders's reputation could still turn sour, just as Cardenas's did.

FEDERAL HOME LOAN BANK BOARD

RICHARD PRATT
CHAIRMAN

RESPONSIBILITY OF OFFICE

Established in 1932, the FHLBB is an independent, three-member board that "supervises and regulates savings and loan associations." It operates the Federal Savings and Loan Insurance Corporation (FSLIC), which pays depositors when institutions fail, and has a $6 billion pool of credit. It also runs the Federal Home Loan Bank System, which "like the Federal Reserve System for banks, provides reserve credit."

Pratt is joined on the board by Republican Andrew DiPrete, and Jamie Jackson, a nominal Democrat who actively supported Reagan's 1976 and 1980 campaigns. Jackson, nominated by Reagan, was formerly executive vice-president of Fidelity Savings and Loan Association of Port Arthur, Texas.

The board operated with a budget of $38 million and 1,463 employees in 1982.

BACKGROUND

If Pratt looks more like a wrestler than a regulator, that's understandable. Tall, husky, bull-necked, Pratt was a starting tackle on the football team at the University of Utah and the heavyweight wrestling champion of New Zealand, where he served a mission for the Mormon Church in the late 1950s. He does not look like someone you might want to argue with outside of a hearing room.

Inside a hearing room he can be formidable too. Congressional staff we spoke with were impressed with Pratt's grasp of the complex issues surrounding banking deregulation—though not necessarily his views on them.

Pratt picked up that understanding over a near 20-year career in the field. A Ph.D. in business administration, Pratt has lectured on, worked for, and consulted to the financial industry. From 1967-69, he was chief economist for the U.S. Savings and Loan League, one of the major trade associations for the industry he now regulates. Since then, he has taught at the University of Utah, and consulted for financial institutions, trade organizations, the State Department and the FHLBB itself. His studies for the State Department have analyzed such issues as: "Alternative Mortgage Instruments in Developing Countries" and "Housing Finance in the Republic of Korea." From 1970-78, he served on the Federal Home Loan Bank of Seattle.

Pratt's view on most of the controversial issues he must address are fairly clear. A strong believer in "deregulating" financial institutions, he told reporters at the time of his nomination: "We've got to work on the long-run problems of assuring a healthy set of mortgage lending institutions which can compete in a financially deregulated world." He makes no bones about being an advocate for the thrift industry. And like many Reagan Administration appointees, he argues that marketplace safeguards built into federal law actually hurt consumers.

With that perspective, Pratt, like other Reagan regulators, can be expected to stress "economic efficiency" rather than government action to more reasonably balance the power of buyers and sellers in the marketplace. Besides stripping consumer safeguards, the cost of that approach is generally increased economic concentration, a trend that "deregulation" is sure to bring. "I think there will be substantial consolidation in the financial markets regardless of what interest rates do," Pratt told us. "Markets are simply changing, the technology has changed and the monopoly profits which regulators used to grant financial institutions by giving them very restrictive territories have been disappearing to a substantial extent."

Born on February 5, 1937 in Murray, Utah, Pratt received his undergraduate and graduate degrees from the University of Utah in 1961 and 1962, and his doctorate from Indiana University three years later.

It was at Indiana, Pratt said, that he picked up his interest in banking. "I thought the problems of the urban economy and so on were fascinating. I worked closely with some professors there that were closely involved [with those issues] and I guess that was the beginning," he said. "Through my contacts in graduate school I had an invitation to join the trade association as an economist. I found that to be a very interesting experience and I followed the industry very closely ever since."

Pratt would not commit himself for staying through his full term. "That's an issue I will have to face," he said. "Right now this is a very busy agency, a typical day ends eight or nine at night and one does that for a certain amount of time, but. . ." Charged with overseeing one of the most devastated quarters of the economy, Pratt's job bears a resemblance to that of an Army surgeon choosing which of the dying he can hope to help. "These are. . .times of crisis and times of trouble and pain for a lot of people in a lot of circumstances," he told us. "But I think that the regulator, like anyone else, takes his best shots. "But I think that the regulator, like anyone else, takes his best shots. I think that I am here because somebody thought I had the judgment to do it. I use my own judgment and do the job as well as I can and will stay as long as I think I am useful.''

A lifelong resident of Utah, Pratt was championed for the bank board post by Senator Jake Garn (R-Utah), chair of the Senate Banking Committee. Pratt was nominated only after the Administration's first choice, California attorney William McKenna, was unable to accept the post for health reasons. Pratt is married with four children.

MAJOR ISSUES

- Pratt has been a key soldier in the Administration's drive to deregulate financial institutions. He backs a broad expansion of the powers of S&Ls, changes that critics say will do little to improve their precarious financial state, will divert funds from the already depressed mortgage market, and will generate a host of conflicts-of-interest and anti-competitive practices as S&Ls move into nonbanking activities, such as real estate, investment and insurance underwriting.

- Pratt is seeking through the deregulation legislation to override state usury ceilings and prohibitions against due on sale clauses.

- Pratt pushed through board approval of unrestricted adjustable rate mortgages, which allow mortgage rates to rise with interest rates and expose borrowers to the risks of substantially increased monthly bills.

- At the same time, though, he has fought to keep down the interest rates paid on savings accounts, claiming that the S&L industry's current losses prevent S&Ls from paying higher rates.

Pratt is a man with a vision. "What I would see evolving are two types of financial institutions which compete fairly broadly for the consumer savers but have different orientations in their lending,'' he has said. "One set primarily related to real estate and home ownership, acting as a full-service financial center for the homeowners, but with commercial powers—the other primarily oriented toward the traditional activities of commercial banking.''

Pratt is also a man with a problem. Record high interest rates are scourging the industry he regulates by forcing up their cost of acquiring money while their assets are tied up in long-term, low-yielding mortgages. Pratt estimated last summer that 80 percent of all savings and loans are losing money; they continue to suffer record declines in deposits. For 1981, net new deposits for all S&Ls declined $25.5 billion. Ten percent of the nation's S&Ls were on the board's list of seriously troubled institutions when the agency decided to stop maintaining the list in July. All-savers certificates, designed to infuse the S&Ls with new funds, have not generated as much money as anticipated. In all, the nation's 4,000 S&Ls lost $5 billion in 1981. "The thrift industry is at present in its worst state since World War II,'' Pratt has said.

Pratt sees the fulfillment of his vision as the solution to his problem. He has hammered out and gathered Administration support for a financial deregulation bill that would allow S&Ls to move out of the housing finance field that has been their historic responsibility. Under Pratt's bill, S&Ls would be allowed for the first time to offer commercial loans, could make consumer loans and commercial real estate loans without limit, and become involved in commercial leasing. When the bill stalled, Pratt in February, 1982 proposed regulatory changes that would give these new powers and the authority to offer money market funds to S&L service corporations.

Pratt rejected suggestions that the rule changes constituted an end run around Congress, which has not moved on the legislation. "I think it coincides with the legislation and dovetails with it very nicely," he told us. "The legislation on the Hill deals with quite a different matter in the sense that it asks for the authority in the financial institution itself whereas this [would cover]. . .the subsidiary corporation."

Pratt acknowledges that the proposals are "certainly no panacea. . .and no major answer to the industry's problems." But he said "it would be a substantial help in the sense that it gives a broader range of activities to the institution in the financial services area in which to make a profit. . .To the extent that these offer an opportunity for a successful business venture that makes the owning or controlling of the savings and loan more attractive and therefore would encourage investment in these institutions. One of the critical issues today is to get American investors interested in housing/finance institutions in this country, which they are not interested in."

But many believe Pratt is using the crisis atmosphere to push through changes that may be ill-advised and will almost certainly do little for the S&Ls' immediate problems.

Said John Wood, president of the National Association of Realtors:

> The solutions proposed by the Administration, the Federal Home Loan Bank Board, and [the Senate Banking] Committee, will not be responsive to a public desperately in need of understandable solutions which explain why they cannot afford even the most basic shelter. . .Succinctly stated, proposals to dismantle the few remaining elements of this nation's housing financial delivery system, with no assurance that the private sector will be able or even willing to meet this challenge, leaves only the hope that a recovering economy will produce the solution. . .

Rep. Byron Dorgan (D-N.D.), a former state tax commissioner, said the "present problems that face the savings and loan industry have been created by the tight money policy of the Federal Reserve Board, yet will allow the dramatic changes in financial institutions to take place much more quickly than otherwise would be possible."

(During our interview, Pratt acknowledged that, "Of course the best and the foremost solution is a decrease in interest rates and stabilization in the rate of inflation." Asked if the Administration's proposed deficits stretching out into the future will hurt the S&L industry, Pratt replied tersely: "I think [the deficits] exacerbate the interest rate situation.")

Originally, in spring, 1981 Pratt and other banking industry regulators proposed an emergency relief bill that would have given them more authority to inject capital into troubled institutions, and would have expanded the FSLIC's line of credit at the Treasury from $750 million to $3 billion. Treasury opposed that latter provision, and it was omitted from emergency legislation passed by the House the following October. Senate Banking Committee Chairman Jake Garn (R-Utah), however, has refused to separate consideration of the relief provisions from his overall banking deregulation legislation. That has tied any efforts to assist the strug-gling S&Ls to the far larger, and infinitely more complex question of assessing the future structure of the financial industry.

Wood's industry, of course, is acutely sensitive to one of the main implications of the Administration's proposal: that S&Ls could provide less money for mortgages than previously. "It could really affect the supply of mortgage money by diverting funds to commercial lending," said one Washington attorney active in banking issues.

Bankers, who are resisting the expansion of S&Ls into their lines of business, argue that the new powers may actually hurt the thrifts' immediate financial posi-tion. "To utilize many of the additional powers. . .specialized thrifts would have to enter entirely new markets in which they currently have no experience," said Llewellyn Jenkins, president of the American Bankers Association. "The com-petitive nature of the markets which specialized thrifts would be allowed to enter, and their lack of expertise in these markets will initially incur substantial losses."

That concern, Pratt argues, is "a little bit like someone counselling a person against receiving a $20 million inheritance from their aunt, because it may cause their moral character to degenerate somewhat."

That fundamental question aside, the bill is loaded down with other goodies for the S&L industry. The bill seeks to preempt for federally chartered institutions state laws that prohibit the use of due on sale clauses which allow lenders to increase rates on existing mortgages when a house is sold. Fourteen states restrict or bar the use of such clauses, according to the Mortgage Bankers Association of America. The bill would also preempt state usury laws. Overriding the usury laws troubles other federal banking regulators, such as Fed Chairman Paul Volcker, who see the move as an infringement on the rights of the states.

In an Administration that regularly calls for a "New Federalism," such a pro-posal is an obvious contradiction. "It's been an issue I think which has caused a lot of soul searching throughout the Administration and I guess the issue is: Are there some items that really totally transcend state boundaries?. . . I guess the precedent in the other area would be interstate commerce and I suppose I would come to the conclusion that if anything is fungible and if there is a national market in any stan-dard commodity it has to be money and regulations which are designed to better thy neighbor or to prohibit consumers from obtaining loans by making credit unavailable or stop the flow of capital between political jurisdictions for the most part are not in the public interest, even in a federalized situation," Pratt said.

The FHLBB has already approved five interstate mergers involving S&Ls. Troubled state S&Ls can easily be converted to federal S&Ls for interstate merger—so there is no current limitation on interstate banking by S&Ls.

So the FHLBB has opened the door to interstate banking—a change Pratt sup-ports, but has said is a decision that should be made by Congress. But, as one S&L economist told the *Wall Street Journal*, "What they have in mind is the auctioning of market entry rights. It will be the only way institutions that want new out-of-state markets can get them. They'll say to Citibank that you can enter this market"—at the price of acquiring a weak S&L.

But the mergers are obviously contracting the S&L industry. The entire Illinois congressional delegation wrote Pratt in March, 1982 to protest the merger of rural S&Ls into larger urban banks. Instead, they said, mergers should "preserve the character of the thrift institution and its distinct role in the community."

That trend toward accelerating merger activity is not welcomed by many segments of the S&L industry. "He has been fairly committed to the notion that the board shouldn't be bailing out poorly managed S&Ls," said an aide at the House government operations subcommittee that oversees the FHLBB. "He has basically screwed the hell out of the managers of the failed institutions by forcing their mergers."

On regulatory matters, though, Pratt has carefully followed the industry line. In April, 1981, the FHLBB allowed S&Ls to tie mortgage rates to market interest rates—so-called "adjustable rate mortgages." Even if the S&Ls need some form of adjustable rate mortgages to meet their funding needs, consumer groups and some congressional leaders argue, the package approved by the FHLBB goes out of its way to strip protection from borrowers. "The direction of change," said Rep. Benjamin Rosenthal (D-N.Y.), chairman of the House subcommittee on monetary affairs, "has been solely toward meeting the needs of the lending institutions."

Specifically, Rosenthal, the Federal Trade Commission's Bureau of Consumer Protection, and numerous consumer organizations criticized the FHLBB for failing to place any upper limit on the heights to which S&Ls can raise mortgage rates. "As a consequence, purchasing a home with an adjustable mortgage, given the present regulations, inevitably involves a gamble that the family's income will rise fast whenever interest rates rise fast, or else that interest rates will never rise fast," said Rosenthal. "Obviously, neither is a good gamble. . ."

"These regulations shift all the risks onto the borrower," said Allen Fishbein of the Center for Community Change, who is leading a coalition of union, community and church groups opposing the regulations. "We think the risks should be more equitably apportioned." In addition to capping the monthly increases, Fishbein believes the FHLBB should require S&Ls to use a standard economic index for computing changes in the rate; the current regulations allow them to use any formula they wish.

Payment increase restrictions, Rosenthal noted, were supported not only by consumer groups but "by both major savings and loan trade organizations as well as by a majority of the several hundred individual savings and loan[s]" that commented on the plan. Rosenthal and consumer groups also criticized the proposal for failing to insure that borrowers receive adequate information about the liability they could face. As the *Wall Street Journal* recently observed: "The message for mortgage borrowers is: Shop around, and watch out."

Pratt rejects the criticism that the FHLBB should have put more restrictions on the adjustable rate mortgage. "I don't think" the lack of restrictions has hurt the market, he told us. "In fact, I would think that it has probably done the opposite. With the deregulation, institutions are working very hard to try and find an instrument which both allows them a reasonable profit and [provides] something acceptable to the consumer. I don't think the wisdom exists in government agencies" to decide which instruments to offer.

Nonetheless, Pratt told us, he "wouldn't be surprised if some standardization occurs through the actions of the market itself." But he has no preference for the standard. "I have some guesses. I think fixed-rate mortgages are going to remain very popular. I think the consumer doesn't really like the interest rate risk, and as long as you pay a fairly good premium to avoid that [these mortgages will remain popular]," he said. Pratt predicted that one alternative "pioneered" by Merrill Lynch may prove "a fairly popular alternative." This "is a variable payment," he said. "However, the additional payment goes to pay off the principal rather than to a higher interest rate."

The adjustable rate mortgages may increase the number of foreclosures, Pratt conceded. "I think the lender obviously wants to and should make credit available to as wide a group as possible. That would argue for being liberal in the underwriting aspect. The other side of that issue is that the more liberal one is in the underwriting, of course, the more foreclosures one will have because you will obviously occasionally pick up someone that was too risky. . . . The public has to realize that some foreclosures will occur and that they are appropriate and that they are in the public interest because they result from a lender trying to serve a broader category of borrowers," he said.

At the same time Pratt has supported increasing the interest rates paid to S&Ls, Pratt has resolutely opposed increases in the rates paid by them. He led the opposition on the Depository Institutions Deregulation Committee to raising the rates paid to passbook savers, and convinced Treasury Secretary Regan to reverse his support, thereby scuttling the proposal. He was the only member of the five-person committee to vote against the lifting of interest ceilings on Individual Retirement Accounts begun after January 1 of 1981. (See Donald Regan profile.)

"[W]e believe that the safety and soundness of all depository institutions requires that the pace of deregulation be carefully metered," Pratt said.

To enhance his ability to "meter"—read "slow"—the pace of interest rate deregulation, Pratt has proposed restructuring the committee, so that it consists solely of the FHLBB chairman, the Treasury secretary and the Fed chairman, eliminating the chairmen of the FDIC and the National Credit Union Administration. "I can't see that he'll push that idea hard," said the House aide. "As long as it's him and Regan and Volcker, he'd still lose."

Pratt also envisions consolidation of the financial regulatory bodies. "There might be some standardization that could be achieved and to a substantial extent I think that it is a public policy question of whether Congress would like to see some special orientation, let's say, remain with the thrifts. If they are inclined in that direction, then probably keeping separate regulatory agencies makes some sense. Ultimately they would like to totally homogenize all financial institutions [so] then there could probably be some substantial regulatory reform. I would think that might take the form of taking bank regulations out of the Federal Reserve, leaving it as a monetary control and economic entity. Having a single charterer and regulator of financial institutions and having a single insurer of financial institutions. I would see that as probably several years down the road but maybe it's a structure that makes some sense," he told us. But Pratt is in no hurry: "If it were to happen now, the thrifts would very quickly become second class citizens in that regulatory structure."

Pratt's resistance to interest rate deregulation, of course, directly contradicts his arguments for the free market on the lending side. Some speculate that he is swallowing his reservations and backing the industry on interest rates—an issue which they see as crucial to their immediate problems —in return for support on his own agenda, broad-scale deregulation.

Pratt has already displayed a clear willingness to deal with the Administration for its support. When he entered office in April, 1981 Pratt backed the S&L industry's assertion that the government should place restrictions, such as reserve requirements, on money markets. After negotiating with Regan—whose former firm,

Merrill Lynch, runs the nation's largest money market fund—for support on his legislation, Pratt came around to Treasury's view that "placing regulatory restrictions on them probably wouldn't be in the public interest," as he told the Senate Banking Committee in October of that year.

Nor, needless to say, would an attempt to erect such restrictions be in the interest of his deregulation bill.

During our interview, Pratt touched on a number of other subjects of interest to savers. Among them:

o He favors increased disclosure of compensation granted to S&L officials. "I think in general disclosure is a positive thing and that it serves to minimize abuse."

o He does not favor disclosure of the amount of federal assistance granted to facilitate S&L mergers. "The number of problems that the FSLIC is facing and has to deal with involves a continual round of negotiations and these negotiations can often make a difference of hundreds of millions of dollars in the use of the public's funds. We believe that our abilities to negotiate the best transactions in the public interest are served by not providing everyone full information about the last deal that we did. We simply would get whip-sawed in those negotiations." In all, the FSLIC spent just under $1 billion on mergers in 1981.

o If Congress does approve direct aid to troubled thrifts it should "be assistance which doesn't reward inefficiency and which keeps the institutions interested in and effectively trying to compete with one another in offering services to the public and that it maintains competition and efficiency. We would prefer to see that over something that takes institutions which are failing regardless of circumstances and just provide them money."

FINANCIAL BACKGROUND

Most of Pratt's contact with the S&L industry came through his work in two consulting firms, Richart T. Pratt, Assoc. (RTP), which he chaired, and JPS Financial Consultants of which he was a partner. From those two firms, Pratt said, he "provided consulting services to savings and loan associations, federal agencies, commercial banks, public utility companies, and numerous non-financial businesses." Pratt received between $15,000 and $50,000 in dividends from the RTP firm last year, and has divested himself of his interest since taking office. He earned another $37,000 from the University of Utah and a total of $4,800 from the Home Savings and Loan Association and Western Mortgage Loan Company for sitting on their boards. In all, Pratt lists assets worth at least $465,000.

Pratt has said he intends to return to the University of Utah after leaving the board.

WHAT OTHERS ARE SAYING ABOUT HIM

- Said one House aide who has met with Pratt: "I would say that in the usual, traditional sense of being in the industry's pocket, he is much less so than recent chairmen. He arrives at his positions from an intellectual conviction rather than loyalty to industry."

- The industry, nonetheless, could not be much happier. William B. O'Connell, President of the United States League of Savings Associations, called Pratt "an exceptional chairman, an exceptional chairman." Smaller S&Ls, which may well be harmed by the deregulation Pratt seeks, are somewhat less glowing in their assessments, but have so far not publicly broken ranks with the industry leaders.

EXPORT-IMPORT BANK

WILLIAM DRAPER
PRESIDENT AND CHAIRMAN

RESPONSIBILITY OF OFFICE

Established as an independent agency in 1934 to assist in "financing exports of U.S. goods and services," the Export-Import Bank does a hefty enough business, supporting exports valued at over $18 billion last year.

In 1982, the agency operated with 351 employees and $4.4 billion in direct loan authority.

BACKGROUND

At 54 Draper had compiled a list of business ventures that rivaled the likes of Jay Gould. His financial disclosure report lists no less than 72 sources of income and property—14 of these sources are given as "over $250,000."

Draper's most successful enterprise has been Sutter Hill Ventures, a multi-million dollar operation begun in 1965 which "organizes and finances companies which show promise for rapid growth." As founder and senior partner in the Palo Alto, California firm, Draper spent 16 years overseeing Sutter Hill's investing in technology intensive forays. Sutter Hill has financed such companies as Qume (acquired by ITT) and Xidex (now publicly owned).

Draper was graduated from Yale in 1950 and received his M.B.A., cum laude, from the Harvard Business School in 1954. After a five-year stint as a salesman with Inland Steel Co., Draper gleaned nuts and bolts business training with his father's investment banking firm of Draper, Gaither and Anderson. In 1962, Draper founded his own small business investment concern, Draper and Johnson Investment Co., a move which foreshadowed the formation of Sutter Hill in 1965.

Draper has been involved in several professional organizations, including positions as director of the National Venture Capital Association and as president of the Western Association of Venture Capitalists. His company directorships are numerous; highlights include the Measurex Corporation, Plantronics, Inc. and Apollo Computer, Inc.

Draper chairs California's Association for American Conservatory Theater in San Francisco. He is also a director of the Draper World Population Fund, founded by his father and dedicated to checking the "rampant population problem."

According to a staff member at Planned Parenthood, the Draper Fund consists largely of "influential people influencing other influential people." In terms of political style they are "very much the old-boy style of network." The Draper Fund is not particularly sympathetic to Ronald Reagan's ideas on family issues. In addition to promoting widespread contraceptive programs— without prescription and for minimal charge—for poor women in third world countries, the fund's Population Crisis Committee supports "making early abortion under safe, medically-supervised conditions widely available." It has also vigorously supported expanding women's political, economic and social rights around the world.

Draper has long been involved in Republican politics—albeit not always successfully. He lost to Rep. Paul N. McCloskey, Jr. in California's 12th Congressional district in 1967. In the 1968 election he enthusiastically supported Richard Nixon. In the 1980 election, Draper donated $15,000 to two Republican funds for support of various candidates in California, according to Federal Election Commission records.

Vice President Bush is Draper's tie-in to Reagan's Washington. Originally co-chairman of the Finance Committee for the Bush for President Campaign, Draper later applied his energies to fundraising for the Reagan-Bush ticket. The two men remain in touch: Draper recalled a recent phone call from Bush who told him, "Gee, you've really aged in Washington". It is unclear whether the trials and tribulations of the beleaguered Ex-Im Bank or the Washington party circuit (Draper considers parties "very important in the business of Washington") have worn Draper thin.

Born in White Plains, New York, on January 1, 1928, William H. Draper III is married with three children. Draper boasts a famous father—General William H. Draper Jr. Described as the general who "emerged after WWII as a crusader for a strong Germany and a revived Japan," General Draper was instrumental in the rebuilding of the German and Japanese economies with the same industrial leaders who supported the dictatorships before and during the war.

MAJOR ISSUES

The Export-Import Bank operates a range of programs aimed at meeting the needs of exporting businesses—from direct loans at lower-than-market rates, to insurance and loan guarantees. These programs attract to American goods foreign buyers who might either buy from other countries that offer export subsidies, or simply could not otherwise afford to buy.

In 1980, two-thirds of all the direct loans offered by the bank went to support seven companies, including Boeing and Westinghouse. Of the 15 largest loans, four went to Boeing: The bank has earned a nickname of "Boeing's Bank." Aircraft loans are far and away the most prevalent type of product loan (over 40 percent of all loans by dollar), followed by loans for nuclear power plants. Commercial aircraft loans outstanding total $8.6 billion; the nuclear industry is the second largest recipient at $5.8 billion.

Facing both high domestic interest rates and heavy export subsidies by other countries, Draper has maintained the bank's major decision is whether to raise its interest rates and remain self-sufficient or to keep down rates in order to be competitive.

Upon confirmation, Draper immediately raised the direct loan interest rates from 8.75 percent to 10.75 percent and initiated a one-time 2 percent fee for each credit authorization. Draper vowed to review every loan application personally to ensure the bank stacked up with foreign competition.

Budget Director Stockman had originally targeted the bank for large cuts in 1981. In criticizing the bank, Stockman maintained it served a small group of corporations and claimed the bank's existence had "not been justified" in terms of attracting foreign buyers. For a few months the proposed cuts were held up as "proof" that the Reagan Administration was practicing a "policy of even-handedness" by cutting subsidies to business as well as to the poor.

Yet, Ex-Im's budget was saved in the legislative branch with scarcely a peep of protest from the executive office—Draper even received a letter of hearty endorsement from the bank's ostensible foe, David Stockman. In March, 1981 the Senate Budget Committee proposed an increase of $250 million in the bank's direct lending authority.

On the House side, the Appropriations Committee recommended $376 million more in direct loans and an additional $500 million in loan guarantee authority for the bank. When the recommendation came to the floor in May, however, an amendment proposed by the Democrats was successful in killing the proposed hikes. The House seemed to have accepted (at least temporarily) the sentiments of Rep. David Obey (D-Wis.) who maintained "there is no reason for us not to ask Boeing, GE and the other privileged characters in our society to share the load."

But overnight Boeing, General Electric and the General Association of Machinists lobbied to reinstate the cuts. The following day, the House conceded to this heavy lobbying, which required over 70 members to change their votes overnight.

Despite this last minute change of heart, the bank remains on very shaky ground. Its survival will no doubt be determined by its ability to stave off operating losses. Many feel the losses are inevitable and Draper may be destined to juggle a program whose days are numbered.

Stockman targeted Ex-Im's direct lending authority again in his 1983 budget, proposing a 13 percent cut from $4.4 billion to $3.8 billion. Though loan guarantee commitments would be allowed to remain steady at $8 billion, the proposed cuts have again mobilized the business community. The nuclear and aircraft industries have founded—and given a $150,000 budget to—a new Coalition for Employment Through Exports, which will press Congress to restore funding to the 1981 level of $5.4 billion. Facing a moribund domestic market, the nuclear industry in particular is dependent on Ex-Im loans for its very survival.

The bank continues to draw heavy criticism for its nuclear power subsidies. The bank is currently negotiating a $1.36 billion loan guarantee package for two nuclear reactors in Taiwan. A staff member of the Center for Development Policy told us "there is no question that nuclear subsidies will be stepped up under this Administration. Nuclear sales are being actively encouraged by the bank and by members of the State Department."

FINANCIAL BACKGROUND

Draper reports assets worth at least $4.55 million. His property and investments include a Texas oil drilling partnership and stakes in a number of high technology firms. In addition to these property holdings, Draper received $223,785 in salary last year—$78,145 from Sutter Hill Ventures and $145,640 from the Hambrecht and Quist Investment Banking firm.

CHAPTER 2

NATURAL RESOURCES

INTERIOR DEPARTMENT

JAMES WATT
SECRETARY

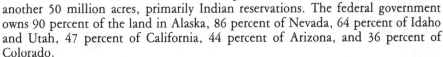

RESPONSIBILITY OF OFFICE

In the East, the Interior Secretary is generally obscure. In the West, though, his name is commonplace, for he administers lands that comprise large portions of their states and controls the federal water which keeps their economies afloat.

The Interior Department administers over 500 million acres of federal land, and holds trust responsibilities for another 50 million acres, primarily Indian reservations. The federal government owns 90 percent of the land in Alaska, 86 percent of Nevada, 64 percent of Idaho and Utah, 47 percent of California, 44 percent of Arizona, and 36 percent of Colorado.

Watt is responsible for administering those lands. As the Government Manual puts it, that responsibility "includes fostering the wisest use of our land and water resources, protecting our fish and wildlife, preserving the environmental and cultural value of our national parks and historical places, and providing for the enjoyment of life through outdoor recreation."

Watt's department includes the Bureau of Land Management, which actually runs those federal lands; the Bureau of Reclamation, which builds water projects to irrigate the arid West; the National Park Service; the U.S. Fish and Wildlife Service, and the Office of Surface Mining.

In title, Watt is responsible for all activities of the department; and indeed almost every major activity of the department during 1981 was identified with Watt by name.

In 1982, the department operated with a budget of $6.2 billion and 52,000 employees. It would pick up another 5,200 employees, along with responsibility for the strategic petroleum reserve and the regional power administrations, if Congress agrees to dismantle the Department of Energy.

BACKGROUND

For James Watt, it was high noon. There he was, the hired gun of the big land owners, come down into the grand ballroom of the Denver Regency Inn on a November morning in 1977 to face off against the feds who had headed West from Washington to lay down the law.

The law in question was the Reclamation Act, which large Western land owners had been profitably evading every since Teddy Roosevelt signed it into law in 1902. Seventy-five years later, Secretary of the Interior Cecil Andrus was whistlestopping through the West to hear what the locals had to say about what was viewed as a truly radical idea: enforcing the law.

Watt was there as president of the Mountain States Legal Foundation (MSLF), a conservative law firm created to combat just those sorts of governmental affronts. Founded in 1976 by the National Legal Center for the Public Interest (which received its primary funding from the right-wing Scaife Foundation and the Fluor Corp.) and conservative brewery magnate Joseph Coors, Mountain States' purpose was to "fight in the courts those bureaucrats and no-growth advocates who create a challenge to individual liberty and economic freedoms."

On the day in question at the Denver Regency Inn, individual liberty and economic freedom were being challenged by a law whose dual, but interconnected, purposes had tantalized and terrified powerful Western interests for three-fourths of a century. The Reclamation Act was not a major political issue in the East, but in the West there were entire squadrons of attorneys immersed in its most dizzying minutiae, and politicians who built their careers around it.

Watt was not one of those, but he understood that water, the control of water, was the root of power in the West, and he was there to tell Andrus that the portion of the law limiting to 160 acres the landholdings of those receiving federally subsidized water was "outdated." But to its original sponsors that was the heart of the 1902 law, which authorized the federal government to build dams and reservoirs to irrigate the arid lands and at the same time to break up the vast landholdings that were already strangling the West. "The purpose, so far as the right to use water is concerned," said the father of the Reclamation Act, Francis G. Newlands, back in 1901, "is to prevent monopoly of lands." That seemed clear enough. But, over the years, deploying generations of steely-eyed lawyers like Watt, the powerful ranchers and farmers had managed to keep their cheap water, and their land.

Though the most litigious, water was not the only issue dividing Washington and those forces promoting development in the West who would later be tagged leaders of the "sagebrush rebellion." Grazing on federal pastures caused similar problems, as did access to energy resources and minerals on public lands. The environmental laws of the 1970s, mandating investment in remedial measures to clean the air and water and restore strip-mined land, created new conflicts between developers, environmentalists and the government.

By the time he joined Mountain States, Watt had been involved in these issues for at least a decade. From 1966 through 1969, he was a lobbyist for the Chamber of Commerce on "mining, public lands, energy, water and environmental pollution," primarily opposing clean air and water legislation. For the next six years, he worked for the Interior Department in a variety of posts, rising to become director of the Bureau of Outdoor Recreation. He spent two years as a commissioner on the Federal Power Commission (FPC), before that agency was folded into Jimmy Carter's Energy Department.

That day in Denver gave a stark demonstration of the forces which propelled Watt from a relatively obscure, contentious Washington bureaucrat to a national symbol. Following the 1976 passage of a law to tighten federal management of public lands, and the Carter Administration's water project "hit list," Andrus's threat to actually enforce the Reclamation Act appeared to many powerful Westerners as the final twist sealing the federal pump that had poured dollars into the desert for more than 100 years.

It was that prospect which prompted the much-publicized sagebrush rebellion, filled the treasuries of organizations like Mountain States, and opened a prominent place in the world for people like James Watt. Much was at stake. The federal government owns 760 million acres of land—primarily in western states and Alaska—which hold substantial portions of the remaining domestic oil, gas and mineral reserves. Federal water projects irrigated almost 12 million acres of western farmland, anually producing crops worth almost $7.5 billion. Efforts by environmentalists and the Carter Administration to change the ground rules governing those resources sent powerful westerners into paroxysms of rage.

When Watt preached the virulent strain of born-again capitalism, oil executives reached for their wallets. "What is the real motive of the extreme environmentalists, who appear determined to accomplish their objectives at whatever cost to society?" Watt once said. "Is it to simply protect the environment? Is it to delay and deny energy development? Is it to weaken America?"

Reflecting those fears, Mountain States' budget quickly grew, from an initial total of $194,000 to $1.3 million in 1981. Anxiously donating large sums to Mountain States and similar organizations were not only conservative ideologues like Coors and Scaife, but scores of energy companies—from Exxon, to Chevron, Gulf, Shell, Amoco and Phillips—to mining and timber giants—like Amax, Boise Cascade, Consolidated Coal and Burlington Northern—with extensive financial interest in the disposition of the resources on federal lands. (See Financial Background section.)

Mountain States and its colleague groups, such as the Pacific Legal Foundation further to the west, pressed the agenda of these firms with urgency. The foundation legally challenged the government's right to restrict grazing on public lands and to withdraw lands from oil and gas exploration as wilderness. It fought the Occupational Safety and Health Administration's right to inspect workplaces for occupational hazards, and the Environmental Protection Agency's (EPA) authority to withhold federal aid to a state that did not institute a required vehicle emission inspection program. It challenged the legality of EPA clean air standards for wilderness and national park areas. It consulted with oil and mining companies concerned about the Forest Service's efforts to increase the amount of wilderness land, and farmers and ranchers terrified by Andrus's threat to dust off the acreage limitations.

Mountain States took on cases not only of broad economic interest to its contributors and supporters, but of more specific concern as well. In one example, MSLF filed an amicus brief in the U.S. Supreme Court on behalf of the Mountain Fuel Supply Company in a case involving the valuation of its assets. Mountain Fuel is a contributor to Mountain States; the chairman of Mountain Fuel sits on the board of Mountain States. The case has almost no conceivable relevance to any "public interest" beyond the financial concerns of Mountain Fuel.

Eventually, the western water interests used the Pacific Legal Foundation to file a lawsuit against Andrus. But during that hearing in Denver, Watt made clear he stood with them in their opposition to the Reclamation Act. At the same time he revealed the philosophy that underpins the sagebrush rebellion.

"While that law may have been practicable when passed," Watt told Andrus, "it was soon understandably ignored by government officials." (One of those officials, presumably, was James Watt, who supervised the Bureau of Reclamation from 1969 through 1972 as a deputy assistant interior secretary.) "Therefore," Watt continued, "those of us who are westerners recognize that the development of our lands has come about because of the consortium of interest of the United States Congress, the Bureau of Reclamation and western water users." (The composition of MSLF reflected that historic triangle. Watt, a former reclamation official, was its chief officer. Wayne Aspinall, the long-time chairman of the House Interior Committee, who protected water projects for decades, sat on its board. And the users provided its funding.)

To Watt, the regulations were more than obsolescent; they were a sinister shade of pink. "[A]lthough the immediate target of these regulations is land under a federal water project," he argued, "the principles which are applied to justify land appropriation can be applied to any private property, for these regulations strike at the very right to private property."

And then, in a single phrase, Watt unconsciously captured the fundamental contradiction of the sagebrush rebellion. Andrus's proposed regulations, Watt continued, "deprive the private individual of the right to acquire and continue to own more *than 160 acres of federally irrigated farm land*." (emphasis added)

To the sagebrush rebels, like Watt, the federal government was impinging on states rights when it sought to manage, or set ground rules for the dispersion of its subsidies. That the subsidies themselves might not be an inalienable right, appears never to have occurred to them. Or as appears more likely, that thought was simply ignored.

Though chafing under federal efforts to manage the subsidies it dispenses—whether access to minerals on public lands or cheap water—the "independent" westerners that Watt celebrates had no desire to see their form of welfare end. In fact, the history of western water politics into which Watt waded on that November day, could be summed in a single word: *more*.

This simple proposition is obscured by noisy declarations of regional pride. "Today," Watt said in 1979 congressional testimony, "we of the West believe that in too many instances our states are being treated like colonies. 'Foreigners'—bureaucrats who seem to be out of control—are making the decisions affecting the land, water and resources which are the foundation of wealth for the West and indeed in many respects, the Nation." With Washington still making those decisions—but in a manner that makes more resources available for development—Watt has declared the rebellion to be defused.

Watt has western roots, though in temperament and experience he is more bureaucrat than cowboy. Watt grew up in the small, isolated eastern Wyoming town of Wheatland. The top student in Wheatland High, he married his high school sweetheart, Leilani Bomgardner. During their senior year they were the king and queen of the prom. Watt sailed through the University of Wyoming graduating in 1960, picked up a law degree there in 1962 (he edited the law review) and then joined the senatorial campaign of former Wyoming Governor Milward Simpson. When Simpson was elected, Watt traded in Wyoming for Washington as a senate aide.

From his father, Watt picked up a conservative viewpoint. Bill Watt, his father, told the *Los Angeles Times* last summer, "I never voted for a winning President until Eisenhower ran. The anger would come out in great bursts of passion after every election. You would see the New Deal, the left wing, taking over. You could see it attracting the teachers in public schools, they were idealists, and they would teach it to the kids. People seemed to want everything handed to them on a platter. Well, I resented that and I guess James picked up his philosophy from me."

After beginning his career as an aide to Simpson, Watt spent three fairly routine years in Washington as a Chamber of Commerce lobbyist, resisting the environmental initiatives that were just beginning to bubble through Congress. In a typical comment on 1967 air quality legislation, Watt argued that pollution limits should be set at the state, not federal, level. "This would allow us," he maintained, "to take advantage of the assimilative capacities of the environment and the other unique characteristics of each locality or region." Watt advocated a similar regime for strip mining.

With a push from the Chamber, Watt joined the Nixon transition. Assigned to coach Walter Hickel, the former Alaska governor whom Nixon had nominated as Interior secretary, Watt successfully shepherded the unsophisticated nominee through the nomination hearings. Hickel then tapped Watt as a $98-a-day consultant. Watt quickly became, as one trade publication put it, "Hickel's eyes and ears on oil, without any formal title."

That relationship prompted a *New York Times* editorial whose tone would be echoed in newspapers across the country 12 years later. Describing Watt as "a former lobbyist for business interests opposed to federal legislation against water pollution and other conservation measures," the *Times* wrote that "public confidence in the concern that Hickel will show for conservation is hardly enhanced by his hiring" Watt.

Watt hung on, though, and in May picked up a title as deputy assistant secretary, overseeing the Bureau of Reclamation and other departments involved in water and power issues. Three years later, he was promoted to head the Bureau of Outdoor Recreation.

In the latter job, Watt reported to Nathaniel Reed, an assistant Interior secretary. Reed found Watt almost impossible to deal with. "He was a very strange, distant, driving, me-first kind of guy, dedicated to succeeding at any cost," Reed told us. "He once told me he wanted to only have a job for one or two years so he could fill his resume."

Eventually, Reed said, "I finally refused to have him in the office." It fell to Reed's deputy, Douglas Wheeler, to be "the buffer between Nat and Jim Watt," as Wheeler put it. Though Reed recalls Watt as "very political, a true believer," Wheeler said "He wasn't as strident as he is now." At the time, Watt was excited by management, particularly about instituting a management by objective system at the bureau. To help design it, Watt hired an old college friend for $60,000 without offering the contracts to competitive bidding. That decision later held up his nomination to the Federal Power Commission (FPC) for almost a year.

To Wheeler, Watt was not an ideologue but an "advocate," who could take the positions expected by his superiors. Wheeler recalls a classic example of Watt's ability to switch sides when necessary. During his final months at the bureau, Watt prepared the department's opposition to the construction of a power dam on West Virginia's New River. (Though the FPC had licensed the dam, Interior hoped to save it with a wild and scenic river classification.) When he joined the FPC in November, 1975, Watt switched sides. "He would protect the river at Interior and dam it at the FPC," Wheeler told us.

Watt was more strident about some things than others. His religious convictions, which became a national issue when he offered a congressional committee an unsolicited prediction on the imminence of the second coming, were already spilling over into his work. Deeply religious, Watt has "a special. . .relationship with Christ," one close friend has said. "He has the gift of speaking in tongues, and there have been times in prayer meetings with James when people have been healed."

At the Bureau of Outdoor Recreation, Watt made his religious feelings well known. Reed remembers "cautioning" Watt after receiving a complaint from a staff member who felt Watt was pressuring him to attend a prayer session. Watt's wife organized prayer meetings for the wives of bureau officials, some of whom apparently felt their attendance would influence their husband's career. "More than one called me and said they were worried they should go," said Matilda Wood, the wife of Roy Wood a special assistant to Watt at the Bureau.

Roy Wood came to Washington as a special assistant in August, 1972, from Atlanta, Georgia, where he had been directing the bureau's regional office. Wood felt certain the move was designed to ease him out of his position, part of a broad Watt effort to consolidate his control over the regional offices. "He [Watt] was disappointed that I had come," Wood said. "He made it clear and I was not comfortable [in the job]." Sometime in January, 1973, Wood recalled, Watt called him into his office to begin easing him out of the special assistant job. After making it apparent he wanted Wood to go, "Watt said 'let's pray about it' and down on our knees we went. . .we prayed on our knees and I could feel that steely knife twisting in my backbone," Wood told us. Watt later called Wood's wife to discuss the situation. "He said he had talked with the Lord and the Lord felt that we should return to Georgia," said Matilda Wood.

Wood left the bureau in February, 1973. "First time I ever met a man in my life I couldn't reason with," Wood said of Watt. "I couldn't reason with him and the Lord both." (Watt, of course, maintains his religious intensity today. When a protester asked him after a February, 1982 speech why he was allowing the oil companies to "rape" America, Watt replied: "Son, you remind me of a bumper sticker I once saw: 'God Loves You and I'm Trying To'.")

With that significant exception, Watt was basically a traditional bureaucrat, working a 40-hour week, peppering his walls with flow charts and angling for advancement. President Ford rewarded Watt in 1975 with an appointment to the FPC. There Watt pushed for the removal of all price controls on natural gas, and succeeded, with his colleagues, in tripling the price ceiling for newly discovered gas.

Reagan offered Watt the Interior secretary job only after Clifford Hansen, a former Republican governor and senator from Wyoming, declined the position, and Sen. Paul Laxalt (R-Nev.) approved of Watt following an interview. Laxalt talked to Joseph Coors, who eagerly signed on, and the two convinced Reagan that Watt was his man.

Born on January 31, 1938 in Lusk, Wyoming, Watt is married with two children.

FINANCIAL BACKGROUND

Watt, an ideologue, is not one of the wealthier members of Reagan's cabinet. He reports no investments worth more than $50,000 and no significant stock holdings of any kind. He earned $73,500 from Mountain States in 1980.

More important in terms of possible conflict are the contributors to Watt's foundation. Though he declined Senate requests at his confirmation hearing to list the contributors, some information is available. Below we print a list of firms included on a 1978 list of contributors of over $500. Parenthetically following some firms is the total donated in 1980, according to information supplied by the companies to a reporter for Jack Anderson.

Amax (about $5,000)
Albuquerque Gravel Products Co.
Asarco Co.
Associated Contractors of Colorado
Boise Cascade Corp. ($7,500)
Boomtown Inc.
Burlington Northern ($4,000)
Bunker Hill Corp.
Chevron U.S.A. Inc. ($5,000)
Climax Molybdenum (an Amax subsidiary)
Consolidated Coal Corp. ($2,000)
Energy Fuels Corp.
Exxon ($5,000)
First National Bank of Arizona
Gulf Resources & Chemical Corp.
Harrah's
Holly Sugar
Idaho Power Co. ($5,000)
Independent Petroleum Corp. of Mountain States
Kemmerer Coal Co. (Gulf, which recently acquired Kemmerer donated $1,000)
Mountain Bell
Occidental Oil Shale
Salt River Project
Sears, Roebuck & Co.
Shell Oil Co. ($1,500)
Sierra Pacific Power Co.
Stauffer Chemical Co.
Teton Exploration Drilling Co.
Tri-State Generation & Trans.
True Oil Co.
Utah Power & Light
Wold Nuclear Co.
Wyoming Machinery Co.
Adolph Coors Foundation ($35,000)
Scaife Family Charitable Trust
Amoco Foundation ($10,000)
Marathon Oil Foundation
John F. Long Foundation

Other recent large contributors include: Arizona Public Service Co., a private utility ($6,000), Phillips Petroleum ($2,500), and Public Service Corp. of Colo. ($8,000 in 1979).

Many of these firms have ongoing relationships with the Department of Interior. In the box on page 125, is an analysis of some of their activities, prepared by the Wilderness Society.

WHAT OTHERS ARE SAYING ABOUT HIM

• Nathanial Reed, Watt's former boss at the Interior Department, said in a 1981 speech that, "My suspicion that vindictiveness may be Watt's guiding principle is supported by the man's attitudes to his opponents. Does he marshal his arguments and try to reason with them? No, he calls them names—'Environment extremists' who would 'weaken America.' What a bankrupt and infantile approach. . .reminiscent of the worst excesses of Watergate, of the McCarthy era. . .Criticism is not treason and the Brezhnev Doctrine has no place at the Department of Interior.''

- California officials involved in the dispute over the four scenic basins hold similar views. ''Watt is vindictive,'' said Deni Greene, director of California's Office of Planning and Research. ''We got the feeling that he wanted to show California.''

- In one of its op-ed page ads, Mobil took out ''A plug for Mr. Watt.'' Concluded Mobil: ''Based on his record, we see Mr. Watt as striving for the production of more domestic energy while providing for a healthy environment. His policy is worthy of support.''

- Cecil Andrus, Watt's predecessor, said that Watt ''ignores the Congress of the United States and the will of the majority of the American people in order to be a developmental zealot of the highest degree. His approach seems to be—if Mobil or Exxon want it, they can have it.''

- Norman Livermore, who ran the California Resources Agency for Reagan and was part of the Administration's environmental transition team task force, told us Watt is ''making it awful difficult in terms of middle ground, which there are on many of these things. . .He's just too strident. He leads with his chin all the time.''

- In all corners of the political world there are angry groups with James Watt horror stories. One of the angriest might be the various natural history associations around the country which produce educational materials sold to national park visitors. The groups donate some of the money raised that way to a special National Park Service fund, designed to pay for publishing educational seminars. Watt dipped into the fund twice last year to pay for two parties that he held at the home of Confederate General Robert E. Lee, a public building in Virginia in which free tours are given by volunteers. That the parties were held there at all—forcing the mansion to be closed in one case—angered many people. That the parties were paid for with voluntary contributions angered even more. ''I think it's absolutely despicable that those funds would be used for that,'' David Thornton of the Everglades Natural History Association told the *Washington Post*, which revealed the entire incident. ''This is the last thing in the world that money should be used for.'' In January, 1982, Watt decided to reimburse the fund with $2,000—in taxpayers' money. In February, 1982, the General Accounting Office concluded that Watt improperly used government funds for the party and should reimburse the Treasury from his own pocket.

DONALD HODEL
UNDERSECRETARY

RESPONSIBILITY OF OFFICE

As the department's number two official, Hodel "assists the Secretary in the discharge of Secretarial duties and serves as Acting Secretary in the absence of the Secretary." That latter responsibility has become particularly important with Watt spending so much of this time on the road raising money for Republican candidates.

During his confirmation hearing, Hodel received a colorful description of his major job responsibility from Virginia Senator John Warner. Warner told him, "I can't help but put myself in your place many years ago when I was No. 2 to a very distinguished man not unlike your boss, but he told me one time that the No. 2 man's greatest value comes when it is Katie block the door, which meant that when I as No. 2 saw he was on a course of action that was wrong, that I had the fortitude to stand in front of the door. . . and you are shooting in that direction, is that correct?

Hodel: I believe so, yes, sir.
Warner: You could go toe to toe with him and eye to eye?
Hodel: Toe to toe and eye to eye.
Warner: And Katie block the door?
Hodel: And Katie block the door . . .
Warner: Mr. Chairman, this man has my vote.

BACKGROUND

Environmentalists, Donald Hodel once said, "clamor for a return to a more primitive life, to choking off our individual and collective aspirations for ourselves and our children."

And: "Over the past several years, it [the environmental movement] has fallen into the hands of a small, arrogant faction which is dedicated to bringing our society to a halt. I call this faction the Prophets of Shortage. They are the anti-producers, the anti-achievers."

Actually, as administrator of the Bonneville Power Administration (BPA), Hodel was a prophet of shortage himself, repeatedly forecasting that some people's "lights would be turned off" unless more and more generating facilities were built. These two views—a passionate commitment to building new electrical capacity, particularly nuclear, and a passionate distaste for environmentalists—guided Hodel's stormy eight-year reign at the Bonneville Power Administration, a federal agency that markets electrical power produced by federal dams in the northwest.

"Let the no-growth proponent explain to parents and their children why the schools must be closed soon because there isn't enough power to heat and light them," Hodel said in a typical 1975 remark. "Let him tell housewives how to operate their homes during rotating blackouts. This is the sort of direct accountability that the no-growthers should have to assume."

Ironically, Hodel was forced to admit in 1977 that layoffs caused by a power shortage the previous winter (which was caused by a drought in fall, 1976) could have been delayed if "extra" electricity from the region had not been sold to California before the drought began. And demand forecasts by the region's utilities for the benchmark year, 1989-1990 have dropped from 30,184 average megawatts in 1974 during the height of Hodel's reign to only 21,888 average megawatts in projections made last year.

Hodel faced direct accountability of another kind in 1977 when Jimmy Carter's election placed Cecil Andrus at the head of the Interior Department, which then oversaw the BPA. Shortly before the inauguration, leaders of environmental groups throughout the Northwest wrote Carter urging Hodel's dismissal. "As Administrator of BPA, Mr. Hodel has actively promoted policies that have favored massively expensive new power plants, rather than workable energy conservation," they wrote. "He has blatantly ignored environmental laws, requiring repeated lawsuits by our environmental organizations—at great expense—simply to force his compliance with basic laws."

They were joined by Oregon Representative Jim Weaver, who said, "Hodel is hell-bent for energy growth at any cost. He embodies the energy philosophy of the past."

An environmentalist himself, Andrus found the case persuasive, and Hodel resigned as BPA administrator less than a year later.

Hodel had begun his BPA career in 1969 as deputy administrator. As he acknowledged in an interview at the time, "The key that opened the door to this job for me was my chairmanship of the Republican party [of Oregon from 1966-67]." Further, the article noted, "Hodel admitted that he didn't know much about the power industry." At the time of the appointment, he had been an attorney for the giant paper company, Georgia Pacific.

Hodel spent three years as deputy administrator before being appointed to the top slot in 1972. There he became a key figure in the region's energy planning. Though Bonneville does not operate any power plants, it does contract for and sell power, and has tremendous influence over the investment decisions of Northwest utilities. "Bonneville played a central role in facilitating an enormous nuclear and coal expansion in the Northwest," said Ralph Cavanagh, an attorney with the Natural Resources Defense Council in San Francisco.

One massive project assisted—and arguably only made possible—by Bonneville is the ill-fated excursion into nuclear power by the Washington Public Power Supply System (WPPSS). In the early 1970s, under a complex agreement with Bonneville known as "net billing," WPPSS began work on five nuclear power plants, whose cost was estimated at $4 billion. Under the arrangement, the BPA agreed to raise its rates as high as necessary— throughout its entire power grid—to cover the debt for the first three plants. (The final two plants were forced out on their own when the Internal Revenue Service ruled that WPPSS bonds could not receive tax exempt status if BPA was purchasing the power.) Hodel "was the principal architect of the net billing scheme," said Mark Reis, a former energy aide to Rep. Weaver, who now directs a coalition monitoring implementation of a 1980 law that amended the BPA's functions. Hodel signed the net billing contracts on two of the plants. According to Reis and other regional energy sources, Hodel also orally promised the utilities investing in the WPPSS 4 and 5 plants that he would purchase their output for the Bonneville system. BPA has not been able to fulfill that promise, and the utilities invested in the two plants are facing financial disaster, as construction costs escalate. Today, the estimated cost for the five plants has soared to $23.8 billion, and WPPSS in February, 1982 terminated construction on the final two plants.

The massive project symbolizes two tenets of the Hodel era at BPA: support for nuclear power and resistance to environmental impact statements. BPA resisted the compilation of an EIS on the Northwest regional power plan, which included WPPSS 4 and 5 until forced by a federal court to do so in 1978. During his speeches, Hodel regularly criticized the EIS process, calling it a "burdensome requirement" and alleging that it has been used "to obstruct the orderly progress of obtaining the power supply this region must have. . ."

Hodel had firm ideas where that power should come from. "Any rational energy policy adopted by the United States will be founded upon nuclear and coal-fired generation," he said in a 1976 speech. "If we can't see to this at the state level, then I see no alternative but federal intervention." Hodel actively campaigned against initiatives in western states to limit nuclear power, and came up with a proposal to use the initiative process to block public challenges to power plant development. As he outlined it in 1975, "One approach might be for the utilities to draw up a comprehensive blueprint providing for the electric energy needs of the Pacific Northwest over the next 20 years or more. . . The package would be placed on the statewide ballot in both Oregon and Washington, with the proviso that, once endorsed by popular vote, further intervention and legal harassment would be foreclosed."

Hodel's resistance to public involvement in energy planning spread beyond this proposal and his aversion to environmental impact statements. In late 1976 and early 1977, Hodel and BPA officials held a series of private meetings with utility officials—to which no public representatives were invited—to map out a new regional power plan. Hodel told one outside group that asked to sit in on one of the meetings that they could attend— but that if they did he would cancel the meeting.

After leaving BPA, Hodel became President of the National Electric Reliability Council, a utility organization formed after the New York City blackout of 1965. Testifying before Congress in that capacity, Hodel moderated his harsh words somewhat, but continued to discount alternative energy sources and to support nuclear power, urging a speedup in licensing during 1979 testimony. In his final years at BPA, while maintaining his support for new capacity, Hodel plugged conservation into his speeches, recognizing perhaps the increased public concern in saving both energy and money. In 1980, Hodel even headed a state commission on alternative energy sources that concluded renewable resources could meet all of Oregon's increased demands through the year 2000. But, typically, he used the press conference releasing the report to back the continued development of nuclear power, saying "We defraud ourselves if we think we can evade that responsibility."

From 1978 until his appointment, Hodel ran a consulting firm that primarily serviced utilities. (See Financial Background section.)

Hodel has old ties to both Reagan and Watt. A long-time Republican activist, Hodel was an alternate delegate to the 1968 convention and served on state Reagan for President committees in both 1968 and 1980. When Bonneville was still in the Interior Department (it was since moved to Energy though Reagan is seeking to return it to Interior), it reported to the assistant secretary for water and power, to whom Watt was deputy from 1969 through 1972.

Born on May 23, 1935 in Portland, Oregon, Hodel was graduated from Harvard University in 1957 and the University of Oregon Law School, where he edited the law review, in 1960. He is married with one child.

FINANCIAL BACKGROUND

In 1980, Hodel earned $33,143 in salary from his consulting firm, whose clients included Pacific Power and Light, Puget Sound Power and Light, Portland General Electric and the Montana Power Company. He also has consulted for a variety of municipalities in the Southwest, for Boeing and for Fording Coal Ltd. of Calgary. Hodel also has small holdings in a variety of stocks and bonds, including common stock in Bethlehem Steel, General Tire and Rubber and J.P. Stevens.

WHAT OTHERS ARE SAYING ABOUT HIM

- Jim Blumquist, another environmentalist who sparred with Hodel from his position at the Sierra Club, said, "Hodel and Watt are birds of a feather."

- Larry Williams, who regularly sparred with Hodel as executive director of the Oregon Environmental Council before joining the federal Council on Environmental Quality staff under Carter told us, "Hodel has a very low sensitivity to environmental issues. . .he blundered very badly in the Northwest in taking on environmentalists, saying they were something akin to communists."

- Senator Robert Packwood, a Republican moderate from Oregon who has occasionally been at odds with Reagan introduced Hodel at his confirmation hearing with glowing praise. Noting that he had known Hodel for 30 years, Packwood said: "I never in my wildest hopes thought we could get Don Hodel back. I never initially put his name forward. I remember talking about what he said as he left the Bonneville Power Administration which was the reason I didn't bother to put his name forward initially— he had given his full measure of service to public employment, and it would be a fair number of years before he came back."

MAJOR ISSUES

It would be difficult to find any Cabinet official in recent memory who has prompted more obscenities, angry speeches and nasty political cartoons than Interior Secretary James Watt.

Garry Trudeau pictures him in Doonesbury with a steam shovel on his desk, proudly running over pigeons in his parking lot on the way to work. Pat Oliphant draws him stepping out of the wilderness in the blazing light of a mission from God—with a can of gasoline on one hand and a chainsaw in the other.

Even Ronald Reagan jokes about him planning to strip mine the rose garden.

When his name was announced at a capitol lawn National Symphony performance the audience booed, not sporadically, but long and lustily.

Over one million Americans signed a petition demanding his removal from office.

The *New York Times* says, "he does not sound like a man to be trusted with jewels or even trees."

The *Los Angeles Times* says, "Watt should be sent back to his legal foundation to plead the case for his clients from the outside again, where he belongs."

Sen. Alan Cranston (D-Calif.) calls Watt a "puppet of the exploiters and destroyers."

Dan Lufkin, a lifelong Republican who headed Reagan's environmental transition team, says Watt's policies are leading to "the destruction of our wilderness land; the corruption of our national parks; the wasting of our irreplaceable resources."

Democrat Morris Udall, chairman of the House Interior Committee, called for his resignation.

Manual Lujan, the ranking Republican on the committee, angrily introduces a resolution to stop Watt from issuing oil and gas leases in wilderness areas.

Almost 60 percent of those surveyed in the mountain states—the area Watt claims to represent—said they weren't happy with his policies.

In just a year, Watt had assumed a sort of mythic proportion, as an uncompromising zealot on a one-man crusade to turn America's priceless heritage of public lands and wilderness over to the oil and mining industries.

That indeed may be Watt's crusade. But it is by no means a one-man crusade, a point often overlooked in the calls for Watt's resignation.

The drives to open up public lands, roll back environmental law and increase industry access to the national forests are long-standing and frequently expressed goals of Ronald Reagan that are unlikely to change even if Watt is removed from office. Reagan's initial advice to him, Watt recalled, was unequivocal: "When I said, 'I want to do this, I want to do that,' he replied, 'Sic 'em'."

As Lufkin's letter indicates, Watt has drawn regular criticism from many environmentally sensitive Republicans for abandoning the party's conservation heritage that stretches back to Theodore Roosevelt. But Reagan had already indicated in his radio broadcasts and newspaper columns of the mid-1970s that he had personally veered off that course long ago.

Consider:

- Like Watt, Reagan frequently has suggested that those who wanted to restrict industry access to public lands were elitists. "Is public land really for the public or for an elite few who want to keep it for their own use?" Reagan asked in a 1978 radio broadcast.

- Like Watt, Reagan has opposed the Forest Service's efforts to increase the amount of wilderness area to be rendered off limits to mineral and energy development. "The unavailability of these public resources to provide jobs, wages, and, yes, taxes, undermines the whole system that has made us prosperous," Reagan remarked in another 1978 broadcast.

- Like Watt, Reagan during the campaign promised to quicken the pace of oil and gas exploration on the Outer Continental Shelf (OCS), complaining that the government was offering areas for lease too slowly.

In a 1981 year-in-review interview with the *Los Angeles Times*, Reagan again defended Watt, charging that "we had environmental extremism that was going beyond all bounds of reason. I felt that way then and I feel that way now. And I think that Jim Watt, he's not going to destroy the environment, but he is going to restore some common sense. . ."

What is most remarkable about Watt is his ability to attract public attention and his seemingly congenital inability to avoid picking fights. Cold, single-minded and arrogant, he has alienated not only the environmental groups considered liberal, but the National Wildlife Federation, whose members primarily voted for Reagan, the two key chairmen overseeing his programs in the House (Udall and Rep. Sydney Yates (D-Ill.)), and the California Republican Party, which last summer urged Reagan to pull Watt off their shores, lest he pollute their electoral prospects for

1982. For refusing to turn over documents regarding his decision on Canadian access to U.S. mineral leases, Watt faced a contempt citation from the House, which was only averted at the eleventh hour through a compromise engineered by the White House.

Many believe that combativeness is impeding the implementation of Reagan's program. This has certainly been the case in the two most contentious proposals of Watt's first year: his plans to greatly accelerate the leasing of the Outer Continental Shelf (particularly four spectacular areas off the coast of California) and his plans to open wilderness areas to exploration and development.

Under the 1964 Wilderness Act, oil, gas and mineral leasing is permitted in federal wilderness areas through the end of 1983. But no drilling has ever taken place within the wilderness areas.

Watt early on announced that one of his goals would be to "open wilderness areas" to development. That declaration made a run-in with Congress inevitable. But Watt's style in carrying out his pledge, escalated the conflict, adding disagreeableness to disagreement, and generating intense congressional opposition, lawsuits between the legislative and executive branch, and charges of improper collusion with his former law firm.

The skirmish began in May, 1981 when in an unprecedented move the House Interior Committee voted to bar Watt from opening the Bob Marshall Wilderness in Montana to natural gas exploration.

After questioning the constitutionality of the move, Watt reluctantly complied with the resolution on June 1. Two days later the MSLF, joined on June 4 by its colleague firm the Pacific Legal Foundation, filed suit against Watt in federal court to overturn his decision. In effect, they argued that Watt should be free to do what he wanted in the first place—ignore the committee's demand. In September, the Justice Department joined in the suit, also arguing that Congress could not prevent Watt from opening the preserve.

Watt's actions raised other questions. In July, Ronald Zumbrun, president of the Pacific Legal Foundation, wrote the Justice Department a "confidential" letter complaining about the manner in which the government was conducting its case. Of its own brief, Zumbrun wrote, "We were informed that the filing of this lawsuit was received with favor by the involved officials of the executive branch." Environmental groups that were parties to the suit accused Watt of "collusion" with his former associates, a charge both Watt and the Justice Department denied.

While that battle was underway, the Forest Service recommended to Watt that he make available for oil and gas leasing wilderness areas in California (near the spectacular Big Sur coastline), Arkansas, and Wyoming (on land that borders Yellowstone National Park). The efforts were resisted not only by Democratic representatives, but Republicans like Richard Cheney of Wyoming, who served as President Ford's chief of staff, and the state's two Republican senators, including the son of Milward Simpson, the man who first brought Watt to Washington. Beyond the policy issues, the potential leases in California's Los Padres National Forest raised questions of propriety as well. An investigation by the *Los Angeles Times* revealed that while at MSLF Watt had personally handled a wilderness area case involving identical legal issues as those revolving around the Los Padres national forest. Further, one of those seeking leases in the California forest was Thomas Connelly, a Denver oilman who contributed to Mountain States.

Watt took his first concrete steps in New Mexico. And there he angered another powerful Republican, Rep. Manuel Lujan, Jr., the ranking minority member on the

House Interior Committee. After Watt issued three leases for drilling inside the Capitan Wilderness—without any public notice and without an environmental impact statement—Lujan was furious. Lujan first threatened a resolution that would permanently bar all oil and mineral leasing in wilderness areas. But the committee approved a declaration barring such leasing through June 1, 1982. Though he had won this legal point in the Bob Marshall case in January, Watt agreed to comply with the resolution, and later extended the moratorium through the 1982 election.

Around that time, though, Watt decided to open five national park recreation areas to mineral leasing, in addition to the energy leasing that had already been approved by the Carter Administration. By Interior Department calculations, the decision will open up over 400,000 acres in five western national parks to mineral exploration. And at the time the agreement with the committee was announced Watt was also seeking to overturn a Carter Administration decision that barred strip mining next to Utah's Bryce Canyon National Park. (Watt's efforts were rebuffed by a federal judge early this year.)

With roguish flair, Watt generated favorable front-page headlines in late February, 1982, by apparently reversing his earlier stand on opening wilderness areas. Watt announced that he would ask Congress to bar all mining and drilling in wilderness areas through the end of the century—which sounded good until some more deliberative legislators pointed out that the *existing* wilderness law would bar such activity *permanently* after 1983. Watt's bill would also allow the President—meaning the secretary of Interior— to open wilderness study areas to development; Congress currently holds that authority.

When slapped with the House Interior Committee resolution, Watt announced that he was "delighted" since he believed "wilderness areas are the last that should be drilled." That might be construed to mean, at the least, that land already under lease should be explored before national parks are carved up in search of energy and minerals. But according to the Wilderness Society, "there are 118 million acres of non-wilderness federal land currently leased but almost totally unexplored." And, according to a recent study conducted for the organization, designated wilderness areas contain only 1.4 percent of the producable domestic oil and just 1 percent of the available natural gas. Those lands now under study for possible inclusion in the wilderness system add only another 4.3 percent of the available oil and 3.1 percent of the natural gas.

Watt's program to greatly accelerate oil and gas development on the OCS provoked even greater pyrotechnics. Politically, Watt himself fueled the fire with a particularly unfortunate decision early in 1981 to reconsider the leasing of four basins off the Northern California coast that had been ruled off-limits for oil and gas exploration by the Carter Administration.

It may simply have been the wrong fight. Prominent Californians from both political parties—from the governor up to the congressional delegation and down to town and county supervisors had already made it clear that they did not want oil rigs sprouting off the spectacular, craggy coasts and quiet communities both north and just south of San Francisco.

"The antipathy toward northern California oil drilling is so much of an emotional outpouring from Republicans and Democrats alike that it goes beyond visual pollution," said Michael Fischer, executive director of the California Coastal Commission. "It has to do with a sense of place being violated."

Watt never understood that, which may explain why he was ambushed. In spring 1981 he told a House committee that while "the central and northern coastal areas are valuable and unique. . .that in itself is not a unique condition.'' To Watt, the four basins, and a fifth area off Southern California, included in the sale were simply the last major offshore areas in the lower 48 states which had not been offered for lease since the 1973 oil embargo.

And they were, virtually everyone involved agrees, a symbol—demonstrable proof of Watt's steely determination to serve as the " 'amicus' for the minerals industry in the court of federal policymaking,'' as he once told Congress.

The basins off Northern California turned out to be a symbol, but certainly of a different kind than Watt had hoped. Watt provoked fierce reaction from Gov. Jerry Brown and local officials throughout the state. The outcry was so sharp that the California Republican Party wrote Watt begging him to reconsider because of ''the short and long-range impact on our Republican candidates for office in 1982 and beyond.'' Then, in July, 1981 three-quarters of the Republicans in the House joined the Democrats in approving an amendment to the Interior appropriations bill that blocked any leasing of the four basins.

Meanwhile, the governor's office had chosen a different point of attack. Since Watt had not taken a final action on any of the four basins, the state sued the secretary to block leasing of 32 tracts in the fifth basin, off the southern coast, which he had formally offered.

In July, 1981, a federal judge permanently blocked the sale of 29 of the northernmost tracts, a stiff legal rebuke to the secretary. Watt promised to appeal to the Supreme Court if necessary, but 11 days later, citing the judge's decision, Watt decided not to offer the four northern basins for leasing after all. Under his own schedule, he anticipated he could not offer them again until 1983.

Watt's defeat at the hands of California presaged serious problems for his ambitious leasing program. In July, 1981 Watt proposed a five-year plan that would open the OCS at an unprecedented rate. Since Congress passed the OCS Lands Act in 1953, Interior has offered to lease about 40 million acres. Watt plans to offer five times as much annually for each of the next five years; about a billion acres in all. ''Development of offshore oil and gas resources is a vital part of the Reagan Administration's energy and economic recovery program,'' he said when announcing the plan in April, 1981. ''The program we are proposing will make more acreage available for leasing, will cut substantially the time now required to start leasing in promising frontier areas, and will use the market mechanism rather than arbitrary government decisions in selecting areas for lease and exploration.'' Virtually every tract on the entire OCS will be offered at least once under Watt's original plan. In 1981, more acreage—almost twice as much as 1980—was leased than ever before.

Once again, the plan drew bipartisan criticism. No one was particularly surprised when Jerry Brown said that Watt's five-year plan ''is a reckless, wanton attack on a precious national heritage that belongs to all Americans.'' But when Alaska's Republican Governor Jay Hammond complains that Watt's department has ''thumbed its nose'' at this state's environmental concerns and joins in Brown's suit against Watt, it's clear that Watt was straining traditional political alliances.

Watt's plan suffered another political rebuff that October, when the Administration was forced to withdraw regulations designed to foreclose state lawsuits such as the one filed by California. The Commerce Department—which Watt had pressured to issue the rules—withdrew them after the House Merchant Marine Committee voted to overturn them. (For more on the regulations, see profile of Malcolm Baldrige.)

Without those regulations, which deny states the right to participate in pre-leasing OCS decisions, Watt's plan is doomed to years of litigation. Just before Christmas, in an internal memorandum obtained by the *New York Times*, Watt ordered important changes in the leasing procedures he had earlier approved. The effect of the changes could be to reduce the amount of acreage actually leased by up to one-third.

These sorts of battles have worried even the oil industry, much as Anne Gorsuch's actions have concerned some more subtle thinkers in the chemical industry. Though obviously pleased with the direction of Watt's policies—Mobil has taken out ads to support the beleaguered secretary—some representatives of the industry fear that Watt's zealotry will ultimately hurt them. That seemed a sound conclusion about Watt's decision to offer more offshore acreage than the industry could hope to evaluate, let alone digest, a plan that could engender significant opposition against offshore leasing in general. At the least, Watt's five-year plan, and the concomitant controversy over state oversight of OCS activities, effectively scuttled the oil industry's proposal to completely exempt offshore drilling from state oversight under the Coastal Zone Management Act. As one oilman told *Fortune*, "I'd feel a hell of a lot more confident if he were a better public-relations man and weren't so abrasive with environmentalists. There is a possibility of a backlash against the oil companies." Concluded the business magazine: "The ideologue at Interior has picked such a fight that the issues are getting lost."

Part of the fight is an unrelenting campaign against the environmental groups that oppose him. Watt's definition of conciliation appears to be refraining from firebombing the Sierra Club's offices. Late in 1981, Watt told top department staff members that he did not intend to meet with any paid representatives of environmental groups, suggesting that they do likewise. Watt said he did not want his aides "wasting government money by talking to national conservation leaders," according to his spokesman. Some of his top aides promptly cancelled scheduled meetings with outside groups. Watt also directed the department to review all service contracts and dues paid to "special interest organizations."

Watt issued the directive after returning from a western trip in which he told a group of farmers that "I don't speak of Republicans and Democrats any more; I speak of liberals and Americans." A few weeks later, when he was testifying on legislation to reform the 1902 Reclamation Act, Watt was tossed a softball question, giving him an on-the-record opportunity to state whether he considered liberals "good Americans."

"I suppose," the Interior Secretary responded, "some of them are." Later on "Meet the Press" he said "Some of my best friends are liberals." Watt often uses his brand of humor to laugh off tough questions or escape tight corners.

When a gas company lobbyist wrote, in an unofficial capacity, to question Watt's comment about liberals, an assistant Interior secretary wrote back to the lobbyist's employer, Enserch Corp. of Dallas, complaining about the question. The Interior Department wrote that "The Secretary is, frankly, surprised at Mr. [Timothy] Donohoe's representation in the attached letter." Enserch then dismissed Donohoe. (Watt later claimed he was unaware of the letter until he read about it in the newspapers.)

Though generally of little concern in the East, water is a key issue with Watt's western constituency. The water needs of western farmers and ranchers that supported Reagan, though, have run against the budget concerns of OMB. The first collision left both sides retreating and claiming victory. The Bureau of Reclamation, which builds western water projects, took a small cut in 1982, which looks better in light of the deep slashes proposed for the primarily eastern-based Army Corps of Engineers. "Watt just threw his body in front of the West," said one water issue consultant.

In the 1983 budget, the bureau made a surprising comeback. Proposed construction appropriations jumped by 21 percent to $667 million. Overall bureau appropriations would rise by 23 percent to $937 million. Funding would be increased on the Central Arizona Project dear to Rep. Udall, chair of the House Interior Committee, and the Central Utah Project. Though "contingency" money is included in the overall budget, no new water projects starts were announced.

With budgetary pressures certain to constrain federal funding for water projects, Watt has moved to assure that he can maximize the political mileage from the dollars that are available. Watt has pulled control over water project funding into his Cabinet Council on Natural Resources and proposed to jettison "principles and standards" established under the Carter Administration to assess the worth of water projects and preserve environmental quality. "Jim Watt will be in a position where he can use pork barrel whenever it becomes politically expedient," said Brent Blackwelder, water policy expert with the Environmental Policy Center.

Watt has also waded into the controversy over the Reclamation Act. Extremely critical of the act while at MSLF (See Background Section), Watt suspended proposed regulations implementing the law as one of his first acts in office. In December, 1981 Watt proposed to Congress to essentially eliminate the social purposes of the act—by raising the allowed acreage limitation from 160 to 960 acres, and eliminating restrictions on leasing and a requirement that recipients of the water live near their farms—in return for raising the price on the subsidized water delivered above the acreage limitation. Of residency, which many supporters believe is the heart of the law, Watt said: "We see this provision as an unnecessary and unwarranted restriction on land owners."

With that proposal, Watt is seeking to strike an uneasy compromise between conflicting factions of the Reagan coalition. Conservatives concerned about the budget can look to the prospect of increased payments from farmers receiving federal water. Large landowners in the West are freed from the legal requirements that drove them to a frenzy under the Carter Administration.

It may turn out to be a less than an equal deal. Watt has proposed various "grandfathering" and special case exemptions to the higher prices that make it "very unclear that anyone will actually pay that price," said Guy Martin, assistant Interior secretary for land and water under Carter. "I think there's real doubt whether those higher prices will actually be paid," he added.

And that is just a sampling of Watt's activities during his first year. Watt has sought to overturn policy in virtually every corner of the Interior bureaucracy. In some cases, this has had valuable results. In one case, he investigated and then moved to close loopholes that allowed oil companies to avoid paying the government hundreds of millions of dollars annually. Watt also sought to raise the royalties paid by the firms to the government on onshore leases, though he is seeking only nominal fees for oil shale leases. Some of the other major activities noted in a year-end review by the Wilderness Society included:

- seeking to stop acquisitions of new federal parkland. Watt sought drastic cutbacks in funding for the Land and Water Conservation Fund, but Congress agreed to only some of the cuts and directed that the money be used for acquisitions.

- requesting that President Reagan revoke a 1972 Executive Order which limits use of off-road vehicles on public lands. Watt has already relaxed regulations on off-road snowmobiling in national parks and is planning to end the ban on motorized boats through the Grand Canyon. (Watt earlier described a Grand Canyon raft trip as "tedious.")

- reorganizing and slashing the staff of the Office of Surface Mining. When the House Interior Appropriations Subcommittee headed by Rep. Yates added a rider to the Interior funding bill prohibiting the use of 1982 dollars for the move, Watt simply ordered the reorganization speeded up so it could be completed with 1981 funds. Watt did reorganize the office; but at the cost of poisoned relations with a key subcommittee chairman.

For all the controversy, Watt remains a potent Republican fundraiser. (In one six-week stretch, he brought in $400,000.) Through the fall, he spent increasing amounts of time on the rubber chicken circuit, urging conservative businessmen to reach down into their wallets and help maintain Watt's vision of stewardship as the law of the land. With these performances Watt calls up memories of his performance as the head of the Mountain States Legal Foundation, searching for corporate succor. But, then, those memories are evoked almost as strongly by Watt's performance as steward of the public lands.

WATT'S CONTRIBUTORS AND THE DOI

Salt River Project (SRP): Agricultural Improvement and Power District
A political subdivision of the state of arizona, and REA coop. It supplies electricity to 330,000 customers in Phoenix and other parts of central Arizona. Operates the Navajo Generating Station, 2,250 MW plant, near Page, Arizona. Land was obtained by trade with Navajo Tribe. The coal comes from mines on Indian land leases at Black Mesa (Hopi and Navajo). Operates Coronado Generating Station near St. Johns, Arizona. Part owner of the Mohave, Four Corners, Craig and Hayden coal-fired generating stations. All use coal from federal land leases and/or Indian land leases and have rights-of-way across federal lands and/or Indian lands. Is especially concerned that visibility standards in the national parks will impair SRP's expansion plans or require limits on pollution emissions at existing plants.

Nevada Power Company: A private (stockholder-owned) utility based in Las Vegas.
Participant in the proposed 2,500 MW Allen-Warner Valley energy system now before DOI. The system would have two power plants in Nevada and Utah supplied by a coal mine on federal leases next to Bryce Canyon National Park. The coal and power would be transported by slurry and power lines requiring extensive rights-of-way permits on public lands.

AMAX, Inc. (Also its subsidiary, Climax Molybdenum, has contributed).
Amax is a large multinational mining company. Its principal interests are molybdenum and coal mining in this country and it has proposed large copper development projects.

Amax has federal coal leases in Wyoming and operates coal mines regulated by DOI's Office of Surface Mining (OSM) in at least four states: Illinois, Indiana, Ohio, and Wyoming. Its Wyoming mine has an application pending before OSM. Amax is planning a coal mine on the Colville Indian Reservation in Washington; their mine would require approval from the Bureau of Indian Affairs. Amax is proposing a large molybdenum mine near Crested Butte which would require rights-of-way permits for federal lands administered by Forest Service (Department of Agriculture) and Bureau of Land Management (Department of Interior) as have its existing mines.

Arizona Public Service Co.: Investor-owned utility company in Arizona.

Owns the Four Corners Power Plant on the Navajo Reservation near Farmington, New Mexico and has all or part of the power plants at Page, Arizona, Cholla, and Coronado, Arizona. The coal for all these plants comes from public and Indian land leases—administered by Bureau of Land Management (BLM) and Bureau of Indian Affairs (BIA). Also has rights-of-way permits for extensive power lines to cross public and Indian land. Has a stake in how visibility standards are set and enforced on National Parks. (Grand Canyon, Zion, Mesa Verde Parks, for example).

Arizona Cotton Growers Association

Involved in the Central Arizona Project (CAP) (a huge multibillion water diversion and irrigation project sponsored by the DOI) but hurt by the fact that under present CAP rules, water for Indian agriculture is given a priority equal to that for non-Indian municipal and industrial water. Non-Indian agriculture, i.e, the cottongrowers, thus have a lower priority in water-short years.

Burlington Northern (BN)

Company based in Minneapolis. Owns the BN railroad, has extensive land holdings along railroad rights-of-way. Much of the land is owned in a checkerboard pattern, sections of BN land alternating with sections of public or private land. Involved in minerals, timber, and real estate development. BN has nominated over 100,000 acres of public coal lands for leasing in eastern Montana and Wyoming. The secretary has to decide on these nominations by early 1983. BN now has rights-of-way permits on public lands. BN has a 25% interest in the proposed Northern Tier Pipeline to bring natural gas down from Alaska to Washington state then across the northern states just south of the U.S.-Canadian border; rights-of-way across public land have been applied for and are essential for the project to be built (under the BN subsidiary Glacier Park Co.). BN has proposed that the federal government trade public coal lands in eastern Montana for BN's forest lands in western Montana. BN also holds oil and gas leases on BLM-administered lands.

Consolidated Coal Co.

One of nation's largest coal companies with numerous mines, mostly in the eastern states, which are regulated by the Office of Surface Mining.

Denver and Rio Grande Western R.R.: Large railroad serving parts of Colorado and Utah. Based in Denver.

Primary revenue-producing activity is hauling coal from the coal fields in northwest Colorado, south central and eastern Utah. Much of the coal is produced on federal coal leases from BLM and the railroad has rights-of-way from DOI. Expansion of business is dependent on additional federal coal leases and federal approval of new lines and rights-of-way. For example, its proposed railroad from

Wellington to Emery, Utah has right-of-way applications pending before the department and the feasibility depends on both existing and proposed mines on existing and proposed federal coal leases.

Energy Fuels (EF) Corp.: Coal company privately owned and based in Denver.

EF operates the largest strip mine in Colorado (Energy Fuels mine) and has a major interest in at least one other, Kerr Coal mine in Colorado. Have nine federal coal leases from BLM and have proposed additional ones, now pending. The Kerr mine has a mining permit pending before OSM. Energy Fuels has been a vociferous critic of BLM's refusals to rush its desired coal leases.

Exxon Company, U.S.A.: Multinational energy company.

Through parent company and subsidiaries, Exxon has numerous federal coal leases in the West. Two coal mines (Rawhide and Caballo) now operate on public lands in Wyoming and a third (South Rawhide) is pending. DOI approval of a mine permit; the existing two mines have applied for new permits to DOI, now pending.

Exxon has thousands of oil and gas leases on public lands and off-shore areas from Alaska to the Gulf coast and off the East Coast—these are administered by DOI. It has 262 oil and gas leases on 226,378 acres in Colorado alone. It also has pipeline rights-of-way, including the Alaskan Pipeline.

In oil shale, Exxon has pending before the Department its nomination of technology for an oil shale leasing program on public lands in western Colorado. Also pending is its proposal that the Department exchange over 10,000 acres of rich publicly owned oil shale land in Colorado for numerous scattered tracts of unmineable oilshale land owned by Exxon. It also has an application to DOI for a major pipeline right-of-way for shale oil in Colorado.

Fluor Oil and Gas Corp.: A subsidiary of Fluor Corp., a giant construction company for energy and industrial facilities based in California.

Fluor has energy and mining interests, and is one of the six-company consortium which owns Peabody Coal Co. Peabody has five coal mines in the west, three proposed, and has extensive public and Indian coal leases from BLM and BIA. The mines are located both on Indian lands and on public lands and at least two permits are pending from OSM. Peabody has many coal mines in the eastern states as well which are regulated by OSM.

Fluor has 15 oil and gas leases on 10,537 acres of public land in Colorado.

Gulf Resources & Chemical Corp.: A subsidiary of Gulf Oil Corp. The parent company, a large multinational energy, minerals and real estate firm will be discussed here.

Gulf is involved in uranium mining and processing on Navajo Indian lands in New Mexico; in coal mining on Navajo lands in New Mexico; and public lands in Colorado and has a proposed mine on public lands in Wyoming; in oil shale, it holds a lease on public lands in Colorado, and it has extensive oil and gas leases throughout the country, including 112 leases on 124,623 acres in Colorado alone. Major revisions to its oil shale mining plan are pending before the department, and it has a proposal in to the department on its nomination of a technology for an oil shale leasing program on public lands in western Colorado.

Kemmerer Coal Co.: A coal company in S.W. Wyoming with a large open-pit mine producing 4.5 million tons per year.

Kemmerer has coal leases on public lands and has a mining permit proposal before the OSM. Its mine is regulated by OSM. In Colorado alone, it has 12 coal leases on a total of 16,257 acres and 36 oil and gas leases on 20,576 acres.

Utah Power & Light (UP&L): An investor-owned utility serving most of Utah and the southern part of Idaho. Based in Salt Lake City.

Utah Power & Light (UP&L) owns three large underground coal mines on federal coal leases (Deer Creek, DesBee Dove, and Wilberg) and has a major mine expansion proposal pending before OSM (Cottonwood). In addition it has undeveloped federal coal leases on the Kaiparowits Plateau in southern Utah and has a controversial proposal to the department, now pending a secretarial decision, to exchange those leases back to the government for federal coal leases in the Central Utah coal field.

UP&L is the major proponent of the Intermountain Power Project which requires DOI approval and has extensive rights-of-way permits for power lines and roads across public lands. UP&L has been a persistent critic of clean air protection for national parks and wilderness areas. UP&L has been found in consistent violation of the coal mining act by OSM and an enforcement action brought by citizens against UP&L is pending before the department.

Montana Power Company (MPC): An investor-owned utility in Montana.

MPC has a subsidiary, Western Energy Co., which owns the Calstrip mine, a large coal strip mine in southeast Montana which produced over 10 million tons in 1978. The mine is on federal coal leases and currently has a permit pending before OSM and will submit additional permit applications within the next year.

Montana Power owns the Calstrip power plant. The plant, located northwest and upwind from the Northern Cheyenne Reservation, has been extremely controversial as MPC fought the air pollution controls required by the tribe.

MPC has numerous permits for rights-of-way across public land.
Occidental Oil Shale: A subsidiary of Occidental Petroleum (Oxy), a multinational energy, minerals and mining firm.

Oxy has extensive coal interests through two subsidiaries: Island Creek Coal, which operates in the midwest and Appalachian states; and Sheridan Enterprises, which operates in the West. All mines come under OSM enforcement. Sheridan Enterprises has a pending permit at its McClane Canyon mine in Colorado, a mine which it operated illegally without a reclamation plan and mining permit. Sheridan has 7 coal leases in Colorado on 15,089 acres.

Occidental Oil Shale has one of the four oil shale leases on federal land in Colorado; major revisions to its mining plan are up before the Department. Its nomination of technology for an oil shale leasing program on public lands is pending before the Department.

Oxy has leases and rights-of-way permits on federal lands.

Pacific Power and Light Company: PP&L serves northern California with electric power; it is an investor-owned utility.

PP&L has a number of Federal coal leases and owns three strip mines—Dave Johnston (Wyo.), Spring Creek (MT), and Antelope (Wyo.)—and two-thirds interest in a fourth, the Jim Bridger mine in Wyoming. All four mines have submitted permit applications to OSM which will be decided in the coming year.

PP&L has extensive rights-of-way permits for power lines and roads on public lands.

Public Service Co. of New Mexico and subsidiary, Western Coal Co.: PSCo of New Mexico is an investor-owned utility company based in Albuquerque.

It owns the San Juan coal strip mine, which is on federal coal leases.

The mine supplies the San Juan power plant.

Tri-State Generation and Transmission: Power supplier to REA coops based in Northglenn, Colorado. It wants to build two more 350 megawatt units at the Wheatland (Wyo.) power plant, which would require more water from the Laramie River Station. In order to increase the reservoir capacity with North Platte River water, TSG&T's agreement with the U.S. Fish and Wildlife Service (an agency in DOI) would have to be amended to provide less protection to the whooping cranes downstream on the Platte in Nebraska.

Adolph Coors Co.: Brewery, ceramics and energy firm based in Golden, Colorado.

Coors owns 106 oil and gas leases on 97,005 acres of public land in Colorado. It owns two coal mines, one of which has a plan pending approval before OSM. The Ceramics Division makes a key component for the TOSCO II oil shale process. The TOSCO company has been a vigorous lobbyist for more public land leasing to oil shale developers.

OTHER PUBLIC LAND LEASE HOLDERS WHO CONTRIBUTED TO MSLF

Amoco—142 oil and gas leases on 152,940 acres in Colorado.

Anschutz—1 coal lease on 2,480 acres and 10 oil and gas leases on 10,895 acres in Colorado.

Chevron—99 oil and gas leases on 89,643 acres in Colorado.

Colorado Interstate Gas Company—36 oil and gas leases on 44,427 acres in Colorado. (Excludes those by parent company, Coastal States Gas Corp., which probably totals over 100,000 acres).

Cities Service—194 oil and gas leases on 166,104 acres in Colorado.

Hawthorne Oil Company—2 oil and gas leases on 1,456 acres in Colorado.

Wm. G. Helis Estate—2 oil and gas leases on 3,113 acres in Colorado.

Husky Oil Co.—77 oil and gas leases on 45,294 acres in Colorado.

Kansas-Nebraska Natural Gas and subsidiaries—45 oil and gas leases on 26,900 acres.

Kennedy & Mitchell, Inc.—1 oil and gas lease on 1,840 acres.

Marathon Oil—12 oil and gas leases on 7,607 acres.

Mountain Fuel Supply—268 oil and gas leases on 174,588 acres.

Northwest Pipeline Co. and subsidiaries—57 oil and gas leases on 42,916 acres in Colorado.

Phillips Petroleum—103 oil and gas leases on 114,335 acres in Colorado.

Santa Fe Minerals—13 oil and gas leases on 15,396 acres in Colorado.

Shell Oil Company—202 oil and gas leases on 190,904 acres in Colorado.

UV Industries—4 oil and gas leases on 2,361 acres in Colorado.

List compiled by The Wilderness Society.

ROBERT BURFORD
DIRECTOR, BUREAU OF LAND MANAGEMENT

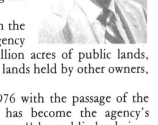

RESPONSIBILITY OF OFFICE

Founded in 1946, the BLM can trace its roots back to the
General Land Office, which opened for business in 1812,
and the Grazing Service, which began operation during the
New Deal.

Little-known in the East, the BLM is a huge force in the
West, where most of the public land is located. The agency
is responsible for managing, and protecting, 417 million acres of public lands,
another 169 million acres of subsurface minerals below lands held by other owners,
and the Outer Continental Shelf.

Its tangled legislative mandate was unsnarled in 1976 with the passage of the
Federal Land Policy and Management Act, which has become the agency's
"organic" statute. The act directs the agency to manage "the public lands in a
manner that will protect the quality of scientific, scenic, historical, ecological, environmental, air and atmospheric, water resource, and archeological values."

Burford oversees a staff of 5,744 and a budget in 1982 of $1.177 billion.

BACKGROUND

A lifelong rancher often described as feeling more comfortable in cowboy boots and
jeans than a business suit, Burford comes to Washington as part of the "Colorado
mafia" that includes his boss, Interior Secretary James Watt, and his close friend,
EPA chief Anne Gorsuch. Gorsuch—with whom Burford has frequently been
romantically linked—was one of a group of conservative legislators that engineered
his election as speaker of the Colorado House of Representatives in 1978. One year
later Burford and 26 other state legislators joined Watt's Mountain States Legal
Foundation in a suit against the federal Environmental Protection Agency for
threatening to cut off federal funds if the state didn't move to control auto emissions. Eventually the state approved a vehicle inspection program and the suit was
dropped.

Burford worked closely with Gorsuch to push conservative causes, including the
elimination of a state women's commission. Burford was considered a cagey and
effective legislative leader who made the most of his country boy demeanor.

Burford is a third generation Coloradoan whose grandfather, as the *Denver Post*
once put it, "came from Kansas in a covered wagon." He owns, and has become
wealthy from, a 10,000-acre ranch about 25 miles south of Grand Junction. He is a
member of both the state and National Cattlemen's Associations, which have regularly pressed for increased grazing access to public lands.

Except for his suit, Burford still looks as if he was sprung from a Marlboro Country commercial. Craggy-faced, gravelly-voiced, and chain-smoking (of course)
Marlboros, he is a shrewdly disarming Western stereotype. He retains the sagebrush
rebel's disdain for Washington. "I think they [Washingtonians] don't have any
true concept of what makes this nation run," he told us. "I mean the perception in
Washington is that: I guess it is probably best described as very similar to that often
reprinted cover of the *New Yorker* that has Broadway and then halfway across [the

country] the Mississippi River, and there is practically nothing beyond the Mississippi River, and Broadway takes up everything. That's the view of a lot of people in Washington, I find. They think this is the center of all action and that the viewpoint that exists within the city is really reflective of the viewpoint of the nation—and it really isn't. Washingtonians think they're very sophisticated people and actually they're not. I don't think they understand nearly as much about the United States as a whole as some of the other people do that come in here. . .with the viewpoints they bring with them.''

Over the past decade, Burford has regularly banged heads with the agency he now directs. In July, 1979, BLM fined him $169 for grazing his livestock ''on public lands without a valid permit.'' Such a violation is extremely rare, local BLM officials later told reporters. Almost exactly one year later, the BLM's area manager wrote Burford again, warning that he had improperly trailed his cattle through a BLM driveway and that ''future unauthorized use of the driveway will constitute trespass actions.''

These incidents were apparently not isolated; as far back as 1971, BLM officials wrote Burford and four other ranchers to delineate an official definition of trespass. That letter followed a meeting with the ranchers ''to discuss the problem of unauthorized grazing.''

Burford clashed with the BLM again in spring, 1976 over the agency's management plan for a range north of Grand Junction where he grazed his cattle. In his report on a March 8, 1976 meeting with Burford, BLM official Terry Brumley wrote: ''Mr. Burford asked about the proposed grazing system and became quite defensive after learning spring grazing would possibly be discontinued. He stated, 'I will fight that system from here to Washington.' Then in retrospect he went on, 'No, I will start in Washington.''' Despite the threat, three weeks later, the BLM reduced his spring grazing allotment by about 60 percent, citing ''a deteriorated range condition [in which]. . .overgrazing is evidenced. . .''

This record, said Debbie Sease of the Sierra Club at his confirmation hearing, ''demonstrates a reluctance on Mr. Burford's part to work with the BLM toward good land management.''

Inside the Colorado statehouse, Burford generally displayed a similar attitude toward environmental issues. With the exception of an 82 percent rating in 1980, his final year, Burford received extremely low ratings from the Colorado Open Space Council, which charts legislators on environmental issues. During 1976 and 1978, he received ratings of zero from the group. After the 1975 session, in which he received a 20 percent rating, the group wrote: ''He does not seem to waste much sympathy on environmental problems.''

Burford received similarly low marks from organized labor, tallying a zero rating in the 1978-80 session.

In our interview, Burford offered a definition of stewardship that few environmentalists would quarrel with. ''I think stewardship in some ways to me was probably expressed by my grandfather when I was six or eight years old. He said: 'Always leave a piece of land in better shape than it was when you bought it, or controlled it, or managed it, or whatever.' And I think—and I've owned what to some people would be a lot of land, it's not a lot of land in the West [See Financial Background]—I don't think I've ever left a piece of land in worse shape when I sold it or left it than it was when I used it or bought it.''

''And that's what you want to do here?'' we asked.

"That's my goal. And when I leave, why, you can go out there and see if I achieved my goal."

Indeed, environmentalists and millions of other voters will soon have their chance to assess whether the policies of Burford and Watt are leaving the public "land in better shape" than when they took office, or indelibly scarring it, as critics contend.

Born in Grand Junction on February 5, 1923, Burford was first elected to the Colorado House in 1974, and served three terms before resigning in 1980. From 1967-1973 he served on various state and federal grazing advisory boards. He has long been active in Republican politics, chairing the Eagle County Republican committee from 1961-1969 and serving on the state Republican Committee for that same period and again from 1975-1981. According to some published reports, Burford was conservative businessman Joseph Coors's first choice for the Interior Secretary job; he may well inherit the position if Watt is forced from office.

Burford was graduated from the Colorado School of Mines in 1944. He has four children, and is divorced.

MAJOR ISSUES

- Burford has reorganized the bureau, giving energy and mineral development increased prominence;

- The Reagan budget cut BLM funds devoted to environmental protection measures while increasing funding for both on and offshore oil and gas development;

- Burford has proposed a series of changes to loosen federal grazing policy, though analysts say much of federal land is already overgrazed.

Despite the intense controversy over the Administration's public land policies, Burford has retained a remarkably low profile. In the decisions to open virtually the entire Outer Continental Shelf (OCS) to oil exploration, or make available vast tracts of land in Alaska, Burford's name has occasionally appeared at the end of a press release offering a throwaway fact or tepid commentary; Secretary Watt has had no interest in sharing the limelight in his crusade to open up the public lands. "It's pretty apparent Watt is hiring people to do what he wants them to do," said one House staffer. "Burford is one of his people."

That in itself is not particularly unusual. Former BLM Director Frank Gregg told us that in the Carter Administration "the BLM had very little significant effect on policies, which was unfortunate because BLM knew the resource best." One Republican Senate Energy Committee staff member said he does not expect too much of a change under Burford. "I think he's more concerned with operation than policy," said Tony Benvetto, staff director of the subcommittee on public lands.

Accordingly, Burford's most significant early action was a departmental reorganization that increased the prominence of the energy and minerals division. Formerly, energy and mineral issues were handled under the lands and resources division. Burford raised the division to equal bureaucratic status and turned it over to Sandra L. Blackstone, a 33-year-old Colorado attorney who had worked for Union Pacific on synfuels development for the past seven years. "My major priorities," said Burford, "are to streamline and make more efficient the process for leasing minerals on the public lands."

Gregg told us he had placed energy development within the lands division "because I wanted the conflict between what we could clearly see coming in energy development, and the interplay of that with renewable resources, to come together in the bureau below the level of the director." Staff members of the House subcommittee on public lands said the elevation of energy development concerns "must have pleased Watt and the mining folks. If Burford wanted to do that, he did a good job."

The BLM's 1982 budget also reflects the shifting priorities. The Reagan budget cut the funds and personnel devoted to wilderness reviews, analysis of environmental impacts for offshore oil and gas leasing, resource inventories, and planning; while increasing funds for both on- and offshore oil and gas development. The 1983 budget continues this trend, both in budget and personnel. "The proposed budget," said Terry Sopher of the Wilderness Society at congressional hearings, "will have the effect of seriously undermining the mandate and intent of the Federal Land Policy and Management Act. There will be no real balancing of resource development with resource protection."

There is no indication that Burford would raise any different concerns than Watt, even if he had a larger policy role. Like Watt, he had been closely aligned with the "sagebrush rebellion" in the past. In Colorado, Burford sponsored legislation supporting the turnover of federal lands to the states that eventually emerged from the Colorado legislature as a bill supporting an interstate study of such a turnover.

Burford told us the sagebrush rebellion was made up of "ranchers, miners, oil people and all the support people that exist within the communities which are mostly dependent upon the income from surrounding land owned by the 'Great White Father.'" When we asked him for the status of the rebellion he said, "It's defused, but it's certainly not dead. And I don't think it should be. I think it keeps the federal government on its toes. A lot of the states out there that have great [public] land masses in them think that they're not listened to in a lot of ways and there will still be some of that perception. There always will be."

Like Watt, once he got to Washington Burford found the prospect of relinquishing federal control of public lands less attractive, stating explicitly at his confirmation hearing that he believed in "federal ownership" of public lands. "I'm a pragmatic politician," he told us. "I don't think that the mass transfer would probably take place. . .I don't think that it is going to happen. . .maybe the mood of the country is such that it will want to return more and more of it [to private ownership]; I don't think it really will. I think that we'll still see a large public lands influence in the West."

Though Burford's views are similar to Watt's, his style is not. Less abrasive than his boss, Burford is a smooth legislative operator who doesn't like to unnecessarily ruffle feathers. Less prone to adverse publicity, he might make a more effective Secretary than Watt, in terms of keeping the lid on potentially unpopular policy shifts. Asked about Watt's confrontations with Congress, Burford told us: "Well, the secretary has a very direct manner and sometimes he's not too political in some of the things he says. But he makes the determination that that's the way he goes, is right down the line and he makes no bones about where he stands on any issue. Some people are able to soften impacts to a certain extent and Jim has been very upfront ever since I've known him and he just continues that way. That's bound to produce some abrasiveness that some might disagree with."

And his own style? "Oh, I think my style is a little different," he replied in his best Western drawl. "I come from a different background and I never had any experience in bureaucracies before. I've been in the legislative branch before for six years and I've been around for a good many years before that and I think that, I guess, you're quieter [with that background]."

Burford brings the longest personal experience to the grazing issue, which Gregg believes set off, more than any other single dispute, the sagebrush rebellion. "The livestock industry was—is—the most effectively organized lobby group around," said Gregg.

Burford, who has been part of that lobby for decades, said shortly before his nomination that while overgrazing might be a problem in some BLM areas, improved management could allow for increased grazing. In September, 1981 he told the Western Governors' Conference, "The public rangeland has the greatest potential for increased production of any resource on the public lands." Overgrazing prompted by federal subsidies was cited by a 1981 Council on Environmental Quality (CEQ) study as a major factor behind increasing desertification of the West. Studies by the BLM and the General Accounting Office indicated that at least a quarter, and perhaps much more, of BLM land, is "declining" due to overuse.

Of the CEQ analysis Burford said, "A lot of conclusions in that study I don't agree with and there are a lot of other people that are pretty knowledgeable not only in the United States but throughout the world community that don't agree with that." Desertification in the West, he said, "really is not one of my big concerns. I think we're going to see forage production and timber production and management, intensive management of ranges, intensive management of forests, of all renewable resources. . .I think that the capacity for. . .increasing production in rangeland is tremendous."

In an Administration overflowing with rhetoric about making the users of federal services pay their way, Burford is a holdout on the subsidies offered to ranchers who graze their herds on federal lands. Extending an argument that might have the federal government open the Treasury to any business facing rough times, Burford defended the subsidy by saying, "I look at a lot of the ranches in the West and I look at the rate that their debt has increased over the past 15 years and if that's a subsidy they need more of it, because most of them are in a pretty tough financial state." Besides, he said, the production of meat was something that "benefit[s] the entire population of the United States."

When we asked Burford if the entire population benefits as much as the individual rancher that is subsidized, he invoked free enterprise to again defend the government hand-out. "We operate on a free enterprise system, a profit system," Burford said. "If that man can't make a profit out there he's not going to stay there. . . . Where a lot of people get confused is they say that's a subsidy to the livestock industry. And in a way maybe it is. Some of the people that run on private lands think so. Even some of the livestock people will say that's a subsidy. But you go out to a lot of those ranchers, they're not making a lot of money and I know that from personal experience because that's where I come out of. I used to make money, but over the past 10 years the livestock business has not been very good."

In July, 1981, Burford issued a series of changes in federal grazing policy that included scaling back the environmental impact statement program, and dividing grazing lands into three categories ranging from "highly productive" to "fair-to-poor." In a form of triage, the most money would be applied to maintaining the bountiful areas and improving the weak areas, while those areas with "economially-limited production potential" would receive less attention.

"[T]he proposed policy," wrote the National Wildlife Federation in a September letter to Burford, "is a retreat from hard-won principles of scientific range management which the BLM has adopted and is in the process of applying to individual cases of conflicting resource use. . . . It undermines the BLM's planning process [and]. . .reduces the role of the interested public in grazing decisions by emphasizing consultation with livestock operators. . . ." Environmentalists maintain that the policy violates the requirements laid down for bureau environmental impact statements by a 1975 federal court decision on a case brought by the Natural Resources Defense Council.

Like Watt, Burford has long supported increasing industry access to wilderness areas. Burford summed his feelings in a *Denver Post* op-ed piece: "The ranchers, foresters and industry have a far greater dedication to land protection than environmentalists credit them with."

Burford expanded that position in our interview when we asked him whether the oil companies have as much concern for the environment as the government does. "It's been forced on them by attitudes of people, the environmental concerns of the people, that they have to have an environmental concern. Whether it is as great as or any greater than the government I don't know how you'd make that comparison, but they've done some terrific work in environmental issues recently—I'm not one who says we should remove all environmental controls because that's not feasible and I don't think would work—but they do have a great concern in it, they've spent a lot of money in it. . .and they are showing that environmental concern. They're people, just like you and I."

Burford has no use for proposals that the U.S. form a publicly-owned competitor to the multinational oil companies to develop resources on public lands, as other nations such as Canada and England have done. Such a move, he said, would lead to "nationalization." Reminded that the proposal does not involve nationalizing anything, he replied: "Yeah, but you're going right down the same line, and I take the attitude that if you think nationalization of oil companies is great I suggest you take a look at the Post Office."

In February, 1982, Burford issued a proposal to speed the release to development of potential wilderness lands and reduce the environmental impact studies of those areas. Voicing a position backed by developers, Burford expressed dissatisfaction with Congress' handling of wilderness designations. "I think Congress should take action on wilderness areas as they come up," he said. "I think they should be allowed a certain amount of time on it and inaction—uh—they should act on it because one committee should not be allowed to control whether an area stays in wilderness or not and that's essentially what you have."

FINANCIAL BACKGROUND

Burford's net worth, according to a March, 1981 Department of Interior filing with the Office of Personnel Management, "is several million dollars." Much of that derives from his extensive land and cattle holdings; he has made a great deal of money buying and selling land. In 1980, Burford sold 400 acres of his property to the National Park Service for $273,248. Several years ago he sold a patch of Eagle County ranchland that became the Vail Colorado ski resort.

Two of Burford's holdings raise conflict of interest questions. When nominated, Burford held permits to graze his cattle on 33,614 acres of federal land. Burford transferred title to his Mesa County ranch to a limited partnership consisting of himself and his three sons. Then, a second partnership, consisting solely of his three sons, was formed to purchase his cattle, BLM permits and a forest service permit, and to lease his interest in the first partnership. "The legal vehicle of two partnerships is being used to allow me to retain interest in the deeded land as an investment for future retirement," Burford wrote in a March 30, 1981 memo to the Office of Government Ethics. At his confirmation hearing, he explained he may wish to purchase "some more cattle, some more leases" when he leaves office, possibly from his sons.

Burford also received about $8,000 in royalties in 1980 from mineral rights that he leased to five companies, including Tenneco. The rights are valued at between $50,000 and $100,000. Burford agreed to turn over the royalties to charity while in office and to excuse himself from any "particular matters specifically involving BLM and any of the companies paying him royalties."

WHAT OTHERS ARE SAYING ABOUT HIM

- "Burford is right in tune with Watt's philosophy," said a staff member at the House Subcommittee on Public Lands and Parks.

- "Mr. Burford's background as a rancher on the public lands should give him a unique perspective and insight into public land grazing issues, but we would be more reassured by this background if it provided evidence that he cooperated with the BLM in devising a workable grazing plan for his allotment," said Debbie Sease of the Sierra Club.

- "Most of the bureau people basically say they are impressed with his sharpness," said Terry Sopher of the Wilderness Society. "But, he's a Watt man. He's not going to break with the secretary on anything."

JAMES HARRIS
DIRECTOR, OFFICE OF SURFACE MINING

RESPONSIBILITY OF OFFICE

Established by the 1977 Surface Mining Control and Reclamation Act, the OSM "is charged with making sure coal is mined in an environmentally sound fashion, and that previously mined-out areas are restored," in the words of an agency fact sheet.

Like the other major regulatory agencies, OSM sets minimum national standards for state programs, which, when approved, assume primary responsibility for enforcement under federal oversight. It also administers the Abandoned Mine Reclamation Fund, which is used to restore strip mined lands.

And like other regulatory agencies, OSM's activities have been snarled by a bewildering web of lawsuits from industry, states, and environmental groups.

The OSM's budget is divided into regulatory activities and the abandoned mine reclamation fund, which is funded by a tax on coal mine operations. While the total agency budget will rise from $131.2 million in 1981 to $137 million in 1982, regulatory activities will decline. Funding for regulation will drop from $74.8 million to $66.4 million. The budget increase is created by the growing revenue of the Trust Fund. Total agency staff will also drop from 1036 employees in 1981 (though Watt left 264 of those positions unfilled) to 657.

BACKGROUND

A professional geologist and former coal company employee who has often charged that the economy was "overregulated," Harris comes to the OSM from the Indiana State Senate, where he was a frequent critic of the agency.

As a state legislator, Harris had a long involvement with the federal surface mining law. He chaired a two-year study committee on developing a state program under the surface mining law and in 1978 and 1979 chaired the advisory committee created to monitor the state agency implementing that program. When he left Indiana, he was chair of the Senate Committee on Natural Resources, which had jurisdiction over strip mining and other resource issues. Indiana submitted its plan for federal approval in March, 1980. It was given partial approval eight months later; Indiana resubmitted on the rejected portions of the plan in September, 1981. The state legislation implementing the plan, which Harris sponsored, condemned the federal strip mining law as "An intrusion into the land use and planning control" functions of the state. Harris, who has voiced such sentiments elsewhere, said he inserted the language to avoid a gubernatorial veto of the measure.

In 1978 Harris sponsored a resolution urging the state to sue the federal government over the strip mining law provisions protecting prime farmland, and allowing the government to determine whether lands were "unsuitable" for stripping. "I felt that land use planning was a function of the state," he said later. The suit, which was joined by several coal companies, was rejected in a unanimous decision by the Supreme Court in June, 1981.

The court specifically rejected the argument that the law stepped on state prerogatives—a key point since the Reagan Administration is planning to devolve to the states increased authority for strip mining regulation.

Some of Harris's other votes in the Indiana Senate are also harbingers of the changes coming in OSM policy. During 1977 and 1978 he voted against legislation designed to encourage farmland preservation. In 1977, he voted against a sunshine bill opening up most agency proceedings to the public and the press; critics believe new Reagan Administration OSM regulations will reduce the opportunity for public input.

But Harris's record, despite the rote Republican bromides against regulation and federal encroachment, is difficult to easily categorize. During his first three years in the Indiana Senate, Harris's voting record, as measured by the Izaac Walton League's ratings, hovered around 60 percent. In his final year, he received a 100 percent rating from the environmental group, the only state Republican to do so. That 100 percent rating included a vote against a bill that would prohibit regulations stronger than federal law requires. He also played the key role in defeating another measure to require that agencies perform economic analyses before issuing regulations. (Under a February 17, 1981 executive order, the Reagan Administration has required that all "major" rules be subjected to "cost-benefit" analysis.)

Harris told us that while he supports cost-benefit analysis, the Indiana bill was too "open-ended" in its requirements.

"On quite a few occasions he has been one of only a few Republican senators voting with the conservationist position on bills before the legislature," wrote Thomas Dustin, the Izaak Walton League's executive director, in a July 9, 1981 letter to the Senate Energy Committee.

Harris's voting record on non-resource issues is similarly eclectic. He sponsored legislation to allow confidential pre-natal care for teenage girls, fought a bill proposing regulatory changes sought by state utilities, introduced a bill to increase the state income tax and said in a farewell interview that "the greatest danger to our system of government is one-issue politics regardless of the issue."

On the other hand, Harris sponsored a bill to repeal the state's direct primary election law, argued against the mandatory use of both safety seats for infants riding in automobiles and motorcycle helmets and successfully pushed through legislation which critics said undermined the merit appointee systems for police and fire departments.

Harris was first elected to the Indiana Senate in 1976 and reelected in 1980. From 1973-74, he served in the Indiana House of Representatives. Before that, he worked as a consulting geologist and spent a year as a surface mine superintendent for the J.R. Coal Company.

Harris comes with a long personal association with the coal mining industry. Both his grandfathers were coal miners, as was his father, who rose to supervisory positions with the Peabody Coal Co. Harris himself worked summers during World War II planting trees for a local strip-mining coal producer as part of what was then considered a reclamation effort. For four years during high school and college, Harris worked nights in a coal mine near his home in Boonville, Indiana.

That experience has given Harris some first-hand sensitivity for the need for a government presence overseeing surface mining. Asked if the free market could guarantee proper reclamation, Harris emphatically answered "No." Since neither the states nor the operators had shown enough responsibility to the problem, he told us, the federal government had properly stepped in. "Just as the states didn't show equal responsibility," he said, "so didn't the operators."

Since leaving the J.R. firm, and throughout his tenure in the state legislature, Harris has been a busy, and successful businessman. From 1969 to 1974, he was president and co-owner of Elberfeld Telephone Co., a rural telephone company. In 1975, he founded Harris Minerals Inc., which drilled for oil and gas. Three years later, in a partnership with W.C. Bussing, Jr., an Evansville developer, he founded Temp-Tek, a cellulose insulation concern. And throughout, often in partnership with Bussing, Harris bought and sold land—some of which raised conflict of interest questions since it involved coal companies under his committee's jurisdiction (See Financial Background.)

Born on March 5, 1929, Harris sought to enter both the Naval Academy and West Point, but was rejected because of an eye problem. He was graduated with a degree in geology from Indiana University in 1951, and is now married with four sons.

MAJOR ISSUES

- The Reagan Administration has targeted OSM for the same treatment it has accorded the other regulatory agencies: sharp budget cuts, siphoning off greater authority to the state and weakening regulations.

- Specifically, the Administration has proposed regulatory changes that would allow weak state programs to receive federal approval; environmental groups, many legislators and even some state officials fear this will force a "race to the bottom" with each state seeking to attract industry with the loosest standards.

- Harris has revised regulations governing inspection and enforcement to sharply reduce citizen participation.

- Even before Harris took office, Watt uprooted the agency with a major reorganization that severely reduces the OSM's presence in the field, limiting the agency's ability to oversee the state programs.

While waiting to see OSM Director James Harris, visitors can thumb through the periodicals in his anteroom—which include Peabody Coal's company magazine, filled with all the latest inside news of picnics and promotions, the journal of the American Mining Congress, and the Mining and Reclamation Council of America's magazine.

If that doesn't offer a clear enough indication of the OSM's new direction, Harris's boss James Watt left no doubt when addressing the National Coal Association in June, 1981: "In this one office, the Office of Surface Mining, we have every abuse of government. What a shame, what a shame. I promise you it will be changed."

Others might consider shameful the years of unregulated surface mining that scarred broad swathes of the midwestern and western countryside and left long, loping hillsides as barren and desolate as moonscapes. In any case, the Reagan Administration, spurred by the coal industry, has targeted the OSM for the same treatment it has accorded the other major regulatory agencies: sharp budget cuts, siphoning off greater authority to the states, and replacing, wherever possible, specific design standards with the less rigid performance standards desired by industry.

In his own words, the new director's primary goal is "to allow the industry to put coal on top of the ground at the least possible cost with sound environmental practices."

OSM is currently rewriting the complex Surface Mining Act Regulations promulgated in March, 1979 by the Carter Administration. The act itself, and the regulations, lay out in considerable detail what the coal operators must do to reclaim the land and protect surface and groundwater resources.

Like the industry, Harris has long been critical of that exacting approach, which is known as a design standard. "We in Washington do not have a corner on mining and reclamation technology and we cannot afford to tie the industry to design standards so rigid that the industry is precluded from building that 'better mousetrap,' " he said in congressional testimony.

But Edward Grandis of the Environmental Policy Center, a Washington group that has closely monitored the OSM since the act was passed, says that "in certain instances mere performance standards are not adequate and design criteria are necessary." Grandis cites as an example sedimentation ponds that hold mine spoils, refuse and toxic wastes, and are currently constructed according to design standards. "Those designs are critical to protect the residents of mining communities," he said. OSM is developing a performance standard for sedimentary ponds.

Industry claims about the rigidity of the regulations are also overstated, Grandis said. "The regulations were not all design in the first place," he told us. "But the regulations that they are trying to remove from design to performance are ultra-hazardous activities like blasting and sedimentation ponds." The changes will make enforcement more difficult, Grandis believes, because "the inspector, whether state or federal is not going to be able to tell by going down a checklist that [the activity] is being done correctly. It will only be apparent after problems develop" that something was being done wrong.

Harris has also indicated a distaste for the regulations requiring mining operators to return the land to its original contour—which Rep. John Seiberling (D-Ohio), a sponsor of the original law, calls "the guts of the act"—and those rules prohibiting the mining of farmland unless it can be restored to its former productivity. Changes in those standards would seem certain to prompt lawsuits.

Just before Christmas, 1981, Harris proposed to rewrite the rules governing enforcement and inspection as well. Harris put out an integrated series of changes that would sharply reduce the ability of citizen groups to press for restoration of stripmined lands. Harris said the rules demonstrated "our commitment to work closely with the states." But the Environmental Policy Center said they demonstrated a "gross denial of the coverage" afforded by the act.

Though the February 17, 1981 executive order requires formal cost-benefit analysis of agency regulations, Harris told us, "I think we're using a common sense rather than a counting approach with regard to cost-benefit." He added that he "didn't think there was any way" to use "accounting" methods to measure the value of many of the office's rules.

And although Watt has said the surface mining act does not need revision, Harris told us "I think there are some areas in which the act is flawed and I would hope in 1983 or so Congress would make some remedial changes." Among the areas Harris would like to see reviewed are the provisions governing surface mining on land designated "prime farmland" and overlapping state/federal enforcement authority.

Perhaps the most significant change proposed so far under the regulatory review has been in the criteria for judging state plans. OSM decided in October, 1981 to allow states to meet the law's requirement for programs "consistent with" the federal law by developing plans "as effective as" the federal program. According to Harris, the change would mean that "the state approach no longer need parallel the approach in federal regulations." Environmental groups have sued over the plan.

Under the old criteria, the OSM fully approved the programs of only three states and gave conditional approval to 13 others.

"I think the previous administration closed the state window and nailed it shut," Harris said. Critics fear the new policy will allow the approval of inadequate state programs.

"We are concerned that the programs that are being submitted under new program standards. . .are going to be essentially weaker than the act and also weaker than the 16 state programs that have been approved," said Grandis.

States that have developed strong programs fear that competing states might lure coal firm investment by offering less stringent regulations. "We want to be sure that the minimum stringent floor is not going to be dropped out from under," Rep. Pat Williams (D-Mont.) told Harris in hearings. "The dropping of the minimum standards would place. . .states that toed the mark in an economic disadvantage."

And the looser criteria may encourage states to weaken existing programs, as Harris appears to be aware. "If [because of the new rules] they [the states] see fit to change those programs to take advantage of some additional flexibility," Harris has said, "they are in a position to do that." "States have already said they will be under intense pressure from the coal industry to go back and weaken them," said Grandis.

"I think Harris is dedicated to severely restricting the role and responsibilities of the federal government in surface mining," concluded a counsel to the House Interior Committee. That effort includes sharp reductions in OSM's field presence. Before Harris was confirmed, Watt announced a massive reorganization of the OSM, which will reduce the total number of agency field offices from 42 to 22. The plan eliminates all five regional offices, all 13 district offices, and cuts the number of field offices from 24 to six, replacing them with 14 state liaison offices and two technical centers. Total personnel would be cut from the current ceiling of 1,001 to the mid-600s. Harris told us he was consulted on the "state office concept," but not on the specific location of the offices. But he has continued to implement the plan.

The OSM reorganization became one of Watt's most controversial actions, provoking an acerbic clash with Rep. Sidney Yates (D-Ill.), who chairs the House subcommittee that handles Interior appropriations. When Yates inserted a rider to the 1982 Interior appropriation barring the use of any funds to move the OSM Denver office to Casper, Wyoming, Watt, one day later, ordered the Denver (and Kansas City) office closed by August—still in the 1981 fiscal year. Watt made the order despite an internal Interior legal analysis which said the move might be illegal, because it used funds Congress had earmarked for other purposes.

Yates's subcommittee went back and added language that would have barred Interior from operating a reorganized OSM in 1982, meaning, one staffer said, "they could go ahead with the reorganization, but in 1982 they'd have to come back to the 1981 structure." But the Senate refused to go along with that provision, and the shift has continued.

The OSM reorganization has drawn criticism from many state officials and even some industry people who fear it will seriously disrupt the agency, and provoke an exodus of technical people unwilling to relocate. One industry lawyer told *Colorado Business*: "The reorganization could have the impact they [OSM employees] said it will. In the interim it's a headless monster." Watt critics said the reorganization was intended simply to weed out current OSM employees, and to make it more difficult for citizens to gain access to OSM officials.

Asked if the reorganization was worth the bitter feelings it stirred up among key House legislators, Harris told us, "You have to look at DOI as an entity and I think you have obstructionist forces in the House who will oppose any reorganization. And if we were to allow them to block this one without showing any resistance to their obstructionist position they might think we were going to lay down and play dead [on other issues]."

Interior officials said the move would put OSM closer to the booming coal industry in Wyoming. But, ironically, when Harris was on a western swing in October, 1981 he had to fly to Denver to meet with coal industry representatives. Aside from Denver, he had been meeting with ranchers—in Wyoming.

That such a major change in the agency could have been made without Harris's participation has fueled questions about his real role in shaping OSM policy. It has been widely speculated that Harris, who on occasion has appeared unaware of the regulatory changes his agency is promulgating, is merely a figurehead and that his deputy, J. Steven Griles, is really running OSM.

"I think Harris has recognized his role as director is to go around and make the industry and states love him,'' said Grandis, who has met with Harris several times. ''Harris has a lot of faith in Griles and realizes that Watt has a lot of faith in Griles.'' Griles formerly worked on the Virginia strip mining plan; like Indiana, Virginia challenged the federal law in the case in which the Supreme Court upheld the OSM law. Harris told us that he considers Griles ''a very capable young man.''

FINANCIAL BACKGROUND

Harris's business affairs are intertwined with two companies he must now regulate, and whose activities he was in a position to influence as an Indiana state legislator.

In March, 1981, the *Wall Street Journal* reported that Harris and his business partner, W.C. Bussing Jr., made two large land purchases from the Peabody and Amax coal companies at what the paper, based on interviews with local bankers and realtors, termed ''bargain prices.''

Harris and Bussing had bought 450 acres from Peabody in 1978 at $390 an acre and 1030 acres from Amax at $250 an acre in December, 1980 just three months before his nomination. Harris and Bussing subsequently subdivided and sold much of the land at prices up to $1,500.

Controversy over the Peabody sale declined somewhat when Bussing revealed that he first became aware of the land's availability through an ad in either an Evansville newspaper or the *Journal*. Several local real estate appraisers subsequently disputed the assertions that the land was sold at a bargain rate.

Amax officials said that the price for their land was relatively low because they wanted to sell it in one block, and that they had unsuccessfully tried to interest other buyers in the property. Amax's appraiser said that he told the company ''the value of the land would be a lot less that way than if they would sell the land a parcel at a time. . .I said they were going to make somebody a lot of money, but they said they weren't in the real estate business, they were in the coal business.''

The circumstances surrounding the Amax sale continued to raise troubling questions, even when Amax officials and Bussing testified at Harris's confirmation hearing to defend the transaction. The picture painted by those officials at the hearing, and by Harris in other public statements, was one of inside manuevering that, if not improper, was at the least unavailable to the average citizen.

Bussing told the Senate Energy Committee that he had first heard about the land's availability in late 1978 from the planning director of the Warwick County Planning Commission. Harris said that he, in turn, first heard about the land from Bussing.

Harris then contacted J. Nat Noland, Amax's chief Indiana lobbyist, according to Noland's testimony at the hearing. Noland set up a meeting between Harris and Gibson Martin, Amax's Indiana real estate chief, who has since left the company. Noland confirmed at the hearing, that on other occasions ''I had several discussions with Mr. Harris concerning surface mining legislation'' including bills relating to strip mining. At the meeting, Martin recalled in press interviews, he told Harris that: ''I will let you have the first shot at buying the land if you meet our price.'' The land did not go on the open market until at least the fall of 1979, up to a year after that meeting.

In July, 1980 Martin wrote Don McCollum, a real estate representative working on the sale to remind him that before he sold the land he should be certain to get back to Harris. The sale was concluded five months later.

"He [Harris] was sympathetic with the needs and problems of the industry and. . .the coal industry is one of the larger employers in his area," Martin said at the hearing. "And in my business career, when I say its easier to do business with your friends, it's always easier to make a deal with someone you know and had past relationships with rather than someone that you don't know or don't get along with."

Harris and Bussing hold an option to purchase another 1,030 acres from Amax at $275 an acre. Harris has said he intends to exercise the option, and has recused himself from all "particular matters regarding Amax" until he has completed the deal. But, as Grandis pointed out at Harris's confirmation, "It is difficult to understand how this can be practically implemented. Any action initiated by OSM that impacts large coal producers will effect Amax."

Harris earned $18,530 in salary and expenses from the Indiana State Senate in 1980 and another $11,490 in fees from the Indiana Farm Bureau for work as a geologist. He reported capital gains totalling between $106,700 and $280,000 largely through sales of stock in his telephone company, and 14 acres of farm land in Kentucky.

Harris shut down his Harris Minerals business. And asked at his confirmation hearing if he planned any more business deals with Bussing while in office, Harris replied, "After my experience over the past four months, you can be assured I won't."

WHAT OTHERS ARE SAYING ABOUT HIM

- "I think Harris is a good guy, but an ineffectual leader," said Grandis. "But he wants to be an ineffectual leader. I don't think he knows what is going on within his office day to day and I don't think he is particularly interested."

- Industry officials were more pleased with OSM's new approach. Representing both the National Coal Association and the American Mining Congress, Robin Turner told a House hearing, "The present OSM administration is making a valiant effort in reforming many of these unreasonable, burdensome and counterproductive regulations."

- Rep. Morris Udall (D-Ariz.), a co-sponsor of the strip mining law had a different view. "Putting someone like Harris in charge of the strip mining program," he told reporters, "is like putting Dracula in charge of the blood bank."

ENERGY DEPARTMENT

JAMES EDWARDS
SECRETARY

RESPONSIBILITY OF OFFICE

Edwards heads one of the most maligned federal agencies. Established in 1977 to consolidate the government's fragmented energy programs, the DOE has suffered from bureaucratic inefficiencies, administrative foul-ups and undue influence by the nation's oil industry. If the Reagan Administration has its way, DOE will soon be dispersed to the bureaucratic winds.

As secretary of DOE, Edwards runs a sprawling bureaucracy of 20,000 employees with a $10.5 billion budget.

Created to respond to the increasing shortages of non-renewable energy resources, and the United States' increasing dependence on foreign energy supplies, the DOE was expected to formulate a strong national energy program to meet present and future national energy needs.

BACKGROUND

Edwards was a practicing oral surgeon in Charleston, South Carolina, when he was appointed county chairman of the Charleston Republican Party in 1964, and entered a life of politics.

After running unsuccessfully for Congress in 1971, Edwards won a seat in the South Carolina State Legislature the next year. He did not forget his roots. One of the bills he introduced in the legislature required citizens to post a $500 bond when they sued doctors or dentists for malpractice.

After two terms in the state senate, Edwards snagged the GOP nomination for governor in 1974, opposing Charles "Pug" Ravenal, a popular Democrat who was heavily favored. Just prior to the general elections though, the South Carolina courts ruled that Ravenal violated residency requirements and barred him from the election. Edwards won the "fluke" election with 50.9 percent of the vote, over former Rep. William Jennings Bryan Dorn who was unable to unite the Democratic Party. The victory made Edwards the first Republican governor of South Carolina in over 100 years.

One of Edwards's outspoken opponents in South Carolina was state Rep. Robert R. Woods (D-Charleston). Woods recalls that from the beginning of his term as governor, Edwards denounced the Equal Rights Amendment, favored the death penalty, and dismissed the idea that government should assist the poor.

"He was one who felt superior to those he governed. Blacks were not able to have a meaningful role or input in government under Edwards," added Woods.

Edwards's views on pollution have long been consonant with those now expressed by the Reagan Administration. In 1968, one state health officer publicly stated that he considered breathing the air in Charleston to be equivalent to smoking at least two packs of cigarettes per day. A few years later the South Carolina commissioner for the Department of Health and Environmental Controls described North Charleston as "a veritable smorgasbord of pollutants." But at his first gubernatorial news conference, Edwards dismissed the need for anti-pollution laws in South Carolina. "They are not needed here in South Carolina where we have the nice breezes to carry off the emissions and dissipate them," Edwards told reporters.

As governor, Edwards was an unabashed supporter of nuclear energy and declared that "the good Lord has given us the resources [atomic energy] to continue the life we are used to in this country. We should take advantage of this resource." Also a proponent of the development of nuclear fuel reprocessing, Edwards supported the construction of South Carolina's Barnwell Nuclear Fuel Plant (the only commercial reprocessing facility in the United States). Although the plant was completed in the early 1970s, neither President Ford nor Carter would sanction commercial reprocessing. Both presidents refused for fear that the plutonium derived from the reprocessing procedure could be used to produce nuclear weapons. Reagan has lifted the ban on reprocessing, but no one has yet sought a license to actually do it.

Proudly calling his state "the nuclear capital of the world," Edwards dismissed these fears saying, "this idea that a high school kid can go into the kitchen and manufacture a plutonium bomb is a bunch of hogwash."

In 1978 testimony before the House Subcommittee on Fossil and Nuclear Energy, Edwards, who had been appointed chairman of the nuclear energy subcommittee of the National Governors Association, was asked whether the people of South Carolina would allow a nuclear repository in their state. Edwards responded that his state was already a repository for nuclear wastes. "I make no excuses for it. I'm not apologizing for it," said Edwards. "Thank God we have these nuclear wastes because if we didn't we would probably all be working in salt mines in Siberia today and we would not be worried about nuclear wastes."

During Edwards's tenure as governor, Chem-Nuclear Services Inc., a low-level waste burial site in Barnwell, grew from a small regional dump to become the nation's major commercial low-level waste disposal site. When Edwards left office, South Carolina was receiving 80-90 percent of the nation's commercially generated low-level radioactive waste. The state's inspection program was criticized by the anti-nuclear Palmetto Alliance organization as infrequent and ineffective.

In 1977 Edwards established the South Carolina Energy Research Institute (ERI) which has been repeatedly singled out by his supporters as one of Edwards's major qualifications for the position of Energy Secretary. Officially ERI was to be broadly "representative of business, industrial, environmental and consumer interests in the energy field." With a steering committee that looked like a nuclear industry board of directors and Ben Rusche (formerly of the Nuclear Regulatory Commission) as director, the ERI recommended a $2.2 million "feasibility" study for a gargantuan 12-reactor park in Anderson County. The park idea was soon dropped, however, but Rusche, a proponent of the breeder reactor and advocate of reprocessing, is currently one of Edwards's top advisers.

Edwards was nominated to head DOE after southern senators, led by Strom Thurmond (R-S.C.), complained that the South had been ignored in Reagan's initial Cabinet selections. One of the few elected Republicans to support Reagan in his unsuccessful 1976 race against Gerald Ford, Edwards had originally backed John B.

Connally in the 1980 race, but helped Reagan carry the state after Connally quit.

Born on June 24, 1927, in Hawthorne, Florida, Edwards received his under-graduate degree from the College of Charleston in 1950 and his dentistry degree from the University of Louisville in 1955. He is married with two children.

MAJOR ISSUES

- A Washington novice, Edwards was often outmaneuvered during his first year in office, but proved to be a determined advocate of the nuclear industry, advancing its interests on all fronts.

- His department's budget protects expenditures on nuclear-related projects, while slashing funding for conservation, solar energy, and other renewables.

- Edwards fought hard to maintain costly synfuels subsidies, despite opposition from the Office of Management and Budget (OMB). Eventually, Reagan backed Edwards.

- Edwards has been the leading force within the Administration promoting the decontrol of natural gas, a move which could double consumer bills by 1985, and swell inflationary pressures.

- Edwards has acquiesced in the Administration's plans to dismantle his agency, though by some accounts he is privately unenthusiastic about the prospect.

For Edwards, it has not been a smooth transition to Washington and the byzan-tine world of energy politics. Often unsure of his facts, occasionally embarrassed in congressional testimony, and regularly outmaneuvered by David Stockman, the hard-driving OMB director, Edwards stumbled out of the starting gate and quickly fell out of favor with White House aides. They reportedly consider him one of the major disappointments in the Cabinet.

Though much of the Administration's energy policy appeared to be emanating from OMB, Edwards's own energy philosophy is right in line with Reagan's: removal of federal energy price controls, a reduced emphasis on solar and conserva-tion, and strong support for the nuclear power industry. The third National Energy Plan, released by Edwards in July, 1981 calls for increased reliance on market forces and expanded development of nuclear power.

The Administration's real commitment to the development of a free, open energy marketplace is viewed as a "mixed policy" by Edwin Rothschild, director of Energy Action.

"Clearly nuclear is getting a lot of constant support while solar and conservation aren't and what they're [the Reagan Administration] saying is free market for all these solar and conservation technologies but subsidies for nuclear and synthetic fuels," said Rothschild.

The Administration's 1982 budget slashed spending for solar and conservation, while increasing nuclear expenditures by 18 percent. Funding was provided toward completion of the long-delayed and increasingly expensive Clinch River Breeder Reactor (See Davis and Brewer profiles), and to help General Public Utilities clean up Three Mile Island.

The 1983 budget continues this trend. Under the Administration's proposal, Clinch River would receive $252 million, $185 million would be devoted toward nuclear waste management, and overall nuclear budget authority would be trimmed by 7 percent to $1.16 billion. Funding for nuclear fusion would remain virtually stable. Expenditures on renewable resources, by contrast, would be virtually eradicated. Solar research would be cut from $524 million in 1981 to $72 million; conservation research from $279 million in 1981 to $18 million; and conservation grants to localities, hospitals and schools virtually eliminated. Certain tax credits to encourage conservation would also be eliminated.

Cumulatively, the cuts reflect a drastic reordering of priorities toward atomic energy. In the 1981 budget, renewables, nuclear and fossil each received about 13 percent of R&D funding; under the 1983 budget nuclear would remain steady at 12 percent, while renewables and fossil would drop almost out of sight at 1 percent. Nuclear expenditures are slated to rise again by 15 percent in 1984 to $1.686 billion, while funding for non-nuclear research would decline 85 percent from its 1980 level to $331 million.

In a recent *New York Times* article, former director of the department's Solar Energy Research Institute (SERI), Denis Hayes, argued that "Edwards's energy budget was shaped by blind bias. Even as the country's most promising energy options are being gutted, a herd of technological losers will be getting fat at the public trough." Hayes, who was asked for his resignation following an argument with DOE over possible staffing cutbacks at SERI, has been a strong and outspoken proponent of solar energy.

A Gallup Poll funded by SERI revealed that out of seven options, solar was the most preferred energy source among Americans. Nuclear energy came in last.

"Unless Congress acts swiftly to protect the solar programs it originally created, America's brightest energy hope—the renewable technologies most favored by the U.S. public—will be set back dramatically," said Hayes.

Edwards also sought funds in the 1982 budget for a federal purchase of the Barnwell plant, but was denied by OMB. Ultimately, Congress gave Barnwell about $10 million for maintenance and research and development though the DOE budget did not request any funding.

Edwards's commitment to supporting the nuclear industry is evident in a June, 1981 interview in the *Orangeburg Times and Democrat* in which he charged that "subversive elements" are using environmentalists to undermine the nation's nuclear energy development. "We are inflicting wounds on ourselves by allowing these strident voices, many of them who wish us harm, to keep us from realizing our potential," he said. Edwards did not identify any "subversives."

A June 21, 1981 editorial in Columbia's *The State* newspaper said the Edwards interview "reminds us of the way the late Sen. Joe McCarthy went about his campaign against alleged communists infiltrating the U.S. government." The newspaper demanded that Edwards back up his charges and noted that since they came from a Cabinet member, the statements "must be taken seriously and considered to reflect the thinking of the Administration." Indeed, Reagan has been making similarly unsubstantiated charges about nuclear opponents for years.

The Administration's free market sympathies has not kept it from upholding the synthetic fuels subsidy program. Though the Synthetic Fuels Corporation was left untouched in the budget cuts, Edwards has run into conflict with OMB Director David Stockman over direct DOE synfuel subsidies.

Edwards was on the verge of awarding government loans and price guarantees to three synfuels projects in spring, 1981 when Stockman refused to sign off on the projects. Involved was a $2 billion loan guarantee to the Great Plains coal-gasification project in Beulah, North Dakota; a $1.1 billion loan guarantee to Tosco

Corporation for a shale-oil project; and price guarantees for a Union Oil Co. shale-oil project.

Stockman and Edwards were bucking in a noisy, increasingly public dispute, when Reagan stepped in on July 29 and approved the $400 million guarantee for Union Oil. Reagan's move saved Edwards in a nasty confrontation with the energy subcommittee of the House Government Operations Committee, which had been demanding to see documents spelling out the financial arrangements the government negotiated with Union Oil. Edwards had refused to provide material the committee demanded, arguing that it involved unresolved confidential negotiations. The subcommittee hit Edwards with a contempt of Congress citation, but with the plans approved, the documents were forwarded to the committee.

Stockman and other White House aides were even more critical of the other two projects, but the White House approved both those subsidies on August 6, 1981.

In the upcoming months, Edwards and the Reagan Administration may face a political battle that will make the synfuels tussle pale by comparison. On August 9, 1981 Reagan's Cabinet Council on Energy and Natural Resources recommended that he press for the decontrol of natural gas prices, a move which could double consumer bills by 1985, and ignite a full-scale political conflagration in Congress. Edwards has been a consistent supporter of decontrol and even claimed credit for being the "leader in bringing about consensus" at the Cabinet council meeting.

Even congressional leaders sympathetic to the oil industry such as James McClure of Idaho, chair of the Senate Energy Committee, have urged that the extraordinarily volatile issue be put off. The Administration ultimately decided to defer the debate until after the 1982 congressional elections, fearing a politically damaging battle. Rep. John Dingell (D-Mich.), who chairs the House Energy and Commerce Committee, has already warned that decontrol will come "over my dead body."

If the issue is delayed several years, Edwards may not be in Washington to worry about it. Shortly before his nomination, Edwards said, "I'd like to go to Washington and close the Energy Department down and work myself out of a job."

Even though abolishing the department was an early Reagan campaign pledge, Edwards changed his tune in questioning from Sen. Henry Jackson (D-Wash.) during his confirmation hearing. Edwards said that what he meant was, "we're going to look at the agency, try to streamline it if we can, increase the efficiency of it and see what we can do to deliver more energy to the American people."

But when the budget picture darkened in the fall of 1981, the Administration floated the idea again. In December, the Administration introduced a plan to dismember the agency. Interior Secretary James Watt—who wanted the entire body—would be given the $3 billion a year strategic petroleum reserve, the naval petroleum reserves, the oil shale program and the regional power marketing administrations. The Justice Department would be handed the cases against major oil companies for overcharging while price controls were in place. The Federal Energy Regulatory Commission would become an independent agency. The big winner in the deal would be the Commerce Department, which would pick up authority for national energy policy, statistics and fossil fuels, assume oversight of a new Energy Research and Technology Administration that would handle the $6 billion nuclear weapons construction program; and direct nuclear, solar and conservation research and the government's uranium enrichment plants.

In its 1983 budget, the Administration maintains the reorganization would save $1.3 billion and "3,800 work years from present estimates of 1982 levels."

Though the DOE has never been among the more popular, or well run, federal agencies, the President's plan hasn't won too many friends either. The Congressional Budget Office says the savings reorganization would produce are minimal, and some legislators are concerned the proposal represents a decreased national attention to energy policy. Even Edwards, according to some press accounts, is unenthusiastic about the plan. He is likely to be one of the first Reagan Cabinet members to leave office.

FINANCIAL BACKGROUND

Edwards left a lucrative dental practice in South Carolina, which netted him almost $200,000 a year, to serve as Energy secretary. As secretary he is taking about a two-thirds cut in pay and was asked to resign from Amvest Corporation prior to assuming office.

Edwards' financial disclosure indicates that his total net worth is over $1 million with the bulk of his holdings in real estate centering around Mt. Pleasant, South Carolina. Edwards has also been a partner in the real estate organization of Edwards & Brock since 1967.

WHAT OTHERS ARE SAYING ABOUT HIM

- "I think it is not an overdramatization to say that this Administration—and, in particular, Secretary Edwards—has declared open war on solar energy," said Denis Hayes, former director of SERI.

- "I don't think that Edwards is running the DOE, I think it's Watt and before that it was Stockman. The person chosen for the DOE is not the person that is really going to be the real key on energy policy. Watt has been the person sitting on the cabinet council on natural gas and on the OCS [Outer Continental Shelf] and those are the two major directions that the Administration is taking on energy, and Watt is in charge of it. Clearly Edwards is second fiddle," said Edwin Rothschild of Energy Action.

W. KENNETH DAVIS
DEPUTY SECRETARY

RESPONSIBILITY OF OFFICE

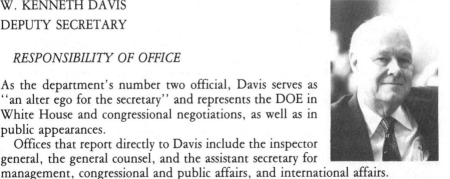

As the department's number two official, Davis serves as "an alter ego for the secretary" and represents the DOE in White House and congressional negotiations, as well as in public appearances.

Offices that report directly to Davis include the inspector general, the general counsel, and the assistant secretary for management, congressional and public affairs, and international affairs.

If Edwards were to become disabled, Davis would take over the department. Davis has a broad policy role, but his long career in the nuclear industry gives him a special interest in that area. Insiders say that Davis could replace Edwards if the secretary leaves as is expected.

BACKGROUND

When it comes to nuclear power, W. Kenneth Davis has been present since the creation. Formerly director of reactor development for the Atomic Energy Commission (AEC), formerly vice-president for nuclear development of the Bechtel Corp., one of the nation's major nuclear contractors, former president of the Atomic Industrial Forum (AIF), the industry trade group, former director of the American Nuclear Energy Council (ANEC), Davis's hands have shaped the nuclear power industry as much as any. After a 22-year hiatus at Bechtel, he moves back into government at a critical juncture for the industry he has devoted his career to building.

Davis, a chemical engineer by training, first joined the government in 1954, as an assistant director of reactor development for the AEC. In private business he worked on AEC and nuclear matters since the late 1940s; first with Ford, Bacon & Davis where he helped design the federal government's Argonne National Lab; and then with the California Research and Development Co., where he worked on breeder reactors and designed the federal nuclear laboratory at Livermore, California.

In the bureaucracy, Davis quickly rose to head reactor development. In the mid-1950s, as the AEC (under steady prodding from the Congressional Joint Committee on Atomic Energy) intensified its efforts to develop a commercial nuclear power industry—expanding expenditures five-fold from 1954 to 1959—Davis became a familiar public figure. Obviously an influential aide, Davis supplied the technical expertise the AEC commissioners needed when summoned before Congress; during one 1957 hearing a total of 24 AEC officials were brought in to testify but only the commission chairman and Davis answered any questions.

Under a variety of research programs, Davis's division evaluated the various forms of nuclear power plants that might be constructed— pressurized and boiling water reactors, fast breeders, sodium-graphite and aqueous homogenous reactors. In October, 1957, Davis declared that the water reactors were the most promising. Since then, water reactors have become the dominant form in the industry. Davis backed the use of enriched, rather than natural, uranium as nuclear fuel. Enriched uranium is now the dominant nuclear fuel. These two decisions guaranteed that other countries anxious to develop nuclear power would be dependent on U.S. corporations and the U.S. government because of complexity and secrecy surrounding uranium enrichment.

In those days, the optimism of Davis and his colleagues was almost boundless, tempered only by concern about nuclear's ability to compete economically at its outset. At a 1955 conference on industrial health, Davis told participants that nuclear power plants should be built as close as possible to consuming areas. "When it [nuclear power] comes," he said, "it will not bring undue safety hazards to plant workers or public." Two and a half years later, in an article written with two AEC colleagues, Davis predicted that by 1967 the "safety of nuclear power plants [will be] established to the point where site selection will no longer be of real concern to the public." Experts now admit that plants such as Indian Point on the outskirts of New York City should never have been built where they were.

In a 1956 article for the *Washington Post*, Davis forecasted 100 million kilowatts of nuclear electrical capacity would be in place by 1980; about half that much of capacity is actually on line today. Davis also predicted that by 1980 nuclear would provide two-thirds of all new generation capacity; the actual figure is 12 percent. And he claimed there would be "significant decreases in both capital and operating costs," though the industry had already shown, in the words of a 1958 issue of *Nucleonics*, "a marked genius for underestimating costs."

Nor would the role of nuclear power be limited to generating commercial electricity. Davis predicted nuclear power would propel both military and commercial ships. He spoke of nuclear process heat for industry and even reactors that would be used to preserve food and shape materials.

Though optimistic, Davis consistently argued for focusing first on research and demonstration projects, rather than launching a full-scale effort to immediately dot the countryside with commercial-scale plants, as some members of Congress—and indeed the press—were pushing with a cold war-generated fervor. Responding to a 1956 *New York Times* editorial on "The Lag in Atomic Power," Davis wrote: "We believe that the immediate job is the development of nuclear-power plants through research, development, reactor experiments and prototype power plants, not the construction of a large number of nuclear-power plants to achieve an arbitrary or competitive goal in terms of nuclear kilowatts."

Private companies began to be part of this process under an AEC Power Demonstration Reactor Program begun in 1955. Under that program, the AEC directly subsidized nuclear power plant construction. One of the first reactors built under the program was the Enrico Fermi plant whose near-meltdown in 1966 was the subject of the book *We Almost Lost Detroit*.

By the late 1950s, a commercial nuclear power industry was taking form: In 1956, the AEC listed four major engineering firms working with utilities to usher in the new age, including Westinghouse and General Electric. Bechtel was not among them, so in July, 1958, the corporation reached out to Washington and hired Davis and some of his top aides to bring them into the nuclear business. Davis went to Bechtel two weeks before John McCone, a former business partner and long-time friend of Stephen Bechtel, Sr., became AEC chairman. "As ordinarily happens," said David Brower, chairman of Friends of the Earth and a personal friend of Davis for 45 years, "they go right to the top to get the best people they can. If you're going to get into the nuclear business, you get Ken Davis."

Davis did his job well. With the help of an AEC contract to build a plant in Dresden, Illinois, Bechtel jumped into the nuclear business. Today, of the 167 nuclear power plants either licensed or in the pipeline, Bechtel has built or designed 60 of them; it is both the architect and construction contractor on about one-fourth of all existing and planned reactors.

Though not one of the more heavily-troubled nuclear contractors, Bechtel's record has its flaws. In 1977, it agreed to pay the Consumers Power Company of Michigan $14 million in damages over operating difficulties at the company's Palisades nuclear plant. A 1973 AEC memo labeled Bechtel's plant in Tarapur, India the world's "prime candidate" for a major nuclear disaster.

A Critical Mass Energy Project study analyzing mishaps at nuclear power plants, reported to the Nuclear Regulatory Commission (NRC) in 1980, found that a plant for which Bechtel was the architect/engineer, the Hatch 1 unit in Georgia, had the most reported incidents relating to equipment failure. Another plant both engineered and built by Bechtel, the Arkansas II unit, in Russellville, Arkansas had the second highest number of incidents. Of the ten plants with the most incidents related to design/fabrication errors, Bechtel was the engineer and construction agent on three of them; it was the engineer on another two. Finally, of the five plants that had six or more "especially significant mishaps"—based on internal NRC classification procedures—two were both engineered and built by Bechtel.

Hiring high Washington officials like Davis, former Treasury Secretary George Schultz, and former Budget Director (now Defense Secretary) Caspar Weinberger, Bechtel has always enjoyed a lucrative relationship with the federal government. At the DOE alone, as of 1981 Bechtel had contracts totalling $250 million, including a $140 million assignment to oversee the cleanup of some uranium mining operations in the West; a $37.5 million contract as architect/engineer on the Waste Isolation Pilot Plant in New Mexico; and a $32.96 million contract as co-architect/engineer on a government uranium enrichment facility under expansion at Portsmouth, Ohio.

Bechtel has used that influence to obtain other favors as well. In the early 1970s, the company developed a plan to enter the uranium enrichment business, which had been until that time a government monopoly. As he was on all nuclear issues, Davis was heavily involved in the proposal, Bechtel sources report.

In May, 1975, Uranium Enrichment Associates (UEA), a consortium headed by Bechtel, sent an unsolicited proposal to the government for its enrichment plant; one month later, President Ford sent to Congress the Nuclear Fuel Assurance Act, which would have not only broken the government monopoly but given UEA a series of subsidies and guarantees that would, according to the General Accounting Office, shift "most of the risks" to the government. After fierce lobbying, Congress eventually rejected the plan. With the government now urging commercialization of nuclear reprocessing, it would not be surprising to see the proposals for commercial fuel enrichment resurface.

Similarly, when Bechtel developed a proposal in the early 1970s to build a slurry pipeline to transport coal from Wyoming to southern utilities, it persuaded congressional supporters to introduce legislation granting the pipelines the right of eminent domain, which would allow the pipeline to cross railroad rights-of-way. Davis's role in the development of this proposal is less clear, but he did head an internal committee studying ways to increase Bechtel's coal business, and he notes in his resume that he was "very active in positioning Bechtel in the coal and synthetic fuels area. . . ."

Bitterly opposed by the railroads, the legislation is still before Congress. After much internal debate, the Administration announced at November, 1981 hearings that it would oppose the plan. Its most strenuous supporter in the internal deliberations, however, was the DOE.

Through it all, though, Davis still holds a special passion for nuclear power. President of the Atomic Industrial Forum (AIF) from 1964-1966, he has headed up numerous AIF committees and served as an honorary director until his appointment. As vice-president of the National Academy of Engineering and a member of the governing board of the National Research Council, Davis has participated in innumerable other energy studies—a true growth industry of the 1970s—including the National Academy of Sciences' massive *Energy in Transition* report.

Despite nuclear power's setbacks in the 1970s, Davis remains a true believer, committed to the development of the breeder and spent fuel reprocessing (Bechtel designed the Barnwell, South Carolina, reprocessing facility and both designed and built the now-closed West Valley, New York plant); downplaying the risks of weapons proliferation those technologies bring (he once called such risks "trivial"); asserting that the industry's problems "have been grossly distorted and inflated by the critics who manage to obtain enormous publicity for wild statements of all sorts"; and disparaging solar energy, which he told the AIF in 1975 was of "no significance whatever in the next 10 to 20 years."

During that 1975 speech, Davis perhaps best summed up his energy philosophy: "We need to proceed as fast as we can to build nuclear power plants. . ." he said. That would require, he noted, "a new spirit of cooperation between government and industry."

Another story captures Davis's devotion. Through most of his life, Davis has been an ardent hiker and skier—his friends call him "65 degree Davis" because he claims to have once skied a slope that steep. A few summers ago, Davis was hiking with a colleague in New Hampshire when he stopped in a camp area to rest. Also in the camp, coincidentally, was Amory Lovins, the well-known anti-nuclear physicist. Lovins recognized Davis and decided to say hello. "I came up to their table and introduced myself," Lovins recalled, "and they reacted as if I said I was the anti-Christ."

Born on July 26, 1918, in Seattle, Washington, Davis received his undergraduate and graduate degrees in chemical engineering from the Massachusetts Institute of Technology in 1940 and 1942 respectively. He is married with three children.

FINANCIAL BACKGROUND

As is the rule for high Bechtel officials, Davis is a wealthy man. His salary in 1980 was $224,305, and he pocketed $63,750 in bonuses when he left the company to take the DOE job. His financial disclosure form shows that he has assets worth at least $4.5 million, and probably a good deal more than that. His Bechtel stock alone—which he sold upon assuming office—was worth more than $750,000. Davis also had large holdings in several oil and real estate partnerships.

The DOE originally sought a waiver that would allow Davis to participate in departmental affairs concerning Bechtel. But when the House Government Operations Subcommittee on Energy and the Environment raised objections, the department agreed to keep Davis out of matters directly affecting Bechtel, such as contracts and lawsuits. Edwards granted Davis a waiver to participate in broader policy decisions that could affect Bechtel.

When assuming office, Davis sold off a number of energy stocks, including Standard Oil of California, Occidental Petroleum and Pacific Gas & Electric—and subsequently divested himself of a second group, including Phelps Dodge, Newmont Mining and General Electric.

Under Bechtel's mandatory retirement policy, Davis has to return to the company by July, 1983 if he wants to return in a management position at all.

WHAT OTHERS ARE SAYING ABOUT HIM

- David Brower, who has hiked and skied with Davis for years, said: "He's always been pretty much the optimist about nuclear power and he's put so much of his life into it he can't reverse. He talked about it with great confidence back in the mid-1950s and he never lost it. I lost mine."

- Noting that Davis is "thought of in the industry as one of their leading strategists," Lovins told us, "It's pretty clear that people like Davis have been responsible for killing the industry and that will be the verdict of history."

- Several congressional staffers said that they believed that Davis had been put at the DOE to watch over Bechtel's interests in energy policy. Though he has recused himself from specific Bechtel contracts, "he probably should still be on the payroll," said an aide at the House Interior Committee.

SHELBY BREWER
ASSISTANT SECRETARY FOR NUCLEAR ENERGY

RESPONSIBILITY OF OFFICE

Usually the department's senior nuclear energy official, the assistant secretary slot has been overshadowed by two equally ardent nuclear supporters in the department's top two positions: Secretary Edwards and Deputy Secretary Davis.

Brewer is responsible for all of DOE's nuclear programs, save for those involved in actually building nuclear weapons, which are handled by the assistant secretary for defense programs. Brewer oversees the department's nuclear waste programs, nuclear research, and runs the government's uranium enrichment services, which enhances uranium for domestic and foreign utilities and for the military.

BACKGROUND

Brewer has been a company man, steadily moving up over the past decade through the government's nuclear bureaucracy. Immediately before taking over the assistant secretary for nuclear energy slot, Brewer headed the nuclear division's Office of Plans and Evaluation.

His responsibilities there included fiscal and policy oversight of breeder reactor development, whose cause he has embraced with passion. Though the much troubled Clinch River Breeder Reactor continues to rise in cost, plagued by management and contracting problems, Brewer remains a staunch supporter. One former Carter Administration official who served on interagency work groups with Brewer told us: "He's pro-breeder to the extent that he's lost sight of the original intention, which is to produce electricity economically." (See Major Issues.)

A nuclear engineer by training, Brewer has been wed to the breeder since he entered government in 1971 as a technical assistant to the director of Reactor Research and Demonstration at the old Atomic Energy Commission (AEC). From 1975-77 he ran the breeder program at the Energy Research and Development Administration (ERDA).

In a written statement submitted at his confirmation hearing, Brewer asserted, "I am recognized as a principal force in defending and salvaging AEC/ERDA/DOE nuclear development/demonstration projects during their most critical and volatile period—1974–present."

In all, Brewer has been involved with nuclear power for almost 20 years. After receiving undergraduate humanities, and graduate engineering, degrees from Columbia University in 1959 and 1960 respectively, he joined the U.S. Navy in 1960; two years later, he took over the Department of Nuclear Reactor Physics and Nuclear Reactor Engineering at the Navy's Nuclear Power Staff, where he wrote classified textbooks. After leaving the Navy, he joined the staff of the Massachusetts Institute of Technology (MIT), working on nuclear research. Along the way, he picked up another M.S. degree, in nuclear engineering from MIT, which he supplemented with a Ph.D. in the same field in 1970.

From 1968-1971, Brewer was a consulting engineer for Stone and Webster, a major nuclear supplier, working on containment design and representing utility clients seeking permits from the AEC. In 1979, the Nuclear Regulatory Commission shut down five nuclear plants after learning that an arithmetical error in a computer model designed by Stone & Webster left their cooling system pipes only one-sixth as strong as they should be, and inadequately resistant to earthquakes.

In public appearances, Brewer is low-key, unconfrontational, and somewhat unflappable, even if plodding in presentation. That style, though, can be surprisingly effective. Case in point: In October, 1981, Brewer was summoned to testify before a hostile subcommittee of the House Interior Committee. As the first congressional hearings on the Reagan nuclear policy, it drew an overflow crowd and a bevy of network cameras. But despite sharp criticism, bitter questions, and repeated interruptions by the panel, Brewer refused to be drawn into a fight. Speaking almost inaudibly, he also managed to avoid giving the press any good quotes—and thereby kept the event off the evening's news. He left the hearing room unscathed.

Privately, the former Carter official explained, Brewer can be considerably different. "He can be quite a fighter," the official said. "He can be fairly aggressive. But deep down, he's just one of your typical hard-case breeder supporters. . ."

Brewer is a member of the American Nuclear Society, an aggressively pro-nuclear organization and once played on the U.S. Junior Davis Cup tennis team.

Born in Little Rock, Arkansas on February 19, 1937, Brewer is married with two children.

FINANCIAL BACKGROUND

Brewer's financial disclosure statement does not list holdings or investments of any kind.

WHAT OTHERS ARE SAYING ABOUT HIM

- After Brewer's appearance before the House Interior Oversight Subcommittee, one aide told us, "For one of those strong supporter types he was very mild-mannered. Not a nut, which is why they [send him up]. . .They don't send up the nuts."

- "He's not a foolish person, he's not unreasonable," said a Carter Administration official who worked with him, "but he's quite single-minded about the breeder."

MAJOR ISSUES

Buffeted by exploding construction costs, relentless safety problems, and its distinctly diminishing attraction for the utility industry and Wall Street, the nuclear power industry is limping into the 1980s. For the Reagan Administration, reversing the industry's fortunes has become a crusade, perhaps its single most cherished energy goal.

"One of the best potential sources of new electrical energy supplies in the coming decades is nuclear power," Reagan said in October, 1981 when announcing a series of policy changes designed to revive the industry. "The policies and actions that I am announcing today will permit a revitalization of the U.S. industry's efforts to develop nuclear power."

Despite that rosy prediction the industry must still wonder whether any amount of federal resuscitation can bring it back from its nearly comatose state. No new reactor orders have been placed since 1978; since 1974, more reactors by far have been cancelled than have been ordered. Massive cost overruns have been the rule on projects around the country.

The Washington Public Power Supply System, for example, has been forced to scrap two of five planned nuclear reactors, after construction costs for the package soared from $6 billion to $23.8 billion. Meanwhile, federal investigators continue to routinely turn up safety problems at the plants in operation; Nuclear Regulatory Commission investigators, for example, say at least eight—and perhaps as many as 46—of the nation's 72 reactors have reactor vessels that are becoming brittle more quickly than had been expected. Solving the problem will require more expensive modifications and costly down-time. NRC chairman Nunzio Palladino recently assailed the nuclear industry for its "failure to achieve. . .quality of construction and plant operations."

"The Reagan nuclear policy is little more than a get well card for a terminally ill patient," maintained physicist Dr. Henry Kendall, chairman of the board of the Union of Concerned Scientists. "The nuclear power industry has fallen ill—gravely we believe—from a host of ailments whose symptoms have been studiously ignored or suppressed for almost two decades by industry and the federal nuclear establishment alike."

The Administration's plan to rescue the nuclear industry has four basic components:

- increasing federal expenditures for nuclear power, including funding the completion of the Clinch River Breeder Reactor, and assisting General Public Utilities with the clean-up of Three Mile Island;

- pressuring the Nuclear Regulatory Commission to speed up licensing of new plants (For more information, see profile of Nunzio Palladino);

- ending the ban on commercial reprocessing of nuclear wastes and providing private reprocessors with a "stable" government market that does not exclude military applications;

- aggressively seeking the export of nuclear reactors.

Clearly, those measures indicate that the Reagan Administration's commitment to reviving the nuclear industry exceeds even its frequently professed determination to rely on the free market for energy decisions. Those two aims have not been easy to reconcile and Administration spokesmen have only perfunctorily tried to do so. Brewer ran into the difficulty in October, 1981 when he told a House oversight subcommittee that "an underlying principle of this Administration's overall policy is to allow the marketplace to be the determinant of future economic developments" and then, just a few breaths later proclaimed: "Our options for energy production, however, continue to require direct Federal involvement. . ."

Budget figures starkly capture the disparity. While proposing to cut 1982 federal expenditures on solar energy and conservation by 67 percent, the Administration proposed an 18 percent increase in nuclear expenditures.

Administration budget proposals for 1983 trimmed nuclear power by 7 percent, while slashing expenditures for renewables and conservation by 31 percent from 1982. The Administration has said it will spend over $100 million to help clean up the Three Mile Island nuclear power plant, still incapacitated after the accident of March 28, 1979.

Those increased federal expenditures also include funding for the completion of the controversial Clinch River Breeder Reactor. Since 1973, the estimated cost of building Clinch River has soared by 450 percent—from $669 million to the current $3.2 billion and the estimated date of completion has steadily receded into the future. In his biographical submission to the Senate Energy Committee, Brewer takes credit for overseeing the breeder's financial operations since at least 1975 and notes that in his earlier AEC job he was responsible for "formulating financial arrangements between the AEC, the utilities, and supply industry" for Clinch River. During congressional testimony in July, 1981, Brewer blamed the breeder's problems on "an evolving and uncertain regulatory climate, massive escalation [of costs] in the general economy, and a debilitating policy debate."

But an investigation by the House Oversight and Investigations Subcommittee, led by Air Force procurement analyst A. Ernest Fitzgerald, put the blame closer to home, citing poor management and performance by the prime contractors. "A fundamental flaw in the management approach to the Clinch River project is the fact that principal prime contracts have been written [by the government] without binding provisions for costs and schedule performance or for meeting specific engineering specifications," Fitzgerald told the committee. "It is clear that with these contracts the prime contractors have no need to perform, much less to excel, and they have not."

In a blistering analysis of the project, Fitzgerald and the subcommittee staff also found major cost overruns, contracts that were "rewritten to make history fit the results," cost estimates with "major uncertainties," and, perhaps most damaging of all, "that no one seems to be looking for or much less investigating contract irregularities, waste, fraud, and abuse." The investigators also said they ran into resistance from DOE employees who said they had been instructed not to cooperate with the investigation. Following these hearings, the breeder's project manager resigned in November, 1981.

The Carter Administration had opposed completion of Clinch River, arguing that it was technologically obsolete and a threat to non-proliferation goals since it used and produced plutonium. Citing nuclear proliferation concerns, the Carter Administration—like the Ford Administration before it—also prohibited the commercial reprocessing of nuclear wastes, which would also produce plutonium.

The Reagan Administration has not only lifted the ban on commercial reprocessing—Davis calls reprocessing "key to the formulation of our high-level waste program"—but offered potential reprocessors the prospect of a guaranteed government market for their product. Asked if that meant wastes from civilian nuclear power plants might be used to build nuclear weapons, White House Science Adviser George Keyworth told reporters the program "excludes no government applications." Edwards has gone even further, telling the federal Energy Research Advisory Board (ERAB), "We are going to be needing some more plutonium for our weapons program, and the best way I can see to get that plutonium is to solve your waste problem. Reprocess it, pull out the plutonium."

With Edwards and other Administration officials warning that government facilities may not be able to produce the plutonium required for the massive military buildup planned for the 1980s, the military sees the used fuel rods lying in pools beside utility plants around the country as a potential mother lode. Said Thomas Cochran, a scientist with the Natural Resources Defense Council and a member of the ERAB: "If you look out to the year 2000 at the inventory of spent fuel in the pools you will be talking in the neighborhood of 300 tons of weapon-grade plutonium, about roughly three times the current inventory and enough for 30,000 weapons.''

The possibility of such use has drawn more flak than any other aspect of Reagan's nuclear policy. ''If the United States starts using plutonium produced in civilian power reactors for making nuclear weapons, nations that have been looking to the United States for consistent leadership in worldwide efforts to prevent the future spread of nuclear weapons will see us doing exactly what we have been urging other nations not to do,'' said Dr. Theodore B. Taylor, a nuclear physicist and former deputy director of the Defense Atomic Support Agency who served on the Presidential Commission studying the Three Mile Island accident, near Harrisburg, Pennsylvania. ''Consumers of nuclear electric power in this country will then be directly participating in the process of expanding the quantities of plutonium in our nuclear weapons stockpile. I doubt that a majority of utility executives or electric power consumers would adopt such new roles with much enthusiasm.''

At a September, 1981 meeting of the International Atomic Energy Agency, a Vienna-based affiliate of the United Nations which monitors nuclear proliferation, Davis was stiffly warned that such a move would increase opposition to nuclear power in Europe. Fearing domestic public reaction, even the American nuclear industry has reportedly blanched at the suggestion. One key Pentagon official told us he didn't ''see any particular problem'' with such a plan. ''The symbolism is not helpful,'' said Richard Perle, the assistant secretary for international security policy, ''but it's nothing more than symbolism.''

Though DOE officials say the plan is only under consideration, other moves raise hints that the Administration is committed to this course. Between 1982 and 1989, the DOE plans to spend $560 million to develop and build a laser isotope separation plant that would upgrade commercially reprocessed plutonium to a grade suitable for military applications. Cochran has calculated that after the Clinch River breeder and other needs have been met by 1989 only 1,000 kilograms of government reactor grade plutonium will be available for treatment in the separation plant. ''So you are going to have a plant that will operate one year, process 1,000 kilograms of—enrich 1,000 kilograms and that would cost. . .$560 million which is about eight times the cost of the plutonium if they just produced it in the [government's] Savannah River plant. It's totally ludicrous. I don't think that is the objective of this program. The real objective is to go after the spent fuel,'' he said.

Reopening the Barnwell reprocessing plant might also point in that direction. After Edwards failed to convince Reagan to purchase the plant, Bechtel, Davis's former employer, began to look at the feasibility of buying and reopening the plant itself. Since the reprocessing capability of the plant is far greater than the plutonium requirements of the breeder and utilities are convinced that economics do not justify using reprocessed fuel in commercial reactors, Taylor told us, ''the only economic rationale for reopening Barnwell is military.'' (Taylor's point is buttressed by a recent DOE study, which concluded that ''at today's uranium prices there is little economic incentive for thermal reactor recycle.'')

''If Bechtel wants to get into the weapons-making business, it would be a very surprising decision,'' added Taylor.

Even without a commitment to diverting civilian wastes to military programs, numerous critics argue that development of the breeder and fuel reprocessing will create a ''plutonium economy'' that will greatly increase the risk of foreign countries, or even terrorist groups, joining the nuclear weapons club. But the Administration rejects that argument out of hand.

Said Brewer at October, 1981 congressional hearings: "I frankly cannot see the connection between a deferral of a U.S. energy program and the laudable objective" of halting nuclear proliferation.

Rep. Edward Markey (D-Mass.), who chairs the House Interior Oversight Subcommittee shot back: "I think that is a fatal and possibly apocalyptic flaw. . ." (For more on nuclear proliferation, see the profiles of James Malone and Richard Kennedy.)

Though presenting the threat of a public backlash, government purchases of spent fuel for reprocessing does offer the civilian nuclear industry a way out of its growing nuclear waste problem. Spent fuel is continuing to accumulate in pools beside reactors around the country, and though none has yet had to close for lack of storage space, that is a possibility in upcoming years. "A DOE takeover of civilian spent fuel would serve as a massive governmental bailout," said Cochran. "It would relieve the industry of its radioactive waste problems, shifting the tremendous financial burden away from the utilities to the American taxpayer."

Independent of the decision on military application of waste, Reagan pledged in his October statement to "proceed swiftly toward deployment of means of storing and disposing of commercial high-level radioactive waste." Davis has said the DOE plans to select the site for a test waste disposal facility by 1985. The 1983 budget requests $185 million in borrowing authority to help finance nuclear waste facilities that the Administration is proposing to operate by levying user fees on utilities.

But other scientists are far less certain that suitable means for disposing of the wastes are ready to be "deployed." "The stark fact. . .is that the technology for radioactive waste disposal is gradually being evolved, and no proven means for safe disposal is available at this time," said Kendall of the Union of Concerned Scientists. "The Administration is apparently proposing to push ahead with the burial of radioactive wastes before an adequate scientific basis can be established for doing so."

Meanwhile, the Administration is doing whatever else can help the industry at home and abroad. Arguing that uncertain government policy has chilled the market for nuclear reactors, DOE officials have gone out of their way to repeatedly proclaim their constancy to nuclear energy. "I fully support continued use of nuclear power and revitalization of our nuclear industry since I am sure it will be needed to meet our growing needs for electric power during the next decades," said Davis at his confirmation.

Davis also discounts fears of a major nuclear accident. Testifying during recent hearings concerning the 1957 Price-Anderson Act, which limits liability in case of a nuclear accident, Davis remarked that since the bill was passed, "we have had a great deal of experience—but very few accidents. The few that have occurred have served to further strengthen our safety systems. As a result we can now predict with greater assurance that the chances of a nuclear accident are far more remote than when the Price-Anderson Act was originally passed."

In case the public misses the point, the department has developed plans to engender a groundswell of support for the nuclear option. In response to a September, 1981 request from Brewer to examine nuclear's public relations problems, Thomas Werner, director of policy and planning, consulted with "leading members of the nuclear energy public information community including the Atomic Industrial Forum, Committee on Energy Awareness, Scientists and Engineers for Secure Energy [SE-2] and others" and drew up a 21-page plan to push nuclear power. Included were proposals to: send out top government officials to speak in favor of nuclear power; bring in for interviews sympathetic journalists such as Hugh Sidey of *Time*, James Reston of the *New York Times* and syndicated columnists George Will, William Buckley and Carl Rowan; hire public relations firms, at $100,000 annually, to place pro-nuclear government spokesmen on talk shows; lobby members of the financial community with "top-level Administration officials;" and to sponsor $200,000 worth of pro-nuclear studies by the SE-2 group. In all, the department estimated that between $1 and $2 million of taxpayer funds would be spent on outside contracts, with additional funds supporting the use of four full-time staff and a $20,000 travel budget.

In a similar vein, the Administration is seeking to help the industry make sales to foreign nations. To induce oil and gas rich Mexico to buy reactors from U.S. companies, the *Wall Street Journal* reported, the DOE has offered to sell it enriched uranium at bargain rates and to establish a joint nuclear research facility. The Export-Import Bank will also be aggressively used to induce potential foreign purchasers. (See profile of William Draper.)

"The business we should be doing abroad—in nuclear plant construction, fuel, and related equipment and services—would go far toward bolstering this country's balance of payments," Davis asserted in a speech in 1981. "It is hoped that, by making a relatively modest investment in nuclear energy, Government will help bring the industry through a period of unusual difficulty and help restore it to a position of world leadership."

This extraordinary government effort to revive a single industry—an effort that has rolled over even the Office of Management and Budget's determination to keep down expenditures—displays an unusual sense of urgency, even desperation, particularly in the speeches of long-time nuclear advocates like Davis. Across the board, the nuclear industry grudgingly agrees that Ronald Reagan is their last best hope; and in their hearts, there is an unsettling fear that even he may not be enough to save them.

JOSEPH TRIBBLE
ASSISTANT SECRETARY FOR CONSERVATION AND
  RENEWABLE ENERGY

RESPONSIBILITY OF OFFICE

Tribble is responsible for encouraging efficient use of the nation's energy supplies and the widespread use of solar and other renewable energy sources. The programs he directs range from research, development and demonstration of advanced technologies to financial and technical assistance,  regulatory programs and technology transfer activities. He also oversees the management of the Solar Energy Research Institute, Regional Solar Energy Centers and manages the alcohol fuels produced from biomass program for the DOE.

BACKGROUND

For the past 25 years, Tribble has held several positions with the Union Camp Corporation of Savannah, Georgia, one of the largest and most complex pulp and paper companies in the nation.

Tribble spent the past seven years as energy coordinator for Union Camp's Unbleached Division, where he was involved in a variety of energy conservation projects—including co-generation and use of biomass—at three Union Camp paper mills. Union Camp has long used co-generation, according to Tribble.

Union Camp's environmental attitude has been less than enlightened in the past. During the early 1970s, the Savannah mill was responsible for an estimated 80 percent of the pollution flowing into the Savannah River. Confronted with that record, the company's director of air and water pollution trenchantly commented: "It probably won't hurt mankind a whole hell of a lot in the long run if the whooping crane doesn't quite make it."

Tribble has been active in Republican politics since the early 1960s, when he became the first Republican elected to the state senate from his district since Reconstruction. Tribble received a degree in engineering from Georgia Institute of Technology in 1942, and worked for a year at Bethlehem Steel Company before joining Union Camp.

Born on August 30, 1920 in Forsyth, Georgia, Tribble is married with four children.

MAJOR ISSUES

- Tribble advocates a "free-market" approach to energy conservation, seeing only a limited governmental role in promoting alternative energy sources like solar, water and wind power. Expenditures in these areas have been slashed, accompanied by projected reductions in personnel.

- The elderly and families on fixed incomes could be forced to choose between eating or heating their homes by the Administration's proposal to encourage conservation by allowing energy prices to increase.

- Tribble sees the Carter Administration's goal of having solar provide 20 percent of the nation's energy by the end of the century as unrealistic, and it is likely that under Tribble's direction government assistance to solar research will virtually disappear.

- Tribble is implementing policies that belittle Congress. He has failed to meet congressionally mandated deadlines, and is instituting the budget cuts that will become, in effect, statutory repeals.

Tribble maintains that rising energy prices, along with tax credits, are adequate incentives for industry to pursue conservation measures, and sees only a limited role for government in promoting the use of solar energy.

President Reagan's budget cuts will have a decisive effect on Tribble's activities, since his budget was slashed from close to $1.5 billion in 1981 to $758 million for FY 1982. For 1983, expenditures on renewable energy and conservation will be cut from $518 million to $101 million if the Administration budget is approved. Virtually eliminated would be conservation research and grants that help fund energy-saving investments, particularly in schools and hospitals. Certain conservation tax credits would also be ended. As of February 1, 1982, Tribble's energy conservation program had 154 employees; if the budget is approved, this will be reduced to 105 by the end of FY 1982, and cut to 29 by the end of FY 1983. These figures are even 50 percent below estimates made by Tribble's own staff of minimum personnel necessary to carry out the department's mission.

Tribble's free-market approach to conservation has met with sharp criticism. Former Assistant Secretary for Conservation and Renewable Energy Thomas E. Stelson in March, 1981 testimony before a congressional subcommittee said: "To say that a cost effective program is a program that can be handled by private enterprise without government leadership and support is to say that one is ignorant of the private enterprise system in the United States."

Tribble maintains that "a right good bit" of market-driven industrial energy conservation is already happening. He cited the paper industry which has sliced its energy use per unit of production by 20 percent, "virtually all because of increases in the price of fuel, very little in response to government programs."

Questioned about the appropriate roles for private industry, financial institutions, and federal and local governments, Tribble said, "I think that industry will do whatever is necessary as it becomes economical."

Tribble asserts that because the federal budget cannot fund all the energy conservation needed in the country, the DOE should see that consumers face market signals—in other words, increased prices—that encourage conservation, and focus federal resources on research and development efforts that provide information to complement the market.

Responding to the research aspect of Tribble's policy, Edwin Rothschild said, "The kinds of research will be that which goes to the largest companies that are doing the most esoteric kinds of research and it won't be for the benefit of those companies that try to compete in the marketplace with their conservation technologies."

While at Union Camp Tribble reportedly looked into the use of solar energy, but found that it wasn't cost-effective yet, an opinion he apparently still holds. Tribble discounts the significance of the past administration's goal of having solar provide 20 percent of the nation's energy requirements by the turn of the century. "Generally, all of the projections that I have ever seen on that kind of thing have been wrong and so we are not trying to make that kind of a goal as definitive as that," said Tribble.

In 1982, Reagan proposed to cut the solar budget from $559 million to $193 million. Both active and passive solar programs were slated to be cut by two-thirds; the photovoltaic research program was to be cut by almost $100 million to $63 million. For 1983, the Administration has proposed to cut photovoltaic again to $27 million; overall solar research would be reduced to just $72 million.

Responding to Tribble's skepticism about the 20 percent goal for renewables' contribution to domestic energy supply, Rothschild said, "If the policies of this Administration continue as they are, I don't think that goal will be reached or that we'll be anywhere close to it." Internal DOE budget analyses prepared under Stelson indicated that even the Carter level of funding would be inadequate to meet that goal.

Last July 30, Tribble met with members of the Energy Conservation Coalition Board and was asked to describe his criteria in evaluating an energy program. According to Renee Parsons of Friends of the Earth, Tribble said one of his major goals is development of electrical vehicles.

"That [his focus on electrical vehicles] is the best example that he doesn't understand conservation well enough, the opportunities with conservation, and the problems with conservation, to be able to set his priorities straight. Anyone who would have as his A-number-one priority something such as the electric car, which is so cost-ineffective so far into the future as to make it almost irrelevant to the situation, is just not prepared to do his job," said board member Bill Chandler of the Environmental Policy Center.

Despite Tribble's stated goal, the Administration has slashed the Electrical Vehicles Program (EVP) along with other solar and renewable energy programs. Originally allocated approximately $40 million in President Carter's fiscal year 1982 budget, EVP was cut by $21 million.

With the cuts, the Administration has made it impossible for the division to fulfill its congressional mandates. In hearings by the House Subcommittee on Energy, Conservation and Power on March 16, 1982, Chairman Richard Ottinger charged: "In all the mandated programs, you are seriously behind. You are in fact in violation of the law with respect to promulgation of standards and the Residential Conservation Service and the compliance efficiency standards, [and] the weatherization money is not out yet." Tribble claimed to be making a "diligent effort" to accomplish these tasks, to which Ottinger sharply replied: "Nothing is being done and no funds are being provided to carry out those obligations."

The Residential Conservation Service is one program that is cut out altogether from the 1983 budget. At the hearings, Ottinger asked: "Have you got an opinion from your general counsel about the legality of proceeding to zero funds for programs for which there is a legal mandate?" Tribble replied: "I certainly do not have anything in writing, but we have had a number of conversations and my impression is that if the Congress agrees with the budget proposals, agrees not to fund something, then that does certainly imply congressional agreement with it not being done." That view is hardly held with unanimity on Capitol Hill.

Tribble's first year performance reveals him as a classic Reagan domestic appointee: managing the dismantling of his own agency under White House direction. While blessing nuclear power, Reagan has clouded the future for solar energy.

FINANCIAL BACKGROUND

Upon his confirmation as assistant secretary, Tribble resigned his position with Union Camp and agreed to divest himself of his financial investments in Anglo-American Corporation of South America and Coastal Caribbean Oils and Minerals, Ltd. Tribble earned $38,885 in salary from Union Camp during 1980.

WHAT OTHERS ARE SAYING ABOUT HIM

- "Secretary Edwards and President Reagan were lucky to have attracted someone with Tribble's background and stature to come and do the job he has. After all the campaign statements they made about dismantling the DOE it was hard to find recruits who were qualified and competent enough to take a job that was going to be demolished," said assistant secretary for conservation and renewable energy under Carter, Thomas Stelson.

- "Tribble does not understand the purpose of the programs he's managing," said Bill Chandler of the Environmental Policy Center. "He just doesn't understand the issues. He's interested in fuel-switching rather than true conservation. And with all the staff reductions, it'll take years to rebuild the talent they had there."

CHARLES BUTLER, III
CHAIRMAN, FEDERAL ENERGY REGULATORY COMMISSION

RESPONSIBILITY OF OFFICE

Created in October of 1977, by the same act that established the Department of Energy (DOE), the five-member FERC succeeded the Federal Power Commission. FERC inherited its predecessor's jurisdiction over the interstate aspects of the electric power and natural gas industries, and the Interstate Commerce Commission's responsibility for regulating oil pipelines.

An autonomous agency within the Department of Energy, FERC is also responsible for ensuring consumers are charged fair and reasonable rates, and for supporting national energy policies which call for increased production of domestic energy supplies, use of renewable resources and conservation. The 1978 Natural Gas Policy Act gave the commission regulatory power over all producer sales of natural gas. FERC rules over an enormously complex, and litigious, domain.

In fiscal year 1982 Butler will be managing a budget of $77 million and approximately 1,650 employees. With the proposed elimination of the DOE, the Administration is seeking to establish FERC as an independent agency. The Administration is seeking only $44 million in 1983 funding for FERC; it expects the agency to raise another $60 million through license fees. It will raise about half that in fees during 1982.

Reagan reappointed Georgiana Sheldon to the commission. She had previously served a three-year term and acted as chairman for the six months that Butler's post was vacant. New to the commission is Anthony G. Sousa, a former executive with the Hawaii Telephone Co.

BACKGROUND

As an attorney Butler has been an active advocate for the energy industry over the past 10 years. He was added to Sen. John Tower's (R-Tex.) staff in 1973 after two years with the Houston law firm of Baker and Botts, which was founded by the grandfather of White House Chief of Staff James Baker. Butler spent three years as Tower's chief legislative assistant, then left to join the Dallas law firm of Kendrick, Kendrick and Bradley. At his confirmation hearing, Butler testified that his experience with the Dallas firm included work for natural gas producers, natural gas pipelines and electrical utilities.

From 1976 to 1979, Butler was a senior attorney for the American Natural Resources (ANR) Company of Detroit, where he worked on arranging loan guarantees and financing for the Great Plains Coal Gasification Project in North Dakota.

Butler returned to Washington in 1979 to serve at Tower's side. During that term, Tower was a consistent advocate for legislation sought by the energy industry in such areas as resource development on federal lands, nuclear wastes, and limiting the windfall profit tax.

During Tower's stint as chair of the platform committee at the 1980 Republican National Convention, Butler worked on the platform's heavily anti-conservation, anti-regulation energy section.

At his confirmation hearing, Butler was grilled by Sen. Howard Metzenbaum (D-Ohio), who complained that the selection of Butler was another in a series of "pro-industry" choices made by the Administration to fill key government positions.

Metzenbaum proposed that Butler refrain from participating in any commission cases involving clients that he or any of his former law associates represented. But Butler agreed only to disqualify himself from a much more narrowly defined group of cases—those before the commission that he or any of his former associates actually prepared while Butler was at the firm of Baker and Botts. Since that was eight years ago, Butler acknowledged that the number of cases his recusal would cover "is probably relatively small." If a former client brought a new case before the commission, Butler said he would not recuse himself.

Butler replaces former Chairman Charles Curtis, who resigned in January 1981. Although Reagan could renominate Butler for a full four-year term when Curtis's term expires in 1983, Butler, who earns $55,387 in his FERC job, said he can't afford to remain a government employee permanently, "despite all the psychological income I get from it."

Born in Midland, Texas, on February 6, 1943, Butler received a B.A. in economics from the University of Houston in 1969 and was graduated with honors from the University of Texas Law School in Austin in 1971. He is married and has three children.

MAJOR ISSUES

- Butler has backed the accelerated decontrol of natural gas, which the Administration is planning to push for some time in the upcoming years. While the legislative debate goes on, Butler has said FERC is pushing independently to raise the price of natural gas. Natural gas decontrol, which would swell producer revenues, and consumer and industry heating bills, will undoubtedly incite a major legislative battle. Butler is trying to avoid that, critics say, with backdoor deregulation.

- Butler has also supported the construction of the Alaskan Natural Gas Pipeline, which is being built by a consortium of energy companies, including American Natural Resources, his former employer. The companies and their bankers convinced the Administration and Congress to revise the 1977 ground rules for the project in several ways that would reduce very substantially their financial risk.

- FERC is proposing to change several rules to improve the financial picture of the utility industry. One of the proposed changes would make it easier for utilities to pass along the costs of construction work in progress.

Butler is in the middle of what could be among the Administration's most bruising political battles: the effort to raise the price of natural gas controlled under the 1978 Natural Gas Policy Act. His views on price controls were made clear in a June, 1981 interview with the *Houston Post*: "Regulating the commodity prices of anything just contributes to shortages and eventually to higher prices," he said.

That view is in tune with the Administration's stance. Reagan's Cabinet Council on Natural Resources and the Environment has recommended that the Administration push for a three-year phase-out of natural gas price controls. Reagan has balked, fearing the political fallout. Butler has predicted that the White House may never introduce a decontrol bill.

Even the natural gas industry is split on decontrol. Gas producers support decontrol because they would profit from the higher prices, while pipeline companies fear that a decrease in demand would reduce the volume of gas they would transport. Consumer groups and many congressional leaders have argued that decontrol would fuel inflation, while doing little to increase supply. Even some utilities, such as Southern California Gas Co., are opposing the FERC price hikes their suppliers are seeking.

The cost of decontrol is extremely controversial. Reagan's Cabinet Council estimated immediate decontrol would raise residential bills about $170 a year; the Natural Gas Supply Association—which supports decontrol—concedes that it would just about double residential bills to more than 40 million American homes. Energy Action, a consumer group, has estimated that decontrol would impose annual direct and indirect costs of $2,600 to a typical family earning $20,000.

Butler maintains that immediate decontrol might actually reduce natural gas prices, arguing that the current phase-out plan may trigger a costly bidding war between pipelines for supplies. "We have tentatively concluded—and we need to do some more work—that quite possibly you can see a situation where natural gas prices would rise to a higher level if the [current law] plays out the way it's scheduled than they would with a complete decontrol bill," he said. But Butler conceded that his theory had not actually been tested with marketplace figures.

While Congress and the Administration grapple with what promises to be an epic legislative battle, Butler and FERC will continue to make the regular, arcane, pricing decisions that form the substance of the price controls. Butler believes "natural gas never should have been regulated at the wellhead," and is doing all he can to administratively speed up decontrol. Beginning in December, 1981, FERC has embarked on a series of actions that could, by some analyses, double the price of 40 percent of the nation's gas by the middle of this year. FERC has proposed a substantial rise in the price of "near-deep" gas—situated from 10,000-15,000 feet deep—a move that Energy Action believes could increase the nation's $40 billion gas bill by a staggering $12-18 billion. FERC is also considering a number of other price increases, including a possible hike in the price of "old" gas—that produced before April, 1977—from as low as 20 cents per thousand cubic feet to as much as $4.

Butler was involved in another struggle over natural gas, as the Administration sought to revise the ground rules governing development of the Alaska Natural Gas Pipeline.

Approved by the Carter Administration in 1977, the 4,800-mile pipeline would transport natural gas to domestic users from Alaska's Prudhoe Bay—which contains about one-eighth of the country's total proven natural gas reserves. Work is underway on all portions of the pipeline except the Alaska segment.

But cost estimates have soared, and the energy companies and banks financing the project pressed the Administration to change the 1977 presidential decision laying the ground rules for the project in several ways that would transfer their financial risk. Among other things, they sought the right to charge consumers for the pipeline's cost before the project is completed and gas is flowing—and whether or not the pipeline is ever finished. Asked Republican Senator David Durenberger of Minnesota: "If Exxon will not risk its assets to gain a substantial profit, why should a small businessman in Minnesota be expected to take on the risk of the project when he has no possibility of the gain?"

In October, 1981, Reagan passed along to Congress the industry's requests for waivers. Butler, whose former employer ANR is involved in the project, was considered one of the plan's strongest supporters inside the Administration. With Reagan's support, and a high-powered, bi-partisan lobbying effort—the consortium hired leading Democrats such as Walter Mondale, Robert Strauss and Anne Wexler, and former Reagan aide Peter Hannaford—the bill passed the Senate in November, 1981, and the House, in a more acrimonious battle, a month later.

Again, while Congress debates the big picture, FERC will make several key decisions of its own, involving the estimated cost of construction upon which to base return, tariff and tax matters. Butler has refused to recuse himself from pipeline decisions, arguing that he was only peripherally involved in the project while at ANR.

Responding to pleas of distress from the utility industry, FERC is also moving in a variety of ways to improve the industry's financial picture. In August, 1981 the agency published proposed regulations to loosen guidelines established in 1976 for allowing utilities to pass along to customers the cost of Construction Work in Progress (CWIP). Under the original guidelines, utilities were forced to meet on a case-by-case basis a strict "severe financial difficulty" test (with exceptions for pollution control or coal conversion expenses) before assessing CWIP. The new rules would replace that system with a generic presumption of financial distress for utilities with poor bond ratings and a large amount of work under construction. Consumer groups expect this would greatly facilitate the imposition of CWIP for power sales regulated by FERC. CWIP has been banned by several states. It has been criticized for forcing today's utility consumers to pay for projects they may never use and to, in effect, invest money without getting any dividends or principal back. Instead, the shareholders reap the profits. CWIP may also provide an incentive for unneeded construction since, as the Consumers Union recently wrote: "If utilities can count on getting needed cash without having to submit to the rigorous scrutiny of the investment community, the result may be poorly conceived or unneeded expansion projects."

In May, 1981, FERC issued an order making it easier for utilities to profit from so-called "phantom taxes"—taxes claimed as expenses in setting rates charged consumers but never paid to the government. Municipally owned power companies protested to the commission that the proposal "will require ratepayers to pay more in compensation for tax expense than the tax liability actually incurred by the utilities." In January, 1982 FERC began a broad investigation of the proper rate of return for the utility industry, and the possibility of setting a standard level for use in rate cases. Said Edward Petrini, an attorney with the National Consumer Law Center: "Implicit in the notion of the study is that [the rate of return] should be higher."

FINANCIAL BACKGROUND

Butler has sold his stock holdings in a variety of energy companies, including Exxon, Mobil, Englehard Minerals and El Paso Co. None of the holdings was worth more than $15,000.

AGRICULTURE DEPARTMENT

JOHN BLOCK
SECRETARY

RESPONSIBILITY OF OFFICE

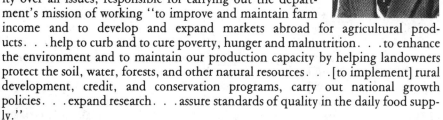

Since its establishment in 1862, the USDA has grown into one of the federal government's largest departments, employing around 89,000.

Block is the department's chief officer, with final authority over all issues, responsible for carrying out the department's mission of working "to improve and maintain farm income and to develop and expand markets abroad for agricultural products. . .help to curb and to cure poverty, hunger and malnutrition. . .to enhance the environment and to maintain our production capacity by helping landowners protect the soil, water, forests, and other natural resources. . .[to implement] rural development, credit, and conservation programs, carry out national growth policies. . .expand research. . .assure standards of quality in the daily food supply."

In 1982, the department operated with a budget of $29.4 billion.

BACKGROUND

One industry lobbyist describes Block as "the classic Horatio Alger story." Since taking over his father's 300-acre farm in 1960, Block made some shrewd business investments and built the sort of modern, 3,000-acre farm which is increasingly common in the dwindling U.S. farm population. In that period his farm's hog production increased from 200 per year to 6,000.

Like many U.S. farmers, Block has turned part of his land over to growing soybeans—a quick profit crop—one that the secretary himself recently identified as ranking among the most soil-erosive grown in this country.

Several newspaper accounts indicate Block was chosen for the USDA position after "a behind-the-scenes power struggle" between the White House and Midwestern congressmen. *The Washington Monthly* reported that Block's "selection was sealed when Senator Bob Dole, the influential Kansas Republican, gave Reagan aides a map of the country marked with the home state of the Cabinet choices thus far. The map, which showed the Middle West, a Republican stronghold, to be conspicuous for its lack of representation, proved persuasive."

The President reportedly would have preferred his former California agriculture aide, Richard Lyng, who settled for the deputy secretary job.

Block's philosophy is perhaps best summed in his oft-used statement, "The best thing for consumers is a good healthy agriculture." This was the same statement frequently employed by Nixon Agriculture Secretary Earl Butz, who was noted for favoring the interests of producers over consumers.

"Philosophically, I'm very close to [Earl Butz] on most issues," Block admits. "I know him. He was a great secretary of Agriculture and I think we're not very far apart. . ."

Block became Illinois's director of agriculture in 1977 and "was one of the better, and more active, state commissioners," according to Carter Agriculture Secretary Bob Bergland.

"I knew him personally, I knew him to be a grassroots farmer," Harold Dodd of the Illinois Farmers Union told us. Dodd was one of the 17 people from the state who accompanied Block on the 1977 Illinois Agricultural Trade Mission to China. "Some things were in the making, but he [Block]," Dodd maintained enthusiastically, "helped turn the tide" in U.S. trade relations with China.

Several former colleagues praised Block for prógrams he instituted as Illinois agricultural chief. Jim Frank, head of the Illinois Division of Natural Resources—a division established under Block—told us that Block was more concerned about erosion than any director he'd observed in years.

As director, Block obtained an executive order from the governor requiring all state agencies to file statements assessing the impact that any construction—roads or otherwise—had on agricultural lands. "I thought it was a nice song and dance at first, and wouldn't amount to much," said Al Sax of the Illinois South Project, a rural advocacy group. "But good people are there and they have carried it forth."

Dodd was complimentary of Block's leadership abilities. "We had split factions between many different organizations and special interests here in Illinois," he said. "John Block had the ability to bridge the gap. . .this is not easy to accomplish."

Since taking over at Agriculture, Block, said Dodd, has been overshadowed by other Administration leaders. "Still Block has not lost my confidence. I think of him as a leader. The unfortunate thing I see happening is that far too many people who don't understand agriculture are not allowing him to make policy on important issues. . .He has my sympathies."

Prior to taking over his father's farm in 1960, Block served three years as an infantry officer and paratrooper in the Army; Block was graduated from the West Point Military Academy in 1957.

Born February 15, 1935 in Gilson, Illinois, Block is married and has three children.

FINANCIAL BACKGROUND

Block is a business success story who holds multimillion dollar farm and property investments, worth over $3.2 million, as well as substantial liabilities.

WHAT OTHERS ARE SAYING ABOUT HIM

- Washington veterans have expressed misgivings about Block's ability to survive in the swirling array of interests involved in agricultural politics. One prominent agribusiness lobbyist told the *Wall Street Journal* that Block risks being "eaten alive" in trying to meet the often-conflicting interests of farmers, packers, retailers and consumer activists.

- "There is no doubt about it," said David Senter of the American Agricultural Movement, "Block will have all he can handle to keep from getting buried by the bureaucratic and political demands of the job."

- "Lyng is really running that department," said a rural lobbyist. "From the very beginning it seems obvious Block has merely been a showpiece—a very attractive figure."

- Another rural lobbyist, Kathryn Lerza of the National Family Coalition, said Block's clean-cut, successful farmer image appeals to farmers. "Block is not a disliked person like Al Haig or James Watt," she said. "The thing about Block is that he sincerely believes his way is the way for all farmers. He expects farmers to achieve profitability in the same way he did. But the conditions are very different now for the young farmer. This isn't 1960."

RICHARD LYNG
DEPUTY SECRETARY

RESPONSIBILITY OF OFFICE

Lyng handles the department's day-to-day administration. But he is a shrewd Washington veteran and is involved in virtually all matters of substance.

BACKGROUND

Lyng has moved easily between government and industry jobs during the past decade. It is well-known that he was the transition team's first choice for the top job at USDA.

As the self-described "alter ego of the secretary," Lyng has in many ways been more visible around Washington than Block himself. And as the Community Nutrition Institute newsletter notes, some consumer groups even favored Lyng over John Block because he "is a familiar face in Washington, D.C. and an open-minded—if difficult—adversary on most issues."

Lyng was president of the American Meat Institute (AMI) from 1973 to 1979 and remained a part-time consultant to the powerful lobby until his appointment in January, 1981.

AMI, along with such industry lobbyists as the National Cattlemen's Association, has strenuously opposed numerous government regulations affecting the meat industry over the years. The major targets for AMI in recent years have been nutrition guidelines and meat additive regulations. Lyng has served as a member of the Agriculture Committee for the U.S. Chamber of Commerce and as a member of the Animal Health Committee for the National Academy of Sciences.

Lyng is a gracious, grandfatherly type. When he appeared at the Consumer Federation of America's (CFA) 1982 annual conference, former CFA president and Carter Administration agriculture official Carol Tucker Foreman, a frequent adversary, praised his accessibility. "There's not a whole lot that Dick Lyng and I agree on," she said. "But he is one of the few officials of the Administration. . .who has agreed" to be here.

Since 1974, Lyng served on the board of directors of Tri-Valley Growers of California, the Chicago Mercantile Exchange and the Refrigeration Research Foundation.

Lyng's first experience in the federal government was as assistant secretary of marketing and consumer services at USDA from 1969 to 1973.

Lyng began his government career under Ronald Reagan in 1967 as deputy director of the California State Department of Agriculture, later serving as director.

Prior to entering government, Lyng was president for 22 years of a family seed company in Modesto, California. He was graduated cum laude from the University of Notre Dame in 1940.

Born on June 29, 1918 in San Francisco, Lyng is married and has two daughters.

FINANCIAL BACKGROUND

Lyng was a part-time consultant for the American Meat Institute in 1980, earning $12,000 in fees. He also received a few thousand dollars in assorted consulting and director's fees from various other small concerns. His income was bolstered by a $9,000 honorarium from an Australian organization called Queensland Graziers. He also maintained steady income from two real estate concerns, each valued at over $250,000.

Prior to taking office, he sold his 1,400 shares in Oscar Mayer & Co.

WHAT OTHERS ARE SAYING ABOUT HIM

- David Senter said Lyng is undoubtedly more business-oriented than agriculture-oriented but is nonetheless pleased with Lyng's considerable knowledge and experience. "Lyng is an excellent administrator," he said. "We feel he is in a good position to handle the day-to-day responsibilities of the department."

- Carol Tucker Foreman, who headed USDA's food and consumer services under President Carter, has had a number of run-ins with Lyng over the past four years. (Lyng once called her "the Ayatollah of USDA" for her aggressive enforcement of meat inspection regulations.) "Lyng is basically a good guy," Foreman said. "We have obviously disagreed on a number of issues, but he will at least talk with you."

- Former Secretary of Agriculture Bob Bergland calls Lyng "a street smart professional. On balance, I think Lyng makes for a good combination with Block since they each appeal to an important constituency [farmers and industry]."

MAJOR ISSUES

- Agricultural experts fear USDA's farm policies and programs are not only unfair to small farmers, and destructive of the farming resource base, but prevent self-reliance among developing nations. Yet Block, a successful large farmer, sees no need to alter the status quo.

- Despite Block's inflated rhetoric in opposition to price supports, he has at times contradicted himself, and Congress has confidently disregarded Block's unfulfilled threats of a presidential veto in restoring dairy subsidies, and padding the budget with other agricultural handouts.

- Nutrition and anti-hunger lobbyists see Block's actions as a threat to consumers and the poor, as food stamps and government nutrition programs shrivel under Reagan's budget cuts.

- The department is dismantling many of the accomplishments of the Carter Administration in food safety and nutrition programs (most of which Lyng opposed as a lobbyist for the meat industry).

- Lyng disputes the findings of Bob Bergland's "farm structure" study, claiming the problems facing the small farmer are due more to inflation than the nature of federal farm programs.

Farm productivity and profitability are Block's avowed priorities. Despite stacks of evidence to the contrary, he is convinced that U.S. agriculture can continue to run on a fast track of technological breakthroughs and enjoy ever-expanding international trade. Both the secretary and the deputy secretary are confident technology, coupled with new management techniques, will come to the rescue of the troubled American farm community. Congress, however, is not anxious to subsidize such discoveries with tax dollars.

Both Lyng and Block supported increased federal funding for agricultural research and are eager to develop techniques to increase utilization of the nation's fragile topsoil and water resources. But this approach is fraught with risks for the long-term health of American agriculture, particularly as federal dollars to support conservation measures erode.

For instance, the program to slow down the rapid pace at which this country's topsoil is eroding—a rate of about 6.4 billion tons annually—have been all but buried by Congress. Though he made soil conservation efforts a priority for Illinois, Block was unable to convince the Administration to beef-up its spending. For 1983, total federal budget authority for agricultural land conservation is slated to drop from $570 million to $428 million; outlays are slated to drop sharply through the mid-1980s. "What this means," a Senate aide told us, "is that the federal government has decided to let the soil just blow away"—which doesn't apparently sit well with the department. Lyng suggested to a gathering of local state legislators in late 1981 that we are paying for our rich defense budget in many ways: "One of those big bombers," he said, "would take care of a helluva lot of soil conservation."

Block made several proposals to Congress to shovel the responsibility for protecting crop land back to the states, with modest federal block grants to subsidize them. Congress has taken no steps in that direction so far. The secretary said the grants, totalling about $10 million, and targeted towards specific states, would "be directed toward encouraging less erosive tillage rather than spending it for more costly structural projects, such as terracing and drainage tiles."

For years terracing and similar methods have been considered as essential to conserving topsoil as the tillage programs. When asked where funding for these types of soil prevention projects are likely to be found, one House staffer said he didn't know. "Those programs are just as important," he said. "Unfortunately they're more expensive."

"Serious measures must be taken soon to safeguard the basic soil, water and fuel resources," warned former USDA Secretary Bergland, ". . .measures that range from more responsible practices in fragile areas to careful thought about the side-effects of national enthusiams that reward short-term advantage at the expense of long-term productivity."

One of these "national enthusiasms" is the government's voracious exporting programs. One of every three farm acres now produces food for export. Critics warn that by increasing international trade the government is encouraging farmers to overproduce and ravage their land with mass production techniques and poor planning. "Farmers think that the volume will make up for low prices," David Senter of the American Agriculture Movement told us, "but the price they pay for not conserving will eventually cost farmers and the nation much more."

"Soil conservation is of national consequence," warned Charles Frazier of the National Farmer's Organization. "Without a responsible program our farmland might some day be a vast desert. This is a problem of national consequence."

The urge toward mass production on the farms has made the small farm something of an endangered species. Bergland lamented the demise of the family farm amid the surge of agribusiness. Block though, seems determined to return USDA to the philosophy of Earl Butz, who once said the small farmer must either "adapt or die."

Block has generally downplayed the findings of *A Time To Choose*, a department study completed in January, 1981 under Bergland which analyzed the structure of American agriculture. Bergland told us that the very structure of the federal agricultural programs are slanted against the small farmer and recommends that—with the exception of the grain reserve— the large farmer be excluded from government subsidies.

Lyng represented Block at several key hearings before Congress on the farm structure report. Lyng disputed most of the major conclusions of the study, which took a highly critical look at the role of federal subsidies in accelerating the consolidation of the farming population into a small number of large farms. Lyng downplayed the impact of USDA's programs on farm concentration, blaming the phenomenon on inflation, which he said makes farm property more ripe for manipulation by speculators.

"At the very least," Bergland said. "We should remove the provisions of law that funnel disproportionate benefits to the largest farmers and outside investors and thereby encourage them to become even larger." Among the benefits cited by the study as going "disproportionately" to large farmers are USDA loans, price supports and marketing orders.

Bergland said that most of our major farm programs were designed at a time "when there was an excess capacity to produce food and fiber" and when the needs of American farmers were more alike. "There is a persistent streak of opinion. . .[which] holds that agriculture never changes," he said.

Bergland considers acceptance of this attitude Block's major shortcoming. Block certainly doesn't see reason for alarm in Bergland's finding that "a whole range of different unrelated persons and firms are increasing their control over one or more of those functions [of ownership, management and labor on farms]."

In fact, while head of the Illinois Department of Agriculture, Block indicated "he didn't think absentee investment was much of a problem," said Sax, who told us that Illinois South Project had pushed for "some restrictions on foreign ownership" but did not find Block very concerned.

Block himself was accused of speculating activity in 1980 when he bought some land in Minnesota. He sold the land, he claims, because it had become too difficult to manage. "Anyway," he said, "people have a right to buy and sell land. . .And I'm a neighbor. I'm from Illinois, not from Saudi Arabia."

Bergland worries that the Administration's policies will make the already bad agricultural concentration problem worse. For instance, he points to the capital gains and inheritance tax revisions in the President's tax package as an incentive for more speculators to enter the farm land market— thereby crowding out already hardpressed beginning farmers. "Let's face it," he said. "Farmland is already a popular tax shelter and this will make it even more so."

Block fancies himself a strict free-marketman in most respects, though he and Congress have bowed to special interest pressures which defend agricultural subsidies. In a trade mission to Europe in May, 1981, Block told a meeting of the World Food Council that the U.S. "will no longer tolerate protectionist trade policies by other exporting nations." Critics said this statement rang hollow in light of recent Japanese auto import restrictions.

Block hedged for a long time on imports of casein, a powdered milk protein. Despite criticisms that a quota on imports would not only be contrary to his free market rhetoric, but would make the product more expensive, Block said that casein imports "materially interfere with the price support program for milk." He said the government could save $380 million per year, which would have been spent for milk price supports if no casein were imported.

The President also supports placing limits on casein imports, but the International Trade Commission, after studying the possibility, ruled against the President as well as the dairy industry, arguing against any constraints whatsoever. It's possible for the President to overrule the commission; however, according to Tom Smith of the Community Nutrition Institute, "it's an unlikely prospect."

Since the Administration pushed a bill through Congress in April, 1981 which eliminated semi-annual milk price support adjustments (depriving the dairy industry of millions of subsidy dollars), Block has stepped carefully around controversial issues like a consumer petition which asked him to restrict regulations on reconstituted milk. When asked in April, 1981 about his denial of the petition at a food conference, Block clearly was caught over a barrel. Elimination of the regulations were seemingly consistent with the Reagan Administration's philosophy—but in this case reconstituted milk, much like casein, would have increased competition, thereby eroding the effect of the government's elaborate price support system.

Block said the Administration is striving to make the dairy program "less government-restricted [and] more of a free enterprise," yet at the same time he told the questioner, "I think we have to be a little careful with how we tamper with something like [the reconstituted milk regulations]. . .The dairy program has worked. . .and if it works you'd better not fix it too much. Don't over-tinker with it all at one time. . .and this is one that I'm not ready to tinker with yet. I hear what you're saying and thanks for the advice. Thanks a lot.''

While Congress was considering the Administration's economic program last summer, Block spoke out strongly against the peanut allotment program. But his remarks were unheeded as the Reagan Administration bargained away proposed cuts in that area in return for Southern votes for the budget and tax packages. Seeking votes, the Administration also agreed to sugar price supports that will cost consumers $1 billion in 1982 alone.

The structure of the farm commodities support system was basically carried over in the farm bill passed in 1981. However the parity index for dairy subsidies, an important determinant in the price the government sets on dairy goods, has been altered and made more receptive to inflationary factors. "Consumers need to know," Lyng said in January, 1982, "that farm prices are way too low; they must be higher.''

During a feisty House Agriculture Committee hearing in February, 1982, Block was accused of underestimating the cost of 1983 farm price supports. Rep. Leon Panetta (D-Calif.) claimed that the Administration, in order to make the deficit appear smaller, intentionally underestimated the projected expenses of the Commodity Credit Corporation by $5 billion. "At some point it would be nice to present the facts as they are," Panetta told Block. "I'd like to see you at least give something that has more honest figures." The Congressional Budget Office projected guarantees of around $7.3 billion. Block had estimated the government would spend only $1.5 billion.

The Reagan Administration's food policy, of course, is having international effects as well. Export sales of U.S. agriculture products are expected to reach about $40 billion in 1982 in the wake of renewed grain trade with the Soviet Union, as well as a number of other promising new contacts with China and various European nations.

Block's public statements about the role of U.S. agriculture products have tempered since the early days of the Reagan Administration when he once referred to U.S. food stocks as a foreign policy "weapon." Since then he has referred to it as a "tool of peace.''

Block has long opposed agricultural trade embargoes, claiming they make "victims" of the American farmer. "Past policy," he explained, "too often has been distorted by the notion that 'trade is aid'—that agricultural exports are an act of charity to be granted or denied with impunity. Agricultural exports are a vitally important part of our national economy.''

The secretary outlined other major problems surrounding trade embargoes before the Senate agriculture committee in February, 1982. A "truly effective unilateral agricultural sanction is a practical impossibility" according to Block because it is impossible to assure that other nations will honor the measure. Block also asserted that a limited embargo "is of no value. The transparency and ineffectiveness of such policy," he told the senators, "would become a source of international and domestic ridicule.''

Given his point of view, it is not surprising that Block had always opposed the Soviet grain embargo and was one of the prime movers in its revocation in 1981. He engaged in a well publicized power struggle with Secretary of State Alexander Haig over who would handle the grain talks with the Soviets. Block and grain industry representatives were concerned that Haig's involvement in the talks would add political complications to the negotiations. The issue was finally resolved to Block's satisfaction when U.S. Trade Representative William Brock was appointed to handle the talks.

Congress added a clause to the farm bill that would weaken the power of food as a diplomatic weapon after 1984, by forcing the President to embargo all products to a given country if he wants to withhold any. Should the President embargo agriculture exports for reasons of "national security or foreign policy," the clause requires that the government compensate farmers for the losses from foreign sales they incur from an embargo.

The Administration's concern about the consumers of farm products is less visible. At a conference of state legislators held in Washington in December, 1981 Lyng joked about a phone call he'd received from a member of Common Cause. The caller wanted Lyng to know she supported the farm bill. "Maybe we should take a second look at it," he joked.

The joke, though, has more than a grain of truth. Nutrition and anti-hunger lobbyists are dismayed about Block's policies.

In spring, 1981 Block told a meeting of dairy executives, "I sometimes wonder if we are going deep enough," with cuts in the food stamps program. New cuts have been proposed for 1983. (See Mary Jarratt profile.)

Nutrition advocates knew they were in for a long four years when Block summed up his philosophy of human nutrition at his nomination hearing:

"I know that they are not the same," Block said, "but hogs are just like people. You can provide protein and grain to a hog and he will balance his ration. He will eat about the right amount of protein to go along with the grain. He will not overeat on the protein or the grain. People are surely as smart as hogs."

Lyng has said he is eager to be a part of the debate as Congress, USDA and the Food and Drug Administration, under the prod of industry groups, reconsider the Delaney Clause, which bans any food additive proven to cause cancer in animals or humans. Lyng has said that if government strictly adheres to the "zero-risk, zero-tolerance" wording of the amendment, the nation could end up with "zero-food."

"When Lyng said that he is grossly oversimplifying the issue for the sake of sensationalism," said Smith of the Community Nutrition Institute, "The law only refers to food additives and nothing else. There is a big difference between what he implies and what the law actually says."

As a December, 1981 General Accounting Office report observed, no tests to determine whether food additives cause cancer and no statistical models to assess the risks these additives pose to human health, have "been developed to the point where many experts totally accept their reliability." Relative risk assessment would likely become a political calculation heavily influenced by food and chemical producers.

Lyng has fought Delaney on numerous occasions on behalf of the American Meat Institute, most recently over the possible risks caused by nitrites in meat. (John Block sided with the AMI on this issue while director of the Illinois Department of Agriculture.)

While at the AMI Lyng often fought then Assistant Secretary for Food and Consumer Services Carol Tucker Foreman, and, at one point, demanded that she withdraw from any mechanically-deboned meat decisions because she made a "prejudiced" statement against the meat industry. He referred to a comment she made before a group of food editors at the White House in 1979: "Their [the meat industry's] position is. . .that the public won't buy [the product] if they know what is in it." Lyng said at the 1982 CFA convention that he did not participate in the deboned meat decision. (See McMillan profile.)

The combativeness between the food industry and USDA under Carter has all but vanished since Block and Lyng took office. The cattle industry has asked the Administration to change beef grading standards in a manner that consumer groups and the restaurant industry believe will give higher ratings to lower-quality meat. Of the department proposal, Lyng said: "Our proposal is trying to be responsive to their [the cattlemen's] request."

Lyng takes a predictable stance on school lunch and nutrition issues, opposing expansion of the school feeding programs "beyond children in real need." (See Mary Jarratt profile.)

Lyng has long opposed nutritional information programs as "federal pre-emption of parents" and is eagerly paring down many of the information programs developed under Foreman.

The undersecretary's stance on food stamps has changed considerably since the days when he personally administered the program for President Nixon. However, in the current political climate, Lyng maintains the program is out of control and needs substantial reductions.

C.W. MCMILLAN

ASSISTANT SECRETARY, MARKETING AND INSPECTION SERVICES

RESPONSIBILITY OF OFFICE

Under the June, 1981 departmental reorganization, McMillan's responsibilities were expanded to include supervision of the Food Safety and Quality Service (FSQS) (now called the Food Safety and Inspection Service) which had previously been under the Assistant Secretary for Food and Consumer Services.

Now, in addition to administering the department's inspection programs, McMillan will be administering safety regulations, a situation which concerns consumer advocates who believe food safety ought to be a separate program.

Former Secretary Bob Bergland established the FSQS in 1977 "to provide assurance to the consumer that foods are safe, wholesome, and nutritious, that they are of good quality, and that they are informatively and honestly labelled; and to provide assistance to the marketing system through purchase of surplus food commodities and those needed in the National Food Assistance Programs."

McMillan also is the chief administrator of the Agricultural Marketing Service which "administers standardization, grading, voluntary and mandatory inspection, market news, marketing orders, regulatory and related programs."

The Food Safety and Inspection Service will operate in 1982 with a budget of $309 million and a staff of 9,808, down 1,000 from 1981. The Agricultural Marketing Service will spend $466 million and employ 4,304.

McMillan was appointed by the President to the seven-member board of the government's Commodity Credit Corporation which was created in 1933 to "stabilize and protect farm income and prices, to assist in maintaining balanced and adequate supplies of agricultural commodities and their products, and to facilitate the orderly distribution of commodities."

BACKGROUND

McMillan has been executive vice president of the National Cattlemen's Association (NCA) for the past 22 years. NCA is a trade association which was known as the American National Cattlemen's Association prior to its merger with the National Livestock Feeders Association in 1977.

The NCA has long fought government regulations as part of an attempt to preserve the profitability of the contracting U.S. red meat market.

"NCA tends to look upon certain federal regulations on meat the way the National Rifle Association looks upon gun control," said Fowler West, staff director of the House Agriculture Committee.

NCA has also opposed various government decisions to preserve public land that NCA contended could be used for agricultural or grazing purposes.

At a March, 1978 Senate hearing, McMillan testified with another NCA vice-president who declared, "Within the administrative and regulatory branches of government, including USDA, EPA [Environmental Protection Agency], FDA [Food and Drug Administration], OSHA [Occupational Safety and Health Administration] and Interior, we are seeing actions and proposals which can eventually result in the socialization of food production and marketing."

In addition to his work at the NCA, McMillan has served in various positions including: the executive committee of the National Environmental Development Association; USDA's Advisory Committee on Foreign Animal Diseases; and the Food and Agricultural Committee of the U.S. Chamber of Commerce.

Prior to coming to Washington in 1959, McMillan was head of agricultural research for Swift and Company, Chicago, for five years. Before that he served six years as an assistant 4-H club agent, a county agent, and a faculty member at Colorado State University. He obtained his B.S. degree in economics from the university in 1948.

Born February 9, 1926 in Fort Collins, Colorado, McMillan is married and has three sons.

MAJOR ISSUES

- Despite numerous findings that marketing orders are anti-consumer, and disrupt free market choices, McMillan is supporting these expensive government subsidies.

- McMillan was put in charge of food safety and quality matters in June, 1981, a situation which most consumer advocates consider a classic case of "the fox guarding the henhouse." He has already weakened several rules in line with meat industry demands.

The Administration's policy on marketing orders has been perhaps the main issue confronting McMillan. Public attention was heightened during 1981 by press reports of disgruntled orange growers in California who complained that the orders kept them from selling their bountiful crops.

It was a scene poignant enough to revive memories of the Great Depression, and recall the words of John Steinbeck, as *The San Francisco Examiner* did: "The works of the roots of the vines, of the trees," wrote Steinbeck, "must be destroyed to keep up the price, and this is the saddest, bitterest thing of all. Carloads of oranges dumped on the ground."

Somewhat less eloquently, the General Accounting Office (GAO) fueled the opposition to the price-setting mechanism by issuing a report in July, 1981 which concluded the order system is totally controlled by agribusiness and "provides little or no consumer protection."

When faced with a question on marketing orders during his nomination hearing, McMillan backed the status quo, saying, "I am a strong believer in the market system, and I think we can do it within the laws and regulations we have."

He also defended the program in a May 19, 1981 USDA press release: "Unlike most fruits, oranges can be 'stored' on the trees and the weekly regulations are intended to spread the total supply over a longer period to stabilize prices and avoid market gluts and shortages."

The GAO report disagreed, saying the orders merely keep prices superficially high and "the law. . .was designed primarily to help the growers."

Not surprisingly, the USDA policy released in January, 1982 recommends little change in the marketing orders for several fruits, vegetables and specialty crops. But the White House's regulatory reviewers are continuing to pressure agriculture to revise its rules, which an agriculture task force concluded in November, 1981 "can impose inefficiencies on the industries affected and reduce consumer welfare." In other words, they cost consumers money.

McMillan has also been busy with food safety and inspection matters since the June, 1981 departmental reorganization, when he was suddenly empowered to authorize changes which the meat industry has been seeking for years.

Former Assistant Secretary Carol Tucker Foreman is especially dismayed to see food safety matters under McMillan's jurisdiction. "It is only in this Administration that the responsibility has been shifted," she said. "And this is contrary to the act, which clearly states that this is a public health area."

"I don't disagree that it is a public health area," McMillan told us. But he said the change was made in order to get all the regulatory functions involving meat inspection under one roof. The public health aspect will be adequately taken care of under his direction, he maintained. "You are talking about a regulatory function," he said. "And it is the appropriate role of my office to handle all matters of a regulatory nature."

That may be a problem itself. McMillan has clearly demonstrated his intention to make USDA more sympathetic toward the meat industry. Several recent USDA rule changes have borne the obvious stamp of McMillan and Deputy Secretary Richard Lyng, both longtime meat industry lobbyists.

Among the most controversial of these is a proposed rule change issued in July, 1981 involving the labelling of mechanically deboned meat products. Existing law requires such products to specify powdered-bone content on the main label. The new rule, authorized by McMillan, proposed to eliminate that requirement and replaced it with one which said producers must list the product's calcium content on the ingredient label, but won't have to say that the meat contains powdered bone.

Tom Smith of the Community Nutrition Institute said, "If the proposals are adopted, they will result in deliberate deception of consumers who purchase the product." Additionally, Smith has contended, meat which contains the powdered bone could pose health problems for certain people.

McMillan has publicly stated he intends to work toward changes in the USDA beef grading standards "so that beef with less marbling can be graded choice." (Marbling, flecks of fat interspersed through the meat, makes meat more tender and flavorful.)

Inspections are another troubled area. The USDA's record in this area remains deficient three-quarters of a century after the publication of *The Jungle*. In 1978, the House Oversight and Investigations Subcommittee concluded that the USDA, "which is responsible for monitoring meat and poultry for residues of chemicals such as pesticides and animal drugs, is doing a poor job of finding residue violations and of preventing. . .the marketing of contaminated meat. The department's two residue monitoring programs. . .are seriously ineffective. The 'in slaughterhouse' monitoring program tests few animals and doesn't look for many harmful chemicals known to occur in meat and poultry. The 'pretest' program, which enjoins growers suspected of marketing violative livestock to submit tissue samples for laboratory analysis, is easily avoided by farmers. Consequently, much of the meat and poultry consumed in this country may be contaminated."

The Reagan Administration's response to this situation has been predictable: weaken the government's enforcement capability.

McMillan has authorized a rule change which will eliminate USDA's policy of publicly labelling meat and poultry plants that do not pass federal inspections as "problem" or "chronic problem" plants. USDA officials claim such plants will now be quietly excluded from inspections rather than embarrassing them with press releases. (If USDA does not inspect, the plant's meat cannot legally be sold.)

The department is proposing legislation to end daily inspection for some meat plants. Instead, plants identified by the secretary would be allowed to "self-inspect" to ensure their compliance with pure food regulations.

To Jim Murphy, chairman of the National Joint Council of the meat inspectors union, the dangers of that approach are obvious. "How many slaughter houses, packing and processing plants can be expected to discard diseased or contaminated meat when the loss means a downturn in profits?" he asked. "Can consumers be assured that the meat and poultry products they buy are safe, wholesome and free of disease under production line speedups and self-inspection systems?"

The meat industry is also pleased to hear McMillan say the Reagan Administration will do all it can to halt further publication of the controversial "dietary guidelines" which were co-published by USDA last year. (See Mary Jarratt profile for more detail.) At least partially in response to such consumer education programs, USDA's own studies show that in the past three years about two-thirds of U.S. families have altered their diets for health reasons to limit intake of fat and cholesterol.

McMillan contends USDA will continue to provide nutrition information but "will now base it on fact and not opinion." Said Foreman: "What that means is that now we're going to get the meat industry's definition of the facts."

FINANCIAL BACKGROUND

As vice-president of the National Cattlemen's Association, McMillan received a $67,000 salary. It was his only major source of income.

WHAT OTHERS ARE SAYING ABOUT HIM

- "Bill McMillan is not a bad guy," Foreman told us. "I wouldn't say he is very smart on some issues. . .he is just one of those guys who is proud of his function as a representative of his industry."

MARY JARRATT
ASSISTANT SECRETARY
FOOD AND CONSUMER SERVICES

RESPONSIBILITY OF OFFICE

Jarratt's responsibilities were altered considerably in a June, 1981 departmental shake-up which transferred the Food Safety and Quality Service out of her jurisdiction and left her primarily in charge of USDA's huge Food and Nutrition Service which administers food stamps and various child nutrition services, including the National School Lunch Program, the Food Distribution Program, and the Women, Infant and Children Program (WIC). WIC "provides specified nutritious food supplements to pregnant and nursing women up to 6 months postpartum, and to children up to 5 years of age."

Jarratt gained two new responsibilities in the reorganization: overseeing the Human Nutrition Information Service (which had previously been a part of the department's research wing) and a consumer adviser's office (which had previously reported directly to the secretary).

The Food and Nutrition Service was established in 1969 and became part of Food and Consumer Services when that division was formed in 1977.

BACKGROUND

Jarratt spent the last six years before taking office as a minority staff member at the House Agriculture Subcommittee on Domestic Marketing, Consumer Relations and Nutrition, working on consumer nutrition issues and the food stamp program. She also served as a staff member of the special House Committee on Welfare Reform during the 95th Congress. Jarratt earned a reputation as a hardline critic of food stamps.

During her tenure with the Agriculture subcommittee, anti-hunger groups described Jarratt a "vociferous" opponent of food stamps. To Republicans on the committee, though, she was a loyal, if pedestrian, soldier. "[I never saw her] get out of line and do or say anything other than what she was told to do" by the committee's ranking minority member, Rep. William C. Wampler (R-Va.), said Fowler West, now majority staff director of the House Agriculture Committee.

Jarratt was the first woman to be named to professional status in the 130-year history of the House Agriculture Committee.

Prior to 1975, Jarratt was an executive secretary to Rep. Richard Poff (R-Va.), and then to William Haley, a member of the National Transportation Safety Board. From 1966 to 1967 she was an assistant to Raymond Bauer at the Harvard Graduate School of Business Administration.

Born in Clifton Forge, Virginia on October 29, 1942, Jarratt received her B.A. in history from Mary Baldwin College of Staunton, Virginia in 1964 and later a degree of business certification from the Katharine Gibbs School in Boston, Massachusetts.

Appropriately for a veteran of the House Agriculture Committee and an official at the USDA, Jarratt has been active in the 4-H. In 1980 she was named a National 4-H Alumni Achievement winner.

MAJOR ISSUES

- Jarratt has long sought to decrease funding for food stamps as a House aide, and now is working to slash the program in a way that will be devastating for the working poor.

- Jarratt advocates block grants for most of the major nutrition programs—a plan which would entail fewer federal dollars, less services and a reduced federal commitment to hunger and nutrition problems.

- Consumer nutrition programs are gradually being phased out under Jarratt along with a number of regulations which were designed to foster better diets among school children. The result, said her predecessor, will be "to let the businessmen into the schools."

Jarratt has been consistent. She toed the conservative line on food stamps as a House aide, and now she is working to carry out the cuts as an administrator.

After working several years in Congress to trim food stamp benefits, Jarratt is particularly pleased by the $1.65 billion in cuts approved by Congress for fiscal year 1982 (over $200 million more than the Reagan Administration requested).

And she is eager to cut more. In its 1983 budget, the Administration has proposed another $2.3 billion reduction in food stamp expenditures. Jarratt is particularly optimistic about "reducing food stamp fraud," an issue which has been most aggressively pursued by Sen. Jesse Helms, the vociferous North Carolina food stamp critic. Helms, a conservative Republican, and Jarratt have more than rhetoric in common; one of her first acts in office was to appoint Helms's close aide, John Bode, as her top deputy.

The proposed second round of food stamp cuts would have a devastating impact on the program. According to the Congressional Budget Office, the cuts would affect 35 percent of all households receiving food stamps. About one-eighth of the households—approximately three million people—would have their benefits eliminated entirely. And the cuts would be focused at the working poor, who would lose 40 percent of their current benefits.

Jarratt's reputation among anti-hunger groups is also consistent. "In public forums [Jarratt] was extremely hostile to any kind of advocacy for food stamp recipients," said Bari Schwartz of the Food Research Action Center. "She would get quite vociferous and claim that anti-hunger groups really wanted to give food stamps away with no strings attached."

Jarratt has a similar view of child nutrition programs. In line with Office of Management and Budget suggestions, she has backed the consolidation of such programs into block grants saying "some money could be saved on reporting requirements."

Ellen Haas, of the consumer division of the Community Nutrition Institute, said converting child nutrition programs to block grants will mean there are fewer services, less money available and a reduced federal commitment to hunger and nutrition problems. Specifically, it would mean "school lunch prices would increase," thereby increasing the burden on low and middle income families which will already be hard-pressed by other program cuts, she said.

For 1983, the Administration is proposing a 9.4 percent cut in child nutrition programs that would eliminate the summer meal program and slash programs that subsidize lunches during the school year. In writing regulations to allow school districts to comply with the first round of budget cuts, the Food and Nutrition Service triggered one of the great public relations disasters of the Reagan Administration's first year—a debacle that arguably revealed with exquisite clarity the Administration's priorities.

In September, 1981, the Agriculture Department proposed regulations to allow schools to reduce the portions served under the school lunch program. And they proposed to let the schools count ketchup and pickle relish as vegetables, and cake and cookies as bread. Reagan backed down in the resulting furor and pulled the regulations. But he has not rescinded the cuts that made them necessary; the 1983 budget shows he is pushing further in that direction. Beyond the cuts proposed for 1983, the budget envisions cuts of $800 million in 1984 and 1985. The Women, Infants and Children nutrition program would be folded into a health services block grant. Cuts in the WIC program have been cited by Dr. William Bithony of Boston's Children's Hospital Medical Center as having a "direct" impact on child malnutrition. In a study by the Food Research Action Center, Bithony said: "The cases I have seen are a direct result of children being dropped from the WIC program." Added Nancy Amidei, the center's director: "The deep budget cuts in the food programs and our contacts with low-income people around the country have given us good reason to fear that malnutrition was becoming a serious problem once again. Now hard evidence is starting to come in."

Consumers will suffer from cutbacks and deemphasis of nutrition information programs, maintains Jarratt's predecessor, Carol Tucker Foreman, who is seeing many of her accomplishments under President Carter dismantled. "This Administration is saying we're going to take care of business interests and some farmers," she said.

The June departmental reorganization took away from Jarratt many vital food safety responsibilities. Critics contend this was part of an industry power play designed to switch most food safety and nutrition issues from Jarratt to C.W. McMillan, the head of USDA's marketing and transportation division (now renamed Food Safety and Inspection Service), and a former lobbyist for the National Cattlemen's Association.

Foreman also noted that Jarratt has announced the end of USDA's free distribution of the "Dietary Guidelines for Americans," issued by USDA and the Department of Health and Human Service, which recommended decreased consumption for salt, fat, cholesterol, sugar, and alcohol, increased consumption of starch and fiber, keeping down one's weight, and eating a variety of foods.

The industry groups that have opposed the publication of the guidelines convinced Jarratt and the Reagan Administration not only to squash the guidelines, but to dismantle the agency which produced them, the Human Nutrition Center. The center's director, Dr. Mark Hegstad, said the move was indicative of the "deemphasis of nutrition in USDA."

In related actions, Jarratt has approved the following changes in USDA's nutrition policy:

- a revision of a school lunch menu planning guide (after protests were voiced by meat industry lobbyists). The revision was ordered because the menu "suggested that school cafeterias might want to explore substitutes for foods high in fat." The revision recommended "a wide variety of foods" in "moderate quantities" instead.

- deciding not to "regulate the availability of saccharin-containing foods sold in competition with the school nutrition programs. . ." Saccharin, a controversial artificial sweetener, has been demonstrated by the FDA to be a low-level carcinogen.

- announcing plans to reconsider USDA's year-old rule restricting until the end of classes the sale of the snack foods at schools. (No formal plan to change the rule has been announced.) Vending machine companies had objected to the rule though a Jarratt assistant claims the action was taken because "school officials and students complained that it would inhibit their fund-raising activities."

"They're saying we're going to let the businessmen into the schools and have direct access to molding the eating of our children," concludes Foreman.

FINANCIAL BACKGROUND

Jarratt's financial statement indicates no source of income other than her job with the House Committee on Agriculture.

WHAT OTHERS ARE SAYING ABOUT HER

- "People say Jarratt is very conservative and that is the reason she got this position," said Dr. Michael Jacobson of the Center for Science in the Public Interest. "But my guess is that she was chosen to be a gopher. . .a doormat compared to some of the really high-powered people in USDA like Richard Lyng and Bill McMillan."

- Foreman echoes Jacobson's statement, saying that Jarratt was "a perfect choice" for the purposes of the new Administration because of her dedication and loyalty to the Administration's determination to strip away consumer protection.

- Jeff Becker, of the Community Nutrition Institute, described Jarratt "as never very dynamic—except when in opposition to anti-hunger groups."

JOHN CROWELL
ASSISTANT SECRETARY,
NATURAL RESOURCES AND THE ENVIRONMENT

RESPONSIBILITY OF OFFICE

The assistant secretary's major responsibility is to set policy for the U.S. Forest Service, the agency that manages the 188 million-acre national forest system. Congress has mandated that these public forests, located in 41 states and Puerto Rico, must be made available for a variety of public and commercial purposes. Uses that have been specifically recognized by law include recreation, mining, timbering, wildlife and fisheries management and water quality protection.

When one use of forest land might interfere with another—for example, if timber cutting was sought in an area with recreational value—the Forest Service is required to balance the conflicting demands and select the combination of uses that would allow the greatest use of the forest, a system known as multiple use.

Though the Interior Department has ultimate authority, traditionally the Forest Service has made recommendations on whether or not to grant drilling and mining leases in both wilderness and other national forest areas and Interior Secretary Watt has promised to abide by them.

Crowell also oversees the Soil Conservation Service, responsible for developing and carrying out a national soil and water conservation program. In 1982, the Forest Service operated on a $2.125 billion budget and employed 28,697 people.

BACKGROUND

After weeks of controversy, Crowell was finally confirmed on May 20, 1981 by a 72-25 Senate vote, one of the largest tallies recorded against a Reagan appointee.

During his March confirmation hearings, critics sharply questioned Crowell's fitness to direct the Forest Service, given his long-stated opposition to the agency's policies, and his background with two paper industry giants, Louisiana Pacific and Georgia Pacific. From 1959 through 1972, Crowell was an attorney for Georgia Pacific, the nation's third largest lumber producer. When an antitrust case forced the company to divest itself of some holdings in 1973, Crowell moved to the newly-formed Louisiana Pacific as general counsel. Louisiana Pacific, the nation's second largest timber company, was until recently the largest purchaser of federal timber.

While with the paper companies and as a member of the National Forest Products Association, a powerful industry lobby, Crowell was often a caustic critic of federal timbering policies. In one speech, Crowell claimed that wilderness advocates were seeking "to minimize the benefits obtainable from the national forests. . ."

Bearing such views, Crowell was greeted by environmentalists with alarm. Despite calls for more intensive hearings, Crowell's nomination was quickly approved by the Senate Agriculture Committee. Senate approval was stalled, though, when charges of possible illegal behavior were added to the complaints about Crowell's environmental record.

Ketchikan Pulp Company (KPC), an Alaska-based subsidiary of Louisiana Pacific, was found guilty in March, 1981 by a federal court in Alaska of conspiring with another firm, Alaska Lumber and Pulp Company (ALP), to restrain trade and monopolize the timber industry in Alaska's Tongass National Forest. Over the past two decades KPC and ALP have bought out or gained control of virtually every logging operation in the Tongass. In the antitrust case, the court found evidence that KPC and ALP used fronts as well as controlled companies and subsidiaries to carry out their conspiracy.

Senators Patrick Leahy (D-Vt.) and Edward Kennedy (D-Mass.), along with Rep. James Weaver (D-Ore.), chair of a House agriculture subcommittee on forests, charged that Crowell knew about the firms' collusive activities. Citing two memoranda from the lengthy antitrust case, Leahy asserted that Crowell was "directly link[ed]. . .to the material facts" of the court's case against KPC.

According to Leahy, a May 2, 1973 letter from KPC executive D.L. Murdey to Crowell indicates, in Leahy's words, "Crowell was aware that on critical matters of log supply, KPC and ALP were cooperative ventures." In the memo cited by Leahy, Murdey wrote to Crowell: "My concern is that I don't feel anything will be gained if

[Clarence] Kramer [of ALP] starts the ball rolling while in D.C. unless it is under your direction. This he agrees with." Summarizing, Leahy said: "This memorandum indicates that John Crowell was in a position of joint leadership and advocacy for the acts to monopolize by the two companies. Certainly Mr. Murdey believed Mr. Crowell to be the central figure in these activities." Another "equally damaging" document, claims Leahy, was a memo Crowell sent to Louisiana Pacific executive H.A. Merlo commenting that KPC use its subsidiary, Anette Timber Company, "to gain access to timber reserves of small loggers under the small business set aside program," as Leahy summarized it.

Wrote Crowell in the memo: "It would seem KPC would have. . .plenty of time to do what might be necessary to qualify ATC as a small business if that seemed at the time to be in KPC's interests."

Crowell repeatedly testified that he had never been involved in the "remotest way with any of the occurrences, negotiations, or contracts out of which the plaintiffs' claims allegedly rose." He said he was never called to the trial because he had "no relevant information material to the contentions of either side." Crowell claims his involvement as general counselor in the affair was "limited to approving selection of defense counsel for the Ketchikan Pulp Company, to receiving status reports thereafter from defense counsel. . .and to participating with such counsel in developing trial tactics and strategy."

Crowell's adversaries in Congress felt their charges were further substantiated, however, when several days later they learned he neglected to disclose his position as assistant secretary for KPC in his initial financial report. Under pressure, Crowell filed an addendum to the report with the Government Ethics Office in May, 1981 revealing that he had acted as secretary to KPC since 1976, and that he held secretarial positions on 16 other subsidiaries of Louisiana Pulp as well.

Crowell said he was not paid for these responsibilities and "failed to make the mental connection and to realize that the scope of the [financial] report might also cover functions and positions of a minor nature and for which no pay was given or received."

"We have here more than just a forgetful memory," charged Leahy, wondering how a "well-trained lawyer" could have "misread all those directions." Both Weaver's and Kennedy's staff are continuing to investigate the allegations.

Born on March 18, 1930, in Elizabeth, New Jersey, Crowell graduated from Dartmouth in 1952 and from Harvard Law School in 1957. After clerking at the U.S. Court of Appeals for the Third Circuit in New Jersey for two years, Crowell joined Georgia Pacific. Crowell is married with three children.

MAJOR ISSUES

- Conservationists are alarmed by Crowell's "dollar return" approach to forestry. He proposes to double the output of timber harvested from national forests, departing from the long-standing policy of "non-declining even flow" in favor of environmentally destructive clear-cutting and forest restructuring.

- Crowell supports California Senator S.I. Hayakawa's bill which would eliminate a mandatory periodic Forest Service review of forests for wilderness consideration, and place wilderness out of regular multiple use review.

- Like Watt, Crowell is a rabid opponent of environmental groups; he maintains most environmentalists' concerns are exaggerated and designed to raise money.

Environmentalists have dubbed Crowell "the James Watt of the Agriculture Department." Indeed, when speaking about environmentalists or exploiting natural resources he sounds much like the embattled Interior secretary. Over the next four years, Crowell told us, he wants "to increase the productive outputs of the national forests, particularly timber, but also mineral and oil and gas."

Already, to the dismay of conservationists, the Forest Service has made recommendations for oil and gas leases in designated wilderness areas in California, Arkansas, Mississippi and Wyoming.

Crowell told the Audubon Society that "much of the over-stated concern by environmental organizations is for the purpose of raising money from a loyal and largely unquestioning membership."

Crowell hopes to double the timber harvest of national forests as rapidly as possible. According to Crowell, the national forests "have not been contributing a proportionate share to the wood needs of the country." Yet many economists and environmentalists question whether the Forest Service actually needs to contribute a greater share to the nation's wood supply. With high interest rates depressing the housing market, timber demand has moderated. According to Peter Kirby of the Wilderness Society, the current market proves that "there is a shortage in timber demand, not timber supply. The sales level should actually be adjusted down to reflect realistic market conditions."

Kirby also maintains that even if the Reagan Administration's optimistic predictions that housing starts will pick up are validated, the Forest Service's proposed 12.3 billion board feet timber harvest increase for fiscal 1983 still exceeds needed supplies.

What's more, the Forest Service in some cases may actually be subsidizing timber sales. In 1976 the Natural Resources Defense Council (NRDC) undertook an examination of the Forest Service's timber sales and found that "in many regions the expenses of timber sales programs. . .exceeded the income from the sales, often by a considerable amount." When asked whether this still was the case Crowell accused us of "reading Barlow's stuff." (Thomas Barlow is a researcher with the NRDC.) "It's wrong." he added. Barlow stands by his conclusions.

More controversy is simmering in the Forest Service because sections of the 1976 National Forest Management Act have come under the scrutiny of Vice-President Bush's Task Force on Regulatory Relief. The task force's main targets are regulations covering clear-cutting—the dimensions and shape of an area where trees can be completely stripped away—and with stream-side cutting—the mandated distance from water courses that foresters must restrain from cutting. While with the National Forest Products Association Crowell advocated loosening the rules, a view he still holds. Environmentalists want tighter guidelines to protect wildlife and other natural resources.

Crowell's McCarthy-like criticisms of environmentalists and the "wilderness concept" echo Watt's rhetoric. In March, 1982 the assistant secretary told a reporter for the *Albuquerque Journal* that he thought both the Sierra Club and the Audubon Society were "infiltrated by people who have very strong ideas about socialism and even communism." But unlike his colleague in Interior, Crowell could not ignore the flak his statement precipitated and was forced to apologize shortly thereafter. He said he was "mortified and shocked" to see his words printed and that he had made "a mistake."

Crowell maintains that from the 89 million acres of national forests designated for commercial use, the potential annual yield is about 35 billion board feet. The

Forest Service has never sold more than 13 billion board feet a year.

To increase output, Crowell wants to depart from the traditional practice of "non-declining even flow" forest management. The Forest Service has always pursued the non-declining even flow procedure, which mandates that the volume of trees harvested may not exceed the growth of a forest. In passing the 1976 National Forest Management Act, Congress endorsed non-declining even flow, but allowed the Forest Service limited discretion to depart from it.

Crowell claims non-declining even flow makes sense only in young or under-stocked forests and firmly believes it should not be practiced in overstocked forests, which he likens to a factory: "Production will eventually come to a halt, if instead of selling the product, you stack it in the aisles of the factory. To keep national forests productive, managers need to liquidate the accumulated inventory." In 1980 Crowell told the Society of American Foresters that non-declining even flow was "absurd."

That's "sheer nonsense" said Rep. Weaver, asserting that old growth forests "are at equilibrium between mortality and new growth. They are not going to fall down and go to waste."

Environmentalists charge that Crowell is trying to maximize short-term gain at the expense of long-term resource management. Jack Usher of the Forest Service's regional office in Portland, Oregon, is skeptical about departing from existing policy. "We have to keep reminding people we are not a national tree farm. The forests have other uses too, such as recreation, wildlife, water production and wilderness." Others point out that the timber companies are pushing for increased access to public forests, because they are depleting their own lands through overcutting and mismanagement.

Crowell's belief "that land allocations are only to be made on the basis of an economic justification," disturbs Sen. Leahy. "Such an approach," Leahy said, "is contrary to the Forest Service practice and the multiple-use Sustained Yield Act which specifically directs the Forest Service not to automatically manage units of the National Forest System for the greatest dollar return."

The Forest Service's proposed 1983 budget devotes the greatest proportions of funding towards mineral activity and timber cutting. Calling the budget request a "mockery of sound and balanced multiple-use management," Peter Kirby of the Wilderness Society told a House interior subcommittee that "because of excess funding for roads and timber sales, the Forest Service will fail to meet its basic multiple-use responsibilities."

Kirby pointed out that about half of the nation's trail system will fall into disrepair due to cuts in funds for trail maintenance; that funding for habitat improvement and protection will be transferred to timber sales supports; and that the budget request virtually eliminates money for soil and water improvement programs.

Crowell's development strategies will also smack against established wilderness policy. In 1979 the Forest Service released its RARE II Report (Roadless Area Review and Evaluation) which studied 60 million acres of roadless, undeveloped national forest areas. RARE II recommended that Congress designate 15 million acres in the forests as wilderness, that 10.6 million be studied further and that 36 million acres be classified as non-wilderness multiple use areas.

In 1980, Congress, drawing from RARE II recommendations, designated wilderness areas in Alaska, central Idaho, Colorado, New Mexico, and in several eastern states. This year Congress will be considering bills for California,

Washington, Florida, Oregon and other states.

In the past, Crowell referred to RARE II while on the National Forest Products Association task force as "particularly ill-conceived" and "outside the planning process mandated by" law.

Crowell now claims to support the majority of Forest Service wilderness recommendations made so far, but he wants to "end uncertainty about and resolve the status of the national forest roadless areas." He supported legislation proposed by California Republican Senator S. I. Hayakawa which would make all areas of the national forest now under consideration for wilderness designation immediately eligible for development—if Congress doesn't act on them by 1985. Hayakawa's bill also could release the 36 million acres of multiple use areas from further wilderness consideraton by the Forest Service. Under a 1974 act, the Forest Service is required to review these lands for wilderness consideration every 10 years.

Crowell told us the 1985 deadline the Hayakawa bill sets for congressional action on potential wilderness areas is not unreasonable because, "the fact that Congress hasn't acted on [a wilderness proposal] would imply that as a satisfactory result."

Speaking to the American Foresters in October, 1980, Crowell categorized as the most valuable "output" of the national forest mining and timber production, followed by cattle grazing, enhancement of water volumes and recreation. Of wilderness, Crowell said disparagingly, "Then the point is reached where substantially all of these objectives are simultaneously abandoned for celebration instead of a concept encapsulated in the term 'wilderness'."

Crowell apparently sees wilderness as single-use purpose for forests, arguing that with "wise management" all forests can be made into multiple-use areas.

The Wilderness Society takes a contrary view: "The wilderness itself has many uses, it protects watersheds and rangelands and provides habitat for wildlife." Peter Kirby of the Wilderness Society summed up his concerns about Crowell by paraphrasing Orwell, "Mr. Crowell strongly holds the view that all multiple uses are equal, but some [uses] are more equal than others."

FINANCIAL BACKGROUND

In 1980, Crowell earned $92,742 in salary from Louisiana Pacific. Upon his confirmation he divested himself of stock holdings worth more than $50,000 in Louisiana Pacific and over $15,000 in Georgia Pacific and agreed to recuse himself on any "specific administrative appeals" brought by either company.

Nonetheless, many remain skeptical of Crowell's ability to avoid conflict of interest problems. At Crowell's confirmation hearings, Brock Evans of the Sierra Club argued "it would be nearly impossible [for Crowell] to make any decisions affecting management or allocation of federal lands which will not affect the financial interest of these corporations."

It will be particularly difficult for Crowell to avoid influencing the fate of KPC, which takes *all* of its product from theTongass. As Weaver has suggested, that puts Crowell in an "absurd" position of either aiding his former employer, or removing himself from some of the major areas of his responsibility, including the Tongass, which is the largest national forest. "It is," Weaver has written, "absurd to expect that this [Crowell staying out of decisions on the Tongass] will actually occur. Were it to occur, it would be absurd to have an Assistant Secretary hobbled in this way."

Crowell also divested of interests in several energy corporations, including Consolidated Natural Gas, Atlantic Richfield, and General Electric, which has a large mining subsidiary. His children continue to hold small shares of General Electric and Exxon.

WHAT OTHERS ARE SAYING ABOUT HIM

- "Installing Mr. Crowell to implement forest policy is a perfect example of letting the fox guard the henhouse," said Peter Kirby of the Wilderness Society.

- "The losses that this country will suffer under such administrators of the public lands as Mr. Crowell and his spiritual comrade-in-arms, Secretary of the Interior James G. Watt, will be irreversible and irretrievable," wrote John B. Oakes, in the *New York Times*.

- "He's a good manager, and a lawyer, he's probably one of the better Reagan appointees. But if he gets in and cuts down all the forests I probably won't like him," said a staff aide at the Senate Agriculture Committee.

COUNCIL ON ENVIRONMENTAL QUALITY

A. ALAN HILL

CHAIRMAN

RESPONSIBILITY OF OFFICE

Established by the National Environmental Policy Act (NEPA) of 1969, the council has been called the federal government's environmental conscience. The three presidentially-appointed members of the council and their staff have two major responsibilities: the preparation of an annual state of the environment report, and oversight of federal compliance with the Environmental Impact Statement requirements of NEPA. When relations between the chairman and the White House are good, as they were under the Carter Administration, CEQ can also play a significant role as the President's government-wide environmental adviser, a role provided for in NEPA. In 1982, with a staff of 15 and a budget of $2.7 million, that is not likely to be CEQ's role.

BACKGROUND

On Alan Hill's desk is a jar filled to the brim with official White House jelly beans; on his shelf is another jelly bean jar, empty now, a souvenir of his days in Sacramento.

Those beans brand Hill as a member of Reagan's California contingent. He spent five years in Reagan's California administration, serving first as deputy secretary of agriculture, and then as assistant to Secretary of Resources Ike Livermore, who has now emerged as a surprisingly strong critic of Interior Secretary James Watt.

In California, Hill became acquainted with Ed Meese, and close to Ed Thomas, Meese's assistant. Hill has said Thomas offered him the CEQ job after Hill called the White House to see if they could arrange anything special for his teenage son who was coming to Washington for a week-long seminar program. "Ed called and he said, 'Hey, we've got this program and we want *you* to do it,' " Hill recalled in an interview with *Not Man Apart*.

That long association has not yielded any demonstrable influence on policy, but Hill said it does guarantee access to the key decisionmakers. Hill sits in on meetings of the Cabinet Council on Natural Resources chaired by Watt and also on regular meetings of an executive office group that includes representatives from the Council of Economic Advisers, the Office of Management and Budget (OMB), White House Chief of Staff James Baker's office, domestic policy staff, the national security adviser's office, and the White House science and technology adviser. Hill personally reports to Meese.

Hill is remembered in California as a competent, friendly, and somewhat dispassionate administrator. During his years in government, he served on a number of commissions and boards, from the San Francisco Bay Conservation and Development Commission to the Tahoe Regional Planning Agency. At the agriculture department, he handled legislative relations and supervised the forestry, mining, oil and gas, and soil conservation divisions. While with the state Republican Committee, he handled much of the planning for Reagan's elaborate first inaugural which took place at the unusual hour of 12:01 a.m. on the morning of January 2.

After leaving the Reagan Administration in 1974, Hill ran unsuccessfully for the state assembly. His largest campaign contribution was $5,000 from a group called "United for California," a consortium of major businesses in the state.

Hill came to CEQ after five years running Hill Building Specialities, a small San Francisco-based business that supplied washroom products. From 1974-76 he worked at another California supply company.

Hill also has a long background in partisan politics. From 1962-65, he served as assistant to the minority leader of the California Senate; from 1965-1969 he handled press and public relations for the state Republican Committee. Hill was marginally involved in Reagan's 1976 and 1980 races, as part of his Marin County campaign committees.

Born on February 1, 1938, in San Francisco, California, Hill was graduated with a degree in political science from the College of the Pacific in 1960. He is married, with three children.

FINANCIAL BACKGROUND

Hill is not among the Administration's more affluent members. He earned $19,170 from his washroom supply business last year and holds a negligible amount of stock.

WHAT OTHERS ARE SAYING ABOUT HIM

- Lou Regenstein of the Fund for Animals said of Hill in May, 1981: "As far as I'm concerned, this is the first Reagan appointment that's not a disaster."

Regenstein told us four months later that, "It's my impression that he's not willing to push very hard for conservation-oriented policies and if he did push very hard he'd probably be in trouble."

W. ERNST MINOR
MEMBER

BACKGROUND

Minor's qualifications for the council are far more political than scientific. A former press secretary for the Environmental Protection Agency (EPA) in Ohio, Minor comes to the council directly from the Reagan campaign committee, for which he handled family scheduling. During the 1968 presidential campaign, Minor handled scheduling for vice-presidential candidate Spiro Agnew; when Nixon was elected, Minor spent three years in the White House performing the same functions. Of his current relationship with the former vice-president, Minor says cooly: "We communicate on his birthday."

After leaving the White House, Minor spent a year with the Republican National Committee (RNC) again working on media relations and scheduling. He made his connection to the Reagan camp at that time, traveling with Reagan "every time he left California" from May, 1971 to April, 1972 on RNC fundraising trips.

With the help of childhood friend William Ruckleshaus, an EPA administrator under Nixon, Minor then landed a job as a press secretary with the EPA in Cincinnati, where he remained until joining the 1980 Reagan campaign. During the fall, Minor served on the EPA transition team, where he ran into his first Washington controversy.

During the transition, Minor recalled a pamphlet entitled "Getting Smarter About Regulation" written by William Drayton, then assistant EPA administrator for planning and management. The pamphlet, based on an article Drayton was publishing in the *Harvard Business Review*, offered suggestions on how to make the regulatory process more flexible—ostensibly an avowed aim of the new Administration. Minor told us he didn't "stop it for the content" but because he questioned its "legality." "In particular," he said, "Drayton had not checked the quotes." Responded Drayton: "*Harvard Business Review* seemed to think it was sufficiently accurate to publish it."

Minor describes himself as an environmental "moderate in the midst of two gentlemen who could be construed as pro-environment [Hill] and pro-industry [James MacAvoy]." (MacAvoy's nomination was subsequently withdrawn.) Minor is not considered an authority on environmental problems. Born on April 25, 1931, in Cincinnati, Ohio, Minor was graduated from Brown University in 1955 and is married with three children.

FINANCIAL BACKGROUND

Minor earned only $11,000 from the Reagan/Bush committee, but has much more extensive stock holdings, worth at least $400,000. Most of these are in two trusts, which include holdings in Exxon, Dow, Tenneco, Texaco, and General Motors.

WHAT OTHERS ARE SAYING ABOUT HIM

- Hugh Kaufman, assistant to the director of EPA's Hazardous Waste Control Division, said of Minor: "He might just have the most experience in environmental management in the CEQ, but he's essentially an old Republican workhorse who worked in the Reagan campaigns. Basically, he's a *good* press flack."

MAJOR ISSUES

- Crippled by budget cuts, CEQ is only a shadow of its former self, with a greatly diminished role in environmental policy.

- CEQ has abandoned most of the efforts begun under the Carter Administration to study toxic substances, atmospheric buildup of carbon dioxide and other environmental problems.

After a devastating round of budget cuts, CEQ is still breathing but you have to listen carefully to pick up a heartbeat. In fact, you have to listen carefully to pick up much of anything in the agency's Jackson Place townhouse. Following budget cuts that reduced the size of the staff from 50 to 16—including the three members and their secretaries—the hallways are quiet and no one seems particularly hurried about anything. The phones can ring for a long time before they are answered.

Faced with a 72 percent budget cut, and an Administration with an expressed distaste for the thrust of federal environmental policy, the council members face the overriding question of finding a way to remain relevant. Under the Carter Administration, CEQ Chairman Gus Speth was a forceful advocate for environmental causes and led a busy staff that produced well-regarded and influential studies on toxic chemicals, groundwater contamination, disappearing farmland, and world resource and population trends for the year 2000.

That's not the role Hill sees for himself. "I've done a lot of thinking about how Gus Speth occupied this office; generally as being spokesman for the environmental community in the Administration. I view my role as trying to reach some balance," Hill told us. Adds Minor: "There's a lot to be said for cutting the council down as the Reagan Administration has done." Indeed; the CEQ has been virtually invisible on all important environmental questions. Through 1981, the CEQ issued only one publication. Even its 1981 annual report was not completed by the spring of 1982. A recent caller inquiring about CEQ publications was told, as he went through a long list of recent studies, that none of them were available from the council anymore; they would have to be purchased from the Government Printing Office.

Hill's was one of the few Reagan nominations not greeted with terror by environmentalists. An open, affable individual, he has arranged several meetings with environmental groups and generally seems to speak their language more than just about anyone else in the Administration. "Some people say oil rigs are pretty," he told us, "they're not. They're functional." And again: "I'll never forget the first time I went up to Eureka [in Northern California] and met with the timber industry. I mentioned the word aesthetic and you'd have thought I said the 'f' word at high mass."

But Hill tempers those sentiments with the usual Administration complaints about government regulation, defending the activities of Vice-President Bush's Task Force on Regulatory Relief and distancing himself from Livermore—who Hill describes as his environmental mentor—in his criticism of Watt. "I think Jim Watt is Jim Watt," Hill says blandly. "No matter how you paint it, he's a very determined individual. . .he's very sharp and very abrasive."

Comments like those symbolize the tact Hill has taken: sympathetic to environmental concerns, but cautious, and unanxious to make waves. In fact, his main job responsibility might well be to be *sympathetic*, to provide a good-natured sounding board where environmentalists can at least make their displeasure known to someone in the Administration who'll agree to have lunch with them. Though friendly, Hill will be close-to-the-vest. One lobbyist who met with him said he couldn't get Hill "to commit himself on anything more controversial than the day's weather." It has not been apparent that Hill, who considers himself a consensus builder, has the commitment, or the burning interest in environmental protection, to face down the very determined opponents of environmental health standards at Interior, OMB, and EPA.

Even if he had the commitment, he lacks the staff support to become a major influence on policy. With the reduced funding, the council will publish little beside its annual report—and even that in reduced form. CEQ's annual reports on the environment have been extraordinarily thorough compilations of the state of air, water, and land resources, as well as the status of toxic and international environmental issues. Frederick Khedouri, OMB's associate director for natural resources, demonstrated the Administration's interest in the annual report when he told the *New York Times* in spring, 1981 that, "In my opinion, the EPA annual report is far superior to the CEQ report."

The EPA does not publish an annual report.

In interviews, Hill and Minor said they view the council's proper role under Reagan as coordinating Administration response to environmental problems that cut across agency lines, such as acid rain and hazardous waste facility siting. The council is attempting to coordinate the State Department and the EPA in the negotiations with Canada for an agreement curtailing acid rain. Canadian officials have become increasingly concerned about the Administration's clean air policies, and openly critical of the EPA's failure to adhere to a 1980 memorandum of agreement between Ottawa and Washington pledging both countries to steps to control the problem.

Officially, the Reagan Administration, like the coal and utility industries, argues that more research is needed before action can be taken. "If somebody was fooling around with some of my basic industries, I'd be up on on a soapbox too," Hill told us. "But our scientists say we don't have enough data on hand to move off on a control strategy."

Though negotiations on the treaty began in summer, 1981 the Canadians have shifted their efforts to Congress, figuring that the Reagan Administration's hostility both to domestic environmental controls and to the Trudeau government's nationalistic energy policies make the prospects dim for a satisfactory treaty. "There is a growing disquietude up there," said one House staffer who traveled to Canada as part of a trip arranged by the Canadian government, "over what they perceive to be stalling tactics here."

Hill hopes to play a similar role in devising an Administration policy for the siting of hazardous waste facilities. "I think the entire question is an emotional issue," he said. "We're going to do something to try to achieve a decision-making method" involving both the states and the federal government. That job is certain to be made more difficult by the EPA's announced intentions to review the regulations governing future hazardous waste disposal.

Hill concedes "it's possible" that regulatory changes may make communities more reluctant to accept the dumping facilities.

Other areas CEQ plans to focus on include:

- Reviewing the Environmental Impact Statement process established under the NEPA, the landmark 1969 law that created the council. Several Reagan Administration officials have criticized the process for holding up needed energy development and snarling the bureaucracy in needless paper. Early in the Administration, Interior Secretary James Watt unsuccessfully sought to remove CEQ's responsibility to ensure that federal agencies comply with NEPA. Said Hill, "If we bury ourselves in paper over less important questions, we're not serving the spirit of the act well."

- Following up on the Carter CEQ's massive "Global 2000" study, which analyzed world resources, population and environmental trends toward the year 2000. That study concluded that if present trends continue, "the world in 2000 will be more crowded, more polluted, less stable ecologically, and more vulnerable to disruption than the world we live in now"—conclusions that raise serious long-range questions about Reagan's plans to roll back environmental statutes and conservation efforts, and to greatly accelerate energy and agricultural production. A followup study called "Global Future: Time to Act" laid out a program for combating those problems, which included increased aid to less developed nations, enhanced attention to international environmental problems, and stepped-up efforts to conserve energy both here and abroad.

Hill says his first priority for following up on Global 2000 is to improve the government's forecasting ability. "I also want to try to involve the private sector in looking at these forecasts and looking at what kind of contribution they could make," said Hill. "The business community had very little response to Global 2000."

Those priorities for the council leave a formidable list of issues raised under Speth that will be dropped. Among them:

- Toxic chemicals. CEQ previously had led efforts to coordinate the government's response to disease-causing chemicals, but Hill says the council will not do "that much [on toxics]." Asked if toxics were a low profile concern for the Administration, Hill responded: "I would tend to agree."

- Export of hazardous substances. Under the Carter Administration, CEQ worked with the White House Office of Consumer Affairs to fashion an executive order restricting the export of certain extremely hazardous products, such as cancer-causing pesticides, banned here. Reagan revoked that order before Hill even got out of San Francisco, and the council is only peripherally involved in Administration deliberations to weaken remaining notification provisions for hazardous exports.

- Atmospheric buildup of carbon dioxide. A major concern of the previous council was the steady increase in atmospheric levels of carbon dioxide—the so-called greenhouse effect that could radically shift world weather patterns by the middle of the next century and turn some major agricultural areas into deserts. Asked about the CO_2 problem, considered by some the most serious international environmental issue of the upcoming decades, Hill said: "I don't know who's taking care of it." But he is not likely to press the concern that increasing CO_2 levels will require a decrease in fossil fuel use. "My basic feeling is that the conservation ethic is wonderful, but it isn't going to make it in the long run. I think we're going to have to produce more energy," he told us.

At a meeting with Hill shortly after his appointment, Lou Regenstein, executive vice-president of the Fund for Animals, raised the CO_2 issue. Regenstein asked Hill what he thought Reagan's reaction would be if Hill told him that the Administration's energy policies—emphasizing the burning of oil and coal—would put so much carbon dioxide into the atmosphere that the resulting warming trend would melt the icecap and flood coastal cities such as San Francisco and Los Angeles.

Hill laughed.

Researchers from Columbia University reported last year that the summer Antarctic ice pack had decreased nearly one million square miles, or about 35 percent, since the early 1970s. From the Woods Hole Oceangraphic Institute comes word that sea levels have been rising ten times faster in the past decade than during the previous 40 years.

"Maybe," said Regenstein, "Reagan's ranch is on real high ground."

NUCLEAR REGULATORY COMMISSION

NUNZIO PALLADINO
CHAIRMAN

RESPONSIBILITY OF OFFICE

Palladino chairs the NRC's five member-board of commissioners. The agency is charged with licensing and regulating the "uses of nuclear energy to protect the public health and safety and environment." It assumed the regulatory functions of the Atomic Energy Commission when that agency was abolished in 1974.

NRC sets standards for building and operating nuclear reactors as well as for handling and transporting nuclear materials.

NRC's "headquarters" are housed in ten separate office buildings scattered about metropolitan Washington, D.C. Five regional offices complete the NRC, which all tolled, employs 3,325 and runs on a budget of $446 million. As this book went to press, Reagan nominated to the commission James Asselstine, a Republican aide at the Senate Committee on Environment and Public Works.

BACKGROUND

Palladino has been with the nuclear industry since its inception. Joining Westinghouse as a steam turbine design engineer in 1939, Palladino was one of a cadre of top engineers sent by the company to work in federal nuclear facilities developing the new technology in the 1940s. Later this pool of skilled employees helped catapult Westinghouse to the forefront of commercial nuclear development. And they helped make Westinghouse the favored firm of the Atomic Energy Commission.

After World War II, Westinghouse first sent Palladino to the government nuclear laboratory in Oak Ridge, Tennessee. After two years as a senior engineer there, Palladino was transferred to the Argonne National Laboratory.

Finally in 1950, Palladino returned to Westinghouse, where he managed the Pressurized Water Reactor Design Subdivision. There he directed the design of the reactor cores for the submarine prototype reactor, Mark I; the Nautilus, the first atomic submarine; and the Shippingsport nuclear power plant, the first commercial nuclear plant. In 1959, Palladino left Westinghouse to chair the Department of Nuclear Engineering at Pennsylvania State University, becoming dean of the College of Engineering in 1966. He remained dean until his appointment as chairman.

Over the years Palladino has been presented with many awards, including an honorary doctorate from Lehigh University. This created a problem for Sen. Alan Simpson (R-Wyo.) during Palladino's confirmation hearing. Simpson was unsure how to properly address the new chairman. When Palladino confirmed that he in fact had not earned a doctorate, Simpson thanked him and decided to call him "Dean Palladino" remarking, "soon after this, they will call you everything in the book."

Over the years Palladino sat on many state and federal committees. He was a member of the Pennsylvania governor's science advisory committee and served as chairman of both the Pennsylvania Advisory Committee on Atomic Energy Development and Radiation Control and the NRC Advisory Committee on Reactor Safeguards. From 1974 to 1980, he served on the board of the Atomic Industrial Forum.

After the Three Mile Island mishap, Palladino was called upon to participate in two task forces. He served on the governor's commission on Three Mile Island, a seven-month investigation charged with assessing the environmental, economic, legal, and social effects of the accident, but which resulted in nothing more than recommendations for further action and study. Palladino also participated on NRC's special task force to evaluate and monitor clean-up activities at the damaged reactor.

Palladino's appointment was somewhat of a disappointment to the nuclear industry. He was not on the list of people industry wanted for the job. One utility chief told the *Washington Post* that Palladino "is maybe too nice for that snakepit."

Born on November 10, 1916 in Allentown, Pennsylvania, Palladino received his undergraduate and graduate degrees in mechanical engineering from Lehigh University in 1938 and 1939 respectively. He is married with three daughters.

FINANCIAL BACKGROUND

Palladino's salary at Pennsylvania State University was $58,350 in 1980 and $20,388 for the beginning of 1981. He also took in small amounts in fees from his work at Scientific Systems, a nuclear products manufacturing firm, where he has been vice-president and a board member since 1968, and from the Electric Power Research Institute, where he worked in the Nuclear Safety Analysis Center. Over the years Palladino has also received commissions from the Nuclear Regulatory Commission, Technical Audit Associates, and other consulting groups.

Palladino holds stock in various banks, school districts, and investment firms. None of the entities in which he holds security interests are in the commercial nuclear field.

Palladino does, however, have a pension with Westinghouse, a major manufacturer of nuclear reactors, which matured when he turned 65 in November, 1981. The White House counsel found that "the interest was not so substantial as to affect the integrity of the service expected of you [Palladino] as Chairman," and therefore will allow Palladino to participate in all matters involving Westinghouse that come before the NRC.

WHAT OTHERS ARE SAYING ABOUT HIM

- "Palladino is fair and honest—one who listens to other points of view. He's the best of the ones [commissioners] I've dealt with," said Commissioner Victor Galinsky, NRC.

- "Considering the other choices the Administration could have made, Palladino's a good choice. I can think of a lot worse. He's no liberal by any means, however he doesn't seem to be doing outrageous things," said an aide at the House Interior and Insular Affairs Committee.

- "He seems to be doing things the industry would like him to. Palladino is Mr. Safety. A lot of people knew he would be tough. A lot think he's competent. He knows his business," said Don Winston of the Atomic Industrial Forum.

- "The chairman is serious about safety issues. He's also serious about the Reagan agenda and I'm not sure the two can be meshed," outgoing NRC Commissioner Peter Bradford told listeners at a Public Citizen forum in March, 1982.

THOMAS ROBERTS
COMMISSIONER

BACKGROUND

Prior to his brief stint from March, 1979 to July, 1980 as treasurer for the Bush presidential campaign, Roberts admits, he had "absolutely no experience with government—other than voting." The Tennessee businessman agrees, in fact, that his appointment was political in nature. "That's the way the system works. Democracy is the only system we've got," he told us.

In February, 1981 many speculated that the Bush ally would actually be nominated for the NRC chairmanship. But Robert's obvious lack of knowledge of nuclear matters quickly convinced the Administration that was a bad idea.

Before joining the NRC, Roberts had a long career as president of Southern Boiler and Tanks Works, Inc., a Memphis-based steel plate fabricator opened by his father. Among its other activities, the company manufactures containment shelters for nuclear power plants. Roberts feels this background, along with his lucrative activity as a private investor, has provided him with both "firsthand experience [in working] daily with relevant [NRC] codes, standards and regulations. . .as well as with sound management principles that have universal application."

Roberts told us he feels capable of making the complicated, technical decisions necessary as an NRC commissioner because "I possess the necessary intelligence to make reasonable judgments."

Roberts attended Georgia Institute of Technology on a Naval Reserve officers training course and was graduated in 1959 with a B.S. in industrial engineering. He subsequently served as an engineering officer aboard a Navy destroyer. Discharged three years later, he joined his father's company in Tennessee. Roberts became chief executive officer of Southern in 1969 and takes credit for greatly expanding it—increasing profits three fold by the time Southern was acquired by Chicago Milwaukee Corporation in 1978.

Born on April 14, 1937, in Memphis, Tennessee, Roberts is married and has three daughters.

FINANCIAL BACKGROUND

Roberts filed an extremely thick financial disclosure statement. A "self employed private investor", Roberts's and his family's various investments and business ventures make him worth over $2 million. He was an overseer for Lloyds of London and the director of Boyle Investment Co., a real estate company. His wife holds stock valued between $15,000 and over $250,000 in various corporations, including: Data Communications, General Electric, Gulf Oil, Halliburton, IBM and Merck. She also has bonds in Maine Yankee and Southwestern Electric Power.

Though he is no longer working with Southern, Roberts will have to recuse himself if the NRC ever deals with containment liners at the plants Southern contracted with while he was there. Roberts still holds a pension plan with the company.

MAJOR ISSUES

- Palladino came down surprisingly hard on the nuclear industry, criticizing it for its "serious quality assurance break-downs," saying that the discovery of so many problems with the industry recently "clouds the high degree of confidence he once had in atomic energy."

- Adhering to the Reagan Administration's commitment to revive the failing nuclear industry, Palladino in his early months of chairmanship, promised to try and license 33 new plants by 1982 "at an unprecedented speed of licensing." In light of recent problems at nuclear facilities around the country, though, Palladino doubts this will occur. Indeed, NRC staffers now acknowledge that at least 19 plants already under construction are likely to be cancelled.

- The NRC's pace in implementing post-Three Mile Island safety and emergency planning requirements has slowed to a virtual standstill under Palladino.

- The Administration is considering amending the law in order to avoid NRC safety licensing of the Clinch River Breeder Reactor, a project that's already been determined as financially unsound by the General Accounting Office.

- In an unexpected move, Palladino called for review and improvements in the "inadequate" International Atomic Energy Agency (IAEA) safeguards under the Nuclear Non-Proliferation Act. He told us the IAEA is still the "best vehicle" we have for controlling weapons proliferation.

Palladino's performance may be one of the White House's biggest surprises of 1981. Appointed by a President who has long believed that nuclear power is safe, serving in an Administration dedicated to expanding its use, Palladino emerged as a surprisingly stern critic of the industry, chiding it for shoddy work and inadequate quality control. As he told the Atomic Industrial Forum in December, 1981, "No amount of regulatory reform will save it [the nuclear industry] from the consequences of its own failures to achieve the quality of construction and plant operations it must have for its own well-being and for the safety of the public it serves." Whether those words came from Palladino's genuine concern or his "horse sense" for public relations, or both, they could not have sat well with a President who has long blamed the government for all of the nuclear industry's problems. The response of the assembled industry leaders might be best described as one of shock.

Around the same time, Palladino sent Congress the unprecedented warning that the international safeguards system established to prevent diversion of nuclear materials from civilian facilities to produce atomic weapons was inadequate. That provided powerful ammunition to opponents of the Administration's effort to increase nuclear exports as a way to revive the sagging domestic industry.

Perhaps the Administration misjudged its man. But events, of course, drive politics. Palladino's crisis of confidence in the industry was spurred by a series of major problems which turned up at nuclear facilities with depressing regularity during 1981. The Israelis pointedly delivered their own vote on the reliability of the safeguards system with their June, 1981 raid on Iraq.

These events, and Palladino's tortured efforts to publicly remain optimistic about the future deployment of nuclear power while acknowledging that the job had been done poorly over the past quarter century, suggested that even the Reagan Administration might not be able to turn the tide of history against the nuclear industry. That doesn't mean, however, that the White House will not continue to try to do so.

In its October, 1981 policy statement on nuclear power, the White House established a task force to study ways to accelerate licensing. That is undoubtedly one of the financially ailing industry's top priorities, but whether a speedup will actually help the industry is another question. An investigation by the House Energy and Environment Subcommittee found that licensing delays were due largely to construction foul-ups and utility financing problems. Nevertheless, Palladino and Congress have endorsed and adopted speed-up proposals which will curtail public participation in the licensing process, even though that is not the actual source of the delay.

Many analysts believe that accelerated licensing will actually hurt the industry, by decreasing public confidence in power plant safety and increasing the chance of a catastrophic accident.

"The events of the 1970s show us where this [emphasis on nuclear development] will lead if the current atmosphere prevails: Pressures to license quickly will build. Warning events like the Browns Ferry fire will happen and be underrated. Concerned professionals will leave the NRC staff. . . More serious events such as Three Mile Island or worse can happen," said Peter Bradford, an out-going NRC Commissioner, in a fall, 1981 speech. "It is not a scenario that is in the industry's interest in the 1980s any more than it was in the 1970s."

In early March, 1982, Bradford told a Public Citizen forum that recognition of these problems was sapping the "vitality" of the licensing speed-up drive. "The commission no longer meets, as it did last spring, ten times a month to seek ways to eliminate a nonexistent licensing backlog," Bradford said.

Adhering to the Administation line during his first months in office Palladino continually promised to try to license 33 new power plants by the end of 1982, at what he called "an unprecedented pace of licensing." In mid-December, 1981, though, he added to the White House's dismay by backing down from this figure.

A push to accelerate licensing could also reduce the level of safety at the plants already operating. "The overwhelming emphasis on speeding up the process of licensing new nuclear power plants," wrote the House Government Operations Committee in a study released in June, 1981, "will have the equally real impact of draining manpower and agency attention from an already inadequate inspection program."

Serious safety problems at reactors continue to turn up with daunting regularity. In at least eight, and possibly as many as 46, plants across the country the steel shells surrounding the reactor cores have been embrittled by radiation. So rapidly is this occurring that NRC officials believe some plants may not be able to operate by the end of this year without risking radiation leakage. "Embrittlement is not going to be a problem we can't cope with," Palladino told us. "We're going to have to resolve this one way or another."

Embrittlement, though, is only one problem that has recently turned up. In another move that rocked the nuclear industry, Palladino suspended the operating license of the controversial Diablo Canyon reactor in San Luis Obispo, California. The object of mass protests (and mass arrests) the plant, built on an earthquake fault line, was kept from opening with the discovery in September, 1981 that the piping used to strenghten the plant's two reactors against seismic stress had been switched due to a blueprint mix-up. Reinforcements that should have been in Unit 1 were in Unit 2 and vice-versa. This extraordinary error compelled Palladino to tell a congressional committee that "after reviewing both industry and NRC performance in quality assurance, I readily acknowledge that neither has been as effective as they should have been."

The chairman's opinion echoes a recent report by the House Committee on Government Operations, which concluded that "high safety standards have not yet been consistently attained by the nuclear industry, or by the NRC."

Palladino would like to take a new look at the entire safety issue, and clarify "both the guidelines for conducting the process and the criteria on which decisions regarding health and safety are made." Specifically, the NRC has issued a February, 1982 study entitled "Safety Goals for Nuclear Power Plants," quantifying the acceptable risks from nuclear power. According to Bradford, the study assumes that the acceptable level of risk for 150 plants over their lifetime would be accidents resulting in as many as 13,000 deaths.

Nuclear critics fear this means the NRC will try to institute vague qualifications for risk assessment, thereby rationalizing nuclear power vis-a-vis other social risks. "There's no clear statement of the use to which a quantitative safety goal would be put," warned Ellen Weiss, attorney for the Union of Concerned Scientists. Experts disagree not only on the probability of an accident but over the destruction that will result.

Though his criticisms have stiffened during his term in office, some of Palladino's doubts about nuclear energy were evident from the start. In an interview with the student newspaper at Pennsylvania State University, he said that neither the NRC nor the utilities are prepared to handle an accident. "I don't think we ever believe that we're going to have an accident. Well," he told the reporters, "we're kidding ourselves."

If an accident were to occur, the liability of the plant owners and operators is limited by the Price-Anderson Act of 1957. The limit was set by the government in order to encourage commercial development of nuclear power. Corporations, fearing liability, would not have ventured into the technology otherwise. Most authorities estimate that the damages from an accident would far exceed the $560 million limit imposed by that law. Further, the General Accounting Office recently disclosed that most nuclear facilities are under-insured because insurance firms are reluctant to extend them coverage.

That reluctance springs in part from industry's repeated claims that the damage that a nuclear accident might cause cannot accurately be estimated in dollars. "If the industry wished to do so, it could easily obtain enough information upon which to make such judgements," countered an attorney for Public Citizen. Several congressional leaders are considering revisions of the Price-Anderson Act that would require industry to purchase more private insurance coverage and would remove or at least greatly increase the liability limit under the act.

In one of his last public statements as an NRC commissioner, Bradford charged that Price-Anderson coverage desperately needs to be raised. "The Price-Anderson Act liability limitations are two decades out of date," he said, "and need to be increased by at least a factor of five, with the amount below the ceiling funded exclusively by industry."

Palladino agrees that Price-Anderson coverage should be increased. Furthermore, he told us "that at a time a nuclear power plant is operated for the first time, it should have enough insurance to cover the cost of such anaccident. It should be reviewed every two or three years so that inflationary factors can be taken into account."

There were not nearly enough funds to cover damages and clean-up at Three Mile Island (TMI): No funding came from Price-Anderson because the government refused to classify the disaster as an ENO—an extraordinary nuclear occurrence. In October, 1981 the Reagan Administration agreed to put up $123 million to help pay for the cleanup. Palladino feels aid is necessary because, "if General Public Utilities [GPU] goes under, the problem won't go away. If the owners were financially in shape to clean it up, we'd put it to them all the way," he contended. Others see the funding as a simple bailout.

Asked at his confirmation hearing for his opinion of what should be done with the waste and other radioactive materials on the site, Palladino replied, "I have no suggestions to dump it [the thousands of gallons of contaminated water remaining in the plant] in the Susquehanna or not."

At the same time, the NRC is considering whether to allow GPU to restart TMI-1, which was shut down for repair at the time of the accident. Opponents of the restart fear that NRC will be moved by GPU's precarious financial position to rush through a restart. The Institute for Nuclear Power Operations, an industry group, recently raised 31 specific operational criticisms it said needed to be corrected at the plant.

Palladino angered anti-nuclear activists on October 30, 1981 by retracting an earlier pledge that the commission would hold off on its restart decision-making at least until 1982. Palladino had thought NRC was legally required to investigate charges that Unit I firemen had cheated on their licensing exam before restart proceedings could be completed. When he learned the contrary, he rescinded his promise. Even so, most critics, citing upcoming litigation, predict restart won't be considered until 1984.

Political and financial pressures may also impel NRC decisions on the long-delayed Clinch River Breeder Reactor. Under the Energy Reorganization Act of 1974, the Clinch River plant must be licensed by the NRC before it can operate. "Every technology that's built is outdated because there's always a better one on paper. . .the first one of anything you build already has behind it better ideas," Palladino told us. "We have far more to gain by building Clinch River now that we're this far along. . .I think it is a worthwhile venture and we ought to proceed with it."

In the past, NRC officials have expressed doubts about the suitability of the Clinch River site as well as the plant design. In 1977, one NRC official told the General Accounting Office that "if the [project] is delayed for two years or more it would be very difficult, if not impossible, for the NRC staff, in its analysis, to conclude that it is cost-beneficial to locate the demonstration reactor at the Clinch River site."

Four years later, with no completion date in sight, that prospect obviously troubles the White House. According to the House Oversight and Investigations Subcommittee, which last summer scrutinized Clinch River (See profiles of Kenneth Davis and Shelby Brewer), the Administration is considering amending the law to avoid NRC safety licensing of the plant, and will attempt to gain for Clinch River an exemption from the environmental impact statement process. Ironically, as a subcommittee report notes, "one of the major objectives of the CRBR project was to demonstrate the licenseability of a breeder reactor."

And as the agency's budget constricts, NRC personnel used to monitor Clinch River "will necessarily be taken out of positions that are responsible for safety in other areas," said Bradford. Roberts told us he disagrees, but could not say where the additional personnel would be found. In March, 1982, the NRC voted 3-2 against an Energy Department proposal to expedite construction of Clinch River by allowing work to begin before permit hearings were held. Palladino and Roberts voted for the proposal.

"The Administration's insistence on subsidizing this technology from Clinch River while starving conservation and solar programs that have proved their worth," said Bradford, "is beyond sober analysis. Indeed, any crew that would forge ahead with a billion taxpayer dollars for Clinch River while flirting with the notion of proclaiming ketchup to be a nourishing vegetable is not a force to be underestimated."

Concomitant with its renewed support of the breeder, the Administration has withdrawn the ban on domestic commercial reprocessing. It has even suggested that the plutonium extracted in those operations might be used for atomic weapons. (See Davis and Brewer profiles.) Of that prospect, Palladino told us, "I am concerned that if we start to violate what we've been preaching in terms of nonproliferation, we're going to set a bad example. And I'm concerned. . .that there may be nations that are trying to get hold of nuclear weapons not for the well being of mankind.'' (Roberts was not prepared to comment.)

Palladino thinks "the best vehicle" for controlling non-proliferation "at least at this moment is the IAEA (International Atomic Energy Agency). . .but that has its problems. We are going to accentuate those problems if we start to put our commercial wastes into nuclear weapons," he warned, "and that concerns me quite a bit.''

As a nation "we should not deny ourselves whatever opportunites we have" to protect ourselves, Palladino explained. But, he said, "there are other ways of meeting those needs and if they are viable I would recommend that they be followed rather than trying to use our fuel that we get from commercial reactors and put it into weapons.''

Specifically, Palladino told the House Interior Committee in a significant November 27, 1981 letter, "The NRC is concerned that the IAEA safeguards system would not detect a diversion [of civilian fuel to military uses] in at least some type of facilities. In addition, we are not confident that the member states would be notifed of a diversion in a timely fashion.'' However in March, 1982 testimony Palladino backed off a bit from this earlier statement, saying he had not meant "to suggest that we believe a clear diversion would be covered up by IAEA officials.'' Long criticized by anti-nuclear activitists as inadequate, the IAEA is the linchpin of the international efforts to control nuclear proliferation while expanding civilian nuclear power trade.

How closely Palladino will accede to the nuclear industry's wishes is unclear. "The role of the NRC is research and safety and should enable us to evaluate plants, not promote nuclear power,'' he told us. On the other hand, he told the avidly pro-nuclear Atomic Industrial Forum, "It's time for the NRC to move closer to industry.''

The make-up of the commission shifted further in Reagan's direction with Bradford's resignation in March, 1982. That leaves Victor Galinsky, a Democrat, and John Aherne, an independent described by one industry spokesperson as "unpredictable,'' as the holdovers, with Palladino, Roberts and James Asselstine. With three Reagan appointees, nuclear critics fear the NRC will align itself more closely with industry and push to ease many existing safety standards and regulations.

Despite his criticisms of the nuclear industry, Palladino remains a staunch supporter of nuclear energy. "I know that these plants can be built well,'' he said. "I know they can be operated safely. But if operating plants are not up to standards, we'll shut them down.'' Some anti-nuclear activists believe Palladino's hard line does not necessarily reflect a legitimate concern about safety, but rather a shrewd political understanding of the context needed to nurture public approval of the expansion in nuclear power sought by the Administration. But if his first year in office has proven anything, it is that Palladino is a difficult man to forecast. He has stunned the nuclear industry, but he recently refused to appear on the McNeil Lehrer Show with a Critical Mass Energy Project anti-nuclear advocate. The NRC will be one of the more interesting agencies to watch under Reagan.

ENVIRONMENTAL PROTECTION AGENCY

ANNE GORSUCH
ADMINISTRATOR

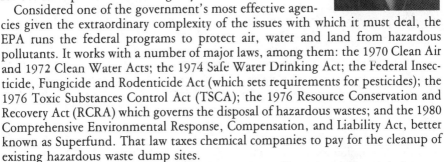

RESPONSIBILITY OF OFFICE

Founded in 1970 under Richard Nixon, the EPA has an uncompromising mission: "To protect and enhance our environment today and for future generations to the fullest extent possible. . ." As Administrator, Gorsuch is responsible for overall supervision of the agency.

Considered one of the government's most effective agencies given the extraordinary complexity of the issues with which it must deal, the EPA runs the federal programs to protect air, water and land from hazardous pollutants. It works with a number of major laws, among them: the 1970 Clean Air and 1972 Clean Water Acts; the 1974 Safe Water Drinking Act; the Federal Insecticide, Fungicide and Rodenticide Act (which sets requirements for pesticides); the 1976 Toxic Substances Control Act (TSCA); the 1976 Resource Conservation and Recovery Act (RCRA) which governs the disposal of hazardous wastes; and the 1980 Comprehensive Environmental Response, Compensation, and Liability Act, better known as Superfund. That law taxes chemical companies to pay for the cleanup of existing hazardous waste dump sites.

As TSCA, RCRA and the Superfund move into effect, they will greatly increase the agency's workload, which has steadily grown since 1970. In 1981, EPA had 9,872 employees and a budget of $1.353 billion. Excluding Superfund, spending on pollution control and research will be reduced at least 10 percent in 1982 and even more sharply in 1983. Staff under the 1983 budget is proposed to drop to 8,129 with an operating budget of about $975 million, (excluding waste water grants and the Superfund trust fund), down almost $400 million since 1981.

BACKGROUND

Quieter than her Colorado colleague James Watt, Anne Gorsuch over the years has proven to be every bit as tough—and almost as abrasive. Her appointment to one of Washington's top jobs—what she has called the "hottest spot" in domestic politics—culminated a rapid ascension through the state Republican hierarchy. First elected to the Colorado House of Representatives in 1976, Gorsuch quickly became a key legislator and a close ally of House Speaker Robert Burford, who now runs the Bureau of Land Management in the Interior Department.

Linking each of these three powerful officials is Joseph Coors, president of the Adolph Coors Co. A devoted financier of conservative causes, including Watt's Mountain States Legal Foundation, and a member of Reagan's kitchen cabinet, Coors was crucial to Gorsuch's appointment. He presented her as a compromise choice when the Administration was deadlocked between two other choices; one of those, Dr. John Hernandez of New Mexico, became the EPA's deputy administrator. "It was a combination of lobbying effort, support of Coors and senators—and that she's articulate and capable," said Freda Poundstone, a Colorado Reagan activist who brought Gorsuch to Washington to help with the transition. Coors' support was not new: Coors Co. was among the two largest contributors to Gorsuch's 1976 race and her successful 1978 bid for reelection.

Though Gorsuch drew respect for her shrewdness and power—which increased markedly after she helped engineer Burford's 1978 election as speaker—she also provoked sharp antagonisms in the statehouse, much as she has done in Washington. "I have a great deal of admiration and respect for her skills as a lawyer," Republican state Rep. Martha Ezzard told us, "but she was not a unifier, she was a divisive force in the Colorado Legislature. My reservation with Gorsuch is her inability to compromise or negotiate. I found her difficult to work with." In an annual skit put on at the end of the legislative session, the Democrats tagged her with the nickname of the "Dragon Lady," a characterization that stuck.

When we asked her why she didn't seek to change her hard image through a speech expressing concern for environmental victims she said she found little value in "a soapbox. . .on victims. No, I really think our environmental concerns are better addressed by getting a job done as opposed to going out and making speeches about horror stories. . . To the extent that it's relevant to our considerations in any one of our initiatives, I think you can expect to see the 'human' element included." That Gorsuch would consider the "human" element of environmental protection relevant to only *some* of her initiatives, would not surprise many people that know her.

Gorsuch left her mark in Colorado in one particularly divisive legislative battle involving the Colorado Commission on Women, a battle so ugly that some Colorado observers believe it was a key factor in her decision not to seek reelection in 1980. As chair of the House State Affairs Committee, Gorsuch led a successful fight to eliminate the commission, which she claimed pushed too hard for the interests of a small group of feminists. The last meeting between Gorsuch, Burford, and women supporting the commission, when the legislators said they were going to eliminate the commision, was extraordinarily bitter, according to one participant. "Some of the hottest women in town were working in it and she reduced half of the group to tears," said the participant. Long after the struggle was over, Josie Heath, who had directed the commission, told a reporter: "She had the opportunity to do so much on several issues—not just the feminist issue. For example, she could have made the difference on hazardous waste but she chose not to. She sat there and told us any woman worth her salt doesn't need the commission; she could make it on her own just like she [Gorsuch] did. But she came from a well-to-do family. All the doors were opened for her. She didn't make it on her own."

As Heath noted, Gorsuch was also deeply involved in legislative battles over hazardous wastes. According to several Colorado sources, she effectively used her committee to delay and obstruct state hazardous waste regulation. Citing the now familiar Reagan Administration arguments about federal encroachment on state rights, Gorsuch in 1980 led the opposition to bills that would have increased the state Public Utilities Commission's authority to regulate toxics and begun a state hazardous waste regulatory program under federal supervision.

Gorsuch so vehemently opposed state involvement under RCRA that after one hearing she upbraided a lobbyist for the Colorado Association of Commerce and Industry—hardly what James Watt would call "environmental extremists"— who had supported such a program.

On other environmental issues Gorsuch occasionally sent off mixed signals, but generally followed an anti-regulatory line. She was the prime sponsor of a vehicle inspection and maintenance bill that defused a clash between the state and the EPA (See Burford profile), but she also helped plan the lawsuit filed by Mountain States Legal Foundation and 27 state legislators against the federal agency during the dispute. And in August, 1981 she followed up on the dispute by asking the National Governors' Association to push for repeal of the mandatory inspection program.

During her tenure, she also voted for bills weakening state land use controls and state strip mining regulation, as well as a measure that would have subjected all state regulations to legislative veto. "Gorsuch did not exhibit in the Colorado Legislature an interest in a balance between economic development and environmental preservation," concluded Ezzard.

Overall, for her four years, Gorsuch received ratings from the Colorado Open Space Council (which rates legislators on environmental issues) of 33, 8, 73, and 72 percent. Though these ratings seemingly indicate improvement, some Colorado observers say the way the council computed the ratings changed more than Gorsuch did. And Heidi Schmidt, council executive director, told us: "One of the major points regarding Gorsuch is not reflected in the ratings she received. That is, she was responsible for introducing severe compromises and/or killing several pieces of environmental legislation in her committee. This was particularly true for legislation governing the disposal of hazardous wastes."

As an overall philosophy, Gorsuch stressed the devolution of environmental decision-making to local governments, a process that many believe will lead to an inevitable process of localities bidding away pollution control to attract or retain industry. Gorsuch still believes in that transfer of power, as evidenced by her comments on the proper federal role in combating noise pollution. An "incinerator truck is only a problem if somebody is there to hear it," she told us. "So the engineering standards for the incinerator truck in eastern Colorado are not nearly as relevant as it might be for New York City. And Congress, and I'm paraphrasing their point [decided]. . .If I live in Colorado I should not have to pay for the same control of equipment as New York City would. I don't quarrel with that."

Gorsuch has always been driven and hard-working, an achiever anxious to advance. (She openly campaigned for the EPA job.) She was graduated from the University of Colorado law school in 1964 and became the youngest woman ever admitted to the Colorado bar. A few months later, she took a Fulbright Scholarship and packed off to Jaipur, India for a year.

When she returned, she went to work for the First National Bank of Denver, and then the district attorney's office in Jefferson County, Colorado. According to some reports, Gorsuch and a friend, Ann Allott, were fired from the job in 1971 because they inflated the amount of child support payment collections their office had made. The official dismissal letters did not list a cause for the firing, and Allott denied the charges. In either case, both then accepted jobs with Denver's district attorney.

In 1975, Gorsuch joined Mountain Bell's corporate law department, specializing in land acquisitions, leasing, and similar work.

Asked why she left Colorado for the EPA job, Gorsuch said: "Because I think this President has an enormous opportunity to change the way this government does business. And in no place is that opportunity more important or more relevant than in the environmental area.'' She said she plans to finish out a four-year term.

Born in Casper, Wyoming on April 21, 1942, Gorsuch was raised in Denver, where her father was a well-known physician. She received her undergraduate degree from the University of Colorado in 1961 and her law degree there three years later. Gorsuch has three children and is being divorced from her husband, David, a Denver attorney. She frequently has been romantically linked with Burford, though she regularly dismisses the reports as ''gossip.''

MAJOR ISSUES

- Gorsuch has proposed staggering budget cuts for 1983 that may cripple the agency's ability to enforce the nation's environmental laws.

- Gorsuch has moved to greatly reduce congressional and public access to the agency, and has entered into what approaches open warfare with career staff.

- Gorsuch and the Administration have backed revisions in the Clean Air Act that would drastically weaken the law.

- They have also proposed substantial revisions in the regulations governing hazardous wastes that will reduce protection on existing sites.

- Funding for the Superfund, designed to clean up abandoned sites, has been slashed and implementation has moved slowly.

- Plans to regulate two carcinogenic chemicals, DEHP and formaldehyde, have also been stalled after agency officials held a series of private meetings with industry lobbyists that may have violated federal law, according to congressional analysts.

- Long-standing proceedings to cancel the registration of 2,4,5-T—a carcinogenic component of Agent Orange—have been recessed and the agency is seeking an out-of-court settlement with its manufacturers.

- Enforcement actions have been reduced since Gorsuch took office, running at a rate of abut one-eighth of the total pursued by previous administrations.

Ann Gorsuch may have already failed in her major goal as EPA administrator: to keep things quiet while she shut off the agency.

Gorsuch is already well on the way toward pulling back the EPA from key programs overseeing hazardous wastes, toxic substances, clean air and clean water. But despite a spirited effort, she has failed to keep the agency out of the public eye.

That may well have been an impossible goal, given the numerous environmental groups that carefully track the agency, and the many career staff members dedicated to the environmental programs she is attempting to weaken. But that failure, as Gorsuch is well aware, endangers her entire regulatory rollback. As public pressure increases, it could also threaten her job.

Gorsuch, a terse, tough attorney whose general litany divulges little to interviewers, has worked to make the agency reflect that personality. In style and substance, Gorsuch rarely gives an inch; she resolutely puffed Marlboros through a conversation about controlling carcinogens. To charges that her budget cuts are crippling the agency, Gorsuch responds that, ''I intend to do a better job with fewer resources.'' To charges that she is weakening enforcement, she responds that negotiation is a more efficient way to clean up pollutants. To charges that she is debilitating strong environmental regulations, she responds, "It isn't a fair inference to say strength equals a better environment. . .or a stronger environmental program." To charges that she is ignoring serious environmental problems such as acid rain, she responds, "I think there's an awful lot that needs to be known about the problem before responsible regulatory action can be taken." To charges that she is delaying pending rules, she responds, "I'd love to have you come and look at that backlog. . . . It's going to be easy to improve on the track record that I received." To charges that she is inaccessible, she responded in December, 1981 that, "no environmental group has requested a meeting with me that has ever been turned down." As the months roll by, Gorsuch's record will form its own response to her assertions.

Gorsuch designed an elaborate peer review process for EPA scientists that would require not only technical papers, but even many public statements to be approved by 11 or more officials. Her top aides minimized contact with congressional oversight committees and carefully controlled them from Gorsuch's inner circle. She slashed, or even eliminated, budgets for public outreach programs and publications. Employees were ordered to reduce public appearances. She left key staff positions unfilled for months. Specific phrases such as "cancer-causing" were reportedly barred from press releases.

Publicly, the Administration even took a back seat on the reauthorization of the Clean Air Act, delaying the release of its position until August and then only divulging 11 general points, rather than a specific bill.

Gorsuch was apparently gambling that without an inviting public target— as, for example, Watt had provided—neither the press, Congress, nor the public would hunt through the dizzying technical, legal and scientific interstices of the EPA regulatory programs for significant changes in policy.

The strategy started to unravel in the summer of 1981. Congressional staffers began to complain that agency officials were uncooperative or uninformed. "Quite frankly," one aide at the House Government Operations Subcommittee on the Environment and Energy told us, "I'm tired of hearing 'nobody knows, we'll reach you later.'" By October, 1981 even Sen. Robert Stafford of Vermont, the Republican chairman of the Senate Environment and Public Works Committee, publicly complained to Gorsuch that "one of the [committee's] great problems. . .is a lack of information as to happenings at the Environmental Protection Agency."

And then came the leaks. In June, 1981 Democratic Representative Henry Waxman of California, who chairs the House Health and the Environment Subcommittee handling the Clean Air Act, released an EPA draft bill for revising the law which he called "a blueprint for destruction of our clean air laws." Stafford felt the same way about the proposals. In late August, about two weeks after Gorsuch articulated the Administration's 11 points, two congressmen released another leaked draft, which also called for a far more drastic weakening of the law than the Administration had publicly said it would seek.

Most damaging to Gorsuch's efforts to keep things quiet was the September leak of a proposed 1983 budget. Going further than even the Office of Management and Budget (OMB) had asked, Gorsuch proposed a massive 20 percent budget cut that would eliminate up to 3,200 employees. Coupled with the original 12 percent cut in Carter's 1982 budget, and the additional 12 percent later requested by Reagan, Gorsuch's 1983 cut would reduce EPA purchasing power by a crippling 60 percent when inflation is taken into account, calculated William Drayton, the agency's former assistant administrator for planning and management. Research activities and programs to control toxic substances were to be particularly hard hit. Making these cuts doubly damaging, Drayton and others reasoned, was that they came at a time when EPA's statutory responsibilities, particularly to control toxic chemicals, were expanding greatly.

"The Reagan-Gorsuch program, if allowed to go ahead, would tear EPA up by the roots," said Drayton. "It would take a new Administration that gave top priority to restoring this institution of public protection seven or eight years to get back to the 1980 level of competence."

Gorsuch disagreed, arguing that she will improve management and increase efficiency through use of such practices as generic consideration of chemicals under TSCA. "I don't equate more dollars with a stronger budget," Gorsuch told us. "I again don't equate more rigorous standards with. . .better environmental quality."

When the OMB proposed even further slashes in the 1983 budget—suggesting an additional 20 percent reduction—Gorsuch was then cast in the unlikely—and, many environmentalists maintain, orchestrated—position of defender of the environment, fighting the additional cuts all the way to the President. Reagan eventually restored about 80 percent of the additional slashes sought by OMB—which still left the agency with greater reductions above the 18 percent cut that Gorsuch volunteered.

Gorsuch told us that she deals as an equal with Budget Director David Stockman. "He doesn't *let* me have personal access," she said. "I am the head of the Environmental Protection Agency. And he is the director of the OMB. And, yes, we transact business. . . . I will say that in my entire life experience synergistic decision-making is always more healthy and more productive than individual decision-making. So strong disagreements generally serve the ultimate outcome of good decisions."

While attracting favorable publicity for her resistance to Stockman, Gorsuch was drawing up a plan to wipe out the agency's career bureaucracy. Internal EPA documents revealed that Gorsuch planned to reduce the agency's headquarters staff by about fifty percent through attrition and firings by June, 1982. "Imagine the impact on the agency's capacity to get its complex, technical work done at all, let alone competently," said Drayton. "Think of the effect on morale." Between 800 and 1,500 employees would be fired under the plan, though the agency was already operating *under* its budgetary personnel ceiling, according to Drayton. Gorsuch has, at least temporarily, backed off from the plan.

Gorsuch's original proposed 1983 budget hit the newspapers only a few days after two top EPA Reagan appointees cleaned out their desks and hit the streets. On September 23, 1981, Nolan Clark, a Washington attorney whom Gorsuch had named to the agency's number three position, associate administrator for policy, resigned, citing "irreconcilable differences between myself and the administrator." EPA sources said Clark left the agency at Gorsuch's behest, after refusing her request to fire a number of career staff members.

That same week, Frank Shepherd, a Miami attorney who had represented General Motors, among other clients, resigned from his position as associate administrator for legal counsel and enforcement.

These departures sharpened public focus on the undeclared war that pitted Gorsuch and her immediate staff against the EPA's career employees. "The morale is pretty low and people are leaving in droves," Steven Jellinek, the former assistant administrator for toxic substances, told us. "The new team has decided it can't trust any of the career civil servants—the professionals and technicians who give facts and information but don't make political decisions."

All these reports led the Senate environment committee to summon Gorsuch to Capitol Hill in October, 1981 for a spirited day of oversight hearings. These hearings generated another round of press reports, particularly since Republicans such as Stafford criticized Gorsuch almost as briskly as did Democrats. "I personally do not believe that the Environmental Protection Agency can continue to function if its staff and budget are cut so drastically," Stafford complained. "Decreases of such magnitude could amount to de facto repeal of some environmental laws. We would do better to repeal these laws outright than to leave them on the books as empty shells."

And a week later, Gorsuch was back on Capitol Hill with her deputy, Hernandez, to answer charges of possible illegality stemming from a series of unannounced meetings between Hernandez and industry groups on the potential regulation of two chemicals suspected of causing cancer and general changes in the Toxic Substances Control Act.

By this time, even some industry groups were becoming uneasy. The automakers complained that the Administration was moving too slowly and devoting too little effort to the Clean Air Act. And though pleased with the new direction Gorsuch was taking, some chemical executives worried about increasing drift. *Chemical Week* headlined its October 21 issue with a photo of a worried Gorsuch and a trenchant headline: "EPA in disarray."

For Gorsuch, the growing press and congressional criticism threatened an overall agency redirection that began with the appointments process. Gorsuch surrounded herself with alumni from major industries that numbered among the agency's most dedicated opponents. Among the key appointments were:

- John E. Daniel as chief of staff. Daniel, the American Paper Institute's chief lobbyist from 1976 to 1980, had spent the last year as the Washington counsel for Johns-Manville, the nation's largest asbestos manufacturer, which paid him $60,000.

- Thornton "Whit" Field, as special assistant for hazardous wastes. A 32-year-old lawyer who represented the Adolph Coors Co. on regulatory issues, Field's knowledge of both hazardous wastes and Washington politics are considered limited; career EPA hazardous waste officials, call him "Twit" Field. Also from Coors came attorney James Sanderson, the first special assistant chosen by Gorsuch, and a key figure in the agency's day to day administration.

- Kitty Adams and Joseph Cannon, both 31-year-old attorneys as special assistants for regulatory reform. Adams worked for the Business Roundtable, an organization of chief executive officers that often fought environmental initiatives, from 1977-1978; since then she has been a consultant whose clients included Dow Chemical ($26,998 in 1980 fees); Allied Chemical ($3,138 in 1980 fees); and Olin ($9,185). She continues to hold stock in DuPont, Minnesota Mining and Manufacturing, and Eastman Kodak. (Adams left the EPA in February, 1982.) Cannon worked in the Washington office of the Houston law firm Andrews, Kurth, Campbell, & Jones. He was also an aide in the 1980 Reagan campaign.

- Robert Perry, an Exxon attorney, as general counsel.

- Kathleen Bennett, a long-time lobbyist for the timber industry, as assistant administrator for air, noise, and radiation. Since 1977, she has lobbied in Washington for Crown Zellerbach; before that she was director of legislative affairs for the Paper Institute, the same job Daniels had. Despite her long background, her knowledge of clean air issues is not held in high regard on Capitol Hill. "She's a lightweight," concluded one staffer at the House Environment and Health Subcommittee.

- Rita Lavelle as assistant administrator for solid waste and emergency response. Lavelle, who will oversee both the Superfund and the RCRA regulations governing hazardous waste disposal, comes from a California firm with a record of improperly disposing of hazardous wastes. Lavelle had been director of communications—head flack—for Aerojet Liquid Rocket Co., a subsidiary of Aerojet-General Corp. of California. According to EPA, Aerojet-General has the third worst pollution record in the state; the state has charged it with improperly dumping up to 20,000 gallons a day of carcinogens and other toxic wastes.

- John Todhunter, as assistant administrator for toxic substances. A professor at Catholic University, Todhunter served on the scientific advisory board of the American Council on Science and Health, a largely industry-financed organization (contributors include Dow, Ciba-Geigy, General Motors, Exxon, Georgia Pacific, Union Carbide, Diamond Shamrock, Shell and Monsanto)—that has downplayed the role of chemicals and pollution in the causation of cancer and other diseases. A 1980 study by the council concluded that 2,4,5-T—a component of Agent Orange that the EPA has been trying to ban—is safe for use. Todhunter has not recused himself from decisions on 2,4,5-T.

With these officials, Gorsuch has fashioned a policy of reticence and even secrecy, resisting the inquiries of congressional committees, avoiding the spotlight, and, on more than one occasion, meeting quietly with industry groups behind closed doors to fashion regulatory policy, possibly in violation of federal statute.

This posture is best exemplified by the Administration's actions on the reauthorization of the Clean Air Act, undoubtedly the major environmental issue of 1981. To the consternation of Congress, and even many industry lobbyists, the Administration publicly stayed out of the Clean Air battle until August. And then, the Administration only issued general proposals— rather than a detailed bill.

Behind the scenes, though, the EPA was considering draconian revisions. One draft EPA bill, leaked in August, 1981, required cost-benefit analysis of all clean air regulations, weakened the program for controlling toxic air pollutants, doubled the nitrogen oxide standard, eliminated the "offset" requirement for new pollution sources built in areas not in compliance with the law, and removed requirements that states set specific emission levels and compliance schedules for polluters.

As part of the Administration's clean air strategy, congressional staffers were being ignored too. Both Senate and House aides complained that the Administration was "doing as little as possible to help us" evaluate the law, and that requests for information went unanswered for months. "Their strategy is to cut down the amount of information and make it more of a political debate," said an aide at the House Environment and Health Subcommittee. (Gorsuch herself misstated the present NOx standard at her August press briefing.)

Indeed, Stafford's hopes of quickly fine-tuning the law have evaporated, and the reauthorization has bogged down in a political morass. On the other side, Gorsuch and the Administration have drawn criticism from some conservative economists for not using the reauthorization process to increase reliance on "market incentives," such as pollution taxes as a substitute for regulation. "I'd like to see what we've got on the books work, and allow for the testing of some of these new ideas on a laboratory basis rather than going out and advocating the imposition of an entirely new scheme," she told us in December, 1981. But in April, 1982—to the approval of OMB's regulatory reviewers—Gorsuch announced a policy to expand the use of economic incentives, such as the "bubble" concept, in place of regulation.

Early in 1982, the Administration finally endorsed changes in the law proposed by Reps. John Dingell (D-Mich.) and James Broyhill (R-N.C.). Particularly helpful to Dingell's auto industry constituents, the bill would double the maximum amount of permissible carbon monoxide and nitrogen oxide pollutants in exhaust, stretch out compliance dates, and give the EPA authority to further loosen emission standards in the future. (Clean air, apparently, wasn't much of a personal priority for Gorsuch either; for her personal car she ordered a four-door diesel Oldsmobile that is one of the heaviest polluters on the road.)

The Administration is developing a similar strategy on the Clean Water Act, the next major piece of environmental legislation due to be reauthorized. While professing their belief that the act is "fundamentally sound," the EPA is drawing up amendments that would sharply curtail the law by extending compliance dates and reducing federal regulation of toxic wastes.

For years, EPA programs to control the disposal of hazardous waste have been mired as well. Progress began to be made toward the end of the Carter Administration when major regulations implementing RCRA were promulgated. Gorsuch, though, has suspended and deferred technical regulations governing landfills, incinerators, and waste storage impoundments. The result will be to increase the number of sites operating under "interim" status—for which the EPA has less authority to tightly regulate. An extremely critical General Accounting Office examination found the interim status program to be understaffed and unable to ensure that facilities are complying with the regulations.

"[The interim regulations] offer very little [protection]," said one EPA hazardous waste official. "But when it was put out we thought the very little wouldn't last for very long."

Other changes have been made in hazardous waste programs as well. Funding for Superfund—passed in 1980 to clean up existing hazardous waste sites—has been slashed; though Gorsuch repeatedly affirms her commitment to the program, implementation has moved slowly and drawn a lawsuit from the Environmental Defense Fund. Gorsuch has also postponed regulations requiring financial solvency of hazardous waste disposers. And the agency has announced it will ask those responsible for "priority" hazardous waste sites to "voluntarily" clean them up before using the Superfund.

Related programs to protect groundwater—which provides drinking water for half the country—have also been slowed. A groundwater protection strategy begun by the Carter Administration has been shelved, and efforts to define maximum permissible levels for groundwater contaminants have been stuffed back into the bureaucracy. "Your lack of action suggests that the Reagan Administration in general and EPA in particular have no real interest in assisting the further protection of. . .groundwater resources," Rep. Toby Moffett (D-Conn.), who chairs the House Environment and Energy Subcommittee, wrote Gorsuch in September. In February, 1982 Gorsuch sought to lift the agency's ban on landfilling hazardous liquids, but reversed herself after intense public opposition.

These and other policy changes led senior EPA hazardous waste official Hugh Kaufman to tell reporters that the agency was being run by a "radical group" dedicated to "stopping the EPA from doing its job as mandated by Congress."

In the agency toxics program, the story is much the same.

Todhunter has quietly met with officials of the Chemical Manufacturers Association to develop broad exemptions to the premanufacture notification provisions of TSCA, the heart of that law. Similarly, Hernandez held a series of six meetings over the summer with the Chemical Manufacturers Association and other chemical industry officials to discuss possible EPA regulation of formaldehyde and DEHP, two widely used chemicals believed to be carcinogenic. Legal analysis by the House Energy and Environment Subcommittee concluded the meetings "may very well" be a violation of the Federal Advisory Committee Act. No public representatives attended any of the meetings. (Gorsuch, incidentally, closed out her first day in office by attending a reception hosted by the Formaldehyde Institute.)

Todhunter is reassessing the models the agency uses to determine a chemical's potential risks to health. "They take the point of view that a chemical has to be convicted beyond all reasonable doubt," said former Administrator Doug Costle in an interview. "They have flopped all the way from the public health point of view to the conservative industry side of you have to have bodies stacked like firewood before you do anything." Gorsuch told us she rejects the idea postulated by many scientists—including President Carter's interagency Toxic Substances Strategy Committee—that there is no known safe threshold level of exposure to cancer-causing substances. "I really wouldn't subscribe [to that] as a general regulatory philosophy," she said. "Anything in excess is harmful. Too much sunlight is harmful."

In yet another major policy change, the agency is moving to settle out-of-court its protracted cancellation proceeding against 2,4,5-T, a carcinogenic, mutagenic herbicide that contains dioxin, generally considered the deadliest substance ever synthesized. And it is backing off efforts to put a cap on the production of chlorofluorocarbons, implicated in the depletion of atmospheric ozone. Plans for controlling, or even banning, asbestos use are also being rethought, and are unlikely to be acted upon; plans to clean up schools where it was used have been stalled.

And on it goes. Enforcement actions referred to the Justice Department are way down over previous years. During previous administrations they averaged 150-200 a year, but in 1981, only 69 cases were sent to Justice, a 69 percent drop from the 252 in 1980. The proposed 1983 budget projects cuts of almost 44 percent from the enforcement budget. Gorsuch also abolished the Office of Enforcement and dispersed its functions to the various program departments, a move that environmental groups predicted quite accurately would diminish enforcement actions. Research and development would be cut 57 percent from the 1981 level.

The list goes on, throughout the agency.

"The danger is not simply that environmental programs will be slowed," said Jonathan Lash, an attorney with the Natural Resources Defense Council, "but that the entire legal and institutional framework for environmental protection will be destroyed, and human beings will suffer death and disease as a result."

FINANCIAL BACKGROUND

As an attorney for Mountain States Bell, Gorsuch earned $41,000 in 1980. For her seat in the Colorado General Assembly, she took home another $14,350. (Gorsuch annually took a leave of absence during the legislative sessions.) Her investments include holdings in farm, coal mining and oil and gas drilling concerns, some of which are in her husband's name. She has recused herself from particular matters involving those firms, or cases brought before the EPA by her husband's law firm. Clients of his firm, though not necessarily on EPA matters, include Amoco Production Co., Firestone, Phillips Petroleum, Rocky Mountain Energy Co., Union Pacific Railroad and Western Crude Oil, Inc.

Gorsuch describes herself as "on leave" from Mountain States Bell.

WHAT OTHERS ARE SAYING ABOUT HER

- With the exceptions of James Watt and William Casey, more people have sought Gorsuch's resignation than that of any other Reagan official. Senator Daniel Patrick Moynihan suggested the idea to her face during the October Senate hearings on her budget proposals; "Thank you for your advice," she responded. Another critic, Rep. James Florio (D-N.J.), also called on her to resign in a sharply-worded statement issued during the final days of his New Jersey gubernatorial campaign. "[S]he already has effectively resigned from the performance of the duties of her office," said Florio. "Overall, her performance in office shows a lack of respect for the environment and the health of the American people."

- Not surprisingly, the Synthetic Organic Chemical Manufacturers Association has a more charitable view. "The big difference," said Ronald Lang, the group's executive director, "is that we can go into the agency with all the facts and people will listen. We know we are being taken seriously and we know we will have an impact."

- A top aide at the House Environment and Health Subcommittee who has met with Gorsuch seconds that assessment—but is less sanguine about its implications for public health. "She is armed with industry arguments; she uses them as blocks in order to stop thought. She's almost dogmatic about it," said the aide. "The most serious concern is her presumption that industry is going to do things the right way. It will protect health and safety and government will act as an auditor. She's got a marketplace mentality; the strong will survive, the rich will survive and the poor will suffer like they should."

AN HONEST BUDGET

Just before Reagan released his 1983 budget, the National Wildlife Federation put out an "Honest Budget" for the EPA. Drawing on internal EPA information and documents, and the skills of several dozen program experts, the budget attempted to calculate what level of resources the EPA would need to efficiently carry out its statutory responsibilities. The total was $2.18 billion, about $800 million more than the agency received in 1981, and more than double what Reagan planned to spend in 1983. Their comparison with the Reagan budget follows:

EPA PROGRAMS: NEEDS VS. REAGAN BUDGET

	1981 Budget		Actual FY 83 Needs		Reagan-Gorsuch FY 83 Budget	
	Permanent Positions	Dollars (000)	Permanent Positions	Dollars (000)	Permanent Positions	Dollars (000)
OPERATING BUDGET						
Hazardous Waste[1]	992	138,872.7	2,386.8	346,838.9	661.3	111,308.5
Toxic Chemicals	775	109,904.1	1,775.1	255,112.1	641.5	72,440.7
Clean Water[1]	2,735	319,876.4	3,446.6	408,784.8	1,827.0	188,277.0
Clean Air	1,932	255,705.1	2,763.8	426,888.2	1,355.0	197,448.8
Pesticides	925	75,943.2	1,237.3	116,674.0	669.8	50,620.6
Other[2]	1,473	237,772.7	1,228.1	313,700.5	1,066.1	146,085.6
Management	2,575	214,802.0	3,711.2	310,750.0	2,178.3	208,479.1
Total Operating	11,407	1,352,876.2	16,548.9	2,178,748.5	8,399.0	974,660.3
Superfund	142	78,000.0	965.0	690,000.0	554.6	275,000.0
Construction Grants		3,304,837.0				2,400,000.0

1. For comparison purposes, the hazardous waste and water quality figures have been adjusted to reflect such things as the subsequent expiration of the conventional solid waste program, the transfer of spill response duties from the water office to the new Office of Solid Waste and Emergency Response, and other minor adjustments.

2. Contains drinking water, radiation, noise, and other minor programs, plus certain special items (such as the conventional solid waste program) that have been subtracted from the hazardous waste and water quality media for comparison purposes (see footnote #1).

SYNTHETIC FUELS CORPORATION

EDWARD NOBLE
CHAIRMAN

RESPONSIBILITY OF OFFICE

Noble is the third chairman of the SFC, which was established by the 1980 Energy Security Act. The corporation, a pet project of President Jimmy Carter, initially was to be funded through the windfall profits tax but Congress scrapped the idea, appropriating about $15 billion for SFC activities over the next four years—the first installment in a projected $88 billion, 10-year program.

The potential cost of SFC would therefore run three times more than the Apollo space program and $10 billion more than the entire federal interstate highway program. It is not likely, though, that all those funds will actually be dispensed.

SFC's billions are to be used to accelerate private sector development of a diversified commercial synthetic fuels industry by providing financial assistance to qualifying synthetics fuels projects. The major types of assistance are price guarantees, purchase agreements, loan guarantees, direct loans, and joint ventures.

As SFC chair, Noble will manage a staff of 200 and a $24 million administrative budget in 1982.

BACKGROUND

Until his appointment to the SFC, Noble was on the board of directors of Noble Affiliates, Inc., an independent energy company with operations in oil and gas exploration and production, contract drilling and heavy trucking. Noble Affiliates, Inc., was established in 1969, combining Noble Drilling (which his father founded), B.F. Walker Truck Lines, and Samedan Oil Corporation (which was named after the three Noble children: Samuel, Edward and Ann).

Between 1956 and 1980, while living in Georgia, Noble developed the 1.5 million square-foot Lenox Shopping Center in Atlanta and started Noble Inns Corp., a motor hotel chain with locations in Georgia, Florida and Ohio. When he returned to Oklahoma in January, 1980 he became director and principal stockholder in the Tulsa Auto Crane Company, which manufactures heavy cranes used by the oil industry.

Over the last decade, Noble has been a major benefactor to conservative causes and think-tanks. He is a 15-year member of the board of overseers for the Hoover Institution at Stanford University, a conservative institute close to Reagan that is primarily concerned with foreign affairs. He has also served as a fund-raiser for the Heritage Foundation.

Noble remains a trustee of the Samuel Robert Noble Foundation, established by his father, Lloyd Noble, an oil pioneer, in 1954. The foundation, originally set up to fund agricultural and cancer research, has become a virtual godparent to the conservative movement.

According to IRS records, the foundation has contributed more than $1.2 million to the Heritage Foundation. Since 1974, the Hoover Institution has received $620,000. Other donations include:

- $120,000 to the Committee on the Present Danger in 1977 and 1979;

- $10,000 to the Institute for Contemporary Studies in 1979, a conservative think-tank in San Francisco which Edwin Meese helped establish. (The group recently released a report urging tighter control by the President over news coverage of the White House.);

- $10,000 in 1978 to the Free Congress Resource and Educational Foundation;

- $47,900 in 1979 to the Institute for Foreign Policy Analysis in Cambridge, Masschusetts, a conservative think-tank concerned with defense and foreign policy issues.

Noble Affiliates Political Action Committee in 1980 contributed $28,725 to Republican candidates for national office, including $2,600 to Reagan. Noble himself contributed $1,000 to the Reagan campaign in 1980 and in the two years before taking office contributed close to $10,000 to other conservative candidates and organizations. While in Georgia, Noble was an active member of the state

Republican Party and served as co-finance chairman of the state's Reagan for President campaign in 1979.

In 1980 Noble ran for the U.S. Senate seat in Oklahoma held by retiring Republican Senator Henry Bellmon. Since he entered the race only two months before the primary, Noble wound up personally financing most of the $800,000 he spent on the campaign. Following his loss in the primary, Noble gave his support to Republican Don Nickles, who won the election in November.

During the campaign, Noble opposed the SFC, calling the corporation "costly and wasteful." He suggested tax breaks be used instead to stimulate synfuels development.

Noble became a leading candidate for the SFC post after heading Reagan's transition task force on the corporation. In April, 1981, Noble reneged on his earlier remarks about the SFC, saying he had "learned a hell of a lot" and was convinced the country needs to develop synthetic fuels because it is "25 to 30 years behind."

The transition team, however, reportedly issued a negative report on government involvement in the synthetic fuels industry.

Born on March 19, 1928, in Ardmore, Oklahoma, Noble received a B.S. degree in geology from the University of Oklahoma in 1951. He is divorced with two children.

MAJOR ISSUES

- Noble, a former critic of the program, must reconcile the massive synfuels subsidy with the Administration's stated desire to turn the energy industry over to the free market. The corporation must make key decisions on how much of their own money applicants will be required to invest in projects that receive government aid.

- Noble has so far avoided comment on the potentially devastating environmental problems posed by synfuels development. Little information is available on many synfuels by-products, but some studies have already turned up evidence of serious birth defects from exposure to synfuel product wastes.

Although the synfuels subsidy program ostensibly runs counter to Reagan's market-oriented economic energy policies, the Administration has not proposed that the program be scrapped. Instead it has suggested that the corporation use strict criteria in dispensing aid and require applicants to put up more of their own money.

Bob Roach of the Environmental Policy Center agrees that one of the first challenges facing Noble is the development of appropriate criteria by which projects can be judged.

"Many of the industries lining up to this new trough of government largess have submitted proposals for projects which don't require government subsidies, are high-risk ventures, and have little if any private financial backing," Roach explained.

In September, 1981 testimony before the House Subcommittee on Environment, Energy and Natural Resources, Noble said the Administration would like to bow out of the synthetic fuels program as early as 1984 and probably won't commit any of the $66 billion Congress had appropriated to spur development of that industry beyond that date. That statement was considered the first clear-cut signal that Reagan, pressured by a swollen deficit, may not ask Congress to extend the synfuels program beyond the first phase.

"Our primary goal is to create and leave behind us a viable private sector synthetic fuels industry; all other goals are secondary," Noble told the congressional subcommittee.

The first synfuels aid should be dispensed some time this year. In March, 1982, the corporation narrowed the list of contenders for its first round of assistance to five projects, including those sponsored by Tenneco, Sohio, and Bechtel. By law, the corporation can dispense up to $14.6 billion by 1984. But until the corporation's board actually decides which projects to fund, as the Administration notes in the 1983 budget, "the Corporation will not be able to develop budget projections of financial assistance with any degree of accuracy."

Noble's abandonment of the Carter Administration's gung-ho attitude toward synfuels, and the worldwide oil glut of 1981, have dampened enthusiasm for the projects. "It's pretty much agreed," said Michael Koleda, president of the National Council on Synthetic Fuels Production, "that synthetic fuels development is going to go ahead a lot slower than we had anticipated." Several members of the House—including Democrat Richard Ottinger and Republican Jack Kemp— have introduced legislation to scrap the corporation entirely.

That the Administration would continue to support this multi-billion dollar white elephant at all is a demonstration of how far it can bend its ideology when the interests of its business supporters are at stake. Projected synfuel prices have shown a remarkable facility for staying a step ahead of world oil prices. In 1972 when world oil prices were $3.50 a barrel, the National Petroleum Council estimated $8 a barrel for synfuels. When prices jumped to $13 a barrel in 1975, Standard Oil of California pegged the price for synfuels at between $17 and $30 a barrel. When Carter pushed through the Synfuels Corp., oil was running $28-$32 a barrel; it projected synfuels at between $32 and $40. Even with oil prices holding steady in the world oil glut, synfuels backers do not expect the plants completed later this decade to beat the price of oil.

It is unclear exactly *why* the estimated cost of synfuels seem to rise in tandem with the world price of oil, but it may be because those preparing the estimates have generally been those selling the oil. According to documents obtained by Canada in its antitrust investigation of the oil companies, Exxon deliberately delayed the development of synfuels in the late 1960s to protect their crude oil interests.

Jonathan Lash of the Natural Resources Defense Council sees Noble's skepticism as healthy. "It may lead him to make more rational decisions of where to put the money. He's saying if the energy industry has concluded that this is not worth doing, economically, why do it? What you end up with after all the subsidizing is a few plants that cannot make an economically competitive product," said Lash. Added Roach: "The pace of development should be more reasonable—slower, and should go through the proper stages of scale-up until we can generate the data base which we need to make evaluations of the relative effectiveness and the problems."

The SFC itself got off to a slow start, hobbled by a dispute between the Administration and Sen. James McClure (R-Idaho), chairman of the Senate Energy Committee. While the DOE feuded with the Office of Management and Budget over granting a $2 billion loan guarantee for a Great Plains coal-gasification project in North Dakota that McClure supported, the chairman held up the nominations for other members of the board. When Reagan personally approved the loan in August, 1981, McClure allowed the nominations to proceed. In September the Senate approved the nominations of Robert Monk, chairman of the Boston Co.;

Victor Schroeder, executive director of Atlanta's Peachtree Center; C. Howard Wilkins, former vice-chairman of Pizza Hut; and V.M. Thompson Jr., chief executive officer for Utica National Bank and Trust Company in Tulsa.

One of the first decisions facing Noble and the new directors was whether to take over financial responsibility for Great Plains and two other synfuels projects now funded by the Energy Department, under a $6.2 billion interim synfuels program. The projects could be transferred by a majority vote of the board.

A McClure-sponsored amendment prohibited SFC from assuming responsibility for Great Plains, but it did take over the other two projects in February, 1982. A month later the SFC threatened to cut off funding for one of the projects because of massive cost overruns. The project, a shale oil joint venture between Exxon and Tosco, received $1.1 billion in federal loan guarantees; its estimated cost has soared from $3.1 billion in October, 1981 to $5 billion by March, 1982. The project was doomed in May, 1982 when Exxon pulled out.

Another critical issue facing the board of directors is the potentially serious environmental problems faced by synfuels development. Environmentalists want assistance criteria to focus on environmental performance, especially since the Reagan Administration is not likely to stiffen any environmental laws affecting synfuels.

Noble skirted the environmental issue during his September, 1981 testimony before the House Subcommittee on Environment, Energy and Natural Resources, stating only that his staff was meeting regularly with the Environmental Protection Agency (EPA).

"It's not comforting to hear them say they'll have to comply with all regulatory standards," said Lash. "There are no regulatory standards explicitly applicable to synthetic fuels," he said, noting that scores of potentially dangerous substances associated with synfuels production are not covered under EPA Clean Air or Clean Water Act regulations and "a big fight" is expected over which synfuels wastes will be subject to EPA hazardous waste regulations. Morever, synfuel use would add carbon dioxide to the atmosphere more quickly than other fuels, exacerbating the "greenhouse effect." But that problem is not regulated by any agency.

Lash contends that most of the potential hazards from synthetic fuels plants have not even been closely studied. But disturbing evidence is already available. An April, 1981 issue of *Science* featured on the cover a cricket with an exta pair of eyes; it had been exposed while in the egg to minute amounts of certain synthetic fuels products and a compound found in synfuel wastes.

FINANCIAL BACKGROUND

Noble, a wealthy oilman, is serving for $1 a year, instead of taking the $175,000 a year salary.

Immediately following his confirmation hearing Noble said he had offered to take the job for $1 a year to defuse the controversies over high salaries at the corporation, which is not covered by federal salary ceilings. Noble, however, has not indicated that he expects his executives to follow his lead. In fact, he has suggested SFC may have to raise its executive pay scale—which usually exceeds $100,000 per year—to attract competent candidates from private industry.

Noble's financial disclosure indicates that his holdings in oil properties, real estate, stocks and other assets are worth at least several million dollars.

Noble, who upon confirmation resigned from the board of directors at Noble Affiliates, has placed his oil holdings in a blind trust.

WHAT OTHERS ARE SAYING ABOUT HIM

- House Energy Conservation and Power Subcommittee Chairman Richard Ottinger, calling the corporation "the very symbol of corporate welfare," said in a February, 1982 statement: "The existence of the Synthetic Fuels Corporation today only confirms the most cynical view of the federal government. For while we make low and middle income Americans suffer increasing hardship in the name of economic recovery, we give out billions of dollars in loan guarantees to Exxon, and Texaco, among America's richest corporations—billions for uneconomic ventures that the private sector won't finance."

CHAPTER 3

HUMAN RESOURCES

LABOR DEPARTMENT

RAYMOND DONOVAN
SECRETARY

RESPONSIBILITY OF OFFICE

The secretary of Labor administers more than 130 federal laws affecting 115 million working Americans. Legally he is required to "foster, promote, and develop the welfare of the wage-earners of the United States, to improve their working conditions and to advance their opportunities for profitable employment."

As secretary, Donovan is charged with guaranteeing workers' collective bargaining rights, upholding fair labor standards, and ensuring workers a safe workplace and freedom from job discrimination. He also is responsible for protecting workers' financial interests under private pension and welfare benefits plans, and under workers' compensation and unemployment compensation programs. In addition, his department conducts job training and public service employment programs.

BACKGROUND

Before his appointment by Reagan, Donovan was one of two principal owners of a New Jersey construction firm that has been accused by a union official of making payoffs to local politicians and to Teamsters Union officials, and has accrued a lengthy list of occupational safety and labor law infractions.

Donovan was the last Reagan Cabinet selection confirmed by the Senate. Allegations by sources in the Justice Department's "protected witness" program that Donovan's company, Schiavone Construction, had ties to the Genovese organized crime family, bought "labor peace," and bribed local politicians with laundered money prompted lengthy hearings into his background. FBI officials testified at his confirmation hearings, however, that they were unable to verify the charges on the basis of a brief, but intensive, investigation. Donovan vehemently attacked the allegations as "scurrilous and untrue," and denounced one of the government-protected witnesses as "murdering slime."

Five Democratic members of the Senate Labor and Human Resources Committee noted in their minority report that they could not support President Reagan's choice for Labor secretary "because of the number and gravity of the allegations against Mr. Donovan," which they described as "almost unique in the history of presidential nominations to the Cabinet." Arguing that Donovan's background made him unfit to oversee efforts to combat labor racketeering, they attempted to block Donovan's confirmation. But the Senate endorsed Donovan by an 80-to-17 margin.

By the end of his first year in office, though, a federal appeals court panel had appointed a special prosecutor under the 1978 Ethics in Government Act to conduct a grand jury probe of newly-surfaced allegations that Donovan and another

Schiavone Construction Company executive made payoffs to officials of Local 29 of the Laborers International Union in New York.

Mario Montuoro, a dissident past secretary-treasurer of the union local, reportedly originally told federal investigators in 1978 of payoffs involving Donovan and subsequently repeated the allegations to New York state investigators during Donovan's confirmation hearings. But his charges apparently were brushed aside by Justice Department investigators concerned that it might interfere with Montuoro's participation in other cases under investigation. Attorney General William French Smith finally requested that a special prosecutor be appointed to look into the matter in December, 1981, fully three months after Montuoro repeated his allegations for a third time in an interview with members of the Federal Organized Crime Strike Force in Brooklyn. Donovan insists Montuoro "is a damnable and contemptible liar."

Aside from its alleged corruption of union officials and connections with organized crime, Donovan's construction firm also has a mixed record of compliance with labor laws, including 57 citations over a six-year period for violations of health and safety regulations involving "a substantial probability that death or serious physical harm could result." The Occupational Safety and Health Administration (OSHA) inspected Schiavone Construction Company sites 49 times during the six years preceding Donovan's appointment and found a total of 135 violations. OSHA officials reported Schiavone's record was worse than average for a firm its size.

Labor Department records indicate that during the 1960s the New Jersey company also failed to comply with provisions of the Davis-Bacon Act, a federal statute requiring that workers on federally financed construction projects be paid locally prevailing wage rates. In addition, six charges of unfair labor practices were filed against Schiavone Construction with the National Labor Relations Board, three of which were sustained. At the time Donovan assumed office, the Labor Department's Employment Standards Administration was investigating 12 complaints against his firm alleging race and sex discrimination, along with a separate charge of sexual harassment.

Donovan's familiarity with workers' concerns derives mainly from his experience as Schiavone Construction's chief labor negotiator. Yet Donovan once intervened to quickly end a strike against a short-lived New York daily newspaper called *The Trib*, in which Donovan and his construction company had invested $370,000. On the second day of publication a sudden strike by delivery truck drivers cut *The Trib's* circulation from 250,000 down to 60,000.

But after a meeting that evening in a bar at the Algonquin Hotel between Donovan and Douglas LaChance, the president of the Newspaper and Mail Deliverers Union, the strike was called off. Two years later LaChance was convicted of labor racketeering and sentenced to 12 years in prison for extortion of over $300,000 in illegal payoffs. Although Donovan's dealings with LaChance were not a factor in LaChance's conviction, the *New York Daily News* has reported they may be under investigation by the special prosecutor appointed to look into the other allegations against Donovan.

During the 1980 presidential election campaign Donovan served as chairman of the New Jersey Reagan-Bush campaign committee. Though formerly a Democrat, he is a long-time political ally of President Reagan and has been a major fundraiser for him. Reagan named Donovan to the post in the face of stiff opposition from both big business and the Teamsters Union, who lobbied hard for their consensus candidate, Betty Southard Murphy—a former head of the National Labor Relations Board.

Born on August 31, 1930 in Bayonne, New Jersey, Donovan graduated from Notre Dame Seminary in New Orleans with a B.A. in philosophy in 1952. He then went to work for the American Insurance Co. in New Jersey, where he worked as an underwriter and bond supervisor through 1958.

In 1959 he joined the Schiavone Construction Co., as a major shareholder and Vice-President. The construction firm did only about $200,000 worth of business in 1959, but by the time Donovan placed his interest in trust, following his nomination as Labor secretary, its annual business ran to about $150 million.

Donovan is married and has three children.

MAJOR ISSUES

- Perhaps more than any other Labor secretary in the past 50 years—Democratic or Republican—Donovan has isolated himself from organized labor, leaving the unions without any effective communication with the Reagan Administration.

- He has also aggressively pushed Reagan's directive to cut government programs and reduce federal oversight of business; the department's Occupational Safety and Health Administration has already withdrawn a series of major occupational health standards for reconsideration.

At least since the passage of the landmark labor legislation of the New Deal era, the Labor Department has served both Democratic and Republican administrations as a sounding board, if not always an advocate, for the concerns of organized labor in the United States. But despite a pledge by Secretary Donovan that he would seek to emulate former Labor Secretary James Mitchell—who was known as the "social conscience" of the Eisenhower Administration—labor leaders feel cut off and alienated from Donovan's Labor Department.

"I don't know a goddamn soul over there," said George Taylor, the AFL-CIO's occupational safety and health director. "I don't have a working relationship with any of them. We don't have any contact with this Administration."

Lane Kirkland, president of the AFL-CIO, has denounced Donovan for failing to consider organized labor's interests before making some "deeply disturbing" decisions on the budget and on regulations that unions consider crucial to protecting workers' health and safety. "He hasn't consulted with us before taking a number of steps that go to the heart of our concerns," Kirkland charges.

Donovan first antagonized labor leaders following a meeting with the AFL-CIO's executive council in February, 1981, when he suggested to reporters that perhaps half of the council supported President Reagan's economic program to some extent. Kirkland, however, quickly corrected him, saying that Donovan was "mistaken" in his estimation of labor's support for Reagan. Donovan's snubs of labor leaders since then have increased animosity between Kirkland and the Labor secretary to the point now, where, according to a Democratic source on the Senate Labor and Human Resources Committee, "Lane doesn't even want to talk to Donovan."

In fact, Donovan so alienated union leaders that Reagan finally felt obliged to designate Vice-President Bush as his top liaison with organized labor at a White House meeting on December 2, 1981. The hastily called conference with union officials came a week after the AFL-CIO held its centennial convention in New York City without inviting either the President, or the Labor secretary, to give the customary address to delegates. Conventioneers instead heard a series of scathing attacks on Reagan's policies by prominent Democrats.

In the months before the convention Donovan had personally involved himself in settling a lengthy major league baseball players' strike, but failed to intervene before or after the Professional Air Traffic Controllers' Organization (PATCO) strike seriously disrupted air travel beginning on August 3, 1981. Donovan's inaction, coupled with Reagan's decision to fire the 11,500 PATCO members who refused to return to work, apparently finally dispelled any lingering hopes American labor leaders had of finding a sympathetic ear in Donovan's Labor Department.

Meanwhile, Donovan further aggravated the situation by filling top posts in his department with political allies, or management-oriented labor consultants clearly antagonistic to labor's interests. Prior to their appointments, both the deputy undersecretary for international labor affairs and the deputy assistant secretary for labor management relations had represented major corporations such as Kaiser Steel and Westinghouse in labor matters. The assistant secretary for training and employment, Albert Angrisani, was a vice president of Chase Manhattan Bank and Reagan fundraiser before he came to the Labor Department. Angrisani now also serves as Donovan's chief of staff, screening all of the secretary's contacts with subordinates and outsiders.

All of this makes particularly ironic Donovan's exhortations for a "closer, more meaningful and productive relationship" between labor and management. "I'm talking about a spirit, a sense of shared pride that transcends ancient grudges and petty grievances, and could lead to a fuller participation by labor in the decisions that affect the working lives of its members, as well as the productivity and quality of their work," he said in one speech. There's no sense of shared anything between Donovan and organized labor, and business leaders, perhaps partly in jest, complained to Commerce Secretary Baldrige that Labor secretary Donovan was more pro-business than he was. (See profile of Malcolm Baldrige.)

While they're developing this new relationship with business, Donovan continued, "labor [should] not dissipate its attention and energy fighting to save every counterproductive clause in every piece of legislation and every program now under review in the Department of Labor." Labor hasn't been much interested in that offer either, seeing the department's policy reversals at OSHA and the Mine Safety and Health Administration as direct assaults on the health and well-being of their members. (See profiles of Thorne Auchter and Ford B. Ford.)

Since taking office, Donovan has zealously carried out President Reagan's admonition to cut government spending and roll back regulations of business. The Labor Department took a 23 percent cut in fiscal 1982—slashing $8 billion from the $34.5 billion budget proposed by the Carter Administration. Particularly hard-hit were job training programs. Reagan has refused to offer any government employment plans to ameliorate post-war record unemployment rates. It is generally assumed that most of the decisions on budget cuts were actually made by David Stockman's Office of Management and Budget (OMB), rather than by Donovan, who displayed little detailed knowledge of Labor Department programs in his testimony before congressional committees.

The Administration's decision to cut back on black lung benefits for miners disabled from inhaling coal dust provoked one of the most heated protests of Reagan's budget cuts. More than 5,000 coal miners marched on the White House in March, 1981, following a rally sponsored by the United Mine Workers of America. Donovan and his assistant secretary in charge of OSHA, Auchter, have also angered workers and their union leaders with a series of moves to revise, rescind or postpone health and safety rules. These included rules lowering the permissible levels of lead in the blood of workers threatened with lead poisoning, and a proposal to require identification of hazardous substances workers face on the job. Under the identification standard, for instance, the Carter Administration proposed that hazardous substances be labeled to advise workers of potential dangers. That proposal was quickly withdrawn by Donovan and Auchter and replaced by one that simply requires "that workers be alerted to the hazards of substances they work with. . . ."

According to Donovan, under previous administrations OSHA "became a national laughing stock" by "descending on companies to inspect everything from ladders to latrines." In a speech before a carpenters' union convention in September, 1981, Donovan suggested that voluntary labor-management committees would be "more reasonable and far more effective" than regular OSHA inspections in maintaining health and safety standards.

Rather than push OSHA rules that can lead to confrontation with major industrial employers, Donovan has focused his attention instead on "sweatshops" run by small employers who allegedly pay workers less than legal wages. Donovan personally joined in "raids" on purported sweatshops in New York and Chicago, without bothering to consult local union officials who have long monitored working conditions in their areas. One such well-publicized raid in New York's garment district proved to be an embarrassing false alarm.

Donovan's tactics have even managed to antagonize some big business leaders. A plan to ease employment discrimination strictures for small contractors doing business with the federal government prompted the Business Roundtable and other groups representing large employers to complain to OMB that small employers were being favored at their expense.

Further proposals by Donovan to water down affirmative action requirements and health and safety rules are likely, along with support for establishing subminimum wage rates for younger workers pegged at 75-85 percent of the standard minimum wage. Unions can be expected to vigorously oppose such moves, as well as proposed changes in regulations to cut wage rates for government building contractors under the Davis-Bacon Act.

Like many other Reagan Cabinet and sub-Cabinet appointees, Donovan discounts organized labor's fears about his announced intention to seek accommodation and cooperation, rather than confrontation with employers. "The people who do not share our philosophy have. . .a distrust of business," he maintains. "They say that we are anti-worker, anti-poor, anti-old, and that the free enterprise system has had its chance to prove that it was responsible and that it has failed. I reject that philosophy. Ronald Reagan rejects it."

Although Donovan and his appointees faithfully follow the President's political line, their inexperience with congressional politics has prompted criticism from both the White House and Capitol Hill. The Republican counsel on the House Education and Labor Committee attributes Donovan's problems to "political naivete," while maintaining that: "He's very sincere, and he does want to get a grasp on the administration of the department. But he doesn't fully have it yet." A Democratic source on the Senate Labor and Human Resources Committee was more succinct in his estimation of the job done by Donovan and his staff during their first six months in office. "They haven't done anything," he insisted.

Another indication of Donovan's inexperience was the White House's refusal to defer to his suggestions on several labor-related appointments, including the selection of his own undersecretary. Donovan pushed to elevate his chief of staff, Albert

Angrisani, to that job, but presidential aides held out for someone experienced in Washington politics. Finally, Malcolm R. Lovell, Jr., a former assistant Labor secretary in the Nixon Administration, was named to the post.

Lovell, an experienced rubber industry lobbyist, has become a frequent stand-in for Donovan before congressional committees and is generally credited with opening up lines of communications between Labor Department officials and representatives of organized labor and big business groups. Should Donovan resign, Lovell is generally expected to replace him in the Cabinet. Donovan may try to get rid of Lovell first.

FINANCIAL BACKGROUND

Like many other Reagan Cabinet and sub-Cabinet appointees, Donovan came to his post from an industry directly affected by the policies of his department. Construction companies, more than most employers, often maintain a running battle with Labor Department officials over health and safety violations, affirmative action requirements, federal contract compliance rules, and collective bargaining disputes. Donovan's firm, Schiavone Construction, apparently had more than its share of these types of problems, with the notable exception of labor unrest.

Donovan was a millionaire when he assumed office, with partnership interests in at least ten separate business and investment groups besides his involvement with Schiavone Construction. In addition, he was a joint owner of oil and gas leases in Texas, Colorado, New Mexico, Louisiana and Kansas. He also owned rental property in Boca Raton, Florida, valued at over $250,000, a racehorse, and a variety of stocks and securities worth well over $700,000.

Allegations aired at his confirmation hearings that Schiavone bought "labor peace" with payoffs to Teamsters Union officials and that the company was "mobbed up" raise serious question about Donovan's self-proclaimed intentions to "root out" organized crime's influence on labor unions. Steven Brill, editor of *The American Lawyer*, wrote that in the course of his two years of research for a book on the Teamsters Union, "the names of Donovan and his New Jersey-based Schiavone Construction Company were mentioned together as a good example of an executive and a company that was paying off Teamsters officials." Brill notes that, "on two occasions, sources provided convincing details of such payoffs."

But beyond any personal involvement Donovan may have with corrupt Teamsters, compounding federal investigators' problems in dealing with labor racketeering are President Reagan's own overtures to Teamsters President Roy Williams and a lesser Teamster official, Jackie Presser. Reagan reportedly shocked Labor and Justice Department officials when he named Presser to his transition advisory team prior to the inauguration. Subsequently, Reagan invited Williams to the White House, even though proceedings were pending against the Teamsters boss in federal court for mismanagement of union pension funds. "Obviously, the President has gone out of his way to give Williams a certain respectability by inviting him to the White House," one federal investigator said, suggesting that such displays of cordiality and the fact that the Teamsters were the only major labor union to endorse Reagan may hinder further investigation and prosecution of corrupt Teamsters officials.

WHAT OTHERS ARE SAYING ABOUT HIM

- "The change in direction at the Labor Department under Secretary Raymond J. Donovan is probably the most radical turnabout of any Cabinet department in the Reagan Administration. Donovan has stripped the department of its advocacy role and—in line with the Reagan philosophy—has begun pulling it back from commitments to employment and worker protection programs," wrote *Business Week.*

- "The Senate vote on Mr. Donovan may be a sign that people are getting just a bit tired of the demands this legalistic, post-Watergate style has been making on public life. . . ," wrote the *The Wall Street Journal.*

- "Using [*The Wall Street Journal's*] logic would impel the President to appoint Don Corleone as attorney general. . ." said Steven Brill, editor of *The American Lawyer.*

- "He's effectively repealed Davis-Bacon through deregulation. We had a chance to make recommendations. . .but they'd already made up their minds," said Ralph Willham, lobbyist for the Sheet Metal Workers International Association.

- "I don't think anyone's running the Labor Department. Donovan's not an administrator," said Arthur Goldberg, a former secretary of Labor and U.S. Supreme Court justice, now practicing labor law.

T. TIMOTHY RYAN, JR.
SOLICITOR

RESPONSIBILITY OF OFFICE

As chief legal officer for the Labor Department, the solicitor enforces laws and regulations intended to protect worker's health and safety, collective bargaining and employment rights. These include fair labor standards, such as minimum wage requirements, and laws that prohibit discrimination in hiring or promotion on the basis of race, sex, religion, age, national origin, or physical handicap.

The solicitor sets prosecutorial priorities for his deputies in nine regional offices considering legal action against employers or labor unions charged with abridging workers' rights. Besides his labor law enforcement duties, Ryan advises the secretary of Labor in developing legislation, regulations and department policies to "foster, promote, and develop the welfare" of American wage earners.

BACKGROUND

Prior to his appointment, Ryan primarily represented management in labor relations matters for the Washington law firm of Pierson, Ball & Dowd. Besides negotiations for employers in collective bargaining and defending management against unfair labor practice charges, Ryan also advised employers fighting union organizing campaigns. Two suits brought by the Labor Department against Ryan's clients were pending when he was appointed. Both arose out of charges that Ryan's clients had failed to report their union resisting activities to the Department of Labor as required by the Labor-Management Reporting and Disclosure Act (LMRDA) of 1959. That law, the Landrum-Griffin Act, requires written reports from all labor unions, employers and labor relations consultants involved in unionization votes. Although unions and employers generally conform to the reporting requirements, labor leaders maintain that many "union busters" who work as management consultants routinely ignore LMRDA.

In July, 1980, a federal judge ruled that an employers' association counseled by Ryan had failed to file reports required by Landrum-Griffin. In that case, then Labor Secretary Ray Marshall sued Ryan's client, the Master Printers of America (MPA), and a federal district court agreed that *Insight*, an MPA publication mailed to employees considering unionization, constituted "persuader activity" that must be reported under LMRDA.

"Even a cursory reading of the enumerated articles reveals that they are unabashedly anti-union," U.S. District Judge Albert Bryan concluded in his written opinion in that case.

At Ryan's Senate confirmation hearing, Graphic Arts International Union (GAIU) Vice-President Edward V. Donahue argued that Ryan's involvement with MPA indicated "he is unqualified to fairly interpret and execute federal labor law. . . ." Donahue pointed out that despite the court ruling in the *Insight* case, MPA still refused to file reports, in organizing campaigns conducted at a Rand McNally plant in Versailles, Kentucky and a Taylor Publishing Co. plant in Malvern, Pennsylvania, apparently on Ryan's advice. Subsequently the Labor and Justice Departments filed a second suit, he noted, alleging that MPA "has failed and refused, after repeated requests and demands. . . to file labor relations consultant report forms designated by the Secretary of Labor. . . ."

Since Ryan took office as solicitor the *Insight* case has been appealed by MPA, while the case involving Rand McNally and Taylor Publishing has been resolved in MPA's favor.

Besides advising MPA to refuse filing consultant reports, Donahue testified that Ryan was directly involved in fighting the GAIU organizing effort at the Rand McNally & Co. plant in Versailles, as an attorney representing both MPA and Rand McNally. The effort to prevent unionization there was "conducted in an extremely virulent and abusive manner," Donahue testified, that prompted the filing of two unfair labor practice charges against the company, in addition to the "failure to report" charge in the Labor Department lawsuit.

The first unfair practice charge alleged that security guards equipped for the first time with handguns had interfered with the distribution of handbills by union organizers. The company responded by posting literature in non-working areas and by instructing guards not to carry pistols.

The National Labor Relations Board (NLRB) drew up a formal complaint documenting a second charge that Rand McNally had engaged in surveillance of employees by demanding samples of their signatures, ostensibly for use by the NLRB. The complaint was withdrawn when the company notified employees they were not required to provide sample signatures to the company. "We can detect nothing in Mr. Ryan's conduct in those organizing drives involving the GAIU, in which he advised companies, which indicates a degree of fairness and impartiality, obviously required [in] the Solicitor of Labor," Donahue concluded, urging the

Senate not to confirm Ryan for the post. Ryan was easily confirmed by the Republican-controlled Senate, but he explicitly agreed to abstain as solicitor from "any determination dealing with persuader activity" and "litigation involving the Master Printers and Rand McNally & Co."

Ryan has represented employers' interests before a variety of Labor Department agencies, including the Occupational Safety and Health Administration (OSHA), the NLRB, the Office of Federal Contract Compliance Programs (OFFCP) and the Mine Safety and Health Administration. He also spent a year as an attorney-adviser to an NLRB member, and has been an adjunct law professor at the Georgetown University Law Center.

Politically, Ryan has been active as a legal adviser in the campaigns of many prominent Republicans, including those of former President Gerald Ford and presidential hopeful Sen. Howard Baker (R-Tenn.). Just prior to his appointment, Ryan worked as a legal counsel to President-elect Reagan's transition team. Ryan's wife, Judith Rush Ryan, is an information officer in the State Department. Born on June 13, 1945 in Washington D.C., Ryan was graduated from Villanova University in 1967 and American University law school in 1973.

MAJOR ISSUES

- Ryan has assumed the lead in revising Labor Department regulations, moving to relax worker health and safety regulations and to ease rules prohibitng employment discrimination by federal contractors based on race, sex, or physical handicap.

- Ryan has refused to initiate legal actions urged by a Senate subcommittee against allegedly corrupt Teamsters Union officials.

As solicitor, Ryan is essentially in a position to become "very much a coordinator of department programs," according to Peter Nash, a Labor solicitor during the Nixon Administration. On the basis of his own experience, Nash says the solicitor can become "as powerful as his intellect, personality and time. . .allow him to be." And according to the *National Journal*, Ryan had developed "a reputation as a 'take charge' person" in Washington, even before assuming his post as solicitor.

At his confirmation hearing, Ryan told members of the Senate Labor and Human Resources Committee that already he had taken charge of a "Departmental Task Force for Regulatory Reform" that was busy with a wide-ranging review of labor regulations. At the same time, Ryan noted that he would head up a "litigation strategy task force" intended to coordinate the activities of the Labor, Justice and Treasury Departments in the well-publicized prosecution of Teamsters Union officials accused of mismanaging union pension funds.

"We're treating it [the Teamsters investigation] with great sensitivity," Ryan told us, adding: "We view it as one of our primary jobs." Yet Ryan has rejected a recommendation by the Senate Permanent Subcommittee on Investigations that the Labor Department institute administrative proceedings against Teamsters President Roy Lee Williams in an effort to remove him from office and from his post as a trustee of the $2.2 billion Teamsters Central States Pension Fund. Ryan has advised Labor Secretary Donovan that "the Labor Department has no authority to seek the removal of Williams or to otherwise challenge his incumbency as President of the Teamsters." Both Republican and Democratic senators dispute Ryan's interpretation of the law, however, and have promised to introduce legislation declaring the

Labor Department's obligation to seek removal of union officials who abuse their posts as union trustees.

"It becomes somewhat natural for the solicitor to become involved in just flat-out policy judgements," Nash said, pointing out that the solicitor has a large staff both in Washington and in regional offices to draw on for research and advice. "Nothing went to the [Labor] secretary or undersecretary without the solicitor's initials" during his term, Nash said.

Arthur J. Goldberg, Labor secretary in the Kennedy Administration and a former U.S. Supreme Court justice, agrees with Nash's assessment of the importance of the solicitor's policy role. "At that level of legal work it's very difficult to draw the line between legal and policy decisions," Goldberg told us. As legal director for the Amalgamated Clothing and Textile Workers Union (ACTWU), Goldberg had a particular interest in one of Ryan's initial legal decisions, since it amounted to a complete reversal of OSHA policy affecting ACTWU members.

In what *Business Week* described as "an unusually bold move," Ryan asked the U.S. Supreme Court in March, 1981 to hold off a decision pending on OSHA's cotton dust exposure rule until his regulatory review task force had a chance to "reconsider" the standard based on their own cost-benefit analysis. Ryan failed to persuade the court to withhold its judgment, however. Instead, the Supreme Court ruled out the cost-benefit argument in June, 1981 by a 5-to-3 vote, holding that Congress already had placed the "benefit" of worker health above all other considerations. (See profile of Thorne Auchter.)

Ryan's involvement in another OSHA case has provoked charges from the Oil, Chemical and Atomic Workers International Union (OCAW) that the solicitor "cut a backroom deal" with an oil company. The charges stemmed from an out-of-court settlement apparently ordered by Ryan a few weeks after he took office. OCAW officials maintain they were denied "meaningful participation" in the settlement of the case, which involved a three-year-old dispute over gas-testing safety procedures at an Amoco Oil Co. refinery in Indiana.

In October, 1973, OSHA had cited Amoco for "inadequate and unsafe gas testing" for "potentially combustible, toxic, and oxygen-deficient atmospheres likely to be encountered" at its Whiting Refinery near Calumet, Indiana. Such testing is crucial in oil refineries because of the highly volatile petroleum distillates processed and stored there.

"This issue of inadequate gas testing is a widespread hazard in the oil refining industry and is of great importance to the 60,000 oil refinery workers represented by our union," OCAW Vice-President Ernie Rousselle wrote in a letter to Labor Secretary Donovan protesting the settlement of the Amoco case and of a similar case against Texaco.

Not surprisingly, Amoco praised the settlement as "reflecting the company position" on safety testing, since all legal charges were dropped against the company and in return Amoco merely agreed to pay a $415 fine. In his letter to Donovan, Rousselle asserts that "the order went out to Chicago from the Labor Department headquarters in Washington that your agency's former resistance to the company's position was to be abandoned and settlements were to be reached even if OCAW objected."

Responding to Rousselle's charges on Donovan's behalf, the Labor solicitor's office wrote back to Rousselle insisting that "in accordance with established procedures, your union was given an opportunity to present its views on the draft settlements before they were signed. . ." Rousselle wrote back to Ryan's office, however, pointing out that "the Regional Solicitor signed the settlement within six hours of when our representative in Washington received the document. The Regional Solicitor did not even allow time for our local union at the Amoco refinery in Whiting, Indiana, to see the document before it was signed."

Besides intervening in OSHA litigation to ease its impact on business, Ryan has also moved to lighten the regulatory load on government contractors. In May, 1981, the Labor Department's regulatory reform group headed by Ryan proposed wholesale revisions of regulations that set wage and anti-discrimination requirements for federal contractors. But unexpected resistance from big-business groups to proposed exemptions from filing written affirmative action programs for small contractors, delayed the proposed changes.

The revisions proposed by Ryan's group would sharply reduce compliance requirements on 12,624 of the 16,767 businesses that now have written affirmative action programs. Ryan would also eliminate a proposal to make contractors responsible for sexual harassment on the job by nonemployees, and ease requirements that federal contractors employ women and minorities in ratios reflecting their work force availability.

Ryan has also reversed the Labor Department's position on job discrimination suits by the handicapped, saying that the Rehabilitation Act of 1973 does not give the handicapped the right to sue federal contractors on their own. Ryan said he will seek to restrict such suits to those approved by his office.

FINANCIAL BACKGROUND

A rewrite of regulations under Ryan's supervision may directly benefit some of his past clients by effectively lowering the wages non-union government contractors have to pay their employees.

Under both the Davis-Bacon Act and the Service Contract Act, federal contractors are required to pay the "prevailing wage" in a locality— usually a higher rate than non-union employers would otherwise pay. As solicitor, Ryan has proposed changes in the regulations used in determining minimum allowable wage rates.

The new rules generally would allow federal contractors to pay lower wages, often below union scale, by setting the rate at what a majority of workers earn in the area, rather than at the top wage paid at least 30 percent of workers there. The revised rules would also relax reporting requirements that aid enforcement efforts. Instead of requiring contractors to submit weekly payroll records, under Ryan's revised regulations they would simply file a brief form to certify that they have complied.

Although a lawyer's convictions cannot always be deduced from those of his clientele, Ryan's background representing employers accused of labor law violations and as an adviser to a non-union employers' group vigorously fighting unionization clearly suggests he is not inclined to represent workers' interests. The key question, two prominent labor lawyers told us, is whether Ryan is intellectually or morally committed to the "union busting" philosophy espoused by many of his clients. Another prominent Washington labor lawyer with Republican ties, who declined to be identified, insists that "his [Ryan's] bias is heavily anti-union."

Besides his $57,000 salary as a management labor lawyer in 1980, Ryan earned $3,000 as a special counsel to the Baker for President Committee. He also took in more than $2,500 in rent of business property in Columbia, Maryland.

WHAT OTHERS ARE SAYING ABOUT HIM

- "We constantly expect them [Ryan and Labor Secretary Donovan] to pull the rug out from under us," said Arthur J. Goldberg, secretary of Labor in the Kennedy Administration and a former U.S. Supreme Court justice, now legal director for the Amalgamated Clothing and Textile Workers Union.

- "Your agency [the Labor Solicitor's office] failed to enforce the law and our people will now risk paying the ultimate price," wrote Ernie Rousselle, vice-president of the Oil, Chemical and Atomic Workers International Union.

THORNE AUCHTER
ASSISTANT SECRETARY FOR OCCUPATIONAL SAFETY AND HEALTH

RESPONSIBILITY OF OFFICE

Established in 1970, the Occupational Safety and Health Administration (OSHA) has been one of the most controversial, and bitterly resisted, federal agencies. Its statutory mandate, laid out in the preamble to the act, is bold and unequivocal: To "assure safe and healthful working conditions for working men and women."

It hasn't generally worked out that way, with OSHA's efforts provoking regular lawsuits from business groups, and complaints from labor that the agency was not moving quickly enough to protect workers. Recently, the Surgeon General noted that nine out of ten American industrial workers are still "not adequately protected from exposure to at least one of the 163 most common hazardous chemicals." The Carter Administration estimated that occupational disease killed 100,000 workers annually. OSHA operated with a budget of $192.5 million in 1982, down from $209 million in 1981, and a staff of 2,260, down from 2,544 in 1981.

BACKGROUND

Since graduating from Jacksonville University in 1968, Auchter has worked at the family construction business, The Auchter Co. of Jacksonville, Florida. From 1968 to 1975, he was a construction supervisor; from 1975 on, he was executive vice-president. His responsibilities included labor relations, public relations and safety and health; but one union leader long familiar with the firm said Auchter "was basically a spokesman for the Auchter Company." OSHA records show that from July 1972 through November 1980, the company was cited with 48 safety violations, six of which were considered serious. Fines totaled $1,200.

P.R. Russ, Jr., a local union official who has known Auchter for 20 years, said that Auchter's experience has been almost entirely on safety, the major concern in construction, rather than occupational health issues. "All of that [occupational disease] stuff is absolutely foreign to him," Russ said.

In 1972, Auchter chaired a governor's task force which wrote Florida's plan for establishing an approved state program under OSHA. Auchter was selected, recalled Baxter Swing, director of workers compensation in the Department of Labor, "because we needed somebody strong from management." Eventually, the state legislature decided not to apply for an OSHA-certified plan. Swing said that funding requirements, "not the quality of the final product from the task force," were behind the legislature's decision.

From 1977-79, Auchter was director of the Northeast Florida Associated General Contractors. One union official who dealt with him there said he took a hard line on union issues. "I think that he, personally, is really anti-union. The relationship with the union company that he's in put him in a different posture," said the official.

Auchter spent two months in 1975 working for the State Senate Rules Committee.

He has also been active in local Republican politics. In 1980, he ran special events in Florida for the Republican Party. "He was the right-hand man to the state chairman," said Tommy Thomas, who chaired Reagan's 1976 and 1980 Florida campaigns. "He did an outstanding job." One reporter who covers Florida politics said the Reagan campaign was pleased with Auchter's work because "he could be in charge or he could take orders."

Auchter is unlikely to make a career of occupational safety and health—he hasn't demonstrated any noticeable interest in the science of the problem—so it may well be that he is using the OSHA spot as a springboard to a political career. He's a perfect candidate for the video age: handsome, glib, and programmed with the basic Reagan buzzwords against big, unresponsive government. "He certainly would have [a political future] if he wanted one," Thomas told us. "He would certainly be a very attractive candidate if he wanted to be one."

Auchter was born on March 6, 1945 in Jacksonville. He is married with three children.

MAJOR ISSUES

- Auchter sharply reduced federal workplace inspections during his first nine months in office.

- He has presented regulatory plans that would further reduce the federal role by allowing some firms to "self-inspect" their workplaces and by exempting three-fourths of all manufacturers from routine inspections.

- Several major occupational health standards—including those governing exposure to lead, workplace noise, and "right to know" about chemicals used on the job—have been watered down.

- Other major proposals, such as the cotton dust and carcinogen rules, are being reconsidered.

- OSHA has certified state plans previously considered unacceptable.

Repeating Reagan's own sentiments during the campaign, Auchter has undertaken a major policy shift for OSHA, from an enforcement-oriented agency toward a sort of federal consulting firm, relying more heavily on efforts by business itself to clean up the workplace. "Consultation and education will be increased and improved," Auchter told a union audience in June, 1981. "The states will play a larger role. We will begin encouraging employers to do self-inspection of their workplaces. And OSHA will become the catalyst to encourage various employer/employee approaches to workplace health and safety." On another occasion, Auchter declared OSHA should be "neutral" between industry and labor.

"OSHA has certainly not been the positive force that Congress envisioned," Auchter told us.

If nothing else, Auchter has been busy. He has made it easier for states—even those with job safety programs of questionable efficacy—to assume leading roles for policing the workplace. He has exempted the vast majority of workplaces from routine inspections, slashed the number of inspections and the fines given out, and proposed to allow certain companies to "self-inspect" their workplaces and avoid OSHA inspections altogether. OSHA, Auchter told us, has been too "confrontational" in the past. That attitude, he maintains, has been "extremely detrimental."

Union occupational health officials, and many health officials within the agency, believe that instead Auchter's policies will be extremely detrimental to the health of working people. "In previous administrations, you get a swing to be pro-union or pro-management, depending on whether Democrats or Republicans were coming in," said one high OSHA official. "These guys are different—they want to stop the whole thing."

"He has been the most negative force on OSHA since its inception," George Taylor, director of occupational safety and health for the AFL-CIO, told us. "I don't think anybody has ever designed to go out and gut the act, in the name of God and Reagan, with the zeal of Auchter." Tony Mazzocchi, former vice-president of the Oil, Chemical and Atomic Workers, and one of the nation's leading experts on occupational health, seconded Taylor's view. "Every other administrator at least said they were trying to carry out the congressional mandate. . .there may have been delays. . .but here is an individual dedicated to dismantling the apparatus," he said. "I just think. . .in the shortest time possible, he's dismantling what has been done over a decade."

Figures on the agency's inspection activities bear that out. Compared to the first nine months of 1980, all OSHA inspection actions were significantly reduced during the similiar period under Auchter's administration. Under Auchter:

- total inspections declined 21 percent;
- serious citations declined 33 percent;
- willful citations declined 75 percent;
- repeat citations declined 48 percent;
- total penalties (in dollars) declined 48 percent;
- complaints filed dropped 26 percent;
- complaints backlogged rose 189 percent.

In the field, the cutback in inspections is obvious. "Nothing is going on. They've cut it back to the quick," said Ed Sadlowski, assistant director of District 31 of the United Steelworkers of America and former candidate for the union's presidency. "They're not making the physical inspections—you don't even hear the OSHA question coming up anymore. . .you don't even see the guys in the plant using it anymore."

Auchter's proposals make OSHA inspection activities certain to further decline in the future. In September, 1981 Auchter announced a "targeted inspection program that exempts firms whose accident rate does not exceed the national average."

In January, 1982 he came out with a proposal—rejected earlier by Congress—to allow selected firms that set up self-policing programs to escape OSHA inspections.

Auchter is more comfortable making these sorts of moves than resolving the complex scientific questions about the agency's occupational health standards. Unlike his predecessor, Dr. Eula Bingham, Auchter has little personal grounding in the science of occupational health. "I'm not a scientist," he told us. "I'm a manager and a regulator." That is reflected in his office, filled with flow charts and management graphs that depict elaborate interconnected circles of decision and the administrative decathlon a proposal must complete before becoming a regulation. He talks about the need "to reprioritize on a regular basis."

According to one high OSHA health official, Auchter has little interest in expanding his scientific knowledge. "Auchter does not want to understand this. It's a nuisance to him. It's time consuming," said the official. "When an assistant secretary has to ask what beryllium is, I think that gives some indication. . .His tolerance for scientific discussion, even translating scientific discussion into lay terms, is very low."

We received a glimpse of that attitude during our interview with Auchter. At one point we asked him what he thought of the estimate prepared by the National Cancer Institute and the National Institute of Occupational Safety and Health which associated up to 38 percent of all U.S. cancer with an occupational exposure. Denounced by many business groups—though largely validated by a business-commissioned review—the study is pointed to by labor as demonstrating the need for strong regulation of cancer-causing chemicals in the workplace.

Auchter told us he thought the "data is probably very soft." And, he said, "It's an estimate, I'm sure there are others." When we pressed a bit further, he acknowledged that he had not read the report.

Four major standards were initially reopened for reconsideration by agency task forces directed by Mark Cowan, a former CIA attorney who began as Auchter's special assistant for regulatory affairs and was later named his deputy. The standards under review govern workplace exposure to cotton dust, lead and occupational noise; the fourth rule, known as the labeling standard, would require manufacturers to inform workers of the chemical identities of the substances with which they work.

A fifth major standard, setting procedures for regulating cancer-causing substances, was reopened in December, 1981. A standard requiring firms to pay employees for the time they spend on OSHA inspections—the "walkaround" rule—was revoked.

One task force participant told us: "The concept of teamwork is good. But the underlying objective here is to weaken and delay. . .Cowan has made apparent that we're going to listen to industry. Industry is going to call the shots on these standards."

Originally, Auchter intended to subject the standards to cost-benefit analysis, in line with a February, 1981 Reagan Executive Order on regulation. Since the Supreme Court was already considering whether OSHA can perform cost-benefit analysis in a case regarding the cotton dust standard, Auchter asked the court to drop the matter and send the standard back to OSHA. "If we sat back and let things proceed with the court," Cowan said in a June interview, "there was a possibility that the cost-benefit would have been decided against us. So we would have been up the creek without a paddle."

Rejecting Auchter's request to drop the case, the Supreme Court ruled against the use of cost-benefit analysis on June 17, 1981. In light of the decision, Auchter began paddling and said the agency would not use cost-benefit analysis for health standards, and instead would employ a four-step process, culiminating in the use of "cost-effective" regulation—which generally means the substitution of personal protective equipment, such as respirators, for engineering controls. The use of such regulation has long been advocated by top Administration officials such as Murray Weidenbaum, chairman of the Council of Economic Advisers and James C. Miller, III, who was executive director of the President's regulatory task force until moving to FTC. Many in Washington believe that Miller was really directing OSHA policy in the early months of the Administration.

Numerous studies have questioned the ability of respirators and other personal protective equipment to provide adequate safety, leading occupational health professionals to consider their use simply another strategem for weakening OSHA. "Respirators are not the solution to cleaning up the workplace," said Dr. Eula Bingham, OSHA director under President Carter. "It is certainly the least effective route because of leaks and the lack of adequate protection. But I expect them to push respirators whether they protect adequately or not."

OSHA has not issued standards on any unregulated toxic substance since Auchter took office, and few expect many to come out under his administration. "We expect a dimunition of the efforts in the previous administration toward more health standards," said Taylor of the AFL-CIO.

In August, 1981 Auchter reissued a watered-down noise protection standard; portions of the lead standard, significantly weakened, were delivered to a federal court in December of that year. In March, 1982 Auchter published a revised labeling standard—which increased employers' ability to claim "trade secret" protection and thereby cut back worker access to the actual names of chemicals they handle.

The rule had been held up at OMB, which had, as its top regulatory official Chris DeMuth told us, "serious problems" with Auchter's proposal. But DeMuth relented under pressure from the chemical industry, which preferred one national rule to those proliferating at the state level.

Auchter's plans to delegate more authority to the states has also run into opposition. In March, 1981 he dropped a case brought by Bingham to decertify Indiana's state OSHA plan. And in July, he rejected petitions by three unions and a Virginia county to withdraw certification for that state's plan. Both state programs are among the three worst in the country, Taylor maintains. A 1979 internal OSHA study of the Virginia program also found serious problems, concluding that the "Virginia enforcement scheme renders the state program substantially less effective than the federal system." In October, Auchter reduced the number of inspectors a state must have to receive federal approval.

Those standards Auchter is not addressing are as important as those he is attempting to weaken. "I don't think they have ignored a single important area," said Frank Mirer, director of health and safety for the United Auto Workers (UAW). "They are deliberately not doing anything." Mirer said standards that need to be strengthened include those governing:

- isocyanates, a lung-disease inducing chemical used in making polyurethane;

- silica, which induces a lung-scarring disease called silicosis;

- chromates; and

- nickel, neither of which "were set with their cancer-causing properties in mind."

The efforts of OSHA's scientific personnel may be chilled by the attempted June, 1981 firing of Dr. Peter Infante, head of OSHA's Office of Carcinogen Identification. Infante was fired after he wrote a letter to the International Agency for Research on Cancer (IARC), criticizing the manner in which an agency working group concluded there was only "limited" evidence that formaldehyde caused cancer in animals. On May 28, IARC director John Higginson dashed off to Auchter a stiff response to Infante's letter. In a letter dated five days later, an attorney for the Formaldehyde Institute wrote Cowan, asking, "How do you control members of the bureaucracy who seem to be operating freely within and without government and who seem to have made a decision and now are advocating a position rather than processing information for the appropriate policy decision-makers?"

Sometime earlier, Cowan had met with representatives of the Institute to discuss their objections to a technical publication on formaldehyde scheduled to be released by OSHA and the National Institute for Occupational Safety and Health (NIOSH). The document recommended that formaldehyde be treated as a potential carcinogen. After the meeting, Cowan wrote Auchter in a confidential memo that the Formaldehyde Institute representatives "presented me with what I consider to be significant evidence leading to the conclusion that the [document] on formaldehyde ought not, at present, be released." Auchter agreed and 25,000 copies of the document with a joint OSHA/NIOSH identification were called to warehouses. NIOSH later issued the bulletin itself. (Several months earlier, Auchter had recalled an agency booklet on cotton dust, alleging it was "biased" against industry.)

Infante's firing sparked congressional hearings. At the hearings, Dr. Bailus Walker, who signed the dismissal letter, testified that he suggested to Auchter that they "simply discuss the issue with him [Infante] and use the informal route," but that Auchter preferred a "formal" approach—firing Infante. In direct conflict, Auchter testified that he had "absolutely not" directed Infante's firing, and that Walker had suggested the idea. "That is totally incorrect," Walker told us later. "The issue of firing Peter was never asked by me."

Rep. Albert Gore (D-Tenn.), who directed the investigation, charged at the hearings that: "To fire this scientist for expressing his scientific opinion on formaldehyde is a blatant effort to rid the government of a competent scientist whose well-founded views happened not to agree with an industry whose profits are at stake." Infante contested his dismissal, and Auchter backed off the efforts to fire him in August, 1981.

But Auchter has continued to take a hard line on formaldehyde itself, despite warnings about its carcinogenicity from such authoritative sources as Dr. Arthur Upton, former director of the National Cancer Institute. "As far as OSHA is concerned," Auchter told us, "formaldehyde is not a human carcinogen at this time." Arguing that "we have certain processes to follow," he said that "for me to fire from the hip [on formaldehyde] would be totally irresponsible."

Auchter's overall effect on OSHA has already been devastating, all of the occupational health experts we spoke with agreed. The threat is more than the standards ignored or the inspectors muzzled. "There is a hemorrhage of OSHA talent," said

Mirer, which will take time to replace. It will be harder to find those people, Mirer continued, because the removal of government pressure has made the companies less anxious to hire occupational health professionals—and that in turn discourages students from specializing in the field. Cuts in NIOSH are weakening the research and educational base of occupational health. "There's no question that the field has been set back from where it would have been," Mirer said. "They won't push us back to before 1972—not in four years anyway. Maybe in eight."

FINANCIAL BACKGROUND

Auchter comes from the construction industry, whose relations with OSHA have never been good. He is a millionaire, with his interests held in large long-held trusts. Between them, the two trusts contain Auchter company stock worth over $1.5 million, as well as substantial holdings in DuPont, Exxon, Pepsico, and RCA. Auchter earned a $45,140 salary from the Auchter Co., in 1980.

WHAT OTHERS ARE SAYING ABOUT HIM

- Steve Wodka, formerly international safety and health representative of the Oil, Chemical and Atomic Workers Union, then perhaps the most active union on health and safety issues, said Auchter "has been put in there with a specific purpose: to dismantle any effectiveness the agency might have."

- Eula Bingham, former OSHA director, holds a similar views. "I can repeat what I said back in September about Reagan—that he would bring the place to a halt. And I think that is what happened. . .the standards that have moved are the ones that the courts have forced. And they are certainly not being vigorously enforced."

- Said one high OSHA official: "For a person who has only a baccalaureate, whose experience with occupational safety and health has been with his dad's construction firm how can he deal with this stuff? I don't think he's going to survive there very long."

- Jack Sheehan, legislative director for the Steelworkers Union told us: "You don't have a sense of vitality about OSHA. You do find them concentrating on the negatives—about what OSHA shouldn't be doing."

- Mark deBernardo, a U.S. Chamber of Commerce labor lawyer, delivered perhaps the most telling assessment of Auchter's performance when he told the *Wall Street Journal*, "A lot of what Auchter is doing is what Mark deBernardo and the Chamber of Commerce have been advocating for a long time."

- Overall though, labor has attracted surprisingly little attention to Auchter. He has not received a fraction of the criticism of Gorsuch or Watt, though he is strangling his agency every bit as effectively. Labor leaders have to bear part of the blame for that; few would argue that they have displayed the verve and doggedness of the groups following the EPA and Interior. But Frank Mirer of the UAW cites other causes as well. "It's only because occupational safety and health is a less broad-based issue than the others," he said. "Really EPA is a much bigger and broader-based agency than OSHA." We asked Mirer if he thought top labor leaders were doing enough to defend occupational safety and health. He paused for a long moment before responding. "I think we're doing qualitatively more than we've ever done before and it should be more than that," he said finally. "I think, given the other issues, we're getting about our fair share. . .but the total amount of political pressure that the unions have been able to bring to bear on the Administration and Congress hasn't been enough."

FORD B. FORD
ASSISTANT SECRETARY, MINE SAFETY AND HEALTH ADMINISTRATION

RESPONSIBILITY OF OFFICE

Established under 1977 amendments to the 1969 Federal Coal Mine Health and Safety Act, MSHA is charged with "preventing and reducing mine accidents and occupational diseases in the mining industry." Under the 1977 act it regulates metal and nonmetal, as well as coal mines. Its responsibilities are to:

- develop and promulgate mandatory safety and health standards;

- ensure compliance with standards;

- work with states to develop safety and health programs.

The agency operated with a budget of $149 million and 2,719 employees in 1982.

The agency is responsible for protecting 235,000 coal miners in 2,335 underground mines and 2,375 surface mines (as well as 1,185 surface facilities); and another 295,000 workers in 977 underground and 922 open pit metal mines (and 461 mills connected to those operations). Until 1981, when Congress transferred the authority to OSHA as a way to weaken enforcement, MSHA also inspected over 12,000 sand and gravel and quarrying operations with 180,000 workers. "OSHA hasn't got the faintest chance of inspecting them," said one MSHA official. "I think they've inspected a dozen since they got the authority."

BACKGROUND

During a 25-year career in Sacramento, Ford B. Ford worked his way from total, to relative, obscurity. From the mid-1950s until his appointment, Ford had worked in the California Legislature, in the executive branch, and for most of the past decade as a lobbyist influencing government in the field of occupational health.

But almost two dozen phone calls to California officials, legislative aides, union lobbyists and reporters turned up only a handful of people who had even heard his name. And those that did recognize him were less than glowing in describing his commitment to occupational health.

Ford picked up his most relevant job experience as chairman of the California Occupational Safety and Health Appeals Board from 1973-1978. Appointed by Reagan, "Ford was clearly the employer advocate on the board," said one high-ranking California occupational health official. "The impression that we always had from those folks was that there was no evidence that OSHA was improving safety and health and that OSHA was going too far."

When his term expired and Gov. Jerry Brown declined to reappoint him, Ford became vice-president of the California Institute for Industrial and Governmental Relations, a firm whose soaring title belied its pecuniary ambitions. Little-known among union and occupational health experts in the state, the firm primarily represented businesses before the appeals board that Ford had chaired. At the time of his appointment, Ford was also a registered lobbyist for the California Rental Association, an equipment leasing trade association, and the Tahoe City Public Utilities District. He also lobbied for the Pacific Coast Federation of Fishermen's Associations.

Ford had helped to establish the appeals board from his post as deputy secretary of the California Resources Agency, a job he held for Ronald Reagan from 1967. In the 1950s, he had held a variety of posts in the California state legislature. Acting postmaster of Bishop, California from 1951 to 1954, Ford also has experience as a construction inspector and a Coca-Cola franchise manager.

Born on November 19, 1922 in Norton, Virginia, Ford received a degree in production management and control from Berkeley in 1948. He is married with two grown children.

MAJOR ISSUES

To display the impact of the Mine Health and Safety Act on life and death in the mines, the United Mine Workers (UMW) union distributes a series of charts. With jagged lines, and bars, they make a clear point: since the passage of the act, the number of mining disasters, the number of deaths per disaster, and the death rate per million tons of coal mined have all declined.

Then came the Reagan Administration.

For the first time since the act was passed, the number of mining deaths rose between 1980 and 1981 from 133 to 153. That was despite a contract strike that kept miners out of the mines for 10 weeks early in the year. During the first 20 days of 1982, another 14 miners were killed.

"This has been terrible," Ford lamented in *Business Week*.

Crocodile tears, says the mine workers union. In fiscal year 1981, under the Reagan Administration, inspections were down 8 percent from 1980, follow-up inspections down 8 percent, citations down 15 percent, and the number of orders issued down 13 percent. To comply with 1982 budget cuts, Ford originally indicated he might cut as many as 700 staff positions. "A cut of this size in a single year will clearly disrupt the agency's already limited ability to protect miners on the job and to carry out education and training functions vital to development of a preventive approach to mine accidents," wrote J. Davitt McAteer of the Center for Law and Social Policy and Dr. Sidney Wolfe, director of the Health Research Group in a letter to Congress.

When the mine workers threatened a strike over the weakening of MSHA, Reagan announced in February, 1982 that he would restore $2 million to the agency's 1982 budget and $15 million to its 1983 budget. But a close look at the budget shows how the President easily can use misleading figures to obscure the Administration's real actions. The purported "increases" merely offsets cuts already imposed by Reagan; when all the numbers are totalled up MSHA would only be back at its 1981 level, and still significantly below what Jimmy Carter had proposed for 1982.

As "Deep Throat" advised, it pays to follow the money. The agency's actual 1981 budget was $152.2 million. Carter proposed a $166.8 million budget for 1982; Reagan in March, 1981 revised that down to $157.5 million. In September, 1981, as part of his across-the-board 12 percent slash in domestic agencies, Reagan proposed to cut the budget back to $138.6 million. Congress rejected that proposal and gave MSHA $149.3 million. So when all was finished in 1982, Reagan's first budget, the agency had $17 million less than Carter had proposed, and $3 million less than it had in 1981. (Reagan would like to give it another $2 million for 1982, which would put MSHA $1 million short of 1981.)

For 1983, Reagan again proposed to cut the agency's funding back to $138.8 million. It was from that total that he "restored" the $15 million, bringing the agency's funding to $153.8 million, $1 million more than the actual total in 1981, and still $12 million less than Jimmy Carter planned to give the agency in 1982.

Ford had also approved a reorganization plan that would, beginning in 1982, require the district offices to handle education and training programs as well as inspections. "The people in the field should be doing inspections," said Mike Buckner, research manager for the UMW. And other UMW officials and mine safety experts are already concerned that the new attitude in Washington is encouraging some mining operations to pay less attention to safety rules. The Reagan Administration's attitude, wrote Wolfe and McAteer, is "encouraging mine operators to believe that federal mine safety regulations are being eased and need not be respected." Five inspectors told Congress in February, 1982 that Ford's clear opposition to vigorous enforcement was "systematically destroying the morale" of inspectors.

Before three major mine accidents killed 24 miners within a week in early December, 1981, the Reagan Administration and some members of Congress had been looking for ways to slow down MSHA. As part of an effort to end what he considered an inappropriate adversarial relationship with the mining industry, Ford had said he was "seriously considering" a plan to allow mine operators to "self-certify that they had complied with safety laws." "This system," wrote Wolfe and McAteer, "would clearly be inappropriate for an industry with a long record of failure to correct violations even when *ordered* to do so." And the Administration was working with conservative senators to cut the agency's inspection budget in half. After initial success, that effort was defeated.

But Ford and the Administration were constrained in what they could do because the 1969 act was unusually specific. "It's much more limited than what [Thorne] Auchter can do at OSHA," explained Buckner. "He has very limited ability to stop those things [that the agency does]."

The UMW will also press the Administration to reduce the permissible exposure limit to coal dust, which causes the debilitating lung disease known as black lung. But, almost needless to say, it is not optimistic about MHSA tightening the standard. The act mandates the number of inspections that must be conducted, and the amount of safety training that miners must receive.

So Sen. Orrin Hatch (R-Utah), who chairs the Senate Labor and Human Resources Committee, is trying to change the act. In a sweeping bill, Hatch would cut the number of mandatory inspections at underground mines from four to two, cut the number of hours of training by up to 75 percent, allow operators to request "penalty-free" inspections, and permanently transfer responsibility for much surface mining to an already-overburdened OSHA. The Administration has not taken a formal position on the legislation, but congressional sources expect the Administration to fall in line behind the bill. The legislation has been stalled by strong union opposition.

Ford's role in all these decisions is unclear. "He readily admits," said Buckner, "he knows nothing about coal mining."

And Ford is hardly one of the Administration's most headstrong, energetic appointees. "I can't imagine him storming into OMB, slamming his books down, and demanding more money," continued Buckner, who has met with him. "He's not your Washington type. He's not going to be able to take all the bitching we're going to deliver and all the screaming industry is going to deliver." We offered Ford a chance to respond to these criticisms of his performance, and his office said he would accept written questions, which we submitted. But he then refused to answer them. Around Ford, the word sinecure has a cozy feel.

FINANCIAL BACKGROUND

Ford reported earnings from the California Institute for Industrial and Governmental Relations of $6,000 in 1980 and $8,000 in 1981. He reported assets worth at least $78,000, most of which consisted of two small houses in Bishop, California.

WHAT OTHERS ARE SAYING ABOUT HIM

- Buckner tells a revealing story. When Buckner met with Ford, the new assistant secretary lamented that when he was in California if he needed Reagan's approval on some matter, he could get it in an afternoon. Now, he sighed, there are so many channels to go through. Moral: Ford's activities at MSHA will be closely watched and regulated by the Administration.

- Beulah Gibson, a 26-year-old coal miner's widow told a congressional committee in March, 1982: "I suggest that Mr. Ford work one day in a coal mine like the one owned by Orville Adkins [where an explosion in December, 1981 killed eight men]. I believe that Mr. Ford would learn in one day that coal production comes first and foremost and is far more important to the company than the safety of its men."

HEALTH AND HUMAN SERVICES DEPARTMENT

RICHARD SCHWEIKER
SECRETARY

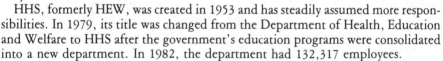

RESPONSIBILITY OF OFFICE

Schweiker describes his job as "awe-inspiring," overseeing a department which "spends more money ($252.9 billion in 1982) than any country in the world except the Soviet Union and the United States."

As HHS head, Schweiker administers most of the health, welfare and income security programs provided by the federal government. The most prominent of these, of course, is the Social Security program. Medicare for the aged and disabled, Medicaid for the poor, and Aid to Families with Dependent Children (AFDC) are among the other programs under his jurisdiction.

HHS, formerly HEW, was created in 1953 and has steadily assumed more responsibilities. In 1979, its title was changed from the Department of Health, Education and Welfare to HHS after the government's education programs were consolidated into a new department. In 1982, the department had 132,317 employees.

BACKGROUND

Schweiker retired from the U.S. Senate in December, 1980, concluding a 20-year career in Congress as a Republican representative of Pennsylvania (eight years in the House, 12 years in the Senate).

For many years Schweiker was considered among the most liberal Republicans in Congress, remembered most for his criticism of the Vietnam War, and opposition to President Nixon's nominees to the Supreme Court—Clement F. Haynsworth, Jr. and G. Harrold Carswell.

Then, Schweiker underwent a rapid reversal in 1976, when Reagan asked him to be his presidential running mate prior to the GOP national convention. Before that time, the two men hardly knew each other. But Reagan strategists felt he needed a moderate politician from the Northeast to balance his ticket. Schweiker eagerly accepted the offer, despite criticism from his liberal colleagues. With Schweiker, Reagan campaign aides were looking to pry the Pennsylvania delegation led by Drew Lewis away from Gerald Ford. But Lewis held firm, temporarily straining his friendship with Schweiker.

Schweiker has been the ranking Republican on both the Senate Labor and Human Resources Committee, and the Labor-Health and Human Services Appropriations Subcommittee, the two Senate units which controlled both authorizing legislation and appropriations for labor, health, education, aging and public welfare matters.

After serving an apprenticeship knocking on doors as a Republican precinct worker in Pennsylvania, Schweiker began his political career in 1960 as a reformer. He successfully ran in the Republican 13th Congressional District primary as an out-sider, challenging John Lafore, the chosen candidate of the county Republican organization. In an interview with the Public Citizen Congress Project several years later, Schweiker criticized the "closed operation" of the local Republicans and argued that the party had failed to attract "young people, community oriented people," instead relying on the wealthy "main line" suburbs. In 1966, citing Schweiker's support for Medicare, Lafore challenged him again. But Schweiker turned him away by a 3 to 1 margin. Two years later, Schweiker unseated two-term veteran Sen. Joseph Clark, castigating the Democrat's "dovish" policies. But the key issue in the race was Schweiker's opposition to gun control (Clark supported such measures), which generated intense support for his candidacy from the pro-gun lobbies.

Schweiker's early voting record included support for many programs in disrepute at the White House today. He backed tougher regulation of flammable fabrics and proposed legislation to increase nutritional education and nutritional labeling on foods. He sought to tighten up the Coal Mine Health and Safety Act of 1969, and proposed to ban the use of lead-based paint in homes. On foreign policy issues, he often opposed the Nixon Administration, rejecting positions today supported by Reagan. Schweiker not only voted against deployment of the ABM system, but held a splashy press conference with three other Republican senators to explain why. (For more on the ABM see profile of Richard Perle.) He voted for measures to cut off funds for the Vietnam War, and long advocated the elimination of the draft. (In 1967, he co-authored a book with four other representatives entitled: *How to End the Draft: The Case for an All-Volunteer Army.*)

After 1976, Schweiker's voting record drifted toward the right. His Public Citizen voting index—which charts votes on key consumer issues—dropped from a 75 in the 94th Congress to a 36 in the 95th Congress to a 29 in the 96th Congress. In his last year in Congress he received a 23. That rating included four separate votes to weaken the Federal Trade Commission, a vote to weaken strip mining regulation, and support for a Jesse Helms amendment to cut legal services funding. He also pushed legislation to weaken the Occupational Safety and Health Administration (OSHA), which estranged him from organized labor.

As ranking Republican on the health subcommittee, Schweiker's record on health issues was mixed in the 96th Congress. While generally supporting "pro-competition" bills and limited federal influence, Schweiker sometimes jumped fences. For instance, in 1978 Schweiker was one of only six Republicans who voted in favor of a bill to authorize $440 million for a National Institute of Health Care Research. (The bill was rejected 30-48.) Again, in 1980, he joined Sen. Edward Kennedy (D-Mass.) in sponsoring a bill that established a "mental patient's bill of rights" enforceable by HHS. Schweiker's liberal stance on the mental health issue was fleeting. Less than six months after supporting Kennedy's legislation, the new HHS secretary allowed the mental health program to be included among the 40 programs originally consolidated for block grants. "It is an interesting little turn-around," a former Kennedy aide wryly noted, "but it is just indicative of how the political winds have changed since the election."

Schweiker was born in Norristown, Pennsylvania, on June 1, 1926. His father owned a tile company, that was later purchased by the National Gypsum Company (NGC). At 17, he enlisted in the Navy, serving in the Pacific in World War II as an electronic technician's mate aboard an aircraft carrier. In 1950, he was graduated from Pennsylvania State University, Phi Beta Kappa. In 1955 he married Claire Coleman, the hostess of the Philadelphia version of the children's television show "Romper Room." They have five children and one grandchild.

MAJOR ISSUES

- Programs, such as Social Security, which were originally targeted as "social safety net" programs, soon fell prey to the budget-cutting force of the Office of Management and Budget (OMB) and Schweiker. Sharp cuts for Medicare and Medicaid are slated in the 1983 budget.

- AFDC cuts hit the poor at a time when they are already absorbing massive cuts in several other areas such as food stamps and school lunch programs.

- Schweiker is pushing to fold numerous HHS programs into block grants that will in many cases merely transfer the responsibility (and the blame) for sizeable budget cuts from the federal government to the localities.

- Schweiker opposes federal funding for sex education or abortions, and is backing new proposals that would require family planning agencies to notify the parents of minors seeking contraceptives.

Schweiker has been waiting for his current opportunity. After the February, 1981 release of the President's economic program, Schweiker said, "This is our last opportunity and best opportunity. If we don't do it now, we never will."

In the beginning of the Administration Schweiker pledged to "maintain the integrity of the Social Security program," deeming it his "highest priority." But later in the spring, Schweiker joined Budget Director David Stockman in calling for Social Security cuts. Congress eventually salvaged most of the proposed cuts and Reagan backed off from the plan, but Schweiker has indicated his desire to pursue further cuts in the future. (See John Svahn profile.)

Most of the major budget cuts at HHS are directed at a broad array of health and welfare programs. One of the most controversial proposals is to place "a cap" on the federal portion of Medicaid payments, supposedly to give states added incentive to crack down on administrative mistakes. (The federal government paid $15.6 billion of a total of $28.5 billion spent on Medicaid in fiscal year 1981.) Schweiker's proposal would have increased the burden on the states by imposing an 8 percent cut in federal funds.

"The impact this 'cap' will have on future years is what has us worried," said David Riemer, director of the Human Resources Committee for the National Conference of State Legislatures. "A long-term reduction of federal services is going to harm some states worse than others. Sooner or later, somebody is going to lose out."

Congress rejected the cap, but approved Medicaid cutbacks totaling $1 billion annually. Medicaid played a key role in Reagan's sweeping "New Federalism" proposal made during the 1982 State of the Union address, with the Administration proposing to buy out the state share of the expenses; in return the states would assume responsibility for AFDC and food stamps. The key question regarding Medicaid was left unanswered with the proposal: Once switched back to the federal government would the benefits be evened out at some national level? That could penalize states with high-benefits and help those that give lesser coverage. Given the Administration's budget posture, of course, it seems likely the balance would be struck on the lower end of the spectrum. Schweiker resisted the plan during the Administration's internal deliberations, fearing that it had not been thought through.

At least one million Medicaid recipients will become ineligible because of changes in the law governing the AFDC program, which qualifies the poor for medical aid. But those are only numbers. The reality of the reductions was portrayed in elegant and poignant simplicity by Spencer Rich and Margaret Engel of the *Washington Post* through the story of Lois Gatewood of Woodbridge, Virginia:

> There is no safety net for Gatewood, a 73-year-old diabetic with failing eyesight, as she precariously makes her way alongside four lanes of busy traffic on her twice-weekly journey to buy insulin.
>
> She cannot afford the $4 cab fare from her trailer home and rarely can find a neighbor with a car to drive her. And, as she discovered when she collapsed in the drugstore one day recently, the Reagan Administration's budget cuts mean she cannot afford the tiny $9.40 bottles of life-sustaining medicine either.
>
> "What's people like us going to do?" agonized the sobbing woman who swooned into a chair at the store out of weakness and anxiety over payment when she learned her Medicaid card no longer was honored and she would not be eligible for the state's medically needy program...Her Medicaid card first was pulled in July, when the annual Social Security cost-of-living increase inched her over the eligibility cutoff. . .

We wanted to ask Schweiker what his response was to the story of Lois Gatewood, among other subjects. But he declined to be personally interviewed. His actions, though, speak loudly:

For 1983, the Administration proposed further cuts of $2.5 billion in Medicare and $2 billion in Medicaid. Sharp cuts were also proposed for childhood immunization programs, raising fears of renewed outbreaks of childhood illnesses. "If the program is not maintained, we can expect a resurgence of disease," Dr. Frederick Robbins, president of the National Academy of Science's Institute of Medicine, has said.

(But Schweiker has managed to overlook some savings. Congress Watch has estimated that Medicaid spends about $125 million on prescription drugs considered ineffective by the Food and Drug Administration (FDA). In the 1981 reconciliation bill, Congress ordered HHS to cease paying for such drugs by October 1. On October 1, HHS unilaterally asked for a 90-day extension. The Health Research Group successfully sued to overturn that decision, but congressional Republicans later added to a continuing resolution a provision repealing the prohibition on paying for ineffective drugs. So HHS continues to spend millions of dollars on pills that don't work.)

State officials have voiced the same concerns about welfare payments. Schweiker's budget reductions made it through Congress intact, leading state officials to wonder where the welfare funds would come from under the new system. The federal government will now offer considerably less support than in the past. The 1983 budget seeks to cut another $1.2 billion from federal welfare costs. It also requires all states to start "workfare" programs.

One prominent study (conducted by Thomas C.W. Joe, a former Nixon welfare official) concluded: "In its stampede to produce federal spending cuts, Congress proposed a method of federal financing in AFDC and Medicaid that is far more devastating to states, and ultimately the poor, than any other policy change proposal thus far." Turning the AFDC program over to hard-pressed states seems certain to force further benefit reductions.

Block grants in the health programs have caused a different concern. Schweiker's program will be providing less overall funding and almost certainly less federal accountability with the remaining grants. Critics worry about heightened tensions between recipient groups at the state and local level leading to a situation which could pit poor people against each other in a scramble for federal dollars. Congress was not receptive to Schweiker's plan to fold 40 federal health programs into four block grants. By the end of the summer, Congress had boiled the plan down to just 21 programs divided among four block grants.

Like most other departments in the Administration, HHS is also facing broad regulatory changes under Schweiker. For instance, in the health field, the Administration has targeted both the health planning system and physician peer review program for abolition.

Each program was formed in the past decade to hold down rising health costs. The planning program is aimed at curbing unnecessary hospital expansion; peer review is intended to reduce use of medical services and facilities under Medicare and Medicaid. The Administration's stand has the avid support of both the American Medical Association and the American Hospital Association. Congress supported the peer review program in the 1982 budget, but the Administration's 1983 budget again seeks the elimination of funds. It also seeks to end federal assistance to Health Maintenance Organizations (HMO). Schweiker was a sponsor of the original HMO Act in 1972.

Schweiker's views on "family" issues are also clearly aligned with Reagan's. In this regard, Schweiker is in stark contrast to his predecessor, Patricia Roberts Harris, who was a strong supporter of sex education and family planning programs.

Schweiker has said "the government should not be in the business of sex education," and has been a long-time opponent of federal funding for abortions. He also opposes Medicaid funding of contraception for unmarried teen-agers. In spring, 1981 he stopped an HHS scientist from delivering congressional testimony which concluded that legalized abortion has reduced abortion-related deaths and disease. To head the department's Office of Adolescent Pregnancy Programs, Schweiker named Marjory Mecklenburg, a long-time anti-abortion activist. And according to an analysis by Planned Parenthood, the department has been dispensing family planning funds at a rate 20 percent lower than that authorized by Congress.

In February, 1982, Schweiker took his furthest step toward reorienting the government's policies in this area. Schweiker proposed rules that would require family planning agencies receiving federal dollars to notify the parents of minors under 18 who seek contraceptives. "We've built a Berlin Wall between the kid and the parents," Schweiker told a congressional hearing in February. "We think that's wrong." But to the plan's many critics—which range from congressional Democrats to the American Medical Association and the American Academy of Pediatrics—the rules would only discourage young people from seeking contraception, meaning more teenage pregnancies and more abortions. "It doesn't take a genius to read the handwriting on the wall," said Rep. Patricia Schroeder (D-Colo.). "The effect of parental notification requirements will be an increase in the number of teen-age pregnancies." Dr. George Ryan, president of the American College of Obstetricians and Gynecologists, has estimated that the proposal will result in "well over

100,000'' additional teen-age pregnancies annually. "This makes no sense on the grounds of health," he said.

These strong sentiments of resistance may ultimately convince the Administration to back off. Schweiker has shown a willingness to retreat in the face of political heat before. Late in 1981, press reports indicated that Schweiker was considering drastic weakening of HHS rules governing health and safety in nursing homes, including standards for infection control and the prevention of communicable disease. But in March, 1982, Schweiker abandoned the effort, saying, "The existing health and safety requirements will remain untouched. I will not turn back the clock." Not that clock anyway: Schweiker still plans to issue rules reducing inspection requirements for homes with a "record of sustained good performance." Those are the rules the regulatory reviewers at the White House were concerned about in the first place. HHS also drew up an elaborate plan to control medical costs relying on various private sector actions spurred through tax credits and benefits. But when virtually everyone concerned—labor, insurance companies, large corporations—rejected the idea, the Administration put it on a shelf. The alternative may have to be the mandatory hospital cost control legislation sponsored by President Carter and abhorred by Reaganites (Schweiker spoke against it at his confirmation hearing). Even Senate Finance Committee Chairman Robert Dole has said Congress might have made a "mistake" in rejecting the plan.

At his confirmation hearing, Schweiker said, "Without hesitation. . . .I would say that I would like to be remembered as the secretary who put preventive health care and preventive medicine at the very top of the federal medical agenda." Against that desire is the record of an Administration that has slashed federal efforts to reduce exposure to disease-causing chemicals; cut the budgets for nutrition programs for children and pregnant women; diminished enforcement and eliminated important regulatory protections at the Food and Drug Administration (See Arthur Hayes profile); reduced immunization expenditures; cut HHS funding for consumer affairs and smoking education; and refused to back stronger warnings on cigarettes, despite the incontrovertible medical evidence of its hazard. (See Everett Koop profile.) Whatever Schweiker's aspirations, it is that record—which stretches beyond his department, throughout the Reagan Administration—that will be judged.

FINANCIAL BACKGROUND

According to Schweiker's financial statement, the combined wealth of his immediate family is in excess of $690,000. Most of this money is tied up in the National Gypsum Company (NGC). His NGC investment is at least $465,000.

Schweiker's association with NGC can be traced to his father's small Pennsylvania tile firm, which was bought out by NGC several years ago. Schweiker retains the large investment in the firm which is partially divided in the names of his wife, Claire, and three of his five children.

(The 1968 "Schweiker for Senator" campaign was chaired by a vice-president of NGC, Drew Lewis, who is Schweiker's close friend and now secretary of Transportation.)

NGC has had a number of run-ins with the federal government in the past decade:

- In December of 1979 the President's Council on Wage and Price Stability announced NGC was not complying with the Administration's voluntary price guidelines.

- NGC has been embroiled in an antitrust case (involving price fixing) with the Justice Department.

- NGC's attempt to sell its cement division to General Dynamics (a major defense firm) has been questioned by the Bureau of Competition of the Federal Trade Commission.

- The tile firm which formerly belonged to his father (and now belongs to NGC) received a stiff penalty from OSHA early in 1980.

In light of Schweiker's recent voting record and his presence in the Reagan Administration, the latter two items are especially troublesome.

The implication of his anti-OSHA sentiments are most striking. Shortly after NGC received the OSHA penalty, Schweiker introduced the "Occupational Safety and Health Improvements" bill. Schweiker's legislation would have exempted most employers from most safety inspections if they filed affidavits claiming low rates of workplace injury. Eula Bingham, then head of OSHA, said the Schweiker bill would exclude 90 percent of the workplaces in America from inspection. One of Schweiker's first personnel changes as HHS Secretary was the firing of Dr. Anthony Robbins, the pro-worker safety head of the National Institute of Occupational Safety and Health (NIOSH). Shortly thereafter, NIOSH, which researches workplace health hazards, was budgeted for a one-third reduction in funds, and is scheduled to be moved to Atlanta.

WHAT OTHERS ARE SAYING ABOUT HIM

- According to close observers, Schweiker is plugged into a White House blueprint which leaves little room for independent action. "If you really look at some of these [HHS] appointments," says one HHS insider, "you don't see the fingerprints of Schweiker on hardly any of them."

- Former HHS head Patricia Roberts Harris speculates that White House aide Robert Carleson is dictating much of the social welfare policy together with OMB. "The law gives responsibility for these programs to the secretary for Health and Human Services," she said, ". . . not to the director of OMB or the White House policy advisers. I will say this—when I was secretary I always obeyed the law."

- Schweiker's experience and knowledge have been questioned by some observers who claim he is not on par with previous appointees. "I never considered Schweiker knowledgeable on the level with Joseph Califano [former HEW head under Carter]," said Betty Duskin of the National Council of Senior Citizens. "I always gave Califano credit for being very bright even though I disagreed with him on many issues. I do not give Schweiker the same credit."

- Anthony Robbins, the former NIOSH head, told us he believes Schweiker "hasn't really thought for himself" since he began his association with Reagan in 1976. "I wouldn't say Schweiker has exactly taken on an ultra-right wing, redneck attitude," he said. "It is more of a big money, big business sort of political attitude."

Robbins noted the circumstances of his firing as an example. Shortly before he was fired an article appeared in a Chamber of Commerce publication charging Robbins with being a "radical activist" with a "radical anti-business posture.'' Robbins, who has an excellent reputation in the health field, also was released from his duties as assistant surgeon general, an action which previously was only taken in cases of gross personal misconduct. The firing came as a total surprise to Robbins, who said all his previous contacts with Schweiker had been ''really friendly.''

''It is hard to make a guy like Schweiker into an evil character,'' Robbins said. ''[Schweiker] is simply the man who has to carry out this Reagan mandate of taking the federal governmental influence out of the private sector. Schweiker is just doing what he's told to do.''

- ''Out of one corner of his mouth he's the leading spokesman for prevention. . . of illness and out of the other corner he is doing whatever possible to destroy preventive programs within his own department,'' said Dr. Sid Wolfe, director of the Health Research Group, citing budget cuts for childhood immunization and smoking education, and decreasing enforcement of the food and drug laws at FDA.

ARTHUR HULL HAYES, JR.
COMMISSIONER, FOOD AND DRUG ADMINISTRATION

RESPONSIBILITY OF OFFICE

Historically, the primary responsibility of the 75-year-old FDA has been to protect ''the health of the Nation against impure and unsafe foods, drugs and cosmetics, and other potential hazards.''

However, Hayes believes the FDA has done its job so well that ''we no longer think about acute hazards. The issues that confront us today are much more subtle, much harder to diagnose and to resolve.''

Hence, Hayes has defined his job responsibility ''to see that FDA encourages development [of new drug therapies], remove unnecessary obstacles to research, and review data promptly, while at the same time affording the needed protection to research subjects as well as to patients who ultimately will receive those drugs.''

Hayes is the chief policymaker in FDA matters concerning drugs, foods, radiological health, veterinary medicine, medical devices and toxicological research.

In 1982, the FDA operated with a budget of $329 million and a staff of 7,159.

BACKGROUND

Recognized as one of the foremost clinical pharmacologists in the United States, Hayes since 1973 has primarily devoted himself to a hypertension clinic which he directed at the Hershey Medical Center, a part of the Pennsylvania State University network. Since 1973, he has also been chief of the Division of Clinical Pharmacology at the University's Medical School.

Prior to 1972, he spent several years as a teacher and researcher in pharmacology at Cornell University Medical College. Hayes had attended school there, graduating from the Cornell Graduate School of Medical Sciences almost a decade earlier. He belongs to 30 professional societies, and in 1980 was the president of the American Society for Clinical Pharmacology and Therapeutics. He has also served on the executive committee of the American Society for Pharmacology and Experimental Therapeutics.

Hayes considers that scientific background essential for his current job. "Do I think the commissioner should have a scientific background? Yes. I have no second thoughts," he told us. "I really think that a strong scientific base is important for the agency, and I think it is important for the leadership of the agency not excluding—indeed most importantly—the commissioner."

Hayes was graduated from the Bellarmine College Preparatory School in San Jose, California in 1951 and went on to obtain an A.B. degree in philosophy in 1955 from the University of Santa Clara, California. He then received both a Rhodes Scholarship and Danforth fellowship and obtained an M.A. (in philosophy, politics and economics) at Oxford University in England in 1957.

Finally, he pursued his medical education, attending Washington's Georgetown University for three years before moving on to Cornell University, where he received an M.D. in 1964. Hayes has served on the editorial boards of half a dozen medical and scientific publications.

Hayes was born July 18, 1933, in Highland Park, Michigan. He is the son of Arthur Hull Hayes, Sr., the former president of CBS Radio. From his father, Hayes has inherited a love of the water. Today, his office is festooned with all things nautical: model sailboats and globes surround his collection of mortar and pestles and a little dish of Hershey chocolates.

"Oh, my father lived on the water for many years," he said. "Or at least near the water and then on the water. And I used to love to sail. And though I was in the Army, not the Navy, I have always enjoyed boats. When we lived in central Pennsylvania it was only a little boat on a trailer; someday, I'd like to do a little bit more here. Any invitation I get to go sailing I accept if I can. I can think of no more way to relax and to reflect in the very best sense than to be out on a sailboat. It doesn't smell bad, it doesn't go too fast, it is not noisy and you don't have to go anyplace to enjoy yourself. You can sit there with the sun and the water and the wind—I know it sounds idyllic—but by God, you're away from the telephone, you're away from the door, you're away from the Hill. And the problem is finding the time to do it."

A slight, slim man, Hayes is soft spoken and unassuming. For all his academic credentials, he fills his conversation with such remarks as "My long suit, if I have any. . ." But he enjoys the hectic Washington work—"I talk to people in industry, I'm not afraid of them. I'm really not afraid of anybody. I don't really feel any pressure cooker here"—and has no plans to leave before 1984. "Unless you know something I don't," Hayes said.

Hayes is married with three children.

MAJOR ISSUES

- With Schweiker, Hayes stopped a Carter Administration program to provide patients with more information about prescription drugs.
- Under Hayes, FDA enforcement actions on both food and drugs have sharply declined.

- Though he came into office suggesting mandatory labeling of sodium content—and is well aware of the deleterious effects of sodium consumption through his research—Hayes eventually issued a voluntary proposal.

- Other labeling proposals have been derailed, though Hayes said action on sugar and fats may be forthcoming.

- Hayes has strongly suggested that he would support a change in the Delaney Amendment, which prohibits carcinogenic food additives; and he has displayed doubts about the underlying scientific methods used to regulate cancer-causing substances in food.

By his own account, Hayes spends most of his time—about equally divided—on drugs and food safety. Those are the contentious, high-visibility, issues within the sprawling FDA that attract the most press, public and congressional attention. Food safety, in particular, Hayes said will receive "very special attention" in his tenure.

Hayes arrived at the FDA without generating the intense opposition of many other Reagan regulatory appointments from Anne Gorsuch to James Miller. But his policies provoked increasing concern through 1981.

Hayes stepped delicately through the first drug dispute he faced involving so-called "paper NDAs."

At the heart of the dispute are the efforts of major pharmaceutical manufacturers to shield the market for brand-name drugs whose patents have expired, and are subject to competition from less costly generic versions.

The FDA had decided to allow generic manufacturers to file "paper" New Drug Applications—which assumed that the previously patented versions of the drug met the agency's requirements to demonstrate safety and effectiveness. This saved generic suppliers from expensive testing, and promoted competition, saving the public and the government money.

But the drug manufacturers sued the FDA in fall, 1980 and won a court decision staying the practice. When the stay expired in February, 1981 Health and Human Services Secretary Richard Schweiker invoked a freeze on generic drug approvals.

In a February, 1981 lawsuit, Dr. Sidney Wolfe, director of the Health Research Group, accused Schweiker of acting "illegally" and "under pressure from large drug companies."

"This is truly an outrage. . .a welfare program for the big drug companies," Wolfe told a House commerce investigations subcommittee which convened several days after Schweiker's "freeze."

Rep. Albert Gore (D-Tenn.) told the House panel that he believed the drug industry had too much influence in the Reagan Administration and expressed doubts that FDA would ever revoke the freeze.

But after Hayes arrived at FDA, an agreement was worked out and the freeze was lifted (the lawsuit was subsequently dropped). At the same time, however, Hayes and Schweiker said they would "advocate changes in patent laws [euphemistically called patent restoration] to help innovative pharmaceutical companies recover the investment they make in developing new therapies. This will serve to correct disincentives to innovative research."

Despite Hayes's statements against inappropriate drug prescriptions, the FDA's only action on the problem has been to eliminate a Carter Administration program designed to combat it. Prior to Hayes's appointment Public Citizen sued Schweiker for suspending already-finalized FDA regulations requiring that patients be provided with written information concerning the safety and effectiveness of certain prescription drugs. This information was to be provided in the form of patient package inserts (PPIs).

"The seriousness of the suspension of this important patient education program is demonstrated by the statement of former FDA commissioner Dr. Jere Goyan," said Dr. Wolfe, "Goyan has told me that he considered the regulations requiring patient package inserts for prescription drugs to be his most important accomplishment at FDA."

Though Hayes has repeatedly criticized doctors for the "frequent and inappropriate" use of drugs since 1975 and admits there are "shocking statistics on adverse reactions," he joined with Schweiker to announce at a December, 1981 press conference that the program will be eliminated for all but the existing three categories of drugs for which they are already provided.

Hayes is defensive about industry charges that the FDA review keeps beneficial drugs off the market. "It doesn't take a genius to realize that to say 100,000 people have died from lack of using a drug for an indication because we didn't approve it for that is like saying that in 20 years Dr. So and So is going to be faulted for all the misery that people have suffered from 1981 to the year 2000 from athletes foot when they could have been cured by aspirin in very large doses. And I say 'But I don't know that aspirin can cure athletes foot.' And they'll say, 'Ah, but a paper is going to come out in the year 2000 that's going to prove that.' Well I'm supposed to be so omniscient—not only prescient—that I know that now. I mean it is clairvoyance at its best. . . . That is just so irrational," he told us.

And Hayes has little patience for those that question the value of laws requiring the agency to certify the efficacy of drugs on the market. "Usually those who question that fundamental tenet of the efficacy law usually do it, I believe, not so much from some general philosophy or principle but because of a specific instance and they think that maybe the answer is not to have it [efficacy] and this never would have happened," he said. "But in fact if you tried to turn back the clock. . . it would mean that drugs were not shown to be effective or you relied on the marketplace or the literature as well as the awareness on the part of physicians and patients about that, and they [the critics] realize that it's much more complicated than they thought."

Nonetheless, the FDA policies are moving in a direction which should please the drug industry. Besides the regulatory changes, FDA enforcement actions for drugs in 1981 dropped 54 percent from the average of 393 annually from 1977-1980. Requirements that antibiotics be batch tested, at the companies' expense, for quality strength and purity, are to be dropped.

Hayes's attitudes on food issues are similar. Food enforcement actions dropped 47 percent in 1981 over the previous four years.

Early in his term at FDA Hayes expressed a willingness to consider labeling requirements for salt. But following a meeting with 200 food industry representatives on June 30, 1981, Hayes said he only favored voluntary labeling of salt content. As director of the hypertension clinic at Hershey Medical Center he saw the effects of high-sodium diets first hand. About 50 million Americans suffer from hypertension (high blood pressure).

It is possible Hayes may have tempered his views on salt labeling under pressure from the White House and the Department of Agriculture—both insisted in mid-April, 1981 that salt labeling remain voluntary.

"I received no pressure from any source in developing FDA's sodium program," Hayes maintained to us. "Essentially there were two approaches we could have tried. One was to start developing regulations to mandate sodium labeling. The administrative procedures to finalize those regulations would have taken literally years. And experience has shown that while proposed regulations are pending, industry is inclined not to take any initiatives." Hayes said that with the voluntary approach "I felt we might be able to see more results, and more prompt results."

Many others are not so sure, and Rep. Gore, chairman of the oversight subcommittee of the House Science and Technology committee, has introduced mandatory sodium labeling legislation. Hayes predicted that "probably in the next couple of months. . .50 percent of everything that's out there" will be complying with his voluntary proposal. "If you make the comparison I think we are going to be—within a year or so of when we first started doing this last summer—where we could have been with that bill," he said in December, 1981.

Sodium labeling is but one of a series of labeling proposals that the Carter Administration was considering in an integrated package. Staffers say that process has been derailed. "I do not want to do something that is so general that it dilutes the parts that we really know are important," Hayes said.

Asked what the next labeling priorities will be Hayes replied, "One of course that there is a lot of question about is the fats; unfortunately every day that gets more complicated rather than less. . . . The other one that I think is very important and therefore is at the top of the priority list for review is sugar. . .I think sugar could be very much like sodium."

Hayes has done little, but has already said much, about revising food safety laws. Schweiker has long favored repeal of the Delaney Amendment (which forbids use of any food additive which has been shown to cause cancer in either animals or man), and Hayes has spoken of more lenient wording, as well as changes in the food safety laws. In an apparent reference to Delaney, he said: "We have to recognize that absolute, 100 percent safety is impossible." Through 1981, the Administration had not issued its opinion on legislation to revise Delaney, but it is likely Reagan will seek to weaken it.

During our interview, Hayes expressed discomfort with some of the guiding principles of past food safety efforts, particularly those for controlling cancer-causing or other disease-inducing substances. "I am not sure that we should, at least in the first instance, make our decisions about safety based on what we can do. I am uncomfortable with the principle translated into policy that whatever you can find, a little bit less than that is zero; since it's zero that we want, if we can't find it it's ok. From a practical standpoint you may be forced into that position, at least for a time, until the technology and the analytic capability catch up. But on the other hand, when you're cutting across the board looking at food safety and you say, 'Well, the methodology for this is terrific, we can find a part per trillion. Therefore, zero would be a part per trillion and one. You just can't find it therefore it's zero'. . . . On the other hand if for something else you are still finding a part per thousand, zero is a part in a thousand and one," he said.

Hayes also has doubts about the animal tests used to establish a chemical's carcinogenicity. "As a scientist I am really not too sure," he said of the tests, which were backed under the Carter Administration by an interagency panel which included the FDA.

Last summer, Hayes approved for use the artificial sweetner aspartame, though an FDA board of inquiry recommended further testing to determine the validity of evidence that the substance may cause brain damage.

On other matters, Hayes said:

- Recruiting top-level personnel for the agency was a problem. "It doesn't pay what they could even make in academia at senior levels; it certainly doesn't pay what they could make with industry or private institutions."

- He may ask for greater legislative authority "in both the areas of food and drugs, and perhaps cosmetics. . ."

- His greatest disappointment was "The fact that. . .this last year we have had to spend so much time on budgets and new suggestions; new cuts or reorganizing what you're going to do. . .with the uncertainty and the consequent anxieties and even demoralizing effect." During March, 1982 testimony, Hayes expressed more dissatisfaction with OMB, explaining that the President's requirement for cost-benefit analysis of proposed new regulations had held up FDA regulations to protect infants from defective infant formula. Citing a case in which over half a million cans of formula had to be recalled by Wyeth Laboratories, Hayes explained "The proposed regulations would have, if followed by the firm, prevented this problem." But the regulations have been stalled since May, 1981 because of OMB's requirement for economic analysis. The defective formula lacked vitamin B6, deprivation of which can lead to permanent brain damage in infants.

- Despite plans that appeared in the press, Hayes said, "I have said from the beginning that I do not have any prediliction for cutting out scientific libraries."

- The FDA should provide "leadership" in reducing patient exposure to radiation through x-rays. "I think we can decrease, without compromising the health benefits, the amount of radiation people are exposed to and we can do this by educating the physicians and patients or potential patients that you have done something that's going to last and is going to become the way medicine is practiced."

- Administration proposals to broaden exemptions for business trade secrets under the Freedom of Information Act would cost the agency "a hell of a lot of money. . . . If there is this extension of the exemptions it will take more people. Is it to be exempted? Do you consider it confidential? There's no question that it's going to be more work for us."

FINANCIAL BACKGROUND

Much of Hayes's research at Hershey Medical Center was funded by Hoffman-LaRoche, the Swiss drug manufacturer which is the world leader in sales of valium.

The firm paid Hayes a salary of $66,958.92 in 1980 and $16,365.24 in the first three months of 1981. It was his primary source of income.

Three months after taking office, Hayes wrote an agency memo indicating that he intended to abstain from any decision concerning Hoffman-LaRoche for one year.

Hayes has for the most part been choosing his words carefully in his public appearances, but his comfortable relationship with the drug industry has sometimes shown through.

For instance, in a speech before the Proprietary Association (an organization of non-prescription, over-the-counter and self-medication drug manufacturers) on May 11, 1981, Hayes cordially vowed to improve relations between his agency and the industry. At one point, he mentioned how helpful his "meetings" with industry representatives have been.

"One of the most useful and enjoyable of those meetings, by the way, was with your President, Jim Cope. He is even helping me with the toughest job before me—finding a house I can afford!"

WHAT OTHERS ARE SAYING ABOUT HIM

- *The Wall Street Journal* reported "it's known that industry executives are pleased by [Hayes's] choice, partly because in 1978 he appeared before a House committee to urge faster handling of new drug applications."

- Former FDA Commissioner Dr. Jere Goyan, who once appointed Hayes to an advisory role, had no particular criticism of Hayes, saying "you can't judge a person by what he is saying. . .you must wait and judge him on what he does."

  Goyan said it is not surprising to him that Hayes had industry financial support at Hershey Medical Center. "You see that in academia all the time," he said.

  He further noted that the Reagan political campaign received large contributions from the drug industry—and therefore was naturally expected to have some influence in this Administration.

  "He who pays the piper calls the tune," Goyan said.

- Hayes has proceeded cautiously in his contacts with consumer interest groups, many of which are still withholding final judgment on the new FDA head. Dr. Michael Jacobson, of the Center for Science in the Public Interest, said that in a recent FDA consumer meeting the commissioner "chose his words carefully" and "seemed to be playing his cards very close to his chest."

  "When I left the meeting I said he seemed like old stoney-face," Jacobson said. "It was a two-hour meeting—and Hayes didn't crack a smile the whole time."

- It remains to be seen how much influence the aggressive, pro-industry officials at USDA will have on Hayes's decision-making on other food issues.

  "Hayes is not as bad an appointment as the Reagan appointees at USDA," said Carol Tucker Foreman, who was assistant secretary of food and consumer services at USDA under President Carter. "He at least seems to have some desire to protect the public health from unsafe foods. . .He may prove to be one of the few bright spots."

JOHN SVAHN
COMMISSIONER, SOCIAL SECURITY ADMINISTRATION

RESPONSIBILITY OF OFFICE

Svahn takes over the Social Security Administration at a crucial point in its history. Svahn has been working together with his boss, Richard Schweiker, and Budget Director David Stockman to develop the Administration's policy. The commissioner's primary responsibility, however, is managing the system, which today includes three programs: Old Age and Survivors Insurance (OASI), Disability Insurance (DI), and Hospitalization Insurance (HI). Ninety percent of all wage and salary workers fall under the system.

More than 36 million retired and disabled workers, their dependents and survivors, are receiving benefits (which are expected to total $174 billion in fiscal year 1982).

Other major programs which come under SSA's purview include the Supplemental Security Income program (SSI) and Aid to Families with Dependent Children (AFDC). Each of these programs is funded by general revenues.

In addition to keeping the system solvent, Svahn's primary concern as commissioner is to maintain smooth administration of services within the huge bureaucracy. During a recent interview he expressed a particular interest in concentrating on improving the efficiency and reliability of SSA's computer data systems as well as promoting public knowledge and understanding of protections, rights and responsibilities under SSA-administered programs.

BACKGROUND

Svahn is a long-time member of the Reagan circle. In the early 1970s he worked on Reagan's California welfare cuts. He eventually became the director of the state's social welfare program (the nation's largest). Svahn worked as an assistant to Robert Carleson, who led Reagan's welfare reform efforts in California and is now writing welfare reform policy in the White House.

When Carleson came to Washington as welfare commissioner in 1973, Svahn followed and occupied the following positions within the Department of Health, Education and Welfare hierarchy: acting commisisioner, Community Services Administration (1973-74) and commissioner, Assistance Payments Administration (1973-75). He served concurrently in 1975-76 as administrator for the Social Rehabilitation Service (SRS) and director of the U.S. Office of Child Support Enforcement. As SRS administrator, Svahn administered the nation's welfare, medicaid, social services and rehabilitation programs with an annual budget of about $30 billion.

After leaving the federal government in 1976, Svahn worked as a private consultant in Maryland.

Svahn was born on May 13, 1943 in New London, Connecticut, and is a graduate of the University of Washington in 1966. He is married with two children.

MAJOR ISSUES

- The Social Security system is at a critical juncture in its history—facing both a near-term shortage of funds and a long-range demographical shift that is drastically reducing the ratio between workers paying into the system and beneficiaries receiving funds from it.

- In 1981, the Administration proposed major cuts in Social Security benefits but was rebuffed by Congress, setting the stage for an ongoing legislative battle in the upcoming years.

- Svahn must also face an increasingly serious administrative problem: the steady deterioration of the SSA's computer capability, which endangers the agency's ability to mail out its checks.

Few federal programs, if any, directly touch the lives of so many people as Social Security. About 90 percent of all workers are either current or future beneficiaries. "Social Security benefits are the only income for 7 million older Americans and the primary source of income for 15 million out of 25 million older Americans," wrote the House Select Committee on Aging in a report in the summer of 1981.

Social Security has been a sleeping dragon in political debate for most of the last decade. But a combination of factors—including the Reagan Administration's efforts last year to reduce benefits—have placed it near the top of the political agenda. The attempt to cut benefits provided Reagan with his biggest legislative defeat of 1981 and set the stage for what promises to be a difficult series of legislative battles in the upcoming years.

The Social Security system faces two distinct problems: a near-term shortage and a long-range demographical shift that will reduce the ratio between workers paying into the system and beneficiaries receiving funds from it. By the year 2030, there will be only two contributors for every recipient compared to a 3.2-1 ratio today and 16.5-1 in 1950. In the short-run is a financial crunch facing the Old Age and Survivors Insurance Fund, which has been running a deficit since 1975. "The one thing that everybody agrees on is that we have a problem in this decade, because if the present law isn't changed, the July 1, 1983 checks for the Old Age and Survivors Insurance Fund [the one that pays old-age benefits] cannot be met in a timely manner," said Robert Myers, former chief actuary for the system, in an interview with the *Washington Post.*

But estimates on the scope of the problem—based largely on economic projections—are extremely volatile. Svahn acknowledged the uncertainty in mid-1981 when he announced "that despite the 1977 Social Security tax increase, the largest peacetime tax hike in history, the system still faces a short-term funding shortfall that could range from $10 billion to $111 billion over the next five years, depending upon the economic assumptions used." Obviously, the policy changes required by a $111 billion shortfall are far greater than might be required by a $10 billion deficit. Svahn and the Administration proposed "that we and the Congress should act to insure the system against that 'worst case' lest we repeat the mistakes made at the time of the 1977 Social Security amendments when relatively optimistic assumptions were used as the basis for congressional action."

But key Democrats such as Sen. Daniel Patrick Moynihan (D-N.Y.) and Rep. J.J. Pickle (D-Tex.), who chairs the House Ways and Means Social Security Subcommittee, argued that the Administration was proposing cuts far greater than needed to restore Social Security's health in order to reduce its overall budget deficit. The

House Aging Committee calculated that the impact of the Administration's legislative changes over the next 75 years annually would cut benefits by an average of $37 billion annually—more than twice the expected annual shortfall. Robert Ball, a Social Security commissioner for Presidents Kennedy, Johnson and Nixon who opposed the proposals, said, "The Administration is, in part, seeking to cut Social Security benefits in order to help balance the general budget." That suspicion helped stalemate efforts to restructure the system last year.

OASI's short-term troubles are directly linked to the nation's economic malaise. With inflation rising swiftly, the fund's expenditures have quickly grown. But wages have not kept up with inflation, diminishing taxable revenues. High unemployment has also kept down revenues. The financial position of the other two Social Security trust funds, disability insurance and hospital insurance, is stronger. Even so, the Congressional Budget Office (CBO) projects problems for the trust funds in only a few years. "CBO projects that unless corrective measures are taken, Social Security trust fund levels could drop to 13.4 percent of annual outlays by the end of fiscal year 1983, and they could be as low as 7.6 percent by the end of 1984," the office wrote in a February, 1982 study. "Though there is no consensus about an acceptable minimum level of trust fund reserves, a year-end figure of 12 percent of the coming year's anticipated outlays falls roughly in the middle of the range of levels that various analysts regard as adequate to guarantee that all benefits can be paid on time."

To deal with the immediate problem—and many argue to reduce social expenditures—the Administration in May, 1981 proposed a series of benefit cuts totalling between $82 and $110 billion through 1986. Reagan's package included a penalty for early retirement, elimination of the minimum benefit, further tightening of disability requirements, and a delay in the next Cost of Living Adjustment. Those proposals owed more to Stockman than to Svahn.

But Svahn was probably glad to be on the outside of that idea. What began as an offensive quickly turned into a full-scale retreat. The Senate voted unanimously to oppose any effort to penalize early retirement. The House Aging Committee termed the package "the most fundamental assault on the Social Security system since its inception 46 years ago." In the budget package, the Administration did convince Congress to eliminate the minimum benefit, which provides $122 a month to three million people. But the outcry was so sharp that the Administration was again forced to back down. In December, 1981 Congress restored the minimum benefit for all those currently receiving it, though the benefit was eliminated for anyone retiring after January 1, 1982. The largest change in the package that ultimately passed was the elimination of postsecondary student benefits funded by Social Security.

By the December negotiations, Svahn was playing a larger role, scurrying back and forth with technical calculations. But it was clear at least to Myers, a well-respected Republican analyst who had served as deputy commissioner for programs in the agency, that OMB was still running the show. In December, 1981, he resigned, sending a stinging letter to Schweiker that condemned both the Health and Human Services staff and OMB. OMB, Myers wrote, "develops policy without regard to the social and economic aspects of the Social Security program—and even the political aspects."

Faced with intractable opposition, the Administration took a time-honored political response and appointed a blue-ribbon commission headed by Alan Greenspan—a conservative economist labeled by Evans and Novak as "Dr. Pain" for his views on how to revive the economy—to study the system. Myers became executive director of the task force. Their report is expected by the end of 1982.

It will be difficult for the Democrats and Republicans on the task force to find common ground. There are significant, philosophical differences between the leading Democrats and the Administration on the issue. The Administration has argued that only benefit cuts can pull the system through its difficult period in the 1980s, until demographics and scheduled tax increases begin to improve its financial picture. In 1980, Democrats such as Moynihan and House Speaker Tip O'Neill have said that interfund borrowing could meet the immediate problems. In 1980 Congress authorized OASI to borrow from the disability insurance fund. Myers has said that, "With complete interfund borrowing, not just stopgap, temporary borrowing like we have now, under very good economic conditions, we could get by for 30 to 35 years." But with the economy continuing to erode, Moynihan and others are less sanguine about the ability of interfund borrowing to do the job.

Rep. Pickle sees the infusion of general revenues as also necessary to meet the short-range problems. But Svahn has said, "We don't want to go to general revenue, because once you eliminate the fiscal discipline of the trust fund and the dedicated tax, it becomes all too easy to finance the program out of the deficit."

Other areas may be more amenable to compromise. Pickle has proposed raising the retirement age to 68, which the Administration has opposed so far, but has indicated may be part of a long-term solution. Pickle is also proposing some benefit reductions for those who take early retirement, but unlike the Administration he would not phase in these cuts until at least 1990, giving beneficiaries more time to plan. The Administration wanted to cut the benefits immediately.

Though its proposals were rejected, the Administration has created the context in which the task force's plans to reform the system will be considered. In that way, its discredited proposals will continue to influence the debate. "A danger exists that the Administration's proposals are so extreme that it may increase the willingness of some Americans to accept cuts they would not have otherwise tolerated," wrote the AFL-CIO in a 1981 statement on the Administration's proposed cuts.

Funding the benefits is not the Social Security Administration's only problem. Delivering the benefits is almost as intractable. After years of neglect, the SSA's computers are a mess, as its top officials freely admit. If Congress had gone along with the elimination of the minimum benefit, the SSA would have had to review all 36 million Social Security recipients in order to find the three million who are receiving the minimum benefits, and then compute how much they should be cut. Incredibly, the process would have had to be done manually. Upgrading the computer system will be one of Svahn's main responsibilities. But the decay is advanced and budgets are tight; it is not an enviable task. In March, 1982, Svahn announced plans to spend $479 million over the next five years to upgrade the agency's computer system. Without the overhaul, Svahn said, the system could hit "the ultimate disaster: the checks don't go out."

FINANCIAL BACKGROUND

Svahn was making over $45,000 a year as a professional welfare consultant. One of his major clients was the State of Maryland.

Svahn told us, "Schweiker really had to twist my arm to get me to come back to the federal government. . .For the amount of hours invested, I can make a lot more money in private enterprise."

His major investment is in two homes (in Sacramento, Cal. and Miami, Fla.) and his only stock venture is a modest investment in Exxon.

WHAT OTHERS ARE SAYING ABOUT HIM

- SSA people have expressed "disappointment" because as one insider said, "People whose job it used to be to advise the Commissioner and Deputy Commissioner are simply not being consulted on a lot of these new measures." Many of them assume Reagan's benefit-cut proposals were made entirely by Stockman, Schweiker, and to a lesser extent, Svahn.

"We're just waiting, hoping and monitoring the situation," one SSA career person said. "Maybe things will get better in the future. But right now we're not sure what is going on."

- Another SSA insider describes Svahn as "unreasonable" and "paranoid" in his contacts with some employees. "He seems unwilling to trust other people's judgment," the source claims.
- Lobby groups are united in opposition to SSA benefit cuts, but there have been mixed first impressions among those who have met with Svahn personally. "Mr. Svahn was personable, positive and showed a willingness to compromise," said Lauri Fiori, a legislative representative for the American Association of Retired Persons. "He obviously had a good grasp of the issues involved in social security."

However, other lobbyists have not been favorably impressed.

"Svahn struck me as an unduly arrogant man," said Betty Duskin of the National Council of Senior Citizens. "It is hard for me to determine whose policies are being implemented in Social Security. But my first impression is that Svahn hasn't taken any initiative as commissioner, but is merely doing what he has been told to do by his superiors."

C. EVERETT KOOP
SURGEON GENERAL

RESPONSIBILITY OF OFFICE

Koop's role is to plan and direct the activities of the Public Health Service, which since its formation in 1944 has been revised and expanded several times.

As surgeon general, Koop reports directly to Assistant Secretary for Health Edward Brandt. The Public Health Service includes three major operating centers: the National Center for Health Statistics, the National Center for Health Services Research, and the National Center for Health Care Technology.

Since 1972, the assistant secretary for health has handled the surgeon general's responsibilities. Koop is the first full-time surgeon general since then. New responsibilities were also turned over to the surgeon general. He will direct the Office of

International Health which was deflated from an independent department of 54 employees in 1981, to a ten-member arm of the surgeon general's office in fiscal 1982.

The surgeon general is "charged by law to promote and assure the highest level of health attainable for every individual and family in America, and to develop cooperation in health projects with other nations."

BACKGROUND

Koop's background as a staunch anti-abortionist was the source of a long controversy which delayed his confirmation for nine months. Officially, his nomination was held up by a technicality which required that the surgeon general be less than 64 years old. (Koop was 64 when nominated.) Congress eventually waived that rule, but not until Rep. Henry Waxman (D-Calif.), who chairs the responsible House health subcommittee, made it clear that he considered Koop an inappropriate nominee for surgeon general.

Waxman was joined in his opposition to the Koop nomination by several newspaper editorials, and pro-choice and women's groups. Critics noted that while Koop had a very distinguished career as a pediatric surgeon, he lacked the necessary public health and administrative background for the surgeon general job.

Of his arduous confirmation process, Koop remembered "many discouraging days" spent waiting for Senate approval "in a strange city with strange tribal rites and mysterious ceremonies. During that long period of frustration, when I wondered why a grown man such as myself should even consider such a trial, I found a few people of great warmth and friendship," said Koop before the Utah Hospital Association in March, 1982. "Chief among them," he continued, "was Senator Orrin Hatch. He was my shepherd for me and my nomination. . . I doubt that he had ever come upon a more confused or depressed lamb until that time."

Koop is considered a pioneer of pediatric surgery and is famous for operations to separate Siamese twins. He was the surgeon-in-chief at Children's Hospital in Philadelphia for over 30 years and is one of the most sought-after doctors in his field.

Clearly, children are his passion. In 1979, Dr. Koop extolled motherhood and all its traditional virtues when speaking to a class of graduating seniors at a preparatory school in Philadelphia. The class consisted of 72 females and one male student. Koop described motherhood as a completion of the "whole vocation" of being a woman. "After all," he asked, "isn't it a very naive concept of feminism to insist that women prove their ability to do all the things that men can do? Men have not tried to prove that they can do all the things that women can do."

Koop also felt it necessary to warn his young audience about the hidden dangers lurking behind the new "freedoms" won by college students in the last decade, such as the abolishment of lights-out time and the advent of coed dorms. "As a result," Koop explained "they [students]. . .can stay out all night, they can play their hi fi at 3 a.m. and they can spend the night in whose room they please. But consider for a moment, that because of this, there is now no freedom to sleep, there is no freedom to study, and there is no freedom for students to be students which is really what they went away to college for in the first place. And after sharing the bathroom with the boys down the hall, you will find that disgust replaces a cherished mystique. . ."

In the past decade Koop has become active in the anti-abortion movement, joining the boards of numerous organizations and recently touring the country promoting a film entitled "Whatever Happened to the Human Race?". During one scene in the movie, Koop stands in a desert surrounded by dolls which symbolize the children not born because of abortions.

Based on only one screening of the film, representatives from the National Abortion Rights Action League (NARAL) found six major factual and legal errors, including a mischaracterization of fetuses at different stages of development, a mistatement concerning the most frequently employed method of abortion, and a misleading depiction of birth defects.

In another highly-publicized 1979 commencement speech, Koop portrayed an old man in the year 1999 looking back on the 1973 Supreme Court decision on abortion. He spoke of a "domino theory" resulting from the decision in which legalized abortion led to "infanticide" and "euthanasia." He also linked this theory to the development of "homosexual and lesbian" test-tube babies which would give the gay population greater political clout.

Koop drew links between communism and abortion in his 1980 book *The Right To Live, the Right to Die.* "And it's no mere coincidence," Koop wrote, "that the modern practice of abortion first appeared as a policy of government in the communist dictatorships, where contempt for the dignity of life is widely demonstrated."

Born in New York City on October 14, 1916, Koop is married with three children. He received an A.B. from Dartmouth University in 1937 and an M.D. from Cornell in 1941. He has been associated with the University of Pennsylvania ever since.

MAJOR ISSUES

- While Koop contends he will not have anything to do with abortion matters, his critics say many of the programs which the surgeon general traditionally oversees have frequently been attacked by anti-abortionists.

- Koop has been heavily criticized as a nominee for surgeon general because he lacks the essential public health administrative experience.

- Koop issued a devastating report on the health hazards of smoking, but the White House, facing tobacco industry pressure, has backed off support of tougher warnings.

As far as pro-choice people are concerned, the major issue confronting the surgeon general's office is how much influence Koop will have over the government's policy toward abortion.

"Not much at all," maintains Laura Genero of the Health and Human Services press office. "There is a real misconception here. The truth is that Koop will really have nothing to do with abortion."

However, critics charge Koop will be in charge of programs which have been frequently attacked by anti-abortionists, such as the Center for Disease Control, the Population Research Center, and the National Institute of Health.

Koop has publicly pledged not to use the surgeon general position to promote his anti-abortion views. Instead, he says he intends to concentrate his efforts on the problems of the elderly and the handicapped.

But NARAL representative Margurite Beck-Rex told us there are many ways Koop might indirectly influence abortion issues. "Koop can encourage other pro-life members at lower levels of the Reagan Administration," she points out. "He can plan with them. He can add the strength of his office—in other words he can add clout."

Beck-Rex also pointed out that Koop's anti-abortion film, "Whatever Happened To The Human Race?" is still in circulation. "The real danger posed by Koop therefore, is his continual identification with the [anti-abortion] movement," she explained. "It's got the imprimatur of the surgeon general."

In fact, Koop mentioned his film—in passing—while discussing post-natal surgery on infants born with congenital defects during a November, 1981 address to members of Our Lady's Hospital for Sick Children in Dublin, Ireland. He prefaced a story about a woman who fought to keep her child, born with spina bifida, alive with: "Last year in Birmingham after presentation of our film 'Whatever Happened to the Human Race'. . .'' Never mentioning abortion, Koop proceeded to tell his audience that surgery often allows such children to survive and lead fulfilling lives. He berated parents who allow their disabled children to die at childbirth: "I am absolutely convinced that the parents who opt to let their child die and only consent to its surgery when it was guaranteed that they would never have to be concerned with the child again will have, if not now, later; the grief, the guilt, the shame, the physical problems and even the mental aberrations that come with the abandonment of one's own flesh and blood."

Koop has also drawn fire from groups such as the American Public Health Association (APHA), which contends he is sorely lacking in public health experience. Genero stresses that Koop is not going to be as powerful as Assistant Secretary Brandt in the health hierarchy (Brandt had the APHA's endorsement), but the organization is still upset.

"This Administration is underplaying the significance of the surgeon general," said Barbara Levine, a spokeswoman for APHA, "They are saying don't worry about this guy, he doesn't have much power anyway."

She said it appears the Administration is molding the office to suit Koop, rather than finding a qualified individual to fill the traditional surgeon general role.

"Koop is a clinician," she said, "not a public health professional. He has plenty of experience dealing with an individual's health needs, but he has no substantial experience in administration of matters like immunization, venereal disease, lead poisoning, and immigration."

Despite his lack of administrative experience, Koop has said he has a good understanding of public health needs. For instance, he believes he is uniquely qualified to be surgeon general because he has traveled in more than 30 countries while participating in international health programs.

However, Levine said Koop's work in foreign countries "involved clinical medicine only, not administrative work. In fact, [Koop] doesn't even list those Third World experiences in his [curriculum vitae]," she said, "which is a good indication that he considered them to be pretty minor."

Nonetheless, Koop's role in international health policy development is expanding, being molded as his term progresses. The International Health Office came under his wing only recently and, according to Linda Vogel, acting director of the office, they are "still trying to figure out how to function and how to do business," given the drastically reduced staff and budget.

Thus far Koop has made several international excursions as representative of the office. In April, 1982 he went to Kuwait. According to a May, 1981 memorandum of agreement, the U.S. is to "provide technical assistance in health. . .[to Kuwait] through establishment of a formal agreement between the two governments for the provisions of that assistance on a reimbursable basis."

"We're like service brokers," says Vogel, explaining that the U.S. will provide personnel from within HHS, as well as representatives from academic and other non-governmental organizations, to give technical assistance to Kuwaiti health officials. The Kuwait government will furnish travel and other expenses incurred by HHS personnel, but there is no mention in the contract about salary reimbursement for the government employees. Koop has also journeyed to Ireland and Mexico.

Since taking office, Koop has assumed a low public profile, mostly addressing private clubs and organizations. But in February, 1982, he made front-page news around the country. Koop delivered a report which contained one of the toughest indictments of cigarette smoking given by a federal official in almost two decades.

"Cigarette smoking," Koop declared, "is clearly identified as the chief preventable cause of death in our society." In addition to the long-established relationship between smoking and lung, larynx, and esophagus cancer, the report linked cigarette smoking to bladder, kidney, and pancreatic cancers.

The reason Koop makes very few public appearances is his candidness, according to one minority Senate aide. "He's a very compassionate person," the aide said, "and he disagrees with the Administration on many issues. If they let him out, he'll talk." In early March, 1982, Koop and Brandt appeared before a House subcommittee to back tougher warning labels on cigarettes; a few days later, the White House, having heard from the tobacco industry and its congressional supporters, pulled Administration support for the bill.

If Koop does disagree with the Administration, he keeps it under his salad during his numerous luncheon addresses and award dinner speeches. Sounding like many other Reagan Administration officials, Koop says the government and the medical community must work together "as partners." At the top of his list of suggestions to achieve such a relationship was "getting the government out of the PSRO business by 1984." The PSRO (Professional Standards Review Organization) is responsible for reviewing how medical professionals use hospital facilities and services in order to hold down medical costs.

Koop talks of developing a stronger "prevention ethic" as another major priority in health care today: "We need to counsel our patients, in the one-to-one relationship in the office, on smoking, on drug and alcohol use, and on nutrition. But we also need to counsel our communities on ways to achieve safer highways, better control over infectious disease, a possible reduction in the incidence of domestic violence, improved home and commercial building safety, and other goals that represent better health and well-being for their citizens. The cost in lives and in dollars is too high for any of us to ignore this. . ." The irony in that statement is both inescapable and tragic: in each case that Koop mentioned—from providing information about nutrition to making the highways safer—the Reagan Administration is frantically dismantling government programs designed to improve health and save lives. Perhaps Koop should give one of his after-lunch speeches in the White House mess.

FINANCIAL BACKGROUND

In 1980, Koop earned more than $136,000 in hospital salary. His income was supplemented by over $45,000 from book royalties and $9,000 in proceeds from his "Life Seminars."

WHAT OTHERS ARE SAYING ABOUT HIM

- In addition to his liberal critics, Koop's nomination was also opposed by the 109-year-old APHA, which is normally neutral on such matters. The *Washington Post*, the *Village Voice* and the *New York Times* also opposed him.

  The *Times* noted that most surgeon generals come from the field of public health. "Dr. Koop has neither worked in the field nor, during his years at Children's Hospital in Philadelphia, shown any interest or influence in it," the newspaper said.

- Former HHS head Patricia Roberts Harris worries that the controversial Koop "will be a divisive force as surgeon general."

  "The surgeon general should not be associated with parochial issues," she told us. "What we need is an administrator who can bring the health profession together. But Koop is identified with a divisive rather than a reconciling role."

EDUCATION DEPARTMENT

TERREL BELL
SECRETARY

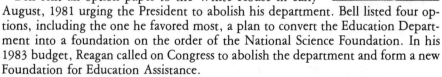

RESPONSIBILITY OF OFFICE

The Department of Education may prove to be one of the most short-lived Cabinet departments in history—which would suit Terrel Bell just fine. Formed in September, 1979, the department came under fire repeatedly from presidential candidate Reagan in the 1980 campaign.

Bell sent an option paper to the White House in early August, 1981 urging the President to abolish his department. Bell listed four options, including the one he favored most, a plan to convert the Education Department into a foundation on the order of the National Science Foundation. In his 1983 budget, Reagan called on Congress to abolish the department and form a new Foundation for Education Assistance.

Prior to 1979, the department had been part of the Department of Health, Education and Welfare (HEW).

By statute, Bell is chief adviser to the President on all federal plans, policies and programs in education. He establishes federal policy on matters relating to elementary and secondary education; postsecondary education; educational research; vocational and adult education; special education and rehabilitation services; education for overseas dependents (in conjunction with the military); and civil rights as it pertains to educational programs.

In 1982, Bell supervised a budget of over $13 billion and 4,400 employees. That represents a sharp decrease from the 5,666-member staff in place when he took office.

BACKGROUND

Bell has a long record in education. In 1974-76 he served as U.S. Commissioner of Education under Caspar Weinberger at HEW. For six months in 1970-71 he served as deputy commissioner. Since then he's been commissioner and chief executive for the Utah System of Higher Education.

In Utah, he was faced with reduced educational funding and increased enrollments. In dealing with that problem he usually decided on cutbacks in programs rather than tuition increases.

As head of the austere education program in Utah, Bell earned the reputation among his colleagues as the "master of compromise."

Born on November 11, 1921, in Lava Hot Springs, Idaho, Bell received his bachelors degree from Southern Idaho College (1946) and graduate degrees from the University of Idaho (1954) and the University of Utah (1961). He began teaching as an athletic coach and science teacher in Eden, Idaho in 1946, but within a year he was elevated to superintendent of another Idaho school district. He has been involved in education administration ever since.

Bell is the author of five books, including a novel called *The Prodigal Pedagogue*, and in 1972 was appointed by President Nixon to the National Council on Educational Research.

He has been a long-time supporter of the Republican Party. He is married with four sons.

Bell is leasing 100 acres of undeveloped land in rural Utah where he is beginning a sod farm together with his sons, in what the *New York Times* termed "a nostalgic return to his roots."

MAJOR ISSUES

- Bell, who only five years ago saw a significant place for federal education programs, now is attempting to convey as many programs as possible to the states (along with sizeable program reductions).

- He supports the elimination of the department as a Cabinet-level agency.

- Many innovative and experimental education programs will be reduced or abandoned as part of Bell's defederalization of education. Basic higher education aid programs are being sharply cut.

- At the same time public education will sustain massive cuts, Bell is actively supporting tuition tax credits which will be of the greatest benefit to the more well-to-do.

- Bell supports parents groups which want to ban books like *Catcher in the Rye*, saying children should have "the right not to read."

Secretary Bell does not mince words.

"This is a states-rights administration," he said in an early press conference.

That statement stands in stark contrast to his views while U.S. Commissioner of Education. Upon leaving that post in 1976, he said, "I came here feeling that education was almost exclusively a state responsibility. My view has shifted. . . Congress and the federal statutes can no longer defer to the states and say 'You take the lead.' The federal government must guarantee certain rights, and in doing so, it should specify the ends of education and provide the financial support to meet those ends." Bell testified in favor of Carter's proposal to form the Department of Education, saying flatly, "We need a U.S. Department of Education."

Bell's nomination was actively supported by Utah Republican Senators Orrin Hatch and Jake Garn, who approve of his recent opposition to "excessive" federal influence in education. Bell, though, was not the first choice of the Administration, which sought to place a prominent black academic, Thomas Sowell of the Hoover Institution, in the job. Sowell turned down the offer.

That tenuous position may explain the alacrity with which Bell has rejected many of the policies he advocated just five years ago and his acquiescence to pressure from both the Office of Management and Budget (OMB) and the Moral Majority for changes in other areas of federal education policy. Among the endangered policies that he had earlier supported are various student loan plans, "impact aid" in federally-affected areas, and aid to vocational, elementary and secondary schools. Bell cut off federal grants to the Rev. Jesse Jackson's "Push-Excel" school project. His public information department asked the conservative American Enterprise Institute (AEI) "to take over control and direction of the [department] magazine," as Dennis Doyle of the AEI put it. (The AEI refused.) And Bell is also, of course, supporting the elimination of his own department.

Ah, but all that still doesn't make the grade for the vocal New Right. Richard Viguerie has called for Bell's resignation; he says the secretary has failed "to stop the flow of federal dollars to radical groups." Viguerie's *Conservative Digest* labeled Bell as one of the non-Reaganite appointees in the government.

And Bell is feeling the heat from another quarter. This pressure undoubtedly disturbs him more. After a cordial honeymoon period, professional educators have become increasingly disturbed by Bell's performance and the Reagan program. Leaders of national education organizations, student groups, and even university presidents generally silent on major issues are condemning the Administration with increasing frequency and harshness. Donald Swain, the President of the University of Louisville, told a congressional committee in March, 1982: "The Administration proposals may return us to an educational era characterized by crude and unenlightened elitism and perhaps will create social problems of major magnitude in our society." Jack Peltason, president of the American Council on Education, has said the proposals aren't "just minor tinkering. This is dismantling the whole structure of student financial aid." Washington education lobbyists scornfully refer to him as a "former public educator," the *Washington Post* reported.

As a lifetime education professional, Bell feels the sting of this repudiation. It may be OMB calling the shots, but it is Terrel Bell taking the return fire. "I think it's true [that he feels hurt]," said Terry Herndon, president of the National Education Association. "Dr. Bell has been a leader in public education for 25 years. He has long personal relationships with people in the field including myself. . .it has to hurt. . .but he's still personally flying the flag [of the Administration]."

Bell is reportedly growing weary of the endless conflicts between the White House, OMB, the far right, and his former colleagues. He will never be pure enough for the Moral Majority, and he is too stained by his acquiescence to the budget cuts to ever be accepted by educators. Bell is a good candidate for an early exodus from Washington.

Bell sought to lump together 44 elementary and secondary education programs into block grants to the states, and cut federal support by about $1 billion. (Congress eventually okayed a package of 33 programs for block grants.)

Bell admits some of the poorer school districts "are going to get hit harder" than others, and added, "I'm concerned about it, but that's just the way it's going to fall."

Critics contend that the block-grant program will pit parents of poor children against parents of handicapped ones in a new scramble at state and local levels for federal aid as well as divert the public's wrath over budget reductions from Reagan's Washington to state and local governments.

The special grants for innovative and experimental programs (such as environmental, metric, consumer, and citizen education) are likely to be drastically reduced or eliminated. Bell had avidly supported many of these programs as commissioner. But when asked about them at his confirmation hearing by conservative Sen. Jeremiah Denton (R-Ala.), Bell said, "I believe that we have too many small categorical programs which provide no reasonable national benefit when compared to their cost and effect."

Bell's predecessor, Shirley Hufstedler, told us that these cuts are part of the theme "through this Administration's policies of an undeclared war on children. . .of a failure of public support for children who are the most in need."

The Administration's 1983 budget seeks not only to cut programs for low-income students, Indians, and the handicapped, but the basic loans and grants that assist students attending college. Overall student aid for higher education would be cut from $6.9 billion in 1981 to $6.55 in 1982 to $4.8 billion in 1983. Pell Grants, which provide direct aid to low-income students, would be cut by a third in 1983 to $1.4 billion; that would cut the number of recipients from 2.2 to 1.8 million.

"The linchpin of public higher education are the Pell Grants," said Jay Hershenson, executive director of the Committee for Public Higher Education in New York State. In New York public higher education alone, over 170,000 students depend on Pell Grants, Hershenson said. "They are especially important to lower and middle income students. The single most devastating proposal Reagan has made is a cut in the Pell Grant program. Since Pell covers the basic cost of education. . . The Pell program more than any other makes the difference between staying in college and having to leave."

The Administration also will seek legislative changes restricting eligibility for Guaranteed Student Loans that would cut expenditures by more than a fourth. In all, these proposals would eliminate assistance to about 2 million people, according to the American Council on Education. "This Administration," charged Charles Sanders, vice-president of the council, "in effect is asking Congress to welch on a commitment that has been clear for 25 years." Bell has also proposed rules to bar loans to students at colleges where the default rate is over 25 percent. Penalties would be applied to schools with a default rate over 10 percent. "Rather than viewing higher education as an investment," said Hershenson, "they are trying to put taxes on students while they are in college. [These proposals] say to the lower income students that their education is not a national priority."

Former Secretary Hufstedler agreed with Hershenson's assessment. "That's the only way I can read it," she said. "It's a reflection of an even deeper policy that the investment in hardware—particularly military hardware—is more important than the investment in human resources."

Thousands of college students descended on Washington in March, 1982 to protest the proposed cuts in student aid in the largest student protest of recent years. Student groups have launched a major lobbying effort on Congress to fight the cuts.

Under the 1983 budget, total federal outlays for education would drop from $15.4 to $13.1 billion.

Reductions in regulations are coming hand-in-hand with budget cuts. Bell withdrew the Carter proposal on bilingual education which would have required most school districts to use native languages to teach children with limited English skills. Bell approved the original bilingual education guidelines as commissioner in 1976.

One form of spending on education which Reagan will seek to increase is aid to private schools through the controversial tuition tax credit. Reagan has long supported the credit and Bell concurs.

Bell admits "tax credits by their nature are not designed to serve low income or perhaps even lower middle class families," but claims those groups are already adequately served by other public education programs. Reagan proposed a tuition tax credit program in April, 1982—even, of course, as he was cutting funds for public education. That obvious inequity may well be too much for Congress to swallow.

Bell will downplay enforcement of civil rights regulations at the department. He has already said he will not press lawsuits for achieving school desegregation through busing. He also will seek to reduce the federal role in enforcing laws against discrimination in the nation's schools and universities. Only six weeks after taking office he told a group of state education officials, "We ought to try to get the federal government, to the extent we can, out of the monitoring and enforcement business. Is there some way we could persuade you to do more so we could do less?"

The secretary was sharply criticized by an NAACP Legal Defense Fund lawyer in July, 1981 for the manner in which we handled a North Carolina desegration plan. The attorney, Joseph Rauh, objected to Bell's "collusive action" with President William C. Friday of the University of North Carolina. The two worked out a behind-the-scenes agreement to desegregate North Carolina's public colleges and universities. The NAACP maintains the agreement is inadequate.

The U.S. district court judge approved the plan offered by Bell and Friday in what Rauh called "a travesty of federal judicial procedure." Rauh intends to appeal the ruling, claiming it does not meet federal criteria issued in 1977 for college desegregation plans.

In December, 1981 Bell sought to revise regulations defining "financial assistance" to free from federal civil rights regulations about 1,000 colleges and technical schools that do not receive direct federal aid, but have students who do. But the Justice Department objected, arguing that the changes would not stand up in court. After a meeting with White House Counselor Edwin Meese III, Bell withdrew the rules in January. But in March, 1982 on the advice of Meese, Reagan personally decided to exempt from civil rights rules colleges where the only form of federal aid is guaranteed student loans.

The Reagan Administration is pleased with Bell's actions and his anti-federal rhetoric. An example of his personal initiative was displayed in March, 1981, when he eliminated 39 high slots in the Education Department hierarchy, reportedly without any specific prompting from the Administration. Shortly thereafter he struck again, firing 75 percent of the department's loan collection staff. Such actions have put him in the good graces of the budget cutters, though he did publicly resist some cuts last fall.

Bell has also been eager to please other sects in the Reagan entourage, including the Moral Majority. Speaking in support of parent groups which have attempted to ban so-called immoral books like *Catcher in the Rye* from school libraries, Bell has spoken of the importance of guaranteeing children "the right not to read."

Bell further appeased the New Right by appointing the Reverend Bob Billings, executive director of the Moral Majority, to the department's Office of Non-Public Education.

Most appealing to the far right, though, is Bell's plan to downgrade the department into a foundation. In an interview with the *New York Times*, Bell explained how the move would limit the federal role in education: "A foundation is not a line entity. Foundations are established to give financial support and to do studies and that sort of thing. They don't regulate and run things." Eliminating the department, Hufstedler told us, "sends a signal throughout the country that [education] is not a matter of national concern. . .The signals throughout are to reduce educational equity, educational opportunity, to diminish support for public education."

The foundation would oversee the education grant programs, conduct some research, and perform civil rights investigations. Civil rights enforcement authority would be transferred to the Justice Department. Congress may resist the changes, which are fervently opposed by virtually all major educational organizations. If all of Reagan's proposed changes go through, Hufstedler said, "it will take multiple administrations [to repair the damage]. One has to recognize just how devastating it really is." And no future Administration will be able to help the young students denied the special programs they need to have a chance at educational success. "You don't recover those children," she said. "They're gone."

FINANCIAL BACKGROUND

Bell, a career education professional, has no significant holdings or interests other than his Utah farm acreage. He earned $64,500 as Utah's education commissioner, and has said he probably plans to take a professor's post after leaving Washington.

WHAT OTHERS ARE SAYING ABOUT HIM

- Bell's friends "say the. . .former machine gun instructor in World War II is an engaging, warm, resolute but inoffensive administrator who, if less than a stirring public speaker, is politically astute and a master of compromise," according to the *New York Times*.

- "Sure, [Bell] is a nice, personable guy. . .but we really wonder if he is in control of his own department. Most of us feel OMB is dictating most of the changes in education. . .Bell is going around the country making all sorts of nice statements about education, but his rhetoric is softer than his actions. It is deceptive," said a minority staff member on the Senate Labor and Human Resources Committee.

- "I'm not so sure that Bell knows what his job responsibility is. It is evident to me that the education policy is being dictated almost completely by the President and OMB," said Arnold Fege, director of government relations for the National PTA.

- Hufstedler told us that she only talked to Bell "very, very briefly." It wasn't from a lack of effort: "I made myself available. . .There was no encouragement whatsoever from the Administration" to talk to the outgoing officials.

NATIONAL LABOR RELATIONS BOARD

JOHN VAN DE WATER
CHAIRMAN

RESPONSIBILITY OF OFFICE

Created by the National Labor Relations Act of 1935, the National Labor Relations Board's responsibility is to "safeguard employees' rights to organize, to determine through [secret ballot] elections whether workers want unions as their bargaining representatives" and to prevent and remedy violations of the act by ordering labor and management to sit at the bargaining table.

The board handled about 60,000 cases in 1980, up almost 300 percent since 1957.

As chairman of the five-member NLRB, Van de Water's responsibilites are largely administrative. "He really doesn't have any extra power," explains John H. Fanning, the former board chairman, replaced by Van de Water, "basically there's just a lot of extra paper pushing. He's got one vote. . .and his staff is the same size as his fellow board members." The board operates on a $113.8 million budget, with a staff of 2,620.

BACKGROUND

A former president of a leading West Coast anti-union consulting firm, Van de Water is to organized labor what James Watt is to environmentalists. When Reagan appointed Van de Water and Robert P. Hunter to fill two vacant board seats on an interim basis—pending confirmation—in April, 1981 the *Washington Post* predicted they would be "shoo-ins" for Senate approval. Unrelenting opposition from the AFL-CIO, especially after Reagan appointed Van de Water acting chairman in August, 1981 though, has blocked Van de Water's approval.

The Senate Labor and Human Resources Committee has repeatedly refused to endorse Van de Water, doubting his ability to render impartial decisions on charges of unfair labor practices.

Testifying at Van de Water's confirmation hearing, AFL-CIO Secretary Thomas Donahue pointed out that even by the avowed standards of one of Van de Water's staunchest supporters, Utah's arch-conservative Senator Orrin Hatch, Reagan's nominee seems unfit to serve on the NLRB. During debate over an earlier NLRB appointee, Hatch spoke resoundingly about the "compelling need to have a board member who is perceived as objective and, most important, independent." "We submit that a man who views it as his mission to thwart [union] organization at every turn is not fit to administer those laws," Donahue said.

Since 1949 Van de Water has run John R. Van de Water Associates Inc., a management consulting firm that specialized in advising companies on how to defeat union organizing campaigns. In some of the campaigns the firm was involved in, the companies distributed virulent anti-union literature. When employees of the Alloy Die Sink Company sought to affiliate with the Aluminum Workers International Union, Alloy hired Van de Water's agency. Subsequently Alloy distributed a flyer, which at both his confirmation hearing and afterwards Van de Water denied writing. It read: "Promises are worth what they cost: NOTHING. Ask yourself—can this union guarantee me specific improved wages, benefits and working conditions? The answer is NO. No union can guarantee anything. . . . Only after the gates of unionism slam shut behind you, does the iron rule of union domination clamp down on you. And then it's too late."

Whether Van de Water Associates wrote the pamphlet is impossible to ascertain. As with most of his firm's activities, records are sketchy. "That's the problem," said one Senate aide, "it's impossible to verify any information on the guy."

Donahue also gave the subcommittee an article excerpting a Van de Water speech entitled "How To Deal With The Union." At one point Van de Water discusses good faith bargaining: "Good-faith bargaining simply means that you listen to the union's arguments with yours. That's all that good-faith bargaining is. You don't have to give one cent." Van de Water did not deny that he gave this speech, but he says it is taken out of context.

Van de Water claims he has only counseled companies on how to comply with the law and proclaims that "never once. . .has there ever been found by the NLRB an unfair labor practice on my part or by any client that I represent."

But NLRB records indicate that statement is untrue. In a November, 1977 case, the board found Van de Water's client, General Telephone Directory Company, to have unlawfully threatened during a meeting at which Van de Water was present that a "promise of a wage increase might be withheld" if employees voted to join the International Brotherhood of Electrical Workers.

The AFL-CIO has also asked the Labor Department to investigate Van de Water's role in a 1976 organizing campaign by the International Chemical Workers Union at Bell Helmets, Inc. That campaign generated unfair labor practice charges against the company, which the NLRB rejected. During the hearings on the case, workers told the NLRB that Van de Water had participated in the company's campaign, and remembered him saying that during a strike the employer could call in replacements and the employees could be permanently replaced; that the union could get employees fired if they didn't pay their dues, and so forth.

The AFL-CIO contends that Van de Water's actions constituted "persuader activities" and that Van de Water failed to report them to the Department of Labor, as required by the Landrum-Griffin Act. The investigation is being taken up by aides to Sen. Edward Kennedy (D-Mass.) and the AFL-CIO, though not formally by the Labor Department.

A 1939 graduate of the University of Chicago and a 1941 graduate of the University's law school, Van de Water ran a law practice in addition to his consulting work. He has served as director of the Executive Program of UCLA's Graduate School of Management, and at the time of his nomination, Van de Water was directing the Executive Education Department at San Diego State University.

In the past Van de Water has served on the Labor Arbitration and Collective Bargaining Law Committee of the American Bar Association as well as the Labor Relations Committee of the U.S. Chamber of Commerce.

Born March 26, 1917, in Long Beach, California, Van de Water is married and has seven children.

MAJOR ISSUES

- In a December, 1981 meeting with Reagan, labor leaders cited Van de Water's nomination as one of the three major obstacles standing in the path of improved relations between the President and the nation's work force. Van de Water's career-long anti-union activity makes him anathema to union leaders.

- Labor leaders feel that under Van de Water the NLRB will take a sharply pro-management tilt.

- Proposals under consideration to curtail NLRB's jurisdiction might raise the board's discretionary dollar standard, thereby removing smaller companies from the reach of the law.

When labor leaders met with Reagan in December, 1981, they cited Van de Water's nomination as one of the three major obstacles standing in the path of improved relations between the President and the nation's work force. Union representatives said the appointment of Van de Water, a man they believe to be staunchly anti-union, is indicative of the new Administration's attitude toward working people, and have called for his resignation.

Such vehement opposition may seem curious to many Americans who have never heard of the National Labor Relations Board. But the NLRB is crucial to labor because its decisions are integral to the overall formulation of national labor policy.

Since its creation in 1935, labor and management have been sparring for control of the board. The decisions handed down by the board are not nearly as bound to precedent as are those from the circuit courts—from which evolves a slow, case-by-case development of policy. The board's political perspective keeps changing, according to Paul Tobias, a long-time labor lawyer, "depending upon the administration in office."

Under Van de Water, the board is expected to take a sharp turn towards management. And as corporate resistance to organizing grows increasingly widespread and labor desperately attempts to expand its power base, especially in the unorganized South, there is a strong likelihood that workers' rights will be infringed, but that the violations will go unremedied.

A number of sensitive, if not volatile issues lay pending before the NLRB. Decisions on thousands of cases are likely to be handed down under Van de Water, setting the tone of labor-management relations for the '80s. Among the more pressing issues before the board involve developing criteria for determining whether a union official has been discriminated against for union activism; delineating the difference between "surface bargaining" and "good faith bargaining"; drawing the fine line between management's rights to keep trade secrets and workers' "right to know" about workplace threats to their health and safety; and defining employees' rights during plant closures; setting forth rights of subsidiaries during secondary boycott proceedings.

When it came into power, the Reagan Administration was handed the opportunity to realign the NLRB. Resignations and term expirations over the preceding year left two vacant seats, ready for Reagan to fill with Republicans, giving the party a three member majority. Under law, three members is the maximum number any one party is allowed on the board. The Republican already in office was Howard Jenkins, scheduled to complete 20 years of service in August, 1983. Joining him are Van de Water and Robert Hunter, a long-time aide to Sen. Orrin Hatch (R-Utah) and head of the team that authored the labor chapter in The Heritage Foundation's book, *Mandate for Leadership: Policy Management in a Conservative Administration*, which sharply criticized the NLRB for being pro-union.

Business sees these new appointments as only rectifying a pro-labor bias. Arthur Rosenfeld, an attorney with the U.S. Chamber of Commerce, welcomed them: "The board's treatment of business has been horrible in the last four or five years," he said. "[It's] everything organized labor could have possibly wanted."

But labor disagrees. Hugh Beins, a Washington union lawyer, said, "It's a crazy thing to say that the board has been pro-union. . .At best, from our view, the NLRB has been moderate in its disposition of cases."

Donahue wondered where the board will turn now. During confirmation hearings Donahue pointed to Van de Water's record as evidence of his belief that union "organization is an evil which management should fight." To labor, Van de Water symbolizes the anti-union professionals—management consultants—that are increasingly used to fight organization efforts.

Leonard Page, counsel for the United Auto Workers, declared: "It's a rather well known secret that employers are using them [management consultants] to fight unions. Yet," he said, "there's no mechanism under the NLRB to deal with them."

A report on anti-union consultants issued in December, 1980 by the House Subcommittee on Labor-Management Relations found "disturbing evidence" that some consultants try to "circumvent and nullify. . .existing worker protections," sometimes going so far as provoking decertification elections to expel unions from workplaces. Many such firms "come dangerously close to justifying whatever means are necessary" to defeat unions, the report concludes. The possibility that Van de Water might play a key role in formulating NLRB policy on management consultants indicates its stance. Page said that with Van de Water as chairman, he "doesn't expect to see much action taken by the NLRB to alter such practices." In fact he expects employers' reliance on management consultant firms to escalate.

Another weapon management uses to fight unionization, according to Page, is the NLRB litigation process. "Probably the biggest problem at the NLRB is its lack of remedies. Historically it's never been able to muster up sufficient remedies," he explained. Cases wind up in the courts and by the time most employers exhaust their appeals the union is too weak to benefit by it. On the average, waiting time on appeals is three to five years, Page said. Often after all litigation procedures have been completed the employer is simply ordered to sit down and bargain with the union. Page and other labor representatives fear more and more employers are using the NLRB as a "stalling ground" to delay union organizing.

Cuts in NLRB's budget might be used as an excuse by board members to skirt cases they prefer not to contend with. At his confirmation hearing Van de Water warned that cutbacks might restrain the board's "operational capabilities," though he hoped he could find savings in other areas like telephone costs and travel expenses. Labor representatives however, fear belt tightening, coupled with the ever increasing quantity of cases on the board's docket, will severely curtail its willingness to employ extraordinary measures such as preliminary injunctions in their proceedings.

Its escalating caseload, expected to exceed 60,000 in 1982, has created pressure to curtail the NLRB's jurisdiction. John Irving, NLRB general counsel during the Nixon Administration and now a lawyer representing management, believes the "board simply cannot afford the luxury of prosecuting every marginal case" and recommends that the NLRB be granted greater prosecutorial discretion. He believes certain priorities must be laid down, and suggests that perhaps exceptions should be made for first offenders, or under circumstances where "believable assurances are given that there will be no more violations."

It is likely that such procedures would damage the NLRB's credibility. "If it became public knowledge that the board would not seek enforcement in any significant number of cases," said Don Zimmerman, a Carter appointee to the board, "the effect on the general counsel's ability to negotiate settlements would obviously be severe."

A different proposal to cut the board's case load calls for revision of the board's "discretionary dollar standard." The minimum standard has not been increased since 1937. Irving contends that "the board ignores the fact that inflation has expanded its jurisdictions and says there is nothing it can do." If the board does not increase its standard to keep up with inflation, he said, "it will find itself with jurisdiction over virtually every private sector labor dispute. Surely the board cannot handle that additional case load."

But if a minimum monetary standard is established, Zimmerman counters that many serious violations of the act might occur in cases involving establishments too small to qualify. "When one or more employees is discharged for engaging in activity protected by the act," he said, "it seems to me of little consequence whether there are 10 other employees in the shop or 200."

Before the NLRB even hands down any significant decisions it's obvious that labor and the new Administration are already at odds. Despite his announced intention to give "full consideration to organized labor's interests and concerns," the President is encouraging byzantine legislative machinations in a desperate attempt to keep Van de Water in office. It's likely that Sen. Howard Baker (R-Tenn.) will introduce a motion to the full Senate to side-step the Senate Labor and Human Resources Committee's refusal to endorse Van de Water's nomination.

FINANCIAL BACKGROUND

Van de Water was worth over $600,000 in 1981. Much of this was held in large property holdings in Hawaii and California. His income was $22,500 from Van de Water Associates; $21,000 in salary from San Diego State University; and another $65,000 from Dible, Inc. for lectures.

Van de Water has recused himself from any cases involving 126 of his former clients, including: the American Council of School Administrators, American Institute of Banking, American Society for Personnel Administration, American Telecommunications Company, Amusement Park Personnel Association, Building Industries Credit Association, California State Banking Department, Caterpillar Corporation of Canada, City National Bank, Coca-Cola Corp. (Western Division), Crest Steel Corp., Diamond Sunsweet Co., Electric Manufacturers Association of Detroit, FMC, First Boston Corp., City of Garden Grove, General Telephone Company, Grumman, Inc., Hunt Wesson Corp., IBM Corp., Lockheed, Inc., Martin Luther King Hospital, National Association of Accountants, Oklahoma Public Personnel Association, Pacific Telephone and Telegraph Company, Paramount Pictures Corp., Royal Aluminum Co., Sales and Marketing Executive Association, San Diego Employers Council, Terminal Data Corp., Texas Christian University, Texas Wholesale Grocers Association, United California Bank, Wang Labs, Western Council of Construction Consumers and Western Insulation Company.

WHAT OTHERS ARE SAYING ABOUT HIM

* "I think of him as a union buster," said Hugh L. Beins.

* "[Van de Water] is a man who espouses the philosophy that 'It is not who is right, but what is right.' I believe, based on my knowledge of Mr. Van de Water, that he is not anti-union," said William C. Demas, Los Angeles Vice President of the Communication Workers of America

VETERANS ADMINISTRATION

ROBERT NIMMO
ADMINISTRATOR

RESPONSIBILITY OF OFFICE

Nimmo is the eleventh administrator to serve since the Veterans Administration was formed by presidential executive order in 1930. The VA has long been the government's largest independent agency with more than 216,000 employees. In 1982, the VA operated with a $24.1 billion budget.

In addition to managing this sprawling empire, Nimmo has "the responsibility to seek full funding for those programs that have been mandated by Congress for the welfare of veterans and their families".

Nimmo's department intimately affects millions of Americans. VA programs provide monthly compensation payments to over 2.2 million veterans with service-connected disabilities. About 878,000 war veterans and another 989,000 relatives of veterans receive monthly pension checks.

Among other major VA programs are:

—education benefits to nearly 773,000 veterans under the GI Bill;

—medical benefits provided by VA's 172 hospitals, 228 outpatient clinics and 102 nursing homes;

—guaranteed mortgage loans to veterans which will total more than $114 billion in insurance commitments by 1982.

BACKGROUND

Nimmo is best remembered in his home state of California as the state legislator who led the successful fight against actress and political activist Jane Fonda's appointment to the California Arts Council in 1979.

Nimmo accused Fonda of treason for her broadcasts on North Vietnam's Radio Hanoi in 1972 when she appealed to U.S. pilots to stop bombing. (Nimmo is an ex-bomber pilot himself, a retired U.S. Air Force colonel who served in both World

War II and the Korean War.) "By the standards under which I was raised and served for 29 years," Nimmo proclaimed, "giving aid and comfort to the enemy is an act of treason. She in fact gave aid and comfort to a country at war with the U.S." Noting that Fonda and Tom Hayden were friends and "advisers" to Gov. Jerry Brown, a presidential aspirant, Nimmo asked: "Do we want the President of the United States to be advised by traitors and collaborators?"

Nimmo has been a rancher and businessman for most of his life. He became politically active in the late 1960s after his close friend, Ronald Reagan, became governor of California.

In 1970 he was appointed by Reagan to serve as U.S. Property and Fiscal Officer, with responsibility for overseeing the federal contributions to California's Army and Air National Guard.

Nimmo represented San Luis Obispo in the state assembly from 1973 to 1976 and in the senate from 1976 until his retirement last year.

He is an active Republican and was the honorary chairman of Reagan's 1980 presidential campaign in San Luis Obispo County.

Born in Balboa, California on February 5, 1922, Nimmo was graduated from the Army Command and General Staff College in 1964. He is married with three children.

MAJOR ISSUES

- Veterans' groups are angered by Nimmo's downplaying of the problem of delayed stress syndrome, prevalent among Vietnam vets.

- Nimmo believes the health hazards of Agent Orange are confined to a skin ailment, prompting additional criticism from Vietnam veterans' groups.

- Funds for a number of VA construction projects have been deferred by the Administration, stirring critical response from a number of congressmen. A large number of other construction projects of VA medical facilities scheduled to begin in 1984 will now be subject to review under new standards.

- The VA took no official position on a proposed new GI Bill, which was recently rejected by the Pentagon. Anxious to buy new weapons, the Pentagon convinced the White House that the expenditures on veterans would be too costly.

Nimmo's selection for the VA post did little to silence the howls of protest to President Reagan's proposed 3.2 percent budget reduction from the budget submitted by President Carter for fiscal year 1982. The cuts would have hit Vietnam veterans the hardest, many of whom were concerned about losing federal assistance for popular vet counseling centers.

Vietnam veterans felt that Nimmo was out of touch with their needs, and demanded that the VA post be filled with a younger veteran. (Carter had appointed Max Cleland, an activist in Vietnam veteran organizations.) The Reagan Administration refused, but appointed Allen B. Clark, Jr., a Vietnam veteran, as Nimmo's deputy. This pleased Vietnam veterans groups because the deputy administrator post has traditionally been a powerful, policy-making position.

But Nimmo then decided to limit the authority of the deputy post—which led to quick conflict. After only two weeks on the job, Clark stomped out of a mid-June, 1981 meeting with Nimmo and went home to Texas, frustrated by his lack of influence on VA policy. Charles Hagel, also a Vietnam veteran, has been appointed to take his place. Vietnam veteran groups are generally pleased by Hagel's appointment.

One of Clark's major concerns was the VA's treatment of "delayed stress syndrome" among Vietnam veterans. While Nimmo has tended to downplay the severity of the problem, veterans groups are demanding more counseling centers and medical treatment. Nimmo has said 95 percent of Vietnam veterans have not been shortchanged by the government "and are doing just fine," a statement which has riled the veterans groups.

"That statement is totally wrong," said John Terzano, director of the Washington office of Vietnam Veterans of America. Terzano has cited a recent Harris poll which found that 70 percent of the American public believes the Vietnam veterans deserve greater compensation from the federal government. He also cited a study by the Center for Policy Research, a New York-based, domestic economic research group which concluded Vietnam veterans have not been adequately compensated.

The powerful veterans groups won a battle against the Reagan budget-cutters in July, 1981. Under pressure from Congress, which increased the funding for the readjustment programs, Nimmo announced the addition of 42 counseling centers.

Nimmo's early statements on Agent Orange, the defoliant which veterans and many scientists believe to cause cancer and birth defects, have also angered Vietnam veterans groups. Nimmo has said "there is no body of medical evidence" to prove the herbicide causes anything worse than chloracne, a skin ailment he characterizes as similar to "teen-age acne."

"I'd say that was an unfortunate statement," said Molly Milligan, a staffer who specializes in Agent Orange issues for the Senate Veterans Affairs Committee. "It shows a great deal of insensitivity to a serious problem."

The Senate recently approved federally funded medical treatment for Vietnam veterans who were exposed to Agent Orange. The bill requires the VA hospitals to give Agent Orange victims priority "ahead of those whose medical problems have no link whatsoever to their military service."

Terzano said he is "a little bit dismayed" by Nimmo's statements on Agent Orange, but is confident Congress will force the VA to move on the problem. There are a number of Agent Orange studies under way to gauge the effects of the herbicide. Among the major agencies involved are: the VA's newly created Agent Orange Research and Education Center, Air Force, Environmental Protection Agency, and the Center for Disease Control.

The VA's study has come under fire from veterans groups because the UCLA scientist designing its protocol has already stated his opinion that there is little evidence to associate Agent Orange with health problems, a view similar to Nimmo's. The VA has refused to dismiss the scientist, Dr. Gary Spivey, but his original protocol for conducting the study is continuing to be revised.

Nimmo indicated to Sen. Alan Cranston (D-Calif.) at his confirmation hearings that he did not intend to let the director of the Office of Management and Budget make unilateral major budgetary decisions that would affect VA programs, assuring Cranston that he would have access to the White House if necessary. Yet Cranston later said there is "legitimate cause for concern" that the Administration's reductions in the VA budget were proposed without VA involvement; Nimmo discussed revisions with OMB only after the "magnitude of the reductions" became clear, Nimmo admitted in a letter to Cranston.

On February 19, 1982, Nimmo announced a major reexamination of VA medical facility construction programs, which would reconsider $2.7 billion in construction. Projects potentially eligible for construction funding in fiscal year 1984 will have to be found valid under "new and defensible criteria;" some of the planned facilities may never be built as a result, Nimmo said.

The Administration has also deferred $91.3 million in funds appropriated for major VA construction projects. This money would have gone to fund five construction projects in D.C., Ohio, New Jersey, and two in California. The New Jersey project is a "long overdue and oft-postponed" facility renovation at the VA medical center in East Orange, involving the correction of various fire and safety deficiencies and the installation of air conditioning. Both Congress and the President agreed that this renovation was needed and justified, but the Administration has now overturned that decision with the deferral. Sen. Cranston has co-sponsored a resolution of disapproval of the deferral which he has said is "premised totally on consideration of ways to eliminate the VA hospital system as we know it today."

Nimmo's attitude on hospitals has angered the politically powerful Veterans of Foreign Wars (VFW). The VFW is worried that Nimmo's rhetoric accompanying his announcement of the reexamination of construction programs for 1984 and beyond is meant to justify "mainstreaming" health care for veterans—contracting out to private hospitals. In an interview, Nimmo had asked reporters, "Does it make sense to spend $280 million for a replacement VA hospital in Minneapolis where we've got 2,000 empty beds already there and where you've got a declining veterans population?" Arthur J. Fellwock, commander-in-chief of the VFW, claims that this statement is misleading on both counts: the purported 2,000 empty beds are in community hospitals, and the VA's own figures indicate no decline in the veteran population in the Minneapolis-St. Paul region. Nimmo maintained in a letter to Cranston that, "My reference to the 2,000 empty non-VA hospital beds in the Minneapolis area merely reiterates the concerns of the Minneapolis Metropolitan Board of Health regarding the size of the Minneapolis replacement project."

But Fellwock is not easily convinced. "Those at the highest levels speak the words of 'mainstreaming' and then tell us we do not understand what we have read," he testified before the Senate Committee on Veterans' Affairs on March 30, 1982. After assuring the committee that the VFW would fight any proposals to mainstream veterans' health care, he made it clear "that if these outbursts by Mr. Nimmo continue, the membership of my organization will have no choice but to seek the resignation of the present VA administrator," prompting applause from the nearly 300 veterans who accompanied him.

Fellwock was also angered by Nimmo's characterization of veterans' benefit programs as social welfare. He quoted Nimmo as saying, "It has long been my conviction, and still is, that public service is the price of citizenship, that people have an obligation to serve their country, and are not necessarily entitled thereby to a permanent social welfare system."

The VA budget proposed by the Administration for fiscal year 1983 is a mixture of increases and decreases. Total outlays of $24.4 billion represent a net increase of $222 million over 1982. Appropriations for readjustment benefits were decreased to $1.69 billion from an estimated $1.94 billion in 1982. Funding for Medical and Prosthetic Research is to be increased by $7.6 million, but is still left below the 1981 level of $144.4 million, and the program will lose 199 employees. The Administration also proposed savings of $135.3 million by eliminating dependency allowances—which provide greater compensation for veterans with families to support—for those veterans receiving service-connected disability compensation at the 30 and 40 percent rate. Thus, a Vietnam veteran (the group most affected by this provision) who was a below the knee amputee with a wife and two children would have his monthly benefit check increased by $19 through an increase in basic compensation rates, and simultaneously reduced by $61 through the elimination of the dependency allowances, for a net decrease of $42 per month.

Nimmo's programs may be facing lean times, but he isn't. Nimmo has garnered a reputation as "the best-tanned member of the Administration," scheduling speaking appearances that allow him to improve his golf game. He ordered the redecorating of his office and the rest of the tenth floor of the Veterans Administration Building at a cost of $46,000. Included in the renovation was an $8,400 bathroom so Nimmo can shower before evening appointments. Some $7,000 worth of the old furniture, which one VA spokesman described as "garish," went to his daughter Mary Nimmo, director of public affairs at the Commerce Department. Another $48,000 redecoration is planned.

Nimmo is not entitled by law to the use of a government automobile, yet the government is paying $7,250 for his ten-month lease on a gas-guzzling Buick Electra. Nimmo has paid a driver over $8,000 in overtime alone since June, 1981; the driver takes him to and from work, another service that Nimmo is technically not entitled to receive. Max Cleland, Nimmo's predecessor, a Vietnam vet who was a triple amputee, drove himself to work.

The trend is clear—as the Administration funnels billions of dollars into military hardware—even resuscitating old World War II-era battleships, it has less money for the men who served on them. This pattern was predicted in 1973 by Paul Starr in his book: *The Discarded Army: Veterans After Vietnam*: "To attract sufficient new recruits and to retain its men, the military has increased salaries and bonuses enormously. This increase in manpower costs produces a natural response to look for related expenses that might be eliminated. As the Pentagon opposed extension of the GI Bill after Korea because of its alleged impact on enlistment, so it may oppose the extension after Vietnam. The recent increases in GI Bill rates, which make the program even more expensive, will probably strengthen the Pentagon's hand."

Starr's analysis has proven prophetic. On March 11, 1982, the Pentagon rejected a proposed new GI Bill that would pay for veterans' education. Defense manpower chief Lawrence Korb said that a task force concluded that "educational benefits are not the most efficient incentive for recruiting high-quality personnel," and that other incentives, such as bonuses, were more effective. Korb said that because of the state of the economy "we cannot afford to spend one unnecessary dollar" on defense. In an obvious and unexplained contradiction, Defense Secretary Weinberger told reporters two weeks earlier: "We have found in all of our studies that it [a GI Bill] is the benefit that is most desired, and it would have the best effect on recruitment and retention." The VA has remained quiet on this issue that involves thousands of veterans.

FINANCIAL BACKGROUND

Nimmo holds some large real estate interests in California and in 1980 he received $36,000 in retirement pay from the state of California (the military department) in addition to his $23,750 salary from the state senate.

WHAT OTHERS ARE SAYING ABOUT HIM

- When contacted at his home in Texas, Allen B. Clark, Jr., said he didn't care to comment on Nimmo. He confirmed a *Washington Post* story that said he had stormed out of Nimmo's office after a misunderstanding in June, 1981 and said it was "in the best interest of everyone involved that I decided to leave."

- Cooper T. Holt, executive director of the Washington Office of the Veterans of Foreign Wars, said he is "deeply disturbed" by the politicizing of the administrator's office in recent years "and the willingness of the incumbent to wholly acquiesce to the dictates of the Office of Management and Budget."

- Nimmo's performance in the California state legislature is described as "fairly undistinguished" by Ted Sell, an editor at the *Sacramento Bee's* Capitol news bureau. "Nimmo represented the agricultural growers in a very safe district," he said, noting that Nimmo took a very conservative, anti-labor stance on agricultural issues. "Nimmo is remembered around California for the Jane Fonda thing," he said, "but that is about it."

CHAPTER 4

TRANSPORTATION
AND HOUSING

TRANSPORTATION DEPARTMENT

ANDREW LEWIS
SECRETARY

RESPONSIBILITY OF OFFICE

The Department of Transportation was formed in 1966 with a primary objective to develop "national transportation policies and programs conducive to the provision of fast, safe, efficient and convenient transportation at the lowest cost consistent therewith."

Lewis presides over eight operating administrations whose jurisdictions include highway planning, development and construction; urban mass transit; railroads; aviation; and safety of waterways, ports, highways, motor vehicles, transportation of hazardous materials, and oil and gas pipelines.

In 1982, DOT will operate with 113,000 employees and a budget of $20.3 billion.

BACKGROUND

When Lewis ran for Pennsylvania governor in 1974, the joke around the state was "Drew who?" Lewis was a powerful and well-known figure in the state Republican Party, a proficient fundraiser and long-time ally of then Republican Senator Richard Schweiker. But Lewis had never held public office; to the voters he was just another pretty face.

Lewis ran a "friendly" campaign against incumbent Milton Shapp, though state Republicans attacked Shapp for corruption in his administration. But Lewis had his own problems on the honesty and integrity front. Shapp accused Lewis of illegal campaign practices when Lewis accepted money from his former employer, Snelling and Snelling, to test out the campaign waters through a Friends of Drew Lewis Committee before he formally filed.

Lewis spent $1 million on the election, half of it raised through loans from F. Eugene Dixon and right-wing financier Richard Mellon Scaife (Scaife donated another $42,500) but Lewis got drubbed, losing by a 54-46 percent count.

Bill McLaughlin, Shapp's legislative secretary recalled that Lewis was a less than charismatic campaigner. "He had this kind of Rotary Club businessman's presentation," said McLaughlin. "I always expected him to have a pointer and a few charts. . .He didn't radiate a pol's kind of personality." McLaughlin said that Lewis did not run a "very aggressive" campaign, and speculates that Lewis may have been a sacrificial lamb, sent out by the Republicans to run a very difficult race against a popular incumbent in the shadow of Watergate.

Pennsylvania has historically been a machine state politically and Lewis made his way to the top through the party bureaucracy. He has been a delegate to every Republican national convention since 1968. He served as a Republican national committeeman from the state. He chaired Pennsylvania's Republican Finance Committee. In 1968, he ran Schweiker's senatorial campaign. In 1980, he served as deputy director of both the Reagan-Bush Committee and deputy chairman of the Republican National Committee.

Lewis remains a powerful force in Pennsylvania politics, with a significant coterie of followers among party regulars. It is common knowledge that Lewis is estranged from the current Pennsylvania governor, Republican Richard Thornburgh. A former federal prosecutor, Thornburgh ran in 1978 as an outsider, aided by large contributions from Senator John Heinz. Lewis and Thornburgh have made a great deal of publicly patching up their differences lately, but veteran Pennsylvania political observers say that privately they just don't like each other.

Lewis is a keenly ambitious man; it is evident in everything he does—from his brisk pace in official Washington, to the way in which he badgers national television programs (particularly during the air controllers strike) to give him air-time. West Virginia Governor Jay Rockefeller, for one, believes Lewis is thirsting after the governorship of Pennsylvania.

But Lewis would be trying to elbow his way up on a crowded escalator. It's unlikely he will challenge Thornburgh for the gubernatorial nomination when his term expires in 1983. Waiting in the wings behind Thornburgh is the state's young Lieutenant Governor William Scranton III. Capital observers say Lewis might have trouble wresting a nomination away from Scranton, with his almost legendary name. Moreover, Scranton is considered something of a Lewis protege. Lewis has told the *Philadelphia Inquirer* that gubernatorial racing was "something I'll never do again." As for Washington, both of the state's senators are Republicans. And it's hard to picture Drew Lewis in the House of Representatives.

Lewis's political aspirations are particularly important to understanding his performance in Washington. He has some background in transportation issues—since 1971 he was one of two trustees handling the Reading Co.'s reorganization under federal bankruptcy laws. (Most of the 1,200-mile railroad system was transferred to Conrail in 1976. Just before Lewis took office in January, 1981, the railroad formally emerged from bankruptcy and in August, 1981 agreed to a government settlement of $121 million for the railroad properties transferred in 1976.) But in Washington he has displayed little interest in the substance of transit issues, concentrating on only a handful of politically sensitive—and publicly visible—concerns. (See Major Issues section.)

Lewis has been a successful businessman. As his Reading experience demonstrates, he has lucratively applied his management skills to troubled businesses. From 1969 to 1972 he served as president and chief executive of Simplex Wire & Co. From 1970 to 1974 he was chief executive of Snelling & Snelling. From 1974 until taking office he ran a consulting firm called Lewis & Associates. Lewis began his business career in 1955 at Henkels & McCoy, Inc., a general contractor in Philadelphia. From 1960 to 1969 he worked for the American Olean Tile Co., a subsidiary of the National Gypsum Co. Before National Gypsum bought it, Schweiker's father ran the company.

Lewis's relationship with Schweiker dates back to childhood. They went to the same high school, the same church, and lived next door in Worcester, Pennsylvania. In 1976, Reagan tapped Schweiker as his running-mate in part to woo Lewis, who controlled the state's 103-member delegation and was committed to Ford. But Lewis refused the advances—temporarily straining relations with Schweiker—and Ford held onto the nomination. After the election, though, Lewis mended his fences, jumped on the Reagan bandwagon in 1977, and handled Reagan's Pennsylvania primary campaign before being promoted to a spot on the national staff.

Born on November 3, 1931 in Philadelphia, Pennsylvania, Lewis was graduated from Haverford College in 1953 with a B.S. in economics and from Harvard Business School with an M.B.A. in 1955. He is married to Marilyn Stoughton, who is now a second-term Pennsylvania state legislator. She is the inheritor of a fortune from her family. (See Financial Background section.) The couple has three children.

MAJOR ISSUES

- Lewis has spearheaded Administration efforts to revive the domestic auto industry at the cost of life-saving auto safety and environmental regulations. Lewis has overseen the revocation of the passive restraint standard, which could have saved the lives of tens of thousands of Americans over the next decade.

- Lewis earned early notoriety by his harsh response toward the air traffic controllers. Scorning negotiations with the union, once it began its illegal strike, Lewis never budged from the hard line laid down by Reagan. Lewis has refused to rehire any of the controllers, jeopardizing the safety of travelers and disrupting the air traffic system through at least 1984.

- Faced with mounting opposition to the increased amount of air traffic at Washington's National Airport and a growing concern about air safety, Lewis has made only a few cosmetic changes in the airport's regulations, wary of stepping on too many congressional toes. Lewis has also withdrawn important aircraft safety proposals.

In a city where the appearance of doing often inspires more accolades than the quality of what is done, Drew Lewis is a man for all motions.

Lewis appears to be constantly on the move. Newspaper profiles begin with a variation on the phrase, "At 7:30 a.m., Drew Lewis reached across his desk. . ." Aggressive and brisk in speech, Lewis has charmed much of the Washington press corps and Congress and impressed the White House with a firm image of decisiveness. The *New York Times* says he is "widely regarded as the most active, visible and influential transportation chief ever." *Time* magazine puts him on the short list of Cabinet secretaries whose performance rates an "A," and calls him a "possible candidate for promotion." The *Philadelphia Inquirer* breathlessly calls him "The Dynamo." Sometimes he walks with "a purposeful stride." Other times he "Bound[s]. . .down three flights at a gallop."

Whew! Lewis is undoubtedly aggressive and vigorous (he pulled 20-hour days during the air controller strike and still looked fresh on TV.) He speaks well, knows how to communicate with Congress—Rep. James Howard (D-N.J.), chairman of the House Public Works and Transportation Committee, speaks well of him—and is a frequently sought after guest for cocktail parties, though he professes not to enjoy them much. And he is good looking, with the crisp features and manicured coiffeur that a good media consultant can build an entire political campaign around.

All of which makes Lewis an attractive political commodity. And none of which has much to do with whether his performance as Transportation secretary has benefited the public

Lewis runs the DOT like a business, viewing his administrators as something akin to vice-presidents running profit centers in a corporation. "Lewis likes to delegate as much as possible," said one analyst in the secretary's office. "The normal type of interference a staff would run for a secretary, under Lewis we don't run." Another analyst who recently left the secretary's office told us that Lewis had, in effect, told the administrators "If you don't embarrass me and you stick to the major dictates of the program. . .I don't give a damn what you do."

That's partly because Lewis isn't much interested in transportation issues (with a few exceptions), staffers say. "I don't have a sense that he cares at all about improving the transportation system," said the former analyst. "I don't think he really cares whether there's a DOT five years down the road." Added the analyst still at the DOT: "He's interested in getting ready for his next job—whatever that may be." For some programs—such as maritime subsidies—that attitude can mean a healthy reexamination, the analyst said. For most DOT activities though, it means abandoning the agency's mission.

Like Reagan, Lewis prides himself on being the chief executive, above the daily fray. "Lewis is a businessman," said the former analyst. "Almost to the point where he is willing to rely more on the options [presented him by staff] rather than thinking it through himself." But Richard Sullivan, chief counsel of the House Public Works and Transportation Committee, said that in their meetings "Lewis knows what he is talking about. He reminds me a lot of [Richard] Daley and Nelson Rockefeller. . .Rockefeller brought in a bunch of technicians, 20 people, but when it came to the crunch he answered the questions himself. Lewis fielded the questions very well."

Lewis surged from the center of the Cabinet pack to the front pages, of course, through his handling of the air traffic controller strike. Together with Reagan, Lewis inflicted on organized labor one of its most devastating defeats in the past generation. Suddenly, tough-guy profiles of Drew Lewis sprouted in papers around the country. The *Los Angeles Times*, beneath a headline that read "Tough Leaders Clash in Controller Strike" wrote admiringly of how Lewis, as a young employee from a Philadelphia construction firm, broke a strike while working in the Azores by air-lifting in 16 Italian technicians.

In the crisis, though, the Administration raised strike breaking to a new level of vehemence. Lewis quickly shoved aside Federal Aviation Administration (FAA) Administrator J. Lynn Helms, who would usually handle such matters, and personally took control of the negotiations, though Reagan reportedly took the hardest line of all.

Through the weekend of August 1, 1981 negotiators tried to patch together a deal, after Professional Air Traffic Controllers' Association's (PATCO) membership overwhelmingly rejected the contract offer made by the government the previous June. But the negotiations stalled. And on the morning of August 3, PATCO took the first step towards its demise by illegally walking off the job.

Reacting with unprecedented harshness, the Reagan Administration thoroughly and unequivocally destroyed the union. Four hours after the strike began, Reagan announced he would fire the controllers if they didn't return to work within 48 hours. They didn't, and he did, and three days later Drew Lewis was already referring to the strike in the past tense. "We're forgetting about the strike that did exist, and we're going ahead in terms of hiring people and figuring out how we operate" the system, he told reporters.

Throughout the subsequent months, Lewis and the Administration steadfastly refused all attempts to find a solution. Three former Republican secretaries of Labor offered to mediate a week after the strike began; the Administration rebuffed them all. The international air traffic controllers federation asked Lewis to reopen negotiations; Lewis replied, "We do not see how it is possible to reopen the negotiations." After the Administration decertified PATCO in October, 1981 labor and some congressional leaders urged Reagan to rehire the individual controllers because, as Lane Kirkland put it, "Any continued vendetta against these workers and their families would not be justice, but revenge." Others argued that Lewis's chief obligation was the safety of the skies for millions of Americans and that if that duty required hiring back a minority of the controllers he should do so. Lewis replied, "We have concluded it would not be worth it [to rehire]. It would not be worth it as a matter of principle." Eventually, in December, 1981, Lewis announced the Administration would allow the controllers to apply for other federal jobs (at a time when the federal work force was contracting) but would never allow them to return to civilian control towers. Said Lewis: The action is "a final decision within the Administration."

So what is left in the dust of what the *New York Times* called the "Execution of a Union?" The Transportation Department says the air traffic system will not return to normal until at least mid-1984, and possibly 1985. The Administration acknowledges it will cost $1.3 billion to train new controllers. Reduction in flight schedules required by the government have removed many of the benefits of airline decontrol and increased fares. At some urban airports, delays are running three to five times the pre-strike rate. According to the National Transportation Safety Board, stress and fatigue may present a long-term safety hazard among the diminished controller work force. And a union that had endorsed Ronald Reagan in the 1980 campaign and had received from him an assurance that he would work in "a spirit of cooperation [with] the air traffic controllers," had ceased to exist.

With the exception of the air controllers' strike, Lewis has, by his own calculation, spent the most time dealing with the controversy over limiting air traffic at Washington's National Airport, a matter of relatively minor moment in the national transportation picture, but of acute concern to the members of Congress and Executive Branch that use the airport.

For the past few years, critics have contended that much of the air traffic at National should be diverted to Dulles International Airport, where the runways are longer, the approach by air is easier, and noisy jets do not disturb Washington residents. But Dulles is 26 miles from the White House, and much less convenient than National.

In 1979, the Carter Administration proposed regulations to limit National traffic. In 1980, Congress passed an amendment delaying the implementation of that plan until April, 1981.

That made it Lewis's problem. Lewis first postponed the April deadline, then issued a July, 1981 proposal that would cap National's annual passenger traffic at 16 million and reduce the daily number of big commercial jet flights. (In a concession to Sen. Russell Long (D-La.), the maximum flight length permitted from National was extended from 650 to 1,000 miles, which would bring New Orleans in under the limit.)

Lewis's regulations would have hurt the upstart New York Air, which was taking advantage of a loophole in FAA regulations to run almost 50 takeoffs and landings a day. New York Air's majority owner is Texas Air—which recruited Rep. Charles Wilson (D-Tex.). Wilson slapped an amendment onto the DOT authorization bill that would increase the takeoff and landing limit by 10 percent. But Lewis reached an agreement with New York Air, and Wilson allowed the Senate to delete his amendment. Lewis's proposal went in effect in December, 1981.

But Lewis's victory does nothing for the safety concerns that spawned much of the drive to curtail National's traffic. "It does nothing about safety at National, the noise and overcrowding," said Eric Bernthal, president of a Coalition on Airport Problems. "It prevents them from getting worse. It puts Secretary Lewis's finger in the dike." But the pressure on the other side will continue to build: Lewis's flight and passenger limits will be reached perhaps as soon as 1984. The issue is sure to return. Meanwhile, the FAA is engaged in a widespread rollback of air safety efforts. (See Helms profile.)

Lewis first earned the President's ear by running the Administration's task force on the auto industry. Lewis made it clear from the beginning of the Administration that he would carry the automakers case for imposing quotas on the increasingly popular Japanese imports. But with other high Administration policymakers resisting formal quotas—in deference to the Administration's ostensible free-trade posture—Lewis and his allies had to settle for "voluntary" quotas with Japan.

Reviving the auto industry—which he has called "vital to our economic well-being"—has been one of Lewis's top concerns. His primary effort to assist the manufacturers has been to roll back federal auto safety standards and stop further fuel efficiency standards. Lewis maintains that auto safety regulations have "hit the law of diminishing returns"—a contention fervently disputed by the insurance industry and safety engineers who point to such examples as a recent study by Yale Professor William Nordhaus, a former member of the Council of Economic Advisers, which concluded that the economic benefits of a crash protection standard (passive restraint) would be ten times greater than its cost.

On April 6, 1981, Lewis's task force on the auto industry released a list of 34 safety and Environmental Protection Agency regulations to be postponed, reconsidered or eliminated. In late May, 1981, Lewis assured a House committee that further deregulation would proceed following careful cost-benefit analysis. But later in the same hearing he offered a more revealing indication of his plans, stating flatly: "I don't see any regulations coming out of my department in the next four years." That remark was so inappropriate as a matter of procedure that National Highway Traffic Safety Administrator Raymond Peck later told people that his boss "deserved to get beat up on" for saying such a thing. The unperturbed Lewis proceeded to approve the revocation in October, 1981 of crash protection standard 208, ten years in the making under previous Republican and Democratic administrations.

Peck's relationship with Lewis is fitful. Peck is not a Lewis man—his ticket to the department was Deputy Secretary Darrell Trent, a campaign official with whom Peck worked during the transition. Lewis has told visitors that Peck was his fifth choice for the job; the first choice was comedian Bob Hope's daughter, a Washington attorney.

In part, Peck's cool relationship with Lewis reflects the split in the department between Lewis's people and Trent's allies. A key Lewis ally is counsel John Fowler, a 33-year-old attorney who, staffers say, has been heavily involved in all matters of policy. A former vice-president of the Reading Co. (where Lewis was a trustee), "Fowler is a critical player on everything in this department. Lewis relies heavily on him."

Lewis has delegated broadly to Peck, and Peck seems to view part of his job to be keeping Lewis from being too closely identified with regulatory decisions that will bring about thousands of otherwise preventable deaths. Of course, Peck's decisions consistently follow Lewis's policy directions. But their personalities clash. Lewis, a businessman with a time-is-money ethic, has little patience for Peck's long-windedness, staffers say. "Lewis won't enjoy the meeting with Peck, for Peck will go on twice as long as he should," said one close observer. (See profile of Raymond Peck.)

Lewis likes the image of a man of action. His wife likes to comment, "Drew may be wrong, but he never hesitates." He has little patience for detail—it slows him down, of course—and he treats his subordinate agency heads with a measure of low key intimidation that keeps them in their place. He is a tough administrator. He has publicly rebuked Peck on personnel matters. When we asked him questions in an interview, he often rolled his eyes off toward the ceiling, after tossing the questions to Peck. But to subordinates, Lewis's "hate" for government (as one put it) is clear. One very knowledgeable official called him, "evil, totally incapable of human emotion, cold as ice beneath a charming, engaging veneer."

In one interview, Lewis's vehemence leapt out. "There's no sense of urgency, no compulsion to get something done," he said of the people in his department. "If I had the time I'd go to every department around here, including my own office and get rid of 10 percent of the people without any loss whatsoever in terms of our ability to serve the public." (Ironic words from an official who prides himself on dismantling safety programs and imposing a do-nothing stance on his air, railroad, highway, and motor vehicle safety programs.) Now staffers around the department wear buttons reading "Drew's drones."

Lewis can be a tough politician too. After retiring Pennsylvania Republican Representative Marc Marks blasted Reagan's economic policies, Lewis gave him a tongue-lashing—and a warning. Marks told the *New York Times* that Lewis "began by asking me what the hell I thought I was up to. He said Meese, Baker and Brock were catching hell, and said he was catching hell, too. He then gave me a little lecture, told me not to worry, that he and others were going to convince the President he had to change his course. . ." Lewis urged Marks to quiet down, telling the congressman: "I want you to know that Meese, Baker, Brock and I have a lot of friends in this town and you had better think about that before you go on saying what you're saying." Lewis denied threatening Marks.

The other area in which Lewis has been personally involved, department sources say, is railroad policy. Lewis is seeking major changes in both Conrail and Amtrak. The Administration is working to sell Conrail to private buyers, but maintains that it must first make the stock more attractive by reducing labor costs. (See profile of Robert Blanchette.) At the same time, Lewis is pushing to slash federal assistance to Amtrak and mass transit, provoking opposition even from conservative Republicans such as Sen. Alfonse D'Amato (D-N.Y.). "What he's doing is called 'kill the program fellows,' " said Anne Canby, outgoing commissioner of transportation in New Jersey. "In the case of public transportation they are forcing us. . .to charge so much that everybody is going to go back to their automobiles." (See profile of Arthur Teele.)

Lewis has mollified some sectors of the public transportation community by proposing to use one cent of a proposed gasoline tax increase to fund capital expenses on mass transit projects. The additional penny would generate $1 billion annually. Reagan has already rejected the proposed increase—which primarily would be used to offset declining gasoline consumption that is crimping the trust fund that pays for interstate highways—but Lewis continues to press the idea. (See profile on Ray Barnhart.)

On maritime issues, Lewis has fashioned a trade off for the heavily-subsidized maritime industry, which now receives more than $2.53 million in federal operating aid per ship. Lewis is proposing to grant shippers antitrust and regulatory immunity that will make it easier for them to join international rate-fixing cartels, share facilities, and even pool cargoes. In return, the future growth of government subsidies will be cut.

Congress has already approved a trial suspension of construction subsidies, which cost $135 million in new obligations during 1981. Operating subsidies, though, will continue to balloon under the 1983 budget, rising from $417 million to $454 million. The 1983 budget document promises that "administrative changes will be made to hold down escalating costs." Those proposals are expected to be unveiled by Lewis in mid-1982.

FINANCIAL BACKGROUND

Lewis, a multi-millionaire, has one of the thickest financial disclosure statements in the Administration. In 1980, he earned $60,783 from Lewis & Associates; $179,167 from the Reading Company; another $19,450 in director's fees from Provident National Corp., Coleman Co., Wawa Inc., Tamaqua Cable Products Corp., and Comcast Inc; and another $80,600 in Trustee fees from Builders Investment Group and Fidelco Growth Investors. His holdings in Lewis & Associates are valued at over $250,000.

The secretary reports moderate holdings ($15,-50,000) in Finsco. Inc., SCM Corp., B.F. Goodrich, and Sears, Roebuck, and Co.

His largest holdings are in 20 different oil and gas ventures, which are valued at more than $800,000 and produced income exceeding $140,000.

Lewis's wife and children are the beneficiary of seven trusts worth almost $5 million as of October, 1980, according to information in the financial disclosure statement.

WHAT OTHERS ARE SAYING ABOUT HIM

- One veteran Pennsylvania journalist describes Lewis as a businessman "who is very heavy on efficiency" and a political money handler who "has a passion for the game." As a prominent political figure in Pennsylvania, Lewis developed a "healthy sense of rivalry" with other Republican heavyweights like Governor Richard Thornburgh and Senator John Heinz. "It is no secret around here that there is no lost love between Lewis and those two," the source said.

  Nonetheless, at Lewis's nomination hearing, Heinz was there as a chief witness. "I've had many occasions stretching back over a decade to work with Drew Lewis in Pennsylvania and on national issues," Heinz said. "And I must say that I believe he is the right man for an extremely difficult job at precisely the right time. . .

- One congressional aide says Lewis's actions are no mystery. "Drew Lewis is a politician," he said. "He will do the politically expedient things and he certainly will avoid rocking the boat. I've heard from several sources that Lewis wants to run for the U.S. Senate eventually.

- Speaking of the cuts in transportation programs, James Howard, chairman of the House Committee on Public Works and Transportation said, "could anyone who has driven over our crumbling highways or ridden on public transit in recent months honestly question the need for more, not less, investment in public transportation?" Howard, however, speaks highly of Lewis and is happy with the working relationship Lewis has established. Lewis has particularly pleased Howard by pushing for an increase in the gasoline tax, which would give the government more money to spend on highways.

RAYMOND PECK

ADMINISTRATOR, NATIONAL HIGHWAY TRAFFIC SAFETY ADMINISTRATION

RESPONSIBILITY OF OFFICE

NHTSA primarily administers the 1966 National Traffic and Motor Vehicle Safety Act, which clearly lays out the agency's responsibilities: "to reduce traffic accidents and deaths and injuries to persons resulting from traffic accidents." It does not, it is worth remembering, provide that those goals be compromised if the auto industry has a bad sales year.

Established under the 1966 Highway Safety Act, the agency also is responsible under the 1972 Cost Saving Act and 1975 fuel economy standards legislation for the national odometer law, setting a uniform national speed limit and promulgating fuel economy standards.

Peck supervised a budget of $194.6 million and a staff of about 640 in 1982.

BACKGROUND

"My prior experience in this particular subject area," Peck noted modestly at his confirmation hearing, "is limited." In fact, Peck's experience in auto safety prior to 1981 consisted of his involvement in an auto accident which demolished his expensive BMW, but left him, his wife and his daughter unhurt because they were wearing seat belts and a child restraint harness.

Far from a hindrance, lack of experience was apparently a requisite job qualification. Peck told us that transition officials "decided [they needed] somebody who had not been previously involved in this precise subject matter." The Republicans, others in the auto safety community explained, hoped in that way to avoid a contentious nomination process.

Peck not only met those qualifications, but also possessed a long record of resisting government regulation—both from within and outside of the executive branch—and the reputation of a tough political infighter, not averse to bending the truth to make a point. At a NHTSA social function a month after taking office he bragged, "I'm the best damned deregulation lawyer in town."

Peck earned his reputation during his first tour of government duty in the Nixon and Ford Administrations. From 1971 through 1974 he served as environmental counsel at the Department of Commerce preparing the department's position on environmental and regulatory matters. In 1974 he became director of the Treasury Department's office of energy regulatory and legislative policy. The next year, he joined the Interior Department as deputy assistant secretary for energy and minerals.

Peck's tenure in government was dominated by the epic struggle between Ford and Congress over strip mining legislation. Twice Congress overwhelmingly passed legislation to curb the mining practices that had stripped hillsides and mountains in coal counties around America. Ford pocket vetoed the bill at the end of the 93rd Congress and rejected a second version in 1975. The House came within three votes of the two-thirds majority needed to override that second veto.

Peck led the Ford Administration's efforts against the bill. "The worst thing that Ray Peck did was organize the two Ford vetoes of the strip mining legislation," said Nathaniel Reed, assistant secretary of Interior from 1971 to 1977. Ford justified his opposition with apocalyptic projections of the bill's impact on the coal mining industry.

But the figures themselves quickly became controversial and were ultimately discredited. "Peck tried to come up with a justification, but there was no serious justification for the figures," recalled an aide to Rep. Morris Udall (D-Az.), chairman of the House Interior Committee. "The numbers were nonsense."

At hearings on Ford's veto, Udall told Peck and the other Administration witnesses testifying: "This is the most dishonest set of calculations I have ever seen in all my years in the committee." An internal Interior Department memo agreed the figures were "mushy."

In rejecting the bill, the White House for example, cited Interior Department calculations that the bill would reduce production by 162 million tons annually; a study done at the Environmental Protection Agency (EPA) estimated the loss would be about 90 million tons and found "double-counting" in the Administration's forecast. And, while Ford argued the bill would eliminate 36,000 jobs, subsequent analysis revealed the losses would not be existing jobs, but rather prospective, future jobs.

At one point during the heated debate, Udall questioned Peck's key role: "I have been sitting here all day, Mr. Peck, and wondering, in my experience around here, the Commerce Department rarely plays any kind of major role in these resource questions. The President has the CEQ [Council on Environmental Quality], EPA, Interior, he has FEA [Federal Energy Administration]. But here is a man from the Commerce Department, the spokesman for big business, dominating a large part of our discussion. Is there any significance to that?"

Peck explained that he had been dealing with the bill since 1971 when the Nixon Administration began looking at strip mining. And he asserted—as he would again in 1981 after eliminating the crucial passive restraint standard—that he "had not spoken with anybody from the industry" on the issue.

Peck told us the suggestion (which came from Reed, among others) that he was responsible for the disputed numbers was, in one of his favorite phrases, "a flat, fucking, lie." "I saw those numbers at exactly the same time that everybody else in the interagency review process saw them. I could not for the life of me tell you now what they were. I could only vaguely tell you how they were collected," he maintained.

Nonetheless, Peck eventually moved to the Interior Department, where he continued to make headlines over his actions in the strip mining controversy. Peck ordered his department geologists not to give technical strip mining information to Congress without clearing the data with him, saying he wanted "to protect the scientific objectivity" of the geologists. Said Reed: "He was the coal industry's man in Interior, their spy."

Challenging the information blackout, then Rep. John Melcher (D-Mont.) said,

"If Peck interferes, it is a disadvantage to Congress and a disadvantage to the Administration because it raises again the whole question of who they are serving, the public or the coal industry."

For Peck that question became moot when Ford lost the 1976 election. Taking a quick swing through the revolving door, he landed at the Washington law firm of Cotten, Day & Doyle, where he represented such clients as the U.S. Chamber of Commerce in a suit against the Interior Department, and Virginia coal operators fighting the regulations that implemented the strip mining act which finally passed Congress in 1977.

Peck went full circle the next year, leaving the firm to become vice-president and director of regulatory affairs for the National Coal Association. He represented the coal association before government agencies, drafted policy positions and wrote articles. One piece on federal public land policies—called "And Then There Were None"—concluded industry would have to become more involved in the regulatory process: "Without such active participation, the process will subordinate virtually all resource development options to the intangible benefits derived from non-development."

Environmentalists remember Peck with a disdain usually reserved for the likes of James Watt. One long-time activist on coal issues called him "a slug." Another said he was "a mad dog."

"Peck is an undercutter of federal law," said one lobbyist at the Environmental Policy Center, the group that worked most intimately with the strip mining legislation. "I can't think of anyone more anti-environmental in the country."

One consultant who served with Peck on a coal policy task force said his views were "so paleolithic" that they were beyond the bounds of discussion. "It was worse than arguing with a blank wall," said the consultant.

A flash of Peck's perspective on environmental issues came out when he told us that he thought "Jim Watt's gotten a bum rap. What is actually being done is not being accurately reflected in the way the activity of the agency is being reported."

Before joining the Nixon Administration, Peck spent seven years in private practice at three New York law firms: Casey, Lane & Mittendorf (1964-1967); Norton, Sachs, Molineaux & Pastore (1967-1968), and Cahill & McPhillips, where he was a partner. Peck was also involved in Republican politics, serving as the New England regional director for the United Citizens for Nixon-Agnew in 1968, and on various local Republican bodies. Peck's route to the NHTSA job was his volunteer work for the transition Legal and Administrative Services Office, which looked at the Justice Department and the independent regulatory agencies. (Other members of the office included Timothy Ryan, who became solicitor of labor and M. Peter McPherson who took over AID.)

"I didn't look for this job," Peck said. "I turned this job down several times. I did not want to get into the government at all." Now in the government, though, he told us "I have no plans of leaving"; but he wouldn't commit to staying through the first Reagan term. Because Peck is known to be under financial pressures, he is not expected to finish his term. After leaving office, Peck plans to go back into natural resource law. "I don't see how I could ever go to work for an auto company," he responded to that suggestion of possible future plans. "I honestly don't see how in good conscience any administrator could talk himself into feeling that there isn't either a conflict or an appearance of conflict, a question of impropriety there."

Born on January 16, 1940 in Orange, New Jersey, Peck was graduated from Holy

Cross in 1961 and received his law degree from New York University in 1964, and a masters of law there two years later. He is married, with a baby daughter.

MAJOR ISSUES

On October 23, 1981, speaking slowly and carefully before the hot lights of almost a dozen television cameras and a room full of reporters, Raymond Peck gave the domestic auto industry what it most passionately sought from the Reagan Adminstration. Peck rescinded Standard 208, which would have required the manufacturers to install "passive restraints"—either airbags or automatic safety belts in their cars. The decision will please the auto companies, but at a steep cost to motorists; as many as 100,000 deaths and 600,000 injuries over the next decade.

Peck eliminated this crash protection standard at a time when deaths on the highway are expected to climb. "How is this different from the time in this country when we had a polio epidemic and a number of our children were killed or crippled," said Dr. Seymour Charles, president of Physicians for Auto Safety. "We've never had an epidemic of any disease in the United States that is of the proportions of the highway epidemic."

In part because of the shift toward smaller cars, highway deaths are rising again, after falling sharply in 1974, the year in which a 55-mile per hour speed limit was enacted. From 46,402 deaths that year, the total rose to over 53,000 in 1980 before dropping to 51,000 in 1981, according to the National Safety Council. There is an injury on the highway every nine seconds. And in recent years, the death rate per mile driven has begun to increase. A NHTSA study projects that if no significant safety improvements are made in vehicles or highway design the death toll would reach 70,000 a year by 1990. One hundred forty people die on the highway every day; that's the equivalent of a major airline crash 365 days a year. In a 1978 Louis Harris poll—conducted for Amtrak not NHTSA—over 80 percent of those responding considered improving auto safety the top transportation priority for the government.

At the least, the measureable cost of the highway epidemic is $60 billion a year. That costs the insurance industry a lot of money, and with its eyes firmly on the bottom line it has become one of the strongest advocates for passive restraints, particularly the airbag. All members of the industry that commented on the rule favored its retention. Peck's decision "condemns to utterly needless death tens of thousands of Americans," said the Insurance Institute for Highway Safety.

From the early days of the Administration—indeed from the time of Budget Director David Stockman's "Economic Dunkirk" memo—the passive restraint standard has been in danger.

At his first press conference, Transportation Secretary Drew Lewis said "the only problem we might have, or question we may have in that area, is going to be the timing of it"—referring to the congressionally revised schedule of phasing in passive restraints for large cars before small cars.

But two weeks later, Lewis postponed the long-delayed standard for another year, setting the stage for its elimination in October, 1981.

"I make no bones about the fact that I and Lewis and Dave thought that it was appropriate to delay the standard," said James C. Miller III, who ran the Admnistration's regulatory review efforts before being appointed chairman of the Federal Trade Commission. "The issue was discussed in Cabinet meetings, sometimes with the President there, and so I don't think that it should come as any surprise that [the department] took action expeditiously.''

From there, it was all downhill. In April, 1981, General Motors announced it was abandoning its airbag research section and staff, and would meet the passive restraint requirement, if it ever came, with automatic belts. And the automaker promptly stepped up its efforts to see that the standard would never be imposed. During the summer, Peck criticized the airbag as being uneconomical, though he said—as he did during the press conference—that he would buy one for his own car.

But, of course, Peck cannot buy one for his own car—nor can any other motorist, since none of the auto manufacturers will even offer them as options on cars sold in America. ''It's frustrating,'' Peck acknowledged. ''It has to be frustrating for anybody standing in this place.''

In rescinding the standard, Peck argued that manufacturers would meet the rule with easily disengaged automatic belts which would be rejected by motorists, blunting the expected safety benefits of the standard and creating a public backlash against the agency that ''could have a far greater adverse effect on the agency safety mission.''

When we asked Peck if rescinding the standard advanced the cause of highway safety, he said flatly: ''I do indeed. If I hadn't thought that, I wouldn't have done it.''

At his press conference, Peck acknowledged that, ''I don't think anyone on my staff agreed with all aspects of this decision.'' In fact, according to agency sources, Peck overruled his entire senior technical staff by completely rescinding the standard. Many NHTSA staff found out the date of the press conference after General Motors did.

At the heart of Peck's decision is the contention that passive belts would not be used by many more motorists than already use the manual belts. The staff, however, told Peck that ''even if the auto makers use automatic belts primarily as the means of complying with an automatic crash protection standard, the standard can have benefits that easily justify their costs.''

Asked by one of the authors at the press conference if his decision would increase the number of deaths on the highway, Peck replied: ''Not by one more death than would not occur if the seat belt in the car involved had been in use.''

Question: ''Based on your research with the amount of seat belts that are in use, will this decision increase the amount of deaths on the highway over the next few years?''

Peck: ''We simply cannot tell. It is a function entirely of whether people who would not otherwise have used their manual belts. . . . There is very little data; there is very little hard evidence. . .''

But the evidence available did suggest that many more people would use the passive belt, meaning that killing the rule would necessarily kill more Americans. From 1975 to 1979 Volkswagon offered automatic belts in Rabbits. Over 80 percent of Rabbit owners who took the option used the automatic belts, compared to about 36 percent for the manual belts, according to observational studies conducted by a contractor hired by NHTSA. In crashes, the observed usage rate for the automatic belt was about 57 percent—still significantly higher than the 29 percent rate for manual belts. No studies were done on automatic belt use for the 1978-79 Chevy Chevette, since only a relatively small number were sold, but a telephone survey by the contractor, Opinion Research, Corp., indicated over 70 percent usage. That compared to an observed rate by Opinion Research of 11 percent for manual belts.

Peck argued that these figures would not reflect usage through the entire car fleet, since the Rabbit particularly had "all of the demographics in favor of usage" and other use-inducing features such as an ignition interlock that would not be required under 208. It was only by assuming that the usage rate for the automatic belt would be far lower than that found in the Rabbit and Chevette—in the range of about 20 percent—that the agency was able to conclude that the costs of the regulation exceeded its benefits to society. Projecting a higher usage rate, Yale Professor William Nordhaus, a former member of the Council of Economic Advisers generally considered a foe of government regulation, calculated the standard would produce annual economic benefits ten times greater than its cost, or about a $10 billion net benefit to society from 1982-1985.

"Peck's statement that the airbags are irrelevant is false because Mercedes and clearly some other companies were going to offer airbags for sale," said Joan Claybrook, Peck's predecessor as NHTSA administrator. "So Peck and the Reagan Administration are responsible for the public's inability to buy airbags. Second, his justification for rescinding the standard is perverted, in that the analysis that was done was primarily of belt systems and ignored the cost-effectiveness of airbags, even though this is a performance, not design, standard.

"The auto companies announced that they would comply with the standard with the most ineffective possible system—a belt that retracts out of the way once it is detached. It's questionable whether that would even meet the requirement of an automatic restraint. Peck used this announcement as an excuse for determining that the standard would not be effective, ignoring all the other systems that the companies could have employed in good faith to comply with the standard," explained Claybrook.

Added Mike Sohn, an attorney for State Farm Mutual Automobile Insurance, which has sued Peck over the decision: "If you think you wouldn't get higher rates [of belt usage] because of the way the belts are designed you should amend the rule to preclude that kind of design, not rescind the standard."

Peck told us, "I believe fairly strongly that it's highly irresponsible of the agency to rely almost exclusively upon technology solutions." He made that remark only a few months after an agency report—using General Accounting Office methodology—concluded that NHTSA technology-requiring regulations had saved 70,000 lives and prevented many more injuries since 1968.

In place of the standard, Peck said he has launched two lobbying campaigns, one aimed at the auto companies, the other at the public.

Peck, who claimed he did not talk about the decision with the auto companies (though he has met regularly with them in Detroit and Washington since taking office), said at the press conference he will launch "a major effort addressed at all levels of the automobile industry, and the manufacturers and suppliers of that industry. . .to identify, demonstrate and offer to car buyers the most advanced safety technology. . ." Development of those technologies, Peck argued, "has been, in effect, forestalled by the pendency of this [the passive restraint] question." When he called the auto companies after he announced his decision, Peck told us, one chief executive officer told him, "you come and get us tiger, it's long overdue."

"What you are talking about [with these technologies] are things that will save maybe 100 or so lives, which is valuable. But when you compare it with what you're throwing away with automatic restraints, there's nothing with even a fraction of the life-saving potential," said Clarence Ditlow, director of the Center for Auto Safety.

In our interview, Peck said he expects an American manufacturer to announce early in 1982 plans to offer airbags; Ford has said it is talking seriously with Peck about offering airbags. "There are budget decisions being made both here and abroad in the first quarter of [this] year which I expect will involve not only further commitments but in some cases final commitments," he said. But, he said, mandating airbags was an "untenable economic proposition," because of the industry's capital shortage. "The economics are such now that mandating airbags from a purely practical standpoint you might as well mandate anti-gravity. . .I keep coming back to the fact that four years ago the money was there. Now it is not."

"They already have a capital investment of $30 million in preparation for manufacturing airbags in 1982 models," said Claybrook. "If they don't manufacture airbags, they actually lose any chance to recoup that investment. If airbags—which are very price sensitive in terms of volume—were mandated for every car, it would be from a purely economic point of view, the cheapest way to put airbags in vehicles."

Peck often speaks about the prospects for voluntary manufacture of airbags with a sort of regulatory macho, warning the auto companies—or just the listener, depending on your level of cynicism—that he is "not easily fooled. . .and not easily fooled more than once. I want airbags throughout the fleet." He told us recent airbag tests on DeLorean cars were "very exciting. . .I hesitate to overemphasize because I'm not a technician but this looks an awful lot to a layman like a quantum leap forward in validating a kind of technology that would be cheaper, more efficient, and probably more effective."

While he would not commit himself to reissuing the standard if the auto companies don't make a substantial commitment to airbags within a year, he told us, "If I don't see very substantial evidence of good faith and recognition of the responsibility to move onto further technological generations of protection within a year, then I'll certainly reassess the question. Actually it could be sooner than a year."

The airbag episode well reflected Peck's style. Unlike James Watt and some other members of the Administration, Peck rarely castigates the auto safety community or auto safety values. His instinct is to keep hope springing eternal by assuring auto safety advocates that he shares their values. (He told us: "There's very little difference—I'd be hard pressed to find one—between the goals of even my predecessor or most of the highway safety community and mine.") He said that he is negotiating with the auto executives to adopt advanced safety technology, and that he is not issuing notices of proposed safety rule-making because he wants to use such notices as a bargaining chip if the auto companies do not come around. . .In the meantime, the months pass by and nothing happens—because Peck and his superiors want nothing to happen. His strategy is to temporize, and to keep his adversaries in the safety community clinging to some hope that his verbal assurances of future development will in some fashion come about. The surprising aspect of Peck's public personality is that he expects his critics to be taken in by such maneuvers: after all, doesn't he frequently confide in them some of his innermost skepticisms about the auto executives?

The strategy doesn't always work, needless to say, and Peck's critics on Capitol Hill are becoming increasingly hostile. In late March, 1982, a bristling Rep. Tim Wirth (D-Colo.), chairman of the House Telecommunications, Consumer Protection and Finance Subcommittee, accused Peck of "taking NHTSA back to the safety mentality of the 1950s and 1960s." A few days later, Republican Senator Jack Danforth excoriated Peck, saying: "I do not think it is in the best interest of the

American people to spend $1.5 million unmaking rules, $6 million not enforcing rules, $32 million to do research and analysis on how not to make cars safer, or $36 million for salaries just to make the highways less safe." Peck received the same treatment on March 25 on the House side when Rep. Adam Benjamin (D-Ind.), who chairs the House appropriations transportation subcommittee, questioned the veracity of airbag cost figures Peck provided, refused to swear him in, and abruptly cancelled the hearing. Instead, he sent Peck more than 200 questions to answer in writing. All of these incidents reflect increasing congressional annoyance with Peck's garrulousness—his tendency to filibuster from the witness table. Even Rep. James Collins (R-Tex.), who supports Peck's policies, said at the Wirth hearing that Peck reminded him of the kind of man who, when you ask him what time it is, tells you how to build a clock.

The Peck campaign directed at motorists follows the line frequently advanced by the auto companies—that unsafe drivers, not unsafe cars, are responsible for mayhem on the highway. But the 'nut behind the wheel' theory was disposed of 15 years ago when scientists pointed out that the cause of injury—unsafe design—was more easily altered than the behavior of drivers.

No one disagrees that there would be fewer highway deaths if more people wore seatbelts; but the insurance industry and auto safety activists argue that a public relations campaign designed to spur manual belt usage is no substitute for regulatory action that would mandate automatic crash protection. Peck's campaign, noted the Insurance Institute for Highway Safety, is only the latest of a dozen such efforts launched since 1968, none of which have ever had any sustained success.

Agreeing was the NHTSA staff, which told Peck: "The chance of raising voluntary manual belt usage with information programs to the point that it would make automatic restraints unnecessary is remote." And the staff also advised Peck that they did "not believe that there is any contradiction between the policy of attempting to increase manual belt usage and the policy of requiring automatic crash protection systems in new cars."

Asked whether he would support a mandatory federal seatbelt law, Peck said, "probably not, just because it would be impractical. It would be foolish." But state requirements "are another whole question," he told us. "We have supported vigorously and have testified in favor of child restraint laws. . .Michigan will be pushing a mandatory seatbelt law and I expect we will be supporting it."

Though none of his other decisions approach the magnitude of the ruling on the passive restraint standard, Peck has worked on matters large and small to bring the agency in line with the wishes of the auto industry, whose antipathy for Washington reached new heights under highway safety activist Claybrook.

Over a dozen NHTSA regulations are being reconsidered at the behest of the industry and the President's Task Force on Regulatory Relief, but it has been on a non-regulatory initiative that the Administration has most clearly displayed its intentions.

In 1980, NHTSA published *The Car Book*, a glossy, handsomely designed guide to the government's crash tests, vehicle recalls, maintenance expenses, and other information. It was an instant success, with car owners requesting and receiving over 1.5 million copies.

But it was also anathema to the auto companies. Following complaints by the companies, NHTSA in April, 1981 withdrew the free public service announcements advertising the book's availability. "We inquired," said a General Motors spokesperson, "and the ads were stopped." Then in August, 1981 NHTSA decided not to reprint or update the publication. Secretary Lewis called it "anti-industry." That summer, Peck said that Lewis told the press there would be no *Car Book* and then Lewis's staff called him and said: "Isn't that right, wasn't that NHTSA's position?" At the time, Peck said, NHTSA didn't have a position.

That would have been the end of the story if not for John Gillis. A NHTSA employee who edited the first edition, Gillis prepared a second *Car Book* using information available in the public record and working on his own time. Investing $30,000 of his own money, Gillis published the book with the Center for Auto Safety and Tilden Press.

Peck, who had earlier said the free market should make the information in the *Car Book* available, was livid over Gillis's entrepreneurial capitalism. Blustering that the action was "immoral," Peck instructed the department's inspector general to investigate Gillis. At a stormy meeting in which Gillis informed Peck the book would be coming out, Peck blew up, shouting at Gillis, threatening him with legal action, and ordering him to appear before him the next morning with the book. Gillis refused, calling instead. By then, cooler heads in the agency had prevailed and Peck was more conciliatory, even denying that he had made any threats the night before and wishing Gillis luck on the project.

That heavy-handed behavior toward staff was not atypical. In February, 1982, Peck sought to place on administrative leave three top agency employees as an example to curtail leaking of agency documents. Not that the three had leaked anything; but the office they supervise had accidentally included a confidential agency memo in the response to a Freedom of Information Act request. Drew Lewis, though, publicly overruled Peck, pointing out that it was inappropriate to punish agency employees for something they didn't do.

Lewis slapped down another Peck idea, in which the administrator displayed considerably more favor for private initiative than he did in the Gillis affair. In November, 1981, NHTSA gave $9,903 to Stephen Jacobs, a Washington public relations consultant, to study the formation of a "private" group to promote highway safety. Four days after he completed the study, Jacobs founded the Traffic Safety Foundation. With the help of two letters from President Reagan and some lobbying by Peck, the group has solicited funds from the auto industry to promote voluntary cooperation between the automakers and the government. That fits in with Peck's aversion to regulation, so he planned to join the foundation's board of directors. Lewis, however, vetoed the idea.

Inside the agency Peck isn't considered much of a manager. He frequently loses things and is chronically disorganized.

Peck has wide swings of temperament. He jokes a lot—the kind of inside humor that circulates among his anti-regulatory allies. He also easily flies into rages as when he called up a nonplussed, veteran correspondent, Helen Kahn, of *Automotive News* to object to her reporting and to declare that henceforth he would make sure his agency's major news announcements would be released after her weekly deadline.

Most upsetting to the auto companies about the *Car Book* was the inclusion of results from NHTSA's crash tests, which they have long opposed as "inaccurate." In September, 1981 Peck announced the agency would no longer report whether new cars pass or fail the tests, which assess the safety of autos involved in collisions. Alleging irregularities in the tests, Peck also threw out the failing test results for the Audi 5000 and Ford's new sports car, the EXP. Ford, of course, has been counting on strong sales of the EXP to help reverse its plunging fortunes. Peck said that pass/fail "tends to mask" significant differences in crash-worthiness between cars within those two categories and that he is "finalizing" a new method of explaining the results.

"You have to have something other than numbers to make it meaningful to people," said Ditlow. "No one understands what '1013' on the test is versus '759.' You're only going to create consumer confusion. Whether you say 'fail' or 'poor,' that creates more of an incentive [for the manufacturer] to improve it." Ditlow predicts that Peck will eventually seek to eliminate the crash tests completely. Peck told us he intends to continue the tests "as long as we have a budget for it and so far nobody's gone after the budget."

Peck's decision on the crash tests, which were initiated by Claybrook, was only one of a series of actions rolling back auto safety efforts begun in the Carter Administration. In other major actions, Peck has also:

- changed government policy on recalls. No longer does NHTSA press the auto manufacturers to publicly announce their recalls, or routinely issue notices themselves. Though Peck denied any policy change, one Ford official told reporters: "I presume the change has occurred as a result of the change in administrations." After unfavorable publicity in August, 1981 Ford agreed to again announce its recalls.

- eased government policy on looking for defects. The changes, involving the increased use of informal investigations, and the refusal to investigate problems identified by only a "small number" of complaints, is expected to sharply reduce the number of full-scale defect investigations, which could then cut the number of recalls. "If you don't look into a problem," said Ditlow, "you can't do anything about it."

- failed to act on several critical safety standards which were ready to be promulgated soon after he took office. These include side impact protection—a mode of crash in which 8,000 motorists are killed annually—and pedestrian protection, in which 9,000 people are killed each year.

- Peck, following Secretary Lewis's plan and General Motors demands, reduced the bumper standard from the popular five mile per hour collision protection levels down to two and one half miles per hour, or walking speed. Both the NHTSA staff studies of 1980 and several insurance industry analyses concluded that the five mile per hour bumper on automobiles saved motorists several million dollars per year, reduced the need to purchase spare parts such as fenders and avoided much time and energy by car owners at repair garages.

- revoked a regulation requiring manufacturers to ensure fields of direct view for drivers, which took the agency 11 years to finally develop.

- reconsidered the Uniform Tire Grading System established in 1980, which has been criticized by most of the tire companies and is designed to help consumers evaluate tires' tread life, traction and heat resistance.

- dropped a proposed standard regarding auto batteries, explosions of which have been linked to up to 10,000 injuries a year.

- dropped a proposal that would have required manufacturers to install a simple warning system that would signal when tire pressure was dropping. Such a rule would not only increase highway safety, but improve fuel economy, said Ditlow.

- announced plans to stop setting fuel-economy standards after 1985, even though a December, 1980 NHTSA study concluded that manufacturers could reach a fleet-wide average of 45-50 MPG by 1990 if the government required them to do so.

- proposed to eliminate a regulation to install a marking system on the odometer that would notify the owner of tampering. Odometer fraud costs consumers billions of dollars each year.

Peck is not looking to take the agency into any new areas. "Frankly, there aren't many areas that you can think of, even if you were to look at an index of research and development, or an index of problem areas, prepared by anyone—the most vigorous and comprehensive rulemaker—where we weren't already out there in some form or another with either an advanced notice or a notice [of rulemaking]," he told us. "There are limits to human ingenuity. If I sat down and said 'Now, where would I want to promulgate a new rule just to satisfy the critics of the agency who say you're not doing any new rulemaking,' I'd have a hard time coming up with an area we're not already moving into."

This sweeping regulatory reversal has come with the implicit aim of reviving the sagging domestic auto industry, a government-wide priority mandated by the White House. "The overall economic health of any industry that is regulated is a factor to be taken into account in regulation because if it isn't. . .then the actual question that is posed by a particular regulation or regulatory scheme may be: do we intend to allow this industry to produce this product. Period," Peck said. "If you don't take costs into account—and I said take it into account—then you run the risk that you're going to make it impossible for anybody but the very large aggregations of capital to participate in the manufacturing of the product. And that could be as unhealthy a situation as an unregulated industry."   But whether the package will actually help the industry is problematic, since imports must also meet the same safety requirements. "Safety is one of the cheapest, easiest things to do," said Claybrook: "Even if they eliminate all of the standards it makes virtually no difference at all in the industry's financial position. This is a philosophical debate about whether the auto companies or the U.S. government, representing the public, should decide the minimum level of safety for the American people." Even Peck agreed that fuel economy and emission control standards had a far greater impact on the industry's finances than the safety rules. And costs to industry are not one of the specific criteria the agency is directed by statute to consider.

Without the government mandates to increase mileage performance, the domestic manufacturers might be in even worse shape—(Peck says that issue is still an open question)—an onimous thought as NHTSA prepares to drop standard-setting in that area. The same can be said for technology-forcing safety regulation.

As Peck told us, the industry has long thought of safety "as a dangerous, if not a counterproductive sales technique," but "we see what I think is a very substantial inchoate demand out there [for safety] which can be capitalized on."

It was to questions about this nexus of lives and dollars that Peck gave perhaps the most revealing answers in our two-hour interview. The first answer demonstrated his feelings about the moral responsibility of the government to promote public health through highway safety, the second his feelings on the industry's responsibility.

When we asked him if he cared "at all what the auto companies do with the savings that the regulatory programs generate?" he told us: "I don't agree with the implicit premise that it's up to government to determine how the economy should invest its money. A more direct question is 'do you think the fact that any money that might be saved. . .should be put back into safety?' I would hope it would be. Do I think that's my responsibility to ensure that it is, or the government's responsibility to ensure that it is? No, I don't. For this reason: significant safety research is going on in all of the companies. We have access to a lot of it. The public has access to a lot of it. I think it would be inappropriate and possibly counterproductive for me to presume to say which dollar should be spent for which purpose."

Later, we asked Peck: If he was the head of an auto company and "felt that you had technology that could reduce the amount of deaths on the highway would you consider it a moral responsibility to use it?"

And he replied: "I would certainly consider it an element to be taken into account in deciding what kind of a car to produce. . . . Again it gets back to what is perceived to be in a company's economic self-interest. . . If you asked the reverse of that question, it's an easier question to answer. [That] is, do you see evidence that companies are deliberately making and selling unsafe cars. I don't see that evidence. Companies have made mistakes. They've made mistakes in design, they've made mistakes in production. Those kinds of errors—whether they're manufacturing defects or design defects—are the price we pay for a highly industrialized, diverse, complicated society which produces a machine as inherently dangerous under the laws of physics as an automobile."

Peck gladly absorbs the responsibility for the Reagan Administration's dismantling of highway safety efforts; he sees it as part of his job to keep the heat from scarring Drew Lewis's image. But Peck's actions reflect the clear directions of Reagan, David Stockman and particularly Lewis, who said early on that he didn't see any standards coming out of his department through the next four years. (See Drew Lewis profile.)

When Lewis is in town, Peck meets with him weekly. And when Peck revokes standards, halts the distribution of comparative information about cars by make and model, slows the research and development program, and concentrates on drivers (through a campaign against drunk driving and the buckle up effort) rather than manufacturers, he is filling in the lines of Lewis's policy direction. Peck is the man with his name on the press releases, but the line of those pulling the federal government back from its legal mission to reduce death on the highway stretches through the secretary's office, cross town, all the way to the Oval Office.

FINANCIAL BACKGROUND

Peck earned $59,261.88 from the National Coal Association (NCA) in 1980.

He remained on the NCA's payroll in 1981 during the transition period, until his confirmation in April. Peck has said he did not make any government decisions during that time, though his principal place of business was NHTSA. But a Freedom of Information Act request revealed several documents that suggest Peck was involved in NHTSA decisions while still employed by the National Coal Association. For example, on February 12, 1981 Robert L. Fairman, acting assistant secretary for administration, wrote Peck to ask whether he wished to buy terminals for an accident reporting system. "If you concur," Fairman wrote, "I will approve the request. . ." On March 9, the director of public affairs wrote Peck on an alcohol safety TV spot narrated by then-New York Yankee star Reggie Jackson, asking "Do you wish to complete the proposed contract or cancel it?" Eight days later, the agency's associate administrator for rulemaking asked Peck in a memo "What course of action do you want the agency to pursue?" on the publication of a tire buying guide for consumers.

The NHTSA inspector general cleared Peck of any impropriety.

WHAT OTHERS ARE SAYING ABOUT HIM

- Ditlow, who has dealt with all of NHTSA's administrators since 1971, said "The guy never gives you a straight answer about anything." For example, he said, when rescinding the passive restraint standard, Peck extolled the 1976 "Coleman Agreement" under which the auto manufacturers agreed to voluntarily offer a set number of cars with airbags. "Coleman put that together in 30 days. What has Peck done in the months since the October press conference?" said Ditlow. "You're dealing with strictly a facade."

- Reed told us "I am very fond of Ray, who has gone amazingly far in life." But, he said, Peck puts "loyalty above all, above thinking." During his years at Interior, that loyalty was to the coal industry; Reed says Peck was known as "Bagge's man"—referring to Carl Bagge, head of the National Coal Association.

- Claybrook also considers Peck duplicitous at best, a flat-out liar at worst. "He attempts to mislead his audience when he's questioned on safety issues," she told us. "He knows the safety belt promotion is a ruse. He doesn't have any scientific basis for what he's doing. He's done a lot of harm in attacking some of the major life-saving programs. The Salk vaccine really pales by comparison to the airbag in terms of life-saving. This is a major public health system and he's treating it like a plumbing contract."

  Peck was slated to debate Claybrook at the Consumer Federation of America's 1982 convention. Peck left early, though, after making his pitch and relinquished the platform to Claybrook, avoiding an exchange. He missed, as he certainly knew he would, a blistering critique of his policies. "They have now officially made NHTSA a wholly owned subsidiary of General Motors," she concluded.

- I know the type," said Jerry Sonosky, a Washington corporate attorney who worked with Connecticut Senator Abe Ribicoff on the seminal auto safety hearings in the mid-1960s. "He's a heel-clicker."

- When Peck went up to inform Rep. James Howard, the New Jersey Democrat who chairs the House Public Works and Transportation Committee, of his airbag decision, Howard told him, "That's fine. Just don't try and persuade me you're in favor of safety."

RAY BARNHART
ADMINISTRATOR, FEDERAL HIGHWAY
ADMINISTRATION

RESPONSIBILITY OF OFFICE

FHWA became a part of the Department of Transportation
in 1966; as chief administrator, Barnhart must be "concerned with the total operation and environment of highway systems, with particular emphasis on improvement of
highway-oriented aspects of highway safety." A staff of
3,454 administered an $8.1 billion budget in 1982.

BACKGROUND

Barnhart has been long active in Texas governmental affairs, serving most recently
as one of three commissioners of the Texas Highways and Public Transportation
Department, and as a member of the board of the Texas Turnpike Authority. The
former body is the policy-making group which governs the multi-billion dollar
Texas highway construction and public transportation assistance programs. The latter group is the state agency responsible for construction and operation of major toll
facilities.

Barnhart was a member of the Pasadena (Texas) City Council from 1965 to 1969
and later served two years in the Texas state legislature (1973-74). He was chairman
of the Texas Republican Party from 1977 until he resigned in 1979 to join the highway commission. A long-time supporter of Ronald Reagan, Barnhart served as co-
chairman of Texans for Reagan in the 1976 presidential primary. He chaired the
Harris County Republican Party from 1975 through 1977.

His speeches are filled with the reflexive Reagan assaults on government. "One
of the gravest threats to the survival of our nation and us as a free people," he has
often said, "has been the increased concentration of power in a centralized, unaccountable, unresponsive federal government." And: "The tragedy is that while
many have foreseen the danger of Washington power, and experienced the consequences in personal and corporate and political activities, most of the nation has not
had the courage to truly come to grips with it, and thus, through acquiescence, has
bred expansion of its destructive powers."

Barnhart displays no doubts about what the 1980 election means: "There are
many—both in the private and public sectors of our country—who have failed to
hear, or refused to believe, the clear mandate of November: that caring citizens will
tolerate no longer the expansion of powers of the federal government and the
accompanying diminishment of personal freedom. Americans want government off
their backs! And Ronald Reagan wants to help lighten the load!"

Barnhart, who was born in Elgin, Illinois on January 12, 1928, received his B.A.
in speech in 1950 from Marietta College, Ohio, and his M.A. in theater from the
University of Houston in 1951.

After receiving his M.A., Barnhart taught at Marietta. In 1956, he moved to
Houston where for 20 years he was engaged in underground utilities construction.
In 1978, he joined the Barmore Insurance Agency of Pasadena.

MAJOR ISSUES

- Barnhart and Transportation Secretary Drew Lewis failed to convince the President to increase the four-cent gasoline tax, which raises questions about future financing of the Highway Trust Fund.

- Under the Reagan Administration's New Federalism proposal, the federal government would pull out of all but the interstate portions of the highway system.

- Funding for highway safety has been slashed in the 1983 budget.

True to his Texas heritage, Barnhart is a zealous advocate of state and local control—and highway travel. He looks upon himself as an "unabashed advocate of the highway mode of transportation"—not a bad niche to have in an Administration dedicated to reviving the auto industry.

"The Federal-Aid Highway Program will consolidate activities, reduce categories, minimize intrusions into the jurisdictions of other levels of government, hold the line on taxes and red tape, eliminate excessive delays and, in short, let the states manage their own money and affairs," Barnhart has said.

Beneath those code words is a familiar pattern of Reagan Administration deregulatory activity. The states have opposed requirements for highway safety improvements, particularly as funding available for construction becomes tighter. In recent years, the states have mounted an effective counterattack. "The states' efforts to convince the FHWA to lower its regulatory requirements or, in some cases, to eliminate them altogether, have been and continue to be largely successful," wrote Gerald Donaldson of the Center for Auto Safety in a January, 1982 study.

The battle has taken place both in regulatory hearing rooms and Congress. In 1976, the states won a major victory when Congress redefined "construction" to include resurfacing, restoration, and rehabilitation of existing roads—the so-called 3R program. In 1978, Congress directed that at least 20 percent of the primary and secondary road money the states receive should go to 3R.

For the states, the 3R program provides a way to avoid both federal requirements for safety improvements, and their own responsibility to pay for routine maintenance. The program allows federal dollars to come in for maintenance—ordinarily a state funding responsibility—when a road has deteriorated to the point where it needs "rehabilitation." And the program allows regional highway administration officials to grant "exemptions" from the safety work required for all new highway construction. The states see the program as a way to stretch their highway dollars into the short-term, politically popular, restoration of rough riding surfaces.

"It awards enormous discretion to the state highway departments to use federal money without any real control by Division Administrators, without any requirement to include crucial safety features in rehabilitation projects, and without any requirements for performance reviews or reporting on safety benefits," wrote Donaldson. "It's a state versus federal thing," added a highway administration official. "It's just symptomatic of the whole thing. They like 3R as opposed to safety because there are no regs on it." And by picking up the tab for what should be routine maintenance work, the program creates a perverse incentive to let highways deteriorate. Wrote Donaldson: "Many states are allowing routine preventive maintenance to be deferred consistently until the highway is qualified for rehabilitation under the Federal R-R-R program."

In his public statements, Barnhart has strongly supported the program, backing the addition of a fourth "R"—reconstruction. But with the House raising serious questions about the way FHWA is implementing the plan, he has been unable to finish regulations governing the program. The FHWA has been trying to issue such rules since 1977, under the Carter Administration. In addition to the House Public Works Committee, the National Transportation Safety Board has excoriated the current proposal.

In April, 1981 the FHWA sent out a trial balloon for pulling back federal oversight even further, asking for comments on regulations that "because of their associated costs and/or controversy, are prime candidates for priority review and possible revision or recision." Among the regulations listed were "Design Standards for Highway." "The general drift of this agency action," wrote Donaldson, "appears to be in the direction of removing all controlling Federal standards which the states claim are unduly burdensome and cost-ineffective." One federal highway safety expert monitoring the FHWA agreed: "Safety as an issue is dead with Barnhart," the observer said.

Early in his administration, Barnhart tried to remove safety as a line item in the agency's budget, but Congress rejected the plan. "I remember having people over in safety research tell me that he said he wanted to see all the [ongoing] projects and that his first reaction was to cut out everything that had safety in the title," said the government source. Outlays for safety grants to states would be slashed to half of the 1981 level under the 1983 budget. Overall safety expenditures, including construction, will drop from $400 million to $100 million in 1983.

"The whole philosophy of the new Administration is that we're only interested in doing things of national concern," said the agency official. "So safety to them is not a national concern. It's part of the general policy. . .[they say] we'll still provide national leadership on safety—as long as it doesn't cost any money."

Barnhart's role in all of this is unclear. According to some agency sources, Barnhart is not heavily involved in the day-to-day decision-making at the agency, leaving the reins in the hands of the agency's long-time executive director Les Lamm. "Ninety percent of the way the operation goes is just left up to the executive director," said the source.

The federal government would dump off another large share of its role in highway construction with Reagan's New Federalism plan. Under that proposal, states would assume responsibility for primary, rural, urban, bridge, construction safety, and assorted other highway grants, leaving the federal government paying only for the interstate portions of the system. For 1983, interstate expenditures will constitute $3.2 billion of the total $8 billion dispensed from the trust fund. (Lewis acknowledged in February, 1982 that under the first three years of New Federalism states would be out from $16 to $18 billion for building and maintaining highways.)

That proposal would seem to be in line with Barnhart's beliefs. "I can see no justification for the federal gasoline tax being used to pave a city street in my town, or installing a storm sewer in yours," he has said.

The New Federalism would also strip the FHWA of half the revenues from the four-cent gasoline tax to help finance the new trust fund established as part of the proposal. Barnhart, along with his boss, Drew Lewis, campaigned throughout the fall of 1981 for an increase in the gasoline fee, which pays for the highway trust fund. Expenditures are now running steadily ahead of revenues, a problem exacerbated by a drop in gasoline consumption.

To broaden support for the tax hike, Lewis proposed to divert $1 billion annually for capital expenses on subways and buses. But Reagan flatly rejected the proposal. "It's dead," said one FHWA spokesperson.

With the rejection of the proposal, it's not clear how the deficit in the trust fund will be filled. But pressure may build for further cuts in the system. Barnhart has said he intends to finish all sections already under construction, but the government is not likely to proceed with new construction on most of the system's remaining gaps (approximately 5 percent) which have hit financial and environmental snags.

Environmental groups believe the complete elimination of these projects would have "a negligible effect on interstate commerce, and would not hurt our existing highway system." In the process, of course, DOT could realize even bigger savings ($3.3 billion in 1982 and $53.8 billion over the next several years).

Among Barnhart's other major proposals are:

- support for repeal of the 55-mph speed limit, leaving such judgments to the states.

- support for modification or repeal of the Davis-Bacon labor law.

Barnhart has so far been agreeable with others in the Reagan Administration though he has strongly indicated he will be willing to fight the Office of Management and Budget (OMB) if it attempts to cut more from his programs than he thinks is necessary.

"I recognize that the highway program has for the last seven years been cut," he said, "and certainly it seems that OMB has had a propensity to look at the highway program." In light of this "propensity," he speculates he "will have to do an awful lot of fighting."

Barnhart has spent most of his career in the construction industry, a major part of the highway lobby. Since taking office he has said he believes "the highway is generally the most effective, efficient, versatile, economic, and convenient method of mobility yet devised."

Barnhart, however, has made strong statements against collusive bidding on highway projects which the Justice Department has been prosecuting under the antitrust laws.

"There have been requests that have come across my desk from the state highway departments seeking relief [relaxation of the period of debarment] for those contractors who have cooperated with law enforcement authorities," Barnhart said. "The letters say, 'Contractor X has assisted us in the prosecution of others, and has paid X dollars in penalties to the state in retribution, therefore we request he be restored to good graces and be allowed to bid on our projects. . . . ' Baloney! A fine does not pay a debt to society. . . nor redeem the damage done to a professional industry. . . . ''

FINANCIAL BACKGROUND

Barnhart earned a $21,000 salary from the Texas Highway Commission in 1980 as well as about $32,000 in commissions with the Barmore Insurance Agency.

He retains a small interest in the construction industry in the form of a firm (Barney's, Inc.) which he began in 1975. The company, however, has been "inactive" for several years and Barnhart claims it is in the process of "liquidating." He claimed a $3,700 salary from the firm in 1980.

WHAT OTHERS ARE SAYING ABOUT HIM

- Barnhart is a mover and shaker who has taken up his new task with great zeal. His former colleagues on the Texas Highway Commission are not surprised. One veteran Texas journalist describes Barnhart as "a kind of a hipshooter," but one who generally "knew his stuff" on the Texas Highway Commission. Barnhart was a very "high profile" figure on the state commission who wasn't afraid to "take a stand on controversial issues" such as the state gasoline tax hike.

- Barnhart has not made a very good first impression among some members of the House Public Works and Transportation Subcommittee on Surface Transportation, especially in his assessment of the 55-mph speed limit. Rep. James Howard (D-N.J.), chairman of the full committee, made an impromptu appearance at the subcommittee hearings in April, 1981 to demand an explanation from Barnhart on a statement he had made in a recent speech. Barnhart admitted that he had called the 55-mph limit "a stinking rule" but said he would nonetheless see that the law was enforced as part of his FHWA responsibility.

    But Rep. Howard was skeptical. He questioned Barnhart's respect for the law, calling the 55-mph limit "a gut political issue. . .in some of our macho-oriented states in the West." Howard went on to cite numerous studies which "clearly indicated" that the speed limit had saved energy and cut down on highway fatalities in those areas where it was most aggressively enforced. Howard concluded that Barnhart's legal interpretation on this issue was "a stinking legal interpretation."

ARTHUR TEELE

ADMINISTRATOR, URBAN MASS TRANSPORTATION
ADMINISTRATION

RESPONSIBILITY OF OFFICE

UMTA was formed in 1964 and brought under the Department of Transportation in 1968. A 515-person staff administered a $3.7 billion program in 1982.

Teele's job is to oversee the UMTA's primary mission: "to assist in the development of improved mass transportation facilities, equipment, techniques, and methods: to encourage planning and establishment of areawide urban mass transportation systems; and to provide assistance to state and local governments in financing such systems."

Traditionally, UMTA's financing responsibilities have included both capital grants and operational subsidies. In more recent years, UMTA has been responsible for implementing and enforcing special programs for the elderly and handicapped as well.

BACKGROUND

Teele, 36, is one of the youngest nominees. He is also one of the very few blacks in a high-level post.

Teele's first direct involvement in mass transit issues took place shortly after Reagan was elected, when he was appointed head of the Department of Transportation transition team.

"To be honest, I thought they were going to appoint me to the defense transition team," he said, considering his nine years in the U.S. Army.

Before coming to Washington, Teele had been a private attorney in Florida for the previous five years. Among his clients were a major sports firm in Daytona Beach and his alma mater, Florida A&M. Teele also performed civic services for both the Florida NAACP and the Florida Voters League.

He served in the Army between 1967 and 1976, accumulating numerous honors as an officer within the United States and in Southeast Asia. Having completed undergraduate work at Florida A&M in 1967, Teele obtained his law degree at Florida State University in 1972. He served his last few years in the military as senior aide-de-camp and special private counsel to the commanding general at Fort Bragg, N.C.

After entering private practice in 1976, Teele did brief stints as a consultant to both the Florida Department of Administration and the U.S. Department of Labor. A registered Republican, Teele served as a national director on the Reagan-Bush campaign committee.

Teele was born on May 14, 1946, in Prince Georges County, Maryland.

MAJOR ISSUES

- Teele is implementing cuts in operational subsidies for mass transit that many urban analysts believe will result in inadequate service and increased reliance upon the automobile.

- Teele has begun reducing UMTA regulations, aiming to limit the federal aid and requirements for programs serving the elderly and handicapped.

UMTA is taking a beating.

In 1982 capital subsidies for mass transit were maintained at slightly reduced levels. But the $1.036 billion operational subsidies program is slated for elimination by 1985.

In its 1983 budget, the Administration has proposed to hold capital assistance funding steady at about $1.7 billion. That would allow funding only of projects to modernize and repair existing mass transit systems; no new systems would be funded. Operational subsidies are being cut from the $1 billion appropriated for 1982 to $640 million in 1983; the Administration projects a $275 million budget for fiscal 1984. No funds will be appropriated for operating assistance after 1984. Reagan hopes to eventually turn over to the states responsibility for both capital and operating funding as part of his New Federalism package.

Teele claims the termination of operational assistance "should have no effect on the transit operators' ability to maintain service." But Congress and many localities are skeptical.

In December, 1981, the American Public Transit Association forecast a "bleak picture" for mass transit because of the budget cuts. A survey of its members revealed that virtually all planned to raise fares to help meet the shortfall—though fare rises inevitably decrease ridership; two-thirds expected to reduce service; and more than two dozen cities planned to end services entirely. The association feared that the funding constraints could accelerate the debilitating spiral of ever-increasing fares and declining ridership.

Teele insists that localities assume more responsibility for their systems. Since operational subsidies began in 1974, labor costs among transit workers have soared commensurately, he said. Teele believes that if the localities are forced to bear funding responsibilities, they will push harder to control labor costs.

But the transit unions say Teele is misinformed. Earl Putnam, general counsel of the Amalgamated Transit Union, said Teele draws his conclusions from data beginning in 1967 which shows transit wages have risen "in excess of the rate of inflation."

Putnam claims the only pertinent period to consider is the time in which the operating aid has been offered—1974 to 1981. While the consumer price index rose 52.6 percent in that period, he says, transit workers' wages rose only 44.2 percent.

Furthermore, he said that Teele's payroll examples do not take into account the high amount of overtime wages paid to transit workers. Most transit systems have chosen to pay more overtime rather than hire more workers, he said. Also, transit wage increases have been commensurate with wage scales of other city officials since 1974.

Critics contend that both capital and operational assistance must be maintained to allow for adequate service.

"Most localities probably can't afford to raise the fare too much further," said Marshall Boyd, a spokesman from the Urban League. "Services are bound to get cut. At this rate, service is eventually likely to be limited to rush-hour commuters."

Teele testified uneasily before a subcommittee of the Senate Appropriations Committee in April, 1982, saying that the phase out of operational assistance would have "individually unique" effects on each city. Defensive and off-balance, Teele refused to make any "broad sweeping generalizations."

"I'll give you a broad sweeping generalization," said Sen. Al D'Amato, a conservative Republican from New York, in his critical questioning of Teele. "[Many cities] are going to have a difficult time maintaining any mass transportation."

The experience of Birmingham, Alabama provides one example of D'Amato's point. Even with UMTA aid, funding problems forced Birmingham to discontinue all bus service on February 28, 1981, making it the largest city in the U.S. without public transportation. Teele has suggested that cities and states raise money to replace the operating subsidies. But in Birmingham's case the state legislature refused to enact any revenue producing measures. Needless to say, the city's need for new revenue measures will only increase in upcoming years as UMTA aid declines. Merchants along downtown bus routes reported a 25 percent decline in retail sales, and a total of some 250 people in the metropolitan area lost their jobs as a direct result of the shutdown. Bus services, reduced by 37 percent, were resumed June 1, 1981 with tax revenues accumulated during the shutdown and will continue until September 30, 1982, when the fiscal year ends. Birmingham may then once again be forced to discontinue its mass transportation program, according to Mayor Richard Arrington, Jr.

Many mayors and local transportation officials have testified in opposition to the elimination of operating assistance. Thomas Volgy, vice-mayor of Tucson, Arizona, told one House committee his city has "made as great a commitment. . . as we can locally," and was "not sure how much longer our public transportation system can last without" continued federal operating assistance. New York City Mayor Ed Koch said the lack of these funds "would compound the difficulties of revitalizing transit systems and sustaining major urban centers." "It will mean a tragic step backwards," said Harvel Williams, general manager of Metropolitan Transit Authority of Nashville, Tennessee.

Other critics have argued that operational subsidies are just good investments because they tend to prolong the life of transit systems through better maintenance. One recent study concluded that by providing capital assistance without operating assistance, transit operators would be more likely "to treat buses like throwaway paper cups, to be discarded rather than fixed up and reused."

President Carter had planned healthy increases in both subsidies as part of his fuel conservation plan. Teele claims to be energy-conscious and stresses the "alternatives" to mass transit such as "ride-sharing programs, jitneys, shared-ride taxi systems, neighborhood transportation cooperatives and other innovative strategies."

All these alternatives, of course, entail use of automobiles.

"This is an ironic situation," said Putnam. "After working since 1964 to increase mass transit and get people out of their cars—the trend now seems to be reversing itself."

Those most dependent on mass transit—the poor, the elderly and the handicapped—may have no feasible alternatives. Teele has also begun an oversight on UMTA regulations, aiming to limit the federal aid and requirements for programs serving the elderly and handicapped. Teele has eliminated 3 of 14 existing UMTA regulations, and further eliminated 20 of 25 regulations that were under development. Teele's program will ask localities to provide "reasonably comparable service" for the elderly and handicapped, meaning localities will no longer be required to make all of their buses and subways accessible. The decision has to be cleared by Secretary Lewis.

Obviously annoyed, D'Amato pressed Teele on a number of other issues at the April appropriations hearing. Uncomfortable in parting from his written testimony, Teele's responses were frequently unsatisfying. D'Amato claimed there was "little done" to set out an agenda for developing managerial skills and the training of new management personnel. Teele said his agency was sponsoring seminars, but D'Amato interrupted him and cited a recent GAO report which concluded that the seminar technique and theory was an insufficient means for increasing management's productivity. "We also talked last year about getting a study of the impact of the removal of operating subsidies," continued D'Amato. "To date I have not received anything." Teele answered that although a number of separate analyses had been carried out, there was no overall study. D'Amato also inquired about a study he had requested last year of whether local taxes and farebox revenues would make up for federal subsidies; Teele was not able to produce that one either.

FINANCIAL BACKGROUND

Teele has been financially successful in his five years as a private attorney. In 1978, he earned approximately $148,076 and the next year $95,603. In 1980, a year which he devoted mostly to Republican campaigning, he earned only $32,716. Teele had a modest stock investment portfolio in 1980 which includes shares in such companies as Alcan Aluminum, International Motor Sports, and North Carolina Natural Gas.

WHAT OTHERS ARE SAYING ABOUT HIM

- Teele was endorsed unanimously at his nomination hearing, but not before Sen. William Proxmire (D-Wis.) expressed some misgivings about the nominee's limited experience:
  ". . .It's as if a young man came to the Redskins' training camp at Carlisle and from the very beginning he was talking to all the players and the coach and when the season opened they made him the head coach. You know that doesn't happen. They say we need somebody who's had a record of coaching before, somebody who understands the game, has something we can judge him by, and you just don't have that kind of background at all. That doesn't disqualify you. You will get overwhelming approval because we never pay any attention to qualifications when we appoint people, but it does trouble me.''

J. LYNN HELMS
ADMINISTRATOR, FEDERAL AVIATION
ADMINISTRATION

RESPONSIBILITY OF OFFICE

The Federal Aviation Administration has historically been in an awkward position. The once independent agency—which was appended to the Department of Transportation in 1967—is supposed to promote the aviation industry and ensure its safe operation. It has been accused on occasion of putting more priority on the former responsibility, but Helms contends that the two responsibiities are compatible because ''by the very nature of pressing for safety, the FAA in fact does promote aviation.''

In 1982, Helms had a budget of $1.6 billion and a staff of 45,000.

BACKGROUND

Helms has extensive aviation experience in both the military and private sectors.

Most recently, he was president of Piper Aircraft Corp. and is credited with restoring the once struggling enterprise to financial success—at the cost of inattention to safety, some contend—in the small aircraft field over the span of just six years.

Helms retired last year a very wealthy man. He received a percentage of the firm's growing profits, and by 1980, according to one industry colleague, he was ''practically making more money on Piper Aircraft than the conglomerate (Bangor Punta) which owned the firm.''

Helms began his aviation career near the end of World War II as a Marine Corps pilot. He remained in the Corps as a test pilot and instructor for 14 years before joining the North American Aviation Co. as director of marketing and sales in 1956. He eventually moved on to various executive positions with the Bendix Corp. and the Norden Division of United Technologies Corp., which specializes in electronic military gear for aircraft.

Helms, a licensed pilot, is a fellow of the American Institute of Aeronautics and the Society of Experimental Test Pilots. He was the first aviator to exceed the speed of 1,000-mph in a combat aircraft.

He is a long-time supporter of the Republican Party and in recent years has received a number of achievement awards from business groups as head of Piper Aircraft Corp.

Born March 1, 1925 in DeQueen, Arkansas, Helms is married with four children.

MAJOR ISSUES

- In his business career, Helms demonstrated a long record of anti-unionism, an attitude that became particularly evident during the PATCO negotiations.

- The safety record of Helms's former firm has been poor, as he attempted to boost production.

- Helms is actively reducing FAA air safety regulations, including a major rule requiring airplane designs to be reviewed every ten years.

The hottest issue facing the FAA in the first year of Helms's administration was the air traffic controllers union August, 1981 walkout. Helms had a small part in the negotiations and generally kept his distance from the fray, letting Transportation Secretary Drew Lewis hold the spotlight.

But his views of the Professional Air Traffic Controllers Organization (PATCO) were evident.

"Helms has a reputation for being hard on unions," said PATCO's Marsha Feldman. "I think his corporate attitude was pretty well summed up when he was quoted as saying 'The chairman of the board does not negotiate.'" Lewis handled most of the negotiating personally, a role which had traditionally been left to the FAA.

Even after PATCO had been crushed, Helms remained unforgiving. In February, 1982, he sent out a memo to field supervisors, ordering them to discipline air traffic controllers who had returned to work after Reagan's ultimatum in August, 1981. Secretary Lewis rescinded the order.

Helms's staunch position was not surprising to those who had dealt with him before. He once attempted to avert a strike at Piper Aircraft by threatening to move the entire company out of the state of Pennsylvania. (He didn't.)

Shortly thereafter he threatened to move the firm again in the midst of a run-in with state authorities. According to Dave Shugarts, an editor of *Aviation Consumer*, the flap arose after "a somewhat unexplained" crash of a Piper aircraft which killed nine state officials. Helms placed the primary blame on the pilot, but state authorities contended the manufacturer was also at fault (a contention which Helms vigorously denied).

In December, 1981 testimony, Helms predicted the air traffic system would return to "normal" by mid-1984 or 1985, at least three years after Reagan dismissed the striking controllers. In January, Helms unveiled a grandiose 20-year, $20 billion plan to revamp the nation's air traffic control system. Relying on increased use of computers and automation, the plan would reduce the number of controllers needed, and would be funded by increased taxes on aviation fuel and plane tickets. "In the final system," Helms told reporters, "one controller will do what three or four did before."

Like most other agency heads in the Reagan Administration, Helms has strongly advocated regulatory weakness and the transfer of more responsibility to states and localities.

In June, 1981, Helms addressed the Aviation Executive Conference. Gathered at the Sheraton Carlton Hotel in Washington were the presidents and chief executives of American Airlines, Eastern, Boeing, Air Florida, McDonnell Douglas, Cessna, and more than a dozen other major corporations and trade associations. Helms made his agenda clear. According to a transcript of the event, he told the business leaders: "I was very serious, unless I get fired, we're going to take the FAA down a different path, and I'd rather we do it of: where [do] you fellows want to go? What you want to do?. . .Hell, everybody in this room is dedicated to safety. We wouldn't be in this business, but we do have to keep the business going, and keep the industry going. No other comments or questions?" Helms asked. None came. "Gents," he said, "let's have a social hour then."

For the airlines, the atmosphere at the FAA under Helms has been very sociable. He has eliminated a number of the FAA's safety proposals, including proposed standards to:

- require the review of the design of airplane types, such as the DC-10 and B-747, once every ten years. The current practice allows airplanes to be manufactured indefinitely under the standards in effect when they are designed, even if those older standards are outdated and do not reflect subsequent improvements in safety technology;

- strengthen seats and seat tie-down mechanisms to ensure that seats do not break off in minor crashes, propelling the occupants about the cabin and blocking exits; and

- require all airplanes to use new tires meeting the significantly updated 1979 standards by 1984, instead of allowing airlines to exhaust their inventories of less safe tires.

- reduce the number of hours that commuter pilots can fly from 70 hours a week to 40 hours to prevent fatigue;

- require the use of less flammable crew member uniforms.

Having withdrawn these proposed regulations, Helms is now looking at existing safety regulations. "We are taking a similar hard look at all our other regulations with the aim of cutting costs and eliminating constraints on aviation," he said.

The Aviation Consumer Action Project (ACAP) protested Helms's actions in June 1981, citing studies by both the General Accounting Office and a committee of the National Research Council which found "the FAA appears to take a passive approach to air safety, slowly writing regulations only after a major air disaster occurs."

ACAP Director Matthew H. Finucane wrote Helms, saying in part: ". . . Never before has an FAA administrator started in office by trying to halt the progress in air safety, rather than trying to speed it up." In April, 1982, Finucane asked the National Transportation Safety Board to investigate the role of FAA laxity in the Air

Florida crash from Washington's National Airport. "The Air Florida crash, the World crash at Logan, and at least one other report of an aircraft skidding off the runway all raise the question of whether the FAA is fundamentally deficient in its supervision of cold weather operations," he wrote. "[W]e also urge you to explore whether budget cuts are affecting FAA supervision of the airlines, and whether the new industry-orientation of the FAA under J. Lynn Helms, as opposed to Langhorne Bond's stated pro-enforcement policies, are causing a decrease in airline and airport supervision."

Helms's dedication to safety has been questioned in the past. Helms once fired an FAA-certified test pilot after he refused to approve one of Piper's new-model planes. The pilot, Bill Kelly, later revealed in an interview with *Aviation Consumer* that Helms had been so eager to get the plane on the market that he participated in some of the test flights himself and at one point gave the in-house tester a special, secret bonus.

"This particular incident indicates two things to me," Shugarts told us. "Number one, that Helms doesn't always play by the rules. And number two, he has shown a propensity to take special actions in the interest of maintaining production."

At his nomination hearing, which lasted less than 30 minutes, Helms was asked only one question about Piper's safety record. It was pointed out that the FAA levied 48 percent of all its air worthiness directives (AD) against Piper Aircraft in 1980, while the firm was still under his direction. (An "AD" is a document of law which orders safety compliance by manufacturers.)

Helms responded by saying his company "produces more new models of aircraft than any other company in history" and, therefore, he could "understand why there would be more AD's."

"His answer indicates to me that he may have placed production as a higher priority than safety," said Shugarts.

Helms will attempt to deregulate the aviation industry on the ground as well. He favors defederalization of the nation's largest airports, which would transfer the primary funding responsibility to the localities. In the process, he wants to relax regulations which, for instance, limit the amount a municipality can charge in airport head taxes. In its 1982 budget, the Administration continues to push the defederalization proposal. Critics fear the inevitable results of these actions will be higher fares and fewer services, especially for flights to rural areas.

Helms's determination to shore up the agency's reputation in dealing with air traffic control problems has been questioned. Allegations have been raised that the FAA has underestimated the magnitude of computer system problems.

In late June, 1981, Helms announced that development of a newly designed air traffic anti-collision system has been completed. He said he "absolutely and firmly" intended to have it in regular operation by 1984, though he has announced no plans to require its use through regulation. Like most Reagan regulators, he plans to rely on voluntary cooperation.

Although work on such airborne, general aviation devices has been going on for decades, Helms is the first FAA chief to proclaim that a system is proven and ready for operation. "I'm sure most of the FAA people wish he hadn't made this decision so soon," said Shugarts. "Nobody in general aviation is likely to buy this device. The general aviation people are just going to laugh at the FAA when they sit down to review this decision because many of them feel it has no real use in the cockpit at this time."

Helms's decision has also raised concern in the industry. Weldon B. Clark, Trans World Airlines director of electronic engineering, said his firm had been preparing to use a different type of anti-collision system which the FAA was developing. Now the airlines must make plans for a new system, which "will delay the implementation of the [anti-collision] system [at TWA] by two or three years," said Clark.

Clark agrees with Shugarts's contention that general aviation fliers won't buy the system, since it is not mandatory. He said he could not understand why Helms approved the system.

FAA officials announced that an important component of the new system (a scanning directional antenna) was developed by the Bendix Corporation, where Helms was an executive from 1963 to 1970.

FINANCIAL BACKGROUND

Prior to taking office, Helms divested himself from 15,940 shares of Bangor Punta stock (the conglomerate that owned Piper Aircraft Corp.).

Nonetheless, his allegiance to the aviation industry is indisputable. He has emerged from a 25-year career in the industry as a multi-millionaire. Piper paid him a salary of $394,046 in 1980.

WHAT OTHERS ARE SAYING ABOUT HIM

- Former FAA head Langhorne Bond believes Helms will be an "excellent" administrator who has the benefit of a "stronger mandate from the Reagan Administration than I ever had under Carter." Helms has pledged to "stay out of the press as much as possible," but Bond knows better.

  "This is a position in which you are going to get ravaged," he said. "You are going to get it from all sides—the industry, the unions and the public. I expect it is going to happen to Helms, too, regardless of what he does."

- How Helms got this position is a matter of speculation. During the PATCO negotiations it was revealed that a "letter of understanding" had been addressed to candidate Reagan in October demanding that he appoint an FAA administrator suitable to PATCO. (The letter was written by PATCO legal counsel, Richard J. Leighton.) In return, the 15,000-member union vowed to support his candidacy. Reagan returned a favorable letter and PATCO subsequently endorsed him.

  PATCO's Marsha Feldman now admits "we did not oppose Helms's name when it was raised for this position," but denies the union had any direct veto power in the decision.

  Bond speculates that Helms was chosen not only because of his qualifications but also because Secretary Lewis wanted a person with "separate military and civilian backgrounds."

  The FAA post was originally offered to Vice-Admiral William D. Hauser, (on the recommendation of Cessna Corp. executive Russell Meyer), but he rejected the offer out of fear for losing his military pension, Bond said.

  Lewis finally settled on the independently wealthy Helms, who indicated that he will donate his FAA salary to charity.

- One House aide reports that Helms apparently "stirred up a hornet's nest" in his efforts to reorganize FAA and cut down on the headquarters staff.

  Among his proposals was a plan to eliminate five of the 11 FAA regional offices (including New York, Chicago, and Los Angeles). Following a storm of protest, his plan was put under review by superiors at the Department of Transportation.

"Helms has an impressive technical background for this position," the aide said, "but politically he has so far appeared to be somewhat less than astute."

- Shugarts of *Aviation Consumer* has been a Helms-watcher for several years. He said Helms has held a grudge against much of the aviation consumer press, dating back to an incident in 1977 when Shugarts published a routine advance story on an upcoming Piper model. Helms, who had requested that the story not appear, became angry and vowed not to speak with Shugarts again. Later, when another aviation publication criticized Helms's treatment of Shugarts in an editorial, the Piper head vowed never to cooperate with that publication, either.

  Shugarts, who actively opposed Helms' confirmation, calls the administrator a "captain of industry." He notes that in a press conference after his nomination hearing, Helms told reporters that since he knows most of the heads of the airlines and the leading manufacturers he would be able to deal with them personally and simply "call them up on the phone" to iron out any problems which might arise.

  Shugarts is greatly alarmed by this "chummy" aproach to aviation administration. He said the FAA has been especially susceptible to this sort of "word of honor" in the past. "I think the classic example is the DC-10," Shugarts said. "That was a case where the FAA and the manufacturer mutually agreed to take the most expedient route to ensure safety. . .and 347 people died for their mistake."

ROBERT BLANCHETTE

ADMINISTRATOR, FEDERAL RAILROAD ADMINISTRATION

RESPONSIBILITY OF OFFICE

FRA was created with the Department of Transportation (DOT) in 1966, just prior to a rash of private bankruptcies which dragged the federal government into the railroad business.

Amtrak and Conrail are Blanchette's main concerns. Amtrak (the National Railroad Passenger Corp.), supported mainly through federal financing, is the nation's most important supplier of intercity rail passenger service. Consolidated Rail Corp. (Conrail) receives federal subsidies for operating freight and commuter trains in the Northeast and Midwest.

In 1982, the FRA managed a budget of $2.4 billion (primarily devoted to Amtrak) and 1,194 employees. For 1983, the Administration is seeking to reduce those figures to $1.3 billion and 700 employees.

BACKGROUND

Blanchette is one of several of Transportation Secretary Drew Lewis's former railroad associates appointed to key DOT positions. Through most of the past decade, he served as chairman of the board of trustees and chief executive officer of Penn Central Transportation Co. Blanchette was responsible for keeping the railroad's freight and passenger services operating throughout its lengthy bankruptcy proceeding.

Blanchette began his railroad career in 1962 as general counsel for the New Haven Railroad. In 1969, he was executive director of America's Sound Transportation Review Organization, an industry group which met for six months to formulate strategies to revive the ailing railroads.

From 1976 until his appointment Blanchette was a managing partner in the Washington, D.C. law firm Alston, Miller, and Gaines.

Blanchette became a registered Democrat in Maryland in 1980 and made a $250 contribution to the Carter/Mondale primary campaign. He also contributed $150 to Republican Governor Richard Thornburgh's reelection campaign in Pennsylvania. (Thornburgh is a long-time political rival of Blanchette's new boss, Drew Lewis.) Blanchette had been a registered independent for most of his business life.

Born July 7, 1932 in New Haven, Connecticut, Blanchette received a B.A. from the University of Connecticut in 1953 where he was a Woodrow Wilson fellow and Fulbright scholar. In 1957, he was graduated from Yale Law School.

Blanchette is married with two children.

MAJOR ISSUES

- Rather than promoting railroads, Blanchette is hastening the demise of most of Amtrak's lines by campaigning for drastic reductions in funding.

- Blanchette is eager to begin the sale of Conrail stock, thereby getting the federal government out of the railroad business.

- Blanchette, like Reagan officials throughout the government, is seeking to weaken safety standards under his jurisdiction.

Conrail and Amtrak have been Blanchette's primary concerns since taking office in March, 1981. DOT legislation to severely reduce services on both government funded railroads has run into stiff congressional opposition.

From the beginning, Blanchette indicated a willingness to compromise on finding a Conrail solution, but he has remained adamant in his desire to see Amtrak funds curtailed.

In its 1982 budget, the Administration sought to cut Amtrak funding to $600 million but Congress refused to go along, and 1982 outlays are expected to total $820 million, still a reduction from $850 million in 1981. Those cuts forced Amtrak to reduce services 12 percent. For 1983, the Administration is again seeking to reduce the budget to the $600 million level; Amtrak claims that those cuts wouldn't allow it to run any trains outside of the Boston-New York corridor.

Blanchette and Amtrak have been engaged in a war of statistics, with Amtrak contending that the FRA head has misled the public into thinking the system is an undue burden on the taxpayer. Blanchette has said he cannot justify continued funding for any of the Amtrak lines other than the heavily used Northeast corridor.

"The rest of these rail lines are as efficient as Napoleon's Army," Blanchette told us. "Amtrak's long haul system is essentially little more than a travelling hotel. . .a remnant of a bygone era."

Amtrak cites the potential fuel efficiency of the train and its increasing importance as the nation moves into an era of fuel scarcity. During U.S. gasoline shortages in 1973 and again in 1979 Amtrak usage rose sharply and as gas prices continue to rise, Amtrak expects Americans to become increasingly reliant upon the passenger railway. Yet Blanchette urges bus travel, claiming it is more fuel efficient.

"Mr. Blanchette must be basing his opinions on erroneous information," counters Amtrak spokesman, Mike Delaney. Delaney points out two recent studies: the first, which Amtrak conducted together with several private organizations, found that 60 percent of Amtrak riders would return to their private automobiles if rail service were curtailed. Twenty-five percent would travel by air—only 15 percent would use buses. The second study, by the U.S. Conference of Mayors, found that between 1946 and 1978, federal subsidies to highways and airways surpassed the railways by a 24-1 ratio.

In light of these findings, a sympathetic House Energy and Commerce Committee concluded that, "government support for Amtrak has been far from excessive, especially in light of the substantial improvements in track and equipment which have had to be made in order for Amtrak to operate a national rail passenger system."

One congressional aide notes that in a recent hearing when Blanchette was questioned about alternatives to Amtrak, he said some people would simply have to get back in their cars. "I'm not sure he really meant to say that," the aide said. "I think it was just a slip of the tongue." Nonetheless, such a statement is not entirely suprising. In the Carter Administration it would have been contrary to the President's policy, but in the new Administration, Blanchette's statement is consistent with DOT's top priority: assistance to the auto industry.

Originally, the Administration planned to sell the most desirable Conrail lines piecemeal to the private sector and abandon the rest. But the plan ran into a congressional wall. "They had no one on their side," said a House aide. "Most of the people in the business sector have been opposed to the piecemeal plan, too. [Drew] Lewis and Blanchette tried to get their support, but the businesses of the Northeast know they stand to lose too much service. Thousands of shippers would get hit hard under that plan. . .and I think that feeling is even shared by the Republicans on the Senate Commerce Committee."

Some critics doubt the commitments of Lewis and Blanchette to the piecemeal plan, claiming they were merely following orders from Budget Director David Stockman. Yet Blanchette has shown a strong commitment to the goal of private railroad ownership. In the early 1970s, he developed a scheme to sell Penn Central to some private buyers, but the government prevented the sale because it probably would have eliminated too many services.

"Blanchette and Lewis know [the piecemeal plan] was an imperfect bill," said Conrail spokesman Obie O'Bannon. "They were feeling the pressure from the Senate and elsewhere and they knew they had to come up with a better plan."

The new plan was agreed upon by House and Senate budget conferees in late July, 1981. It was decided that if Conrail fails to meet a "profitability" test, the secretary of Transportation may sell it piecemeal after October 30, 1983. However, if the railroad is deemed profitable, it can be sold only as an entity, but only until June 1, 1984. Thereafter, Lewis can sell it piecemeal if he has not found a buyer for the entire unit. In order to make the Conrail stock attractive to private buyers, Blanchette has continued to encourage internal changes: removal of carrier rate limitations, elimination of commuter services, and reduction of labor protection costs. In its fiscal 1983 budget, the Administration proposed no federal funding for Conrail in 1983 and 1984.

The proposed labor changes have been the most controversial. One union president claims Blanchette and the Administration "could set collective bargaining back 50 years" by overriding the railroad workers hard fought labor agreements through government fiat. The act directs Conrail to enter into labor agreements that will cut its costs by $200 million annually.

Blanchette, with the advice and help of top railroad industry and labor officials, has proposed a number of weakening changes in rail safety statutes, regulations, and inspection policies. Blanchette describes the proposal for changes in the FRA's Railroad Safety Program as an "historic labor/management accord," but it is an accord which heavily favors the railroad industry, and which barely disguises its blatant disregard for safety with the rhetoric of budget-cutting measures and the reform of "onerous" regulations.

The 1970 Federal Rail Safety Act established minimum national track and freight car safety standards, and established a program through which the federal government provides 50 percent of the funds for 86 state inspectors.

The rail safety program is only now beginning to show its effectiveness. The total number of reported railroad accidents (excluding grade crossing accidents, still the largest single cause of rail-related fatalities, with 623 deaths in 1981) declined by about 30 percent between 1980 and 1981, and total injuries from all railroad accidents decreased from 62,246 to 52,877 in the same period. Fatalities declined from 1,417 to 1,283. A number of states have shown remarkable improvement. The number of derailments in Tennessee (which ranks 7th in the nation in transportation of hazardous materials) decreased by 35 percent between 1978 and 1979, another 35 percent in 1980, and by 41 percent again in 1981.

Now Blanchette wants to weaken the program that made these advances in safety possible. One of the most important regulatory changes he is seeking would reduce train brake inspections currently required every 500 miles to every 1,000 miles. Patricia Goldman, a member of the National Transportation Safety Board, told a Senate committee in April, 1982 that the relaxation of those requirements, "without a realistic expectation of voluntary compliance by the industry or effective monitoring of compliance by the FRA will lessen the present level of safety and will result an increase in the number of brake-related accidents."

Blanchette is also proposing to allow railroads to operate with as few as five good ties for each 39-foot section of track. Goldman maintains that these proposed standards "do not provide an adequate margin for safety [and] will increase the likelihood of a derailment and subsequent catastrophic release of hazardous materials."

Accidents involving hazardous materials evoke the greatest concern in connection with the proposed regulatory changes. In the past decade, rail accidents involving hazardous materials have resulted in over $45 million in damages, 2,188 injuries and 44 deaths. The figures since 1978 show a fairly steady decline in each of these categories, but as the brake and track standards are relaxed and the number of state inspectors cut back, this trend will likely reverse. The result may be more accidents like the 1980 incident in Kentucky when ten tank cars containing vinyl chloride, chlorine, acrylonitrile, and toluene derailed in a residential area near Fort Knox. The four tank cars carrying vinyl chloride caught fire, two of them exploded, and a cloud of toxic vapor forced the evacuation of over 7,500 people.

The most devastating proposal is to eliminate federal grants for the state railroad safety programs. (Instead the federal government would hire 20 new inspectors and four new clerks.)

This state participation program has been effective in maintaining track and safety standards. In Florida, in the seven-year period between the enactment of the federal program in 1970 and the time when Florida's Department of Transportation assumed inspection in October, 1978, federal inspectors had not fully covered all of Florida's 6,262 miles of railroad track. In 1981, state inspectors covered 6,366 miles of track, listing 5,935 defects which were eventually corrected by the carrier.

Thirty-one states currently participate in the program, providing 47 percent of the nation's railroad track and equipment inspection force. Eliminating federal funds for these programs "would set us back over a decade," stated William Druhan, representing the National Conference of State Railway Officials at the April hearing.

In written testimony, J.R. Snyder, chairman of the Safety Committee of the Railway Labor Executives Association, the labor group which assisted Blanchette with the safety proposals, actually condemned parts of the plan. "The System Safety Plan represents a significant backward step in reducing accidents and injuries," wrote Snyder.

Snyder sees the proposals as part of an overall abandonment of railroad safety goals. "The FRA is embarking on a plan whereby violations discovered by the FRA inspectors will not be subject to citations and penalties as required by all of the railroad safety laws. Rather, the FRA will now permit a defect to exist until such time as the railroad has the opportunity to correct it," he wrote in his testimony. A.W. Westhall, who delivered Snyder's testimony, asserted that federal inspectors have been instructed not to impose fines if they discover a violation. Enforcement figures bear out those feelings. In 1979, the FRA collected $7.5 million in civil penalties. In 1980, the figure was $15 million. Under Blanchette in 1981, the FRA collected a total of only $1,329,697.

FINANCIAL BACKGROUND

Blanchette has indicated he will disqualify himself from any actions involving his former legal clients, including Seaboard Coastline Railroad and Richmond, Fredericksburg and Potomac Railroad.

He has represented a diverse group of firms including Occidental Petroleum, Detroit Steel and RCA. His annual salary totalled about $153,000 and he held modest stock investments in AT&T, Bristol Myers, Pfizer, Subaru, Texaco and several other companies as well as larger holdings in Baltimore municipal bonds. He reports assets of at least $400,000.

WHAT OTHERS ARE SAYING ABOUT HIM

- "We don't really hold Lewis or Blanchette responsible for many of the decisions which are being made," said Jim Kennedy, general counsel to the Brotherhood of Railway and Airway Clerks. "David Stockman is clearly running the show. . ."

- Amtrak supporters think Blanchette has a "one track" mind. "Blanchette is vastly more concerned with running freight rails," said an Amtrak spokesman. "I don't think he truly understands the essential need for passenger rails, especially in times of fuel scarcity."

- The report issued by the Blanchette-led America's Sound Transportation Review Organization was hailed by one trucking industry lobbyist as "the railroad industry's letter to Santa Claus." The report demanded congressional action to bring railroad subsidies into line with those of the heavily subsidized highway and waterway industries.

- "It took several years," said an official of the Association of American Railroads, "but Congress has eventually honored many of the demands which Blanchette and his panel originally made in 1970." The Staggers Act of 1980 was "culminating legislation" which gave the railroads increased rate flexibility in order to improve their financial status, the official said.

HOUSING AND URBAN DEVELOPMENT DEPARTMENT

SAMUEL PIERCE
SECRETARY

RESPONSIBILITY OF OFFICE

Pierce is directing the steady dismantling of many programs with roots in LBJ's Great Society. HUD was created in 1965 to advance federal solutions to the monumental problems of inadequate housing, urban decay, and troubled neighborhoods.

Pierce's position is to oversee "the principal programs which provide assistance for housing and for the development of the nation's communities. . .to encourage the solution of problems of housing and community development through states, cities, counties and other units of general local government. . .to encourage the maximum contributions that may be made by vigorous private homebuilding and mortgage lending industries to housing, community development, and the national economy; and to provide for full and appropriate consideration, at the national level, of the needs and interests of the Nation's communities and of the people who live and work in them."

Pierce oversees around 14,300 employees and administers a $14.6 billion budget, up from $14 billion in 1981. New budget authority, however, will plummet from $33.5 billion in 1981 to $13 billion in 1982. In 1983 budget authority is scheduled to drop to 685 million.

BACKGROUND

The only black in the Reagan cabinet, Pierce is a veteran of both the executive branch and several corporate boardrooms. The *Wall Street Journal* reported that he was chosen in December, 1980 "after word went out from the transition office to Republican politicians to come up with some black candidates." But Pierce clearly has considerable personal qualifications for the job.

A lifelong Republican, his federal experience dates back to President Eisenhower's first term, when he served as an assistant to the undersecretary of Labor. Pierce also served as counsel to a House Antitrust Subcommittee, before serving two years as a judge of the New York State Court of General Session.

In 1961, he became the first black to join a major New York law firm, Battle, Fowler, Jaffin, Pierce, and Kheel, where he practiced until 1970. He rejoined the firm in 1973 and remained until tapped by Reagan. In 1964, he became the first black to join the board of a major corporation (U.S. Industries). Since then he served as a director of several other major companies including Prudential Insurance, General Electric, and International Paper Company.

When asked whether he thought large corporations have too much power in the United States, Pierce was momentarily taken aback. "That's an interesting question," he said. "I hadn't thought about it that much." After a few seconds, though, Pierce said he believed corporations "have been very helpful for the country on the whole. True, they have done things that haven't been proper on various occasions, as proved by the many convictions and findings of fault under the antitrust laws. . . .But on the whole I think they've been a very important part of this country. . . .I think they've helped a lot. . . .I think that as long as they stay within the bounds of the various antitrust laws and other laws we have, that's the way we control our corporations. . . . I would not like to see us exclusively a nation of small businesses, because I do not think we would be able to compete in world markets. In fact, I think we're having a tough time now because other nations, I believe, are giving their companies too much help. Japan has given a great deal of help to its companies—the same with West Germany. So I think that our companies, to compete in the world market today, have to be strong, and the size that they are. I think if they're doing something wrong, it's up to us to pass the laws that will block them."

On banks, a corporate presence he must deal with in his current job, Pierce is more expansive. He told us he disagrees with "a lot of their practices. I disagree with the redlining practice. I wish it could be cut out completely. In some states they're pretty effective at controlling it. . . .The trouble with banking is you have to judge who you have to give the money to. When we get into this area of subjective judgement, it's always hard. Because it's very difficult to say you're doing this because a fellow's black, or Puerto Rican, or what have you. They can give you good reasons usually. And that subjective judgment with the subjective rationale usually makes it very difficult to say they're doing something wrong; but I don't like redlining. I wish they'd get rid of it immediately. . . . I would like to see more effort put into getting rid of redlining nationwide."

In 1970, Pierce was appointed general counsel of the Treasury Department, a position he held until 1973. He is best remembered for his work on the Lockheed bailout.

Pierce has been an avid Republican. In 1972, he campaigned for Richard Nixon and made several speeches for the incumbent President.

Pierce grew up in Glen Cove, New York, a racially integrated community on Long Island. He often mentions how his career was aided by his education in that integrated environment. In fact, Pierce believes "the best way to achieve integration, is to integrate living. If you integrate living, you integrate schools because most schools are based on a neighborhood system. . . . I think our efforts should be to get blacks into all communities.''

But like the Administration, Pierce is cool towards school busing. "You'll find that a lot of black people don't like busing. That's something you'll find people—both black and white—don't like. I do know that people don't like to go a great number of miles everyday. They don't like to get their kids up at six in the morning in order to get them to school by 8:30 or whatever it is. They feel as though it is very hard on their children. Black people feel that.''

When asked if he was concerned about the Justice Department's decision to stop bringing housing discrimination cases in tandem with school discrimination cases, Pierce said such a measure would "bother" him. (See William Bradford Reynolds profile.)

Although he has never been a high profile figure in the civil rights movement, Pierce serves as a trustee for a fund-raising arm of the NAACP. The secretary told us he doesn't think there is any one recognized voice speaking for blacks: "Take Vernon Jordan and Benjamin Hooks. I think they reflect a lot of black thinking, there's no doubt about it. But, I don't think there's any more a black leader than a white leader. . .I think you have to get a cross-section of black leaders. Even they don't speak completely for blacks. . .I noticed in the past a lot of Presidents of the United States, when blacks were having a problem, would call up the head of the NAACP and think he had the solution. Well, no one person does.''

Republicans have an ambivalent attitude toward black voters. The Reagan Administration clearly has not been willing to moderate its policies—particularly in the civil rights area—to attract blacks and some Republican leaders have suggested writing them off altogether. But other more moderate Republicans realize that the party has to reach out to new constituencies if it is ever to become a governing majority.

Pierce believes Republican success in attracting black voters will hinge on "philosophy" and economics. "I compare this time very much to the time Roosevelt came into office. When Roosevelt came into office virtually all black people were Republicans. And as a matter of fact in 1932, if you go back and get the records, you'll find that the vast majority of blacks voted for Hoover against Roosevelt. Then in the next four years they changed because of economics, not civil rights. Economics caused them to change.

"We are in a very similar posture, in my opinion, right now. When you look at the statistics for unemployment—black youth, 50 percent; and black adults, 17-something percent—these are remarkable. We're sure we're in a recession, but to an average black person this is depression right now. This is hell. If—and it's a big if—we are able to turn around this economy so that the economy is moving and these people begin to get a bite of the pie again. . .I think they'll be going more toward the Republican Party. . .When we were spending more money than ever before in 1979 and 1980, you'll find that black unemployment was going up. They'll [blacks] begin to see that, we'll be able to tell them that. . .and they will back the Republican Party. . .There's only one way that movement could be stopped: If we were to butcher civil rights.''

Many black leaders, though, believe that is an accurate description of Reagan's current civil rights policies. In February, 1982, the Leadership Conference on Civil Rights accused the Reagan Administration of adopting a "cave man" ethic on civil rights. Attorney General William French Smith subsequently characterized the Leadership Conference's report as "inflammatory and inaccurate." (See profile of

Smith.) Pierce told us he couldn't agree or disagree with Smith because he hadn't read the report.

Pierce did concede that there have been several "mistakes" made by the Administration on civil rights, citing the Bob Jones tax break fiasco as an example. Still, the secretary told us he believes the President when he says there will be "no backsliding" on civil rights. "I believe he means that. We're trying to get the implementation, the mechanisms to assure that. If we do that, and we're able to keep civil rights at the current level or better, I think we'll get a lot of black people into the party. . .or to come back in the party. . .But if you backslide too far on civil rights, I think you'll lose them. The blacks have fought too hard for civil rights to go down the drain right now."

If high unemployment continues, Pierce said it is "possible" for uprisings like those that occurred in the '60s to erupt again. He hoped the Administration would "turn unemployment around" before that point is reached and, as yet, senses no turbulence brewing. "I sense a lot of blacks feel as though they're carrying the brunt of the trouble. . .that the rich people should bear more of the burden. Some complain that defense should be cut more. But, there's a long distance between [that feeling and] the turbulence that happened in the '60s," he told us. We asked Pierce whether *he* thought defense spending should be curtailed. He responded: "Well uh, I'd rather. . .I'd like to reserve on that. . .I don't want to get into that."

When people say the President "hates blacks or that he's turning against the poor," Pierce thinks Reagan "takes it at heart. I really don't think that's him at all." When asked whether top members of the Justice Department share what Pierce sees as the President's commitment to civil rights, Pierce hedged, visibly uncomfortable. "It's hard for me to say, I don't know, but in time I will know very well. I don't want to make a comment prematurely. . .I want to watch these things. I think it's premature to say that things are being done intentionally to try to hurt or to push the progress that has been made on civil rights. . ."

Pierce found it difficult to predict whether he would remain in his post with the Administration for four years, hinting that decisions in areas other than housing and urban policy might determine his decision. "I really don't have any intentions of leaving right away," he told us. "I don't know, really, what the future will bring. That depends on many factors. It hasn't happened, but if something changed, for example, that I could not absolutely take in my heart, that I believe has just really gone completely distant, I think I'd have to quit because I just couldn't be loyal to a team when I just felt that they've gone too far. . ."

In 1978, the *Nation* identified Pierce as the man the FBI had hoped would take over leadership of the civil rights movement once they had "discredited" Martin Luther King, Jr. In a January, 1964 memo entitled "Samuel Riley Pierce, Jr.," the FBI's William Sullivan wrote that "King must, at some propitious point in the future, be revealed to the people of this country, to his Negro followers, as being what he actually is—a fraud, demagogue, and moral scoundrel. . .When this is done. . .the right kind of a national Negro leader could at this time be gradually developed so as to overshadow Dr. King and be in the position to assure the role of leadership of the Negro people when King had been completely discredited." Pierce was the man Sullivan had in mind. J. Edgar Hoover approved the scheme, but there is no evidence the FBI actually approached Pierce. Pierce has denied any knowledge of the plan.

Pierce was born on September 8, 1922 in Glen Cove, New York. He received his B.A. degree in 1947 from Cornell University (where he was a star football halfback) and his law degree in 1949 from Cornell Law University. His undergraduate work was interrupted by World War II, when he served three years in North Africa and Italy as the only black in the Army's Criminal Investigation's Division in the Mediterranean theater.

He was admitted to the New York bar in 1949 and served the next four years as an assistant district attorney. He was then appointed assistant U.S. attorney for the Southern District of New York before moving on to the Department of Labor in 1955.

Pierce is married with one daughter.

FINANCIAL BACKGROUND

When Pierce fought with the budget cutters to save the UDAG program, he was hailed by some as a savior of the urban poor. Other interests also benefit from the program though. One of the major beneficiaries of the UDAG program this year will be Prudential Insurance, which will put up a new office building in Newark, New Jersey with the help of a $9 million UDAG grant. Pierce, of course, has served on Prudential's board of directors for several years.

Pierce is sometimes willing to go against his former corporate colleagues as well. For instance, at one point last spring, he aggressively opposed a budget cut favored by his former conglomerate, General Electric, which is among a cadre of large firms which has mounted a campaign to wipe out the Federal Housing Administration (FHA) as a competitor in the mortgage insurance field. Yet it was Pierce who fought David Stockman to raise the FHA's insurance ceiling.

In the year before taking office, Pierce earned $280,000 from his law firm. His stock portfolio has been termed "superconservative," comprised of dozens of modest investments in reliable, steady-yield stocks. He reports assets greater than $800,000.

WHAT OTHERS ARE SAYING ABOUT HIM

- In the early months of his term at HUD, Pierce kept a very low profile, prompting several critics to contend that he was hiding his ignorance of the issues. HUD employees dubbed him "Silent Sam," and one *Wall Street Journal* report said the Reagan Administration was displeased with Pierce's performance in Cabinet meetings because he appeared detached and unresponsive. One Administration insider speculated Pierce was merely occupying space on the Cabinet while awaiting Reagan's nomination to the Supreme Court when the first vacancy occurred. Pierce's friends, however, claim he is quiet by nature and "like any good labor negotiator, [he] does a lot of listening before he speaks."

- Pierce's law partner Theodore H. Kheel gives a glowing review of the HUD Secretary: "[Pierce] is a rare human being. He has the ability to walk a tightrope or deal with a variety of situations and come out with the respect of everybody."

- At the NAACP's national convention in July, 1981, Pierce told a cool audience that he would "build a bridge over troubled waters." However, according to one NAACP attendee, most of the members were not especially impressed by

Pierce's reassuring words. "Pierce is just not aware of the needs of black people in this country because of the kind of Madison Avenue environment he's been in for so long," the NAACP source said.

DONALD HOVDE
UNDERSECRETARY

RESPONSIBILITY OF OFFICE

The undersecretary's responsibilites are much the same as those of the secretary. Hovde is primarily in charge of "the day-to-day functions of the secretary's office." In Pierce's absence, Hovde would serve as acting secretary.

In the early months of the Administration, Hovde gave several speeches around the country (as well as in Europe) on behalf of Pierce. Secretary Pierce also placed Hovde in charge of a special department task force to study ways to crack down on waste, fraud, and mismanagement.

BACKGROUND

Hovde was owner and president of Hovde Realty, a commercial and investment real estate brokerage firm in Madison, Wisconsin for 26 years. One of the largest developers in Dane County, Wisconsin, Hovde has also headed the 122 Building Corporation, a real estate investment holding company. He was also national senior vice-president of Partners Real Estate, Inc.

Hovde capped a long-time membership in the National Association of Realtors by becoming president of the 760,000-member organization in 1979. The association contributed $5,000 to Reagan's 1980 campaign.

Hovde is a past president of the Madison Chamber of Commerce and helped organize a local council which worked toward stimulating inner-city redevelopment. He also served as chairman of a local fund-raising drive to create a major housing facility for the elderly.

In 1980, he was regional chairman of the "Realtors for Reagan" committee.

Hovde earned a Bachelor of Business Administration degree in finance at the University of Wisconsin in 1953. He was commissioned in the U.S. Army the same year, earned his pilot's wings in 1958, and served in the Army Reserve until 1963, achieving the rank of captain.

Born on June 3, 1931 in Madison, Hovde is married with five children.

FINANCIAL BACKGROUND

As a former president and government lobbyist for the National Association of Realtors (NAR), Hovde is now in a position to strongly influence policies which concern this politically-active group.

In 1980, Hovde listed earnings from his various business activities totaling about $47,000 and in addition he had numerous partnership investments in Madison-area properties. He reports assets worth at least $2 million. He also reports substantial liabilities.

WHAT OTHERS ARE SAYING ABOUT HIM

- Despite Secretary Pierce's lack of experience in the housing field, most observers believe he will still maintain a tight rein over housing policies, and it is doubted that Hovde will hold too much sway over Pierce.

- "I don't see Hovde as a guru at HUD," said Bill Kamela, spokesman for the National Urban League. "With his NAR background, he may not exactly be a friend of the low-income person, but I don't know how much influence he will really have on policy. There are a lot of career people at HUD who have been there a long time and have seen a lot of these assistant secretaries and undersecretaries come and go. . .and I'm not sure they will really pay that much attention to these new people."

- HUD program analyst Alan Ripskis said, "[Pierce and Hovde] are intelligent men, but they are amateurs when it comes to government administration. . .I really think they want to do something about this waste problem, but they don't know what the hell to do because they're still trying to learn the system."

MAJOR ISSUES

- New regulations in block grant programs will make cities less accountable for the federal money they receive. Many observers believe the money is less likely than ever to go to those in need, and instead will be diverted by municipalities to other uses.

- The Administration is pushing for a new vouchers system that will replace the current section 8 housing program. Housing experts predict the vouchers program will exacerbate the difficulties of the poor. Already cuts in section 8 will affect more than 125,000 poor people.

- Pierce predicts enterprise zones will be the "major urban initiative" for the '80s although most agree that the cities most in need of rejuvenation will be unable to afford the program.

One of the centerpieces of the Great Society's war on poverty, HUD has been on the frontier of the Reagan Administration's war against social expenditures.

At first many thought Pierce would sit by quietly and watch Budget Director David Stockman erase his agency. Dubbed "Silent Sam," Pierce was quite conciliatory during his first months in office. But of late, especially since Stockman was wounded by the *Atlantic Monthly* episode, Pierce has stiffened his spine.

Pierce explained his frequent "conflicts with David [Stockman]": "We're good friends, but we have fights about things—that's the way it is. We see things differently at times."

In the heat of the battle Pierce predicted that Stockman's proposed cuts would devastate housing and urban development, precipitating "rent strikes, riots, vandalism, and irreparable damage." Pierce managed to salvage several key HUD programs but not without great compromise.

One major program the Administration proposed annihilating was the Community Development Block Grants (CDBG), a program designed to stimulate neighborhood projects and housing rehabilitation. Although Pierce managed to recover most of the funds for CDBG—in one of his "biggest fights" with Stockman—Paul Bloid of the Center for Community Change said it still represents "a major gutting of the program."

CDBG monies are divided into two categories: the small cities program, which provides to areas with 50,000 residents or less; and the entitlement program which covers the more populated regions. CDBG is one of the few programs whose rules are subject to congressional veto and the recently released proposals governing the small cities program have run into stiff opposition from many in both houses. "We feel the regulations proposed by HUD are inconsistent with the law," David Yudin, a Democratic counsel on the Senate Housing and Urban Affairs Subcommittee, told us.

If the legislators approve the regulations as written, HUD grant recipients will be much less accountable for the money they receive. For instance, HUD will no longer strictly define who the targeted low and moderate beneficiaries are, but will turn that responsibility over to the state or local agencies. States will also be allowed to develop their own standard for reporting the success of the programs they implement and will operate under significantly loosened distribution rules. "It's like a big guessing game for states and localities," warned Bloid, who fears grants will be used simply to supplement municipal budgets, rather than to develop neighborhoods. "The regulations are strictly an OMB agenda," he contended, "and Pierce is party to them by virtue of his silence."

HUD has not yet released CDBG entitlement regulations. But housing experts are fairly confident they will resemble those set down for the small cities program. "The small cities regulations are probably a preview for the entitlement regulations," Reggie Todd of the National League of Cities predicted. "We lose what we need—a balanced regulatory approach."

Pierce thinks the proposed regulations would benefit the CDBG programs. "I think we can certainly change them," he said. "I think it's sufficient to watch the program to see if it goes all right. . .I'm not worried about it."

The other grant program Pierce saved from total abolition is the Urban Development Action Grants (UDAG). UDAG funds are used to stimulate private investment in hotels, shopping centers, and other projects that, as the *Wall Street Journal* says, "mayors and developers like."

UDAG funds have been criticized for underwriting projects for some of the richest corporations in America, such as General Motors (GM). In February, 1981, HUD approved a $30 million UDAG grant to help General Motors build a new Cadillac assembly plant in Detroit. The grant, along with hundreds of millions of dollars of other state and federal subsidies, will pay for the complete elimination of the neighborhood, known as Poletown, where GM wanted to put the plant. Approximately 3,500 people and 150 businesses were forced out by the project. GM had threatened to leave Detroit if the city did not come up with a suitable site for its new plant. "Any company may well play the game," Pierce acknowledged. "But, from the evidence we have, I am pretty sure we saved jobs at a time when the automobile industry was rough on people who worked for them. . .it's one of those things where I was pretty satisfied we did the right thing on it. I will agree that most of the time we shouldn't worry about General Motors or Cadillac."

"Everybody's interested in UDAG," Pierce explained. And that, he told us, was the driving force behind his struggle to save the program. "When I came here and started to talk to members of Congress—every one of them, Republican, Democrat, liberal, conservative, whoever it was, the only thing they ever talked about to me was the UDAG program. They all said it was the greatest program in the world."

When it became apparent Stockman was set on UDAG's abolition, Pierce brought the conflict directly to the President, who agreed to maintain a skeleton UDAG. "David always wanted to get rid of that program," Pierce told us. "He was not alone—there were others who wanted to get rid of UDAG. Last year we had to carry our appeal to the President and the President decided to keep it for one more year." The program was cut by 33 percent.

The President's decision was greatly influenced, Pierce maintains, after meeting with local government officials: "He had state legislators, mayors, and other officials come into see him. Reportedly, the only thing all of them agreed upon was UDAG. They thought UDAG was an excellent program and I am sure this helped to influence the President to keep the program for another year."

Both UDAG and CDBG are meant to stimulate local economy, thereby indirectly aiding the local poor by providing jobs, housing assistance, and so forth. More often than not, those who benefit the most are local merchants, corporations, contractors, and others not in dire need. Loosening federal oversight is expected to only exacerbate the problem.

"When these responsibilities are turned over to the local authorities there is a loss of commitment," said Bill Koustenis of the National Community Action Agency. "At least in the past we've had this national commitment to poor people. But when HUD gives up authority like this, the poor people lose a powerful ally." Block grants, Koustenis believes, "amount to throwing money at a community without ensuring that the community leaders are held accountable."

While Pierce fought ferociously to save block grant programs, he's applauding moves to dismantle programs that directly aid the needy. The Housing secretary enthusiastically supports phasing out the section 8 program which subsidizes housing costs for low-income people and advocates replacing it with a voucher system. Virtually no new subsidized housing starts are funded by the 1983 budget.

Vouchers, lauded by both Pierce and a presidential housing commission as a major housing aid priority for the future, would give payments directly to needy families—practically eliminating all other federal housing programs. Under the present program, money is provided to landlords who have agreed to participate in the program, an attempt to guarantee enough affordable housing. With a voucher system, prospective tenants would be forced to find their own shelter, without the protection of rent ceilings. "It's just not going to happen," said Bloid. "There won't be enough [low cost housing] to go around." Under the proposed 1983 budget, 117,000 families would receive vouchers. The average voucher given to a family will be $2,000. A recent study by the Pratt Institute Center for Community and Environmental Development found that the voucher program would intensify the financial difficulties of the poor.

"Our housing programs, particularly section 8 programs, are one of the big reasons that our outstanding debt for housing will be a quarter of a trillion dollars by the end of 1982," said Pierce, although he told a gathering of the National Association of Housing and Redevelopment Officials that section 8 is still "one of our most effective means of providing housing for lower-income families." He told us section 8 "was a way of making a lot of money for a lot of rich people."

Already the amount of rent recipients must contribute under section 8 has been increased from 25 to 30 percent of their total income. This increase, Pierce said, will allow HUD to spread the available funds among more people.

But the 10 million poor people affected by housing cuts are hardly in a position to sacrifice. A study by the Americans for Democratic Action (ADA) found the impact of the subsidized housing cuts "will be to make an already bad situation worse. It means that 125,000 people faced with displacement from their homes or living in bad housing will be unable to obtain decent, affordable units."

Replacing section 8 with a voucher system is also likely to strip away the political backing of the real estate, banking, and other powerful lobbies that previously had a stake in section 8 funding, leaving a program with only the poor as a constituency. This, many argue, will make the program's funding more vulnerable. Pierce discounts that prospect. "I think 'necessity is the mother of invention,' " he told us, "and when this system comes I think there are going to be new lobbies and they're going to be even stronger." He points to the increased political clout of the elderly in recent years as an example.

Pierce doesn't ever see the federal government completely out of the housing business. "There are some areas of government building that I think we have to stay in because, for a variety of reasons, private builders won't go into them," he explained, "I mean housing for the handicapped and the elderly. I guess they just can't get the money out of it that they can with other kinds of building. So, we're going to stay in that area. It's an area I think we have to stay in because the private sector just doesn't want to get into it." The budget for the housing loan program for the elderly and handicapped was cut by 50 percent in 1983.

But Pierce displays a Reagan-like faith in the private sector. "This country went a long time before it even had these kinds of [housing] programs. Prior to the Depression years, there were no programs like this, yet all the people in America were housed, and it was all through the private sector," he said. "So there is a precedent for its happening, and we believe that will continue to happen."

Before stepping down as HUD housing commissioner, Philip Winn strongly supported reduced subsidized housing starts and increased tenant/rent contributions. "The results," he argued, "will be a system which will have all tenants in similar circumstances paying the same rent, regardless of the program under which they receive assistance."

But the ADA study concluded that less assistance "amounts to a proposal to give at least 20 percent rent increases to the 'truly deserving needy' at a time when their other resources are also being diminished and their costs of living are rising far more rapidly than those of the rest of us."

Instead of constructing new low-income housing, Pierce would like to see existing structures rehabilitated. Pointing to the empty buildings in his home city, New York, Pierce said, "They're perfectly good structures, but nobody lives in them. . .we can rehabilitate a lot of these buildings and it will be for voucher people, it will be for poor people. So we're not completely out of supplying housing."

The moribund housing industry is hanging its hopes on the Reagan economic promises. The Administration is encouraging more private investment in the housing market and has rejected pleas for public assistance.

Pierce too is hoping for the great economic turnaround: "I think, that when you really look at the building in this country, it has not really been the government, it has been the private sector. We're really private sector builders. The thing that really stops us from getting building done right now is the high rate of interest. If interest rates were reasonable, I wouldn't worry about the amount of government building because it wouldn't make that much difference."

Pierce has been working closely with New York Representatives Jack Kemp and Robert Garcia on a plan for urban enterprise zones, which Pierce says will "probably be the major urban initiative of the Administration." Enterprise zones supposedly would create incentives through state, local, and federal tax breaks and other benefits for businesses to locate in distressed urban areas. The 1983 budget allocates $310 million to finance pilot projects beginning in 1984.

In March, 1982, President Reagan announced formal plans for up to 25 pilots. In order to qualify, an area must have an unemployment rate of one-and-a-half times that of the national average and a poverty rate 20 percent higher than national averages.

In order to lure business into the targeted areas—chosen by the secretary—at least 75 percent of the corporate income taxes will be rolled back in the zones and capital gains taxes would be eliminated. To stimulate hiring, a 50 percent tax credit is proposed on wages paid to disadvantaged employees. "Looking at it very practically," Pierce told us, "you're going to have to give some kind of incentives to get investment into these neighborhoods. There are a lot of areas, or sections, where investors just won't go in without some kind of incentive."

The irony behind this plan, according to Todd, is that the cities in need of the zones are those in no position to distribute the tax breaks industry is demanding, despite federal assistance. "State budgets are so tight to begin with, why should they be prepared to make additional tax breaks for corporations that under the present Administration already have any type of break they want?" he asked. "It's like pulling on a loose string."

Early enterprise zone proposals featured proposals to waive minimum wage standards in the targeted neighborhoods. The version before Congress does not include any plans to do so. Pierce who told us he "disagrees with a lot of things [Stanford economist] Thomas Sowell says"—including his theory that the minimum wage has increased black unemployment—does not think Congress will allow a waiver. "But," he said, "the way it was proposed was that it would be up to the state and local governments to decide whether it would be waived or not. It could be. The law could say that the particular federal government agency responsible for its enforcement could waive it and that's the way it would work, but I don't think Congress is going to go for it anyway."

Pierce thinks the Administration will proceed cautiously with enterprise zones. "We want to gain experience. As we gain experience, we can answer a lot of these questions and maybe even change our legislation to make it more effective. . .I think we have to go slowly, put them in various parts of the country under different circumstances, so we can get a feeling of how it works."

While HUD officials are looking towards increased private sector involvement as a means of upgrading neighborhoods, it is deemphasizing the role local community, neighborhood, and consumer groups play in the process. In the 1982 budget HUD eliminated the Neighborhood and Consumer Protection Office—a public information and technical assistance program for housing and community development. Pierce argues the move was necessary to reduce the amount of local involvement at the federal level and vice-versa. "I think the cities are where the neighborhood groups should be working out their problems and needs. I think we had a little trouble here, once these neighborhood organizations had access to Washington. It caused a lot of trouble with mayors and city governments. I think that local people should work together. And, we do give access to cities at HUD. If we gave access to neighborhoods, I think that would be going too far. . .I think you've got to have a little order."

Such a hierarchy "is absolutely not in keeping with reality," one HUD analyst told us. "The mayor is not always doing the people's will. I could give you hundreds of examples." The bureau functioned "to teach the 'state of the art' of the sophisticated skills local people need," said Geno Baroni, a former HUD assistant secretary who headed the consumer office. "Housing is no longer raising the country barn, today people need to understand mortgage equity, bonds, loans and a lot of other technical things in order to learn how to put the job together. . .They won't learn these things under the Reagan Administration."

Hovde, keeping carefully in line with Secretary Pierce's publicly stated positions for the most part, runs a waste, fraud, and mismanagement task force formed in July, 1981 to "establish policies and develop procedures to improve program monitoring." Thus far little has emerged. Perhaps this is because the HUD inspector general, according to Cushing Dolbeare of the low-income housing coalition, "has already been doing a good job of cracking down on graft and abuse, and has established a reputation of competence."

"The problem," she said, "lies as much in the structure of HUD programs as in attempting to find fraud and abuse. There is only so much the inspector general can do within the existing structure." Andy Mott, vice-president of the Center for Community Change, says HUD's new approach to Community Development Block Grants will "increase the chance of fraud by virtually eliminating federal enforcement."

HUD program analyst Alan Ripskis is also skeptical about HUD's campaign to eliminate waste. (Ripskis is editor of an underground HUD newsletter, *Impact Journal*.) "[The new HUD leadership] probably has the best intentions," he said. "But every new administration makes big noises about how they are going to diminish fraud, and I really don't see any indication that this one is going to do anything different."

Ripskis calls the CDBG block grant situation "the first loss in the [new HUD administration's] war against fraud, waste and mismanagement."

Ripskis said he has been attempting to bring examples of fraud and waste to the attention of HUD leaders for years, nearly always with negligible results. In May, 1981 he sent an open letter to Secretary Pierce pointing out severe waste in the department's contracting system. He told the secretary about a HUD inspector general audit of a random group of contracts which found that about two-thirds of the money had been wasted. "The way the entire HUD contract system is structured," Ripskis said, ". . .is designed to punish rather than reward a conscientious GTR [government technical representative] trying to accomplish his job properly."

In August, 1981, a month after Pierce announced his crackdown on waste, Stockman sent Pierce a letter congratulating him on his new debt collection posture: "You're the first Cabinet member to announce such a positive change in debt collection policy, and I wanted you to know we're grateful to you for taking the lead. . ."

Most agree that the new federal housing policies will result in even less efficiency and reduced effectiveness. "They're just paving the way for the total dismantling of HUD," said a Senate aide. "Next year Stockman can take HUD's record to Congress and tell them how useless it is and recommend that they do away with it."

The secretary foresees no such scenario. Unlike the Energy and Education Departments, Pierce thinks housing programs will still need a Cabinet department even "when we complete the New Federalism program."

Despite his efforts to heighten his profile, Pierce's stature in the Administration is still modest. Take these two incidents. Pierce was present at a gathering of mayors in the White House last year. The President arrived, shaking the hands and slapping the backs of everyone present including his housing secretary, with the cheery greeting, "Hello, Mr. Mayor, Hello, Mr. Mayor." Several seconds after he shook Pierce's hand, Reagan stopped and said, "Oh, Sam, I'm sorry. I didn't mean it."

Then at a press briefing to describe the agency's 1983 budget, Pierce was asked what White House Counselor Ed Meese had in mind when he said, a few days earlier, that the Administration shortly planned to announce a major housing initiative. Said Pierce: "You've got me."

INTERSTATE COMMERCE COMMISSION

REESE TAYLOR
CHAIRMAN

RESPONSIBILITY OF OFFICE

Since 1887, the ICC's regulatory influence has burgeoned, wrapping the trucking, bus, and railroad industries in a web of often anti-competitive regulation dominated by the industries themselves.

Taylor takes over after the Carter Administration's 1980 Motor Carrier Act and 1980 Staggers Act began untangling this government regulation by private cartels.

Today the 11-member ICC regulates all interstate surface transportation, including trains, trucks, buses, inland waterways, coastal shipping, and freight forwarders. There are several vacancies on the commission. (See Major Issues section.)

In 1982, the agency operated with a budget of $78.5 million and 1,450 employees.

BACKGROUND

Taylor, a Nevada lawyer, is a close friend and former law partner of influential Sen. Paul Laxalt (R-Nev.). Taylor has been an active member of the Nevada State Bar since 1967, working heavily on regulatory matters pertaining to public utilities and transportation companies. He has frequently represented trucking and transportation companies in state regulatory proceedings.

Taylor campaigned for Laxalt in 1966 (when he ran successfully for governor) and in 1974 when Laxalt won his Senate seat.

In 1967, Gov. Laxalt appointed Taylor as chairman of the state Public Service Commission, which regulates trucks, railroads, and utilities, where he served for four years. Taylor also served on the Nevada Tax Commission as well as the Governor's Cabinet and Civil Defense Advisory Council.

In 1979 Taylor lobbied in the Nevada State Legislature on behalf of several taxicab companies and was instrumental in preventing local drivers from owning their own cabs. According to the *Las Vegas Sun*, Taylor said the proposed state legislation to allow more competition in taxi services would be "terribly unfair" to fleet owners.

In his younger days, Taylor practiced alongside William French Smith as an associate with the Los Angeles-based firm of Gibson, Dunn and Crutcher, where from 1952 to 1958 he engaged almost exclusively in labor relations law, representing management.

Somewhat a "jack-of-all-trades," Taylor spent the next eight years consecutively making a movie in Europe, setting up a sparkplug distributorship in Las Vegas, working part-time in Beverly Hills as a panel board salesman for Minuteman Missile installations, and practicing as a part-time attorney.

Taylor owes his nomination to his close relationship with Laxalt, but also apparently to the approval of the Teamsters Union, one of the few unions to endorse Reagan during the 1980 election.

Allegations that Taylor's nomination was political payoff to the union were raised by *Common Cause* magazine a few days before Taylor's nomination hearing in June, 1981. That article reported that Frank Fitzsimmons, then president of the Teamsters Union, asked Teamsters attorney Ed Wheeler to find an ICC chairman. Wheeler told *Common Cause* that he chose Taylor and then consulted Laxalt who was "enthusiastic" about the nomination.

As to the Teamsters' endorsement, Taylor has since said that he "didn't solicit it or want it" and also claims that he hardly knew Wheeler. Conversely, Wheeler told *Common Cause* writer Florence Graves he has known Taylor "for years."

"One of these men had to be lying," Graves said. "If there is nothing wrong about this nomination like everybody says, then why did at least one of these men have to lie about their relationship?"

Former ICC Chairman Marcus Alexis, who has discussed the matter with Taylor, speculates that Wheeler "may have been trying to impress his clients" by saying he was responsible for Taylor's selection. Alexis called it a "calculated mistake" by Wheeler.

But Graves doubts that explanation. She thinks it is more likely that she happened to catch Wheeler "somewhat off guard." She said the reason "the Wheeler connection" hadn't been uncovered earlier is that Wheeler had previously refused to speak with reporters.

Despite the *Common Cause* allegations, Taylor breezed through his Senate nomination hearing in 33 minutes. He denied there had been any political payoff to the Teamsters and said he was merely selected because of his political allegiance to Reagan and recommendation by Laxalt.

Born in Los Angeles on May 6, 1928, Taylor obtained his B.A. from Stanford University in 1949. He earned his law degree from Cornell University in 1952 and was admitted to the California bar two years later. He headed the Nevada Reagan for President committees in both 1976 and 1980. He was a member of the steering committee for Reagan's between-campaigns front group, Citizens for the Republic.

He is married to Jolene V. Taylor and has three children from a previous marriage.

MAJOR ISSUES

- Taylor is putting the brakes on trucking deregulation. A joint congressional committee has charged that Taylor "abandoned the goal of a freely competitive trucking market and has moved to reverse the progress toward deregulation. . . ."

- White House support for Taylor's policies is uncertain. Though the Administration professes to back deregulation, White House aide Michael Deaver, openly hostile to deregulation, exercises influence over trucking policy. His public relations firm represented the California Trucking Association.

- On railroad deregulation, Taylor has been much less vocal. Railroad people are worried he might try to re-regulate the railroads, as he has the truckers.

Like many statutes involving regulation, the 1980 Motor Carrier Act was written to minimize immediate political pain by maximizing the agency's leeway in implementing the law. That made it easier to get the bill through Congress; but it also opened the way for a reversal in course with the appointment of officials like Taylor, committed to slowing deregulation as much as possible within the latitude afforded him by the law.

Trucking deregulation is undoubtedly the issue upon which Taylor's nomination will be ultimately judged. He's already angered many members of the Reagan Administration, as well as the Democratic deregulators who wrote the law. Taylor asserts that his predecessors at ICC interpreted the law too broadly, maintaining that Congress set out to reform, not to deregulate, the trucking industry.

That's not how most congressional leaders read the law they wrote. In a January, 1982, report the Joint Economic Committee charged that Taylor "has abandoned the goal of a freely competitive trucking market and has moved to reverse the progress toward deregulation which has recently been made. This policy," the report continues, "contradicts the intent of Congress embodied in its passage of the 1980 Motor Carrier Act."

One Senate aide who was a principal draftsman of the Carrier Act, admits that Congress passed a version vague enough to allow for "fuzzy" interpretations in several key areas. This, he believes, allows Taylor to scrutinize the law more closely than its authors intended.

Taylor insists he is only following the law as written, and his detractors are people who "expect me to enforce the bill they wanted, not the one that passed." The Carter Administration's ICC had moved quickly to implement the law. Already truckers across the nation are feeling the impact of those actions. Since formal deregulation 5,122 new companies have registered with ICC and freight bills have been reduced 10 to 20 percent as of early 1982, according to the *New York Times*.

Fierce competition and reduced rates are exactly what deregulators intended the law to bring. "It all depends upon what you perceive as good and what you perceive as bad," explained one Democratic congressional expert on the issue. "Truckers have incredible salaries with respect to other sectors of the economy. Before deregulation everybody was trying to keep shippers in business, no matter how inefficient they were."

There was virtually no competition among truckers before the 1980 law. Over the years organized labor and large truckers closed off the industry with the help of government regulations that effectively locked out small trucking firms through restrictive route allocation and price-fixing rules.

In the months following his confirmation Taylor weeded out avowed deregulators within ICC and brought to his personal staff a lawyer, Paul S. Dempsey, who has written articles in legal journals critical of deregulation, especially free entry—the ability of a company to enter a market easily. According to the ICC press office, Dempsey's appointment was only temporary. He took a leave of absence from Denver University where he is a law professor and returned in December, 1981. Others speculate that increasing political pressure prompted Dempsey to leave.

"Dempsey's views are indicative of Taylor's," said Joe Cobb of the Council for a Competitive Economy, "or else Taylor never would have brought him on board."

One of Dempsey's articles appeared in 1979 in the *Transportation Law Journal* sharply criticizing the deregulation of airlines: "Like a pack of ravenous sharks," Dempsey wrote, "the CAB [Civil Aeronautics Board] has attacked its prey in a deregulatory frenzy. The ultimate tragedy however, may well be that communities, carriers and passengers must suffer the irresponsible and ill-conceived policies of a misguided majority of the CAB."

Alexis has said the ICC, while under his direction, has already "dragged its feet very, very considerably" in implementing deregulation. Under Taylor, he believes the already slow deregulation process will be "slowed to a crawl."

Former CAB Chairman Alfred E. Kahn recently led a panel of deregulators condemning Taylor's policies before the Joint Economic Committee (JEC). Kahn said that under Taylor, ICC had begun to interpret its legislative mandate "in a more protectionist, anticompetitive manner."

In his speeches and testimony, Taylor defends his slowdown with an extended metaphor that compares the deregulation of the trucking and railroad industries to the ascent to the surface "of the marketplace" of two divers long encrusted in "the murky depths of regulation." As Taylor puts it: "The critical part of the entire operation is the ascent itself. Both divers [the trucking and railroad industries] have been dislodged from the bottom and can be brought up to safety. But if they are jerked to the surface in one fell swoop, they will suffer from the bends and will undoubtedly be resubmerged for decompression. The challenge is to bring each diver up to a given level, allow him to decompress at that level, and then bring him up some more."

In its report, the JEC scored Tayor's policies on six counts. The Committee criticized Taylor's ICC for:

- disallowing rate reductions. Taylor has focused his rate concerns on "predatory" pricing, a preoccupation which led conservative economist Thomas Gale Moore of the Hoover Institute, a member of Reagan's ICC transition team, to comment that "the arguments about predatory pricing are simply a method of preventing price competition."

The 1980 act allows carriers to change their rates 10 percent without commission approval. It also phased out antitrust immunity for some forms of collective rate-making. Both procedures were liberalized a good deal further under the Carter ICC, which allowed carriers to experiment with a variety of rate discounts including across-the-board percentage reductions, volume discounts, discounts to specific shippers, and "multiple tender" discounts.

But with Taylor in the driver's seat, the ICC has put the brakes on this activity. Since September, 1981 it has issued a series of mandates restricting trade, including a blanket order rescinding existing permissions for individual discounts, rejecting arguments that discounts might be justified by cost factors.

- requesting more regulators. At a time when all other regulatory agencies are being slashed, Taylor is seeking to increase his enforcement budget. Said Kahn: "Enforcement [means] prohibiting price competition."

- imposing burdensome hearing requirements. Oral hearings, which some feel may discourage prospective applicants by requiring them to travel and appear before an administrative law judge, are being used again, after the Carter ICC had reduced their use.

- issuing narrower grants of authority. The commission has generally narrowed the routes that it grants, restricting the routes that truckers can run. Said Alexis: "Quantities [of grants issued under Taylor] may be similar, but the quality of grants has deteriorated. . ."

- failing to appeal recent court decisions slowing deregulation.

In October, 1981 Taylor's efforts in these areas were boosted by a decision of the Fifth Circuit Court in New Orleans. Much to the dismay of deregulation advocates, the American Trucking Association successfully narrowed the broad entry guidelines established by the ICC before Taylor's chairmanship. But that's okay with Taylor, who voted not to appeal the decision in a 2-2 commission split that ruled out further legal action.

Taylor's critics believe the ICC should have challenged the court's ruling. Kahn claims that "there are elements of this decision which seem to be flagrantly anti-competition, and I would think the commission would appeal it."

- proposing restrictive standards. Taylor has formally proposed replacing the "public convenience and necessity" standard used in granting routes with a "fit, willing and able" standard. Such a standard, argued Alexis, "would in fact be more restrictive than the present standard. . .and would be a step backwards."

Congress isn't the only government entity critical of the regulatory slow-down. In early March, 1982, the Federal Trade Commission released its evaluation of the Motor Carrier Act. "The study shows that deregulation is working better than its opponents charge, but not so well as its backers had hoped," wrote Chairman James C. Miller III in a *Wall Street Journal* article. Miller suggested that, "Resolute initiatives by the ICC to further the goal of deregulation would help clarify the scene."

White House support for Taylor's policies is uncertain. President Reagan has publicly stated his support for deregulation, but close Reagan aide Michael Deaver holds different views and has exercised his influence over trucking policy. Deaver's public relations firm represented the California Trucking Association, which vigorously fought deregulation of intrastate trucking in the late 1970s.

Deaver halted the nomination to the ICC of William K. Ris, a Senate Commerce Committee staffer responsible for drafting the Carrier Act, after a June, 1981, meeting with California Trucking Association Director Thomas C. Schumacher, Jr.

The newest ICC appointees are Republican Malcolm Sterrett, a former vice-president of the United States Railway Association and Frederic N. Andre, former

Commissioner of the Indiana Bureau of Motor Vehicles. To fill a Democratic seat, the President tapped J.J. Simmons, a New York oil company executive, called by one Senate aide, a "Republican's Democrat."

The ICC by law can have up to 11 commissioners, with no more than six from one political party. Since 1977 no more than seven have sat on the commission. The new Reagan Administration has been sharply criticized for packing the committee with Republicans.

"The best hope for deregulation lies with the Senate Commerce Committee," Alexis said. "[Chairman] Bob Packwood has to get control of the committee. Hopefully, Packwood will consider a 'sunset' of the ICC's authority over the trucking industry. The best solution is to take away Taylor's jurisdiction over trucking. . .it is the only way to avoid the truckers' continued undermining of the ICC."

While the trucking industry is pleased with Taylor's selection, the railroad industry is less optimistic. Alexis said the railroad executives will not be expecting too many favors from Reagan because it is rumored "they met during the campaign and formed a war chest for President Carter." Moreover, Alexis said, the trucking industry "has always played the political game more adroitly than the railroads," and generally tends to get more political favors.

Alexis said the Transportation Department will conflict with the ICC as much over railroad, as trucking policy. Transportation Secretary Drew Lewis is pushing hard for deregulation of the railroad shipping rates as part of his plan to make Conrail stock more attractive to private buyers. Lewis has formally asked the ICC to "abandon its efforts to establish guidelines for setting rates charged by railroads for transporting coal."

Taylor has been tougher on the railroads than his predecessor. Sen. Wendell Ford (D-Ky.) obviously sensed this during Taylor's nomination hearing when he requested the delay of an upcoming coal rate hearing which affected the shippers in his state. Ford said he didn't want the ICC to vote on the petition until Taylor had a chance to review it.

Congress passed the Staggers Act, the railroad's deregulation mandate, in 1980. Implementation has moved much slower than with trucking. Some of the delay has been attributed to the painstaking care rulemakers must take to insure that prices are regulated where there is no competition—often in the shipping of grain, coal and other bulk commodities—while allowing prices to be competitive where there are alternative means of transportation, such as in the shipping of food.

The chairman's first review of the Staggers Act came in a public oversight hearing in early November, 1981. At that time he said, "The Staggers Act and our implementation of the act has been successful, in our view, in removing unneeded regulatory burdens while retaining the protection afforded by regulation where there is an absence of effective competition."

There are not as many potential forms of competition in the railroad, as in the trucking industry. This makes the deregulation process much more sensitive for railroads. As one Senate aide explained, "When there's only one rail going up a mountain to a coal mine, there's little room for competition. Many railroads are by nature monopolistic."

Coal producers are worried that railroad deregulation will produce skyrocketing shipping costs that will price them out of world markets. Some of the more crucial rules in the Staggers Act, especially in the coal shipping arena, have yet to be ironed out by the ICC.

The Coal Exporters Association and the National Coal Association maintain that deregulation will cost the U.S. a big chunk of the export business. In fact some domestic coal buyers warn that higher rail transport will force them to import coal from other nations. Railroad representatives claim that such predictions are alarmist, and that competition will keep down prices.

In another move bound to influence rates, late in March, 1982, ICC announced the elimination of 30-year-old regulations that provided formulas for distributing business during railroad mergers. Essentially, the regulations were meant to protect the smaller railroads affected by merger activity. The ICC predicted that deregulation would, in effect, give shippers new freedom to improve their services. Transportation analysts viewed the change as largely beneficial to large carriers and detrimental to smaller ones that are dependent upon the connecting traffic. Such concerns apparently carried little weight with the ICC, which emphasized "that the commission's primary concern is the preservation of essential service, not the survival of particular railroad companies."

It probably won't be until late summer, 1982 before the remaining Staggers Act rules have been clarified. Still to be settled is ICC's authority to limit the amount rates can rise under the maximum rate regulations.

Taylor has been relatively quiet on railroad issues. The slow pace at which policy has emerged from his office has made the railroad people uneasy. They're afraid he might attempt to re-regulate the railroads, as he has the truckers.

The railroad industry is in some ways like a mirror image of the trucking industry. Railroads, having little competition to contend with, would largely be free to set rates as they choose without some regulation.

FINANCIAL BACKGROUND

Taylor earned a good portion of his $82,100 lawyer's salary in 1980 by representing trucking interests in Nevada. He represented most of his clients before the Nevada Public Service Commission and "occasionally" before the ICC.

He also received over $60,000 in royalties last year from his interest in land under lease to the Standard Oil Company of California (Socal). Taylor inherited the land several years ago and claims that he has "not taken an active part in the management of the property or the oil and gas production."

WHAT OTHERS ARE SAYING ABOUT HIM.

- *Common Cause* writer Florence Graves describes Taylor as "affable, mild-mannered, and fairly undistinquished." At the beginning of her interview with Taylor, he said his lawyer had advised him not to talk about the sensitive issues surrounding his nomination. Three long-winded hours later he apparently decided he had said enough.

CHAPTER 5

LEGAL AFFAIRS

JUSTICE DEPARTMENT

WILLIAM FRENCH SMITH
ATTORNEY GENERAL

RESPONSIBILITY OF OFFICE

As attorney general, Smith heads the Justice Department and serves as the federal government's chief attorney and law enforcement officer. His department represents the U.S. government in all litigation. In exceptionally grave or important cases before the Supreme Court, Smith himself will act as court lawyer.

With over 4,000 attorneys, the Justice Department is the largest law firm in the country, representing U.S. citizens by "enforcing law in the public interest."

Smith oversees both the department's criminal law functions—including the FBI (which, unlike other divisions, reports directly to Smith)—and civil divisions. In practice, Smith spends most of his time as the department's spokesman both at the White House and on Capitol Hill, and giving speeches. As one high official in the department put it, Smith is "Mr. Outside," while his deputy, Schmults, is "Mr. Inside."

In 1982, the department operated with a budget of $2.64 billion and a staff of over 54,000.

BACKGROUND

Urbane, judicious and discreet, William French Smith is a Los Angeles attorney who has operated in some of the most prestigious corporate board rooms on the West Coast, leaving the public little more than a whisper of his existence. A Harvard law school graduate; a life member of both the General Society of Mayflower Descendants and the Sons of the American Revolution; and a very wealthy businessman. In any room where the few hundred men and women who run the country were gathering, Smith would be assured a seat.

A society lawyer who has built his entire career on a network of connections, he is also assured an invitation to Washington's most prominent social gatherings, which he and his wife have eagerly attended since they arrived in town. To Smith, parties are the bedrock of his office. He seems more comfortable around the soft clinking of cocktail glasses than the hard rap of a gavel. "You can get to know people better, which makes communication better," Smith told the *New York Times* at a bash for tennis star Bjorn Borg. "I think that's a very important attribute of Washington." In April, 1982, Smith became the first Cabinet secretary with two private dining rooms. He installed the second dinette—at a cost of $4,300—so that he and other top department officials could have their guests in for "working lunches" without bothering others in the original dining room, according to his spokesman, Art Brill.

Smith is learning that indiscretion in his social life can cause some trouble. He was sharply criticized in early 1981 when he attended a birthday party for his long-time friend Frank Sinatra, who has been accused of ties to organized crime. Smith countered that he was "totally unaware of any allegation about Frank Sinatra's background."

As attorney general, Smith is getting his first taste of both criminal and civil rights law. For 34 years he was a corporate lawyer in Los Angeles's largest firm—Gibson, Dunn, and Crutcher, which is rapidly expanding with 280 partners, and offices from San Jose, California to London and Paris to Riyadh, Saudi Arabia. The firm specializes in representing management in labor disputes. Its notable clients include the defense contractor Textron, Saudi Arabia, the United Arab Emirates, and Times-Mirror, owner of the *Los Angeles Times*. Smith's personal clients have included Southern California Edison, Metromedia, Inc., Pacific Lighting Corp., California Federal Savings and Loan, Irvine Co., Occidental Life, Inc., Pacific Resources, and, of course, Ronald Reagan.

Smith has been Reagan's close personal friend, business adviser, and attorney since the early 1960s. Together with a group of other wealthy men, later known as Reagan's "kitchen cabinet," Smith encouraged his client and friend to run for governor in 1966.

Smith was behind Reagan's rise to wealth. He and other Los Angeles multi-millionaires like Justin Dart, Holmes Tuttle, and William A. Wilson arranged the financing for Reagan's campaign at a time when the candidate received little income other than royalties from his array of B-movies. (Reagan's job with the General Electric Theater had ended in 1962.)

After Reagan gained the governor's seat, Smith and others in the "kitchen cabinet" put together a series of deals that made Ronald Reagan rich. In one transaction, Reagan sold most of a rocky 290-acre "ranch" in the Santa Monica mountains, the Yearling Row Ranch, which he had bought in 1951 for $275 an acre, to Twentieth Century Fox for $1.9 million, or $8,178 an acre. The company then sold the land to the state at a much lower price. (Two years later Reagan signed legislation—vetoed by his predecessor—that gave film studios such as Twentieth Century a massive tax break on their film inventories.)

The remaining 54 acres were bought by a subsidiary of Kaiser Aetna, Santa Rosa Ranches, for $165,000 as part of a trade that left Reagan with another ranch. Later a cryptic firm called 57th Madison Corporation bought the land from Kaiser for about the same price, effectively reimbursing Kaiser. Two *Rolling Stone* reporters in the mid-1970s tracked down 57th Madison and found it was actually owned in part by Jules Stein, co-founder of the movie-record-television conglomerate Music Corporation of America (MCA).

As it turned out, Stein, a long-time friend, probably owed Reagan one: In the mid-1950s MCA was able to branch into television production, largely through the efforts of then Screen Actors Guild President Reagan, who helped Stein obtain a guild waiver. The Yearling Row sale and other land deals left Reagan with about $2 million.

Later Reagan, through Oppenheimer Industries, which locates tax shelters for wealthy investors and is owned by Stein's stepson, purchased beef cattle from ranches in Wyoming, Nevada, and Montana. Until 1980, Smith was also a partner in Oppenheimer.

Smith's investment decisions were so shrewd that in 1970 Reagan, by then a millionaire, paid no state income taxes. After that news became public Reagan denounced the Sacramento press corps, which, he said, "demeaned itself a little by engaging in invasion of privacy. They knew that someone illegally provided the information from the Franchise Tax Board."

In 1974 *Rolling Stone* reporters Howard Kohn and Lowell Bergman went to Smith in search of some answers about Reagan's murky financial dealings. Smith wouldn't budge. When they asked him if he himself had ever been involved in a conflict of interest, Smith replied: "I've always tried to remove myself from situations that might invite a conflict. But in any situation where you're a friend of someone, you're just not sterile."

Shortly after his election in 1966, Reagan appointed Smith to the University of California (UC) Board of Regents. Smith is a UC alumnus, and a seat on the regents board is one of the most prestigious positions in the state. But the appointment was more than just a favor to Smith: Reagan at that time was trying to persuade a recalcitrant UC board to implement tuition for the first time in the university's 102-year history, a move Reagan claimed was necessary to make student activists "more responsible."

Smith stepped up to the challenge. Together with another Reagan regent, Edward Carter, he engineered a smooth compromise. Over lunch the pair convinced several regents to change their "no" votes on tuition that morning to "yes" votes in the afternoon. The governor got his way.

"Smith is thorough," says Fred Dutton, a former UC regent now practicing law in Washington, D.C. "He's efficient. He moves quietly. You don't even know he's at work, then he'll spring a coup d'etat."

Smith moved quickly to gain the chairmanship of the UC board in the early '70s and set a hardline tone toward student activists. He supported Reagan's decision to call the National Guard into Berkeley in 1969, when protestors were sprayed with tear gas. As chair of the board in the early 1970s he led the regents' successful effort to fire UCLA lecturer and Communist Party member Angela Davis. Though he didn't support affirmative action, Smith backed UC in the controversial *Bakke* case, when a white male challenged UC Davis Medical School's race-conscious admissions policy.

During his term on the regents, Smith has ardently supported UC research on agricultural mechanization projects. That support has generated a conflict of interest lawsuit against Smith and several other regents filed in a California Superior Court by the California Rural Legal Assistance, an organization that Reagan has long sought to eliminate. The suit charges that agricultural firms in which Smith, and other regents, have financial interests have used mechanization projects developed at UC.

Smith's business dealings while on the regents raised eyebrows on another occasion. In the early 1960s, the Irvine Company developed the town of Irvine in Southern California and donated 1,000 acres to UC to build a campus there. During Smith's tenure as board chairman, the company applied to the regents for approval to expand the town.

Smith, who lobbied the board to adopt the resolution, was also the Irvine Company's attorney—a connection that did not escape the board of regents. Despite loud protests from much of the board, and Smith's decision to abstain from the vote, the resolution squeezed through on support from Reagan and his appointees.

Smith did not resign from the regents after his appointment as attorney general, prompting an anti-nuclear weapons group to file suit against him, charging that state law prohibits officials from holding both state and federal offices. But it is doubtful that a regent seat falls under that law. The same group, the UC Nuclear Weapons Lab Conversion Project, filed another conflict of interest suit against several regents, including Smith, contending they have ties to industries that profit from nuclear weapons research and development. Smith, a strong supporter of retaining UC management of two federal nuclear weapons laboratories—in Livermore, California and Los Alamos, New Mexico—is considered a key obstacle in the way of activists, including Gov. Jerry Brown, who want to break those ties.

Smith has been characterized as a businessman, as well as lawyer. With good reason. From 1967 until his appointment, Smith served on the board of Pacific Lighting Corporation, a holding company with 23 subsidiaries in California, Hawaii, Florida, Australia, the Netherlands, Indonesia, and Canada. He joined Pacific Telephone and Telegraph's board in 1969; Pacific Mutual Life in 1970, Crocker National Bank in 1971, and Jorgenson Steel (owned by kitchen cabinet members Earl Jorgenson and William Wilson) in 1974. He also served on the boards of Pullman Inc., and the AAA of Southern California. Smith is a member of the California Roundtable, an elite organization of conservative businessmen.

Smith also has had a hand in California's lucrative agribusiness. He owns several acres of land in Madera County, California. The land is managed by W.D. Fowler and Sons, a subsidiary of Pacific Lighting. Another former subsidiary of Pacific Lighting, Blue Goose, caused Smith some embarrassment at his nomination hearing.

Blue Goose relied heavily upon undocumented workers for citrus harvesting outside Phoenix, Arizona. According to Don Devereaux, who organized farmworkers in the area, conditions at Blue Goose were "terrible." Blue Goose "used almost entirely Mexican nationals [as workers] who had to live on the ground without housing, toilets, or drinking water. And the pay was substantially less than minimum wage," Devereaux told us.

Pacific Lighting, where Smith was a director, took Devereaux and several other organizers to court for obstructing Blue Goose's operations by publicizing the workers' plight. During his 1981 nomination hearing, however, Smith maintained that the employment practices of Blue Goose "to the best of my recollection did not come to my attention."

The most heated controversy over Smith's nomination surrounded his membership in the all-male Bohemian Club in San Francisco and the California Club in Los Angeles. His membership in the restrictive clubs—neither admits women and the California Club has admitted no blacks—struck many as inappropriate for an official who is charged with ensuring equal justice for all. "Membership in organizations like these suggests to many an insensitivity to the consequences of discrimination on women and various minorities," Sen. Alan Cranston (D-Calif.) told the Senate Judiciary Committee. "As our nation's top law enforcement office, our attorney general has a unique responsibility to demonstrate the fairest and most impartial attitudes and to symbolize justice and equality in all his actions."

In recent years a number of nominees for federal positions have resigned their membership in discriminatory clubs before taking office, including former Attorney General Griffin Bell. Smith refuses to give up his memberships.

The nation's chief law officer can be expected to continue attending weekend retreats at the Bohemian Grove, 75 miles north of San Francisco, where he and hundreds of other wealthy lawyers and businessmen put on skits, drink freely, listen to political commentators—and play. One reason cited for excluding women from the club is the members' propensity to trot around *al fresco*, and, sometimes, to dress up as women. Smith's favorite spot in the Grove, according to sociologist G. William Domhoff, is Mandalay Camp, "known for its gin and lemon juice drinks, its Welsh Rarebit dinners and plush furnishings well beyond what other camps have to offer." Smith shares the camp with such notables as Stephen D. Bechtel Jr., chair of Bechtel Construction; Richard P. Cooley, chair of Wells Fargo Bank; Jack Horton, chair of Southern California Edison; and George Schultz, vice-chairman of Bechtel Construction Company.

Until his appointment to the Justice Department, Smith had generally succeeded in avoiding public controversy. In fact, except for his role with the UC regents Smith's name rarely seeped into the California press. As Jack Anderson noted in 1981, Smith didn't even make *Who's Who* until the current edition.

Perhaps one reason Smith has escaped attention is his reluctance to take public stands on contentious issues. "Of every nominee in the last eight years that I have been here. . .I have never found anyone who had fewer answers to more questions than this nominee," Sen. Joseph Biden (D-Del.) told the Senate. "He was almost totally devoid of an opinion at all. His is the ultimate corporate lawyer. He hardly says anything, other than his rank, name and serial number."

But to those who have worked with him, Smith is a man who clearly states his views. "He's not a man who is out pounding the table," said UC regent Stanley Sheinbaum. "But he will not fudge his views or hold back. He'll let you know where he stands."

Despite his resistance to publicity, in 1973 he granted an interview with the *Los Angeles Times* in which he set forth the premise of his political philosophy: "The radical or revolutionary goal of our American system was to place power at the bottom and let it filter up. It seems to me that the true liberal approach, which I favor, is one that aims at keeping power at the bottom, with as little as possible filtering back to the top.

"There are two characteristics that tend to keep power at the bottom. One is citizen participation. The second, overlapping the first, is the necessity of keeping final decision-making in the *smallest* possible group that is capable of making effective decisions," he said. His remarks about the importance of citizen participation are particularly ironic nine years later, as he attempts to curtail citizen access to the federal government by weakening the Freedom of Information Act and opposing environmental and other citizen groups' standing in challenging federal actions in court.

Aside from his early support of Reagan, Smith has had a long association with Republican Party politics. He was a member of the Republican State Central Committee (1954-56), chair of the California delegation to the Republican National Convention in 1968, and the delegation's vice chair in 1972 and 1976; and he was vice chair of the Nixon-Agnew Finance Committee in 1968.

Smith has also been a member of the advisory board to the Georgetown University's Center for Strategic and International Studies, a conservative research group concerned primarily with foreign affairs.

Born August 26, 1917, in Wilton, New Hampshire, Smith received his undergraduate degree from the University of California at Los Angeles in 1939 and a law degree from Harvard three years later. He is married with four children.

MAJOR ISSUES

- Smith is seeking to politicize the federal judiciary by urging the courts to respond to the "groundswell of conservatism evidenced by the 1980 election."

- His record on civil rights has been dismal, prompting a leading coalition of civil rights groups to charge that "power and prejudice hold sway" in the Justice Department. He fought an extension of the Voting Rights Act with tough provisions, but later lost when the White House agreed to a compromise that was widely supported by civil rights leaders.

- On crime, Smith has focused his efforts on street violence (only a small fraction of which falls under federal jurisdiction), food stamp fraud, and evaders of draft registration. He has paid less attention to corporate crime, which costs consumers billions of dollars each year.

- At the top of Smith's list of post-Watergate reforms to be eviscerated is the Freedom of Information Act. His proposed amendments would significantly curtail the types of information the press and public could obtain from the federal government.

- While cracking down on illegal immigrants and their employers, Smith has thrown out a goodie to business groups: a guest worker program under which 50,000 Mexican nationals would be admitted to the United States annually and issued temporary worker permits.

During his first months in office, Smith was criticized for his low profile, which many observers said indicated a lack of leadership, and his department's sluggish policy-making. One White House official, quoted by *Business Week*, called the attorney general a "somnambulist." In June, 1981, Robert Pear of the *New York Times* commented, "Mr. Smith seems temperamentally ill-suited to the type of bureaucratic infighting that attends the formulation of policy in Washington."

Smith's slow start was deceiving. Within weeks after those negative appraisals, Smith pulled a coup d'etat: During the second half of 1981 his department initiated dramatic and far-reaching changes in both criminal and civil law—changes that have alarmed civil libertarians. "The Justice Department's policies are completely insensitive to civil liberties," said David Landau, Washington lobbyist for the American Civil Liberties Union (ACLU), "a major retreat in the area of civil rights."

Smith's dramatic moves during the last half of 1981 set forth a clear pattern for the Justice Department for the next three years. What is less clear is who controls the department's policies. Observers speculate that Justice is merely reflecting White House policy, particularly because of Edwin Meese's concerted interest in criminal law. Others say Smith may follow White House advice, but point out he would not act any differently on his own.

But Smith's remarks have substantiated observations that the White House has more influence over Justice Department policies than in the Carter Administration. The Justice Department, Smith told the *Los Angeles Times*, no longer needs to be operated as "an independent isolated and pure bastion free of White House influence. . . .We really are much more collegial now."

In an effort to alter the role of the nation's judicial system, Smith has begun a campaign to curb the role of federal courts in areas such as abortion, school busing, and affirmative action. During an October 29, 1981 speech before the Federal Legal Council, a group of high-level federal attorneys, Smith asserted that judges had reached too far into the arena of policy-making. "We will attempt to reverse this unhealthy flow of power from state and federal legislatures to federal courts—and the concomitant flow of power from state and local governments to the federal level," Smith said. "The groundswell of conservatism evidenced by the 1980 election makes this an especially appropriate time to urge upon the courts more principled bases that would diminish judicial activism."

Smith's criticism of the federal court system reflects a growing resentment among the right over court decisions upholding legalized abortion, ordering school desegregation plans, and banning state-sponsored prayer in schools. As the *ABA Journal* editorialized after his speech: "The Reagan Administration is not the first, nor probably the last, to be dissatisfied with court decisions. Within this century liberals railed against the invalidation of social legislation under the rubric of substantive due process. Now conservatives rail against 'judicial activism.' "

Smith, the American Bar Association warned, may be "spelling out more frankly than usual the desire of many administrations to politicize the federal judiciary and constitutional law." Constitutional scholar Laurence Tribe of Harvard Law School, quoted in the *New York Times*, called Smith's speech "extraordinarily platitudinous and somewhat Neanderthal."

The Justice Department's efforts to rein in the federal courts will focus on its courtroom arguments—as defendant, plaintiff or amicus curiae—and on selecting appointees to the federal bench "who understand the meaning of federal restraint," Smith said. These include such men as recently appointed federal appellate judge Robert Bork, a major critic of antitrust law best remembered as the official who fired Archibald Cox during the Saturday Night Massacre in 1973. In addition, Smith said he will press for court restraint through specific Justice Department policies such as opposing "outmoded and exotic" antitrust theories, and opposing "the distortion of the meaning of equal protection by courts that mandate counterproductive busing and quotas."

The big question looming in the minds of legal scholars and, indeed, much of the working law profession, after Smith's speech was whether Smith would support legislation trickling through Congress that would limit the jurisdiction and remedies of federal courts on specific social issues. Introduced by lawmakers on the right, these bills would accomplish directly what Smith appeared to want to accomplish indirectly.

"Under the theory of this legislation," commented John Shattuck and David Landau of the ACLU in writing about an anti-busing bill initiated in the Senate, "any special interest group that disagrees with an interpretation of the Constitution by the Supreme Court would need only find a simple majority in Congress willing to pass legislation curtailing federal court jurisdiction in that area." ABA President David Brink said passage of these bills would "raise the most serious constitutional crisis" since the Civil War.

Towards the end of 1981 and into the beginning of 1982, leaders of the New Right movement stepped up their pressure on the President to address some of those sticky social questions. In a February, 1982 issue of *Conservative Digest*, publisher Richard Viguerie urged Reagan to "put yourself on the side of social issues as the debate begins in Congress on subjects like busing, school prayer. . . quotas and affirmative action."

Reagan finally responded three months later. Smith released two letters—one questioning the constitutionality of legislation in the Senate that would prohibit federal courts from reviewing state laws that permit "voluntary" prayer in public schools; another letter gave a muddled review of anti-busing legislation that left both sides satisfied. The same week Reagan announced his support for a constitutional amendment to permit prayer in public schools.

The Administration took the safest course, while keeping to the letter of its campaign promises. By supporting a constitutional amendment that would be time-consuming and difficult to enact—it requires approval by two-thirds of both houses of Congress and by 38 states—Reagan is unlikely to be faced with the situation where he actually has to expend precious political capital that he needs for his budget battles in Congress.

On the busing question, Smith purposely left the issue confused: While the *Washington Post* said "the Justice Department gave its blessing to an anti-busing bill" the *New York Times* commended Smith for "politely objecting" to the legislation. "He never really endorsed it, but he never really said straight out that it was clearly unconstitutional," said ACLU lobbyist Landau. The bill, sponsored by Sen. Jesse Helms (R-N.C.) and Sen. J. Bennett Johnston (D-La.), would restrict the remedies a court could employ to correct segregated school systems by barring them from ordering students to be bused more than five miles or 15 minutes from their homes. Smith created the confusion by saying "careful examination of these provisions indicates that they are constitutional" at one point in the 16-page letter, but at another he said: "Congress cannot impose mandatory restrictions on federal courts in a given case where the restriction would prevent them from fully remedying the constitutional violations." Smith said restricting lower federal courts was constitutional but restricting the Supreme Court was not. (The legislation is intended to restrict both.) "We're happy," said Landau, "in that we got a good statement [from Smith] on Supreme Court jurisdiction."

And while leaders on the right also commended Smith, the *Post* noted that without a restriction on the Supreme Court, "the legislation becomes relatively toothless, allowing the Supreme Court to call the shots on busing just as it does now."

With Smith running the Justice Department, blacks and other minorities are experiencing a sense of deja vu: battles which they fought, and thought they had won more than a decade ago are now resurfacing. This time, though, civil rights groups find themselves on the defensive, attempting to protect their hard won gains against aggressions from the federal government.

"Civil and human rights occupy a low rung on the totem pole of this Administration's concerns," NAACP President Benjamin Hooks said at a news conference in February, 1982. "I have a chill run across me as I look at the systematic, pervasive attack [on civil rights]. We're having to fight all over again—not to secure new rights, but to hold on to the ones we have gained." Hooks is also chairman of the Leadership Conference on Civil Rights, an umbrella organization of more than 160 civil rights groups which in early 1982 released a 75-page report detailing the department's dismal civil rights record.

The stinging report accused the Justice Department of cooperating "in the corruption of the legal process by allowing its decisions to be shaped by appeals from politicians not based on law." The basic qualities of "fairmindedness and fidelity to the law are lacking at the department," the report said, "power and prejudice hold sway."

Smith's performance has raised doubts in even so loyal a Reaganite as Housing and Urban Development Secretary Samuel Pierce, the only black in Reagan's Cabinet. In an interview Pierce seconded Smith's repeated characterization of Reagan as an unbiased man. When we asked Pierce if he thought "the top leadership in the Justice Department shares the President's commitment to civil rights," the secretary paused, then said: "This is a hard thing. . . .It's a hard thing for me to say. I don't know. But in time I will know very well."

The civil rights debate during the Administration's first year in office focused on extension of the Voting Rights Act. The act has become so much a part of the American political firmament—a milepost of the nation's commitment to equal rights for all—that it is generally considered part of that select group of statutes almost beyond political debate.

Recognizing that political reality, the White House signalled to members of the House that the President would sign a widely supported extension of the act, which the House passed in October, 1981 by a vote of 389 to 24. The legislation, however, had one important modification: It prohibited state and local officials around the country from employing any voting procedure that *resulted* in discrimination against blacks or other minorities. That standard was stiffer than one that had been in effect since a 1980 Supreme Court decision that required those challenging a voting system to prove that the state or local officials consciously *intended* to discriminate.

Smith, after learning that the White House had agreed to the House version, contacted the President and persuaded him to retract his promise, arguing in favor of the intent standard. "Quotas would be the end result" if the House bill was enacted, Smith has contended. "The test would be triggered whenever election results did not mirror the population mix of a particular community, and could gradually lead to a system of proportional representation based on race or minority language status," he asserted in a March, 1982 commentary.

Proponents of the provision, however, argued that "intent" is difficult, and often impossible, to prove. Thus the act could rarely be enforced. Both sides acknowledge that discriminatory voting practices are still prevalent in many regions of the country. As to Smith's assertion that the standard would result in quotas, earlier Supreme Court cases have "made it clear that there is no right to a 'quota system' or proportional representation, and that the only right that anyone has is the right to an equal opportunity to run in a fair election," Drew Days III, assistant attorney general for civil rights under the Carter Administration, testified before a House subcommittee in July, 1981. The NAACP called Smith's assertion "a scare tactic."

Smith also objected to a provision in the House bill that indefinitely required several states and localities to obtain federal preclearance for any changes in their voting procedures because of their records of past discrimination. "Progress. . .under the Voting Rights Act has been painstakingly slow," Arthur Flemming, then-chair of the U.S. Commission on Civil Rights told a House sub-committee in supporting that provision. "Moreover, voting discrimination has not been eradicated in many jurisdictions." But Smith pressed for only a 10-year extension of that provision.

Singed by the explosive outcry over his Administration's refusal to endorse the House legislation and his handling of the tax exemption fiasco (See White House chapter)—coming after numerous other statements and policies that suggested a disinterest in minorities—Reagan in May, 1982 agreed to a compromise version of the Voting Rights Act. The compromise, which was roundly supported by civil rights leaders, adopted the "results" standard but makes clear that there is no requirement for proportional representation. The provision that certain jurisdictions with a history of voting discrimination preclear changes was extended for 25 years.

Evidently the compromise is part of a nervous campaign by the White House to improve the President's image among minority and civil rights groups. On the same day agreement on the Voting Rights Act was announced, Reagan and his wife, Nancy, surrounded by reporters and TV crews, visited a black family living in a Maryland suburb who had had a Ku Klux Klan cross burned on their front lawn five years earlier. Reagan had read about the family, the Butler's, in the newspaper that morning—where it was reported that a federal court had finally awarded them several thousand dollars in damages—and White House aide Michael Deaver immediately arranged the visit. It was a successful public relations splash: TV stations ran the film on their nightly news, and on the front page of the *Washington Post* the following day Reagan's voting rights compromise and his visit to the Butler's ran back to back.

Although only a small fraction of street crime falls under federal jurisdiction, it has remained near the top of Smith's agenda. In one of his first major actions after assuming office, Smith set up a task force on violent street crime, headed by former Attorney General Griffin Bell and Republican Gov. James Thompson of Illinois. Smith readily embraced the task force's recommendations to implement preventive detention, longer sentences, and a weakening of the exclusionary rule. Justice Department officials helped draft a federal criminal code reform bill sponsored by Sen. Strom Thurmond (R-S.C.) now lying dormant in the Senate. (See profiles of Lowell Jensen and Rudolph Giuliani for details.) Smith's frank remarks before the National District Attorney's Association in July, 1981 indicated the direction he intended to take: "Simply put," said Smith, "we intend to ensure that more criminals go to jail."

Food stamp fraud is also on the top of Smith's agenda. In September, 1981 he set up a task force to investigate illegalities in the anti-poverty program and announced that he would act upon the group's recommendations. "We now have very strong indications that fraud of the worst kind has permeated the food stamp program, and we are going to use every effort to identify those possible then prosecute them and put them behind bars," Smith said during an ABC interview.

The department also is focusing efforts on prosecuting young men who, for whatever reason, did not register for the draft and continue to fail to register after notification. Failure to register is a felony punishable by a $10,000 fine or up to five years in prison. Smith estimated in early 1982 that there would be "hundreds" of prosecutions. "If we can't handle everybody, we'll handle as many as we can," he said.

But Smith takes a more understanding approach to violent and illegal corporate behavior. He and his top officials rarely express concern about corporate crime, which a Senate Judiciary Committee study has estimated costs consumers roughly $200 billion annually. Neither has the problem merited a task force. Smith's attitude toward harmful corporate behavior was perhaps most clearly revealed when his department successfully blocked a proposed revision of the federal criminal code that would have made it a felony for businesses and corporate executives to knowingly endanger human life by violating health, safety, and environmental regulations. Such a provision was originally proposed several years ago as a deterrent to dangerous corporate practices, such as Hooker Chemical Co.'s dumping of toxic chemicals in New York's Love Canal, which resulted in serious illnesses and birth defects among families in the surrounding neighborhood. At the Justice Department's urging, the Senate Judiciary Committee in late 1981 refused to endorse the provision, which, curiously enough, had been the result of a 1979 compromise reached by Smith's peers on the Business Roundtable and the Carter Administration.

In the area of antitrust, Smith has made a number of public statements indicating that the Justice Department will ease enforcement activities. In June, 1981 he told the District of Columbia Bar that "bigness in business does not necessarily mean badness. . . The disappearance of some should not be taken as indisputable proof that something is amiss in an industry. . ." Smith's assurances have been picked up and mimicked by several other top Administration officials, and most observers have cited those public statements as a factor in 1981's merger boom. (See profile of William Baxter.)

The Administration has taken a sledgehammer to a number of post-Watergate reforms that it claimed it only wanted to fine tune. At the top of Smith's list is the Freedom of Information Act (FOIA), a vital tool used by reporters, scholars, public interest groups, businesses and other citizens to obtain undisclosed federal documents. As Katharine Graham, board chairman of the *Washington Post* and president of the American Newspaper Publishers Association put it: "No single statute has ever given the citizens of democracy a better window on their government. The Freedom of Information Act says to Americans— and to the world—that the business of government in a democracy is the people's business." Through the FOIA the public has gained access to information about faulty and dangerous products, about hazardous chemical dumps and nuclear waste sites, about fraud in government programs, about abuses by intelligence agencies. After obtaining information under the act, public interest groups forced the banning of dangerous products such as red dye #2 and the recall of Ford Pintos with faulty gas tanks. A local government blocked the dumping of hazardous chemicals into its citizens' drinking water after FOIA requests produced evidence of illegal dumping by a corporation. The revelations during the 1970s—much of it through the FOIA—of FBI and CIA spying on innocent citizens with unpopular political views led to support for stronger oversight of the intelligence communities.

But Smith says the act, as amended in 1974, is costly to enforce (although the Justice Department's contested $45 million estimate of what it costs each year to comply with the act is less than half what the Pentagon spends yearly on marching bands); that it impedes law enforcement; and that it leads to the disclosure of trade secrets. Because the act has been used in ways not originally intended by Congress, said Smith, "informants are more reluctant to share information with enforcement agencies, foreign intelligence services are more reluctant to share information with U.S. intelligence agencies, companies are reluctant to provide reliable information to the government, and other impediments to effective government are created."

In May, 1981, Smith issued a memorandum to federal agencies announcing his department's intention to defend their denials of information requested under the FOIA unless the agency's denial lacked a substantial legal basis. In effect, Smith's new guidelines changed a Carter Administration policy of "when in doubt, disclose" to a Reagan policy of "when in doubt, conceal."

Five months later the Justice Department released its plans to amend the act in testimony before a Senate committee. Calling the act "a highly overrated instrument" for ferreting out questionable government activity, Assistant Attorney General Jonathan Rose proposed changes in the law that would significantly curtail the types of information the press and public could obtain from the federal government.

First, the changes would broaden the exemption of business records from disclosure. Currently the law protects "trade secrets and commercial information obtained from a person and privileged or confidential" from disclosure. The Justice Department wants to change that to cover any information whose release "could impair the legitimate private competitive research, financial or business interests of any person." Business could designate which information fits that definition.

"This would include virtually any information that reflects adversely on a corporation's product or activities," according to an analysis written by attorneys Katherine Meyer and Diane Cohn of the Public Citizen Litigation Group, "such as data obtained by the Food and Drug Administration showing that a widely-used food additive is unsafe, information obtained by the Department of Transportation indicating that a certain model car or tire is defective. . . ."

In 1978, the House Subcommittee on Government Information concluded in a report that the current exemption has given adequate protection to trade secrets, which the Administration claims have been disclosed through the act.

A second exemption the Administration seeks to broaden covers law enforcement records. The current law protects records, that if disclosed, would "interfere with enforcement proceedings." The Administration's amendments would provide a blanket exemption for all information which is "relevant to or used in an ongoing investigation or enforcement proceeding." The word "ongoing" is particularly troublesome to users of the act because an agency that doesn't want specific information disclosed could simply leave a case in "open" status.

In addition, according to Meyer and Cohn, access would be closed off to information such as the National Highway Traffic Safety Administration records collected in the course of investigating defective cars and tires; Nuclear Regulatory Commission records on investigations of safety violations or discharges of radioactive materials; and Food and Drug Administration reports on investigations of unsafe or ineffective drugs.

Also exempt under the Administration's changes would be:

- FBI records from "foreign counter-intelligence, organized crime and terrorism files."

- Documents "created for personal convenience of any government employees or official" such as journals, telephone logs, desk calendars, or research notes. "Such materials are often nothing more than an extension of an individual's own memory," the Administration said in its fact sheet.

- Finally, the Administration is seeking complete exemption for the CIA through proposed changes in the 1947 National Security Act.

Smith has taken a personal interest in federal immigration policy—perhaps not surprisingly considering his background with agricultural interests that employ Mexican nationals. In July, 1981 Smith proposed a "guest worker program" under which 50,000 Mexican nationals would be admitted to the United States annually and issued temporary worker permits. They would have to pay social security, income and other taxes but would be ineligible for welfare, federally assisted housing, food stamps, or unemployment—an arrangement that John Shattuck of the ACLU called "denial of equal protection."

The program, which is opposed by labor organizations such as the AFL-CIO, was clearly a goodie for business groups who are opposing Administration-backed legislation that would impose fines on employers who hire illegal immigrants. The principal bill, sponsored in the Senate by Sen. Alan Simpson (R-Wyo.) and in the House by Rep. Romano Mazzoli (D-Ky.), would impose fines of up to $2,000 on employers, a provision that U.S. Chamber of Commerce has said "will breed greater disrespect for our laws."

Smith also supports fines on employers who knowingly hire illegal immigrants. But he has recommended excluding "the smallest employers, who account for only a small portion of the nation's workforce, but are a large share of the nation's employers, and for whom regulatory requirements would be most burdensome." Smith also favors tighter restrictions than the Simpson-Mazzoli bill provides for granting legal status.

Smith may not be the sort of attorney general found in the office at 9 p.m. or a particularly deep thinker on matters of constitutional law, but he is a smooth operator. And he is dedicated to translating Ronald Reagan's views into a new direction for federal legal policy. The guideposts for that new direction have long been evident. Anyone who saw Ronald Reagan speak during his first campaign in California of "city streets [that] are jungle paths after dark" would not be surprised by Smith's emphasis on violent crime. Anyone who was there in March, 1966 when Reagan blew up before a black audience and stomped off the stage, yelling that his opposition to civil rights legislation did not make him a racist, would not be surprised by the Justice Department's turnaround on civil rights—or its denial that the new policies represent a disinterest in minorities. None of those views cause Smith any problems. Fred Dutton, a former Kennedy Administration official who served as a University of California regent with Smith, summed up his colleague's view of the world succinctly: "Smith's philosophy is that a small central establishment of a few people who have proven successful should run the rest of our lives."

FINANCIAL BACKGROUND

Smith slips easily into the list of millionaires in the Reagan Cabinet. Together with his wife, Smith's net worth is at least $2.9 million.

According to his financial disclosure statement, he received a $325,000 salary from Gibson, Dunn and Crutcher and nearly $115,000 in various fees from companies where he served as corporate director, including Pacific Lighting Corporation, Pacific Telephone and Telegraph Co., Crocker National Corporation, Pacific Mutual Life Insurance Co., Earle M. Jorgensen Co., and Pullman, Inc.

In addition to an array of smaller holdings, Smith lists investments of between $100,000 and $250,000 in Town and Country Associates, 5900 Luther Lane Ltd., and Woodpark Associates II; between $50,000 and $100,000 in Teledyne, Inc., Cottonwood Station Associates, Ltd., Trails East Associates, Ltd., Hunter Hill Associates, Ltd., and Plano Associates Ltd.; and between $15,000 and $50,000 in Archer Daniels Midland Co., Dresser Industries, Inc., Emerson Electric Co., Earle M. Jorgensen Co., Fluor Corporation, Gannett Co., Inc., Geokinetics Inc., Houston National Gas Corp., Missouri Pacific Corporation, Moore McCormack Resources, Inc., Newmont Mining Corp., Northrop Corporation, Northwest Industries, Inc., Southern Pacific Company, Times Mirror Company, Transamerica Corp., Washington Square Associates, Ltd., Sherman Associates, Ltd., and M. R. Anadarko, Ltd.

His wife has over $250,000 invested in General Electric Company; between $100,000 and $250,000 in Southland Royalty Co.; between $50,000 and $100,000 in Phillips Petroleum, Panhandle Eastern Pipelines, Permian Basin Royalty Trust, and Southland Royalty Co.; between $15,000 and $50,000 in American Telephone and Telegraph, Beneficial Stndard Corp., Earl M. Jorgensen Co., Northrop Corporation, Southern Union Co., Standard Oil of California and So. Union Production Co.

In late 1980, six days after his nomination, Smith obtained a $50,000 tax deduction when he invested $12,900 in a gas tax shelter called Blackhawk Energy Partners Ltd., which his spokesman said he inadvertently left off his financial disclosure statement. In 1981, Smith personally invested in another tax shelter, Yale-Quay Energy Partners, that permitted him to write off $4 for each $1 paid in 1981, and $2 for each $1 paid in 1982. When he invested $16,500 in Yale-Quay in 1981 he received a $66,000 tax deduction under the "intangible drilling costs" provision of the tax code.

But, as a confidential investment summary obtained by the *Washington Post* reveals, Yale-Quay was a questionable investment likely to be challenged by the IRS, and the 35 investors had to sign an agreement acknowledging that risk. Yale-Quay's operations began in February, 1982 on 198 acres of land in Payne County, Oklahoma.

WHAT OTHERS ARE SAYING ABOUT HIM

- UC Regent Stanley Sheinbaum said of Smith: "I would hardly call him a civil libertarian."

- David Landau, ACLU's Washington lobbyist, described Smith after meeting with him: "He's polite. He listens to your side. But he'll give very little indication of where he will come down on an issue."

- Smith's long-time associate, California businessman Edward Carter, called him "considerably right of center, but he isn't dogmatic."

- After Smith's nomination hearing, Senator Joseph Biden (D-Del.) commented: "I was gravely disappointed by Mr. Smith's inability to answer even on a general philosophical level questions we put to him. . .I felt that in many cases his reluctance to answer was not based on natural reluctance but upon the fact that he was unfamiliar with the issues."

AT THE CENTER OF THE WEB

Draw a line through any conceivable diagram of California farming interests and sooner or later you come back to William French Smith. Start at the Crocker National Bank where, until his appointment as attorney general, Smith served as director. Crocker is the nation's number two agricultural lender, with close to $460 million in outstanding farm loans. It was also the largest stockholder in Del Monte, until R. J. Reynolds bought the fruit and vegetable giant. Now Crocker is the sixth largest stockholder in the larger conglomerate.

Crocker is also the top stockholder in Standard Oil of California (SoCal) which has an extensive farming operation in the state's central valley; it has an interlock with the oil company's board. Also on the SoCal board are two board members from Bank of America—the nation's largest agricultural lender, with almost $1.6 billion outstanding—in which Crocker owns almost one million shares itself.

Getting dizzy? Bank of America has substantial holdings in Getty Oil, another major California farmer, and has interlocking boards with DiGiorgio Fruit Company—the Cadillac of California agribusiness; Pacific Lighting, where Smith was a director; Union Oil, which also has California farming interests; and Newhall Land and Farming. The bank owns large chunks of stock in both Castle and Cooke, and Carnation, two more big money food companies.

But back to Newhall. Newhall, a major landowner, lists as its legal counsel Gibson, Dunn & Crutcher, Smith's former law firm. It also has board interlocks with DiGiorgio, Union Oil, and Pacific Lighting and Pacific Telephone and Telegraph (both of whose boards included one William French Smith), and Wells Fargo, the nation's fourth largest agricultural lender.

Wells Fargo holds over one million shares in both SoCal and R.J. Reynolds and has substantial holdings in Bank of America, Tenneco (another oil company dabbling in California agriculture), and Getty Oil. It also has interlocks with Castle and Cooke, Southern Pacific, Pacific Lighting, Del Monte and Pacific Mutual Life Insurance (which holds almost $900 million worth of mortgages and included William French Smith on its board of directors). The fifth largest shareholder in Wells Fargo is the Crocker National Bank, with whom, you will recall, we began this little trip.

Where do we go from here? To Pacific Lighting, which, despite its name, owned until last year 2000 acres of apple and peach orchards and a 405 acre citrus grove in California, and used to have a subsidiary called Blue Goose Growers which produced and distributed food. Pacific Lighting has interlocks with Bank of America and Southern Pacific. The largest stockholder in Pacific Lighting is the Western Bancorporation, a banking and holding company which has interlocking boards with Del Monte, Pacific Mutual Life, Southern Pacific, and SoCal. Smith had substantial stock holdings in each of the latter two companies (his stock is now in a blind trust). The largest stockholder in the Western Bancorporation is Bank of America.

Southern Pacific, probably the state's largest private landowner, has direct board links with Pacific Lighting, J.G. Boswell, and Tenneco. Boswell's board interlocks with the nation's number three agricultural lender, Security Pacific Bank. Security Pacific has interlocks with Carnation, Getty Oil, the Superior Farming Company, and two companies on whose boards sat William French Smith: Pacific Lighting and Pacific Mutual.

As far as Smith is concerned, this could go on interminably but one more connection is worth mentioning. Smith retains his seat on the Board of Regents of the University of California—perhaps the main strand in California's agribusiness web. The university has interests in just about everything connected with California farming, from Southern Pacific to the Bank of America. Sometimes it has a more direct interest, as when it plopped down a campus in the middle of land owned by the Irvine Company, which instantly created the basis for a new town that the company wanted to build around it. Irvine was one of Smith's personal clients at Gibson, Dunn and Crutcher. Both Smith and Reagan's friend William Wilson (who is now our new ambassador to the Vatican) are defendants in a suit by California Rural Legal Assistance charging UC's board with conflicts of interest in authorizing farm mechanization research projects that benefit their ranch and farm holdings.

EDWARD SCHMULTS
DEPUTY ATTORNEY GENERAL

RESPONSIBILITY OF OFFICE

Officially, Schmults serves as Attorney General Smith's traffic cop, overseeing the department's day-to-day activities.
In practice, largely because of his federal experience,
Schmults has an exceptionally influential role in policy formulation.

After a bureaucratic reshuffling in early 1981, Schmults's
position became number two in the department. Under the Carter Administration,
the deputy attorney general—who at that time handled criminal matters—and the
associate attorney general—directing civil functions—were equals. Now these
responsibilities have essentially been reversed, in part to accommodate the
backgrounds of Schmults, a corporate lawyer and Giuliani, a criminal prosecutor.

Giuliani, the department's number three official, now reports directly to
Schmults, as do the tax, civil rights, civil, and land and natural resources divisions.

BACKGROUND

Like his boss, William French Smith, Schmults is a shrewd corporate attorney whose
phone number can be found on the rolodexes of numerous top executives. But
Schmults has one advantage over Smith that has shaped his influential role in the
Reagan Justice Department—federal experience.

Schmults's long career with the Wall Street firm White and Case, which began in
1958, has been punctuated by appointments to the Treasury Department and later
to the Ford White House. In 1973, Schmults came to Washington as general
counsel to the Treasury Department. The following year he was appointed
undersecretary at Treasury, where he directed the department's law enforcement
activities, including the Customs Service. Schmults was also director of the
Securities Investors Protection Corp., U.S. Railway Association, and the Federal
Financing Bank. He was part of an effort to coordinate the activities of U.S. agencies assigned to crack down on drug trafficking at the southwest border.

Coming out of a corporate life, Schmults's first Washington experience was a
jolting one. "The shock of coming down as a Wall Street corporate lawyer. . .and
finding myself in the middle—literally in the middle, though I think I came in near
the end—of the whole Watergate turmoil," still stands out in his mind, he told us.
"It was an unbelievable period to be here. My father said 'what do you want to go
down with those scalawags for?' because by the time the appointment finally came,
everyone had resigned—[H.R.] Haldeman, [John] Ehrlichman, and [John] Dean. I
said 'I think it's going to be a pretty interesting time.' Absolutely fascinating, it
really was."

Schmults got a personal taste of those tumultuous years. Only three months after
arriving in Washington, Schmults invoked executive privilege on President Nixon's
behalf when Sen. Joseph Montoya (D-N.M.) asked him in a private meeting
whether the Treasury Department knew that the President had wiretapped his
brother, F. Donald Nixon, according to the *New York Times*.

As undersecretary at Treasury in 1975, he also served as executive director of the Emergency Loan Guarantee Board, which administered $250 million in loan guarantees to the financially troubled Lockheed Corp.

During that period it was revealed that since 1970 Lockheed had dispensed some $37 million in bribes and extortion payments to foreign officials in Saudi Arabia, Germany, Holland, Spain, Japan, and other countries. (Later, that figure was raised to $220 million.) During a 1975 congressional investigation, Schmults testified he was aware that Lockheed was paying "foreign consultants," but did not know they were illicit payments. Neither had the loan board investigated the company's practices.

Schmults said at the time that he did not intend to punish Lockheed by refusing to extend further guarantees or by collecting on the company's outstanding loans until the government had developed a policy on overseas payments. "I don't think the fact that they have government guarantee means that Lockheed shouldn't be able to play by the same rules as other U.S. corporations," he told reporters at the time. "That would be standing the loan agreement on its head." Lockheed had contended its officials were acting under customary business practices, although its internal documents showed Lockheed taking uncustomary planning initiatives for bribing of influential persons in those countries.

Schmults told Congress he was "in the process of working with Lockheed to develop their internal corporate controls." During that testimony Schmults condemned corporate bribery, which, he said, is "doing incalculable harm to American business in the view of the American public." But, he added, "I am talking about bribes to government officials now, not. . .things that people can argue about whether they are bribes or. . .legitimate payments."

When Schmults joined the Ford White House as deputy counsel in 1975, he was assigned to help organize a task force on questionable overseas payments, after more than 80 companies had been caught making foreign bribes.

Acting on the task force's recommendation, President Ford in 1976 submitted legislation to Congress requiring U.S. companies and their foreign subsidiaries and affiliates to report all significant payments abroad. The bill took a softer approach to corporate bribery than the Foreign Corrupt Practices Act, which passed the next year outlawing corporate bribery of foreign officials and authorizing the Securities and Exchange Commission to enforce accounting regulations that require publicly held corporations to keep accurate books and records on all transactions. Now Schmults is seeking to significantly weaken that act.

Schmults's experience on regulatory issues during the 1970s has made him a particularly appealing candidate to the Reagan Administration. As Ford's deputy counsel, Schmults specialized in regulatory reform and was on the ground floor of the bipartisan effort to deregulate the trucking and airline industries—efforts that came to fruition under Carter. (The Reagan Administration, though, is retreating on trucking deregulation and has effectively grounded airline deregulation through its handling of the air traffic controllers' strike.)

While at the White House, Schmults co-chaired President Ford's Domestic Council Review Group on Regulatory Reform, which was generally critical of government health and safety regulation. In a 1977 issue of *Business Lawyer*, Schmults recommended a congressionally approved "master plan" for submitting government regulatory activities to "systematic re-examination and reform according to a mandated time schedule," and a regulatory budget, which would put a ceiling on the amount of money the federal government could spend on regulatory agencies *and* on the regulatory costs it could impose on business.

Schmults pursued his interest in regulation when he was appointed to the council of the Administrative Conference, a governmental advisory body formed in 1964 to study the efficiency and fairness of federal administrative processes. He remained a member until his appointment to the Justice Department.

Although the conference focuses on procedural and organizational aspects of the federal government, when the topic of regulatory reform came up, Schmults "favored the deregulatory approach in economic areas, but took a good deal more modest approach in the area of health and safety," said council member Joan Bernstein, general counsel of the Department of Health and Human Services under Carter.

"I think accountable people ought to be making more of these decisions," Schmults said in an interview. "That's the tension with administrative agencies. They were created by the Congress to deal with problems [in which Congress] didn't have the expertise, so they were going to leave it to a group of experts. And I still think that principle is sound. But I think there are some important decisions that we should not let Congress pass off to unelected people. . . I think we ought to demand that our laws be drafted more carefully."

After his stint in Washington, Schmults returned to White and Case. There he was sought out for his expertise in banking and securities law, and he spent much of his time smoothing the way on mergers and acquisitions.

Schmults's clients have included prominent members of the investment industry (Salomon Brothers, Fiat Credit Services, and Bache, Halsey, Stuart, Shields, Inc.), the insurance industry (Prudential Insurance Company of America, Metropolitan Life Insurance Company, and Connecticut General Life Insurance Company), and even corporate America's most elite lobby group, the Business Roundtable.

Although it attracted little attention during his nomination proceedings, Schmults is a member of two clubs that do not admit women—the Downtown Association of New York and the Metropolitan Club of Washington, D.C. Schmults refused to resign from either. However, he said he was letting his membership in the New York club expire for financial reasons.

Schmults is a skillful corporate lawyer who straddles fences without giving any hints where his personal convictions lie. "I don't have a personal agenda," he said during an interview. "I'm working for the President and helping him and the Attorney General carry out his policies."

But it is clear that Schmults has little patience for the cacophony emanating from the right and pressing the Administration to address sticky social questions like abortion and school prayer. The right blamed Schmults, among others, for that initial omission. *Conservative Digest* has labeled Schmults a non-Reaganite, "weak on the Reagan agenda." We asked Schmults if that criticism has affected his decisions. "No, no," he replied with a hint of disdain for Richard Viguerie and Co. in his voice. "If you start to let things like that affect your decisions, it's time to get back into private law."

Schmults has been an ardent supporter of Gerald Ford, and in the 1976 campaign he screened running mates for the presidential candidate. He also is a good friend of White House Chief of Staff James Baker, another Reagan official who is disdained by the right.

Schmults was graduated from Yale University in 1953 and Harvard Law School in 1958. Born February 6, 1931, in Paterson, New Jersey, Schmults is married with three children.

MAJOR ISSUES

- Schmults is the Justice Department's point man in the Administration-wide effort to weaken the Foreign Corrupt Practices Act (FCPA).

- He has testified in support of legislation that would force victims of constitutional violations by federal officials to sue the government, rather than the individual offender.

- Schmults is involved in the department's efforts to weaken the Freedom of Information Act (FOIA).

- In the area of civil rights, Schmults has proven himself a loyal Reaganite.

Just five years after he organized a White House task force on overseas bribery, Schmults began serving as the Justice Department's advocate in the Administration-wide effort to blunt the Foreign Corrupt Practices Act.

Ironically, Schmults wants to weaken the accounting requirements in the current law, which require companies to keep fair and accurate accountings of all their financial transactions abroad. If those procedures had been in place in the early 1970s, Lockheed's illicit payments to foreign officials in the early 1970s might have been detected much sooner by federal officials. During the summer of 1981, Schmults testified in support of the "Business Practices and Records Act," introduced by Sen. John Chafee (R-R.I.), a carefully crafted piece of legislation that only requires companies to record financial transactions in "all material respects," and would make legal any payment which is "customary in the country where made and the purpose of which is to facilitate or expedite performance by such foreign official of his official duties."

The General Accounting Office has said the "materiality" standard is ineffective in preventing bribery. Schmults testified that the Chafee bill would help remove some of "the unnecessary and unfair burdens and uncertainties faced by American international business, yet it would also retain the direct criminal prohibitions necessary to deter or prosecute those business activities that could have the greatest adverse impact on our foreign relations."

Schmults added: "Rather than require businesses to report in detail their legitimate financial activities, it makes more sense to brand concealment of illicit payments as a separate criminal offense."

The Chafee bill evoked a much different reaction from Sen. William Proxmire (D-Wis.), author of the Foreign Corrupt Practices Act: "Make no mistake about it, S708 is a probribery bill. If S708 passes, that means Americans can once again do business overseas by bribery. Companies will once again wink at slush fund bookkeeping."

Before FCPA was enacted in 1977, Proxmire says much competition abroad "was conducted on the basis of bribery, not price and quality of product." Because of American corporate bribery abroad, Proxmire maintains, "our image as a democracy was tarnished, we suffered severe foreign policy setbacks in Japan and in Europe, [and] third world emerging democracies were corrupted. . .''

In an interview Schmults explained his views about the law. "I don't think bribery is good any place. Clearly that is something that is very difficult to detect, requires normally undercover operations and all this sort of thing. Nobody ever comes in and tells you that they're making bribes, it's very hard to find evidence of this. But bribery is bad, per se. On the other hand,. . .I [have] come to believe that the FCPA. . .was really exporting our criminal law. While I'm still opposed to bribery overseas, I am in favor, and the Administration is in favor, of amendments that draw a reasonably bright line. I don't defend even the grease payments when you pay customs officials to get their boats unloaded. . .

"Here's an example, I'm not going to characterize it as legitimate or illegitimate, but it's a very serious problem. You've got a contract to build a dam, let's say, someplace in a foreign country. And you need barges to get your equipment up to where the dam is going to be built, and you have to go up a river. Everybody's got their equipment there so you have to get the barge operator to take your equipment up there. People are concerned that it is more than a grease payment if you have to pay the harbor master to sort of get your barges on schedule, so they can go up to wherever you're going. I don't defend that; I don't think that's good. . .[But] quite frankly, I would not make that conduct illegal. I think we're going to lose too much for this country if we do that. . .If you don't allow a little play in the joints here—by play in the joints I think we ought to draw a brighter line in the FCPA which can make the sort of conduct we saw in the Lockheed and some of these other companies bribing government officials to actually get contracts [illegal]. In many cases they were actually competing against other American businesses, so the argument that we couldn't compete with foreign businesses I never thought was a particularly solid argument in those days," said Schmults.

"But I think now the world's changed a good bit and we no longer have the dominant construction companies, there is tough competition all over the world. We've got to take another look and see that we've drawn that line in the right place and wherever we do draw it, it ought to be brighter. You'll never get me to defend bribery in any country, because I think it's bad from a moral standpoint. On the other hand. . .one has to be concerned about the ability of people to draw international/domestic lines. Something you permit overseas might not always sound like a good idea domestically. . ." And on and on. Schmults rarely delineates a clear personal position on any mattter.

Schmults also has testified in support of a bill that would force victims of constitutional violations by federal officials to sue the government, rather than individual officials. Schmults claimed the amendment to the Federal Tort Claims Act would free federal employees from the threat of individual liability that might prevent them from taking forceful actions necessary to carry out their responsibilities. "The specter of personal lawsuits," Schmults testified before a Senate subcommittee in November, 1981, "depresses morale, chills vigorous and effective public action, and unfairly burdens the conscientious public official in executing his or her federal duties." At the time of his testimony, roughly 2,000 lawsuits were pending against federal officials.

But lawyer Mark Lynch, who represented former Nixon National Security Council analyst Morton Halperin in suing Henry Kissinger over wiretaps, said individual liability is a necessary deterrent. "This bill would have made Nixon and Kissinger unaccountable," he told the *Washington Post*. "To say that proper law enforcement activity is being chilled by [individual liability] suits is a lot of nonsense. The

FBI has carried out some of its more aggressive and imaginative investigations in the past few years."

Schmults has been involved in another Administration effort to weaken government accountability programs: revision of the Freedom of Information Act (FOIA). In May, 1981, Schmults told the Second Circuit Judicial Conference that the act was being used in unintended ways, "interfered unduly with important government activities," and had been a financial burden on federal agencies. Schmults helped draft the Administration's legislation weakening the act. (See profile of William French Smith.)

"I'm for Freedom of Information Act as such," Schmults said in an interview. "But I'm really not for jeopardizing law enforcement or intelligence activities and I think people rely too much, they think the FOIA is a real tool to keep rogue law enforcement agencies in line. I really don't think it is, if you're talking about the real world. I think we're talking about intelligence oversight committees, better executive oversight and things like that."

He added: "We find in the judges area, when the FBI goes out to do a background check people are very reluctant to say lawyer x is an alcoholic, they're afraid the fellow is going to wind up being a judge and somehow the information is going to get out that they charged him with being an alcoholic. So we find the ABA in their ratings, in their committee on the judiciary, frequently is able to get much better information about the quality of the people, and the sort of personal problems that they have, than the FBI does. I say that's a problem."

Schmults said the intelligence agencies should be completely exempt from the act. "It sort of boggles my mind that our intelligence agency is subject to the Freedom of Information Act. . .I think it's just absolutely the opposite of what intelligence is all about, which is secrecy. I think we have to look for other mechanisms to prevent, and to control; we want to be sure we're on top of it, managing through politically accountable people, our intelligence agencies."

Although the right has branded Schmults a "non-Reaganite," his record on the civil rights questions that have come across his desk suggests otherwise. He was one of the initiators of the Administration's decision to reverse a long-standing IRS policy denying tax exempt status to private schools that practice racial discrimination, a move that opened Reagan to charges of racism. According to a *Washington Post* report on the debacle, when Rep. Trent Lott (R-Miss.) inquired about the Administration's position on two cases before the Supreme Court in which private schools were challenging the policy, Schmults responded that the department would argue against granting the schools the tax breaks, a position it had taken for years. But in mid-December, 1981 Schmults, either on personal instructions from Reagan or after examining the President's campaign promises, made preparations to change the policy and contacted his counterpart at the Treasury Department, Deputy Secretary R.T. McNamar. Several weeks later the Administration announced it was reversing the policy.

Contrary to claims by the White House's advisers, and reports by the press, Schmults said he knew the reversal would evoke an outcry and "called it to the attention of just about everybody." He refused to say if this included his good friend, White House Chief of Staff James Baker, who had maintained he wasn't informed of the change in time to assess its potential political damage.

"Certainly there were, I think, reasonably accurate predictions made of what the outcry would be," said Schmults. "That whole thing is extremely unfortunate, it's extremely unfortunate in a couple of respects. One, the principle involved: race, which is a tremendous problem in this country and it's understandable that there's tremendous sensitivity to it. Second, the two-step process was extremely unfortunate. As you look back on it, dealing with a case which we got all wrapped up in it here and the time schedule for filing. . .and the proposal of the legislation.''

(After the vehement public reaction to the reversal of the IRS policy, the Administration proposed legislation to Congress which would replace the existing policy with a similar rule. Then Reagan argued that he simply wanted an elected body, Congress, to make the decision rather than agency bureaucrats.)

"What's really unfortunate,'' Schmults argued, "in my own view, is that the principle got blown away in the political outcry and the charges of racism. I thought it was a very important principle. As a citizen now, not as a government official, I guess I am more concerned—it goes to my philosophy of government—about what I would call faceless bureaucracies than I am about misdeeds by politically accountable people because we can throw politically accountable people out of office, we can get at them, we can elect them or not elect them, we can impeach them. . .The bureaucracy I think is extremely tough to deal with as a citizen and you really can't get at it, who is making the decisions. . . . And I really thought the IRS. . .I remained persuaded that there's no authority in the law for an agency, rather than Congress, to make those decisions.''

Schmults said the impact of the fiasco was "unfortunate. I think it was adverse. . .I think we really have to do a better job of explaining what it is we are trying to do here. We've got to reach out more and try to have more contact with leaders of the civil rights groups. . .To some extent you get so tied up in the paperwork coming across your desk. . .that you forget that you ought to spend a large part of your time getting out around the country talking to people, so they can talk to you.

"It's not to say we're going to be changing our policies, but I think we can do a better job explaining them. . .We think we are vigorously enforcing the civil rights laws in finding liability; what we're talking about—where most of the differences come—is how you fashion the remedy. What sort of remedies are appropriate and fair to all people. And there we have some sharp differences,'' he said.

There is "wide agreement'' that many civil rights remedies don't make sense, he insisted. "Forced busing is an example. I personally believe quotas are another question. I think it's a very serious question in our society whether we ought to discriminate in favor of someone who may not have been discriminated against and discriminate against someone else who's done nothing wrong. If you've been discriminated against you ought to have a remedy: get hired, or get back pay, or get promoted, or whatever it is. But, we simply don't see any basis for making [an employment] choice on some sort of a quota. You ought to base it on which one of you two is the most qualified.''

Despite court approval of such plans, Schmults, with Assistant Attorney General William Reynolds, has attempted to block federal actions that promote school desegregation. "There are many alternatives to forced busing,'' Schmults said at his nomination hearing. "The location of new schools in border areas, the creation of uniquely excellent schools which will attract students voluntarily and the breakdown of unlawful housing segregation. . .''

In July, 1981, Schmults, without consulting the attorneys on the case, approved a desegregation plan for North Carolina's state college system that was significantly weaker than plans previously rejected by the Carter Administration. Under Carter,

North Carolina had agreed to goals for minority enrollment at the state's predominantly white campuses and made promises to improve the traditionally black campuses. But, Education Secretary Terrel Bell's agreement with North Carolina, approved by Schmults, rejected those measures in favor of a more lenient plan. Said David Tatel, former head of the Department of Education's civil rights office, "The [Reagan Administration] settlement doesn't read like a desegregation plan. It reads like a joint U.S.-North Carolina defense of everything the system did."

We asked Schmults whether, given the differing approach to remedies, he could foresee bringing in support from the established civil rights community. After a long pause he said, "I don't know. I don't know. I would like to think—it's just going to be difficult. I think if we can promote a better understanding of what it is we're trying to do the differences would still be there, but I would hope that the criticisms and the attacks, and indeed in some cases our responses, would be to talk about which direction is best and which programs are best rather than to have them be personal and not civil. I think we can raise the level of debate."

In an interview, Schmults explained his ideas on some other Justice Department issues.

- *Antitrust:* "I've always thought the antitrust laws were to provide the widest variety of goods and services to consumers at the lowest price. . .Back in the late 1960s [there was] a great concern about the corporate conglomerates. If you look at the studies. . .you found that those things weren't anticompetitive. The market took care of that pretty well. A lot of those great conglomerates we were worried about really didn't do very well; they couldn't run these diverse businesses. Now what do you see—you see people selling off businesses. So we think we're enforcing the antitrust laws. I know that you probably all think that [William] Baxter's not antitrust, he's pro-trust. I think Baxter's a pretty tough antitrust guy, he believes we ought to look to see what's going to benefit the consumer. He thinks there's a lot of antitrust activity that's gone on that in fact results in higher prices, and that the lawyers have captured the antitrust business and developed all these esoteric theories that really don't affect prices very much."

- *Environment:* Schmults conceded that few cases had been coming into the land and natural resources division from the Environmental Protection Agency. "I have looked at that situation. I think there's going to be, we believe there will be some improvement. . . She's [Carol Dinkins] doing what she can do to improve the situation. I believe it is going to be improved. I think we're going to see more activity here. . .I get a little worried whether we're talking about numbers or quality or extent, but I suspect we're going to see more activity over the coming year."

- *Reining in the federal courts:* "That's not just an academic exercise. We think—and we're going to try to persuade courts through the arguments we make—that they ought to exercise where appropriate greater judicial restraint. . . There are areas that ought to be left more to our politically accountable areas of government, mainly the legislature."

- *Drug enforcement:* "We've got the DEA [Drug Enforcement Agency] reporting to the FBI now. The FBI for the first time in the history of this country is into the drug business. They were never willing to do that; Hoover was afraid of corruption. We've got hundreds of joint DEA operations going on now. . .We've got the military in for the first time. . .we've got Navy E-2C planes flying around the Carribean; we're getting intelligence from the Navy and Air Force. You talk about Florida—those planes aren't flying into Florida now. . .We're moving judges down there, we've got prosecutors going in, we've got more DEA agents, we're removing financial assets. We've got a major effort underway to remove the financial assets out of this drug business. . .We're seizing marijuana now measured in the millions of pounds."

FINANCIAL BACKGROUND

According to his financial disclosure statement, Schmults received a $285,000 salary from the White and Case law firm and has over $250,000 invested in the firm, which is being paid out to him since 1981 in six-month, $45,000 installments. He also has between $15-50,000 invested in Cedar Glen Associations, owner of section 8 federally-subsidized apartments in Massachusetts, and in Centennial First 1980 (oil and gas) Drilling Program.

In addition, Schmults has between $50,000-$100,000 invested in Putnam Restaurant Co., a fast food franchise in Greenwich, Connecticut, and less than $15,000 in Wall Park Investors, which acts as a limited partner in a capital venture fund.

WHAT OTHERS ARE SAYING ABOUT HIM

- Democrats on Capitol Hill have expressed concern about Schmults's approach to criminal and civil law enforcement. Said one staff member of the Senate Judiciary Committee, "He's very insensitive to civil liberties."

- William Taylor, director of the Center of National Policy Review at Catholic University Law School remarked: "Schmults is forswearing the use of remedies in civil rights cases that the Supreme Court has authorized or mandated. . . His actions are inconsistent with his responsibilities."

- But, adds Joan Bernstein, who worked with Schmults on the Administrative Conference: "He's one of the more moderate people I've seen in Republican Administrations."

- Philip Buchen, legal counsel to President Ford and Schmults's boss during his stay in the White House, called him "unflappable. . .very cool and calm, even in times of crisis."

RUDOLPH GIULIANI
ASSOCIATE ATTORNEY GENERAL

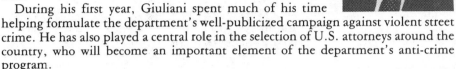

RESPONSIBILITY OF OFFICE

As the department's number three official, Giuliani oversees the criminal functions: including the Criminal Division, the U.S. Marshals Service, the U.S. Attorneys, the Bureau of Prisons, and the Drug Enforcement Administration.

During his first year, Giuliani spent much of his time helping formulate the department's well-publicized campaign against violent street crime. He has also played a central role in the selection of U.S. attorneys around the country, who will become an important element of the department's anti-crime program.

The White House also considered Giuliani for Jensen's position heading up the criminal division. Jensen is a long-time friend of White House Counselor Ed Meese, while Giuliani's nomination was pushed by his friend, federal Judge Harold Tyler, a prominent Republican. Rather than operating as an equal to Deputy Attorney General Schmults, as would have been the case in previous years, Giuliani is in the number three spot.

In addition, the responsibilities of the associate and deputy attorney generals were reversed to accommodate the backgrounds of Schmults, a corporate attorney and Giuliani, a criminal prosecutor.

BACKGROUND

Guiliani loves to tell the story of his father, an intensely proud Italian-American who walked the streets of New York late at night, refusing to heed warnings that he was asking for trouble. The senior Giuliani insisted that his late-night walks were an inalienable right.

"He would not submit to not being able to walk," Giuliani told us. "When he was 69 his friend dropped him off at the subway to go home and two fellows jumped him. Before his friend could try to help him, one of them had run away and. . .[my father] had broken the [other] fellow's jaw by hitting him with his fist and then hitting him with a garbage pail.

"Then the last two years when he was alive—he was sort of wobbly because he had cancer which really infected his whole body—he'd go out walking at about 10:30 or 11:00 at night and scared the living daylights out of my mother. She used to try to get me to stop him from doing it. I would call him on the phone and tell him 'don't do it, go out walking in the middle of the day.' He would tell me 'I would rather die than have to be afraid, and if they kill me, they kill me.'"

The stubborn resistance of his father, who ran a restaurant in Brooklyn, helped shape Giuliani's tough attitude toward criminals, an attitude that hardened during his years as a U.S. prosecutor in New York City and has grounded his policy-making role at the Justice Department. But, Giuliani said, he never thought of himself "as going into law enforcement. I see myself as a lawyer."

After receiving his law degree from New York University, Giuliani from 1968 to 1970 worked as a law clerk for Federal Judge Lloyd F. MacMahon in the Southern

District of New York. He then became an assistant U.S. attorney in the same district.

In the elite, Ivy League world of the Southern District office, Giuliani's working class background made him one of the few attorneys that local police implicitly trusted during sensitive investigations. "I've always felt very close to policemen and federal agents," said Giuliani. "I've always enjoyed working with them. They seem to do more living than observing in comparison to other people."

During his tenure at the U.S. attorney's office Giuliani worked closely with the New York City police force. The most serious problem facing the city police at that time, he said, was "systematic corruption. . . The thing about New York City—until the early '70s at least—there was systematic corruption. You could not be honest if you wanted to be, and there were many people who wanted to be.

"Many people would go into the police department with tremendous motivation," he added. "They wanted to help. They wanted to accomplish all sorts of things and then they would get into a squad where if you weren't dishonest you were thrown out of the squad."

Giuliani was young, intelligent and self-assured, often to the point of being pompous. Said one friend: "He's incredibly bright and everyone has been telling him that since he was a kid."

Those on the right side of Giuliani describe him as affectionate, warm, even charming—"sensitive and understanding," said his long-time friend Robert Leuci. Those we talked to who have crossed him, however, use different words to describe him, like "vindictive" and "hot-tempered."

Giuliani earned Robert Leuci's trust in the early 1970s during a memorable police corruption case. Leuci, then on the Special Investigating Unit (SIU) of the New York City police agreed to cooperate with federal officials and spy on colleagues who were accepting bribes, selling drugs, and pocketing recovered cash from arrested criminals.

The celebrated case, sparked by an investigation from the Knapp Commission, has been dramatized in the 1981 film "Prince of the City," a reference to Leuci's connections with cops and criminals alike throughout the city.

Leuci, who had illicitly pocketed about $18,000 by the time he signed onto the investigation, at first confessed three of his more minor misdeeds— he eventually confessed to many more—and was granted amnesty. Bugged with a mike and transmitter device for nearly 18 months, he recorded illegal activities by his fellow narcotics officers, armed with a promise from federal officials that his partners, also close friends, would not be indicted.

After the investigation began, Giuliani, then a greenhorn in the U.S. attorney's office, was assigned to the case. Giuliani's initial task was probably the most difficult—gaining Leuci's trust. "My first reaction," Leuci told us, "was that Rudi was one of those Italian-American WASP's—you know the kind I mean? He looked very young and inexperienced. He didn't talk much during the initial meeting [involving Leuci and several federal officials], and I wasn't much impressed."

But later, said Leuci, "as he talked to me, I realized that everything he saw in that room he had remembered. He knew exactly what buttons to push in me." Giuliani quickly became close friends with Leuci. But Leuci also saw the other side of Giuliani. Certain that his friend wasn't telling all, Giuliani repeatedly tried to persuade Leuci to confess more.

"Sometimes Rudi would come down on me for refusing to say what I had been involved in," said Leuci. "He would argue at this certain pitch, and then get into a rage for about 20 seconds—while I just cowered.''

Leuci finally did confess all, and in doing so also implicated his partners. While he was granted further amnesty, they were not. In all, 50 fellow SIU officers were indicted: about a dozen were successfully prosecuted by Giuliani. Two of Leuci's partners under investigation committed suicide, one went insane.

Leuci, who has retired from the police force, is promoting ''Prince of the City,'' a film Giuliani calls ''dramatically accurate, factually inaccurate.''

We asked Giuliani if systematic corruption was still pervasive in local police forces. ''I could tell you the answer to that better four years ago,'' he said, ''even two years ago. I tend to think that now that does not exist. There's a certain level of corruption. I'm sure there's crooked policemen who shake people down, [and] take money, but I don't think there are paths where they're collecting money from the bookmakers and then handing it out to everyone who *has* to take it. I don't think there's organized narcotics corruption like there was seven or eight years ago, and part of that is because they're afraid another policeman will testify against them. Ten years ago there was no possibility that one police officer would testify against another police officer. There was total assurance that even if the other police officer was honest he would certainly never testify against a fellow police officer. They were putting their own guise of friendship ahead of their obligation to enforce the law.''

During his five years with the Southern District U.S. attorney's office, Giuliani prosecuted several other well-publicized cases. In one case Brooklyn Congressman Bertram Podell was accused of accepting bribes of over $40,000 from a Florida airline in return for pressing the Civil Aeronautics Board to grant the company an air route between Florida and the Bahamas. Podell was subjected to Giuliani's fiercer side during his prosecution.

The trial, according to the *New York Post*, came to an end with ''dramatic suddenness in the ninth day. . .after a morning of devastating cross examination'' by Giuliani wore down Podell and he pled guilty to charges of conspiracy and conflict of interest. At one point during the trial Giuliani literally threw the book at Podell. ''The way that he was claiming the money he received was not a conflict of interest was that he had two law firms—one in which he was a partner and one in which he was not a partner—and therefore all the money that was being paid to him for his lobbying efforts for this airline was going to the law firm of which he was not a partner,'' said Giuliani. ''Well, there was no evidence anywhere that there was such a law firm, we went through a whole list of things. Did you ever have any stationery? Did you ever have any clients? Can you give us the names of the clients? And finally I said 'of course all law firms are listed in Martindale-Hubbell, aren't they?' And he said, 'yes, that's right.' We had a Martindale-Hubbell hidden under the counselor's table. . .So I took it and I *threw* it on the table and I said 'find it!'

''This was a very funny scene because he pulled out his glasses to find it and he put his fingers through one of the lenses and knocked it onto the floor. Then he opened it up and I said, 'well, Congressman you're reading it very quietly, none of us can hear you, why don't you read it louder? Now, do you find another law firm?' 'No.' 'I can't hear you.' And he said'*no*.' That helped convince him to plead guilty,'' Giuliani said.

''It was a typical case, though, of what happens to politicians when they get into the criminal process—they are so used to lying their way out of [things]. They're in a debate with their opponent, how do you get out of it? You lie about it. If your opponent doesn't have the fact there to stick right in front of you [you can get away with it]. And that was [Podell's] pattern of behavior—to tell the most absurd lies, not realizing that, 'my God, this is a different process, somebody else has facts to show that I'm lying.' ''

In another case, Giuliani conducted an undercover investigation of the federally-funded Model Cities Program in East Harlem. ''We caught the number two person in the Model City Administration,'' he said, who had been accepting bribes. ''He wore a wire for a year and wiped out the entire leadership of the Model City Administration, all the lawyers he dealt with. It was easy. He just sat there and recorded conversations. He didn't have to even trap anybody. He just sat there and listened and we recorded it.'' The investigation led to the convictions of a city council candidate, a real estate agent, a lawyer and four businessmen, among others, who were accused of bribing Model City officials in return for contracts, as well as Model City officials.

To Giuliani, undercover operations are the key to success in public corruption cases, and, in fact, he confided to us that he has always wanted to conduct such an investigation of the New York State Legislature and Congress, both of which he implied needed some shaking up.

''I used to think when I was a prosecutor that one of the things that would have been very useful is if we would have caught one or two lobbyists for income tax evasion or some serious crime, get them to cooperate and run an undercover investigation the way we did in the New York City police department. Congress really needed that. And the New York State Legislature needs that.

''I used to think about getting a lobbyist either to deal with the New York State Legislature or the Senate or the House of Representatives because I thought there was a good deal going on there, particularly after the Podell investigation—I never thought he was alone, the only one who did something like this. We've investigated situations where congressmen were allegedly being paid [off] for private immigration bills. I used to think that [it was] more than just one congressman: There was a system going on there and we were looking for a way to get in there and we never found the right person the way we did in the police department or the Model City Administration. . .The construction industry could probably use a couple of well placed undercover agents,'' he said.

''That's why I get troubled by some of the congressional reaction to Abscam. I think there are some things that should have been done differently, a little more carefully. The need for undercover investigation, controlled properly, is absolutely vital to getting at corruption and the knowledge that this could happen—even if it isn't happening now, it could happen a year from now, two years from now—keeps people from organizing systems of corruption, keeps them careful of who they're going to talk to, how they're going to deal with it,'' he added.

From the special prosecutions unit, where he specialized in public corruption, Giuliani was transferred to head the attorney's narcotics division, where he worked on several major drug cases. ''There were times in New York when I thought—back in the early '70s—that, although morally and philosophically I was very troubled by the idea of decriminalizing drugs,'' he said, ''that it might be the practical, necessary thing to do—the problem was getting so bad. The only way to protect innocent citizens, because government couldn't deal with the problem at the level that it was at, would be to decriminalize it, regulate it or whatever, some system of doing it differently. The thing that changed my mind about it and gave me more hope, I guess, was in the middle '70s when we were successful in getting the Turkish government to burn down the poppy fields, which cut down the large amount of heroin coming in. . .Heroin addicts were diverting themselves to other things. And because the numbers had diminished, law enforcement had a more manageable problem to work with. They had much more success in going after organized crime figures and big operators like Nicky Barnes and Frank Lucas—the big black operators who ran Harlem, getting drugs from organized crime but actually being street distributors of it. It really disrupted the heroin trade. So I think that though the heroin trade is still a problem, it's not the emergency it was ten years ago."

What about cocaine and marijuana? we asked. "I'd rather see us, if we could do it, have our society take a stand against using dangerous drugs; drugs that have an intoxicating, bad effect on people," he said. I still don't think we're at the point where we have to cave in to it and I think we're doing a better job in the last couple years dealing with the drug problems both as a law enforcement matter and as an educational matter. I think people are turning off to drugs more today than they were four or five years ago."

After working the crime beat for five years Giuliani has developed his own ideas on the root of the high crime rates in American cities. "A lot of it turns on your prejudices, biases, your background," he said. "I think a lot of the reasons people advance as the principal reasons, I would see as one reason among many, like poverty, unemployment. A lot of people see that as almost a major reason for crime. If there's high unemployment there will be more crime. That has sometimes been true, sometimes not true.

"New York City has decreased the number of police officers by 8,000 in five or six years," he continued. "If more police stop crime, then the opposite of that should be that crime should have increased dramatically in New York with 8,000 less police officers. That's a lot to lose. Crime has not increased dramatically in New York which says to me that [the number of police] is not going to dramatically change it either.

"Higher prison sentences? We've been giving higher prison sentences. We've been putting people in jail for longer periods of time and still we have, if not an increase in crime, it's been remaining pretty steady. I think that all of those things would have some effect on it, but I think that it goes deeper than that," he said.

"I'll give you my own personal reason. As a society we don't respect the law the way we used to, and the way some other societies do, and that's why we have more crime, certainly more violent crime. I think we have more crime in general than many other Western societies and even communist governments. I don't think we have the same respect for the rule of law that we used to have 40 or 50 years ago, and that others of our peers have. I think that cuts through our society, not just violent crime—which is generally the lower economic level, the middle economic level—I think that's true throughout our society. We have a great tendency now to set our own laws."

Giuliani attributed that trend to "the breakdown of other controls on us—the family, church, neighborhoods, town—all of those don't have the controls on us they did 40 or 50 years ago. So we look to law enforcement to solve the problems, and it was never equipped to solve the problems. Law enforcement can't teach values."

He added: "We don't want a pervasive government. We don't want an authoritarian government. An authoritarian government could solve the problem caused by the breakdown of these other systems. If we could take a child away from the home—because we didn't like the way the home was structured—at six months—we didn't think the parents were teaching the values that fit into

American society or Chinese society—take the child away and put it in a camp and bring it up for five years. . .statistically we'd have a much better chance of bringing up a child that had inculcated the values of our society, that didn't break the law, that didn't commit acts of violence, that learned how to deal with it in other ways. We don't want a government like that, and we shouldn't have a government like that. So I think we make a mistake when we talk about the problems of crime constantly looking to government because we don't give government the tools to solve the problems. We don't want to do that. I think the breakdown in these other institutions that used to function before have contributed to a higher level of crime."

That applies to crime across the board, he said. "I don't think that the reasons for crime in our society are so different as among the person who evades his income tax and the person who bops someone over the head—the effects of that are different—but I don't think the reasons for that are as different as a lot of people think. It's the same breakdown for the respect for the rules of law and in the way that person was brought up."

In 1975, Giuliani came to Washington under the wing of Deputy Attorney General Harold Tyler. As associate deputy, Giuliani during 1976 congressional testimony bemoaned recent budget cuts in federal law enforcement activities. "I would agree with you and any other member of the committee," he told then Rep. Charles Rangel (D-N.Y.), "that would attempt to try and reverse what has been a trend in the last three or four Congresses of cutting our budget for resources for U.S. attorneys."

After leaving Washington in 1977, Giuliani joined the New York law firm of Patterson, Belknap, Webb and Tyler (the latter being Giuliani's former boss Judge Harold Tyler) where he worked until 1981. Giuliani was born in New York City on May 28, 1944.

FINANCIAL BACKGROUND

According to his financial disclosure statement, Giuliani received $160,000 as a partner with Patterson, Belknap, Webb and Tyler. He owns no stock. His principal clients at the New York law firm were the New York News, Inc., Aminex Resources Corp., the Tumpane Co., American Telephone and Telegraph, Beneficial Management Corp., Applied Human Resources, Adelphi Business Institute, National Training Systems, Cooper Rolls Royce, Elliot Cuker, Albert A. Terranova, Eliot Weisman, Kalmin Redner, Abbey Victoria Hotel, Standard Metropolitan Shipping Corp., and Constantine Gratsos.

WHAT OTHERS ARE SAYING ABOUT HIM

- One Justice Department attorney who has been on Giuliani's wrong side described him as "thin-skinned, hot-tempered and ineffective in individually dealing with people."

- Robert Leuci said of his friend and former associate: "If he doesn't step on too many toes, he'll go far at Justice. . .He's young and ambitious."

- However, Giuliani is already developing a reputation at the department for being, as one Washington reporter put it, "too much of a loose cannon."

- His reputation among his former colleagues in the Southern District office, though, remains unscarred. Said New York attorney Elliot Sagor, who worked with Giuliani for several years: "He is aggressive, dynamic and tough in the best tradition of prosecutors." Paul Curran, Giuliani's superior in the Southern District U.S. attorney's office, recalled that every case Giuliani prosecuted resulted in convictions.

D. LOWELL JENSEN
ASSISTANT ATTORNEY GENERAL, CRIMINAL DIVISION

RESPONSIBILITY OF OFFICE

Jensen is charged with developing and enforcing federal criminal statutes "in a vigorous, fair and effective manner"—excluding laws that fall under the jurisdiction of the department's tax, civil rights and antitrust divisions. He guides the development and refinement of the government's criminal law enforcement strategies, and helps determine where the federal government will focus its criminal resources.

Sections that fall under Jensen's jurisdiction include organized crime and racketeering, narcotics and dangerous drugs, internal security, fraud, public integrity (of government officials), and international criminal cases.

In 1982, Jensen manages a budget of about $33 million, up slightly from 1981 levels.

BACKGROUND

It's no secret that D. Lowell Jensen owes his nomination to his long-time association with White House Counselor Ed Meese. Jensen has spent his entire legal career as a prosecutor in California's Alameda County. He joined the county as a deputy district attorney in 1955, became an assistant in 1966, and was appointed district attorney in 1969. He successfully ran for that office three times after his initial appointment. He left his district attorney position upon coming to the Justice Department.

Meese was a deputy district attorney there from 1959 to 1966 and since then the two have maintained a close personal friendship. Together, Meese and Jensen prosecuted several hundred University of California (UC), Berkeley students during a 1964 mass trial held in a Berkeley auditorium. The students had been arrested during a Free Speech Movement sit-in at Sproul Hall led by Mario Savio.

According to the Alameda County's current district attorney, John J. Meehan, an associate of Jensen's at that time, Jensen masterminded the massive arrest, ensuring that enough evidence was obtained to successfully convict more than 700 students. Over a period of about 12 hours—through one full night and into the next morning—Berkeley police officers, at Jensen's direction, collected photos and identification from each demonstrator.

"The arrest was very carefully orchestrated," said New York University Law Professor Stephen Gillers, who was arrested at the sit-in. "It was clear that a lawyer, rather than a police official, was behind it."

During that trial Jensen was the classically cool prosecutor, Gillers told us. "He was not outrageous like his boss [District Attorney J. Frank Coakley]. He didn't make speeches for the press. He just did his job, laid out the proof and won."

In another celebrated trial, Jensen successfully prosecuted Black Panther leader Huey Newton on a murder charge in 1968, but the conviction was later overturned because of judicial error.

Even after assuming the largely administrative position of district attorney, Jensen continued to keep a hand in criminal proceedings. He prosecuted Symbionese Liberation Army (SLA) leaders Joseph Reniro and Russell Little, who were convicted of the murder of Oakland school superintendent Marcus Foster, and he was the chief prosecutor in the case against William and Emily Harris, who pled guilty before a grand jury in the Patricia Hearst kidnapping case.

Jensen says the SLA murder case was the most challenging of his career. "If there was any case that merited my [personal] participation, it was that one," he told us. "It was a case with a great deal of significance for the community."

Understandably, the silver-haired, low keyed prosecutor earned the reputation as a strict law and order man in California. During his term as Alameda County district attorney, Jensen lobbied heavily for tougher state criminal laws, often on behalf of the California District Attorneys' Association. He was behind the state's adoption of a determinate sentencing law in 1976 and he helped draft legislation to abolish the use of "diminished capacity" (insanity) as a defense in criminal cases. Though that defense was not abolished entirely in California, the legislature did curtail its use.

Jensen is a long-time proponent of capital punishment. During a California court case in 1972 challenging the state's death penalty law, Jensen filed a brief supporting it. When the law was struck down, Jensen helped draft legislation implementing a death penalty provision which would meet constitutional requirements. That legislation passed but was superseded by a 1978 California ballot initiative restoring a stiffer death penalty law.

In at least one case which Jensen prosecuted, the defendant was sentenced to death. The defendant was convicted in the early 1960s of killing a prominent druggist but was never executed; by the time his case had failed all appeals in the early '70s, the state's death penalty law had been wiped off the books.

Jensen has been an active proponent of victim-witness programs, particularly in rape cases. Victim-witness programs provide help and support to both the victims and witnesses of crime. With a $1 million grant from the Justice Department's Law Enforcement Assistance Administration (LEAA), an agency which Congress began phasing out in 1980, he helped establish the first significant victim-witness program in the country. Representing the National District Attorney's Association, during congressional testimony in 1979, he argued for inclusion of victim-witness programs in LEAA's reauthorization legislation.

Despite Jensen's lobbying and administrative experience, courtroom drama still puts the light in his eyes. "It's easier to convince a jury than a subcommittee," he told us, "basically because jurors are in a structured setting: if you prove the truth before them [they will back your position]. With a legislative body, you're dealing with much more difficult areas of policy choice."

Jensen has been active in the California District Attorney Association and he served as the association's president in 1979-80. He is a "law and order Democrat," he says, though not active in party politics.

He was graduated from UC Berkeley in 1949 and UC's Boalt Law School in 1952. Born June 3, 1928 in Grigham, Utah, Jensen is married with three children.

FINANCIAL BACKGROUND

According to his financial disclosure statement, Jensen has no major investments and in 1980-81 only received income from salary as district attorney ($54,000 annually) and honoraria for speaking as a panelist for the Continuing Education of the Bar ($700) and as a lecturer at Northwestern Law School ($300).

WHAT OTHERS ARE SAYING ABOUT HIM

- Jensen has a good reputation among both colleagues and adversaries in California. Richard Moore, Alameda County counsel and long-time associate of Jensen's, called him "an outstanding criminal attorney, a very intelligent and able individual. He has a wonderful touch with a jury." Like others we spoke to about Jensen, Moore agreed that Jensen "is not one to go easy on criminals."

- Said John Meehan, Alameda County's current District Attorney and former associate of Jensen: "Jensen is probably the finest trial lawyer this office has ever had."

- Alameda Superior Court Judge Stanley Golde, a liberal who represented the UC student demonstrators arrested in the 1960s and who says he disagrees with Jensen on many points of criminal law, said: "He's not a crazy, hysterical, ranting conservative. . . . He is a hard, but fair, prosecutor."

MAJOR ISSUES

- For an Administration baptized and blessed by business, corporate crime—which cost consumers billions of dollars a year and results in untold illnesses, injuries, and death—is not a top priority. Following that agenda, Giuliani dropped criminal charges against four aerospace executives accused of fraud and conspiracy.

- The Justice Department is seeking to weaken statutes governing white collar crime. Giuliani, moreover, insists that "sufficient and substantial" resources already are being devoted to the problem of white collar crime.

- Despite its pledges about fighting street crime, the Administration is cutting back on assistance to state and local law enforcement— claiming that "public safety is primarily a state and local responsibility."

- At the same time the Justice Department has pressed for tougher sentencing and criminal procedures that much of the established law community says will violate the constitutional rights of Americans, while doing little or nothing to combat crime. Those measures include weakening the exclusionary rule, preventive detention, and capital punishment.

- Ignoring large numbers of crimes committed each year with firearms, Reagan has supported efforts to weaken the 1968 Gun Control Act.

On May 14, 1981, in a meeting that went unreported for one month, Rudolph Giuliani listened to McDonnell-Douglas's general counsel argue that his company and four of its top executives had been unfairly singled out in a Justice Department case charging them with fraud and conspiracy. The department had indicted the aerospace firm and executives in November, 1979 on charges they made $1.6 million in secret commission payments on the sale of DC-10 jetliners to Pakistan and other countries in the early 1970s.

In June, the two prosecuting attorneys on the case, who were excluded from the meeting, blew the whistle on Giuliani's back-door approach. With that disclosure and the events that followed, Justice Department observers caught a revealing glimpse of the Administration's attitude toward corporate crime.

Once the meeting hit the press, the Administration assigned internal investigators to look into the propriety of Giuliani's actions. They later cleared him of any wrongdoing.

Undeterred by the damaging publicity, and in a move sources close to the case called unprecedented, Giuliani in September dropped all criminal charges against the four McDonnell-Douglas executives. Acknowledging that the department had a well-substantiated case against the four, Giuliani contended their prosecution was unfair. "It's one thing when you're talking about the corporation and dollars, and another when you're talking about people's liberty," he said. "In reviewing the case, I had real doubt they knew they were committing crimes in 1973. It appeared to be an ex-post facto application of the new morality."

So Giuliani instead went forward only with the charges against the corporation. A federal judge slapped McDonnell Douglas with a $55,000 criminal fine and $1.2 million in damages arising from a companion civil suit, also filed by the department. The unusual settlement moved one Justice Department attorney close to the case to remark: "The corporation was permitted to buy off the criminal liability of its officers."

Other sources close to the case say Jensen had initially recommended going forward with the prosecution of the officers but was overruled by Giuliani.

Philip Heymann, head of the Criminal Division under Carter, was suprised by Giuliani's move. By reopening the McDonnell Douglas case, he said, "you are doing something for a large and powerful corporation that you would never do for anyone else." The Giuliani meeting had been arranged by Sen. John Danforth (R-Mo.), whose brother is a director on the company's board.

For an Administration baptized and blessed by business, corporate crime is not a top priority. Justice Department officials do not give ringing speeches about weeding out corruption in the executive suites that end up on page one of the *New York Times*: instead they focus on muggings and food stamp fraud. The Administration is seeking to weaken the nation's foreign bribery law. It has scuttled a legislative proposal that would make it a felony for businesses and corporate officials to knowingly endanger lives by violating environmental, health, and safety regulations. It has virtually shut off enforcement of the environmental, occupational health, and mine safety laws. In doing so, the Reagan Administration has set a tone of tolerance for corporate criminals.

With a criminal law background, Giuliani is not as sanguine about the nature of corporate behavior as, for example, Attorney General Smith or John Shad, chairman of the Securities and Exchange Commission. But Giuliani's focus is more on how business corrupts public officials. Those are the kinds of cases in which he made his name; and, during our interview, public corruption cases were what he focused on. Giuliani's biases were most clearly revealed when he told us that in a bribery case, "as a trial decision, if I was going to try that case, I would want to try it with the businessman testifying against the congressman, rather than the congressman testifying against the businessman.''

Corporate crime costs society billions of dollars each year, even excluding the deaths, illnesses and injuries, and damage to the environment caused by illegal corporate behavior. A Senate judiciary subcommittee recently estimated that faulty goods, monopolistic practices and similar law violations cost consumers between $174 and $231 billion each year. Illegal overcharges by fifteen major oil companies from 1973-1976 totalled $10 billion, according to the Department of Energy. During the 1970s Lockheed Corporation admitted to illegal payments, mostly foreign bribes, of more than $220 million. In contrast, the largest robbery ever was a $5.4 million theft in 1978 from the Lufthansa airport warehouse in New York City. The largest welfare fraud case, disclosed in 1978, involved $240,000.

''I see a real close connection between corporate crime, individual white collar crime—like income tax evasions, general fraud and con operations—and [public] corruption,'' said Giuliani. ''I think all of that together is a very big problem in our society. It's like a circle. It helps in some ways to create the levels of violent crime we have. . .If we had less white collar crime we'd have less violent crime.''

But the federal control of corporate crime has been limited—and remains so under the Reagan Administration. A 1979 Justice Department study found that ''generally penalties imposed on top corporate management are quite lenient, particularly if one looks at them in relation to the gravity of the offenses committed. . .Few members of corporate management ever go to prison, even if convicted.'' The same study, which examined the largest 582 publicly held corporations, found that about two-thirds of them had violated the law, some of them many times. ''Serious and moderate violations were extensive,'' it said.

The Justice Department sent a signal that it might be diminishing attention to the entire area of white collar crime when the 1982 budget cut in half the number of economic-crime specialists stationed in U.S. attorneys' offices outside of Washington. In their two years at work, the specialists had uncovered such crimes as fraud by owners of a nursing home chain in Oregon, arson in Pittsburgh, and Medicaid fraud in Detroit. A Justice Department study in December, 1980 called the specialist program ''a promising approach'' to fighting white collar crime.

Even in the specific area of public corruption, Giuliani's passion, the Administration is seeking to loosen federal law by pushing for repeal of a 1978 law requiring the appointment of special outside prosecutors in serious criminal cases against top federal officials.

''By enacting these extraordinary and unprecedented procedures'' in the special prosecutor provision of the Ethics in Government Act, Giuliani testified before a Senate subcommittee, ''Congress singled out certain persons and crimes for investigation and prosecution in circumstances in which investigation and prosecution would not normally proceed. The effect is to subject public officials with extremely vulnerable reputations to the stigma and expense of criminal investigations in circumstances where, absent the statute, criminal investigations would probably not be warranted.''

Giuliani told us that, although data collection on white collar crime could be improved, he does not see a need for increasing resources to enforcement activities in that area. ''I think there is sufficient and substantial devotion of resources to the whole area of corporate crime, white collar crime, tax evasion, public corruption. A big chunk of the [FBI's] resources are now devoted to fraud and corruption. And if you look at the U.S. attorneys' offices, I would almost say that we've almost overdone it in the sense that we're spending time on cases that don't get made. . .The area in which we could improve is targeting those resources better—because we don't have the kind of statistics we should have."

Jensen and Giuliani emphatically deny that the department's emphasis on violent crime means that white collar crime enforcement has taken a back seat. "We just have a new and distinct emphasis that the federal government should have responsibility vis-a-vis violent crime," Jensen told us.

Giuliani said the emphasis on street crime "was to balance what wasn't being done" in past years. "When I came here it seemed to me that we're doing a great deal—in terms of devotion of time and resources—to organized crime. . .We were doing a lot more in all of the areas of white collar crime than we did back in [the Ford Administration]. What we really needed—what really had broken down—was how do we help state and local law enforcement deal with some of the serious emergencies they have."

The Justice Department's well-publicized campaign against street crime—only 6 percent of which falls under federal jurisdiction—has taken on the zeal of a Manhattan project. In one of his first actions in office, Smith appointed a distinguished eight-member task force chaired by former Attorney General Griffin Bell and Illinois Gov. James Thompson, to study violent street crime and within months of their final report he initiated several far-reaching legislative changes to federal criminal law. Smith, Giuliani, and other top Justice officials—along with White House Counselor Edwin Meese and the President—have taken the fight against street crime to the public in regular speeches.

"We will use this, what Teddy Roosevelt called a 'bully pulpit' of the presidency, to remind the public of the seriousness of this problem and the need to support your efforts to combat it," Reagan told the International Association of Chiefs of Police on September 28, 1981. "I believe that this focusing of public attention on crime, its causes, and those trying to fight it, is one of the most important things that we can do."

But what that means in substantive help is unclear. Outlays for criminal justice assistance to state and local government will decrease from $318 million in 1982 to $162 million in 1983. Though much of that is due to the phase-outs, begun under previous administrations, of grant programs, the Justice Department is not in a hurry to fill the void. "Public safety is primarily a state and local responsibility," said the Administration's 1983 budget report. "This Administration does not believe that providing criminal justice assistance in the form of grants or contracts is an appropriate or effective use of federal funds. For this reason, budget authority is not requested in the 1983 budget for the juvenile justice and delinquency prevention program, or for any other general law enforcement assistance programs for states and local governments."

Jensen maintains the Administration's assistance will come through better coordination between U.S. attorney's offices and local police forces. Giuliani says the Administration is doing its part to combat street crime by stepping up its drug enforcement activities.

At the same time, as part of its campaign the Justice Department is backing legislative changes in criminal law. But much of the established law community says the changes offer the public a false hope because they will do little or nothing to prevent crime. What these changes will do, say critics, is expose citizens to violations of their constitutional rights. Of the 64 recommendations made by the Attorney General's Task Force on Violent Crime, the Administration embraced only the least expensive and, to civil libertarians, the most alarming measures.

The Justice Department has proposed a series of legislative changes—some based on the task force report, others not—following that tack, including:

- Easing of the exclusionary rule, which, under the 4th Amendment, prohibits admission in court of illegally seized evidence. Jensen told a Senate committee in fall, 1981 that the exclusionary rule has resulted in too many "unjustified acquittals of guilty defendants." But studies show that a weakening of the rule will not have much impact on crime. A 1979 General Accounting Office survey of over 2,800 criminal cases found that only four-tenths of 1 percent of the cases were dropped due to 4th Amendment search and seizure problems.

  The Administration, Jensen testified, favors legislation to allow federal courts to permit illegally seized evidence to be admitted "if the search or seizure was undertaken with a reasonable good faith belief that it was in conformity with the 4th Amendment." That change, said ACLU lobbyist David Landau, would "invite police abuse and lawlessness." New York University Law Professor Stephen Gillers, a member of the Committee for Public Justice, said he doesn't expect an immediate impact from a weaker exclusionary rule. But, he said, in the long run, "as the police begin to adjust to more relaxed, responsive courts, they may begin to do things they know violate the intention of the law." Legal observers are still unsure whether the Administration's "reasonable good faith" test would stand up in court.

  The American Bar Association (ABA) also supports retention of the exclusionary rule. "An examination of the empirical data does clearly reveal that the exclusionary rule is not responsible for hordes of criminals going free," said Richard Gerstein, chair of the ABA's task force on crime. He cited it as one of several "apparently simple solutions to crime [that] not only pose constitutional problems but also offer false promise."

- Curbs on federal habeas corpus laws, which permit state prisoners to challenge their convictions in federal courts. Legislation proposed by the Justice Department would prevent federal courts from even considering a prisoner's habeas corpus petition until a specified period after all appeals had been completed, and would limit the issues that a federal judge could consider in reviewing such petitions. Landau called the proposed legislation "another in a set of ineffective proposals" which would do little to combat crime, while curtailing the rights of defendants.

- Revision of the 1878 Posse Comitatus Act, which prohibits the use of Army and Air Force personnel in domestic law enforcement. The Administration wants to use the military to crack down on drug trafficking—a proposal that arouses concern from civil libertarians who say using the military for these purposes runs counter to the aims of a civilian democratic society. Even the Pentagon is uneasy about the set-up.

- Preventive detention—the denial of bail to persons "who are found by clear and convincing evidence to present a danger to particular persons or the community." The Administration is seeking such a provision in its criminal code reform bill in the Senate.

  The ABA has endorsed preventive detention to keep potentially dangerous criminals off the street. But others say the change will mean further infringement of constitutional rights. "My experience," said D.C. Circuit Judge David Bazelon, "convinces me that it is well-nigh impossible to predict dangerousness with any accuracy. It has been estimated that, in order to be sure of jailing *a single individual* who would engage in violence while on bail, we would have to detain as many as four to ten people who would not have. Before we incur the substantial financial and constitutional costs, we should consider less onerous measures'' like adequate supervision of individuals out on bail.

- Changes in the law to permit confidential information obtained by the Internal Revenue Service to be used to fight organized crime, another precedent that worries civil libertarians.

- Capital punishment. The Administration—with Jensen at the lead—is pushing for the passage of a federal capital punishment law. In June, 1981 Jensen told the Senate Judiciary Committee that the Justice Department supports the legislation sponsored by Sen. Strom Thurmond (R-S.C.) which would revive the death penalty for federal crimes such as treason, espionage, and the murder of the President, Vice-President and certain other high government officials. A 1972 Supreme Court decision invalidated all existing state and federal death penalty provisions. But Jensen contended the new legislation will "pass the constitutional muster." The Thurmond bill sets up a series of sentencing procedures designed to prevent "arbitrary" and "capricious" application of the law, behavior the Supreme Court had found unacceptable.

A number of studies have concluded that the death penalty does not necessarily act as a more significant deterrent than long-term sentences to violent crimes, a fact that Jensen acknowledges but chooses to discount. "While sociological studies have reached differing conclusions," he told a Senate committee in May, 1981, "common sense tells us that the death penalty does operate as an effective deterrent for some crimes involving premeditation and calculation."

Jensen said he believes "society [has] a right to exact a just and proportionate punishment on those individuals who deliberately flout its laws."

Henry Schwartzchild, director of ACLU's capital punishment project, argued that the Thurmond bill is unconstitutional. "The death penalty in principle violates the ban against cruel and unusual punishment under the 8th Amendment and violates the due process caluse of the 5th Amendment and the equal protection clause of the 14th." The reintroduction of the death penalty, he added, "must mean unavoidably that the United States will execute innocent persons."

But the White House rejected other aspects of the task force report. One recommendation, prison construction, was considered too costly. A second, tighter gun laws, would alienate a vociferous element of Reagan's constituency.

The task force suggested the federal government disperse $2 billion over four years to build more prison facilities. Already, overcrowded conditions in prisons have led to prison riots in recent years, and correctional authorities fear more uprisings—particularly if the state and federal governments begin sending more criminals to jail. "The Reagan Administration wants more prisoners," said James Goodman of the Committee for Public Justice, "but they don't want to spend money on prisons. That shows that they're not even willing to be responsible for their rhetoric."

Even Giuliani was disappointed at the White House's response to that proposal. "I think it was a good recommendation," he told us. "But I can't really assess from this budget and with all of the other problems that we face what kind of priorities we should have. If I was sitting outside of the Justice Department, within the criminal justice system, I would agree with the task force that if we're going to spend money that's the thing to spend it on." But, he said, "we don't just need more prisons, we need different kinds of prisons and correctional facilities than we've had in the past. At least from law enforcement's point of view, we could make a very big difference if we could convince people that spending money on prisons made sense. I think we could have a very big turnaround in the crime rate.''

Giuliani said a system ''like the federal prison system for most states as a model would be very useful'' with varying grades of security, depending on the severity of the prisoners' crimes.

''You don't want [life-term prisoners] with other prisoners who are going to be let out in society again, but at the same time you have levels of secruity that ratchet down from that that permits you to treat people, depending on their problem, in different ways,'' he said, ''and also [be able] to reenter someone in society in a sensible way—not just take them out of the penitentiary and stick them in the street. That's crazy! By having different levels of security and various ways in which a person can be freer in his movement, get out into society as he is reentering, you help the reentry process.''

He described one federal correctional institute in Miami which he visited recently. ''It was August and it was boiling, it must have been 110 degrees out. It is a very nice facility, it looks like a community college campus. It has a pond in the middle, it has four or five low buildings, two-story buildings that are red brick. It's not beautiful, but it looks like a typical southern, western, community college campus. There's grass, people [wear] colorful uniforms. The [administrator] said, 'We had a lot of trouble when we put this up because we air-conditioned the building—people in the community were outraged that we spent money on air-conditioning the building that some of them—the poor in the community—couldn't afford.' I said 'My God, they don't really mean that! They don't really mean that they want us to take prisoners, put them in those cells for two or three years at 150 degrees, which is what it would be inside the cells, and then let them out again.' Maybe they wouldn't mind if we put them in and left them there forever, and we locked the key and that was it. But we don't do that to someone who got convicted of a bank robbery and didn't shoot someone for the third time. We don't do that to an income tax evader.

''We don't do that to most criminals, we don't put them away forever. And if we're not going to put them in forever, then we want them to come out and rejoin society in a way that reduces the possibility that they're going to endanger innocent people. And all the people in the community want that. They don't really want those people sitting in 150 degrees for three years and then let them out to walk around plantations—they would be maniacs!

''A lot of people criticize that as coddling criminals. I think if we can get them to think about it differently: that these are all people who are candidates for coming out and walking next to you on the street, you want them to come out with a better chance of not committing a crime. . .then we might get people to spend more money not just on the physical facilities but on making the physical facility a place that reduces the amount of people who commit crime, not increase it.''

The White House also disregarded a task force proposal to tighten the 1968 Gun Control Act, which despite its name, simply requires the licensing of gun dealers and identification for gun purchasers, and restricts the sale of guns to convicted felons. The Task Force recommended that the law be changed to ban the importation of parts for Saturday Night Specials.

Instead, Reagan has supported legislation in the Senate to substantially weaken the 1968 law. To top it off, Reagan, a member of the National Rifle Association, formally proposed the elimination of the Bureau of Alcohol, Tobacco and Firearms, charged with enforcing firearm laws, and plans to transfer its gun oversight activities to the Secret Service. The Treasury Department, which administered the bureau, has admitted that the plan would result in far fewer inspections of gun dealers.

According to the task force report, about 10,000 Americans are murdered each year by criminals using handguns. In 1978 firearms were used in more than 300,000 cases of murder, robbery, and aggravated assault. Even Giuliani disagrees with loosening the law.

"I don't think control or tighter controls on rifles and so forth will make much difference on the level of crime. I *do* think tighter controls [on handguns] or at least clearing up the loopholes in the 1968 Gun Control Act—my guess would be that it would have a beneficial effect. And it's worth trying. Then if it doesn't, you could loosen it up, but it's worth trying. I don't see a good rational argument for not doing it. I don't know what we'd gain by either leaving things the way they are in terms of handguns or loosening up on handguns." But that is precisely what the Administration-backed gun bill, sponsored by Sen. James McClure (R-Ida.) and Rep. Harold Volkmer (D-Miss.), would do by repealing key provisions of the 1968 act.

Another aspect of the task force's report which the White House has so far failed to adopt—though officials say the measure is under study—was a mandatory waiting period after the purchase of a handgun "to allow for a mandatory records check to ensure that the purchaser is not in one of the categories of persons who are proscribed by existing federal law from possessing a handgun," such as ex-convicts.

Giuliani agrees with that proposal. "Twenty-one days is almost a minimum waiting period," he said. "I'd almost prefer to have it longer—a month—because I know how long it takes to check FBI files. But I can't imagine any sensible person wanting an ex-convict who has committed a violent crime before to possess a handgun. We have a law now that says you have to fill out a form saying you are not an ex-convict. Now why we let that law rest on the credibility of the ex-convict is just silly. That has to be a loophole in the law. . .I can't see what legitimate rights of anyone would be violated by a waiting period."

Giuliani is pessimistic about the potential benefit of a national ban on handguns. "It's too drastic a change for our society," he said. "Right now we're a society with too many guns. If we tried to go too drastically to that, we'd end up with an illegal market. . .I still think there should be a legitimate way that people who want guns should be able to get them—a process to prove they're responsible people who should possess guns like this and they don't want them for any illegal purpose, but to protect themselves."

But, he conceded, "The level of accidents and mistakes from handguns outweigh the number of times people legitimately have to defend their lives with it."

Giuliani contends the Administration's decision to fold the Drug Enforcement Admin. into the FBI will improve the federal government's narcotics enforcement and help reduce violent crime—an estimated 50 percent of all street crimes are drug related. "The FBI wasn't involved in drug enforcement previously," said Giuliani, "I thought for all the wrong reasons. I've heard that Hoover didn't want the FBI in drug enforcement for two reasons 1) it tended to lead to corruption and it offered great temptation for the agents and he didn't want to take that chance and 2) because the success rate was not as great as the kinds of cases the bureau concentrated on under Hoover. Those are two terrible reasons. . .So we've got our biggest [law enforcement] agency not working on one of our biggest problems and because they're afraid the agency will be corrupted." He added, though, "drug enforcement does offer more temptation for corruption than other forms of law enforcement.''

Reagan's anti-crime program has a familiar tinge—as in other domestic areas, he is offering cheap and simple solutions to a costly and complex problem. Street crime is pervasive in American cities, almost regardless of location, size or composition. People are understandably scared, and by playing upon those fears with tough rhetoric, Reagan has scored political points.

But beneath the glib rhetoric, the Administration is pursuing programs that offer little hope for significantly reducing street crime, at a tremendous loss in civil liberties. First, street crime is primarily a state and local responsibility—and the Administration is cutting federal assistance to localities. Second, concentrating on tougher sentencing and criminal procedures is not efficient—only six percent of serious crime results in arrest. And the Administration's gun policies will make it easier for criminals to obtain firearms.

At the same time, a wide array of critics say the Administration's cuts in social programs will exacerbate the problem. "It's only common sense that if your food stamps get cut off and you're in a bind," said Goodman of the Committee for Public Justice, "the chances for committing a crime go up." A study commissioned by Congress's Joint Economic Committee reported that each 1 percent rise in unemployment is accompanied by a 4.3 percent increase in such crimes as robbery, burglary, homicides, and drug offenses.

But Jensen maintains there is no contradiction between the Reagan Administration's cuts in social programs and its battle against crime. "The necessary relationship between dollars expended on social programs and the crime rate is more conventional wisdom than one you can document," he said. "I look at it from the point of view of the criminal justice system in a relatively narrow sense—the ability to apprehend, the ability to adjudicate, and the ability to correct. That's a very hard, direct way of looking at it." To Reagan, "it's obvious that deprivation and want don't necessarily increase crime. The truth is that today's criminals, for the most part, are not desperate people seeking bread for their families. Crime is the way they've chosen to live."

WILLIAM BAXTER
ASSISTANT ATTORNEY GENERAL, ANTITRUST DIVISION

RESPONSIBILITY OF OFFICE

Baxter's division is generally considered one of the government's most elite units. It has a budget of $43 million, and a staff of 830, up from the days when William A. Day opened the department with five lawyers and four stenographers in 1903, but down from the last year of the Carter Administration. Asked what would be the perfect budget, Baxter replied with a smile: "That's like asking me for the right price of carpets." Baxter is charged with "enforcement of the federal antitrust laws," essentially the Sherman and Clayton Acts.

BACKGROUND

After a brief stint at the Washington law firm of Covington and Burling in the late 1950s, Baxter has spent the last 20 years teaching at Stanford Law School, and consulting for a variety of businesses and trade associations, including Exxon, the American Petroleum Institute, Hoffmann-LaRoche, and Levi Strauss. He has consulted for the Federal Aviation Administration on aircraft noise and served on presidential task forces on communications and antitrust policy.

Baxter has been in recent years a forceful proponent of the views made popular by the Chicago school, a conservative group of lawyers and economists based at the University of Chicago who argue that antitrust law has unnecessarily placed roadblocks before business practices that could benefit consumers. They, and Baxter, reject the notion that industrial concentration presents inherent anticompetitive problems.

But Baxter has gone further than most critics of antitrust law, asserting in 1979 Senate testimony that "the thesis that large corporate size yields overweening political power" is not even "remotely true." In a late March, 1982 panel discussion he reiterated the point, remarking that "No one in his right mind could possibly suppose there was a connection between the concentration of economic markets and political power." In an August, 1980 American Bar Association debate on the Federal Trade Commission, though, Baxter contradicted himself and acknowledged the power of business lobbies. "What really got the FTC in trouble was that it took on some of the central powers of the American political system," he said. "For example, the television networks. You just do not mess with the television networks."

On another occasion, he said he would not have brought the famous GM/DuPont case. And he said, "I'm not sure what an oligopoly is. We have no coherent theory of oligopolistic behavior." Baxter has said he can "envision a world" in which 100 companies each have 1 percent of every market. In his view, antitrust's legitimate aims are narrowly defined: "Free market competition—unhindered by either private restraints such as. . .price fixing or unnecessarily anticompetitive public regulatory restraints—is the whole object of antitrust law and competition policy."

In a March, 1982 interview with the *Wall Street Journal*, Baxter blasted the Supreme Court for ignoring these theories, calling rulings "rubbish," "ludicrous," and "wacko." The court's rulings, Baxter said, are wrapped in "such a confused and self-contradictory welter of language" that they do not yield "the faintest idea of what the antitrust laws mean." The Warren court, he asserted, was not trying to protect competition through antitrust enforcement, but rather "to impose higher costs on [big companies] and penalize them for their large size."

At his confirmation hearing, Baxter summed up his view of the economy: "I have a fairly deep-seated conviction that companies will always—I should not say always, but almost invariably—act to maximize what they perceive to be their profit opportunities at any particular point in time. In a free market economy, that generally results in favorable outcomes and should not be interfered with."

Baxter didn't always hold such views. In 1968, he served on President Johnson's Task Force on Antitrust Policy, known as the Neal Commission after its chairman, Phil Neal, dean of the University of Chicago Law School. The task force concluded that current antitrust laws were unable to deal with the growing problem of concentrated industries, which according to "an impressive body of economic opinion and analysis. . .precludes effective market competition and interferes with the optimum use of economic resources." The task force recommended new legislation to deconcentrate the most concentrated industries; it also backed new legislation "prohibiting mergers in which a very large firm acquires one of the leading firms in a concentrated industry." (The report also recommended weakening the Robinson-Patman Act, a law Baxter still opposes.) Asked about the disparity between those positions and his views today, Baxter told one acquaintance that he wasn't experienced then, and hadn't really thought through his views. He was 39 at the time.

Baxter's stay at Stanford, according to one account, was "controversial." While chairing the school's admissions committee in the mid-1970s, he was a staunch opponent of affirmative action. Many faculty members also believe he prevented, "through an intense lobbying effort" the granting of tenure to a leftist legal economist in 1976. One student who studied under him recalled for the *American Lawyer*: "He seemed to have a presumption that anything business does is okay. It was more protrust than antitrust."

In some respects, Baxter's views have changed significantly since his earlier teaching days. Al Kramer, a former student now active in antitrust law told us that Baxter formerly believed that the division should lay down clear broad rules of what kind of behavior would be permissible; businessmen would "behave rationally" and make the most efficient economic decisions within those rules. At that time, Kramer said, Baxter felt "the worst thing" was a rule of reason, case-by-case approach. Now, however, that is the approach he advocates; rejecting *per se* condemnations of many activities considered by previous division chiefs inherently anticompetitive. (See Major Issues section.)

Born in New York City on July 13, 1929 Baxter moved to California in 1939 when his father entered the gold mining business.

Baxter earned his undergraduate and law degrees at Stanford in 1951 and 1956, respectively. He lives in Washington with Carol Treanor of Stanford's Center for Advanced Study in the Behavioral Sciences. Baxter, divorced, says he has not remarried because to do so would raise his tax bill.

MAJOR ISSUES

- Baxter assured himself a place in antitrust history by negotiating a settlement to the massive AT&T case and dropping the government's 13-year-old proceeding against IBM. The IBM decision, in particular, signaled a sharp retreat on government antitrust policy.

- Baxter's remarks looking favorably on large corporate mergers, many analysts agree, have helped set off a roaring merger wave, with over $82 billion in acquisitions being completed in 1981, a total $38 billion larger than the previous annual high. Baxter opposed legislation to restrict oil company acquisitions.

- Baxter ended the Justice Department's opposition to special interest legislation that would keep foreign governments from suing domestic drug companies for price fixing. At the outset of his career, Baxter worked for one of the companies on a domestic variation of the case; Attorney General Smith's former law firm still represents one of the defendants in other domestic litigation on the case.

In less than a year, William Baxter has already done what many might have thought impossible: made antitrust a front page issue.

Actually, Baxter didn't do it alone. He was joined by other leading officials of the Reagan Administration who trooped before assorted conventions of attorneys to assure America's boardrooms that Washington no longer viewed corporate bigness as badness. And he was given plenty of help by acquisition-minded companies that took full advantage of the new leniency to enter into unprecedented bidding wars that turned even some of the most conservative stomachs in Congress.

"It is true, in a sense, we are going to turn back the clock on antitrust because there is an awful lot of rubbish that has been passed around under the name of antitrust, an awful lot of pari-mutuel handicapping, and within the limits of my ability to do anything about that, I do indeed intend to turn back the clock and get rid of that kind of antitrust," he told the American Bar Association antitrust section during its annual meeting in April, 1981.

As corporate acquisitions raced along at a record pace, Baxter became one of the most controversial Reagan appointments. When he settled the long-running cases against American Telephone & Telegraph (AT&T) and International Business Machines (IBM) on a single memorable day in January, 1982, Baxter became a national figure overnight.

The AT&T settlement was perhaps the most spectacular antitrust agreement since the government broke up Standard Oil 70 years ago. Requiring the divestiture of as much as $80 billion in assets, the agreement cut a fresh path through a thicket of political and regulatory disputes. For years, Congress and the Federal Communications Commission (FCC)—prodded by the steadily advancing antitrust case—have been trying to decide how to restructure AT&T, which was chafing at restrictions that prevented it from entering the burgeoning field of information services.

At his first press conference in office, Baxter vowed to litigate the case "to the eyeballs," and the final agreement essentially satisfied the conditions that he originally laid out during that April, 1981 press conference. Baxter hoped to separate the regulated portions of AT&T business— primarily local service—from its unregulated activities, to prevent the firm from subsidizing its unregulated products with guaranteed revenues from its regulated monopoly unavailable to competitors. As Baxter explained in House testimony after the agreement was completed, "The most straightforward and effective way to eliminate AT&T's incentives and abilities to exclude competition from potentially competitive telecommunications markets is to require the divestiture of its regulated local exchange monopolies from these portions of AT&T that engage in competitive and potentially competitive activities."

The January 8 agreement broadly followed those directives—with significant concessions to AT&T. AT&T agreed to divest its 22 local operating companies, and was allowed to keep Western Electric, Bell Labs, and its long lines division, which will still be regulated by the FCC. It also kept the highly-profitable Yellow Pages. Left open were the crucial questions of how many companies those 22 units will be consolidated into, how to value the assets transferred between AT&T and the non-independent locals, and how to compensate local ratepayers for inventions developed at Bell Labs partially with revenues from local calls. AT&T has since proposed to form seven regional companies.

Most political attention has focused on whether the agreement will force a sharp increase in local rates. Baxter says the decree "will have absolutely no effect, zero," on local rates; AT&T says it won't change the way rates would have increased in any event; the FCC says the agreement will probably hurt the local units; and the local companies are predicting significant increases. That issue is sure to keep the agreement in the public eye for months to come.

AT&T's willingness to surrender its local operating companies demonstrated that it feared worse treatment at the hands of the trial judge, federal district court Judge Harold Greene, who had indicated he believed the government had proven violation of the antitrust laws by AT&T. But there was a carrot whose lure was even more potent than the company's fear of the stick. AT&T saw enormous profit potential in the field of telecommunications technologies, which the settlement freed it to enter. AT&T is now contemplating new ventures that range from cable TV and video Yellow Pages to systems that allow different kinds of computers to communicate with one another.

Baxter had originally designed the settlement as a modification to a 1956 consent decree in a previous government antitrust case against AT&T, a procedural move that would keep Greene from reviewing the terms of the agreement. But Greene objected, and although a New Jersey federal court had approved the settlement, the case was eventually returned to his jurisdiction. Baxter, in turn, has threatened to restart the case if Greene tries to alter the terms of the settlement.

It is understandable that Baxter is protective about the agreement. For him, the settlement is a considerable personal triumph. It generally adheres to his ideological beliefs. It insures him a place in antitrust history. And it represents a victory over formidable forces in the Administration that would have preferred to see the whole thing go away.

Since both Attorney General Smith and Deputy Attorney General Schmults recused themselves because of prior business associations with AT&T, Baxter was the top official on the case. So it was Baxter on the firing line when the White House began having second thoughts. Over Baxter's heated objections, the Administration in summer, 1981 backed Senate legislation that would allow AT&T to establish subsidiaries to compete in its unregulated markets, rather than requiring divestiture. Baxter had written the Office of Management and Budget arguing that the legislation would undermine the law suit.

The suit faced more direct challenges. The Defense Department asked Baxter to drop the proceeding because of potential national security disruptions, and a White House task force studying the telecommunications industry also reportedly asked the President to order Baxter to drop the suit. At one Cabinet meeting, Baxter said he discussed the case directly with the President.

In mid-summer, Baxter appeared to wilt. On July 29, he backed down and said he would drop the case if pending communications deregulation legislation passed Congress. But after the Senate passed the legislation, Baxter stiffened and said further amendments would be needed before he would end the case.

Those statements, along with the disquieting signals from Judge Greene and doubts in the House about the adequacy of the Senate-passed legislation, are what made AT&T realize a settlement might be its best hope. Serious negotiations began shortly before Christmas. Baxter concluded the negotiations during a ski vacation in Utah, with aides calling him every morning and top AT&T officials calling every night. In flamboyant style, Baxter whooshed off the slopes on Tuesday, January 5, met with a division attorney who had flown out with a draft of the agreement, approved the text, and flew back to Washington. Three days later, the agreement was signed.

That the 13-year-old case against IBM was dropped the same day, Baxter said, was nothing more than "serendipity." From the start of his tenure, Baxter was critical of the IBM case. "I don't think it has been well handled by the government," he complained early on. "I don't think it has been well handled by IBM. I don't think it has been well handled by the judge." After dismissing the case, Baxter said the government's chances of victory were but one in 10,000.

Those remarks were sharply disputed by federal Judge David Edelstein, who had handled the case. Edelstein angrily told the *Wall Street Journal* that Baxter's remarks were "self-serving" and "absolutely appalling." Baxter's criticism of the case, Edelstein said, was an attempt "to disguise his myopia and misunderstanding of the antitrust laws and this case specifically."

In March, 1981 Judge Edelstein urged Congress to investigate the dismissal, citing Baxter's failure to disclose consulting work he had done for IBM in a previous antitrust case. Baxter admitted that he was paid $1,500 six years ago by a law firm representing IBM "to assist them, in a limited way, in selecting economists to serve as experts and as expert witnesses in the litigation." He said he did not disclose the work in his Senate confirmation hearing because it was "so trivial." But Judge Edelstein said: "the apparent failure of Mr. Baxter to disclose this relationship itself creates an appearance of impropriety." A few weeks later, the *Wall Street Journal* disclosed that IBM paid Baxter's salary during the 1968-69 academic year, in an arrangement which allowed him to study math and computer courses and then prepare a paper for the company on "how they could sell more computational equipment to the legal profession," as Baxter explained in a February 25, 1981 deposition for a private antitrust case. Baxter further fueled the controversy by actively lobbying for IBM in Europe, where the computer giant is facing an antitrust case from the European Economic Commission (EEC). Meeting in both Washington and Paris, Baxter has pressured EEC officials to curb their case.

Antitrust experts expect the Justice Department's unilateral declaration of surrender in the IBM case to be more reflective of Baxter's future direction than the AT&T case, which involved a specialized set of cross subsidies complicated by the government regulation that is anathema to many Reagan officials.

Through the first nine months of 1981—even before the Mobil-Marathon Oil-U.S. Steel drama began—over $60 billion in mergers were recorded, twice as much as during the same period in 1980 and $16 billion more than had ever been recorded for an entire year. The total for 1981 hit $82.6 billion, an 86 percent increase over 1980's record. During one stormy congressional hearing, Sen. Howard Metzenbaum (D-Ohio), former chairman of the Senate antitrust subcommittee, charged Baxter with deliberately ignoring the antitrust laws. "I honestly believe you're a person who violates the law and does it with a kind of presumptuousness and arrogance that is almost unbelievable for an official of the government," Metzenbaum said. In less strenuous tones, the concern about the Reagan Administration's digression from 75 years of antitrust policy was echoed by leading Republicans.

From the start, there was no doubt that a sharp reverse in course was underway. Upon entering office, Baxter made clear that he was not worried about the rash of large mergers in recent years. "I do not believe that any particular degree of concentration in an industry necessarily indicates an antitrust violation and I am not sympathetic to the view that concentrated industries as a rule should be broken up," he told the Senate Judiciary Committee during his confirmation hearings. Of conglomerate takeovers, he announced: "I am not convinced by the evidence that I have seen that conglomerate mergers, or mergers generally, have increased economic concentration to dangerous levels." The oil company acquisitions, he said, may well be beneficial since the mining firms can use the "large infusions of capital" the oil companies can provide. Over the summer of 1981, the department nimbly avoided issuing an opinion on whether Mobil could purchase Conoco. Such signals have provided the political context for the current merger wave, most analysts agree, including one of Baxter's predecessors, John Shenefield, who has to go to great lengths to rein in clients made euphoric by Baxter's almost anything goes attitude. Concluded *Business Week*: "The proposed. . .takeover by Mobil Corp. of Marathon Oil Co. is the kind of corporate deal that just would not have been floated before Ronald Reagan became President, legal advisers to the nation's biggest companies agree."

Faced with this merger wave, Baxter has stuck to his guns, repeating his contention that antitrust enforcement should "not. . .be unduly influenced by the overall size of pending transactions or the fact that, at least in terms of money changing hands, merger activity is greater now than it recently had been." Baxter has acknowledged that "some mergers occur for reasons no more significant" than corporate empire building, but he does not consider that necessarily an antitrust problem. Said Baxter in December, 1981 testimony: "Some have argued that we should abandon this objective analysis and adopt other, more stringent approaches in the face of what is termed by some the current merger 'wave.' I believe that we cannot do so, and should not try to." Baxter opposed in December, 1981 testimony one response to the current "wave," a bill introduced by Senate Commerce Committee Chairman Robert Packwood (R-Ore.) and other representatives to temporarily bar oil company acquisitions such as Mobil's proposed takeover of Marathon. (See Financial Background section.)

Pressed on these stands, Baxter adopts the cloak of a skeptical academic, arguing that the evidence to act simply isn't available. Baxter, in a characteristic response, said he had "no data" to determine whether his statements have contributed to the increase in merger activity. When asked by a congressional panel if a Mobil-Marathon merger would set off a wave of similar acquisitions, Baxter retreated behind a similar response, saying, "I have no confident belief that there will or will not be other acquisitions if this is or is not approved."

Baxter uses that posture to defer judgment—and action—on almost any subject. Asked about Commerce Secretary Malcolm Baldrige's famous remark that American business managers have been "too fat, dumb and happy in the past 10 years," he said he would "want to look at the empirical data"—although exactly what data would nail down such a conclusion is unclear. For antitrust enforcement, the practical result of this attitude has been a stand-aside attitude that encourages acquisitions.

Baxter sees no need for revising any of the basic antitrust statutes— though he wouldn't mind if the Robinson-Patman Act were eliminated. In a 1980 ABA debate he stated flatly: "I would like to see the FTC [Federal Trade Commission] lose all its antitrust jurisdiction. I think it's done a deplorable job with it over the years." He sees no reason to stop the FTC's line of business reporting which offers "items of data that have never been available before." Nor does he see the need to tighten up tax code provisions that allow companies to deduct the interest paid on debt incurred during mergers and which permit mergers effected by stock swaps to go through tax free. "I don't have any doubt that the availability of tax free exchanges causes mergers to occur that wouldn't occur and probably increases the number of mergers that don't confer any social—rather than private—benefits," he said. "It's not at all clear to me that that's good or bad." Besides he said, the matter is a tax policy problem not an antitrust question. He holds the same view about purchasing decisions influenced by tax-deductible favors, such as the three-martini lunch. Rather than a competition problem, he sees that as "a conflict of interest between the people making the buying decisions and the people they're buying for."

Baxter is not shy about expressing his views, though the points sometimes are buried beneath economic jargon. In December, 1981 he told an incredulous, though confused, Senate Small Business Committee that allowing many mergers to go through would help small business, by preserving "the flexibility and incentives that are crucial if small business is to flourish." And, he argued, small businesses themselves benefit by being bought out. "There comes a point in the life of many successful small businesses when the individuals responsible for its successes can best reap the true value of their efforts by merger with another firm," he said.

Baxter has been critical only of "horizontal" mergers—the kind which involve direct competitors, such as Mobil and Conoco. His views supporting vertical mergers—such as a DuPont/Conoco marriage—or conglomerate mergers— such as a Seagram/Conoco combination—are passionate and long-held. In 1969 he called Attorney General John Mitchell a "populist" for overzealous criticism of conglomerate mergers.

Most people used other names for John Mitchell.

Baxter's views on vertical mergers and other "vertical" arrangements— made between producers and distributors in the production chain—are equally radical. "In my view, there is no such thing as a vertical 'problem,'" he said in April, 1981 congressional testimony. ". . .The courts have created blanket prohibitions on the use of vertical contractual devices which, as useful business tools, can facilitate the flow of commerce. . ." Baxter has said that not only will Justice avoid such cases itself, but that it will seek to overturn current case law by filing amicus briefs on behalf of private defendants in vertical antitrust cases.

As long as vertical mergers had no effect on horizontal activities, Baxter said, "I wouldn't draw any line at all." Asked if he would mind if General Motors bought Goodyear, he replied, "I wouldn't mind if a significant auto company acquires a significant tire manufacturer."

"Starting out saying vertical price fixing is good for the consumer is kind of nutty," Jerry S. Cohen, former chief counsel for the Senate Antitrust Committee told us. "I just don't know what the hell he's talking about."

While at Stanford, Baxter worked for Levi Strauss, the jeans manufacturer, in a vertical case brought against the company by the FTC. The FTC's 1978 victory prevented Levi from restricting sales only to retailers that would not discount their jeans. One economist has estimated that the suit has saved consumers $75 million a year. (There is no official FTC estimate.) Baxter estimates that he spent about 75 percent of his consulting time in 1978 working for Levi on the case, and a subsequent suit brought by the California Attorney General.

These kinds of cases will monopolize most of Baxter's time. Though he feels there's "a lot of anticompetitive behavior" involved in some labor agreements, given the division's workload he has no present plans to begin any actions in that contentious field. Nor does he have any plans to take action against state licensing boards, though he acknowledges the anticompetitive problems they can pose. The same is true for Defense Department procurement policies. And although he doesn't "think it is a terrific idea" to continue antitrust immunity which allows

U.S. airlines to participate in rate-setting for routes over the North Atlantic, he is unlikely to expend much political capital on the issue. All of which reflects a curiously passive posture vis-a-vis anti-competitive restriction that he ideologically opposes.

On other issues, Baxter said:

- he is satisfied with the department's current information procurement power.

- while he hasn't devoted much attention to sanctions policy, he is considering measures that would "destablize patterns of [anticompetitive] behavior." One example might refer to bid riggings. Most bid-rigging occurs in hotel rooms at the appointed spot for bid opening; it might be better to have bids mailed in, he said.

FINANCIAL BACKGROUND

During the summer of 1979, when the gas lines were long and public patience with the oil companies was short, Congress considered legislation to restrict the companies from buying other firms with the funds pouring in from decontrol of domestic oil. The man the American Petroleum Institute (API) sent to testify against the bill was Baxter, then a professor at Stanford Law School. "I don't think there is any particular reason to believe there will be a rash of acquisitions as a result of [the oil companies] augumented cash flow," he told the Senate Judiciary Committee.

Baxter estimates that he spent 20 percent of his time that year consulting for the API; he was paid $11,562.50 for his testimony. Another 10 percent of his time was spent designing antitrust seminars for Exxon.

Over two years later, in December, 1981, Baxter appeared before the House and Senate Commerce Committees to oppose similar legislation that would place an 18-month moratorium on acquisitions of second-tier oil firms by the nation's largest 20 petroleum companies. Asserting that "merger activity in general is an important and healthy feature of a capital market," Baxter said that oil company purchases of existing oil reserves would spur economic efficiency. "Those assets will once again find themselves in the hands of those who can deploy them most efficiently and with the greatest good to the greatest public," he said to a skeptical panel of representatives.

Other consulting clients in 1979 included Visa and Levi Strauss. Of his association with Levi Strauss, which began in 1977, Baxter says, "My involvement was over a broader range of problems and over a sufficiently longer period of time that I really came to be fairly close to the management of the company." During 1980, he received $8,812 in consulting fees from Levi Strauss. Other major clients that year included Northrop and Fairchild Industries. Baxter received a $51,200 salary from Stanford Law School in 1980.

Besides the oil company acquisition issue, Baxter has been involved in another controversial case which raised concerns about both conflict of interest and improper political influence. The dispute involves a suit against five major American drug companies by four foreign countries, including West Germany, India, and the Philippines. The suit charges the companies with fixing the price of certain antibiotics marketed worldwide during the 1950s. It grows out of domestic litigation stretching back 30 years.

In 1978 the Supreme Court ruled that the foreign governments could sue the companies in U.S. courts. Since then, the American companies have been trying to convince Congress to pass legislation nullifying the decision. Those efforts failed, in part because of opposition by the Carter Justice and State Departments. But the bill was revived in 1981 in the Senate Judiciary Committee.

On April 20, 1981 Baxter testified before a hastily called session of that committee and pronounced that "the Department of Justice does not oppose [the bill] from an antitrust enforcement perspective." The State Department was not invited to testify. Three weeks later, the Judiciary Committee approved the bill. And three weeks after that, the four nations settled out of court with the drug companies. "The pending legislation drastically weakened our bargaining position," Doug Rigler, who represented the Philippines in the case told us. "It undercut us." Added Paul C. Sprenger, who represented West Germany, "It cut the value of our case probably into a fifth of what it should have been."

Rigler maintains that Baxter has a "taint" in the case because he represented Upjohn, one of the defendants, in a similar case while he worked at Covington and Burling in the late 1950s. Pfizer, another defendant, is represented in ongoing U.S. litigation by Gibson, Dunn & Crutcher, the former law firm of Attorney General Smith. "There's no logical legal reason for supporting the bill unless one assumes that total non-enforcement of the antitrust laws is a valid position," said Sprenger.

WHAT OTHERS ARE SAYING ABOUT HIM

- One Stanford faculty member told the *American Lawyer*, "He's like an android. He wears this mask of the economic man, underneath which is a stewpot of the usual right-wing prejudices."

- Speaking at hearings on the Reagan Administration's proposal to eliminate the FTC's antitrust arm, Harvey Goldschmid, professor of law at Columbia University, said the Administration's "permissive" signals on antitrust will spark "a great deal of impermissible conduct." Said Goldschmid, "Questionable mergers and acquisitions may be only the tip of the iceberg. Anticompetitive problems in distribution take much longer to surface."

WILLIAM BRADFORD REYNOLDS
ASSISTANT ATTORNEY GENERAL, CIVIL RIGHTS DIVISION

RESPONSIBILITY OF OFFICE

Established in 1957, the Civil Rights Division "secures effective enforcement of civil rights laws." The Division enforces federal laws and presidential executive orders that prohibit discrimination on the grounds of race, national origin, religion, sex and age in employment, education, housing, credit, voting, public accomodations and facilities and federally-assisted programs. It works largely on overseeing the 1964 Voting Rights Act, school busing and affirmative action cases and guidelines.

The division houses 170 attorneys, 243 other employees and has a 1982 budget of $18.2 million.

BACKGROUND

A corporate super-lawyer whose salary tops $229,000, Reynolds has been a partner in the Washington firm of Shaw, Pittman, Potts and Trowbridge since 1973. The firm, known for its pro-nuclear stance largely represents utilities and airlines; it also regularly churns out high government officials in Republican Administrations. Reynolds "has a good reputation in his law firm, but, of course," as one Justice Department attorney said, "it hasn't been in the civil rights field."

During the Nixon Administration, Reynolds gained the experience which he says qualified him for his current job, working for Solicitor General Erwin Griswold. But contrary to the Justice Department's official biography, he did not personally compose Supreme Court briefs on civil rights cases. According to his supervisor, "He was the junior man in our office—an assistant staff attorney. The briefs therefore don't reflect his thoughts, just his writing."

Springing from a politically well-connected family, Reynolds likely caught the Administration's eye through the prompting of Griswold. "I recommended him for another position," Griswold told us, "but they offered him this one." Supposedly Reynolds wanted to head the Justice Department's Civil Division. According to Senate sources, Reynolds was offered his job only after the Administration was unable to find a black candidate it could agree on. "I don't think he has very broad experience in civil rights matters," said Griswold. "But then stop and think about it for a moment: do you think they [the Administration] are going to appoint someone with extensive civil rights experience to head that division?"

Reynolds has led a gilded life. He comes from a wealthy family—his mother was a Dupont. His appointment angered civil rights activists who say he has never experienced discrimination and therefore doesn't understand it. "There is no discrimination in Palm Springs," said Robert Plotkin, a career attorney who quit the division in August, 1981 in protest to Reynold's confirmation. Reynolds performance on the job has angered civil rights activists even more.

A graduate of Phillips Exeter Academy, a prestigious preparatory school in Andover, Massachusetts, Reynolds received his B.A. from Yale University in 1964 and graduated second in his class from Vanderbilt Law School in Nashville, Tennessee, where he edited the law review. While a law student, Reynolds worked a summer in the U.S. Attorney's office in Nashville. He clerked for the New York law firm Sullivan and Cromwell in the general practice division before moving to the Solicitor General's office in 1970.

Born June 21, 1942, in Bridgeport, Connecticut, Reynolds is married with one son and three daughters.

MAJOR ISSUES

- Reynolds has reversed division policy in virtually every civil rights area, in some cases perhaps violating clear direction from Congress and the courts.

- Reynolds says the division will no longer pursue class action suits in job bias cases.

- Reynolds rejects the use of affirmative action goals and timetables, which he labels "quotas." He is looking for a test case to overturn the *Weber* decision encouraging their voluntary use.

- Reynolds has indicated that he may actually go so far as to charge reverse discrimination against employers who use these systems.

- Reynolds has foresworn the use of busing in school segregation cases, a course that many civil rights attorneys maintain is illegal.

- Reynolds drew sharp criticism from division attorneys for his role in the Administration's decision to grant tax breaks to racially segregated schools.

Reynolds has become the focus of heated debate in the civil rights community, with division attorneys dubbing him chief of the new "anti-civil rights" department. "They are trying to overturn a whole tradition of dealing with civil rights issues and to undercut everything that has been done in the past," one Justice Department career attorney told us.

These strong words are borne out by sharp changes in department policy on affirmative action and busing. The division has renounced class action suits in job bias cases and instead plans to pursue such complaints on a case-by-case basis; critics say the inevitable administrative overload from that policy will slow affirmative action to a crawl.

Combined with the recession of a government policy denying tax breaks to racially segregated schools, the dismissal of Arthur S. Flemming, the long-term Republican head of the U.S. Commission on Civil Rights, and the Administration's support of revisions that could significantly weaken the Voting Rights Act, the activities of Reynolds have led the National Urban League to condemn the Administration for a "betrayal of basic civil rights protections."

"Taken together," said the new league president John E. Jacobs, "these and other steps can only be interpreted as attempts to dismantle the process of desegregating America."

Meanwhile, the elimination of class action suits, "will mean that individual women will have no protection under the law," said Eleanor Smeal, President of the National Organization of Women. "Since women are at the bottom of the pay scale, few will be able to afford the expensive court costs. Those fortunate enough to defend their rights will find overloaded courts and will probably never get justice."

A leading opponent of goals and timetables—which he calls "quotas"—Reynolds says he prefers to aim for "broad performance standards." As he said in House testimony, "We will no longer insist upon or in any respect support the use of quotas or any statistical formula designed to protect nonvictims of discrimination or give them preferential treatment based on race, sex, national origin, or religion." Said Reynolds in a January, 1982 speech: "By elevating the rights of groups over individuals, racial and sexual preferences are at war with the American ideal of equal opportunity for each person to achieve whatever his or her industry and talents warrant."

"Reynolds is woefully ignorant in many of the areas he is deciding upon," said William Taylor of the Leadership Conference on Civil Rights. "He hasn't read the studies in relevant areas. Clearly he is arrogant in his actions." (Reynolds admitted in an interview that he has never heard of the 1961 Federal Plans for Progress—a voluntary affirmative action program for federal contracts. Its failure spawned federally mandated goals and timetables.)

"You [Reynolds] know better than the Supreme Court how to interpret the Constitution. . .You lecture civil rights groups, yet you have been in your present position for less than a year, and you have come to it with very little experience in civil rights. On the basis of this limited experience, you are prepared to do away with remedies that were achieved by civil rights groups only after great sacrifice and suffering, remedies that have been enacted by Congress, approved by the courts and that have brought about the progress that has been achieved in this country in the past 15 years,'' said Rep. Don Edwards (D-Calif.), chairman of the Judiciary Subcommittee on Civil and Constitutional Rights. ''You promise new, more effective, remedies but you do not tell us what they are.''

These policy changes, combined with the Administration's public statements, will derail affirmative action, Arthur Flemming told one interviewer. ''Unless people in public office indicate that they believe that you must use affirmative action in order to achieve equal employment opportunity,'' he told the *New York Times*, ''equal employment is just going to be rhetoric and you are not going to see any real results.''

Reynolds tries to project the image of a careful legal analyst, interpreting the law more conservatively than those predecessors the Administration considers activist. In fact, Reynolds is an activist himself, radically breaking away from established legal precedent and government policy. ''Reynolds approaches the job as a technician. He's a lawyer, a good lawyer and as any good lawyer, he cites those cases which support his position; there's no prosecution involved. He's wedded to the notion of legal precedent but he's really much more of an activist,'' said former division attorney Robert Plotkin.

Reynolds faults at least two of the past decade's Supreme Court rulings on affirmative action. He believes that the court ruled wrongly in the *Bakke* case in which it decided race could be a factor in college admissions as long as no rigid quota system exists. He is also seeking to overturn the Court decision in the *Weber* case which held that a company and a union could set up a voluntary affirmative action plan with a quota.

In his December 17, 1981 press conference, Reagan cheerfully admitted his ignorance of the *Weber* case. When a questioner explained the case, Reagan replied, ''If this is something that simply allows the training and bringing up so that more opportunities are there for them in voluntary agreements between the union and management, I can't see any fault with that. I'm for that.''

That remark stunned Reynolds who had just made a big press splash by telling an interviewer that he was looking for a test case to overturn *Weber*. The White House quickly retreated and issued what has become a Washington staple—a ''clarification''—of the President's remarks. In the clarification, the White House explained that Reagan didn't disagree with the Justice Department on the case and that both found ''this racial quota unacceptable.''

In a historic twist, Reynolds recently announced that the department may now charge an employer with reverse discrimination. ''It seems to me that if it's discrimination, it works as much against the situation when you're discriminating against males and whites as opposed to females and blacks,'' Reynolds explained.

Jane P. Flemmings, executive director of Wider Opportunities for Women, spurns Reynolds's commitment to reverse discrimination. ''White males have been discriminated for for centuries,'' she said. ''What we're trying to do is change that so everyone has opportunities.''

Since his confirmation, Reynolds has worked with the Department of Education to keep Title IX provisions barring sex discrimination in federally-funded schools from extending to employees as well as students. The Carter Administration had argued in the courts that it should protect employees as well. Reynolds also settled a blatant case of sex discrimination against the New Hampshire police with kid gloves. (Though New Hampshire's state police had never hired a woman officer, Reynolds approved a consent decree in September, 1981 that did not require any numerical hiring goals or timetables, just "best efforts" to recruit women.)

Like Reagan and his superiors at the Justice Department, Reynolds staunchly opposes busing, claiming it has caused white flight, eroded urban tax bases, and created inferior schools. Reynolds has reversed Justice Department stands in ongoing cases to sidestep busing in favor of voluntary methods, such as the creation of high quality "magnet" schools. In doing so, however, he is veering away not just from court-ordered authorizations (as with affirmative action) but from court-ordered *mandates* for desegregation cases. "By limiting desegregation remedies to voluntary methods, Reynolds is in direct contravention to the oath he took when he assumed office," charged Taylor of the Leadership Conference. "In fact, in some cases, he is breaking the law."

Throughout his confirmation hearing, Reynolds repeatedly said that he would enforce the civil rights laws that were on the books. "The Department's responsibility is to enforce the laws as written," he said. "I will, if confirmed, religiously adhere to that philosophy in seeking to carry out my obligation to provide rigorous and even-handed enforcement of the civil rights laws of this country."

But, said Taylor, "By making desegregation always voluntary, Reynolds is breaking the oath he took when he assumed office." Drew Days, III, Reynolds's predecessor added, "To refuse busing in all cases is unconstitutional."

In addition, Reynolds rejects an approach used by the Carter Administration to simultaneously bring combination suits attacking housing and school desegregation. In Yonkers, New York the public school systems had allegedly been segregated not only by a series of school board decisions but also by the placement of federally-subsidized housing projects. "It's ridiculous to rule out any remedy in advance, such as not using busing and housing together," said Days.

The civil rights community believes Reynolds's "creative solutions" signal a return to the "separate but equal" philosophy ruled unconstitutional in *Brown v. Board of Education*. In a memo, Reynolds's assistant Robert D'Agostino recommended that the Yonkers case be shelved. Arguing that the Yonkers case was a "new attempt to remake America through coerced residential integration," D'Agostino asserted that "blacks because of their family, cultural and economic background are more disruptive in the classroom on the average. It appears they would benefit from programs for the emotionally disturbed."

Approximately 120 of the 170 division attorneys signed a petition protesting the memo, but Reynolds did not repudiate it. He did, however, reprimand department lawyers—he assumed one of them had leaked the memo— and finally issued a moratorium on business conversations outside the department. Reporters must now speak to a designated spokesman.

Reynolds drew another angry staff letter for his role in the Administration's decision to restore tax exemptions to discriminatory private schools. Over 200 employees—more than half of the division—signed the January, 1982 letter, which said that Reynolds's actions in the decision "cast serious doubt upon the division's commitment to enforce vigorously the nation's civil rights laws." In response, a Justice Department spokesman said protesting lawyers were "welcome to leave." Reynolds prepared a legal analysis used by the Administration to support the policy change, which department lawyers in the letter said, "violates existing federal civil rights law, as expressed in the Constitution, acts of Congress, and federal court interpretations thereof." Reynolds subsequently testified in support of the decision before the Senate Finance Committee.

Although part of the executive branch, by tradition the Justice Department has been viewed as more independent of White House control than other departments. In the wake of Watergate, the Carter Administration forbade the White House from communicating with anyone at the Justice Department, except the Attorney General or his deputy. This was to insulate Justice Department decisions from political interference. Since Reynolds has assumed office that policy seems to be interpreted more liberally.

At one point, then-White House political affairs director, Lyn Nofziger, sent Reynolds a letter on a pending busing case in Seattle, writing, "Surely if we are to change the direction of this country, mandatory busing is a good place to start. I thought that was what Reagan wanted." According to press reports, the White House later reprimanded Nofziger for his memo.

Inviting further political comment, Reynolds now requires division attorneys to have both Senators preclear complaints before they are launched in their state. "This is totally out of keeping with Department of Justice policy," said William Robinson of the Lawyers Committee for Civil Rights Under Law. "They are inviting political comment in a matter that should be strictly nonpolitical."

Reynolds has created a civil rights division characterized by insensitivity to desegregation and affirmative action, and dogmatic in its attitudes toward its own employees' freedom of expression. "If he [Reynolds] has a private philosophical hangup that is impeding his ability to uphold the law on civil rights," said Richard Seymour of the Lawyers Committee, "he just shouldn't do that job."

FINANCIAL BACKGROUND

By any account, Reynolds is a wealthy man. His assets, added with those in the name of his family, are worth at least $1.7 million, according to his financial disclosure form. He reports income from his partnership as $229,278.

His portfolio includes holdings of over $250,000 in DuPont and General Motors; a trust fund which also contains holdings of over $250,000 in each of the two companies, stock in Phillips Petroleum valued between $100,000 and $250,000; and smaller investments in DuPont, Burroughs Corp. and IBM in the names of his children.

At his law firm, Reynolds represented General Public Utilities and Metropolitan Edison Co., the firms involved in Three Mile Island; Union Electric Co., Emerson Electric Co., Communications Satellite Corp., American Management Systems, Inc., and B.F. Saul Real Estate Investment Trust.

WHAT OTHERS ARE SAYING ABOUT HIM

- "I think it's clear," said Benjamin R. Civiletti, attorney general during the last 18 months of the Carter Administration, "that the Reagan Administration as a matter of policy has retreated from effective civil rights enforcement. In my view that is a tragic withdrawal from the progress that has been made in equal rights in the last twenty years."

- "The problem now is that they are totally result-oriented and willing to take short cuts, and you find yourself being directed to reach a solution that will justify their new position," said one Civil Rights division attorney. "They are chipping away at the very heart of the civil rights system, and they are doing it effectively."

- William Taylor, of the Leadership Conference on Civil Rights, said he was surprised "how brazenly the Reagan Administration has changed positions on cases already in the courts. They're not making any pretense of paying respect to consistency."

- "What is going on," said Michael H. Sussman, a lawyer who left the division in May, 1981 to protest its policies, "is that you have a bunch of people [Reynolds] who don't pay attention to the view of their staff and, more importantly, they don't pay attention to the law."

- "There is new and increasing racism in this country. . .manifested in the way some feel they can treat blacks and minorities. You [Reynolds]," said Rep. Harold Washington (D-Ill.) at a committee hearing, "have pursued a policy of active reversal. The signals you have sent to the country make you somewhat accountable for what's going on. It suggests to racists that they can return to business as usual without fear of government retribution."

CAROL DINKINS
ASSISTANT ATTORNEY GENERAL,
LAND AND NATURAL RESOURCES DIVISION

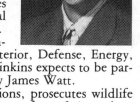

RESPONSIBILITY OF OFFICE

As Dinkins explains, her staff's "function is to serve as trial lawyers for the United States in disputes involving the general areas of land and natural resources." That involves both defending the U.S. government in environmental cases, and prosecuting violators of environmental statutes.

Most of the division's work comes from the Environmental Protection Agency (EPA); the Departments of Interior, Defense, Energy, Transportation, and Commerce; and the Forest Service. Dinkins expects to be particularly busy defending the decisions of Interior Secretary James Watt.

In addition, the division handles federal land acquisitions, prosecutes wildlife smugglers, and in conjunction with the EPA sues the owners of unsafe hazardous waste disposal sites. The division has a staff of 200 lawyers and a budget of about $16 million.

BACKGROUND

Dinkins comes to Justice from the Houston law firm of Vinson & Elkins (V&E), a virtual farm team for top federal appointees. V&E, the nation's third largest law firm, counts John Connally among its senior partners. And it has also produced Reagan's assistant treasury secretary (John Chapoton) and Carter's Energy Department general counsel (Lynn Coleman). V&E has deep ties with the energy industry: Its major clients include Gulf Resources & Chemical, Houston Natural Gas, Superior Oil, and Texas Eastern.

Dinkins, who became V&E's first woman partner in January, 1980, handled environmental and land use cases, largely representing coastal developers who needed permits from various federal agencies.

One of those clients was Perry Bass, a wealthy oilman with links to Connally, who was appointed head of the State Wildlife Commission by Republican Governor Bill

Clements in April, 1979. As head of the State Parks and Wildlife Commission, Bass ran into considerable embarrassment when a *Houston Post* investigation of Army Corps of Engineers records revealed that in 1975 he constructed, without permits, 97 dams and dikes near a piece of his ranch property that damaged 3,200 acres of wetlands and wiped out large numbers of fish. Bass built the dams to improve grazing vegetation on his property. Despite the damage, the Corps agreed in a settlement negotiated by Dinkins not to prosecute Bass. Bass agreed to tear down the dams—except for the largest one, for which the Corps issued an after-the-fact permit. Of the incident, Dinkins says today, "I thought it was silly for the press to rake that up years after that had happened and my client had done everything the Corps had asked to make it right."

In March, 1979 Clements placed Dinkins at the head of a nine-member commission charged with preparing a state coastal management plan that would meet the requirements of the 1972 Coastal Zone Management Act, a job she cites as evidence of her environmental credentials. Under the law, states with approved plans for managing development and protection of their coastlines are given the right to review federal actions that "directly affect" their shores for "consistency" with the plan.

Dinkins stepped into an effort that had been going on for years. An earlier plan developed by State Lands Commissioner Bob Armstrong had been rejected by then-Governor Dolph Briscoe, under opposition from the oil and chemical industries, which felt it would have added to their permitting problems. As head of the commission, Dinkins was "cautiously acceptable to the environmental people and was certainly acceptable to industry people," said Armstrong.

The commission worked quickly and Clements forwarded Dinkins's revised coastal plan to the federal government in June, 1979. Though federal officials say it was in some respects more manageable than the Armstrong plan, its provisions governing wetlands development were considered inadequate and the federal government refused to certify it.

After negotiating with the Commerce Department for two years, Clements decided in May, 1981 to withdraw from the coastal management program. Dinkins told us she was with Clements when he made his decision and that she had advised him to withdraw.

In 1980, Clements again tapped Dinkins to head a panel studying flooding along the Clear Creek watershed, southeast of Houston.

Before joining V&E in 1973, Dinkins was an adjunct law professor at the University of Houston and an associate at the university's Institute of Coastal and Marine Resources. Dinkins, who received her law degree from the university in 1971, and her undergraduate degree from the University of Texas in 1968, is considered a tough and creative attorney.

Her environmental background is less revealing. She is a member of the Environmental Defense Fund, the Natural Resources Defense Council, and the National Wildlife Federation (all of which she joined in 1980), though she told us she joined the groups "to be on the mailing list." She also served on the "Environmental Protection Committee" of the Interstate Oil Compact Commission, an organization of oil and gas producing states.

Overall, Armstrong said, "Dinkins is a 'B-minus' environmentalist as opposed to the 'D-minus' that are in Interior, and an 'A-minus' pro-industry person. But she will at least recognize the laws are there and if someone is really flagrant or gross she'll do what's right and enforce the laws. She's a bright lawyer whose only weakness is she gets on the wrong side of the issues because she sides with her clients.''

A native Texan—she was born in Corpus Christi on November 9, 1945—Dinkins is married to a partner in the Houston firm of Butler, Binion, Rice, Cook & Knapp. With her ties to Governor Clements, it would not be too surprising for her to return to Texas politics, perhaps in a race for state attorney general. ''I don't have my eye on political office,'' she told us, ''but when I got out of law school I didn't know there was such a thing as assistant attorney general for land and natural resources. I'm not foreclosing anything.'' She has two children.

MAJOR ISSUES

The Land and Natural Resources Division's impact on policy can either be significant or quite minimal, depending upon its willingness to accept its client agencies'—primarily EPA and Interior—interpretation of the law. In speeches, Dinkins has suggested that she has little inclination to challenge the agencies, as her predecessor James Moorman did on several occasions. ''We're in litigation, not management,'' she has said. An internal memo for division attorneys reaffirmed the point.

''The philosophy of the Moorman lands division was that you weren't entirely dependent on your client,'' said Khristine Hall, who left the division in May, 1981 to join the Environmental Defense Fund. ''That's all gone now.''

That policy shift is significant, for it indicates Dinkins will not forcefully challenge the other environmental agencies for failing to aggressively enforce their laws. Under Moorman, a special litigation unit had been established to ''look at things that EPA and Interior didn't do,'' says Hall, who worked in the unit. Initiatives generated by that unit include the highly successful hazardous waste and wildlife smuggling programs, and an energy unit that hoped to become involved in legal problems hindering solar and conservation development. Though supportive of the hazardous waste and wildlife programs, Dinkins has ended the energy program.

Similarly, Dinkins appears inclined to grant the agencies greater leeway in determining the government's position in court challenges. ''Moorman was willing to take a hard look at positions he was asked to defend,'' said Peter Coppelman, a division attorney who left to join the Wilderness Society. ''The clear impact of what Dinkins is saying is that that is not going to be how the Justice Department is going to function on a regular basis.'' In one telling incident, the EPA kept out Justice Department attorneys from private meetings with industry groups aimed at settling a case brought against the agency's hazardous waste permitting regulations. Dinkins only reluctantly lodged a complaint with the EPA. ''Any other lands division in the past,'' said one former attorney, ''would have told EPA to go to hell on it.''

This subservience to agencies that are apparently dedicated to crippling the laws they are bound to enforce has discouraged many attorneys who came to the division when Moorman was proclaiming it to be the city's largest environmental law firm. ''If you assume the Justice Department is not going to take an active role in shaping policy, it's going to have a very limited role. And it looks like the worst is yet to come,'' said Coppelman, who stays in touch with friends inside the division. Other sources close to the division say Dinkins has made some efforts to prod EPA, but is extremely limited in what she can do by the White House's approval of that agency's current course.

Dinkins is stoical about staff morale, acknowledging that some division attorneys feel pointedly uncomfortable defending James Watt and Anne Gorsuch and will probably leave. "As a lawyer they shouldn't be representing people they don't feel comfortable with," she said.

In any case, Dinkins already has made clear that her views are not too far from those of agency heads seeking to roll back federal regulations, or to turn over increased environmental responsibilities to the states. Echoing a current Getty Oil television commercial, she said in a May, 1981 speech that, "When the law in its zeal, seeks to remedy every ill, to resolve every conflict, it becomes a burden so heavy that liberty is stifled and society suffers." Three days later, in a Washington speech, she entreated the National Forest Products Association to join with her in defending the Administration's deregulatory goals: "We will fully and enthusiastically defend actions of the new heads of agencies charged with reduction of regulations as they fulfill President Reagan's program to reduce the unnecessarily heavy regulatory burden this country now faces."

Unlike many other Reagan officials who share those feelings, Dinkins presents those sentiments in a non-threatening manner, devoid of zealotry and sprinkled with apparently legitimate personal concern about hazardous wastes and other environmental problems. "Her personal style is not confrontational," said Coppelman, who has met with her several times. "She's not a nut. But the difference in outcome on policy from having Carol Dinkins and a James Watt is next to nothing." Still there is a question of degree and some sources suggest Dinkins is "appalled" by how far Watt and Gorsuch are redirecting their agencies.

As do regulatory officials at the EPA and Occupational Safety and Health Administration, though, Dinkins would like to turn over more of her responsibilities to the states. "Clearly, many environmental problems, aspects of air and water pollution, for example, require federal resolution; but if we carefully review the allocation of responsibility that has evolved in the last decade, I think that we shall discover that much of the current environmental law could be given back to the states," she has said.

In an interview, Dinkins conceded that while "in the abstract it's a good principle" to increase the state role, "very few of the states have a large litigating unit. They may not be able to take up much of that burden." But she told us she expects the states to move more heavily into environmental litigation for several reasons. "These are exciting cases to work on," she said, which would attract attorneys. The cases also draw publicity, which would attract attorney generals with an eye on future elections. And, she says, "I think that industry people will encourage them to have a state program" because it is "easier to deal with the states." (To help the states develop their programs, Dinkins has organized a workshop on hazardous wastes for state litigators.)

Under Moorman, the division began an aggressive hazardous waste enforcement unit of its own, bringing landmark cases against the Hooker Chemical Co. and other major polluters for such sites as Love Canal, New York. Soon after taking office, Dinkins merged the hazardous waste unit into the larger environmental enforcement section, a move which drew criticism from some environmental groups but is discounted as a managerial move by others. Dinkins said she "absolutely" felt jail terms were appropriate for some polluters, and that she would continue to seek to pin liability for cleanup on dumpers under the Superfund law. "We are committed to try to find responsible parties," she said. "The fund simply can't clean up everything." Dinkins said she considers hazardous wastes the top environmental problem facing the country. "There are a lot of areas I think we have regulatory overkill in," she said, "But there are other areas where I don't think we've done everything we need to do, such as hazardous wastes."

A very significant change is in the division's attitude toward the legal standing of private groups seeking to sue the government and the awarding of attorneys fees—two issues of paramount concern to environmental groups and other citizens that expect to be regularly in court defending the nation's basic environmental laws against the Reagan Administration. "I have already issued a directive to the attorneys in the division to be aggressive in challenging standing," she told us. Without "standing to sue" citizens cannot get into the courtroom to argue their case.

The division has been so aggressive that it challenged, and successfully kept out of a case between James Watt and a California water district, the Environmental Defense Fund—which sought to intervene on *behalf* of Watt's attempt to raise water prices.

"I think it's going to anger the courts," said Coppelman of Dinkins's new policy. "It's just a way to harass environmental groups."

Similarly, Dinkins has taken a tough line on the awarding of attorneys' fees. In a case involving EPA coal emission regulations, a Justice Department attorney agreed in August, 1981 to the award of $30,000 in an unsuccessful case brought by the Sierra Club legal defense fund. Two weeks later, a Dinkins aide called the Sierra Club attorney and told him that Dinkins had overruled the request. The dispute is currently in court.

FINANCIAL BACKGROUND

As a partner in V&E, Dinkins earned $131,454. Her clients included Amoco, Dow Chemical, and Texas Eastern Transmission Corp., a pipeline company; her work for these firms generally consisted of seeking permits for oil drilling or other activities. Asked if she was usually successful, Dinkins said: "That's how come they hired me."

Together with her husband, Dinkins reports assets largely in bank accounts and land holdings, totalling at least half a million dollars.

WHAT OTHERS ARE SAYING ABOUT HER

- Dinkins draws high marks as a talented, meticulous lawyer. One federal analyst who negotiated with her on Texas's coastal plan said, "We had a very good working relationship with her. She seemed very up front with us, no B.S."

- Tony Roisman, who headed the division's hazardous waste section until it was eliminated in the reorganization, said, "The division is running very smoothly. There was a quick transition. She's on top of things, very supportive."

- Ken Berlin, who worked with Dinkins for several months as head of the division's wildlife smuggling section before leaving to join the Audubon Society summed up the consensus on Dinkins when he told us: "If she were writing the laws from scratch, it might be different. But she'll uphold the law."

REX LEE
SOLICITOR GENERAL

RESPONSIBILITY OF OFFICE

Lee considers his position as the U.S. government's representative to the Supreme Court "the most challenging job in the world for a lawyer."

In this capacity, he "decides what cases the government should ask the Supreme Court to review and what position the government should take in cases before the court; he supervises the preparation of the government's Supreme Court briefs and other legal documents and the conduct of the oral arguments in the Court and argues most of the important cases himself."

The solicitor general also decides whether the United States should appeal cases it loses before lower courts.

The court agrees to hear about 80 percent of the cases requested by the solicitor's office, as compared to less than 10 percent of private requests.

BACKGROUND AND MAJOR ISSUES

Lee's opposition to the Equal Rights Amendment (ERA) led to a surge of opposition to his nomination.

The author of a book criticizing the ERA, Lee also worked with the Mountain States Legal Foundation (MSLF) and the state of Idaho to fashion a lawsuit challenging Congress's authority to extend the deadline for the amendment's ratification.

In December, 1981, a federal district judge in Boise ruled for MSLF and Idaho, declaring that Congress had no right to stretch out the ratification date to 1982, and that states did have the right to rescind their approval. After the decision, John Runft, the MSLF attorney who argued the case, told reporters that the lawsuit had its origins at the MSLF.

Until his appointment as solicitor general, Lee served on MSLF's Board of Litigation, which evaluates and must approve any cases which the foundation proposes to become involved in. Lee recused himself from government decisions on the Idaho case.

Lee recalls the case as one of "the ones that I was most prominently involved in" at MSLF. "The laboring was done by John Runft, and I was his consultant, his idea person; he had others, but there were things that he ran by me and in certain instances I would do first drafts of portions of the brief," Lee said.

In his book, Lee argues that the ERA presents "risks...[that] are not worth running because the need for massive change is not great. Indeed, massive change is the biggest risk." Current law prohibiting sex discrimination, he argued, has reached the point where "we are at the fine-tuning stage."

Lee grounds his argument in a fear of judicial activism, stressing that court decisions will determine the actual scope of the amendment. "Neither during the present preratification period nor, if ratified, for decades after can anyone on this planet know what the ERA will mean," he wrote.

Lee offers some predictions, though. Under the standard of judicial review he considers most likely, he is "convinced that laws prohibiting homosexual conduct and coeducational dorms'' will be struck down. And, he argues, ''there is a strong argument that rape laws cannot withstand the theoretical demands of that standard, the proponents' preferences notwithstanding.''

With the exception of nullifying rape laws, Lee suggests that ERA proponents would favor those interpretations. ''For a few people, the answer [on whether the amendment's benefits justify its risks] will be easy because there are no horribles in the parade. Constitutional legalization of homosexual conduct and coed dorms is exactly what they would like. For most people, however, these would be unwanted results and would therefore cause serious concern,'' he wrote.

At his confirmation hearing, Lee's critics argued that the book ''misstates'' both the intent of the amendment and the coverage afforded by current law.

Said Iris Mitgang, chair of the National Women's Political Caucus: ''The books'—Lee's—selective reading of the legislative history of the ERA, disregard of many state ERA cases, and the mischaracterization of the current state of law reveal a somewhat disingenuous attempt at a dispassionate evaluation of the ERA. Therefore, they raise cause for concern.''

Said Judith Lichtman, executive director of the Women's Legal Defense Fund: ''That well-developed body of law praised by Dean Lee leaves sex discrimination complainants and defendents alike at the mercy of the subjective conclusions of the predominantly male judiciary, which without guidance attempts to resolve the individual cases before it.''

Critics at his nomination hearing traced Lee's anti-ERA views to his Mormon background. Since 1977, Lee has been dean of Utah's Brigham Young University (BYU) law school and is active in the Mormon Church. The Mormon Church has stridently opposed the ERA.

''We could naively hope that his views change for the better,'' said Teddie Woods of Mormons for ERA, ''but that is not likely until he is directed to change his views by. . .the Mormon Church.''

In a statement submitted to the Senate Judiciary Committee, one Mormon woman said church officials told her they encouraged Lee to write his book. Cheryl Dalton, a Mormon woman who supports the amendment, described in her statement a meeting of October 4, 1980 with Gordon Hinckley, head of the church's powerful Special Affairs Committee. ''It was made clear to us that Hinckley not only had prior knowledge of the manuscript, but that Mr. Lee was encouraged through Church lines to write the book critical of the Equal Rights Amendment,'' Dalton wrote. ''Mr. Hinckley spoke of the necessity of getting the book to press quickly.'' The book was published in 1980 by the BYU Press.

Lee told us that, ''I was not asked to write that book by anyone. I think it would have been perfectly proper if I had been. If someone either at the church or somewhere else had said to me, 'Look, we need a good statement from a lawyer's point of view as to what's wrong with the Equal Rights Amendment, will you do it?' In fact, that was not the way it happened. It was entirely my own idea and no one other than my own intimate associates there at the law school even knew I was working on it.'' Hinckley did not see the manuscript, Lee said, ''until the time it was in final manuscript and submitted to the printers.''

''I did do this,'' Lee continued. ''I was so astounded by that [statement at the confirmation hearing] that I called him [Hinckley] after my hearing was all over. And I read him the letter and what he told me was a bit inconclusive. He said, 'I remember meeting with them.' He said, 'I am sure I would not have told them that we had asked you to write it because that in fact is not the case.' But he said, 'I don't remember what was said, but it is possible that they might have inferred that' '' the church encouraged the writing of the book.

In a second book entitled *A Lawyer Looks at the Constitution*, Lee fleshes out his views on the case for what he and other conservatives call "judicial restraint." Lee argues that the "general approach that courts should bring to their task is one of restraint—of upsetting the legislative judgment only in those instances where the error is quite clear and where the balance scales quite clearly disfavor the policy-makers' judgment."

Lee sees an essential role for the courts, though, as "the most appropriate safeguards of constitutionally guaranteed minority rights." As he wrote in the book:

> Whether a substantial number of his constituents agree with the positions taken by the President (or a member of Congress) is quite relevant to the adequacy of his performance. Whether a substantial number of American citizens agree with judicial interpretations of the Constitution is less relevant to the adequacy of the judge's performance. Indeed, in light of the fact that the Constitution usually protects minority rights, additional levels of insulation between the popular will and the stewards of constitutional meaning is not only acceptable but required.

Nonetheless, Lee said that he believes, "There is a solid basis for the argument that on a case-by-case basis in some instances Congress may have certain powers to cut back the jurisdiction of the courts."

Lee was particularly encouraged by the Supreme Court's January, 1982 ruling in the case of *Valley Forge Christian College* vs. *Americans for Separation of Church and State*. Lee called the decision a 'linchpin'' of the Administration's campaign against judicial activism, "a really significant victory." The 5-to-4 decision greatly curtailed the ability of citizen organizations to sue in the federal courts over government aid to religion, but the implications are wider. Justice William Rehnquist wrote in the decision that citizen groups have no "special license to roam the country in search of governmental wrongdoing and to reveal their discoveries in the federal court." He added, "The federal courts were simply not constituted as ombudsmen of the general welfare."

Lee himself feels that too many "fundamental rights" have been created by the courts, and that the Reagan Administration, while not necessarily working to eliminate some of those already created, "will resist any opportunity to expand them."

Because of prior involvements, Lee recused himself from two recent cases that raised the judicial activism issue. One, of course, was the ERA ratification case. The other was the Bob Jones University case involving tax exemptions for schools that racially discriminate. On January 8, 1982, the Justice Department asked the Supreme Court to dismiss the case as moot because new Reagan IRS policies would grant the schools tax exempt status; but after a federal appeals court in February blocked the exemptions, the Justice Department decided to ask the Supreme Court to hear the case after all. Its new brief, however, reversed previous policy and asserted the government did not have the authority to deny the tax exemptions. In a highly unusual move, Lawrence Wallace—who filed the brief because Lee recused himself—added a footnote disassociating himself from the new position. Wallace had defended the IRS decision to deny the exemptions before the court the previous September. (See profiles of Ed Meese, James Baker and Mike Deaver.)

Wade McCree, Lee's predecessor in the solicitor general's office, cautioned against extrapolating the recent *Valley Forge* decision into a campaign against activism in the courts. "I would avoid making a judgment based on a single case," he told us. But the pressure to mount such a campaign is present. Richard Viguerie's *Conservative Digest* recently criticized Lee for "publicly water[ing] down a strong speech by Attorney General Smith opposing judicial activism, by announcing that the Justice Department would not seek to overturn existing activist rulings."

Lee is beginning his second term in the Justice Department. He served as assistant attorney general for the Civil Division under President Ford from 1975 to 1977, before returning to BYU, where he had been the founding dean of the university's J. Reuben Clark Law School since 1971. Lee has taught constitutional and antitrust law.

Lee's association with the school dates back to 1960, when he obtained his B.A. degree there. He went on to the University of Chicago Law School where he was graduated first in his class in 1964.

With the help of his cousin, then Secretary of Interior Stewart Udall, Lee was hired as a law clerk for U.S. Supreme Court Justice Byron White in 1963.

He joined the firm of Jennings, Strouss, Salmon & Trask in Phoenix, Arizona, as an associate in 1964 and in 1967 became a partner.

Born on February 27, 1935, in Los Angeles, California, Lee is married and has seven children.

FINANCIAL BACKGROUND

Lee earned $49,083 from BYU in 1980. He earned more than $57,000 that year in additional consulting fees for several law firms, the states of Nevada and Arizona, and the Mountain States Legal Foundation, which paid him $499.50 in 1980 and $760.50 in 1981.

Lee worked with Stewart Udall on the class action suit brought by the Utah, Arizona and Nevada residents against the government over illnesses the residents believe are a result of fallout from atomic tests conducted in the desert decades ago. Lee said he has not yet been paid for his work on that still-pending case because "they don't have any money. The other clean thing would have been for me simply to say 'Forget it, I don't want anything.' I can't do that because I'm a poor boy and I've got hundreds of hours of my life wrapped up in that. What we did was agree on an amount in the event of recovery," he said. He has recused himself from government policy in the dispute.

WHAT OTHERS ARE SAYING ABOUT HIM

- Maida Withers, a Mormon woman who teaches at George Washington University, knew Lee as an undergraduate at BYU. "He was considered a liberal then," said Withers, who has actively supported the ERA. "But if you want to play with the church you don't have any choice. If you want to be an apostle: you're one, going to be a Republican, and two, you're going to be a conservative."

FEDERAL TRADE COMMISSION

JAMES C. MILLER III
CHAIRMAN

RESPONSIBILITY OF OFFICE

Miller takes over one of the oldest independent federal agencies at one of the most difficult times in its history. Established in 1914 "to prevent the free enterprise system from being stifled, substantially lessened or fettered by monopoly or restraints on trade or corrupted by unfair or deceptive trade practices," the Federal Trade Commission (FTC) has lately stifled, lessened, and fettered itself. Twice in 1980 it was forced to shut down for lack of funds while Congress debated its future. Eventually, it became the first independent agency to have its rules subjected to a congressional legislative veto.

The FTC Act of 1914 provides the agency with its basic authority to regulate "unfair methods of competition" and "unfair or deceptive acts or practices." It enforces that authority through a Bureau of Competition, which handles antitrust matters; a Bureau of Consumer Protection, which watches over advertising, product reliability, and marketing abuses; and a Bureau of Economics, which conducts research on the structure of the economy. In 1982, the agency had a budget of approximately $68 million and 1,380 employees. For 1983, the Administration has proposed an 11 percent budget reduction.

As chairman, Miller is specifically responsible for administration of the commission, including supervision and direction of the staff-which develops the proposals upon which the commission acts—and the hiring of commission employees (with the exception of several top employees whose appointment must be agreed to by the full commission upon recommendation of the chairman).

BACKGROUND

Miller has spent virtually his entire career opposing federal regulation, which in other times would make him a somewhat unusual choice to head one of the relatively more aggressive and effective federal regulatory agencies.

"All institutions in society have certain imperfections," he said when we asked him about business's behavior. "Churches are not perfect, labor unions are not perfect, even voluntary associations are not perfect. . . . I feel that the operating hypothesis is that markets are competitive, that there isn't this 'power' to affect outcomes, that the market works pretty darn well to discipline firms. . . along the question of predatory pricing, the literature cries out in its paucity on documented cases of predation. . . . On the question of pollution, that is really a problem of property rights. And you know, I mean an economist probably would say as a first cut, the problem, the imperfection that exists is because the collective as a whole is reluctant to assign and enforce property rights, the use of rivers and so forth. . . .

But surely I mean businessmen and women must sit around the table and make decisions about pollution and surely, you know, I think most businessmen and women that face the option 'Gee, we can legally pollute but the result will be that we kill people and even if we don't, even if we would not be held liable for that,' they as a moral issue probably take that option [not to pollute]," he said.

Until his appointment at the FTC, Miller was serving in a pair of high-visibility low-accountability posts: administrator of the Office of Information and Regulatory Affairs at the Office of Management and Budget (OMB), and executive director of the President's Task Force on Regulatory Relief. Under a presidential executive order of February 17, 1981, OMB—and Miller in practice—was given unprecedented authority over regulatory decisions by federal agencies. From these positions, Miller directed the suspension, recall, or elimination of hundreds of regulations. "Right now," he told a business conference in the summer of 1981, "we're only at the tip of the iceberg. There's a lot more to do to achieve substantial regulatory relief for our economy."

Miller's stay at OMB was extremely controversial, with congressional critics charging that his office has served as a back-room "conduit" for industries anxious to escape federal regulations, but less anxious to have their advocacy appear in a public docket. At OMB, Miller refused to publicly log his meetings with outside parties.

In a June, 1981 analysis which disputed the legality of the executive order, the Congressional Research Service wrote that "the very nature and design of the order is an affront to. . .due process. . .and renders it unconstitutional on its face."

Under President Ford, Miller served in similar positions at the Council of Economic Advisers, the Council on Wage and Price Stability (COWPS), and the Administration's Regulatory Review Group. From his post at COWPS, he regularly intervened against rules proposed by other federal agencies—such as the Occupational Safety and Health Administration's (OSHA) attempt to regulate carcinogenic coke-oven emissions—on the grounds that the regulations were inflationary. He also became a relentless advocate of "cost-benefit" analysis—the requirement that agencies demonstrate that the benefits of a regulation to society exceed its cost to industry.

"His major contribution," said one Capitol Hill staffer familiar with Miller's work, "has been to translate a rather abstruse part of neo-classical economic theory into public policy." Miller's efforts were crowned with success last year when the Reagan executive order mandated that regulations "not be undertaken unless the potential benefits to society from the regulation outweigh the potential costs to society." Like other conservative economists, Miller has long advocated the use of "personal protective equipment," such as respirators, as a substiutute for engineering controls that remove pollutants from the workplace. Miller has pushed for these devices for so long that he is practically an apostle of earplugs.

Most of the economists manage to go through their whole lives without actually wearing the equipment they would impose on workers. Miller, though, wore a respirator during a visit to a coke-oven while at COWPS. Workers and industrial hygienists have pointed out that respirators are extremely uncomfortable, and considerably less effective in practice than they appear to be in laboratory tests. Miller acknowledged the drawbacks under cross examination during a 1976 OSHA proceeding at which he recommended the use of respirators for coke-oven workers exposed to carcinogenic emissions:

Q: Is it a fair statement to say that coke-oven workers do not wear respirators and do not want to?

Miller: On our visit [to a coke-oven facility], Dr. Fair emphasized that in the summer it is very hot and it is very uncomfortable wearing these things.

Q. You could not talk with me right now like you are if you had a respirator on. Is that not correct?

Miller: It would be rather muffled.

In all, Miller said, during his visit to the coke-oven, he wore his respirator "10 or 20 percent" of the time.

The experience, apparently, did not alter his views. Regarding the complaints of workers about the inconvenience of the masks, Miller recently commented: "Perhaps we should rename the agency the Occupational Safety, Health and Comfort Administration."

Like most regulatory critics, Miller regularly says he does not oppose the goals of health and safety regulation, just the way they are implemented. But for all his regulatory analysis it's hard to think of an example where he has ever advocated stronger regulation. During an interview he told us, "Most of the relevant and needed regulations are on the books in some form or another." We pressed again for any specific areas where he thought regulation needed to be strengthened: "I don't want to say that there are particular gross areas that are neglected and at the same time I don't want to say that there are not particular situations that need to be addressed. There are. But I just don't have a catalogue of those in my head right now," he replied.

Miller agreed that the Administration's polices of cutting regulatory budgets and directing agency resources toward reexamining existing rules will mean fewer regulations. "The result of this process," he said, "is going to be much more cost-effective regulation. I think of where I come from in terms of what things need to be regulated, how they need to be regulated, just measuring the number of regulations is probably not the best way of determining how the regulatory process has worked."

During the Carter Administration, Miller exiled himself to the American Enterprise Institute, a Washington based business-oriented think-tank, where he continued to write and testify against federal health and safety regulation sometimes in tandem with Murray Weidenbaum, now chairman of the Council of Economic Advisers. Miller had done an earlier stint there, and at the Brookings Institution, in 1972. From September, 1972 until June, 1974, he taught at Texas A&M University; in 1968 he taught at Georgia State University. From 1969 to 1972, he was a senior econmomist at the U.S. Department of Transportation.

Miller is generally considered an ideologue. A fervent believer that government should stay out of business's way, he speaks of "economic efficiency" with the reverence of an artist describing the Sistine Chapel. Prone to wearing ties with profiles of Adam Smith—de rigueur among the knights of the free market in Reagan's capital—he attributes his economic view to his years working in a grocery store and then running a grass-mowing business while growing up in Conyers, Georgia. Conyers honored its favorite son with "Jimmy Miller Day" on December 19, 1981.

On a personal level, Miller is not nearly as strident as his ideology, but one veteran newsman said: "Underneath that soft appearance is a core of steel." When not using the inelegant elocution of a hard core economist, concerned about "maximizing consumer welfare," he often plays the country boy, spicing his remarks with such observations as, "Back in Georgia, you didn't go squirrel hunting in a cornfield and you didn't go looking for rabbits up a tree.''

Miller has hired a media consultant to help him project ''more of the Georgia country boy that we know around the office and less of the Ph.D.,'' said Neal Friedman, head of the FTC's public relations office. Working with Miller on ''his television performance,'' his speeches and ''maximizing his time'' while on the road is Merrie Spaeth, a former White House fellow who performed similar duties for William Webster at the FBI. Friedman said Spaeth is supposed ''to sort of take what he [Miller] is and develop that.'' Such as the chairman's television manner. ''He started out as stiff,'' said Friedman, ''[We're working] to make him more comfortable, to teach him some of the tricks of the trade, so to speak.''

Miller is something of a prankster. At the FTC Christmas party—shortly after his controversial remarks about advertising substantiation (see Major Issues)—Miller turned up in an airline pilot's uniform, complete with a cap that read ''Fly By Night Airlines.'' During a recent TV appearance he conducted a mike check by sonorously intoning ''James C. Mil-ler, the third.'' When he finished he said: ''I've spared my son the designation as the fourth.''

Miller was born in Atlanta on June 25, 1942. He was graduated from the University of Georgia in 1964 and received his Ph.D. in economics from the University of Virginia in 1969. He is married with three children.

Miller wouldn't commit to staying through his seven-year term, though he said he ''probably would'' if Reagan remained in office. ''Should President Reagan not—well, for whatever reason—if there was a new Administration and they didn't want me to be chairman. . .I have a fairly strong feeling that new Presidents ought to have the option of appointing their own chairman of an agency and I would certainly give a great deal of consideration to stepping down for that reason.''

MAJOR ISSUES

- Miller has suggested the agency back away from its ad substantiation program, a proposal criticized even by many leaders of the advertising industry.

- Miller has also criticized the agency's product defects program, which has won over $125 million for consumers stuck with defective goods.

- Like other Reagan officials, Miller has called for substantially loosening the scope of the antitrust laws, and a focus solely on clear cases of collusion and mergers between direct competitors.

- Miller's transition team report on the FTC suggests reallocating the agency's resources from policing the marketplace to intervening before other government agencies to fight regulation of business.

- Miller has filled the agency's key staff slots with conservative economists who share his view that government oversight of business often generates ''economic inefficiencies'' that harm consumers.

A few months after Miller took over as FTC Chairman, Michael Pertschuk, his precedessor and now a minority member of the commission, addressed the Utah Advertising Federation in Salt Lake City. With some bemused sympathy, Pertschuk told the crowd that ''within the first few months of Chairman Miller's reign, I see signs and portents that he may very well be entering (from the right) the same political tornado that we were sucked into from the left side of the political spectrum.''

Normally, a group like the Utah Advertising Federation, it could be safely assumed, would feel more comfortable with James Miller's view of the world than that of Michael Pertschuk, an activist chairman who tussled with the advertising industry over ads aimed at children. But in this case Pertschuk was speaking to an audience that could sympathize with his message.

Miller had instantly acquired a reputation in the advertising industry as something of a loose cannon with a remarkable performance at his first press conference. Trying to reify his economic ideology into specific policy, Miller managed to alienate consumers, advertisers, and just about everyone short of fellow travelers in the camp of economic efficiency.

Arguing that "Consumers are not as gullible as many regulators think they are," Miller suggested he would seek to move the commission away from its standard requiring advertisers to substantiate their claims. Combined with his remarks about antitrust and product defects, those statements immediately plunged Miller into controversy.

Since 1971, the FTC has required advertisers to back up their claims by disclosing, upon request, data and studies showing that they have a "reasonable basis" for making their claims. That Republican-chaired commission, under the Nixon Administration, said this was necessary because advertisers had refused to voluntarily disclose the information consumers needed to make rational purchasing decisions.

Once the program was in full swing, the claims of advertisers across the board came under close scrutiny. By 1978, the FTC had taken action against 22 companies, including the three major auto firms, General Electric, Sears, and General Foods. Close to 80 others were ordered to use adequate substantiation data. But the biggest impact was deterrence. A 1978 staff report to the commissioner concluded that more and more advertisers, faced with the prospect of an FTC investigation were making significant "institutional changes" in order to substantiate their claims.

So when Miller announced that he had "strong reservations" about the ad substantiation standard, even advertisers were taken aback.

Said Ralph Alexander, executive director of the National Advertising Review Board, an industry self-policing organization: "I don't think there is any particular problem [with the ad substantiation]. A responsible advertiser isn't going to make up things. . .I think everyone has learned to live with it."

Said Kent Mitchell, vice-president of General Foods: "Removal of substantiation requirements would remove the guarantor of advertising legitimacy on which consumers and advertisers now depend. It would place the ethical advertiser at a pronounced disadvantage: his message would no longer be distinguishable from those of the unscrupulous."

Faced with this reaction, Miller beat a hasty retreat in public, qualifying his criticism and suggesting he had been misinterpreted. But he does not have to move publicly, or obtain commission approval, to effectively dismantle the program. "All he has to do is not enforce the standard," said Peter Barash, staff director of the House subcommittee that oversees that FTC. "Or he can claim that there is not enough money to enforce it. He doesn't have to formally repeal any rule."

Part of that strategy is already underway. Miller proposed cutting the advertising practices' budget almost a third for 1982. And he is considering consolidating the commission's three advertising divisions into a single office more tightly under his control.

Since most of the program's actual work consists of the staff informally requesting advertisers to substantiate their claims, Miller can simply order the head of the Bureau of Consumer Protection to chill the staff's efforts. That the new bureau chief is Timothy Muris, a conservative lawyer long critical of the FTC who worked for Miller at OMB and on the transition team, makes that only more likely. Miller's remarks alone will probably embolden advertisers who might have voluntarily changed their policy to avoid an FTC lawsuit.

Despite the public rebuff, Miller's views on advertising remain radical. When we asked Miller if "there was any way that it can help consumers if an ad is misleading," he replied "not in isolation" and proceeded to offer a defense of why the government efforts to prohibit such advertising should be limited. "Since the way we deal with institutions—since the best we can do is to deal with them with a hatchet rather than a scalpel or even smaller surgical instruments—we have to think at the margin of the effects both pro and con. . .If our methods of dealing with false and misleading advertising are so strenuous in some dimension that the result is to restrain the communication of useful information we have to make the decision at the margin whether additional forays into this area are going to help consumers. . . ." Past the margin for Miller was the FTC's proposal under Pertschuk to control advertising aimed at children. Miller said he thought children of 5, 6, and 7 could respond to "some kinds" of ads. "I have three children and when they were that age I observed their behavior closely and I had no problem with the advertisements that were on TV," he said.

At the same press conference, Miller expressed doubts about the FTC program to reimburse people stuck with defective products. An extraordinarily successful effort, the program in the past few years has won for consumers $70 million in reimbursement from Chrysler and $35 million from American Honda for defective fenders, and $30 million from Ford for defective pistons, among other decisions.

Miller's problem with the program, he explained, was that it could "deprive" people of the opportunity to buy "not as high a quality product."

Those views were developed in the Reagan Administration's transition team report on the FTC, which Miller chaired. "It is important to emphasize," the group wrote, "that we should expect to find some imperfect products. Avoiding defects is not costless. . . . Those who have low aversion to risk (relative to money) will be most likely to purchase cheap nonreliable products. Those who have a greater aversion to risk will be most likely to purchase more expensive and more reliable products." Stripped of the economic jargon, that last statement roughly translates into the undeniable verity that rich people can afford higher-quality products than poor people can. That argument ignores the main issue, which is the sale of a product with defects that were not part of the way in which the product was offered for sale.

All of these themes came together in Miller's March, 1982 testimony on the FTC reauthorization. Miller rallied the commission—with Pertschuk dissenting—around a narrowed definition of unfairness that would force the commission before moving against an ad or business practice to show that: consumer injury was "economic" and "substantial;" the "injury from the alleged unfair act or practice. . .outweigh[ed] its benefits;" and that "the harm [was] one which consumers could not reasonably have avoided." On his own, without any concurring commissioners Miller proposed a further drastic reduction in the deceptive standard, suggesting that the commission be required to prove intent on the part of advertisers before acting against such ads.

"To the best of my knowledge," Pertschuk told the Senate Commerce Committee the same day, "not a single advertiser, advertising agency or advertising medium or any of their trade associations has urged upon the Commission or Congress the statutory redefinition of deception. No previous Chairman or any individual Commissioner suggested it. It is my understanding that no other present member of the Commission supports it." The results of Miller's proposed changes, Pertschuk said, are not hard to predict: "Make no mistake of it. Amending, redefining and complicating the Commission's statutory authority would serve the interest only of those fringe advertisers tempted to shave the truth, dissemble, spawn half-truths, and make claims based on flimsy, hoked-up tests."

In challenging the deception standard, Miller borrowed a technique frequently employed by Reagan: making policy by anecdote. Among the cases he has cited as FTC abuse of the standard was a complaint brought against Clairol in 1941 and one brought against a deodorant manufacturer in 1943. In raising the cases, Miller omitted the dates.

When we spoke with him, Miller raised the idea that FTC advertising regulation may "cost the consumers more by restraining the transmittal of information." When we asked for examples, Miller ducked. "Well, it's something that's very hard to document in a quantitative way," said a man who for his entire professional life has urged regulators to reduce all variables to numbers that can be tallied in a cost-benefit analysis. "I mean. . .there's anecdotal stuff around, there's common sense-type arguments—to the extent that you put companies in substantial jeopardy when they make factual claims and there exists uncertainty about how we will interpret those factual claims it certainly biases the company to rely more on imagery and puffery. . .in terms of transmitting factual information." Any proof of that, we asked? "I can't point to you, I could probably ask my staff to come up with some anecdotal evidence; I've talked to people in the advertising community who confirm that, yes, that's the way their thought processes work."

Also singled out for sharp criticism in the transition team report was the FTC's antitrust efforts. The report—still the most comprehensive guide to Miller's long-range plans as chairman—insists the FTC should "concentrate its resources. . .on horizontal collusion cases." That echoes the view taken at the Justice Department by Miller's like-minded colleague William Baxter.

The report recommends diminished attention to cases involving vertical restraints and mergers, and conglomerate mergers, asserting in the latter instance that "such mergers tend to generate efficiencies. and the Commission should be wary of standing in their way." Expanding that point, the report says that "The anticompetitive effects [of mergers] should be weighed against possible efficiencies created by the merger." That specifically contradicts the Supreme Court's 1967 ruling in the *FTC* vs. *Procter & Gamble Co.* case, in which it concluded "Possible economies cannot be used as a defense to illegality." The report also criticizes the agency's "shared monopoly cases"—erroneously, since the agency has brought only one shared monopoly case, that against the big three cereal manufacturers in 1972. (The case was brought by a Republican FTC, while Miles Kirkpatrick, a Republican antitrust scholar, was chairman.) And the report suggests backing away from the Robinson-Patman Act, which protects small businesses against unfair competition.

In our interview, Miller maintained that some previous FTC antitrust efforts had diminished competition. "I think [that's true] of some of the Robinson-Patman enforcement in the past. . . .I did not believe that the theory under which the cereal case was brought would have enhanced competition. I felt that it reduced it.

The oil case I have the same view about," he said.

Miller has buttressed these points in 1981 public statements, whose intent, numerous analysts have suggested, can hardly be lost on acquisition-minded companies and their attorneys:

November 19: "Mergers, or the threat of takeovers, pressure managers to use resources efficiently and in response to the demands of consumers."

December 1: "In my view, mergers play an important and often procompetitive role in our society."

December 9: "[I]t is axiomatic that a decision to acquire another company reflects a decision that the acquisition of those assets is a better use of the firm's capital than competing uses."

Miller told us he didn't think those statements, and similar ones by William Baxter of the Justice Department, contributed to the increased levels of mergers. "Perhaps at the margin," he said employing one of his favorite words, "but I mean if anything, the acquisition. . .that passes antitrust muster is something we shouldn't be saying is good or bad."

Miller, not surprisingly, would like to keep a voice in antitrust policy. Before Miller took over the FTC, Stockman proposed to eliminate the agency's antitrust authority by wiping out its budget for that activity. "I do not anticipate calling for the elimination of our antitrust authority," Miller told us. "There is a relevant kind of case—a binary case—that's better handled by the Justice Department: you fixed prices or you didn't, you put 'em in the slammer or you don't and the other cases which are much closer calls. . .for which I think the strongest argument [for the FTC involvement] is the panel of experts to judge close cases, rule of reason cases." Miller has called for a blue-ribbon panel to look at the state of antitrust enforcement.

From the start, Miller's views on antitrust have drawn bipartisan reproach. Even senators generally unfriendly to the FTC, such as John Danforth (R-Mo.) have told Miller that these views indicate "a singular lack of interest in the enforcement of the antitrust laws." Republic Senator Slade Gorton of Washington held up the floor vote on Miller's nomination out of concern over his antitrust policies.

The heat turned up another notch in December, 1981 when the FTC ruled on Mobil Oil's attempt to acquire Marathon Oil. Though it challenged the acquisition, the commission informed Mobil, over the objections of Pertschuk and Republican Patricia Bailey, that it might drop the suit if Mobil let go of Marathon's "transportation, storage, and marketing assets." That would leave Mobil with what it wanted in the first place: Marathon's crude reserves.

Congressional critics immediately charged that the plan offered Mobil an unprecedented "blueprint" for concluding the merger. In congressional testimony Thomas Campbell, the new director of the Bureau of Competition, was unable to cite another case in which the FTC had offered such guidance. Nonetheless, Miller expects to continue to push for similar decisions in the future. "I think we owe it to the courts and anyone else to be as specific as we can in terms of revealing our thinking on these things," he said.

The FTC challenged LTV's attempt to take over the Grumman Corp., an effort LTV eventually dropped after Grumman fiercely resisted. In January, 1982, with Miller voting in the majority, the commission voted 3-1 to drop its antitrust case against the big three cereal manufacturers. An FTC administrative law judge had already rejected the commission's contentions in the case.

Under Miller, the agency's historic independence may be compromised. In summer, 1981 the agency split 2-2 on a request from the Regulatory Relief Task Force that it "voluntarily" submit its regulations to OMB for review. Miller, the architect of the OMB review process, seems certain to support the task force's requests.

The transition report reveals another change Miller may bring. The report makes clear that he is planning a fundamental reallocation of agency resources, from fighting anti-competitive marketplace activities to battling other federal agencies seeking to regulate business. Noting that the "agency's economists in recent years have spent most of their time analyzing imperfections in the marketplace," the report suggests instead that they "analyze imperfections in regulation"—as the OMB staff now does. With the information, the report continues, the FTC could expand its program of intervening before other agencies "to highlight the inflationary impacts of proposed rules and regulations."

Currently the FTC intervenes before such bodies as the Federal Reserve Board to increase the amount of credit information available to consumers, and the Interstate Commerce Commission to press for accelerated elimination of industry-supported government rules that keep up trucking prices. Miller supports trucking deregulation—he has consulted for the FTC on the issue—but judging by his record, the more likely targets for agency economists in his administration will be the health and safety agencies. Such a move would be a radical shift in the agency's emphasis.

Said one former top Bureau of Competition official: "The danger to the commission from Miller's ascension is that he will use public resources to create a public American Enterprise Institute and the law enforcement responsibilities of the commission will be neglected entirely." Miller said he would intervene in health and safety regulatory prodeedings "to the degree that we can say something about competitive effects."

Miller's commitment to that goal will be tested by three flatly anticompetitive government interventions supported by the White House: reimposing IATA cartelization over North Atlantic flights, and protecting maritime subsidies and agricultural marketing orders. "We are looking for an appropriate forum in which to say some things about IATA and competition in the airlines generally," Miller said. "We will be making comments on [legislation regarding maritime subsidies]. On marketing orders, I would anticipate—you realize that the 1980 act keeps us out of certain agricultural things—consistent to the degree that we can comment on that I would anticipate having comments."

Miller also plans basic changes in the agency's relationship with business and the public. Two recommendations in the transition report would sharply cut public access to the agency. The report recommends, as did OMB in its original budget proposal, the elimination of the FTC's regional offices, which provide much of the agency's public outreach. Cuts proposed in the 1983 budget would eliminate four of the agency's 10 regional offices.

It also suggests elimination of the agency's intervenor funding program, which aides citizens and small business that otherwise lack the funds to participate in agency proceedings. That funding was ended in the 1982 budget. On public participation funding, Miller said, "I start from the following perspective: Public participation I think is a very, very useful institutional device where agencies are likely to be captured." Those agencies likely to be captured are "where you have an agency regulating a single industry," he continued, such as the Civil Aeronautics Board ("that agency was in a sense very much captured"), the Interstate Commerce Commission, the Federal Maritime Commission and the Agriculture Department. But agencies such as the FTC or the Environmental Protection Agency that regulate a broad spectrum of interests are not likely to be "captured," Miller believes. In any case, "As I think most any impartial observer will tell you. . .the influence that the staff has overwhelms the influence all the other parties have," he said. When staff information should be supplemented by outside studies, those needs should "be filled by other means," Miller concluded.

At the same time, the report supports increased access for business groups. "What is critical for a new commission, symbolically and in terms of real policies, is to create a perception on the part of the private sector that its input is respected," the study notes. During his tenure at OMB, Miller met almost exclusively with business groups, including the U.S. Chamber of Commerce, the Chemical Manufacturers Association, General Motors, Ford, and the National Association of Manufacturers. To head the FTC's congressional liaison office, Miller selected a former lobbyist for the Grocery Manufacturers of America.

As part of the increased reliance on industry, Miller's transition report advises the FTC to "rely more heavily on the monitoring of industry self-regulation and less on the setting of industry-wide standards." In recent years, the commission has moved aggressively to consider industry-wide standards affecting such groups as funeral directors, used car dealers, and advertisers.

Miller, the first economist to head the FTC, will also support a greater role for the agency's economists. That will be part of a redirection of agency efforts from what he terms "social theories" to the promotion of "economic efficiency"—presumably through opposition to governmment regulation, and a more lenient attitude toward mergers. "The danger in this focus on regulation," said the former Bureau of Competition official, "is that this will be the primary work or only use of those resources, as opposed to using them to enforce the merger laws or go after potential monopolists."

Miller's appointments to key staff positions reflects the ascension of economists. As director of the Bureau of Consumer Protection, Miller selected Muris, an economist as well as an attorney. He is also one of the FTC's most extreme critics. In a 1981 book on the agency, he suggested "a five-year moratorium on budget increases. . .a freeze that, given inflation, would effectively halve the agency." Muris also urges use of cost-benefit analysis, and concluded "there appears no harm. . .and some chance for benefit" from abolishing the agency's adjudicatory authority in antitrust cases. As director of the Bureau of Competition, Miller selected Thomas Campbell, a young economist/attorney who received his Ph.D. in economics from the University of Chicago, which has been the leading force in developing the "bigness is not necessarily badness" theme trumpeted by the Administration. As director of the Bureau of Economics, Miller chose Robert D. Tollison, an economics professor from Virginia Polytechnic Institute who served on the Administration transition teams for the FTC and environmental policy.

A more touchy situation for Miller will be the agency's efforts to break down the anticompetitive self-regulatory practices of the professions. Philosophically, Miller supports such efforts. But the lawyers and doctors are sure to make their opposition known to the Administration, which is sure to be sympathetic. The transition report reflects his ambivalence, concluding that the "Commission should pursue such activities with vigor," but avoid action "where there is evidence that [a] state has weighed the competitive consequence of the practice at issue." Miller has testified against efforts by the professions to be exempted from FTC oversight.

With Miller sitting in the chairman's seat and one of its most fervent opponents, David Stockman, running the Administration's budget, the FTC is likely to face some very difficult years. Miller only halfheartedly defends the agency from Stockman's celebrated comment that "If you eliminated the FTC, the world would never know the difference."

"Probably in terms of the aggregate benefits and costs imposed by the FTC given its track record at the time, I wouldn't disagree with that statement," he said. "I would disagree with it today and he would probably retract the statement today."

And there is no budget cut that Miller could not live with. Reagan plans to cut the FTC budget steadily throughout the 1980s, but Miller doesn't see the agency ceasing to function at any budget level. "You've got marginal benefits and marginal costs for any kind of activity and where these lines cross. . . it is a continuum of activities that the Federal Trade Commission or most other regulatory agencies could get involved in. And I've heard some people say if you had a $50 million budget that's tantamount to shutting down; or if you have a $25 million budget that's tantamount to shutting down. It means, no, it doesn't mean that you're shutting down, it means you're doing fewer things. Realistically. . . even whatever the skill of management— given the skill of management—you're going to be able to do less things on $25 million than you could do with $50 million and less with $50 million than you could do with $60 million," he said.

Partially because of the budget, Miller expects that under his direction "there will be less numbers of regulations issued by the Federal Trade Commission." Miller said he "thinks" he can get FTC lawyers to work harder. But such "management" initiatives are the hubris of each new incoming Administration—and in this case an oft-used smokescreen for debilitating budget cuts. When we asked Miller how a representative group of business executives might sum up his tenure at some date in the future, he said, "I would hope they would say Miller is doing a good job, the FTC is a respected institution, we feel like we're being treated fairly, but also Miller's effective."

Miller's true constituency—the people who buy the products produced by those leaders—are likely to remember him as the only chairman who ever proposed to statutorily diminish the agency's powers, the man that the Administration trusted to shut off the FTC during the era of Reagan.

FINANCIAL BACKGROUND

Miller comes from OMB under a cloud. During a stormy congressional hearing in June, 1981, he ran into stiff questioning when he asserted that his private meetings with industry groups did not cover regulations affecting those industries that were later reviewed by the task force. In a written submission to the House Subcommittee on Oversight and Investigations, Miller reported that most of the meetings dealt with nothing more specific than "support for regulatory relief."

But as Rep. Albert Gore (D-Tenn.) noted, the timing of several meetings opened that claim to question. Miller, for example, met with the Chemical Manufacturers Association on February 23, 1981—one month before the presidential task force ordered the review of regulations governing the disposal of hazardous wastes. Miller maintained that the subject of hazardous wastes did not come up during the meeting. Gore was skeptical to the point of incredulity.

Gore, the subcommittee, and the Congressional Research Service were concerned that industries could short-circuit the regulatory process through private meetings with sympathetic OMB officials such as Miller. In the context of an FTC chairmanship, that makes Miller's potential conflict more ideological than economic.

During 1980, Miller received a salary of $46,807 from the American Enterprise Institute; he earned another $22,507 from Economic Impact Analysts, Inc., a consulting firm for which Miller is chairman of the board. His clients included General Motors, Carborundum Company and the U.S. Civil Aeronautics Board.

As chairman, Miller stirred more controversy when he accepted a trip to Australia in March, 1982. The trip was paid for by the Advertising Federation of Australia, which includes many U.S. advertising agency giants obviously interested in Miller's views on a number of issues. Miller accepted the trip after the FTC's general counsel orally advised him that it didn't create any impropriety. "Let me tell you how it came up," Miller said. "First of all, I really haven't had a break since the election, literally the election." So it was a vacation, we asked? "No it was not. I haven't had a break," he repeated. "And I was asked to go to Australia and my first reaction was that would be nice, I've never been to Australia, I'd really like a break, but I can't expect the American taxpayer to send me to Australia." On the other hand, Miller told us the trip gave him "an opportunity to visit my brother who I haven't seen in several years. . .[and] was a combination of business and pleasure.

"I was damned tired," he said a few moments later. "I wanted a break and this looked like a good break to take. And I did it and that's it."

Miller met with government officials, and spoke to the U.S. Chambers of Commerce in Sydney and Melbourne but no consumer groups during the trip. That fits into his domestic pattern: none of his speeches through March, 1982 have been to consumer groups.

WHAT OTHERS ARE SAYING ABOUT HIM

- George Eads, a former member of the Council of Economic Advisers and a long-time friend of Miller's (he recommended Miller for his first government job), said "I don't think they have nearly as much respect for the agencies, and the professionals within the agencies as they should. I'm disappointed in Jim's general approach to the process of getting people to do things, which is to show them you've got the power to make them do it. I'm not totally surprised though."

  Eads, who has been critical of the regulatory agencies in the past, thinks the current efforts at OMB go too far: "I am disappointed in the tack they are taking with the executive order. I think they are politicizing the regulatory oversight process to an unfortunate degree."

- Pertschuk remained relatively quiet during the first few months of Miller's reign, but in January, 1982 he sharply criticized Miller's policies in two speeches. Of Miller and his key appointments, Pertschuk said: "their simplistic faith in the benign workings of the unfettered marketplace has an Alice-in-Wonderland quality about it."

- "He's a dedicated ideologue," said one congressional staffer who knows him. "There's no negotiating with him."

- Testifying against Miller's nomination, Mark Green, the former director of Congress Watch, said, "to appoint a pro-corporate cheerleader the head of an agency policing corporations is like making prisoners warders. The selection of people such as James Miller to this consumer agency is tantamount to repealing the 1914 FTC Act without bothering to go to Congress."

- One long-time Miller associate expects some frustrations for him at the commission. "The conflict with Miller at the FTC will be that he philosophically would be interested in deregulating the professions, but the Administration won't support it; he's less interested in the other stuff—mergers and so on—that the Administration considers priorities [for the FTC]."

LEGAL SERVICES CORPORATION

BOARD MEMBERS

RESPONSIBILITY OF OFFICE

In 1974, Congress established the Legal Services Corporation as a private, non-profit organization to insulate legal assistance for the poor from political pressures. The program was formerly carried out by the Federal Office of Economic Opportunity and the Community Services Administration. The Corporation is governed by an eleven-member Board of Directors, appointed by the President with the advice and consent of the Senate. With funds provided through Congressional appropriations, the Corporation distributes grants to some 320 legal services programs operating in about 1,200 neighborhood offices throughout the fifty states, the District of Columbia, Puerto Rico, the Virgin Islands and Micronesia.

As created by Congress, the Corporation operates under a number of restrictions. For example, the Hatch Act, which prohibits government employees from participating in partisan political activities, applies to Legal Services Corporation attorneys. In addition, programs which receive money from the Legal Services Corporation cannot provide legal assistance in school desegregation, non-therapeutic abortion, and armed forces desertion cases, or in cases involving certain violations of the Selective Services Act.

The Legal Services Corporation funds full-time staff attorney programs, and low-fee "judicare programs" in which private attorneys handle cases on a volunteer basis.

In 1981, the Corporation operated with a budget of $321 million, funding 6,200 attorneys. Both these figures sharply declined in 1982. (See Major Issues.)

BACKGROUND

President Reagan has frequently appointed as heads of agencies people who oppose their purpose. The Legal Services Corporation fared no differently. Below are profiles of two board members expected to be the most active. A weekly trumpet of the new right, *Human Events*, heralded these appointments as "a big plus for conservatives. Not only is it now probable that some of the most bizarre grants can be turned off, but the new board is likely to revise the astonishing regulations drawn up by the old board which made it virtually impossible to shut down some of the more dangerous legal services programs."

WILLIAM J. OLSON

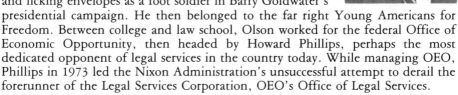

After serving a two-month stint as acting chairman of the Legal Services Corporation Board of Directors in early 1982, Olson was not nominated as permanent chair. A thirty-two-year old lawyer who friends dub an "affable conservative" and the more strident *Human Events* terms a "stalwart Reaganite," Olson has been active in Virginia politics and has worked on some publications issued by the conservative American Enterprise Institute.

Olson's political baptism consisted of knocking on doors and licking envelopes as a foot soldier in Barry Goldwater's presidential campaign. He then belonged to the far right Young Americans for Freedom. Between college and law school, Olson worked for the federal Office of Economic Opportunity, then headed by Howard Phillips, perhaps the most dedicated opponent of legal services in the country today. While managing OEO, Phillips in 1973 led the Nixon Administration's unsuccessful attempt to derail the forerunner of the Legal Services Corporation, OEO's Office of Legal Services.

Phillips now heads the Conservative Caucus's Committee to Defeat Legal Services. Located in Falls Church, Virginia, the group has spent $200,000 in a vigorous lobbying effort to scrap the program. As for the Legal Service Board appointees, including his former employee, Phillips has no comment. "The Conservative Caucus has not involved itself in support or opposition to President Reagan's nominees to the Legal Services Board," he told us. "Our position is the Legal Services Corporation ought to be eliminated and that President Reagan is to be faulted for not having vetoed the continuing resolution which carried for its authorization and appropriation."

After leaving OEO, Olson entered the University of Richmond Law School graduating in 1976. He is a partner with the general practice law firm of Smiley, Murphey, Olson, and Gilman in Washington, D.C., which specializes in litigation before the Postal Rate Commission. The firm represents the March of Dimes Birth Defects Foundation and the Third Class Nonprofit Mailers Alliance.

Olson, according to James McClellan, chief counsel of Senate Judiciary's Subcommittee on Separation of Power, "is very active in pro-life activities and in the conservative movement generally. . . .He doesn't hesitate to let his views be known and let the chips fall where they may." He worked with the American Enterprise Institute on studies of tuition tax credits and national health insurance.

Although Olson has made few formal statements on the Legal Services Corporation, Congressional observers expect him to be the Administration's hatchet man on the board. Olson headed Reagan's transition team on the Legal Services Corporation and many suspect his final report recommended scuttling the Corporation. Olson has steadfastly refused to disclose the report. "If it is true Mr. Olson supported the position to abolish the Legal Services Corporation, then the public should know about the contents of the Team Report and the position taken by its chairman," said Susan Kellock, executive director of the Equal Justice Foundation.

Born on November 23, 1949 in Paterson, New Jersey, Olson received his undergraduate degree in 1971 from Brown. His wife, Jan, is executive director of the House Republican Conference, chaired by Jack Kemp (R-N.Y.).

WILLIAM F. HARVEY

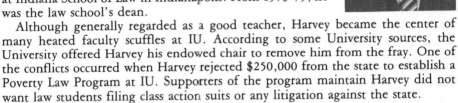

Serving on the board of advisers to the Pacific Legal Foundation's College and Public Interest Law Program—a recruiting and training program for the Foundation—Harvey was named chairman of the Legal Services Corporation's Board of Directors until the board meets in October, 1982. He takes a straight, hard conservative line on all social issues in which he has expressed public positions.

Harvey has taught law for 21 years and is now a professor at Indiana School of Law in Indianapolis. From 1973-79, he was the law school's dean.

Although generally regarded as a good teacher, Harvey became the center of many heated faculty scuffles at IU. According to some University sources, the University offered Harvey his endowed chair to remove him from the fray. One of the conflicts occurred when Harvey rejected $250,000 from the state to establish a Poverty Law Program at IU. Supporters of the program maintain Harvey did not want law students filing class action suits or any litigation against the state.

While dean, Harvey authored and helped pass a state rule requiring applicants to the Indiana bar to have taken prescribed courses. Critics say this "core curriculum" mandated many of the most business-oriented courses. Subsequently most Indiana law schools have integrated the courses into their curricula.

In another move that sparked dissent, Harvey supported an Indiana University Semester-in-Washington program, administered by the right-wing Lincoln Center for Legal Studies. When IU law professors got wind that an outside group would be running a program which granted IU credit, they requested information about the Center and its funding. The Center refused to disclose the information, so after one semester, the faculty rejected the program. The Center, located in Arlington, Virginia, is directed by a colleague of Harvey's, former IU law professor Bill Stanmeyer.

As for political positions, Harvey told one interviewer that he "has always been a supporter of Reagan." In 1981 Senate Judiciary Committee testimony, he opposed court ordered busing as a means of school desegregation. During the Indianapolis school *de jure* segregation case, Harvey served as counsel to a school district that was fighting busing. He also wrote briefs for the state in opposition to the countywide school desegregation remedy. In this effort, he opposed legal services organization which was supporting busing.

In a 1978 *Human Events* article, Harvey took to task a government policy denying tax breaks to racially segregated schools—recently stirred up by the Reagan Administration's own floundering on the issue. He blasted the policy, saying it had no moral or legal foundation.

On behalf of the Pacific Legal Foundation, Harvey also wrote a brief for the Supreme Court in the controversial reverse-discrimination suit brought by Allen Bakke against the University of California Medical School at Davis. Harvey argued the quota system ruled constitutional in the case was "illegal, immoral, unconstitutional, inherently wrong and destructive to a democratic society." The Pacific Legal Foundation supported Bakke, the white applicant in the case.

A prolific writer, Harvey has authored 13 volumes on civil procedure and evidence and recently contributed an article to *A Blueprint for Judicial Review*, a book critiquing the American legal system underwritten by the arch-conservative Free

Congress Foundation. Harvey's contribution focused on rolling back federal regulations. Another article in the report called for the elimination of the Legal Services Corporation.

A 1959 graduate of Georgetown Law School and 1954 graduate of the University of Missouri, Harvey clerked for the Honorable John A. Danaher (1960) on the United States Court of Appeals for the District of Columbia, and for Hon. Thomas Quinn (1959) on the District of Columbia Court of Appeals.

Born on November 20, 1932 in Eldon, Missouri, Harvey belongs to the bar in Indiana, Virginia, and D.C. He is married with two children.

MAJOR ISSUES

From bitter experience in California Ronald Reagan knows how a determined legal service corporation can force an Administration to tailor its aims to the laws. In his haste to turn around the state bureaucracy in Sacramento and implement budget cuts similar to those proposed today, Reagan sought to take some legal shortcuts. When he did, he ran into the federally-funded California Rural Legal Assistance, which took him to court on several occasions and won important cases, including one overturning proposed cuts in the state medicaid program.

With that history, few congressional analysts were surprised when Reagan added to his attack on the social programs of the Great Society an effort to eliminate the Legal Services Corporation. The Administration understood that the nonpartisan, nonprofit corporation—designed by statute to help the poor secure their legal rights—might help the poor defend themselves against slashes in federal assistance programs.

Reagan initially sought to eliminate federally supported legal services in his 1982 budget. Despite heated lobbying by the Administration, Congress refused to eliminate the LSC, but did trim the corporation's funding 25 percent (to $241 million), and place new restrictions on its activities. Legal services attorneys can no longer advocate before legislative bodies, press equal opportunity cases for homosexuals, or file class action suits. Nevertheless, in its 1983 budget, the Administration has once again recommended scuttling the program.

"Our position is now, as it has been, that the Administration does not want a legal services program. . . ." wrote presidential Counselor Edwin Meese III in a letter to House Republican leader Robert Michel last year.

Reagan's intention to abolish the seven-year-old LSC became clear in March, 1981 when he proposed that the states provide legal aid to the poor through social block grants. Congressional critics argued that it would be illegal for the Administration to turn LSC money over to the states. As the law stands now, states can receive money from the corporation only if the LSC board decides that legal services would not otherwise be adequately provided. Congress included that provision in the act creating the LSC because many states—with California under Reagan's leadership a case in point—tried to jettison local legal services programs in the late 1960s.

"Those block grants would inexorably eliminate the whole function in this country that legal programs serve," said Rep. Robert Kastenmeier (D-Wis.), who heads the House subcommittee overseeing the LSC. "I'm not optimistic that legal services would survive given the pressure of limited resources through block grants."

The grants were part of a two-part strategy. The Administration's plan was to eventually allow the states, through local bar associations, to pay private lawyers to represent the poor. This would have delivered a crippling blow to the current system where most legal services for the poor are provided by full-time LSC lawyers. Furthermore, states that have tried such systems have found them incapable of handling more than a fraction of the cases now handled for 1.5 million poor people a year by 6,000 LSC attorneys, according to the American Bar Association.

Although the LSC dates back only to 1974, federally funded legal services have been provided since 1965, when the Office of Economic Opportunity set up its first legal aid programs.

Legal aid lawyers spend much of their time counseling and handling routine civil cases: utility cutoffs, Social Security eligibility, bankruptcy, divorce and family law, housing and consumer complaints. But in the past 15 years they have also shouldered and won class action suits on abortion funding restrictions, eviction rules, treatment of migrant workers and illegitimate children, and similar poverty-related problems. While these sweeping class action suits make up only one percent of all LSC cases, they are the major burr for conservatives, who contend that the legal aid lawyers are using government funds to spur social reform.

"Whatever the issue, be it OSHA, busing, transsexual benefits claims, election law, expunging arrest records, private schools, conscription, and even national defense, the poverty lawyers are being subsidized at public expense to propogate their private views of what is good for the poor and what is good for the country," thunders Howard Phillips, national director of the Conservative Caucus.

But Dan J. Bradley, outgoing president of the LSC, said the class action suits are the most cost-effective way to tackle broad problems. "If you have a problem affecting a large number of people—a rent control ordinance, for instance—it is simply more efficient to have one lawyer file on behalf of all affected eligible clients than to tie up two hundred lawyers with two hundred suits," noted Bradley. "The legal issue is identical whether it's one suit or two hundred."

Last year, the LSC hit its target of providing two attorneys per 10,000 eligible clients. The corporation still hasn't come close to covering the demand for legal assistance, although the program is known for its tight management. Less than two percent of the LSC's $321 million 1981 budget was spent on administration and overhead; the rest went to client services. "We are still, though, turning away seven out of eight eligible clients due to lack of resources," said Charles Dorsey, chairman of the Project Advisory Group, a national organization of legal aid employees.

"Without this program," echoed Senate Minority Whip Alan Cranston (D-Calif.), "the poor people of this country would be deprived of access to our system of justice. . . .It is a very vital part of the American system of Justice."

And the American public seems to agree. An April, 1981 CBS/*New York Times* poll indicated that 83 percent of those polled supported the same level of funding or an increase for legal services for the poor, while only 13 percent favored a decrease in spending. Even among those who "generally approved" of Reagan's economic program, 80 percent favored the same level of funding or an increase for legal services.

The Administration's jaundiced view of legal services has met strong resistance from legal aid lawyers, the American Bar Association, and legal service supporters in Congress.

Eliminating the LSC, said ABA President David Brink, "would effectively deny access to justice to the bulk of this nation's poor. . .[terminating the LSC] in the long term, would cost this nation far more than any immediate dollars served." A petition supporting the LSC was signed by 52 business leaders including, Robert

Anderson, chairman of Atlantic Richfield; Roy Anderson, chairman of Lockheed Corp.; John Filer, chairman of Aetna Life & Casualty Co.; Reginald Jones, former chairman of General Electric; Thomas Murphy, former chairman of General Motors; and Irving Shapiro, former chairman of DuPont.

To shore up his position for the 1983 budget battle, Reagan took steps to cement his control of LSC. During the Christmas 1981 congressional recess, he made recess appointments for ten of the 11 LSC board seats. The White House argued that the nominees could make binding decisions until confirmed by the Senate—a position legal service advocates dispute. Eventually, in March, 1982, Reagan made nine permanent appointments. In addition to Olson, Sandstrom and Harvey, Reagan named:

- George Paras. A Sacramento business lawyer and former judge for California Third District Court of Appeals (appointed by then governor Reagan), Paras opposes affirmative action and is lobbying the California Senate to eliminate government-mandated affirmative action programs. Paras, who admits knowing little about the LSC, says he favors having the legal profession, not the government, provide aid to the poor.

- Robert Sherwood Stubbs. A Missouri native and executive assistant to the attorney general of Georgia, Stubbs has directed the state's defense against numerous legal services units, including a challenge to conditions in Georgia state prisons.

- William Earl. A late appointment, Earl works largely on environmental issues with the Miami firm of Peeples, Earl, Moore & Blank.

- Howard Dana Jr. Reagan's campaign manager in Maine, he helped legal services attorneys win a suit in the Supreme Court, forcing the state to pay for legal fees in some civil rights cases.

- Clarence McKee. A black Washington attorney who worked with legal services programs in college, he believes private attorneys should have more of a role in aiding the poor.

- Harold DeMoss. A Houston, Texas, lawyer specializing in real estate and oil and gas law.

- Ann Slaughter. She has worked with organizations helping crime victims for the past ten years.

Reagan still has two more slots to fill on the board.

CHAPTER 6

NATIONAL SECURITY

DEFENSE DEPARTMENT

CASPAR WEINBERGER
SECRETARY

RESPONSIBILITY OF OFFICE

Weinberger presides over the largest department in the
federal government. With nearly 1 million civilian employees housed in the world's largest office building, the
Pentagon far outstrips every other agency in physical size.
Only the Department of Health and Human Services, which
oversees a myriad of entitlement and health programs, has a
larger budget than the Pentagon's, which in fiscal year 1982 will reach $218.9
billion.

The Defense Department, established in 1949 as the successor to the National
Military Establishment, is responsible for providing forces to deter war and protect
the national security. These forces include the Army, Navy, Marine Corps and Air
Force—consisting of about 2 million men and women on active duty.

Under the direction of the President, who is designated the military's
commander-in-chief under the Constitution, Weinberger directs all aspects of the
Defense Department and serves as the President's chief adviser on military matters.
Weinberger has also been a visible public spokesman on both national and international security issues.

BACKGROUND

In the cavernous office of the secretary of Defense an intricate master switchboard
stands ready to connect the office with the White House, each leg of the nation's
strategic triad, military commanders around the world. In front of the switchboard,
on the secretary's desk, sits a much less obtrusive jar of jellybeans.

The jellybeans mark the office's current occupant, Caspar Weinberger, as a
Reagan man, a veteran of the hectic California years when Reagan transformed
himself from citizen politician to a national hero of the right.

Physically, Weinberger seems better suited for the jellybeans than the control
board. A short but solid Harvard-trained lawyer who reads Shakespeare,
Weinberger is a gracious host who somehow acts calm and unhurried despite his
harried schedule.

When Reagan named his old buddy Weinberger to manage the largest peacetime
military buildup in the republic's history, the right went into a frenzy. After all,
Weinberger was best known as "Cap the Knife," the hard-eyed budget director
who prided himself on cutting military expenditures as much as social programs.
"At a time when those in charge of the Pentagon need to be able to muster the
nation for a call to arms, Ronald Reagan has given us a man of little military experience and with a reputation for cutting budgets," moaned conservative columnist
William P. Hoar shortly after Weinberger's nomination.

If any of them had dug through the records of Weinberger's days as Nixon's budget man and come across a statement he made at the American Enterprise Institute (AEI) in 1972, they would have groaned. Sounding more like Ted Kennedy than Ronald Reagan, Weinberger told the group:

"The identification of a threat to security does not automatically require an expenditure in the defense budget to neutralize it. The nation's total resources being limited, it is necessary to consider what is being given up to meet the threat. Some may feel it more important to invest money in education or health than to provide what they consider remote contingencies in the national security field. The defense budget, in short, must be seen not only in terms of what we must defend ourselves against but what we have to defend. The more we take from the common wealth for its defense the smaller it becomes."

But the right was wrong. Even in the face of massive budget deficits that have sent Wall Street running for cover, Weinberger has successfully faced off Stockman and defended nearly every tank, missile, and machine gun, every esoteric, gold-plated weapon system that has come across his desk. On arms control, on Poland, on trade with the Soviets, Weinberger has taken a harder line than even the most virulent hawks in the Administration.

But to some extent Weinberger's reputation, and indeed some of his own rhetoric about military spending, is misleading. Hawks would have been less uneasy—and doves more alarmed—had they closely scrutinized Weinberger's actual performance as budget director. For, even then, Weinberger considered the military something of a sacred cow. And while he bragged of holding the line on defense spending in one breath, he argued for the development of new and costly weapons systems—including the B-1 bomber and the Trident submarine—in the next.

In the AEI discussion ten years ago, for example, Weinberger vehemently argued against further cuts in the $76.5 billion military budget. His budget plan for fiscal year 1974, which set a spending ceiling and called for the elimination of dozens of Great Society programs—most of which he considered worthless in the fight against poverty—also included a military budget that was the largest since World War II.

"He is one of the few genuine anti-communist cold warriors in Washington," said Admiral Gene LaRocque, director of the Center for Defense Information, who participated in that AEI discussion and debated Weinberger about the necessity of curbing spending on several military programs (all of which Weinberger adamantly defended). "He believes this [cold war] stuff and now he's in a position to do something about it."

Weinberger seems to take a certain delight in disproving the right's predictions about him. Despite his serene manner, the secretary's words are nonetheless sharply militaristic. When we asked what he considered his most shocking experience upon taking over the Pentagon, Weinberger stumbled a moment, muttering about the immensity of his new domain. Then, he said:

"Well, let me put it this way. The principal shock was to find out, through daily briefings, the extent and size of the Soviet build-up and the rapidity with which it had taken place—in all areas, land, sea and air."

It is understandable that the right cringed when Weinberger's name popped up for the top Pentagon spot. Even as a young state legislator in Sacramento during the 1950s Weinberger was considered a "liberal" Republican. He was the ring-leader of a group of dynamic, young Republicans who rode into office determined to clean up the state government. "He was the kind of Republican who believed in moving forward," said A. Alan Post, who served as California's widely respected legislative analyst from 1949 to 1977. Together Post and Weinberger orchestrated an investigation of California's corrupt liquor licensing practices that resulted in the prosecution of public officials and a reorganization of the state's liquor licensing procedures. Weinberger pursued that case, said Post, "with all the vigor he had at his command."

But if Weinberger's zeal earned him kudos with voters, it also brought acrimony from conservatives. During an unsuccessful bid for the state Attorney General post, broadcaster Fulton Lewis, Jr. accused Weinberger of being the state Communist Party's candidate. Lewis had apparently extrapolated from a commentary in the Communist Party press praising Weinberger for being "smart enough to assess correctly the force of the oft-mentioned political winds blowing in the land today." Though Weinberger won a retraction, the damage had been done. As state Republican chair, Weinberger later infuriated conservative Republicans—some of whom, like Holmes Tuttle and Henry Salvatori, became financiers of Reagan's gubernatorial campaign—when he favored Rockefeller over Goldwater in the 1964 presidential race though as chairman he professed neutrality. During that year Weinberger also helped block the far right from gaining control of the central committee.

Worse, though, Weinberger supported former San Francisco Mayor George Christopher over Reagan in the 1966 gubernatorial primary before joining Reagan's campaign in the general election. So it was no surprise that Weinberger, who actively campaigned for an appointment, was initially passed over for the state finance director position. But when Reagan's initial choice quit after a year of havoc, the job went to Weinberger.

Once on the Reagan team, Weinberger's politics quickly began to reflect the character of his boss. "He became a very skillful apologist for what Ronald Reagan wanted," said Post, who himself was asked to become Reagan's finance director but turned down the position. (At one point Weinberger had come to Post asking him how he could get the finance director post. "I told him I couldn't help him," said Post.)

With California legislators, Weinberger earned a reputation for being less than honest in his attempts to shore up support for the governor's initiatives. "He was more brilliant, unquestionably than [Verne] Orr," his successor, explained Post, but far less candid. "He would tend to elaborate in a way that was not necessarily true. He was more inclined to fabricate a rationale that was specious. He acted like a good lawyer taking the side of his client."

Former Republican Assembly Leader Robert Monagan noted that because Weinberger had served in the legislature and was thoroughly conversant with the state government by the time he became state finance director, "Cap chose to ignore the legislature a little bit." Monagan was part of a group of state Republican leaders that recommended Weinberger for the finance job.

Weinberger presided over economic policies best described as erratic. In the wake of familiar campaign promises to cut taxes, Reagan in his first year enacted the largest state tax increase in American history. When the hike left the state with an embarrassing surplus Reagan, with Weinberger as his principal spokesman, insisted on highly touted "rebates"—which were directed at a different sector than the tax hikes—and left the state in the hole, forcing Reagan to raise taxes again. Weinberger's proposed 1970 finance plan included another tax hike. (The per capita tax burden in California during the Reagan administration doubled, and left behind a burgeoning state surplus that led to the state's widespread tax revolt.)

Weinberger's next government service, this time in Washington, changed his credentials once again to a "liberal" Republican. Richard Nixon in 1969 delivered a consumer message to Congress saying "the time has now come for the reactivation and revitalization of the Federal Trade Commission (FTC)." At that time the commission was smarting from criticism that it had devolved into a consumer complaint bureau, with no systematic method for consumer protection. So Nixon plucked Weinberger out of California, where he had earned a reputation, as Nixon put it, for being able to "get good fiscal trends going," and gave him carte blanche to revitalize the FTC.

During a six-month spree, Weinberger reorganized the commission along its two major functions—creating the Bureau of Competition, to handle antitrust matters and the Bureau of Consumer Protection as the commission's consumer protection arm. He also successfully skirted civil service rules in purging the agency—and paved the way for more activist blood—by abolishing the jobs of attorneys he wanted to fire, then offering them unattractive positions or convincing them to "retire". Only 13 of the 31 top level staff members survived.

During his reign, the FTC issued a damning report on automobile quality control and warranty performance. The Weinberger commission urged stronger regulation of the automobile industry and the creation of an automobile regulatory agency that would set minimum quality performance standards.

The conclusion irked GOP conservatives and added to Weinberger's reputation as a liberal. But, as current FTC Commissioner Michael Pertschuk remarked, "I doubt that Caspar Weinberger [today] would claim his early intellectual off-spring, born in that era of high consumerism." As Pertschuk notes, nowhere in the pages of the report "does one find so much as a discussion of the costs of providing such protection or of the trade-offs between such costs and benefits to consumers." In contrast, the Reagan Administration, as part of its regulatory "reform" program, has required that the benefits of proposed regulations outweigh their costs.

Weinberger is credited with carrying out Nixon's stated goal of reviving the FTC, though Weinberger's current boss no doubt wishes Nixon and Weinberger simply let the agency fall further into inaction.

It was in his third Washington post, as director of the Office of Management and Budget (OMB)—he also briefly served as deputy director—that Weinberger earned the sobriquet "Cap the Knife" for his willingness to stand up to even the most powerful backers of federal programs. But that respected reputation had another side: At OMB Weinberger was known for being somewhat single-minded, often riding roughshod over representatives of federal programs even when they presented valid arguments. "I couldn't make up my mind whether he was a deep man or just stubborn," remarked one former high OMB budget officer.

He also played hardball with Capitol Hill. When Congress refused to keep spending on social programs down, Weinberger chastised them in the press. When that didn't work, he used the controversial technique of impounding federal funds, a tool which Congress later banned and which Weinberger's current boss in the Oval Office has sought to reinstate.

Nixon later appointed Weinberger Health, Education and Welfare (HEW) secretary. Together with his successor at OMB, Roy Ash, Weinberger continued controlling spending on social programs through impoundment. In fiscal year 1973 $1.1 billion in federal health funds alone were impounded. Particularly hard hit were schools in the health professions which were already facing a severe financial squeeze from low enrollments. The American Association of Colleges of Podiatric Medicine, among others, sued both Weinberger and Ash; a federal judge later ordered release of the funds.

Weinberger's attempt to curtail or end a number of HEW programs earned him the wrath of liberals in Congress, civil rights activists, and groups representing the poor and aged. But most of Weinberger's attempts were frustrated by those groups in the Democratically-controlled Congress. Ironically, during his term, the department grew more rapidly than under his predecessors.

On regulatory issues Weinberger's record was vastly different. Unlike any of his predecessors, Weinberger took a bold stand against the politically powerful pharmaceutical lobby and imposed the first federal price ceiling on prescription drugs used in government medical programs. He twice asked Congress to enact legislation limiting the tar and nicotine in cigarettes, and took on a stiff anti-smoking position that not even the White House fully supported.

Weinberger also introduced Nixon's proposal for a national health insurance plan in 1974. The Administration plan was in large part a response to more comprehensive health legislation already in Congress, such as that proposed by Sen. Edward Kennedy (D-Mass.) which Weinberger asserted had "huge unsupportable costs" and was objectionable because of its plan for "heavy involvement of government."

Weinberger also argued in favor of a negative income tax for the poor to replace a number of welfare programs. "Principally," he said, this plan "gets money to those who need it directly and quickly, just as a tax cut puts money into the economy [without dictating] to people what priorities they should have in their personal budgets."

Weinberger resigned his job at HEW in 1975, saying he wanted to move back to California where the climate would relieve his wife's arthritis. He joined Bechtel Corporation of San Francisco, a large federal contractor, in a newly created position of "special counsel"—part of the construction corporation's strategy of recruiting former bureaucrats to direct in-house engineers and managers. Weinberger followed George Schultz, former secretary of Labor and of the Treasury, among others.

Weinberger was elected vice-president and director of the company. Away from government during these years, Weinberger told us, he "earned a comfortable living and had a generally easy life." Weinberger's sympathies for Arab nations in the Middle East can be traced to his tenure at Bechtel, which constructs joint public works projects with Saudi Arabia. Weinberger often traveled to Saudi Arabia and worked with top officials from that country. "When I was at Bechtel," he told the *Washington Post*, "I nearly always went to the ambassador's house and he would have some of the [Saudi officials] there. It was just informal. But it did give you an opportunity to learn quite a bit about the country and about the thought and about the way in which they viewed the U.S."

Reagan's nomination of Weinberger to the Defense Department post came as a surprise to close observers. William Van Cleave, a staunch hawk and professor of international relations at the University of Southern California who is considered an expert on defense issues, headed Reagan's transition team on military matters, but was passed over in favor of Weinberger, a Reagan budget adviser. Van Cleave reportedly received a chilly reception when he met with Weinberger and urged him to adopt his transition team's report.

Although he has juggled the budget figures for both a state and the federal government, Weinberger's background is law. A Harvard Law School graduate, Weinberger worked for the San Francisco law firm of Heller, Ehrman, White and McAuliffe during the late 1940s and again in the 1960s.

In January, 1981, Weinberger's only substantial knowledge of military issues stemmed from his two years at OMB, when he handled the Pentagon budget, and his experience, nearly 40 years ago, in the Army, when he pulled combat duty in the Pacific and became a member of General Douglas MacArthur's intelligence staff.

Weinberger apparently is enjoying the trappings of his new office. During the summer of 1981 he took his family to Bar Harbor, Maine five times—at government expense. According to records uncovered by Rep. Les Aspin (D-Wis.), Weinberger used the 89th Military Airlift Wing, which provides top officials with transport for official business, to take his family on vacation—at a cost of about $20,000. "The Pentagon budget isn't just for national security," said Aspin. "It also involves billions for housing, for food. . .and for lots of mundane matters—including, we see now, summer trips to Bar Harbor."

Weinberger responded to Aspin's complaint by asserting that being in the national chain of command he needed to be close to a communications network. But as Aspin staff member Warren Nelson pointed out, even with such considerations Weinberger's predecessors had managed to take their vacations without a military escort.

Weinberger is an avid reader of Shakespeare, as well as British history and biography. He describes himself as a "frustrated journalist," having been editor of the *Harvard Crimson*, a stringer for the *Economist* and a regular book reviewer for several San Francisco papers. He has said he wants to write a biography of William Pitt, "mostly because he became Prime Minister of England at 24." His heros, however, are Winston Churchill and Theodore Roosevelt. As for a book about his experience in government, Weinberger told us: "I suspect that everybody who has been in these kinds of positions commits some kind of literary mayhem and I may do something along that line."

Born August 18, 1917, in San Francisco, California, Weinberger was graduated magna cum laude from Harvard in 1938 and received his law degree there three years later. He is married with two children.

FINANCIAL BACKGROUND

Weinberger is one of at least 10 Reagan cabinet officials worth more than $1 million. According to his 1981 financial disclosure statement, Weinberger listed a net worth of at least $2.2–$3.5 million, including over $350,000 invested in Bechtel Group, Inc.; $50–100,000 in Bechtel Equipment, from which he has divested, and between $50–100,000 in International Harvester. Weinberger did not set up a blind trust.

His $1.1 million income included a $469,466 salary from Bechtel Petroleum, Inc.; $39,605 from Bechtel Trust; $20,800 as a director of Quaker Oats Company; $27,250 as a director of Pepsico, Inc.; $10,350 as director of Illingsworth Morris Ltd. of England; and a $4,932 pension from the state of California, as well as various honoraria. Weinberger resigned all his directorships upon taking office.

WHAT OTHERS ARE SAYING ABOUT HIM

- Weinberger's lack of experience in military affairs worried several Senators during his confirmation hearing. One congressional expert on military matters told us Weinberger "came in knowing very little and though he is still not a recognizable expert like [Robert] McNamara, [Harold] Brown, [James] Schlesinger or [Melvin J.] Laird, all of whom had some sort of prior experience—his knowledge has improved. But you can still see in his answers a lack of detailed knowledge."

- Certainly, Weinberger's actions this year have been as drastic and troubling to opponents—perhaps more so—than, say Interior Secretary James Watt or U.N. Ambassador Jeane Kirkpatrick. Yet unlike these and other confrontational personalities in the Reagan administration, Weinberger has not drawn streams of hate mail or calls for his resignation. Indeed, many adversaries find him palatable, even likeable. Said Stan Norris of the Center for Defense Information: "I never get terribly incensed about Weinberger; he doesn't affect me the way [Richard] Allen or [Richard] Pipes [of the National Security Council] does. He is kind of an enduring bureaucrat who has a congenial personality and is always polite."

- Despite his lack of experience in the area, Weinberger often ventures into foreign policy areas, a proclivity that has brought him into conflict with Secretary of State Alexander Haig more than once. "He is more willing to discuss foreign policies than other secretaries I can remember," said one long-time Senate aide who works on military issues. "He feels comfortable with it and discusses it. In the past a Defense secretary would say 'That's a foreign policy matter' and refer you to the State Department."

- After Weinberger's nomination, conservative columnists Rowland Evans and Robert Novak wrote disapprovingly: "No defense secretary has been less familiar with defense problems since Charley Wilson in 1953 (when the hardware was simpler and the dangers more distant)."

FRANK CARLUCCI
DEPUTY SECRETARY

RESPONSIBILITY OF OFFICE

Carlucci manages the day-to-day operations of the Defense Department, leaving Weinberger free to handle major policy matters. Much of his effort over the last year has been aimed at improving the Pentagon's acquisition process.

If the President is incapacitated or inaccessible, Carlucci is number three in the line of authority to launch a nuclear weapon, following the Vice-President, and Defense Secretary Weinberger.

BACKGROUND

Frank Carlucci has a decidedly dual identity.

To Washington insiders he is the consummate number two bureaucrat—honest, loyal, and strikingly efficient at managing the day-to-day operations of sprawling federal agencies. He has survived and moved ahead under both Republican and Democratic presidents with shrewd maneuvering that has set him apart from the legions of high-level federal bureaucrats in Washington. He has a knack for getting his name in the press, as he demonstrated in 1981 with his 32 ''Carlucci initiatives'' on procurement reform, recommendations that had been kicking around for years and were by no means results of his own brainstorming; or the time he volunteered to be the first to take a lie-detector test during a Pentagon search for the source of leaks to the press. Whether defending at the embattled Office of Economic Opportunity (OEO), directing emergency assistance to hurricane victims, or signing Pentagon memos, Carlucci makes himself appear indispensable.

In other parts of the world Carlucci is considered by some a cunning and devious CIA operative who has been involved in coup d'etats and assassination plots in several Third World countries. By his own account, he has been accused of plotting the assassination of Patrice Lumumba in the Congo, the overthrow of Allende in Chile and Abeid Karume in Zanzibar and of Goulart in Brazil. The Italian Communist Party asserted he was behind the Moro kidnapping. The Portugese Communist Party devoted an entire book to accusations against Carlucci.

Carlucci laughingly denies he was ever a CIA spy, a reputation he earned during his tenure as a foreign service officer. ''Moscow propaganda has consistently labeled me an 'expert in subversion,' '' Carlucci said at his confirmation hearing. ''It is they who are the experts in subversion.'' Indeed he seems almost proud of the accusations, as well as his various displays of bravado as a foreign service officer. After all, these were at one time what distinguished him from dozens of other foreign service officers vying for headier government posts.

In none of these cases have the charges been irrefutably proven. But if Carlucci, as he maintains, was never involved in any of the CIA's covert intrigues during the 1960s, he at least seemed to regularly pop up in the vicinity of some of the agency's sleazier operations. In 1959 he was transferred from his post as vice consul and economic officer in Johannesburg, South Africa to the Congo, which was then torn by bloody internal strife while gaining independence from Belgium. Carlucci befriended Congo Premier Patrice Lumumba, and one time successfully interceded with the premier on behalf of 35 imprisoned Belgians. With a pat on the shoulders, so the story goes, Lumumba turned the Belgians over to Carlucci ''to do with what you like.''

But Lumumba was considerably less welcomed by various elements in the Eisenhower White House at that time. He had allegedly received money from the Belgian Communist Party, had appointed a left-leaning cabinet, and at one point appealed to the Soviet Union for military aid. According to the 1975 Church Committee report, during Carlucci's tenure in the Congo the CIA, possibly at Eisenhower's direction, plotted Lumumba's assassination. However, Lumumba, slipping away from rumored death traps, was later captured and reportedly killed by Congolese opponents.

At the time of Lumumba's death Carlucci was arrested by the pro-Soviet Antoine Gizenga, leader of Lumumba's government-in-exile. There in Stanleyville, in the dead center of the African continent, halfway between Cairo and Capetown and surrounded by tropical rain forests, Carlucci spent nearly a week under house arrest. He managed to slip past guards and escape once but was recaptured. Rather than embroiling themselves in a conflict of international dimensions, Gizenga officials put Carlucci on the next plane out.

During his stay in the Congo, Carlucci once earned kudos for bravery when he came to the aid of a carload of Americans that had collided with a bicycle, killing the rider. With anti-American sentiment in the country growing, an angry mob began gathering around the vehicle. Carlucci jumped in and tried to distract the crowd, which beat and slashed at him; and was only saved when a bus driver pushed through the crowd to help. He was stabbed in the back of his neck.

Carlucci also befriended Lumumba's successor, the West-leaning Premier Cyrille Adoula. Even that relationship lent Carlucci a measure of notoriety. During a state luncheon at the White House in 1962, Adoula asked, "Where is Carlucci?" The embarrassed whisper trickled from President Kennedy on down the table, "Who the hell is Carlucci?" Carlucci, who was then working on the State Department's Congo desk, was finally found across the street, eating a modest lunch with other junior state department officials, and was rushed to the White House just in time to save face for the humiliated President.

In 1964 Carlucci was assigned U.S. consul to Zanzibar, the African island off the cost of Tanzania. One year later he was declared persona non grata and given 24 hours to leave. The charge: According to the Tanzanian government—which by then had merged with Zanzibar—Carlucci, together with U.S. embassy counselor Robert Gordon in Dar es Salaam, were plotting the overthrow of Zanzibar leader Abeid Karume. *Time* maintained that a phone conversation between Gordon and Carlucci had been tapped and the message misconstrued.

From there Carlucci was transferred to Rio de Janeiro, where he arrived only months after a CIA-backed military coup against the elected Goulart regime and at a time when the agency was continuing to funnel aid to the ruling junta. He remained in Brazil, as the U.S. Embassy's counselor for political affairs, from 1964 until 1969, when his old wrestling partner from Princeton, Donald Rumsfeld, brought him back to become his deputy at the Office of Economic Opportunity.

But that wasn't the end of Carlucci's overseas duties, or the controversy. Between 1975 and 1977 he served as ambassador to Portugal, at a time when the CIA was shoring up conservative elements there with money and manpower to prevent the Communist Party from coming into power. During that period Carlucci led a minority of policymakers who argued—against Secretary of State Henry Kissinger—in favor of supporting Portugal's leftist military government in 1975 "as long as appearances of democracy remained extant," as one official said. Carlucci's position eventually gained the White House's support. According to a press report later denied by the State Deparment, Kissinger complained during a meeting, "Whoever sold me Carlucci as a tough guy?" Carlucci devised a U.S. military assistance plan for Portugal; and at one point, in a heated exchange of cables, managed to prevent Kissinger from implementing a virtual aid embargo against the independent socialist government. The most satisfying aspect of his experience there, said Carlucci, "was watching the Portuguese people move from the brink of communism to equilibrium."

The Portuguese Communist Party is convinced Carlucci played more than a passive role in that process.

During that period Carlucci, as he puts it, "became the favorite whipping boy" of the Portuguese Communists, who released a 167-page book, *Dosier Carlucci CIA* which accuses him, among other exploits, of helping "subvert the revolutionary process initiated in Portugal." On the blue soft-back cover, Carlucci, with only his nose, eyes and forehead pictured, peers into the distance. Inside, the manuscript recounts numerous accusations against Carlucci: "It will take some time for our people to know about the high price that the country paid for the activities that [Carlucci] developed in Portugal." The book recounts an article in the West Berlin magazine *Extra* which said Carlucci directed plans for a CIA-backed coup d'etat planned while he was Portuguese ambassador. "The newspapers," the book continues, "then published a scene that Portuguese eyes increduously watched: In Portuguese barracks, an American ambassador was driving a tank! It was his tank, it was his material, and the fact that it was neither his army nor his country did not disturb the diplomat."

To the Portuguese Communists, Carlucci's subsequent appointment to the number two spot at the CIA by President Carter confirmed their theory. "What should one think of the president of one country whose representative to the president of another country afterwards becomes director of the spying service?" Carlucci, of course, maintains the accusations are false, a point about which he carefully reminded us when he let us borrow the book.

Carlucci insists most allegations of CIA abuses are overblown. Those abuses that did occur in the past, he says, are anomalies. "My analysis of CIA abuses is that they originated one of two ways," he told us, "either as a result of political direction—and most of them originated that way—or as a result of one particular unit in the CIA which didn't really report to anybody."

Carlucci's experiences in Washington have had far less intrigue though in some respects as much controversy. He was promoted to OEO director after Rumsfeld left in December, 1970, and was thrown into the center ring of a battle between then Governor Reagan and the OEO-funded California Rural Legal Assistance (CRLA). During the course of that struggle, Carlucci, in Reagan's estimation, shifted from traitorous ally of ultra-liberals to a talented and forceful negotiator. That shift was not suprising—Reagan won an overwhelming publicity battle against CRLA thanks to Carlucci.

Reagan's vendetta against CRLA had begun when the state-wide legal services program sued him on behalf of the rural poor to block his cuts in social programs. (Many of those cuts were initiated by state Finance Director Caspar Weinberger.) OEO Director Rumsfeld, acting on a 1970 federal task force's conclusion that "while not perfect, CRLA is an exemplary legal services program," approved a 12 percent increase in CRLA funds in a new one-year grant. Reagan, invoking his powers under federal anti-poverty law, vetoed the grant. In July, 1970, five months before Carlucci's promotion to OEO director, Reagan appointed a right-wing director, Lewis Uhler, to head the state OEO and conduct a further investigation of CRLA that would produce evidence to sustain the veto.

Uhler's staff produced a 283-page report charging that the federal poverty lawyers were inefficient, incompetent, encouraging prison riots, and otherwise instigating "radical" and "revolutionary" actions. The report was, as conservative columnist James J. Kilpatrick described it, "about as objective as a nonpartisan evaluation of the Chicago Police Department by Eldridge Cleaver." Carlucci, caught between congressional CRLA supporters who would be confirming his appointment as OEO director and the White House, which wanted to accommodate Reagan, appointed three retired state supreme court justices, all Republicans, to review Reagan's investigation.

Several months into the Carlucci investigation, a copy of the federal investigators' report was leaked to the press. The report accused Reagan's state OEO of using federal funds to harass and destroy federal poverty programs. The following week

Reagan held a press conference and released a personal letter to President Nixon, accusing the federal investigating team of engaging in mere "fun and games" and charging Carlucci with attempting to "curry favor with the 'poverty law establishment' and to appease certain ultra-liberal members of Congress."

Despite those results, Carlucci did not automatically override Reagan's veto. Instead, internal Republican politics came into play. The White House, which needed Reagan's support for the upcoming 1972 Republican convention, wanted appeasement. So Carlucci flew to California just in time to escape Freedom of Information Act requests seeking release of the federal team's report. Meeting with Governor Reagan and CRLA officials—and working out details with Ed Meese—Carlucci came to a compromise that would both keep CRLA alive and pacify Reagan. Under that agreement, Reagan got a "clear news-jump" and money for his own legal service program; CRLA got another year of life. "We all emerged friends," Carlucci told us, "and the program is alive and well today."

But CRLA officials didn't realize what they had agreed to until it was too late. The press release engineered by Reagan inverted the federal team's findings, saying that CRLA had actually been found *guilty* of numerous charges which, the release said, necessitated "the imposition of stringent controls on future operations." Although a few afternoon papers discovered the deception and reported it, the damage had already been done. Reagan has since extolled Carlucci for his role in the controversy.

Carlucci moved from OEO to the Office of Management and Budget, where he began his first of three tours of duty as Weinberger's deputy. While Weinberger became better known as "Cap the Knife," Carlucci, who filled in the details of Weinberger's budget cuts, could have been called "Carlucci the Cutter."

In 1972 he was appointed to run another show: the clean up operations in Wyoming Valley, Pennsylvania in the wake of Hurricane Agnes. There, in a well-equipped mobile home, he reigned as federal "czar" (the actual technical term for his role), dispensing federal aid and listening to selected citizens' complaints, cases which came to be known as "Carlucci specials" and as such received personal attention, however trivial.

It being an election year, Carlucci conducted a well-orchestrated public relations campaign for the Nixon Administration's efforts in the devastated area. At one point his aides said they were churning out about a dozen press releases daily. He was also painfully sensitive about any possible bad publicity, or nosy reporters. As Jack Anderson reported upon returning from a tour of the area: "Trailing my car I later learned were two of Carlucci's agents who had been assigned to find out where I went, what I said, and whether I left any reporters behind."

In between his glorious days running the show—at the OEO, in Wyoming Valley, or in Lisbon—Carlucci remained Weinberger's number two man, first at OMB and then at the Department of Health, Education and Welfare. His frank and easy going style provided a moderating complement to Weinberger's often single-minded approach. Department heads often preferred to deal with Carlucci at OMB—he understood the subtle political ramifications of cutting popular programs. Weinberger might also have understood, but he never let on. "Carlucci was easier to deal with," said one former OMB associate.

Though Carlucci went on to become deputy at the CIA and then at the Defense Department after returning from Portugal, he says he considers his work in domestic programs most rewarding. "I enjoyed the social area," he said, "you're better able to see your accomplishments." An odd comment for a man who served an Administration that was more interested in tearing down social programs than building them, and even in that was relatively unsuccessful.

At the CIA, Carlucci pressed for legislation that would exempt most CIA records from Freedom of Information Act requests, and now that he's out from the Carter Administration which favored reining in the CIA, he admits he favors reduced restrictions on CIA activities within the United States. "I think the 'domestic surveillance' issue is a kind of red-herring," he told us. "I don't think the CIA should be engaged in domestic surveillance nor do I think it wants to. I do think the CIA needs to have the capabilities to recruit in this country. . . and ought to have access to organizations which facilitate recruitment. But that is a long way from saying the CIA ought to engage in domestic surveillance." He added the CIA should be permitted to operate domestically in hot-pursuit cases.

"The issue of domestic surveillance is not whether the CIA should engage in domestic surveillance, it is whether the executive order should be written in such a way to give them the flexibility to do the kinds of things I'm talking about," he said.

Admiral Stansfield Turner, who has publicly criticized the Reagan Administration's announced intention to relax restrictions on the CIA, insisted Carlucci followed the Carter Administration's line, though he was not always in agreement. "He was honest and loyal," Turner told us. "If he went left and I went right he would fight and scream and holler. But once I made up my mind, he was entirely loyal."

However, on some issues Carlucci draws a personal line. Three different times during his career he said he was prepared to resign if decisions did not go his way. Though he would not disclose those incidents, he did lend us a bit of his philosopy: "We all lose battles in government every day. With most of them you just roll with the punches. But at a certain point you have to say 'this is just too large or too important an issue, or I feel morally convicted on this issue.'"

Born October 18, 1930 in Scranton, Pennsylvania, Carlucci was graduated from Princeton in 1952 and attended one year of the Harvard Graduate School of Business Administration in 1954, in between which he served two years in the Navy, his only experience with military matters. He made an ill-fated career start with the Jantzen Company, a swimsuit manufacturer, before joining the foreign service. Carlucci is married with three children.

FINANCIAL BACKGROUND

According to his financial disclosure statement, Carlucci's only income outside his salary as CIA deputy director were dividends from family holdings in Dow Chemical, American Broadcasting, Marriott, DeBeers, Wisconsin Southern Gas, U.S. Air, Fidelity Fund, Sabine, and interest from various savings accounts. His wife receives a salary from Coopers and Lybrand.

WHAT OTHERS ARE SAYING ABOUT HIM

- Among Washington insiders, the response to Carlucci is predictable. "He is a noted manager," said one Senate expert on military matters. "He handles day-to-day management and can be expected to stay out of foreign policy matters."

- "Around here he is perceived as a good manager," said an aide to the House Armed Services Committee; "though he has created overexpectations," with the Carlucci initiatives on procurement reform. "He doesn't have an in-depth knowledge of the implications [of his proposals] or the subtleties involved."

- And while the left in countries like Portugal have accused Carlucci of being a CIA operative, the right has also made some disparaging remarks about him. "Frank Carlucci is [a] radical," wrote far-right columnist William P. Hoar, "he favored and promoted a guaranteed annual income program; supported socialized medicine and the Legal Services program; fawned on Marxists like Patrice Lumumba in the Congo and Salvador Allende in Chile. . . ."

FRED CHARLES IKLE
UNDERSECRETARY FOR POLICY

RESPONSIBILITY OF OFFICE

Ikle is the "principal staff assistant to the secretary of Defense for policy as it relates to matters concerned with political-military affairs, such as arms limitations negotiations, intelligence analysis and collection requirements, communications, command and control, the use of outer space" and NATO matters. That makes Ikle, in title, the lead department official on arms control issues as well as nuclear proliferation, areas with which he has long been concerned. He runs what has been called the Pentagon's "little state department."

BACKGROUND

Scholarly and removed, but keenly ambitious, Ikle is well suited in ideology and temperament for his current job of revising the Defense Department's world view. Once considered an eclectic though hardline thinker on arms control and international relations—he wrote in 1973 that, "Toward each other as a people, Americans and Russians harbor practically no feelings of hostility"—since leaving the government in 1977 Ikle's statements have the unswerving tone of yet another reconstructed cold warrior: joining the Committee on the Present Danger, issuing warnings that the U.S. was becoming militarily inferior to the Soviet Union, and declaring that Soviet policies are guided by "the unchanged motivation to expand the Communist empire." Always a hawk on strategic issues, Ikle has helped, in a modest way, to propel the steady rightward drift in political attitudes toward the Soviet Union.

It was the first significant stirrings of those feelings rising in opposition to Henry Kissinger's vision of detente that brought Ikle to national prominence in the early 1970s. After the conclusion of the SALT I agreement, the Nixon Administration agreed under pressure from critics led by Sen. Henry Jackson (D-Wash.), who charged Nixon with giving away too much at the bargaining table, to clean out the Arms Control and Disarmament Agency (ACDA). ACDA had handled a leading role in the negotiations.

In a purge orchestrated by, among others, James Malone, now at the State Department and Richard Perle, now an assistant to Ikle, the White House in 1973 dismissed or transferred the entire senior staff, cut the agency's budget by a third, and reduced its staffing by about 25 percent. Ikle, a Jackson candidate, was brought in to pick up the pieces. Perle, then a Jackson aide, told us he "helped persuade" Ikle to take the job.

From the White House's point of view, Ikle was the perfect man for the job. A thinker with little patience for administration or bureaucratic infighting, Ikle would not resist Kissinger's efforts to consolidate his personal control over arms negotiations. Nor was he likely to press for more stringent arms controls than the Administration was prepared to seek.

Ikle fulfilled the White House's expectations.

From the outset of his tenure in July, 1973, ACDA's diminished role was apparent. Unlike his predecessor, Ikle did not hold the concurrent position of chief SALT negotiator. That went instead to a State Department official. And the agency's influence on policies brought to the negotiations "went into a tremendous decline," as one former high-ranking ACDA official put it.

According to former ACDA officials, Ikle turned over most of the management of the agency to his deputy, John Lehman, Jr., an ambitious conservative who is now secretary of the Navy. Described as "humorless," "too serious," "academic," "cold, very cold," "complicated and insecure" and "high-strung, taut as a fiddle" by former colleagues, Ikle was a diffident figure to most ACDA employees. Uneasy with public appearances, but anxious to advance, Ikle forced himself into public speaking, associates recall. In his speeches he was a perfectionist, "working long and hard on the language." One aide recalls that Ikle would frantically "still be changing the language [of testimony] in the car on the way up to the Hill."

Before assuming the ACDA job, Ikle was a persistent critic of the prevailing strategic doctrine of Mutual Assured Destruction—or MAD—which posited that the best way to deter a nuclear attack was to retain the capability to wipe out the enemy's population in a massive second strike. A Soviet leader, the thinking went, would have to be irrational to precipitate such a cataclysm.

That doctrine, Ikle wrote in an influential January, 1973 *Foreign Policy* article, "rests on a form of warfare universally condemned since the Dark Ages—the mass killing of hostages." That gruesome reality, he wrote, was obscured by policymakers in "layers of dehumanizing abstractions and bland metaphors."

> Thus, 'assured destruction' fails to indicate what is to be destroyed; but then, 'assured genocide' would reveal the truth too starkly. . .Tomas de Torquemada, who burned 10,000 heretics at the stake, could claim principles more humane than our nuclear strategy.

Ikle pressed those views throughout his ACDA stay. In a swan song speech made after Ford lost the 1976 election, he concluded: "We cannot indefinitely shirk the duty of devising a new approach to prevent nuclear war, an approach less fragile and inhuman than the continuing threat of mutual genocide."

Ikle offered but a few alternatives to MAD doctrine, all of which were circumscribed by his explicit acceptance of an ongoing arms race. In his *Foreign Policy* article he suggested the development of "smart bombs" which could more precisely target military and industrial, rather than civil targets (this proposal helps explain his later defense of the cruise missile); the development of arms "invulnerable" to attack—perhaps "buried thousands of feet underground"—that would strip the incentive for surprise attacks; and the renunciation of the "dogma of speed," which would allow the U.S. to conclude an agreement with the Soviets "to replace the Doomsday catapults invented in the 1950s with arms that are incapable of being launched swiftly" and would thus reduce the risk of both a surprise attack and "accidental war."

"I could not quite understand what he was pushing," said Paul Warnke, Ikle's successor at ACDA, analyzing the article. "It was sort of the idea that you couldn't rely just on deterrence, but I couldn't see quite what. . .his alternative was. His approach is much more theoretical, and in my opinion not very practical."

As a strategic theorist himself, Ikle expressed acute awareness of the limitations—indeed, of the delusions—built into the elaborate calculations that produced government doctrine on nuclear war. "Our entire structure of thinking about deterrence lacks empiricism," he said in a 1974 speech. "We work with simplistic abstractions and are not too troubled by the discrepancies between these abstractions and the possible reality, a reality that is so hard to imagine." In a memorable remark he noted acidly that nuclear war planners worked "on the rule: what you can't calculate you leave out."

Actually, he asserted in another 1974 speech, quite a bit had to be left out in those calculations. "We are not only unable to express the human meaning of nuclear war—the only meaning that matters—we are also unable to express the full range of physical effects of nuclear warfare, let alone to calculate these effects. . .the damage from nuclear explosions to the fabric of nature and the sphere of living things cascades from one effect to another in ways too complex for our scientists to predict. Indeed the more we know, the more we know how little we know." Instead, he said planners took "refuge" in "superstitions" and an "imaginary order" measured in "megatons, missiles and MIRVs."

Ikle broke from the evolving Ford Administration line on "limited" nuclear war, a concept also backed by President Reagan in recent remarks about the possible outbreak of nuclear hostilities in Europe. While Defense Secretary James Schlesinger was promoting the concept with evangelical zeal, Ikle observed in 1974 testimony that "there is a danger that people may be misled into believing that limited nuclear wars are somehow safe, and an extension of our military capability." But three years later, in Senate testimony, Ikle moved closer to Schlesinger's position, acknowledging that "The United States must not, in the face of any nuclear attack, no matter how restrained, be forced by doctrine or weapons to choose only between surrender or destruction of most of the civilized world."

At the same time he pointed out "the risk of escalation would be enormous. . .no responsible leader would pretend to himself that a limited nuclear war could be safely controlled."

For all of these sobering remarks about the dangers of nuclear war, Ikle's major contribution to Ford Administration arms control policy was working with then-Defense Secretary Donald Rumsfeld and the Jackson-Perle forces to scuttle Kissinger's efforts in the winter of 1975 to conclude a SALT II agreement. Ikle was particularly concerned about proposals to limit the cruise missile. (See profiles of John Lehman and Richard Perle.)

Ikle and ACDA played a larger role in the Ford Administration's nonproliferation policy. Ikle consistently opposed reprocessing of spent fuel, was ambivalent at best about the need for the breeder reactor, and repeatedly stressed the hazards of uncontrolled international nuclear commerce. Just before the election, Ford presented a plan to defer domestic use of plutonium as a nuclear fuel, while seeking to slow the development of reprocessing abroad and funding a "demonstration" reprocessing project here to assess the possible risks. In the interagency task force that produced the policy, ACDA opposed any reprocessing at all, calling it an "unacceptable proliferation risk," according to an internal report. (Ikle, nonetheless, supported the policy in his public statements.)

Ikle continues to hold these views. In 1979, he defended the Carter Administration non-proliferation policy—which had been bitterly criticized by the nuclear industry, and now by the Reagan Administration, as too restrictive—as "essentially" a continuation of the Ford policy. In that article he laid blame for the "irresponsible behavior" that had scattered nuclear materials and technology to the far corners of the globe on government subsidies that underwrite nuclear development, "strong vested interests" working to advance reprocessing and other hazardous technologies, and an "insouciant lack of realism about the functioning and capabilities of the International Atomic Energy Agency [IAEA]."

Ikle is believed to be a moderating force on Administration non-proliferation policy. In an internal memorandum during the policy review process, the Pentagon warned "against undue reliance on the IAEA by those responsible for national security." Implicit in the new policy is that IAEA safeguards will prevent the diversion of civilian nuclear materials to military use. In their statement, the Pentagon expressed "reservations about the effectiveness of IAEA safeguards [and] the weakness of the IAEA as an international institution."

After leaving the government in 1977, Ikle became chairman of the Conservation Management Corporation, joined the boards of several other corporations and continued to spin out articles on national security topics. In a 1978 article for *Fortune* he argued that the Soviets were passing us in both conventional and nuclear capabilities. Arms control, he wrote, "would not transform the present adverse trends."

Needed instead, Ikle concluded, "needless to say," were increased defense expenditures; greater freedom for the CIA to engage in "overt and covert actions abroad"; increased cooperation with China; and pressure on the Japanese to step up their defense budget. In that and later pieces, Ikle stressed the need for expanding the industrial base available for military production. "By devoting 1 to 3 percent of the defense budget during the next few years to industrial preparedness," he wrote in 1980, "we could place ourselves in a position to expand swiftly the current $150 billion military effort to a trillion-dollar level" needed for an "all-out mobilization."

And he called for a tough response to the Soviet invasion of Afghanistan, though he was, as often, vague on exactly what that should constitute. "By 'normalizing' the invasion of Afghanistan, the West—and the Third World— will make other invasions of 'socialist' Third World countries a normal event, opposition to which would not be expected. Brezhnev's 'common law' will thus have been extended to cover a Soviet invasion of Yugoslavia, South Yemen, Ethiopia, Mozambique, Angola, Cuba (if the Soviets can marshall sufficient military power) and, of course, Iran, once 'socialist construction' has begun there," he wrote in January, 1980. "We in the United States must marshall the strength to back up the self-defense of all independent nations in the Middle East."

In another recent article, he argued that a possible military conflict with the Soviet Union over the oil resources of the Middle East, could end in the subjugation of the entire western world. Wrote Ikle:

The fact that America's military preparations and spending have lagged behind Russia's for so many years would begin to tell in such a confrontation. In such a local war, the United States would be pushed into retreat by superior conventional forces, and globally it would confront Soviet nuclear capabilities in many respects more formidable than its own. Now the notion that America's nuclear forces could somehow deter the Soviet Union from fully exploiting its conventional military advantage would suddenly be revealed as a delusion. If such a crisis reached this point, where and how could the United States and those of its allies who remained steadfast halt the retreat? What remaining resources—military, economic, and political—would prevent a follow-up offensive to subjugate what would be left of the Western world? Napoleon and Hitler did not halt while they were victorious.

It is with such apocalyptic visions in mind that Ikle will formulate national defense policy.

Born in Switzerland on August 21, 1924, Ikle received his masters and doctorate degrees from the University of Chicago, finishing the Ph.D. in 1950. After four years at Columbia University, he joined the Rand Corporation, a military-oriented think-tank. In 1962, he went to Harvard as a research associate at the Center for International Affairs, where he met Kissinger. After a three year stint as a political science professor at MIT that began in 1964, he rejoined Rand as head of its Social Science Department. He remained at Rand until tapped by Nixon to run ACDA.

At the time of his nomination to the defense job, Ikle sat on the Council on Foreign Relations, the American Enterprise Institute's Advisory Board on Foreign Policy, the International Institute of Strategic Studies, Georgetown University's Center for Strategic and International Studies, the Committee on the Present Danger and several other foreign policy groups. From 1977-1979, he ran the Republican National Committee's Advisory Council on International Security.

He is married, with two daughters.

FINANCIAL BACKGROUND

Outside of government, Ikle worked as a consultant. He headed a firm called Transat Energy, Inc.; he lists as major clients two Swiss firms for whom he performed studies on transportation of coal, and "energy resource properties." He received another $5,500 in fees for sitting on the board of Zurich Insurance Companies.

At the time of his appointment Ikle and his wife held stock worth between $15,000 and $50,000 in: Atlantic Richfield, Texas Instruments, Dome Petroleum, Credit Swiss, Nestle, and Sandoz. The family divested itself of the first two, but held onto the latter four stocks.

Ikle also reported holdings of between $5,000 and $15,000 in: Aquitaine of Canada, Texas Utilities, Ciba-Geigy, Jelmoli, Gulf, Hercules, Kennecott, RCA, Standard Oil of California, and Tesoro Petroleum. He has divested of the last four stocks.

WHAT OTHERS ARE SAYING ABOUT HIM

- Every former ACDA official we contacted considered Ikle an inefficient administrator, who turned over the actual running of the agency to Lehman. "Ikle was hardly a figurehead," said one former official. "But the contacts with Secretary Kissinger and the National Security Council was more Lehman than it was Ikle." Added another former high official: "Ikle was not an administrator. He was introspective."

- On the spread of nuclear weapons, however, Ikle took a keen interest. "He was a zealot on non-proliferation," said one official who worked with him. "Under Ikle a lot of important work [in the field] was done."

- He was also an intense individual who raced along "at a metabolism at about five times the rate of a normal person," said one former high-ranking associate. "He walks at 200 paces a minute. He eats like a swarm of locusts, but he doesn't gain weight because he burns it up." Ikle usually "started a conversation in the middle" the associate recalled, "because he assumed you knew what he had been thinking for the previous 15 minutes. Then you had to race to keep up with him."

MAJOR ISSUES

- Weinberger is directing the largest peacetime military buildup in the history of the republic. In all, the redirection of government funds from virtually every domestic program to the military will be a human and economic resource shift of historic magnitude. Yet it is still not clear that the Pentagon has a coherent strategy for protecting American security. The emphasis is on expansion, without clear direction.

- The Pentagon's $1.6 trillion five-year "rearmament plan" could inflict serious damage to the economy. Carlucci, however, insists that "sacrifices are necessary if we are to preserve our freedom and foreign policy goals."

- The Administration's five-part, $222 billion strategic program is designed to enhance the nation's ability to fight in "limited" or even protracted nuclear wars with more precise and less vulnerable weapons systems. Taken together, many critics say the package is a destabilizing force that will bring the country closer to the brink of nuclear war.

- With the prospects of a faster spiraling arms race, the forces opposing nuclear weapons are growing on both sides of the Atlantic. The peace movement is particularly active in Europe, where Reagan's decision to develop the neutron bomb—and his careless comments about "limited" nuclear war—touched off a storm of protest.

- Nuclear war is not the only gruesome conflict for which the Pentagon is preparing the country. For the first time since 1969, the U.S. government plans to produce a stockpile of chemical weapons.

- With his easy access to Reagan and frank hardline talk, Weinberger has exerted unusual influence over foreign policy. He has taken a tougher stand than the State Department on trade with the Soviets and East Europe. But he is less anxious than Secretary of State Haig to see direct U.S. military involvement in Central America.

Weinberger and Carlucci have the responsibility of directing the largest peacetime military buildup in the history of the republic. Over the next five years, the Pentagon will grow fat, while virtually every domestic service provided by the government will shrivel.

In all, it will be a shift of resources of historic magnitude. The Administration's planned $1.6 trillion five-year rearmament plan reflects an average annual increase in the Pentagon's budget of 7 percent—and possibly more—over inflation. The portion of "controllable" federal spending devoted to the military will increase from 54.2 percent in 1981 to 77.8 percent in 1985; the share of the total federal budget set aside for the Pentagon will increase from 25 percent to at least 37 percent. In 1983 alone, the Pentagon has requested $258 billion in total obligational authority, money spent or committed during that year, an increase of 13.3 percent over inflation from 1982.

If the Pentagon receives the congressional okay it will buy, through fiscal year 1984 alone: 62 MX missiles, 18 B-1 bombers, 207 Pershing II nuclear missiles and 305 ground-launched cruise missiles, 90 air defense systems, 10 submarines, 2 nuclear aircraft carriers, 3 reactivated battleships, close to 30 new warships, over 1,000 fighter planes, over 3,000 tanks and 3,500 other types of armored vehicles, more than 11,000 helicopters, and some 100,000 assorted missiles (both conventional and nuclear).

All of which is crucial, Weinberger told us, because "we have not invested the amounts necessary to keep our strategic forces modernized. As a result, we have to do it now, and it is very expensive to do it all at once, rather than over a number of years."

For the military the days of making difficult choices and picking program priorities are fast coming to an end: so far, they've been able to get Weinberger's blessing on nearly every weapon system they can scrounge up. "I don't have any idea what this Administration's defense policy is," said Rep. Les Aspin (D-Wis.) of the House Armed Services Committee in a *New York Times* interview. "And I read the posture statement and I still don't know. And I listen to Fred Ikle and I still don't know. To paraphrase Will Rogers, I think this Administration has never seen a weapons system that it didn't like."

That criticism has come from all political sides. In reviewing the Administration's first year, conservative commentator Walter Laquer of Georgetown University's Center for Strategic Studies, commented that "a strategy is not in sight, only occasional comments, gestures, and reactions— sometimes conflicting, often inconsistent."

In his report to Congress, Weinberger laid out this aim: "Our long-term goal is to be able to meet the demands of a worldwide war, including concurrent reinforcement of Europe, deployment to Southwest Asia, and support in other potential areas of conflict," which is a far more ambitious strategy than that forwarded by previous Pentagons. But critics say that aim is so broad that it obviates the ability to develop a realistic strategy given the level of resources available, even under the most optimistic assumptions. As Jeffrey Record, a senior fellow at the Institute for Foreign Policy Analysis has noted, "Barring a return to conscription and a comprehensive restructuring of the American economy for the purposes of war, the Weinberger-[John] Lehman strategy will serve simply to widen a longstanding gap between U.S. military commitments and capabilities."

Economists on both sides of the political spectrum are uneasy about the impact of this large scale rearmament on the president's economic recovery program. During congressional testimony in October, 1981, economist Lester Thurow said that such a military expansion will set off a bidding war for scientists and engineers. In their 1982 annual report, Reagan's Council of Economic Advisers warned of production bottlenecks, inflation in defense sectors, and a crowding out of private investment from the plan. And former Reagan adviser Simon Ramo, a founder and former director of TRW, Inc., wrote these frank comments in 1980: "Capital investments made on behalf of military R&D and production leave less capital to invest in non-military lines.''

Defense analysts like Robert deGrasse and Paul Murphy of the Council on Economic Priorities have similarly noted: "By further focusing research and development on increasingly esoteric military problems, we risk continued deterioriation of the technological base which supported U.S. economic growth during the past decade.''

In 1980, the Pentagon sponsored a panel discussion by representatives of such reputable economic forecasting firms as Wharton EFA, Data Resources, Chase Econometrics, and Merrill-Lynch, which concluded that "[b]ottlenecks will develop in key industries at [real military] increases in excess of 10 percent and, in fact, bottlenecks may even inhibit completion of planned defense programs on schedule and at programmed cost. . .'' The 1983 Pentagon request, with a 10.5 percent growth in actual spending, begs for just those problems.

But neither Carlucci or Weinberger seem to give much weight to these concerns. "I just can't believe our nation cannot afford a strong military,'' Carlucci told us. "Sure, it is going to require some sacrifices but I think those sacrifices are necessary if we are to preserve our freedom and foreign policy goals. If you argue against that, then you have to change your foreign policy goals and you have to recognize that we are not going to be the world power we think we are—which is a perfectly legitimate option. But it ought to be arrived at consciously.''

Weinberger, though, appears not to even think sacrifice is a necessity. "Our hope is, our feeling is, if we cut taxes then the economy will be stimulated,'' he said, making defense spending a smaller piece of a larger pie. So far, that hope has been unrealized.

Most economists concerned about the level of defense spending worry about its influence on the deficit. Last year, Wall Street, concerned that the Administration was not serious about narrowing the deficit, nearly dropped out of the Reagan camp over military spending. In 1982, major business leaders publicly began to press Reagan to heel "Cap the Shovel." "I wouldn't accept the thesis that the defense budget caused the deficit," said Carlucci, noting that the 1981 budget for Health and Human Services is larger.

Sensing these doubts, David Stockman, who had let the Pentagon slip through the initial budget process unscathed, in summer 1981 proposed cutting the department's proposed fiscal 1982-1984 budget—planned at $657.2 billion— by $30 billion. Weinberger vehemently resisted, arguing that Stockman's cuts would lead to cancellation of vital weapons systems, while the procurement of others would have to be delayed or stretched out, ultimately increasing their cost. Reluctantly, the Defense secretary offered an $8 billion cut. The President's compromise $13 billion figure—2 percent of the total proposed budget—was a clear victory for Weinberger.

In the battle, Weinberger took no chances that Reagan would drown in detail. When Weinberger went in to brief President Reagan on the impact of Stockman's proposed budget cuts he carried with him 32 cartoons. It seems the secretary's staff was told to come up with visual portrayals, rather than their usual charts and graphs to show the impact of potential cuts. Carlucci reviewed most of the material before it got to Weinberger. One chart used three different mushroom clouds to indicate the difference between the military budget Carter left behind, Weinberger's proposed defense level, and the effect of Stockman's $30 billion cut (a much smaller cloud).

To demonstrate the impact of Stockman's proposed Air Force cuts, a fighter-bomber was drawn—with its nose cut off.

Stockman has called the Pentagon a "swamp" of waste and inefficiency, an assertion that Weinberger publicly rejected. The Pentagon "is not a swamp," he said. "It's very dry land. There is not that degree of waste or inefficiency in what we're doing."

When we asked Weinberger about Stockman's remark he replied: "In that article I think Dave must have been referring to the Pentagon of the past. In any large organization, and this is one of the largest in the world, always there will be areas where you can do things or make improvements. I'm never going to say yes I'm finished, all the waste has been eliminated. What bothered me about that [article] was some implication that we were not making major efforts right now and succeeding in major efforts to reduce the waste, the duplication, the overlap."

In fact, Weinberger implies that he has rooted out most of the waste and mismanagement that has kept the General Accounting Office (GAO) busy churning out reports on the Pentagon for years. "We've found waste and we have reached it, but it's just not as big a story" as those about existing Pentagon waste, he told us. "It's not an interesting, large newspaper story. If you can find—as Senator Proxmire occasionally will—a warehouse full of World War II shoes that haven't been used—that's a big story. We cut out $3.5 billion within the first few weeks we were here and nobody noticed." (That figure refers to the Pentagon's rejection of claimed contractor costs that had been questioned by auditors.)

But, Weinberger cautions: Don't expect to actually see a savings from better management. Weinberger and Carlucci prefer the term "cost avoidance." "Because we need so much more of everything, the savings that we have don't net minus, they reduce the plus but they won't net minus," Weinberger told us.

Despite Weinberger's claims, the GAO—which has estimated that waste and mismanagement inflates the Pentagon's budget by $10 billion a year—continues to release its usual round of reports on how the Pentagon can cut waste with such titles as "Improved Management of Fleet Suppliers, Spare Parts, Can Save Millions Without Affecting Readiness" and "DOD Can Save Millions by Improving Management of Air Force Inventories." Weinberger says he finds the GAO reports "very useful."

In early 1981, Carlucci released a set of 32 proposals designed to improve the Pentagon's notoriously abused acquisition system, including multi-year procurement, more realistic budgeting for complex weapons systems and paperwork reduction. Carlucci insists the department also will try to put an end to the widespread problems of "buy-ins," when a company submits an unrealistically low bid in order to win a contract and later lets the price accelerate, forcing the government to cover the excess costs. (For details, see DeLauer profile.) As Pentagon officials readily admit, the initiatives are not original. In fact, the bulk of them have been floating around Congress and the Pentagon for decades. "There's nothing new in the Carlucci initiatives," said a long-time Senate aide who works on the issue. "These proposed reforms have surfaced every year since the 1950s. But it will be news if they actually follow through with them—that will be an accomplishment."

As part of his drive to improve the efficiency of the Pentagon's acquisition process, Carlucci sent a letter to major defense contractors explaining the Administration's proposed changes and asking chief executive officers to "direct an effort within your company to eliminate costly and unnecessary practices." The responses to his letter were generally supportive of the reforms, particularly multi-year procurement. And, of course, the responding executives assured Carlucci·that, as one letter said, "every attempt is being made to eliminate costly and unnecessary practices within our organization."

Ironically, the entire Pentagon budget might be considered a buy-in. Now that Congress has approved the first year of the Administration's military program and has adopted their version of the size of the Soviet threat, senior military planners are indicating that $1.6 trillion is probably not enough. "A defense increase considerably steeper than what the Administration now proposes" will be necessary to close the gap between U.S. and Soviet forces, Ikle told a Senate subcommittee in March, 1982.

During the same month, the Pentagon announced a record $114.5 billion increase in the projected cost of 44 major weapons systems. The new cost estimates, said a Pentagon spokesman, reflect "a lot of extra capabilities and quantities," more realistic pricing, and the inclusion of costs of some future systems.

Ikle's confession came two months after the disclosure of an estimate by DeLauer at a high-level meeting that the Pentagon would require $750 billion more than the Administration originally estimated.

The real test of the Pentagon officials' commitment to "efficiency" is whether they have the wherewithal to cut off weapons systems they consider unnecessary. "We have too many weapons systems in the budget for the resources available," conceded Carlucci. "So we're trying to kill some systems so others can be realistically funded." But, he said, "I had not anticipated the full degree of political pressure such as there is in Defense Department programs. They seem to be more politically sensitive than many social programs."

Carlucci lamented to us about his attempt to cut one weapon program. "Before I even had a chance to read the [service's] recommendation, I had five phone calls from the Hill" demanding the program be saved. "One member even said 'We'll tear your budget apart'" if the program is killed. "I've had company heads sit right there," he said, pointing to our chairs, "and say to me 'I know you're going to kill my system, well, then I'm going to start working the Hill.' I could almost trace the steps of the contractor from door to door."

The Pentagon's big bill, of course, is for the President's five-part, $222 billion strategic program, announced October 2, 1981, to improve the nation's nuclear war-fighting capability. The package includes plans to:

- Develop a fleet of 100 B-1 bombers, to be deployed beginning in 1986. These intercontinental bombers would be capable of carrying both nuclear and conventional bombs, or cruise missiles. In addition, research and development efforts will continue on the highly touted, top secret Stealth bomber, with deployment expected by 1995.

- Deploy 100 MX missiles, half what Carter proposed, and place them in a still to be decided basing mode. A final decision on what to do with the missiles is expected by 1983. Reagan discarded a plan, forwarded by the Carter Administration, to shuffle the missiles between shelters in Nevada and Utah.

- Develop the Trident II (or D-5) missile to replace the current Trident missile now in Trident submarines. The current Trident I missile (C-4) model carries eight warheads; the Trident II will carry seven large or 14 smaller nuclear warheads. The Trident I has a range of 4,800 miles, while the Trident II will have a range of 6,500 miles and be more accurate. The Administration will also continue the Trident submarine program.

- Improve the command, control and communication system so it can survive all types of nuclear war, and be able to continue relaying messages between the Pentagon and the Strategic Air Command and other command posts to each of the three legs of the strategic forces—air, land, and sea.

- Improve defensive systems: upgrade radars, replace five squadrons of F-106's with F-15's, increase research and development money for Anti-Ballistic Missile (ABM) systems, and dramatically expand civil defense. In addition, Weinberger told Congress, "we will buy at least six additional AWACS airborne surveillance aircraft. . .to augment ground-based radars in peacetime and to provide surveillance and control interceptors in wartime."

Reagan's strategic package came under immediate attack from the arms control community. Gerard C. Smith, director of the Arms Control Association, told Congress after Reagan's announcement: "The only purposes which these new weapons can serve are apparently to bolster our self-confidence and to make it more feasible to fight a protracted nuclear war." Private military analysts have estimated that about 17,000 new warheads will have to be produced over the next decade in order to arm the nuclear systems Reagan wants to build. The U.S. currently has over 26,000 nuclear warheads, according to the Center for Defense Information, compared to the Soviets' approximately 16,000.

Most alarming about the President's strategic package, said Stan Norris, a senior analyst for the Center for Defense Information, is its focus on highly accurate, sophisticated weapons—particularly the MX and the Trident II—which bring closer implementation of Carter's Presidential Directive 59, the top secret plan that presents a range of nuclear options, including limited and protracted nuclear wars. These weapons, particularly the Trident, are also considered destabilizing because they enhance our ability to launch a first strike at the Soviets. "What's dangerous is when people begin to believe that these weapons are attaining some sort of perfection," said Norris. "Reagan and Weinberger are only advancing the mystique about nuclear weapons and depriving the U.S. of money and resources for conventional weapons. And that of course, reduces our options. If you have five weapons, four of which are nuclear, what kind of options does that leave?" With an arsenal full of highly accurate nuclear weapons, these critics argue, military leaders believing a nuclear war can be "limited" are more likely to launch a nuclear attack.

Although the program itself consists primarily of delivery systems—launch pads for nuclear weapons and related facilities—it provides a potential for a massive increase in the U.S. nuclear weapons inventory. According to Smith, the Administration's program suggests that about 5,000 new theater and strategic nuclear weapons will be added before the end of the decade. Whether these new weapons will actually be added to the U.S. arsenal or replace existing weapons is still a question.

"It is difficult to see what contribution this expansion of nuclear bombs, and warheads will make to our security," said Smith, director of the Arms Control and Disarmament Agency under Richard Nixon.

In testimony Weinberger has alluded to the possibility of fighting a nuclear war. In addition to deterring nuclear and conventional attack, and preventing coercion or blackmail of the U.S. or its allies, Weinberger said the Administration's objective, "if we fail to deter [would be] to limit further destruction and to deny an adversary any hope of meaningful gain. . .and to deny his politico-military objectives at any level of conflict."

The Administration's strategy of developing a nuclear war fighting capability also includes a $4.2 billion seven-year civil defense program "to provide for survival of a substantial portion [up to two-thirds] of the population in the event of a nuclear attack." Only $133 million a year was being spent previously. The Federal Emergency Management Agency is developing plans to relocate the residents from 380 "high risk areas" in the United States—which includes missile fields, bomber bases, and 319 cities—to shelters.

The prospect of this large-scale program is particularly alarming to arms control activists who say civil defense in a nuclear war is a costly and dangerous myth. (OMB, which opposed the plan, calculated it would actually cost $10 billion.) The plan is based on the premise that the U.S. will have a week's notice of a nuclear attack, an unlikely prospect say critics. And as two physicians, H. Jack Geiger and Eric Chivian, note in their list of "Ten Illusions of Civil Defense," even if major evacuations of 380 high risk areas was successful, overcoming panic and traffic jams, the Soviet Union could simply retarget its missiles. The agency's secondary plan, placing the population in fallout shelters, would be similarly faulty—these shelters would reach 1472 degrees within five miles of a nuclear strike and would "become a crematoria in which people are simultaneously dry-roasted and asphyxiated," as Geiger notes. Besides these there are a host of other problems that no amount of civil defense can effectively handle: medical facilities would be destroyed; food and water supplies would be low; infection would be rampant; and, as the Congressional Office of Technology, Assessment noted in 1979, "cancer deaths and those suffering from some form of genetic damage would run into the millions over the 40 years following an attack."

The plan has also scared the general public, leading more and more people to believe that the Reagan Administration actually thinks it can fight, and win, a nulcear war. Deputy Undersecretary of Defense T.K. Jones, the Pentagon's in-house civil defense zealot, added to those jitters when he told the *Los Angeles Times* that, in the case of a nuclear attack on the United States, "everybody's going to make it if there are enough shovels to go around." Assistant Secretary of Defense Richard Perle was subsequently dispatched to Capitol Hill to tell nervous congressmen that Jones did not speak for the Defense Department on civil defense.

Underlying Reagan's strategic program is the vague and generally misused "window of vulnerability" theory, a phrase that has been manipulated for a variety of ends, most recently by Reagan officials. Accurately applied, the term refers to calculations by Pentagon officials of the number of U.S. nuclear warheads that could survive a Soviet first strike and be able to retaliate.

Recently Pentagon analysts concluded that between 1982 and 1987 there would be a significant drop in the number of surviving warheads—caused by Soviet increases and improved accuracy in missile deployment, and U.S. slowdowns in some areas. Despite this drop, however, the number of surviving missiles would still be high enough to inflict enormous damage on the Soviet Union.

Reagan officials have latched onto the phrase and blurred that distinction. When we asked Weinberger about it, he said the window of vulnerability "is the period of substantial imbalance in the strategic forces between the Soviets and ourselves." The window he maintained, will be open the widest in the mid-'80s, "the balance is at its worst then," he added.

"As we bring on new systems, and it takes a long time," Weinberger said, "we can narrow, and eventually close that window. The addition of cruise missiles that are part of the President's program will help close it more rapidly than anything else because we can get those on line sooner." The strategic program is designed to double the number of survivable nuclear warheads by 1991.

Many arms control experts argue that the "window of vulnerability" is a misnomer. The U.S. is no more vulnerable in a first strike than it was in the 1970s. For a number of reasons, Norris calls the proposition that the Soviets can knock out enough U.S. missiles to prevent a fatal retaliatory strike "fantasy." The Soviets, he said "would have to send over missiles with incredible coordination and precision."

As former ACDA director and SALT II negotiator Paul Warnke points out, well over two-thirds of American strategic forces are on the other two legs of the U.S. triad, sea and air. "Only a sudden fit of insanity could prompt a problem-ridden try at a preemptive strike on a fraction of our retaliatory force," Warnke told the Senate Foreign Relations Committee in November, 1981.

Though it is widely agreed that the two superpowers are in rough parity, Weinberger insists the Soviets have strategic superiority. Even Carlucci acknowledged: "I see some sort of parity now. Cap's more pessimistic." But that is not the issue, Carlucci insisted. "The issue is where we're going to be in 1985." The Administration continues to issue figures on the Soviet buildup, based on CIA estimates, that ostensibly show the Soviets are outspending the U.S. on defense. Those figures, experts have pointed out, are, in fact, skewed assessments of Soviet spending levels.

As Richard Stubbing, former deputy chief of OMB's national security division, wrote in a *Washington Post* commentary: "We are told, for example, that we spend about 5 percent of our gross national product on defense, while the Soviets spend 12 to 14 percent on theirs. We are not reminded, of course, that our GNP is twice that of the Soviet Union's. We are told that in 1980, the Soviets spent 50 . . . , percent more than we did on defense, or that over the past decade their military outlays outpaced ours by more than $300 billion. We are not reminded that defense spending comparisons in the real world include outlays of American and Soviet allies and that the publicly available evidence in this area, as in others, tells a very different tale."

As Stubbing notes, while the margin has no doubt narrowed, the United States and its NATO allies outspent the Soviet Union and its Warsaw Pact allies on defense by more than $300 billion over the past decade.

Weinberger insists he is looking only for parity with the Soviets, not superiority. "We must regain a sufficient degree of strength that will enable us to deter aggression," he told us.

In addition to the weapons systems proposed on October 2, 1981, the Reagan Administration is going ahead with the production and stockpiling of the nuclear weapon commonly known as the neutron bomb, a weapon avidly backed by Richard Perle, a department power on arms control issues. Though Weinberger claims that the U.S. is not deploying the neutron bomb outside the United States, "nor do we have any plans to do so," the Administration's decision touched off a storm of protest in Europe.

Understandably. The neutron bomb was designed primarily for use against Soviet tanks—as Weinberger notes, it would be "an effective counter to the vast imbalance of tanks we face and would allow artillery units to operate in much closer support of infantry and armor than possible with the weapons which are now deployed." Thus, as opponents of the weapon have noted, the most likely battlefield for their deployment is Europe, most notably West Germany. Carter had decided to produce the weapon but, after finally obtaining the support of the West German government, changed his mind.

Because the neutron bomb has a higher radiation ratio and somewhat lower blast and heat ratios than the standard fission warheads now deployed, its use limits damage to structures while escalating the dangers posed to humans. "There is some notion that this is a weapon which can enter a building, work its way up to the fourth floor, kill everyone in sight, and then retrace its steps, leaving the building intact," Weinberger told the American Legion. "Of course, this is absurd." Yet, in a very simplistic sense, that is one of the principles behind the weapon, and one that has stirred opposition to it.

Weinberger asserts that the real strength of the neutron bomb is its "more focused and narrow" range of destruction. That is what concerns opponents of the bomb like Norris: "It's not much different than the weapons already there [in Europe]. But if the military thinks it can be used in a precise, surgical manner, then that lowers the threshold level," he said, referring to the point at which a decision is made to employ nuclear weapons.

Four months into the new Administration, President Reagan succeeded in convincing Congress to adopt another controversial weapon: poison gas. The $20 million amendment passed in May, 1981 would equip a new chemical weapons factory in Pine Bluff, Arkansas, marking the first time since 1969 that the United States would produce chemical weapons. In seeking support for the amendment, Weinberger wrote to Sen. John Tower (R-Tex.), chair of the Senate Armed Services Committee, saying that failure to equip the plant for chemical weapons development would be "tantamount to unilateral disarmament and is, consequently, an extraordinarily risky course to pursue."

While Carlucci manages the nuts and bolts of rearmament from within the Pentagon, Weinberger has galavanted around the globe, doing battle with the State Department over control of U.S. foreign policy. Under Ikle, Weinberger has established what is known as the Pentagon's "little state department." With his easy access to Reagan and his frank hardline talk, Weinberger has exerted unusual influence over foreign policy.

Around Washington, the journeys of Haig and Weinberger abroad have become known as "competing trips." Though both are avid cold-warriors, Secretary of State Haig wants to build an anti-Soviet strategy around a strong, and content, European alliance. He has been careful to assuage European fears by quietly promoting arms control talks between the two superpowers and, though he says he opposes the construction of a $10 billion Soviet pipeline that will supply the West Europeans with natural gas, he does not support pressuring the allies to halt the project, or banning American corporate subsidiaries from taking part in it.

But Pentagon officials, led by Weinberger, have taken the toughest stand against the project, arguing that the U.S. should prevent the corporate subsidiaries from taking part, even if it means alienating the allies. "The pipeline," Weinberger told us, "will have the effect of giving the Soviets $10 billion a year in hard currency which they will turn immediately into military advantage and military gifts of arms to other countries." Added Perle in an interview: "In the absence of an influx of hard currency from the pipeline, the Soviets would be forced into making some difficult choices about the allocation of scarce resources. Their ability to expand their defense industrial base would be limited."

In statements that go beyond the traditional purview of a secretary of Defense, Weinberger has urged further restrictions on Western trade and credit to the Soviets. The Pentagon was the lone dissenting voice in the Administration's decision to pay off loans owed by Poland to U.S. banks rather than allowing the country to default.

Primarily, though, Weinberger is trying to halt the flow of Western technology to the Soviets. "We have added enormously to the Soviet technological base in the past few years," he said. "And I think that while a lot of people are interested in increasing trade, we ought to look very carefully at the benefits some of these things give the Soviets from a purely military point of view." The Pentagon is developing stricter guidelines for the sale of U.S. equipment to the Soviets and Eastern Europe. And Perle, an influential and effective voice in inter-agency councils, would like to go even further. "I think a well designed program of economic sanctions can both damage the development of the Soviet economy and slow the growth of their defense industrial base. I think it would be justified even in the absence of Poland, but in the Polish context it seems to me the choice ought to be easy," he told us. "I think an essential total cutoff in technology and large scale industrial projects [is called for]. We ought to consider and work with our allies to restrain credits to the Soviet Union. . .In the long term we have to investigate on an ongoing basis the possibility of the imposition of a grain embargo." Though agricultural interests criticize the grain embargo as ineffective, Perle maintains, "at various times, depending on the state of the world grain market and the Soviet harvest, curtailment of grain sales can be an effective policy." Asked if he was advocating a total cutoff in trade, Perle replied: "Trade in consumer products, I have no objection to that."

Whether the Pentagon will actually campaign to limit American interaction with the Soviet Union to washing machines and refrigerators is unclear. But Weinberger and his aides have undoubtedly displayed more vigorous interest in the subject than any Pentagon in recent memory.

The Pentagon's policy has differed with the State Department's over others parts of the world as well. Weinberger was quick to dampen an assertion, made by Haig, that the Pentagon should prepare for military intervention in El Salvador. Instead he prefers a steady infusion of U.S. military aid to the ruling junta. He is also wary of plans, hinted at by Haig, to blockade Nicaragua and Cuba and cut off an alleged flow of arms to Salvadoran guerrillas. Navy Secretary John Lehman also raised doubts about a blockade.

In the Middle East, Haig has been an ardent defender of Israeli interests, while Weinberger sought to arm that country's Arab foes, like Jordan, which is in line for some F-16 fighter planes.

Other issues Weinberger and Carlucci are facing include:

- Manpower. A number of military experts have said the military's expansion, combined with a sharp decline in the pool of young men and women, will lead to reinstitution of the draft. Both Weinberger and Carlucci insist that plans for a peacetime draft are not in the offing. "I don't see any need for it," Weinberger told us. "The volunteer forces are working very well, and we're getting all the numbers we can handle."

- Mobility. Weinberger wants a military that can intervene quickly and effectively around the world. "We must be prepared for waging a conventional war that may extend to many parts of the globe, if persistent local aggression by superior forces cannot be turned around," he said in a May, 1981 speech. As part of that plan the 1982 defense budget included $5.5 billion to improve the Rapid Deployment Force, which is designed primarily to protect the Persian Gulf. In addition, the Pentagon has embarked on a plan to construct or expand a string of U.S. military bases along the Indian Ocean.

- A similar strategy is being pursued in Latin America, where the U.S. is conducting classified discussions with several governments in the area on ways to expand the number of military facilitites available to the U.S. military.

- Allied defenses. Weinberger has pressured U.S. allies to follow the American lead in boosting their military spending. A Pentagon report issued in July, 1981, stated that the U.S. "appears to be doing somewhat more than its fair share of the NATO and Japan" defense. Cooperation has been slow in coming and has met resistance among populations in Europe.

As usual, the Pentagon's far-reaching decisions are being implemented with a minimum of public discussion. Even now, as the public begins to seriously question the need for Reagan's massive "rearmament" plan, the Pentagon is trying to wrap a veil of secrecy over more of the department's activities. In February, 1982 the *Washington Post* disclosed that Weinberger has been pushing the White House to implement a new secrecy classification— one for information that if disclosed would not cause damage to the national security. According to a memo obtained by the *Post*, Weinberger said the new classification, "Restricted," was critical to "the effective safeguarding of a range of information that is not now generally classifiable."

The Restricted stamp—to be added to current classifications of Top Secret, Secret, and Confidential—would be applied to "information, the unauthorized disclosure of which reasonably could be expected to cause the loss to the United States of a technological, diplomatic, intelligence, cryptologic or military advantage and which requires protection in the interest of national security." The key phrase in deciding which materials to classify would not be "damage to the national security" but rather "the loss of an advantage to the United States." The new stamp was not enclosed in the Administration's first classification changes, announced in early 1982.

We asked Weinberger if, with the Pentagon making critical decisions that will dramatically affect the lives of Americans, he would encourage military generals to speak before citizen forums. "We don't have any bars on them at all," he replied. "They have a natural professional reluctance not to do very much of it. They aren't required to do anything. For instance, my father told me a reputable lawyer never got his name in the paper. They tend to talk primarily to professional groups."

In the end the Reagan defense budget appears to substitute quantity for strategy. Rather than determining what it considers our national defense priorities, and then calculating the most efficient ways to meet those needs, Reagan has sought to bury those questions beneath mounds of dollars. Even the *Army Times*—no knee jerk liberal publication—called the 1983 budget "indiscriminate": "The Pentagon seems to be saying 'We want it all.' " When all the money has been spent, we will undoubtedly have a lot more destructive power; whether we will be any more secure is less clear.

RICHARD DELAUER

UNDERSECRETARY FOR RESEARCH AND ENGINEERING

RESPONSIBILITY OF OFFICE

DeLauer directs the Pentagon's acquisition of weapons systems, including their research, development, testing, and procurement. He is the Pentagon's chief contracting officer, officially signing off on all weapons systems purchased by the Defense Department. DeLauer also oversees the military's command and control systems, telecommunications, and intelligence activities.

He directs the Defense Advanced Research Projects Agency, the Defense Communications Agency, the Defense Nuclear Agency, and the Defense Mapping Agency. The assistant to the secretary for atomic energy reports to DeLauer.

Much of DeLauer's efforts in the coming years will be focused on directing the build-up of a military-industrial complex capable of sustaining the President's military expansion.

BACKGROUND

DeLauer has been a leading actor in the military industrial complex his entire career life, giving him a distinct advantage over other top Pentagon officials with little or no experience in military matters. He is a textbook example of the iron-triangle syndrome, moving from the military to a major defense contractor and back to a civilian post at the Pentagon. Even when he was on the outside looking in, DeLauer was an important part of the Pentagon's decision-making machinery.

After a lengthy military career, DeLauer in 1958 joined TRW, Inc., a major military contractor. There he directed what are now some of the building blocks of the U.S. strategic program. He guided TRW's development of the Titan ICBM (intercontinental ballistic missile) program in the early 1960s. Later, he was appointed director of TRW's entire ballistic missile program, which included the Minuteman, as well as Titan I and II.

DeLauer was TRW's golden boy, having been one of the central figures behind the company's rise to a formidable military, space, and electronics firm, with one quarter of its net sales coming from government contracts. In 1965 he became vice-president and general manager of the Systems Engineering and Integration Division, and, in another step up the corporate ladder, became vice-president and general manager of TRW's Systems Group in 1968. He was elected an executive vice-president of TRW in 1970 and to the firm's board of directors two years later. As the executive in charge of TRW's systems and energy activities, including the defense, space, energy, and equipment divisions, DeLauer helped the company move into the energy business.

"It's simple," DeLauer said of TRW's ability to get its share of the federal government's energy contracts. "We're good engineers and we get good scientific technical people. We knew how to work the government marketplace. We just examined it like we would any other market, and we stayed in what we knew how to do."

A feisty and forthright man who loves a good debate, DeLauer is the consummate Southern California aerospace executive, peppering his speech with the usual acronyms and defense establishment jargon. For instance, he likes to consider himself a "systems engineer," in contrast to his predecessor, William Perry, whom he describes as a "technologist." "My role in the last 15 to 20 years has been manager of large programs or large organizations," said DeLauer.

His eyes light up when he talks about the nuts and bolts of military hardware, or the successes of his alma mater, TRW. Nowhere is there a sense that he is talking about weapons of war; he might as well be discussing microwave ovens. When we asked him for his thoughts on recycling spent fuel from civilian nuclear plants for military applications, an issue that falls under his purview, his reply was a matter-of-fact, "I think we ought to use all our resources the best way we can." When we pressed about the ethical question of making utility consumers unwilling, but direct, participants in the nuclear arms race, he said: "I'd like to take a look at it. I haven't looked at the reprocessing question for weapons yet on that basis."

DeLauer has been on the inside of policy formulation at the Pentagon for several years, as a member of the highly influential Defense Science Board. This board appraises the merit of major weapons systems of the future. As early as 1974, for example, the board's public records indicate its members were working on the highly secret stealth technology.

Through the Defense Science Board, industry can influence Defense Department policies while the department, in turn, can signal to industry its future directions. DeLauer was an active member of the board, and in 1977 served as chair of the board's Acquisition Cycle Task Force, the conclusions of which set the stage for many of the so-called Carlucci initiatives outlined in 1981.

In 1977, DeLauer, then executive vice-president of TRW and chairman of the American League for International Security Assistance, Inc., testified in favor of relaxing restrictions on arms sales. "Rather than running wild," he told a congressional committee, "military exports are the subject of extensive controls which in fact tend to stifle the ability of the industry to compete in the international marketplace. Approvals are required at every step of the way and it often requires months or years of working the halls of bureaucracy to obtain the necessary clearances and approvals."

DeLauer reacts defensively to remarks that he perpetuates the defense establishment's "iron triangle"—that tightly-knit group of industry executives, congressmen on military committees and Defense Department officials that flow back and forth, dominating the country's military planning and squeezing out alternative perspectives.

"While [this problem] is important and it exists," he told us, "it has been portrayed in the wrong light. And as a consequence we've ended up with an ethics bill that has precluded the government from getting good people. I'm in my terminal assignment. I leave here and I'll retire. If I had to be worried about post service employment it would be very difficult."

Anybody that looks at the problem in an abstract way, he said, "would say 'here we are with a requirement for good people and somebody to do this and this, here is what we want the guy to be—experienced, has knowledge of the thing, some background in it.' If you were going to hire him to sell silk stockings or furniture or something you would go out and recruit in an area that met your requirements. Now, where in the hell are you going to recruit, except from people who know the business?

"Academia doesn't. They can have one piece of it, they can handle the technical aspects of it, but they can't handle the business aspects of it. And we are in a business. It is $200 billion worth of taxpayers' money that has got to be spent in the best way," he said.

Gordon Adams, author of the *Iron Triangle*, a study of the military establishment, agreed that it is difficult to find candidates qualified to fill positions such as DeLauer's in sectors other than the defense industry. "He is 50 percent right," said Adams. "But the other half not covered by his argument is how you safeguard the public interest when the whole series of thinking that goes into strategic policy-making is highly concentrated in companies like TRW and government. When people move from those types of companies into government, this risk of shared perceptions and shared biases is enormous.''

In the iron triangle, questionable connections are inescapable. For example, DeLauer's former employer, TRW, has received several million dollars in DOD contracts for work on the MX missile, which after much input from top Pentagon officials became a key element of Reagan's strategic program announced in October, 1981. DeLauer is chairing the executive committee studying ways to base the MX missile.

DeLauer has found that running the Defense Department has its own challenges. ''It's like working for a corporation with 600 members on the board of directors over there on the Hill—500 some odd representatives with their staff and 100 senators and their staffs. It was much easier when you only had 10 members of the board that might call you up. Then you have the Administration, which is kind of like the chief executive's office—which is exactly what it is—you got guys helping them that want to make the chief executives look good. So you got the same problems as you do in a normal company.''

DeLauer was nominated for his post by former Reagan science adviser Simon Ramo. ''I had doubts about taking it,'' said DeLauer. ''I had almost decided not to take it when things changed at TRW in a way that changed my mind. I really didn't want to come back here as a terminal assignment. I wanted to retire the year later and be kind of an elder statesman for a while.'' Watching DeLauer talk about his job with obvious relish, and listening to his lively and polemic monologues, that statement seems exaggerated.

DeLauer's military career stretches back to 1940. He began as a young aircraft designer for the U.S. Navy, and then moved on to become an aeronautical engineer officer for 15 years. After serving in the Navy, he signed up with the Air Force's ballistic missile program.

By the time TRW, Inc. hired him in 1958, DeLauer was a highly trained and promising engineer, having received in addition to hands-on military training an A.B. in mechanical engineering from Stanford in 1940, a B.S. in Aeronautical Engineering from the U.S. Naval Postgraduate School in 1949, and an aeronautical engineering degree and Ph.D. in aeronautics and mathematics from California Institute of Technology in 1950 and 1953 respectively. A copy of his Naval school thesis, ''Experimental Heat Transfer at Hypersonic Mach Numbers'' is on file at the Library of Congress.

He can claim an unusual honor for another of his publications. His 1965 book, *Fundamentals of Nuclear Flight,* predicts a grandiose future for nuclear rocketry: ''On all counts it seems likely that this will be the most exciting time in mankind's long climb from the Precambrian seas toward the distant stars. Nuclear energy, that other amazing discovery of our times, will almost certainly play a major role in this expansion.'' Apparently, more than DeLauer's UCLA students read the textbook—the Soviets translated it and brought back a few copies for their own use.

Born September 23, 1918 in Oakland, California, DeLauer is married with one son.

MAJOR ISSUES

- DeLauer's efforts to funnel resources into the military industrial establishment in order to fulfill Reagan's massive rearmament plan include longer range contracts with industry, promises to keep abundant contract money flowing, and expansion of the Pentagon's working relationship with colleges and universities. Still, some experts predict trouble, with shortages of both labor and capital.

- DeLauer will implement the Pentagon's proposals to reduce acquisition costs by cutting government red tape, experimenting with multi-year procurement, and implementing more realistic pricing and funding mechanisms.

- The military's communications, command and control system (C³) will be upgraded to cope with prolonged nuclear exchanges, another move which critics say could lull American leaders into resorting to nuclear weapons in the belief that such a war could be won.

- The Pentagon attempted to block Justice Department proposals to break up AT&T, but reluctantly agreed to the settlement finally reached between the two and is now pressing for consolidated control of AT&T's local phone companies.

- DeLauer in the future will have to address whether spent fuel from civilian nuclear reactors should be recycled for military use.

The Reagan Administration plans a $1.6 trillion military buildup over the next half decade. DeLauer's job is to ensure a sufficient defense industrial base exists to support this ambitious armament program. Unquestionably, his efforts will require diverting capital and human resources from the civilian sector into military programs.

Publicly, defense contractors are gleeful about the Administration's decision to funnel them billions of dollars in increased spending.

Privately, though, many predict trouble: shortages of skilled labor, antiquated plants and machinery, and over-reliance on foreign sources for critical raw materials—particularly at the subcontractor level—could frustrate the Administration's plans. A 1980 congressional report, completed *before* Reagan's massive military budget increases, concluded that the defense industrial base is unbalanced—''while excess production capacity generally exists at the prime contractor level, there are serious deficiencies at the subcontractor level.''

To alleviate the problem the Pentagon strongly supported the accelerated depreciation scheme included in the 1981 Reagan tax package, a tax break geared primarily to large, capital-intensive corporations and designed to encourage capital investment. ''This is something you should be taking advantage of right now,'' DeLauer impressed upon defense contractors in 1981.

Meanwhile, Pentagon officials continue to nudge the defense industry into expansion with promises that it will be a reliable customer and won't back off its promise to spend billions more on military contracts each year.

DeLauer has taken a personal interest in the Pentagon's efforts to divert human resources toward the military-industrial complex. ''If there is any weakness in our system vis-a-vis the Soviets,'' DeLauer said during his nomination hearing, ''it is the number of people coming out of our universities who are qualified to carry on the very highly complicated and innovative work that is necessary for us to keep a qualitative edge.'' The Pentagon is particularly concerned about the shortage of experts in microelectronics, propulsion technology, computers and information processing, and oceanography.

DeLauer has approved a number of small programs to bring colleges and universities further under the Pentagon's wing, including a DOD-university forum to discuss the skilled labor shortage and ways to better employ universities in military research. "I've been working my heart out talking to them, meeting with them. We've got a fellowship funded [for graduate students], instrumentation program funded [to modernize university contractors' laboratory equipment], and I am trying to encourage companies to have part of their research and development programs done in universities that are near them," said DeLauer. In addition, military research money flowing onto college campuses has surged.

DeLauer also has asked the U.S. aerospace industry to conduct joint research and development programs with private firms within the NATO alliance. "They can help to establish cooperative relationships on a sound business basis to the mutual advantage of the industrial base of the alliance and NATO's military forces," said DeLauer.

Another measure to encourage investment in production equipment is selective multi-year procurement, formally proposed by the Administration as part of the Carlucci initiatives in early 1981. Generally the Pentagon must renew individual weapons contracts with a company each year. Multi-year procurement would permit the Pentagon to sign contracts covering up to five years for a given weapons system. Administration officials argue that the program allows contractors to plan further in advance, take advantage of economy-of-scale buying, borrow funds less often, and make investments necessary to improve productivity. "Clearly, buying more sooner will have economic benefits," said an aide to the House Armed Services Committee. "The Carlucci initiatives attempt as best they can in a finite number of dollars not to stretch out programs. There's no way to tell how realistic they are until way down the line—after the Administration is gone." The Pentagon claims multi-year procurement could result in average dollar savings of 10 to 20 percent. It is generally agreed, however, that only those weapons systems with little risk of production problems or cost overruns should be covered by multi-year contracts. Therefore weapons will be selected for multi-year contracting on a case-by-case basis. In 1981 only a handful were involved.

Multi-year procurement has a severe drawback—an overall reduction in congressional oversight. Without the ability to review and renew these contracts each year, Congress can be locked into troublesome projects, and will lose some of its ability to change the Pentagon's direction. "The important point about multi-year contracts," said Stan Norris of the Center for Defense Information, "is that. . .the plan deprives Congress of its role to reexamine programs each year."

In return for giving the defense industry the multi-year procurement it has long desired, DeLauer says he is going to require defense contractors to "review their overhead structure and corporate staff functions with the objective of reducing and/or eliminating unnecessary layering or duplicative efforts."

For years the federal government has fallen victim to "buy-ins", in which a defense contractor submits an unrealistically low bid for a specific weapons system and then lets the costs escalate once the contract is in hand. In order to reduce such major cost overruns, the Pentagon will press each of the military services to improve their independent cost estimating capabilities and budget "to most likely or expected costs, including predictable cost increases due to risk," according to the Carlucci memorandum outlining the Administration's procurement reforms.

It's a "positive effort," said one long-time House expert on military matters, "but I don't think the Carlucci initiatives or anything like it can eliminate buy-ins." He said the Pentagon's program may help in the short-run, "but when you talk about programs to be completed near the 1990s, like many of the Administration's, you're just talking about funny money."

Despite these highly touted reforms, the Administration in its first year accepted an unrealistically low cost projection for one of its major weapons purchases, which it then tried to pass off on Congress—the B-1 bomber. The projected cost of the B-1 fleet literally doubled between the period it was reconsidered by the Air Force in early 1981 until Congress forced the Pentagon to provide a more realistic assessment later that year. (See profile of Verne Orr.)

In fact, information leaked to the press in early 1982 suggests that the cost of the entire defense program may be sharply underestimated. The *Washington Post* revealed that during secret Defense Resources Board discussions on January 7, 1982 DeLauer estimated that the Pentagon would have to spend up to $750 billion over the $1.6 trillion already planned by the Reagan Administration to meet its armament goals.

DeLauer is also charged with overseeing the Administration's modernization of the military's command, communications, and control network(C^3)—which includes ground-based radars, early warning satellites, land-based and airborne command centers and an elaborate communications network—with serious consequences for U.S. strategic doctrine.

The C^3 network has evolved into a system that can detect a nuclear attack, confirm it, and then relay the President's orders for retaliation. Until recently, the underlying premise of the system has been that any nuclear exchange would be massive but brief. The Reagan Administration, however, is preparing a system that can survive and conduct a prolonged nuclear war. As Secretary Weinberger told Congress: "We will initiate a vigorous and comprehensive R&D program leading to a communications and control system that would endure for an extended period beyond the first nuclear attack."

Critics of the Administration's strategic program argue that developing a system that can survive a prolonged nuclear exchange will lull American leaders into believing that a nuclear war can actually be fought and won. It will, they say, also prompt the Soviets to make similar improvements in their system.

Much of the military's communication system, of course, is dependent on American Telephone and Telegraph (AT&T). During the first year of the Reagan Administration, Pentagon officials opposed Justice Department efforts to split up the communications giant, claiming it would disrupt the military's communication network and threaten national security. "There are distinct advantages to having the capability and muscle of AT&T," DeLauer told us. "It is very comforting to know that if we've got a problem to be solved on communications AT&T has the capability to handle it."

However, after the Justice Department and AT&T reached a settlement forcing the company to divest itself of its 22 local phone companies, DOD reluctantly said it could live with the agreement but would prefer that the local companies be consolidated in as few units as possible. DeLauer told us a "Pacific Telephone by itself, a Potomac Telephone by itself and so on" could hurt national security.

Under the settlement, AT&T was permitted to keep its manufacturing arm, Western Electric, and its research facilities, Bell Telephone Laboratories—much to the relief of the Defense Department. In an interview with the *Wall Street Journal*, William H. Taft IV, the Pentagon's general counsel, said AT&T's ability to hold on to these two arms "was always our biggest concern, much more than divestitures of local companies."

In the coming years, DeLauer will have to address questions raised by the Reagan Energy Department: Should spent fuel from civilian nuclear power plants be reprocessed for use in military weapons? Reagan legalized the reprocessing, which was banned under the previous two administrations. Although DeLauer left open the possibility, he insisted the military has adequate material on hand to fulfill the Reagan strategic program without turning to civilian spent fuel. The practice is not necessary, he said, "unless we have an accident, and something happens with one of the generating plants. We have plenty of fissionable material. You know, you can resalvage the stuff out of old warheads."

FINANCIAL BACKGROUND

According to his financial disclosure statement, DeLauer received a $332,000 salary from TRW, Inc.; a $12,633 directors fee from Ducommon, Inc., a metal and electronics distributor; and a $25,175 directors fee from Cordura, Inc., a publishing and financial services firm. DeLauer had been director of Ducommon since 1974 and Cordura since 1976. He resigned from all three positions upon assuming office. He also received $13,300 retirement pay from the U.S. Naval Reserve.

In addition, DeLauer owned over $250,000 worth of stock in TRW, 2 percent of the firm's stock, and more minor investments in Ducommon and Damson Oil Exp., all of which he has sold. He has retained holdings, each worth less than $15,000—in Cordura Clover Run Project (natural gas exploration) and Husky Oil Co.

WHAT OTHERS ARE SAYING ABOUT HIM

- "DeLauer has been inside the iron triangle all his life," said Gordon Adams, author of *Iron Triangle*. "He has a unique strength inside the Defense Department because he has the most experience of any of the high level officials."

- "He is certainly qualified for the job," said an aide to the House Armed Services Committee. "But his R&E [Research and Engineering] shop has not been much of a player in a lot of decisions," he said, noting that the recommendations of the staff on basing the MX missile had been overruled by the President and Weinberger.

- DeLauer's operation has also been downgraded because of Defense Secretary Weinberger's decision to further decentralize the Pentagon and give more autonomy to each of the military services. "Now these services have a lot more to say about weapons procurement," said one congressional aide.

GEORGE V. ORR, JR.
SECRETARY OF THE AIR FORCE

RESPONSIBILITY OF OFFICE

Orr is the civilian director of the 580,000-member Air Force. Established by the National Military Act of 1947, the Air Force is responsible in conjunction with the other services for preserving the peace and security of the United States.

In 1982, Orr manages a total budget of $65 billion.

BACKGROUND

About the closest Verne Orr ever got to managing an air fleet before his current job was when he pencilled in the operational costs for Governor Ronald Reagan's personal jet. Orr has never served in the Air Force; his active duty during World War II was with the Navy.

"It's not quite accurate to say I wanted this job," Orr told us. "It's more accurate to say I wanted to be a service secretary and had expected that if I got my wish it would possibly be the Navy since the Navy was the only place I had experience. . .But I don't have to fly a plane in order to pick 12 people around here that I think are capable leaders and eliminate the thirteenth that doesn't seem to measure up."

Orr is more closely associated with a different transport fleet: Chryslers. When Orr got out of the Navy and was looking for a job, his father, then a vice-president of Chrysler Motor Corp., resigned and bought a dealership with his son in Pasadena, California. As a partner in that operation Verne Orr learned the art of selling and the skills of financing that would later advance his career. But a business connection—his friendship with Holmes Tuttle, owner of a Southern California Ford dealership—was Orr's entree to public office.

Tuttle, a principal financial backer of Reagan and a member of his kitchen cabinet, convinced the governor-elect in 1966 to appoint Orr director of the sprawling California Department of Motor Vehicles. It wasn't a particularly glamorous job; in fact it could be said that Orr's only claim to fame during his tenure there was that each year Californians received their license plate tags with his name printed on the upper corner of the envelope.

But either Orr's performance was impressive enough—or his connections to Tuttle significant enough—to merit a more influential spot in the gubernatorial administration. He served briefly as director of the state's Department of General Services and then moved into the state finance director post in 1970, after Caspar Weinberger left to join the Nixon Administration in Washington.

With his conciliatory manner and unpretentious personality, Orr smoothed the feathers of state legislators that had been ruffled by his more contentious predecessor. "Orr came in as an outsider," said former Republican Assembly Speaker Robert T. Monagan, comparing Orr to Weinberger. "He didn't have a know-it-all attitude. He was willing to sit down and listen. He was a tough budget cutter, but he was also very realistic and was willing to reach an acceptable common ground."

In the evenings, Orr frequently stopped by the office of the powerful chairman of the revenue and taxation committee, Assemblyman Bill Bagley. "I'd say what did you bullshitters talk about today and we just tossed it around a little bit," Orr told Reagan biographer Bill Boyarsky. "I'd try not to be stuffy."

Orr did not appear as bright as Weinberger, but he did have a more important asset—credibility among the state's legislators. "Although he made it perfectly clear he was a team player he was nevertheless the sort of person who would lay it on the line very straight," said A. Alan Post, who served as California's legislative analyst for nearly 30 years. Weinberger, on the other hand, had a propensity to stretch the truth to gain support for the governor's programs. "Verne was totally loyal to the governor," said Post. "He was just a little more careful not to stray away from the facts."

"I tried to play very honest with them," Orr told us. "For example, in the legislature I would never go up and say 'Ronald Reagan will sign this or he will veto this'. That wasn't my privilege. . .I went before them when times were bad and would say that times are bad—no fakery."

He was also more willing than Weinberger to listen to the facts. Despite the counsel of professionals in the state government, Weinberger and Reagan had refused to acknowledge that withholding of state income tax was necessary to sound government revenue collection. Orr, however, heeded the advice of the civil servants below him and finally convinced the governor to support withholding after explaining during a cabinet meeting—using charts and diagrams drawn on butcher paper—how the state came up short at the end of each year under the current tax collection system.

During Reagan's tenure, per capita state income tax doubled—despite his highly touted "rebates"—and the state government continued to grow at a rapid pace, despite Orr's tight-fisted budgeting. Orr was running the budget during some of Governor Reagan's many tax hikes, including raising sale and bank incorporation franchise taxes in 1972.

Orr fit well into the Reagan mold. A wealthy businessman who likes to reminisce about the good ol' days as if they were a series of Norman Rockwell portraits strung together, Orr is a likeable character with an unaffected view of the world. It's hard to imagine Verne Orr generating any animosity, even in the tough play of California politics. When we interviewed him, he was relaxed and thoroughly amiable, one leg plopped over the arm of his chair. His simple brown suit and department store tie, clearly worn through the years, were not the attire of millionaires, though his investments put him well into that category.

He told us he worries about the growth of corporate power, that economic concentration is not a healthy trend for American society. But neither does he feel compelled to do anything about it. "There has been constant amalgamation," said Orr. "The poor corner drug store finally lost out to Dart Drugs. The grocer lost out to Safeway. Now you're getting it in spades when Mobil tries to buy Montgomery Ward or whomever, so you're getting super corporations.

"As a person interested in society, I'm sorry," he said. "I liked it when it was an independent merchant who contributed to his community. He was really interested in the school board, he wanted to know about the city council. Now you get a manager who serves three years there, then he's moved to a little bigger store as a promotion and he never gets the same interest in the community that the private merchant had. I regret that. . .But, you know, sitting here you and I, the three of us can't change it. We can sit here and be sorry about it, but that isn't going to keep Mobil from buying Sears and Roebuck, or whatever they want to buy."

If Orr gladly served a gubernatorial administration that favored big business over the general population, he at least was candid about it. In 1974 Orr, in remarks quoted in the Los Angeles Times, summed up the Reagan record in California: "It is natural that the type of special interest group that puts you there [in office] is the one that you're going to listen to more closely. In our case, it was the conservative groups, the business groups, that put this administration in. They are our constituents."

After leaving Sacramento, Orr taught government finance courses at the University of Southern California's Graduate School of Public Administration. In 1977, he also set up a small real estate partnership with his son, and continued to carry on a number of lucrative business deals.

In a move that shocked the state's liberals and academic establishment, Gov. Jerry Brown in 1977 appointed Orr to the University of California's (UC) Board of Regents. Brown, who was then waving the banner of austerity in government, insisted that he wanted Orr on the board "to send the message to the university that we want to keep a very tight rein on spending."

Orr could not have had a more reluctant greeting from the board members, who still retained sour feelings over his actions as finance director. Orr and Reagan had constantly harassed UC's administration to cut its budget requests. When the university refused, Orr did it himself. Liberal regents on the UC board considered Orr anti-research and unwilling to support the institution's quest for academic renown. One regent was quoted as saying of Orr's nomination: "It's like sending in a tank to do a grenade job."

In a 1972 appearance before the UC board, Orr had charged the university with undermining Reagan's cost-cutting initiatives by inflating enrollment figures and crying poverty while paying its top officials lucrative salaries. He pointed out the the UC president's $53,000 salary, was higher than Governor Reagan's, at $49,000. He insisted the governor had been elected "with a huge mandate from the people" to cut expenses. "We reject completely the philosophy that this university has deteriorated or that the only way it can grow greater is from the constant infusion of dollars." Orr told us he still thinks the university is "loose financially."

Many student leaders were more optimistic about Orr's nomination. One of the reasons he was called "anti-research" was that he sympathized with students' concerns that professors were focusing on research at the expense of student contact and instruction. He once proposed requiring instructors to spend a certain number of hours each week in contact with students. He also supported UC students when they successfully sought $1 million to improve undergraduate instruction.

"I just don't think that the students are getting their money's worth," said Orr. "The professor is off doing his thing that he'd rather do, writing his book or getting his graduate students to do his procedures. . .I think we need go back to classroom teaching." Although William French Smith was permitted to keep his UC regent seat, Orr was forced to resign as a UC regent when he accepted the Air Force appointment. Said Orr: "Let me tell you how funny that is. It depends on the [congressional] committee you go before. The attorney general, William French Smith, is still a regent. His committee didn't request him to resign. The Armed Services Committee, who confirmed me, insisted I resign, isn't that odd?" (UC receives a number of research and development contracts from the Pentagon.)

Orr managed Reagan's finances in the 1976 campaign, and again in 1980. "In this [most recent] campaign what happened was that, as you remember, on the night of the New Hampshire primary [Reagan] fired [campaign manager] John Sears. And he announced that he had spent $13 million of the $17 million that he was entitled to spend for the whole thing—he had been through one primary and had 25 or more to go. About a week later I got a call from Ed Meese [saying] we need somebody to come in and help budget." Orr later managed to raise nearly $500,000 in private contributions to fund the President-elect's transition team, and came under heavy criticism when he refused to disclose the names of the donors.

Despite his long-time association with Reagan, Orr says the two did not become "socially" close. "Governor Reagan does not make social friends with his people and I applaud him for it. I don't do it either. I became very close to him on a working level; we had meetings with his cabinet about four times a week, two of them were lunches. Ed Meese sat at his right, I sat at his left for two lunches a week for five years—you get to know a man pretty well. But the only time I have ever been at his home for entertainment or official parties was when he was having a cabinet officer—and he would have a dinner party for 30 to say farewell or welcome to a new one.''

Born November 12, 1916 in Des Moines, Iowa, Orr received a B.A. from Pomona College in California in 1937 and earned a masters degree in business administration from Stanford University in 1939. He is married with two children.

MAJOR ISSUES

- As part of Reagan's plan to improve the nation's capability to fight and win a nuclear war, the Air Force is developing a fleet of 100 B-1 bombers, an addition that critics say is costly and unnecessary.

- The Air Force also will produce at least 100 MX missiles and implement the White House's final decision on how to deploy them. That decision could have profound implications for future arms control agreements and for the nation's security.

- Although Orr doesn't foresee nuclear conflict, he said he can foresee the possibility of more "Koreas or Vietnams." He excludes El Salvador from that category, and says direct U.S. intervention there would be viewed as "gunboat diplomacy" by Latin Americans.

- In tactical weapons systems, Orr faces the problem of a spare parts shortage and decisions on what to do about faulty weapons systems that the Pentagon has already funded.

Within the framework set by Reagan's strategic program, Orr is responsible for developing an Air Force that can fight, and win, a nuclear war. "I have said that the principal reason for the United States to maintain a strategic triad is deterrence, but a deterrent force without war-fighting capability is hollow," Orr remarked in a 1981 *Air Force Magazine* commentary. And, like the secretaries of the other military services, Orr is charged with preparing his forces to perform in both limited, and prolonged, nuclear exchanges. "Forces capable only of a massive final act of defiance and destruction are, in fact, destabilizing," he argued.

Two of Orr's most important decisions in that area have already been made—by Defense Secretary Weinberger and the White House. President Reagan proposed as part of his strategic package announced October 2, 1981 the construction of 100 B-1 bombers and 100 MX missiles. President Carter had cancelled the B-1 fleet in 1977, concluding that the plane was unnecessary and too costly. The expensive and sophisticated B-1 will replace the aging B-52 bombers, which are popularly termed "older than the pilots operating them." But critics of the B-1 point out that it won't be effective any longer than improved versions of the B-52.

In his annual statement, released in January, 1981, Carter Defense Secretary Harold Brown, stated that "with. . .improvements, the B-52 force can remain effective into the 1990s," the same time by which the B-1 is expected to become obsolete. Improvements to the B-52 fleet would include equipping the planes with cruise missile platforms so that nuclear warheads could be launched from outside Soviet airspace.

The Administration is developing a B-1 model that is expected to escape radar detection to a greater extent than the model Carter rejected. In addition to developing the B-1, the Administration still plans to deploy over 4,000 cruise missiles on

B-52's, at a cost of $12-13 billion. Whether the B-1 or the B-52 can successfully penetrate Soviet airspace may be an irrelevant question, say many experts, because the low flying cruise missile can be launched from bombers outside Soviet airspace and still escape radar detection.

The B-1 had nearly dropped out of the dossiers of Pentagon planners when the Reagan Administration revived it. "The B-1 is the Dracula of weapons systems," said Stan Norris, senior analyst at the Center for Defense Information. "The Carter Administration had already tried to drive a silver stake through its heart, but it's alive again with the Reagan Administration."

Orr has argued that "as the current U.S. bomber force of B-52's and FB-111's gradually loses its ability to penetrate the imposing Soviet air defense system, there is a corresponding decrease in our operational flexibility and our warfighting capability." The B-1, he asserted in *Air Force*, "will not only update this most flexible portion of our strategic triad, but also will provide a complementary role in lower orders of conflict, which have, in my judgment, a much higher probability of occurring."

Arms control proponents view the B-1 element of the Administration's strategic program as the least menacing. Unlike missiles, bombers can be recalled once they are launched. As Gerard C. Smith, director of the Arms Control Association, testified before Congress in fall, 1981: "Bombers do not drive the arms competition. . .They are relatively benign from a nuclear arms control point of view. They offer no first strike or counterforce risks."

Rather, the key question surrounding the B-1 is whether its expense can be justified when modified B-52's can perform the same functions. The projected cost of the B-1 has more than doubled since the Pentagon began reconsidering it early in 1981. Rockwell International initially put the cost of 100 planes at $11.9 billion; the Pentagon by early spring was saying $15-19 billion, and in congressional testimony finally put the figure at close to $20 billion. But even that figure lost its credibility when the General Accounting Office released a report charging that the Pentagon had left off about $2.26 billion when calculating the final cost.

Including inflation, the Congressional Budget Office, in a November 6, 1981 letter to Senator Patrick J. Leahy (D-Vt.), ranking minority member of the Senate Appropriations Committee, put the total cost of the B-1 fleet at $39.8 billion, an estimate that takes account of investment costs *only* and does not include life-cycle costs. "The B-1 bomber will be obsolete before it is deployed," said Leahy, "I do not believe we can afford a $40 billion flying Edsel."

The disclosure of the Pentagon's understated figures proved particularly embarrassing to the Administration, which had declared it will eliminate so-called buy-ins from the contracting process. Buy-ins occur when contractors submit unrealistically low bids to win a contract and then let the costs rise, sticking the Pentagon with huge cost overruns. "The B-1 was a textbook case of buying-in," said Gordon Adams, author of *Iron Triangle*. It shows, he said, "that the Administration's reported reforms to prevent cost overruns are not being followed in practice."

While production of the B-1, scheduled for deployment in 1986, continues, the Administration is betting all its chips for the long run on one replacement, the advanced technology bomber, better known as "Stealth." The top secret bomber, which the Pentagon says will be designed to be invisible to radar (and therefore able to penetrate Soviet airspace undetected) is only at the drawing board stage. The Stealth, as Norris commented, is "still a paper airplane." But Northrop, the plane's producer, claims the first Stealth can be developed by 1988, a date

Weinberger later revised to "the 1990s." Although costs of the Stealth are classified, public reports estimate the full program will range between $30-35 billion.

Although the President in October, 1981 announced his intention to build and deploy 100 MX missiles—half what Carter had proposed—over the next decade, Orr will have to recommend by 1984 how the missiles should be based. Reagan has scrapped his original plan to put the first 40 missiles in super-hardened silos that formerly housed Titan missiles.

Reagan's plan to temporarily house the first MX missiles in hardened silos had come under heavy criticism from military hardliners who agreed that the missiles would still be vulnerable to destruction in an attack, even with the added protection. Liberals, on the other hand, had chided the Administration about its "window of vulnerability" theory, which Reagan had seemingly debunked by his decision to leave the new missiles vulnerable to attack.

In announcing his strategic program, Reagan also scrapped a Carter proposal to randomly shuffle the missiles between 4,600 shelters located in Nevada and Utah. The plan had been stiffly resisted in those states by key political allies of Reagan.

So the Pentagon is left to choose among other basing plans. The decisions will center primarily on three options: deploying the missiles on a "Big Bird" aircraft, which would be in constant transit; deep underground basing on the south side of mesas; or ballistic missile defense systems to be placed around missile sites. But those are by no means the only choices. Other possibilities have included hiding the missiles on ships, dirigibles, and trucks, or basing them close together in dense packs.

Arms control proponents are particularly concerned that the Administration will opt for a ballistic missile defense or anti-ballistic missile (ABM) system—considered the most likely option and one into which Reagan is already pouring substantial research and development money.

The deployment of a large-scale ABM system could abrogate the SALT I treaty. Arms controllers say ABM systems spur the arms race and create a false sense of security that will bring closer the likelihood of national leaders resorting to nuclear war (See Profile of Eugene Rostow). "A world where Soviets and Americans were deploying thousands of ABMs," Smith testified, "will make the present seem to have been a peaceful, stable state of nuclear affairs."

In an interview Orr called the ABM treaty "the funniest kind of treaty in the world. It's a treaty against defense. I would think that our treaties would be against offense. . ." Of course, to supporters of the treaty that is its genius—a nation that lays vulnerable to a retaliatory strike is much less likely to strike first than a nation whose military leaders felt they could fend off incoming missiles with ballistic missile defenses.

Although Orr is charged with maintaining an Air Force that can fight—and win—a nuclear war, he adamantly rejects predictions of nuclear conflict. "And the reason that I don't foresee nuclear conflict is. . .we had gas—I was a baby during World War I—but we had gas. We didn't use gas in World War II, we didn't use it in Korea, we didn't use it in Vietnam. Now, it wasn't because we didn't have any. Obviously tremendous strides must have been made in the lethality of gas between 1918 and 1942. And why didn't we use it? I think quite frankly because both sides knew that the other side had it and that it was so awesome they didn't want to start it for fear of retaliation.

"Now I look on nuclear that way. I think with both sides possessing it there is a very good chance it won't be used, because the first people to use it know it is going to come flying back tenfold. But I'm not that optimistic that we won't have some Koreas or Vietnams or something that may break out in the conventional sense.''

Like El Salvador? we asked. ''I doubt it in El Salvador,'' Orr said. ''One of the differences in El Salvador to me is that the people in Vietnam—and I haven't studied the Vietnam War—but the government, and I think the people, wanted intervention. But most of South and Central America still looks on us as gunboat diplomacy. I don't think that the average person down there thirsts to see United States Marines land on the beach.''

Despite Orr's optimistic prediction about nuclear conflict, in his *Air Force* editorial he chillingly described the type of war he is preparing his forces for: ''This future clash of armies may simultaneously involve conventional, chemical, biological and nuclear weapons. This modern battlefield will be a rapidly changing one in which the level and method of warfare will be in constant flux.''

In the conventional arena, Orr faces more mundane questions, such as spare parts and airlift requirements. The Air Force has told Congress that with the current stockpile of spare parts none of its weapons systems has the capability to fight for more than 30 days. That problem developed during the 1970s, according to Richard Tuttle of *Aerospace Daily*, from the Air Force's stress on modernization, bringing in new, ultra-sophisticated aircraft, at a time of tight budgets, leaving fewer resources for spare parts. Tuttle says Reagan's massive budget increases will help, though it will take years to correct the problem.

There is little new in the Air Force's planned tactical weapon system. The service will continue to order from its prepared menu of F-15's, F-16's, A-10's, AWACS planes, TR-I's cargo planes and air-launched missiles.

Like its sister services, the Air Force is plagued with its share of expensive delays and production problems in costly weapons systems. The most publicized since Reagan took office, was the Maverick missile. The Air Force wanted to buy 61,000 of these heat-seeking missiles, but when *Washington Post* reporter Morton Mintz investigated the program and disclosed that the Pentagon planned to pour $5 billion into a missile that tested poorly even in favorable conditions, the Air Force announced it was delaying the program. Orr insisted the events were ''coincidental.''

Pressure against cutting or halting faulty or unnecessary weapon programs, Orr conceded, is enormous. ''The play is harder [in Congress than in the California Legislature]. I did not have in the state of California any players working with the legislature who had billion-dollar contracts at stake, as McDonnell Douglas, Boeing, Lockheed, TRW, and all these people do,'' he said. As for the contractors themselves, he said: ''They can play very hard. There is a great deal of money at stake.''

And as the dollars pouring into arms increase so do the stakes. Even once the Reagan five-year rearmament plan is completed, it will be difficult to slow the momentum of rising military expenditures. The Air Force will have a new fleet of B-1 bombers and modernized B-52's, and will be well on its way towards developing a new, more sophisticated, and more expensive, plane to penetrate Soviet air defenses. Similarly, its prized F-15 Eagle will obsolesce as more advanced fighters earn the Pentagon's financial support. Perhaps nothing illustrates this spiral like these remarks by Orr: ''Most of the stuff we've got gets to be obsolete in a short time. . .I am just amazed: I go down to a base and they have—is it an F-101?—yes, an F-101 which just looks to me—because I'm not an expert pilot by any means—it looks like a gorgeous plane, all sleak. And we send it up there to shoot at it! It's an old plane that has become a drone, a target! And it wouldn't be too many years if we just stopped building new stuff until the old ones would be not much better than target material."

FINANCIAL BACKGROUND

Orr's 1980 take home salary was limited to $15,542 from the Reagan-Bush campaign, and $9,047 from Reagan's transition team, $1,600 as adjunct professor at the University of Southern California; and a $7,043 retirement pension from the state of California.

But Orr's actual income was substantially higher. Together with his wife, Orr has well over $1 million invested in over 50 different firms including:
Hughes Tool Co.
Aetna Life Insurance Co.
Phillips Petroleum
Sears Roebuck, and Co.
Times Mirror
Mesa Petroleum Co.
AT&T
Continental Oil
Bausch & Lomb, Inc.
American Hospital Supply
E. Systems Inc.
Lear Siegler Inc.
Schlumberger Ltd.
Rowan Cos. Inc.
Sundance Oil Co.
Stanley Words
Trans America Corp.
Central Telephone Co., Illinois

He has since divested from any holdings listed on the DOD Statistical List of Contractors. Since July, 1977, Orr served as president of Orr Enterprises, Inc., and as a partner in Orr Enterprises real estate investment operation, based in Pasadena, California, both of which will be "inactive" during his tenure at the Defense Department.

He also served as director of the non-profit Huntington Memorial Hospital and Huntington Institute of Applied Medical Research.

WHAT OTHERS ARE SAYING ABOUT HIM

- "At first industry was wary," said Richard Tuttle of *Aerospace Daily*, "because of his background as a car salesman. But he's a quick study and he's earned their respect."

- Orr has succeeded in that, despite his background and lack of military experience, said an aide to the House Armed Services Committee, "because he is surrounded by a technically competent core of people."

JOHN MARSH
SECRETARY OF THE ARMY

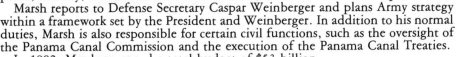

RESPONSIBILITY OF OFFICE

Marsh is the civilian in charge of the 784,000-member active
duty forces of the U.S. Army; the 398,000-member National Guard; and the 252,000-member Army Reserve. In
terms of personnel, the Army is the largest of the four
services. The mission of the Department of the Army,
created in 1947 as the successor to the Department of War,
is to organize, train, and equip active duty and reserve forces for the preservation of
peace, security, and the defense of the nation, with a focus on land operations.

Marsh reports to Defense Secretary Caspar Weinberger and plans Army strategy
within a framework set by the President and Weinberger. In addition to his normal
duties, Marsh is also responsible for certain civil functions, such as the oversight of
the Panama Canal Commission and the execution of the Panama Canal Treaties.

In 1982, Marsh managed a total budget of $53 billion.

BACKGROUND

Mention the word revolution to John Marsh and he's likely to jump into a lengthy
treatise on his favorite subject, the American War for Independence. He'll talk
about the "golden age," those 12 years preceding the war when the ideas of the
American Revolution were discussed and debated—taxation without representation, trial by jury, quartering of British soldiers. He'll describe the battle of
Yorktown, which "was not just a battle, [but] was a bridge between two political
events, the Declaration of Independence and the Constitution of the United
States." He'll muse about the U.S. Army that fought that war, a mixture of
uniformed Continental Army soldiers and ragged volunteer militia men who "embodied the cause of the revolution."

On one wall of his oblong Pentagon office hangs the photo of a log cabin, a
reproduction of an early settler's home, surrounded by 450 acres of mountain land
Marsh owns in Rockbridge County, Virginia. In the background of the photograph
is Signal Knob Mountain, for which North and South armies fought for control during the Civil War. But Marsh points to the far wall, where a painting of a familiar
scene from the American Revolution hangs. "That's one of my favorite pictures,"
he explains. "That's Washington's army going into Valley Forge on the 19th of
December, '77. You could track the army into Valley Forge by the blood on the
soliders' feet. . ."

To Marsh, the American Revolution represents everything a war should be—a
struggle flush with untainted idealism and virtue, where a clean line divides the
good guys and the bad guys and where the good guys, of course, win. "The
American Revolution was unique," he told us, comparing that struggle for freedom
with those over the past decades in Third World countries. "In most revolutions,
the idealism that leads to it seems to be frustrated or captured at some point. The
genius of the American Revolution was that civil government was always maintained and representative government continued in each of the colonies. You
didn't have the chaotic breakdown that so frequently accompanies revolutions. Our
revolution in many ways seemed to be based on reason.

"To the extent that [Third World revolutionaries] want certain freedoms and
representation of legislative bodies," Marsh continued, the struggles are similar.

"Their origins go back to the same ideas and aspirations that you had in the American Revolution. But we were very fortunate in the manner in which we were able to put it together."

Marsh's ideas are shaped by a Rotarian patriotism that he carries over to American foreign intervention today. To Marsh, U.S. involvement in Vietnam represented a benevolent expansion of American ideas. "If you look at the track record of this great country since World War II we have made mistakes, there is no question about it. But we have sought to be a source for the development of individual and economic freedom. And where the American flag has gone, if you look at some of the things Jack Kennedy said for why we went in, our causes and our motives for where we have intervened have had a certain idealism with them that you don't find in the Soviet Union."

Indeed, Marsh was a strong supporter of the Vietnam War during his eight years, from 1963 to 1970, as a congressman from Virginia's 7th district. In a 1966 speech on the House floor, Marsh asserted that troops were sent into Vietnam "to achieve peace and freedom." But at the same time Rep. Marsh was critical of the secrecy that shrouded policy-making over Vietnam. In 1971 Marsh told Lynchburg Jaycees: "The whole episode reeks with the arrogance of power exercised by a selected few, rather than decisions made by the elected. The tragedy is the contemptuous disregard this little clique of planners had for the people of the Nation they were expected to serve."

Marsh said he also believes the war dragged out needlessly. "More aggressive action to wind down the war should have been taken in 1965 by President Johnson in the nature that President Nixon took in 1972—moves against North Vietnam, the bombing of Hanoi, the mining of the harbor at Haiphong—that would have ultimately led to the Paris peace accords," he told us. In addition, he said, "we should have mobilized elements of the Guard and Reserves, which we did in '68 in a very modest way."

But most importantly, says Marsh, "in a democratic society if you are going to prosecute [such] an effort you must mobilize public opinion in support." Reflecting his almost naive idealism for the American Revolution, Marsh sincerely believes that once the public is informed and understands American motives in overseas interventions, they will rally in support. "I think support will flow from understanding; once you make the information available and people become informed, support will flow from that. The problem in Vietnam was that we didn't get out sufficient information where they understood what vital interests Vietnam represented."

What about U.S. intervention in El Salvador, which the public overwhelmingly opposes? "I think the steps that you see that relate to circumstances occurring in El Salvador, the type of information in the reports both by Secretary Haig and Secretary Weinberger and others will be helpful to the development of that [support]. I believe that people, once they understand those circumstances, the long-range impact of U.S. interests in Central America; and secondly when they realize the nature of the sources of infiltration there—the indirect role the Soviets are playing, and the Cubans—I think those will be the types of things that will cause American accord to flow for American policy," he told us.

Press accounts of government troops massacring civilians in El Salvadoran towns, Marsh conceded, damage the Administration's attempts to formulate that support. "It simply makes the necessity of apprising people even more important as to what the U.S. position is and what the truth of the facts are that might be reported in the press. I'm not in the position to address that," Marsh said.

When we asked Marsh if he thought the issues in El Salvador were important enough to risk the lives of his two sons, both in the Army, he replied: "Both of my two sons are associated with the military service and are willing and able to go where the Army sends them. Our policies as a country have been determined by a senior national leadership and if they are selected to go, they will go."

Like his boss, Ronald Reagan, Marsh gets nervous around polarized perspectives. He prefers harmony over discord. As the only lawyer in a small town in the Virginia apple country, population 2,200, and a citizen active in the local Jaycees, Marsh clearly is uncomfortable with the divisions that mark contemporary America. Even his eight years on Capitol Hill didn't make much of a dent. He says of the peace demonstrations during the 1960s: "I like to think that because of 1) my training in the law and 2) what I perceive as the role of the congressman, that these types of peaceful demonstrations are a form of free speech and people have the right to demonstrate. But to me it indicated frustration that flowed from lack of understanding and a lot of the policies we pursued."

Perhaps his most revealing remark was made while showing us the Army streamer for the Civil War, a struggle he is not fond of because it was "divisive." The Civil War streamer, he said, "is blue and gray—which symbolizes the reunion of the two forces. I had forebears who were in the Confederate Army, but I would not have been offended if they had been all blue, that's a gesture."

The Blue Ridge Mountains and Shenandoah Valley towns that comprise Marsh's former congressional district were once home to Abraham Lincoln's parents, Marsh likes to point out, and even though Lincoln is identified with the North, "I'm very proud of Lincoln. Lincoln, had his parents not migrated, would have been from Harrisonburg, Virginia; I grew up in Harrisonburg. I've always felt that Lincoln was the grass roots advocate interpreter of Jeffersonian democracy."

Marsh maintains that he would have been Thomas Jefferson's congressman in those days. "Jefferson never served in the federal Congress but my seat was first contested between James Madison and James Monroe, Madison won."

As a congressman, Marsh was a staunch conservative. Though he was elected a Democrat, his voting record was further to the right than his old Capitol Hill friend and the Republican President he would later serve, Gerald Ford. In 1968, the liberal Americans for Democratic Action gave him a "zero" rating on his voting record.

As a member of the House Appropriations Committee, Marsh found pleasure in trying to slow LBJ's Great Society programs, which he says "created a revolution of rising expectations that could not be met." When the Department of Housing and Urban Development (HUD) was created to aid troubled cities, George Mahon, the tight-fisted Democrat from Texas who chaired the House Appropriations Committee, appointed Marsh to the subcommittee controlling HUD's budget, even though Marsh's district was less than 30 percent urban, far below the national average, and he had accumulated a record opposing federal social programs.

But Marsh does like to assert that he, a conservative southerner, voted to reseat Adam Clayton Powell, an outspoken black congressman from Harlem who was accused of misusing congressional funds during his tenure as chair of the House Education and Labor Committee. Powell, who regained his House seat after the Supreme Court overruled a congressional vote "excluding" him from Congress, claimed the accusations were racially motivated.

In telling that story Marsh conveniently omits two other votes considered even more important by Powell's former special assistant, Chuck Stone, now senior editor at the *Philadelphia Daily News*. On January 10, 1967, Marsh twice voted against Powell, first against a motion by Morris Udall to seat him while his conduct was investigated, and then in favor of a Gerald Ford motion not to seat him. "The vote we considered a key was the Gerry Ford one," said Stone. "Anybody who voted against the Udall motion and for the Ford motion is a categorical, flaming racist." The vote Marsh today refers to was when he voted against a March 1, 1967, measure to expel Powell.

When we asked Marsh what he would like to be remembered for as a congressman, he gave a magnanimous reply about working very hard at representing his constituents and spending a great deal of time in his district. Then, however, he launched a detailed discourse on his work for the American bicentennial. Sitting in his Pentagon office, surrounded by paintings and artifacts recording the American Revolution, a twinkle in his eye and the bicentennial star as a tie pin, Marsh recalled introducing the original legislation on celebrating the American bicentennial in 1963: "People ask 'why did you introduce legislation for the bicentennial in '63 when the Declaration wasn't until '76?' And I point out to them that the revolutionary period in American history is considered to be a block of 20 years. It was during the first 12 years, the 'golden age', that the ideas of the American revolution would be discussed and would be debated."

Marsh served on the bicentennial planning commission, and as recently as 1981 was giving planners of the Yorktown bicentennial a tour of the battlefield, pointing out where the shots were fired and which ridges saw the clash of troops.

After Marsh dropped out of the Democratic Party, which by 1970 he considered too liberal, and decided not to run for reelection, he exiled himself in a Washington law firm, where he remained until 1973, when the Pentagon asked him to become its chief lobbyist. Ten months later, in the closing days of Watergate, he joined Vice-President Ford's staff as assistant for national security affairs. When Ford became President, Marsh moved up as well, becoming counsel with a Cabinet rank.

Together with another Ford protege from Capitol Hill, Donald Rumsfeld, Marsh emerged as a key White House power. Marsh and Rumsfeld represented a sharp contrast to the aides running the Johnson and Nixon White Houses. One *New York Times* reporter wrote: "They have a strong respect for the full range of public institutions and private interests. Both are accessible. . ." Of Marsh, the reporter commented, "He is not the typical White House aide, aggressively seeking power and influence. [He is] as folksy as a lawyer from the Virginia apple country is expected to be. He is friendly and open and seems a little harassed by the hectic daily routine that has been thrust upon him."

In the new spirit of openness, Marsh chaired a Ford committee which reorganized the intelligence community's relationship with Congress. "I think that's helpful," said Marsh. "We have to recognize that elected representatives enjoy a special status and there are times in the execution of their duties that there is a very clear need to know on their part, and where that exists, that information should be made available to them. Our genesis is in the Congress of the United States. This is something that we constantly need to remind ourselves of, those of us in the Executive Branch."

After leaving the White House, Marsh became a partner in the Richmond law firm of Mays, Valentine, Davenport and Moore where he remained until former President Ford asked President-elect Reagan to hire him as secretary of the Army.

In 1977, Marsh joined a committee formed to rally support for ratification of the Panama Canal treaties, accords which Ronald Reagan vigorously opposed in the

1976 campaign. The bipartisan committee formed by President Carter included such luminaries as A. Averill Harriman, George Meany, George Ball, and Henry Cabot Lodge. Marsh now considers himself "an independent associated with the Republicans."

Marsh is an Army man from way back. He joined the Army in 1944, and served active duty with the U.S. occupation forces in Germany. He was an officer in the Army Reserves from 1947 to 1951 and the Virginia National Guard from 1951 to 1976, when he was forced to retire. He served one month in Vietnam, while he was a congressman, and toured with various battalions there, though he never fired his weapon.

Born August 7, 1926, in Winchester, Virginia, Marsh received his law degree from Washington and Lee University in Lexington, Virginia, in 1951. He is married with three children.

MAJOR ISSUES

- Though many experts expect the Army, faced with an expanding labor needs and a shrinking pool of young people, to find it difficult to fulfill Reagan's plans for military expansion without implementing a peacetime draft, in the short run unemployment is swelling the service's ranks.

- The Army's ambitious modernization plans have resulted in numerous cost overruns and delays, yet Marsh is continuing to order up a menu of expensive and sophisticated weapons systems.

- In order to improve the Army's ability to fight in all parts of the world, a new combat doctrine has been imposed calling for faster and more flexible war-fighting capability.

- For the first time since 1969 the U.S. military will begin producing chemical weapons.

The big question facing Secretary Marsh is whether the Army can find enough qualified soldiers to fill the Administration's ambitious military expansion plans without instituting a draft. A secret Army report leaked to the press in July, 1981 hinted that the 96,000 troops needed to meet the Administration's goals by 1987 could not be achieved without some type of conscription. Though the report did not use the words "draft" or "conscription", it did state, referring to the Army's objective of building an 870,000-member force by 1987: "This growth is necessary to support substantial force structure increases and will require extraordinary manpower policies to include significant augmentation to the Volunteer Concept."

Marsh, like other Pentagon appointees, has publicly insisted that he will try to meet the Army's requirements with an all-volunteer force. Implicitly, though, Marsh, Weinberger and others have left open the possibility of a peacetime draft if the all-volunteer concept fails to fulfill their objectives. "The all-volunteer Army is a national policy which we must seek to execute," Marsh told us. "Given certain tools and resources I think we can do it." The draft was replaced by the volunteer service in the early '70s in the wake of public resistance growing out of the Vietnam War.

Reagan's planned military expansion parallels a decline in the pool of 17 to 21 year olds. Moreover, the weaponry soldiers must use is becoming increasingly complex at a time when there is a nationwide shortage of trained personnel in a number of technical fields. The military is trying to attract recruits through better pay and benefits; Congress in 1981 passed a large pay raise for enlistees, increased enlistment and reenlistment bonuses, and, increased educational benefits "that will enable us to attract the college-bound youth," said Marsh.

As a candidate, Reagan said he opposed a peacetime draft and the draft registration program implemented by Carter in 1980. However, the Administration has made no moves to alter the Carter plan.

The Army exceeded its recruitment goals during 1981, both in terms of numbers and educational levels, in part, Marsh concedes, because of the poor performance of the economy and high unemployment rates in the private sector. In April, 1982, as the economy faltered, the Army reported it was exceeding recruitment goals by 25 percent and for the first time would be accepting only high school graduates.

Ironically, if the President's economic program works, and new jobs open up in the private sector, the military could have more difficulty meeting recruiting goals. "But we don't want to ride on the backs of unemployment" in order to meet Army enlistment goals, Marsh insisted. Other reasons for improved recruitment, according to Marsh and other experts, were improved public attitudes about the military, as well as better pay and educational benefits.

"This is going to be a hot issue," said one aide to the House armed forces subcommittee on manpower. "If the economy turns up and if we go ahead with increases in the size of the military, filling their ranks is going to be a concern." That assessment was seconded by the President's Council of Economic Advisers in its 1982 annual report. Already some Republicans favor a draft as a means to rebuild the military, while some Democrats support it as a means to more equitably distribute military service, a burden now disproportionately borne by low-income men. "Some members would like to go back to the draft," said another aide to the House Armed Services Committee. "But it's just not politically feasible at this point." The Administration appears to agree.

During the 1970s the Army undertook an intense modernization plan that included buying a series of highly sophisticated—and expensive—tanks, missiles, helicopters, guns, and electronic equipment. The cost of many of these programs has leapt out of control, forcing the Army to stretch out their procurement in order to meet budget levels. But that move simply added to the cost. The costs of operating and supporting these new weapons systems once they are in the field is expected to be enormous.

In October, 1981 the General Accounting Office (GAO) released a report studying the impact of continuing with 14 of the Army's major systems—which together represent half of the Army's total procurement budget during the next five years.

"Fielding all 14 new systems during the next decade is likely to seriously strain the Army's available long-term operation and support resources," the report concluded. In its 1983 budget, the Army plans to go ahead with all but two of those systems (one of those, the Standoff Target Acquisition System will be replaced by another system; the Roland missile will be discontinued). "Most all of these systems will require more people with higher skills at a time when competition for personnel may be more intense. They will also require more fuel and ammunition, imposing an increased logistics burden," said the GAO report.

Many of the systems can also be expected to escalate in cost. For example, the M-1 tank, the Army's top priority weapon system, and a favorite target of the GAO, was estimated to cost $1.45 million each in May, 1979, when the contract was awarded to Chrysler's tank division. Now the price tag has reached $2.7 million each. The Army wants more than 7,000 of them. The sophisticated tank, which will replace many of the simpler and less expensive M-60 tanks has a number of mechanical difficulties, and breaks down intermittently.

The M-1 transmission is so delicate, in fact, that the Army is developing a companion vehicle called the Armored Combat Earthmover or ACE, to do part of its work. ACE, essentially a fast moving bulldozer that costs $1.1 million each, will dig protective battlefield positions in which the M-1 can hide. The Army, however, insisting that the M-1's "militarily significant" problems have been corrected, will continue fielding the weapon. In testimony before a Senate subcommittee Army Undersecretary James Ambrose called the M-1 "the best tank in the world" and said, "Contrary to what we have read in the newspapers, the cost controls have been excellent."

In cost overruns and technical problems, the M-1 is similar to a number of other Army weapon programs included in the 1982 and 1983 budgets: the AH-64 Apache advanced attack helicopter, whose cost has risen from $10 million a piece two years ago to $16 million each; the Patriot air defense system, which has risen from $5.5 billion in fiscal year 1980 to $7.8 billion in 1982; and the Viper, a shoulder fired antitank rocket, which General Dynamics proposed to the Army in 1976 with a price tag of $78 each. Now each Viper will cost the Army $1,000 each. The Blackhawk helicopter leapt from $2.8 million each in 1979 to $4.7 million each.

The Reagan Administration rejects theories forwarded by a growing number of analysts such as James Fallows, author of *National Defense*, that the U.S. military should rely less on building a few expensive, complicated, and problem-ridden weapons and instead concentrate on developing larger numbers of basic, more practical systems. Currently, the Pentagon is concentrating on maintaining a qualitative edge over the Soviet Union rather than gaining a quantitative edge in many areas. "[T]he argument that the cost [of equipment] is unnecessarily high because of 'gold plating' or because the technology is too complex is unfounded," Marsh said in his 1983 budget statement before Congress. "Technology is expensive, but we need it to survive and to be effective in battle because we cannot redress the quantitative imbalance. . .We owe our soldiers equipment that increases the likelihood of success in combat."

The Army is on the threshold of implementing a new combat doctrine— expected to improve American ability to intervene militarily in other parts of the world—in which troops will rely on a more freewheeling, agile style of war. According to a strategic blueprint called "Airland Battle 2000", the Army is adopting "a style of waging war in which agility, deception, maneuver, and all other tools of combat are used to face the enemy with a succession of dangerous and unexpected situations more rapidly than he can react to them. . .No longer will the outcome of the battle be decided by attrition between lines drawn up as in a football game. . .Picture a soccer game as opposed to football. Each element maneuvering in what appears to be an independent, uncoordinated effort. In reality, it is a highly coordinated plan of action." The doctrine is expected to be implemented through increased use of fast, lightweight land vehicles, sophisticated electronic weapon systems and troops working together in smaller groups.

Airland Battle 2000, which Deputy Secretary Frank Carlucci has praised, depicts a futuristic battlefield. The report includes plans for heavier reliance on automation, particularly robots, which can help fill the manpower gap by performing chores such as repairing vehicles, forging paths through mine fields and planting mines behind enemy lines. It also suggests the possibility of electrically powered vehicles and aircraft that use laser attacks.

Other sharp changes are underway. For the first time since 1969 the U.S. military will begin producing chemical weapons. In what Sen. Mark Hatfield (R-Ore.) chair of the Senate Appropriations Committee, called an action of "sheer madness" that could launch "the country on a system that could bring disaster to the earth," Congress in 1981 appropriated $23 million to equip a new chemical weapons factory in Pine Bluff, Arkansas. Production of chemical weapons ended in 1969 and since then Presidents Nixon, Ford and Carter opposed its resumption.

The Pentagon, however, claims production of chemical weapons is necessary to counter the Soviets. In the Army's 1983 posture statement Marsh called the Administration's decision to go ahead with chemical weapons "a deterrent that is critically needed when viewed in the context of the Soviet Union's formidable and expanding offensive capability to wage chemical warfare and their willingness to use this capability as evidenced in Afghanistan." Further, Marsh maintained, "the very real potential exists, as a result of the linking of lethal mycotoxins to the 'yellow rain' attacks in Southeast Asia, that the Soviets are using biological weapons in direct violation of the Biological Weapons Convention and the Geneva Protocol."

In the absence of a chemical and biological disarmament accord the Army argues, the U.S. needs a "credible" stockpile to "deter" others from using chemical and biological weapons against the U.S. or allies. In its 1983 budget, the Pentagon has requested money to purchase an initial supply of "binary projectiles." In addition, troops are being trained to fight in a chemical-weapon war.

One senior Pentagon official in early 1982 told *New York Times* reporter Drew Middleton that, although talk of using "poison gas frightens people. . .it could be considered a cheaper substitute for nuclear warfare that would do far less damage outside the battlefield."

The Army also will be directing research and development on the Ballistic Missile Defense system included in the President's strategic program. One type of system is intended to destroy nuclear warheads by nuclear bursts after they have entered the atmosphere. Through another system, called overlay defense, on which the Army is continuing research and development, warheads above the atmosphere would theoretically be intercepted and destroyed by non-nuclear means.

FINANCIAL BACKGROUND

According to his financial disclosure statement, Marsh received a $95,225 salary from the law firm of Mays, Valentine, Davenport and Moore, where he worked until his appointment. His major clients included Financial General Corp. of Washington, D.C.; American Marine Underwriters, Inc. of Miami; National Medical Care, Inc. of Boston; Campbell Taggart, Inc. of Dallas; the Airlie Foundation of Airlie, Virginia; Pocantico Hills of New York; and Intercontinental Consolidated Companies of Houston.

Since 1978 he also served on the board of directors of A-T-O, Inc., a multinational company based in Ohio that manufactures such products as fire protection equipment, mining and construction equipment, and electronics. He received a $15,000 fee for that effort. Marsh also served on the board of directors for the First and Merchants National Bank of Arlington, Virginia since 1977 and the Webster-Heise Corporation of Phoenix, Arizona since 1980.

WHAT OTHERS ARE SAYING ABOUT HIM

- Edward Luttwak, a senior fellow at Georgetown University's Center for Strategic and International Studies, and a frequent critic of the Army's past performance said: "I am not interested in the politics of individuals, I'm interested in the study of warfare. But I can tell you this, in my experience, Mr. Marsh is the first [Army] secretary interested in the operational function of the Army, what the Army would potentially have to do on a battlefield." Marsh is interested in the "preparation of warfare;" rather than "bureaucratics," Luttwak added.

- Marsh is expected to be an effective advocate for Army programs. Said an aide to the House Armed Services Committee: "Jack Marsh is good for the Army. The Army, compared to the other two services, has suffered from the lack of an articulate spokesman before Congress."

JOHN LEHMAN, JR.
SECRETARY OF THE NAVY

RESPONSIBILITY OF OFFICE

Better known around the Pentagon as SecNav, John Lehman is responsible for the policies and control of the Department of the Navy, which in 1982 has about 553,000 men and women on active duty. Also under Lehman's purview is the 192,000-member Marine Corps.

The mission of the U.S. Navy, which was founded on October 13, 1775 as the Continental Navy of the American Revolution, is to protect the U.S. with its sea forces and "maintain freedom of the seas."

Traditionally a sinecure for retiring statesman, Lehman has transformed his office into a mapping room for American military strategy around the globe.

In 1982, Lehman managed a budget of $69 billion.

BACKGROUND

There is something of the story of the times in the tale of John Lehman's meteoric career. It is in some respect a typical Washington story: a bright, ambitious young man serving powerful, prestigious officials while accumulating power and prestige of his own. But in it is also the resurgent tide of militarism in the nation's political thought, a current that has washed away the stain of Vietnam and carried him into high office at a tender age.

Twice in the past seven years, Lehman—though still not 40 years of age—has come before the Senate as the President's nominee for vital national security posts. Though the views Lehman expressed did not change much, the two occasions could not have been more dissimilar.

In 1975, with the backwaters of Watergate and Vietnam still rippling, Lehman faced exacting questioning from an openly hostile Senate Foreign Relations Committee when President Ford nominated him as deputy director of the Arms Control and Disarmament Agency (ACDA). Hawkish on Vietnam and the Soviet Union, skilled at bureaucratic infighting, and a veteran of Henry Kissinger's National

Security Council (NSC), Lehman seemed to the White House a perfect complement to Fred Ikle, the professorial ACDA director that Nixon had installed after purging the agency in 1973. (See profile of Fred Ikle.)

Lehman, though, almost never made it to ACDA. Skeptical about his commitment to arms control and piqued by his antagonism toward Congress, the committee grilled Lehman, summoned several other witnesses (including Ikle), and only reluctantly forwarded his nomination. Spiced with sharp language and angry accusations, the encounter was a classic confrontation between the Democratic Congress and the secretive foreign policy apparatus ruled by Henry Kissinger.

When Lehman returned in January, 1981 as Ronald Reagan's nominee to be the youngest secretary of the Navy in this century, the world had changed. Sympathetic Republicans, not Democrats, ran the Committee on Armed Services which heard his testimony. And those Democrats that did appear were less interested in Lehman's views on the prerogatives of the Executive, or the need for arms control, than assessing his stands on how to strengthen the Navy. No one suggested that it might already be strong enough, or at least might not need more money in a time of austerity; such views had apparently passed out of the bounds of political propriety. The result was 90 minutes of powder puff questions and fulsome praise culminating in a unanimous approval of his nomination.

Lehman's first confirmation hearing offers more insight into his views and character. The hearings portrayed a man who took a hard line not only against the Soviet Union, but against the public's role in setting foreign policy as well.

Lehman ran into the most trouble over his undiplomatic attack, at an informal January, 1971 gathering on former Foreign Relations Committee Chairman William Fulbright. At the time, Lehman was Kissinger's congressional liaison at the NSC, which he joined in 1969 as an aide to Richard Allen. Arranged by the American Foreign Service Association in the hope of smoothing over the acrimony between National Security Council and Congress, the meeting blew up when Lehman said Fulbright had a "mischievious" attitude toward the Administration and accused Senate staffers of leaking confidential material to the press. A few days later, the incident landed in the *Washington Post*.

At his confirmation hearing, Lehman acknowledged the remarks about Fulbright, but said he "did not, I repeat, accuse anyone on the Foreign Relations Committee or the staff of leaking information." On that point he was directly contradicted by three staffers who attended the meeting and testified at his confirmation.

Making the incident even more troubling for Lehman was testimony suggesting the outburst was not an isolated incident. Harrison M. Symmes, a former deputy assistant secretary of state for congressional relations who worked with Lehman in 1970 and 1971, wrote the committee that, "In all of my official associations with Mr. Lehman during that period, I found him to be a zealous proponent and advocate of White House attitudes toward the nature and extent of executive power."

Added Symmes at the hearings: "I found he had an overzealous and overenthusiastic approach to control of information and I found that he generally distrusted people like me who were career bureaucrats or who in his opinion were perhaps too liberal in their outlook toward the Constitution of the United States." Nor, Symmes reported, did Lehman have much use for Congress. "[H]is attitude was generally that the committee will not get access to the kind of information they are asking for," he said. "In these kinds of dealings it seemed to me that he was taking a personal responsibility upon himself that exceeded his actual position in the superstructure and that exceeded even what some of his superiors might have wanted him to do in terms of tactfulness and in terms of negotiation."

Similar questions were raised by Lehman's doctoral dissertation, which was ultimately published in 1976 as a book entitled, *The Executive, Congress, and Foreign Policy, Studies of the Nixon Administration*. In a bizarre spectacle, Ikle was hauled before the Senate Foreign Relations Committee not to talk primarily about Lehman's views on arms control, but to explicate his dissertation, which examined battles between the Nixon Administration, particularly the NSC, and Congress over foreign policy in the late 1960s and early 1970s.

Lehman's commitment to arms control, far from passionate, was also questioned. Sen. Claiborne Pell (D-R.I.) told Lehman that he had "made calls within the Government to the ACDA and to the State Department and also to the people who have left both those organizations. I have received one reply with no comment on your nomination. I have not received one reply supportive of it. All I received, except for one neutral, were negative."

Eventually, Kissinger himself had to bail out his embattled former employee, cabling from Aswan that Lehman "would be a great asset to ACDA." The committee cleared him by a 9-6 vote, and the full Senate, by a voice vote with only a handful of members present, went along.

That association with the NSC served Lehman well at ACDA. After SALT I was concluded, Kissinger had downgraded the agency, seizing more of the arms negotiation authority for himself, and Lehman had better access to the NSC than his boss, Ikle. Lehman also had ties to SALT critic Sen. Henry Jackson (D-Wash.) and his aide, Richard Perle, now an assistant secretary of defense. Not an administrator, Ikle left much of the day-to-day agency business to Lehman, whose hardline views alienated many of the staff—who were already suspicious about his role in the 1973 purge of the agency. Of his role in the personnel shakeup, Lehman says today, "Did I have a role in personnel recommendations. . .right after the '72 election? Sure I did and I think it really improved the Arms Control Agency. I think we have the right to have Republicans in a Republican Administration. . .While Paul Warnke purged nearly every Republican with no exception that I am aware of out of the Arms Control Agency when he came in, somehow when Republicans fire a whole bunch of Democrats that was a purge. I never heard the word purge used in the press about Warnke's wiping out the Republicans."

"He was a real super conservative hawk who was out to gut the agency," one high ACDA official who worked with Lehman told us. "I think he was a very destructive force." Said another ACDA official: "He was actively working to slow things up—out of conviction."

"He was an agent provocateur," said one former high government official involved in SALT. "Lehman was a guy who creatively lied, to make trouble."

Though Kissinger supported his nomination, Lehman later opposed Kissinger's efforts to conclude SALT II in late 1975 and early 1976. Working with Ikle, Perle, and then Defense Secretary Donald Rumsfeld, Lehman helped persuade Ford to step back from the negotiations. "It was pretty obvious there was a de facto alliance between Perle, Jackson, Ikle and Lehman," said one former Kissinger associate. ACDA's hard line hamstrung Kissinger's efforts to conclude the agreement, another high government official from the period told us. "As a result [of the purge] the State Department ended up being the furthest to the left on arms control debates. What you really want is to have ACDA to be to your left, so you're not the softy. If you're secretary of State you should have someone to your left. When the ACDA people—Ikle and Lehman— are hardline, that puts Kissinger on the left part of the spectrum and that was one reason why. . .you couldn't get SALT II or Vladivostock agreements," said the official.

"I had many problems with many of the drafts that Henry at various times carried around with him," Lehman told us. "One of the issues that I strongly opposed internally in 1976 was banning the use of Tomahawks [cruise missiles] on ships. I still think that would have been a fundamental mistake and ultimately that was disapproved and thank God, because now we got them and it is one of the most effective conventional weapons for war at sea that I can see right now." Critics of deploying Tomahawks aboard ships argued that because the missiles can carry nuclear warheads as well as conventional ones and are easily concealed, they would make the monitoring of strategic arms agreements difficult.

Many believe that whatever influence ACDA exerted over arms control policy—and until the winter of 1975-76 it wasn't much—was due to Lehman's efforts. "Without Lehman," said the Kissinger aide, "Ikle wouldn't have amounted to a whole lot because John was the man who made that place function." (See profiles of Fred Ikle and Richard Perle.)

Looking back at that period, we asked, did Lehman think the Nixon and Ford Administrations overestimated the goodwill of the Soviet Union? "Certainly some of my colleagues on the NSC staff did. I wouldn't want to name anyone," he said. "I think that I would put more of the blame on Congress during that period for killing the chances for detente because I think Kissinger and Nixon looked at it very realistically and very hopefully. But Congress relentlessly kept knocking [down defense expenditures]. . .and we never really could carry out the defense rebuilding leg that the detente policy stood on."

Despite Kissinger's recent public accusations that the Reagan Administration's foreign and military policies are too soft, Lehman still holds his former boss in high esteem. Kissinger's commentaries in the *New York Times*, Lehman said, "are a much fairer representation of Henry Kissinger's views than some of the attacks that have been made on him by the right. I worked very closely with Henry now for 13 years and those articles are the Henry Kissinger I know, not the one that the right wing has pilloried in the press."

During his ACDA tenure, Lehman did make some strong public statements about nuclear proliferation, which he termed at his confirmation hearing "the single most unrecognized threat to our security today." In 1976, Lehman testified against the reprocessing of commercial nuclear wastes—a move now strongly supported by the Reagan Administration—as a measure of dubious economic value that would "vastly complicate the problem of keeping reliable controls on potential proliferating states." In the agency, though, Lehman spent little time on nonproliferation, concentrating on arms control negotiations and internal organizational issues.

"I am as concerned today as I was at ACDA about the growth of proliferation," he told us, "but there is a fundamental difference in philosophy under Ford and under Reagan compared to Carter's approach to it. We believe the biggest source of the rush to proliferate is the growth of instability in the world. People don't go and make that sacrifice unless they feel their security is very definitely being threatened: Pakistan, Taiwan, Korea, the countries that have been reported in the press to be pursuing nuclear technology, not to mention Iraq and Libya, if they felt they were part of a basically stable world system in which U.S. security commitments to them by treaty and otherwise [would be honored], had a fairly peaceful world, then competition for scarce resources would not make available the kind of magnitude of funds that are necessary to pursue it. . . .As important as IAEA [International Atomic Energy Agency] controls and technology transfer are, we have found—we tried to keep it away from the Russians and we certainly had an even larger incentive to do that—we couldn't keep the technology from seeping out. If we don't do the one and establish security and [instead] just try to hold back the seep of technology in the scientific world we're doomed to failure.''

Lehman was swept out of office by Carter's election, but landed lucratively as president of the Abington Corp., a D.C.-based firm that consulted for the Pentagon and military contractors. Lehman kept his name in military circles by serving on advisory panels to the Republican National Committee, and the Reagan campaign. He chaired the drafting committee that penned the hardline defense section of the Republican platform.

And he continued to write about arms control and national defense. Lehman had been writing about arms control since the mid-1960s when he co-edited two books on the subject. In an introduction to a collection called, *Arms Control For the Late Sixties*, Lehman asserted that nuclear weapons could be a stabilizing force on world politics: ''[I]t is arguable that the power balance of the last twenty years, marked by the severest conflict of ideas the world has known since the Reformation and sustained by the most powerful states in history, owes its relative stability in no small measure to the existence of nuclear weapons.'' In a 1981 *Strategic Review* article, Lehman referred to ''the immense utility, both destructive and psychological, of nuclear arms.''

Out of office, Lehman became part of the shadow government dogging the Carter Administration's efforts to conclude SALT II. He joined the Committee on the Present Danger. And he criticized the Carter Administration's maneuvers, writing in 1977 that, ''The most serious obstacle to achieving a sensible SALT outcome has been the takeover of virtually all key second-tier appointments in State, Defense, and the National Security Council by. . .[a] clique of personalities drawn from an extremely narrow end of the Democratic Party spectrum. . .'' Four years later, he felt secure enough in the treaty's demise to entitle his latest book *Beyond the SALT II Failure*.

Lehman has the eclectic touch of a born politician. An academic who can wade through the catechisms of strategic theory and recite Navy minutiae with a room full of admirals, he is also a lieutenant commander in the Naval Reserve who has, in the words of a blurb used to introduce one of his articles, ''flown most of the strategic and theater attack aircraft in the U.S. inventory.'' Not even his appointment as SECNAV, as the lingo goes, kept him from his tour of duty at Virginia's Ocean Naval Air Station in summer.

He also knows how to touch the hearts of the hawks who now direct American foreign policy with tough talk that exudes a sensuality of power: ''Where once the use of American power, including military power, inspired excitement, optimism and even a sense of destiny, for a long while Americans have been embarrassed rather than excited by the prospect of exerting power abroad. In such exertion we saw entanglement, not a sense of mission; we discerned risk, not opportunity.''

In the photos they distribute, Lehman's press operation makes sure you're aware of the two sides of their boss. One photo has him dark-suited, listening attentively behind a desk; the other captures him with wind-blown hair, ruddy in a flight jacket with two insignias. One reads John Lehman, LCDR; the other Mr. John Lehman, SECNAV. A man on the move, and not one likely to retire from the political arena after his current tenure in the limelight is completed.

It all adds up to an unusually visible Navy secretary, who has overshadowed his less colorful colleagues at the helm of the Army and Air Force. As his aides readily admit, that helps out in the squabbles among the services at budget time, a process that Lehman once described as "fratricide." As Lehman complained in his 1976 book: "It was persistently vexing to the White House during the more difficult legislative struggles on such matters as ABM, the aircraft carriers, the Trident missile submarine, and the B-1 bomber to find that the very best position papers against aircraft carriers circulating on [Capitol] Hill, for instance, were traced back to the Air Force. The best position papers against proceeding with the B-1 bomber were prepared by the Navy."

If those problems are still present, Lehman is now more diplomatic. (See Major Issues section.)

Born on September 14, 1942 in Philadelphia, Pennsylvania, Lehman has a long academic background in international relations, with an undergraduate degree from St. Joseph's College (1964), a graduate degree from Cambridge University (1967) and a doctorate from the University of Pennsylvania in 1974. (By then Lehman was serving as a member of the U.S. delegation to the Mutual Balanced Force Reduction talks in Vienna.) Lehman spent 1967-69 as a staff member at the University of Pennsylvania Foreign Policy Research Institute, the director of which introduced him to Kissinger and Richard Allen and thus began his Washington career as what one Kissinger aide called "Dick Allen's gopher."

Married with two young children, Lehman is not one to spend long hours at the office. He's usually out by six, aides say.

MAJOR ISSUES

- Lehman, in a sharp break from past policies, is seeking clear maritime superiority, a costly endeavor that critics say will heighten world tension.

- The naval aspect of the Reagan strategic program accelerates the arms race in dramatic fashion. The plan includes the continued development of Trident submarines and the Trident II missile, which critics consider "the most destabilizing first strike weapon ever built."

- Lehman made waves last year when he publicly scolded two major contractors for "rip-offs" and "preposterous claims."

- Despite Lehman's far-reaching policy changes, the action that has received the most attention was his recommendation to retire 82-year-old Admiral Human G. Rickover, the outspoken czar of the nuclear Navy.

John Lehman is infatuated with the Navy. His sea blue Pentagon office is dotted with naval paraphenalia: the painting of a naval battleship, a plastic model of a Navy fighter plane, a small submarine that sits in a plastic case on one table. At noon, the clock on the wall chimes twelve bells. When he talks of dominating the seas, he grits his teeth and his blue eyes harden.

Lehman refused to accept any other job with the Reagan Administration; he "lobbied all of the President's staff," until he got the Navy post, he told us. "I did not feel any great pressure to rejoin the government, and in fact it was a fairly heavy shift in income. But I felt so strongly about the Navy—that it was undervalued as an asset and was being dismantled by the Carter Administration [which was] halving the ship building program. Just from the time I started working with Kissinger the fleet had shrunk from about 1,000 ships down to 460, and I thought that was disastrous for American stability and world security."

Now Lehman insists he wants nothing less than maritime superiority over the Soviet Union. Nearly all of his speeches include this favorite declaration (which is inevitably boldly underlined): *"Our national goal must never be less than clear maritime superiority."* In one speech, before the Propeller Club of Washington, D.C., Lehman's nautical machismo reached new heights: "Simply put, we must be able to put the Soviet fleet on the bottom if they attempt to interdict our free use of the sea."

In an interview, Lehman expanded the point: "Nobody is saying that we are trying to get overall military superiority. No one, that I have seen, has suggested that we are going to try to match [the Soviets'] 180 land divisions. We're ceding them superiority there. We are attempting to reestablish parity at the strategic level, we are attempting to get clear maritime superiority. I don't think maritime superiority is something we can negotiate on."

To Lehman, U.S. dominance of the seas is essential for world stability. He plans to implement that philosophy by building a 600-ship Navy—up from 460—that will span the globe by the end of the decade. "I came through [government] experience with the fundamental belief that for the free world naval stability, maritime stability, conventional naval stability were the key towards stabilizing the balance and taking the pressure off the nuclear arms race," he told us.

"We're dependent on the sea lanes," he explained, "as opposed to the Soviet Union which is a land power. We have never sought to challenge their overwhelming land superiority. Similarly, because we're a maritime alliance and power, we believe we should have naval superiority. They don't need it for their security, we do.

"It seems to me that if we could establish that stability it would deny the temptation of any numerical superiority [the Soviets] might gain at the nuclear level to try to translate that into political aggression."

Lehman's plan to build the Navy from 460 to 600 ships, with 15 battlegroups, will be staggeringly expensive. The Navy's shipbuilding budget will *double* if the Administration succeeds in getting its 1983 request, leaping from $8.9 billion in 1982 to $18.6 billion in 1983.

The Reagan plan for 1983-87 envisions the addition of:

- 6 Trident submarines

- 17 attack submarines

- 2 aircraft carriers

- 18 cruisers

- 10 amphibious ships

- 80 escort and auxiliary ships

The Congressional Budget Office has estimated that the shipbuilding plan will cost $25 billion a year over the next six years.

Not including personnel, the cost of a battlegroup which centers around a Nimitz class nuclear aircraft carrier is projected to be $16.8 billion in 1982 dollars, according to Lehman. These groups, of which the U.S. now has 12, will be comprised of escort ships, air defense cruisers and submarines clustered around one huge aircraft carrier and would roam the seas, capable of taking on Soviet forces in their own waters and of launching nuclear-tipped cruise missiles into the Soviet heartland.

Lehman's scheme represents a sharp break from previous military policy and could drastically alter the nature of American military presence around the world. Lehman wants to increase U.S. Naval forces in the Pacific Ocean and rejects contingency plans of previous administrations to transfer ships from the Pacific to support Europe during a war. Strategically, that plan means U.S. forces would pay less attention to protecting Europe's central front and oil supplies in the Persian Gulf, say critics such as Robert Komer, undersecretary of defense under Carter. Komer told the *Washington Post* Lehman's plan "could lead to a strategic disaster. . .playing right into Soviet hands." Komer has called Lehman's strategy "neoisolationist," pointing out that, including NATO forces, "we have a 600-ship Navy."

Lehman's blueprint even concerns some that favor building a 600-ship U.S. fleet. Both Senators William Proxmire (D-Wis.) and Gary Hart (D-Colo.), members of the Senate Armed Services Committee, argue that the Navy should direct its resources to a larger number of simpler, smaller ships, rather than sophisticated, high priced nuclear carriers that require large escort teams and are more vulnerable to attack by Soviet submarines. "The aircraft carrier may be the glamour girl of the fleet, but if we continue committing all our resources to this policy, there will be no fleet to reign over," said Proxmire. "The reason is simple economics. We are pricing ourselves out of a Navy by building these new vulnerable aircraft carrier task forces. Instead we should be building more, smaller, less vulnerable vessels that can be at more than one place at one time."

But it is also clear that Lehman believes naval dominance is valuable for more than defense. "The sea is the Soviets' greatest vulnerability—a place where geography greatly disfavors them. As a consequence, it is here that our superiority must be strongly maintained, enhanced, and exploited," he has said.

Lehman's speeches and testimony are replete with references to improving the Navy's ability to fight a war; deterring conflict is parenthetical. In his 1983 posture statement for example, Lehman said: "Although our national security objectives are oriented toward defense, we cannot rely solely on tactically defense capabilities. . .our forces must be offensively capable. . .Using the inherent flexibility of our naval forces, we will fight on terms more advantageous to us, capitalizing on Soviet geographic disadvantage, and keeping the Soviets concerned with threats all around their periphery."

And reasserting U.S. maritime dominance over waters considered vital to American interests will not necessarily come about peaceably. As a display of renewed strength, the U.S. Navy in 1981 launched military exercises along the Gulf of Sidra, a region which Libyan leader Muammar el-Qaddafi considers his country's territory. (In 1980 with U.S. hostages being held in Iran, President Carter had banned the Navy's 6th Fleet from conducting its missile-firing exercises in that area, though the Navy had previously used the contested region.)

In the midst of the Navy's exercises a pair of Libyan war planes challenged two Navy F-14's and fired on one. The pilots of the F-14's downed both Libyan fighters. Critics of the Administration's decision say Reagan was trying to bully Qaddafi or provoke him into launching an attack, a charge the Administration denies.

Lehman models himself after Alfred Thayer Mahan, the renowned turn-of-the-century naval strategist who postulated that a maritime nation should seek to project its naval power to the most distant corners of the earth. But in one respect, Lehman wants to prove Mahan wrong. "Mahan also believed that democracies were unwilling to pay the price of continued naval power. . .This particular view is one which we must all work together to disprove in our own case."

Until the recent buildup of the Soviet sea forces, which many naval scholars say was largely in response to rapid expansion of U.S. strategic and nuclear forces during the 1960s, the U.S. Navy was master of the seas in the post-world War II world. Today that gap has been substantially narrowed. Though the U.S. still exceeds the Soviets in total tonnage, Russia has about 647 warships while the U.S. has about 460. Much of the Soviet fleet, however, consists of old, diesel-powered submarines.

To some extent, Lehman said, he hopes the Soviets will play catch-up as the U.S. expands its fleet. "If they take money out of building strategic nuclear missiles to build up their fleet to try to catch up with us," he said, "the world is going to be a better place. I hope they do that, and moreover, because of geography I don't think that adding numbers to their fleet affects us a great deal as long as we have the kind of. . .fleet [we want] built around about 15 battlegroups that can take advantage of those geographic realities that they can't change no matter how big they build their fleet."

The ultimate aim of U.S. military and foreign policy vis-a-vis the Soviet Union, said Lehman, is "to reach an equilibrium where the use of force is not a tempting threat for the Soviets. If one wants to step back and be a wholly objective commentator, one would say 'and also the U.S. would not be tempted to use force.' But I'm not objective and I don't think we are the threat to world peace. I think the best way to do that is to make it clear to the Soviets that things like aggression in Afghanistan and Poland and elsewhere do not have a pay-off."

Admiral Hyman G. Rickover, considered a father of the nuclear Navy, has a different perspective on the U.S. fleet, particularly submarines. "I see no reason why we have to have just as many [subs] as the Russians. At a certain point you get where it's sufficient. . .You can sink everything on the oceans several times over with the number we have and so can they," he told a congressional committee in early 1982. "There's got to be some judgment used and these are very expensive things. They take up a lot of time and money and taxpayers' money, too."

Of Lehman's plans for a 600-ship Navy, Rickover said: "It's very difficult for me to answer that question. But, in general, I think we are over-arming altogether because here you have a situation where weapons get more powerful, more destructive, and then you need more; and something seems to be illogical about that."

Lehman's quest to expand the Navy is reaching into the past as well as the future. He has requested funds to overhaul and reactivate four World War II battleships. One of those ships, the New Jersey, mothballed since 1969, is undergoing a $326 million renovation in Long Beach, California. A second, the U.S.S. Iowa, termed a "rust bucket," by some congressional opponents of its reactivation, is undergoing a $407 million rehaul. Two others, the Wisconsin and Missouri, are in line.

Although the ships are expected to last only 15 more years, the Navy has latched onto them as a symbol of its new readiness. The ships will be equipped with cruise missiles. In a typically virile hyperbole, Lehman said of the Navy's plans to modernize these ships,"[They] will provide a massive capability, a capability to be reckoned with by any potential adversary."

Despite production problems and cost increases, the Navy is continuing with its plans to acquire a fleet of F-18 fighter jets. Originally envisioned as an inexpensive companion to the sophisticated and expensive F-14, the plane has grown in cost and complexity. Passing even the F-14 in price, the plane now runs $25.6 million, though the Navy claims that is due to inflation.

Lehman is directing the sea-based element of the Reagan nuclear program, which includes continued production of Trident ballistic missile submarines— at the rate of at least one per year—and the development of a larger, more accurate sea-launched ballistic missile than is currently in use, known as the Trident II or D-5. The Trident II missile, which Rep. Thomas J. Downy (D-N.Y.), a member of the House Budget Committee's defense task force, called "the most destabilizing first strike weapon every built, far more than the MX," will enable American submarines to reach any target in the Soviet Union, including hardened silos.

The Administration concedes the Trident II is a counterforce weapon, able to knock out Soviet missiles in hardened silos. Critics like Downey say the missile's sole significance will be "to initiate nuclear war by delivering a uniquely effective first strike against the Soviet Union's deterrent forces." Fired from submarines near the Soviet Union, the Trident II would be an effective surprise attack weapon, giving the Soviets no more than 10 minutes warning.

Gerard C. Smith, ACDA director under Nixon and now chairman of the Arms Control Association, echoed similar concerns in congressional testimony: "The likely consequence of our development of a counterforce missile will be greater instability of the nuclear balance in a crisis. The same analysis applies to the Trident II missile. We can only expect eventual Soviet production of improved counterforce submarine missiles of its own. It seems unwise, therefore, to pursue a program that will end by putting more targets in the United States at greater risk."

More worrisome, still, said Smith. and less noticed by the public, is the Administration's plan to deploy several hundred nuclear cruise missiles on our regular submarines. "If implemented," he said, "this program will create an essentially new strategic nuclear force. It is a step which should not be undertaken without the most careful consideration of its grave consequences for our security."

Beginning in 1984, the Administration plans to deploy Tomahawk nuclear land-attack cruise missiles on ships, and general purpose submarines. During 1982 the Navy deployed conventional Tomahawks. Critics say the program will frustrate attempts to monitor arms control agreements that might be reached in the future. (See profile of Eugene Rostow.)

All of Lehman's far-reaching policy changes, though, did not generate as much controversy as his recommendation approved by Reagan to forcefully retire Admiral Rickover. The 82-year-old outspoken admiral, who directed the Navy's nuclear propulsion program, had been the object of attacks by two powerful contractors, General Dynamic's Electric Boat Division, and Tenneco Corp.'s Newport News Shipyard, both of which Rickover had publicly lashed for cost overruns and shoddy production. Lehman claimed that his decision to retire Rickover was based on his belief that "we need to put a younger man who can be available, perhaps, for the next decade in that job to give the stability that is so necessary."

Lehman even refused Rickover's request that he continue active duty as an adviser at the Navy Yard, though he did provide Rickover an office there on the condition that he be out within six months. Weinberger had initially offered Rickover the position of adviser to the President on civilian nuclear materials; Rickover declined.

"The secretary of the Navy has said, well, I'm losing my marbles or something," Rickover said of his retirement. "The secretary of the Navy has said that I'm being replaced for 'actuarial' reasons. If all government officials were replaced strictly on an actuarial basis, we would lose some of our most effective legislators and administrators because anybody over 69, the average lifespan of a U.S. male, should be replaced."

It has been speculated that the pressure of defense contractors, like General Dynamics and others Rickover has lambasted for waste, mismanagement, and malfeasance was one force behind Lehman's decision.

Rickover ended his 59-year Navy career with one more spectacular splash. In his January, 1982 farewell testimony to Congress, Rickover said that the arms race is out of control and that we are on a careening path to self-destruction through nuclear war. "What difference does it make?" he asked. "Some new species will come along. They may be wiser." Rickover said he was "not proud of the part" he played in fathering the nuclear Navy and called for immediate disarmament accords. Rickover also took the opportunity to jab the Pentagon: "To increase the efficiency of the Defense Department, you'd first have to abolish it and go back to an Army, Navy, and Air Force."

When we asked Lehman for his reaction to Rickover's characterization of the arms race, he replied caustically: "I think that is nonsense."

In fact, Lehman has a quite different perception of the nuclear arms race, and nuclear war. He believes that a nuclear exchange does not necessarily have to result in mass destruction, and that nuclear war can be limited, an assertion that alarms arms control proponents who say national leaders are more likely to resort to nuclear war if they believe it can be contained. "The fact is," Lehman told us, "I'm bound to carry out the law of the land and part of that law which the courts will enforce is the NATO treaty which includes an article under article 5 that binds us to treat any attack on a NATO country as an attack on the United States. Part of that body of law are the decisions carried out to implement article 5 made by the NATO Council, which has for 35 years included responding with a limited response rather than an all-out armageddon response.

"I have had trouble," he continued, "particularly since it seems to come mainly from the left-wing people who argue against limiting a response to [a nuclear] attack, that it should be all out against women and children. The irony is that the anti-defense people that argue against improving our strategic defenses, argue against accuracy, argue for staying with inaccurate weapons to kill people. They are arguing to have a response against any Soviet attack that is only targeted on women and children and civilians in the Soviet Union. And that seems to me to be morally deplorable and logically indefensible."

Lehman earned accolades from Capitol Hill, the press, and much of the top Navy brass—and the indignation of much of the military industry—when in August, 1981 he accused major contractors like General Dynamics and McDonnell Douglas of "rip-offs" and making "preposterous claims" on the Navy. Lehman told the National Press Club that he "will not subscribe to the notion that the government always pays," and promised to countersue firms that attempt to "take advantage of the inherent disadvantage that the taxpayer suffers in the arena of corporate litigation."

Lehman was provoked primarily by two issues. The first was the crash of a $38 million F-18 plane after a British air show in 1980. The manufacturer, McDonnell Douglas, said the plane belonged to the Navy, and was a Navy loss. Lehman, however, argued the plane was on a promotional trip and had been piloted by a McDonnell Douglas employee.

The second, and most publicized, issue was over production problems at General Dynamics Electric Boat plant, which supplies the Navy's nuclear submarines. The company had tried to stick the Navy with a bill for production problems that had accumulated but later backed off after Lehman threatened to go elsewhere to buy submarines and in one case passed over Electric Boat on a submarine contract, even though Electric Boat submitted a lower bid than that accepted.

During his first year in office Lehman successfully overcame two challenges: persuading Weinberger to adopt the goal of naval superiority (even if it meant ceding the Soviets superiority in other areas) and obtaining the backing of Congress. Given his forceful personality and Washington experience, Lehman didn't have much trouble getting what he wanted from Weinberger. But it was a flush year, with enough of an increase in the military budget to keep all the services happy. "With some minor exceptions on pay matters, I cannot say that we in the Navy have suffered any lobbying against us by any of our sister services. And I know we have not done any against them. Quite naturally, though, [in-fighting] is a problem that is far more evident in a bear market than a bull market," he said.

In 1982, however, the atmosphere is markedly different and the defense budget is receiving closer scrutiny after the Administration's revelation of massive future deficits. But Lehman still insists he can get what he wants: "I'm pretty confident that we will sustain the kind of consensus we've got in Congress to carry this out. This will be the big year of tests: We're at the height of alarm over the state of the economy and the cuts—actually the growth I might underline—in social services. And we're asking for two nuclear aircraft carriers and two Trident submarines and we're laying this groundwork down for Congress: 'If you are serious about rebuilding the Navy, here's the way to do it at the lowest possible cost.' So they've got to face up to the problem."

Whatever the prospects for success, Lehman's budget is guaranteed the protection of an impermeable White House escort on the way up to Capitol Hill. He is a newcomer to the Reagan clique, but it's become clear that his harsh rhetoric and ambitious plans have found more than one sympathetic ear inside the Reagan Administration. He even has the exclusive jar of jelly beans garnishing his coffee table. "Well," he explained to us, "there is quite a sweet tooth in this Administration for the military."

FINANCIAL BACKGROUND

According to his financial disclosure statement, Lehman did, as he remarked, experience "a pretty heavy shift in income" when he rejoined the government. As president of Abington Corp, a defense consulting firm, Lehman received a $180,000 salary and had investments in the firm of over $250,000 which he was in the process of selling at his appointment.

He also received minor consultant fees from the Department of Energy-owned Los Alamos Scientific Laboratory and Sandia National Laboratory and a $4,000 fee from Smithkline Co.

From 1977 until his appointment, Lehman served as president of Intruder, Inc., listed as an "aircraft operator," director of the Philadelphia-based Foreign Policy Research Institute, and director of the Washington, D.C.-based Transco Energy, Inc.

In addition to Abington Corp, Lehman listed over $400,000 worth of investments in an Abington Pension Trust in firms including AT&T, Pennsylvania Power and Light, Moran Energy, Texaco, Parker Drilling; and direct investments in five different real estate partnerships: Clay County Mining Co., Lake of Four Seasons Lts., Van Antwerp Apts., Summer Whitehurst Ltd., and L III Associates.

WHAT OTHERS ARE SAYING ABOUT HIM

- When Lehman was nominated for his ACDA post, Stuart Symington, presciently as it turned out, told the Senate: "If this gentleman is confirmed, the SALT talks are dead." According to Evans and Novak, who devoted a column to the "vicious fight waged backstage for months" over Lehman's nomination, "When Symington demanded reassurance from Kissinger that he really wanted Lehman, [congressional] network allies inside the State Department hinted that perhaps Henry ought to drop this hot potato. But Henry was adamant. . ."

- One former high ACDA official who worked with Lehman told us, "He's a guy with a tremendous amount of moxie. In some respects he's ruthless, but I don't mean that in a derogatory way. He sees a goal and he goes after it without regard for anything else. . .I don't know what it would be like to be on the other side of an argument from him, but it probably wouldn't be very pleasant."

RICHARD PERLE

ASSISTANT SECRETARY FOR INTERNATIONAL SECURITY POLICY

RESPONSIBILITY OF OFFICE

As part of the Pentagon's "little state department" Perle has responsibility for relations with NATO, the European allies, and the Soviet Union; international economic and technical matters; and, his primary interest, arms control negotiations. An effective Washington insider, Perle can be expected to play a significant role in all of these areas.

BACKGROUND

More perhaps than anywhere else in the world, in Washington knowledge is power. If you know, really know, what is going on, and you have a forum to use that information, you can call the tune.

For a decade, Sen. Henry Jackson (D-Wash.) and his right-hand man Richard Perle called a two-step. Over time, the steps became familiar. Inside the executive branch, the hardest-liners would be on the verge of losing a crucial battle in the interagency deliberations over arms control with the Soviet Union. A document—a crucial memo forecasting impending military peril if the position were not changed—would find its way into Perle's hands. Some time later, the memo might reappear, in a column by Evans and Novak, or a *Wall Street Journal* editorial, or in a closed door session of Jackson's subcommittee on arms control that would leave Administration witnesses with chattering teeth, a scowl of disgust, and perhaps, just a touch less enthusiasm for negotiating an agreement with the Soviets.

It was an insider's game—lean, tough, and focused. "Richard deals only with a few players inside the beltway," said one Senate source who knows him well. "His coin of the realm is the smarmy inside political detail. Richard's skills have been those of a salon politician, like Paris in the 19th century; he is not a retail politician."

In his unsuccessful bids for the presidency, Jackson had not proven much of a retail politician either, so, the two almost naturally came together. Jackson was a resolute hardliner who had immersed himself in the guts of the national security bureaucracy since the late 1950s and long understood the importance of having friends at the sensitive vantage points where the papers crossed. Perle was the young intellectual who "fights people, not just issues" and considered the Soviet Union "another Hitler's Germany" as his former friend, Dimitri Simes, the executive director of the Soviet and East European research program at Johns Hopkins University, put it. In 1979, Perle devoted an entire article to drawing parallels between Britain's appeasement of Hitler in the 1930s and the West's policies towards the Soviets today. "I think we're kidding ourselves now, as we kidded ourselves then," he said in a 1979 debate. "As the Soviets have broken through each successive barrier we have persuaded ourselves that it is something else that matters."

Perle's was an effort driven by a passionate distrust of the Soviet Union, an unshakeable belief that they had always managed to bend arms control agreements to their advantage and always would. SALT, he once wrote, "is a bizarre symbiosis between our tendency to harbor illusions and the Russian practice of nurturing them." To that view, U.S.-Soviet arms control is an unequal contest, with the U.S. virtually doomed to lose by the openness and susceptibility to public opinion of our system. When Perle describes the natural advantages he believes the Soviets bring to the negotiations, his tone approaches envy. "I think they have some inherent advantages," he told us. "There is a temptation in this open society of ours to try to produce agreements; they are popular. . . .The Soviets know everything they need to know to plan their negotiating strategy, while we have to make guesses about where they're headed. We have an open, free, and often critical press that becomes a source of pressure on our government. . .and we need to sustain public support for the kind of programs [we institute], while the Soviets are not burdened with the need to satisfy public opinion."

For most of the decade, Jackson and Perle staged a virtuoso performance. They soured the triumph of SALT I for Henry Kissinger and worked with allies in the executive branch to stop Kissinger from concluding SALT II. They bloodied the Carter Administration's chief SALT negotiator in a brutal confirmation brawl, and then launched steady rear-guard actions against the SALT II negotiations. They pushed, scratched, clawed, and left a lot of bitter feelings, even among their allies. "When you work with Richard Perle," said one Republican staffer who has worked for Barry Goldwater and Strom Thurmond, among others, "it's kind of a one-way street. It's just give. Richard's a very strong, very opinionated guy; there's not much room for compromise."

The give and take of Congress, the endless compromise of legislation, usually washes out the ideological rigidity of those who work there. Not Perle. He remains an ideologue, focused on the Soviet Union. "I think his views are set in concrete," said Simes, who has frequently talked, argued and debated with Perle since emigrating from the Soviet Union in 1973. "His definition of arms control is that which would change the balance of power to the benefit of the United States." Another Senate aide, who has knocked heads with him for years, sums up Perle's views succinctly: "He thinks we should run an arms race with the Russians and win."

Unlike some of his fellow travelers on the far right side of the national security spectrum, Perle doesn't come out and say things like that. He is smooth, very bright, well-spoken, and described by Simes and other adversaries as a "brilliant debater, highly effective.'' But in conversation, beneath the measured words, is an unbending hard line.

What do you think are the aims of the Soviet Union's foreign policy? we asked him. ''I think it's quite clear that the aims of their policy is to increase the extent to which decisions made anywhere in the world are made consistent with their interests.''

Do you see, we continued, any interest at all on the part of their leaders in having us cease to exist as a national entity? ''I think the Soviet Union would like to see us weakened or neutralized [to the point] where we were not a factor in their decisions.''

What should be the aim of our foreign and military policy toward them? ''I think we have to try to contain the capacity of the Soviet Union to use military force to achieve its political goals.''

How do the Soviets react to tough talk? ''I think what the Soviets respect and even desire most is straight talk. . . .They want to know what we're prepared to do and they expect us to regard them as an adversary. I think they're frustrated more than anything else by confusion and vacillation. They found Carter very difficult to deal with; he was so mercurial. . . .I think they prefer conservatives, hardliners, if you will.''

What do you think is Ronald Reagan's greatest strength in dealing with the Soviets? ''The simple, straightforward, clear understanding that the Soviet Union is indeed an adversary. . . .he's under no illusions about either their ultimate purpose or ours.''

In his own way, Perle had as little doubt about who his adversaries were, and even fewer compunctions about dealing with them. ''He's extremely vindictive, and narrow-minded,'' said Simes, whose friendship with Perle cooled as his support for arms control grew. ''If Perle perceives that somebody is a political enemy he will go all the way to fight that person. If he believes that someone is a political ally, he will stay with that person to the end.''

Simes is in a position to know. In June, 1979, Time Inc. gathered some of the leading experts on arms control to a seminar for its editors. After Simes had spoken in favor of the SALT II treaty, he overheard Perle comment to a group of Time editors that, considering Simes's background, it ''was unusual'' for him to take positions that coincided with the stand of the Soviet Union. ''The implication was that there had to be some sinister reason,'' said Simes.

Another natural ally of Perle's confirmed that he questioned Simes's motivations. Robert Gordon, a Massachusetts businessman who served as executive director of the Union of Councils for Soviet Jews—a nationwide organization devoted to helping Soviet Jews emigrate—told us that ''Richard questioned whether Dimitri Simes was loyal to this country; he raised various aspects of Dimitri's career and relationships.''

Gordon said that at one point Jackson's other close aide, Dorothy Fosdick, talked to Nechemiah Levanon, an aide to Israeli Prime Minister Begin on Soviet issues, and requested that they pressure the union to cut back its dealings with Simes. ''When I talked about it with Richard he confirmed that,'' Gordon said. ''Perle was very hard on Dimitri Simes.'' Fosdick said she never made such a call.

At the Time debate, Perle lashed out at West German Chancellor Helmut Schmidt for supporting the SALT II treaty. Using language particularly offensive for a German leader, Perle accused Schmidt of ''appeasement'' towards the Soviets.

"What I think we are witnessing in Schmidt's latter day enthusiasm for this treaty is in part political pressure on West Germany. . . .I find that's a lamentable development in Europe—that America's closest ally should feel obliged to strike the position that he's now striking in order to deal with internal political difficulties and in order to maintain a suitable relationship with the Soviet Union. I don't see how that differs substantially from the kind of appeasements that we've seen historically," Perle said.

Gordon himself received some of that treatment in 1979, when he sparred with Perle over the Jackson-Vanik amendment. Originally passed as part of the 1974 trade bill, the amendment prevents the U.S. from granting most-favored nation status to countries that restrict emigration, a measure aimed at loosening Soviet restrictions on Jews that wished to leave. In 1979 testimony, Gordon left open the possibility that the union would accept changes in the amendment; even Vanik felt the Soviets should receive recognition of what was at the time an improved emigration record.

"When I remarked to Perle that Vanik was seeking some changes, he said 'Was he lucid? Did he hold onto the topic? Was he rambling?'" Gordon told us. Then Perle turned on him: Perle "informed me that I was working with the enemies of Soviet Jews, that I was a traitor to Soviet Jews," said Gordon. Vanik told us, "Perle was pretty rough [on me]. He was very rigid about it."

"Richard is a very tough guy and is willing to bring up any kind of dirt that might change your opinion of someone," Gordon concluded.

"Richard, in my view, has two personalities," said a Senate aide who has known him for a decade. "There's a very courtly, almost diplomatic in a European sense, manner. . .he can be a very ingratiating, very charming sort of person. . . .There's another side; it is dark—partly that his face itself literally becomes dark, the lines under his eyes, the visage becomes kind of dark; it's a very intense, humorless, compulsive personality that will not let go."

The darkest side of Richard Perle came to the forefront when President Carter nominated Paul Warnke to run the Arms Control and Disarmament Agency (ACDA) and head the SALT negotiating team.

Jackson and Perle appeared spoiling for a fight. Their man, James Schlesinger, had been passed over for Defense Secretary. And Warnke, whose commitment to SALT was well known, was anathema to them.

With Evans and Novak leading the drumbeat, and Paul Nitze of the newly-formed Committee on the Present Danger weighing in with testimony that some considered savage, the Warnke nomination turned into a donnybrook. The Jackson forces successfully planted the idea that if they could generate more than 35 votes against Warnke, the Senate would likely reject any treaty he could bring home.

In March, 1977 the Senate approved Warnke as SALT negotiator by a 58-40 count. That vote gave added weight to the 23-page memo Jackson and Perle had delivered to the White House a month earlier. Rejecting Kissinger's approach, the memo instead urged a far tougher line in the negotiations. "It was a well-written, well-reasoned memorandum—provided you start off with the premise with which they started off, which is that what we ought to try and do is establish strategic superiority," said Warnke. "Obviously I don't accept the premise." Neither did the Carter Administration, though its first "deep-cut" SALT proposal reflected Jackson's influence, if not the specifics of the memo.

"It was a wish list, a formula for an ideal agreement," said one Carter Administration Defense Department official. "Anybody can write those; it's like playing tennis without a net. I remember the day it came in. We said, 'Great, now all Richard Perle has to do is go off and negotiate it.'"

The Soviet rejection of that proposal may have been exactly what Perle expected, and was seeking. Perle maintains that he is merely seeking meaningful agreements in place of the "cosmetic" solutions pursued by Kissinger. But skeptics argue that Perle puts forward proposals so unbalanced as to make Soviet acceptance impossible. Such has been the Soviet response to the "zero option," another negotiating position heavily influenced by Perle. Once arms control has proven to be a dead end, this analysis of Perle's views continues, the U.S. can engage in a massive buildup that the Soviets will be unable to match.

"I think basically they see arms control as being totally unilateral: anything that controls the other side is fine, anything that interferes with what you might want to do is bad," Warnke said of Jackson and Perle. "Consequently no arms control agreement could possibly be negotiated that would be satisfactory to them. The fundamental premise on which you have to negotiate an arms control agreement is that it has to be something which is beneficial to both sides."

Perle himself told us, "It's not in our interest to sign agreements that do not entail a *significant improvement* in the strategic balance." (Emphasis added.)

To the eyes of many in the Senate, the Warnke episode reflected the last great hurrah of the Jackson-Perle team. Around late 1977, an organized counter-effort—centered around Senators Hart, Culver, McIntyre and Bumpers, among others—came together to support Carter's arms control efforts. The Republicans meanwhile, were developing independent stands of their own. By the time Perle was the subject of a June, 1977 profile in the *Washington Post* Sunday Outlook section—heady stuff for a congressional aide—his power may have already peaked. The intensity of his efforts had not diminished; but Perle and Jackson no longer had the field to themselves.

When Perle first met Jackson, the senator had as much running room as he wanted. It was summer 1969, and Perle had come to Washington as a staffer to an organization established by Dean Acheson, Paul Nitze and Albert Wohlstetter to promote the anti-ballistic missile (ABM). Wohlstetter was Perle's connection: Perle had met the hardline strategic planner's daughter at Beverly Hills High School and become friends with the older man. Today, Perle cites Wohlstetter—along with Jackson and Reinhold Niebuhr—as among the major influences on his thinking.

After a few months with that group, a forerunner of the more influential Committee on the Present Danger formed in the mid 1970s, Perle followed Nitze to the Defense Department, where he was working as a special assistant to the secretary. In the fall, an opening popped up on Jackson's subcommittee on national security and international operations, and the senator, who had met Perle during the ABM fight, offered him the job.

Perle launched into the ABM battle with his customary vigor. "I was honored to hear the rumor from staffers that Perle had a dartboard with my picture on it in his office," said Tom Halsted, who headed a group opposing the ABM called the Council For A Livable World. Halsted is now director of the Physicians for Social Responsibility, an organization of doctors and scientists devoted to fighting the nuclear arms race.

If the ABM brought Jackson and Perle together, it also eventually split the two from the Nixon Administration. Jackson had been the Administration's key supporter in the battle over building four ABM sites, which eventually divided the

Senate 50-50 on a proposal to delete the plan from the budget. But two years later, in SALT I the Administration negotiated the number of potential ABM sites down to two, and later one. "He [Jackson] had invested his personal prestige and political capital to win Senate approval of four ABM sites of several hundred launchers each and felt betrayed because only one site with a hundred launchers could now be built," wrote Peter Ognibene in his 1975 biography of Jackson, *Scoop*.

Working with Perle, Jackson got his revenge. Jackson knew he could not block the treaty. But he proposed a stiff amendment that called on the U.S. to abrogate the treaty if the Soviets deployed any missiles that threatened our forces, even if permitted by the treaty. Eventually, in watered-down form, the amendment was approved by a 56-35 vote as an injunction that future negotiations "not limit the United States to levels of intercontinental strategic forces inferior to" the Soviet Union and instead be based on "the principle of equality." (See Major Issues.)

That was the beginning. The other response to SALT I was to root out the ACDA officials who had negotiated it.

The role of Jackson and Perle in the purge of ACDA that followed the 1972 election is not written in stone anywhere. People rarely acknowledge their roles in such unpleasant undertakings. But, among those in the arms control community, there is virtually unanimous belief that Jackson and Perle were at the center. After Gerard Smith resigned as ACDA head, Nixon in 1973 appointed Fred Ikle, an introspective, bookish Rand Corp. strategic thinker to run the agency, largely on Jackson's recommendation. "I helped persuade him to take that job," said Perle of the man who is now his titular boss. (See Ikle profile.) Of the other personnel actions—which led to the dismissal of many top officials and a reduction of ACDA's budget and influence—Perle is more circumspect. In his book, Ognibene reported that "In the early months of 1973. . . . Perle bragged to several people that he and Jackson were responsible for the purge." But later, after the Watergate hearings had unearthed the White House enemies list Perle backed off and "began denying there was a list or that he and the Senator were responsible in any way for the purge," wrote Ognibene. Only two members of the original SALT delegation survived: Harold Brown, and Perle's former employer, Paul Nitze.

Raymond Garthoff was one of those purged. Fluent in Russian, and a 12-year veteran of the State Department at the time the delegation was cleared out, Garthoff had served as executive officer and senior adviser from the State Department on SALT I. "It's my understanding," said Garthoff, expressing a view seconded by other sources from the period, "that Jackson told President Nixon when the two of them were talking alone in the Rose Garden [in September, 1972] that he thought there ought to be an entirely new SALT delegation."

After Garthoff was recalled from the delegation and returned to his post as deputy director of the State Department's Bureau of Politico-Military affairs, he went to see Perle. "He told me there was nothing personal about it, that they had not asked for my head personally. He did not deny that Jackson wanted a whole new delegation. . . . He [Perle] did not show any particular contrition [about my dismissal]," Garthoff told us.

Kissinger did little to defend ACDA. Ever sensitive to bureaucratic nuance, he saw the opportunity to downgrade a potential rival and to tighten his grip on arms control policy. But his failure to check the growing influence of Perle and Jackson cost him dearly just two years later.

In the view of one well-placed Capitol Hill aide, the influence of Perle and Jackson over arms control policy in that period soared "largely because of forfeit."

Distracted by other events, and weakened by Watergate, in this view, Kissinger never mounted an effective counter-attack against Jackson and Perle.

Left without effective opposition, Jackson and Perle worked with their allies in the reconstituted ACDA—Ikle, and particularly his deputy John Lehman—to influence the Administration's internal debate. "The pattern would be allegedly that John Lehman, working with the tolerance of Fred Ikle, who was a limp and ineffective director, would be allied with Richard, and as the anti-Kissinger position on SALT would be about to be defeated in Executive branch councils, a 'smoking gun' would come to Perle, " said one Senate aide involved in the debate.

In his second volume of memoirs, Henry Kissinger pays a backhanded compliment to the extraordinary sources developed by Jackson's office. "When I testified before Jackson," Kissinger wrote, "I often found myself in the anomalous position of being confronted with secret documents from the Joint Chiefs of Staff that had never been seen in the White House." Kissinger's memoirs overflow with bitterness toward Jackson and his staff. Jackson, Kissinger wrote, "was aided by one of the ablest—and most ruthless—staffs that I encountered in Washington. They systematically narrowed whatever scope for discussion existed between the Administration and the Senator by giving the most invidious interpretations to Administration motives; they were masterful in the use of press leaks."

So they were, with public pressure kept up by Evans and Novak—particularly through one memorable December, 1975 column that literally may have grounded a last-ditch effort by Kissinger to conclude the treaty—Jackson, Perle, Ikle and Lehman, joined significantly by Defense Secretary Donald Rumsfeld, convinced Ford to shelve SALT. Ford didn't need that much convincing; he saw the shadow of Ronald Reagan looming on his right as the primary season approached. "I'm sure they were not naive," said one Ford Administration official who backed the treaty. "They knew that Ford would be nervous about getting reelected and they figured they had some leverage there."

That episode captures what some on Capitol Hill see as the essence of the Jackson-Perle strategy: to ensure that no treaty would ever be completed. Unsure of their ability to actually defeat a treaty on the Senate floor, Perle and Jackson focused their efforts on intimidating the Administration in power into never signing a treaty.

Those efforts were redoubled when Jimmy Carter took office. After the Russians threw the Jackson-influenced "deep cut" proposal back into Cyrus Vance's face and more serious negotiations commenced, Jackson's subcommittee on arms control dragged top Administration officials onto the Hill for executive sessions on the most intimate details of the negotiations. "We must have severely encumbered the ability of the Administration to negotiate with all the shit that was going on," said one Republican aide who fought SALT II.

From Perle's point of view, the pattern was the same as SALT I. Administration officials would be minutely cross-examined on the progress of the negotiations; a few days later any damaging statement would turn up in Evans and Novak. But the ballgame had changed. "There was a stable of people who knew strategic issues," and were willing to fight Jackson, as a Senate aide put it.

And they were willing to fight Perle. After some remarks at an executive session by Secretary of State Vance turned up in an Evans and Novak column in fall, 1977, Sen. John Culver (D-Iowa) began the committee's next executive session on November 7 by demanding an investigation of the leak. "He let all 128 guns fly in a denunciation of whoever this dastardly person was, and all the time he glared at

Richard Perle. Culver was apoplectic," said one eyewitness. "Perle was livid about it."

Perle got his fingers burned by another leak a few months later. CIA Director Admiral Stansfield Turner urged Jackson to fire Perle, after Perle was revealed to have accepted top secret CIA reports on SALT from a disaffected CIA analyst named David Sullivan. Turner fired Sullivan and reportedly urged Jackson to get rid of Perle. But Jackson held firm, and the Administration— and its congressional supporters—backed off. "In that case they decided we would not take the leaking of classified material seriously," said one Senate aide. "They didn't want to take on Jackson."

Perle and Jackson never were forced to prove they could defeat a SALT II treaty. The taking of American hostages in Iran and the Soviet invasion of Afghanistan killed it without a senatorial shot being fired.

Perle pursues all issues with a single-minded focus on the Soviets. He fervently watched for Israeli interests and was a strong supporter of Soviet Jews, through such efforts as the Jackson-Vanik amendment. Now Perle is pursuing a hard line on trade with the Soviets, even in an Administration with deep ties to the business community. He adamantly opposes the Siberian natural gas pipeline (See Larry Brady profile) which could generate hundreds of millions of dollars in contracts for some U.S. companies. A few days before we spoke to Perle, the U.S. Chamber of Commerce—whose invaluable foot soldiers were credited by White House aides with carrying Reagan's budget and tax package over the hump in Congress—wrote Reagan to oppose further efforts to stop the project.

"I wasn't much surprised," Perle told us. "[Pepsico President] Don Kendall is running that organization now and his view on these matters are well known."

Were you disappointed? we asked him. "No, not really. I don't think it makes much difference one way or the other. . . .I doubt that a single member of Congress will change his view about the pipeline [because of] the statement issued by the Chamber of Commerce. . . .[and] in the end, I believe the Administration is prepared to stand up to criticism in those sectors [whose] narrow economic interests are adversely affected by our policy, that is undertaken in the greater national interest."

It will be interesting to watch Perle's progress through the Executive Branch. By some accounts, he has Weinberger's ear and is one of the handful of top Administration policymakers on arms control. But he has a reputation as a maverick, an open field runner who feels chafed by bureaucracy and protocol. "I think one way of looking at Rich is that he is basically an anti-institutionalist," said one Senate aide who knows him well. "You know, there are conservatives who believe the Republic is made up of institutions which provide stabilization. Perle isn't one of those; he never really showed any affection for or sense of Senate traditions."

Perle already displays some annoyance with congressional aides who view their job (as he did) as dogging the Executive's actions. "Obviously it's very important to work closely with the Executive Branch. The Executive can't accomplish very much in the face of opposition and resistance on the Hill," he said. "There's a certain amount of frivolous interaction and I think there's altogether too much of that. Staff people who will write 200 questions and expect you to devote hundreds of hours of staff time and so on. . . . ."

Born on September 16, 1941 in New York City, Perle took his B.A. in international relations from the University of California, Los Angeles in 1964 and his M.A. from the politics department at Princeton University three years later. Perle studied at the London School of Economics, though he did not receive a degree there.

Before coming to Washington he spent two years with Westinghouse Electric Corp.'s defense and space center as a senior political analyst. After leaving Jackson's staff in 1980, Perle worked until his appointment as a consultant, mostly to the Abington Corp. run by his friend John Lehman.

Married with one son, Perle is reported to be an excellent cook.

MAJOR ISSUES

(See profiles of Eugene Rostow, Edward Rowny and Paul Nitze.)

FINANCIAL BACKGROUND

For Perle, who had subsisted during the previous decade on the relatively more modest earnings of a Senate aide, 1980 was a lucrative year. He earned $140,000 from the Abington Corp. headed by John Lehman (See Lehman profile) and another $91,000 in consulting fees from Northrop, TRW, Tamares Ltd. of London and the Systems Development Corp. Perle has three property holdings in Washington worth over $200,000 and a few small stock holdings.

WHAT OTHERS ARE SAYING ABOUT HIM

- Said one Republican aide who worked with him: "He's tough. He's a very conscientious guy; strong in his beliefs. But Richard is abrasive."

- Said a Democrat who worked against him: "Richard's the kind of person you can have a nice conversation with. I'm not sure you're going to change his mind."

- Another Republican aide believes Perle was a product of his times. "If Richard Perle was to go to work for Henry Jackson today he would be a footnote, instead of a participant. Jackson is in essence without a cause today." That may not be entirely true, but it's close. When we went to Jackson's office to talk about Perle, they said they were no longer monitoring the Defense Department as closely as in the past; they felt certain it was in good hands with Perle.

- One former government official familiar with Kissinger's thinking said "Kissinger feels the hardliners don't understand what is a sophisticated way to contain the Soviet Union. . . . He thinks that to be belligerent, to dismiss any thought of arms control and have only one track toward the Soviet Union is not the way to control the Soviet Union. [He feels] that if you follow the kind of line of the Jacksons and Perles that you are apt to lose public support for strong defense because [they think] it's our fault, not the Russians."

ARMS CONTROL AND DISARMAMENT AGENCY

EUGENE ROSTOW
DIRECTOR

RESPONSIBILITY OF OFFICE

Established by Congress in 1961 with the rather optimistic mission of not only formulating and implementing arms control policies, but also disarmament policies that will promote the national security, ACDA's influence has fluctuated over the past two decades. The principal decisions and initiatives on arms control have been volleyed between

ACDA, the secretary of State, and the "mini-state department" within the Pentagon, which reports to the undersecretary of defense for policy, depending upon the individuals holding these offices.

ACDA is charged with preparing and participating in discussions and negotiations with the Soviet Union and other countries on strategic arms limitations, such as SALT; mutual force reductions in Central Europe; nuclear proliferation; and chemical weapons limitations. The agency also monitors the flow of conventional arms trade throughout the world.

In addition to directing the agency, Rostow is responsible for advising the White House on the arms control implications of weapons decisions.

In 1982 Rostow will manage a budget of $16.7 million and a staff of 164.

BACKGROUND

In 1978 political commentator Ronald Reagan named a series of radio editorials after Yale Professor Eugene V. Rostow, beginning with "Rostow I" and ending with "Rostow VI". Describing Rostow as "a man of unquestionable liberal credentials—there is no way Eugene Rostow could be called a hawk or a tool for military interests"—Reagan quoted extensively from a Rostow address in an effort to demonstrate that opposition to the SALT II treaty was not limited to the right.

Only, perhaps, to a man in Reagan's foreign policy sphere would Eugene Rostow appear to be on the left side of the political spectrum. A neoconservative Democrat and a former high-ranking official in the Johnson Administration, Rostow resolutely defended U.S. involvement in Vietnam, publicly fought SALT, and was a founding member of the unabashedly hardline Committee on the Present Danger.

Despite that record, Rostow agrees with Reagan's description of his politics. "I certainly would!" he retorted when we asked him if he would describe himself as Reagan did. "We don't have any popes in the liberal movement. Nobody can rule me out of the liberal fraternity—I don't recognize anybody's authority to do that. Liberalism has nothing to do with foreign policy. Liberalism has to do with attitudes towards freedom, liberty and order."

"Order" is a common theme of Rostow's, underlying both his opinions about America's role in the world and his attitude toward the Soviets. The Soviets, he says, are the principal culprits behind the current disruption of world order. Rostow considered American intervention in Vietnam, part of an "effort we were making in all parts of the world to recreate some kind of system of order."

In an interview, Rostow made similiar remarks about world order and El Salvador: "Now, the issue in El Salvador is not who has the best land reform program, and that was never the issue in Vietnam. The problem is whether there are violations going on of the rules of world public order which are universal, and there are. We should be focusing on those [violations]—arms coming into El Salvador, from Cuba, from Nicaragua, via Nicaragua, via Honduras and so on. That is a violation of the [U.N.] charter and that is what we are opposed to."

Like other conservative intellectuals who made up the core of the Committee on the Present Danger, Rostow has a long and reputable background in both government and academia. The credentials add weight to his frequent criticisms of arms control efforts and detente. He served as an adviser to the Department of State from 1942 to 1944. He was a law professor at Yale from 1944 to 1949; and then served for one year as assistant executive secretary to the U.N. Economic Commission for Europe. In 1950 he returned to Yale as a law professor and within five years had become dean, a position which he held until 1965. After serving in the Johnson State Department from 1966 to 1969 he returned to Yale in 1970 as Sterling Professor of Law and Public Affairs.

Rostow is firmly entrenched in conservative policy groups. At the time of his appointment, he was chairman of the executive committee of the Committee on the Present Danger; vice-president of the Atlantic Council of the U.S. in Washington; director of the Atlantic Institute in Paris; director of the National Strategy Information Center in New York; adviser to the Institute for Foreign Policy Analysis in Cambridge, Mass.; an associate to the Ethics and Public Policy Center; and director of the Coalition for a Democratic Majority.

Actually it might be said that Rostow's only claim to that liberal label is his name: His father, a Russian immigrant, and his mother, born in the U.S., named him after the renowned socialist Eugene V. Debs. His two brothers were named Walt Whitman Rostow and Ralph Emerson Rostow.

Rolling back and forth in his rocking chair, eyeglasses in hand, dressed in a three-piece suit, a pocketwatch chain draped across his vest, Rostow is the portrait of an erstwhile professor."He's very much the 19th century gentleman," said a Senate expert on arms control. "He's charming." He speaks with the pomp and aloofness of an Ivy League scholar, with the dehumanizing abstraction of a strategic thinker.

Rostow demonstrated that characteristic during his confirmation hearing, with an exchange startling even in a Capital becoming inured to talk of nuclear war. Sen. Claiborne Pell (D-R.I.) asked Rostow: "Do you believe that there is such a thing as limited nuclear war?" Rostow replied: "The practical answer, I suppose, would be that since 1945 and the shock of those first explosions no one has used nuclear weapons in conflict." Then this exchange took place:

Pell: In the event of a full nuclear exchange between the Soviet Union and the United States, do you envision either country surviving to any substantial degree?

Rostow: [I]t depends on how extensive the nuclear exchange is. . .Japan, after all, not only survived but flourished after the nuclear attack. . .

Pell: My question is, in a full nuclear exchange, would a country survive?

Rostow: The human race is very resilient, Senator Pell.

Pell: Oh, the race is; but I asked if either country would survive.

Rostow: Well, there are ghoulish statistical calculations that are made about how many people would die. . .some estimates predict that there would be 10 million casualties on one side and 100 million on the other. But that is not the whole population."

With his skeptical views on arms control, Rostow spent much of the 1970s fighting the efforts of the agency he now heads. Rostow worked through the Committee on the Present Danger, which sprung out of conversations between Rostow and lobbyist Charls Walker, who now directs the committee. Said Rostow: "I had been chairman of a foreign policy committee for the Coalition for a Democratic Majority," a group of conservative Democrats who had become frustrated with liberal trends in their party during the late 1960s and early 1970s. "We reached the conclusion that we weren't getting very far and what was needed was a bipartisan effort. The problem was not simply to save the soul of the Democratic Party but to reach the public at large."

The committee sought public support, through press campaigns and newsletters with such titles as "Why the Soviet Union Wants SALT II" and "Countering the Soviet Threat," which urged a rapid U.S. military expansion to counter "the Soviet drive for dominance." At that time considered by many Carter officials in power as being dominated by "knee-jerk anti-Soviets," blaming the Russians for everything from national liberation movements to the Arab oil embargo, the group's rhetoric is common fare in the current Administration. That is not surprising: Ronald Reagan was one of the first members of the committee and at the beginning of his Administration, 32 of his top appointments could be found on the committee's membership rolls. (See list following Major Issues.) Basking in the victory of the Reagan forces during a post-election speech at the committee's annual dinner Rostow said: "Respectable people cannot dismiss us as cranks, crack pots, and lunatics. After all, we too write sedate federal prose, and wear the old school tie."

The committee's defense strategy for the 1980s sounds nearly identical to the Administration's plans: a nuclear expansion that includes additional Trident submarines, a fleet of B-1 bombers, deployment of MX missiles in vertical launching silos, additional cruise and tactical ballistic missiles, production of the neutron bomb, and expanded civil defense planning. But in early 1982, the Committee on the Present Danger complained the Pentagon's planned build-up was not enough. The committee urges "containing" Soviet or proxy aggression against U.S. interests around the world, an oft-heard theme of Reagan Administration officials today and has said the U.S. "should resume production and stockpile of arms for rapid transfer to endangered friends and allies."

The Committee on the Present Danger helped create the climate for the current military expansion. But it also mustered forces for a battle it never had a chance to really fight: ratification of the SALT II treaty, an agreement that Rostow likes to call "a soft bargain, a hard sell." By many accounts the committee was even more effective in generating opposition to the SALT II treaty than Sen. Henry Jackson (D-Wash.) and his allies in Congress.

"The ultimate absurdity," Rostow wrote in *Commentary* in February, 1979, "is the claim that SALT II would limit or reduce either arms or arms expenditures. The one thing the 1972 Interim Agreement on Offensive Strategic Arms [SALT I] did not do was limit Soviet arms development or expenditures, or the growth of the Soviet nuclear arsenal."

To Rostow the history of arms control is a history of failure. The post-World War I arms limitation agreements, he says, lulled the U.S., Britain, and France into letting their navies slide. Those agreements not only failed to prevent World War II, he maintains, but "helped bring on World War II, by reinforcing the blind and willful optimism of the West, thus inhibiting the possibility of military preparedness and diplomatic actions through which Britain and France could easily have deterred war."

Indeed, Rostow considers only one arms control agreement in modern history as successful, and that was completed one and a half centuries ago—the Rush-Bagot Agreement of 1817 between Great Britain and the United States which limited naval power on the Great Lakes.

Paul Warnke, former ACDA director and SALT II negotiator under Carter, thinks that his long-time adversary's analogy between Hitler's Germany and Soviet Russia today goes too far. "In my opinion he overestimates both the military threat and the political threat. I don't think the Soviets are as competent as he thinks they are. So I don't get quite as obsessed with the fact that they are out to get us. I certainly feel that they would like to be the most important world power, they would like to be the dominant country but I don't think they have any realistic expectations of achieving that. [Rostow] thinks more in terms of their willingness, and in fact their desire, to achieve domination over the rest of the world by force."

We asked Rostow how he felt when he saw Jimmy Carter kiss Soviet President Leonid Brezhnev at the end of the SALT II agreement. "In the transition period" for Reagan, he said, "I wrote a study on how to deal with the Russians. As we discussed it and I presented it to [President Reagan], I summed it up in part saying 'Mr. President I advise three things. First, nothing for nothing— even the things in your campaign, don't give them up for nothing. Secondly, LBJ's rule was a good one—with the Russians, you always have your right hand extended, your left hand up. And third, I hope I never get up in the morning and pick up the paper to see a picture of you kissing Brezhnev.' He laughed and said, 'I promise you, I won't even kiss Mrs. Brezhnev.' "

Rostow's writings during the 1960s portray the Russian-American relationship as a love affair gone awry, due largely to the post-World War II behavior of the Soviet government. "We wanted. . .to continue our wartime association with the Russian people and with the Soviet Union," he wrote in 1968. "We had fresh memories of wartime comradeship in arms, of hands across the Elbe, of the Soviet contribution to the victory over Hitler. We recalled other ties and similarities between our two peoples: the traits of generosity, of spontaneity and frankness. . .There was also, let us not forget, much genuine sympathy in the United States for the March Revolution in 1917 and for the ideals which it proclaimed. There was more than a little initial sympathy for the October Revolution. . ."

It was not surprising, wrote Rostow, that in 1945 many Americans envisioned a peaceful future based on the new United Nations and Soviet-American cooperation. But, he said, "these hopes were soon disappointed," after the Soviets took control of East Europe. Now the United States must bear the burden of checking continued communist aggression around the world.

When William Whitworth in the late 1960s was questioning officials in the Johnson Administration for his *New Yorker* article, "Naive Questions About War and Peace," he said the only high ranking member of the Johnson Administration he could find who continued to believe the Vietnam War was necessary and was willing to publicly defend it was Eugene Rostow. Then the number three official in the State Department, undersecretary for political affairs, Rostow was the brother of the hawkish National Security Adviser Walt Rostow. "Our interest is not to protect democracy as such but to deter, prevent and defeat aggression," he told Whitworth.

In a 1968 address to the Indianapolis Junior Chamber of Commerce, Rostow expressed impatience with opponents of the war: "[T]he destructive element in American concern about Vietnam is resistance to the bleak fact that the protection of our national security requires not a sprint, a one-shot effort followed by the relief of a withdrawal, but a permanent involvement in the politics of every part of the globe, based on a strategy of peace that seeks to achieve order and to make progress possible."

In a similar address to the Women's Forum on National Security in February, 1968, he had these sharp words: "However much we dislike the burden of responsibility, the U.S. will not again abandon the defense of our national interests to chance. . .we shall have to continue to exert ourselves [against communist aggression]. . .In theory, there may be better places to fight than Vietnam, in fact we have no alternative."

Rostow's remarks today reflect an unchanged attitude about Vietnam. He said his only regret is that Johnson was held back from a full commitment and instead resorted to fighting a "border war. It was probably a mistake also," he told us, "to make such a fuss about endless peace offensives."

Rostow is both a legal scholar—having taught constitutional law, antitrust law, and international law—and an economist. He has described his primary interest as "the intersection of law and economics, the area of public policy concerned with regulating the economy." Despite his title in the Johnson Administration, he was also the senior economic official in the State Department.

That interest lured Rostow into the legal quagmire of telecommunications policy, for which he was lucratively rewarded through the 1970s as a consultant to American Telephone and Telegraph (AT&T). In 1967 President Johnson appointed a 16-member task force to conduct a sweeping study of the telecommunications industry. Rostow was named chairman. The task force concluded that AT&T should retain its switched network as a "natural monopoly, regulated as a public utility. . ." Competition, said the task force, should be confined to areas outside the network, such as point-to-point private line service. But, if the company's network was opened to competition, they argued, national security would be threatened.

Rostow has been bearing that message ever since—through attempts by Congress and the Justice Department to break up the communications giant. In 1975 as AT&T's consultant he prepared a lengthy memorandum for a House subcommittee on communications called, not surprisingly: "The Case for Congressional Action to Safeguard the Telephone Network as a Universal and Optimized System." AT&T has vigorously resisted government decisions that opened services such as long distance to competitors like MCI Communications Corp.

Testifying under subpoena in December, 1981 in the Justice Department's antitrust case against AT&T, Rostow said that the company was not guilty of anticompetitive practices. On the contrary, he asserted the company was reluctant to compete. "I found AT&T to be a very timid and cautious company, conscious of all the risks, political and otherwise, of being too active and too vigorous." AT&T allowed itself "to be nibbled at far more actively than I and others in their advisory groups thought wise," he said. AT&T settled in the case after the trial judge indicated he believed the Justice Department had demonstrated anticompetitive behavior. (See William Baxter Profile.)

Rostow has since put aside his consulting business and his teaching career to take over an agency that he has nettled for the better part of a decade, an agency whose mission in Rostow's estimation has little chance of success. In the end, of course, arms control is a matter of perception as much as precision; as important as verification and the definitions of heavy bombers are the perceptions of whether we need to limit our military arsenal, whether the Soviets would launch a nuclear strike if they thought they had the chance, whether the world is careening along an arms race that threatens its survival. We had a chance to see Rostow's views at the end of our interview, when he walked over to his desk and pulled out some political cartoons sent to him by his son.

The cartoons were by the famous British political cartoonist of the 1930s, David Low. Rostow handed one across the desk for us to look at. Low had drawn the nations of the world on a skimpy raft he christened "collective security." Around the raft were the raging waves of an unrestricted arms race. As we were walking from the office we asked Rostow whether he thought we were on the raft or in the water. He laughed. "On the raft," he said. And then he turned back into his office, perhaps to ponder the 5,000 nuclear weapons Ronald Reagan would add to the nation's arsenal over the next decade and the waves even one of those might produce.

Born on August 25, 1913 in Brooklyn, New York, Rostow received his undergraduate, law, and masters degrees (among others) from Yale, in 1933, 1937 and 1959 respectively. He is married with three children.

FINANCIAL BACKGROUND

According to his financial disclosure statement, Rostow had a modest $54,687 annual salary as a professor at Yale. His big money came from AT&T— $175,753 in 1980—for which he has consulted for about a decade. He also received a $16,703 annuity from Teachers Insurance and Annuity Corporation of New York in 1980.

At the time of his appointment, Rostow was a director on the South Sacosta Corp. of Texas and the Petro Development Corp. of Delaware.

WHAT OTHERS ARE SAYING ABOUT HIM

- Rostow's commitment to achieving strategic arms accords with the Soviet Union has been strongly questioned by many in the arms control community. Jeremy J. Stone of the Federation of American Scientists wrote during his confirmation proceedings: "[H]e wants to dramatically improve our military posture through arms control if he is to have any at all. . .He wants to . . . 'restore world public order.' This would certainly be nice. But who has previously thought this a prerequisite to nuclear arms control, much less a goal of arms control?. . .If arms control will await the restoration of world public order, it is going to be long in coming and then be quite unneeded. Arms control is, after all, agreement between adversaries."

- Said Herbert Scoville, Jr., former deputy director of the CIA and now board director for the Council for a Livable World, in a prepared statement to the Senate Foreign Relations Committee: "[T]he director of [ACDA] must have a deep appreciation of the part arms control can play in our overall security structure. . .He must recognize that arms control is not a game in which we must beat the Soviet Union; instead he must seek ways in which both nuclear superpower can have mutual gains. . .So far an investigation of Professor Rostow's past has produced no evidence that he has the experience or the philosophy to serve as the chief government spokesman for promoting our national security through arms control."

- "[A]s chairman of the executive committee of the Committee on the Present Danger, Gene has performed yeoman service in alerting the nation to our long-term competition with Moscow," said Sen. Jackson at Rostow's confirmation. "I believe that Gene Rostow fully appreciates the need to articulate the American view and vision for a peaceful world while building and protecting the west's bargaining position for a genuine, mutual, verifiable arms reductions."

- Said former ACDA director and SALT II negotiator Paul Warnke, a long-time Rostow adversary: "I think he does [have a commitment to arms control]. But his approach is so unrealistic as to virtually amount to an abdication of arms control efforts."

EDWARD ROWNY
U.S. SPECIAL REPRESENTATIVE FOR ARMS
CONTROL AND DISARMAMENT NEGOTIATIONS

RESPONSIBILITY OF OFFICE

Rowny is the Administration's chief negotiator at the Strategic Arms Reduction Talks or START (previously Strategic Arms Limitation Talks or SALT). He has the rank of ambassador, and is the number two official at ACDA.

Rowny initially was considered for the top spot at ACDA, and was favored by key Senate leaders Jesse Helms (R-N.C.) and Charles Percy (R-Ill.) But Reagan had already promised the job to Rostow. Rowny was so certain that he would get the top ACDA position, in fact, that on his financial disclosure form he typed "Director" under the slot "Position for Which Filing." That was later crossed out and replaced in handwriting by "Special Negotiator."

BACKGROUND

Efforts at nuclear arms limitation have been based on the premise that within the acute competition between the two superpowers there exists one very critical point of agreement: Neither side can afford continuing an arms race nor the resulting risk of nuclear confrontation. "We have championed arms control," said Jeremy Stone, director of the Federation of American Scientists, "for more than 30 years as a solution to the dangers of the arms race—not as a solution to the problems of the Russians."

That's not the way Rowny sees it. An Army general who has commanded troops in two wars, Rowny regards arms control negotiations as a continuation of the super-power conflict, a forum in which to defeat the Soviets. So far, he maintains, the Soviets have been the clear winners at the bargaining table. "We took our lumps three times, in SALT I, the ABM and SALT II, we should be wary of risking too much on a fourth go-around," he wrote in his new book, *The Problems of Negotiating SALT.*

On the fourth go-around Rowny is prepared to run an arms race with the Russians, one that will bring Moscow to the bargaining table with the realization that they cannot hope to outbuild the U.S. "They know that in the long run, once they get us into a race, they can't win," he told us. "It's been a one-way race. We have twice the gross national product the Soviet Union has, are spending one-half the GNP they are on defense, there's no objective reason why we can't spend more if we have to. One of the things they want to accomplish is to keep us quiet and keep us from getting into a race." He said the U.S. has already tried "all these ways of having the Soviets come down by showing a unilateral example and by being reasonable."

These days Rowny is particularly pleased with his new boss, who did not shrink from entering that race with full force. In announcing his five-part nuclear arms program in October, 1981, Reagan "showed he was going to be firm no matter what, no matter how tough the depression—recession then, now there's talk of depression—but no matter how bad the unemployment, we've got to take care of our national defense, and that takes first call," said Rowny.

It's a familiar gospel to Rowny, one he has been preaching since he resigned from the SALT II delegation in 1979 to protest that the treaty weakened the United States' strategic position. "You will note," he said at the National Defense University in 1980, "that to this point I have had little to say about arms control. I have done this because my six and one-half years with SALT have led me to the conclusion that we have put too much emphasis on the *control* of arms and too little on the *provision* of arms." (Emphasis in original.)

Rowny repeated that prescription at his nomination hearing: "Either the Soviets come down of their own volition—and they have shown very little readiness to do so—or we have to go up in order to convince them that they have to come down." To which Sen. Claiborne Pell (D-R.I.) replied: "Your prescription really is not so much for arms control here as it would be for an arms race."

Rowny concedes that a high level of defense spending comes at a cost to a nation's economic health. "Japan is a good example of that," he said. "If you don't have to devote resources to take care of your defenses and you can depend on somebody, then you can put a greater number of resources to underwriting your products that you're going to export and that sort of thing, and become better off economically."

Like a successful military strategist, Rowny has sought an intimate understanding of his enemy: not only their tactics and strategies but their convictions and ways of thinking, their points of strength and areas of vulnerability. He has studied the Soviet system, speaks the language, and purports to know how the Russians think. "You have to understand the Soviets," he explained. "You have to study them, and you have to learn their language. You have to learn what they're after, you have to recognize the great disadvantages we're under in terms of making an agreement and the great advantages they have.

"We as a country have pulled into a shell. We just don't study Russian history anymore; we don't study the Russian language. It's all dried up. We're mirror-imaging; we're living in a vacuum. We believe that we have certain ideas and principles and therefore the other side must have them because that's the only sensible thing to do."

The Soviets, Rowny maintains, do not share American concern about increasing world stability, or decreasing the risk of nuclear war. "They're different," he said, "and we don't realize it. We believe that because we're in favor of reductions that the Soviets are going to beat a path toward us. Nothing is further from their philosophy." He added: "I don't think they really believe they have a better system. But they certainly are more dedicated in one way or another. They're making tremendous sacrifices, their standard of living is not nearly what ours is. Our housewife doesn't spend three and a half hours in line just trying to get daily food, which is what happens—and then not too much variety at that—in the Soviet Union. . . . It wouldn't take too much more on our side in order to match them, and we're starting."

Rowny, said one former Pentagon official who has worked with him, "fundamentally objects to negotiating with the Soviets." A former member of the SALT II negotiating team added: Rowny views the Soviets as "untrustworthy, imperialistic, and threatening. It's not a realistic view to that degree—he thinks they're responsible when it rains, sleets, or snows, for every evil in the world."

Perhaps that is what first endeared him to Sen. Henry Jackson (D-Wash.) the Senate's most active, and unbending, opponent of arms control accords with the Soviets. (See profile of Richard Perle.) Working behind the scenes, Jackson had

Rowny pulled off his position as chair of NATO's Mutual Balance Force Reductions (MBFR) Group in Belgium in 1973 to replace General Royal B. Allison—whom Jackson had successfully purged as the Joint Chiefs of Staff's (JCS) representative to SALT.

Allison ran afoul of Jackson at a Senate hearing where the senator attempted to trap Allison into criticizing the SALT I agreement he had just helped negotiate. Jackson hoped to pick up fuel for his fight against SALT I; but Allison wouldn't budge.

After Nixon's re-election according to Peter Ognibene, author of *Scoop*, Jackson went directly to JCS chairman Admiral Moorer, and demanded that Allison be relieved of his position on the SALT team. "Moorer resisted at first," wrote Ognibene. "But when Jackson threatened to block any promotion or assignment for Allison which required Senate action, the admiral capitulated." One former SALT negotiator recalled that after Jackson succeeded in eliminating Allison, it was the Navy's turn to pick a JCS representative to SALT. Moorer routinely sent the name of an admiral to the White House for confirmation. He received back an abrupt reply explaining that the White House had already decided on an Army general—Rowny.

It was within that atmosphere of back-door arm-twisting that Rowny took his seat on the SALT delegation. He spent the next six years pushing Jackson's position (which invariably meant advancing arms limits which the Soviets would reject because they left the U.S. ahead) and feeding information to Perle and Jackson. When he resigned in 1979 to protest the SALT II treaty he joined forces with Jackson and the Committee on the Present Danger, led by Paul Nitze and Eugene Rostow. After the invasion of Afghanistan, when it became clear the treaty would not be ratified, Rowny argued that the U.S. should not abide by the terms of SALT II. Even Reagan has been careful not to breach the accord.

Carter's decision to reassign Rowny to the SALT delegation after his Administration took office was a less than subtle attempt to appease Jackson, a fact not lost on Rowny's new colleagues. He was known as "Jackson's man," sent in to do Jackson's bidding. "Everybody recognized that Ed was extremely unlikely to support a treaty," said a Carter Administration official who worked on SALT. "The people in Geneva found him difficult to work with." Carter would have probably been better served by writing off Jackson and his proxies from the start.

Rowny's first, and last, real display of support for the Carter Administration's arms control efforts not surprisingly was for a Jackson-backed initiative—the March, 1977 comprehensive proposal, based in part on a memo Jackson sent Carter shortly after his election. (See Perle profile.) The comprehensive proposal, which Rowny helped draft, had little to do with the 1974 Vladivostok agreement between the two superpowers that had laid the foundations for SALT II. It was, without doubt, a lop-sided proposal designed to enhance the United States' strategic position. As *Time* correspondent Strobe Talbott writes in his study of SALT II, *Endgame*: "In the comprehensive proposals, the U.S. was seeking substantial reductions in existing Soviet systems in exchange for marginal cuts in future American ones. Had it been negotiable it would have been a very good deal indeed for the U.S."

But it was not negotiable; in Moscow the Soviets rejected the comprehensive proposal abruptly and sent Cyrus Vance back home with his tail between his legs. Rowny still calls the March '77 proposal a "great missed opportunity" and insists that if the Carter Administration had been more tenacious, the Soviets would have finally agreed to it. "I was sorely disappointed that the first time the Soviets said 'no' we said 'okay, no' and we walked away," he told us. "There's no doubt in my mind whatsoever that the Soviets would have come around. I think they would have much preferred that to subsequently having SALT II and having it rejected."

After that episode Rowny served as team spoiler, fighting the American delegation every inch of the way. "I don't think that General Rowny was really interested in any kind of available compromise," said chief SALT II negotiator Paul Warnke. "His views would have required that the Soviets give up in every respect where the asymmetries favored them and allowed us to preserve every instance where the asymmetries favored us."

During the negotiations in Geneva, recalled one member of the SALT delegation, "Rowny and his [Soviet] counterpart mainly lectured to each other." Another SALT negotiator recalled that with his Soviet counterpart Rowny was "stiff, at arms length. They didn't communicate very well and, though the Soviet generals are stubborn too, it was largely Rowny's fault." None of the SALT II negotiators we asked could recall any part of the treaty that Rowny successfully negotiated.

Even the Joint Chiefs of Staff, which Rowny officially represented, were more flexible than he. As one top Pentagon official said: "I didn't get the impression the JCS was fighting [the Administration's SALT efforts] and I never got the impression that Rowny had their support." Another top Carter Administration official working on SALT added: "Ed was more of an independent force. He didn't regard himself as the ambassador of the Joint Chiefs of Staff institutional views." Indeed, after Rowny's resignation the JCS called the treaty a modest but useful contribution to the nation's security, provided it was carried out in conjunction with a nuclear modernization plan.

But the JCS, recalled one Pentagon official, "treated Rowny delicately. I think they were concerned about his close connections with Jackson [a key Pentagon ally]. Rowny was under the protection of Jackson."

One SALT delegate said it became apparent to him that Rowny was not going to support the treaty fully 18 months before it was signed. But Rowny sat through the initialling of the accord in Geneva and then, amidst much fanfare, he resigned from the delegation and retired from the Army "so I could testify. . .against ratification of the SALT II treaty," as he said during his nomination hearing. And that he did, giving Perle and Jackson added ammunition in their attempts to defeat the treaty. After his resignation, Rowny served as an adviser to Sen. Jesse Helms (R-N.C.), a noted hawk on Capitol Hill. During Reagan's 1980 campaign, Rowny co-chaired the candidate's Defense Advisory Committee. During the transition he was adviser for European Affairs and Arms Control for Reagan's Interim Foreign Policy Advisory Board and headed the Central Intelligence Agency's transition team.

Rowny's objections to the SALT II treaty—primarily centering on the Soviets' "unilateral right to 308 launchers for heavy ICBM's" and the exclusion of limits on 375 Soviet backfire bombers—have been called "irrelevant" by others who worked on the treaty. "We have more warheads," said one Carter Administration Pentagon official, "that are more accurate. They'll do the job."

But Rowny insists that SALT II gives the Soviets political advantages. In explaining that, he used an analogy in which two primitive adversaries are confronting each other—each has a sword, but one has a longer and sharper weapon. "Whoever has the longer sword, for one thing, has the greater advantage psychologically and he intimidates his opponent. He looks intimidating to the Third World, particularly with people like the Soviet Union who are great students, and understand what force is all about. Force is the ultimate arbiter, but it's best use is its nonuse. If you have force and you don't have to use it then you really achieved your objectives. This goes back to. . .Sun Tzu and the Chinese military strategists up through Clausewitz and [the Soviets] understand this, and they understand the value of having force. So the object of who has the greater sword, the larger sword, has first of all this psychological idea, that in a crisis the one side will feel intimidated and the other side will feel bold and aggressive. We don't want either one," Rowny said.

"So it's very difficult for a defensive country to prepare itself for these eventualities when another country is on the move and they intend to stay on the move. They believe that they have an ideological mission to spread their type of government around the world," he added.

Rowny maintains the Soviets have strategic superiority—during his nomination hearing he calculated they achieved superiority "somewhere between the last quarter of 1980 and the first half of 1981"—which provides a backdrop to Soviet aggression. "What they want to do is achieve their political goals and that in any kind of a crisis situation they want to say, 'look we've got the threat here and you had better come to terms,'" he said. "I think it's very much going on in terms of Poland for example. . .being able to stave off anyone that might want to" come to the Poles' aid, he said. "It's a backdrop to what they're doing in Southeast Asia. . ."

During an interview in April, 1982, Rowny backed off his claim that the Soviets have clear superiority. But, he said, "They certainly have an edge in those things which count most. What I mean from count most is that from our point of view we want to deter and we want to have stability in times of crisis. They have the destablizing weapons: they have more of these heavy ICBM's, they have a larger number of ICBM's, and more throw-weight and so on and they have a greater number of the destabilizing systems and since we are trying to have deterrence. . .deterrence to that extent is weakened.

"The best proof I have of this is the $220 billion program we have in defense. If we didn't believe that we needed this the President wouldn't be putting forth these programs and the people wouldn't support it. As to who has superiority, or what this is, it's a question of what you want to do with it. If we wanted to turn our SLBM's [submarine-launched ballistic missiles] and bombers out and destroy Russia, no problem, we've got plenty. We don't want to do that. If we want to have enough to deter the Soviet Union we have to have enough forces of the right type or have them come down so there's a better balance of the forces of the right type, these are the types of questions that ought to be addressed in this debate" on nuclear weapons, he said.

Though Rowny said he does not see nuclear war as the Soviets' major intention, he has said that Moscow would not shrink from using nuclear weapons. "The people in official positions write and believe that nuclear weapons are part of the arsenal, that nuclear weapons exist to be used," he said during his confirmation hearing. "They believe that they can, through their civil defense measures—and largely through dispersion of population— limit their casualties. . ." Ominously, he omits the fact that similar statements emanate from Administration officials like Navy Secretary John Lehman who has referred to the "tremendous utility of nuclear weapons, both destructive and psychological"; T.K. Jones, deputy undersecretary of Defense, who has quipped that enough shovels to go around would solve the nation's civil defense needs in the event of a nuclear war; or indeed American nuclear doctrine itself, under which the U.S. is preparing its forces to fight in various types of nuclear war.

When Rowny was appointed to the SALT II delegation in 1973, he had a long standing interest in arms control. He wrote his thesis on the topic as a graduate student at Yale in the late 1940s and served as chair of NATO's Mutual Balance Force Reductions Groups (MBFR) in Belgium in the early 1970s. Those talks sought to limit NATO and Warsaw Pact troop levels in Europe.

But to arms control skeptics like Jackson, Rowny's greatest asset was his military training. The son of a Baltimore shipbuilder, Rowny spent an active 38 years in the Army. He had no doubt that he would spend his career in the military, he said, "after I made a trip to Germany in 1936 when I was a junior in college. I took part of a year to study abroad and I went to Nuremberg and then later to East Berlin and saw the Nazi youth on the move, the torch light parades and all that, and I said I'm within a year of graduating college but there's going to be a war so I'd better learn something about it. So I came home and finished college and went to West Point. The United States' part in it fortunately was postponed four years until I graduated. I graduated two years after Poland was invaded by the Germans, but just five months before Pearl Harbor," he said.

During World War II, Rowny commanded troops of the 41st Engineer Regiment in Liberia, Africa and later a regimental task force of the 92nd Division in Italy. In 1945 he became a strategic planner for General George Marshall.

When the United States entered the Korean War, Rowny became official spokesman for General MacArthur, helped plan the Inchon invasion, and fought in a total of seven Korean campaigns. Rowny, then a lieutenant, served with Alexander Haig, then a lieutenant colonel.

In Vietnam Rowny had a different kind of duty: He established the Army Concept Team in 1962, which tested and evaluated new Army plans for counterinsurgency operations.

The following year he was routed to Washington to help direct American efforts in Vietnam, and was appointed special assistant for tactical mobility. From 1965 until 1969 Rowny was stationed in Germany, first as commander of the 24th infantry division, then as deputy chief of staff for logistics at U.S. Army headquarters in Heidelberg and finally as deputy chief of staff at the U.S. European Command headquarters in Stuttgart.

After a year as deputy chief of research and development in Washington Rowny in 1970 assumed command of the I Corps in Red Cloud, Korea for one year before chairing the MBFR working group in Europe.

With a military background, he is impatient with the sways of public opinion. He considers the current peace movement a misguided and overstated whim. "There's nothing wrong with more attention being put to an awful thing to contemplate, provided it's done in the end in a responsible way. We're all concerned about the prospect of nuclear war and these people are just discovering the thing exists. To the extent that they feel they have to put pressure on us, they are misguided. We're not the problem, the problem is the Soviet leaders," he said.

"We're creatures of our own assumptions," he said. "We put up a hypothesis and we hear some people repeat that. And in a democracy, you do have a plurality of opinion, you tend to hear those things which some people want to hear because of their assumptions. What you don't hear—and again this is one of the fundamental weaknesses of a democracy—you don't hear the silent majority. You don't hear the more responsible viewpoint. . . ."

Born in Baltimore, Maryland on April 3, 1917, Rowny received a B.S. from Johns Hopkins University in 1937, was graduated from West Point as a second lieutenant in the Corps of Engineers in 1941. In 1949 he received two masters degrees in civil engineering and in international relations from Yale and in 1977 received a Ph.D. in philosophy from American University. Between 1979 and 1981 he was a fellow at the Wilson Center, Smithsonian Institution where he worked on a comparative analysis of U.S. and Soviet negotiating, and a director of the National Strategy Information Center in New York until he assumed the ACDA post. He is married with five children.

FINANCIAL BACKGROUND

According to his financial disclosure statement, Rowny has between $50-100,000 in a Merrill-Lynch trust and in a Fidelity Daily Income Trust. He owns stock worth between $15-50,000 in IBM and between $5-15,000 in Coherent, Inc.; National Semiconductor; Ranger Oil, Ltd.; and Virginia Electric Power. He has between $1-5,000 in Geico Corp.; Asarco, Inc.; and Spectra Physics, Inc. He sold stock worth between $1-5,000 in General Dynamics in May, 1981.

WHAT OTHERS ARE SAYING ABOUT HIM

- "Ed Rowny's idea of a good treaty is one he has dictated to the Soviets," said one former SALT II negotiator.

- "Rowny has always pushed proposals which are clearly non-negotiable," said another former member of the SALT II delegation. "I'll be very surprised if any of his proposals would result in an agreement." On the prospects for completing a START agreement, this former official added: "In my experience in negotiating, the Russians' approach will be to try to get SALT II codified first. They like to lock in on the first step before taking the next step. My guess is that in their conservatism they'll want to take it one step at a time."

- Several arms control experts we interviewed agreed that although Rowny's positions are nearly identical to that of Nitze, he is considered a far less competent negotiator and a less reputable strategic thinker. "Rowny is not near as smart as Nitze. He has that sort of gut feeling, while Nitze reaches [his position] intellectually," said a former SALT negotiator.

- Though former ACDA chief Paul Warnke disagrees with Rowny's views on arms control, he was cautiously optimistic about the prospects of Rowny completing an arms accord. "Responsibility does sometimes generate responsibility. When you find that you are to come up with some type of agreement rather than just be the critical gadfly on the sidelines you begin to take more of a personal interest in it."

- Other experts are more pessimistic: "Left to his own devices," said Jeremy Stone, director of the Federation of American Scientists, "General Rowny would not, we think, ever reach agreement with the Soviet Union—even in cases where agreement would be considered sensible to virtually all Americans—because of the excessively hard bargains he would attempt to drive."

- "A great many men talk about principles," said Sen. John Warner (R-Va.) at Rowny's confirmation hearing, "but fewer abide by them. Before us today, Mr. Chairman, is a man who was willing to lay his career on the line in order to stand up for his principles. . . I consider him to be a great American and I am grateful that he would accept this nomination."

PAUL NITZE

AMBASSADOR, LONG-RANGE THEATER NUCLEAR FORCE NEGOTIATIONS

RESPONSIBILITY OF OFFICE

Nitze heads up the U.S. delegation seeking to negotiate limits on "theater" nuclear weapons in Europe. Pressed by a groundswell of public opinion in the U.S. and Europe, Reagan made his first major arms control proposal in these negotiations—the so-called "zero option" that Nitze is attempting to turn into a treaty. (See Major Issues section.)

BACKGROUND

In the four-decade Washington career of Paul Nitze, there have been many dramatic moments, many days spent at the very heartbeat of history. But for this political generation, none left such an imprint as his performance on February 9, 1977 before the Senate Committee on Foreign Relations.

For those who move in the tightly circumscribed, collegial, world of arms control and strategic doctrine, the performance of Nitze that morning was a watershed, an event that placed people on one or the other side of a clear, deep, fissure.

Nitze had come before the committee to oppose President Carter's nomination of Paul Warnke to head the Arms Control and Disarmament Agency (ACDA) and to negotiate SALT II. Nitze had worked with Warnke in the mid-1960s when Warnke was general counsel to the Defense Department and later assistant secretary for international security affairs and Nitze was McNamara's deputy. Representing the newly formed Committee on the Present Danger, Nitze was the star witness of the forces opposing Warnke. Sen. Henry Jackson (D-Wash.) and his right-hand man Richard Perle (See Richard Perle profile) were determined to turn Warnke's confirmation into a referendum on the future of SALT.

Nitze lent an air of dignity, of history, to their effort. A conservative Democrat, former investment banker, a senior official in prior administrations of both parties, Nitze for over 30 years had been an influential hardliner favoring high levels of defense spending and tough bargaining with the Soviets on arms control. Through his longevity alone, he was a familiar figure on Capitol Hill, and even among those who disagreed with him, he was respected for his technical mastery of arms control and his analytic skills.

That Nitze took a different view than Warnke on the Soviet Union and strategic doctrine was well known. What surprised most in attendance— including people who would consider themselves Nitze's friends—was the intensity of his attack.

"I am concerned," Nitze began, "that Mr. Warnke, who has spoken with such certainty on matters of military requirements, weapons capabilities, and strategy, may nevertheless not be a qualified student or competent judge of any of these matters. It is claimed that he is a superb negotiator. I am unfamiliar with his successes in this area."

From that point, things deteriorated. Of Warnke's stand on one point of strategic doctrine, Nitze said: "I don't believe he understands anything about this, nor do I think he is being honest or consistent in saying what his views are." Warnke's views on another matter, Nitze said, were "absolutely asinine."

"The vehemence of his opposition to Warnke at a personal level was a surprise," said one Carter Defense Department official friendly with Nitze. "It seems to me not characteristic."

Another former government official, who worked with Nitze on SALT I, was less charitable. "You cannot think of where anybody of his [Warnke's] stature has been so viciously attacked at a confirmation," said the official.

Almost everyone who deals with Nitze describes him as fair, engaging, even charming, and certainly more of a subtle thinker than Perle or Jackson. Even Warnke believes that "Paul thinks differently from Perle or Jackson. . .he is a more thoughtful man. He has given a great deal of thought to the entire question of strategic nuclear doctrine. I don't agree with his conclusions, but they are, I think, considerably more sophisticated than the idea of an all-out competition in which the Soviets finally cry 'Uncle' and yield us strategic nuclear superiority."

Why then the uncharacteristic attack? Some friends speculate on unspecified personal animosity between Nitze and Warnke; some say Nitze genuinely believed that Warnke was deliberately misrepresenting positions he had earlier held and therefore couldn't be trusted; others cite Nitze's intensity, his passion on the issue, and his unflagging belief that arms control was weakening the western world. "I know him well, I thought he was the wrong man for the job," Nitze said in an interview. "I still think I was right," he said and laughed. But why such a harsh attack? "I tried to restrain myself, but some of the Senators wouldn't let me; they put me in a box. If I were to answer the questions truthfully, they forced me to lose my usual tact. And after I had seen what had been done to me, I asked for permission to change the record and they wouldn't give me permission." (One aide involved in the hearings said he was unaware of any such request; in any case, the aide pointed out, Nitze's remarks were made in open session where they were reported by the press.) Other observers look at more personal reasons. "He's a bitter man," argued the official who worked for him. "He has the bitterness of the prophet scorned."

Nitze's long and distinguished career has not rewarded him with a position at the top of the official pantheon; he has served next to the seats of real power, but no President has called upon him to sit in them. After the Democratic convention in 1976 nominee Carter relied on four senior Democratic experts to brief him on defense policy. Three of them received high posts in Carter's Administration—Harold Brown became secretary of defense, Cyrus Vance the secretary of state, Warnke took the ACDA post. The fourth was Paul Nitze. It has been a long road to the negotiating table in Geneva for Nitze, one filled with repudiation, political exile, and now, sweet vindication. After graduating from Harvard University in 1928, Nitze joined the investment banking firm of Dillon, Read and Co., rising to become a vice president. With independent means, he turned to government service, entering the Roosevelt Administration in 1940 as an aide to Navy Secretary James Forrestal, whom he had met on Wall Street. Nitze headed the Metals and Minerals Branch of the Board of Economic Warfare in 1942 and directed the Foreign Procurement and Development Branch of the Foreign Economic Administration (which included Lend-Lease operations) in 1943. The following year, he was appointed vice chairman of the Strategic Bombing Survey, later touring Germany and Japan to assess the effects of the air war.

In 1946, Nitze shifted to the State Department, where serving successively as deputy director of the office of international trade policy, deputy to the assistant secretary for economic affairs, and—in 1950—director of the policy planning staff he helped draft and oversee the Marshall Plan to rebuild Europe. Nitze said his greatest triumph "was converting Secretary Marshall's speech—just a three paragraph idea—into a detailed plan."

In the latter capacity, Nitze headed a group that drafted the legendary National Security Council Directive No. 68 in response to President Truman's request for a review of U.S. security policies. The basic reasoning, Nitze explained many years later was that, "as the Soviet Union developed its nuclear capabilities, there would be an increasing risk that they would support or cause aggression." Approved by Truman prior to the outbreak of the Korean War, NSC-68 called for a tripling of military spending to strengthen conventional as well as nuclear forces, and is now regarded by historians as one of the opening shots of the cold war. At the time, Nitze was a leading supporter of the development of the hydrogen bomb.

But in those days, even so dedicated a cold warrior as Paul Nitze could be considered soft. And when the Eisenhower Administration came in it was convinced by conservative Republican Senators not to appoint him as assistant secretary of defense. When we asked Nitze what he considered his greatest disappointment, he paused for several moments and then came back to that time. "In a way [it was] when I got fired from the government in 1952, when the Eisenhower Administration came in, I was too liberal for them. They decided they couldn't see their way to supporting me for confirmation for assistant secretary of Defense. . .In any case at that time I thought I might like to run for public office. So I did all the things that I thought might be appropriate for making myself available as a candidate for the Senate from the state of Maryland: held babies, gave speeches at firehouses, escorted all the Democratic politicians in the state who contributed money. Finally I received a telephone call from the local Democratic leader—he wanted to know whether Mrs. Nitze wanted to run for any of three offices. He made no reference to me," Nitze said with a laugh.

So Nitze left government in 1953 to head the Foreign Service Educational Foundation. But he continued actively to promote strong U.S. defense policies as a consultant to the Gaither Committee appointed by President Eisenhower. The post-Sputnik Gaither Report saw "the prospect of a missile gap" advantageous to the USSR and "recommended that we accelerate our missile and radar warning programs."

Throughout the period, Nitze's tone was steady, strident and uncompromising. He did not blink at the prospect of using nuclear weapons. "Perhaps we must always stand ignominiously by as we did in the Hungarian crisis," he said in a 1957 address. "I really do not believe that it need always be so. We have been putting almost all of our research and development effort on the weapons we would require in a big war. The day may soon come when we can and should transfer a substantial portion of that effort to the weapons and tactics which would pay off in a limited war." A few months later he declared, "If we must engage in military action, it is to be hoped that that action can be limited in scope and in the weapons used. If conventional weapons cannot by themselves restore the situation, certain types of situations may require tactical atomic weapons as well."

During the period, Nitze became one of the first—if not the first—strategic thinker to raise the specter of a window of vulnerability, the concept that dominates Reagan Administration nuclear weapons policy. As Nitze explained in a 1956 *Foreign Affairs* article, the theory holds that no nation would launch a nuclear attack "unless they believed that the power of their initial atomic attack and its immediate effects on the enemy would be substantially one-sided." In other words, if the Soviets developed the ability to disable the U.S.'s retaliatory capacity with a surprise first strike, they might be tempted to launch such an attack. It is that fear currently prompting replacement of the Minutemen missiles— considered increasingly vulnerable to such a Soviet attack—with an MX missile in an as-yet-undetermined basing mode.

With their retaliatory capability crippled, Nitze wrote, the nation's leaders would face "a truly agonizing decision." Its forces "may still have the capability of destroying a few of the enemy's cities. But the damage it could inflict would be indecisive and out of all proportion to the annihilation which its own cities could expect to receive in return." In such a situation, the theory holds, the President would face a choice between surrender and mass suicide. (See Caspar Weinberger profile.)

Nitze's views fit well with the virile, muscle-flexing foreign policy of John F. Kennedy. In 1961, Nitze returned to government as Kennedy's assistant secretary of defense for international security affairs. In that post, Nitze worked on the first arms control agreement with the USSR—the partial nuclear test ban treaty. Moved to Navy secretary in 1963, he was commended by Sen. Jackson during confirmation hearings for taking "a hard, tough position in dealing with the enemies of this country."

In arguing at the hearings for a policy of flexible response, Nitze again emphasized that "Certain types of situations may require tactical atomic weapons" as well as conventional forces.

Nitze was promoted to deputy secretary of Defense during 1967—the height of the Vietnam War. According to Nitze, his responsibilities were confined to detailed management of the Pentagon and he at one point "cautioned against our massive intervention in Vietnam."

Out of government again in 1969, Nitze founded, with Dean Acheson and Albert Wohlstetter, the Committee to Maintain a Prudent Defense Policy. A forerunner of the Committee on the Present Danger, the group effectively lobbied for the Nixon Administration's plan to deploy four Anti-Ballistic Missile (ABM) sites. Ironically, only a few years later, Nitze played a key role in negotiating the treaty limiting ABM deployment.

After a few months with the committee, Nitze returned to government, joining the SALT I delegation as a representative of the Defense Department. According to Henry Kissinger's memoirs, Nitze favored a tough U.S. bargaining position—a near halving in numbers of U.S. and Soviet long range nuclear tipped missiles.

In his book on SALT I, chief negotiator Gerard Smith wrote that of the negotiating team "Paul Nitze seemed under the most strain." Concerned about the Soviet advantage in "throw-weight"—missile payload—Nitze "tended to grow less sanguine about SALT prospects. He constantly pushed in Washington and probed while abroad to see if the scope of the negotiation could not be increased to include controls over throw-weight." The Soviet throw-weight advantage would be raised regularly by SALT critics throughout the 1970s.

According to one Nixon Administration official intimately involved in the SALT I negotiations, Nitze was "agnostic about what you could do" with arms controls. When it became clear SALT would not address his throw-weight concerns, this official said, Nitze turned his attention to the ABM portion of the treaty, working effectively on the fine print of the final agreement that was produced. "He has the engineering mind," said the official. "He really likes the technical aspects." (Indeed, Nitze is very fond of the orderly measured music of Bach.)

During the negotiations, Nitze was "very persistent and very dogged," Raymond Garthoff, the delegation's executive secretary told us. "It was largely due to his efforts that we got the Soviets to go as far as they did" on the radar controls imposed by ABM treaty. "I think he's a very effective negotiator," Garthoff continued, "but to the extent that he feels something is of cardinal importance he might in a given instance be too adamant." Though others in the Administration have expressed doubts about the treaty (See Major Issues section), Nitze told us he believes "it's basically sound. In fact, I think the treaty is sounder now than it was when we initially negotiated it."

Nitze reluctantly went along with the final SALT I treaty of 1972, which limited the numbers of Soviet and U.S. missiles, but partly in ambiguous or unilateral statements. In 1977, Nitze complained that the Soviets had interpreted the ambiguities differently than Kissinger had earlier—to their benefit. Defending his assent to the treaty, Nitze claimed that "we could not get the Soviets to agree to any clearer language" with Congress pressing hard for an agreement.

Nitze took part in early SALT II negotiations but resigned in 1974, claiming that President Nixon was so anxious to secure a new arms agreement which might distract public attention from the Watergate scandal that he was making damaging concessions. Nitze already had reason to be bitter about the scandal. Earlier in the year, Defense Secretary Schlesinger had recommended Nitze's reappointment as assistant secretary of Defense for international security but Watergate politics reportedly kept Nixon from agreeing to the nomination. The White House was said to be wary of antagonizing conservative Senators who considered Nitze "anti-Air Force" (some called him a "McNamara-Whiz Kid recycle") and whose support might be necessary to prevent impeachment of the President.

It was against that backdrop that Nitze worked with Eugene Rostow to form the Committee on the Present Danger. Nitze was, by far, the most visible member of the Committee, giving the heavyweight testimony and gathering the most press notices. "Nitze had, rightly, a great deal of credibility," said the Carter Defense official. "He spent a lot of time, presented detailed information and was available to the press. One of his characteristics is that he has the ability and the experience to devote himself fully to work on these issues. He's a class act; he operates at a level of discourse not many in this city manage."

For all his technical sophistication, though, Nitze clearly still sees the world in black and white hardline terms.

While opposing Warnke, Nitze laid out his credo on arms control, a view that makes the U.S. akin to innocent idealists, facing an adversary determined to twist every comma and clause to the cause of international revolution. "[T]he United States—in my view, properly—is intent on strategic arms control arrangements designed to neutralize strategic arms as a factor overhanging international politics, while I believe the Soviet Union to be intent on strategic arms arrangements calculated to afford the Soviet Union a strategic preponderance on the basis of which they can aspire to lay down the direction of world events to Soviet advantage, and, step by step, to achieve eventual Socialist triumph."

That feeling came out when we asked Nitze—just back from the bargaining tables in Geneva—whether the Soviets were more or less interested in arms control than they were a decade ago. As usual, he responded in an historical perspective. Arms control has "been an important part of their foreign policy for years. Back from the very beginning. . .this has been one element of their political program, to identify themselves as peacemakers. . .The program. . .has at least two aspects with [the other] being the decision they made in February, 1946—it was to be crystal clear that he [Stalin] was adopting a different program for demobilization after World War II than were we." Of the current anti-nuclear weapons movement, Nitze said "there's been a strong feeling about the nuclear weapons since the very first days that the explosions at Hiroshima and Nagasaki were announced in the papers;" but his own views were more vividly etched by his subsequent characterization of the movement as "the idea of nondefense."

Nitze takes a more businesslike view of nuclear weapons. After he told us that he had directed the investigation of the effects of the weapons on Hiroshima and Nagasaki, we asked him what feelings that left with him. "It had an enormous impact," he said. "Went to all the hospitals, saw the survivors; measured the effects. I think all of the work on the effects of nuclear weapons is based upon the work that we did." Any philosphical thoughts, we asked? "It left me with the feeling that it's an important thing to do what one could [to keep that] from occurring again and the question is: how do you prevent that?. . .And that in turn goes to the issue of whether or not it's possible to avoid having the problem of whether it's better to be red than dead become a real issue."

Nitze nevertheless believes that further arms control negotiations with the Soviets can be fruitful which actually makes him something of a moderate in an Administration with officials who would just as soon drop the entire idea. Nitze told the House Foreign Affairs Committee in 1974 that, "in the long run it may be possible to negotiate an equitable and useful agreement to control offensive strategic weapons." Such an agreement would come only slowly and "will require continuous work." The ideal agreement, he told the Senate Foreign Relations Committee in 1977, "would be if we were willing to give up many of the systems that we now have, provided we can really get comparable action on the part of the Soviet Union." In a 1980 *Foreign Affairs* article, though, he said the completion of an agreement limiting theater nuclear weapons—which he is now negotiating—was an "unlikely prospect."

Natty, adroit, and precise, he is the embodiment of the patrician school of diplomacy. Twirling his glasses, speaking of Roosevelt and Harriman and William Bullitt ("I go back a long way," he said. "I was involved in the decision—indirectly involved in the decision—by Mr. Roosevelt to recognize the USSR and to appoint Mr. Bullitt as our first ambassador [in 1933]."), he conjures up a world of statecraft unabridged by public opinion or economic pressures. "The contractors try" to influence military decisions, he told us, "but their influence is very small and much less than the public or President Eisenhower in his famous remarks gives them credit for." (For another view, see profile of Frank Carlucci.)

With those jarring exceptions in 1952 and 1974, Nitze has operated through his four-decade public career almost beyond the reach of partisan politics. Perhaps it is because he has never held elective office—never had his views judged by voters with concerns and beliefs and backgrounds different than he—that he has been so unwavering in his beliefs. From Harvard to Wall Street to Washington, he has maneuvered always in the upper crust of American society and in his words the public outside of that thin sphere seems far away, barely visible.

"I've seen a number of movements of public opinion in which the views are deeply held and forcibly expressed," he replied when we asked about the growing concern over the nuclear buildup. And in his tone, it was clear: this too shall pass; and when the noisy public clamor has blown on like a brief summer storm, the decisions will remain in the hands of men of affairs, men of state, men like Paul Nitze.

Born January 26, 1907 in Amherst, Massachusetts, Nitze holds a B.A. cum laude from Harvard (1928). At the time of his appointment, he chaired the Advisory Council of the Johns Hopkins School of Advanced International Studies, was a director of Schroder's, Inc., and a member of the Atlantic Council. Nitze resides in Maryland and is married to Phyllis Pratt. He has four children.

FINANCIAL BACKGROUND

Nitze's financial disclosure form is a worldwind tour through the upper reaches of the Fortune 500. According to his statement, he is worth at least $5.5 million and the actual figure is probably much higher. With his wife, his portfolio includes investment of $250,000 or greater in: Revlon, Inc; Dorsey Corp. (a glass/plastics containers manufacturer); American Security Corp.; Loews Corp.; Exxon Corp.; Mobil Corp; Standard Oil of California; Standard Oil of Indiana; Freeport McMoran Inc. (a mining concern); and Asarco Inc. Nitze and his wife reported investments greater than $100,000 in: U.S. & Foreign Securities Corp.; Teledyne Inc.; IBM; Union Oil of California; Reynolds Metals Co.; the Washington Post; Investment Properties Associates (a real estate firm); an apartment renting partnership in Susquehanna, Pennsylvania; a racing boat construction firm and a family farm in Bel Alton, Maryland.

Nitze earned just over $40,000 in director's fees in 1981, from serving on the boards of Twentieth Century-Fox, Aspen Skiing Corp., Schroders Inc. and the American Security Corp. He received $4,084 in social security payments.

WHAT OTHERS ARE SAYING ABOUT HIM

- Most people we spoke with carefully distinguished between Nitze and Richard Perle, the other leading opponent of SALT II now in the Administration. Said one former high government official still heavily involved in the arms control debate: "They're both zealots and they both see everyting in terms of the Soviet Union. But Nitze's more technically sound than Perle. And Perle is always speaking through somebody else; Nitze commands attention and he speaks for himself."

- Said a Senate aide: "Nitze, unlike Richard, is very much an institutionalist; he's very orderly."

- Pulitzer prize winning historian Barbara Tuchman said recently "A rough equivalent. . .[to] the appointment as chief delegate to the Geneva talks of the high priest of the hard line, Paul Nitze. . .would be putting Pope John Paul II in charge of abortion rights."

MAJOR ISSUES

- The background of the key policymakers in the Reagan Administration's arms control apparatus, their anti-Soviet rhetoric, and the Pentagon's plans for a massive peace-time military build-up have left much of the public doubting whether Reagan has any real interest in reducing nuclear arms.

- Rostow has renamed the SALT process START, but those negotiations are only beginning to get underway 18 months after Reagan took office.

- Responding to displays of anti-American sentiment over the nuclear weapons issue in Europe and concerns expressed by the West European governments, President Reagan came forth with the "zero-option", a proposal for limiting medium range nuclear weapons in Europe. Paul Nitze is leading the negotiations on that issue with the Soviets in Geneva.

- Rostow told us that the Administration's position on the ABM Treaty, up for review in 1982, will depend on its decision on how to base the MX missile, a key shift in emphasis suggesting the Administration may consider defending the MX with an ABM system

At first the layers of cold war rhetoric and military expansion plans lining the Reagan agenda nearly strangled the prospect of arms control. And, though public pressure has kept the issue alive, its standing on the White House's list of priorities remains low. Indeed, through most of its first year the Reagan Administration appeared hostile to the concept of arms accords with the Soviet Union. Some Administration officials like Assistant Defense Secretary Richard Perle and Rostow have suggested they consider arms control talks with Soviets a futile exercise.

The Soviets, Perle said in an interview, "have found it possible to exploit our desire for arms control to accomplish political purposes, to create the impression that we and they were involved together in a collaborative program of moderation at a time when in fact they were building, rapidly building, their military forces." Likewise Rostow maintains the Soviets took advantage of U.S. good nature during the SALT process to reach for nuclear superiority: "So far it hasn't been an arms race for the last 10 years. They've raced and we've slept." Neither, of course, has their boss ever put much stock in arms control. During the 1980 campaign Reagan was fond of telling audiences that he was going to send the still unratified SALT II treaty back to the Russians so fast "they will think we have a new postal system."

Reagan has staffed the key arms control spots in the government with men who, like him, steadfastly opposed the SALT accords between the U.S. and the Soviet Union—Rostow, Rowny, and Nitze at ACDA and Richard Perle in the Pentagon. While officially Rostow heads the Administration's arms control efforts—flanked by his two top negotiators, Nitze for the ongoing talks on the intermediate nuclear forces in Europe and Rowny for the upcoming strategic arms talks—most close observers agree that Perle is a chief architect of Reagan's arms control policies. And, of the various currents pushing arms control policy in the Administration, Perle is considered the least supportive of arms control agreements with the Soviets. "He says he is not against arms control in principal," said a former friend, Dimitri Simes, director of the Soviet-East European program at Johns Hopkins University's Foreign Policy Institute. "But he thinks arms agreements inevitably lull the U.S. into a false sense of security."

Still, some critics hold out hope that the Administration will complete arms accords with the Soviets, particularly as domestic public pressure rises. Said a former top foreign policy official who served under Presidents Nixon and Ford: "I think you have to be careful [about predicting failure]. When people start negotiating they suddenly get more interested in getting an agreement than they are in the abstract".

Most disconcerting to many arms control supporters is the Administration's insistence on linking Soviet behavior to nuclear arms talks. Rostow, in particular, has insisted that strategic arms control negotiations—which he immediately renamed START, Strategic Arms Reduction Talks—cannot begin until the Soviets end their various forms of intervention into other countries, though Reagan appears to have discounted that.

Reflecting his legal background, a frequent theme of Rostow's speeches is that the Soviets must agree to abide by international law (specifically Article 2(4) of the U.N. Charter, which forbids the threat or use of force against the territorial integrity or political independence of any state) before the U.S. will negotiate. (He insists that U.S. intervention in Vietnam during the 1960s and in El Salvador today are "legal.") "The notion of having arms control agreements in the nuclear stalemate so as to make the world safe for conventional war and for guerrilla wars and wars of national liberation is nonsense," Rostow told us. "It explodes in your face."

Because the United States has agreed to provide a nuclear guarantee "against conventional attacks on our supreme interests", Rostow said, "there is no way of drawing an impermeable line between conventional warfare and nuclear warfare. Therefore, in order to eliminate nuclear war, you must eliminate war itself."

That argument, say critics of linkage, points up Rostow's unrealistic approach. "If you're going to link arms control with your evaluation of Soviet behavior, you'd better forget about arms control," said former ACDA director and SALT II negotiator Paul Warnke. "Linkage is a false issue," added Herbert Scoville, a former high official in both the CIA and ACDA. "You don't go into arms control agreements because you want the Russians to be good boys. You need it even more when they're bad boys."

Of course, linkage now centers on Poland. When the Soviet-backed Polish government cracked down on the Solidarity union, jailed its leaders and implemented martial law, Reagan stopped START, before it had even begun. When we asked Rostow if he expected START to get underway in the near future he replied, "Yes, I hope so. It depends on the course of events in Poland." As this book went to press, Reagan had said formal START negotiations could begin as early as June, 1982.

Warnke disagrees with linking the Polish situation to arms control talks. "Poland, in my opinion, should not interfere with the SALT process. This is the sort of thing of which we disapprove. We resent it. The Soviets shouldn't do it. But it is expectable and it's within the bounds of the kind of conduct that is bound to occur when you've got two superpowers who are trying to protect what they regard as their basic interests."

The Reagan Administration's huge nuclear weapons buildup—particularly its decision to develop the neutron bomb—and its expressed lack of interest in nuclear arms control were at the root of a series of mass demonstrations throughout Europe during the late summer and fall of 1981. Rostow dismissed the protests as representative only of the fringe left. Moreover, Moscow, he said, "is trying to exploit" the European peace movement. "It didn't invent it; it's not running it, but it's active. If you look at the list of the groups in England who are managing the affairs, a large number are public communists," he told us.

Ironically it was those "misrepresentative" displays of popular disapproval of American policy, and the resulting pressure on NATO governments, most experts say, that pushed the Administration into forwarding its first major arms control proposal—the zero option, which centers on limiting European-based NATO and Soviet nuclear missiles. That initiative, presented in a November, 1981 speech by President Reagan, "could not have been expected a year ago or nine months ago," said the Arms Control Association in a statement released immediately after the

President's address. This "shows that the Administration takes very seriously the climate of public opinion in Western Europe. Indeed, it is hard to believe that the speech would have been made at all without the pressure from West European governments and publics." Perle, who has been described as the architect of the proposal, insists that the European peace movement "didn't play much of a role" in the Administration's choice. "The proposal was adopted because it was militarily sound," he told us. "That is, if accepted it would produce a more stable military environment. We hoped naturally, it would appeal to some of the demonstrators, particularly to those demonstrators who are genuinely concerned to bring about arms control on both sides."

Actually, the zero option had friends throughout the Reagan Administration's arms control apparatus. The Europeanists working in the State Department liked it because it would quiet NATO fears that the U.S. was not interested in arms control, and it would give the U.S. a leg-up in its propaganda war with the Soviets for European public opinion. Hawks like Perle inside the Pentagon liked it because, as Warnke observed, "they thought it was so unachievable as virtually to amount to no negotiations."

Under the zero option, Reagan offered to forego so-called "modernization" plans to deploy in Europe 572 Pershing II and ground-launched cruise missiles (GLCM) capable of reaching the Soviet Union, if the Soviets agreed to dismantle all their existing SS-4, SS-5, and SS-20 missiles. The decision to deploy the American missiles on European soil had originally been made by the NATO allies in 1979, in response to the threat posed by Soviet deployment of the SS-20, a highly accurate, mobile missile.

Reagan's zero option proposal was generally welcomed as a positive sign by arms controllers. "This was the first encouraging recognition by the President that emphasis should be put on constructive negotiations to limit nuclear arms rather than building a U.S. nuclear war-fighting capability," said Admiral Gene LaRocque, director of the Center for Defense Information. Scoville agreed: "The zero option was the first statement Reagan and his Administration made which recognized there was something to be gained by getting rid of nuclear weapons."

Scoville and Warnke agreed that as a starting position the zero option was a reasonable proposal; that is, if the negotiators are willing to make compromises. "If you look at it as a position of take it or leave it, [the zero option] is a sham," said Scoville. "On the other hand it is a perfectly satisfactory position" with which to begin negotiations.

Simes of Johns Hopkins University described the zero option as a gamble. "Because it is so one-sided, the Soviets can counter with equally unreasonable proposals. So we could end up with a *real* zero option: zero deployment on our side because of European opinion, and zero reduction on theirs."

As was generally expected, the Soviets rejected the zero option soon after Paul Nitze and his delegation arrived in Geneva. Their repudiation of the American proposal was understandable; it would require the Soviets to dismantle not only SS-20's aimed at Europe but also those targeted at China, a Soviet enemy, and other Asian regions, and to dismantle the less threatening SS-4's and SS-5's which it has deployed for some 20 years. In return the U.S. would drop plans for a future deployment of missiles. In essence, the plan proposes trading 572 prospective U.S. missiles for some 600 Soviet missiles already in place. "Not a single state that is concerned about the security of its people would agree to this in our place," declared Soviet President Leonid Brezhnev.

Although the U.S. currently does not deploy medium-range land-based missiles in Europe, NATO could respond to a Soviet attack with American forward-based bombers and submarines, as well as British and French nuclear forces. Counting those forces in its tally, the Soviets insist that an essential equivalence exists in medium-range nuclear weapons in Europe. The Reagan Administration maintains that the Soviets have the edge. In February, 1982 the Soviets presented a counter-proposal to the zero option which called for cuts in the "approximately 1,000 units on each side" to 600 units by the end of 1985 and 300 "toward the close of 1990."

After the Soviets had presented their proposal, which the U.S. promptly rejected, Rostow told a House subcommittee that the Soviet proposal: "would effectively kill NATO's Pershing II and GLCM modernization program, while permitting the Soviets to produce an unlimited number of SS-20's and deploy them in the eastern USSR."

So far, the prospects for a settlement in the Geneva talks appear slim. When we asked Rostow in March, 1982 if he saw any progress in the ongoing talks he had one word: "None." He expanded on that before Congress: "The Soviet Union is not yet convinced of the need to negotiate seriously. Until it comes to accept that necessity. . .it will continue to conduct INF [Intermediate-range Nuclear Force] negotiations not as part of a quest for stability and peace. . .but as a tactical effort to divide the United States from Europe, Japan and from its other allies and vital interests." Meanwhile development of the Pershing II and ground-launched cruise missiles continues.

Responding to the upsurge of concern across the country over the nuclear arms race, Reagan in May, 1982 proposed that each side cut its long-range ballistic missile warheads by one-third. As expected, Reagan discarded SALT II and pro-posed a plan that would leave the U.S. in a significantly stronger strategic position than the Soviet Union. "There has to be some rough equality or parity in such a sensitive area for a proposal to be acceptable to both sides," former Secretary of State Edmund Muskie said in the Democrats' response to Reagan's announcement. "I don't think the Soviets will unilaterally disarm."

Each superpower has roughly 7,500 ballistic warheads—which can be launched from land-based intercontinental missiles or submarines. So a one-third cut would leave each with about 5,000. But the catch is that Reagan stipulated that no more than one-half of each side's remaining ballistic missile warheads could be land-based. The Soviet Union is far more dependent on land-based missiles than the U.S.—over 70 percent of its forces are land-based compared to 30 percent of U.S. forces. Thus, while the Soviets would be forced to dismantle some 3,260 warheads, the U.S. could even add a few. Under the plan the U.S. could still build the MX missile, the Trident II, the B-1 bomber, deploy the cruise missile, and in short con-tinue a massive addition to its nuclear arsenal.

In deference to the hardliners at the Pentagon, such as Perle, Reagan also pro-posed a second "phase" of negotiations, that would seek "an equal ceiling. . .on ballistic missile throw-weight at less than current American levels." That too would require the Russians to make far greater cuts than the U.S.; the Administration has estimated that the Soviets' land- and sea-based ICBM's have three times as much throw-weight as the corresponding American weapons.

Brezhnev responded to the proposal by calling for an immediate freeze on nuclear weapons production as soon as the START talks begin.

Critics fear that the Administration's tough bargaining stance is a deceptive way to avoid completing an arms control accord: "What troubles me," said Muskie, "is that it may be a secret agenda for sidetracking disarmament while the United States gets on with rearmament—in a hopeless quest for superiority in these things."

The insistence of Administration officials, reflected in START, on measuring "equal numbers of similiar forces," particularly land-based forces, in negotiations rather than "equal aggregates" dims prospects for any type of nuclear accord with the Soviets. That approach, says the Arms Control Association, among others, completely overlooks the different geographies and military strategies of the negotiating powers.

It is like trying to balance their apples against our bananas—and vice versa—without looking at the entire basket of fruit. "If you try to suggest that we aren't doing enough then you try to emphasize the respects in which the other side is ahead. If you try to make what I regard as a more objective view you look at the totality," said Warnke.

For example, Reagan Administration officials frequently point out that the Soviet ICBM (intercontinental ballistic missile) force is stronger than that of the U.S. But, as Warnke points out, "we have approximately 30 percent of our strategic forces in ICBM's, about 50 percent in the submarine-launched missiles, and about 20 percent in the strategic bomber forces. The Soviets, because their submarine launched missile technology has never been as good as ours and their submarines are not as good as ours, still have something like 75 percent of their resources in the land-based ICBM's."

Warnke illustrated the absurdity of the Reagan approach with an example from the conventional balance of forces in Europe, where the Soviets have an immense advantage in tanks. "Do we really need as many tanks as the Soviets? Do we really feel that at some point the raving hordes of NATO are going to pour over the border and invade the Soviet Union? The answer is no—that we are essentially optimized for defense. So what we ought to do is compare their tank force not only with our tank force but with our anti-tank capability. And the same is true when it comes to the strategic balance—only more so, because there what you are trying to do is create a stalemate."

He added: "If you feel as I do that the only purpose of strategic nuclear weapons is to see to it that the other side can't use theirs," he said, "then you wind up with very different conclusions than if what you say is we have to be prepared to fight, survive and win a nuclear war," as the Reagan Administration asserts.

The throw-weight, or total payload issue will also be sticky. Sen. Henry Jackson (D-Wash.) and Perle have consistently argued that the Soviets' heavy missiles should be singled out for stronger limits, a move the Soviets have fiercely resisted. Reagan accepted that posture for "phase two" of START. (The Soviets have relied more on heavy missiles, while the U.S. intentionally opted for smaller, more accurate missiles. Henry Kissinger once remarked, "We could have had heavies too if we'd decided to go that route ten years ago," wrote *Time* reporter Strobe Talbott in his book *Endgame*.)

"Throw-weight is not near as important as the number of weapons," said Warnke, "and we still have an appreciable lead there. We have close to 10,000 [central] strategic warheads, they have approximately 7,000. Now the fact that their warheads are bigger isn't really relevant because once you get up to a certain explosive power all you are really talking about is how deep the hole is where the high school used to be. But everybody is dead anyway."

Though the Reagan strategic arms package as announced in October, 1981, does not breach the unratified SALT II agreement, it does establish several potential roadblocks to future strategic arms accords. One key issue which to a large extent has escaped public discussion, is the cruise missile. If the Reagan plan goes forward, the U.S. will build almost 9,000 of these small, mobile and highly accurate missiles which can carry conventional or nuclear warheads. (About 10 percent are now planned for nuclear roles.) Of those, about 4,000 will be deployed on B-52 and B-1 bombers, over 400 will be set for ground-launched deployment in Europe, and several thousand more will be installed on ships and submarines. The Soviets, who have not yet developed comparable cruise missiles, view them as means by which the U.S. can assert nuclear superiority and consider them as dangerous as either the MX or the Trident missiles.

Cruise missiles will make verification of weapons agreements extremely difficult because they are easily hidden and can carry nuclear or conventional warheads. Alan B. Scherr, president of the Lawyer's Alliance for Nuclear Arms Control commented: "If we deploy cruise missiles now we will be tying the hands of our nuclear arms negotiators in the future." Reagan's START proposal said nothing about cruise missiles.

Another implication of the strategic arms package is the potential basing mode for the MX missile. Ballistic missile defense, one proposal the Administration is considering, could require abrogation of the ABM (Anti-Ballistic Missile) treaty of 1972, widely considered the principal success in U.S.-Soviet arms control efforts. Such a system would protect MX missiles in concrete silos by launching rockets to destroy incoming missiles. Nixon and Brezhnev negotiated strict limits on such systems because they felt ABM deployment would greatly accelerate the arms race. As former Secretary of State Dean Rusk has explained it: "Any schoolboy knows that the presence of such ABM's on both sides would simply cause each side to multiply its offensive missiles to the point where ABM's could be smothered or used up before the main strikes are delivered." In addition, it was feared that leaders in countries under ABM protection would be more willing to resort to nuclear weapons.

Sen. Carl Levin (D-Mich.), ranking minority member of the Senate Armed Services Committee, said any decision to break the ABM treaty would be an "action which could have great disadvantages for our defense because Soviet ABM systems, if deployed as a result of our abrogation could seriously weaken the effectiveness of our own missiles. . . And our European allies would question our commitment to continuing the arms control process."

Rostow's remarks on the ABM treaty, up for review in 1982, have not been encouraging. "Review of the treaty," said Rostow at his confirmation hearing, "should not be pro forma, but searching." Indeed, Rostow told us that the fate of the ABM treaty depends on the outcome of the Administration's MX plans rather than vice versa. "The scope of that review," he said, "will depend on future military decisions about the MX and how to deploy it and so on."

Perle said the treaty "precludes us from pursuing some potentially interesting approaches to the defense of our strategic forces." And, he added, "If we come to the conclusion that the effective way to defend our strategic forces is by deploying defenses beyond the limits permitted under the treaty, then I think the treaty would cease to be in our national interest."

Rowny called the ABM treaty "a good treaty for its time. The question is whether it will have enduring value. If we don't get an offensive agreement. . .then the defense agreement makes no sense." He explained that with an analogy of two warriors in primitive times, each with a shield and sword. "We say, 'all right, let's throw away our shields.' It makes some sense to do that if the two swords are the same length and the same sharpness. But if we throw away our shields and one of us has a sword that is twice as long and twice as sharp as the other then we ought to go think about having some shields again. The better thing is once you've thrown your shields away—now that's overdrawn because we haven't given up our defense completely, some limited defense is possible under the ABM treaty—but basically speaking, we're both defenseless against ballistic missile attacks and if you're going to reduce arms, it's great to reduce defenses if you also reduce the offensive."

In addition to the intermediate-range force talks and START, the Administration is expected to propose opening talks on a treaty to eliminate chemical weapons in all countries. Meanwhile, the Army is going ahead with its plan to start producing a new generation of nerve gas bombs in 1984.

In Congress a resolution calling for a freeze in the levels of Soviet and American nuclear arsenals is gaining bipartisan support in both houses. The resolution urges the United States and Soviet Union to "pursue a complete halt to the nuclear weapons race" and says the two sides themselves should decide when and how to achieve "a mutual and verifiable freeze."

Immediately after the resolution was announced in March, 1982 the State Department denounced it, saying the measure would "freeze the United States into a position of military disadvantage and dangerous vulnerability."

The Soviet Union has been quick to latch onto this new public sentiment sweeping through the United States and Europe, and has proven an astute player in the propaganda tug of war. When Reagan—in what at first glance appeared to be burst of generosity—proposed the zero option, the Soviets not only came back with a proposal for deeper cuts on both sides but also announced in early 1982 that they were unilaterally suspending deployment of new nuclear missiles in European Russia. Soviet President Brezhnev announced that the self-imposed freeze would last either until an arms agreement had been reached or until NATO began "practical preparations" for deploying the 572 American-built missiles on European soil. He said further that the Soviets intended to dismantle some of their medium-range missiles, and he proposed a U.S.-Soviet freeze on long-range cruise missiles until strategic arms talks could resume.

Brezhnev's proposal was accompanied by a threat of retaliatory actions "that would put the other side, including the United States itself, its own territory, in an analogous position," if NATO goes ahead with the deployment of the 572 missiles. It has been speculated that Brezhnev was hinting he might deploy nuclear missiles on Cuban soil.

Reagan, who reportedly knew in advance that such a proposal was in the works, immediately rejected the idea of an arms freeze as "neither evidence of Soviet restraint nor is it designed to foster an arms control agreement." Many congressional leaders remarked that Reagan had reacted too hastily. Others took Reagan's abrupt reaction as one more sign that he is not serious about arms control.

As the INF talks stall and arms control officials continue to push for an arms buildup, the American public support for nuclear arms reduction is growing. In fact, next to its environmental policy, the Reagan Administration's attitude towards arms control may be its greatest misrepresentation of public opinion. A December, 1981 Gallup Poll revealed that by a margin of 4 to 1, Americans would support a move by the Administration and the Soviets to reduce their nuclear stockpiles by half. A California Poll indicated that by a margin of 2 to 1 Californians favor a proposed ballot measure calling for a bilateral freeze on the production, testing and deployment of nuclear weapons. Similar initiatives are being put on the ballot in other states.

Opposition to the nuclear arms race has spread into the Catholic Church—which views nuclear weapons as a moral issue—and the established medical community—which has publicized the fact that medical response to a nuclear war would be futile. "I wish there had been similar public concern and similar public support in 1978 and 1979," lamented Warnke.

Ironically, though, much of the recent public protest over nuclear arms was probably sparked by the White House. "They've done arms control a great service by some of their careless statements," said Warnke. "It scared people, when government officials start talking in terms of limited nuclear war, then all of a sudden people begin to think" about the realities of such a war.

Rowny called the current movement against nuclear weapons "unbalanced." A certain amount of fear, he said, "is always necessary. . .but to engender an inordinate fear that somehow because these weapons are around we're all going to perish from them I just think is irresponsible. . .If you're going to do that, that goes to the second and more important problem: So what? So how do we get rid of these weapons and how do you avoid war? So far, our government, under various administrations have been pretty successful—36 years, we haven't had a war. Many people argue we haven't had it because we've had the nuclear weapons. Second, we've had it cheaper. A lot of people don't realize that if you got rid of all these nuclear weapons and then tried to match the Soviet Union conventionally it could cost us six to seven times as much. Nuclear weapons are cheaper—that's why we had nuclear weapons in the first place. Now, I'm not arguing that we should keep nuclear weapons for that purpose, but the arguments that you used to hear that this all costs money is a false argument."

He added: "Part of these current movements that I abhor is this nonsense—and really irresponsible business—of getting school kids involved. They had Ground Zero Week and last Sunday night they had three experts on the radio: 'What do you think about nuclear war?' [they were asked.] 'I think it's bad.' 'What do you think the U.S. ought to do about it?' 'I think we ought to throw away all our weapons.' 'Who do you think is ahead?' 'Ah, we both have too many.' The three experts were 7, 8, and 9 years of age. We laughed and ridiculed the Amy Carter approach to public policy and now we're not only putting our policy in the hands of opinion makers at 7, 8, and 9, we're traumatizing these people, engendering a fear there which is not responsible."

But remarks by Administration officials indicate that they are going to redouble their propaganda efforts to regain some of that public opinion that was lost to the peace movement. "If we sit here and do nothing to correct any misconceptions that are maintained in public information, of course" the peace movement will affect public policy, Rostow told us. "I often thought that the Soviet propaganda victory about the so-called neutron bomb, which is neither neutron nor a bomb—was totally undeserved. But they won the victory because we never did answer it adequately and sensibly."

THE COMMITTEE AND THE ADMINISTRATION

Founded in 1976 to trumpet a call to arms against the growing military might of the Soviet Union, the Committee on the Present Danger has found a comforting echo in the rhetoric of Ronald Reagan. Reagan, a member of the organization, has appointed 32 members of the organization to key staff and advisory positions in his Administration. Three of these officials (an asterisk is placed beside their name) have left the government, but the group's imprint on the Reagan Administration is unmistakeable and probably unprecedented.

In March, 1982, the committee issued a report chiding the Administration for its "minimal" defense program which they claimed leaves the U.S. nuclear triad "clearly inadequate." The committee called for Reagan to move more rapidly toward the goal of spending 7 percent of the GNP on defense. Such criticism is probably not unwelcome in the White House; it offers Reagan the chance to appear as a relative moderate before a public and Congress increasingly skeptical of the Administration's defense spending plans.

Committee on the Present Danger
Members in the Administration

Ronald Reagan
President of the United States
Kenneth L. Adelman
U.S. Deputy Representative to the
United Nations
*Richard V. Allen
Assistant to the President for
National Security Affairs
*Martin Anderson
Assistant to the President for
Policy Development
James L. Buckley
Under Secretary of State for Security
Assistance, Science and Technology
W. Glenn Campbell
Chairman, Intelligence Oversight
Board, and member, President's
Foreign Intelligence Advisory Board
William J. Casey
Director of Central Intelligence
John B. Connally
Member, President's Foreign
Intelligence Advisory Board
Joseph D. Douglass Jr.
Assistant Director, Arms Control and
Disarmament Agency
John S. Foster Jr.
Member, President's Foreign
Intelligence Advisory Board

Amorella M. Hoeber
Deputy Assistant Secretary of the
Army for Research and Development
Fred Charles Ikle
Under Secretary of Defense for Policy
Max M. Kampelman
Chairman, U.S. Delegation to
Conference on Security and
Cooperation in Europe
Geoffrey Kemp
Staff, National Security Council
Jeane J. Kirkpatrick
U.S. Representative to the United
Nations
John F. Lehman
Secretary of the Navy
Clare Booth Luce
Member, President's Foreign
Intelligence Advisory Board
Paul H. Nitze
Chief Negotiator for Theater Nuclear
Forces(TNF)
Edward F. Noble
Chairman, U.S. Synthetic Fuels Corp.
Michael Novak
U.S. Representative on the Human Rights
Commission of the Economic and Social
Council of the United Nations

Committee on the Present Danger
Members in the Administration

Peter O'Donnell Jr.
Member, President's Foreign Intelligence Advisory Board

Richard N. Perle
Assistant Secretary of Defense for International Security Policy

Richard Pipes
Staff, National Security Council

Eugene V. Rostow
Director, Arms Control and Disarmament Agency

Paul Seabury
Member, President's Foreign Intelligence Advisory Board

George P. Shultz
Chairman, President's Economic Policy Advisory Board

R.G. Stilwell
Deputy Under Secretary of Defense for Policy

Robert Strausz-Hupe
Ambassador to Turkey

Charles Tyroler 2d
Member, Intelligence Oversight Board

*William R. Van Cleave
Chairman-Designate, General Advisory Committee, Arms Control and Disarmament Agency

Charls E. Walker
Member, President's Economic Policy Advisory Board

Seymour Weiss
Member, President's Foreign Intelligence Advisory Board

Edward Bennett Williams
Member, President's Foreign Intelligence Advisory Board

Source: New York Times.

* Have left the government

NAIVE QUESTIONS ABOUT WAR AND PEACE, 1982

In the late 1960s, when William Whitworth sat down Eugene Rostow, then a high-ranking State Department official in the Johnson Administration, to ask some pointed, if fundamental, questions about the country's foreign and military policy for his *New Yorker* article "Naive Questions About War and Peace," Rostow's responses had a remarkably similar ring to his speeches today. With the onslaught of communist aggressions, Rostow asserted, the world was witnessing a large scale breakdown in public order, from the Middle East to Southeast Asia—even Europe risked the threat of "neutralization." The Vietnam War, said Rostow, was part of an effort the U.S. was making "in all parts of the world to recreate some kind of system of order."

Rostow, now director of Reagan's Arms Control and Disarmament Agency, still feels it imperative that the U.S. intervene to check Soviet and allegedly Soviet-backed "disruption of world order." El Salvador, he says, is an example of that disruption. But, while Rostow's view of America's role in the world hasn't changed, the ground has shifted beneath him. In the 1960s, the U.S. had unquestioned nuclear superiority, and the Europeans welcomed the protection of their powerful ally's nuclear umbrella. During the 1970s, the Soviets, virtually all experts agree, reached nuclear parity with the United States. Faced with the prospect of a new generation of weapons on their own soil and new warheads facing them from Soviet lands, much of the European public has begun to question the need for America's nuclear guarantee, preferring instead a drastic reduction in nuclear arms on both sides.

A growing community on both sides of the Atlantic is demanding that policy-makers look again at the almost incomprehensible destructiveness of their nuclear stockpiles, weapons which would produce disasters beyond historical antecedent or even imagination. Now the Soviets and the U.S. government are locked in a bitter propaganda competition for the hearts and minds of the European—and, increasingly, the American—public in the arms control debate.

American strategic doctrine has changed as well. During the 1960s, each side acknowledged that the other had the capability to destroy its nation as a functioning society. That historically unprecedented destructive power was considered sufficient to deter either side from launching a nuclear weapon—or indeed a conventional attack—at the other.

Since then, nuclear weapons have become increasingly precise, as have the strategic doctrines guiding them. The world of strategic thinkers is a rarefied one, in which discussions of hundreds of millions of casualties takes place in ordinary, almost casual, tones. Strategic thinkers perform elaborate, elegant calculations: "If we do this, they will do that, but if instead we. . ." All elegant; perhaps logical. But its relationship is questionable to the reality of crushed cities and burning bodies that would follow a nuclear exchange.

The Mutually Assured Destruction (MAD) doctrine that held each side's population hostage during the 1960s has evolved into a doctrine, embodied in President Carter's Directive 59, that envisions the possibility of fighting both "limited" and "prolonged" nuclear wars. The Reagan strategic program is designed to prepare American military forces, as well as the public through civil defense, for both those scenarios.

With his hard line towards the Soviets, his predeliction for finding a Soviet lizard under every rock around the globe, and his casual comments about the use of nuclear weapons, Ronald Reagan has made arms control an issue on Main Street, U.S.A. Communities around the nation are demanding that both sides freeze nuclear weapons development. Over 100 legislators in Congress have joined them. Reagan has rejected the calls.

Within this new atmosphere we took some similarly fundamental questions to Rostow, searching for his views on the future of the U.S.-Soviet relationship. We asked the same questions of one of his colleagues in the Reagan Administration, Richard Perle, the assistant secretary of defense for international security affairs, a leading shaper of the Administration's arms control policies and one of the leading opponents of both SALT I and SALT II; and Paul Nitze, negotiater on the zero option in Europe. We also spoke with Paul Warnke, former ACDA director and SALT II negotiator, the bete noir of the forces that Perle and Rostow so forcefully represent.

Following are their answers:

On Soviet intentions in the nuclear age:
Perle: The Soviets take nuclear war a good deal more seriously than we do. And, despite what they now say, their doctrine is replete with discussion about how to conduct a nuclear war. Whether they feel they can win is an impossible question to answer.

Warnke: I think the Soviets are genuinely concerned about where this competition is heading. For political reasons as well as concern about their own people, they can't contemplate a nuclear war. They are far more sensitized to the destruction of war than we are. The last time there was fighting in the continental United States they were using muskets at Gettysburg. The Soviets have gone through World War I and World War II in their own country. They lost 20 million Russians in World War II and principally Russians, not just Soviet citizens. Some people say that since they are used to that they are much more apt to contemplate war—well, that has not been my experience. I think that anyone who has seen a war never wants to see another one. It's the people that haven't ever fought, that have never seen the destruction that takes place that can be brave as hell.

Rostow: The infinitely greater risk [than Soviet use of nuclear weapons] is the danger of nuclear blackmail. . .and I think we're witnessing it now. That's what the controversy over the SS-20s [nuclear missiles] is about. It puts intense pressures on the Europeans, the Japanese too, arising from the existence of the SS-20s in their numbers. And [the Soviets are trying to] press to paralyze, neutralize Europe on that basis, at a time when the United States strategic nuclear guarantee is in doubt. . .That's the idea, and that's what they are trying to achieve.

On the concept of "limiting" or "winning" a nuclear war:

Perle: I would hope that if deterrence fails and nuclear weapons were used that we would find ways to minimize the number of such weapons [used] and bring the war to a rapid termination short of an all-out nuclear exchange.

Rostow: The practical answer I suppose would be that since 1945 and the shock of those first explosions no one has used nuclear weapons in conflict. . .

Warnke: No, I don't think it is possible to win a nuclear war. It is conceivable that if you have just the use of the tactical battlefield weapon that you might win in the sense that it is conceivable you might discourage the other side from continuing. I think that is probably what President Reagan, and Secretary Haig, had in mind when they talked about 'limited nuclear war'. . .If you feel as I do that the only purpose of strategic nuclear weapons is to see to it that the other side can't use theirs then you wind up with very different conclusions than if what you say is we have to be prepared to fight, survive and win a nuclear war.

On the prospects of a nuclear weapon being fired in the next decade:

Perle: It's very difficult to say. If we do our job properly, then we can hold that prospect to a very low level.

Warnke: Unless the two of us totally abandon arms control efforts and go in for an unrestricted competition, it seems to me that the greater risk is that some third country will use it against a fourth country. It seems to me there is no circumstance where the Soviets could have a realistic gain from initiating strategic nuclear war. If you look at it from the standpoint of people who are mean and tough, but not crazy, why would they possibly do it?

Rostow: I think there is always a chance. But the infinitely greater risk we face is the pressure of nuclear blackmail. Well, I put in parentheses the possibility of Iraq or Libya, that's always a possibility, and that is one of the reasons why proliferation is such a serious subject.

On the "Atoms for Peace" program (A plan proposed by President Eisenhower in December, 1953 which advocated the spread of peaceful nuclear technology throughout the world):

Warnke: It turned out to be a poor idea, with no conceivable gain that is worth the risk that has been done. I'm not saying that I was wise enough at the time to recognize it. At that time people thought that nuclear power was the wave of the future, and that there was no other way to go, it was going to be essential for the functioning of the world economy. That turned out to be a mistake. The problems it creates are immense and the risks it creates of giving a nuclear weapons capability makes it a bum idea.

Perle: I think [the program] was probably a bad idea. There are certainly inherent risks in the diffusion of plutonium around the world.

On the impact of the peace movement, here and in Europe:

Perle: There is no question that Moscow is involved in encouraging anti-U.S. demonstrators wherever they can, and in promoting their view of arms control wherever they can. But there would be some popular concern in Europe even if Moscow were not playing up to it. [In the U.S.] there has always been an enormous gulf between public perceptions of arms control and the judgments and perceptions of the experts. The experts have understood from the very beginning, for example, that arms control was unlikely to produce cost saving. Yet I think if you polled the public on the reasons why arms control is desirable, a high percentage would identify the savings of resources. . . I frankly don't think that the level of public interest makes very much difference, in terms of our ability to successfully negotiate agreements. If the Soviets are prepared to be accommodating, we can find agreements that the public accepts.

Rostow: Of course [ballot initiatives here calling for a U.S.-Soviet freeze on nuclear weapons have some resonance with the public]. You are asked if you are in favor of peace between the U.S. and the Soviet Union, of course you say yes. I would, too. Do you think a freeze [is a good idea]? Well, you'd have to know a little about the present state of things before you can answer that very rationally. I have great respect for the public and it always makes sense if you give it enough information. If we sit here and do nothing to correct any misconceptions that are maintained in public information of course the peace movement will have an impact. I often thought that the Soviet propaganda victory about the so-called neutron bomb. . .was totally undeserved. But they won the victory because we never did answer it adequately and sensibly.

Warnke: After I left the government in 1979 I had made in excess of 75 speeches out of Washington, so I was in just about every part of the country, and I would say the general reaction then was polite and interested but almost indifferent. That is quite different now. When U.S. officials start talking in terms of limited nuclear war then all of a sudden people begin to think—particularly the Europeans. I think the European movement against nuclear weapons has had its impact in this country.

On the strategy of linking Soviet behavior with arms control talks:

Rostow: In my view there is no way of separating the problem of conventional war from the problem of nuclear war. The notion of having arms control agreements in the nuclear stalemate so as to make the world safe for conventional war and for guerrilla war and wars of national liberation is nonsense. It can't work, it explodes in your face. . .Therefore, in order to eliminate nuclear war, you must eliminate war itself. [The Reagan Administration delayed initiation of strategic arms reduction, or START, talks after the Soviet-backed Polish government implemented martial law.]

Warnke: Obviously to some extent linkage is a fact of life. I think back to August of 1968 and at that point we were almost certainly going to announce the beginning of the SALT talks. And Mr. Brezhnev was going to make a simultaneous announcement in Moscow. That turned out to be the day that the Soviets marched into Czechoslovakia. Now, obviously under those circumstances I can make a logical argument that we should have gone ahead with the SALT talks anyway. As a political matter, it was totally infeasible. Similarly, after Afghanistan it would have been senseless for President Carter to present the SALT II treaty to the Senate because it would have lost.

Poland, in my opinion, should not interfere with the SALT process. This is the sort of thing of which we disapprove, we resent it, the Soviets shouldn't do it, but it is expectable and it is within the bounds of the kind of conduct that is bound to occur when you've got two superpowers who are both trying to protect what they regard as their basic interests.

On the future of nuclear arms control:

Perle: I think we have to keep trying. The problem is not so much the current political atmosphere, it's the decade of not having achieved [meaningful] arms control largely because the Soviets have been unwilling to agree to measures that would produce a restraint on the growth of their forces. . .I think you have to keep trying by putting forward some proposals but I think it will take a change in attitude in Moscow to realize these proposals.

Warnke: I expect that within the next ten years, the pendulum will have swung, reality will have begun to break through and we will in fact be moving towards very substantial reductions in nuclear arms. By that point those that feel there is a political utility in [nuclear arms] will have been disabused and the idea that somehow we can gain a first strike capability that will enable us to dictate to the Soviet Union will have proven to be a chimera. . .Also, we're going to find that just budgetary pressures will have an impact. . .Total [nuclear] disarmament? Not within my lifetime certainly, and probably not within yours. But a very, very substantial reduction, yes.

Rostow: I'm rather an optimist about all this in some way, if we're reasonably rational and lucky.

Nitze: I have no crystal ball. But I will tell a story about that. When I was director of the policy planning staff of the State Department, I asked members of the staff to conduct a study of the prospects of our being able to avoid a nuclear war in the indefinite future. They came back and [said] they thought considering history and the general problems involved they thought the chances were low. I then asked them what the chances of being able to conduct ourselves correctly, what are the chances of being able to avoid such a war for 10 years. They came back with a percentage estimate—I can't remember what it was—but in any case it was high. And I said if we manage to avoid nuclear war for 10 years what are the chances of avoiding it for the next 10 years, are those chances increased by the success of avoiding it for 10 years? They came back with the estimate that that would be increased. And therefore, I said it seems to me the policy point is clear: try to reduce the dangers of nuclear war within the relevant future time period as best you can. . .You just get depressed [if you worry] about the long-term future.

STATE DEPARTMENT

ALEXANDER HAIG
SECRETARY

RESPONSIBILITY OF OFFICE

President Reagan declared early in his administration that the secretary of State would be the chief formulator and spokesman for U.S. foreign policy, eclipsing the national security adviser.

Haig is responsible for the overall direction, coordination and supervision of U.S. foreign relations and for the inter-departmental activities of the U.S. government overseas. He is the first-ranking member of the Cabinet, a member of the National Security Council, and third in the line of presidential succession after the Vice-President and Speaker of the House.

In 1982, Haig oversees a budget of about $2.5 billion and a staff of over 16,000.

BACKGROUND

Haig was involved in some of the seedier aspects of the Nixon era—government wiretapping, CIA intervention in Chile, the Watergate tapes, the secret bombing of Cambodia. Though he has never been found guilty of a crime for his five tumultuous years in the White House, as were others who served Nixon, Haig has left a trail of unanswered questions. (When Sen. Paul Sarbanes (D-Md.) asked Haig at his nomination hearing to give "some indication" of his "value judgment" on the abuses that occurred during that period, Haig responded: "[T]here were tremendous abuses on both sides, honest differences between honest men. This is what government is all about, even when there are seamy aspects of government. Nobody has a monopoly on virtue, not even you, Senator.")

For the first 50 years of his life—until his appointment as NATO commander in 1974—Haig only followed orders. He has spent most of his career as a devoted and indispensable aide-de-camp. Waterboy and confidante, messenger and adviser, Haig has always been lured toward power.

To those closest to him, Haig's raw ambition must have been apparent since he was a child. He grew up in Philadelphia during the Depression; his father, a lawyer, died when he was 10, leaving his mother with three children and not much money. His father's death, Haig has said, convinced him that "whatever hopes I had for my own future were going to have to be shaped largely by me." He applied to West Point as a young man, was turned down, and asked his uncle to pull some strings. He was finally accepted and graduated 214 in a class of 310.

As a 23-year-old second lieutenant fresh out of West Point, Haig slipped onto the small personal staff of General Douglas MacArthur, becoming administrative assistant and aide-de-camp to MacArthur's chief-of-staff in Japan. Thus began his swift rise up the military's bureaucratic staircase. Within three years he was assigned aide-de-camp to General Edward Almond, commander of the Xth Corps in North Korea.

Twenty years later, when staffers on Henry Kissinger's National Security Council would complain about their duties, Haig (then Kissinger's deputy) would retort: "You guys don't know anything," as one former staff member, Roger Morris, recalls in his book *Uncertain Greatness*. Then Haig would tell them about the time he caught pneumonia after wading through deep waters holding General MacArthur's sleeping bag aloft.

Or about the time a Chinese advance in the Korean War forced Almond's troops to evacuate: Left behind at Almond's villa was his treasured tile bathtub which Haig said he had built "by local North Korean labor—That damn thing was a labor of love." Disgusted at the thought of a "Chinese general taking a bath in General Almond's tile tub," Haig, amidst heavy gunfire, ran back and tossed a grenade into the tub so that "no commissar would ever wallow in it."

When the Korean War ended, Haig began less colorful pursuits. After completing his graduate work at Georgetown University and working a year on European and Middle Eastern affairs in the International Plans and Policy Division at the Pentagon, Haig in 1963 was appointed military assistant to Army Secretary Cyrus Vance, on the recommendation of Joseph Califano, then Army general counsel.

When Vance became deputy secretary of defense under Robert McNamara, Haig piggybacked along, becoming McNamara's deputy special assistant.

Haig did his requisite six-month duty in Vietnam in 1967, commanding battle troops for the first—and only—time. He earned a Distinguished Service Cross at the battle of Ap Gu, was promoted to colonel, and, avoiding the sticky Pentagon bureaucratic battles flaring up over Vietnam, detoured to West Point as an instructor upon his return. There, Colonel Haig insisted that his cadets march with their fingers cocked at the second knuckle, their thumbs pointed straight to the ground, and their elbows locked. "It's my way of putting a signature on a unit," he has said. In 1969 when National Security Adviser Kissinger decided he needed a good military man as a first deputy he asked each of the services for nominations. Haig, coming on high recommendations from the Army, as well as both Califano and McNamara, got the job.

Haig was the ideal counterweight to the group of often high-minded thinkers Kissinger had brought onto his staff: His appointment assured the Joint Chiefs of Staff that Kissinger would not stray too far from Nixon's conservative foreign policy agenda.

He also lent a measure of order to the undisciplined staff. "He disciplined my anarchic tendencies," wrote Kissinger in *Years of Upheaval*, "and established coherence and procedures in an NSC staff of talented prima donnas."

In the early months of the Nixon Administration Lawrence Eagleburger was Kissinger's chief confidante and right-hand. But when he left after less than a year on the job, Haig stepped into that role. His experience in the military became as valuable to Kissinger as Eagleburger's experience in the State Department had been. "In some ways Haig was savvier about the ways of the bureaucracy than Kissinger," said one of Kissinger's former aides, "and about using levers of power. Haig had been around longer. He also had a much more personal, direct understanding of the military, which Kissinger didn't."

To others on the National Security Council staff, Haig was known as a guy who got things done; not a particularly deep or original thinker but industrious and hard working. "He was not a conceptual thinker," said one top staff member. When we asked this source if at that time he expected Haig to rise to a position of power such as secretary of State he replied: "Never."

Haig's hardline convictions, Morris agrees, "were seldom sophisticated. He could argue for harsher terms in secret negotiations with Hanoi, for example, by recounting a story of how his men had once entered a village where an apparently harmless old man blew himself up along with one of Haig's troopers with a concealed grenade."

But neither was Haig a simple executor of Kissinger's will. "He had his own views; there was plenty of disagreement between Haig and Kissinger, but [Haig] was disciplined," said another former top NSC official. As former Nixon speechwriter William Safire wrote in *Before the Fall*, Haig "was a military staff man who would lay out options for his commander, offer opinions when asked, then put his complete loyalty and penchant for orderliness behind whatever decision his superior made."

More than that, though, Haig tolerated his boss's condescending requests and quick temper. After two decades in the military, Haig had become inured to such abuse—besides, he knew what it took to get ahead.

"Haig had an office adjacent to Kissinger," recalled a former Kissinger intimate. "When Kissinger went off to social events in the evening he left Haig with piles of paper work to finish by the next morning. Haig would work long hours [into the night] and then was back in early in the morning."

All the while, though, Haig was carving out his own niche, first vis-a-vis Kissinger, later with Nixon. Morris once described Haig to a reporter as "Stalin to Henry's Lenin."

"I could not help noticing that Haig was implacable in squeezing to the sidelines potential competitors for my attention," Kissinger writes in his memoirs. "He was not averse to restricting the staff's direct access to me or at least making himself the principal intermediary to the outside world. . . At the same time, I am sure, he was not above presenting himself to my subordinates as the good guy tempering my demanding, somewhat unbalanced, nature. He worked assiduously at establishing his own personal relationship first with [H.R.] Haldeman and [John] Ehrlichman, then with Nixon."

Haig's long hours in the West Basement eventually paid off with Nixon's favor. "Haig's always down there while Henry's off having dinner in Georgetown," Nixon remarked to aides in 1970.

As Haig's personal access to the President grew, so did his competitive relationship with Kissinger, a situation that Nixon encouraged. A former Kissinger aide said: "Nixon tried to play Haig off Kissinger." Nothing better demonstrates the pettiness of that competition than the squabble between the two during the president's visit to Moscow in 1974—after Haig had become White House chief of staff—over who should get the bedroom closer to Nixon.

But in the early months on the NSC, Haig was nothing more than Kissinger's waterboy, pushing papers and handling tasks that Kissinger found distasteful. One of those duties was passing orders to the FBI to place "technical surveillance"—wiretaps—on government officials and news reporters in the name of national security. In the earliest days of the Administration, Kissinger, Nixon, and FBI Director J. Edgar Hoover had discussed the possibility of using wiretaps to catch leaks of sensitive information. (The White House itself had already put one tap on columnist Joseph Kraft's home telephone.) But William Beecher's May 9,

1969 *New York Times* report on the secret bombing of North Vietnamese camps in Cambodia launched them into action.

The first to be tapped was NSC staffer Morton Halperin, whose liberal background made him immediately suspect. Two other staff members, both Democrats, were on the first list of those tapped: Helmut Sonnenfeldt, later to become one of Kissinger's closest advisers, and Daniel Davidson. (Haig later testified that Sonnenfeldt came into his office "almost weekly. .and [said] he was sure he was being tapped." Haig of course denied it.)

Haig was charged with delivering the names of those staffers Nixon and Kissinger wanted tapped to William Sullivan, Hoover's assistant director. When Haig dropped off the first list of names to Sullivan, Sullivan wrote a memo indicating Haig had asked "on the highest authority" that "technical surveillance" be placed on the homes of the four officials. "He stressed that it is so sensitive it demands handling on a need-to-know basis, with no record maintained," Sullivan wrote "Instead he will come to my office to review the information developed, which will enable us to maintain tight control of it." Haig testified before a Senate committee in June, 1974 that Kissinger "asked me to go over and see Mr. Sullivan, who apparently was designated by Mr. Hoover to be the point of contact in the Bureau, and to lay out parameters under which the system would be established and reports rendered to Dr. Kissinger and the President." Haig implied that Kissinger's participation in the program was designed to gain the trust of the White House and, particularly, Hoover, who considered the NSC staff (and by extension Kissinger) too liberal. "Dr. Kissinger at the outset of this program," said Haig, "was very concerned that he and we were suspect because of the character of the staff that we had put together and I feel quite frankly that part of Henry's own mental discomfort with proceeding with this thing was an effort to vindicate these men and to assure those who had suspicions, the [FBI] Director."

During the episode Haig would sort out for Kissinger's perusal the masses of transcripts and summaries produced by the tapes. "I would open them," Haig testified in a civil suit later brought by Halperin against Kissinger, "and pass them to Henry, if they were significant."

The list of those to be tapped rapidly broadened to include 13 government officials, many of them surprising, indeed: key Nixon campaign aide John Sears, staff member Winston Lord (today chairman of the Council on Foreign Relations and a very close friend of Kissinger) and Nixon speechwriter William Safire. Four reporters—Henry Brandon of the *Sunday Times of London*, Hedrick Smith and William Beecher of the *New York Times* and Marvin Kalb, CBS's diplomatic correspondent—were also tapped during the one-and-a-half year operation, code-named June.

Haig told a Senate committee during his nomination hearings last year: "I was not involved in the decision to wiretap. . .I was assured that the program was legal. . .I never decided which individuals were to be tapped. On several occasions I was asked by Dr. Kissinger to identify individuals who had access to specific information, and I [did]."

That defense is backed by other White House aides. And in Halperin's suit a federal district court dismissed Haig as a defendant because of his "inactive role and. . .lack of oversight authority."

On the other hand, it is not clear that Haig has always told the truth about the taps, or that he felt any remorse about the decision to wiretap. In a congressional investigation of the incident, Haig backed Kissinger's testimony when he said he was "astonished" to find that William Safire's phone had been tapped. That contradicted testimony by the FBI's Sullivan that Haig had delivered the message to tap Safire's phone.

Safire wrote that Haig later told him the taps "don't give me gas pains." Indeed, during his nomination hearing, Haig never denounced the use of taps, instead he said that their use would not "make good sense. . .in today's environment, largely as a result of all the controversy associated with that incident." He still maintains the Nixon taps were legal.

On the Vietnam War, Haig also took a consistently hard line. He was involved in Nixon's decision to secretly bomb Cambodia. "I supported the President's decision to order those raids and I was involved in planning them," he said at his confirmation hearing.

Haig said at his confirmation hearing that the Vietnam War was "one of the most profound mistakes in the history of our country, not the war itself but the way in which it was fought." One former Kissinger aide told us Haig was "very hawkish" and thought Kissinger was soft on the war. Haig consistently argued for more drastic military operations against North Vietnam and Viet Cong camps in Cambodia.

In his first volume of memoirs, Kissinger insists that Haig was the force behind the Christmas bombing, when American B-52's resumed heavy raids over North Vietnam, including civilian areas, after peace talks had stalled in December 1972. "I favored resuming bombing on the scale of that before the October self-imposed restrictions, over all of North Vietnam but using fighter-bombers over the populated areas. Haig, on the other hand, favored B-52 attacks. . .on the ground that only a massive shock could bring Hanoi back to the conference table. Nixon accepted Haig's view. I went along with it," Kissinger wrote.

Haig made several trips to Cambodia, often to soothe Cambodian leader Lon Nol, and in so doing became a crucial link between the White House and Southeast Asia. "He was vital in defining the relationship between the White House and Lon Nol, between the White House and the U.S. Embassy, between the White House and reality," wrote William Shawcross in *Sideshow*, an account of the Cambodian bombing. Haig's version of reality was generally rosier than the one painted by independent observers and congressmembers and their staff who visited the region.

The bombing and subsequent invasion across Cambodian borders, without the knowledge or consent of Congress, infuriated some members of the NSC staff. Shawcross writes that William Watts, staff secretary, at one point told Kissinger he objected to his decision to send U.S. troops into the Fish Hook—a peninsula of Cambodia that juts into Vietnam—and stalked out to resign. When he later met up with Haig, the colonel insisted he could not resign; telling Watts: "You've just had an order from your commander-in-chief!" "Fuck you, Al," said Watts, "I just did [resign]." As Shawcross writes: "For Haig to refuse any order was unthinkable."

Haig also had a hand in the White House's plans to overthrow the Allende government in Chile—an incident about which numerous questions still remain. On September 15, 1970—a week after Chileans elected socialist leader Salvador Allende Gossens to the presidency—Nixon instructed the CIA to play a direct role in organizing a military coup d'etat. Progress reports were relayed to Haig.

According to a Senate report on the episode, "Between October 5 and October 20, 1970 the CIA made 21 contacts with key military and Carabinero (police) officials in Chile. Those Chileans who were inclined to stage a coup were given assurances of strong support at the highest levels of the U.S. government, both before and after the coup."

Both Kissinger and Haig have testified that the White House, exactly one month later, on October 15, resisted further coup efforts by the CIA because it looked like it would be unsuccessful. However, after that date the CIA passed guns to a group of Chilean military officers, who twice unsuccessfully attempted to eliminate the major obstacle standing in the way of Allende's overthrow—General Rene Schneider, Commander in Chief of the Army, who firmly opposed any illegal attempt to block Allende's confirmation. On Oct. 22 Schneider was killed during a botched kidnapping attempt by a different group.

CIA officials have contradicted Haig's and Kissinger's testimony, saying they were in regular contact with the White House after October 15. In fact, the calendar of one of the CIA's contact men on the mission, indicates he met with Haig on October 19, the date of the first attempt to kidnap Schneider and three days before the general was killed. Haig has testified that he does not recall the meeting. Three years later in September, 1973, Allende was overthrown and killed. A Senate investigating committee was unable to find clear evidence of direct U.S. complicity.

Like his comments on government wiretapping, Haig appeared during his nomination hearing to have no compunction about the CIA's activities in Chile. During questioning on the episode Senator Paul Tsongas (D-Mass.) asked Haig: "Would you say that the decision arrived at in the White House on September 15 [1970] to engage in an attempt, a military attempt, to prevent Allende from taking power violates article 18 of the OAS [Organization of American States] charter?"

Haig replied: "It is clearly not. It is in contrast to the spirit of that charter. But, again, it has got to be viewed in the context of a host of other counter pressures and other countervening imperatives. And I don't think you, Senator, or anyone in this room would want a rigid legalistic preoccupation which does not assess exigencies of the moment or particular events which represent American interests." Reagan reportedly has approved a similar covert destabilization plan for Nicaragua.

In 1972 Haig received his first reward from Nixon when he was promoted to a four-star general—over 240 other military officers. He left the White House when he was appointed Army Vice Chief of Staff in January, 1973, only to return four months later when Nixon was grasping for someone he could trust as chief of staff during his final days.

Haig's supporting part quickly broadened into a leading role. "As Nixon became immobilized by the ordeal around him and consumed by the effort to save his job, Haig ran the White House," wrote Leon Jaworski in *The Right and The Power*. "It is not altogether unlikely that in the final days of the Nixon Administration Haig ran the country. He was our thirty-seventh and a half president." Haig is also credited with convincing Nixon to resign after all hope of avoiding impeachment had run out.

Haig's name has been connected with the Nixon White House tapes and the infamous 18 and a half minute gap. At his nomination hearing he insisted that he "never personally listened to a tape (other than a brief portion of one that President Nixon played at a Cabinet meeting to demonstrate the poor quality of the recordings). . .I never physically had any tape in my possession. . .I still have no knowledge of the origin of the 18 ½ minute gap."

The truth of Haig's story remains unknown: Nixon prevented the Senate committee conducting Haig's nomination hearing in 1981 from obtaining access to the tapes.

Then there is Haig's involvement with Howard Hughes's $100,000 contribution to the Nixon campaign, which was funneled through Bebe Rebozo. On that matter

Haig testified that his only involvement was to give Rebozo the name of an attorney to employ after the IRS indicated it was beginning an investigation into the Hughes contribution.

And it has been suggested that Haig might have cut a deal with then President Ford to obtain a pardon for Nixon, a charge that Haig denies. "At no time did I ever suggest an agreement or 'deal' that Mr. Nixon would resign in exchange for a pardon from Mr. Ford," Haig testified at his nomination hearing.

Despite the questions that still surround Haig's involvement during these years, the Senate, after six-days of nomination proceedings, confirmed him on a 93-6 vote. "The press had created the expectation that we had to find a smoking gun," said one Senate aide, "that if we could not actually prove he was guilty of anything then he was suitable for the job." The smoking gun was not found, particularly on limited time and with limited evidence, some of which—such as the Nixon tapes—was unavailable.

In 1974, President Ford appointed Haig Commander-in-Chief of the United States European Command. Shortly after, he also became Supreme Allied (NATO) Commander in Europe. Because of his activities in the Nixon White House his assignment was bitterly resisted throughout Europe. But, said Admiral Eugene J. Carroll, who worked under Haig, he rapidly "turned around those feelings and commanded the respect of Europe's top leaders. He held the alliance together." Carroll is now deputy director of the Center for Defense Information, an organization generally critical of Reagan's military policies.

But Haig's relationship with the American president was a different story. He regularly clashed with the Carter Administration, with mixed results. In 1978 Haig successfully fought for the responsibility of coordinating French and Belgian military action with U.S. airlift support during the insurrection in Zaire's Shaba province. Nominally, the Commander-in-Chief of U.S. Readiness Command should have been in charge of the operation.

During the Iranian revolution Haig was less successful. Not only was he completely cut out of the picture but his top deputy was sent into Iran over his objections. According to one official close to the situation, Haig should have been given the responsibility and "was basically bypassed during the whole Iranian situation."

Haig's most fierce disagreements with Carter stemmed from the President's indecision on whether to modernize the theater nuclear forces in Europe, a move which at that time most of the NATO governments favored. (That modernization is now under discussion by the U.S. and Soviet Union in arms control negotiations.) In 1979 Haig resigned as NATO commander and retired from the Army.

As a boss and commander, Haig's tactics are said to be much like those of his mentor, Henry Kissinger. Said one former aide: "He can be extremely demanding and critical, then turn charming, warm and personal—whatever it takes to motivate and lead."

In December, 1979 United Technologies, Inc., a $9 billion conglomerate and the nation's third largest defense contractor, hired General Haig—a man with close Pentagon ties—as company president. Haig maintained he would not involve himself in government procurement contracts, which account for one-quarter of the corporation's business. Company chairman Harry J. Gray personally courted Haig for the job, expecting the general to succeed him when he retired in 1985.

During his term as president, United Technology's sales jumped from $9 billion to $12.324 billion. Half of the increase was due to the sales generated by two companies purchased shortly before Haig arrived.

Running a large corporation, though, clearly was never to be the end of the line for Haig. He considered running for president in 1980 but was stopped by lack of support and poor health—in April, 1980 he underwent triple bypass open heart surgery. In July, while still United Technology president, Haig served as a Connecticut delegate to the Republican Convention. At his nomination hearings, when Sen. Paul Sarbanes (D-Md.) asked him if he still held ambitions for the presidency, Haig replied "Not at all," the standard response for presidential aspirants looking at primaries several years off into the future. After the president was shot last year, Haig stunned the American public when he bolted onto national television and declared that he was in charge. It doesn't seem unlikely that Haig would like a chance to direct the White House palace politics that have hobbled him in his current post.

Haig's redundant and jargon-ridden speech has become a common joke. The National Council of Teachers of English awarded him the 1981 Doublespeak Award for such colorful phrases as "careful caution" and "caveat my response."

Born December 2, 1924 in Philadelphia, Pennsylvania, Haig is married with three children. Haig was graduated from West Point in 1947 and Georgetown in 1962.

FINANCIAL BACKGROUND

Haig made a healthy living as president of United Technologies, with a $415,519 salary in 1980, a bonus of $390,000 payable in 1981, and $41,250 in disability payments during his surgery. He also received a $44,000 pension from the Army; $14,062 for his directorship with Chase Manhattan, $874 directorship fee from Texas Instruments, and $17,500 directors fee from Crown Cork and Seal, all of which he resigned from upon taking office. During 1979, Haig was a director of ConAgra.

He has $100-250,000 invested in Professional Park Associates, a professional office building site in Farmington, Ct., and received fees for various speaking engagements. He divested his over $250,000 in United Technology stock upon taking office.

WHAT OTHERS ARE SAYING ABOUT HIM.

- A former top foreign policy official who has worked closely with Haig said that although Haig has never been a brilliant foreign policy-maker, "in an Administration where conceptual thinking is rare Haig stands out as a conceptualist."

- A former Kissinger intimate who has known Haig for over a decade said: "Haig has a style of rhetoric, a delivery, that is somewhat emotional and somewhat given to overstatements."

- After Haig's nomination had been confirmed by the Senate, Minority Leader Robert C. Byrd (D-W.Va.), one of six senators opposing Haig's appointment, said Haig's background shows he "lacks a fundamental understanding of and sensitivity to the designated and distinct roles and responsibilities of the executive and legislative branches of the government."

- "I'm just concerned," said Sen. Claiborne Pell (D-R.I.), who reluctantly voted to confirm Haig, "that he might be more likely than another man to seek a military solution to a problem. But he's no more hawkish than any other nominee that Reagan would send up."

WALTER STOESSEL
DEPUTY SECRETARY

RESPONSIBILITY OF OFFICE

Stoessel's initial position in the Reagan State Department was undersecretary for political affairs, assisting Secretary of State Haig in policy formulation and managing the department's day-to-day dealings with foreign governments. But when William Clark was promoted to national security adviser at the beginning of 1982, Stoessel moved into the number two position at State. It is unusual for a career foreign service officer, like Stoessel, to hold the deputy position; his appointment was viewed as a gesture by Haig to careerists in the department.

As deputy, Stoessel is responsible for representing Haig in his absence, chairing a committee of the National Security Council, representing the United States overseas, coordinating the interdepartment operations abroad, guiding American efforts in multilateral negotiations, and making recommendations on personnel and ambassadorial appointments. Because of his long foreign policy experience, Stoessel can also be expected to wield significant influence over policy formulation.

BACKGROUND

Walter Stoessel has been called the model diplomat—a dashing and gallant entertainer with a wide circle of prominent friends; a calm and discreet negotiator who can be trusted with the most sensitive of missions. The silver-haired statesman has spent most of his career life in diplomacy, serving as U.S. Ambassador to Poland, the Soviet Union, and West Germany.

But Stoessel's special interest is Soviet affairs. He served two years at the American Embassy in post-World War II Moscow, at a time when the two countries were terminating an uneasy alliance. He returned to study at the Russian Institute at Columbia University, and in the mid 1950s, he directed the State Department's Office of Soviet Affairs through some of the chilliest days of the cold war. He became the American embassy's number two official in Moscow in 1963, just two years after the Cuban missile crisis had brought the two superpowers to the brink of war.

Stoessel returned to Russia as U.S. Ambassador in 1974—in the era of detente—and helped negotiate a U.S.-USSR agreement limiting underground nuclear test explosions. Unlike his predecessor, Stoessel had personal access to the Kremlin and met informally a number of times with Soviet President Leonid Brezhnev.

Until recently, Stoessel has taken a consistently moderate approach to Soviet relations. Former U.S. Ambassadors to Moscow, Malcolm Toon and Foy Kohler both used the same word to describe Stoessel's views: "realistic." "He's certainly not a famous hardliner," Kohler, who puts himself in that category, told us.

During the 1970s Stoessel was optimistic about the future of Soviet-American relations, and he publicly defended detente against its critics. When the *Washington Post* denounced the U.S.-USSR General Agreement on Contacts, Exchanges and Cooperation because it appeared to condone the Soviets' domestic policies and gave the U.S. less leverage in future negotiations, Stoessel, then assistant secretary of State for European affairs, responded:

"[Your editorial] reflects a misunderstanding of the purpose of the agreement. . . .Our objective. . . .was to arrange a pattern of exchanges in various sectors of the cultural, informational and other fields which affords an acceptable balance of reciprocal advantage. We believe that the exchange programs over the past 15 years have contributed significantly to our foreign policy goal of improving relations with the Soviet Union on the basis of mutual benefit."

In a 1976 interview with the *New York Times*, as he was stepping down from his ambassador post, Stoessel said: "It's hard to be very certain, but I feel that the detente relationship. . . .is rooted in sort of fundamental factors on both sides, for the Soviets and for ourselves, and that those factors will continue to operate."

Propelling the easing of tensions, he said, is a fear on both sides about nuclear war: "I think there is a concern on both sides to try to put some kind of limitation on strategic arms." In addition, he said the Soviet leadership is interested in technology trade and "I think we are interested also in more trade as a way to get the Soviets more interested in a normal relationship, building this web of interests which I still think is valid, although it's very long-term business."

Contrast those remarks with a speech he gave as a Reagan Administration official during the fall of 1981 in Brussels: "The Soviet Union has in recent years carried out an unprecedented conventional and strategic military buildup far in excess of its legitimate defense needs. The buildup has continued through a period when the West pursued a policy of detente. . ." In the same speech, in which he had nothing positive to say about U.S. relations with the Soviets, he added: "Soviet behavior is a serious and growing threat to our own security and to the basic principle on which a human and rational international system must be based."

Stoessel's first experience as ambassador was in Poland, from 1968 to 1972. (An avid athlete, Stoessel decided the Warsaw embassy did not meet his needs so he had installed a wooden paddle tennis court and a swimming pool.) While in Warsaw, Stoessel was charged with a delicate task—secretly paving the way for reopening talks between the United States and mainland China. Though Henry Kissinger claims credit for personally engineering the historic breakthrough embodied in the Shanghai Communique in which the United States affirmed "the ultimate objective of the withdrawal of all U.S. forces and military installations from Taiwan," the Chinese first extracted that agreement, though informally, in Warsaw—from the U.S. ambassador to Poland.

It all started in a topless fashion show in December, 1969 in Warsaw's Palace of Culture, reported *Look* foreign editor J. Robert Moskin. "The throb of the big Yugoslav band, the titillation of the Communist models in their peekaboo clothes. And then, in the confusion when everyone was leaving, a handsome silver-haired American approached the interpreter for the People's Republic of China and made contact," wrote Moskin. "He discreetly told the man in Polish that he would like to talk with his boss, the Communist Chinese charge d'affaires."

Discretion is Stoessel's professional forte, and that is perhaps why he was designated to make the first attempt at resurrecting talks with the Chinese that had died several months before. He gained entree: "The following week," he told Moskin, "I heard from them. They said, 'you wanted to see the charge so come and see him.' I went to the embassy, which was probably the first time an American ambassador had been in a Chinese embassy since 1949." For the Chinese the time was right—with the Soviets posing a growing threat, the Cultural Revolution winding down, and the U.S. withdrawing troops from Vietnam. Lei Yang, the Chinese charge d'affaires, agreed to begin talks in January, 1970, leading later to Kissinger's visit to Shanghai, and, in 1972, Nixon's visit to Peking.

According to documents obtained by Jack Anderson in 1980, when Lei indicated that China's aversion to U.S. military support of Taiwan was "firm and unswerving," Stoessel replied: "The limited United States military presence in Taiwan is not a threat to the security of your government and it is our hope that as peace and stability in Asia grow, we can reduce those facilities on Taiwan we now have." Stoessel had succeeded in smoothing the thorniest controversy between the two countries.

From 1976 until his appointment to the Reagan Administration, Stoessel served as ambassador to Germany, easing often strained relations between Helmut Schmidt and Jimmy Carter. He had previously been in Germany as a political officer to the U.S. High Commission in the early 1950s.

Stoessel also served as special assistant to President Eisenhower's foreign policy adviser (1956); executive secretary at the Department of State (1960–61); political adviser to the Supreme Allied Commander in Europe (1961–63); and deputy assistant secretary of State for European affairs (1965–68).

Born January 24, 1920 in Manhattan, Kansas, Stoessel received his B.A. from Stanford University in 1941, and entered the Foreign Service the following year, serving briefly in Caracas, Venezuela before entering the Navy. He attended Harvard's Center for International Affairs in 1959 where he studied under Kissinger. Stoessel is married with three children.

FINANCIAL BACKGROUND

According to his financial disclosure statement, the only income Stoessel received in 1980 was a salary from his ambassadorship and interest and dividends on various stockholdings. His and his wife's stocks include, in the $5,000–15,000 range: Southern Bell Telephone and Telegraph, American Home Products, Emerson Electric, El Paso Co., Georgia-Pacific Co., Caterpillar Tractor Co., Amax Inc., IBM and Southern Pacific. In the $15,000–50,000 range: Atlantic Richfield, Schlumberger Ltd., Gulf Oil Corp., and various housing bonds.

WHAT OTHERS ARE SAYING ABOUT HIM

- Inquiries about Stoessel evoke general praise from the foreign policy community. David Newsom, undersecretary for political affairs under Carter, said: "He's by nature relatively quiet. He's well-regarded as a professional in the foreign service because he deals with problems in a calm, deliberate fashion and he interacts well with people."

- Former ambassador to the Soviet Union Malcolm Toon, who has known and worked on and off with Stoessel for about 30 years, said Stoessel's good relationship with a wide range of representatives and senators will be an asset to the Reagan State Department.

- Another former ambassador, Foy Kohler, who represented the U.S. in Moscow from 1963–65 compared his former deputy to another young foreign service officer, Malcolm Toon, during their early career years. "Stoessel was always the quieter, less outspoken [one], more of what people think of as diplomatic."

LAWRENCE EAGLEBURGER

UNDERSECRETARY FOR POLITICAL AFFAIRS

RESPONSIBILITY OF OFFICE

Eagleburger joined the Reagan Administration in 1981 as assistant secretary for European affairs, but he was promoted to undersecretary, Stoessel's original position, when Stoessel moved up to take the deputy's spot. As undersecretary for political affairs, Eagleburger participates in the formulation of foreign policy and coordinates the department's activities with other U.S. agencies here and abroad.

He is the State Department's number three official.

BACKGROUND

Through much of the 1970s, while Secretary of State Henry Kissinger was shuttling to the Middle East, soothing allied leaders and fashioning detente with the Soviets, his trusted aide Larry Eagleburger was at home minding the store—and Kissinger's image. As his top assistant, Eagleburger shielded Kissinger from meddlesome Congressmen, set straight critical journalists, and tracked down embarrassing leaks.

He has been described as "Kissinger's Kissinger," "Kissinger's alter ego," and "Kissinger's enforcer." Invariably his name appeared in newspaper clips only alongside Kissinger's. A career foreign service officer, Eagleburger has publicly said little on foreign policy, except as a Kissinger aide. But that taint is enough for the far right: Eagleburger's appointment to the Reagan State Department evoked howls of protest from congressional hardliners, in whose minds the name Kissinger conjures up sinister images of detente and SALT.

In appearance, Eagleburger is hardly the image of a high-level diplomat. Those who know him say his health is invariably poor. He doesn't watch his weight, he smokes incessantly, and he is high-strung. "He has a lot of nervous energy," said another former top Kissinger aide, William Hyland. Eagleburger didn't last long at the tense Kissinger National Security Council (NSC) in 1969; within several months he had physically collapsed and was ordered by doctors to take a less strenuous job. "He worked himself too hard," said Hyland. Recently, Eagleburger was hospitalized with phlebitis.

Eagleburger's association with Kissinger began in 1969, when he served as the State Department's liaison to the NSC. At that time Eagleburger was a 38-year-old career Foreign Service Officer with overseas experience in Honduras and Yugoslavia. He had been a staff expert on European affairs for Walt Rostow's NSC under Lyndon Johnson and, most recently, had served as special assistant to Undersecretary of State Nicholas Katzenbach. Kissinger hired Eagleburger to help hire staff, keep schedules straight and acquaint him with the State Department.

He proved to be a much more significant force. In fact, Eagleburger was instrumental in developing Kissinger's power base, bringing in a team of ambitious intellectuals and helping to guide his boss through the maze of Washington's foreign policy machinery. "Eagleburger knew State inside and out," one former Kissinger associate told us. "He knew the players over there [at the State Department]. Eagleburger helped Kissinger set up the NSC staff, organizing it and staging the coup d'etat that made the council the premier force" in the Nixon Administration's foreign policy-making.

During the early months of Kissinger's reign Eagleburger was one of the few aides to gain his trust, and he quickly became Kissinger's closest confidante. It wasn't until Eagleburger left the NSC in 1969 that Alexander Haig began taking on that role. According to others on the council, Eagleburger spoke his mind, and frequently challenged his boss, a quality that Kissinger appreciated. "He was very much not the compliant yes-man," one source remarked. "Kissinger respected that." Kissinger said the same in his book, *Years of Upheaval*: "[Eagleburger] stood up to me when necessary."

As Kissinger's confidante, Eagleburger was privy to some of the White House's darker secrets. He knew of Nixon's drinking problem and that, in fact, the President had been drunk during highly sensitive deliberations over what to do after a North Korean plane in April, 1969 shot down a Navy reconnaissance plane—during those discussions Nixon and Kissinger considered using B-52 bombing raids, and nuclear weapons, against North Korea, as Seymour Hersh reports in his upcoming book on the Nixon White House excerpted in the *Atlantic Monthly*. Eagleburger knew that colleagues on the NSC had been wiretapped at Kissinger's direction and, according to Hersh, he even told one staff member, Roger Morris, that his phone had been tapped. He knew that another staff member, Morton Halperin, was being squeezed out. Halperin's liberal political views made his loyalty suspect to Nixon, Attorney General John Mitchell and FBI Director J. Edgar Hoover, among others. In fact, there is no evidence that Halperin was disloyal. But, as Hersh writes:

> Larry Eagleburger added to the rumors. . .by confiding to Roger Morris that Halperin's name had shown up on an intercept by the National Security Agency of a Japanese Embassy transmission. The NSA reported that Halperin had been discussing sensitive negotiations over the future status of Okinawa with Japanese officials in Washington, who had cabled the conversations to their foreign office in Tokyo. Morris got the impression from Eagleburger that the White House could have made a case against Halperin for treason. (Halperin acknowledges holding private talks with the Japanese; such talks, he says, were also held during the Johnson Administration, and were always considered to be part of the normal bargaining process.)

Eagleburger missed most of Kissinger's exploits at the NSC. By the end of 1969, his health in shambles, Eagleburger had left Washington for a more relaxing post in Brussels, as counselor for political affairs to the U.S. Mission to NATO. In 1971, he returned to Washington, but not to the White House. Instead, he served as deputy assistant to the Defense Secretary for two years. But when Kissinger took up residence at Foggy Bottom in 1973— thereby moving the seat of foreign policy power back to the State Department—he surrounded himself with a coterie of loyalists; Eagleburger was one of those.

At State, Eagleburger proved as useful to Kissinger as he had been at the NSC. As Kissinger's executive assistant, he kept the wheels oiled between the department, Capitol Hill, and the White House. He was Kissinger's bullhorn to the rest of the State Department, and to Gen. Brent Scowcroft at the NSC. The *Washington Post* in 1974 described Eagleburger as the "linch-pin between the how-to-do-it and the get-things-done echelons. . ." One top official described him as primarily a "domestic troubleshooter;" at times he also met with foreign officials.

Though in his memoirs Kissinger does not describe Eagleburger as a "close friend" (as he does another top aide, Winston Lord), associates say Eagleburger had a unique relationship with Kissinger. One former official told us Eagleburger was considered the best person to bear bad news to Kissinger; he suffered through Kissinger's short temper with good humor; and he was able to nudge Kissinger into altering his views.

In *Years of Upheaval*, Kissinger recounts one incident that dramatizes their relationship. It took place in Moscow during the 1973 Middle East war, when Kissinger woke up to discover that an important cable to Washington had been delayed. Eagleburger, who had been assigned the task of transmitting the message, recalled the incident later in a letter to Kissinger:

"Unbeknownst to me, you walked in at that moment and obviously heard what I was saying. . .There was a bellow along the lines of: 'What, the cables aren't out yet?!' I looked up to find you standing in the middle of the room with smoke issuing from nose, eyes, and ears, and no one else. . .in sight. . . The single exception was Winston Lord, who was sort of huddled in a corner, but—God bless him—prepared to hang around for the pyrotechnics and to clean up the blood (mine) when it was all over. . ."

Though Eagleburger obviously retains a sense of humor about the incident, Kissinger still describes it as "far from funny."

Eagleburger was also Kissinger's public defender. When two Anthony Lewis columns appeared in the *New York Times* in early 1975 criticizing the secretary of State for letting the Vietnam War drag on by propping up regimes in Vietnam and Cambodia that could "never stand by themselves"—and questioning Kissinger's commitment to humanitarian aid to those countries—Eagleburger sent a stinging reply. Calling Lewis's columns—and another by William Safire—"unfair, offensive, distasteful and painful," Eagleburger implied the columnists had been uncouth, even unpatriotic, for questioning the personal motives of the secretary of State. "My point is that these articles attacked the motivation, not the actions of the Secretary of State," he wrote. "They impugned the loyalty and integrity of his person, and ignored the fact." Lewis, in particular, had questioned the motives of Kissinger, who Lewis said, "would rather have war than an indigenous settlement because the latter would show the futility, the cynical brutality, of what he has been doing all these years in Indochina."

To Eagleburger, these attacks on Kissinger amounted to nothing less than McCarthyism. "More than twenty years ago, as a student at the University of Wisconsin, and a member of the Republican party, I fought Senator McCarthy because of his vicious attempt to corrupt the American political process," Eagleburger wrote in his response. "It will ever be to the credit of the *New York Times* that it stood against him. Yet now, regrettably, that same great and influential newspaper is prepared to be the vehicle for attacks which bear a strong resemblance in tone, content and tactics to the sordid phenomenon it once courageously opposed."

Eagleburger ended his acerbic letter with this closure: "I would like to emphasize one point: It is I—and I alone—who initiated, drafted and sent this letter. Secretary Kissinger has not seen it, nor is he aware of its existence."

Generally, however, Eagleburger acted on his boss's instructions. In 1974 when CBS correspondent Daniel Schorr was producing a television version of Seymour Hersh's *New York Times* exposes on the CIA's clandestine activities in Chile, he interviewed Ray Cline, who had recently resigned as State Department chief of Intelligence and Research after a falling out with Kissinger. Cline insisted that both the CIA and the State Department had opposed covert action in Chile and charged Nixon and Kissinger with operating together "on an Olympian plane" in pursuing a policy that the experts opposed.

The next day, a Saturday, Schorr mentioned to Kissinger that Cline had confirmed CIA operations against Chilean President Salvador Allende and had pointed the finger at Kissinger and Nixon. On the following Monday, Schorr writes in his book *Clearing the Air*, he received a call from Eagleburger. " 'Would you be able to come back to the Department and see me?' he asked in a mock German accent. 'Heinrich has instructed me to show you some interesting captured documents.' What Eagleburger showed me were three top-secret papers, written in 1970 and 1973, listing various recommendations for opposing Allende—bribing members of Parliament to vote against his election, subsidizing opposition parties, and working with the Chilean military." Each of the documents, wrote Schorr, "bore handwritten remarks by Cline, generally supporting strong action and scoffing at the doubters."

Eagleburger, however, did not try to disprove Cline's charge that Kissinger was behind the covert activities in Chile. "He [Eagleburger] just acted as a mailboy," Schorr told us, and didn't want to volunteer any other information.

In another episode in 1975, Eagleburger defended Kissinger's foreign policy machinery from an inquisitive congressional panel, the House Select Committee on Intelligence, better known as the Pike Committee for its forceful chairman Rep. Otis G. Pike (D-N.Y.). The dispute began when the committee voted to declassify U.S. intelligence information on the 1974 Cyprus crisis and then invite comment on it during a closed session. But the Administration refused to provide the data; and Eagleburger issued instructions preventing a middle-level official, Thomas D. Boyatt, then chief of the State Department's Cyprus desk, from testifying about his opposition to Kissinger's policy. (Eagleburger said his policy barring junior and middle level officials from testifying about their policy recommendations was a move to ensure their "candid advice" would remain confidential; Pike noted that he thought Kissinger was trying to protect himself, not his employees.)

Some committee members said the State Department's decision to withhold classified information from the panel was an attempt to cover up failures in intelligence gathering and policies. "They never intended to give this committee classified information with respect to the Cyprus invasion nor the coup in Portugal because they clearly realized. . .if this committee could ever unravel the mess, many heads would roll," said Rep. Ronald Dellums (D-Calif.). During a heated appearance before the committee Eagleburger received some piercing remarks. "You remind me of a sideshow magician," said Rep. Morgan F. Murphy (D-Ill.). "You won't give us policy or the facts. It's just this mumbo jumbo. . ."

Later, however, Eagleburger negotiated a compromise with the committee that was a clear victory for Kissinger. Boyatt's criticism would be mixed into a general report to the committee where they would be indistinguisable from others' comments on the policy. But Boyatt still could not testify. (After the debacle, Boyatt was exiled to Santiago, Chile as a counselor to the U.S. embassy, and later to Upper Volta, Africa as ambassador.)

Eagleburger was also involved in defending Kissinger against a contempt citation issued by Pike's committee over the release of other classified material. The contempt charge was eventually dropped after another compromise was reached. The final Pike Committee report, an incisive and devastating examination of the intelligence community, deplored Kissinger's "passion for secrecy," and accused him of putting forth a "new doctrine that can best be characterized as 'secretarial privilege.'"

In 1977 Carter appointed Eagleburger ambassador to Yugoslavia, where he served until he entered the Reagan Administration. The Yugoslavs were particularly fond of Eagleburger: As a young foreign service officer there in the early 1960s he had been dispatched by the U.S. embassy to help the victims of an earthquake in Scopia, the capital of Macedonia. He set up a tent in the middle of a muddy field and for several weeks distributed aid and helped the residents rebuild their town. When he returned as ambassador in the late 1970s the Yugoslavs had coined their own nickname for him: "Lawrence of Macedonia."

But he was welcomed in Yugoslavia for another reason. His more hardline predecessor had incensed President Tito by pressuring the Yugoslavian government to stand up to the Soviets. By the time Eagleburger arrived, relations between the U.S. and Yugoslavia were at a low ebb. Eagleburger, on the other hand, publicly was more tolerant of the country's ties with the Soviets. "He understood Yugoslavia and the complexities of its relationship with the Soviet Union," said State Department official Mark Palmer, who served as political counselor to the U.S. embassy under Eagleburger.

Kissinger and Eagleburger are still friends, and, indeed, Eagleburger told the Senate Foreign Relations Committee during his first nomination hearing as a Reagan appointee, that Kissinger "has a great deal of experience and intellect that can be offered to all of us in government, in giving us at least his ideas on how issues ought to be handled, and I would intend to talk with him about those and to consult him on occasion." Needless to say, that statement did not please right-wing senators like Jesse Helms (R-N.C.), who opposed both Eagleburger's initial appointment and his promotion.

Though conservative on foreign policy matters, Eagleburger seems uncomfortable with the anti-Soviet rhetoric that emanates from right-wing elements in Congress (and indeed from the President) if only because of the damage it causes to relations with European allies. During his second nomination hearing Eagleburger noted that Reagan's objectives of establishing a new basis of relationship with the Soviet Union had "led to some fairly harsh rhetoric over the course of the first year. I think that that rhetoric, while it disturbed relations, and I admit it, with a number of our Western European allies, the message got through to the Soviet Union."

Of criticism coming from the right (not to mention Kissinger), that the U.S. had not responded harshly enough to the Polish crackdown, Eagleburger said: "Several columnists have decided to become the latest version of hairychested tub-thumpers on the subject to prove their manhood, if I may, without really thinking through the consequences of some of those sanctions."

During his first year in the Reagan Administration Eagleburger reportedly clashed with hardliners in the Pentagon and on the National Security Council staff. He does not get along with Richard Perle, a tough assistant secretary of defense who plays a key role in arms control policy. As an aide to Sen. Henry Jackson (D-Wash.), Perle was a leading opponent of Kissinger's SALT efforts. (See profile of Richard Perle.) Reportedly neither Perle nor Eagleburger will attend meetings in the other's office.

Born on August 1, 1930 in Milwaukee, Wisconsin Eagleburger received a B.S. and an M.S. in political science from the University of Wisconsin, Madison. As a young man he worked for Earl Warren in his unsuccessful 1948 bid for the presidency. He is married with three children.

FINANCIAL BACKGROUND

According to his financial disclosure statement Eagleburger has minor investments in Safeguard Business Systems, Quotron Systems, Inc., and the Webster Cash Reserve Fund. He also owns a condominium in Daytona Beach Shores, Fla. worth between $50-$100,000. Aside from interest on his holdings and a salary as ambassador, Eagleburger received no other income, according to the statement.

WHAT OTHERS ARE SAYING ABOUT HIM

- We asked Paul Warnke who knows him personally, to compare Eagleburger's view of the world with that of other Reagan foreign policymakers. "Far more sophisticated," he said. "I think he certainly feels that the Soviets present a menace, but I don't think the way he feels the way you should deal with them is to try to paint them into a corner and hope that somehow they are going to collapse."

- In his second volume of memoirs, Henry Kissinger says of his former top aide: "Eagleburger's skill was the management of men and organizations. . .he understood the foibles of his colleagues without succumbing to their parochialism."

MAJOR ISSUES

- Haig has attempted, unsuccessfully, to develop a consensus among the American public and U.S. allies that the Soviet Union is the greatest source of international insecurity today. In a strategy to contain what the Administration sees as Soviet-backed aggression, the U.S. is pumping arms into volatile regions and embracing right-wing authoritarian regimes, while the Pentagon flexes American military muscle around the globe.

- In Latin America, Haig is scrambling to produce evidence that would justify U.S. military intervention in El Salvador. He insists the Salvadoran civil war is a result of Soviet-backed meddling; while other Latin America experts assert that it is an indigenous uprising, the result of decades of political and economic repression. Additionally, the Administration is reportedly supporting covert action to destabilize the leftist government in Nicaragua.

- The Europeans have been reluctant to support the Reagan Administration's attempts to squeeze Moscow economically and bully it militarily. Among the people of Europe, Reagan's confrontational rhetoric and nuclear weapons buildup have resulted in widespread protest.

- Despite hardline posturing, the Administration was unable to prevent, or later cut off, the Polish government's crackdown, demonstrating the difficulty of transforming its confrontational rhetoric into reality. Now Reagan's right-wing supporters are calling Haig "a pussycat."

- In Africa, the Administration has pursued an anti-Soviet strategy by embracing the anti-communist and apartheid-practicing government of South Africa, and is supporting elimination of the Clark Amendment, which prohibits sending American aid to Angolan opposition groups opposing that country's leftist government.

- China is the big winner of the Administration's anti-Soviet drive in Asia, and has been informally promised American military aid.

At his nomination hearing, Haig stressed that Reagan's foreign policy would be built around three qualities—consistency, reliability and balance.

To be accurate, he should have added another: simplicity. Like the one-page memos on which Reagan relies for far-reaching domestic policy decisions, like the anecdotes he uses to rally public support for those decisions, Reaganomacy began as a skin-deep version of complex international issues

Its underlying premise is that the Soviet Union is responsible for all instability and violence around the world; from the Middle East to Africa to Latin America the Soviets are busy peddling arms and ideology in their drive to dominate the world. As Reagan put it during the campaign: "Let's not delude ourselves. The Soviet Union underlies all the unrest that is going on. If they weren't engaged in this game of dominoes, there wouldn't be any hot spots in the world."

Within this tidy world view, America's role is to lead its friends and allies in a global crusade to contain Soviet-backed aggression, to funnel arms to regimes that proclaim their aversion to communism, to flex American military muscle around the globe, and to squeeze the Soviet bloc by curbing Western trade and credit. Once America begins to provide this kind of sturdy leadership and to regain its preeminence in world affairs, the theory goes, a consensus of support will once again flow from the American public and U.S. allies. "We can do this," said Haig, "by demonstrating, as we are doing in El Salvador today, that a government bent on making necessary reforms will not be overthrown by armed intervention supported by Moscow or its surrogates." The Administration is acting, he said, "to restore confidence in American leadership through a more robust defense of U.S. ideals and interests."

But accord did not flow, either from the American public or U.S. allies. Neither were as convinced as Haig and Reagan that the Soviets were bent on taking over the world. American friends in Latin America such as Venezuela and Mexico were dubious about alleged Soviet interference in Central America and have grown increasingly uneasy about American involvement there. Our European allies have begun to wonder if El Salvador was becoming another Vietnam; France even expressed its support for the leftist guerrillas. Within the U.S. the American public displayed dissatisfaction with Reagan's Central American policy through polls and public demonstrations. "What is troubling," commented former State Department spokesman Hodding Carter III, "is a world view which not only sees the red hand everywhere, but which has an unlimited notion of our responsibility to counter it."

It is a telling note that Haig began his second year in office confronting a dilemma that doesn't have a niche in the Reagan Administration's world view: a battle between two American allies, Great Britain and Argentina, over a remote group of islands in the South Atlantic.

LATIN AMERICA: Since he took office, Haig has been itching for a stronger U.S. military presence in El Salvador. With his vehement insistence of Soviet-Cuban-Nicaraguan intervention, critics say, Haig has transformed an indigenous popular rebellion against decades of economic and political repression into a showplace for superpower posturing, complete with cameras and reporters from around the globe. When his rhetoric failed to turn the tide of public opinion and polls showed that the Administration's El Salvador policy was costing the President valuable political capital—Haig began rummaging for "evidence" of Cuban and Nicaraguan interference.

The first was the infamous "white paper." The report, which the State Department claimed drew on "captured guerrilla documents and war materials, and was corroborated by intelligence reports," sought to present "definitive evidence of the clandestine military support given by the Soviet Union, Cuba, and their communist allies to Marxist-Leninist guerrillas now fighting to overthrow the established government of El Salvador."

Nearly four months later, the *Wall Street Journal* interviewed Jon Glassman, the State Department official largely responsible for the document. Glassman admitted that the paper was replete with errors. For example, Glassman admitted that in decoding the documents he probably misidentified the authors, whom the State Department had claimed were leftist guerrilla leaders. Moreover, the quantity of arms the white paper insisted were involved was 20 times higher than what the captured documents actually listed. In short, as John Dinges, co-author of *Assassination on Embassy Row*, who had unearthed many discrepancies by translating the materials himself, commented: "These. . .documents. . .provide conclusions that fall far short of the Administration's portrayal of El Salvador as an arena of U.S.-Soviet confrontation." Although Haig insists that the white paper is still valid, the State Department no longer refers to it.

That route closed, Haig tried another tack. In spring, 1981 he told the House Foreign Affairs Committee that El Salvador's civil war was part of a "four-phased operation" being conducted by the Soviets. The first phase, he said, was "the seizure of Nicaragua, next is El Salvador, to be followed by Honduras and Guatemala. . .I wouldn't call it necessarily a domino theory. . .I would call it a priority target list—a hit list, if you will—for the ultimate takeover of Central America."

Others who, unlike Haig, have spent extended periods in Central America, discount the hit list theory. Former U.S. Ambassador to El Salvador Robert White said of Haig's assertions: "It's easier to fight Soviet imperialism where it's absent than where it's real." Said another expert on El Salvadoran affairs, Larry Birns of the Council on Hemispheric Affairs: "Rather than seeing the El Salvador situation as a situation where a significant part of the population has come to the conclusion that no social justice can be attained through the existing regime, and rather than inducing the current [U.S.-backed] government to make significant concessions in order to satisfy the population, the Administration has decreed that we need tough governments in the area to fight a supposed Soviet threat."

In another attempt to bolster his case, Haig in early 1982 trotted out a 19-year-old Nicaraguan—recently captured in El Salvador—as evidence of systematic Nicaraguan support for leftist Salvadoran guerrillas. To the embarrassment of the Reagan Administration, the young student, at a State Department-sponsored press conference, recanted earlier confessions he had made of Nicaraguan involvement. Moreover, he charged that American officials had threatened to return him to the Salvadoran town where he had been arrested and tortured by brutal Treasury Police if he did not "confess."

"An official of the U.S. Embassy told me that they needed to demonstrate the presence of Cubans in El Salvador," the Nicaraguan, Orlando Jose Tardencillas Espinosa, told reporters. "They gave me an option. They said I could come here, or face certain death. All my previous statements about my training in Ethiopia and Cuba were false."

Nicaraguan officials asserted that Tardencillas, swept up in the cause of the revolution, had left Nicaragua surreptitiously and joined the Salvadoran guerrillas. With the devastating press conference over—and Tardencillas on his way back to

Nicaragua—a red-faced State Department spokesman, Dean Fischer, remarked simply: "You win some, you lose some."

Haig's case for sending U.S. troops to prop up the Salvadoran regime has been further weakened by regular press accounts of civilian massacres by government troops and right-wing death squads linked to the government. In late 1980, for example, four American churchwomen were raped and murdered; six National Guardsmen have been charged. To the dismay of friends, relatives, and others, Haig suggested that the four nuns could have been shot while running a roadblock. In succeeding months hundreds of men, women and children in countryside villages and city slums known or thought to be sympathetic to leftist guerrillas have been slaughtered. In March, 1982 four members of a Dutch television crew were slain by government troops as they, together with leftist Salvadoran guides, were on their way to film in rebel-controlled territory. On the day of the murder a right-wing death list with the names of 35 journalists was found in a San Salvador radio station (the Dutch journalists were not on it).

These developments have had a marked impact on Capitol Hill, prompting Congress to require that Reagan certify the El Salvadoran government was making progress on restoring human rights before sending further U.S. aid. But Reagan had no qualms about making that certification and in February, 1982, tripled U.S. military aid to the El Salvador government from what Congress intended to send in 1982—from $26 million to $81 million. Shortly after his certification, government troops poured into a San Salvador slum, murdering 19. In responding to charges that government troops conducted that mass murder, Thomas O. Enders, assistant secretary for inter-American affairs, told the Senate Foreign Relations Committee that the Administration could not prove or disprove this, adding "the guerrillas did nothing to remove [civilians] from the path of battle."

Disclosures of civilian murders have also affected American public opinion. A *Washington Post*-ABC news poll conducted in March, 1982 revealed that 6 in 10 Americans opposed the Administration's sending of 55 U.S. military advisers to El Salvador and over 70 percent opposed sending American troops to Central America.

Despite public and congressional opposition, Haig still refused to rule out the possibility of sending in troops. "We have not ruled out anything, and we're not going to, a priori, in a very dynamic ongoing situation," he told the Senate Foreign Relations Committee in early 1982. He added the U.S. would do "whatever is necessary" to prevent rebel guerrillas from overthrowing the Salvadoran government. Haig "doesn't care about listening to Congress," said Rep. Thomas Foley (D-Wash.), majority whip, 'I think we are playing a macho game in El Salvador."

Public uneasiness over U.S involvement in El Salvador is likely to increase with the outcome of the March, 1982 election, boycotted by leftists, in which a coalition of right-wing factions joined together to dominate the government, leaving only a small role for Christian Democrat Jose Napoleon Duarte, president of the outgoing, U.S.-backed civilian-military junta. While the Administration and many members of Congress considered Duarte a "moderate," they admit that the newly emerging leader, Robert D'Aubuisson of the rightist National Republican Alliance, spells trouble. He has been linked to death squads and terrorist activities, and opposes reform. Former Ambassador White called him a "pathological killer." But the Reagan Administration, though clearly distressed by the outcome of the election, is preparing to work with him anyway. In an ironic note, Eagleburger said after the election: "What government is formed is basically an issue for the Salvadoran people."

During his first year, Haig also busily waged his own guerrilla campaign against Nicaragua. It started as a war of words with the country's leftist Sandinista regime: Haig charged them with "harboring international terrorism and abetting violence in another country" by supplying arms to Salvadoran guerrillas. In the first months of the Administration, the U.S. suspended $90 million in economic aid to Nicaragua.

From there relations deteriorated. In the last months of 1981 U.S. destroyers were dispatched to the Gulf of Fonseca, which is bordered by El Salvador, Honduras and Nicaragua, to watch for Nicaraguan arm shipments to El Salvador. Several months later the *Washington Post* disclosed that Reagan had approved a $19 million plan to form a CIA-backed paramilitary force to disrupt the Nicaraguan government. The Administration has not denied the report. "This is only the latest in a long series of reports, all undenied by the Administration, of planned covert activity against Nicaragua," said Rep. Michael Barnes (D-Md.), who introduced legislation to bar such action. "It is hard to imagine that we would do anything so stupid."

The evidence supporting Haig's claim of large Nicaraguan arms shipments to Salvadoran guerrillas is weak. Birns maintains Nicaragua stopped supplying small caches of arms to the guerrillas in late spring, 1981 as the political stakes grew and shipping them without U.S. knowledge became next to impossible. "The guerrillas have obtained arms through the international market and they also have the capacity now to produce their own arms," he said. American journalists in El Salvador have reported that the guerrillas are ill-equipped and short on ammunition—in sharp contrast to well-armed American-backed government troops.

The White House has also considered building a naval blockade around Nicaragua to intercept arms coming in from Cuba. Even Navy Secretary John Lehman is wary about that option.

In a mirror of his attempts to prove outside agitation is responsible for the Salvadoran war, Haig has been scrambling to demonstrate to Congress and the public that Moscow is running the show in Nicaragua. In March, 1982 then Deputy CIA Director Bobby Inman and John Hughes, deputy director of the Defense Intelligence Agency, conducted a public briefing—complete with pointer and slides of aerial reconnaissance photos— to demonstrate Soviet military involvement in the country, and to prove that Nicaragua is marshalling the largest military force in Central America to threaten its neighbors. The two officials patiently explained their evidence, bit by bit. (They had even rehearsed it sometime earlier for Haig.) "Now, we show a MIG-17 configuration here, but there's a question mark behind it. . .because we believe that soon either [Soviet-built] MIG-17's or MIG-21's will be delivered to Nicaragua. . . ."

The following day, however, a senior Nicaraguan official pointed out that the chief evidence in the briefing—the lengthening of airstrips "to accomodate heavy jet aircraft"—was originally proposed by a U.S. government-financed study conducted during the reign of Anastasio Somoza. A spokesman for the Agency for International Development confirmed his assertion. The Nicaraguan government also denied U.S. charges that 50 Nicaraguan pilots are being trained in Bulgaria and Cuba to fly Soviet-built MIG fighters, and asserted that Nicaragua's army is no larger than the forces under Somoza.

Gary Trudeau captured the absurdity of the Administration's valiant attempt to "educate" the public about Soviet intervention in Nicaragua in a Doonesbury comic strip:

"This is an aerial view of just one of the dozens of Cuban-style army bases being built in Nicaragua today. Notice the Soviet-style training ground with Romanian-backed Nicaraguans in North Korean-made sneakers doing Cuban style push-ups. . .Notice, too, the Soviet-style Cubans wearing Czech-inspired fatigues having lunch with Cuban-trained Nicaraguans in the Bulgarian-built mess tent.''

"Great photos, general. What's that they're eating?''

"Soviet-style pizza.''

Further to the south, the Administration has dropped nations' human rights records as criteria in choosing its Latin American friends and has embraced what im-partial observers believe are the hemisphere's most notorious human rights violators: Guatemala, which Amnesty International said was ''conducting a govern-ment coordinated campaign of terror;'' Chile, where Amnesty says human rights conditions have ''sharply deteriorated;'' and Argentina, where thousands have mysteriously disappeared. (See James Buckley profile for details on military aid to these countries.) Instead, the State Department has emphasized it will use ''quiet diplomacy'' to encourage these countries to change their ways.

Within the first months of the Administration, Haig reshuffled the State Depart-ment Latin American machinery, firing experts and replacing them with loyalists who have little experience in the region. The key actor is Enders, assistant secretary of State for inter-American affairs. Enders has served as Ambassador to Canada, charge d'affairs in Pnom Penh during Nixon's bombing of Cambodia, and was assistant secretary of State for business and economic affairs under Ford. He does not speak Spanish and had no direct experience in Latin America or the Caribbean.

EUROPE: Nineteen eighty-one was a tense year for U.S.-European relations. An anti-American mood surfaced in several European capitals. The U.S. and its allies seemed to disagree on almost every significant international issue, from American policy in Central America to trade with the Soviets and East Europe. Headlines prompted by such commentators as Henry Kissinger proclaimed the NATO alliance to be in disarray, ''facing a paralysis of will,'' said one. Even former NATO com-mander Haig found it difficult to hold back the avalanche.

The root of popular discontent in Europe was Reagan's bellicose cold war postur-ing and careless references to nuclear conflict. The Europeans, who had felt two world wars ravage their continent, understandably felt trampled by the Reagan Ad-ministration's rush to out-bluster and out-muscle the Soviets. ''There is a growing feeling that we are moving inexorably toward a nuclear war in Europe,'' Admiral Gene R. LaRocque, director of the Center for Defense Information, said at a con-ference on the subject, held during the spring of 1981 in the Netherlands. ''It seems unfair that nuclear war will be fought over and in the nations which have nothing to say about whether nuclear weapons are to be used.''

Within months of that conference Reagan announced—without consulting the allies—that the U.S. would begin production of the neutron bomb, a weapon prin-cipally for use in conflicts on European soil. Later he startled Europe again by sug-gesting that a nuclear weapons exchange in Europe would not necessarily lead to a full-scale nuclear war between the two superpowers.

Haig himself stoked the fires of fear in Europe when he noted in congressional testimony that NATO has contingency plans to launch a ''demonstration'' nuclear explosion as a warning to the Soviets not to invade West Europe. Such an explosion would ''demonstrate to the other side that it is exceeding the limits of toleration in the conventional area,'' he said.

During fall, 1981 some 600,000 demonstrators poured into the streets of London, Paris, Brussels, Rome, and Amsterdam to protest the nuclear buildup. Reagan officials have routinely dismissed the protestors as "pacifists" who only represent the fringe left. Reagan asserted the Soviet Union was underwriting the demonstrators. But Haig's public relations tour of Europe at the height of the discontent suggested that the Administration viewed it much more seriously. Haig flew across the Atlantic in September, 1981 in an effort to convince the Europeans that Moscow, not Washington, was endangering world peace.

In Berlin, where thousands of protestors chanted "Haig go home," he delivered his pitch for unity: "Too many are prophesying a future devoid of hope, indecisive, unable to cope with the challenge of the '80s, and the everpresent critics of NATO are once again acting as though the alliance were about to crumble."

Even NATO officials were perturbed by the Reagan Administration's virulent rhetoric. After Haig's Berlin visit, NATO Secretary General Joseph Luns criticized the Reagan Administration for allowing "the impression, albeit false, to grow that it is reluctant to pursue the subject [of arms control] and is preoccupied with the pursuit of military supremacy." Luns also took the opportunity to chide Reagan for his decision to go ahead with producing and stockpiling neutron weapons. "In all frankness, that decision was not an example of tact in the conduct of international relations," he said, referring to the Administration's failure to consult NATO on the decision.

Europe's display of outrage appeared to have some impact; late in 1981 the tide began to turn. In his first major foreign policy speech since taking office Reagan stressed his desire for peace, and offered a proposal to the Soviet Union for nuclear arms control in Europe. The President's zero option proposal was greeted with relief in some sectors of Europe and skepticism in others. The Sunday after the plan was announced, tens of thousands of peace demonstrators marched in the streets of Amsterdam. "There is a real danger that in the struggle for propaganda advantage with the Soviets," LaRocque commented after Reagan's speech, "the true concerns and interests of the Europeans and others will be overlooked." (For more on arms control, see Eugene Rostow profile.)

At the official level the European governments were resisting Reagan's attempt to integrate them into his strategy of curtailing trade with the Soviets. Many West European countries, particularly West Germany, have a comfortable trade relationship with Soviet bloc countries that they are unwilling to relinquish. West Germany, for example, in 1978 signed a 25-year agreement with the Soviets committing them to a wide range of financial and industrial partnerships. In many European capitals, Reagan's strategy is seen as counterproductive and insensitive to the mutually beneficial economic relationship between the two blocs. (They also point out the U.S. has been unwilling to give up its lucrative agricultural exports to the Soviets.) Haig and other "Europeanists" at State, such as Stoessel and Eagleburger, have taken a moderate position in the internal Administration debate on how far to push the allies. Weinberger and Kirkpatrick have taken a much harder line.

After the Polish crackdown in December, 1981, Reagan imposed a ban on exports of oil and gas equipment and technology to the Soviet Union and asked European leaders to take similar steps. Though they joined in Reagan's criticism of Moscow and the Polish regime they refused to second the ban and instead imposed their own, more moderate, diplomatic and economic sanctions. Weinberger and Kirkpatrick argued that the Europeans should be coerced into taking stronger action by a U.S. threat to declare Poland formally in default on its huge borrowings from

Western banks, a move that would wreak havoc on the European banking community.

Haig argued successfully in the first round of debates that the U.S. should not force a default on the Polish debt. In notes of a staff meeting obtained by the *Washington Post*, Haig said a default could mean "the collapse of the West German economy." The effects of default, he said, would be "very far-reaching and unpredictable. One of the effects: ruin East-West trade."

On the Siberian natural gas pipeline, in which British, French, West German, and Italian companies are involved, Haig has opposed European participation but has rejected Weinberger's calls for stronger pressure on the allies to pull out of the project. Although Haig says he agrees that the Europeans will increase their dependence on Soviet energy supplies and will provide Moscow with hard currency that could be diverted to military hardware, he insists that the Europeans' position is firm and further pressure will only fracture the alliance. (See Robert Hormats and Larry Brady profiles for more on pipeline.)

The future of European relations with the U.S. appears to rest both on Haig's continued ability to win these internal debates, and on a concerted Administration effort to complete an arms control agreement with the Soviets.

SOVIET UNION AND EAST EUROPE: As expected, Reagan's Soviet policy has centered on bluster and bluff. Reagan set the tone during his first White House press conference when he asserted that the Soviet leadership reserved "the right to commit any crime, to lie, to cheat," in order to reach their goal of world-wide communism. His Administration has linked hostilities in the Middle East, Africa, Latin America, and elsewhere to Soviet meddling. And in a diplomatic deja vu, "containment" of the Soviet Union, a catchword of the '50s, has become the dominant theme of American foreign policy.

Though Reagan officials routinely exaggerate the intentions and capabilities of the Soviets, at times their cold war rhetoric reaches levels of hysteria. After hearing this belligerent posturing for close to a year, George Kennan, a Soviet expert and former ambassador to Moscow whose post-World War II writings provided the intellectual basis for containment, was prompted to speak up. The prevalent view of the Soviet Union, he told a Dartmouth College audience in November, 1981, is "so extreme, so subjective, so far removed from what any sober scrutiny of external reality would reveal that it is not only ineffective but dangerous as a guide to political action." He said the "endless series of distortions and oversimplification, systematic dehumanization of the leadership of another great country, and routine exaggeration of Moscow's military capabilities and of the supposed inequity of its intentions" would imperil chances for "a more hopeful world."

While Reagan rolls out a familiar cold-war routine, Haig has been adding a few interesting new twists. During his first month in office he began a campaign—which continued through most of the year—to pin the blame for international terrorism on the Soviet Union. The Soviets, he said, as part of a "conscious policy," are "training, funding and equipping" international terrorists. Despite his repeated assertions, top CIA officials later said Haig's charges were based on 10-year old testimony by a Czech defector. Officials at the State Department's Bureau of Intelligence, according to the *New York Times*, later warned Haig that there was no hard evidence for his assertion.

Haig also tried to convince Congress and the public that the Soviet Union is waging chemical warfare in Asia. But with little more than single leaf and stem sample he was unable to convince skeptics. A United Nations investigation into the charge was inconclusive. So in early 1982 Haig released a 31-page report which Stoessel said demonstrates "the Soviet Union and its allies are flagrantly and repeatedly violating international laws and agreements" on chemical weapons. But a senior Administration official conceded to the *New York Times*, "We still don't have the kind of hard, direct evidence that would remove all doubts."

Although he says Moscow is a super-powerful instigator of "international insecurity" that must be contained, Haig acknowledges—and, indeed, gloats over—the decline in Soviet strength. He cited the labor movement in Poland as a sign that "we are witnessing an historic unraveling of Marxist-Leninism on the Soviet model." In August, 1981 he said the "economies of Moscow's Eastern European allies are in various stages of decline. The Soviet economy itself may have lost its capacity for the high growth of the past. Ambitious foreign and defense policies are therefore becoming more of a burden." That contradiction led Frank Church, former chairman of the Senate Foreign Relations Committee, to comment: "There is something schizophrenic about the Reagan Administration's obsession with the Soviet Union."

But the Reagan Administration has found its propaganda war difficult to translate into substantive action against the Soviets. Economic and political reality continues to intervene. In April, 1981, Reagan responded to the agriculture lobby and lifted a 15-month grain embargo against the Soviets that was imposed after the invasion of Afghanistan. His efforts to restrict U.S. business sales to the Siberian pipeline project have been resisted by the U.S. Chamber of Commerce.

But the starkest example of the Administration's limitations in controlling Soviet behavior was its reaction to the Moscow-backed Polish regime's crackdown in December, 1981. As the Polish workers' movement escalated during the year and the Soviets became visibly concerned, the State Department sent repeated warnings to Moscow. On March 5, it warned that the USSR faced "gravest consequences" if it intervened in Poland. On September 18, after Warsaw released a letter from the Soviet government which called for a crackdown on the workers, the State Department vehemently warned that the action constituted meddling in Polish affairs. On December 14, the day after the Polish regime declared martial law and arrested union leaders, the White House suspended all pending aid to Poland and warned of "grave" results if the repression continued.

One week later Reagan imposed a series of mild sanctions against Poland and on December 29—citing Soviet responsibility for the repression—he announced he was banning the sale of oil and gas equipment to the Soviets. At the same time the Reagan Administration urged the Europeans to drop their plans for participating in the construction of the Siberian natural gas pipeline which would transport Soviet energy supplies to Western Europe. The Allies refused to go along with Reagan's request and plans were made to procure from other sources the parts for the project which Reagan restricted. Though the American actions are likely to delay the pipeline, they won't stop it. (See Larry Brady profile.)

The Administration was also limited in the economic pressure it could place on the Polish regime. Though the Poles owed several billion dollars to Western banks, a declaration of default would, as Haig successfully argued in White House debates, cause a crisis in the international banking community.

Haig's inability to turn rhetoric into reality has put him in hot water with the right. The conservative weekly, *Human Events*, called Haig a "pussycat" who has failed to "put some spine into our foreign policy." Somehow, the publication's editors said, this "combative warrior. . .has. . .been transformed. . . The Secretary loves to bluster about the Soviets, but when it comes to urging actions short of war, his advice is remarkably restrained."

Haig has reacted to right-wing groups, and hardliners within the Administration, in blunt remarks during State Department staff meetings. Notes on these meetings, obtained by the *Washington Post*, quoted Haig saying: "Everybody got his rocks off on Poland and demonstrated their masculinity in their recommendations to the President."

Of criticism by the right he said: There is a ". . .need to educate the Jack Kemps of the world." And he seemed to expect more trouble: "Same thing started in right-wing press on Eastern Europe," the notes quote him as saying. "Now we're going to bail out the Romanians. If you don't differentiate between USSR and rest of Eastern Europe, you'll drive Eastern Europe into the hands of USSR."

MIDDLE EAST: Secretary Haig arrived in the Middle East in April, 1981 determined to capitalize on what he called the "strategic consensus" developing between American friends in the region—Israel, Egypt, Jordan, Saudi Arabia. That consensus stems, he asserted, from a common fear of Soviet-backed aggression in the volatile region.

"I'm speaking of the collapse of the Shah of Iran, the Iran-Iraq conflict, the Soviet invasion of Afghanistan, the dynamics of the Horn of Africa and the two Yemens—that all of these things were a fact of life that have impinged upon the perceptions of the nations in the area with respect to the Soviet threat," he said.

But the message he received during that April tour was much different. Saudi Arabia and Jordan insisted that Israel was the primary threat to stability in the region, while Israel warned against increasing U.S. arms sales to its hostile Arab neighbors. In short, the Middle East nations were more concerned about each other than about the Soviet Union.

Yet Haig continued to insist that a strategic consensus was in the offing; and he maintained that the nations' differing perceptions of who posed a threat to the region were not contradictory. "Precisely the opposite," said Haig upon his departure from Saudi Arabia, "they are interrelated, mutually interrelated problems. . .the failure to achieve progress in the [Middle East] peace process offers the Soviet Union waters in which to fish."

To pull friendly Arab nations into this strategic consensus, the Administration (to the consternation of Israel) is offering arms. After Haig returned from the Middle East, the White House formally proposed the sale of AWACS (Airborne Warning and Control System) aircraft to Saudi Arabia, and several months later managed, with Reagan's personal intervention, to block a congressional veto of the sale. Israeli Prime Minister Menachem Begin publicly voiced strong opposition to the deal.

In Congress the sale was opposed by both staunch Israeli supporters—who feared the Saudis would use the equipment in hostilities with Israel—and lawmakers who were concerned that the sophisticated AWACS equipment would fall into enemy hands. Senate Minority Leader Robert Byrd of West Virginia argued that the sale would transfer "the mantle of client state" to Saudi Arabia, angering Arab radicals and further endangering the shaky Saudi monarchy.

The Administration also promised sophisticated arms to Egypt and the Sudan, which fears a military threat from Libya. That commitment was reiterated after Sadat's assassination. (In November, 1981 the press reported that the Administration had agreed to provide a military umbrella against the Soviet Union in the event of an Egyptian attack on Libya.) Sadat's death lent new urgency to the Administration's drive not only to arm its friends in the region, but also to publicize its military support. So Reagan launched a massive display of American military strength in the region. "Bright Star," a joint military exercise with Egypt and Oman, included the use of two Army airborne battalions, Air Force B-52's and U.S. Marines. "It is important to demonstrate that it is not fatal to be an American ally," Haig said.

Later, on a visit to the Middle East, Defense Secretary Weinberger, who has regularly indicated that he considers the Arab nations more valuable to the Administration's strategic consensus plans than Israel, told Jordan's King Hussein he favors the sale of F-16 fighters and mobile Hawk missiles to Jordan, which was on the verge of purchasing Soviet weapons. During that trip, Weinberger also repeated his request to Saudi Arabia for access by the Rapid Deployment Force to installations there. The Saudis, worried that such an American presence would aggravate internal dissent, refused. However, the monarchy did agree to participate in a joint Saudi-U.S. committee that would coordinate military actions.

While Weinberger tantalizes the Arabs with weapons, Haig has been soothing the Israelis with words, assuring them that the U.S. will not abandon its commitment to their security. In early 1982, when relations between the two countries were at a low ebb, President Reagan himself got into the game with a "Dear Menachem" letter. "I am determined to see that Israel's qualitative edge is maintained," he cooed. "Recent press reports have presented incorrect and exaggerated commentary regarding U.S. military assistance policies for the Middle East." He signed it simply, "Ron."

Despite its jitters over the Administration's military embrace of its Arab foes, Israel is no bit player in Haig's campaign to build a strategic consensus. In September, 1981 Haig and Israeli officials began discussing plans for a "strategic cooperation" beween the two countries. An initial agreement was signed two months later that called for joint naval maneuvers and air exercises in the Middle East. But the agreement put off more sensitive questions such as storage of U.S. military equipment in Israel.

Tensions between the two nations have also mounted over Israeli military actions, to which the Administration did not quite know how to respond. After Israeli jets destroyed an Iraqi nuclear reactor in June, 1981 the U.S. temporarily suspended delivery of F-16 fighters to the country and supported a United Nations resolution condemning the attack. The following month Israeli jets bombed Beirut, killing and injuring hundreds of civilians, and began a series of attacks on other Palestinian Liberation Organization strongholds. Weinberger sharply criticized Israel's military actions; Haig pressed for a cease-fire. Five months later, the Israeli Knesset voted to annex the Golan Heights; Haig called in the Israeli ambassador for talks, and Weinberger condemned the move as "provocative." Meanwhile, Haig will seek to continue the Camp David peace process left behind by Jimmy Carter.

AFRICA: In May, 1981 the State Department announced that the U.S. would "open a new chapter" in its relations with South Africa. In return, the South Africans would cooperate in combating alleged Soviet influence in the region and work to attain an "internationally acceptable solution" to Namibia, long an occupied territory of Pretoria. A new policy of "constructive engagement" will replace the confrontational relationship between the two countries, the State Department said.

It was a telling signal of the Reagan Administration's approach to foreign policy on the African continent and, indeed, around the globe: Human rights are destined to play second fiddle to anti-communism. For years South Africa's apartheid policies had been the object of public criticism from U.S. presidents. But Reagan has sympathetic words for the Pretoria government: "Can we abandon a country that has stood by us in every war we have ever fought, a country that is strategically essential to the free world in its production of minerals that we all must have?" Reagan asked during a CBS interview.

The Reagan Administration reversed a policy prohibiting military officers to enter this country on official business. During spring, 1981 senior South African military officers quietly slipped into the United States for private meetings with Chester Crocker, assistant secretary of state for African affairs and U.N. Ambassador Jeane Kirkpatrick.

With that blanket of protection in place, South Africa in 1981 invaded both Angola and Mozambique in search of rebels who have been fighting to wrest control of Namibia from a South African-backed regime. At the same time, South Africa has economically pressured neighboring Zimbabwe in an effort to weaken the Mugabe government. The Reagan Administration did not condemn any of these actions.

In shifting U.S. policy towards South Africa, Reagan has strained relations with black African nations that were friendly during the Carter Administration. During the summer of 1981 a congressional team met with leaders in Nigeria, Angola, Kenya, Somalia, and Zimbabwe, all of whom expressed dismay at the Reagan Adminstration's rapprochement with South Africa, said a House committee aide who accompanied the lawmakers.

Within South Africa, foreign policy analysts have noted that the Pretoria government's racial policies have ossified as the Administration's approach softens. "The tilt by the Reagan Administration toward South Africa has been reflected in a tilt toward the right in Prime Minister Botha's internal policies," David Anderson, an expert in African affairs and assistant secretary-general in the Commonwealth Secretariat in London, wrote in *Foreign Affairs*. Arrests of black dissidents, closings of black newspapers and bannings have been stepped up. Promises for limited reform the government made two years ago have been dropped.

The congressional team which visited Africa talked to black and colored citizens in South Africa who blamed the government's harsher treatment on Reagan's policies. "The mood there has changed radically over the past year," said the House aide, who also had accompanied a congressional mission to southern Africa in 1980. "There's a feeling there that the West has betrayed them. The people in South Africa are angry at us. The government is arresting union leaders, political leaders, journalists—they feel they can do anything now that they have Reagan's blessing."

At the same time, popular protest in South Africa has continued, with protest rallies, school boycotts, and strikes. The Administration's policy, said one congressional expert on African affairs, "is undermining any hope for peaceful change in that country."

The anger which the Administration has evoked over its South Africa policy has overshadowed its success in moving toward a settlement in Namibia. Although in 1978 South Africa agreed in principle to a settlement plan for Namibia which would include internationally supervised elections and a constitutional government, its refusal to agree on specifics deadlocked the negotiations shortly before

Reagan took office. The Administration has wooed South Africa back into negotiations with its closer relations and offers to expand trade. But whether the Reagan Administration's strategy can lead to a settlement in Namibia is in question. Pretoria is reluctant to support elections where the rebels have a chance of winning.

"The consensus in this office," said an aide to the House subcommittee on African affairs, "is that there is a 25 to 55 percent chance of success. South Africa has domestic problems in making concessions towards a Namibia settlement—there's a strong right-wing faction in the South African government."

While courting South Africa and Zaire (another key strategic interest with open-door economic policies and a dismal human rights record), the Reagan Administration has chilled relations with governments it considers ideologically unsuitable. Relations with Tanzania and Mozambique have deteriorated. U.S. aid to Tanzania was slashed in half. But Angola has been the chief focus of the Administration's anti-communist crusade in Africa. Reagan has pressed Congress to eliminate the Clark Amendment, which prohibits covert aid to opposition groups in Angola, where a large contingent of Cuban troops are stationed. At one point the State Department favored linking the Namibia settlement to the withdrawal of Cuban troops from Angola. (The Angolan government claims the Cuban troops are stationed there to protect the country from South African aggression.) Congress has refused to rescind the amendment.

But the Administration has run up against a formidable opponent in its Angolan policies—American oil companies operating there. Gulf Oil in particular has pressed the Administration to moderate its stance. Reflecting that pressure, the U.S. Export-Import Bank in August, 1981 approved loans of roughly $80 million for further U.S. investment in oil development in Angola.

Libyan strongman Colonel Muammar el-Qaddafi has been a consistent target of Reagan invective. A well-armed and unpredictable ruler that even the Soviets are reluctant to call an ally (though they supply him with arms), Qaddafi is an internationally recognized agitator. But many observers caution that Reagan's persistent pressuring may prove counterproductive. Within months of taking office Reagan expelled Libya's diplomatic mission from the United States, citing Qaddafi's support for terrorism and meddling in African affairs. In a move that Reagan called "impressive," U.S. Navy fighters during the summer shot down two Libyan jets after they had shot at the Americans for flying over Libyan waters. The U.S. claimed they were international waters. In December Reagan Administration officials captured headlines by claiming, without disclosing its evidence, that five Libyan terrorists had entered the U.S. on instructions from Qaddafi to assassinate Reagan and other top aides; and a week later Reagan banned American travel to Libya and urged U.S. oil companies and 2,000 U.S. citizens residing there to leave.

ASIA: China was the big winner on the Asian front of the Administration's anti-Soviet campaign. Haig has made a determined effort to woo the Chinese and "keep China pro-West." Closer U.S.-China ties, Haig said, are a "strategic imperative" in the face of a growing Soviet threat. As part of that strategy the State Department has lifted trade curbs against the People's Republic of China and during a stop in Beijing in June, 1981, Haig announced that the U.S. had agreed in principle to sell arms to China.

But Haig is walking a delicate line between America's new friendship with China and the Administration's ideological affinity for Taiwan. Over the loud objections of China, right-wing factions in the Administration and Congress are pressing for improved relations with Taiwan, which Reagan himself frequently advocated during the campaign. Plans for a sale of advanced aircraft to the island nation were eventually dropped after warnings from China. Even proposals to sell Taiwan spare military parts ran into opposition from Beijing. So far Haig has played a balancing game, soothing both China's and Taiwan's concerns while promising weapons to both.

Elsewhere in Asia, the Reagan Administration's performance has been predictable, bolstering traditional anti-communist allies regardless of their human rights records. Most revealing was a remark by Vice-President Bush while visiting President Ferdinand Marcos of the Philippines, notorious for suppressing opposition.

During a dinner toast for Marcos, Bush said: "We love your adherence to democratic principles." After the remark was publicized one opposition leader commented: "Mr. Bush didn't seem to know what he was talking about."

JAMES BUCKLEY
COUNSELOR

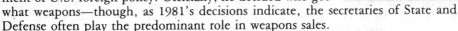

RESPONSIBILITY OF OFFICE

Buckley was appointed counselor in early 1982; prior to that he served as undersecretary of State for security assistance, science and technology. In that post, Buckley, one of four undersecretaries in the State Department, was charged with ensuring that military aid was used as an effective instrument of U.S. foreign policy. Officially, he decided who got what weapons—though, as 1981's decisions indicate, the secretaries of State and Defense often play the predominant role in weapons sales.

As counselor, Buckley will serve as a general troubleshooter, but because of his experience the first year he is likely to continue playing an influential role in security assistance.

BACKGROUND

When James Buckley rose to address a meeting of the Aerospace Industries Association early in 1981, his presence no doubt pleased the Connecticut businessmen in attendance. Their trusted political ally, fresh from a loss at the polls, stood before the gathering of aircraft manufacturers and arms dealers not as Connecticut's most prominent also-ran, but as a leading member of the Reagan State Department, one with the power to boost their sales and earnings records.

After two electoral defeats—first in his 1976 bid for re-election to the U.S. Senate from New York, and a 1980 effort to become Connecticut's junior senator—Buckley seemed destined for political obscurity. Instead, he now sits in the inner circle of the country's foreign policy elite.

James Buckley and his siblings were weaned on wealth, conservatism, and strict Catholic discipline. Their father, William Buckley, Sr., was an attorney who made his original fortune off Mexican oil. In 1921, after Buckley had organized the American Association of Mexico to lobby against U.S. recognition of the new regime, the government expelled him as a "pernicious foreigner." Rather than accomodating himself to the nationalist regime, Buckley had chosen to lose oil properties worth some $1 million.

In 1919 the senior Buckley told a Senate committee what he thought of Mexican democracy: "The truth is that it does not matter what a great majority of the Mexican people think. The mass of people have not the ability to think clearly, and have not the knowledge on which to base convictions, or the public spirit to act on them." After his expulsion, Buckley transferred the operations of his oil firm, Pantepec (now Pantepec International) to Venezuela.

That was the kind of elitist philosophy which William Buckley doggedly injected into his children as they grew up in New York.

No doubt if William Buckley were alive today he would be proud of his children. His eldest son, John, took over the family's oil empire. (The experience in Mexico had not deterred William Buckley: At his death in the late 1950s, he had large holdings in oil and gas operations around the world.)

F. Reid Buckley became a celebrated author. The caustic William, Jr., of course, has for years been a prominent spokesman for the right, as a columnist and as editor of the *National Review* (one of Reagan's favorite magazines), and as founder of both the Young Americans for Freedom and New York's Conservative Party.

James became vice-president of the family's Catawba Corporation, an oil "consulting firm" that in reality controls several oil and drilling companies. But in 1970, at the suggestion of his brother Bill, James made his political debut as the Conservative Party candidate for New York.

In a race where his two opponents criticized U.S. involvement in Vietnam, the staunchly conservative Buckley appealed to both Republicans and many blue collar Democrats supporting the President's policies. When conservative turned-liberal Republican Charles Goodell, the incumbent, and Democrat candidate Richard Ottinger denounced Nixon's bombing of Cambodia, Buckley called it "a damn successful operation."

Buckley also had the advantage of all-American good looks combined with a down-home, sincere demeanor—a formula he once called his "Boy Scout syndrome."

But more importantly, he had Nixon's support and flush campaign chest. Buckley raised more than $1.9 million, 28 percent of which was funneled through such obscure Washington-based political action committees as "Committee to Keep a Cop on the Beat," the "League of Middle American Women," and "Protectors of Our Land."

Pulling in just under 40 percent of the vote, James Buckley became the first third party senator since 1940. The day after the election the *New York Times* called Buckley's victory a "step backward for New York. . .If Mr. Buckley comes to appreciate the fact [that nearly 61 percent voted against him] he may. . .modify his views to give this state true representation."

Brother Bill was also quick to remind James of his shaky mandate. On election night, James Buckley, flush with victory, declared, "There is a new conservative politic and I am the voice of that politic." When told about the remark, Bill retorted, "Who in the hell does he think he is? La politique nouvelle, c'est goddamn moi!"

Despite the pleas of the *New York Times*, Buckley did not modify his views and in the Senate he consistently applied the Tory line to both domestic and foreign issues. In the past Buckley had professed his deep concern for the environment—one magazine affectionately referred to him as a "nature nut." (In

1982, in fact, Buckley wrote an article supporting measures to protect endangered species in the environmental journal, *Amicus*.) But on the floor Buckley was reluctant to support measures allocating federal money to environmental programs unless it was a measure to relieve industry of clean-up costs.

On other domestic issues, Buckley's views were less ambiguous. He favored cutting taxes and government spending, state control of welfare, and less government regulation. He sponsored a bill prohibiting the installation of ignition seat-belt interlocks in automobiles, and an amendment providing reimbursement of businesses that successfully defended themselves against complaints by the Consumer Product Safety Commission (both amendments failed). In 1974, he sponsored legislation to decontrol natural gas which would cost consumers $9.2 to 11.2 billion in 1975 alone. Buckley also supported a constitutional amendment making abortion illegal, except in cases where the mother's life is in danger.

During the height of New York City's financial crisis in the mid-'70s, when Gov. Hugh Carey and Mayor Abe Beame were pleading for federal assistance, Buckley publicly suggested that the city declare bankruptcy.

But Buckley also liked to maintain an image of a principled public servant. He was the first conservative representative outside the Democratic Party to call for Richard Nixon's resignation after Watergate.

On foreign and military issues, Buckley has always been a hawk. In 1960 he had said communism is "the greatest threat which world civilization has ever known." Eleven years later he was still talking about the "driving, disciplined, fanatic force of communism. . ." In a 1971 address to the National Press Club, Buckley spoke of the necessity of maintaining a dominant world military capability. "Once we begin backing down under pressure here and there around the globe, we will court disaster of a third world war." Keeping with that view, he opposed congressional efforts to legislate an end to U.S. involvement in Vietnam.

Of CIA covert action in Chile during the early 1970s, Buckley said in 1976: "[I]t was only by virtue of covert help by the United States that these free institutions were able to survive in the face of increasingly repressive measures by the Allende regime."

He was one of two senators to vote against the anti-ballistic missile limit that was part of President Nixon's accord with the Soviet Union; he considered SALT a giveaway of American interests; he said detente threatened the liberty of the West; and he voted against both the War Powers Act putting a congressional check on military operations initiated by the President, and the Mansfield Amendment cutting the number of U.S. troops in Europe. Buckley denounced Nixon's trip to China and the restoration of relations with that country.

"Unfortunately," Buckley wrote in his 1975 book, *If Men Were Angels*, "when with an excess of exuberance, Richard Nixon rushed to Peking and raised his glass in extravagant toasts to the high priests of Communist China, and then went on to Moscow to pay the same honors to the Soviet leaders in the Kremlin, he undercut the perceived moral basis of a foreign policy which Americans could understand and support, and for which in times of test they were willing to sacrifice."

Not surprisingly, given those feelings, Buckley repeatedly called for the resignation of Henry Kissinger as national security adviser, who he claimed was keeping President Ford from heeding the advice of the Pentagon. Henry Kissinger, said Buckley, "is destined to be an albatross around the President's neck." Now he works with one former Kissinger intimate, Lawrence Eagleburger, and reports to another, Alexander Haig.

On the subject of conducting "limited" nuclear warfare, Buckley made these remarks during a 1972 debate: "We ought to begin to give ourselves the ability to strike selectively at military targets, not cities, so that a President in a crisis would have the fullest range of options and we could keep the killing, whether of Americans or of the enemy, at a minimum. . .[L]et's assume there is something that is in the border of accidental. You could lob something over towards Moscow just to remind the Russian leadership that you are alert.

"I think this is the area where selective use of nuclear weapons is possible and desirable."

Though elected as a Conservative, Buckley worked through Republican channels in the Senate and was admitted to the Senate Republican Conference. Buckley's charm, combined with his prominent name, made him one of the most sought after speakers at Republican fundraisers. "Buckley has potential that puts him behind Spiro Agnew in 'star' qualities," wrote L. Clayton DuBois in the *New York Times* after Buckley's first year in office. "On the podium he is all grace and sincerity in a way that can't be put on, and with none of the invective of Agnew or the proud polysyllables or theatrics of William F. Buckley. In short, he is very likeable."

The Reaganites find him particularly likeable. In the frustratingly moderate world of the State Department, the White House can count on Buckley as a loyal and trustworthy marshal. After all, he told *Time* magazine several years ago that the politicians he most admired were Ronald Reagan, George Bush, and John Tower.

Buckley's most valuable tie to right-wing circles was his position as a policy director of the Institute of American Relations, a Washington-based think tank established in 1974 by John Carbaugh, a foreign policy aide to Sen. Jesse Helms (R-N.C.). The institute, among its many activities, has financed at least one trip by Helms to the South American dictatorships of Argentina, Chile and Uruguay. The organization also bankrolled a 1979 visit by two Helms aides (one was Carbaugh) to London during the sensitive negotiations over majority rule in Zimbabwe. The aides reportedly urged white minority leader Ian Smith to resist compromise, prompting the British government to file a formal protest with the U.S. State Department.

After his 1976 electoral defeat to Democrat Daniel Patrick Moynihan, Buckley was kept on a retainer with Catawba Corp., and served on the boards of directors of several corporations. He ran for a Senate seat from Connecticut in 1980—but was defeated by another Democrat, Christopher Dodd.

After receiving his B.A. degree from Yale in 1943 and his law degree from Yale Law School in 1949, Buckley practiced law with the Connecticut firm of Wiggin and Dana until 1953, when he became an officer and director of Catawba Corp. He is an avid bird-watcher, and once considered a career in ornithology.

Born March 9, 1923, in New York City, Buckley is married with six children.

MAJOR ISSUES

- The doors of the U.S. military store have been thrown wide open— restrictions on arms sales have been dropped, and U.S. military assistance around the world is on the rise. U.S. arms exports in fiscal year 1983 may top the all time record, at $30 billion.

- Pakistan, previously dropped off the U.S. military sales customer list because of evidence that the country's ruling regime was developing nuclear weapons, is now receiving U.S. military aid and will buy sophisticated F-16 aircraft.

- Chile and Argentina, once boycotted for their dismal human rights records, will also be in line for U.S. military aid after the Administration certifies their records have improved.

- Military assistance to El Salvador's ruling junta continues to escalate.

- In a startling shift of U.S. policy, the Reagan Administration has agreed in principle to sell arms to China.

- Sophisticated weaponry that the Reagan Administration is selling to Saudi Arabia, Venezuela, Pakistan, South Korea, Egypt, Israel and Jordan are likely to generate spiralling arms races in those volatile regions and will divert resources from U.S. defenses.

As the Reagan Administration's chief arms merchant, Buckley has been as busy as a department store clerk during Christmas rush. The doors of the U.S. arms shop have been thrown wide open—displaying everything from jeeps and trucks to sophisticated jet fighters—much of it on generous financing terms. Restrictions imposed by Buckley's predecessors have been lifted, and customers from every continent are rushing in to claim their share. During his first year in office, Reagan recommended over $25 billion in arms sales to Congress.

Though arms exports rose during the last half of Carter's tenure—after a sharp drop in 1977—Carter declared that the U.S. "will henceforth view arms transfers as an exceptional foreign policy implement. . ." Reagan in July, 1981 said that the U.S. views "transfer of conventional arms. . .as an essential element of its global defense posture and an indispensable component of its foreign policy."

In May, 1981 Buckley announced the Reagan Administration intended to reverse the Carter Administration's announced policy of restraint in foreign arms sales. Restrictions on sales to "nations whose behavior—in the case of human rights—or intentions—in the case of nuclear proliferation—we disapprove of" has harmed U.S. security, he asserted. Buckley told the Aerospace Industries Association in Williamsburg, Virginia: "While these well-intentioned efforts have had little detectable impact on such behavior or intentions, they did lead at times to the awkward result of undercutting the capabilities of strategically located nations in whose ability to defend themselves we have the most immediate and urgent self-interest."

The net effect, he charged, was that the United States now has "far fewer nations in a position to work with us in defending the common interests and deterring threats by the Soviet Union and its surrogates."

Already the U.S. is the world's no. 1 arms merchant. Official government and private American arms sales now reach over $17 billion a year, up from $1.8 billion a decade ago. U.S sales account for one-third of the $30 billion a year arms sales to the Third World. The Soviet Union and other Eastern bloc nations pick up an equal percentage, with the NATO countries accounting for most of the balance. Buckley will try to boost America's chunk of that business, which many observers say will cut into NATO's share, not the Soviets, as intended. Reagan has eliminated the Carter-imposed ceiling on the total value of U.S. arms transfers authorized each year, dropped a prohibition on developing weapon systems solely for export, and dropped the prohibition against sales of weapons not yet deployed in U.S. forces.

Buckley's authority in the area of arms sales is considerable. As an aide to Sen. John Glenn (D-Ohio) of the Senate Foreign Relations Committee remarked: "Once Haig assigns Buckley responsibility, it's his baby. Buckley becomes the key decision-maker, not Haig."

During his first year, Buckley devoted most of his energy to obtaining military aid for Pakistan, just two years after Carter had cut it off, charging the government with secretly developing nuclear weapons. In spring, 1981 he flew to Islamabad, the Pakistani capital, to negotiate a $3 billion aid agreement with the country's military leaders. The package—which accompanies a U.S. pledge to supply the regime with F-16 aircraft—is one of the largest security deals yet unveiled by the Reagan Administration. "The whole Pakistan issue was sort of Buckley's," Glenn's aide told us. "It was clearly a Buckley show."

Buckley claims that Pakistan's strongman, Zia ul Haq, has become a key U.S. ally in the region because of the fall of the Shah of Iran and the Soviet invasion of Afghanistan. But a second factor behind the Pakistan deal is U.S. anxiety over domestic unrest in Saudi Arabia. Pakistan is already an important guardian of the ruling Saudi elite, maintaining some 3,000 troops in the oil-rich country. News reports indicate that Zia, in return for U.S. aid, may add several thousand soldiers to his Saudi presence.

"There can be no pretext that Pakistan would be defending Saudi Arabia against Soviet aggression," said Jeff McConnell, author of a Center for International Policy report on Southwest Asia. "The Pakistanis are to be connected with the Saudi National Guard which protects the royal family, not the nation."

Several weeks after his return from Islamabad, Buckley appeared before the Senate Subcommittee on Energy and Nuclear Proliferation seeking an exemption to the 1977 Symington Amendment, which forbids U.S. aid to nations developing atomic weapons.

During the course of an acrimonious hearing, Buckley responded gingerly to congressional attacks. He told skeptical senators he "was assured by President [Zia] himself" that Pakistan was not developing an atomic warhead. He quietly qualified that remark, however, by drawing a semantic distinction between nuclear warheads and "the nuclear option."

In light of the voluminous evidence detailing Pakistan's weapon program—Senator Alan Cranston informed his colleagues earlier that Zia is building an underground atomic test site—Buckley's comments troubled anti-proliferation legislators.

His "assurances" appeared even less convincing when the Associated Press obtained a State Department cable dispatched over the July 21 weekend—three days before Buckley's testimony. The secret cable identified Turkey as the base of a "covert purchasing organization" established to funnel electronic inverters into Pakistan. Inverters are used in the construction of atomic bombs.

"We have strong reason to believe that Pakistan is seeking to develop a nuclear explosive capability," the State Department warned. "We also have information that Pakistan is conducting a program for the design and development of the triggering package for nuclear explosive devices." The text of the July 21 cable conflicts sharply with Buckley's Senate testimony.

In the 1982 military assistance package, the Reagan Administration won the right to sell arms to Pakistan and two other countries previously boycotted because of their dismal human rights records—Chile and Argentina. Military assistance to two other human rights violators, El Salvador and Guatemala, has been expanded. At the same time Congress agreed to repeal the ban on arms sales to those countries, it added a provision to the foreign aid package passed in December, 1981 requiring the Administration to certify that El Salvador was "making a concerted and significant effort" to control human rights violations, was achieving "substantial control" over its military forces and was making "continued progress" in reform efforts. The certification process, however, failed to slow U.S. military assistance to El Salvador's ruling junta: in early 1982 the Administration tripled its military aid to the country.

In defending the elimination of restrictions on arms to Argentina before a House Appropriations subcommittee, Buckley was asked about the wealth of evidence pointing up anti-Semitism in that country—synagogue burnings, televised anti-Semitic speeches by Argentine generals and the widely-acclaimed reporting of exiled journalist Jacobo Timmerman.

Buckley was hard pressed to respond. He had not read Timmerman's book, and based much of his rebuttal on the findings of a 1980 report by the U.S. dominated Organization of American States.

Nonetheless, on the day after his damaging encounter with the subcommittee, Buckley telephoned House Foreign Relations Committee Chairman Clement Zablocki, just hours before his committee cast a crucial vote on the proposal. Buckley—reportedly citing no evidence—assured Zablocki that the Argentine junta did not condone attacks on the country's Jewish citizens. Largely as a consequence of Buckley's appeals, Zablocki backed the White House. Zablocki's support was an important factor in the Administration's narrow victory. "It let people off the hook on the anti-Semitism issue," says Connecticut Congressman Sam Gejdenson. "That was its most important role."

Pakistan is not the only country slated to receive advanced military aircraft under Reagan's open-shop policy. During his first 15 months in office fleets of F-16's were sold to Venezuela, South Korea and Egypt. Now Jordan may be in line for the sophisticated fighter, a result of Defense Secretary Weinberger's visit to that country in early 1982. The Administration also proposed selling sophisticated fighter planes to Taiwan.

The most controversial arms deal of 1981, of course, was sale of five airborne warning and control system (AWACS) aircraft to Saudi Arabia. Fierce lobbying by Buckley, Haig, and Reagan himself during the fall of 1981 successfully blocked a Senate veto of the sale. The House—where most members were concerned that the sale posed a security threat to Israel and could ultimately leave the AWACS in unfriendly hands if the shaky Saudi monarchy fell—voted against the sale. However, a majority vote by both houses is required to block proposed arms sales.

Congressional critics of such sales say the military forces of those countries cannot quickly or effectively absorb such sophisticated weaponry as the F-16—an ability that Buckley has claimed would be heavily weighed in determining who will get arms.

But critics are also concerned that massive arms sales will hurt domestic defenses. Both the Air Force and the Office of Management and Budget argued that the sales could increase the cost of planes delivered to American forces. An internal April, 1981 memo by the Defense Department's Office of Program Analysis and Evaluation said that aerospace companies were raiding American military forces "for officers able to provide the training and support commitments that accompany such sales. . . . This may be very good for G.D. [General Dynamics—manufacturer of the F-16], but it seriously threatens U.S. Air Force F-16 support capability."

Such sales of sophisticated aircraft to Third World countries, moreover, are likely to generate a spiralling arms race in those areas and to fuel regional tensions. As Andrew Pierre, a former State Department official and currently a researcher at the Council on Foreign Relations has pointed out, if Venezuela buys F-16's it will pave the way for the sale of sophisticated fighters to other Latin American countries.

When Pakistan buys F-16's, India may seek offsetting aid from the Soviet Union or France. In the Middle East, the U.S. government is continuing its heavy arming of Israel and, at the same time, selling sophisticated weapon systems to its Arab foes, Saudi Arabia, Jordan and Egypt.

In a startling shift in U.S. policy the Reagan Administration has agreed in principle to begin arms sales to China, a move designed to isolate the Soviet Union—and an ironic one in light of Buckley's fierce opposition to opening relations with China when he was a senator in the early 1970s. Many foreign policy experts say that arms sales to China would substantially diminish U.S. influence over that country and could prove a dangerous strategy in the long run. Former Secretary of State Cyrus Vance told the *New York Times*: "We played the China card in a no-trump, and there is not much left."

Other measures to increase American arms sales are underway. Buckley is leading Administration efforts to repeal the Clark Amendment. Passed in 1976, the amendment bans aid to anti-Marxist guerrillas in Angola. Rep. Howard Wolpe, (D-Mich.) chairman of the House subcomittee on Africa, said the repeal would "have disastrous consequences for our relations with Angola. . .[and] would be viewed throughout the African continent as further evidence of a new tilt toward South Africa." Congress refused to repeal it during the Administration's first year.

In May, 1981 Buckley announced that the Administration is rescinding the "leprosy letter" which instructed U.S. officials overseas not to assist U.S. businessmen seeking arms customers. "Henceforth," said Buckley, "U.S. government representatives overseas will be expected to provide the same courtesies to firms that have obtained licenses to market items on the U.S. munitions list as they would to those marketing other American products."

To further expedite arms transfers abroad, the Administration is extending record amounts of military aid. During 1981 military aid totalled $1.1 billion; Reagan requested four times that, $4.7 billion, in fiscal year 1982, and dramatically increased the total of "forgiven loans."

Buckley also persuaded Congress to set up a revolving fund, the Special Defense Acquisition Fund, financed by income from previous weapon purchases. Congress put a cap of $300 million on the fund in fiscal year 1982 and $600 million in fiscal year 1983. The fund permits the President to provide military aid to U.S. allies without undergoing standard procedures for congressional review, presumably in times of crisis. "Buckley's proposal amounts to a slush fund, a dangerous precedent for U.S. foreign policy," warns human rights activist Larry Birns, director of the Council on Hemispheric Affairs.

Over the past decade arms sales have become the chief tool of diplomacy for both the United States and the Soviet Union. As each side pours sophisticated arms into clients' borders the destructive capabilities of developing nations grow. Carter tried, with limited success, to dam some tributaries of the river of weapons. The Reagan Administration has opened the flood gates. Said Sen. Alan Cranston (D-Calif.), "Reagan's policy on arms sales is to spew them everywhere."

FINANCIAL BACKGROUND

Like most millionaires, James Buckley does not like to lay out his financial holdings for public scrutiny. In 1975, he denounced a request by the *New York Times* to disclose his financial interests as "an invasion of privacy". Such requests, he said, "clearly breach the line between the most generously defined limits of legitimate concern over potential conflicts of interest and unabashed curiosity." Only later, "in light of [the following year's] election," did he make a limited disclosure.

During his 1980 campaign for the Connecticut Senate seat, Buckley made public his 1979 tax return "under protest," in response to a challenge by his opponent, Christopher Dodd. The return showed a combined adjusted gross income of $207,000 for him and his wife.

Most of Buckley's wealth is tied up in the family's oil empire. After World War II, his father set up the Catawba Corp., which has since been owned and run by the Buckley family. Catawba, ostensibly a "consulting firm," actually controlled a number of publicly owned oil and mining corporations around the world by ensuring that the board of directors of those firms were dominated by Catawba officials.

The firms, which included Pantepec International, Pancoastal, Canada Southern, Magellan, United Canso, and Coastal Caribbean, explored regions in the U.S., Canada, Venezuela, South Africa, Australia, Spain, the Spanish Sahara, Israel, Fiji, Thailand and the Philippines.

In 1976, the Securities and Exchange Commission (SEC) launched an investigation in response to charges by Coastal Caribbean stockholders that the Catawba was secretly extracting fees and royalties from its corporation. John Buckley in 1978 resigned his positions with the Catawba-controlled corporations and cut off Catawaba's ties with them. The following year a new Buckley corporation, Minex, Inc. was formed.

The SEC completed its investigation in 1981 and forced four Catawba officials, including John, to pay $175,000 to Coastal Caribbean and three other former Catawba energy concerns.

James Buckley's financial disclosure statement reveals that he was a director of Catawba—which he indicated is involved in "mineral and real estate investments"—from 1979 to 1981. His duties included "advice on corporate strategy, reorganization and planning."

According to his 1981 financial disclosure statement, during 1980 Buckley again had an income of well over $200,000, including a $60,000 retainer fee from the family-owned Catawba Corp., a $10,500 directorship fee from Donaldson, Lufkin and Jenrette, a New York brokerage firm, a $1500 directorship fee from Alliance Capital Management Corps., a trustee fee from Alliance Dollar Reserves, and various honoraria.

Buckley's financial holdings include between $100-$250,000 worth of stock in Catawba and in Coastal Caribbean Oils and Minerals Ltd., and over $250,000 in Hempt Royalty Trust and Magellan Royalty. Upon taking office, Buckley sold his $100-$250,000 interest in the CBT Buckley Family Common Trust, a fund that has holdings in such firms as Exxon, Textron Inc., Citicorp, American Telephone and Telegraph Co., Gulf Canada, Ltd., Southern Co., CSX Corp., Beker Inds Corp., Coca Cola Co., Adolph Coors Co., McDonalds Corp., Proctor and Gamble Co., Universal Leaf Tobacco Co., International Telephone and Telegraph Corp., Modular Computer System, IBM Corp., and Burroughs Corp. He sold his interest in the fund because of possible conflicts arising from activities by the latter four firms, and has indicated he will disqualify himself from any decisions relating to those firms because of his wife's and childrens' interests in CBT. He also resigned his directorships which, aside from those mentioned, included Borealis Exploration Ltd., a Canadian oil and mining firm, and Taconic Petroleum Co., AIG Oil Rigs, World Shipping and Trading, all of New York.

He has smaller holdings in Canada Southern Petroleum, Ltd., Borealis Exploration, Catawba Corp., Cognitronics Corp, Ltd. (a small computer firm) and North European Oil Royalty Trust. His holdings have been put in a blind trust.

Buckley's wife and children, with tens of thousands dollars of holdings in many of the same firms, are themselves quite wealthy.

WHAT OTHERS ARE SAYING ABOUT HIM

- Buckley has had trouble gaining the respect of some congressional leaders who are well versed in American foreign policy. William Woodward, foreign policy aide to Rep. Gerry Studds, (D-Mass), a member of the House Foreign Relations Committee, told us: "There is not any great respect for his knowledge or his expertise in foreign affairs at this point. In that sense he is not going to be an effective Reagan spokesman until people begin to have a feeling that he really knows what he's talking about."

- But Buckley apparently wields significant power within the State Department. "He obviously has a certain status and reputation based on his Senate experience," said an aide to Sen. John Glenn (D-Ohio), a member of the Senate Foreign Relations Committee. "He can deal with Haig more as an equal than can some of the other people in the department. Plus, there is a certain amount of trust between him and Haig."

    When asked if the public will begin associating Buckley's name with the wealth of arms flowing into the Third World, Glenn's aide responded: "If they don't already, they should."

RICHARD KENNEDY
UNDERSECRETARY FOR MANAGEMENT

RESPONSIBILITY OF OFFICE

Kennedy's job as undersecretary for management grants him the rather pedestrian responsibilities of keeping the Foggy Bottom bureaucracy in paper clips and the embassies stocked with gin and hors-d'oeuvres. His real influence comes as U.S. Representative to the International Atomic Energy Agency, an ambassador-level position from which he has carved out a strong role in Administration nonproliferation policy. When James Malone was dispatched full-time to the Law of the Sea negotiations in March, 1982, Kennedy became the State Department's lead official on proliferation concerns.

BACKGROUND

When you talk to people in the nuclear field about Richard Kennedy, they don't first mention his crisp, authoritarian demeanor, his gift for gab, or his record of backing the nuclear industry on matters from reactor safety to nuclear proliferation—though all those points eventually come up.

What they talk about first is his love for travel. Travel at the taxpayers' expense.

Kennedy exercised his wanderlust as a charter member of the Nuclear Regulatory Commission (NRC), appointed by President Ford on the recommendation of Henry Kissinger. Known as "the Colonel," Kennedy served as a top aide to Kissinger on the National Security Council in the early 1970s.

The NRC opened its doors on January 19, 1975. On February 22, Kennedy was off to Paris, Vienna and Rome at a cost to the taxpayers of $2,009, according to NRC records obtained by the Critical Mass Energy Project under a Freedom of Information Act (FOIA) request. Seven months later—after stops in seven domestic cities—he was back in Europe, for 16 days in Austria, Belgium, Germany, France, England and Scotland, at a cost of $1,981.

Through October 6, 1978—the years covered by the FOIA request—Kennedy spent $41,065 on travel expenses—far more than any other NRC Commissioner. In all during those four years he made 43 trips to such spots as Paris, Vienna, Rome, Berlin, Scotland, Honolulu, Brussels, London, Switzerland, Amsterdam, Tokyo, Tokai, Hong Kong, Taipei, Seoul, and San Juan. From 1975-1978, he averaged 45.75 days on trips; his annual travel bill was $12,564.

Kennedy's wanderings dominated the NRC's travel expenses. In 1977, for example, Kennedy's $17,040 travel tab was almost 60 percent of the commissioners' total bill. A year later, Kennedy spent over 88 percent of the total commissioner travel expense.

When he touched down in those far-flung cities, Kennedy generally spoke to industry groups (he addressed the Atomic Industrial Forum (AIF) no less than five times in 1976 and 1977). And he did not disappoint them.

In those frequent speeches, Kennedy clearly laid out his stands on nuclear issues, an area in which he openly admitted at his confirmation hearings in 1974 "my experience. . .as you recognize, is somewhat limited." Kennedy joined the newly formed commission just before widespread and vocal public opposition began to make nuclear power one of the most contentious issues facing the federal government. That was not what Kennedy, winding down from a 30-year military career, had bargained for. "He was totally indifferent about the position at NRC," recalled Richard Pollock, former director of the Critical Mass Energy Project.

But he was predictable. "He was the most pro-nuclear person in the history of the commission," Pollock said.

Those views radiated from his speeches. "As a regulator, whose job it is by law to assure that nuclear power facilities are built and operated safely," he was fond of saying, "I will state with confidence that nuclear facilities are safe and that every effort is being made to keep them so." To AIF in 1976 he announced: "There are many areas in which the national interest and the self-interest of the nuclear industry overlap." Speaking to the Kansas City Rotary Club in 1978 he declared flatly—in words that echo harshly against the recent comments of Reagan-appointed NRC Chairman Nunzio Palladino—"The performance of nuclear plants has been impressive." After the Three Mile Island accident, Kennedy repeatedly stressed the safety of nuclear power.

And he exhorted the industry to do the same. Kennedy regularly prodded the nuclear industry to expand its public relations efforts. As he warned a gathering of New York state utility executives in 1976: "It is an educational effort without which the public's decisions on nuclear power may be made on the basis only of incomplete information and often emotional argument. A question you might ask yourselves is whether you can wait until you too are looking down the ballot box before you take the steps needed to educate the public and their elected representatives at all levels of government on the facts of nuclear power."

At the NRC, Kennedy took a special interest in nuclear proliferation. His positions were clear: that the United States should not try to restrict the international flow of nuclear commerce, and that the NRC's role in setting export policy should be as restricted as possible. Both of those stands are reflected in the Reagan Administration's nonproliferation policies. In fact, Kennedy's NRC speeches are a virtual roadmap to the Administration's nonproliferation course.

Though the NRC is an independent agency with statutory authority over nuclear exports, Kennedy felt its exporting decisions should be subjugated to foreign policy interests determined by the State Department, according to former agency staff members and other sources. "The NRC as an agency, has a statutory mandate to make certain independent determinations in the area of nuclear exports," he told the AIF in March, 1977. "But it obviously should not, and cannot, have its own set of nonproliferation principles which differ from overall national policy." The Reagan Administration is considering proposals to transfer the NRC's authority over exports to the State Department.

On few nonproliferation subjects are Kennedy's views not a matter of record—and a matter of concern to those active in the field. He rejects efforts to combat proliferation by controlling the sale of U.S. technology and nuclear materials. "A policy which puts its primary emphasis on denial in my view is doomed to inevitable failure," he said in 1980. Instead, he explained in another speech, "I have long felt that the United States can maximize its influence to secure its nonproliferation goals only if other nations perceive us as a reliable and predictable supplier of nuclear fuels and equipment."

Though he avoided direct criticism of the Carter Administration efforts to more tightly control nuclear commerce—perhaps in the hope that Carter would renominate him to the NRC after his term expired in 1980—Kennedy's remarks grew increasingly acrid as foreign nations anxious to pursue nuclear programs and domestic manufacturers eager to supply them chafed under the program.

"We know that the problem of nuclear proliferation will not be solved by unilateral actions by a single nation or even by a group of suppliers alone," he said in Buenos Aires in May, 1980. "Nor can it be solved through a system of export controls alone. . . . For we would surely be driving other countries to obtain through other means that which we might try to withhold. Furthermore, it would be contrary to our own interests to turn our backs on the energy needs of others." He assured a group in Montevideo, Uruguay on the same trip that while "The proliferation issue is unique to nuclear energy, but the avoidance of civilian nuclear power will not remove the risk of further proliferation. . . . Future proliferation will be avoided or limited only by reducing the apparent incentives for and increasing the penalties against the development of nuclear weapons." And he stressed reliance on the international system of safeguards designed to prevent the diversion of nuclear fuels to weapon use, a system under increasing criticism. (See profiles of Nunzio Palladino and Fred Ikle.)

Many in the field see efforts to limit or completely avoid reprocessing of spent fuel, which produces plutonium, as an obvious prerequisite to controlling proliferation. (Forceful articulators of that point of view in the past have included Ikle, now undersecretary of Defense and John Lehman, now secretary of the Navy.) Not Kennedy. As he told the Brazilian group, "the energy value of plutonium will be a resource which should be exploited, presumably in breeder reactors, to achieve the most effective use of our uranium reserves."

On the most contentious nuclear export during his tenure at the NRC—the shipments of fuel to the Tarapur plant in India—Kennedy twice voted to send the fuel, before joining in the unanimous commission vote against shipment in May, 1980. But, as he wrote in his opinion: the decision "seems a classic case of the proverbial 'biting off one's own nose to spite his face'. . .I would support a subsequent decision by the President to authorize these exports by Executive Order." Carter eventually followed that advice, and the sale was upheld in the Senate by a two vote margin.

At the time of his appointment to the NRC, Kennedy had been working for Kissinger as a deputy assistant for planning at the National Security Council (NSC). Kennedy first joined the NSC in 1969 as a senior staff member. There he served with Alexander Haig. "We had been acquainted for many years before that," he said at his brief confirmation hearings in February, 1981. "We are close in terms of our professional as well as our personal contact." When Haig traveled, Kennedy reportedly used his office.

Essentially an administrator, Kennedy rose in time to become de facto number three behind Kissinger and Haig at the NSC. When those two were in Paris completing the Vietnamese peace negotiations, Kennedy served as their go-between to the White House. Mostly, Kennedy handled odd jobs. "He was very well-versed in the bureaucracy, the technicalities of the budget," said one veteran of the period. "He picked up on a lot of things that fell between the different offices—such things as the budgetary and bureaucratic implications of [various proposals]. He operated across the boundary lines that had been established by the staff." Others remember Kennedy working on the "reconstruction" plan for North Vietnam that was originally to accompany the peace accords.

Before joining Kissinger's staff, Kennedy spent five years working his way up through the bureaucracy of the Defense Department's Africa region office of the International Security Affairs division, eventually becoming director. That was the culmination of an Army career that also included such classically bureaucratic stops as an assistant to the assistant of the Secretary of Defense, an assistant to the assistant secretary of the Army as well as a tour through Iran as chief of the military assistance programs there.

Kennedy retired from the Army in 1971 with the rank of colonel.

Kennedy ran the Reagan Administration's NRC transition team and was apparently considered for a post there, before the decision was made to avoid recycling a nominee that would carry the taint of Three Mile Island before Senate confirmation hearings. Haig then offered Kennedy his current job, which by definition, offers the opportunity for plenty of travel.

Born on December 24, 1919, in Rochester, New York, Kennedy was graduated from the University of Rochester in 1941 and received an M.B.A. from Harvard University in 1953. He also attended the U.S. Army Command and General Staff College and the National War College. He is married with no children.

FINANCIAL BACKGROUND

In his financial disclosure form, Kennedy reported compensation greater than $5,000 from Pacific Sierra Research and International Energy Associates, Ltd. of Washington, for whom he served as a consultant. That firm lists as clients: the Departments of State and Energy, Union Carbide, Urenco (the European uranium enrichment consortium), Westinghouse, Pennsylvania Power and Light, the Edison

Electric Institute, Exxon Nuclear, Bechtel, Allied General Nuclear Service, British Nuclear Fuels Ltd., General Electric, Japan Atomic Power Company and the Kansai Electric Power Co. (a major Japanese utility).

Together with his wife, Kennedy holds stock worth between $5,000 and $15,000 in: American Brands, Burroughs, Occidental Petroleum, Southland, Richardson Corp., AT&T, and General Motors. They have smaller holdings in Uniroyal, Pan Am, Boeing, Baird Corp., and Sears Roebuck. He reports holdings of between $15,000 and $50,000 in Eastman Kodak.

WHAT OTHERS ARE SAYING ABOUT HIM

- Richard Pollock, the former Critical Mass director who filed the FOIA request on Kennedy's travel said, "The man is lazy, he likes to have fun, likes to be a big shot." Pollock recalled that the FOIA request drew calls from congressional staffers, from other NRC commissioners, from members of the Council on Environmental Quality, all of whom considered Kennedy's jet-setting something of an outrage. Fittingly at the time the request was filed, Pollock said, Kennedy was in France. After the request went in, Kennedy toned down his behavior. "One of the commissioners told me, 'Your request reformed Dick Kennedy'," Pollock said.

- Don Winston of the Atomic Industrial Forum said the AIF is not focusing on nonproliferation policy, instead it is concentrating its efforts on passing nuclear waste disposal legislation in Congress, without which, he said, an export policy is impossible. Meanwhile, he said, the U.S. is being beat out by other countries supplying nuclear power projects. "You have proliferation no matter what you do," he said. "It's a question of who [which country] runs it, or who gets a crack at running it."

JAMES MALONE

AMBASSADOR AT LARGE, LAW OF THE SEA NEGOTIATIONS

RESPONSIBILITY OF OFFICE

After a year in office, Malone lost his job as assistant secretary for oceans and international environmental and scientific affairs, which he had held concurrently with his law of the sea responsibilities. The *Washington Post* reported that he was booted from the job because of dissatisfaction over his performance; *Business Week* and the State Department official statement said the change was made merely to allow Malone to concentrate more on the Law of the Sea negotiations, which were picking up speed in March, 1982, the time of the move.

BACKGROUND

Few Reagan nominees attracted as much congressional attention as James Malone—for good reason. Malone fits the classic description of a fox in the henhouse: a long-time opponent of the goals of the office he ran during 1981, he has made his living serving those that it regulates.

That, of course, aptly describes many of the officials dispatched by the White House to the far corners of the federal bureaucracy. What heightened congressional concern in Malone's case was the extraordinary sensitivity of his job, and the literally apocalyptic potential of a lax proliferation policy.

A former official of the Arms Control and Disarmament Agency (ACDA), Malone entered the Reagan Administration from the Washington law firm of Doub and Muntzing. There he represented three foreign nuclear utilities: Taiwan Power Co., a government-owned utility; and Tokyo Electric Power Co. and Kansai Electric Power Co., two major Japanese utilities.

Precisely what services Malone performed for these firms remained unclear through his stormy nomination hearings. In a foreign agents registration submission filed with the Justice Department on February 8, 1979, William Doub, a former Atomic Energy Commissioner, of the firm explained: "James L. Malone has rendered services directly in furtherance of the interests of the Taiwan Power Company. He has had personal contact with officials of the Executive Branch and Congress to protect the rights of Taiwan Power Company relating to its generation of nuclear power, particularly in relation to proposed legislation related to Taiwan and amendment of the Existing Agreement for Cooperation."

But during the confirmation proceedings, Malone said the statement was not quite accurate, and that he only "observed and reported" on government and congressional actions for the utilities. "The statement was couched in an overly broad phraseology," he said. "There was some consideration that I might be engaged in that type of activity initially, but I did not engage in that type of activity at any time."

While Malone was at ACDA, Taiwan covertly sought to construct a reprocessing plant that could produce weapons-grade plutonium, but eventually was dissuaded by the Ford Administration. Taiwan's current nuclear ambitions are unclear. Former ACDA nonproliferation officials told us that Taiwan's dependence on American enriched uranium for its ambitious commercial nuclear power program makes it receptive to U.S. pressure to stay out of the nuclear club.

But intelligence officials are concerned that Taiwan is part of a triangular effort—with South Africa and Israel—to develop nuclear weapons. Cited in a recent report by the *New York Times* were Israeli assistance to Taiwan in developing a rocket capable of delivering atomic payloads; Taiwan assistance to South Africa in developing processes to produce weapons-grade enriched uranium; and South Africa's agreement to supply Taiwan with 4,000 tons of uranium over the next six years. In addition, Taiwan is researching the laser isotope enrichment process needed to upgrade commercially reprocessed plutonium for weapons use.

At his confirmation hearing, Malone stated flatly, "We have no reason to believe at this time that Taiwan is a proliferation risk." The Export-Import Bank is currently offering Taiwan an extraordinarily generous loan to cover the purchase of two nuclear plants from American companies. "It is a very special arrangement for Taiwan, which has a lot of friends in this Administration," said one industry official.

Malone formally represented the three clients until December, 1980. (He applied in April, 1980 to deregister as foreign agent for Taiwan.) A month before he left the firm, Malone began serving as chairman of the Administration transition team handling nuclear nonproliferation issues—an overall subject of obvious interest to his clients. "Clearly, to avoid the appearance of professional impropriety," wrote John Glenn and three other senators in a dissenting view on Malone's nomination,

"Mr. Malone should not have dealt with issues of concern to his clients on behalf of the incoming Administration."

The transition team report—which called for a radical loosening of American nonproliferation efforts—also contained recommendations of more specific interest to Malone's clients. Stating "there should be no concern about those industrialized nations with substantial and expanding commitments to nuclear power, e.g., Japan, and the Federal Republic of Germany," the report recommends a "U.S. commitment to assist in the development of. . .a reprocessing facility in Japan. . ." A consortium of Japanese utilities—including both of Malone's former clients—have been seeking the necessary U.S. approval to construct such a plant. The report also recommends that, "Requests for retransfer [of American supplied fuel] for reprocessing in the United Kingdom and France will be approved without linkage to other issues." (For more on the transition report, see Major Issues section.)

With their attention pricked by these conflicts, Senate Foreign Relations Committee Democrats, led by Glenn, pressed Malone for a specific statement that he would recuse himself from decisions affecting his former clients. But Malone resisted in an unsuccessful struggle that held up his nomination. At first Malone suggested that since he had "terminated my relationship with the firm there could not be any conflict of interest." Pressed by Glenn, Malone retreated on April 1, writing that "I may determine it is appropriate to disqualify myself. . .for the above three companies for a period of time." Finally, two days later, Malone agreed to recuse himself from specific matters affecting the three firms; as well as another client, General Atomic Co., the principal U.S. exporter of research reactors and fuel; and any "major policy issue affecting Japan." But throughout, Malone refused to provide the senators with a list of his law firm's clients, saying he did not have access to the information. That, Glenn pointed out, meant Malone would effectively self-police the State Department's policy of avoiding cases involving clients of his former firm. The senators' fears were subsequently borne out. In May, 1982, the Senate Foreign Relations Committee revealed that while in office Malone has lobbied on behalf of Taiwan's Export-Import loan.

Malone began his nuclear career at ACDA, joining as an assistant general counsel in 1971 and rising to the position of general counsel in 1973 during a Nixon orchestrated purge of the agency that simultaneously redirected the agency toward a more hawkish role in arms negotiations and downplayed its influence. According to several agency sources, Malone helped direct the shakeup, which removed several of the agency's top officials and reshuffled several career bureaucrats. Malone was "the finger man" in the purge, one high-ranking former ACDA official told us. After the purge, the White House installed as ACDA Director Fred Ikle, who is now undersecretary of Defense for policy.

At ACDA Malone paid little attention to proliferation issues, contemporaries recall, concentrating instead on mastering the intricacies of the ongoing SALT II negotiations. "He had the reputation of being a hawk," said one former official. "He basically believes in national security through the build-up of arms." Most of all, former ACDA officials recall, Malone was interested in Malone. "He was very pro Jim Malone," said another former ACDA official who worked with him. "He was an ambitious man." Others described him as careful not to deviate from what he considered prevailing policy.

Along with Deputy Director John F. Lehman, Jr., now secretary of the Navy, Malone was part of Ikle's inner circle. He was rewarded for his performance with a lame duck appointment in December, 1976 as U.S. delegate to the Conference of the Committee on Disarmament with the temporary rank of ambassador, a move whose major significance was considered to be its impact on Malone's resume.

After Carter took office, Malone became a consultant for Nuclear Regulatory Commissioner Richard Kennedy, a friend to the industry. Kennedy now serves as undersecretary of State for management, and has replaced Malone as the key figure in Administration nonproliferation policy.

In 1978, Malone joined Doub and Muntzing, where he worked until January, 1981, when Reagan tapped him as acting director of the ACDA. There Malone was involved in a second purge, in which 15 more employees were let go.

Born in Los Angeles, California on December 22, 1931, Malone was graduated from Pomona College in 1953 and received his law degree from Stanford in 1959. Malone was a Development Officer at Beloit College from 1959-1961 before joining the University of California, Los Angeles, where he served as assistant law school dean through 1967. With stops at Willamette University as Law School dean and the University of Texas as a visiting lecturer, he finally joined the federal government as an attorney at the Federal Maritime Commission in 1970. He is married, with three children.

FINANCIAL BACKGROUND

Malone earned $44,000 in 1980 from Doub & Muntzing, and another $1,200 in consulting fees from Cypress International, Inc., an Alexandria-based military contracting and international risk assessment consulting firm. Though Malone told the Senate Foreign Relations Committee he could not provide a full client list for the firm, a number of clients are available through public sources. These included:

- Allied General Nuclear Services, the owners of the mothballed Barnwell reprocessing plant, and therefore acutely interested in U.S. reprocessing policy.

- National Agricultural Chemicals Association and the Pesticide Producers Association. More, perhaps than any other industry, pesticide manufacturers are concerned about government efforts to restrict the sale abroad of products considered unsafe. Early on, Reagan rescinded a Carter executive order that would allow the government to ban some hazardous exports; now the State and Commerce Departments are investigating ways to weaken even the existing statutory requirements to simply notify foreign governments of domestic regulatory actions.

Other Doub & Muntzing clients include Barringer and Co. of Memphis, Tennessee; the Board of Trade of Kansas City; Campbell Taggart, Inc. of Dallas, Texas; the Clayton Brokerage Co. of Clayton, Missouri; CSR, Ltd. of Sydney, Australia; El Ganadero of Puerto Rico; and Morrison-Knudsen Co., of Washington, D.C.

Malone and his family hold two trusts consisting of government bonds and stock in AT&T and Texaco administered by the Arizona Bank and valued at over $250,000.

WHAT OTHERS ARE SAYING ABOUT HIM

- Opposing Malone's confirmation, Sen. Alan Cranston (D-Cal.) wrote, that ''Malone has already demonstrated his insensitivity to conflict of interest issues by his performance during. . .the transition.'' Citing Malone's former foreign nuclear clients, Cranston continued: ''Inevitably these foreign interests will be viewed with considerable sympathy in Mr. Malone's development and execution of general nonproliferation policy, even if the nominee is barred from participating in specific license applications of former foreign clients.'' The only ways to avoid the conflict, Cranston concluded, was either to remove nonproliferation from Malone's purview, or keep Malone out of the State Department.

MAJOR ISSUES

- In a major policy shift, the Reagan Administration is now supporting reprocessing of nuclear fuel at home, and abroad in those countries that it does not feel ''constitute a proliferation risk.'' The policy is considered by many dangerously lax, more concerned about propping up the nuclear industry than controlling proliferation.

- The Administration is considering further changes in nonproliferation policy including the consolidation of all nuclear export authority in the State Department, a move that many say will subjugate proliferation concerns to short-term foreign policy goals.

- In an effort to be seen as a ''reliable supplier,'' the Administration is working out country by country arrangements on nuclear matters that some congressional aides see as an effort to bypass congressional review.

- Stunning delegations from around the world, the Administration in early 1981 announced it would not sign the proposed Law of the Sea Treaty as planned. Malone, the new head of the U.S. delegation, launched an intensive review of the entire document, aimed at finding ways to address the concerns of multinational mining firms dissatisfied with the provisions covering mining of the seabed.

As expressed in the transition team report, Malone's views on nuclear proliferation are close to those of candidate Reagan, who once declared that proliferation was not ''any of our business.'' They are also in tune with those long-expressed by Richard Kennedy. The report rejects the Carter Administration's efforts to slow the spread of sensitive nuclear technology. It instead urges the Administration to support fuel reprocessing both here and in industrialized Western nations ''posing no risk'' of proliferation and to assume a role as a ''reliable supplier'' of nuclear products. At the same time, the report recommends strengthening the executive branch's direct control over proliferation policy by stripping the semi-independent ACDA and Nuclear Regulatory Commission (NRC) of their roles in the exporting process.

''Denial of nuclear supply and other sanctions have proven to be weak instruments for preventing nations from acquiring capabilities for explosives manufacture,'' the report asserts. ''The United States should make every effort to restore its credibility and reliability as a nuclear supplier. . .Accordingly, the policy of denial of U.S. nuclear supply should be applied only to countries posing a threat to U.S. international security interests.''

Malone's report also called for revisions to the Nuclear Nonproliferation and Atomic Energy Acts to sharply limit the government's ability to impose conditions on foreign nations using U.S. fuel for their reactors. Further, he proposed to transfer into the State Department the authority now held by the NRC to approve nuclear export licenses and that of the Energy Department over requests to retransfer or reprocess U.S.-supplied fuel. ACDA's role in the export licensing review process would also be transferred to the State Department, and vested, along with the NRC, the Energy Department, and existing State Department authority—including that held by the Bureau of Politico-Military affairs—in a new assistant secretary for nuclear affairs.

These far-reaching proposals would have turned existing nonproliferation policy on its head. "A few words summary of it [the report] would be that the Nuclear Nonproliferation Act is out, that we are back to business as usual, and that we should sell nuclear technology around the world as we see fit," said Sen. John Glenn (D-Ohio), a principal author of the law, at Malone's confirmation.

When Reagan issued his proliferation position in July, 1981, it did not go as far as Malone's transition report or Kennedy's previous statements. That reflected, some in the arms control community believe, a moderating influence of, among others, Fred Ikle, who displayed a keen concern for nuclear proliferation as head of ACDA under Nixon and Ford. (See Ikle profile.)

Reflecting the transition report, the statement asserted the need to "reestablish this nation as a predictable and reliable partner for" nuclear commerce and promised that the "Administration will. . .not inhibit or set back civil reprocessing and breeder reactor development abroad in nations with advanced nuclear power programs where it does not constitute a proliferation risk." But it was silent on amending the Nuclear Nonproliferation Act, and said nothing about transferring additional authority over nuclear exports to the State Department.

Still, the statement represented a major redirection of government policy toward the position of the nuclear industry, increasingly dependent on foreign sales to offset the stagnant domestic market. Arguing that the policy "signals a return to nuclear boosterism," Rep. Edward Markey (D-Mass.), chairman of the House Interior subcommittee on oversight and investigations, said, "For the President to endorse the plutonium breeder reactor, plutonium reprocessing and the sale of nuclear technology throughout the world constitutes a policy that is certain to advance rather than restrict the spread of nuclear weaponry."

Encouraging reprocessing in advanced nations, many analysts in the field believe, will have a cascading effect on the spread of that technology to less reliable countries. "Obviously, we're establishing the fact that we don't have a problem with reprocessing," said an aide at the House subcommittee on international economic policy. That may make other suppliers more willing to pass along the technology to countries that they consider "reliable", even if we don't, he said.

If the July, 1981 statement were the end of the Administration's proliferation deliberations, that would be cause enough for concern about increasing the membership in the "nuclear armed crowd." But until his reassignment Malone was still seeking further changes. In an October, 1981 internal memo, he again proposed transferring the NRC authority to the State Department, weakening or eliminating laws requiring recipients of U.S. nuclear facilities and fuel to permit international inspection, and repeal of the Glenn-Symington amendment, which cuts off American aid to nations moving toward the production of atomic weapons. "Proliferate and be damned?" was how the *Economist* summed up the package.

Malone was keen to bring the NRC's authority into the State Department not only to expand his bureaucratic turf, but to more closely integrate the sale of nuclear supplies into American foreign policy, making such sales similar to weapons deals.

"It's not a good idea," said Charles Van Dooren, long-time director of ACDA's nonproliferation activities. "You need to have some independence for the agency [making the decisions] within this technical field." In a study, the General Accounting Office agreed.

The other proposed changes, said Glenn, would leave American nonproliferation policy "toothless." Faced with this opposition, the Administration has not pressed the plan. Indeed, its publication may have contributed to Malone's demise.

Malone made the Administration's general feelings clear in a September, 1981 speech to the Uranium Institute in London. "We put overwhelming and all but exclusive emphasis on the proliferation dangers of nuclear technology," he said in reference to the Carter policy. "At the same time, our government was insufficiently inclined to face up to the ineluctable fact that nuclear energy can and must make an important contribution to continually expanding world energy needs."

While the legislative moves are considered, the Reagan nonproliferation policy is being tested in four key areas:

- In September, 1981, the Administration reached agreement with Japan, allowing it to reprocess increased amounts of U.S. fuel at the experimental Tokaimura facility that had been strongly opposed by the Carter Administration. "The agreement gave the Japanese just about everything they wanted," said an aide to Sen. Glenn. The Administration also gave the go-ahead for the eventual construction of a much larger commercial plant;

- Also in September, 1981 the Administration turned over to South Africa title to 80 tons of low-enriched uranium, though it did not grant an export license for the fuel, since South Africa has also refused to accept international safeguards. It did, however, allow South Africa to sell some of the fuel to other nations. South Africa complicated the situation in November, when it obtained a shipment of enriched fuel from an unknown source—presumed to be China—that would allow it to begin operation of two 1,000-megawatt plants this year.

- In October, 1981 the Administration announced it would allow Brazil to sidestep the penalty clause in a contract with the U.S. that prevented it from buying nuclear fuel from foreign suppliers. Waiving the penalty allows Brazil to buy the fuel from other countries without allowing the full international inspection required under the Nonproliferation Act;

- Throughout the fall of 1981 the Administration held apparently fruitless negotiations with India aimed at ending the 18-year-old agreement under which the U.S. supplied fuel and technology for the Tarapur reactor built by Bechtel. Though willing to cancel the contract, the Administration is seeking to maintain international inspection of the facility. India is balking and may unilaterally renounce the agreement; such a move would be a dramatic blow to the entire international safeguards regime.

These policies, strewn with exemptions, waivers and country-by-country considerations have generated confusion and consternation on Capitol Hill, with some legislators concerned that "the Administration is trying to establish a de facto policy outside congressional review," as one Senate Republican aide put it.

Malone entered the public eye with a thud the week before his nomination hearings, when then Deputy Secretary Clark appointed him to head the U.S. delegation negotiating the Law of the Sea Treaty. Malone replaced acting head George H. Aldrich, who, along with the other top diplomats on the delegation, was summarily dismissed on March 7, 1981. Two days later Malone announced that the Administration planned to review its stand on "the entire text" of the 320 clause treaty, which would govern naval right-of-way, deep sea fishing, research, and most contentiously, mining of the sea floor.

Malone's announcement followed by one week a sparse State Department statement that the Administration would not adhere to previous agreements to complete the treaty at the session beginning March, 1981. Instead, under Malone, it launched a widespread review that stretched out past not only that session, but a subsequent August gathering in Geneva.

Generally supported by the military—though that backing moderated in the Reagan Administration—the treaty has been resisted by the international consortia of oil and mining companies formulating plans to mine the manganese and cobalt-bearing modules on the ocean floor. They fear the treaty provisions that established the seabed as the "common heritage of mankind." As his expert adviser during the treaty talks, Malone appointed Leigh Ratiner, a former lobbyist for one of the leading industrial participants, Kennecott Copper. In March, 1982, Ratiner presented the department with a $100,000 bill which triggered State Department and Senate Foreign Relations Committee investigations.

At April, 1981 hearings on the Administration's sudden withdrawal from the treaty process, which stunned the international delegations that expected to conclude the eight-year negotiations in 1981, Malone listed as areas of U.S. "concern" virtually all of the complaints raised by the mining and oil firms against the treaty. Charging that it "places under burdensome international regulation the development of all of the resources of the seabed," Malone asserted the treaty would force U.S. companies to transfer "proprietary information and technology," to the Third World, would create a government system biased to the Soviet Union, would allow the international institution established to oversee seabed mining to "eventually monopolize production of seabed minerals" and would allow revenues from the operation to fund "liberation movements like the PLO."

Testifying two weeks later, Republican former chief negotiator Elliot Richardson obliquely criticized Malone by noting "the remarkable persistence of distortions of the draft convention by critics apparently less interested in getting a good treaty than in scuttling any treaty whether satisfactory or not." Refuting Malone's assertions point by point—without mentioning him by name—Richardson concluded: "Fortunately. . . the attacks on the text have a positive aspect. . . They. . . invite their own refutation by the kind of retort I have just made; namely that the text does not say—or was not intended to say—what the critic has alleged."

Since the U.S. delegation demurred during its review, little was accomplished at either the New York or Geneva sessions in 1981. That the broad changes the U.S. is seeking in the provisions governing seabed mining will be acceptable to the other delegations is unlikely. At that point the Administration and the mining firms that have its ear will likely have to decide whether they want to live with an imperfect treaty or take the chance of either scuttling the entire process or refusing to sign a final document. Without a treaty of some kind, Richardson believes, the consortia would not feel secure enough to invest in seabed operations.

Acknowledging those fears, in February, 1982, the Administration announced it would return to the negotiations and seek basic changes to give the treaty a "pro-development thrust." But though the U.S. scaled back its demands, it won only a few of its points, and the treaty was approved with the U.S. voting against it. (The Soviet Union abstained.) Malone's next step is unclear, since major companies, such as U.S. Steel still vehemently oppose the treaty, but other western nations such as Japan and France find it acceptable.

ROBERT HORMATS
ASSISTANT SECRETARY, ECONOMIC AND BUSINESS AFFAIRS

RESPONSIBILITY OF OFFICE

Hormats has overall responsibility for formulating and implementing State Department policy on foreign economic issues—resources and food, international energy issues, trade, international finance and development, aviation and maritime affairs, and telecommunications. Hormats has spent most of his time organizing U.S. participation in summit meetings—he worked on the Cancun and Ottawa summits in 1981; international energy issues, particularly the Strategic Petroleum Reserve plan; and East-West economic relations. He also works on trade and investment issues, along with representatives of the Treasury and Commerce Departments and Trade Representative Bill Brock. During Law of the Sea negotiations, he has responsibility for aspects relating to the seabeds.

Because of his good relationship with Secretary Haig, Hormats reportedly plays a key role in formulating international economic policy.

BACKGROUND

Robert Hormats was only 26 years old, and fresh out of Tufts University's Fletcher School of International Law and Diplomacy, when he came to work for Henry Kissinger's National Security Council (NSC) staff in 1969. He's been at the upper echelons of power ever since. Like hundreds of other young men and women that pour into Washington each year, Hormats was sharp, well-educated, and ambitious. But something more has enabled him to survive as a political appointee through four presidential administrations—he holds moderate views, has a thorough understanding of Washington interplay, and never makes waves.

"He was extremely quick, not only on substance but also on those very delicate bureaucratic issues," said Dr. C. Fred Bergsten, who hired Hormats onto the NSC staff after contacting his alma mater and asking school officials to send him their best student in development studies.

Hormats came on as the NSC's expert for Third World issues. He had the proper academic background: a pending Ph.D. in international economics, a year of study in Tanzania (and a summer in Kenya) and a knowledge of Swahili, among other languages. His association with Haig began during his years on the NSC.

When Nixon drained power from the NSC to a new Council on International Economic Policy in 1971, Hormats's role in that area diminished. But at the same time he picked up other duties which paved the way for advancement up the NSC ladder and eventually into the State Department.

As an NSC staff member, Hormats helped organize currency realignments after Nixon abruptly took America off the gold standard in 1971. He also worked on normalizing economic relations with China.

In 1974 Hormats was promoted to senior economic adviser, where he served Henry Kissinger, General Brent Scowcroft and later, Zbigniew Brzezinski.

In that capacity, Hormats helped negotiate a response to the Portuguese financial crisis, when the country's Socialist government desperately sought, and obtained, a loan from the U.S. government to remain solvent. He also helped organize an 11-nation consortium in 1976 to bail out the financially troubled British government when the pound sterling plunged in value.

Hormats has attended every economic summit meeting since Rambouillet in 1975. He smoothed U.S. participation at the Rambouillet, Puerto Rico and London economic summits as the NSC's top economic adviser; the Bonn and Tokyo economic summits after he became deputy assistant secretary of state for economic and business affairs in 1977; and was a member of the U.S. Delegation to the Venice economic summit after becoming deputy U.S. trade representative in 1979.

As deputy to U.S. trade representative Reubin Askew, a post he held until his appointment to the Reagan State Department, Hormats was chair of the interagency Trade Policy Review Group, which studied ways to improve America's trading position.

Part of Hormats's secret for survival is the relatively nonpartisan nature of the field he has pursued. Hormats's public statements have not changed much over the past 12 years, but neither has the official U.S. line on international economic policy. Hormats been a consistent proponent of unfettered trade—reduction of both protections and restrictions on business activity here and abroad.

The goals he expressed to us as a Reagan official were no different than what he has worked for over the last decade: strengthening economic ties between the Western powers; opening up more foreign markets for American business; developing unified restrictions among the allies on the export of technology to the Soviet Union; creating a "mutually beneficial" relationship with the developing nations; and strengthening the position of oil importing nations through stockpiling and increased energy development.

His themes have been in general harmony with the Reagan line. Governments, he said in 1978, need "to be considerably more aware of the inflationary implications of. . environmental protection, health and safety regulations, minimum wages, agricultural policy and import restrictions." He told the Senate subcommittee on international finance the same year that U.S. taxation of foreign earnings hinders U.S. trade and overseas investment: "We are presently the only major trading country which taxes the foreign earnings of its citizens. We must make sure that this taxation does not cripple the ability of American businessmen to compete in foreign markets."

During the same testimony he said the State Department should expand its export assistance program—which then consisted largely of using Foreign Service officers to promote U.S. exports and offering help to U.S. businesses through its overseas posts. He said those functions should be supplemented with government-funded research programs, federal subsidization of American business participation in trade fairs, and by asking larger firms already in foreign markets to help small and medium sized companies become exporters.

Hormats generally opposes import restrictions as a means to protect U.S. industry. "In those rare cases where protective action can be justified, the actions are to be temporary, progressively reduced and linked to plans to phase out obsolete capacity," he has said.

One place where Hormats has sought at least voluntary restrictions is in Japan's auto industry. In fact, Japan's protected markets and export subsidies have been a constant source of irritation to Hormats over the years.

As deputy U.S. trade representative, he visited Japan, and according to his former boss Askew, "stressed the importance of accelerated and intensified Japanese efforts in the areas [of encouraging Japanese companies to build parts plants in the U.S. and permitting increased access to Japan's auto market] to assist the U.S. auto industry through this difficult period of adjustment."

"We made the point very strongly in Japan," said Hormats, "that in the future Japan should rely primarily on domestic demand rather than externally led demand."

Hormats scored some significant points with future Reaganites after Carter's visit to the Venice summit in 1980 when he expressed relief that the summit leaders had finally addressed, in addition to the need for near-term fiscal and monetary restraint, "the necessity for effective 'supply-side policies' to increase the share of investment in gross national product, to raise productivity, to reduce rigidities and distortions sometimes caused by regulatory policies, and to permit resources to shift from declining to expanding sectors."

But other of Hormats's views have enabled him to get along with the more moderate sectors of the foreign policy community as well. He has long backed the provision of aid to Third World countries as a supplement to private sector development. "There's a place for both," he told us. As a member of the Development Coordinating Committee of the International Development Cooperation Agency, he said he intended "to play an active role in supporting a vigorous aid program," to offset the huge energy-driven debt built up by developing countries. "[We should] insure that they don't have a deteriorating financial condition which would both have a financial impact on the financial system and on the trading system," he said.

Though he was hand-picked by Haig, Hormats's nomination was one of several initially blocked by Senator Jesse Helms (R-N.C.). Helms dropped his opposition after his staff met with Hormats. "Mr. Hormats. . .was unknown to me," Helms wrote to Senate Foreign Relations Committee Chair Charles Percy (R-Ill.). "My staff has met with Mr. Hormats at my direction and found him forthcoming in his understanding of the needs and concerns of American businessmen faced with unfair foreign competition."

Hormats's willingness to bend to divergent administrations has its limits. When asked if he would serve Ted Kennedy, the answer was an adamant "no way."

Born April 13, 1943 in Baltimore, Maryland, Hormats has been a guest scholar at the Brookings Institution, a fellow at the Council on Foreign Relations, and a senior consultant to the Commission on Critical Choices for Americans, a Rockefeller organization. He was graduated from Tufts University in 1965, received his master's degree the following year, and completed his Ph.D. in International Economics at Tufts University's Fletcher School of Law and Diplomacy in 1969.

MAJOR ISSUES

- Reagan has abruptly told the developing nations that they will receive less foreign aid and should rely instead on "the magic of the marketplace," opening up markets and improving the climate for private investment. Though this strategy may help U.S. firms, critics say it does little for the poverty-stricken nations of the world.

- In a strategy Hormats claims will help both developing countries and American business interests, the Administration has taken a number of steps to encourage commercial investment abroad in a period when high unemployment is rife at home. The cornerstone of that policy is Reagan's Caribbean Basin Initiative, presented by the Administration as a means of thwarting revolutionary movements in Central America.

- The Reagan Administration has reacted sharply to Canada's attempts to gain control of its energy industry and foreign investments in other sectors of the economy.

- The White House imposed trade sanctions against Poland after the country's Soviet-backed government imposed martial law, but agreed to pay U.S. banks' unpaid Polish loans rather than declare the country in default.

- European export subsidies have become a source of irritation to Hormats, who publicly warned that such measures could sour relations between the U.S. and its Western allies.

By the time the delegates from about a dozen developing countries arrived in Cancun, Mexico in October, 1981 to meet with Ronald Reagan and other leaders from industrialized nations, their hopes for beginning talks on developing a "new international economic order" were modest. One week before the 22-nation summit, Reagan gave clear indication that he was not interested in discussing any such plan for closing the gap between rich and poor countries. Developing nations promoting that approach, he said, "simply want a policy of take away from the haves and deliver to the have-nots."

Instead, Reagan told the World Affairs Council in Philadelphia, the developing nations should seek "human fulfillment—an ability by all men and women to realize freely their full potential to go where their God-given talents will take them." In other words, as he had informed the International Monetary Fund (IMF) and World Bank members just weeks before, the Third World should "rely on the magic of the marketplace."

Despite those discouraging remarks, developing countries hoped for some progress at Cancun. In particular, they hoped that pressure by America's European allies—France and Great Britain—would persuade Reagan to support the establishment of a World Bank affiliate that would help oil-importing Third World countries develop indigenous energy sources.

They were wrong. Reagan blithely dismissed the proposal, and in nearly the same breath, refused to endorse any global negotiations held in the United Nations, a forum in which the Third World has greater influence than the World Bank, the traditional forum for such dialogues.

Reagan's message at Cancun reflected his earlier statements that the developing nations should rely less on aid and more on stimulating international trade by opening up markets and improving the climate for private investment. Hungry for aid to construct public works and meet short term payments, protective of their infant industries, and wary of unchecked foreign investment, many developing nations were angered by the American president's lectures extolling the virtues of multinational capitalism. As Larry Birns of the Council on Hemispheric Affairs put it: "Private investment does not produce dams or much needed community projects. It takes public loans, public assistance." (See profile of Donald Regan.)

Hormats, who organized U.S. participation at the summit, conceded that not all the attendees agreed with the President's stand. But, he told us, "It was a pragmatic line, and a lot of developing countries today are more interested in trade opportunities and private investment."

That was not the message he heard at Cancun, say observers who attended. In fact, said one foreign journalist, the mood at a press briefing for foreign reporters before the summit was hostile—with Hormats making "aggressively condescending" remarks about Third World development problems and reporters chiding him for ignoring the real needs of developing countries.

But in one form or another senior officials continue to use rhetoric similar to Reagan's Philadelphia speech when he compared his policies to the proverb: "Give a hungry man a fish and he'll be hungry tomorrow; teach him how to fish and he'll never be hungry again."

"People [in developing countries] need capital equipment—not to be taught the rudiments of fishing—they already know that," an Indian journalist remarked at a State Department press briefing. "This whole idea of teaching them how to fish is a ploy to downgrade the financial needs of developing countries."

Those needs are acute. Growth is faltering and payment problems—once rooted in energy imports—have now been exacerbated by the U.S. government's tight monetary polices and resulting high interest rates in international markets. Each percentage point increase in the U.S. prime interest rate costs the developing nations $4 billion, according to economist C. Fred Bergsten.

Demand for IMF loans to cover payments are at an all time high. But the Administration will not support expansion programs for the multilateral banks—in part due to the political difficulty of justifying any increase in U.S. commitments with an austerity program at home. However, neither will the Administration abandon the institutions. As Hormats told us: "There is room for both [private and public assistance]." And, as officials like Hormats well know, private sector investment in Third World countries generally requires some form of public assistance.

The Reagan Administration, in a strategy officials claim will help both developing countries and American business interests, is determined to "facilitate U.S. private sector involvement in LDC's (lesser developed countries)," Hormats has said. Initial steps toward that goal included tax breaks on personal income earned abroad and attempts to weaken the Foreign Corrupt Practices Act (See profiles of Lionel Olmer and John Shad).

Other efforts are underway. The Administration has broadened the operating authority of the U.S. Overseas Private Investment Corporation (OPIC) to allow it to support private investment in middle-income developing countries. Previously OPIC assisted U.S. investors in about 80 lesser developed countries by helping locate local investment opportunities and providing loans and loan guarantees, and insured U.S. investors against political risks such as expropriation and damage from war or revolution.

The bill Reagan signed into law on October 16, 1981 enables OPIC to insure U.S. investors in middle income countries as well, such as Brazil, South Korea, Taiwan, Portugal, and Turkey; and authorizes the agency to give U.S. investors insurance against losses from "civil strife"—defined as violent action by political organizations seeking to influence the government.

Hormats said the Administration will also attempt to negotiate bilateral investment treaties with developing countries that want American investment. "Such treaties would enhance the attractiveness of investing in those countries by establishing a common frame of reference and legal base," he said.

In February, 1982, President Reagan finally unveiled the most highly publicized aspect of his Third World policy—the Caribbean Basin Initiative, known around the State Department as CBI. The plan was proposed not as a humanitarian gesture, but as a means to thwart revolutionary movements, like those in El Salvador, within the borders of Central American nations considered friendly. The centerpiece of the program, which Reagan personally outlined before the Organization of American States, is a proposal to expand the range of U.S. imports from Central America that are duty free. Currently 87 percent of those products are duty free, but because the others include fruit and leather—goods produced by American industries and unions—the plan is expected to face a tough fight in Congress. Another element of the CBI that will meet resistance from a Congress faced with massive deficits and cuts in domestic programs is a supplemental $350 million economic assistance package for the Caribbean nations which would increase total aid to the region by 96 percent over 1981 levels.

Reagan also proposed "significant" tax incentives to encourage U.S. firms to invest in Central America at a time when domestic unemployment is reaching alarming rates, and many firms are already seeking a reprieve abroad from higher labor costs in the U.S. Before Reagan's announcement, the AFL-CIO Council passed a resolution agreeing that the flow of aid to the Caribbean needs to be increased, but added that proposals for "one-way free trade and additional incentives to United States firms for investing abroad should be rejected."

Hormats denied that promoting foreign investments will hurt Reagan's economic program by encouraging businesses to spend their tax savings overseas rather than on expanding productive capacity and producing jobs at home. "The amounts of investment abroad are really not all that great," he said. "There's going to be a lot more investment here." In 1978 assets owned by American foreign affiliates totalled $490 billion.

State Department officials readily acknowledge that the U.S. government stands ready to use its political muscle to aid American business abroad. "[W]hen a firm has decided to invest abroad, the U.S. government will provide maximum support: such as making available information on market prospects, facilitating contacts with appropriate officials and supporting company efforts to resist unfair treatment," Hormats assured the International Insurance Advisory Council in May, 1981.

"In those countries where they exist, we will encourage removal of unjustified impediments and disincentives to foreign investment—for example, in the tax and regulatory area," he added. In sum, Hormats told us, "If there is a problem with a country, we will go in on [the company's] behalf."

Already Canada is feeling that pressure over its National Energy Program (NEP) which aims to increase Canadian ownership of the country's energy industry to 50 percent by 1990. The government's move to "Canadianize" the energy industry—about 28 percent of the oil industry is currently owned by Canadians—will affect primarily American corporations, which dominate that segment of the Canadian economy.

Also straining relations between the two governments is Canada's Foreign Investment Review Agency (FIRA), which has been given the power to screen applications by foreign investors to determine whether the investment will be of "significant benefit" to Canada. FIRA also has the power to extract "undertakings" from a potential investor, which might require a firm to hire a specified level of Canadian management and labor, or transfer patents to Canada, or limit its imports.

The U.S. has not taken kindly to the measures, and the public platitudes traditionally used by American officials about the close friendship binding the two neighbors have devolved into sharp denunciations of Canadian policy. Hormats told us the Canadian investment restrictions "are past the limits" of what is acceptable. "If they do it, they simply encourage other countries to do it," he said. In March, 1982 a Commerce Department official warned that the Reagan Administration may take retaliatory action against Canada.

Aside from public warnings, Reagan Administration officials have met privately with Canadian officials in an effort to persuade them to back off at least some of their actions. One high-level Canadian official told us he fears the Reagan Administration will pressure his government to retreat from their investment policies as the price for progress on a treaty limiting U.S. pollutants that have produced acid rain in Canada. In a more formal move, the Administration has challenged Canada's FIRA policies under the General Agreement on Tariffs and Trade (GATT). GATT was established to govern trade between nations, not investment. Neither are nations prohibited under international law from deciding who can invest within their borders. But Reagan Administration officials are arguing that Canada's investment policies "distort" trade.

Similarly, Hormats will champion the cause of American farmers vis-a-vis Japan and Western Europe. He says he will take a tough stand against the European Economic Community's practice of subsidizing grain and flour exports, which, he said, "enables the EEC to undersell U.S. suppliers in third country markets." Additionally, he said he will defend American access to European markets: "Any restriction on our access or impairment of our negotiated rights would be viewed with extreme seriousness in this country."

Import restrictions and export subsidies used by many European governments prompted Hormats at the end of 1981 to make an unusually blunt speech in which he said he fears a souring of relations between the U.S. and its allies across the Atlantic. In the speech, before the Mid-America Committee in Chicago, Hormats charged that the European governments were using trade restrictions that hurt the U.S. as a means to solve their domestic economic problems. The continuation of such measures, Hormats warned, could spread to other areas and result in "a downward spiral in world trade and investment" that could lead to "poisonous effects" in the political and military relationships between the U.S. and its allies.

The Reagan Administration has been reluctant to use food as a weapon in international conflict—primarily as a gesture to American farmers. Early in his presidency Reagan lifted a grain embargo against the Soviet Union which had been imposed by the Carter Administration after the invasion of Afghanistan. Hormats, a high level official in the Carter Administration when the embargo was imposed, told us: "I don't know that I would have used [an embargo], but I wasn't involved in the decision. . .I think food embargos should be used only in extraordinary situations."

Although the Administration did not embargo food supplies after the imposition of martial law in Poland, it did halt Commodity Credit Corporation (CCC) credits and guarantees to that country. The CCC has financed close to half of all U.S. agricultural sales to Poland over the last 25 years.

After Poland's regime declared martial law the Pentagon said Poland should be declared in default on the full $1.6 billion it owed U.S. banks and the CCC. The State Department and Treasury Department disagreed, and in the end prevailed. When much of the Polish government's debt became due after the imposition of martial law, the White House instructed the CCC in early 1982 to pay off the U.S. banks that had made the loans. The decision had political, as well as economic, motivations, as Hormats told the Senate Committee on Agriculture, Nutrition and Forestry in March, 1982: "The NATO allies are in firm accord that one of the most effective common tools to keep sustained pressure on Poland and indirectly on the Soviet Union is to continue to insist that the Polish government repay its debts. . .These payments divert scarce foreign exchange from the purchase of imports needed to run the Polish economy. Accordingly, insistence on payment increases the economic pressure on Poland. This, in turn, means more pressure on the Soviets. . .An official declaration of default—while not legally absolving Poland of its obligations to repay—could give the Polish government an excuse to stop making repayments," he said.

Other sanctions Reagan ordered against Poland included suspension of Polish aviation privileges in the U.S., suspension of the right of Polish fishing boats to work in American waters, and a further restriction on the sale of high technology equipment to Poland. The White House's decision to deny a request for a $65 million loan by Romania in February, 1982 could signal a tougher attitude towards such aid to the Eastern bloc countries.

At the same time, the Reagan Administration has loosened economic restrictions against other human rights violators. In July, 1981, then Undersecretary Myer Rashish told the Joint Economic Committee the Administration intended to reverse a U.S. policy of opposing loans by international development banks to four notoriously repressive South American military regimes—Argentina, Chile, Uruguay and Paraguay. Rep. Henry S. Reuss (D-Wis.), chair of the Joint Economic Committee, called the Administration's move "immoral and illegal," asserting that it violates a 1977 law which prohibits the U.S. from supporting development loans to countries engaged in systematic violations of human rights.

As deputy U.S. trade representative under Carter, Hormats supported legislation authorizing bank ownership of export trading companies which "would make available new financial resources as well as new networks of contacts" to help small and medium sized businesses get into the exporting business. Such trading companies would provide export services such as financing, transportation, warehousing, packaging, and marketing. The Reagan Administration is supporting the Carter legislation with several minor changes. Hormats told us he supports the legislation as one option for improving the volume of U.S. exports. "We have been losing a number of contracts not because our products aren't competitive but because financing isn't competitive."

That legislation passed the Senate in 1981. One House expert on the issue said some representatives believe the bill would create "an unfortunate breach of the separation between commercial banking and straight business commerce. It is inappropriate for a financial intermediary to get into the business of owning export trading companies because it exposes banks' assets to the risky business of selling goods and it diverts limited bank assets." Others have expressed concern that bank ownership of such companies raises serious antitrust implications. Jonathan Brown of the Public Interest Research Group expressed that concern in a 1980 letter to Rep. Fernand St. Germain (D-R.I.): "Bank ownership of export trading companies is a false solution to an important national concern—stimulating small business exports. It would be a sad irony if a few giant banks were given a powerful new anticompetitive tool in the name of helping small business."

In addition, the Administration has proposed trimming taxes for U.S. exporters beyond that already provided by the Domestic International Sales Corporation program.

The White House was backed into a tight corner early in 1981 when it came under pressure from U.S. auto manufacturers to limit Japanese auto exports to the United States. Rather than breach its highly touted free trade policies, Reagan opted for "voluntary" restraints by the Japanese. It's likely the pressure on Japan to limit its exports was considerable. As Hormats once said, "Japan negotiates in a way which almost tends to force other countries to apply pressure to it. It seems not to move unless overwhelming pressure is applied, and then only at the last minute, and then only the minimum amount necessary."

The State Department also is seeking "voluntary" restraints on the part of the Western allies and Japan in exporting technology to the Soviet Union. "One of our major goals," said Rashish, "has been to eliminate the transfer of Western equipment and technology which contributes significantly to Soviet military capabilities. There is a need to strengthen multilateral control on the transfer of technology." The challenge the Administration faces in seeking these objectives is whether it can be done without allowing East-West trade "to become a source of dissension and division in the alliance," as Rashish put it. (See profile of Lawrence Brady.)

The Administration's tight monetary policies, which have forced up interest rates worldwide, were a source of irritation at the seven-nation Ottawa summit during the summer of 1981. Despite the abhorrence of Reaganomics, Reagan to a large extent prevailed. "The President walked away with the prize," Rashish told the *Washington Post*. "If you read the communique it sounds like a Reagan economic policy statement."

Indeed, through skillful public relations, Reagan managed to divert public attention away from the severe conflicts underlying that summit. But, as Bergsten commented, the success was short-lived: "Whatever pose was adopted by officials, West European silence could not be sustained in the face of hostile public opinion throughout the continent."

FINANCIAL BACKGROUND

During 1980, Hormats received income only from his salary as deputy U.S. trade representative. According to his financial disclosure statement, Hormats has modest stock holdings ($1,000-$5,000) in Pennsylvania Power and Light, American Heliothermal Corp., Beneficial Corp., Federal Energy Corp., First Chicago Corp., Houston Oil and Minerals, Lomas and Nettleton, Solaron Corp., and Solar Control Corp. He has between $5,000-$10,000 in National Municipal Trust, Browning Ferris Inc., and Ensearch Corp.

WHAT OTHERS ARE SAYING ABOUT HIM

- Unlike Rashish, the White House considers Hormats a team player. As *Washington Post* reporter Hobart Rowen described his relationship with the White House: "Hormats impressed President Reagan in personal dealings with his knowledge of foreign leaders and grasp of issues in briefings prior to the Ottawa heads-of state summit."

- Being a survivor of Democratic and Republican administrations, Hormats has maintained friendly relationships with both sides. His predecessor, and former boss Julius Katz, calls him "very knowledgeable and skillful in dealing with

people. . . His instincts lean towards liberal trade and international cooperation—He's in the mainstream of what U.S. [international economic] policy has
been for the last 40 to 50 years.''

- ''Hormats has broadened his scope of knowledge over the years,'' said his first
  boss, C. Fred Bergsten. ''But if you traced his attitude over the last five years or
  so I don't think you could find much difference.''

UNITED NATIONS

JEANE KIRKPATRICK
U.S. AMBASSADOR

RESPONSIBILITY OF OFFICE

Kirkpatrick represents the U.S. government in the U.N.'s
157-member General Assembly and on the 15-member
Security Council. On the Security Council, the U.S. is one of
five member nations with veto power over council actions.

Established at the end of World War II, the United
Nations is the successor to the embattled League of Nations,
which the United States never joined. The world body includes a network of agencies that handle issues ranging from poverty, malnutrition and disease to educational, scientific and cultural exchanges. The U.N. also provides peacekeeping
forces to volatile regions, such as the Middle East.

Although unsuccessful in ending armed conflict between nations during its lifetime, the U.N. has provided a means for bringing public pressure to bear on
nations that defy the codes of international law, and, more recently, a forum for
lesser developed countries to express their grievances against the industrialized
nations.

In 1980, the United States contributed about $866 million of the organization's
$3.6 billion budget.

BACKGROUND

Having bolted from the Democratic Party to socialism and back again, Jeane
Kirkpatrick in the early 1970s settled into a political niche that she and her like-
minded academic colleagues fondly refer to as ''neoconservatism.'' Though still
formally a Democrat, Kirkpatrick's biting anti-Soviet prose and her tender embrace
of right-wing dictators sympathetic to American strategic interests made her attractive to the Reagan foreign policy team.

Kirkpatrick came to Reagan's attention in 1979, while she was a professor at
Georgetown University, by way of an article she wrote for *Commentary*, an anti-
Soviet, pro-Israel journal. The article, ''Dictatorships and Double Standards,''
which snidely criticized Jimmy Carter's human rights policies, appeared just as
Reagan was gathering election-time ammunition to support his policies toward

Latin America and other Third World regions. Carter, she wrote, "continues to behave. . . .not like a man who abhors autocrats but like one who abhors only right-wing autocrats."

In a lengthy argument that was long on polemics and short on substantiation, she terms regimes such as that of former Nicaragua President Anastasio Somoza and the shah of Iran—"traditional rulers in semi-traditional societies" that "were not only anti-Communist, they were positively friendly to the U.S." The Sandinistas in Nicaragua and the Ayatollah Khomeini in Iran (whom she mistakenly characterized as a Soviet client), she argues, are more repressive than their predecessors and, worse, threaten American security.

In phrases that no doubt endeared her to Ronald Reagan, Kirkpatrick discounted "historical forces" as a basis for revolutions in the Third World. Instead, like a truly loyal cold warrior, she pointed to Soviet expansionism as the root. And she affirmed America's duty to intervene in the Third World to protect its interests from this Soviet threat. "A posture of continuous self-abasement and apology vis-a-vis the Third World," she concluded, referring to Carter's foreign policy, "is neither morally necessary nor politically appropriate."   Richard Allen passed the article onto Reagan who, according to Allen, read the piece and commented, "I'm going to borrow some of her elegant phraseology. Who is she?" Reagan promptly dropped Kirkpatrick a fan letter and invited her onto his foreign policy advisory committee in spring, 1980. In later interviews, Kirkpatrick seemed surprised Reagan had read her article, noting that it was a scholarly piece. During the summer months she prepped candidate Reagan for debates on international issues, and in the fall she became part of his foreign policy task force, where she advocated that he support military aid for the El Salvadoran junta. In January, 1981, after her appointment to the U.N., a similar Kirkpatrick piece appeared in *Commentary*, this time focusing on Latin America, in which she said the Carter Administration "brought down the Somoza regime." (She describes the Somoza period as featuring "limited repression and limited opposition.")

The article brought replies such as one from a former National Security Council staffer, who described it as "superficial, polemical, filled with innuendos unbecoming an Ambassador and laden with factual errors." Another reader wrote, "As a scientist I spend quite a lot of time analyzing facts, unfortunately Jeane Kirkpatrick does not. . .Ambassador Kirkpatrick's rewriting of history. . .reminds me of a book I once read by George Orwell."

This is Kirkpatrick's first significant government post. After receiving her master's degree in political science from Columbia University in 1950, she worked as a research assistant to Evron Kirkpatrick in the State Department's Intelligence Research Bureau. They married after she went on to study at the Sorbonne in Paris. She spent most of the next 18 years raising three sons while teaching part time and writing her dissertation. She earned her doctorate from Columbia and wrote the first of her six books while in her mid-40s. Her books include *The New Presidential Elite* (1976), *Political Woman* (1974), *Leader and Vanguard in Mass Society: A Study of Peronist Argentina* (1971), and *Dismantling the Parties: Reflections on Party Reform and Party Decomposition* (1978).

When she met Evron Kirkpatrick he was a ranking Humphreyite, having moved to Washington with Sen. Hubert Humphrey (D-Minn.) after serving as his campaign manager when he ran for mayor of Minneapolis. Jeane Kirkpatrick was also swept into the Humphrey circle, a position that was by no means new to her. Her father, an oil drilling contractor, had been a staunch party Democrat and, though she had flirted with socialism in college, Jeane's political views as a young woman reflected her upbringing.

Her appointment conjures memories of another U.N. ambassador, Daniel Patrick Moynihan, also a neoconservative Democrat and academic who served a Republican administration.

Like many other mainstream Democrats, the Kirkpatricks during the late 1960s grew increasingly dissatisfied with the party, where liberalism was spreading from bread and butter issues to social and cultural values. The anti-war and black power rhetoric of the 1960s and the conspicuous presence of "Jerry Rubin's. . .Gay Lib, and advocates of legalized abortion" at the 1972 convention—as she once wrote—underlined the cultural cleavages between Kirkpatrick's faction, who still clung to flag-waving patriotism and traditional family values, and the most liberal wing of the Democratic Party. To Kirkpatrick and her clique, the nomination of George McGovern was the last straw.

From her scholarly roost, Kirkpatrick was quick to belittle the Democrats' "New Politics," as she called them. In a 1973 *Commentary* article she wrote: "The New Politics has roots in the tradition of civil disobedience. Its dominant style is moral outrage, tinged with violence. Tolerance is less highly regarded than rectitude, compromise is less important than moral consistence. . .The good guy of the old political culture is the law-abiding, hard-working tax-paying provider. The good guy of the new political culture is the outcast (together with his champion.)"

New Politics, she said, grew out of the humanitarianism and liberalism of the New Deal era but "grew and changed almost imperceptibly into a new political ethic that disdained the Old Politics and Old Politicians, preferred the nation's enemy, apologized for rioters, shielded black extremists, understood young revolutionaries. . ."

Offended by the new direction the Democratic Party was taking in the late 1960s and early 1970s, she and other frustrated prominent Democrats— including Henry Jackson, Michael Novak, Austin Ranney, Daniel Pat Moynihan and Ben Wattenberg founded the Coalition for a Democratic Majority and later earned the label "neoconservative." "We affirmed the validity of the American dream and the morality of the American society," she wrote in 1979. "They [the McGovern wing] adopted the characterizations of intellectuals. . .who described the U.S. as a sick society drunk on technology and materialism."

But she remained a Democrat, and even supported Jimmy Carter, though she rapidly grew discouraged with his policies, and publicly attacked his foreign policies. Astonishingly, she still considers herself a "liberal" on domestic issues: "I'm very pro-labor. I'm very pro-union. Guns leave me pretty cold, too," she said in a 1980 interview. In a 1979 article that appeared in a Republican magazine she explained that she refused to become a Republican because the party was insensitive to the goals of the welfare state: "The problem is that the Republican Party has not articulated any inclusive vision of the public good that reflects concern for the well-being of the whole community." Yet she has chosen to serve an Administration that represents an extreme version of what she dislikes in Republicans.

Though today she talks about the "extreme of women's liberation fervor," Kirkpatrick's earlier writings have ardent feminist strains. In a 1974 study of women in public office, *Political Woman*, a work commissioned by the Center for American Women and Politics at Rutgers University, Kirkpatrick, in examining the dearth of women in political office concluded that "both a cultural and social revolution is required before women achieve de facto political equality."

For example, she wrote, "it would be necessary to abandon the notion, still supported by some influential religious denominations, that men are the natural governors of society, that women are unfit for political (or religious or social) leadership, that men are inherently better suited to authoritative positions either because they are more rational and/or less emotional and/or more stable and/or better able to face forceful challenges.

"It would be necessary to abandon these beliefs as well: that there is something ineffably incompatible between femininity and the pursuit of power, that feminine women neither desire or seek power, that femininity is inexorably associated with the submissiveness of female to male, that, in a woman, the desire for power is a signal of alienation from her true identity, that women who participate in power processes are, in fact, unfeminine, that women are (and should be) less assertive, persistent and competitive, more private and less likely to engage in public affairs than men, that women will devote themselves largely to the home and family, that children fare better if cared for by a full-time natural mother, that normal women will find their principal satisfaction in family roles. . .that the satisfactions available from the dutiful performance of these roles will be adequate to a lifetime, and that for all these reasons women will not develop the skills and careers most closely associated with politics."

She added that sexual discrimination in law employment practices, education, and elsewhere is "intolerable," and said the government should appoint more women to "conspicuous and high positions." Government policy, she said, can "help women win equal access to the professions which are mostly closely related to politics by continuing to refuse public support to universities and related institutions that discriminate against girls and women." However, she stopped short of support for affirmative action quotas, which, she said, sacrifice other values such as equal opportunity.

A political scientist by training, Kirkpatrick has written primarily on American party politics. Her only major study on Third World issues was a book on Peronist Argentina titled *Leader and Vanguard in Mass Society*, in which she characterized the Peronist movement as "a clear-cut example of a Caesarist movement in a technologically advanced society." In this early work can be found the seeds of the distinctions she draws today between authoritarianism (right-wing dictatorships) and totalitarianism (left-wing dictatorships). She calls Peronism "neither democratic nor totalitarian. . .(but) can be conceived as a continuation of traditional Latin politics under conditions of mass society." Kirkpatrick has always been a cerebral sort. As a 10-year-old in Duncan, Oklahoma, she saved her allowance to buy a thesaurus and she says she taught herself to read. After receiving an A.A. at Stephens College in 1946 and an A.B. at Barnard College in 1948 she began work on her master's degree in political science at Columbia University, which she received in 1950. She received a Ph.D. from Columbia 18 years later. Even as an envoy to the U.N. she maintains the demeanor of a skeptic scholar. With perpetually raised eyebrows and a sharp tongue, she is ever ready to indulge in polemics. She has also been known to lecture delegates, and congressmen, as if they were her pupils.

Yet she is far from detached. During the 1970s she regularly used scholarly journals to rail against political antagonists. And she has been an active resident scholar at the American Enterprise Institute (AEI), a powerful and influential "educational" institution funded by major corporations that provided many of Reagan's officials.

Before her appointment, Kirkpatrick, in addition to her position at AEI, was a Georgetown University Leavy professor and a member of Georgetown's Center for

Strategic and International Studies. She was on the board of trustees for the Robert
A. Taft Institute of Government in New York; and a board member of the hawkish
Committee for the Free World and Committee on the Present Danger, the Founda-
tion for Democratic Education, Inc. and the Ethics and Public Policy Center. She is
also a member of the International Political Science Association and the American
Political Science Association, which her husband, Evron, heads.

Born November 19, 1926 in Duncan, Oklahoma, Kirkpatrick is married with
three children.

MAJOR ISSUES

- Kirkpatrick has used her power on the Security Council to protect South Africa
  from U.N. sanctions, leading to concern that the country will feel free to use
  military force to back its racial policies.

- Similarly, Kirkpatrick has protected Israel from U.N. imposed sanctions
  encouraging the hardliners within that government.

- Kirkpatrick's embrace of South Africa, which has angered black African
  nations as well as members of Congress, and of notorious human rights
  violators in Latin America is a sharp departure from previous American policy.

- Following up on threats by Kirkpatrick, the Administration has attempted,
  and convinced Congress in some cases, to cut U.S. funding of U.N. agencies to
  which it ideologically objects.

- Kirkpatrick's acerbic style is alienating many U.N. delegates and angering
  members of Congress.

With Kirkpatrick wielding the U.S. veto on the Security Council, South Africa
and Israel both can count on strong protection against the sanctions the U.N. has
imposed on them in recent years. Though many Congressional liberals conscious of
the Jewish vote are relieved that Israel, a favorite whipping post of the Third World
bloc, is being defended, they are alarmed by American support of South Africa.

But an overriding concern is that this American shelter has given South Africa
and Israel license to employ military force against their enemies without fear of
international repudiation. Both countries have launched military attacks in 1981;
neither was substantially punished by the world body after Kirkpatrick intervened.
In fact, her most impressive diplomatic victories that year were her efforts to
moderate U.N. resolutions condemning the actions of South Africa and Israel.

Kirkpatrick set the tone for her tenure at the U.N. during her maiden speech
when she reproached delegates who had voted to deny South Africa a seat in the
General Assembly. In February, 1981, when South Africa sentenced to death three
members of the black liberationist African National Congress for their roles in a
bank and police station raid, Kirkpatrick managed to block what would have been a
call for amnesty for three "freedom fighters" in favor of a bland resolution expressing concern for the lives of the three young men.

Breaking a 19-year custom—which served as a symbol of disapproval of South
Africa's white-ruled apartheid system—Kirkpatrick the following month met with
top military intelligence officers from South Africa. "My experience as a scholar
leads me to believe that the best way to approach a problem is to listen to diverse
views," she said of the meeting.

After the meeting, the Congressional Black Caucus called for Kirkpatrick's resignation. "We think it was a dangerous precedent to set," said caucus spokesman Ronn Nichols. "It indicates the Reagan Administration's desire to open dialogue with the South African government in the face of its racist apartheid policies."

Later, after abstaining from a vote in September, 1981 condemning South Africa for its invasion of Angola, Kirkpatrick told the press: "The United States has diplomatic relations with South Africa, let's be perfectly clear about that. South Africa's political system has some good elements in it. It's a democracy for whites, and a dictatorship for blacks. We should work through peaceful means to maximize our values."

Upon assuming office, Kirkpatrick stated that she "will do everything I can to prevent [anti-Israel] resolutions and policies from being adopted." She has proven herself an ardent and moderately successful Israeli defender in the international forum. Kirkpatrick says she is a firm supporter of the Camp David peace accords, but her sympathies in the Mideast conflict are clear. When she was asked what the U.S. plans to do to safeguard the rights of Arabs in the territories occupied by Israel she replied: "I don't call them 'occupied territories,' you see. I call them the West Bank."

Even critics of Reagan's foreign policy on Capitol Hill applaud Kirkpatrick's effort to stem the tide of gratuitous U.N. resolutions attacking Israel that inevitably flow out of the General Assembly every year. But there is also concern that she is providing too large an umbrella for Israeli actions, giving hardliners in the Israeli government a license to break international law without fear of reproach.

When a Security Council resolution expressing condolences to the Nigerian government for the deaths of three of its soldiers in the U.N. peacekeeping force in Lebanon turned into an anti-Israel declaration, Kirkpatrick stood firm until all selective finger-pointing at Israel was dropped. After the incident a French TV documentary dubbed her "Reagan's Iron Lady."

After Israel bombed Iraq's nuclear reactor in 1981, Kirkpatrick managed to engineer a compromise that miraculously avoided sanctions against Israel. During an hours-long session with the Iraqi foreign minister in then Secretary General Kurt Waldheim's office she produced a final resolution, adopted unanimously by the Security Council, that was no more than a hand slap. The statement "strongly condemned" the attack as a violation of the U.N. charter and called upon Israel to "refrain in the future from any such acts or threats." Iraq, the Security Council stated, was entitled to "appropriate redress for the destructions it has suffered."

But even that mild reprimand was more than Kirkpatrick could bear. A widely circulated press photo showed her wearily indicating her vote supporting the resolution—her hand flopped in the air, her elbow unable to make it off the table, her shoulders slumped in despair. After voting she leaned back in her chair and sighed: "I feel sick."

Later, in early 1982, Kirkpatrick vetoed a Security Council resolution that proposed unspecified measures to chastise Israel for its annexation of the Golan Heights. She also opposed a resolution in the General Assembly that urged member nations to "cease forthwith individually and collectively all dealings with Israel in order to totally isolate it in all fields." Besides calling the resolution "profoundly objectionable," Kirkpatrick, in a typical remark, said it was "filled with mischief."

Under the Reagan Administration, the words *human rights* have taken on a new meaning, and Kirkpatrick has been one of the chief architects of the revised definition. Now right-wing regimes espousing anti-communist dogma are considered "authoritarian,"—less repressive and worthy of U.S. support; while leftists, such as the Sandinistas in Nicaragua are termed "totalitarian," and have been ostracized by the Reagan Administration. That distinction has prompted human rights activists such as former Assistant Secretary of State Patricia Derian to bubble with anger. "What the hell is 'moderately repressive'—that you only torture half of the people, that you only do summary executions now and then?" Derian asked during a TV interview in responding to Kirkpatrick's philosophy. "The idea that we must somehow stand closer to dictators—people who are cruel to their people is absurd."

In a murky article in a 1981 issue of *World Affairs*, and in a speech before the Council on Foreign Relations, Kirkpatrick attacked the Carter Administration's human rights policy as one of "rationalism and purism, of private interest and public vices." She has said the proposed expansion of the U.N. Universal Declaration of Human Rights "took on the character of a letter to Santa Claus" claiming as universal "every political, economic, and social right yet conceived."

While traveling through Latin America in 1981 Kirkpatrick met with Chilean leader General Augusto Pinochet, high on the list of human rights violators maintained by groups such as Amnesty International, and at a news conference in Santiago described her conversation with him as "most pleasant." She also expressed the Reagan Administration's desire to "fully normalize our relations with Chile." The President of the Chilean Commission for Human Rights, Jaime Castillo Velasco, was among several dissidents who were forced into exile after Kirkpatrick's visit when they signed a letter protesting the jailing of labor leaders. Castillo said Kirkpatrick's overtures had emboldened the military government to crack down on dissidents.

Kirkpatrick refused to meet with human rights activists in either Chile or Argentina during her visit, sending aides instead. Castillo finally obtained a meeting with Kirkpatrick in New York after his exile. He described their conversation as "candid and cordial."

Kirkpatrick has repeatedly threatened to revoke U.S. contributions to specific U.N. agencies that run counter to Reagan Administration ideology. "[A]gencies which engage in mischievous ideological struggle against the fundamental principle of the United States and its friends should know that the patience of the American people is running very thin," she said during her confirmation hearing. The State Department has followed up on that threat by revoking, or attempting to revoke, funding from several voluntary programs, including:

- Cutting off a U.S. contribution of $500,000 to the Voluntary Fund for the U.N. Decade for Women. The fund provides development seed money for the poorest of the poor, the 40 least developed countries. Although the fund is now connected to the U.N. Decade for Women in name only, the Administration cut off funding because of what it considered a anti-Israel, pro-Palestinian Liberation Organization stance of the mid-decade conference. No money was restored by Congress.

- Cutting off the $400,000 U.S. contribution to the U.N. Trust Fund on South Africa, which provides money for legal assistance to victims of apartheid. Congress, however, restored the funding.

- Slashing the U.S. contribution to the U.N. Environment Program, claiming that UNEP had discriminated against Israeli contractors when planning for its expanded facilities. Congress restored the $7.85 million appropriation.

- Zeroing out funding for the U.N. Institute for Training and Research, which trains third world diplomats just beginning service. Congress also restored that money.

- Cutting out funding for the U.N. Fellow Program, which Congress restored.

In addition, the U.S. voted against any funding increase for the U.N. Food and Agriculture Organization. The U.S. has objected to what it calls the confrontational rhetoric of the agency, and it has taken issue with the agency's goal of providing a "safety net" of food assistance to poor nations—a plan the Administration says perpetuates inappropriate agricultural policies. "I am concerned. . .that she would favor withdrawal of U.S. financial support from the specialized agencies of the United Nations," said Sen. Joseph Biden (D-Del.), a member of the Committee on Foreign Relations. "Such a carrot and stick approach to our diplomatic seat at the United Nations may return the U.S. to an era of contentious squabbling with other nations, that has proved neither productive nor effective in pursing our interests and foreign policy objectives."

Attempts by the developing countries to open discussions on a program to transfer wealth from the rich to poor nations through large increases in foreign aid, global cartels, and other means have met sharp resistance from the Reagan Administration. Inside the U.N. Kirkpatrick is holding the defensive line. When the developing countries in fall, 1981 released a blueprint on opening such talks, Kirkpatrick said the plan ran "completely contrary" to the position of the Reagan Administration. The Administration has objected to any such discussions taking place in a forum such as the General Assembly, where the one-nation, one-vote rule would give the Third World bloc an overwhelming majority. (See profile of Robert Hormats.)

Although the Third World's recent proposal called for a one-nation, one vote conference of all nations that would make decisions on the "basis of consensus," the U.S. is still fearful of being publicly isolated in disagreements. Instead the U.S. prefers forums such as the International Monetary Fund or the World Bank, where it predominates by virtue of its financial weight. Kirkpatrick, acting as chief negotiator for the industrialized nations, will seek a compromise with the representative of the 120 developing nations, Mohammed Bedjaoui of Algeria.

But to the U.N. delegates, objectionable actions taken by Kirkpatrick over the past year pale in comparison to her style, which has been labeled "professorial," "condescending," and "acerbic." Reporters have left press conferences with the feeling that they had just attended a college lecture. She has upbraided black African nations for wanting to pass resolutions condemning South Africa. At one meeting of several Third World delegates in her office, Kirkpatrick reportedly got up and left before they had finished speaking. She has publicly decried the rhetoric commonly used by world delegates, calling it imprecise, overblown or "filled with mischief."

In October, 1981, when a group of Third World countries released a document accusing the United States of threatening world peace and prosperity, she promptly sent a letter to 40 of those nations—those she considered American friends—and asked them to explain their support for the document, which she called a pack of "base lies and malicious attacks upon the good name of the United States," full of "vicious and erroneous language."

Her tone in the letter was that of an incredulous school teacher: "Your excellency, I think you no more believe these vicious lies than I do and I do not believe they are an accurate reflection of your Government's outlook. And yet what are we to think when your Government joins in such charges, for that is what you have done in failing to disassociate yourself from them.''

Neither has she minced words with congressmen. At one point Rep. Don Bonker's (D-Wash.) Subcommittee on Human Rights and International Organizations sent her a letter commending her for a human rights speech in which she said the Soviet Union as well as right-wing regimes should be pointed up as a violator. The letter, however, gently pointed out the Administration's own contradictory policies on human rights. Kirkpatrick subsequently zipped off a stinging reply to Bonker and his committee. The closing salutation, which did little to mitigate the tone of her letter, was almost humorous: "With Best Wishes for a Merry Christmas and a Happy New Year.''

She has also shocked observers with complaints about her job, in one interview saying she'd rather "have more time for contemplative pursuits.'' When Bonker's subcommittee asked her to present a short synopsis on current U.S. policy at the U.N. she instead launched into a lengthy tirade about her busy work schedule.

Kirkpatrick has surrounded herself with aides of similar foreign policy persuasion. Her chief counselor, Carl Gershman, is former head of the militantly anti-communist Social Democrats-USA and was a strong supporter of South Africa-backed Unita leader Jonas Savimbi. Her ambassador to the economic and social section, Jose Sorzano, is a staunchly conservative refugee from Castro's Cuba. Her deputy, Charles Lichenstein, is a former CIA officer and was a special assistant to both Nixon and Ford. Joe Shattan, her speechwriter and researcher, and a specialist on Soviet-Egyptian relations, is former policy director of the Coalition for a Democratic Majority. And Marc Plattner, her economic adviser, is a neoconservative who has frequently attacked the left in his writings. Kirkpatrick often sends her deputies to sit in for her at the General Assembly.

During a speech before the American Legion in early 1982, Kirkpatrick called the United Nations "a very dismal show'' that worsens conflicts rather than resolving them. "Conflicts, rather than being solved there, are in fact polarized, extended and exacerbated. They are much harder to solve rather than easier to solve, generally speaking.'' Kirkpatrick's acerbic style has already gone a long way in exacerbating that polarization.

FINANCIAL BACKGROUND

According to her financial disclosure statement, Kirkpatrick received a $35,125 salary from the American Enterprise Institute and a $39,135 salary from Georgetown University. She and her husband have joint savings accounts that total as much as $250,000.

WHAT OTHERS ARE SAYING ABOUT HER

- "The criticism around her has been more over her style than substantive issues,'' said a House aide who works on U.N. issues. "She's arrogant and condescending.''

- Said one journalist who covers the United Nations: "She acts like a tired and tenured professor that no longer has to work at it. She doesn't call up any animosity, but one feels a certain sdness or pity for her. . .She's in way over her head.''

- *Washington Post Magazine* writer James Conaway commented that Kirkpatrick "seems to have replaced Richard Allen in the Administration as the resident intellectual on foreign policy.''

AGENCY FOR INTERNATIONAL DEVELOPMENT

M. PETER MCPHERSON
ADMINISTRATOR

RESPONSIBILITY OF OFFICE

Established in 1961, AID administers most of the government's foreign economic assistance programs. It is considered the "economic arm of the State Department," and as one AID brochure put it, "a tool of U.S. foreign policy."

AID divides its programs into two general categories—development assistance targeted at the poorest countries and "Economic Support Fund" aid earmarked for countries "whose well-being is important to the security of the United States." (Israel and Egypt receive over half the aid in the latter program.) The distinction is actually somewhat artificial: security and political considerations are rarely excluded from assistance decisions. In 1979, AID was taken out of the State Department and placed under an independent agency, the International Development Cooperation Agency (IDCA), along with other international assistance programs "to more effectively integrate the various foreign assistance organizations' policies into a more central body." The director of IDCA, on paper at least, reports directly to the President.

AID operated with a budget of $4.4 billion and 5,251 employees in 1982.

BACKGROUND

The man Reagan appointed to head AID has served as general counsel for the Reagan transition team, helping to hire other Reagan appointees. Before this, McPherson directed the Washington office of an Ohio-based law firm, Vorys, Sater, Seymour and Pease, specializing in international and corporate tax issues.

McPherson lobbied on tax issues for both the International Agricultural Development Service (IADS) which works with Third World countries on agricultural issues, and the Ohio Association of Manufacturers. IADS was established by the Rockefeller Foundation in 1975 and still receives its core funding from the foundation. In 1980, IADS received $112,000 from AID. According to IADS President Colin McClung, McPherson worked on legislation regarding taxation of Americans working overseas for non-profit institutions.

In the mid-1970s, McPherson served as special assistant to President Ford, assisting in the selection of presidential appointees—including ambassadors and judges. Earlier he worked for the Internal Revenue Service, as an international corporate tax law specialist.

McPherson attributes his interest in foreign development to his experience as a Peace Corps volunteer in Peru. "It was through the Corps that I developed an international perspective," he said recently. "Without that, it's unlikely I would be AID administrator today." McPherson also worked in AID's private enterprise office in Lima, Peru.

From 1977-80, McPherson was a member of the presidential Board for International Food and Agricultural Development (BIFAD), an AID advisory body on agricultural research and training. McPherson was a member of the board's Joint Committee on Agricultural Development, which brought together university, corporate, congressional, and AID officials. He is remembered as an active member of the board.

McPherson has a "down home" manner common to several Reagan officials. At a recent press conference he referred several times to his father, a Midwestern farmer, to lend credence to his views that Third World countries have to increase prices paid to farmers: "Farmers have to get more profits," he said, "if they're going to produce more."

McPherson was born on October 27, 1940 in Grand Rapids, Michigan. He is married, with two sons.

MAJOR ISSUES

- Under McPherson, AID will become more directly tied to U.S. foreign policy, and particularly to the promotion of U.S. exports, than ever before.

- Though he had private doubts, McPherson did not challenge the White House's decision to cast the only vote against the proposed World Health Organization code for marketing infant formula.

- McPherson has established a Bureau of Private Enterprise and is steering AID into direct export assistance functions for U.S. multinationals. One grant to the Philippines was awarded only on the condition that a U.S. firm receive the contract it supported.

AID primarily serves two functions: it helps U.S. corporations invest and trade in the Third World, and it attempts to snuff out radical change in the Third World by lending money for economic advancement and population control.

"The money ends up in U.S. pockets," says the AID biweekly news report, *World Development Letter*, explaining that, "a large percentage of money spent has gone to U.S. business and Americans for goods or services they render Third World countries."

McPherson acknowledged this corporate feature of AID lending in an article entitled "Altruism Pays Dividends," which appeared in *Enterprise*, a magazine of the National Association of Manufacturers. Foreign aid, McPherson wrote, "creates new markets for U.S. exports (or expands existing ones). Ninety percent of U.S. development loans comes back to the nation in the form of new or increased exports."

The other function of AID—political stabilization—is also addressed in the agency's *World Development Letter*. "Extreme poverty, overpopulation, environment degradation, disease and periodic famine are still the lot" in most Third World countries, the newsletter notes. "These conditions breed increasing violence, riots, terrorism, urban guerilla warfare and border strife." Economic aid is necessary to alleviate these problems that spill over into the United States; the newsletter suggests in a chauvinistic tone: "In our own backyard we have already felt the impact of Third World overpopulation and poverty in the massive immigration of Latin Americans into the United States."

Although AID's assistance has never been granted solely on the basis of need, under the Reagan Administration its use as a foreign policy tool is likely to be more "blunt" than ever before, as one congressional aide put it. "We're putting more emphasis than ever on encouraging policy changes in governments [we give aid to]," acknowledges McPherson.

With these new changes, AID's priorities will transfer from "aid for the poorest of the poor to aid for entrepreneurial corporations to create markets in these countries," the aide said.

At his confirmation hearing, McPherson laid out some change in emphasis he planned to institute at AID:

> I think, that we are interested in concentrating resources in significant targets of opportunity. Clearly, Jamaica and Zimbabwe are countries on which we need to concentrate. If we could help significant economic development in Jamaica, it would have political and economic impacts throughout the Caribbean, and probably would flow over to Central America as well. [The conservative business-oriented administration of Edward Seaga, which replaced a socialist government in Jamaica, has been warmly supported by the Reagan Administration.]

The creation of IDCA under the Carter Administration was seen as a move to "de-politicize" AID somewhat, by removing it from the immediate orbit of the State Department. But IDCA, as one international development official said, "exists only on paper right now."

And in any case, McPherson, who has also been appointed the acting director of IDCA, has promised to consult carefully with Secretary of State Alexander Haig. As he said at his confirmation hearing: "As you know, IDCA legally reports to the President of the United States. But, as a practical matter, there is going to be, and already has begun, a careful coordination between AID and the Secretary of State. I had a lengthy and most productive discussion with the Secretary a week ago Tuesday. It is his interest that I report to him."

To some, McPherson may be simply formalizing a relationship that has guided AID activities in the past. "That's not a great departure," Eugene N. Babb, the agency's former top agricultural development official told us. "Carter said, 'If you don't have a good human rights record, we're not going to give you aid.' The Republicans say, 'If you don't agree with our kind of [economic] policies we won't give you aid.'"

Babb resigned from AID in May, 1981 along with Dr. Stephen Joseph, the agency's top heath official, in protest of the Administration's "no" vote on the World Health Organization's (WHO) proposed code for marketing infant formula. The U.S. was the only nation to vote against the code, which was strongly opposed by the baby-food industry and the Grocery Manufacturers of America. AID, along with the State Department and the Department of Health and Human Services, sets U.S. policy on WHO issues.

Babb said he discussed his opposition to the "no" vote several times with McPherson. "He was well aware of our position and he was basically in agreement with us," Babb said. "The pressure for a no vote was coming from the White House." According to Babb, McPherson at one point tried to get an abstention instead of a vote against the code, "but the White House demanded a no vote." In the end, McPherson acceded to the White House's decision.

In general, McPherson has said, he plans to steer AID programs along the course set by the Administration's domestic policies—which means increased reliance on private business. "This administration is committed to increased opportunities for the private sector in AID programs," he said.

Toward that end, he has established a new Bureau for Private Enterprise and named as its head Elise R.W. DuPont, wife of Delaware Governor Pierre S. DuPont. For the past few years she has been a corporate lawyer, and her resume reveals no particular involvement with development activities. "Before I resigned," said Babb, "I had a number of meetings with Elise. She was very noncommittal. She had no clear idea of what she wanted to do or what the Administration wanted to do."

But McPherson has since laid out in greater detail what the increased reliance on business will mean. "Our new emphasis seeks a partnership of government and the private sector in the total development process—not just the involvement at the implementation stage," he said in congressional testimony.

In one case, AID extended a $300,000 grant to the Philippines to help pay for a feasibility study on the construction of a new steel mill on the condition that "a U.S. firm be awarded the feasibility study contract." U.S. Steel not only received the contract, McPherson explained, "but also an additional $4.8 million contract from the government of the Philippines."

McPherson has moved AID into a more direct export assistance role on other fronts. In what he called "a departure from tradition" AID is diverting commodity credits allocated to Egypt to help that country purchase hydroelectric equipment from Allis Chalmers. As McPherson noted in a speech to a business group that "represents an extension of the concept of U.S. foreign assistance."

In his first months at AID, McPherson has also restated his longexpressed desire to increase the role of private voluntary organizations, such as religious charities, in AID programs.

AID's 1982 budget was cut by the Administration from the $4.8 billion proposed by the Carter Administration to $4.4 billion. Hard hit by the cuts was the agency's central office; congressional aides expect McPherson to delegate more decision-making power to the field offices. For 1983, the Administration has proposed a $300 million increase.

Overall, one Democratic House aide said, McPherson has been something of a pleasant surprise. "Given the present Administration, given their foreign policy goals, given their total disregard for the poor, the appointment of McPherson is a hell of a lot better than what we could have gotten."

FINANCIAL BACKGROUND

McPherson earned $81,000 from his law partnership in 1980. His financial statement indicates no significant investments.

WHAT OTHERS ARE SAYING ABOUT HIM

- Said David Kinley of the Institute for Food and Development Policy, "I heard Mr. McPherson speak last January. He emphasized strongly that the private sector had a major role to play in the developing countries, and that AID should help to facilitate that. But I disagree. There are inherent dangers in allowing multinational corporations and agribusinesses to get involved to a greater degree in the food systems of developing nations. Inappropriate technology, greater disparity between the rich and the poor, all work to create more, rather than less, obstacles to local independence and growth."

- "Mr. McPherson is a strong advocate for international aid. He's interested and active. He quickly comes to grips with the issues. He's effective. He sees a need to assist developing countries. He has a wide range of contacts and friends in the White House. He's worked under two different terms, two different presidents," said Fred Johnson a BIFAD agricultural economist.

- Eugene Babb, who knew McPherson while he served on BIFAD, said McPherson "will adhere to the party line" but that "He has a good knowledge of development and he worked at the grass roots, so he has strong humanitarian instincts in helping people in the Third World." On development issues, Babb said, "I would call McPherson a liberal. I think the man is a closet liberal within the Administration."

CENTRAL INTELLIGENCE AGENCY

WILLIAM CASEY
DIRECTOR OF CENTRAL INTELLIGENCE

RESPONSIBILITY OF OFFICE

The CIA was established by the National Security Act of 1947 to provide the U.S. with a means of objective fact-gathering to bolster vital national security interests. Since its inception it has played a major role in U.S. foreign policy, but often not as the objective policy tool originally envisioned.

As director of the CIA, Casey is responsible for providing an overall intelligence gathering and disseminating service for government departments, collecting and disseminating foreign intelligence, "including information not otherwise obtainable," conducting counterintelligence activities outside the U.S., and in an elastic clause which has been used to expand CIA authority, "performing such other functions. . .related to intelligence affecting the national security. . ." In the 1947 Act the CIA was explicitly forbidden from operating within the U.S. unless in conjunction with the FBI and with the express consent of the attorney general. But as congressional committees revealed in the 1970s, the CIA has often been guilty of abuse of power.

The CIA's budget and personnel figures are kept secret, but it is certain that both have received sizeable increases since the Reagan Administration took office.

BACKGROUND

William Casey was sitting in his spacious corner office in the Executive Office Building, just a few yards from the White House. He looked prosperous in a finely-cut, expensive, suit and a green silk tie. Casey had just arrived from meetings at the

Pentagon. Outside, waiting in his anteroom was strategic arms negotiator General Edward Rowny, who had made the cross-town trip from the State Department to see him. On the phone was Charles Percy, chairman of the Senate Foreign Relations Committee. In a short while Casey was due in the Situation Room for a meeting of the National Security Council. Then, lunch at the Metropolitan Club.

After a long and lucrative career, Casey had arrived at the very pinnacle of power in Washington. Generals came to his office; powerful senators sought his counsel and support. Casey had held other high government posts, made a fortune as a Wall Street lawyer, and successfully steered Ronald Reagan's presidential campaign to victory—he had directed economic intelligence for the Office of Strategic Services (OSS) during World War II. He had a lot to be proud of. So we asked him what he considered the greatest triumph in his long career. He replied with a chuckle: "If I get out alive. . . After you've been shot down. . . I'd say the thrill is to be still here."

It was almost an unconsciously revealing answer. For each of the high government posts that Casey proudly displays on his resume—chairman of the Securities and Exchange Commission (SEC), undersecretary of State for economic affairs, Export-Import Bank president—Casey has had to suffer through extensive confirmation hearings in which his previous business dealings and government actions were critically examined. There has been plenty to examine: Casey has been involved in a number of civil suits charging him with misleading investors or plagiarizing written material; his activities at the SEC during the Watergate era raised questions—even his testimony at those hearings became an issue as other facts were uncovered.

Casey is almost universally described as quick, sharp and even brilliant by those who work with him. CIA General Counsel Stanley Sporkin, who also worked with Casey at the SEC, calls him "brilliant, ballsy, gutsy" and marvels at his ability to work long hours and dissect problems.

And Casey has never been hesitant to wade into controversy. When Richard Nixon was trying to drum up support for his proposed anti-ballistic missile (ABM) system, Casey founded a Citizens Committee for Peace with Security which backed the plan by taking out large newspaper advertisements around the country—which claimed that a public poll showed overwhelming support for the ABM. Later it was revealed that 55 of the ad's 344 signers had defense industry connections. The manner in which the poll was taken was subsequently criticized by six past presidents of the American Association for Public Opinion Research. Asked about the claim at his SEC confirmation hearing, Casey said: "The use of headlines to attract attention and dramatize the thrust of the statement is rather commonly accepted in American society." Soon after the ad appeared, Nixon appointed Casey to the advisory committee of the Arms Control and Disarmament Agency.

He's also been willing to bend with the times. In his only bid for electoral office, Casey ran as a liberal Republican, stating flatly, "I am not a conservative." At the time, Casey was challenging conservative Steven B. Derounian for the 1966 Republican nomination for the third congressional district in New York. When Barry Goldwater and William Buckley expressed astonishment at Casey's assertions, Casey shot back: "Derounian. . .and his right-wing friends have cooked-up a Birch-like smear. . ." (Buckley pointed out that James Lester Wick, the late editor and publisher of the right-wing *Human Events* had chosen Casey as the executor and trustee of his estate after looking for "the most conservative lawyer in the United States." But Buckley and Casey have patched things up; at the 25th anniversary party for *National Review*, Casey took noisy umbrage at *60 Minutes* reporter

Morley Safer's suggestion that there was a "good Bill Buckley and. . .[a] bad Bill Buckley." Sitting on a couch with Henry Kissinger, Casey interrupted Safer's questioning of Kissinger and blurted: "What about—what about—what about the bad—what about the bad Dan Rather? And what about the bad, who's that guy, Mike Wallace? Bad Bill Buckley!")

Today, Casey talks disparagingly of economic relations with the Soviet Union. "One thing we've done on my watch, we've pulled together a composite, a full picture of the degree to which the increasing power and sophistication of the Soviets weaponry—which has required us to think about spending $50 billion for new missile systems and planes and everything else—the extent to which that has derived from their acquisition of our technology," he told us. "The accuracy above all—the MIRVing of the weapons—has come from our equipment. Not that the Soviets mightn't have gotten it at some point, but they got it a lot faster and a lot cheaper. They got a free ride on our R&D to a great extent. It's kind of dumb, costly and dangerous to us."

But while serving as undersecretary of State in the halcyon days of detente, Casey had a different message. In an April 27, 1972 address to a conference on East-West trade at the University of Georgia law school, Casey said, "We are seeking to build and expand East-West trade as a pivotal element in a structure of peace. We see economic interdependence as a great force for peace." Casey went on to advocate the development of "cooperative" energy projects of the kind the Reagan Administration is today frantically pressuring Western European nations to abandon. (The Administration has spent months unsuccessfully trying to persuade its European allies not to build a pipeline to transport Siberian natural gas.) "Different countries have different needs and different types of natural resources to develop. This presents the opportunity for development projects along cooperative lines. *Examples are gas companies going in to build pipelines and liquefaction and shipping facilities*. . .U.S. firms with technology, equipment, and markets, have the opportunity to work on large aggregations of ores, oil and gas deposits, and great forest resources. Projects of this kind can contribute to Soviet needs and bring out products that satisfy outside. . .requirements," Casey said. (Emphasis added.)

In some ways, Casey has been preparing his entire adult life for this job. He has long links to the intelligence community. During World War II, Casey served as an assistant to David Bruce, one of the founders of the OSS, where he earned a Bronze Star for his work organizing French resistance actions supporting the Normandy invasion. In 1944, he became chief of American Secret Intelligence Operations in Europe. After the war, he served as associate general counsel of the Marshall Plan, and he was there at the birth of the CIA. "I really wasn't, in a direct sense, active in the founding of the CIA," Casey said in an interview. "However, I was secretary to a committee of the OSS in London which General [Wild Bill] Donovan [head of the OSS] asked to study the European intelligence agencies with a view to learning and recommending what kind of a permanent intelligence agency might be established in the United States and I did a report on that and as a result of that I worked with General Donovan in preparing his recommendation to President Roosevelt and the Joint Chiefs of Staff about the establishment of a permanent U.S. intelligence agency. And that was during the war, '44. Then a little later, there was a committee formed under the Truman Administration to study and formulate recommendations on how the United States should operate a clandestine intelligence service. I was one of five members of that committee and I worked on that for four or five months. And then later on there was a committee [that] did another report which really was the substantive foundation for the CIA and then the legislative process started." The CIA now, Casey added, "is much larger than any of us at that time had envisioned. It's evolved into much more because at the time most of us didn't envision the kind of technical capabilities that have been developed over the years."

As a private attorney and the author and editor of business manuals which advised readers *How to Build and Preserve Executive Wealth* and similar pursuits, Casey kept up his links to the intelligence world. In 1962, Casey was a founding director of the National Strategy Information Center, a right-wing group with ties to the CIA that regularly issues warnings that "America is in fact becoming a second class military power," as co-founder Frank Barnett put it in 1971. In 1974, he served on the Murphy Commission which looked at U.S. foreign policy-making; two years later President Ford appointed Casey to the President's Foreign Intelligence Advisory Board, where he worked with Lionel Olmer, now undersecretary of Commerce. (See Olmer profile.) There, Casey focused on the board's recommendation that the CIA undertake a "competitive analysis" of Soviet strength. The subsequent "Team B" analysis commissioned by then-CIA director George Bush doubled estimates of Soviet military spending. (Members of Team B included Paul Nitze and Richard Pipes, now the Soviet specialist at the National Security Council.) At his CIA confirmation hearing, Casey said that Team B "demonstrated the value of some form of competitive analysis."

Casey's confirmation hearing for the post of SEC chairman offered a preview not so much for his confirmation hearings for the CIA position, but for the subsequent investigation of his financial dealings. As in the summer of 1981, more information about Casey's financial dealings seeped out as the hearings went on. Sen. Adlai Sevenson (D-Ill.) questioned a merger that a company founded by Casey completed in Louisiana, rather than California (which was the alternative), to avoid the jurisdiction of the Commissioner of Corporations of California. The commissioner had sought to hold a public hearing, to inquire if the terms were fair to all stockholders. Casey replied: "I do not think there's anything I can find to criticize if grown-up men decide they want to consummate a transaction quickly and they do not need the protective services of the California securities commission."

Casey was also asked about an October, 1961 prospectus written for Advancement Devices, Inc., where he was chairman. Advancement Devices was offering the stock to repay $100,000 that Casey had loaned to the company. The letter was written by Charles J. Thornton, who had once been barred by the SEC from working in the securities industry. Casey acknowledged that the letter was "an outrageous prospectus." Casey settled out of court for $8,000 with one investor who lost his $10,000 investment when the company went bankrupt less than a year later.

But Casey's later performance was most accurately presaged by his presentation of the facts surrounding a plagiarism case in which he had been involved a decade earlier. In the case, Casey agreed to a $20,500 settlement with Harry Fields, an author who charged Casey was plagiarizing two and one-half pages of a manuscript on tax matters. Casey, then on the editorial board of the publishing firm, Institute for Business Planning, had rejected Fields's manuscript.

At Casey's confirmation hearing on February 10, 1971, Sen. William Proxmire (D-Wis.), inquiring about the Fields case, asked Casey whether the transcript of the trial had been sealed. Casey told Proxmire that was true. "I can tell you how that developed," Casey said. "My lawyer, the fellow that represented us in this case, tells me that the plaintiff's attorney had made some inflammatory remarks in his summation about big corporations exploiting the work of his poor clients. After the matter had been settled, the plaintiff asked the judge if he could get a copy of this summation that his lawyer had made. Apparently the judge didn't like this; and he said that since the case had been settled and there would be no appeal and no need to transcribe the record, that he was ordering the record sealed."

Eight days later, though, J. Braxton Craven, Jr., the federal judge on the case, wrote Proxmire, flatly denying *Casey's* contention. "The sealing of the transcript of the trial from public view was not done at my initiative." In fact, a transcript of the case shows that sealing the transcript was Casey's idea. As recounted by Proxmire at March 9, 1971 hearings on Casey's nomination:

The judge was asking the parties whether they agreed with the destruction of the interrogatory submitted to the court:

The Court. Do you agree, Mr. Casey?

Mr. Casey. Yes, I do and I wonder if we can go further.

The Court. I think that is enough.

Mr. Casey. Well, I don't agree. I would like to have the record sealed entirely.

In February, Casey also testified that Judge Craven "called in the two attorneys and he said to them that the verdict was not supported by the evidence in the case, and that he would set it aside, and he recommended that the parties get together and settle it." But Craven flatly refuted that statement in his letter to the committee, writing that he "did not indicate that I would set the verdict aside and order a new trial unless the parties got together and settled the case" and that he did "not recall telling the two attorneys. . .that the verdict was not supported by the evidence."

Casey's personal role in the plagiarism is unclear. In a 1957 letter to Harry Fields, Casey maintained that the plagiarism had been done by a young attorney, John Cuddahy, who had been hired "to write fresh material." Casey wrote that he was "greatly indignant" when he learned about the theft. But in a 1960 pretrial deposition quoted in the *Wall Street Journal*, Cuddahy denied that his job was to write fresh material: "I couldn't write fresh material. It would be a fraud if I said I could." Instead, Cuddahy said, his job was to take articles given to him by Casey and an associate and turn them into new copy: "Material was given to me. I digested the material and wrote," he said. Cuddahy said Casey had never expressed any "indignation" about the incident.

If the specifics of the case were of relatively minor concern for a presidential appointee, Proxmire felt Casey's handling of the case—both before the court and the committee—were extremely revealing of his personality. The case raised questions not only of Casey's judgment, and his veracity as a witness, but also of his temperament. Proxmire read into the record a section of Casey's pretrial deposition in which Casey was accused of striking the plaintiff's attorney:

Mr. Garfield [the plaintiff's attorney]. Did you ever pay Mr. Fields [the author] $250 a month or 250 cents.

Mr. Casey. No, I didn't. The 250 cents isn't necessary. . .God damn, if you're not a gentleman, I will kick your ass out of here. You just kick that 250 cents out of here or you and I will have a hell of a lot of trouble. . .

Mr. Garfield. Then you certainly didn't pay him 250 cents, did you?

Mr. Casey. I told you not to try that again, or don't try that again or there will be more violence in this God damn office. . .

Mr. Garfield. I want the record to show that Mr. Casey struck me in the face.

Mr. Donnelly [Casey's lawyer]. I dispute that and I want the record to show that is a completely false statement.

Casey told Proxmire, "I don't believe I struck Mr. Garfield. . .I haven't struck anyone since high school." But Proxmire remained disturbed by the incident, remarking a few moments later—after Sen. Bill Brock (R-Tenn.) defended Casey as a "man of integrity"—that "I am wondering if we should not take into consideration a man's temperamental qualities when we consider his qualifications for a quasi-judicial position."

Later that day, the Senate Banking Committee approved Casey by a 9-3 vote, with Proxmire, Adlai Stevenson and Harrison Williams (D-N.J.) voting against him. In his dissenting view, Proxmire contended: "Casey. . .is the wrong man to be Chairman of the Securities and Exchange Commission. . .Mr. Casey has cut corners when he considered it to be necessary to business profit. He has wheeled and dealed his way into a personal fortune, sometimes at the expense of his clients."

Controversy followed Casey at the SEC. Though he stayed on the fringe of the Watergate scandal that oozed through all corners of Nixon's Administration, Casey played a part in two related matters involving Robert Vesco and International Telephone & Telegraph (ITT).

On Monday, April 10, 1972 former New Jersey State Senator Harry Sears and Larry Richardson went to Washington to see Maurice Stans, the finance committee chairman of the Committee to Re-elect the President (CREEP). Vesco had hired Sears in December, 1971 as associate counsel for his company International Controls; Richardson was the firm's president.

The SEC had been investigating International Controls since March, 1971. As the investigation deepened, Vesco grew increasingly worrried. In January, 1972 Sears persuaded Attorney General John Mitchell, whom Sears had met in the 1968 campaign, to call Casey and complain about the "excess zeal" of the SEC investigatory staff led by Stanley Sporkin. Casey sent Mitchell an internal SEC memo detailing the staff's findings to that point; Mitchell gave it to Sears, who gave it to Vesco. But the investigation continued, and in April, Vesco dispatched Richardson and Sears to Washington with $200,000 for CREEP and a message for Stans: Stop the SEC investigation.

After dropping off the money, Richardson left town. Sears went on to meet with Mitchell: Mitchell got Sears an appointment with Casey for later that day. Sears met with Casey twice more, once in May and once again during the GOP convention in August. There, "Sears. . .received what he thought was an understanding from Casey that the entire Vesco. . .matter would be given a thorough review. . .," as Robert Hutchison wrote in *Vesco*. But whether or not that review was conducted, Casey subsequently told Sears that the case would continue.

Pressure, meanwhile, was building up from other sources. White House Counsel John Dean had begun calling Casey in the summer of 1971 to inquire about the case, according to Casey's testimony at the subsequent trial of Stans and Mitchell on obstruction of justice charges resulting from the incident. Casey testified that on November 2, 1972, just a few days before the election, Dean asked Casey if scheduled depositions of two of Vesco's secretaries "couldn't be postponed to the following week in order to remove the risk of anybody being tempted to take whatever information came out of that examination and use it. . ." Casey said he would check and called Sporkin. Sporkin insisted that the depositions go on as scheduled and Casey held firm, denying Dean's request.

Vesco had another card he hoped to play. Vesco had been the principal investor in a Casey company called Multiponics, buying over one-third of the stock. Multiponics would continue to cause Casey trouble all the way through his investigation by the Senate Intelligence Committee, and a Vesco aide suggested to the financier at the time that Casey was guilty of violating the Securities Act of 1933 through "fraudulent representations." But Vesco never got to threaten Casey, for the chairman never gave him a private meeting.

All of Vesco's maneuverings did not stop the case. Though the White House was clearly unhappy, Casey and the other commissioners did not back off from the investigation. Casey spoke of his role in the case proudly at his Export-Import Bank confirmation hearings in 1973. Casey's steadfastness on the case may help explain Sporkin's devotion to him through all the accusations that have been raised.

Three weeks after the election, on November 27, 1972, the SEC filed its civil fraud complaint charging Vesco and 41 other defendants with diverting $125 million of stock sales to their own use with another $100 million "unaccounted for." Two paragraphs later, the complaint made a vague allusion to "other large sums of cash. . .transferred among and between Vesco and his group. . .and other parties." An earlier draft of the complaint had contained a direct reference to the transfer of $250,000 believed to be the funds that Vesco had funneled to Nixon's campaign. Sporkin's investigators had doggedly tracked the money's movements. But before the complaint was filed Stans asked SEC General Counsel Brad Cook—who Casey had assigned to oversee the case as the political heat increased—if the reference could be modified; Cook subsequently recommended it be deleted.

At Casey's confirmation hearing in December, 1973, for the position of Ex-Im Bank President, Proxmire questioned him about the deletion. Casey told Proxmire that he did not modify the complaint, he simply "approved the complaint," after telling Cook that "whatever you and Sporkin. . .agree to is satisfactory to me." The disputed paragraph, Casey said, "did not soften the charge at all. That addition merely added a paragraph to a very extensive complaint to recite some information about the movement of cash from the Bahamas to Mr. Vesco in New Jersey. That was a matter involving $250,000 in a case which was a $250 million case. I did not consider it a matter of major significance, and I did not concern myself with it." For Cook, the paragraph turned out to be a matter of major significance: though he was appointed to succeed Casey, he resigned after admitting that he lied under oath about his discussions with Stans. It was a bitter end to the Vesco story for Cook, who had resisted pressure from Sears to drop the case.

Casey's relation to the IT&T affair was more tangential. As part of the SEC's investigation of insider trading on IT&T's 1969 acquisition of the Hartford Insurance Group, the agency had subpoenaed 34 boxes of internal IT&T documents. On September 21, 1972 a special investigations subcommittee of the House Commerce Committee chaired by Rep. Harley Staggers (D-W.Va.) asked Casey for the documents. Casey refused, arguing that SEC staffers were still working on the case. Two weeks later, on October 3, Casey met with Dean at the White House to discuss the request. Dean said he would talk to the Justice Department about the matter and the next day, Casey later testified in congressional hearings, Deputy Attorney General Ralph Erickson called Casey to request the documents. Two days later, Casey notified Staggers that he had transferred the documents to the Justice Department, out of the committee's subpoena reach. At his Ex-Im confirmation hearing, Casey defended his actions, pointing out that, "I did nothing on my own. Everything was done by formal decision of the commission acting unanimously." In 1973, Erickson testified that he took the files under pressure.

Casey resigned from the Ex-Im in January, 1976 and joined the law firm of Rogers & Wells, which included his colleague in the Nixon Administration, former Secretary of State William Rogers. At Rogers & Wells, Casey continued to be involved in controversial activities.

In April, 1976, the Internal Revenue Service (IRS) notified Mobil Oil that its payments to the Indonesian government under proposed oil production contracts would not qualify as foreign income tax and therefore couldn't be credited against their U.S. income. On May 19, Indonesia hired Rogers & Wells to represent it with the IRS; Casey became involved on June 30. On July 8, Casey met with Treasury Secretary William Simon and Charles Walker, the assistant secretary for tax policy. The following day Walker wrote to IRS Commissioner Donald Alexander, asserting his belief that the Indonesian government "with the advice of New York legal counsel" had made the necessary changes in its contracts to qualify for the foreign credit. Walker wrote Alexander that he "assume[d]" the ruling would "be expedited by your office." Five days later, Casey and another Rogers & Wells attorney met with the assistant IRS Commissioner, John Withers, and on July 29, Casey sent Withers additional information. Eventually in 1978, the IRS approved the foreign tax credits for the oil companies operating in Indonesia.

When Patrick Tyler, an investigative reporter with the *Washington* Post, revealed these details on January 7, 1982, the Justice Department convened an investigation into Casey's actions. Casey had not registered as a foreign agent for Indonesia, citing the "attorney exemption" that frees attorneys from the requirement if their actions do "not include attempts to influence or persuade agency personnel or officials other than in the course of established agency proceedings, whether formal or informal." Three months later, on April 8, Attorney General William French Smith cleared Casey of any impropriety. "At all times, the fact that Mr. Casey was representing Indonesia was made clear to those officials with whom he was dealing," Smith said. "The evidence does not support a conclusion that at any time Mr. Casey sought to persuade or influence officials to change any agency policy. . ."

Another Casey client was SCA Services, Inc., a Boston-based hazardous waste firm with extensive operations in New Jersey—and alleged links to organized crime. When the SEC accused the firm's officers of looting several million dollars for their own use, SCA brought in Rogers & Wells to represent it during the proceeding. In 1977, the SEC reached a consent decree with SCA that required them to add outside directors to their board and to have an independent counsel examine their financial operations. SEC sources told reporters at the *Post* and the *Wall Street Journal* that Rogers & Wells brought in Casey to help negotiate the settlement. Sporkin told the *Washington Post* that he did not "remember" Casey "being in that case." Casey includes SCA on his client list.

At two congressional hearings, SCA was identified by an FBI informant and law enforcement officials as a company with extensive links to organized crime. At hearings on May 28, 1981 before the Oversight and Investigations Subcommittee of the House Energy and Commerce Committee, New Jersey State Police Lieutenant Colonel Justin Dintino testified that SCA was involved in the organized-crime controlled system of "property rights, backed by threats and acts of violence" which eliminated competition in the New Jersey garbage industry. Dintino testified that SCA had acquired several solid waste companies in 1972 and 1973 headed by known organized crime figures. Similar charges had been made at a December 18, 1980 hearing by FBI informant Harold Kaufman.

In his initial financial disclosure filing with the Senate Intelligence Committee, Casey did not disclose his work for either Indonesia or SCA. Nor did he disclose a number of other financial dealings. In its subsequent December, 1981 report on Casey, the committee wrote that, "The written responses by Mr. Casey were deficient in several respects. The original answers omitted at least nine investments valued at more than a quarter of a million dollars, personal debts and contingent liabilities of nearly five hundred thousand dollars, a number of corporations or foundations on whose board Mr. Casey served, four civil law suits in which he was involved in the last five years and more than seventy clients he had represented in private practice in the last five years." Among the clients omitted, in addition to SCA and the government of Indonesia, were South Korea, Kennecott Copper, and Merrill Lynch, the stockbrokerage house run by Donald Regan. (For more on Rogers & Wells's relationship with Merrill Lynch see profile on Donald Regan.) The initial list of Casey's clients supplied to the committee in January, 1981 and the full list are reprinted in the Financial Background section.

The Senate investigators also looked into Casey's involvement in civil litigation involving Multiponics, the firm in which Vesco had invested. Multiponics, incorporated in Delaware in 1968, consisted of 43,000 acres of farmland in Louisiana and nearby states assembled by the company's founders including Casey. According to court records, Casey was the largest single investor in the land.

In October, 1968, the firm distributed a circular to private investors offering $3.5 million in stock. The circular did not inform the investors that Multiponics had assumed the mortgage debts of all the other founders—totalling more than $2.7 million including $301,000 of Casey's debts. Multiponics went bankrupt in 1971 and disgruntled investors sued in 1974. Citing the failure to report the debt and similiar omissions, a federal judge, Charles Stewart Jr., of the Southern District of New York, ruled on May 19, 1981 that the firm's founders (including Casey) had "omitted and misrepresented facts." But on November 11, 1981, Judge Stewart reversed his ruling, saying a trial should be held to hear Casey's claim that he "was not directly involved in the management of the company" (as his attorney Arnold S. Jacobs put it after the first decision). In the first case, evidence was presented that Casey was the largest investor, the firm's legal counsel and its corporate secretary. But Jacobs said Casey was "a passive investor." And in a statement submitted to the Senate Intelligence Committee Casey said "his position was largely ceremonial."

But evidence contradicting those claims was uncovered by Michael Kramer of New York magazine. Kramer reviewed the 1971 bankruptcy proceedings and found that Casey had stated, in sworn trial testimony, that he had spent "a considerable amount of time" on Multiponics affairs; that he "read the minutes [which discussed the offering circular] regularly and followed the affairs of the corporation;" and that he thought "I kept very much on top of the important things that the corporation was doing. . ." One of the company's other directors said in a sworn affidavit that "The Offering Circular was prepared by William Casey and Lawrence Orbe [another Multiponics director]." Nonetheless, the Senate Intelligence Committee concluded that "the available evidence indicates that Mr. Casey had no active role in the preparation or legal review of the offering circular which the plaintiffs claim was false and misleading."

When the case surfaced in the summer of 1981, Reagan called the allegations "old news." And though some White House aides wavered in their support of Casey during the Senate investigation, Reagan (in public at least) remained steadfast. Reagan owed Casey quite a bit. When Reagan dismissed campaign manager John Sears on the night of the 1980 New Hampshire primary, Casey came in to rebuild the divided and depressed organization. It was Casey's first crack at running a national campaign, but as he told one reporter "I've been involved in every Republican campaign since Wendell Willkie."

Born on March 13, 1913 in Queens, New York, Casey was graduated in 1934 from Fordham University and earned a law degree in 1937 from St. John's University. From 1950 until 1971 he was a partner in the firm of Hall, Casey, Dickler and Howley (and its predecessor firm). Casey is married with one daughter.

MAJOR ISSUES

- Casey is expanding the scope of the CIA's covert activities while minimizing review by officials outside the intelligence community. The White House has approved a CIA plan to destabilize the Nicaraguan government; and covert operations aimed at overthrowing the governments of Cambodia and Cuba are being considered or have begun, according to watchdog organizations. But the mechanism for approving these kinds of operations is still unclear.

- Under an executive order signed by Reagan, the CIA for the first time in its history is authorized to conduct covert operations inside the United States. The executive order also permits increased surveillance of Americans and domestic organizations.

- Casey is seeking complete exemption for the CIA from the Freedom of Information Act, a law which he described as a "cancer" on the intelligence community.

- Acting on a request by the Reagan Administration, Congress has passed a law making it a felony to disclose the names of U.S. intelligence operatives; one critic called the bill an "Official Secrets Act."

- Deputy Director Bobby Inman (who has since resigned) asked scientists to voluntarily submit their work to censorship to prevent further leakage of U.S. technology to the Soviet Union.

- Casey says that the KGB's activities within the United States is "far flung. . . but we don't know what many of [these agents] are doing."

The headlines that appeared in the press during the first months of Casey's administration were telling: "CIA is on the Rebound," "Casey Promises to Revive Morale, Minimize Restrictions," "Casey Lighting a Fire under the Burnt-Out CIA." In between congressional inquiries into his business dealings Casey, an activist director, has found time to implement far-reaching policy changes at the CIA, permitting the agency to expand its scope of covert activities with a minimum of review by officials outside the intelligence community.

"The CIA," Casey said during his nomination hearing, "suffers institutional self-doubt. . .the morale of much of the agency is said to be low. Too often the agency has been publicly discussed as an institution which must be tightly restrained, stringently monitored or totally reorganized."

If the morale of the agency was low before Casey took office, it wasn't because the CIA had actually been "tightly restrained, stringently monitored or totally reorganized." The highly touted reforms implemented after congressional investigations disclosed a wide range of past abuses—from assassination attempts overseas to spying on American citizens at home—were indeed modest. The agency still carries out covert operations, though the 1974 Hughes-Ryan amendment requires a "presidential finding" that each operation is "important to the national security." Congressional experts have argued that Congress, in passing the 1947 National Security Act, intended the CIA to be an information gathering bureau—the law does not specifically authorize covert operations. A provision authorizing the agency to perform "other functions" for the President was used as the legal basis for covert activities. The Church Committee, which completed its investigation of the intelligence community in 1976, seriously considered proposing a prohibition on covert activities, but later decided to recommend permitting them under "extraordinary circumstances" when there is grave endangerment to national security and overt action won't suffice.

Under legislation passed in 1980 the President is required to tell the House and Senate Intelligence Committees in advance of covert operations. But there are some loopholes. If he determines it "essential" to the national security not to inform the full committees he can tell only eight congressional leaders. And there is a further loophole in the preamble to the law under which the President can fail to notify *anyone* in Congress in advance for the most sensitive operations, as long as he subsequently reports them.

In that same legislation, the committees to which the President must report covert operations was reduced from eight to two.

Casey favored the reduction of oversight committees: "There were too many committees in the past but they've been consolidated," he told us. And he favors an even further reduction. "I'd like to see it unified, have a joint committee, so we'd have one set of people to deal with. I'd only have to testify once instead of twice."

When we asked Casey if, in his estimation, the CIA had ever abused its authority, he replied, "Not during my watch." Then he added: "You know, I'm not going to make a judgment on that. People at the agency—people working there—feel the alleged abuses of power have been greatly exaggerated. They, most of them, feel that some of them were valid and proven. Many of them were alleged and never proven. And in fact some have been alleged and have been litigated as not ever having occurred. And they feel keenly that. . . the proof or disproof of the allegation never catches up with the attention given the original allegation. They feel that they've been substantially reduced—which is not to say that there have not been abuses, abuses to be corrected, and that problem is present in any organization."

Casey has devoted much of his attention to bolstering the agency's covert capabilities. (But at the beginning of our interview, Casey laid out these ground rules: "I don't talk about covert operations. We have the authority to do them as authorized by the President, we report them to Congress. But apart from that I don't talk about them, they don't exist.") In a July, 1981 press interview, then CIA Deputy Director Bobby Inman said the agency had already begun building up its covert operations branch, the Directorate for Operations (DDO), which had been trimmed back since the Vietnam War. Inman claimed DDO's resources "had been drawn down below a safe level" over the past decade.

There already are signs of increased activities planned by DDO. Late in 1981 the press disclosed that the White House had approved preparations for a $19 million operation to destabilize the leftist Sandinista regime in Nicaragua. The White House did not deny the reports. According to the Center for National Security Studies, a watchdog group, covert operations aimed at overthrowing the governments of Cambodia and Cuba are being considered or have already begun, while operations begun during the Carter Administration—the provision of weapons to Afghanistan, and attempts to overthrow Libyan ruler Muammar el-Qaddafi, have been expanded.

During his nomination hearing, Casey was asked his opinion on the Murphy Commission's recommendation that covert action "should not be abandoned but should be employed only when such action is clearly essential to vital U.S. purposes and only then after careful high-level review. Covert action should be authorized only after collective considerations of their benefits and risks by all available 40 Committee members. In addition, covert action should be reported to the proposed joint committee of Congress on national security or to some other appropriate congressional committee." (Casey served on the commission.) Casey responded that the recommendation "generally reflects my view." Asked to expand on that, he told the committee: "Well, what I had in mind when I inserted the word 'generally' was the condition there that covert action should be used only when it is of the greatest importance. . . .There are some things now, I think when we are thinking about strong covert action when you try to intervene in the internal affairs or to influence an election, as we did in Italy in 1948, I think that kind of thing you only do when it is of the highest interest to the United States and when the President and the appropriate authorities perceive it to be. . . .Now, there are other things of lesser nature. . . .that I do not think we had in mind in framing that language." What those "lesser" things might be remain unknown to the general public; Casey refused to elaborate at that open session.

At that hearing Casey defined "covert action" as a secret operation with "nonacknowledgeability." Clandestine activity, he said, is "one that is secret, that is not necessarily nonacknowledgeable."

To head the DDO, Casey hired a businessman, Max Hugel, anticipating that the division's agents would begin relying more heavily on corporations and other commercial enterprises for cover overseas. As he told the CIA staff in a July, 1981 speech: "I believed that [Hugel's] business record. . .had given him broad insights and experience in dealing abroad. I thought this would be valuable in managing a team of experienced professionals and in giving drive and thrust to the rebuilding of capabilities which need rebuilding and to pursuing new directions in collecting intelligence through the private sector."

The decision to hire Hugel almost cost Casey his job. In July, Hugel resigned only hours after the *Washington Post* revealed that two former stockbrokers accused him of participating in stock fraud. Even conservative senators such as Barry Goldwater (R-Ariz.) condemned Casey's judgment in hiring the inexperienced Hugel, and some in Congress felt that decision itself was proof enough that Casey should not be trusted with the CIA director post.

"This person [Hugel] was coming along," Casey told us. "I think he would have been quite good. Now I might have made a mistake in pushing him too far too fast. I perhaps should have made him spend a year in the business to get the right feel for it. There wasn't any strong dissent. Well I tell you most of the dissatisfaction was on the part of old timers, retirees who kind of agitated a lot about it, made publicity about it, fearing that it was some kind of desecration that somebody without specific experience, without having been brought up in the business and put in charge—and this person had a lot of international experience, so he brought a lot to it. And I, you know, you make mistakes, in appointments one can't bet it right all the time. It became a very conspicuous mistake and there was a lot of criticism for it.''

CIA General Counsel Stanley Sporkin also defended Hugel, saying: ''You must remember he never had a real opportunity to serve in that position. It wasn't a question of any failure on the job. It was a question of an old and outside problem that dislodged him.''

Another sign of Casey's increased emphasis on covert activities came in a subtle bureaucratic move. During that July speech Casey told employees that John Stein, Hugel's successor at DDO, would be charged with ''strengthening counterintelligence, covert action, and paramilitary capabilities,'' while his deputy, Clair George, directed the clandestine service (espionage). As Jay Peterzell of the Center for National Security Studies explained: ''It was the clearest indication to date that the perennial competition between collectors and operators would be resolved in favor of the latter in Casey's CIA.''

It is still unclear what mechanism the Reagan Administration uses for reviewing covert operations. Early in the Administration, the White House quietly suspended a part of a Carter Executive Order that required review by all members of the Special Coordinating Committee (SCC)—previously the 40 Committee—which included officials outside the intelligence community. Under the SCC those officials included the Attorney General and the director of the Office of Management and Budget. Inquiries into what replaced that committee have been dodged by the Administration. When we asked Casey if he had devised a system to replace the Special Coordinating Committee, he replied, ''Oh yes.''

What approval system is there? we continued. ''Same thing,'' he said. ''There's an NSPG planning group chaired by the President, in his absence by the Vice-President and everything goes through there.'' Casey went on to list a number of officials on the group, such as the secretaries of State and Defense and (occasionally) the Attorney General. Later, however, Casey's office told us he was ''wrong'' about the additional members and refused to answer any further questions on the topic. The National Security Planning Group, a committee of the National Security Council, according to other accounts includes the secretaries of State and Defense, and the top three aides in the White House—Ed Meese, James Baker, and Michael Deaver. But according to a White House source cited by David Wise, co-author of *The Invisible Government* and a close follower of the CIA, operations are approved by another NSC panel, a senior inter-departmental group (SIG). There are three SIGs, one for military, foreign policy and intelligence. The intelligence SIG is chaired by Casey. If that panel has been designated to covert operations, then, as Wise notes, ''the CIA would be in the position of approving its own operations.''

The most dramatic visible change in the CIA's activities was implemented on December 4, 1981 when Reagan signed an executive order permitting the agency to conduct covert operations within the United States for the first time in its history. The move was a sharp departure from the previous law. As Rep. Don Edwards (D-Calif.), chairman of the House subcommittee on civil and constitutional rights, has pointed out, when ''the CIA was established by the 1947 law, Congress specifically did not want that agency, an international organization with a secret budget and secret personnel, to spy on Americans here at home.'' Testifying before

Edwards's subcommittee, John Shattuck, Jerry Berman and Morton Halperin of the ACLU and its companion group Center for National Security Studies said: "Against an overwhelming record of civil liberties abuses by the CIA, the FBI, NSA and other intelligence agencies, exhaustively documented by responsible committees of both the House and the Senate, President Reagan's order represents an exercise in Orwellian doublespeak. While the Order asserts that its 'procedures shall protect constitutional and other legal rights' the procedures in E.O. 12333 authorize a wide-ranging assault on civil liberties.'' Under the order, the CIA is permitted to conduct covert activities in the U.S. that are not "intended to influence United States political process, public opinion, policies or media.'' Carter's executive order on intelligence had expressly prohibited domestic covert operations. The word "intended" is particularly troubling to the ACLU "since intended or not, [these operations] could adversely impact on the U.S. political process and the media.''

That provision was weakened substantially from an earlier draft that permitted the CIA to infiltrate *and* influence American organizations without a court warrant. The earlier draft also asserted that the President had inherent authority to authorize wiretaps and electronic surveillance without a court order. Those provisions were dropped only after strong pressure by both the Republican-controlled Senate Intelligence Committee and the Democratic-controlled House committee.

Reagan's order permits "undisclosed participation in organizations within the United States" when "in accordance with procedures established by the head of the [intelligence] agency concerned and approved by the Attorney General.'' Agents are authorized to influence the activities of organizations comprised of foreigners and which are "reasonably believed to be acting on behalf of a foreign power.'' (An example might be an Iranian student organization.)

The executive order also permits secret collection of "significant" foreign or counterintelligence provided it is not "undertaken for the purpose of acquiring information concerning the domestic activities of United States persons.'' Carter's executive order had permitted domestic gathering of "information concerning corporations or other commercial organizations or activities that constitute foreign intelligence" and "information concerning persons who are reasonably believed to be acting on behalf of a foreign power.'' (He had no restrictions on gathering counterintelligence information.) Thus, Reagan has eliminated the restriction on subjects about which the CIA can gather information within the U.S.

According to the ACLU, the primary focus of this change "appears to be the ability of the CIA to use informants and pretext interviews to gather foreign intelligence information from Americans who don't want to share information with the CIA.'' They cited a hypothetical case: "A prominent American travels to Iran shortly after the revolution. Upon his return he refuses an invitation to meet with the CIA. However, he is discussing his trip with journalists and at university meetings. The CIA sends a professor to a private meeting to take notes and reports back or sends a person pretending to be a reporter to interview the traveler.''

The new order permits physical surveillance of Americans traveling abroad if it is to collect "significant information that cannot reasonably be acquired by other means.'' (The Carter order had limited such surveillance to persons suspected of being agents of a foreign power.)

The Reagan order also broadens the range of situations in which the CIA is permitted to employ local law enforcement agencies. That practice was barred under the Carter order "except as expressly authorized by law.'' Reagan's order permits assistance unless "precluded by applicable law." Former Senator Frank Church, whose congressional committee during the 1970s conducted an investigation of the intelligence community, said in 1981 congressional testimony that this provision is "pregnant with problems. I don't know whether our memories are sufficiently long in this country so that we learn from experience, but there was a good reason for restricting the CIA in this regard," he said. "Its close cooperation with local police departments led to abuses in the past—serious abuses. The CIA has no business involving itself with local police. It was an agency established—let us not forget—to collect and to assess and to evaluate foreign intelligence. It was meant to operate abroad. We have the FBI at home and we have our hands full watching the FBI to make certain that it does not transgress upon the liberties of the people. We don't want a secret police developing in this country."

In addition, under the Reagan order the intelligence agencies are permitted to conduct mail surveillance of U.S. citizens inside the country and abroad without a warrant if the attorney general finds there is probable cause to believe the target is an agent of a foreign power.

In an interview we asked Casey why the CIA required authority to carry out domestic activities in the U.S. He replied: "We don't carry out domestic activities in the U.S. except for the long established overt requests for help—which has always been and has never been challenged. Our operation is exclusively foreign intelligence. There are two areas which caused all the hullabaloo about operations in the United States and—and really they're FBI operations in the United States. As I said before we're responsible for finding out about what we can find out about KGB and other intelligence activities—Cuban and others. You get these leads abroad when they connect into the United States, we have a fellow who knows the whole story and to hand that over to a cold FBI guy isn't very effective so there is the authorization to cooperate, to work for the FBI and provide our know-how through the FBI, with the consent of the attorney general.

"Now, you can call that operating in the United States but it's a necessary extension of operation abroad and is entirely focused on foreign intelligence. The other thing is when we find people in the United States who want to help or we find foreigners in the United States in the U.N or other places who happen to be in the United States and they can be instrumental in some activities that are focused on foreign intelligence, we are authorized to work with them. We're not authorized to work with them in anyway that's going to impinge on United States public opinion, or anything else. It's a great extension of reality to say we're operating in the United States in those matters."

Under the executive order, the CIA is, as Casey noted, required to work domestically in coordination with the FBI in the collection of foreign and counterintelligence and in conducting counterintelligence activities. But "special activities," or covert operations, are a different matter. As the executive order states, "no agency except the CIA. . .may conduct any special activity unless the President determines that another agency is more likely to achieve a particular objective." Thus, the CIA's domestic covert operations must be conducted unilaterally.

That alone is troubling to former CIA Director Admiral Stansfield Turner: "The CIA is not trained to operate within the constraints of American law," said Turner. "The FBI is. You're being unfair to a CIA officer when you put him in that environment where he's more likely to make a mistake." Turner also warned that the executive order raised the danger of excessive spying on American citizens and unwarranted "intrusion into the lives of Americans" with "very little to be gained" in intelligence collections. Turner also cautioned of risks that the "CIA would be overzealous in the domestic arena" and that "information gained about Americans might be utilized for domestic political purposes."

Casey brushed aside his predecessor's charge that the executive order would result in spying on innocent U.S. citizens. "We have no intention of spying on American citizens," he said. "We've taken great precautions to make sure we're not doing it inadvertently."

The CIA has also proposed a change in the federal criminal code that would exempt agents from criminal prosecution while on approved missions outside the United States. Thus an agent that, for example, engages in bribery or a narcotic transaction while undercover would not be prosecuted in U.S. courts. "What we did want to do was to make it clear that no liability would attach when someone has proper authorization to engage in such activities," said CIA General Counsel Sporkin. "We were concerned that someone could be improperly charged with a crime. That is the basis for the suggested change, it's strictly a technical matter." But one Justice Department intelligence official, quoted in the *Los Angeles Times*, warned that the change would permit CIA agents to "freely engage" in otherwise illegal activities without Justice Department authorization. The change is part of revised version of the federal criminal code lying dormant in Congress.

Casey is also seeking a full exemption from the Freedom of Information Act (FOIA) for his agency. Already the FOIA provides a broad exemption for intelligence material, the disclosure of which would cause "identifiable harm" to national security. Information requested generally comes back with lines and even pages deleted. Despite that limitation, FOIA requests over the last decade have provided the public with information about CIA abuses—such as the surveillance and monitoring of student dissidents, professors, and political groups within the U.S.—and valuable historical information, such as documents on the nuclear accident that occurred west of the Urals in the Soviet Union during the 1950s which were not released previously because the Atomic Energy Commission (which was then promoting civilian nuclear power) thought it would be embarrassing to the U.S. civilian nuclear program.

But Casey considers the act a "cancer" on the intelligence community: "This country will not be able to maintain an effective secret intelligence operation for long if it has to co-exist with the Freedom of Information Act," he told us.

Casey said the fundamental problem is that "people who commit to undertake work in which their lives and their reputations may be at risk if their activity is disclosed, aren't going to take the risk if they think the files are wide open. And then, more important, our case officers aren't going to be willing to take the responsibility to ask people to do that if they can't ensure them protection. Now, you've got to make a balance: which do you want? [And] it's a perceptual thing. We're the only country in the world that invites anybody, including our adversaries, to poke around in our files. We get a large percentage of our information from liaison relationships with the British and other intelligence agencies around the world. That makes them very nervous, reluctant to provide information and we're sure they withhold information for fear it's going to pop out of these files and destroy their sources, or come into the public view and embarrass them and so on. So we don't know what we're not getting but we know we're not getting everything that we had been getting."

He added: "The Freedom of Information Act is not the mode of oversight, the proper mode of oversight is congressional committees—confidential disclosure of everything to them—and that process is in operation and it works, and I think we are happy with it, satisfied with it. The other part of the equation is what a historian or a journalist gets under the Freedom of Information Act; it's usually. . .a piece of paper with great big areas splotched out. Of course, experienced foreign intelligence officers can make a pretty good guess at filling it in but a historian or a journalist—they don't know what they've got. It's just as likely to mislead as it is to lead. So, it just doesn't pay, it hurts and it doesn't pay and it isn't necessary to achieve the oversight to keep the intelligence activities in line.''

Casey complained that the act is an ''enormous drain on our resources. We have to use our experienced people—at least 4-5 percent of our experienced operational people have to go through and make judgments on what the other side could deduce or get out of what would be released. Our experience is that you can't have a clerk read these things exclusively—if I were a KGB and I had to read it what would it mean to me, what would I learn, what would I get out of it.''

Acting on a request by the Reagan Administration, Congress has passed a law making it a felony to disclose the names of U.S. intelligence operatives, even if the information is gleaned from public sources. Though ostensibly introduced in response to the groups which regularly list the names of CIA operatives abroad, the law will result in the prosecution of working journalists and whistleblowers, as well as members of watchdog groups who have ''reason to believe'' the disclosure would impair or impede U.S. intelligence activities. Jack Landau, director of the Reporters Committee for Freedom of the Press, called the bill ''an Official Secrets Act.'' It ''assumes damage is done'' just by disclosing an agent's name, he said.

In testimony before the House Select Committee on Intelligence Landau cited a number of cases where the law would act as a cover for CIA wrongdoing: ''News stories that reveal that an intelligence agent was involved in a conspiracy to assassinate a foreign leader; or was involved in an attempt to overthrow a foreign government in Latin America; or was involved in some type of grotesque medical experiment on human subjects'' would prompt prosecution. It is often critical to the credibility of a news story, he added, that the actual identity of the subject of misconduct be revealed.

Landau also questioned the premise of the law: ''One is forced to speculate that if a reporter can find out the identity of a CIA agent. . .then certainly the KGB or another foreign intelligence agent can find out the same thing with ease.''

Journalists are not the only profession uneasy about the CIA's new preeminence. Leaders in the scientific world were livid when Inman suggested that scientists should voluntarily submit their work to censorship to prevent further leakage of U.S. technology to the Soviet Union. Inman told scientists at the American Association for the Advancement of Science (AAAS) convention in January, 1982 that scientists should submit their work to U.S. intelligence agencies for clearance both ''prior to the start of research and prior to publication.'' To William Carey, executive officer of AAAS, that would be ''no less than a nightmare.'' Scientists, he told the *Washington Post*, don't want to be subject to ''the whims of unknown people inside the walls of the military, not just about immediate problems but potential ones.'' These individuals, he said, would ''resolve questions where there is doubt on the side of censorship rather than the freedom of scientists.''

Casey sees it differently, though he was careful not to criticize the scientists who denounced Inman's proposal. ''Properly, scientists always react to any infringement on their flow of knowledge, because they're receiving as well as giving out, and they'd all like to see. And it's important that they not be unduly circumscribed. What Admiral Inman called for was that some of their exchange of information—the Soviets get more out of it than we do—we send somebody over there on a student exchange, we'll send a 23-year old student [studying] poetry. . .and they'll send a 45-year old fellow who has a background in inertial guidance systems who somehow lands in just the university where our foremost expert in inertial guidance is. What's happening on that now is that the National Academy of Sciences has put together a committee and they're studying this problem and they'll try to formulate some guidelines or recommendations which would do whatever the national interest seems to call for—balancing the interests of the proper, good flow of information that promotes and encourages our scientific development and at the same time doesn't constitute a leaky sieve."

To Casey, the reason that the CIA must reassert itself is clear. In the U.S., he says, the KGB is active, but largely invisible: "We know there is a lot we don't know. In general we know the [KGB's] activity is far flung, we know the number of people working on it in the United States is very large, but we don't know what many of them are doing." Abroad, the enemy is similarly threatening: The ultimate aim of the Soviet Union's foreign policy toward the U.S., he said, pulling out a map of the world splotched with red, "has not changed for 60 years—to establish world communism, to achieve dominion, to achieve greater influence." And, Casey told us, U.S. intelligence currently doesn't have much success in ferreting out Soviet secrets. "We'd like to, we try to find out what they're doing," he said. "It's very important that we not be technologically surprised. But they are much more successful than we are in closing off the information."

He considers mechanisms designed to increase the agency's accountability—such as the FOIA—a debilitating hindrance to its anti-communist efforts. He wants to build a forceful, secretive, and indeed, invisible apparatus. "For a long time there were no books written on the CIA. When the dam broke, there got to be a lot of them," he said. "Now, I'm sorry to say there's been the first crack in the dam on the NSA. . .[one book has] just been written."

The question observers are asking is: How far is Casey's CIA really going in expanding its operations at home and abroad? Because the agency's budget, personnel and operations are shrouded in secrecy, it is, of course, difficult to tell. Inman's resignation in early 1982 was the clearest indication that major changes are underway. Inman, a former NSA director, could hardly be called soft on matters of national security. He strongly favored exempting the agency from the FOIA, and expanding its covert activities as well as its analytic staff. He is so well respected in the intelligence community that many in Congress preferred him to be Reagan's CIA director (a state of affairs which probably contributed significantly to Casey's congressional difficulties).

But Inman told the Senate Intelligence Committee in early 1981, he did not favor spying on Americans at home: "The job of the CIA is abroad," he said. Later, he told the press he might resign if "repugnant changes" were adopted. When he resigned, close observers took it as a sign that whatever was going on inside Casey's CIA, Inman did not want to be around to claim responsibility for it.

FINANCIAL BACKGROUND

Assessing Casey's financial dealings has been an ongoing process. The original list of clients at Rogers & Wells that Casey provided the Senate Intelligence Committee contained less than half as many names as the list he provided during the committee's subsequent investigation. In its December report on Casey, the committee said that Casey told them he had mistakenly supplied a list of only his clients for the previous two years which he had already supplied to the Office of Government Ethics, though the Committee's questionnaire calls for clients of the previous five years. Casey's original list, and the revised list follow:

Original Client List

Diamond Distributors, Inc.
Bear, Stearns & Co.
Capital Cities Communications
Est. of Jos. E. Ridder, Dec'd
Charles Atwood
Cox & Company
John Foglia Sr.
Kephart Communications Inc.
Environmental Research & Technology
Fidelity Management & Research
Anthony G. A. Fisher
Sidney Colen
Jeremiah Burns, Inc.
Resource Asia
Parr Meadows Racing Association Inc.
Robert Ross
Litco Corp. of New York
Long Island Trust Co.
Promenade Magazines, Inc.
Dr. Irving I. Dardik
Mitchell P. Kobelinski
Fitch Investors Service, Inc.
Armor Products Inc.
Jack Farber
Lauraine G. Smith
Nassau County
King Kullen Grocery Stores
Energy Transition Corp.
Andrew Duell
Milton Zipper
Saudi American Lines Company
The Institute for Economic Affairs
Gladding Corp.
The Wachenhut Corporation
Philip J. Sagona
Housatonic Valley Paper Co.
Servo Corporation of America
Semiconductor Specialists Inc.
S.G. Warburg & Co. Ltd.
Korvettes Inc.
Edward Swanson

Florida Condominium Corp.
The Alternative Educational

REVISED CLIENT LIST

(List of Clients furnished by Rogers & Wells
with respect to which William J. Casey,
who was then affiliated with the firm,
had billable time or otherwise received credit
during the period 1976-1981.)

Alexander & Alexander
The Alternative Education
American Society of Allied Health Professions
H. W. Anderson Products
Armor Products Inc.
Associated Press
Charles N. Atwood
Parley Augustsson
BRS Inc.
Virginia Bacon
Banque de Paris
Ford Bartlett
Bear, Stearns & Co.
Bessemer Trust Company
Sidney B. Bowne & Son
Elwood D. Boynton
Broad Hollow Development
Jeremiah Burns, Inc.
Caesar's World
Capital Cities Communications, Inc.
Central American Pipeline
City of New York
Sidney Colen
Continental Hotels Corporation
Covert & Associates, Inc.
Cox & Company
DWG Corporation
Deak & Co Inc.
Diamond Distributors, Inc.
Andrew Duell
E.T.P.M.
Energy Transition Corp.
Environmental Research & Technology
Jack Farber
Fidelity Management & Research Corp.
Film Corporation of America
Anthony G. A. Fisher
Fitch Investors Service, Inc.
Florida Condominium Corp.

John Foglia
Connie Francis
Mr. and Mrs. Abraham Friedberg
Fulbright & Jaworski (D.C.)
Gamble-Skogmo
Gladding Corp.
Government of Indonesia
Graphic Controls Corp.
Estate of Leonard W. Hall
Housatonic Valley Paper Co.
The Institute of Economic Affairs
International Crude Oil Refining Inc.
Kennecott Copper
Kephart Communications, Inc.
King Kullen Grocery Stores
Mitchell P. Kobelinski
Koren-DoResta
Korvettes
Nicholas Krapf
Litco Corporation of New York
Lockheed Aircraft
Long Island Forum for Technology
Long Island Trust Company
Dominique Maillard
Mastercraft Corp.
Merrill Lynch Hubbard
Merrill Lynch International Bank
Merrill, Lynch, Pierce, Fenner & Smith
Miles Laboratories, Inc.
Moore, Schley, Cameron & Company
U. V. Muscio
NAB Manufacturing Company
NVF Corporation
Nassau County
National Telephone Company
Newfoundland Refining
New York State Employees Retirement Fund
Norse Petroleum A/S
Old Lane International
Owens-Illinois Glass Mfg. Co.
Oyster Bay Foodtown
PAN AM World Airways
Parr Meadows Racing Association
Pertamina
Peter Piffath
J. T. Potter
Maxwell M. Powell
Promenade Magazines, Inc.
Pullman, Inc.
Republic of Korea

Resource Asia
Reynolds Construction Company
Estate of Joseph E. Ridder
Robert Ross/East-Europe Domestic International Sales Corp.
SCA Services, Inc.
Philip J. Sagona
Saudi American Lines
Scientific Life Systems (Dr. Irving Dardik)
Howard Sears, Jr.
Semiconductor Specialists, Inc.
Servo Corporation of America
Shaheen Natural Resources
Abraham Shames
Sharon Steel Company
Sloan Valve Company
Lauraine G. Smith
Edward Swanson
Tennessee Partners, Ltd.
Ter Bush & Powell, Inc.
Trubin, Sillcocks, Edelman
Twentieth Century Fox
Walter Van der Waag
Joseph F. Virdone
Wachenhut Corp.
S. G. Warburg & Company, Ltd.
David Westerman
Wilmer, Cutler & Pickering
Milton Zipper

Casey's financial disclosure form, listing assets and liabilities was also revised as the year went along. In his January 8, 1981 filing with the Office of Government Ethics, Casey and his wife listed assets of at least $3.085 million, including holdings of $100,000 or greater in: Prentice Hall, C&D Associates, Capital Cities Communications, Philip Morris, Raychem Corp., Amarex, Inc., Apache Corp., Dome Petroleum, Kerr McGee, Southland Royalty, Standard Oil of Indiana, Superior Oil, and Schlumberger Ltd. The couple reported holdings of $50,000 or more in Georgia Pacific, Data Point Corp., IBM, Englehard Minerals & Chemicals, Atlantic Richfield, Mesa Royalty Trust Unit, Halliburton, Intel Corp., and two trusts related to Southland; with smaller holdings in Exxon, Alcoa, DuPont, Amax, Armco, and other firms. He listed no liabilities, nor any gifts.

In August, 1981, though, Casey amended his filing to add 10 additional assets worth more than $145,000, and several liabilities (loan guarantees) worth $472,000 as well as a direct liability of $18,000. A few weeks earlier Jeff Gerth of the *New York Times* revealed that Casey had received as a gift a $10,000 interest in Penverter Partners, a computer technology firm. Casey was given the stock by Carl G. Paffendorf, who described himself as a frequent business associate.

Unlike his two predecessors, George Bush and Admiral Stansfield Turner, who placed their holdings in blind trusts, Casey has kept control of his stocks. "I don't see why I should be picked on," Casey said when we asked about his decision. "The law is the law; it's a clear cut law as to what you have to do with your stocks and I'm complying with that law. I, as a matter of fact, don't play any role in my investments. I have an investment adviser. . . for 20 years and he makes all the investments, particularly when I was at the SEC and earlier jobs. At that time I had a blind trust. The SEC was somewhat different because everyday I had to act on matters affecting large corporations. Here, nothing like that has come to me. People have said just because I might get a lot of information I could use [I should establish a blind trust]; well, that isn't the standard. The whole Congress gets a lot of information, loads of people, many people in the CIA get a lot of information."

Before assuming office, Casey also served as a director of Long Island Trust Co., Capital Cities Communications and the Long Island Lighting Co. Each of those firms annually paid Casey more than $5,000 in director's fees.

WHAT OTHERS ARE SAYING ABOUT HIM

- For a few hot days in July, 1981 it looked like Casey's career at the CIA would be a brief one. Enraged by his appointment of Hugel, and prompted by steady leaks of questionable financial activities by Casey, the Senate Intelligence Committee began to speak openly of demanding his resignation. On July 23, Chairman Barry Goldwater told the press that "The damage done by Mr. Hugel's appointment is. . .sufficient. . .for Mr. Casey to decide to retire or the President to have him retire." But Casey made a strong lobbying effort on his own report, and in only a few days those kinds of comments had vanished. A week later, Sen. Jake Garn (R-Utah) was telling reporters that "Mr. Casey had acquitted himself very well."

When the Senate Intelligence Committee's report on Casey finally came out in December, 1981, it concluded with the bland observation that "no basis had been found for concluding that Mr. Casey is unfit to hold office as Director of Central Intelligence."

- Casey's admirers, of which there are also many, speak highly of his intelligence and stamina. No one has ever said Casey isn't shrewd. His friend Leo Cherne of the Research Institute of America said at Casey's nomination hearing "that it would be difficult, if not impossible, to find a lifetime experience coupled with wisdom, courage and probity equal to that which William J. Casey will bring to the office of Director of Central Intelligence. . . ."

A CONVERSATION WITH WILLIAM CASEY

On April 16, 1982, Ralph Nader, Nina Easton and Ronald Brownstein sat down with William Casey for a one-hour interview in his Washington office on the fourth floor of the Old Executive Office Building. Though Casey discussed his views on a broad range of national security issues, he laid down one ground rule at the beginning of the session: He would not talk about covert activities. "We have the authority to do them as authorized by the President, we report them to Congress. But apart from that I don't talk about them, they don't exist," he said. Following are excerpts from that interview.

Q. Because of your long association with intelligence issues, when you came on board according to the press reports, there was some surprise that the seeming opposition to you was within the agency—usually this is directed at somebody who has never had any background, who people think is an outsider not familiar with what the issues are. Did that surprise you?

A. Well, let me say this. I never sensed any opposition. I've had good support and good relationships from the very beginning. I think I was welcomed because they felt I had some feel for it. Now, there was some resistance, dissatisfaction, not widespread mind you, when I appointed somebody [Max Hugel] to run what I feel was a key job. And that blew up, got some bad publicity. A very good man. I might have made a mistake in moving him in at that level though I think he would have been useful, either there or elsewhere. But it just didn't work out for him. I knew when I did it that this would be the kind of thing which would create some mild controversy. But the fact that I did it knowing that it wouldn't be universally popular was really a measure of my confidence in what this fellow would do. When I made the decision, as far as I could detect—everybody was comfortable. Whenever you bring somebody new in at the top who kind of alters the way of doing things a little bit—lower level career employees may be concerned.

Q. President Reagan said recently—when he stated that in some way the Soviets were ahead of us in nuclear capabilities—that he didn't see why the American people shouldn't know what the Soviet government already knows. Would you subscribe to that notion in the intelligence area—that is, if the Soviets know—let's give you a very simple example, if the KGB is doing something in this country, of some significance, do you think the American people should be told about this—following that principle that they know so we should?

A. No, I do not follow that principle. That is a fallacious principle. There will be times when it is the right thing to do; when it is proper that the American people should know. There are also times when if we tell the American people what we know, we no longer know it; we lose a source. In those circumstances, we believe that the major priority, and by statute it has to be, I'm charged with protecting sources and methods, and if I have to hand out information that the very possession of which will disclose to the Soviets that we're getting that kind of information and therefore they will stop us from getting that kind of information, then I think we're going to withhold it.

Q. Have you confirmed by your own analyses that the Soviets have superiority, and as of when did they pass us?

A. To start out, that is a matter of judgment. Some people judge it one way, some people judge it the other way. I don't think you know. As for when they passed, when they gained parity—and they say everybody admits we have parity, for a time everybody thought we were stronger. I think it's around ten years ago everybody says they came up to parity and they've been building while we haven't, and on that basis you can argue superiority. And superiority is really a matter of definition. If you're able to hurt them very badly no matter what they do then maybe they won't do it. In that sense some people think that's sufficient security, other people think it's not. All we try to do is measure what they've got and make judgments as to what they're doing, what their strategy is and doctrine is, with the respect to the ways they will use it and why they're building what they're building.

Q. You sound like you're personally more comfortable with parity—

A. I'm much more comfortable with safety. I think in the missile crisis of '62 when we had superiority we told them to lay off and they did. I think that's a more comfortable position to be in but I'm a realist. We're not in that position now and I don't see that we're likely—certainly on my watch, in my lifetime—ever to attain that.

Q. You know, there is an impression that we're so far ahead of the Soviets in technology and electronics that they're always here trying to get our latest technology and that they have nothing that they are ahead in that we need. I don't think that's accurate—

A. We don't think it is.

Q. So, is there a program—you know quid pro quo, where we try to find out what they're doing and we try to find out—

A. We'd like to, we try to find out what they're doing. It's very important that we not be technologically surprised. But they are much more successful than we are in closing off that information.

Q. Are you satisfied with our government's surveillance over what the KGB is doing in this country?

A. Never satisfied. It's quite good. That's the FBI's job primarily. Our job is to find out to the extent we can in the Soviet Union and other countries abroad what we can find out about Soviet operations. It's worldwide, since their major activity has become that of acquiring American technology and they acquire probably most of it from advanced countries, Western Europe and Japan, we are quite active in gathering that kind of information and we've gathered quite a good deal of it. But you never know what you don't know.

Q. You haven't met your counterpart [in the KGB], have you?

A. No.

Q. One always envisions that if there is an invasion from Mars that the KGB and CIA would find something in common to work on—is there anything in the world that the KGB and CIA have worked on?

A. Not in my experience, not in my experience.

Q. What is the CIA's policy about using underworld figures or other illegal organizations in its operations?

A. Underworld figures? We don't use them.

Q. Never?

A. I think way back—not way back—10 or 12 years ago, there was some relationship with Mafia figures. In World War II there was a relationship with [Charles "Lucky"] Luciano and the Sicilian invasion, which was a large mistake, but I don't know how we came down on it. No, we don't want to, we don't think it's productive to use them. It would backfire. You know, there is the fact that there are various organizations abroad who have information you might like to have [but] it's not prudent [to use them].

Q. Are you worried about friendly foreign intelligence agencies operating in this country, abusing the rights of people who live here? Are there examples of that, and how do we deal with that problem? Particularly in the tradition of political asylum, which this country has always been in the forefront of—

A. Well, you mean the right of asylum being used to plant agents? Is that what you're saying?

Q. No, no. People come to this country as refugees and they are followed by a whole variety of foreign intelligence agents. There have been reports in the press, and some observers have thought that this is becoming more expansive, more frequent—

A. That's principally an FBI problem—operations by foreign intelligence agencies in this country. We really don't watch friendly intelligence agencies that much. Abroad we try to find out what we can about the operations of unfriendly agencies and we kind of feed that to the FBI so they can handle it here. We don't do that abroad. To the extent that friendly foreign intelligence agencies operate here, it is an FBI problem.

Q. They don't work through the CIA here? There's no common liaison?

A. No, well there could be, if we came across it and it was a foreign intelligence matter—we'll pass it. What I'm saying is that we don't work at that. Our relationship with friendly intelligence agencies is to cooperate with them abroad and get information through their channels. We don't try to monitor what they're doing.

Q. What happens when multinational corporations overseas have objectives that are contrary to government objectives, particularly in your area? There are two questions in this area: Do you think that there is a problem of their wielding too much power over our foreign policy? And second: Is there some sort of liaison that occurs between State, Defense, your agency to try to anticipate those kinds of problems?

A. I haven't encountered those kinds of problems. Do they wield too much power? I haven't encountered that. As a matter of opinion, all policy decisions evolve out of a mix of influences. Whether multinational corporations influence decisions as compared to others, has not struck me one way or the other. It hasn't reached me. I've had nobody come in and bother me from a multinational corporation to influence my decisions. The contact we've had with them is we do have an organization called the Domestic Collection Division which seeks information overtly from any American who may agree to let us have it. And there are some multinational corporations who have such capabilities. By way of illustration: When the oil companies were asked to pull out of Libya, the head of the Domestic Collection Division contacted a number of them to see what we could find out, what information and observations they had about the state of affairs when they worked in Libya. It happens that we don't have much of an eye on Libya,. . . .many, many sources there could be included and that's the nature of our relationship with multinational corporations. . .Some people might believe that just getting information from them might affect us, that they might influence it by coloring what they tell us. If they have any reason to do so they might not tell us what they know of their understanding of the state of play in Libya or the state of play in the development of military related technology in Europe—or Soviet efforts to get it. I think we're capable of a kind of cross-checking and filling out of the kind of information we get.

Q. Pentagon officials are very concerned about trading with the Soviet Union and some American companies were trading either directly or indirectly in a way that transferred sensitive technology or advanced technology to the Soviet Union.

A. We are at cross purposes lots of times, when they want to do business and we think the nature of the business will assist our adversaries either economically or technologically. And certainly the oil companies were not happy about getting out of Libya. But they all came. They resisted and they complained and they didn't like it. Certainly there have been situations where the Administration has taken action to cut off trade to Poland and other places, then on the pipeline. But on the whole I found the corporations that we talked to have been pretty positive. We're having a problem right now on the GE technology, on the compressors for the Siberian pipeline, a very complicated legal thing but they're all prepared to follow the government's lead by and large and again, they just don't think that far [in advance], it's a big piece of business.

Q. A person in your position must always be concerned that he's getting the information he needs worldwide in order to avoid being surprised that something is going on that you wouldn't approve of. Administratively, have you set up any systems to ensure that the flow of information is coming to you to your satisfaction?

A. We work very hard at that. I have a good strong deputy who is very experienced and knowledgeable about the whole range—has spent his whole lifetime there. I have strong division directors. I meet with the chief executive once a week. I meet with my deputy everyday, and talk about whatever comes up. I meet with the principal geographic chiefs of intelligence gatherers. I talk to them once a week. I have a meeting with the National Foreign Intelligence Board, which is the heads of all the agencies, Army, Navy and so on—I meet with them regularly. I get a report from each division head weekly which I read carefully. We have an Intelligence Oversight Board, where anyone can go and complain if they see something amiss that comes back to, that gets looked at. We have a very energetic inspector general program looking on a regular cycle at all the units. So I think there is a very substantial degree of effort and oversight to try to spot things that are likely to go overboard. You can't make a guarantee.

Q. What about systems to avoid letting employees use their knowledge to their own business advantage once they get out like—Wilson and Terpil, the two former CIA agents who have been charged with exporting explosives to Libya and training terrorists?

A. There's a limitation on that. We've tried to improve our hold on that. I think what you've got to start off there recognizing that the Wilson-Terpil situation involved two or three people out of many—these fellows retired almost 10 years ago—so over that period of time several thousand people have retired and behaved properly. There's a code of ethics on what people are supposed to do when they retire. The Wilson-Terpil thing is sort of a product of the fact that there are mercenaries in the world and there is a trade in technology—communication technology and so on. Some of these mercenaries come out of the Army, some of them come out of the FBI, some of them come out of local police forces, maybe some of them come out of the CIA. And we don't think you can restrict—if you try to restrict or tie up the post-employment activities of

former CIA people too severely it means that you're not going to get an inflow
of talent in the early stages. You're likely to suffer—and that's a tradeoff you've
got to evaluate. Our basic feeling is that anything Congress wants us to do we'll
cooperate with. We think that if there are going to be post-employment restrictions that the CIA should not be singled out, that they should be applied across
the board—military, State Department, anybody else who has foreign contacts
that can be exploited.

Q. On the information question again, do you think then that there are
employees, or occasional employees or connections around the world that are
doing things that you might not approve of? Do you feel like you have a
handle, that there is nothing going on that you would not approve of if you
knew about?

A. How would I know that?

Q. Do you feel secure?

A. I'm never secure. I can't afford to be secure. I don't know. I do know of
employees that have left the service and taken employment that I wouldn't
take—that I think most of our people wouldn't take. But I haven't any control
over them, and as far as I know they are honorable people and they think they
are doing something useful and it's a matter of opinion.

Q. The one time we made a Freedom of Information request to your agency, it was
very useful, because we got the materials on that nuclear disaster in the west of
the Urals that occurred in the '50s. And without that, that could not have been
documented, I don't think. You did come forward with it, with the usual blank
spaces and all, but the fact of the matter was you came forward. And it occurred
to me at the time: "Why would something like that have ever been kept
secret?" Because it was a disaster—Oak Ridge says it was an explosion, Los
Alamos said it was a chronic leak—but I think that would have been very useful
for the American public in the '50s to know, that there was this kind of disaster
in the Soviet Union.

A. I think that's a very good question. And you're probably right. I think the
proper way to handle that is to sanitize it so that we can put the information out
without disclosing our sources. We're facing that problem all the time. That's
not a Freedom of Information Act question, it's a question of public policy in
disclosing information, and our ability to sanitize it so that the damage of the
disclosure is not going to offset the value of the disclosure.

Q. It was some 20 years before it came out, and our understanding of why it was
not disclosed by your agency was because the Atomic Energy Commission,
which was by then promoting civilian nuclear power, thought it would be
embarrassing to the U.S. civilian nuclear power project—that is, people would
get worried about nuclear waste and transportation. That doesn't seem to be an
appropriate reason—

A. I think that's a bad reason and if that's the kind of thing that went on, we
should have addressed it. Whatever ways there are of controlling, in an
emergency, nuclear power, should be appropriately made known.

Q. Exactly, it's like what they say about Three Mile Island—it's a learning experience. This was a learning experience overseas.

A. It's one of the hardest things, no question, about how you get information to the public that it needs and should have, how you balance the need of the public and the desirability of the public knowing what confronts them with the concurrent need to protect sources so you can keep on getting the information. We have this on the Central America thing. We went to the [congressional] committees and we laid out the information we had and it was overwhelmingly compelling, convincing. Still the media said "you haven't proved it." We said, "We can't prove it to you; if we prove it to you we're going to lose the information." So we're kind of at an impassse.

Q. Do you think the media's skepticism has anything to do with the way the white paper was discredited in parts subsequently?

A. Well, the white paper happened to have been accurate. They picked up a little bit and they scored a propaganda success in discrediting it. Subsequently, Castro told the vice-chairman of the Social Democratic Party in Germany that the statements in the white paper were essentially correct and accurate.

Q. Is there some sort of rule on the way records are opened up?

A. You have a 30-year rule, like the British have Official Secrets Act. There are, I can't give you chapter and verse, there are rules. You are required to look through all information to see what could be released to the Archives and under that requirement—we figured it would cost us $22 million with all the people that would entail—to look through all the classified information. . .between now and 1985. $22 million and the experience shows we would have released two percent of it. It was a great big effort that really yields very little.

Q. In a time of constraining budgets, is there any thought to consolidating some of the many arms of the intelligence community?

A. No. I think the judgment is that intelligence is relatively cheap, particularly the analytical part of it and it's good protection to have different approaches, different analytical groups who are analyzing competitively, recognizing all kinds of possibilities to deal with.

Q. You're one of the few people we've asked this question to who can answer from personal experience. Which President do you think best handled the Soviet Union?

A. Well that's easy. Ronald Reagan.

Q. Apart from Ronald Reagan. The answer has always been the same, which we'll tell you after you tell us.

A. I would think the answer would be Nixon. Is that what everybody said?

Q. No, Truman.

A. Well, yes, that's probably. . .yes, I guess. Truman did well. Truman quickly took a strong position. I say Nixon because Nixon opened China as a counterbalance and he looked them right in the eye and said he was going to take some action he thought necessary in Vietnam; I think a good action, at least he had the courage to deal forthrightly with the Soviets. And he worked out the ABM Treaty.

Q. Someone once said that the Soviets operate overseas more out of fear than aggression, out of a deepset insecurity in its position rather than a desire to, you know, to sweep the world, crusade—particularly now with its inability to feed itself. How do you respond to that?

A. That type of view is held by people who used to tell me that Castro was acting to defend Cuba and I'd say, that's why his first effort to subvert another country was Bolivia. . .

CHAPTER 7

THE WHITE HOUSE

EDWIN MEESE, III
COUNSELOR TO THE PRESIDENT

RESPONSIBILITY OF OFFICE

Holding Cabinet rank, Meese is Reagan's chief policy adviser. He runs cabinet meetings, supervises assistant to the President for Cabinet Affairs Craig Fuller, oversees the domestic policy staff, and attends meetings of the National Security Council. Until William Clark replaced Richard Allen, Meese also supervised the national security adviser. But the prospect of reporting to the President through his former colleague was obviously unattractive to Clark, and so he now has direct access to Reagan.

BACKGROUND

Ed Meese was having a beer in Washington's Mayflower Hotel during the hot summer days of the 1980 campaign when the subject of the People's Park demonstrations in Berkeley came up.

Those are sharp memories for Meese. He grew up in Oakland, just down the road. In a more placid era, he took his law degree from Berkeley. A decade later, when the protests of the '60s first began spilling into the streets, he was a deputy district attorney for Alameda County, whose sheriff department quelled the Free Speech Movement protests and arrested hundreds of students. And when campuses across the state exploded in the late 1960s, he directed Governor Reagan's hardline response.

Nowhere was the hard line more apparent than at Berkeley, during those People's Park demonstrations of 1969. Today, the park is uninspiring: a vacant, scraggly garden plot encroached on by a parking lot. But a decade ago it was the scene of pitched street battles between the students and street people who wanted to use it as parkland, and the city, which had development in mind. In one of those battles, a 25-year-old local man, James Rector, was shot and killed by a deputy sheriff's shotgun.

Lowell Jensen, Meese's long-time friend and associate in the Alameda County district attorney office, and now the assistant attorney general for criminal affairs at Justice, recalls the death as "a tragedy." "People's Park was not handled properly" by the police, he told the *Washington Post*. It had never even been proven, Jensen said, that Rector had thrown anything at the deputies.

But when Rector's name came up in the Mayflower Hotel, Meese said simply, "James Rector deserved to die."

You can almost hear Ed Meese saying that, not with anger or malice, or even with passion, but evenly, with certitude. Given the chance by Martin Schram of the *Post* to disown the statement, he didn't. Instead he expanded his remarks: "It was largely the work of a relatively few skillful manipulators on the campuses who got the rest of the students riled up. . . My concern was for the individuals who wanted to study and who were interfered with by people who sought to impose their views on all of the people."

Meese helped formulate, and later directed, Reagan's response to campus disorder; first, as legal affairs secretary and, beginning in 1969, as chief of staff.

Brought to Reagan's attention by his tough response to the Berkeley demonstrations and his lobbying efforts on behalf of the California District Attorneys' Association, Meese expanded the legal affairs office from a narrow cubbyhole focused on clemency to a sprawling fiefdom that influenced all aspects of criminal justice policy. At his appointment to the clemency job, Reagan described Meese as "a believer in capital punishment as a deterrent to crime." While Meese held the job, Reagan refused the clemency plea of Aaron Mitchell, who was executed in April, 1967.

As Reagan's chief of staff, Meese displayed the talent for conciliation and synthesizing options for which he is most renowned. "Our job," he said in a characteristic 1970 interview, "is basically to prevent clashes or people feeling that there's no communication."

Nothing so captures Ed Meese as his reaction to the protests of the 1960s. One friend described Meese's family as "the prototype of Norman Rockwell America" and through his career Meese has shown again and again how he cherishes the value that underpins that vision of America: respect. Respect for the flag. Respect for authority. Respect for law and order.

When tens of thousands of students—and indeed millions of other Americans—questioned those values, Meese, like many others, could not accept that the beliefs he held in his stolid heart were really being questioned, or that authority—the cop on the beat in journalist Jeff Stein's analogy—was suddenly seen as the enemy. Even today Meese still talks about undesirable and anti-education elements fomenting the demonstrations.

That vision of the world (perhaps not dissimilar to James Watt's dichotomy of "liberals and Americans") still animates Meese's perceptions. In mid-1981 he attacked the American Civil Liberties Union as being part of a nationwide "criminals lobby" that thwarts law enforcement. Even the White House press office felt it necessary to disassociate the President from that statement. Again given a chance to disown, or even temper, the statements in a subsequent interview with the *Washington Post*, Meese instead rushed forward: "It's important that the public know that there are forces who have as one of their activities an ongoing lobby opposed to law enforcement, and there is really no comparable citizens' group that represents the law-abiding citizen, other than the District Attorneys' Association and Police Officers' Association."

Meese has similar feelings about legal services. During the early 1970s he was at the center of the Reagan governorship's effort to destroy California Rural Legal Assistance (CRLA), part of the overall Legal Services Corporation now targeted for elimination by the Reagan presidency. From the time he took office, Reagan was plagued by the CRLA, which challenged a number of his actions in court, and in a 1967 lawsuit overturned Reagan's cuts in the Medi-Cal program. In 1970, Reagan declared war on CRLA by naming Lewis Uhler to head the state Office of Economic Opportunity, which administered the legal services program at that time.

A former classmate of Meese's at Yale and Berkeley who came on recommendations by a former state public relations director for the John Birch Society, Uhler produced a 283-page report alleging numerous CRLA improprieties. Citing these findings Reagan vetoed funding for the agency in 1971. Ultimately, the report was reviewed by a three-judge panel appointed by federal Office of Econ. Opportunity Director Frank Carlucci (now deputy secretary of Defense). They found the report did not "furnish any justification whatsoever for any finding of improper activities by CRLA."

Eventually, Carlucci and Reagan—with Meese acting as mediator—came to an agreement that allowed the governor to claim a public relations victory, but gave CRLA its funding. Today, Meese still talks favorably about the Uhler report and Uhler still talks favorably about Meese. "He never backed down," Uhler told Connie Bruck of *American Lawyer*, who wrote the most detailed and revealing profile of Meese so far published. As another friend told Bruck: "Ed wasn't just carrying out the Governor's bidding in the CRLA fight. . .he clearly sees CRLA as turmoil-makers rather than deliverers of legal services."

Outside of the criminal justice arena, Meese's views are not as well exercised, and, associates say, not as well developed. He is reported to be more liberal than the President on abortion. In a *Meet the Press* interview during the transition, he asserted (as Reagan himself does) that busing and affirmative action have not worked. But since taking office Meese has presented only what seems to be the Administration point of view, excepting those occasions where he offered gut-level remarks about the criminal justice system.

"He's a very malleable person," former Reagan campaign director John Sears told us. "I don't recall he had very strong views." Though Meese ran the issues office of the campaign, Sears said he cannot recall a single "major policy initiative from Meese while I was there."

It was the performance of Meese's issues office that precipitated the crisis that ended Sears's relationship with Reagan. Unhappy with the quality, and quantity, of the material Meese was producing, Sears established his own policy operation, and Sears's associates suggested to Nancy Reagan that Meese be shifted to some other position.

That conflict was part of the ongoing struggle in the Reagan campaign between the eastern political professionals led by Sears and the California group headed by Meese, Michael Deaver and Lyn Nofziger. Sears forced out both of the latter by the opening of the primary season. Letting go of Deaver, in particular, had been difficult for Reagan. But letting Meese go was inconceivable. Instead, on the night of the New Hampshire primary, in 1980, Reagan promoted Meese to chief of staff, brought on William Casey as campaign manager, and unceremoniously dumped Sears out into the snow.

From that point on, there was no doubt about Meese's position at the top of the Reagan hierarchy, at least until his bewildering performance in the second half of 1981. During the transition, Meese so obscured his boss that he felt compelled to reassure the press that Reagan "is really running things."

As Meese's first prolonged performance in the full glare of national publicity, the transition highlighted both his strengths and weaknesses. Sprawling and elaborate, the transition was the most expensive ever. Despite the expenditure of about $3 million, and a staff at least 50 percent larger than Carter found necessary, the Reagan effort quickly acquired a reputation for missed deadlines, lost reports, and an isolated, disinterested chief executive.

That reflected both the disorderliness of Meese as an administrator and his increasing—and eventually damaging—encouragement of press reports that portrayed him as "President Meese." Though he passionately collects and composes organizational charts, Meese is passionately disorganized. From the days in Sacramento, aides recall, "Stuff would come to him and stop. He's not a good administrator because he doesn't delegate." Sears holds similar memories from the campaign, and White House staffers refer to his briefcase as a "bottomless pit." All of that seemed painfully evident in the remarkably full-born bureaucracy of the transition.

But the transition also reflected Meese's primary strength. Playing a crucial role in the selection of the Cabinet, Meese helped assemble a group that satisfied traditional Republican constituencies, while mollifying the far-right and supply-side advocates with key sub-Cabinet posts. If supply-siders were unhappy to see Donald Regan as Treasury secretary they were placated by the placement of Norman Ture and Paul Craig Roberts beneath him. If hard-liners could not comprehend the selection of Caspar Weinberger as secretary of Defense and Frank Carlucci as his deputy, they were at least quieted by the appointments of John Lehman and Richard Perle to top positions beneath them. And so on.

Born on December 2, 1931 in Oakland, Meese comes from a family of local political prominence. His father was the county tax collector for 25 years; his grandfather an Oakland city councilman. After graduating from Oakland High School, Meese trundled off to Yale, where he picked up a degree in public administration in 1953 and then returned home to earn a law degree at Berkeley in 1958 after spending two years in the Army. Meese remained in the military reserve until 1976, retiring with the rank of lieutenant colonel.

After graduation, he joined the Alameda County district attorney's office, where he remained a deputy district attorney until tapped by Reagan to join him in Sacramento. When Reagan left office in 1975, Meese joined Rohr Industries as vice-president for corporate administration. Rohr hired Meese to help handle its sticky dispute with Bay Area Rapid Transit (BART), which was suing the firm over defective subway cars. Eventually, Rohr agreed to pay BART $15 million. Meese left Rohr in 1976, a year in which the company lost over $52 million.

After a brief stint as a private attorney, Meese landed at the University of San Diego. There, with the help of a large grant from the right-wing Sarah Scaife Foundation, he established and directed a Center for Criminal Justice Policy & Management. Meese kept up his ties with Reagan, of course, sitting on the board of Citizens for the Republic—the organization that ran Reagan's campaign between the 1976 and 1980 primary seasons—and participating in the plans for 1980. Meese remains honorary chairman of the center's board of advisers, and with his continuing interest in criminal justice has kept a close eye on the activities of the Justice Department. It has been rumored that he may eventually replace William French Smith as attorney general, though it seems unlikely Reagan would force out such a long-time associate before he was willing to leave. Meese is married, with three children. His son graduated from West Point in 1981.

FINANCIAL BACKGROUND

In 1980, Meese earned $13,500 from the University of San Diego, which he supplemented handsomely with another $59,940 in consulting and legal work. That included his payment as "legal counsel" to Citizens for the Republic, and his position as "consultant on political campaign staff, policy and operations" for the Reagan presidential campaign.

Virtually all of the Meese family's stockholdings are in his wife's name. These include holdings of between $5,000 and $15,000 in: AT&T, Central Illinois Power, Consolidated Edison of New York, and Exxon; as well as holdings between $1,000 and $5,000 in Monarch Machine & Tool, Safeway, Southern California Edison, Southern Pacific, Sterling Drug, Texaco, and a number of utility bonds.

WHAT OTHERS ARE SAYING ABOUT HIM

- One prominent former lobbyist on criminal justice issues in California disputes the notion that Meese does not have strongly held views. "I think he does have strong convictions," said the lobbyist, who sparred with Meese in the mid-'60s. "I suppose they are those of the people who believe you can change the world at the end of a gun."

- Raymond Procunier, who ran the California Department of Corrections, holds a similar view. Meese, he told Connie Bruck, is "for people being locked up. He's against sin and in favor of motherhood."

JAMES BAKER, III
CHIEF OF STAFF

RESPONSIBILITY OF OFFICE

As White House chief of staff, Baker is responsible for keeping things moving through the White House bureaucracy. Baker serves as an appointed member of the National Security Council, attends most Cabinet meetings, and is also responsible for White House press operations.

While insisting that his most important job is to be "an honest broker" of information for the president, Baker accepted the post only after being given written assurances that he would share policy and administrative responsiblities with presidential Counselor Edwin Meese III and Deputy Chief of Staff Michael Deaver.

"I know that most policy decisions are made in the Oval Office with two or three people sitting around, and I'm going to be one of those people," Baker told the *Washington Post* shortly before Reagan was inaugurated.

On paper, Baker has the largest domain of the big three. He supervises the offices of legislative affairs, public liaison, personnel, political affairs, intergovernmental affairs, communications, press, and the White House counsel. Baker's assistant, Richard Darman, along with Meese's aide Craig Fuller are sometimes considered part of a "big five" that run the White House.

BACKGROUND

James Baker, III is a direct descendant of one of the founding fathers of Houston, Texas. His great-great-grandfather helped establish Baker & Botts, now one of the dozen largest law firms in the country. Later his grandfather, "Captain" James A. Baker, founded and became chairman of the South Texas Commercial Bank, which since has become the Texas Commerce Bank.

Like his father before him, the third James A. Baker is an alumnus of both Hill (prep) School in Pennsylvania and Princeton University, where he played varsity tennis and rugby. After graduation in 1952, Baker joined the Marine Corps for two years as a junior officer and then went through law school at the University of Texas, earning a degree in 1957.

An anti-nepotism rule at Baker & Botts kept Baker from joining his father's firm, but he soon became a partner in a closely related firm—Andrews, Kurth, Campbell and Jones. There, Baker spent the 1950s and '60s as a highly regarded corporate lawyer, eventually becoming managing director of the firm, while at the same time savoring his family's position at the pinnacle of Houston society, in the "Tex-prep" social strata.

Yet Baker, hard-working and ambitious, apparently felt constrained in the role. Eventually he chose to break one of the cardinal rules of decorum in that rarefied realm—stay out of politics.

Baker rose to the inner sanctum of the White House little more than a decade after his first venture into Texas Republican politics. That came at the urging of then Texas Congressman George Bush, a new-found mentor, who was Baker's tennis partner at the Houston Country Club.

Before meeting Bush, Baker claims to have been "totally apolitical," although nominally a Democrat. But soon Baker became Harris County manager of Bush's ill-fated 1970 U.S. Senate campaign. Bush received only 46 percent of the statewide vote, but Baker's efforts garnered 61 percent of the votes cast in Houston. That experience not only deepened Baker's skills as an effective fundraiser and political tactician, but also convinced Baker that he was "absolutely, totally, pure Republican."

Baker has been continually involved in politics since. He worked as finance chairman for Texas Republicans in 1971-72, and directed President Richard Nixon's re-election campaign in 14 counties along Texas's, Gulf Coast during 1972. Under the Ford Administration, Baker served nine months as undersecretary of Commerce before joining Ford's re-election campaign staff as a delegate hunter shortly before the 1976 GOP convention.

Baker's success in rounding up enough delegates to stem a rising Reagan tide at the 1976 convention convinced Ford to make Baker his manager for the remainder of the campaign. (Baker's walkie-talkie code name at the 1976 convention was "Miracle Man.") At the time Ford was trailing Carter by about 10 points in the Gallup poll, and Baker is generally credited with boosting Ford to within just 1 percentage point of Carter's final vote total.

Although Ford and then Vice-President Nelson Rockefeller backed Baker after the election to succeed Rogers Morton as national Republican Party chairman, Baker withdrew his name from consideration for the post after Reagan made clear that Baker would be unacceptable to Sun Belt conservatives. Baker's withdrawal statement explained that he feared his candidacy "would not contribute to the unification of our party, which. . .is the overriding goal." Smoothing over the differences between the Reagan and Ford factions in the GOP was important to Baker, in part, because he needed the support of Reaganites in Texas when he ran for state attorney general in 1978. For his own campaign manager Baker shrewdly selected Reagan loyalist Frank Donatelli, a former head of the far-right Young Americans for Freedom.

Throughout what proved to be the most expensive campaign ever mounted for the office, Baker stressed his devotion to tough law enforcement policies. Even while acknowledging that the state attorney general has little to do with enforcement of criminal laws, Baker issued a 37-page, five-point "plan to fight crime," advocating: a war on drugs, fixed-length sentencing, swifter and more certain punishment, tougher parole requirements, and stricter juvenile justice.

At the same time Baker emphasized his opposition to federal government environmental, energy, and voting rights regulations, complaining about federal "encroachment." And in a speech before a group of nonunion building contractors, Baker noted his "strong support" for the state "right to work" law, while pointing out that he had "fought hard" as undersecretary of Commerce for a veto of the common situs picketing bill. Baker explained that he opposed that labor law reform because it "would have put a hammerlock on the construction industry."

Although Baker managed to raise nearly $1.5 million for his campaign for attorney general—much of it from big oil interests—he proved to be a much less adept candidate than campaign organizer. Even with Bush, Ford, Jack Kemp, John Connally, and Ronald Reagan all campaigning for him, Baker lost.

Baker later attributed the loss to the difficulty he had in distinguishing his positions from those of conservative Democratic opponent Mark White. "I'd geared my whole campaign to running against Price Daniel Jr., a liberal," Baker told the *Washington Post*, "[but] White beat him in the primary."

A year later Baker was back on the national political scene managing his old friend George Bush's campaign for the Republican presidential nomination. From the start Baker informed Bush staff members that he would allow no tactics or rhetoric that would needlessly antagonize Reagan. He now maintains that getting Bush the vice-presidential nomination was "always a fallback, always a possibility" in his mind.

Bush was the surprise winner of the first skirmish of the primary campaign, winning a large number of delegates in Iowa party caucuses. But Baker and Bush were outmaneuvered in New Hampshire by the Reagan camp, and shortly afterwards Baker advised Bush to drop out of the campaign. Bush hung on until shortly before the June, 1981 primary in California.

Eventually Baker accepted a special assistant's position in the Reagan organization, helping Reagan prepare for his debates with Jimmy Carter and John Anderson during the general election campaign. Baker denies allegations made by some Bush staffers that he had made a deal with the Reagan people even before Bush dropped out of the race.

Two days after the election Reagan asked Baker to serve as his chief of staff. Nancy Reagan, Michael Deaver, and political consultant Stuart Spencer reportedly had agreed that Baker would be the best man for the job more than two weeks earlier.

Baker was born on April 28, 1930 in Houston, Texas. Baker's first wife died of cancer in 1970, leaving him with four sons. He later married Susan Garrett Winston, a widow with three children of her own. She was a close friend of Baker's first wife, and worked in Bush's unsuccessful Senate and presidential campaigns.

FINANCIAL BACKGROUND

James Baker, III was born into a position of wealth, power, and status accrued through family legal, banking, and corporate interests in Houston. Baker estimates the value of his immediate family's assets, including those of his mother, at about $7 million.

Most of Baker's non-investment income came from his partnership interest in Andrews, Kurth, Campbell & Jones, a large Houston law firm that primarily represents corporate clients. His income there totaled $105,442. Baker also received $15,600 in fees for serving on the board of directors of three corporations, including Texas Commerce Bancshares, Inc. (a large bank holding company); and Herman Bros., Inc. (one of the ten largest Anheuser-Busch beer distributorships in the country).

Curiously, Baker bought into the beer distributorship during the heated 1980 presidential campaign along with Robert Strauss, then chairman of the Carter re-election effort. The two Texas political rivals were brought together in the business deal by former vice-chairman of the Republican party Richard Herman, the largest stockholder in the company. Baker has been replaced on the company board by L.E. Greenberg, a trustee for Baker's financial interests.

According to his financial disclosure statement, Baker's family has large holdings in many major oil companies including: Exxon Corp.; Mobil Corp.; Atlantic Richfield Co.; Standard Oil of California; Kerr McGee Corp.; and Standard Oil of Indiana. Baker's family members also have financial interests through trusts in many other major corporations including: Merck & Co.; Freeport Minerals; American Home Products Corp.; Black & Decker Manufacturing Co.; Oklahoma Gas & Electric; Louisiana Land & Exploration Co.; Harris Corp.; and Houston Industries, Inc.

The Baker family also has large interests in two closely held corporate ranches—the Garrett Ranch, Inc., and the Winston Ranch, Inc. Baker continues to hold his position as a director of the Winston Ranch corporation.

WHAT OTHERS ARE SAYING ABOUT HIM

- Baker's reputation is as a classic political operator, according to all the people we spoke with.
  "Baker's supposedly amazingly competent—a real, level-headed, down-to-earth, pure political technician," notes Nicholas Lehmann, editor of the *Texas Monthly*.
  "My socks were charmed off by Jim Baker," said Tony Kornheiser, a reporter for the *Washington Post* who profiled him.

- "When you're dealing with Jim and he says, 'Yes,' you can go home with it," said a leading House Democrat.

MICHAEL DEAVER
DEPUTY CHIEF OF STAFF

RESPONSIBILITY OF OFFICE

That title, and the rather mundane list of responsibilities that go along with it—scheduling for the President, handling the office of the First Lady and the office of the military assistant to the President—is misleading. Titularly Baker's subordinate, Deaver is an equal member of the big three who advise the President on all things. With his unique personal relationship with Reagan, Deaver is in some ways the most indispensable member of the White House staff, the "glue that holds this place together," as press officer David Gergen put it.

BACKGROUND

The quintessential Michael Deaver story, of course, has Ronald Reagan playing a lead role.

The scene: Reagan's California ranch.

The time: Thanksgiving weekend, 1979.

The players: Deaver, campaign manager John Sears and two of his aides, and Ronald and Nancy Reagan.

The group had gathered, only two weeks after Reagan had formally announced his candidacy, because the campaign was already showing signs of disarray. Two of the key players, Sears and Deaver, were no longer on speaking terms.

The problems had begun early. Deaver, dissatisfied with the way things had been run in 1976, had floated in 1978 a campaign structure that would place him as campaign manager and Sears as a subordinate running a steering committee. Sears was furious. Finally, at a Christmas meeting, an arrangement was worked out that placed Sears as first among equals with Ed Meese and Deaver.

But the uneasy arrangement made conflict inevitable. Sears was unhappy with the quality of issues papers coming out of the West Coast office run by Meese and Deaver. He set up his own issues operations in the East. He was incensed that Deaver was spending money, even hiring staffers, without his approval. A series of fund-raising concerts that Deaver had arranged were a bust. And Deaver, drawing on his long personal relationship with Reagan, wasn't shy about telling Sears when he thought Sears was wrong—even if Reagan happened to be present.

So they had come to California to see if anything could be worked out. It was an agonizing afternoon recounted later in numerous newspaper accounts. The two sides twisted in interminable conversation that made only one thing clear: the campaign wasn't big enough for the both of them. Finally, Nancy Reagan, perhaps Deaver's closest ally, told her husband, "honey, you're going to have to make a choice."

Reagan hesitated. Deaver didn't. He stood up instead and resigned, for the good of the campaign, he said. When he had left the room, Reagan returned and sneered at the triumphant Sears team, "Goddamn you guys, the biggest man in this room just left."

In his hour of triumph, then, Sears was still more than a bit insecure. With good reason. In trying to weed Reagan away from Deaver, and ultimately Ed Meese, Sears was asking the elderly candidate to strip away a part of himself.

Ultimately, of course, it was Sears who left the campaign, ignominiously dismissed after the New Hampshire primary. And it was Michael Deaver, welcomed home in the cold of the primary season, who took up White House residence, in an elegant room adjoining the Oval Office that used to be Jimmy Carter's study.

It is difficult to find an entire story, or even a quote longer than a sentence, about Michael Deaver without Ronald Reagan's name in it. Deaver has been a shadow, a surrogate son, a confidante and comforter for the President. The "keeper of the body" during the campaign (he saved Reagan from choking on a peanut during the 1976 campaign), he is the staffer who looks after Nancy's interests. The man who was at Reagan's side when he was hit by an assassin's bullet. The aide most likely to sip an after-hours cocktail with the President. A man who can take off the gloves and tell the President what he really thinks.

If you had to tell Reagan something he wouldn't want to hear, staffers say, you'd want Mike Deaver to break the news.

Deaver has spent so much of his adult life in Reagan's shadow that he has left few footprints of his own. A graduate of San Jose State University. An IBM trainee, who dropped out, cleaned out his bank account and bounced from London to Africa to Australia before running out of funds. A neophyte operative in California Republican politics. And then an appointment in 1967 to Reagan's Sacramento staff as coordinator of state administrative activities. In California, Deaver performed his now familiar roles, supervising Reagan's personal residence, keeping an eye on the personal staff, undertaking some liaison with the legislature and the federal government. The quintessential aide.

When Reagan left the governor's mansion in January, 1975, Deaver joined with another aide, Peter Hannaford, to form a public relations firm. Deaver and Hannaford, Inc., began with one celebrated client: Ronald Reagan. They wrote his newspaper column and radio show, got him from place to place giving speeches, and geared up the candidate for his 1976 challenge to Gerald Ford. For their work in the 1976 campaign—Deaver was chief of staff, and Hannaford served as research director—the firm was paid $50,000.

When the 1976 campaign fell short in Kansas City, Deaver and Hannaford helped pick up the pieces, churning out the speeches and columns and keeping Reagan's name in the press. And they both joined the steering committee of Citizens for the Republic, the Reagan front group established with funds left over from the 1976 campaign. Also on the steering committee were Meese, Sears, and Martin Anderson.

Over the years, Deaver and Hannaford picked up a number of other clients, some of whom proved embarrassing for Reagan during the 1980 campaign. Deaver and Hannaford represented the Association de Amigos del Pais, a group of rightwing Guatemalan businessmen seeking resumption of U.S. arms sales to their government. (They ended their contract in November, 1981.) They took on similar chores from a group of Argentinian businessmen. And they pushed the interests of the government of Taiwan, at the same time they were writing Reagan columns and speeches urging a closer U.S. relationship with that country. When the conflict bounced into the newspapers, Reagan said he had known of the contract for years and had "no objection."

Supplementing these foreign interests with corporate clients—such as Dart, Pacific Mutual Life Insurance Co. (whose board included William French Smith), 3M, and Rockwell—and conservative groups such as the Pacific Legal Foundation and the Institute for Contemporary Studies (whose board included Meese and Caspar Weinberger)—the firm doubled in size between 1979 and 1980.

Since Reagan took office, Hannaford's stock has soared. He has all of the right names in his rolodex, and those anxious to win the ear of the inner circle have sought his services. New clients obtained in 1981, according to the *Washington Post*, included the consortium building the Alaska Natural Gas Pipeline (See profile of Charles Butler), Tosco Oil, a firm fighting to preserve its $1.1 billion synfuels loan guarantee from David Stockman (Stockman lost), General Motors and Trans

World Airlines. Reconstituted as the Hannaford Co.—Hannaford bought out not only Deaver's interest, but also subsumed the international consulting business run by Richard Allen. The firm is now one of the 40 largest public relations outfits in the country. Between 1980 and 1981, the firm's net income more than doubled, from $861,000 to $1.752 million.

Hannaford helped arrange the interview between Japanese journalists and Nancy Reagan that led to Allen's dismissal. Despite the involvement of his old associate, Deaver pushed for Allen's removal as soon as the incident became public.

That, perhaps, reveals Deaver's depth of loyalty to Ronald Reagan, a loyalty that can transcend more practical considerations. Deaver didn't think David Stockman should stay on either, though cooler heads realized that the loss of David Stockman in November, 1981 would mean chaos in January, 1982 when the budget was due.

And why shouldn't Deaver be loyal to Ronald Reagan? Reagan has taken Deaver worlds away from Bakersfield, from the corporate ladder at IBM, from the small-town chamber of commerce that better suits his modest bearing, receding hairline and button-down crispness.

Deaver travels in a different world now, and holds broader expectations. That was most clearly demonstrated when he revealed just before Christmas 1981 that he would leave the Administration because he couldn't get by on his $60,662 annual salary. "I have no money left," he told the *Washington Post*. "We are living on our savings." Sympathetic staffers passed around the White House a jar for donations, suggesting "A Penny a Day Helps Deaver to Stay." It would be a lucrative time for Deaver to set off on his own; as long as Reagan is in office, his services would surely be sought—and handsomely paid for—by those seeking to influence the President. Even if Deaver leaves, chances are good that he will return if Ronald Reagan chooses to run again in 1984.

Born on April 11, 1938, in Bakersfield, Deaver was graduated from San Jose State in 1960. He is married with two children.

FINANCIAL BACKGROUND

Deaver earned a $43,000 salary from the public relations firm in 1980, and another $13,542 from the Reagan campaign. Deaver sold his 40 percent interest in the firm to Hannaford in installments that were completed in July, 1981.

At the firm, Deaver stayed away from the controversial foreign clients. According to his financial disclosure form, he handled the 3M Corporation, Rockwell International, California Grocers Association, California Architects, TD Materials, Fireman Fund Corp., and the California Trucking Association.

The California Trucking Association still has a friend in Deaver. Deaver has consistently opposed the appointment to the Interstate Commerce Commission (ICC) of strong deregulators opposed by the trucking industry. Deaver first scuttled the nomination of Constance L. Abrams, an ICC attorney, and then blocked William K. Ris, a former Senate Commerce Committee aide backed by the Transportation Department.

WILLIAM CLARK
ASSISTANT TO THE PRESIDENT FOR NATIONAL SECURITY

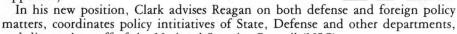

RESPONSIBILITY OF OFFICE

Clark moved up to position of national security adviser in early 1982, after serving 11 months as Secretary of State Alexander Haig's deputy. He replaced Reagan's first choice, Richard V. Allen, who resigned in January, 1982 (See Appendix).

In his new position, Clark advises Reagan on both defense and foreign policy matters, coordinates policy intitiatives of State, Defense and other departments, and directs the staff of the National Security Council (NSC).

Often in the past the national security adviser has been the focal point of the President's international policy, overshadowing both the secretary of State and the secretary of Defense. Reagan insisted early in his Administration that the secretary of State would be the chief foreign policymaker, while the national security adviser would maintain a low profile. Although Allen, as Reagan intended, wielded only minimal influence over foreign policy, Clark's close relationship with the President will allow him to play a much greater role.

The National Security Council, established in 1947, statutorily includes the Vice-President, and the Secretaries of Defense and State; with the chairman of the Joint Chiefs of Staff as military adviser and the director of the CIA as intelligence adviser. It is chaired by the President.

BACKGROUND

It may seen somewhat implausible that a man who attended Stanford University on an athletic scholarship for two years before dropping out with low grades, who flunked out of Loyola Law School, who failed his first attempt at the bar exam, could become a governor's chief of staff, a state Supreme Court justice, the number two official at the State Department, and the President's national security adviser. But that, in a nutshell, has been William Clark's career.

Rarely has a candidate for such prominent, and sensitive, positions had so much to be modest about. Clark's only political experience before becoming Reagan's cabinet and executive secretary in California was as Reagan's campaign chairman for Ventura County. Clark spent two years running Reagan's staff in Sacramento. Then, not long after Reagan promised to "take the cronyism out of judicial appointments," he appointed Clark—a staunch conservative with an undistinguished record as an attorney—to the Superior Court in San Luis Obispo County.

That appointment, and his promotion to the California Court of Appeals in 1971, were simply primers for Clark's appointment to the State Supreme Court. After a disappointing show by Reagan's first appointment to the state's highest court, Chief Justice Donald Wright—who often joined the liberal majority—Reagan wanted a right-wing judge he could count on to tame the nation's most activist court. Clark was his man.

"This was Governor Reagan's idea at all three levels," Clark told the *San*

Francisco Examiner in a 1977 interview. "It never crossed my mind that I would be a judge."

Clark's nomination to the State Supreme Court horrified legal scholars, who were outraged that so unqualified a candidate would even be considered for a spot on the prestigious court. The state Commission on Judicial Appointments confirmed Clark's nomination on a 2-1 vote. The two supporters were Attorney General Evelle Younger, himself a Republican whose candidacy had been backed by Reaganites, and the senior judge of the State Court of Appeals, Parker Wood of Los Angeles, who had served as an appeals court judge with Clark.

The lone dissenter was Chief Justice Wright, who stated, "As of now, he is not qualified by education, training or experience to be confirmed."

Although Clark has built most of his career on political cronyism, his performance has generally been adequate, workmanlike if unspectacular. After the Loyola Law School dean, Father Donovan, approached him during his third year of night school and suggested that he should consider another profession, Clark dropped out, spent two years as an Army counter-intelligence agent in Europe, and then earned enough credits to take two stabs at the bar exam. When he finally passed, he returned to his birthplace, Oxnard (in Ventura County) and, as he put it, "waited for the phone to ring." Eventually, he became a financially successful trial lawyer. As Governor Reagan's cabinet and executive secretary he gained a reputation for solid managerial skills. And, on the State Supreme Court he proved himself a capable, if extremely conservative, justice.

"He was a more competent justice than we expected, although that's still not saying much," said Ephraim Margolin, past president of the California Attorneys for Criminal Justice. "We thought he would fall flat on his face but he didn't. He was a very run-of-the-mill justice. He was not too talented, he never developed any legal theories of his own, but he wasn't flaky either."

"Most people would acknowledge that Clark has done a much better job than expected," University of California law professor Preble Stolz, author of a newly released book on the California Supreme Court, *Judging Judges*, told us. "He had a very trenchant style."

Because of inexperience Clark relied heavily on his research staff, which many legal observers say were responsible for his generally well-written opinions. "Clark was candid. . .about his dependence on staff," Stolz wrote in his book. "He rarely did anything without consulting them and he evidently saw himself as a team leader rather than a sole decisionmaker with assistants whose role was quite subordinate and relatively inconsequential."

According to Stolz, Clark was well-liked by the court family—bailiffs, secretaries, and legal staff. "[H]e knew their names and bantered with them in the halls with genuine interest in their welfare. He was considerably less at ease with his colleagues."

"Less at ease" is a polite way to describe Clark's relationship with the most liberal factions of the court, Justice Mathew Tobriner and Chief Justice Rose Bird. Like Clark, Bird was relatively young, inexperienced and owed her appointment to her loyalty to a governor (She was a close protege of Gov. Jerry Brown and first served on his Agriculture and Services Agency). The open hostility and suspicions that sprung out of infighting between these factions (and included Justice Stanley Mosk who, though a liberal voice on the court, clashed personally with Bird) severely marred the reputation of California's Supreme Court, once considered the nation's most distinguished.

The conflict between Bird, who, said Stolz, "just disregarded people who disagreed with her and had a regrettable tendency to hold grudges" and Clark—who often "spoke his mind more freely than is usual for justices, sometimes rather ill-temperedly"— came to a head in 1978. During November of that year Bird faced a confirmation vote. During that year, also, the court handed down a decision on a politically sensitive case, *People v. Tanner*, which reviewed the state's "use a gun go to jail" law. Tobriner wrote the majority opinion which Bird joined, overturning the law, with Clark writing a dissent which Bird claimed used citations designed to embarrass her and expose her as soft on crime before the electorate. On election day the *Los Angeles Times* reported the still undisclosed 4-3 decision on the case. In a December 20 memorandum Clark suggested that the case had not been filed before election day for political reasons: "In conscience, it must be clear to all on the court that the *Tanner* case was signed up and ready for filing well in advance of November. The question remaining appears to be why it was not filed." Although he later conceded that he had no evidence for his claim and that the case was not ready for filing in November for technical reasons, his charges paved the way for an investigation of the Supreme Court by the Commission on Judicial Performance.

The commission's public hearings the following June did not result in any clear conclusions, but it did expose the inner workings of the court through private memos in which the justices attacked each other personally and even accused each other of lying. (The court later overturned itself on the *Tanner* case, with Clark writing the majority opinion.)

For the most part, Clark's voting record on the California bench was predictable. He supported reinstatement of the death penalty and other tough criminal laws. "Protecting the rights of a criminal defendant is a value we all share," he told the *San Francisco Examiner*. "But indefinitely expanding the defendant's rights must make it virtually impossible to convict the guilty and, therefore, ultimately impossible to protect the victim." Clark has also been described as a strict constructionist, subscribing to the opinion that the courts should interpret laws rather than "make" them through decisions.

But in 1976 Clark, in a departure from his normal rulings, joined in a unanimous decision holding that the Los Angeles school board was obligated to take action to eliminate racial segregation, whether or not the segregation was intentional.

Reagan's nomination of Clark as the number two official at the State Department was considered a move to plant a White House spy on Secretary of State Haig, who is not considered a team player. Clark, still on the California Supreme Court at the time of his nomination, admitted early on that he had no foreign policy experience.

During his nomination hearing, Clark shocked senators and the foreign policy community when he could not identify the leaders of South Africa (P.W. Botha) or Zimbabwe (Robert Mugabe), or the NATO countries that don't want long-range nuclear missiles based on their soil (Belgium and Netherlands). He bowed out of answers to other questions, claiming lack of knowledge, and could only speak very generally on major foreign policy questions. The foreign press immediately jumped on Clark—an Amsterdam daily called him a "nitwit" and a Johannesburg paper labeled him the "Don't Know Man."

His confirmation was opposed by all Democrats on the Senate Foreign Relations Committee, except Alan Cranston (D-Cal.). The dissenters wrote that "Justice Clark's forthrightness [about his lack of foreign policy knowledge] simply could not compensate for his inability to articulate any rationale for his inclusion in the highest ranks of those charged with guiding this country's foreign policy in a dangerous area.''

Clark's chief asset is his insider status with the Reagan team. On Governor Reagan's staff he worked with Edwin Meese III, then legal affairs secretary, Michael Deaver, who was his chief assistant; and Lyn Nofziger, then Reagan's press secretary. Over at the Defense Department is Caspar Weinberger, a close friend.

As executive secretary in Sacramento, Clark devised a favorite Reagan governing tool, which began as an interim measure, was employed eight years in Sacramento, and is still in use in the White House today—the mini-memo, a report to Reagan which boils down complex issues to one page. Clark explained the memo's origins during his confirmation hearing: "Upon arriving in Sacramento Governor-elect Reagan asked Mr. Weinberger and me to look at [the state government's] organization, its faults and defects, which he had campaigned on. . . .'' But, he said, they were faced with huge reports, still on Reagan's desk, covering the critical issues they had been asked to address—"I did not have the time to read them. It was obvious, with all due respect to the former governor, that he had not been able to read them either. . . So I put out an order. . . stating that for at least an interim period no memorandum to the governor would exceed one page.''

The departments, said Clark, "screamed, saying that no problem could be reduced to one page. My answer was if you can't get it on one page, you are unable to understand your problem.''

Early in life, Clark considered becoming a priest and in between Stanford and Loyola Law School, he spent a year in a seminary of the Augustine order. Born October 23, 1931 in Oxnard, California, Clark is married with five children. He bought a 900-acre ranch in San Luis Obispo County in 1965 which has since been his home.

FINANCIAL BACKGROUND

According to his financial disclosure statement, Clark received a $82,000 salary while a California Supreme Court Justice. He has at least $160,000 in investments—nearly all in real estate, including a ranch in Shandon, California and a professional building in Paso Robles, California. His wife and children have investments in Clarkland Company, a family-held corporation involved in ranch realty and land management, and his three sons are involved in a cattle and grain partnership called Clark Brothers.

WHAT OTHERS ARE SAYING ABOUT HIM

- "Just because Clark doesn't have expertise doesn't mean he can't get it," said one scholar who follows NSC matters. "He can channel different views to Reagan—but that assumes the President wants different views.''

- "Clark's lack of knowledge is not a hindrance," said White House reporter Saul Friedman of the *Philadelphia Inquirer*. "In fact, it may be a help: As he learns he inquires, he brings a fresh approach.''

- Sen. Claiborne Pell (D-R.I.) said of Clark after his nomination hearing to become deputy secretary of State: "I found Justice Clark to be a thoroughly engaging, agreeable and honorable person. He has a strong grasp of administrative procedures and would have made an excellent nominee as Undersecretary for Management.''

EDWIN HARPER

ASSISTANT TO THE PRESIDENT FOR POLICY
  DEVELOPMENT

RESPONSIBILITY OF OFFICE

Harper moved into the job in March, 1982, after his
predecessor Martin Anderson left office in February.
Ironically, part of Anderson's frustration grew from the
preeminence of the Office of Management and Budget
(OMB)—where Harper was deputy director—in setting
domestic policy.

That is not the way the system was designed. President Nixon created both the
Domestic Council and the Office of Management and Budget with the intent that
the former would develop policy and the latter would implement it. That line is
easier to draw in a proclamation than in practice, and by virtue of its larger staff,
superior computer capability, and control of the bureaucracy's life-giving numbers,
OMB has generally been the dominant institution.

In 1977, President Carter abolished the Domestic Council and replaced it with a
Domestic Policy Staff directed by Stuart Eizenstat (who did have a significant role in
policy development). Reagan reorganized it again, gave the director a new title, and
cut the staff.

Harper's aides staff the six Cabinet Councils that Reagan created to develop and
coordinate policy for a variety of domestic agencies.

BACKGROUND

Harper comes to the White House from OMB, where he served as David
Stockman's deputy. It could be argued that he left the Administration's real
Domestic Policy Staff—since virtually all important domestic initiatives have
originated in OMB—but the new appointment gives Harper a promotion and a
chance to step out of Stockman's shadow.

As Stockman's number two, Harper devoted his attention to the
Administration's celebrated fight against waste, fraud and corruption. Harper
chaired the "President's Council on Integrity and Efficiency." From the start, the
council appeared to be motivated more by ideology than management. Ignoring
such items as the $126 million the Army wastes every year managing its inventory
(according to the General Accounting Office), Harper expended all of his energies
in the area of "Flics, Flacs and Foldouts"—previously known as audiovisual aids
and publications. Cutbacks in the area are expected to total $100 million—about
what the Pentagon annually spends on marching bands—but those "savings" have
been selectively pursued.

Although a moratorium was announced in April, 1981 on all new publications,
Harper's efforts focused almost exclusively on agencies such as the Environmental
Protection Agency (EPA) and National Highway Traffic Safety Administration
(NHTSA) which have come under heavy fire from the Reagan Administration for
their regulatory activities. NHTSA's enormously popular *Car Book*, a guide for auto
consumers, has been discontinued, but some publications managed to slip through
Harper's "moratorium." On August 20, 1981 the Commerce Department pub-

lished a new guide for businesses hoping to export energy technology to Soviet bloc countries—ironically at the same time the Administration was pressuring its European allies not to build a pipeline to transport Siberian natural gas to Western Europe. One Commerce Department official told us the moratorium "has been lifted for the Commerce Department." Another asked: "Is there a moratorium on new publications?" Although some publications have been granted special exemptions from the moratorium, this pamphlet was not among them. Other pamphlets with such riveting titles as "Growing American Bunch Grapes" remain available.

The "pick and choose" of going after publications was revealed in a testy exchange Harper had with reporters:

Reporter: Here is a 16-page printed program for Easter at the White House 1981. Signed by Nancy Reagan. . .What is your estimated cost of this waste?

Harper: I have no idea. It is the first time I have seen the pamphlet.

Reporter: How. . .could you have overlooked this incredible thing?. . .Could you explain that Ed?

Harper: I don't know. . .We will have to find out and get back to you with information about that. . .

Reporter: You will get back to me? How are you going to get back to me? You don't even know how to get back to me.

Harper's boss, David Stockman, has often claimed that the Defense Department harbors billions of dollars in "waste, fraud and abuse." It is curious that the council has done little on this problem. When asked why the council had not set up a special task force on the Defense Department, an OMB staff member who worked with Harper's council insisted, "It's better to attack the problem as we have done. We choose an area like travel management—the Department of Defense gets investigated just like everyone else. We include them in all our efforts."

Others complain that Harper failed to do his homework. After he publicly ridiculed six publications in an open forum, one astute observer noted that two of the publications were required by law, one was printed because the state of New Jersey had sued to have information on certain food safety materials made available and two others came in at a cost of 2 cents each to produce. One government publications officer told us Harper's council was "Not sure what they are doing. Should have planned a lot better. . .Going off half-cocked. . .Didn't do the legwork."

As his role at OMB indicates, Harper is not an idea man. That can be useful as a counterpoint to someone like Stockman ("Stockman is wrapped up in his new world vision," one OMB staffer told us. "People were glad to see a management type like Ed Harper come to OMB. He provides a grounding in reality."), but it is not the traditional role of the domestic policy adviser. Harper will be more of a paper-pusher than his predecessors, but because he is a smooth bureaucrat he may ultimately be more influential than Martin Anderson, who was rarely involved in Administration decisions.

Harper's government experience is all in the budget area. Upon completion of his doctoral degree requirements at the University of Virginia in 1968, Harper spent a year with the Bureau of the Budget (OMB's precursor) as special assistant to the director for resources planning. In December, 1969 President Nixon appointed Harper his special presidential assistant for domestic budget planning.

After Harper left this post in December, 1972, an embarrassing incident came to light in which he was implicated. Paul R. Jones, Nixon's chief re-election liaison to blacks, claimed that on one occasion his business had received a $75,000 federal grant from the Office of Minority Business Enterprise by submitting a special plea. Applications for these funds were filtered through Harper, who denied any shady role in the deals. When asked about the $75,000 request for funds Harper said he could not remember the incident but if he did receive the request, "my policy would have been to send it to the appropriate agency and would have said 'for your consideration,' period. I never made any recommendation."

Following his stint in the White House, Harper took a series of jobs in the private sector. He spent two years as vice-president of INA Corporation and then joined Certain-Teed, a building material concern, in 1975. In 1978, Harper was named vice-president of Emerson Electric in St. Louis.

As for his appointment to the OMB post, Harper was personally selected by Edwin Meese, III. Harper's most important function there, as one OMB staffer told us, may have been "offsetting the gracelessness of Dave Stockman."

Born on November 13, 1941 in Belleville, Illinois, Harper is married and has two children. He received his undergraduate degree from Principia College in 1963, and his Ph.D. from the University of Virginia. Before entering government he taught for two years at Rutgers University in New Jersey.

FINANCIAL BACKGROUND

Harper earned $175,750 from Emerson Electric Co. He reports assets worth at least $81,000, including those of his wife and children.

WHAT OTHERS ARE SAYING ABOUT HIM

- All of the people we spoke with commented on Harper's management—as opposed to policy development—skills. "Stockman's the big idea man," said a Republican aide at the House Government Operations Committee. "Part of the deal for Harper is to dampen Stockman's influence."

MAJOR ISSUES

Sometime in the fall of 1981, Rep. Trent Lott (R-Miss.) wrote a letter to President Reagan urging him to reverse a long-standing Internal Revenue Service (IRS) policy denying tax-exempt status to private schools that discriminate on the basis of race.

Lott, a conservative Southerner, had a pressing personal interest in the matter: several Mississippi schools, including one in his district, faced the loss of their tax-exempt status for practicing racial discrimination. He was so concerned in fact, that he had designated himself a sort of chief congressional spokesman for two other schools, Bob Jones University in South Carolina and the Goldsboro Christian Schools, Inc. in North Carolina, both of which had appealed to the Supreme Court after federal appeals courts ruled that they were not entitled to the tax exemption.

Lott had good reason to believe that Reagan would be sympathetic to his plea. During his campaign the President had promised to overturn the IRS policy. As it turned out, Lott was right. Next to the presidential correspondence log's summary of the letter, which indicated that Lott had explained the two cases were before the Supreme Court and had urged Reagan "to intervene in this particular case," Reagan scribbled: "I think we should." The summary with Reagan's comment somehow reached Lott, who forwarded copies to the Justice and Treasury Departments.

Within the White House Ed Meese, oblivious to the outrage he was about to generate, directed the staff work and met with Treasury and Justice officials on reversing the policy. He didn't tell the other two senior aides who made up the powerful "troika" of Reagan advisers—Jim Baker and Mike Deaver—what he was up to.

Thirty-six hours before the policy was to be announced, Baker learned about it in a phone call from the Justice Department. Furious that he had been bypassed on such an important issue, Baker brought up the matter with Meese the following day at a staff meeting. Meese assured both Baker and Deaver that the decision was simply one more perfunctory reversal of a burdensome Carter-imposed regulation.

In fact it was not. When Reagan Administration officials announced on January 9, 1982 that they were reversing the IRS policy and would ask the Supreme Court to dismiss the cases as moot, they were altering a policy set forth by the Nixon Administration in response to a federal court injunction—upheld by the U.S. Supreme Court—against granting tax exemptions to schools engaged in racial discrimination. The policy had been a major victory for civil rights.

The reaction to the Reagan Administration's announcement was swift and damaging. On other civil rights questions the Administration had adroitly mitigated perceptions that Reagan was unwilling to protect minorities from discrimination. The tax exemption case exposed the Administration, and Reagan himself, to widespread charges of racism. "I have not yet had occasion to call the Reagan Administration racist," said Benjamin Hooks, executive director of the NAACP after the announcement, "but this latest series of retreats on discrimination puts them mighty close." Said one White House correspondent: "I'm not sure any of those guys understood the history of this thing. Baker sensed [its sensitivity] but even Baker didn't know the history."

Within the White House, "operation salvage" was launched in an attempt to save face for the President. Baker quietly told friendly reporters that it was a Meese operation, and that if he had seen it soon enough he would never have let it through. Deaver, distraught over how the incident had damaged Reagan's image, told reporters the policy shift was a result of sloppy management, not Reagan.

"This President is the most fair-minded man I've ever known," Deaver told the *Washington Post*. "All of those involved failed to see the sensitivity of the issue. It's a shame his reputation has to be tarnished by faulty staff work."

At the same time, Deaver urged the President to submit legislation replacing the IRS rule. Thus Reagan could assert that he simply had not wanted bureaucrats formulating social policy that Congress should address—knowing full well that the conservative-dominated Senate would never pass such a bill.

Within a week, Reagan publicly confessed that he was "the originator of the whole thing," and claimed the decision was simply ill-timed, that he had planned all along to submit legislation replacing the rule.

Personality and performance are always clearly defined in crisis, in the White House as anywhere else. The tax exemption fiasco highlights both the problems Reagan's senior advisers face, and their individual roles in the White House. Meese, an uncomplicated conservative, grabbed the issue from his like-minded friends and huddled it through the White House machinery, insensitive to the political fallout that would occur. Baker, a politically savvy adviser who charts Reagan's ups and downs, immediately recognized the sensitivity of the issue and was quick to blame it on Meese. Deaver, whose blind loyalty to Reagan often skews his judgement, lied to reporters to protect the President.

To Ronald Reagan, who once said he "would have voted against the Civil Rights Act of 1964," the issue went straight to his heart; he did not give a second thought to reversing the IRS policy. "This thing hit a vein of sympathy in Reagan," said one White House reporter. "He still stands for all the things that have been considered racist since those days."

For his senior advisers, an overriding, though unstated, responsibility is to protect Reagan from himself. The same Reagan rhetoric and campaign promises that appealed to the interests of a select few can be politically hazardous when put into action by a leader charged with protecting the interests of the many. The tax exemption question is a case in point. Reagan's position on the matter had been stated in his campaign speeches, and indeed in the Republican platform.

Another example is Reagan's belligerent anti-Soviet rhetoric. While during the campaign those words evoked cheers and applause from like-minded audiences, from the Oval Office they evoke visions of nuclear war and give rise to mass arms control demonstrations.

But Reagan still sees himself as governor of the few. "He has certain ideologies," said Saul Friedman, White House reporter for the *Philadelphia Inquirer*. "If it doesn't fit into his prediliction, his ideas, he discards it." His decisions are based on a general impression of the world that he has developed, not the product of rigorous discussion or debate on the issue at hand. "He is not an intellectually curious man," said Loye Miller of *Newhouse News* service. "He does not go out of his way to get himself exposed to other ideas."

It is no accident that the most politically damaging decisions of his presidency have been made by Reagan himself. One is the tax exemption case. Another is Reagan's decision not to raise taxes in the 1983 budget. Reagan actively backed by Rep. Jack Kemp, rejected advice from nearly his entire circle of advisers to implement some type of tax—the most widely supported was a higher excise tax on liquor, cigarettes and various luxury items—as a means to cap the swelling federal deficit. Reagan's stubborness on that issue—in the face of deficits that will reach more than $100 billion a year—has jeopardized his support from key Republican leaders and members of the business community, as well as providing ammunition to his many critics.

In sharp contrast to Jimmy Carter who muddled himself in detail—reporters still laugh about the stack of documents several feet high that he studied before his decision to cancel the B-1 bomber—Reagan only wants an ankle-deep version of complex issues. In California, William Clark devised the mini-memo for use by Governor Reagan, in which the details of an intricate state issue would be condensed to one page. Reagan reportedly still uses mini-memos to make decisions on federal issues. His counselor, Meese, told a Los Angeles audience in March, 1982 that he tries "to relieve the President of some of the details, but always to make sure he is the one to make the decisions."

Reagan is the President that governs by anecdote. More often than not, his stories are exaggerated, even untrue. In supporting his cuts in the food stamps program, for example, Reagan told Sen. Bob Packwood (R-Ore.) this story: "You know a person yesterday, a young man went into a grocery store and he had an orange in one hand and a bottle of vodka in the other, and he paid for the orange with food stamps and he took the change and paid for the vodka. That's what is wrong." Later an Agriculture Department official, Mary Jarratt, responded in congressional testimony that change from a food stamp transaction is limited to 99 cents. "It's not possible to buy a bottle of vodka with 99 cents," she said. After a year in office, Reagan's misstatements of fact—some would call them lies—had already become legendary.

Reagan has a long history of such misstatements. Reporters regularly report Reagan's errors of fact, but tend to treat them as bloopers, evidence of Reagan's lack of familiarity with the programs under his control and the decisions being made in his name. Rarely pointed out is that the "errors" are always of the same kind: designed to make Reagan look better, or his opponents look worse. Reagan doesn't "accidentally" state that unemployment is higher than when he took office; he twists numbers to make it appear that unemployment is lower. When he was running for his first term as governor—promising, then, as now, to clean up the welfare state—he didn't underestimate the number of Californians receiving welfare. Instead he exaggerated the total by 200 percent.

It's a phenomenon that, try as they might, his advisers cannot control. As one White House reporter noted: "You see growing incidence of bloopers even as it becomes more of an issue." But there is no doubt that it is damaging the Administration's credibility. When we asked a number of reporters what they considered the chief weakness of the Reagan White House, a common response emerged: Ronald Reagan himself.

But in general, the important details of the government are kept out of Reagan's hands. Reagan delegates, preferring to run his show corporate style, and act as the chairman of a board of directors. "I have been asked many times how Reagan goes about making a decision," John Sears, who has managed two Reagan campaigns, wrote in the *Washington Post* four months before Reagan's election. "The answer is that his decisions rarely originate with him. He is an endorser. It is fair to say that on some occasions he is presented with options and selects one, but it is also true that in other instances he simply looks to someone to tell him what to do. . .if his advisers are adequate there is nothing to fear from President Reagan."

During his first year in office, three men emerged as Reagan's most influential advisers, the troika—Counselor Ed Meese, Chief of Staff James Baker and Deputy Chief of Staff Michael Deaver, who despite his title operates as an equal to both Baker and Meese. While David Stockman, James Watt, William French Smith and other Cabinet members sketched in the lines and colors of Reagan's amorphous program, the troika regulated the flow of their information and ideas to the President.

Each morning at 7:30 the three meet for breakfast, before Reagan is awake, and discuss the issues that Reagan will have to address that day. Later the three brief him in the Oval Office. Though Reagan met fairly regularly with the full Cabinet—37 times in 1981—he rarely made decisions without first meeting with the troika.

Of the three, Meese most closely reflects Reagan's views. He is raw Reaganism, without the smoothed edges of a James Baker; and he is a favorite of the right, someone they know they can count on, a "solid Reaganite." His statements rarely have the polish that coats more sophisticated Reaganite speeches. In a March, 1982 address to the Civil Defense Association, for example, he called nuclear war "something that may not be desireable." During a White House meeting he insulted major environmental leaders—including prominent Republicans—with comments like "Solar won't amount to much—what can a few windmills provide?" Left to their own devices, Meese and Reagan would probably drive the Administration off the edge.

Meese's principal interest in the White House has been law and order issues, and he's been a regular spokesman for the Administration's tougher criminal policies. But he has also been a powerful representative for specific business interests. During internal discussions on the 1982 budget, when Samuel Pierce, secretary of the Department of Housing and Urban Development was arguing against Stockman's plan to phase out urban development grants, he was surprised to find an ally in Meese. As Rowland Evans and Robert Novak wrote in *The Reagan Revolution*, Meese "had been convinced by real estate developers in California that 'leveraging' federal funds was a good idea." He prevailed, and the funds for the program were increased in the Administration's budget request. Meese also guided through the American auto industry's request that Japan implement "voluntary" quotas on its exports of automobiles to the United States.

The word during the first months of the Administration was that Meese was the most influential of Reagan's senior advisers. He was the only one of the three with Cabinet rank. He occupies the West Wing office once filled by National Security Adviser Henry Kissinger and later Zbigniew Brzezinski. In a departure from previous Presidents' policy, the National Security Adviser Richard Allen reported to Meese, not the President. So Meese's purview included both domestic and national security matters. Reporters jokingly referred to him as "deputy president" and even "President Meese," and remarked on his extraordinary power in the White House.

That reputation hit a peak in August, 1981 when Meese failed to wake the President to tell him that two Navy jets had been fired upon over the Gulf of Sidra and had retaliated by shooting down the two attacking Libyan planes. Perhaps Meese was starting to believe his press notices. While his decision to let the President sleep during what could have turned into an international crisis spawned a new wave of "President Meese" stories, at the same time it undercut his reputation, as both the press and officials inside the Administration began questioning his judgement. During a *Washington Post* luncheon in early 1982, Meese was introduced with the remark: "I know that if there is another Libyan episode, Ed Meese will wake up the President." Meese didn't disagree. Meese violated a cardinal rule of show business: never upstage the leading man. He has never fully recovered from the incident.

More important, though, Meese is an inept administrator, a condition which readily became apparent over the months. His disorderly nature and penchant for tedious procedures, a familiar characteristic in California, dragged the White House from day one. "Meese is slow," said one White House correspondent. "He frustrates the hell out of everyone." To top it off, Meese seemed to be spending more time making speeches to obscure business groups on the West Coast than churning out ideas. He was addressing audiences in sunny California and Hawaii while the staff huddled in wintry Washington over the Polish crisis and the 1983 budget.

Perhaps his greatest failure was appointing men whose most significant qualification was ardent Reaganism to head the key two offices that reported to him— Martin Anderson at the Office of Policy Development and Richard Allen at the National Security Council.

There's no doubt that Anderson was loyal to Reagan. He alone supported the President in rejecting tax hikes to moderate the deficit. But his office contributed next to nothing to the Administration's domestic policy, a result of lack of organization, a lack of access, and lack of expertise. Of so little use was the domestic policy office that when Reagan was pondering whether he should fire Stockman over the *Atlantic Monthly* fiasco, one senior adviser remarked to a *Time* reporter:

"Hell, he's our entire domestic policy staff. What are we going to do without him?"

Anderson solidly supported the President's supply-side single-mindedness though from a distance. When asked about the supply-siders' influence within the White House during the September tax increase offensive, Jude Wanniski replied: "Let me just say this: when Marty Anderson left the White House last week he sat down with the President at his going-away party. That was the first time since the election that Marty sat down with the President." Anderson resigned in March, 1982.

His successor, Edwin Harper, regarded as a more efficient administrator than Anderson, has reorganized the staff. shoving aside officials who are weak on policy substance and promoting those with some expertise. "Harper is a technocrat who will keep things moving,'.' said one White House reporter. But, with budget-cutting still the Administration's primary domestic policy, the office of policy development can be expected to continue playing a limited role in White House decisions.

The office, which has been substantially scaled down from the Carter years when it was an important force, is now primarily a support mechanism for the six "cabinet councils," devised by Meese as a means for top officials to thrash out policy. Cabinet councils, which consist of cabinet secretaries from the affected departments, have been formed for commerce/trade, economic affairs, food/agriculture, human resources, natural resources, and legal affairs.

In practice, the councils have not become the focus of presidential decision-making as they were billed. In 1981 Reagan chaired only 12 council meetings, and he meets with them less in 1982. Instead domestic policy is discussed in more infor-mal forums, like the legislative strategy group, which includes the three top aides, as well as staff secretary Richard Darman, director of Cabinet administration Craig Fuller, and the assistant for legislative affairs, Kenneth Duberstein (who replaced Max Friedersdorf).

Neither was the national security office a productive element of the White House machinery during 1981; Richard Allen spent most of his energy fighting with Haig and responding to charges that he had acted illegally in accepting custody of a $1,000 check from Japanese journalists that was intended for Nancy Reagan. At the same time his sometimes acerbic and arrogant manner irritated others on the White House staff. Reagan announced early in his presidency that the national security adviser would have a low profile and take a back-seat to the secretary of State. Allen was put in the basement office and did not have regular access to the president. To supplant Allen's weak National Security staff, Meese devised the National Security Planning Group consisting of Haig, Defense Secretary Caspar Weinberger, Vice President Bush, CIA Director William Casey and the three top White House aides. Allen was designated "note-taker" at those meetings.

Allen, however, was an ideologue who wanted to influence policy. He hired a staff that reflected his views and, while not developing any significant initiatives on foreign policy matters he routinely ran head on into Haig. The bickering between the two continued through most of Allen's year in the White House, reaching the point when Haig announced to the press that an unnamed White House aide (obviously Allen) was waging "guerrilla warfare" against him. Meanwhile the con-tradictory statements emanating from the State and Defense Departments escalated.

Despite Allen's embarrassing performance, Meese was his strongest backer, while Baker and Deaver both pressed for his removal. With little choice left, Meese finally ordered an FBI investigation of Allen's acceptance of the $1,000 check. Though cleared of any wrongdoing, Allen was forced to resign at the end of 1981. When Clark came on as national security adviser, Meese lost authority over that area.

Deaver is the President's hand-holder. He sees to Reagan's personal needs and comfort. An amiable public relations man, Deaver also minds the first family's image. His tool is Reagan's daily schedule, which he sets. Through that, Deaver can control not only what the President does and who he sees, but also what the public sees him do. He's been particularly concerned with trying to "correct" perceptions that Reagan is unfair, racist, and unfeeling, an effort consistently thwarted by Reagan himself. But Deaver lacks the insight to catch sensitive decisions before they get into the pipeline. He rarely gives his views on policy substance. "He's not an issues person, though from time to time he tells the President how to approach issues," said Friedman. Another White House reporter remarked: "Deaver likes to avoid responsibility for decisions." Of the big three, Deaver is the least accessible to the press.

Baker, considered a dangerously moderate Bush-type by the far right, has the keenest political insight of Reagan's top advisers. He is the President's chief legislative strategist, the one who keeps count on members of Congress. Baker is the most accessible both to reporters—he's usually the unnamed "senior adviser" quoted in the press—and to congressmen. Reportedly he has a policy of returning before the end of the day every call he receives from members of Congress.

To Democrats and moderate Republican leaders, Baker is the most sensible voice in the White House. He sided with Stockman during discussions on the 1982 budget in arguing for smaller increases in defense spending. He was a vigorous proponent of implementing excise taxes to bring down the deficit and restore the faith of many traditional Reagan supporters that had begun expressing doubts. And he has sought to moderate the cuts in some social programs.

But to the Moral Majority and friends he is that Ivy League-Wall Street-Big Business kind of Republican that Richard Viguerie says he so despises. The right-wing press has sent warnings to Reagan that the "Bakerization" of the White House is stifling his Administration's program. In a May, 1982 letter to a financier of conservative causes, Reagan defended Baker against the carping of the New Right.

Baker has become the far right's whipping boy because they cannot attack the main source of their frustration—Ronald Reagan. Over the years, Reagan has demonstrated himself clearly in support of their goals, but he recognizes there is only so much he can devote attention to. And given the choice between the social agenda of the New Right and the "Robin-Hood-in-Reverse" needs of big business and Wall Street, Reagan has invariably come down on the side of big business. Reagan may well get to the new right's "pro-family" package—he certainly will give it rhetorical support—but he is not likely to vigorously support their efforts if he, and his aides, perceive that it will impinge on the preeminent goal of increasing the after-tax income of the top income earners and business.

On a day-to-day level, Baker's influence is growing. But when it comes down to the crucial decisions, he is still an outsider who has little influence over Reagan's thinking: he, of course, lost on both the defense budget and tax question.

Clark, who joined the White House at the beginning of 1982, came into the national security adviser's post with little knowledge of foreign affairs other than his year as Haig's deputy at the State Department. But he has the requisite ingredients to become a powerful force in Reagan's decisions. He has a close relationship with Reagan from his years as chief of staff in the California governor's office. They are personal friends of similar intellect and interests. As Deaver told the *Los Angeles Times*: "These two guys more than anybody else in the White House would rather be riding off into the sunset on a horse than doing anything else—that's what makes them different."

That relationship gives Clark direct and regular access to the President. As one senior adviser remarked to the *Los Angeles Times*, "Reagan runs a lot of things past Clark, and when Clark wants to see the President he just goes in."

Like Meese, Clark is a solid Reaganite, but unlike Meese he is an efficient administrator. As deputy secretary of State, he functioned capably despite his astonishing lack of knowledge in foreign affairs. He headed an interagency group on El Salvador, coordinated policy for the Law of the Sea conference and headed a committee on ambassadorial appointments. He also traveled to South Africa to discuss the Namibian settlement. Understandably, though, he was kept off Capitol Hill where his lack of knowledge would have been embarrassing during congressional hearings.

"Ultimately," said one White House reporter, "Clark will not be a conceptualizer or initiator of foreign policy ideas, but he will have a lot of influence as a coordinator." In that, Clark occupies a unique position. He spent nearly a year earning Alexander Haig's trust and soothing his tempers. When Reagan, in a move to head off Haig's maneuvers for power, appointed Bush to head a "crisis-management" team that would handle both domestic and foreign crises, Haig was furious and ready to resign. But Clark calmed him down, and even got Deaver to mollify him over breakfast. The crisis management team has still not met, though not for lack of crises.

Clark, in addition, has been friends with Weinberger since they served together in Reagan's gubernatorial administration. Thus he can be a forceful mediator between the two men. "So far he's been successful at banging their heads together," remarked one Washington reporter. When Weinberger and Haig both scheduled trips to the Middle East without consulting each other or the White House until it was too late to change plans, Clark stepped in and reproached both. Then he convinced Reagan to issue a directive requiring that future trips first be cleared with the White House.

More importantly, however, Clark's job is to get Reagan more involved in foreign policy. During his first year, Reagan's superficial understanding of national security matters was evidenced in press conferences, where he became visibly shaky each time a technical national security question arose. It was also clear that Reagan did not fully understand the implications of his initial decision, later reversed, to base MX missiles in hardened silos.

Clark briefs Reagan each morning—a practice that was halted about midway through Allen's tenure—often bringing in experts from the Pentagon and State Department to expand on the issues he presents.

Reagan also meets regularly with the National Security Council. Many observers say Clark's lack of expertise is not a hindrance in his new post, in fact it may help. And because he is no expert, he is unlikely to clash over policy matters with Haig and Weinberger. He will operate as the post was intended—as coordinator and adviser.

With that said, however, Clark is a tried and true Reaganite, a conservative hardliner. After Reagan complained about leaks of sensitive memos and policy decisions, Clark in January, 1982 issued a directive requiring that all contacts between journalists and Administration officials "in which National Security Council matters on classified intelligence information are discussed" first be approved by "a senior official." Baker, who was in Houston when he learned that Clark's order was going to be released, expressed concern over the press's reaction to it, and asked Clark to delay the order. Clark disregarded his advice and issued the order anyway, telling staff members he didn't think "press considerations should be involved in this."

The guidelines did generate a storm of controversy. Several weeks later the White House retreated, and the President issued a substitute directive requiring officials who read material to be digested by the NSC to sign a cover sheet, acknowledging an understanding of the laws governing the release of classified information and agreeing to cooperate with an investigation into unauthorized leaks.

Clark was also a driving force behind Reagan's executive order expanding the government's secrecy authority. The order eliminates the standard for "identifiable" damage to the national security, in effect reversing a 30-year trend towards more open government and changing the operating standard to when in doubt—classify. Before the order was promulgated, Rep. Glenn English (D-Okla.), chairman of the House government information and individual rights subcommittee, conducted a hearing on the proposal, saying it could provide a "blank check" for an unprecedented level of government secrecy. Clark, and Attorney General William French Smith refused to testify or send representatives.

But Clark is credited with taking a relatively pragmatic approach to other matters. He has urged Reagan to tone down his cold war rhetoric and to try to coopt the nuclear freeze movement rather than confront it, hence Reagan's comment to freeze proponents during Ground Zero week: "I'm with you."

He'll try to file the sharper edges of Reagan on foreign policy matters, just as Baker tries to smoothe them on the domestic side. The product may be a sugar-coated Reaganism, a more palatable version. Inside, though, the ingredients are the same. For they are true believers, too, loyal to the President and ready to use their political skills to advance his program.

CHAPTER 8

OTHER AGENCIES

ACTION

THOMAS PAUKEN
DIRECTOR

RESPONSIBILITY OF OFFICE

Action was created by President Nixon in 1971 as a means to exercise a tighter rein on the Peace Corps and VISTA, which were subsumed into it.

Action now includes VISTA, the Foster Grandparents Program, RSVP (Retired Senior Volunteer Program), the Senior Companion Program, and the National Center for Service Learning. In 1979, President Carter designated the Peace Corps as an autonomous agency within Action. Congress, largely in reaction to Pauken's nomination, made the Peace Corps independent in December, 1981 legislation.

As Action director, Pauken is responsible for "administer[ing] and coordinat[ing] the domestic and international volunteer programs sponsored by the Federal Government, which are linked by a commitment to a 'bottom-up' development process which fosters self-reliance and utilizes available human and economic resources to overcome conditions of poverty." For 1982, Action has a budget of $132.7 million and a staff of 310.

BACKGROUND

Though Action is hardly among the most powerful federal agencies, Pauken's nomination proved to be one of Reagan's most controversial. The flap arose over Pauken's career as a military intelligence agent during the Vietnam war.

Since the Peace Corps has long rejected applicants with intelligence backgrounds—to avoid allegations that it was serving as a cover for American spying—Pauken's nomination seemed to many singularly inappropriate.

His nomination was approved unanimously by the Senate Committee on Labor and Human Resources but was held up by the Senate Committee on Foreign Relations. Sen. Alan Cranston (D-Calif.) led the opposition to Pauken, saying he would not approve the nominee unless the Peace Corps were removed from Action's jurisdiction. (Under current law, Action handles Peace Corps recruiting.)

In his confirmation testimony, Pauken sought to minimize his intelligence background. But subsequent investigation led Cranston to conclude that, "Pauken has been less than candid in his representations and dealings with the committee in several respects."

In that regard, three points were particularly important. Pauken told the committee he "happened" to be assigned to military intelligence. But, Cranston wrote in a letter to committee Chairman Charles Percy (R-Ill.), "his enlistment records (according to Defense Department sources) indicate that he requested this assignment."

Pauken described his Vietnam experience as being focused on "research and analysis." Said Pauken: "I served as a Province Intelligence Officer in the [Mekong] delta, and I served as a Senior Analyst for Strategic Research Analysis." But Pauken's military records for November 1, 1968 through May 31, 1969 describe his duties as "Team chief in a unilateral clandestine intelligence collection operation. . . ." For the next three months his duties were described as, "Team chief of an intelligence collection team engaged in covert intelligence operations." In an October 11, 1969 statement, Pauken described his duties: "Simultaneously, I continued to develop the covert intelligence program of the team I headed."

In an interview with the *Washington Post*, one of Pauken's former colleagues who requested anonymity, said their "duties included reviewing agent assets, dispatching agents on intelligence gathering missions, recovering the agents after the mission, debriefing them and reporting back their intelligence to operational units."

On the key issue of whether Pauken worked with the CIA, the record is less firm. Several officers who served with Pauken told the *Post* that a province intelligence officer's duties would routinely include contact with the local CIA agent, but Pauken has denied any such contact. His military records, however, indicate he worked on "several joint classified projects. . .with other intelligence agencies in the Saigon area."

Pauken refused to discuss this, or any other issue with us. He said: "As far as I'm concerned, your report is already written."

Cranston managed to delay consideration of Pauken's nomination until May, 1981. By then, the Foreign Relations Committee had taken up a Cranston-sponsored bill to totally separate the Peace Corps from Action. (See Major Issues.)

More than Pauken's military career is controversial. Pauken has been "a perennial political candidate" for the past several years in his home state of Texas, as one observer put it, running hard-fought, sometimes ugly, campaigns. Since 1976, Pauken has tried and failed in three races—the first for state senator, the second and third for U.S. representative from the Dallas area. Pauken lost all three bids by slim margins.

In both congressional campaigns, Pauken opposed incumbent Congressman James Mattox. "They were two bitter campaigns," said Jean Wicker from the Dallas Democratic headquarters. "Pauken resorted to typical Moral Majority tactics."

Among those tactics were accusations that Mattox was "anti-family and pro-homosexual;" Pauken even persuaded a popular evangelist preacher to attack Mattox.

Mattox raised questions about Pauken's campaign finances but a subsequent Federal Election Commission (FEC) investigation cleared Pauken.

The FEC ruling came on April 24, 1981, just days before Pauken was confirmed. With attention focused on the nominee's intelligence background, the lawsuit's dismissal went unnoticed by the press.

The major allegations Mattox raised were that Pauken knowingly accepted campaign contributions funneled through a non-profit (and legally "charitable") organization which shared the same address as Pauken's home; and that Pauken failed to report or register the name of the same organization as a principle or affiliated campaign committee.

The primary source of these allegations was a film entitled "Whatever Works" that Pauken personally produced and starred in. The film attacked activists Jane Fonda and Tom Hayden, portraying them as ruthless radicals bent on revolution at any cost.

The film was produced by Texas Forum Inc., the non-profit firm based in Pauken's home. The firm's officials included his former campaign manager and former legal counsel. Mattox presented a series of newspaper clips that indicated Pauken used the film extensively on his campaign tour. The film was also rented to numerous Dallas-area civic and business groups during the campaign. Mattox contended that the proceeds from these showings went illegally to Pauken's campaign.

When contacted, a staff aide to Mattox said the congressman did not care to comment about the race or the suit, having no desire to "rekindle the feud."

Pauken, a lifelong conservative Republican, was the national chairman of the College Republican National Committee in 1965 (at the age of 21) and gave numerous speeches on college campuses defending the government's Vietnam policy. He graduated from Georgetown University in 1965 with a political science degree and did two years of graduate political science work there.

In 1967, he enlisted in the Army and served three years in military intelligence, receiving an Army Commendation medal for his service.

After leaving the Army in 1970, Pauken was appointed associate director of a White House Fellowship program. It proved a brief stint.

Pauken was expelled by the Nixon Administration after he wrote a highly critical magazine article entitled "A Look Inside Russia" for *U.S. News and World Report* in August, 1971. He had toured Russia as part of a White House program, but had not been authorized to write about the experience.

Pauken was severly criticized by his program director shortly after the story appeared. In a White House memo dated August 6, 1971, the director, David C. Miller, Jr., said: "The Fellows and I view the actions of Tom Pauken as disloyal, selfish and immature. . ."

He was released from the program a few days later.

Pauken then returned to Texas where he obtained his law degree at Southern Methodist University in 1973. He has been in private practice since, and has maintained his allegiance to the Republican party.

Born on January 11, 1944 in Victoria Texas, Pauken is married with five children.

MAJOR ISSUES

- As a former military intelligence officer, Pauken's association with the Peace Corps has raised serious questions, prompting Congress to pull the Corps out of Action.

- With the VISTA program slated to be phased out, and the loss of the Peace Corps, Pauken may be left in charge of a skeleton operation. Congress might decide to abolish Action completely.

Pauken has vowed to leave Peace Corps' decision-making to its director, Loret M. Ruppe, another Reagan appointee whose only "qualification," critics say, is that she once ran a United Way campaign in a tiny Michigan town. But the Corps has been pilloried by the far right with *Human Events*, charging that its 20th anniversary celebration in June, 1981 attracted "virtually every anti-Reagan freak around."

Sen. Cranston's legislation to sever the Peace Corps from Action passed the Senate in 1981. It also passed the House and was signed into law by the President on December 29, 1981.

At the same time, Reagan plans to phase out VISTA by 1984. Reagan is eager to get rid of VISTA because of business complaints that volunteers were becoming "too political" and organizing tenant unions, welfare recipients, and other groups. VISTA issued guidelines barring volunteers from participating in political demonstrations even during off-hours, but backed down in part in January, 1982 when faced with an American Civil Liberties Union lawsuit. The final rules did not cover off hours.

In lieu of VISTA, Pauken is promoting non-paying programs within local communities. (VISTA workers receive subsistence stipends and in the past have entered communities other than their own.) Pauken will call his low-cost alternative "Young Volunteers in Action," a corps of high school and college-aged people working within their own communities. They will be required to be totally non-political. Critics say this program will amount to offer little in place of VISTA.

"If you take the profile of your typical VISTA volunteer—they're about 25 or 30, locally recruited, low-income person—all walks of life, all ages to take part in meaningful full-time volunteer work, which, because of legislation, [has to be focused] for anti-poverty," said Mimi Mager, executive director of Friends of VISTA. "This program which he is proposing as the alternative is people from 18-22 who will work 8-10 hours a month. Where a VISTA volunteer has to make a one year commitment, these are only four months. There's no anti-poverty focus to the program. One proposal has kids passing out volleyballs."

A hardball hard-right politician, Pauken has compiled hit lists of existing VISTA projects he considers "pro-leftist." Pauken first passed out a list at the National Press Club in May, 1981 of projects he considered "questionable" because of alleged "partisan political postures." All of the 32 projects had previously been approved by Action's state and regional offices and by the Governor of each state involved. Pauken said the projects may be suspended.

A few weeks later Pauken distributed another list of 39 VISTA projects he considered "pro-leftist" at a meeting of a coalition of far right groups known as the Kingston Coalition, according to congressional testimony by Katherine Mountcastle, who attended the meeting. According to Mountcastle, Pauken told the group that "many VISTA volunteers work with pro-leftist groups that need to be eliminated."

When Rep. Louis Stokes, (D-Ohio) wrote Pauken in late June, 1981 to question the inclusion of a VISTA project on the "hit list," Pauken responded: "Let me assure you that there is no such list established for the purposes of targeting projects for investigation and/or elimination." Pauken wrote the letter in July, after both his National Press Club and Kingston Coalition appearances.

When Jack Anderson summed up the events in a December, 1981 column, though, Pauken acknowledged the existence of a list, though he again denied it was a hit list. "There simply is no VISTA 'hit list' or list of 'targeted' groups. I am personally aware of only one list of 32 VISTA projects," he wrote Anderson.

Samuel Brown, Action's director under President Carter, says the elimination of VISTA is in direct conflict with Action's legislative mandate.

"Pauken wants the middle class to promote the welfare state," Brown said. By closing down VISTA, Pauken is attempting to "defang the poor people who have been helped by the program and put them in subservience."

"Pauken does not understand the thrust of the neighborhood and citizen's movements," he said. "He wants to take the power away from the people."

Without the Peace Corps and VISTA, Action would become a shell of its former self. Pauken is proposing to gear its remaining resources toward older Americans' projects (such as Nancy Reagan's pet Foster Grandparents Program), troubled youths and Vietnam veterans.

"[Pauken] has thrown the focusing of funds on anti-poverty programs out the window," said Judy Wagner, staff consultant of the House Education and Labor Subcommittee on Select Education. "His alternatives are appalling because they are unrelated to poverty."

Wagner said she cannot understand why the Administration is starting veterans programs within Action and at the same time has tried to cut Veterans Administration funds. Brown maintains voluntary veterans programs could much easier be organized within that agency than Action.

But Mager sees another plan in the veterans program. "The idea is to find 'successful' Vietnam vets. . .bankers, doctors, real estate developers, lawyers and give them to a soapbox to stand up and say 'Look at me, I'm successful.' It's not to do the kinds of things VA counseling centers are doing. . .It's a way for young Republicans who are going to run for Congress or some other office someday to get public exposure," she said.

Ultimately, many critics see this as the beginning of the end for Action as an independent agency.

"[Congress] may well decide to close Action after Peace Corps and VISTA are gone," Wagner said. "There would be no justification for keeping the Action agency around just for the sake of allowing Reagan to fill it with political cronies. Without Peace Corps and VISTA it would be a useless agency. The remaining programs can just as easily be transferred to other existing agencies."

FINANCIAL BACKGROUND

Pauken, the "perennial candidate," listed only $17,388.07 in salary from his law practice last year. It would appear his patience has paid off, as he will more than triple that salary in his government position this year.

WHAT OTHERS ARE SAYING ABOUT HIM

- Pauken's predecessor, Sam Brown, said he agrees with Sen. Cranston that since Pauken would be ineligible to apply for a staff position at Peace Corps, it is ludicrous that he can be appointed director of the agency which oversees the corps.

  "As far as I'm concerned," said Brown, "this just gives ammunition to the people who want to kill Peace Corps."

- Noting that Peace Corps workers are sometimes accused of working for the CIA, "which often puts them in personal jeopardy," Sen. Rudy Boschwitz (R-Minn.) said Pauken's "association with the Peace Corps as director of Action would be clearly inappropriate. His appointment would unnecessarily endanger our Peace Corps volunteers overseas."

COMMODITY FUTURES TRADING COMMISSION

PHILLIP JOHNSON
CHAIRMAN

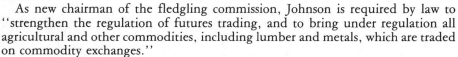

RESPONSIBILITY OF OFFICE

Since its creation in 1974, the CFTC has been a source of irritation to members of the futures industry who have said the commission personnel have lacked experience and imposed too many regulations.

The CFTC succeeded the Commodity Exchange Authority (CEA), which had been in the Department of Agriculture, and became an independent agency with expanded responsibilities. It now regulates all commodities, whereas the CEA only had regulatory authority over some.

As new chairman of the fledgling commission, Johnson is required by law to "strengthen the regulation of futures trading, and to bring under regulation all agricultural and other commodities, including lumber and metals, which are traded on commodity exchanges."

The purpose of such regulation is to "prevent price manipulation, market corners, and the dissemination of false and misleading commodity and future information affecting commodity prices."

In 1982, the agency operated with a budget of $19.5 million and a staff of 510.

BACKGROUND

The futures industry generally could not have been more pleased with President Reagan's selection for chairman of the CFTC. Johnson was a partner in the Chicago law firm of Kirkland & Ellis, where he has specialized for 15 years in the Commodity Exchange Act and its regulations.

His experience has primarily been confined to agricultural futures at the Chicago Board of Trade. Yet, according to Clayton Yeutter, president of the Chicago Mercantile Exchange, Johnson is "probably the most respected commodities lawyer in the world."

Johnson has been a prolific writer on commodities issues. His two-volume legal treatise entitled *Commodities Regulation* has been released by Little, Brown and Co. The *Wall Street Journal* reported the work is "expected to be a standard reference work for the profession."

Over the past six years, Johnson has also written dozens of articles concerning commodities law in several prominent law journals, virtually all of them reflective of his deregulatory philosophy toward commodities.

His writings reflect his deference to the self-regulatory mechanisms of the exchanges. In one 1975 article, he lauds the exchanges for establishing voluntary codes of behavior and argues that they felt "It was only 'good business' to weed out those members of the industry whose activities threatened public confidence in the markets." He is critical of what he sees as the CFTC's "doubts [about] the ability or willingness of exchange members to reach impartial decisions when a claim is made against a fellow member."

Wrote Johnson: "Long-time observers of exchange proceedings tend to feel, on the contrary, that members are the harshest judges of other members."

Many other observers, from the General Accounting Office (GAO) to Senate and House investigators, do not share such a sanguine view of the exchanges.

In a January, 1976 article, Johnson called the agency he now heads "a bold experiment in whether the regulation of an American industry can be conducted more efficiently and more uniformly under a centralized leadership." The industry, Johnson argued, "can be expected to support the CFTC's" preeminent role in futures regulation "since fragmented and conflicting regulatory cross-currents would, in the long run, be injurious to the industry and its orderly growth."

Those same skeptics would argue that the industry supports the CFTC's dominance of futures regulation out of fear not so much of fragmentation as stricter regulation at the hands of other federal bodies less amenable to its arguments.

Johnson has served as a member of the CFTC's advisory committee on the Definition and Regulation of Market Instruments and was also on CFTC's State Jurisdiction and Responsibilities advisory committee.

He served as chairman of the American Bar Association's (ABA) Committee on Commodities Regulation since its creation in 1976. He also was a member of ABA's Section of Corporation, Banking and Business law. Johnson has lectured extensively on the Commodity Exchange Act to groups such as: the Federal Bar Association, the Bureau of National Affairs, American Law Institute, the Futures Industry Association, the Chicago Board of Trade, and the American Bar Association.

He is also a member of board of directors of the Futures Industry Association, which is the commodity industry's national trade association.

Born on June 13, 1938, in Springfield, Ohio, Johnson is a graduate of Indiana University, where he received an B.A. degree with honors in political science and philosophy in 1959. He was graduated from Yale Law School in 1962 and served as managing editor of the *Yale Law Journal*. He is married with four children.

MAJOR ISSUES

- Congressional criticism of the CFTC reached a new peak in early 1982, as two committees and the GAO questioned whether it was capable of effectively regulating commodities markets, and indeed, whether it served any useful purpose at all.

- Nonetheless, the agency continues to authorize new futures, particularly in financial instruments. Critics consider these new contracts—such as a future based on the rise and fall of the stock market—idle speculation that drains capital away from more productive uses.

- Despite the conclusions of the GAO and other analysts that self-regulating futures markets are not performing adequately, the CFTC approved a plan Johnson drew up while a private attorney to establish a new national self-regulatory body.

In the near future, Johnson may be forced to spend a good portion of his time defending the CFTC against legislators skeptical about the need for its continued existence.

Critical House and Senate hearings in late February, 1982 focused on the commission's viability and, more pointedly, on its repeated failure to exercise its regulatory responsibilities, even when crises in the markets seemed to call for intervention.

For the CFTC, legislators have few kind words. Said William Roth (R-Del.), chair of the Senate permanent subcommittee on investigations: "The facts uncovered in our investigation show a continuing pattern of criminal activity which has gone on almost unfettered since the creation of the Commodity Futures Commission. . .The evidence shows that at least $200-million a year is being soaked up, bilked by the con artists operating under the guise of legitimate commodity investment firms, and the result has been the victimization of thousands and thousands of Americans, both young and old."

After three days of hearings, Roth concluded, "I wonder why it may not make some sense to consolidate this commission with the Securities and Exchange Commission (SEC)." Staffers, though, explain there is virtually no chance the House Agriculture Committee would agree to such a step. Commodities dealers passionately resist the idea that the CFTC, with whom they have enjoyed a traditionally cozy relationship, would cede authority to another government agency less wedded to the dealers' views of proper government oversight.

Johnson countered CFTC critics in his statement before Roth's subcommittee with the assertion that "the area of so-called 'commodity' frauds, which in the main, are little more than garden variety confidence games. . ..are no part of the huge commodity futures industry, which this commission is charged by law to regulate."

But the findings of a recent GAO audit belittle Johnson's rosy assessment. The GAO found CFTC ineffective, and lax in its enforcement of trading regulations.

"Federal laws that are supposed to protect commodity investors are instead used to shield criminals, and commodity markets that are supposed to be 'self-regulating' aren't enforcing their own rules," concluded the GAO.

CFTC "regulation is so weak that swindlers deliberately sign up with CFTC so local law enforcement authorities can't go after them," wrote the agency.

Two serious disruptions in commodities markets in recent years have focused congressional attention on the often obscure CFTC. In 1979, there was a severe wheat futures crisis, and the following year a silver market debacle, brought on by an attempt by the billionaire Hunt brothers and several Arab investors to corner the market. The disaster sent the price of silver plummeting from an all time high of $50 an ounce in January to $5 an ounce on March 27.

After the Hunt scheme failed, at the request of Congress, the CFTC and SEC conducted a study of "Silver Thursday." The 500-page report concluded that the erratic behavior of silver prices could repeat itself if manipulation by another "wealthy speculator or foreign government" occurred again.

In a supplement to the silver market report, CFTC Commissioner and former Chairman James Stone introduced a detailed plan to improve CFTC effectiveness, which noted the need to place "reasonable limits on speculative futures positions." If such regulation had been in place at the time of the Hunt speculation, it would have "helped prevent the accumulation of such large positions and resultant dislocation," Stone wrote.

It is doubtful, however, that the CFTC, under Johnson's leadership, will take such steps. As Johnson told one representative: "In the area of margins there is a different perception between the CFTC and SEC on the subject of the role that the government should play in the establishment of margins.''

The CFTC has long sparred with the SEC over the gray areas not clearly within either's jurisdictional bounds. One of Johnson's first acts was to meet with John Shad, the newly-appointed commissioner of the SEC to negotiate jurisdiction over futures and options based on the rise and fall of the stock market.

"I've been an outspoken advocate of the CFTC having exclusive jurisdiction over futures trading," Johnson told us over the summer of 1981.

The rapidly growing area of financial futures has been at the heart of the CFTC-SEC dispute. The SEC tends to look upon them as securities, while the CFTC seeks total jurisdiction over them as commodities. The futures industry has been eager for the CFTC to assert authority over the financial futures (which include such items as Treasury bills, notes, bonds; Government National Mortgage Association (GNMA) certificates; commercial paper and foreign currencies) because of the SEC's history of more aggressive regulation.

In December, 1981 Johnson and Shad reached agreement in the long-standing dispute. Under the truce, the SEC would regulate stock market options; the CFTC stock market futures. For investors, the two instruments are virtually identical, but they will be regulated under very different regulatory regimes.

The agreement did not solve all of the CFTC's jurisdictional disputes. It still claims overlapping jurisdiction with the SEC over some financial instruments, such as options to buy foreign currencies. And the Federal Reserve Board, to the commission's displeasure, is asserting that it has the authority to set the margin requirements for stock futures. On the first stock market future approved by the CFTC—which was based on the Value Line Index of 1,700 stocks—the Fed decided that the margins imposed by the Kansas City Board of Trade were adequate. But, Fed Chairman Paul Volcker wrote Johnson in a February 16, 1982 letter, "We do plan to monitor closely the development and operation of. . .stock index futures contracts. . .so that we can reach an informed judgment. . .as to whether imposition of a formal rule with respect to margin requirements would be appropriate."

Johnson has long been recognized as a staunch supporter of self-regulation by the futures industry. In fact, he was one of the primary architects of the proposed National Futures Association which would allow the industry to regulate itself. Johnson served as the organization's secretary/treasurer from 1976 to his appointment. CFTC turned down such proposals in the past, but approved a new version in September, 1981. (Johnson recused himself from the vote.) Congress has authorized the CFTC to charter a self-regulatory organization. The private groups goals are to simplify federal regulation and at the same time to establish some controls over futures brokers who are not subject to regulations for the CFTC or other regulatory bodies. The self-regulatory plan was condemned in July, 1981 by the Justice Department in a report which concluded that it "might well inhibit vigorous competition." Industry proponents of the plan were caught off guard by the rebuff from the Reagan Administration, but convinced the CFTC to approve their association.

FINANCIAL BACKGROUND

Johnson's primary source of income was his law firm, Kirkland & Ellis, where he earned $248,914 in 1980. He also received $2,500 in book royalties.

WHAT OTHERS ARE SAYING ABOUT HIM

- Alas, it appears not everyone in the futures industry was thrilled with the selection of Phil Johnson. Incredibly, his own client, the Chicago Board of Trade (CBT), was not in favor of his nomination.

    "It was well-known that Leslie Rosenthal [chairman of the CBT] was not crazy about Johnson," Michael Caughland, former CFTC director of policy review told us. "Phil was looked upon as a very independent guy who wasn't afraid to tell Rosenthal the things he didn't want to hear sometimes."

- Several sources told us that Johnson may prove to be surprisingly independent despite his background with CBT. In fact, some speculate that his background may be a very positive factor if he pursues enforcement as aggressively as he says he will. (That may explain why Rosenthal opposed Johnson's nomination.)

- Karen Freiberg, agribusiness editor for the *Kansas City Star*, wrote: "The Chicago Board of Trade, although it does not say so publicly, may not want someone quite so tuned in to its inner workings to become a possible opposing power."

CONSUMER PRODUCT SAFETY COMMISSION

NANCY HARVEY STEORTS
CHAIRMAN

RESPONSIBILITY OF OFFICE

The commission was formed in 1972 as an independent agency to "protect the public against unreasonable risks of injury from consumer products; to assist consumers to evaluate the comparative safety of consumer products; to develop uniform safety standards for consumer products and minimize conflicting state and local regulations; and to promote research and investigation into the causes and prevention of product-related deaths, illnesses and injuries."

Accidents with household consumer products kill 30,000 Americans and injure another 36 million annually at a cost of about $9.5 billion, according to the CPSC.

Together with four other commissioners, Steorts has "responsibility for mandatory product safety standards, where appropriate, to reduce the unreasonable risk of injury to consumers from consumer products."

This responsibility includes "authority to ban hazardous consumer products."

The commission operated in 1982 on a lean budget of $34 million and with 569 employees.

BACKGROUND

Steorts's most relevant qualification for the CPSC position is her experience as special assistant to the secretary of Agriculture for consumer affairs during the Nixon and Ford Administrations. She began her government career in 1971 as a White House aide, involved in Nixon's executive branch reorganization.

Then, in 1973, she was assigned to help Agriculture Secretary Earl Butz form a consumer office (the office won praise from consumer groups throughout the late 1970s for its work in the Carter Administration—but has now been demoted by the Reagan Administration to a lower status).

"[Steorts] put together a successful governmental outreach program under very difficult circumstances," maintained Sandra Willett, executive vice-president of the National Consumers League. Willett said Steorts accomplished "about as much as she possibly could" under Butz's conservative rule.

Other consumer advocates have not been so complimentary.

A consumer activist who dealt with Steorts in the early 1970s called Steorts "a cupie doll who tried to soft soap everybody on Butz's policies," though Steorts "was generally less ideological then someone like Barbara Keating-Edh." (Keating-Edh was the ultra-conservative leader of Reagan's CPSC transition team.)

Columnist Nicholas von Hoffman once described Steorts as "a shill for the industrialized, processed and packaged pseudo-food of mass production agriculture."

Steorts left government in 1977 to begin her own consulting firm, Nancy Harvey Steorts and Associates, which guided businesses on consumer affairs. Among her activities was working with Procter and Gamble on the promotional activities surrounding the centennial of Ivory soap. At her nomination hearing, Sen. Strom Thurmond (R-S.C.) called her firm "a Washington firm which advises industries, businesses and government on consumer issues and their effect on public and corporate policy."

"Consumerism has been my business for a long time," she told us.

Steorts also served on several advisory groups during the past few years including: CPSC's National Advisory Committee on Flammable Fabrics (which she chaired) and the Executive Committee and Board of Trustees of the Food Safety Council (an industry-sponsored group devoted to finding "better ways to make food safety decisions").

Also, in the months prior to her confirmation as head of CPSC, she worked as a consultant to Virginia H. Knauer, special assistant to President Reagan for consumer affairs. Steorts told us she actively sought the CPSC job, and spoke to Ed Meese, Pendleton James, Virginia Knauer, and political adviser Elizabeth Dole before getting the nomination.

Steorts is a graduate of Syracuse University, where she was honored as the most outstanding student in her class. In 1980, she received Syracuse University's highest alumni award, a medal for Excellence in Government.

After graduating from Syracuse in 1959, Steorts went on to hold a variety of business jobs in public relations, home economics, and real estate before entering government in 1971.

Steorts was born on November 28, 1936 in Manilus, New York. She is divorced and has one daughter.

MAJOR ISSUES

- Many consumerists doubt Steorts's ability to fight to keep CPSC alive and fear the skimpy budget allocation will breed a "self-fulfilling prophecy" of doom for the agency's independent status.

- Steorts surprised many observers by voting with the commission majority that banned formaldehyde foam insulation.

- Steorts says she will stress information and education over compliance—a prospect which many critics fear will take the enforcement "bite" out of the agency.

- Steorts will stress voluntary compliance over mandatory rules.

The major issue at CPSC is whether Steorts can put together a program which will convince Congress to reauthorize it as an independent agency in 1983. The Reagan Administration has made it clear that it would prefer to fold the agency into the Commerce Department, the government's institutional advocate for business, but CPSC still enjoys considerable support in Congress.

"I believe this agency should be independent," Steorts told us flatly.

"And I believe her when she says that," said Ellen Haas, of the Community Nutrition Institute, who knows Steorts from her days at Agriculture. "Nancy tries very hard. She is sincere and her inclinations are good. The problem is that she doesn't have the wherewithal to fight her superiors. That is the big question now at CPSC. . .whether she can mount a counterattack to keep the agency alive."

Early indications have not been promising.

In one of her first acts she decided against asking for an additional appropriation to compensate for job severance costs within the agency. Hence, the severance pay for the 25 percent personnel reductions must come out of the already slashed $34 million budget.

"OMB didn't want the additional appropriation," said Ron Wainrib, coordinator of the Consumer Product Safety Network. "And [Steorts] wasn't about to question OMB."

Wainrib is uncertain whether Steorts can (or if anybody could) accomplish much with CPSC's meager budget allotment. He fears the budget which Congress has approved for CPSC will create a "self-fulfilling prophecy."

"When it comes time to reauthorize the CPSC budget Congress will ask why it didn't accomplish more," he said. "And of course, the reason will be that CPSC simply didn't have adequate resources to work with in the first place." The budget cuts, said Mike Lemov, former chief counsel to the House Oversight and Investigation subcommittee, "will virtually cripple this agency."

In all, the 1982 budget cuts forced the agency to dismiss nearly 200 of its 750-member staff and to eliminate half of its regional offices. Despite the cuts, Steorts spent between $8,000 and $10,000 refurbishing her office, a move which caused her considerable embarrassment in the press.

Steorts told us the work, which included painting, the installation of new carpeting and drapes, and the construction of a new entrance, "was really what I would call maintenance."

"When I came here," she said, "this office was literally filthy." Sitting on a couch in her office she pointed toward a closet on the near wall. "Those doors," she told us, "had bloodstains on them.". To be sure that we heard correctly, we asked her about the walls again a few weeks later at the Consumer Federation of America's annual conference. Steorts told us again there were "bloodstains on the panels," adding, "I have no idea how it got there."

"Preposterous," says the office's former occupant, Susan King, who chaired the commission under Jimmy Carter.

The remodeling didn't help Steorts's relations with agency staff who were watching their associates lose their jobs. Relations got worse when she ordered staffers to take annual leave for any lunches that last longer than a half hour. And when she ordered her driver, to wear a coat and tie—which he said he couldn't afford—staff had to scramble to buy the man a suit, after she had reportedly hinted she might fire him if he didn't spruce up his wardrobe.

Citing these, and more substantive, problems, Commission Executive Director Richard Gross resigned in October, 1981. Gross wrote Steorts that "You must learn to trust the staff. They are not wild-eyed or doctrinaire. . . Your persistence in relying on outsiders—consultants and interlopers from other agencies, supposed experts and the like—in preference to professionals in line positions within the agency has already alienated senior management."

On a number of occasions, Steorts has indicated a new direction for the CPSC which will improve relations between the agency and business. "In the past, the corporations saw the CPSC as an adversary," she told us. "I think it's changing. . .it's going to do nobody any good to have an adversary spirit."

On another occasion, she explained, "it is my ambition to forge a union between government and industry as a sort-of protective shield to protect the interest of our mutual client—the American consumer." As she interprets the Reagan mandate, it reflects "a new determination across the country to slow down government, to decrease government regulation and to make government more responsive to its people," as she said in a November, 1981 speech. Steorts told us she "senses" that feeling "from being there, being with the people, talking to industry. . ."

Asked about polls that show the public believes the commission is not doing enough to protect consumers, she said, "I think they are asking us to be more responsible. And there are ways that we can be more responsible without regulating."

In part, this will entail a more lenient policy toward recalls. Steorts stresses the importance of keeping recalls "voluntary". She notes that industry has been very cooperative with the CPSC in past years (less than 1 percent of products recalled in recent years were done so "involuntarily"). However, consumer advocates feel it is important that Steorts maintain and utilize when necessary CPSC's authority to mandate recalls.

And there is evidence that the new emphasis on "voluntary" compliance is encouraging businesses to skirt the law. In 1981, company reports of safety problems—required by law—dropped to 121 from 231 in 1979. Steorts and the other commissioners were stunned at a January 7, 1982 meeting to learn that almost 24,000 infants were injured using baby walkers in 1980. The problem was not reported by industry. Said Commissioner Stuart Statler: "It's a sad state of affairs that it takes a government agency to tell an industry it has a problem."

The movement from mandatory to voluntary standards is as evident within CPSC as it is in most sectors of the Reagan Administration. Under heavy lobbying pressure, Congress decided in the summer of 1981 that the CPSC must defer to industry and private groups before dealing with hazards. Mandatory rulemaking can only take place after the commission has decided that a voluntary proposal submitted by industry is unacceptable. And even after the rule is finished, Congress still has the right to veto it.

Steorts told us several times she would regulate "if necessary." Through 1981 the commission did not find regulation necessary. It voted unanimously in October, 1981 to weaken its standards governing power lawnmower safety. And on a tie vote, it rejected a staff proposal to ban reversible caps used on prescription drugs.

But the key issue facing the commission was not decided until 1982: what to do about formaldehyde foam. Installed as insulation in about 430,000 American homes, the foam produces a vapor that has caused headaches, nausea, eye problems, and skin irritation. Most important, it is also carcinogenic, according to numerous studies.

How the commission voted on formaldehyde, in the face of a furious formaldehyde industry lobbying effort that dissuaded the Occupational Safety and Health Administration (OSHA) and the Environmental Protection Agency (EPA) from acting expeditiously on it, was expected to give a clear indication of Steorts's willingness to confront industry if necessary.

Steorts told us "There are some situations where the consumer will not even be aware of the degree of the problem and in those areas we have a strong responsibility to protect them." Particularly, she said, chemical hazards fall into that category. But the agency budget for handling chemical hazards such as formaldehyde and asbestos in consumer products has been slashed. "It's going to take us longer to do things and we're not going to do anywhere near as many," said Peter Preuss, the CPSC's associate executive director for health sciences.

The formaldehyde industry pressed for some program of increased disclosure as an alternative to regulation. By her own words, Steorts should not have been receptive to that idea; and indeed she wasn't.

In a stunning 4-1 vote on February 22, 1982, the commission banned formaldehyde insulation. Steorts voted in the majority, stating: " I have concluded there is not a voluntary solution to this problem. . .No standard— voluntary or mandatory—can assure the consumer of an installation of ureaformaldehyde foam insulation. . .that will adequately reduce the risk. . ." That surprising vote left the Administration in an embarrassing position. An independent regulatory commission had looked at the evidence and found formaldehyde an unreasonable health risk, but two executive branch regulators at the EPA and OSHA—more closely attuned to the White House's political interests—had refused to act. The inference is not difficult to draw.

FINANCIAL BACKGROUND

As a consultant for such corporate giants as Procter and Gamble, Steorts has maintained a steady income since leaving government service in 1977. In 1980, she earned $24,707 salary from her consulting firm and an additional $12,000 for her work with the Republican National Committee and President Reagan's Inaugural Committee (she was vice-chairman and director in charge of "candle light dinners").

WHAT OTHERS ARE SAYING ABOUT HER

- Wainrib said he is taking a "wait-and-see" attitude toward Steorts, though he admits her early comments have not been especially promising.
  "She is quoting the Heritage Foundation report almost verbatim," [offering advice to the incoming Administration] he said.

- Willett, of the Consumers League, said she wants to "keep things positive for now," but was not exactly encouraged when she attended Steorts's swearing-in ceremony in early August, 1981. Steorts was sworn in by conservative Sen. Strom Thurmond (R-S.C.) and "the reception looked like a gathering of an industrial trade association," she said.

- John Bell, the former CPSC spokesman, was given one hour to clean out his desk and leave on Steorts' first day at the CPSC. Understandably, he does not have a very high opinion of her. "Steorts does not have appropriate experience for this job," he said. "About the only thing she has done within the federal government relating to consumers was at the Agriculture Department. And that was for Earl Butz. . .which isn't saying much."

FEDERAL COMMUNICATIONS COMMISSION

MARK FOWLER

CHAIRMAN

RESPONSIBILITY OF OFFICE

Despite its low profile, the FCC affects virtually all Americans and will make some of the Reagan Administration's most difficult and controversial decisions.

Charged with overseeing all communication "by wire and radio" the FCC licenses radio and television stations, and regulates "common carriers" like American Telephone & Telegraph.

Initially set up as the Federal Radio Commission in 1927 to impose order on the chaotic radio industry, the FCC itself was created by the Communications Act of 1934. As new communications technologies have been developed, the scope, complexity, and importance of the commission's activities have steadily increased.

The heart of its responsibility is the enforcement of Congress's requirement that broadcasters granted a license to use the limited resource of the public airwaves have a responsibility to broadcast in "the public interest, convenience, and necessity." With that admonition in mind, the FCC enforces the Fairness Doctrine, which requires broadcasters to cover controversial issues and to include contrasting points of view in that coverage.

Those who receive an exclusive license to broadcast from the federal government on a specific frequency do so in a fiduciary, or trustee, capacity. That obligates them to be representative in their programming of the views of others in the community, who are excluded from broadcasting because it is technically impossible for more than one person to broadcast on a single frequency at the same time. Trustee obligations imposed by the FCC include the requirement that they cover controversial issues in a balanced manner and that they ascertain community communication needs.

The chairman and the six other members of the commission are appointed by the President for seven-year terms and subject to Senate confirmation. In addition to chairman Fowler, President Reagan has nominated Mimi Weyforth Dawson, a former aide to Sen. Robert Packwood (R-Ore.), a leading proponent of rolling back FCC regulation; and Henry Rivera, a corporate attorney from Albuquerque, New Mexico and Stephen Sharp, an attorney close to Fowler who had been serving as general counsel. Reagan also renominated James H. Quello, a Democrat originally appointed by Richard Nixon.

In 1981, the commission operated with a budget of $80.4 million and a staff of 1,977; in 1982 those numbers were dropped to $76.9 million and 1,862 respectively. An independent agency, the FCC is statutorily obligated to report directly to Congress.

BACKGROUND

A journeyman communications attorney, Fowler comes to the FCC with few credentials beyond his association with the Reagan campaign team. During both the 1976 and 1980 campaigns, Fowler was Reagan's communications counsel. He also apparently became close with kitchen cabinet member (and now director of the International Communication Agency) Charles Z. Wick; at his swearing in ceremony in May, 1981 he took the time to publicly thank Wick for snaring him the job.

Outside of the campaign, though, Fowler was neither particularly well-known, nor well-respected. A partner in the D.C. communications law firm of Fowler & Myers, Fowler had "no big guns as clients," in the words of one trade publication. He primarily represented smaller, southern broadcasting companies, often in matters before the FCC. Since 1978 he also had been chief counsel for the Virginia Association of Broadcasters.

"I think it would be fair to characterize him as not among the most distinguished members of the communications bar," said one Washington communications attorney. "He was certainly not a well-known figure in the field."

Another attorney, who has been prominent in the Federal Communications Bar Association and had been involved in a case against Fowler told us: "I was not in the least bit impressed by his ability. . .he came out of left field to be chairman. He was nothing in the bar. There were a thousand lawyers who had more stature."

Fowler is involved in a messy malpractice suit brought by a Florida group that had hired Fowler's firm to represent them in applying for an FM station. The group was originally denied their application, but eventually given the station by an FCC review board. Before the malpractice suit was filed, Fowler had sued them for failure to pay a $14,000 legal bill.

Fowler had been a partner in his own firm since 1975. Before that, he worked for Smith and Pepper, a Washington communications firm with Republican ties.

While in high school and college, Fowler worked part-time as a radio announcer. After graduating from the University of Florida in 1963, he spent two years as an announcer and sales representative at an AM station in Melbourne, Florida before entering the University of Florida law school in 1965. He was graduated in 1969.

Born on October 6, 1941 in Canada, Fowler holds dual citizenship through his mother, an American citizen. He is married with two children.

MAJOR ISSUES

- Saying that "we are at the end of regulating broadcasting under the trusteeship model," Fowler argues that broadcasters should be freed of many of their responsibilities to broadcast in "the public interest." He pushed through the commission's legislative recommendations to eliminate the Fairness Doctrine and the equal opportunity provision.

- Fowler has been involved in a series of regulatory changes that reduce the amount of information available to community groups seeking to challenge broadcasters at license renewal time.

- Like the Justice Department, Fowler argues that "bigness is not necessarily badness" in communications policy, and that the FCC should not worry about concentration in the broadcasting or telecommunications field.

- Accordingly, he supports the elimination of many of the rules designed to reduce concentration: the 7-7-7 regulation, and the prohibitions preventing networks and local broadcasters from owning cable systems.

Mark Fowler may well be the James Watt of the broadcasting world. An unabashed industry advocate, he offers at the slightest provocation homilies about the evils of government interference whose fervor, industry trade officials told us, is often embarrassing to them. Fowler embraces a sense of stewardship for the public airwaves remarkably similar to that expressed by his more well-known counterpart managing the public lands.

That definition of stewardship is best captured in three words: let industry decide. "[T]he Commission should, so far as possible, defer to a broadcaster's judgment about how best to compete for viewers and listeners because this serves the public interest," Fowler told an appreciative audience at the International Radio and Television Society in September, 1981.

Operating as a licensee on the public airwaves, broadcasters have long been considered trustees, using a limited public resource—the broadcast spectrum—in a manner that should benefit the public. But Fowler says that concept is outdated.

"I believe that we are at the end of regulating broadcasting under the trusteeship model," he said in his September speech. "Whether you call it 'paternalism' or 'nannyism' it is 'Big Brother' and it must cease."

With that stark conflict between the historical notion of stewardship and Fowler's plans for rolling back government oversight of the public airwaves, the FCC will be the scene of some of the most basic—and far-reaching—regulatory disputes of the Reagan Administration. Although the FCC has changed little since 1934, recent technological advances in the electronic communications industry have left the commission panting behind proliferating questions on how to regulate the exploding, and increasingly overlapping, industries of telephones, televisions, computers, and satellites.

The commission must now make key decisions that will determine the structure and control of the expanding cable television industry and the nascent technologies of low power television and direct satellite broadcasting, all of which someday might threaten the dominance of the three networks. It must also continue to oversee the fundamental restructuring of American Telephone & Telegraph (AT&T) as it reaches out into the burgeoning markets of information services opened by its antitrust settlement with the Justice Department. (See profile of William Baxter.)

What's at stake in these deliberations, says Rep. Timothy Wirth (D-Colo.), chairman of the House Telecommunications Subcommittee, is nothing less than the "control of information in a democratic society."

Decisions made by the Fowler FCC could determine for a generation and beyond, who will control, and who will have access to, these technologies as they move toward the marketplace.

In both the telecommunications and broadcasting fields, the FCC—and Congress, which is rewriting the nation's basic communications law—face two fundamental questions. The root issue in both is control. Will the existing communications giants be allowed to control the new technologies? And will those firms that transmit the information be allowed to control its content as well?

In an interview, Fowler told us: "If we just allow the businessmen to compete in serving the needs of the people—in quality, cost, and convenience—the one who will get the most audience will be rewarded. Whatever interests the people is in the public interest." Accordingly, he added, his major goal is "to promote an unregulated, competitive environment, and to eliminate all unnecessary regulations. This will allow the marketplace to determine what it wants."

But what Fowler and his supporters in the broadcasting industry see as unnecessary regulations, media access advocates see as a thin line of protection ensuring some degree of accountability among the broadcasting and telecommunications giants. "What Fowler is doing is a systematic stripping of protections for the general public through a series of coordinated minor and major alterations of the regulatory process," said Andrew Jay Schwartzman, executive director of the Media Access Project (MAP).

Others argue that letting the marketplace alone allocate access to the airwaves will stifle diversity. "The information and entertainment supplied by such a profit-making system has to go where the money is—there can be little concern for providing services to the public that do not return a profit," said John Wicklein, former dean of the Boston University School of Public Communication and associate director of the Corporation for Public Broadcasting.

Fowler maintains that the promise of all the new broadcasting technologies has made what he calls the justification for regulating the airwaves—the perceived scarcity of broadcasting opportunities—obsolete. "In addition to new UHF stations," Fowler has said, "broadband technologies like cable and other video services dramatically have undermined the case for regulating in the name of scarcity."

But Fowler's critics point out that the promise of those technologies remain just that—a promise—and that most communities are still dependent on traditional, and limited, television and radio offerings. The largest cable operator, for example, still has only 1.4 million subscribers; nationwide just 17.4 million, or about one-fifth of all homes, are wired. "The reason for regulation is still the scarcity of the spectrum and the fact that not everyone can participate," former FCC Chairman Charles Ferris told us. "The overall environment is not competitive, to justify the removal of all regulation." And diversity of broadcasting outlets, in any case, does not assure diversity of programming or access.

Critics point out that the new chairman has yet to demonstrate a real commitment to expanding competition as he contracts regulation. Already, the FCC has rejected a proposal, which it had supported under Ferris, to narrow the channels on the AM radio band, a move that would allow hundreds of new stations to operate. Broadcasters had feverishly lobbied against the change.

Though he proposes to let the market assure diversity, Fowler flatly rejects a true market solution: ending the exclusivity of the license. There are many ways this could be done. The government could get out of the allocation business entirely, letting broadcasters bid for the right to use the public airways. Or it could end the 24-hour monopoly, splitting licenses among various firms (in England licenses are shared between one licensee that broadcasts during the week and another that transmits on weekends) or increasing public access, through such mechanisms as Audience Network, which would set aside a certain amount of prime time for public use. Fowler dismisses all of these ideas.

With remarks that sound as if they spun by the Justice Department's antitrust speechwriters, though, Fowler has repeatedly stated his commitment to expanding the opportunities available to both AT&T and the networks. "I do not believe that past players, players with impressive records and innovative plans, should be arbitrarily excluded from new markets," he told the Oregon Association of Broadcasters in a major June, 1981 speech. "As a matter of communications policy, bigness is not necessarily badness; and the public interest is not inconsistent with the profit motive."

Fowler has translated those sentiments into more specific policy in both broadcasting and telecommunications policy. He opposes the current rules barring the networks from owning cable stations or systems and local broadcasters from owning local cable systems; he says the "7-7-7" rule limiting any one firm to owning no more than seven AM, seven FM and seven television stations, "makes little sense." In July, 1981, the commission unanimously approved a massive merger between Westinghouse and the giant Teleprompter.

Fowler backed Senate legislation that would allow AT&T to offer unregulated services by establishing wholly-owned subsidiaries—rather than forcing them to divest those functions as the long-standing Justice Department antitrust suit has sought. In a statement that offers AT&T even more than the Senate legislation Fowler told us, "I think there is no reason why AT&T could not be involved in programming. If there is any problem at that time [after AT&T is involved] we could do something about it. But how terribly arrogant of us to determine beforehand whether companies are going to be dangerous or not."

Those comments reflect Fowler's view that the FCC should not address potentially anti-competitive problems. "If an unhealthy concentration, an unhealthy economic condition comes up, another department—the Justice Department—can deal with that," he said.

Many communications analysts consider that view transparently disingenuous. "The problem with that is that you end up having too few voices," said Samuel Simon, director of the National Citizens Committee for Broadcasting. "Essentially by letting the networks get involved in these new technologies you intensify the power of the gatekeeper to control what information society gets, and sees, and hears."

Allowing the networks to enter the cable area, MAP's Schwartzman maintained, could destroy competition in that growing field. Last summer, the FCC granted CBS a waiver allowing the network to own and operate cable systems serving less than 90,000 subscribers—the first waiver granted since the networks were barred from cable 12 years ago. "You do not take someone who has a vast amount of monopoly power as a result of regulatory protection [like the networks] and then announce there is a free market in which they should compete," said Schwartzman. "They'll just eat up the little fish. . .They are equipped by virtue of their money machine for broadcasting to overwhelm those who are already in cable, and to deter potential entrants."

In the upcoming months, Fowler's FCC will make the decisions that will shape the structure of direct broadcasting satellite (DBS), a potential competitor to both the networks and the cable operators. Commerce Secretary Malcolm Baldrige has urged the FCC to promote early development of the technology and Fowler, to the consternation of the broadcasters, appears inclined to agree. Fourteen firms, including CBS, RCA (the corporate parent of NBC), Western Union, and Comsat have entered interim applications to begin work on DBS service. The FCC will have to decide whether to grant interim permits to begin satellite construction before 1983, when the North American nations will hold their next conference to divvy up satellite channels.

Broadcasters fear that the satellite systems will steal viewers and advertising business, a fear which was heightened when several applicants submitted plans to the FCC in summer, 1981 for satellite channels that will carry advertising. In a meeting with the broadcasters, Fowler dismissed their concerns by suggesting that they enter the satellite business themselves.

Wicklein of the Corporation for Public Broadcasting, and other media reform advocates, argue that if the system is to fulfill its promise the satellite operators should be treated as "common carriers" like AT&T and barred from providing the content that is transmitted through the system. "The temptation of the carrier to bar other [information] providers or favor its in-house producers of content would be just too great," said Wicklein in congressional testimony. "DBS satellites, if operated as common carriers, could add to the diversity of voices that can be heard regionally and nationally." Added Simon: "Those who send out information ought not to be able to decide what information gets out." Several of the DBS applications, including those from the networks, seek to generate as well as transmit programming.

Low-power television, which would serve local areas, is also in limbo. Swamped by applications for licenses—from groups ranging from community organizations and unions to Sears—the FCC sought and received authority from Congress to use a lottery to choose among the competitors. Congress directed the commission to weight the lottery competition toward groups that have historically been under-represented in media ownership. But the FCC rejected the lottery and developed a system that will give preferences only to minorities. Moreover, the plan imposes no ownership limitations—so an unlimited number of stations could be owned by one applicant, and there are no restrictions on cross ownership. Like DBS, the broadcast industry has fought the development of low power TV.

While the debate over these emerging technologies continues, the FCC is stripping away many of the regulations governing existing broadcasting. In June, 1981, the commission voted to reduce the forms required for license renewal—the basic information available to local groups seeking to challenge broadcasters—from several pages to a single postcard, lacking all but the most rudimentary data. Fowler has proposed to eliminate the rule requiring broadcasters to keep public files of complaints, and the annual financial reporting requirements. Fowler also supported Sen. Packwood's successful effort to extend the term of licenses for radio and TV stations and install a lottery for choosing among competing license applicants as part of the reconciliation bill. And he wants to cut back commission review of applicants' backgrounds as part of the licensing procedure; that would lessen commission efforts to increase minority ownership of media outlets.

Most importantly, in September, 1981 Fowler guided through the FCC a legislative package that recommended the elimination of two pillars of government communications policy since World War II: the Fairness Doctrine and the equal opportunities provisions of the 1934 Communications Act.

Established in 1949 and unanimously upheld by the Supreme Court 20 years later, the Fairness Doctrine requires broadcasters to balance coverage of controversial issues with opposing viewpoints. It has long been bitterly opposed by the broadcasting industry, and lately by the advertising industry with corporate clients eager to buy the broadcast equivalent of Mobil's op-ed energy pieces. The equal opportunity rules require stations that give time to a candidate for public office to give equal access to all other qualified candidates.

Fowler said the rules present "a large burden on freedom of speech." "I don't trust the government to make First Amendment decisions," Fowler told us. "The government should not be involved in that at all—unless there is a clear and present danger or if the programming is obscene. The government should not be able to suggest or dictate what shall be presented or not presented on TV."

But supporters of the Fairness Doctrine and the equal opportunity provisions say that its elimination will only allow the broadcasting industry, and the large corporations that can afford to purchase airtime, to dictate what shall be presented on TV.

"In terms of political reality, the broadcasters will have the absolute right to decide which candidates are given coverage, and they will be able to support any candidate they want," said Simon. "Imagine how that will fundamentally change the political structure of this country. We'll have three parties: ABC, CBS, NBC."

Similarly, the elimination of the Fairness Doctrine almost certainly would make the networks and local broadcasters more receptive to issue-oriented corporate advertising. Currently, many local stations and the networks themselves (with the qualified exception of ABC) refuse issue advertising, largely for fear of triggering fairness provisions.

If that fear was removed, Leonard Matthews, President of the American Association of Advertising Agencies, told *Television/Radio Age* it would "encourage more stations to accept this kind of advertising in a general way, and it would also tell advertisers who have been thinking about doing this sort of thing that the opportunities are now there."

Media reform groups say the inevitable outcome of that process is an auction of ideas, allowing only those with the resources to buy time on the public airwaves to set the national agenda. "The effect would be to permit a tremendous increase in the unrebutted presentation of business point of view," said Schwartzman. "This would amount to turning over the most effective tool for shaping public opinion to one side."

Fowler's FCC also will make complex decisions involving AT&T, though the agency's role in telecommunications was significantly reduced by the Justice Department's settlement with AT&T. (The FCC was not consulted on the agreement.)

The agreement came even as AT&T was begining to implement the FCC's 1980 "Computer II" decision, which first freed the world's largest company to compete in unregulated markets. Under that decision, AT&T was to offer its unregulated products—such as data processing and computer services—through a separate subsidiary, dubbed "Baby Bell."

The use of a separate subsidiary—rather than divestiture—to prevent anticompetitive activities was seconded by the Senate, in a 90-4 vote in October, 1981 approving communications deregulation legislation. But the legislation was expected to have a much tougher time in the House, where Wirth's subcommittee had released a massive study that concluded competition in the telecommunications industry was considerably less brisk than deregulation supporters had claimed. Despite the inroads of competitors like MCI Communications Corp., for example, Bell still holds over 96 percent of the long-distance market. Combined with the disquieting signals from the judge, and Baxter's belief that the Senate bill offered insufficient justification to drop the antitrust case, the House's skepticism brought AT&T to the bargaining table in December, 1981.

Though obviously diminished in importance by the settlement, the Computer II decision remains of interest to AT&T's potential competitors, since the FCC still regulates AT&T's long distance service. "Certainly there has to still be a means of preventing cross subsidization between 'long lines' and 'Baby Bell' because of the monopoly power that is still maintained by the Bell System [in long distance service]," said John Chapman, general counsel to the Computer & Communications Industry Association. "You still have the cross subsidization problem but [without the local companies] not on the same scale."

AT&T says it will continue to hatch Baby Bell, though it "expects" the FCC may want to review the entire plan. AT&T's competitors have been after the FCC to review the plan since it was announced, contending that the separate subsidiary safeguard was an illusion. In a detailed critique, published in fall, 1981 the General Accounting Office (GAO) agreed. After a two-year study, the GAO in September found both the structural safeguards established in Computer II to prevent anticompetitive actions, and the FCC's plan for monitoring them, vastly inadequate. The FCC's "separate subsidiary approach. . .does not go far enough. . .in providing for organizational restructuring and separation of the activities of the dominant carrier [AT&T]. . .[and leaves] a significant potential for internal cross-subsidy and a host of other anticompetitive actions," wrote the GAO. Further, the agency concluded, "[T]he Commission has moved too quickly toward implementing the separate subsidiary regulatory approach before many essential costing, accounting and depreciation problems have been resolved." Nor had the commission, according to the GAO, determined the staff and organizational needs that would "give the approach credibility and a realistic chance of success."

Former Chairman Ferris finds the GAO's conclusions compelling. "I think Computer II was the minimum amount of separation that could be accepted and it was the maximum we could get through the commission," he said. "The more insulation the better. No less, certainly, can be tolerated."

Ironically, even the Justice Department—while supporting the separate subsidiary concept before Congress—argued in a brief filed in the case brought by the computer industry that the safeguards established under Computer II were inadequate, relying on "unproven, indeed undeveloped regulatory tools." Their doubts were more forcefully expressed by the terms of their settlement with AT&T.

FINANCIAL BACKGROUND

According to his financial statement, Fowler took in $68,090 from his law firm in 1980, which in the words of one communications lawyer, puts him "in the middle class of broadcast attorneys." In 1978, he earned $46,656 from his firm; and only $30,710 in 1979.

Fowler's client list was unspectacular, ranging from the International Television Corporation of South Burlington, Vermont to Mid South Media, Inc. of Florence, Mississippi.

Fowler's former firm is being dissolved, with its assets sold to a Washington firm without an FCC practice and his two partners joining the firm of Becker, Gurman & Lucas. Fowler has agreed to abstain from matters brought by his former partners, and those involving former clients.

WHAT OTHERS ARE SAYING ABOUT HIM

- "His views are absolutely wild, way out," concluded one prominent D.C. communications attorney, who doesn't think much of Fowler. Said the lawyer: "During all the years I was involved in active work with the bar, he was way down on the list, a low man on the totem pole."

- Many broadcasters are more happy with Fowler. After the commission urged the repeal of the Fairness Doctrine and equal time provisions, NBC Chairman Grant Tinker said, "In challenging broadcasters to participate in the new communications marketplace, Chairman Fowler presented a thoughtful, clearly defined proposal for fundamental changes in broadcast regulation."

- One public interest advocate who has met with him said Fowler "showed some mastery of the issues. But the important thing for me and for others is that he seems not the least bit interested in listening. He's really not plugging into what people have to say."

- Wrote Les Brown, editor of *Channels* magazine and former television reporter for the *New York Times*: "I fear Mark Fowler because he doesn't know what he's talking about and is eager to turn his words into action."

GENERAL SERVICES ADMINISTRATION

GERALD CARMEN
ADMINISTRATOR

RESPONSIBILITY OF OFFICE

Gerald Carmen supervises an agency that described itself in one of its annual reports as "a service and business conglomerate functioning as the government's landlord, builder, procurement agent, engineer, data processor, and historian." With an annual total management budget on the level of $4 billion, GSA employs 35,000 people to help manage the business of the federal government.

The operations of GSA are grouped into several services. The largest of these is the Public Buildings Service, which is responsible for the design, building, leasing, protection and maintenance of federally controlled buildings. The Federal Supply Service is responsible for procurement of materials and services, from rubber bands to civilian aircraft (70 percent of GSA's procurement is for the Department of Defense). The Federal Property Resource Service supervises the acquisition and management of the stockpile of critical and strategic materials (including tungsten, industrial diamonds, and $30 million worth of opium for use as a painkiller in the event of a nuclear holocaust), and conducts the sale of surplus stockpile material, proceeds from which totalled over $67 million in fiscal 1981. The Transportation and Public Utilities Service administers the transportation needs of the government. Preserving and managing the records of the United States government is the responsibility of the National Archives and Records Service, while the Automated Data and Telecommunications Service coordinates the government's telecommunications and data processing.

Other programs operate from the administrator's office itself, including the Consumer Information Center Program, which publishes the free Consumer Information Catalogue, the Office of Small and Disadvantaged Business Utilization, and the Office of Acquisition Policy, which establishes acquisition goals and objectives and serves as the overall coordinator for acquisition policies and programs.

BACKGROUND

Carmen has lived in Manchester, New Hampshire all of his life, channeling his energies into business and Republican politics. He established a wholesale automotive service business in 1959, building it over a period of 20 years into a statewide chain. For Carmen, selling cars "was a tool to give me the free time to do what I wanted to do— spare time or whatever you want to call it was always devoted to my real love, politics and political science. I used politics for relaxation," he told us. "I'd work in my occupation. . .and the rest of the time I spent in politics. So I was working 16 hours a day, seven days a week; it was split. I come down here, and the requirement of this job is the same, except it's in one thing. Which can be a little bit grinding sometimes; I don't have the relaxation.''

A delegate to the 1964 and 1980 Republican National Conventions and a member of the Republican National Committee, Carmen was the senior Northeast adviser for the Reagan presidential campaign, and directed Reagan's successful New Hampshire primary effort. He went on to become director of political programs and analysis for the Reagan-Bush Committee. He also served as transition team leader for the Department of Housing and Urban Development, a post for which he had direct experience, having served as the first chairman of the New Hampshire Housing Authority.

On February 26, 1981, a year after the New Hampshire primary, the President called ''and chatted with me for a few moments about the day and its importance,'' Carmen told us, ''then [he] asked me if I would like to run GSA. Like anyone at that time in history or that moment. you'd say you were honored and glad to accept the job. That's about how I got here.''

Carmen must be one of the few Washington officials who sees the agency as ''very exciting.'' ''I wouldn't take the job if I wasn't fascinated by it,'' he told us. ''Even though it wasn't in the broad policy issues that I think we all like to talk about and be involved in, I found it to be very, very exciting. . .I'm sort of having the time of my life serving my country [and] serving the President.''

His personal style heavily influences the working atmosphere at GSA. ''My office door is never closed,'' he said. ''I like to walk around the halls. I could tell you stories of when I first got here, because of the agency's past condition, the place really had a siege mentality to it. The doors were closed, some people weren't talking to other people, you'd get in the elevator and nobody would talk to each other—which I thought was strange, coming from a small town.''

Describing himself as a ''hands-on manager,'' Carmen told us that the short-term mission at GSA ''is to get our house in order, start managing what we can as best we can. . .[F]rom the standpoint of trying to make the government smaller and more manageable [and] less costly to the taxpayer, these are things that should be done, and they're right in tune with our Administration. I believe. . .that our job of being here is to prove that we can make government work.''

Carmen said he has not contracted Potomac fever, and that he sorely misses his home state. When his time as administrator is completed (''I expect to stay as long as the President wants me. That could be eight years, you know.''), he plans to return to New Hampshire to write, perhaps about his experience at GSA.

Born July 8, 1930, Carmen was graduated from the University of New Hampshire in 1952. He is married with two children.

MAJOR ISSUES

- With its extensive procurement powers and responsibilities, GSA could set innovative standards of efficiency, safety, and product quality. The GSA could also play a more active role in providing the public with the vast amount of information it has compiled about the quality and comparative costs of the wide variety of materials it procures.

- Waste and fraud remain serious concerns. The GSA was not fully purged by the highly-publicized prosecutions of its own officials and business contractors in the late 1970s; Carmen says he is ''doing the best he can'' about this kind of corruption in the GSA, but he is more concerned about (and probably more effective) in dealing with waste.

- Carmen should be credited for increasing GSA's efficiency, tightening up management practices and cleaning up corruption in the agency. But at least one GSA program will be damaged by his cost reduction efforts, the National Archives and Records Service. A 16 percent budget cut was recently implemented at the Archives, eliminating almost 100 jobs and threatening a possible restriction on hours and services vital to scholars.

Although it is not a regulatory agency, GSA can propel valuable technological change through the standards it sets for federal procurement. GSA has already begun such an exemplary function with its Public Building Service (PBS). In the mid-1970s, the PBS constructed two demonstration energy-efficient buildings to promote energy conservation. Since then it has designed 15 other buildings, and the energy needs of existing federal buildings are being reduced through a variety of techniques. In the six-year period between 1973 and 1979, energy consumption in GSA-controlled buildings decreased by 26 percent, despite an increase in space.

GSA has also set a good example in its procurement of motor vehicles in the Transportation and Public Utilities Service. In fiscal 1980, the GSA Interagency Motor Pool sold many of its larger cars and station wagons and bought 15,000 fuel-efficient vehicles. Federal employees using government vehicles and credit cards are required to use self-service pumps to save money. A possible next step for innovation in the transportation area would be the procurement of cars with airbags. Were GSA to take the initiative and install such systems in government vehicles, casualties and related costs would be reduced and airbag production would be stimulated for wider adoption. Currently no auto manufacturer offers airbags in cars sold in the U.S. With his automotive background, Carmen seemed to think such an idea was interesting when we mentioned it to him, but it remains to be seen whether he will act on it.

GSA's other purchases are extensive and diverse. Out of total procurement expenses of $3.085 billion in 1980, GSA spent approximately $200 million on copy machines, $23 million on projectors and cameras, $10 million on calculators, and $4 million on disinfectants. It's understandable to assume, as Carmen did before he came to Washington, that the federal government had everything it could possibly need. "I just somehow had thought they had just bought everything there was to buy," he told us. "I never thought it was being utilized properly, but I thought it was there." Carmen was greatly surprised at the "old and tired" condition of the government assets and property. "They haven't financed their plant, so to speak," he said.

GSA obtains many products through a competitive bidding process, while others are obtained by multiple awards, which are negotiated rather than bid. "[When] you get into multiple awards, you develop problems that make you wonder whether you're achieving the best we can," Carmen said. The problems include bias against small businesses, overpricing, and the lack of specifications (such as energy efficiency). GSA continually reviews multiple award schedules to determine if competitive procurement would be more efficient. "In my opinion," said Carmen, "we've got a long way to go to really do our best there."

Until the Reagan Administration arrived, seven testing laboratories assisted GSA in its procurement policies by providing information on product quality. Carmen closed these labs for an annual budget savings of about $3 million. "It really wasn't a broad enough approach," he told us. "I though we were better off trying other routes and where we did need labs, certainly the universities and other facilities were there for us to utilize." Still, he admits, "quality assurance has been a problem, is still a problem, but we're working on that, [particularly] in assuring that the government gets what it thinks it has purchased. . ." Carmen also wants to get away from writing unique sets of specifications for products. "The more you can move to commercial type items, I think the better off we'll be."

From these testing programs, GSA has accumulated a large body of information—about performance, reliability, energy efficiency, and other consumer concerns—regarding products which consumers purchase: gardening equipment, paint, household appliances, air conditioners, light bulbs, and other items. GSA has traditionally used this information only in setting its own procurement policies, without making the data available in a usable form to the public.

Through Executive Order 11566, issued October 26, 1970, and which to date has not been amended, superseded, or revoked, Richard Nixon ordered the GSA to create a Consumer Product Information Coordinating Center that would "promote the development, production, and public dissemination of government documents containing product information of possible use to consumers, including other government agencies. . ." Consumers have a right to such information, the order continued, since it has been "accumulated in the process of purchasing items for government use with tax dollars."

The vague wording of the order created some disagreement over what kinds of information should be published. The publishing of generic information, such as what to look for in a toaster, would be valuable to consumers without stirring up too much opposition in industry. Publication of brand name information, while it was potentially even more valuable to consumers, worried many manufacturers. The executive order was based on an interagency report which explicitly stated that "[release] of available test reports giving brand name information would be controversial. . .Nonetheless, this committee believes that such data can and should be released subject to appropriate caveats. . ."

The controversy was never resolved and has since been conveniently forgotten. The Consumer Product Information Coordinating Center gradually devolved into the Consumer Information Center, which has consistently ignored these provisions of the executive order and has never published information on competitive products.

The phrase "scandal-plagued agency" will probably haunt the GSA for years to come. In the latter half of the 1970s a pattern of scandals was exposed which included bribery of government officials, payoffs, contracts paid for but not done, and procurement of shoddy products. Investigations by the Justice Department resulted in the indictment of over 90 GSA employees and contractors.

Carmen has made efforts to eliminate this corruption. The GSA maintains a list of debarred vendors; Carmen told us that "we debarred better than three times, I think, the number of debarments and suspensions that had ever been done before, in this year." He is also fostering a good working relationship with the inspector general's office. "When I first got here," he said, "they looked at his office as sort of the enemy—that office against the rest of the agency. You could feel it throughout the entire agency. . .That no longer exists here. He sits in on our meetings, we talk about pre-award audits rather than just post-award audits, we counsel together. Hopefully by taking what he has to offer at the front end, we can avoid a lot of the problems that we had in the past."

With evidence that the problems were not all eliminated, we asked Carmen: "Knowing what you know about what went on in the past, do you think it's still going on, some of it is still going on, pockets that geographically have this kind of corruption?"

Carmen answered calmly: "If this was a private sector business and you said to me, do you have some waste or corruption, I would say yes, and I would say we're always working to eliminate it. Going back to the scandals that went on in GSA, I'm convinced that GSA was more of a symptom of what's wrong with the entire government than it was with just GSA. . .So that's an ongoing problem that you have to be alert to. Whether it's still going on now, we deal with it in a little different way. The best I can do in running this agency is to try to eliminate it when it's there, try to give it the kind of leadership that lets people know we won't tolerate it, and then when it does appear, make sure that we handle it decisively in such a way as it becomes at least a symbol or deterrent for other people who might be considering it." His next comment was the closest to a direct answer: "We understand. . .that we can turn over a rock at any time and find something perhaps wrong underneath it and no one should think that because I'm here all of a sudden the problems have gone away at GSA. That's not the case at all."

So we posed the question again: "Is it your assessment in terms of corruption and fraud that the level of it is partially down, not down at all, or substantially down from 1976-77?"

Carmen answered us in terms of improved morale at GSA. "I do think that people here now are starting to enjoy working in a place that has some integrity. And that protects you from others who would injure it because they are injuring their fellow workers. I was told a story several months ago about one of the people here who wouldn't go to church on Sunday. . .because their friends would ask them questions about working in a place like GSA, which is notoriously bad. They don't have that problem anymore, and I'm hoping, especially for those who had it both ways, that they enjoy working for a place that has a reputation for integrity."

The question was posed for a final time: "Does all this mean to say that you think the level of corruption is down now?"

"What it means," said Carmen, "is that that question assumes some knowledge of the level then and the level now. I don't think I can answer it that way. I can only answer the fact that we're doing our best to stop it from happening again. And I can't tell you what the level was in those years."

Carmen would rather talk about other subjects. "When you cluster this waste, fraud and abuse, it's the waste that intrigues me," he said. Carmen's plans are for the most part short-term. Space is an important issue for him. When he learned that the Marriott Corporation allotted its employees 135 square feet of space, he made plans to reduce the allotment of GSA employees from 220 square feet to something around 180 square feet, and eventually down to 145.

And Carmen practices what he preaches. He does not occupy the traditional administrator's office, an enormous and elegant room adjacent to the smaller board room where the Teapot Dome payoffs were made, but has moved to a much more modest room down the hall (which, he dutifully pointed out, is still twice as large as the governor of New Hampshire's office).

In his quest for efficiency and better management practices, Carmen laments the high turnover among GSA employees. "One of the things that GSA lacks is people that remain in their field; it doesn't have to be a lifetime, but it can be a number of years. But the promotion process seems to be that you come into one job and once you get there you start planning on your next, rather than doing your job. Here you very rarely have the head of a group, an executive that has gone up in GSA from the ground up, as you would in the private sector." Carmen speaks fondly of Japanese management. "The Japanese system when you take the culture out of it," he told us, "is very much an entrepreneur system. It's really American in many ways. A lot of their leaders are really owners who are still in the business—70, 80 years old but they're still running the company. The American system is almost like the bureaucracy, where people float in and out of these industries on their career paths."

But more than inefficient management is often to blame for the large amounts of waste. Take the leasing of office space. Currently the GSA leases 87 million square feet of office space, of which about two million square feet are vacant, or about 2.5 percent. GSA is always making efforts to fill vacant leased space.

But it has been difficult at times to fill vacant space, and even when filled the terms of the lease may waste millions of taxpayers's dollars. Perhaps the most notorious example is that of Buzzard's Point, a building in a distant section of southwest Washington, D.C.

The Securities and Exchange Commission (SEC) asked GSA in 1975 for a new headquarters. GSA arranged for the Buzzard's Point building through a lease-construction agreement with the construction firm of Southwest Joint Venture. The "advantage" of a lease-construction agreement is that it requires only the first year's rent to be listed on the budget for the year construction begins, instead of reporting the building's total cost. In this case that total cost turned out to be $11 million.

After construction was completed, the SEC refused to move in, as did the Agency for International Development and portions of the Treasury Department when GSA tried to place them in this poorly constructed building. The government payed $2.7 million per year in rent as Buzzard's Point sat vacant for two years. Finally parts of the FBI and Department of Defense moved in, demanding alterations which GSA provided for an additional $2 million through a sole-source contract with Westwood Construction, which happened to share the same address as Southwest Joint Venture.

So in the past five years, the federal government has spent $13.5 million in rent on a building which cost a total of $13 million. The lease on Buzzard's Point was renewed for another five years in April, 1981 at the same basic rate; by 1987, then, the government will have spent over $27 million in rent for a $13 million building that it still won't own.

GSA currently lacks the legal authority that would allow it to enter a lease arrangement that ends in ownership. Carmen hinted that he would like to take some action on this. "I'm convinced that many of our leases could be purchase options. At the end of 20 years, we end up with a bag full of receipts; I think in many cases we could end up owning the building," he stated.

"I'm also convinced that the fact that we can't buy is an advantage for someone who wants to lease a building," Carmen continued. "It determines some of the prices, so that we need the option [of buying]. It doesn't mean that we're going to buy a lot of buildings. It's roughly a 50-50 situation now, I think 57 percent [of government employees were in federally owned buildings]. We think that by

1990-95 we can get about 80 percent of the government back in federal buildings, without a massive building program.''

Carmen's efforts to run GSA on a cost-efficient basis may sometimes go too far. The National Archives is a case in point. Faced with a 16 percent budget, it has fired almost 100 archivists and support personnel. ''They're running the Archives like a business that has run on lean times, and that's a mistake,'' commented Samuel R. Gammon, executive director of the American Historical Association. The rate of declassification of government documents has been reduced by 69 percent, and the Archives has already stopped its interlibrary microfilm loan service. The processing of new federal documents has all but halted, it is possible that researchers may soon be charged admission, and there may be future cuts in hours and services. Carmen said the Archives will have to ''get along with less, like everybody else.''

Not all of Carmen's actions are motivated by purely economic concerns. In late April, 1982 Carmen ordered 24 Senior Executive Service personnel based in D.C. to take new jobs by May 23; 17 of these jobs were outside Washington. In one case, a husband and wife were ordered to separate cities, Philadelphia and New York. Carmen said he was trying to strengthen GSA's regional offices.

Not everyone believes that. GSA sources said a number of the reassignments were meant to drive out of their jobs certain employees whose performance had not satisfied Carmen. One of the managers who was transferred called Carmen's action a ''blatant and overt case of reprisal and retaliation.'' Several of the people who were transferred to other cities were hired during Democratic administrations, and three employees at GSA said they had seen or heard of a list of GSA ''liberals'' that was composed earlier in the Reagan Administration, a charge Carmen denied.

FINANCIAL BACKGROUND

Carmen received $25,900 for his work in the Reagan for President campaign. He also listed compensation in excess of $5,000 as president of Car-Go Home and Auto Centers, Inc.

Carmen's assets total over $600,000, mostly in the form of real estate. One piece is worth over $250,000, and two others worth at least $100,000 each have buildings which together draw $10,000 in rent. His liabilities are in the form of bank loans for at least $115,000.

WHAT OTHERS ARE SAYING ABOUT HIM

- ''I have always been extraordinarily critical of most federal operations,'' said Frank Silbey, an investigator with the Senate Labor and Human Resources Committee, ''but I have never seen a guy try harder and more sincerely. Carmen is an unassuming man who has not let his job go to his head, and is head and shoulders above anybody in that office before. He's the first administrator to give the place some hope, and one of the best appointees I've ever seen in government.''

- ''Within a year, he has attempted and is attempting to make the agency function as a business,'' commented Dan Clements, the lawyer who started the GSA prosecutions in 1977 and the only Democrat on the transition team at GSA. ''I mostly approve of what he has begun to do; my overview is he hasn't gone far enough, especially in looking at multiple awards and sole-source contracts. But I'd certainly give him the benefit of the doubt, that this is just a function of time.''

GOVERMENT PRINTING OFFICE

DANFORD SAWYER JR.
PUBLIC PRINTER

RESPONSIBILITY OF OFFICE

Sawyer manages one of the largest job printing organizations in the world and, according to Sawyer, the largest industrial employer in the Washington, D.C. area.

Established in 1860, GPO's original purpose was to serve the printing needs of Congress. The Printing Act of 1895 made mandatory the use of GPO by the Executive and Judicial Branches as well. The Printing Act also established the Joint Committee on Printing (JCP) as the congressional committee that oversees the GPO.

GPO's purpose is twofold: to provide the three branches of the federal government with printing, binding and distribution services; and to distribute the publications that GPO prints through the Superintendent of Documents Division, which includes bookstore operations, the depository library system, and the general sales program.

In 1982, the GPO operated with a budget of $119.5 million and a staff of 6,500. Yearly billings for printing and binding are in excess of $700 million.

BACKGROUND

Before coming to Washington, Sawyer was a successful entrepreneur and Republican activist in Sarasota, Florida. As a member of the Sarasota Jaycees, Sawyer said, he learned "how to organize and how to motivate yourself and other people." A successful entrepreneur, he was founder and president of Sawyer and Associates Advertising, Inc., the largest full-service advertising agency on Florida's west coast; founder and publisher of *Sarasota South*, a monthly community news magazine; and a founding director of First Presidential Savings and Loan of Sarasota. All these activities had "just gotten to be too much," he told us, so he sold the ad agency (for which he received $269,600 in liquidating distributions) and the publications to a vice-president of Foote Cone and Belding (an advertising agency in Chicago), planning to spend his time raising horses and just "winding down for a couple of years."

Having been a delegate to the 1980 Republican National Convention, as well as financial chairman of the Sarasota Republican Party and a member of both the National Advisory and Florida's Regan for President Committee ("Ronald Reagan," he said, "is the only politican in my life I have worked for for free."), Sawyer was in line for some kind of Washington reward. President Reagan interviewed him the day after the inauguration, and by mid-February his job prospects were narrowed to the GPO and a few other positions. "I didn't know anything about GPO at that time," he said, "I'd rather have gotten Charles Wick's job [as head of the International Communication Agency]." But Ed Meese offered him the public printer job in March; Sawyer sold all but three of his horses and moved to Washington. He said he expects to stay for the rest of President Reagan's term.

Born in New York City on November 11, 1939, he attended the University of the South in Sewanee, Tennessee, but never graduated. He is married with three children.

MAJOR ISSUES

- Sawyer has focused more on controlling GPO costs than expanding public access to GPO documents. Among his proposals has been the elimination of virtually all of GPO's regional bookstores, a measure Congress rejected.

- In recent years, the price of GPO documents has skyrocketed (the *Congressional Record* has jumped in price from $45 in 1978 to $208 today), further diminishing public access to government information.

- While instituting a hiring freeze at the agency, and planning to force half of its workers to take payless furlough days every two weeks, Sawyer has padded the top of the GPO bureaucracy with ten new political positions drawing salaries totalling over $330,000.

- Sawyer told us he thought the senators and representatives on the congressional Joint Committee on Printing "should all resign" because they scarcely paid any attention to overseeing the GPO.

Predictably, Sawyer has approached his new job as a businessman, which may turn out to be both his greatest asset and most serious shortcoming. In the last three years, GPO's Superintendent of Documents Division, which includes the general sales program, lost nearly $20 million; in the first six months after Sawyer took over, it made $1.1 million.

At a cost, though. While Sawyer would like to be remembered as "the public printer who made GPO cost-effective and efficient"—a development no one would oppose—he seems to place that far above his primary mission of cheaply and conveniently informing the public of the policies and activities of its government.

Sawyer told us he would like GPO to be self-sustaining and emphasized the importance of the strong and unprecedented marketing program he is initiating. No previous Administration—Democratic or Republican—has made a concerted marketing push.

With the appointment of Donald Fossedal—the first marketing director in GPO's history—this marketing effort may help to increase public awareness of the GPO's wide-ranging information offerings. But the potential of the marketing program is offset by other policies, which reduce public access to GPO documents. The real question facing the GPO and Congress in the upcoming years is where to place the agency on the continuum of economic efficiency and public service. Undoubtedly by raising prices and cutting services the agency can be put on more of a self-sustaining basis; the main question is how much of the GPO's public service function should be sacrificed to improve its financial performance.

One of Sawyer's first proposals was to close 23 of the 27 GPO bookstores through the U.S. No overwhelming economic motivation existed for such a move; nationwide, the bookstores returned a profit in 1979 and 1980, and suffered only a slight loss in 1981. Sawyer's rationale was that the bookstores serve only a five or six mile radius, their function could be absorbed by GPO's mail order program, and closing the bookstores would save an estimated $1 million annually that could be invested in the marketing program. In addition, he reasoned that 83 percent of GPO's business is "captive business," which wouldn't be affected by closing the bookstores. "Any time you tell a businessman he can eliminate 100 percent of the expense and hold on to 83 percent of the business, it is the kind of deal he is looking for," Sawyer told the House Appropriations Committee in February, 1982.

But the Joint Committee on Printing vetoed Sawyer's proposal, reaffirming Congress's belief in the bookstore program as an essential component of public access to government records.

While downplaying the bookstores, Sawyer is quick to emphasize the depository library system. In this system, approximately 1,300 libraries receive free copies of all GPO publications. Sawyer sees new technologies increasing the libraries' role in the future. "In the next ten years it will be all data base," he said, "CRT is coming."

But the depository libraries have serious drawbacks as a means of widely disseminating information. Even if everyone was near a depository library, how many people have the time to spend in such travel? The system for the most part serves the needs of librarians and scholars. And the nearly 100,000 other libraries not included in the system must buy their publications like everyone else—not an easy task in a time of dwindling municipal budgets and rising publication costs. Instead of being content to supply libraries, another view more consistent with Sawyer's role as public printer would be that people need to get these publications directly for their own use and benefit.

Sawyer expressed his admiration for the Consumer Information Center (CIC) in Pueblo, Colorado. Part of the General Services Administration (GSA), the CIC was described by Sawyer as "more aggressive" than the GPO in their marketing. The CIC distributes between 15 and 20 million catalogues annually. In January, 1982, GPO suspended mass distribution (600,000 copies) of its monthly select publication list, the only program bearing any resemblance to the CIC's "more aggressive" marketing efforts. The alternative GPO suggested, "for those who want more comprehensive information about sales publications," was subscribing to the *Monthly Catalog of United States Government Publications*—at a cost of $90 per year.

Access to publications, of course, is influenced by their cost. By law, prices for government publications are "based on the cost as determined by the Public Printer plus 50 percent." While the original definition of "cost" was circumscribed around printing and binding, the GPO has incorporated more and more factors—such as personnel costs, warehouse costs, handling charges, and postage—into the formula over the years. Prices to the consumer have increased accordingly.

Other factors contribute to the price increases. Paper prices skyrocketed through the mid-'70s, in part due to the widely-acknowledged practice of price-fixing in the paper industry. (A May 4, 1978 front-page *Wall Street Journal* story stated that "the paper industry is acquiring a reputation as the nation's biggest price-fixer.") Although he headed two companies that published 13 successful magazines, Sawyer said he was "not knowledgeable on the topic" of paper price-fixing. Increased postage rates have also hit GPO hard; GPO's postal bill in fiscal year 1981 was $15.5 million. Assuming that a "big customer can get better service," Sawyer intends to "argue, fight, claw, and scratch" over the postal rate issue, adding that he "would love to go to something like Federal Express," a step he is not specifically barred from taking.

Congressional decisions have also pressed the GPO. A provision of the 1980 Federal Paperwork Reduction Act gave the Office of Management and Budget discretion over what publications the GPO should publish. Congress previously covered the expenses of the GPO's General Sales Program with direct appropriations, with any revenues it produced returned to the Treasury. But in 1977 Congress placed general sales on a self-sustaining basis, forcing prices to rise again. While Sawyer does not oppose total congressional subsidization—"If Congress wants to say publications A-Z will be available free, fine."—he is not actively pursuing such a policy change. There are indications that JCP Chairman Sen. Charles Mathias (R-Md.) is becoming more interested in the pricing versus accessibility of government documents, especially the *Congressional Record*.

Although Sawyer is not pursuing congressional subsidization, he is seeking other legislation that may save both money and valuable publications. Unsold GPO publications are generally sold as scrap or destroyed. In fiscal 1977, GPO sold about eight million copies of documents, worth about $9 million, as scrap paper. Among the documents destroyed were over 1,000 copies of the "Report of the Watergate Special Prosecution Force" and 5,250 copies of "Toward Cleaner Water." Sawyer is pushing legislation that would allow GPO to sell such publications at a 40 percent discount, or eventually to give them away free, neither of which it can do under current law.

The problems of cost and access become painfully clear with the *Congressional Record*. Printed every night at the GPO, an old red-brick building on North Capitol Street, D.C., this daily account of congressional activities cost $45 a year in 1978, and subscriptions totalled 5,606. The price increased in January, 1979 to $75; by March, 1980 subscriptions dropped to a little over 5,000. The cost jumped again in January, 1981 to $135, and again only nine months later to its present price of $208; the latest subscription count is 4,458. But Sawyer is not concerned about this cost, which clearly deters most people from subscribing. Most of the *Record's* subscribers, he said, are business people, trade journalists, lawyers—people who can afford the price "and end up writing it off anyway." Raising the price of the *Congressional Record* doesn't affect them, so even though subscriptions will decrease as the price continues to rise, he argues that revenue should remain level. Caught in this circular argument, the *Record's* price will almost certainly continue to rise and subscriptions will drop in a self-perpetuating spiral.

Sawyer is not timid in laying blame for the major cause of GPO's price increases. To Sawyer it is not energy costs, not paper prices, not postage increases, but the cost of labor. When asked what surprised him the most when he came to Washington, Sawyer replied: "How much our journeymen make an hour [$14.62]. If I had known that, I'd have never gone to college. There is a guy here who went to high school with me in New York City and with overtime he makes more money than I do."

The unions get such wages for their printers, Sawyer said, by "end-running" him and going to the Joint Committee on Printing. To which one union official responded: "Our printers at the GPO can't strike, so they have the alternative to appeal to the JCP as a final arbiter. If that's an end-run, so be it."

In addition to these wages (which Sawyer maintained were the highest wages paid to printers in the U.S.), printers were receiving huge overtime payments. The GPO has about 100 employees on Capitol Hill who assist the members of Congress with their printing and binding requests. Sawyer implied that these employees have scheduled jobs to help their friends at GPO earn overtime. On a Friday, for example, they may schedule a job which they claim must be done by Monday, when in fact the job could have been completed during regular operating hours, Sawyer maintained. Since Sawyer became public printer, overtime payments have been sharply reduced.

The GPO is a very labor intensive business. "We have too damn many people on the payroll—period," Sawyer told us. So he instituted a hiring freeze at GPO in September, 1981. With some exceptions. Sawyer has added ten political appointees to the payroll, at an annual cost of over $330,000. None of these positions had previously existed.

Sawyer argues that he came into an agency where only two of the top six officials remained ("I stopped the place from hemorrhaging," he told us), and other necessary positions, like congressional liaison and public affairs, did not exist. He justified his actions before the House Appropriations Committee: "I think it is ludicrous to expect me or anyone else to come in from the outside, with no prior government experience, to march into an agency with 6,000 some-odd-plus people, to take control and do it all by my little lonesome."

But those moves stood out in stark contrast when Sawyer announced on March 25, 1982 that he was planning to furlough, one day every two weeks for six months, about half of the agency's emloyees. For the affected employees this would mean a 5 percent annual pay cut. Sawyer cited a reduced volume of printing work—generated by smaller agency printing budgets—as the reason for the furloughs. One union official said that the furloughs were a "shot from the hip" and not well thought-out, adding that Sawyer should have sat down at the table and negotiated with employees some possible solutions beforehand, instead of immediately releasing the story to the press.

In late April, 1982 the GPO began contract negotiations with the unions representing over half of GPO's employees. Sawyer's first offer was that the union members take a 22 percent pay cut. "We laughed all the way back to the office!" said George Lord, chairman of the Joint Council of Unions.

Sawyer also said that some of GPO's business is being siphoned off to over 200 private printing plants authorized by the JCP to do government printing. Sawyer would like to absorb this additional printing business. "We can get these agencies' work done quickly," he said. "We have the capability to do it, we can do anything. We can process 1,600 jobs a day. [We're operating] nowhere near capacity." Sawyer told us that it "is virtually impossible to determine" what percentage of capacity the GPO is utilizing. "While we do have some equipment that is not being used, we do not have the manpower to run it," he said. "It can be said, however, that the GPO operates at approximately 83 percent of its personnel capacity as it is estimated that 17 percent of personnel are on leave or absent on any given day." Sawyer further hinted that the GSA has a printing plant in Atlanta, Georgia that is soliciting bids from other government agencies, an activity illegal under Title 44, the section of the U.S. Code that covers the GPO.

Sawyer is also outspoken when it comes to the Joint Committee on Printing. Asked if he felt the members were active enough, he quickly responded: "I think they should all resign." They're all good people, he added, but as senators and representatives the JCP was low on their list of priorities, and for that reason the JCP was not only failing to serve its intended purpose but was actually hurting the GPO. He said the JCP should "get out of our way."

He also accused some members of the JCP as having potential conflicts of interest, since the workers and 22 unions at GPO are voters whose political favor they seek—''Yet they looked me over for conflicts of interest,'' he said.

Although the JCP is supposed to function as a board of directors for the GPO, Sawyer said that unlike a board, the JCP does not meet monthly, does not choose a chief executive officer (Sawyer) and can't fire him, does not set policy, and is not responsible and accountable for financing. Instead, Sawyer would like GPO to be a semi-private autonomous organization with a truly functioning board of directors. ''GPO needs an oversight committee,'' he admitted, ''but JCP is not it.'' Having displayed such candor, he laughed and asked, ''Can you get me a job?''

Anthony Zagami, general counsel for the Joint Committee on Printing, also laughed a bit when he heard of Sawyer's remarks. ''I'm a little taken aback by that, but probably every public printer has felt the same way. Like any president of a corporation, he might feel like he can do it all and his way is the right way, and that the board of directors is not sensitive to the day-to-day issues. But JCP serves as a sort of check and balance, while at the same time allowing the public printer a lot of autonomy to do what he thinks is necessary. Because JCP is not a legislative committee but is basically a regulatory committee, it meets only once or twice a year. But we have developed an effective polling procedure whereby major policy decisions are developed at a staff level, and statements are sent to each member of the committee for their votes.''

FINANCIAL BACKGROUND

Sawyer's assets are considerable. His salary as president of Sawyer and Associates Advertising, Inc, was $99,540, and he received additional compensation in excess of $5,000 for consultation and services from each of eleven businesses in Florida and the First National Bank of Venice, Florida. When he sold Sawyer and Associates Advertising, Inc., he received liquidating distributions of $269,600. He also received $25,592 as payments on a promissory note valued at $250,000.

He has interests in an office building in Sarasota of at least $250,000; in Waterfront Mobile Home Condominium for at least $50,000, for which he receives at least $1,000 in rent a year; and in a building lot in Sarasota of at least $15,000. He has 50 percent ownership in a 5-acre tract on the Isla de Providencia in Colombia, South America valued at at least $1,000.

He has stocks valued in excess of $165,000, including stocks in the Boeing Company, General Motors, Central and Southwest Corporation, Gulf Oil, Portland General Electric, Buckbee Mears Co., and Sierra Pacific Power. He has purchased five limited partnerships at a total value of $52,500, and various municipal bonds for a total of $35,700. He has an additional $45,000 in certificates of deposit and mutual funds, and has at least $15,000 in gold and silver coins.

WHAT OTHERS ARE SAYING ABOUT HIM

- ''I think he's been making an honest effort to shape that place up,'' said Anthony Zagami. ''There have been a number of problems in the past, in terms of hiring practices and discrimination and inefficiency, and Sawyer has come in with a businessman's approach and really attempted to deal with these things. The whole marketing program is a new thing, and I think it will work.

The people deserve to see exactly what's available, and until now they haven't really known. I think it's going to have a good effect."

- "I've been impressed," said Rep. Lynn Martin (R-Ill.), a member of the Joint Committee on Printing. "I think that as a private businessman he brings an enthusiasm to wanting to make something work better. He seems to be a very fast learner. He struck me as being solid without being rigid, and he has to be the one without the other. I think he can do it."

OFFICE OF PERSONNEL MANAGEMENT

DONALD DEVINE
DIRECTOR

RESPONSIBILITY OF OFFICE

As director of OPM, Devine oversees the personnel system of the federal work force. He is charged with administering and enforcing the civil service laws, including the merit pay system, performance appraisal program, and equal employment laws (with the assistance of the Equal Employment Opportunity Commission). He advises the President on federal personnel matters, and is responsible for implementing Reagan's directives. He also has the fiduciary responsibility to administer the retirement, life, and health trust funds for federal employees.

President Carter's Executive Order 12107 of December 28, 1978 created the Office of Personnel Management as an independent agency, transferring to it many of the functions of the former Civil Service Commission. OPM conducts the recruitment and examination of applicants for all GS-1 through -15 positions, and administers the Senior Executive Service for the classification and assignment of persons in top management-level grades, GS-16 through -18. OPM also conducts federal employee development and training programs. The Office of Government Ethics at OPM collects and reviews financial statements submitted by high-level federal employees.

Sen. William Roth (R-Del.) stated at Devine's confirmation hearing that "directing OPM is like managing the largest work force, not only in this country, but the entire Western Hemisphere. The federal government now has almost three million employees. Many countries, including Ireland, New Zealand, Albania, and El Salvador do not have even three million citizens."

Approximately 5,500 people work at OPM itself. OPM operated in 1982 with a $15.4 billion budget. Requested outlays for 1983 were $16.5 billion.

BACKGROUND

Only in a government at war with its own employees, where political appointees view themselves as the French at Dien Bien Phu, could a man like Devine be appointed to run the OPM.

A favorite of the far right, Devine is currently on leave from the University of Maryland, where he has been an associate professor of government and politics since 1967. He has a long background in conservative electoral politics. His first foray into the political arena was in 1970, when he was political strategist in James Gleason's successful campaign to be Montgomery County's first county executive. He subsequently served as a special assistant to two extremely conservative congressmen: Rep. Phil Crane (R-Ill.) in 1972 and Rep. John Ashbrook (R-Ohio) the following year. Ashbrook challenged Nixon in the 1972 primaries because he thought the President was too liberal.

Devine took part in a similar challenge in 1976 as Reagan's campaign manager for the state of Maryland. Devine announced his candidacy for governor of Maryland in 1978, but then backed off and ran for comptroller. He suffered a resounding defeat at the hands of the popular Louis Goldstein. An alternate delegate to both the 1976 and 1980 Republican National Conventions, Devine was a regional political director and deputy director of political planning and analysis for the Reagan/Bush Committee in 1980.

At the request of 1980 Reagan campaign manager William Casey and pollster Richard Wirthlin, Devine prepared a memo titled "A Winning Strategy for Ronald Reagan." "Reagan must drive home four issues to win the 1980 election," wrote Devine: "First, there must be an aggressive supply-side, increase-production economic policy which emphasizes job-creation, tax cuts, and increased further income for all workers. The appeal. . .should criticize Carter's performance using his own 'misery index.'

"Second, Reagan must show he will restore America's position in the world as a respected power, without evoking a too-aggressive image. . .There should be an intelligent anti-communist thread oriented around the very serious international disorder created by Carter's incompetence and Soviet ambitions.

"Third, Reagan must stress his accomplishments as Governor of California. . .

"Finally, the more difficult political issue of right-to-life must be faced. . .nothing says this issue must be played excessively or emotionally; rather, reason should be the most characteristic aspect of this appeal."

Devine concluded his recommendations on a rousing note: "The key is to reach out to the BCEC [blue collar, ethnic, Catholic] voter and switch his allegiance from the New Deal Democratic coalition to the Reagan Republican coalition. There is a trend in this direction already underway. As a matter of course, a successful switch of the BCEC voter will create what we political scientists call a realigning election, which will set only the seventh new era of American politics. Then the stage is set to fulfill Ronald Reagan's promise to 'make America great again.' "

From the 1980 campaign, he acquired a position as transition team leader at OPM. Devine's appointment to a permanent position at OPM was clearly a concession to the ultra right-wing, a bone thrown to the howling Richard Viguerie and company. His cause was helped considerably by an Evans and Novak column championing his appointment and concluding, "Can Reaganism without Reaganites survive as a government policy?"

Devine's status as a staunch Reaganite cannot be challenged. He is a former director of the American Conservative Union and was an advisory board member of Young Americans for Freedom from 1961 until his appointment. He is also a former director of Life-PAC, an anti-abortion group, and has consulted for the National Right-to-Work Legal Defense Foundation, an organization that is strongly anti-union. In a November 20, 1976 *Human Events* article, Devine cautioned conservatives against forming a third party and advocated changing the name of the Republican Party to the Conservative Republican Party.

Devine could be planning a return to Maryland politics. In November, 1981 he sent out a letter on OPM stationery to various Maryland conservatives, extolling his performance at OPM. "At OPM I am proud of our record after only seven months in office," he wrote, citing his achievements in helping to "get the bureaucracy under control." "People here [at OPM] expect him to bail out and run for Congress," said Karen Boyd, president of the American Federation of Government Employees (AFGE) local at OPM.

Devine has demonstrated a strong streak of paranoia, sensing himself surrounded by "liberal" bureaucrats anxious to frustrate the Administration's goals. When Devine became director he installed extra security doors in his office. Guards were allegedly posted there the day the reductions-in-force (RIF) notices for OPM employees were issued. At the first few meetings of political appointees at OPM, according to two former senior staff members, aides were assigned to patrol outside the conference room to write down the names of any civil servants found lingering in the corridor.

Devine views the people at OPM with a moral eye. According to OPM employees who know his thinking, Devine thinks the people there dress sloppily, and use too much profanity in the halls. He believes too many of them live in sin, and he is upset at the number of women who have supposedly had abortions. Devine declined to be interviewed.

Devine received his Ph.D. from Syracuse University in 1967, his M.A. from the City University of New York in 1965, and a B.B.A. in management from St. John's University in 1959. Born April 14, 1937 in Bronxville, New York, he is married with four children.

MAJOR ISSUES

- Devine reduced the Federal Employees Health Benefits Program (FEHBP) to "a shambles," reducing benefits while raising premiums in a battle with unions that led to calls for his resignation.

- A General Accounting Office study concluded that projected savings from the RIFs ordered by the Reagan Administration were as much as $1 billion too high. The RIFs are also overturning equal employment opportunity gains.

- Devine proposed a new executive order to change the eligibility requirements for charities participating in the Combined Federal Campaign. Federal employees would have been prohibited from contributing through payroll deductions to advocacy groups and charities related to abortion services.

- Devine has surrounded himself with political appointees, many of whom one congressional aide characterized as "utterly incompetent," and has virtually ignored career personnel, resulting in often poorly informed decisions and plummeting morale at OPM.

In an address at a convention of the American Society for Public Administration in Detroit in April, 1981, Devine spelled out what separates the political appointee from the civil bureaucrat, quoting Max Weber: "The honor of the civil servant is vested in his ability to execute conscientiously the order of superior authorities." Maintaining this "distinction between policy and administration," Devine said, would aid in carrying out "a reform of the system which cuts back on the size of government and the functions it performs. . . ."

Continuing a trend from the Carter Administration of turning previously career positions into political ones, Devine has given high level jobs to a number of Reagan campaign veterans. According to agency sources Devine dictates policy, slighting the advice of the most experienced career personnel.

He has alienated not only the senior career staff, but the bulk of the agency as well. He is said to avoid talking to practically anyone at OPM. "He has created a climate where people work out of a defensive crouch," observed Murray Comarow, an expert on executive organization who served in the Nixon Administration, "No modern corporation moderately well-run would dream of treating its people the way he does." Among the jokes making the rounds at OPM: What's the difference between OPM and the Titanic? The Titanic had an orchestra. What's the difference between OPM and a Boy Scout troop? Adult leadership.

Lack of sound counseling may be partly to blame for Devine's creating "chaos" in the Federal Employees Health Benefits Program (FEHBP). As representative of federal employees, Devine has the power to negotiate contracts with the insurance carriers, including the authority to direct benefit changes or terminate a health plan. The funding reserves for this program, which provides health coverage for ten million federal employees, retirees and dependents, were known to be in serious trouble as early as March, 1981. Yet, Devine did not even get around to acknowledging the financial crisis until August. If the problem of the dwindling reserves had been faced in March, OPM and some of the major health insurance carriers could have begun to work out an orderly solution.

Late in August Devine called an emergency meeting of insurance carriers, claiming a government funding shortage of $500 million and calling for an immediate reduction in benefits. Devine later amended the deficit to $440 million, using these figures as evidence that benefits would have to be reduced as part of congressionally mandated budget savings for fiscal 1982.

In past years, Congress has appropriated to the health fund the amount recommended by the Administration. Devine said this amount had been underestimated, creating the shortfall. Without asking for guidance from Congress, which could have appropriated the necessary funds and instructed Devine to negotiate some less drastic changes with the carriers to build up funds slowly over the next few years, Devine decided to cut benefits. "His fundamental mistake," said an aide on the House Compensation and Employee Benefit Subcommittee, "was going after this major benefit program without seeking one single solitary piece of advice from Congress."

In September, Devine ordered a 6.5 percent reduction in benefits, including the elimination of abortion benefits from all federal health plans, an action motivated less by financial concerns than ideology. Abortion benefits cost less than maternity benefits or even some broken-limb benefits. At least one union, the National Treasury Employees Union (NTEU), was given only 24 hours to accept this directive or have their health benefit plan canceled. Faced with this ultimatum, the NTEU acquiesced but reserved the right to sue.

AFGE sued to have the abortion benefit restored. Devine said he would agree to abide by the court's decision, but when the court ruled in favor of AFGE, Devine reneged on the deal and began an appeal. He has since changed his mind again and dropped the issue.

Devine demanded further benefit reductions of 4 percent in October, 1981. Each health plan was given two days to submit its reductions: "the failure of any plan to submit an acceptable offer on or before the deadline," warned Devine, "will be construed as an election by that plan not to participate in the FEHB Program in 1982 and termination notices will be issued forthwith." AFGE sued Devine over these cuts and in late October a federal judge ruled that the benefit reductions were illegal since "this alleged budgetary crisis was in fact non-existent or of no legal significance," as Jim Rosa, general counsel for AFGE, summarized it. "For Mr. Devine to talk about budgetary constraints," continued Rosa, "is to act as if he has decided from on high that the President's budget has been or must be adopted by Congress." But OPM appealed and a three judge panel overturned the decision. Benefits will drop 16 percent in 1982.

Vincent Connery, president of NTEU, thinks Devine is motivated more by anti-union sentiments than by budgetary concerns. In testimony before the House Sub-committee on Compensation and Employee Benefits, Connery told of a meeting he had with Devine, in which Devine said "he doesn't believe taxpayers should be used to provide employee benefits, and that workers who want these benefits should purchase them on their own. . . . There is no doubt in my mind one whit that this current Director of OPM wants to destroy this program [health benefits]. . . .and that he wants the unions out of this thing." Both Connery and Kenneth Blaylock, president of AFGE, called for Devine's resignation.

OPM has been in the middle of one of the most wrenching Reagan Administration initiatives: the effort to cut and reorder the federal work force. Critics have argued that the RIFs at many departments are designed less to save money than to disorder the agencies and deter them from their statutory missions.

In 1981, Reagan announced that RIFs would save $1.6 billion the next year. But a General Accounting Office report released in February, 1982, using the Office of Management and Budget's (OMB) calculation methods, showed that these estimated savings were at least $572 million too high, and could be overstated by as much as $1 billion. "OMB officials," the report stated, "could not provide any documentation to support their projected savings or the extent to which they con-sidered offsetting costs." Rep. Geraldine Ferraro (D-N.Y.), who requested the report, said the projected savings "were unrealistic and undocumented from the beginning." Robert Hartman of the Brookings Institution said that in some areas "they're using reductions as a policy weapon."

This is certainly true within OPM itself. On March 4, 1982, the first specific RIF notices went out to about 390 employees in OPM's Central Office bargaining unit. In the February, 1982 OPM Bulletin, Devine stated that "discontinuous furloughs and a reduction-in-force will be used to keep OPM within its congressionally man-dated budget." Devine was telling a different story to Congress, however, testifying that "the planned RIF is a result of OPM's reorganization."

This kind of double talk is hardly unusual for Devine, who employed similar methods with great effect during the health benefits dispute. But the real impact of the RIFs may be found in a January 5, 1982 internal memo to Devine from one of his political appointees, Assistant Director for Planning and Evaluation Michael Sanera.

The RIF "will adversely affect those organizations which. . . .are operating effectively and economically," wrote Sanera, "effectively reduc[ing] any programmatic benefits. . . .One of the arguments being put forth for conducting a RIF at OPM is to improve organizational efficiency," the memo continued. "We think quite the opposite result is a far more likely occurrence.

"To date, OPM has not followed its own guidance to other agencies in the. . .bulletin entitled Personnel Actions During Budget Reductions," the memo acknowledged. Sanera outlined alternative strategies to accomplish the necessary budget reductions, including furloughs, eliminating overtime, freezes on promotions and monetary rewards, restricting equipment rental, and normal attrition. But Devine apparently was not interested in such measures; agency sources say he scrawled "this should not see the light of day" across the original memo.

Blaylock charged that OPM "is conducting a senseless and unnecessary reduction-in-force which will severely disrupt that agency and adversely affect all the other government agencies. . . .It's obvious to anyone who can think rationally that the RIF at OPM is solely political and phoney."

Fulfilling the old adage of "last-hired, first-fired," the RIF at OPM and at other federal agencies is adversely affecting employment gains made by women and minorities. Female employees at OPM accounted for 69.7 percent of those who lost their jobs in the first round. A survey covering 40 federal agencies conducted by a task force chaired by Rep. Michael Barnes (D-Md.) found that in low grade level jobs women and minorities were not disproportionately affected. But the discrepancies increased with the grade scale, with women administrators being RIFed at a rate over twice the average for all employees, and minority administrators laid off at a rate three and a half times the average.

In October, 1981 hearings, Rep. William Clay (D-Mo.) questioned Devine's commitment to equal employment opportunity. Devine stated that OPM's "primary mission under the law is to administer the federal merit system," and insuring that "selection and advancement should be determined solely on the basis of relative ability, knowledge and skills after fair and open competition which assures that all receive equal opportunity."

Clay went on to quote from Devine's book, *Does Freedom Work?*, in which Devine writes: "In order to end the antagonisms already created by affirmative action plans and to avoid the increasingly possible specter of groups fighting for their fair share of positions in factories, on construction sites, in offices and at colleges and universities, the EEOC [Equal Employment Opportunity Commission] probably should be abolished and all affirmative action plans revoked."

"Is that still your position, Mr. Devine?" Clay asked.

Devine: As I pointed out to the Senate where that section was also read during my confirmation hearing, that book is a work of philosophy. It is not a program for action and it's certainly not a program for action for an officer of the government.

Clay: Whose philosophy is that? Yours?

Devine: That's my philosophy, yes.

Clay: And your philosophy contradicts with your actions?

Devine: The Senate didn't believe it did.

Clay: But the Senate speaks for itself. I'm asking you what you believe, sir.

Devine: I was unanimously confirmed and there were no objections on either side of the aisle to my confirmation.

Devine is one of those Reaganites who argues that discrimination is largely a problem of the past. "I am committed to following the law," he testified at his confirmation hearings in March, 1981. "I think, however, that we have engaged in the whole question of affirmative action in a much too combative way. . .[I]t was necessary in a certain period of our history to go through use of government force to move from a totally unacceptable racial situation in this country to a more humane and balanced one. But I think that period is past. I think that the opportunities before us are opportunities to develop a truly harmonious system of racial relations in the United States."

Devine has also attacked the Combined Federal Campaign, a fund-raising program established by President Kennedy in 1961 that enables federal employees to contribute to charities of their choice through payroll deductions. The campaign was originally intended to include only health and welfare organizations, but U.S. District Court Judge Gerhard Gesell ruled in January, 1981 that the government had illegally excluded the Puerto Rican and NAACP Legal Defense and Education Funds, saying that the wording of the original executive order was too vague to bar them from the campaign. With that door opened, 20 additional charities were admitted to the campaign in June, including the National Black United Fund, National Organization of Women Legal Defense and Education Fund, and the Native American Rights Fund. Many federal employees for the first time found it worthwhile to take payroll deductions, as giving increased dramatically.

This sort of activity seems to fit right in with the President's voluntarism, as well as Devine's own philosophy. In a 1977 *Modern Age* article criticizing government welfare programs, Devine wrote "The supporter of the welfare state insists that there is one right way to organize welfare, that it is the duty of government to find that single way, and that once it is found it is the function and moral responsibility of the state to follow that path—using coercion where it is necessary to achieve justice as defined by those with political power."

Yet Devine has attempted just such a definition of what constitutes a charity. A draft executive order prepared by OPM in the fall of 1981 proposed that members of the Combined Federal Campaign be again limited to the health and welfare agencies considered "traditional" and "nonpolitical," meaning that it does not seek to influence the outcome of elections or engage in lobbying. Also, eligible charities could "not provide any abortions, euthanasia or abortion-related or euthanasia-related services or counseling." Devine wrote in a memo to the White House: "In brief, if we do not want public monies in support of groups that provide abortions or abortion counseling and referrals, we should put this in the executive order to give it legal status." These criteria would have eliminated from the campaign Planned Parenthood and all the organizations previously mentioned.

In response to the outrage and controversy the draft order provoked, President Reagan signed in March, 1982 an executive order that does not eliminate any charities from the campaign. The order does give the United Way authority to run local campaigns. The United Way receives 90 percent of donations not designated for a specific organization (60 percent of all contributions are "undesignated") and has a history of excluding charities for political reasons, most recently cutting off funds for a Catholic family service agency in Amarillo, Texas where the Catholic bishop was encouraging employees at the nuclear weapons plant there to quit their jobs.

Though the White House dodged the issue it left the door open for Devine to take the heat. The executive order grants Devine the power to "establish criteria for determining the eligibility of voluntary agencies" through the prescription of "such rules and regulations as may be necessary to implement" the order. Many charities fear that some of the restrictions originally sought by Devine will reappear in the new regulations, which have yet to be issued.

FINANCIAL BACKGROUND

On his financial disclosure form, Devine listed his income as associate professor at the University of Maryland as $31,000. He received $10,000 for his work on the Reagan/Bush Committee and another $5,300 for his work on the Administration transition. The National Right-to-Work Legal Foundation paid him $216 for counsulting work.

WHAT OTHERS ARE SAYING ABOUT HIM

- "What we are faced with here is an appointed official whose mindset rests firmly in the nineteenth century," said Vincent Connery. "To characterize Mr. Devine's actions as completely lacking in integrity and good faith is to be overly generous. . . I think his appointment is a tragedy. He's saved only by his natural glibness, his unmitigated gall, and his undoubted White House support. This guy is a real highbinder, no question."

- "I think he's just in over his head," said Thomas Tinsley, former director of the Civil Service Commission's Bureau of Retirement. "[But] I've never seen anyone like him. If I had attempted to do some of these things, I would have been in jail."

- "I went out on a limb trying to accommodate him," said Kenneth Blaylock concerning negotiations on the abortion coverage in health plans. "I thought we had built a relationship, but the guy didn't understand that you have to keep a deal. As far as I'm concerned, his credibility is gone."

- "He's taken on a position that's very unpopular among federal workers," said James Cowen, chief counsel on the Senate Civil Service, Post Office, and General Services subcommittee. "He's done a good job in that sense. Generally, many of his appointments have been qualified individuals; I think this is a reflection of Devine's own capabilities."

SECURITIES AND EXCHANGE COMMISSION

JOHN SHAD
CHAIRMAN

RESPONSIBILITY OF OFFICE

Established in 1934, the SEC is an independent, quasi-judicial agency governed by five commissioners—two Republicans, two Democrats and a fifth commissioner of the President's party. The act "assigns to the commission broad regulatory responsibilities over the securities markets, the self-regulatory organizations within the securities industry, and persons conducting a business in securities." Its overall aim is to provide "fullest possible disclosure to the investing public and [to] protect the interests of the public and investors against malpractices in the securities and financial markets."

In addition to Shad, Reagan has placed on the commission Bevis Longstreth, a corporate lawyer with the New York firm of Debevoise, Plimpton, Lyons and Gates.

In 1982, the agency will operate with a budget of $81.6 million, an increase of $3 million over the 1980 level. For 1982, the SEC is budgeted for 1,860 employees, down from 1,928 in 1981.

BACKGROUND

Mergers are John Shad's business. A lucrative business at that. For the past 18 years, Shad ran E.F. Hutton Group Inc.'s merger and corporate financing department; in 1980 the department handled $5.6 billion in mergers, including the union of Dart and Kraft. As his resume proclaims, "Mr. Shad has personally assisted scores of companies in consummating billions of dollars of corporate financings and mergers."

Occasionally, Shad offered other investment bankers his perspective on how to run a successful acquisition. One such speech, to the Practicing Law Institute in 1969, gave a broad sampling of Shad's views. "The conglomerates," he observed, "often show up as the most aggressive buyers; they are in the business of acquiring companies, and their top managements often devote their full time to this activity. Conglomerates are also the easiest ones to work with, for they are well staffed and thoroughly experienced in such transactions."

Companies searching for a suitor were advised to look close to home. "The selling company's major competitors, customers, and suppliers should also be carefully reviewed, for it is generally within these groups that the greatest operating advantages can be realized through a merger. It is also within these groups that potential antitrust problems are encountered. . .Ideal merger prospects should not be lightly dismissed simply because of the possibility of such problems—which are often surmountable."

It is all very down to earth, very businesslike and precise. Government rules are obstacles to be overcome, to be surmounted, in a manner entirely accordant with law. It is the view of a practical, but creative, man. When he found "financings and mergers" he had negotiated as a young investment banker were being held up "because of legal and tax problems," he decided to go to law school at night with his wife. "We decided it was more interesting to go to law school together in the evening than to watch television," he explained at his confirmation hearing. "It has proven very helpful."

Shad was apparently very good at what he did. He was rewarded well financially, rose in rank through E.F. Hutton to the post of vice-chairman of the board and was named Investment Banker of the Year by *Finance* magazine in 1972.

Shad comes to the SEC after a 30-year career on Wall Street. In 1949, he started out as a securities analyst at Arnold Bernhard & Co. After a year there he moved to Shields and Co., and then Reynolds and Co., and then Textron, Inc., and then Shearson, Hammill & Co., where he rose to the position of general partner in 1960. But in 1963 he jumped to E.F. Hutton as a vice-president.

Six SEC enforcement actions had been launched against companies with which Shad was involved. But SEC General Counsel Ralph Ferrara determined, in a letter to the Senate Banking Committee, "From a review of the available documents in these cases, it appears that Mr. Shad's conduct was never a matter of question in any of these proceedings. Moreover, it appears that none of these proceedings involved persons under Mr. Shad's supervision."

At the time of his appointment, Shad sat on the boards of directors of the following companies: A-T-O Inc., Katy Industries Inc., Kaufman and Broad Inc., the Pratt-Shad Foundation, Scudder Duo-Vest, the Scudder Duo-Vest Exchange Fund, Sheller-Globe Corp., and the Triangle Pacific Corp.

He had also been involved in Republican politics for more than 30 years, since working with the New York Young Republicans in 1948. Shad has contributed to and solicited funds for every Republican presidential candidate since Dewey. In 1978, he was a trustee on the Republican Senatorial Trust. In 1979, he headed Reagan's New York finance committee. Over the past eight years he has contributed between $500 and $5,000 to the campaigns of Richard Nixon, Gerald Ford, Reagan, Howard Baker, James Buckley, Alfonse D'Amato, Jacob Javits, Robert Packwood, John Tower and James Thompson of Illinois—Republicans all.

All this helps to explain Shad's entree to the Reagan circle. Shad is also close to William Casey, who ran Reagan's campaign and now runs the CIA. Shad has said he was offered the job by a "close friend of the President" but has declined to identify the individual, presumably Casey. Shad refused to be interviewed.

Born on June 27, 1923 in Brigham City, Utah, Shad has adopted New York as his home. (He was introduced at his confirmation hearing by both of New York's senators.) Shad was graduated from the University of Southern California in 1947, Harvard Business School in 1949, and New York Universty Law School in 1959. He is married with two children.

MAJOR ISSUES

- Shad is carefully following an industry line on key legislative and regulatory decisions. He is actively working to eliminate the central provisions of the Foreign Corrupt Practices Act, a law prompted in part by revelations of corporate bribery unearthed by earlier SEC administrations.

- Shad has made the promotion of "capital formation" his major priority, downplaying the agency's traditional role of policing the marketplace and protecting investors.

- To further that aim, he has proposed numerous regulatory changes, including a package of revisions that would reduce the information companies would have to make public.

- Shad has also worked to approve the sale of stock market index options and futures, high-risk instruments that many in Congress consider to be deceptive for small investors and a drain on productive uses of capital.

John Shad is in the mainstream of Reagan Administration regulatory appointees. Coming from a lucrative career in the industry he now regulates, Shad believes his agency has been too adversarial and entrepreneurial in the past, and that a new attitude is necessary.

"I will do my best to help," Shad told the Securities Industry Association's annual convention in December, 1981, "to help peel away the excessive regulations that have accumulated over the past 50 years."

John Shad is also in the mainstream of Reagan Administration economic appointments. He talks about the "disincentives to save and invest" built into the tax and regulatory structure. And he has a kind word for the massive mergers that rolled through the economy at a record rate in 1981. "Today," he told one interviewer, "acquisitions are often more efficient than internal growth. . .Capital formation is also enhanced to the extent that the acquirer employs the acquired resources more efficiently or profitably."

Actually, there is no evidence that acquiring companies manage resources any more profitably than the companies they acquire. In fact, the most detailed study ever conducted on the subject, by Massachusetts Institute of Technology Professor David Birch, concluded that, "Conglomerates tend to acquire the faster growing independents"—firms that were well managed in the first place. Once acquired, though, these firms grow less quickly than the ones which remain independent.

No matter. For Shad, it is an article of faith that most "major mergers [produce]. . .a net economic gain by and large."

It would be difficult to imagine Shad coming out any other way. His resume, after all, proudly highlights his successful experience in the billion-dollar world of high finance acquisitions. As a veteran of 17 corporate boards of directors, it is equally hard to imagine Shad embracing the efforts of his predecessor, Harold Williams, to open corporate boardrooms to more outsiders. And indeed Shad rejects that notion. "For the most part, the boards of American companies are composed of outstanding individuals," he proclaimed with fraternal pride in one interview.

"I am on seven New York Stock Exchange-listed companies' boards," he explained at his confirmation hearing. "I know that boards do not function well as debating societies. I know you need well-informed men who are willing to devote their efforts to assisting a company in a keenly competitive environment. . .If we are going to keep demanding more and more time, more and more legal exposure, very successful men who have something to bring to companies are not going to be willing to serve on boards."

Those assessments conjure up a vision of a world in which men of business make important fiduciary decisions, unencumbered by too much liberal social baggage. That view comes through even more clearly when Shad speaks of his top priority at the SEC: not policing the markets, not promoting corporate responsibility, but "improving the capital formation process." It is a view focused on the gritty business of business, and Shad is likely to judge other goals by how they affect that priority.

Consider in that light Shad's announced enforcement priority, insider trading. It is a logical focus for Shad, for the examples of malfeasance brought into the spotlight by some of the massive mergers of early 1981 were felt to shake the confidence of small investors in the market. "Few of us would play in a game in which, we were told, the dice were loaded against us," Shad said. Public confidence in the fairness of the markets, he explained, "is an essential element in the capital formation process."

So Shad, along with his enforcement chief John Fedders, came out of the blocks hard on insider trading. "We're going to come down with hobnail boots to give some shocking examples to inhibit the activity," Shad said in one interview, that generated a stiff headline: "SEC Chief Plans Insider Trade Curb." Insider trading cases were filed involving the attempted takeovers of Santa Fe International Corp., St. Joe Minerals, and other mergers.

But sometime during the fall of 1981 the publicity focus shifted. Perhaps Shad came to believe the "shocking examples" would inhibit small investors as well as inside trading. In any case, Shad began to describe the markets as "the broadest, most active and efficient, and the fairest. . .the world has ever known.

"Abuse of inside information is a very serious problem," he said in his December talk to the securities industry, "but it is the exception, not the rule. It is as wrong to overstate the problem as it is to ignore it."

Insider trading remains their top enforcement priority, though. Fedders told us that insider trading cases constituted 31 percent of all new cases brought in 1981, as compared with only 10 percent of the new cases opened in 1980. Fedders also supports tougher measures against inside traders: "The fine has to be greater than the gain," he said, suggesting the commission may soon propose a 300 percent penalty.

Other enforcement veterans told us that the focus on insider trading has "signalled that they're going to give away three-fourths of their jurisdiction"—corporate fraud, questionable payments, tax shelters and so on. "These guys are just putting blinders on," said one knowledgeable source. "They don't understand that unless you maintain your enforcement level, the markets will get away from you and become corrupt." Fedders argued that the commission has been "misinterpreted." But other securities lawyers argue that it is the *impression* of laxity that influences behavior—and Shad and Fedders have done little to dispel the impression.

On many other SEC issues Shad has found the balance that accords with the promotion of capital formation easier to determine. Shad has strongly supported weakening of the Foreign Corrupt Practices Act of 1977, passed in the wake of corporate bribery and slush fund scandals the SEC helped expose. (For the enforcement division led by Stanley Sporkin that ferreted out many of those scandals, Shad has faint praise. "The Commission's Enforcement Division has been praised by some as the best in government—and criticized by others as overzealous and heavy-handed," he has said on numerous occasions, in something less than a ringing endorsement. Fedders has used that assessment as well. Though he told us, "Stanley, I admire, I praise everything he's done. We only disagree on one thing: basketball," we suggested that by seconding the complaints without rebutting them he was implying he agreed with Sporkin's critics. "I think that's a fair response," Fedders said. "But today am I going to make that criticism? I'm not that much of a fool.")

The changes are necessary, Shad maintains, because "the Foreign Corrupt Practices Act has spawned unintended difficulties for American commerce abroad, and uncertainties concerning compliance with the accounting provisions."

Shad backs two major changes in the act. In a move that defies the usual bureaucratic order of things, he would like to turn sole jurisdiction for enforcement over to the Justice Department. (Currently the SEC shares the responsibility.) Shad also wants to revise the accounting provisions that are at the law's center.

Both of these proposals have been sharply criticized. The act's supporters say that removing authority from the SEC—an independent agency—would vest too much responsibility in political appointees at the Justice Department, who might be more receptive to Administration pressure for lax enforcement. "Relinquishing the power also sets a dangerous precedent that could weaken the SEC," said a staff member at the House Energy and Commerce Committee, which oversees the SEC. Former SEC Chairman Williams has said that the accounting changes backed by Shad would amount to wiping out the law.   Shad has also supported the elimination of the Public Utility Holding Company Act of 1935, a centerpiece of New Deal legislation. Prompted by the pyramid scandals of Samuel Insull and other notorious financial escapades in the 1920s, the act forced utility holding companies to receive SEC approval for mergers, new stock issues, and other major financial actions. But with the utility industry under financial stress, Shad now believes "the statute has served its basic purpose, and that continued federal regulation of utility holding companies is unnecessary and inappropriate." The proposed legislation would eliminate government oversight, but it could allow the utilities to stretch beyond their traditional services into everything from insurance to telecommunications.

New opportunities for increased economic influence would also become available to banks under Administration legislation that would allow them to enter the securities business. Shad has supported the Administration's efforts. "Our financial institutions have outgrown their suits of regulatory armor," he has said. "They are bursting at the seams. The time has come to simplify and rationalize the system."

But Shad has also been protective of the securities industry's interests, stressing that the banking affiliates which the legislation would create to handle certain kinds of securities "be subject to the same rules, regulations, and tax treatment as all other broker-dealers." Shad supports Treasury Secretary Donald Regan's proposal that brokers who "engage in no greater securities activites than those permitted the banks be afforded the opportunity to set up separate banking affiliates." And he shows less enthusiasm than Regan for totally dismantling the wall between banking and commerce erected by the Glass-Steagall Act. "While it is clear that the federal securities laws, deposit insurance and improved bank regulation have addressed many of the earlier concerns," he said in Senate testimony, "it would be unwise to ignore the lessons of history. This is particularly true with respect to what the Supreme Court has called 'the more subtle hazards that arise when a commercial bank. . .enters the investment banking business.' A complete demolition of the Glass-Steagall wall would lead to a sharp increase in the number and complexity of the conflicts of interest that are inevitable when a financial institution performs a variety of different functions."

On regulatory issues also, Shad's position is clear. "I believe industry can regulate itself better than the government can," he has said. From the day of his confirmation hearing on, Shad has been complaining about "overcompliance" with SEC reporting requirements that can create negative publicity for companies. Negative publicity, of course, can discourage investors—with good reason—but Shad has proposed regulatory changes to reduce the information companies must supply. In February, 1982 the SEC dropped a rule requiring companies to report all pending environmental litigation involving the government. It is considering a proposal that would exempt up to 500 of the 9,000 firms that now file annual disclosure forms from that public responsibility. Under the rule changes, the requirements for 10-K forms—the basic annual disclosure document—have been simplified so that "annual reports to shareholders can be used to satisfy some, if not all, of the 10-K requirements," Shad has said. It has also withdrawn a rule requiring companies to disclose certain information about their relationship with independent auditors. Perhaps most importantly, in February, 1982, the agency approved a pilot program to allow approximately 1,300 large corporations to issue stock offerings on virtually a moment's notice by filing one long-term statement of its plans. Shad calls the basic package "integration."

And—again in the interest of spurring capital formation—the SEC voted in January, 1982 to cut in half the net capital a securities firm must hold. The SEC voted to allow the firms to hold only two percent of customers' debts in assets, as opposed to the current requirement of four percent. (The change will give major firms an estimated $500 million to use as they wish.) In 1980, the commission proposed reducing the requirement to 3 percent, but the securities industries held out for the lower figure and with the change in administrations got its way.

The practical effect of the new emphasis on capital formation became apparent again in a stunning SEC decision involving Citicorp. Fedders told us he believed, "If you're engaged in deregulation, there has to be stronger enforcement." But according to documents obtained by Jeff Gerth of the *New York Times*, the agency's enforcement staff concluded that the bank had improperly shifted $46 million in profits from areas where taxes are high to the Bahamas, where taxes are low. The staff determined that the "practices and procedures" of the scheme, and efforts to hide the practice from various governments, "were done pursuant to policies laid down by senior management in New York." But, following a recommendation from Fedders, the commission declined to bring a civil action against the bank. Wrote Fedders in a staff report: "I do not subscribe to the theory that a company that violates tax and exchange control regulations is a bad corporation, and disclosure of illegal conduct should be forced as a prophylactic measure." As one enforcement veteran told us, "If somebody told an audience what the SEC did nobody would believe them."

Fedders told us he was "proud" of the Citicorp decision and "looked forward to all the documents coming out," so his recommendation would be better understood. But the SEC has denied Freedom of Information Act requests for the documents. Fedders disowned another assertion in the documents that since Citicorp "had never represented to stockholders or investors that its senior management had 'honesty and integrity' it had no legal duty to disclose breaches of these basic norms," as the *Times* wrote. "There's nobody in this building that subscribes to that," Fedders asserted. "I would agree, though, that that sentence has caused John and me" difficulties.

Fedders is defensive about the case, and anxious, it seems, to change the image it has quickly brought him. "It's ridiculous," to say the SEC has "gone limp" on corporate fraud, he told us. Fedders, a former college basketball player at Marquette, frequently uses basketball imagery. "I think we've got the cases in the mill" to change people's opinion, he told us. "I'm on a run."

Meanwhile, Shad negotiated an agreement with Phillip Johnson, chair of the Commodity Futures Trading Commission (CFTC), that ended the two agencies' jurisdictional dispute over regulating futures and options based on the rise and fall of the stock market. Under this agreement, the CFTC will handle futures, and the SEC options. The two instruments differ in technical terms, though the practical effect for small investors is about the same.

Ironically, critics of the proposals believe the new instruments will hurt capital formation by draining funds away from more productive investments. Some legislators, led by Rep. John Dingell (D-Mich.), the irascible chairman of the House Energy and Commerce Committee, are trying to push through legislation to temporarily ban stock market futures or options, but the passage of such a measure is unlikely.

In general SEC rules governing disclosure, sales personnel, and the use of inside information are much tougher than CFTC requirements. But many analysts fear that the two agencies will be forced to engage in a race to the bottom—loosening their standards to avoid putting the industry they regulate at a competitive disadvantage.

Shad maintains that what the CFTC does is its own business. "We have clearly defined criteria under the securities act," Shad told the *Washington Post*. "What somebody else does is outside our jurisdiction."

This spirit of interagency cooperation has extended to a more troubling question. In June, 1981 Rep. Tim Wirth (D-Colo.) and Dingell disclosed a June 13, 1981 Administration report that said the SEC had agreed to submit its regulations for clearance to the Office of Management and Budget (OMB) before issuing them publicly. After the publicity, Shad said he would not send the rules to OMB.

But doubts about his independence from the White House persist. Some congressional aides believe Shad views the SEC as "an arm of the Reagan Administration"—a view that is particularly interesting since Reagan's transition team on the agency suggested the appointment of commissioners who would strengthen Administration "control of the commission."

FINANCIAL BACKGROUND

Wall Street has been good to John Shad. He enters government service a very wealthy man. He is one of the richest men in the Reagan Administration.

Upon taking office, Shad sold his E.F. Hutton stock to a subsidiary of Morgan Stanley Inc. for $7.8 million. Other assets held by Shad and his wife were placed in five trusts. These holdings are worth at least $4 million more.

In addition to his E.F. Hutton stock, Shad's trusts contain holdings of $50,000 or more in the following firms: Citicorp, Clark Equipment, Data General Corp., Deluxe Check Printers Inc., Eastman Kodak, Exxon, Georgia Pacific, Hyster Co., IBM, Intel Corp., Eli Lilly & Co., Payless Cashways, Pfizer, Raychem, Raytheon, Sigma Aldrich, Schlumberger, Tymshare, Inc., Wang Laboratories, and Atlantic Richfield.

A variety of other stocks, worth at least $350,000, are listed in the name of his children. These include most of the firms that appear in the trusts, as well as other blue-chippers such as General Motors and AT&T.

In addition to E.F. Hutton, Shad reported compensation greater than $5,000 (all in directors fees) from: A-T-O, Katy Industries, Kaufman and Broad Inc., Triangle Pacific Corp., and the Sheller-Globe Corp.

APPENDIX

CASUALTIES OF THE FIRST YEAR

Over the one and a half years of the Reagan Administration that this book chronicles, four of the President's top 100 officials resigned. Two lost their jobs in the wake of controversy over allegedly unethical actions in office, though the reason they were forced out appeared to be rooted in their poor performances as well. One was squeezed out after he ceded too much bureaucratic turf to competing departments; another resigned voluntarily after failing to gain enough turf. Following are brief backgrounds on these men and why they became the casualties of the first year.

RICHARD ALLEN
NATIONAL SECURITY ADVISER

A week before Christmas, 1981, a group of Administration officials, congressmen and conservatives gathered at the Mayflower Hotel in downtown Washington to pay tribute to Richard Allen. In reality, "The Friends of Dick Allen" were sending a blunt signal to the White House, which had recently put Allen on administrative leave, to leave their man alone. Allen was, said Heritage Foundation President Ed Feulner, "one of our own."

By that time Allen, who had come into the White House saying he was going to take a low profile in contrast to his predecessors Zbigniew Brzezinski and Henry Kissinger, had captured the rapt attention of the Washington press corps—though not for his foreign policy initiatives—and had become an acute source of embarrassment to the White House. His friends' efforts at the Mayflower Hotel that day proved futile; in early 1982 Allen's administrative leave became a permanent one.

Press attention focused on Allen after it was disclosed that he had accepted and failed to report $1,000 that Japanese journalists had tried to give Nancy Reagan after a brief interview. Allen had helped arrange the interview through one of his former Japanese business associates. An FBI investigation into the matter, requested by Allen's key White House ally, Counselor Ed Meese—concluded that there was no evidence "that the money was intended for Allen or was kept by Allen for a corrupt purpose." Allen had claimed he forgot about the money.

But that wasn't the only questionable action Allen took while in the White House. He also accepted two wristwatches, valued at about $270, from those same Japanese friends for whom he had arranged the interview with Nancy Reagan. In addition, Allen raised suspicions by initially claiming on his financial disclosure form that he had sold his consulting business, Potomac International, in 1978, and then later revised that to January, 1981.

Still later the press revealed that former Reagan speechwriter Peter Hannaford, who purchased Allen's interest in the firm, had been paying Allen monthly installments, and that Allen had continued to meet with some of his former firm's clients on auto import issues—including executives from Toyota and Nissan Motors, the makers of Datsun—as a Reagan Administration official.

Neither was the $1,000 the first spark of controversy over Allen. In fall, 1980, while Allen was an adviser on Reagan's campaign, *Wall Street Journal* reporter Jonathan Kwitny, following an earlier story in *Mother Jones*, raised a number of questions about Allen's business relationship with Japanese clients. As a member of the President's Commission on International Trade in 1970, Allen had written several letters to a Japanese business consultant warning of a rise in protectionist sentiment in the U.S. and recommending that this friend, David Fleming, begin a lobbying effort on behalf of the Japanese in Washington. After Fleming got a $120,000 contract with Nissan through that recommendation, Allen wrote to him demanding half the fee "inasmuch as your introductions to Japan were arranged by me."

In addition, a Grumman Corp. official had charged in Senate testimony that Allen, then a White House aide, pressed the company to contribute $1 million to the 1972 Nixon reelection campaign, after Allen arranged for the sale of Grumman's advanced reconnaissance plane to the Japanese government.

As the charges mounted Allen resigned from the Reagan campaign on Oct. 30, 1980, where he was serving as the candidate's chief foreign policy staff aide. He joined the team on November 6, two days after Reagan's election, with Reagan telling a press conference, "we find absolutely no evidence of wrongdoing whatsoever." It was a convenient maneuver to diffuse the controversy just before the election.

Allen was the Right's principal spokesman in internal Reagan Administration debates on national security matters. (The "Friends of Dick Allen" reception was noticeably devoid of more moderate elements of the White House machinery and Congressional Republicans.) He had served as a foreign policy adviser to Nixon's 1968 campaign and later joined the National Security Council but left after both personal and political conflicts with Kissinger. His often acerbic personality and far-right foreign policy positions also brought him into visible conflict with key members of the Reagan Administration, particularly Secretary of State Alexander Haig.

Allen received a B.A. and an M.A. degree from Notre Dame and during the 1960s served as a staff member of two conservative think tanks: Georgetown University's Center for Strategic and International Studies and Stanford University's Hoover Institution on War, Revolution and Peace. From 1972 to 1981 he ran his own consulting firm, Potomac International.

MARTIN ANDERSON
ASSISTANT TO THE PRESIDENT FOR POLICY DEVELOPMENT

The real scope of Anderson's job at the White House was an object of speculation. Although officially described as the chief policy adviser to the President on economic and domestic issues, his shop, the Office of Policy Development, appeared to be merely idling in the shadow of Budget Director David Stockman during 1981. In early 1982 Anderson resigned from the Administration, frustrated at his lack of influence over domestic policy.

An academic for most of his life, Anderson is best known for his scholarship on social welfare and urban affairs. In his work he contends that federal and state programs have "virtually wiped out poverty in the United States." In his book, *Welfare: The Political Economy of Welfare Reform in the U.S.*, he also argues that government aid to the poor has created a "poverty wall" that discourages welfare recipients from attempting to join the workforce.

Anderson is a familiar face in the poverty debate. He first went public with his views in 1964 with a book criticizing urban renewal. His writings captured the attention of Richard Nixon, who enlisted Anderson as a White House aide in 1969, where his major task was the development of the all-volunteer Army plan.

Frustrated with the Nixon White House, Anderson in 1971 returned to the academic world as a senior fellow at Stanford University's Hoover Institution, a think-tank closely aligned with Reagan. He served as an adviser to Reagan in both the 1976 and 1980 campaigns.

While in the Reagan White House, Anderson and his staff helped fill in the details of the Stockman agenda by devising a plan to stiffen eligibility requirements for the fedeal welfare plan, Aid to Families with Dependent Children. Also emerging from Anderson's office in 1981 (and clearly influenced by his aide Robert Carleson, Reagan's welfare director in California) were "workfare" plans and a four-month limit on the time during which a portion of a recipient's income can be "disregarded" in fixing eligibility. Anderson also worked on Reagan's plan for urban enterprise zones.

That Anderson did not gain more influence in the White House was not surprising to close observers and friends, like Dr. William Walsh, a member of Reagan's transition team. "Marty Anderson is extremely brilliant," said Walsh well before Anderson's resignation, "but also very low profile. He would never go public with anything even if he did have any differences with anybody in the Administration. Furthermore, I think Marty would just go home if he found himself in a situation where he didn't have as much influence as he expected." *Washington Post* reporter Martin Schram, a long-time Anderson watcher, said Washington critics should not try to compare Anderson with previous policy chiefs, like Carter's Stuart Eizenstat. "The job is different for Martin Anderson," Schram said. "The whole situation is different within this Administration. The emphasis is on budget cutting and Stockman has naturally taken a more dominant role."

MICHAEL CARDENAS
ADMINISTRATOR, SMALL BUSINESS ADMINISTRATION

The White House asked for Cardenas's resignation in February, 1982 after he had been the subject of two inspector general investigations. The first began after the SBA awarded a contract to build an aqueduct for the Interior Department to an Hispanic owned Fresno firm after the SBA field staff had recommended that the $10-14 million contract go to a different firm. The firm that lost the contract maintained that Cardenas, also an Hispanic businessman from Fresno, had improperly influenced the deal. But the inspector general cleared Cardenas of any wrongdoing. The inspector general investigated similar allegations made after the awarding of another SBA contract.

But Cardenas's problems went much deeper. During his reign he succeeded in alienating both members of the small business community and the SBA staff. According to SBA staff, Cardenas ruled with an iron grip. And, although Cardenas was the highest ranking Hispanic in the Administration, Hispanic business groups didn't think much of him either, complaining that he was insensitive to their needs.

Cardenas opened his own accounting firm in Fresno in 1967, the Michael Cardenas Accountancy Firm, which primarily catered to small business owners. In 1979 his firm merged with Fox and Company, a national accounting firm based in Denver. He had been an active supporter of the Republican Party since the mid-60s when he became involved in both the Reagan for Governor and Nixon for President campaigns. In 1970 he headed a group of central California Mexican-Americans for Nixon's re-election. he worked on Reagan's campaign in both 1976 and 1980. He had also served on SBA's regional advisory council in San Francisco and later in Fresno.

Cardenas's experience with small business dated back to the 1950s when he worked as a barber in his father's shop while studying business administration at California State University, Fresno. He later opened his own barbershop.

MYER RASHISH
UNDERSECRETARY OF STATE FOR ECONOMIC AFFAIRS

Like other top officials in the Reagan State Department, Rashish's nomination was vigorously opposed by far-right senators such as Jesse Helms of North Carolina. But unlike others Rashish never developed the kind of relationship with Secretary of State Haig that would enable him to overcome that opposition.

In title Rashish was the principal economic adviser to Haig, responsible for develping the State Department's views on international energy policy, international financial affairs, North-South economic relations and trade. In practice though, Rashish's subordinate, assistant secretary Robert Hormats, rapidly filled that role. At several points during 1981 rumors seeped into the press that Haig was dissatisfied with Rashish's inability to shore up State Department control over trade issues.

Rashish's appointment to the Reagan Administration came as a surprise even to former colleagues. He had served as chief economist for the Democratic-controlled House Ways and Means Committee during the late 1950s; and in the Kennedy State Department as special assistant to the undersecretary for economic affairs during the early '60s. He helped draft one of Kennedy's most important pieces of international legislation, the Trade Expansion Act of 1962. Later he served as a consultant to another Democrat, Hale Boggs of Louisiana, and then from 1971 to 1976 he was a consultant to Democrat Abraham Ribicoff of Connecticut. Though many who have worked with Rashish describe him as a nonpolitical technician, one long-time colleague remarked: "I always thought he was a liberal Democrat."

But Sen. Helms challenged Rashish's nomination for a different reason. Though appointed as the State Department's chief advocate for American exporters, Rashish as a private consultant during the 1970s helped at least one foreign business compete against American industry. He lent advice to a consortium of French, German, Spanish, and British companies, called Aerobus Industrie, which manufactures and markets civilian aircraft, on how to cut in to the market of such manufacturers as Boeing, Lockheed, and McDonnell Douglas. To Helms, that was heretical: "The sales of aircraft made in the United States to foreign purchasers is a major means of redressing unfavorable balance of payment problems for the United States," Helms said. "The simple fact is, sales of U.S. transport aircraft abroad produces a substantial amount of money for U.S. industry."

Rashish attended Boston Latin School and received his undergraduate and graduate degrees from Harvard University.

ACCESS

Following are the office phone numbers for all the officials profiled in the book. All phone numbers (unless otherwise noted) have a 202 area code.

Thorne Auchter	523 9362
James Baker	456 6797
Malcolm Baldrige	377 2112
Ray Barnhart	426 0650
William Baxter	633 2401
Terrel Bell	426 6420
Robert Blanchette	426 0710
John Block	447 3631
Lawrence Brady	377 1455
Shelby Brewer	252 6450
William Brock	395 3204
James Buckley	632 0410
Robert Burford	343 3801
Charles Butler	357 8200
Frank Carlucci	695 6352
Gerald Carmen	566 1212
William Casey	351 6363
William Clark	456 2255
John Crowell	447 7173
W. Kenneth Davis	252 5500
Michael Deaver	456 6475
Richard DeLauer	697 9111
Chris DeMuth	395 3864
Donald Devine	632 6106
Carol Dinkins	633 2701
Raymond Donovan	523 8274
William Draper	566 8144
Lawrence Eagleburger	632 2471
James Edwards	252 6210
Roscoe Egger	566 4115
Ford B. Ford	235 1385
Mark Fowler	632 6600
Rudolph Giuliani	633 3752
Anne Gorsuch	382 4700
Alexander Haig	632 4910
Edwin Harper	456 6515
James Harris	343 4237
William Harvey	272 4040
Arthur Hayes	443 2410
J. Lynn Helms	426 3111
A. Alan Hill	395 5080
Donald Hodel	343 5183
Robert Hormats	632 0396
Donald Hovde	755 7123

Fred Ikle	697 7200
Mary Jarratt	447 7711
Lowell Jensen	633 2601
Phillip Johnson	254 6970
Jerry Jordan	395 5036
Richard Kennedy	632 1500
Jeane Kirkpatrick	(212) 826 4524
C. Everett Koop	245 6467
Rex Lee	633 2201
John Lehman	695 3131
Drew Lewis	426 1111
Richard Lyng	447 6158
James Malone	632 1554
John Marsh	695 3211
C. W. McMillian	447 4256
Peter McPherson	632 9620
Edwin Meese	456 2235
James Miller III	523 3711
Ernst Minor	395 4506
Robert Nimmo	389 3775
William Niskanen	395 5046
Paul Nitze	632 4924
Edward Noble	822 6300
Lionel Olmer	377 2867
William Olson	272 4040
Verne Orr	697 7376
Nunzio Palladino	634 1481
Thomas Pauken	254 3120
Raymond Peck	426 1836
Richard Perle	695 0942
Samuel Pierce	755 6417
Richard Pratt	377 6280
Donald Regan	566 2533
William Bradford Reynolds	633 2151
Thomas Roberts	634 1459
Eugene Rostow	632 9610
Edward Rowny	632 4153
Timothy Ryan	523 7675
James Sanders	653 6605
Danford Sawyer	275 2034
Edward Schmults	633 2101
Richard Schweiker	245 7000
John Shad	272 2000
William French Smith	633 2001
Beryl Sprinkel	566 5164
Nancy Steorts	634 7740
David Stockman	395 4840
Walter Stoessel	632 9640
John Svahn	245 6764

Reese Taylor	275 1912
Arthur Teele	426 4040
Joseph Tribble	252 9220
Norman Ture	566 5847
John Van de Water	254 9258
James Watt	347 7351
Murray Weidenbaum	395 5042
Caspar Weinberger	695 5261

INDEX

DATE DUE			

DEMCO 38-297